P9-AFM-650

Carte Blanche

A Quarter Century of Wine Tasting Diaries and Cellar Notes: 1974–1999

ALBERT GIVTON

Turnagain Enterprises Ltd.

Printed in Canada

First edition: August 1999

Givton, Albert

Carte blanche, a quarter century of wine tasting diaries and cellar notes, 1974-1999

1. Wine tasting. 2. Wines and wine making. 1. Title
   ISBN 0-9685612-0-9

Acknowledgements

EDITOR:	Val Wilson
EDITORIAL ASSISTANTS:	Dorothy McFee and Carol Maye-Norman
COVER PHOTOGRAPHY:	Wildman Photography
VENUE FOR COVER SHOOT:	Park Royal Hotel
GRAPHIC DESIGN AND TYPESETTING:	Graffiki Design
PRINTING:	Broadway Printers

Other publications by Albert Givton

Wine Wise
An indispensable guide to buying wines in British Columbia
Brighouse Press 1988 ISBN 0-921304-00-5

The Wine Consumer magazine
A wine-buying guide for Canadians, published quarterly, 1985 to 1990: 6 volumes, 24 issues

Turnagain Enterprises Ltd.
Suite 601 - 1401 West Broadway
Vancouver, British Columbia, Canada V6H 1H6
Voice (604) 737-1312 Fax (604) 737-1317
carteblanche@intergate.bc.ca

To present and future
students and passionates
of the exciting
world of wines—wherever they may be.

Wine knows no borders.

Dedication

To
Harry Waugh

Jean-Michel Cazes
Gerard Chave
Jean-François Coche-Dury
Pascal Delbeck
François Faiveley
Bruce Guimaraens
Joe Heitz
Rémy Krug
May-Eliane de Lencquesaing
Christian Moueix
Christian Pol Roger
Bruno Prats
Belle and Barney Rhodes

In Memoriam

Gerard Jaboulet
Bernard Ledun
Dr. Haskell Norman
Peter A. Sichel
Bernadette Villars

Table of Contents

Preface

Introduction i

Diary 1 1

Diary 2 40

Diary 3 59

Diary 4 86

Diary 5 116

Diary 6 139

Diary 7 169

Diary 8 198

Diary 9 230

Diary 10 254

Diary 11 281

Diary 12 314

Diary 13 338

Diary 14 360

Diary 15 390

Diary 16 417

Diary 17 452

Diary 18 486

Performance of Selected Châteaux of Bordeaux 510

Diary 19 512

Selected Cellar Notes 532

Photos Three Sections

Index of People 663

Index of Wines 671

Preface

WHY CARTE BLANCHE?

A wine consumer's advocate, I speak from a position of absolute independence from any connection—past or present—to the commercial side of wines. I am completely free to express my views about wines, with no underlying motive or interest.

I have never been associated, in any capacity whatsoever, in the production, ownership, distribution or retailing of wines, nor involved in directorships, auction houses, or any other business ventures related to wines. I am driven by pure passion, and by the desire to follow my fascination for learning and teaching about the wonderful world of wines.

Over the past 25 years, I have been given the opportunity to experience, first-hand, many of the greatest wines ever produced—and to witness the tremendous changes that have occurred in the taste of wines, winemaking methods, and the growing global interest in the subject.

As I wrote about my early wine tasting experiences, I had no thought of ever publishing my notes. As time went by, I saw that on the "inside," the world of wines included some very interesting players. In addition to making notes about my tastings, I began to detail information about people in the business, wine production, and how wine "politics" were starting to influence the wines themselves. I gradually realized that I would one day publish these observations and comments—to create a work to serve both present and future generations.

Comments, reviews, and vintage reports from my wine newsletter, The Wine Consumer, *(a total of 24 issues, published quarterly, from 1985 to 1990), are not included in* Carte Blanche. *Excerpts from those newsletters were published in 1988 in my first book,* Wine Wise, *now out of print.*

Most of my experiences and remarks about individuals mentioned in this book are a matter of public record. Only a very few personal thoughts about specific personalities shall remain untold.

ABOUT TURNAGAIN ISLAND

The name "Turnagain Island" appears often in the Wine Diaries and Cellar Books. Turnagain is an island off the Sunshine Coast in British Columbia where we have a summer residence—and where we have shared many fine bottles over the years, by ourselves and with friends.

THE SPELLING OF NAMES

Given the size and magnitude of Carte Blanche, *spelling errors may have occurred in a few names, for which we humbly apologize.*

Introduction

From War to Wine

Thursday, June 8, 1967

The battle over Jerusalem is subsiding. Both Egypt and Jordan are suing for a cease-fire. The general staff is now concentrating on the Syrian front and on the Golan Heights. The Jordanian Legion is withdrawing East of the Jordan River, over the bridges near Jericho.

The battle over East Jerusalem is being conducted on four fronts. One is to the north of Jerusalem. The second is on the Ramallah Road and the thrust east to Jericho to block the escape of the Jordanian Legion, both led by the 10th ("Harel") mechanized brigade.

The third, the penetration in the centre—including the old city of Jerusalem—is being conducted by the crack Reserve 55th Parachute Brigade, commanded by the legendary Colonel Mota Gur. Two of my best friends are serving in the 55th Parachute Brigade. One is a paratrooper in the pioneer battalion of the 55th Airborne, and the son of my parents' dear friends, who are Holocaust survivors. My friend is killed by a sniper on the second day of the war, near the Mandelbaum Gate (until the war, an official crossing between East and West Jerusalem, similar to "Checkpoint Charlie" in Berlin). Another childhood friend is serving in the artillery support battalion of the same brigade.

The fourth—my brigade, the 16th ("Jerusalem") Infantry—is concentrating its efforts to the south of the city, and in a thrust to Hebron—site of the Tombs of the Patriarchs, past Bethlehem, and Gush Etzion, a group of four settlements that fell to the Jordanians in the War of Independence of 1948.

How the War Began

Like everybody else in Israel, the war started for me on Monday, June 5, 1967, at 7:45 a.m. I was getting ready for work, a ten-minute walk from my home. Having been released from the army in October 1966, after 26 months of compulsory military service, I had found a job at the central Bank of Israel, in the statistics section of the "inspector of banks" department.

As usual during those days of heightened tension in May and early June 1967, everyone was glued to the radio. Suddenly the music stopped. "Here is an announcement from the office of the army spokesman. 'Our air force and land forces are advancing toward the border with Egypt in order to repulse several large attacks by the Egyptian army.' " These words were followed by codes to various Reserve units for immediate mobilization. These messages continued for about 30 minutes. Not hearing my code, I rushed out to work. Political analysts and experts suggested that this would be a skirmish with the Egyptians, and that King Hussein of Jordan would not move against Israel along the West Bank and the Jerusalem fronts.

When I arrived at work, everyone was listening to the radio address to the nation by the newly appointed defence minister, General Moshe Dayan. People were worried, and no one was in the mood to work. A radio blackout masked details of the fighting that early Monday morning. Some co-workers switched on Radio Cairo, which was transmitting in Hebrew, and heard the Egyptians boasting that they were advancing on all fronts and would soon reach Tel Aviv—and that we would be thrown into the sea.

No one believed that, but we were very concerned. Everyone had a son, brother, father, husband, or friend on the Egyptian front, where the bulk of the Israeli army was concentrated.

Prime Minister Levi Eshkol's voice was trembling, and anything but reassuring in his radio addresses to the nation during those long weeks of uncertainty. Could we withstand a simultaneous attack on all fronts—with no allies, no Reserves, and not enough armour and fighter planes? We were alone. We felt isolated.

And what about chemical warfare? During the weeks of partial mobilization preceding the war, we had been issued special antichemical injections. Poison gas and Jews don't make a very good combination…

At 11:20 a.m. that fateful Monday morning, all hell broke loose in Jerusalem. First, a shower of heavy and medium mortar shells landed all over the city. Then, 106 millimetre recoilless rifles and heavy machine guns fired down upon us. The intense shelling was coming from Mount Scopus, the Mount of Olives, and from the wall surrounding the Old City. Young King Hussein had decided to join the fray in order to get a piece of the pie once Israel was dismembered. I realized, at that point, that I had to join my unit.

I ran to my parents' home, zigzagging among the exploding shells and hiding behind solid stone buildings. We lived on the Jordanian border, in an apartment hotel owned by the Assomptionist monks. It had been converted from a pilgrims' hostel. This building, called Notre Dame de France, was operated by the priests, who rented rooms at reasonable rates to people of modest means. A portion of this imposing building, which faced the New Gate of the Old City wall, had been occupied by the Israeli army as an observation post since the end of hostilities in the War of Independence of 1948.

The shelling and fighting in Jerusalem went on without reprieve, and I realized that I would not be able to join my unit. I therefore went up to the army observation position on the roof of Notre Dame, and asked the local commander if he could use a radio operator who had been isolated from his unit. Upon verifying my identification, he let me man the post's radio as a second operator; I spent the first two days of the war in jeans and a white T-shirt, defending not only my country and city, but the actual building in which my parents and I lived! I was stationed on the roof, and they were sheltered in the basement.

As a radio operator, I started to hear details of the fighting. I understood, early on, that in two massive strikes that Monday morning, the Arab air forces had been decimated. Without an air force, and in desert and open-country warfare, the outcome of the war was—for all intents and purposes—decided.

On the third day, the shelling in Jerusalem subsided, and while the paratroopers were forcing their way into the Old City and the Wailing Wall, I managed to join my brigade. I belonged to the Signal Corps company of the 16th Infantry Brigade. It was a special brigade, made up almost exclusively of Jerusalemites, the reason being that until 1967, Jerusalem was surrounded by the Jordanians on three sides. If quick mobilization were necessary, there was always the danger that Jerusalem's western approaches could be cut off, thereby hindering Reservists from other parts of the country from joining their units.

I hitched a ride with elements of our Signal Corps company and several senior officers to join the bulk of our brigade, which was already in Gush Etzion, on the road to Hebron. Arriving very late on the night of Wednesday, June 7, I tried to find a place to sleep, absolutely exhausted after three days of constant shelling. I entered a small bunker that seemed fairly comfortable, and noticed two other soldiers already on the floor fast asleep. I lay down beside them and immediately fell asleep. I woke up at dawn, opened my eyes, and realized to my horror that the two soldiers were not Israelis but Jordanians—and that they were not asleep, but dead!

During their hasty retreat, the Jordanians had abandoned several British-made Centurion tanks, similar to our own but with a different calibre gun and a different radio. The commanding officer of our Signal Corps company instructed me and a friend to climb onto the tanks, remove the radios, and replace them with our own GRC radios. These radios each weighed over 150 pounds. While unloading the radio from the second tank, my friend slipped and fell off the tank, dropping the radio on my right knee. Thus ended my "Six Day War"—on the fourth day of the war. I was taken by ambulance to Hadassah hospital in Jerusalem; my knee had swollen to the size of a cantaloupe. After two days in hospital, I was released on Saturday, June 10, the last day of the war—the day the Golan Heights were conquered, in the north of Israel, on the border with Syria.

When I arrived home, my mother had aged visibly. She told me the dreadful news that my paratrooper friend had been killed. I went to see his mother. What could I say? I had survived the war and her son, an only child like myself, had not. It was a most depressing and difficult moment.

Discovery in a Deli

Four days after the end of hostilities, the corps of engineers cleared a minefield and opened a passage to East Jerusalem, the relatively modern part of the Jordanian side of the city, which faces the Damascus Gate to the north. I was still dressed in battle fatigues and hobbling on a cane when I came across a deli in East Jerusalem.

I noticed a number of wines in the window display, and made my way into the store. The shopkeeper had a worried expression on his face. I asked him if he spoke English, and he said "a little." I said I wasn't there to threaten him, but just to look around and maybe buy a few souvenirs. When I enquired about his selection of wines, he said he had purchased the deli from a Christian Arab a few months before the war. Being a Moslem, he didn't drink alcohol—he was selling off his wines and liquor. He also told me he didn't accept Israeli currency because he didn't know its value yet, but asked if I had American dollars. I replied in the affirmative. He was eager to bargain.

As I looked around, my eye caught an interesting square bottle on which was inscribed: "Rocher/Eau de Vie de Danzig." This was the famous Danziger Goldwasser, a liqueur with tiny gold leaves floating in it. I noticed that the wax capsule was embossed with the words "3eme Republique." From school, I knew that the Third Republic fell in 1940, when France signed an armistice with Nazi Germany. I asked him how much he wanted for this bottle. "Five dollars," he replied. I told him that there was a lot of junk floating in it, and that it was all dusty and dirty and old—I would give him two dollars. We finally agreed on three.

Then I saw an interesting slender bottle of Gewürztraminer from Alsace, produced by Preiss-Henny. I also noticed bottles of Pommard and various other wines. This was all new to me, of course, because I had never tasted fine wines. But, over the years, my father had told me stories about his travels through the capitals of Europe between the two World Wars, when he lived for a while in Bucharest, Prague, and Vienna, and visited Paris, Warsaw, and Budapest. He told me that he had tasted various Cognacs and Champagnes—including his favourite, Veuve Clicquot—and also fine Burgundies, Alsatian wines, and red Bordeaux.

I selected five bottles in that little deli, plus the bottle of Danzig liqueur, and after haggling for about ten minutes, we agreed on US$30 for the lot. When I walked through the door of our flat, my father was stunned. "Where on Earth did you find these treasures?" I told him the story. Over the next few months, he and I enjoyed these fine bottles about which I knew so little and he so much. This was my introduction to the world of fine wines.

Family History

My parents met in Alexandria, Egypt, the city of their births. French was the language spoken by both their families. Since Napoleonic times, French has been the language preferred by most European residents of the city. I was born in Cairo in 1945… a great vintage year. We emigrated from Egypt in 1950, while King Farouk still ruled, and settled in Jerusalem, Israel, arriving there in a roundabout way via Marseilles, France; Israel and Egypt were in a state of war at that time.

Although my father never played an instrument himself, he had a great ear for music; it was he who encouraged me to play the cello, which I have done since the age of 11. My mother's side of the family, however, was rather more musical, albeit two generations removed. My great-grandfather, Armand Lemisiano, was a tenor who participated in the Gala Performance of the opera *Aida* by Verdi, composed for the occasion of the opening of the Suez Canal. The performance took place in Cairo in 1871, after which my great-grandfather returned to Germany with two of his three daughters, and continued his singing career there for a few years, in Tropau, Regensburg, Chemnitz, and at the Königliches Theatre Wiesbaden, as a heldentenor. His third daughter remained in Egypt, having fallen in love with and marrying an Egyptian Bey (a title of Ottoman nobility, Egypt at that time being under the rule of the Ottoman Empire).

Several years later, a widower, and no longer able to perform on stage due to an injury, Great-grandfather decided to settle in Alexandria. The two daughters joined him; one of them was my maternal grandmother.

Post-War Travels

After the Six Day War, I looked for a new place of residence, as my room in Notre Dame had been damaged by a shell that went in through the window. All my belongings had been destroyed or damaged—with the exception of my cello; fortunately, it had been leaning behind a heavy cupboard that suffered the brunt of the explosion. Several months after the war, I left Israel for Montreal and New York. I returned 26 months later, in May 1970, in the middle of the War of Attrition with Egypt along the Suez Canal, and entered the Hebrew university as a student of Political Science and International Relations. During Reserve duty in 1971 and 1972, I also served twice along the Suez Canal and Bir Gifgafa Airfield.

One evening, in the summer of 1971, I was invited—by a friend who had received tickets from the Ministry of Defence—to attend a performance of the ballet *Giselle*, featuring the world-renowned dancer Margot Fonteyn, and the great Rudolph Nureyev, who had defected from the Soviet Union and who was performing in the West. We were seated one row behind Prime Minister Golda Meir, who was surrounded by her bodyguards and members of her family.

Among them was her son Menachem, who had been my cello teacher at the Rubin Academy of Music in Jerusalem for a period of two years prior to my military service. He recognized me, and after a short chat, invited me to join them for a glass of wine at the reception after the performance. This was my second opportunity to taste fine wines, because during my two years in Montreal and New York, I barely had enough money to live on, and whatever money I was earning, I was sending home to my parents.

In June 1973, I completed my studies at the Hebrew university, and returned to Canada that August—this time taking my parents along with me. We settled in Vancouver. Before my departure, I had managed to obtain a release from Reserve duty on the Barlev line (Suez Canal), where units of my old 16th Infantry Brigade were assigned during the high holidays of the Jewish New Year and Yom Kippur.

Little did I know then, that six weeks later, in early October, a war would explode in the Middle East and that part of my brigade—including one full infantry battalion—would be decimated in the first few hours of the Egyptian army's crossing of the Suez canal. The tragedy was double. First, of course, was the loss of so many lives; second, because it was a Reserve unit, many of the men were older, married, and had families. That war created many widows and orphans. Had I stayed in Israel and served on the Canal, my fate would probably have been sealed.

Early in the morning of October 6, 1973, Yom Kippur, my father had a heart attack and was taken to a Vancouver hospital for emergency treatment. While I was waiting in the Emergency Room, I heard two nurses talking about a war in the Middle East. The radio confirmed that war had indeed erupted. I was torn between going back to Israel and staying in Canada with my ailing father. At that early stage, I decided that the best thing to do was to stay put. In any event, when I phoned a contact in New York to find out if it was possible for me to fly back to Israel, I was told they were only flying back doctors and high-ranking officers, and ammunition, electronic equipment, and weapons. The war went on without me. It lasted almost a full month—with horrendous cost in human lives on both sides. Thankfully, my father survived his heart attack.

LIFE IN VANCOUVER, BRITISH COLUMBIA, CANADA

I found a job at a bank as a foreign exchange dealer, and planned to continue my studies at the University of British Columbia, where I had been accepted for a Masters program in Political Science and International Relations.

In August 1974, I married Carol McGregor, and my fervour for wine began to bloom. Carol and I enjoyed travelling, good food, and fine wines. I started shaping a modest wine cellar. At the time, Vancouver was a desert for the wine enthusiast. With its liquor monopoly, no wines of any interest could be found locally.

I had taken a job with a pharmaceutical firm, which was headquartered in Montreal, as their western representative. On my business trips back to Montreal and New York, I would purchase fine wines from the Quebec liquor monopoly and from various wine shops in the New York City area. Simultaneously, I started to read about and taste wines—I realized there was a lot more to wines than I had previously thought.

Wine became an overnight passion. I was fortunate to discover this zeal during "Wine-Gate," the wine scandal in Bordeaux in 1973 -1974. Along with the oil crisis and the depression that followed, the world was awash in great wines—selling at ridiculously low prices. Reading avidly about wines and tasting as much as I could, I realized what a golden opportunity I had to buy many fine wines, and to create a nice wine cellar.

I also understood early on that the best wines were finite commodities. Therefore, I did not buy the ordinary, everyday table wines that were available locally. On my trips through Eastern Canada and New York, I started to acquire rare wines—including Château Petrus 1970, at Macy's Wine Cellar in New York, retailing for $18 per bottle, and 1966 Château Cheval Blanc, for $12 per bottle. I also bought my very first full case of wine: 1966 Château La Lagune, from the Quebec liquor monopoly. It was, and still is, a superb wine.

In early 1975, I gathered a group of friends at our home in Vancouver for a tasting of the finest wines available locally. We had a dozen participants at that first tasting, and found it fascinating; but because of the poor selection of the local liquor monopoly, we could only taste a rather limited number of wines. This type of tasting was held on three occasions during 1975.

In December 1975, the British Columbia liquor monopoly finally entered the 20th century with a specialty wine shop in downtown Vancouver. I walked into the store one day shortly after it opened, and found such treasures as 1970 Château Palmer, selling for $10.50 per bottle; Château d'Yquem 1967, $27.40

a bottle; La Tâche 1972, from the Domaine de la Romanée-Conti, $22 per bottle; 1970 Hermitage "La Chapelle" from Jaboulet, retailing for $12.50 per bottle; Château Trotanoy 1964, at $19 per bottle; Château La Mission Haut-Brion 1959, at $30 per bottle; et cetera. I bought as much wine as I could afford.

I continued collecting wines and organized a few tastings for a group of friends through 1976. By that time, our group had grown to about two dozen participants. In January 1977, I founded "Le Tastevin" wine club, to educate myself and other people about tasting wines.

To England and Back

In April 1977, my wife Carol and I moved, with our two-year-old son Michael, to London, England, for several months. London became the base for our visits to the vineyards of France. During our stay in London, I met Harry Waugh, a gentleman in the true sense of the word. Harry became my first and most important wine mentor.

I returned to Vancouver in October 1977, restarted Le Tastevin, and ran it successfully for two decades. At its peak, we had over 100 members—plus a waiting list—and a substantial wine cellar from which we drew wines; we held, on average, six tastings annually. My philosophy with Le Tastevin was to expose our members to eclectic wines from around the world—every country, every region. Our tasting framework was straightforward: we started each tasting with a Champagne or aperitif wine, then moved on to the "subject" tasting—which usually included eight to 12 wines from a certain grape varietal, region, vintage, et cetera—then we tasted a dessert wine. Over 20 years, the members of Le Tastevin have had the opportunity to taste wines from the simplest to the rarest, from every corner of the globe.

Changes in the World of Wine

Over the past quarter of a century, we have witnessed dramatic improvements and fundamental changes in the world of wines. What worries me about the new, impeccable methods of winemaking is the loss of individuality and "terroir" character of leading producing-regions and individual estates—in order to satisfy a new trend. For instance: creating Haut-Médocs with too much Merlot, thus producing charming, fleshy, early maturing wines that are impeccably made—but that even the most experienced taster could not identify at a blind-tasting as being Haut-Médocs. Or the new "super Tuscan" wines, superbly crafted, but not Italian! The concept of terroir—regional character, varietal, or style—is being sacrificed to satisfy the demand of inexperienced wine collectors who follow, like sheep, the tasting notes and scores of the new "super" wine writers.

Of course, modern living includes smaller spaces, limited cellaring facilities, and impatient people who are not willing to wait for ten or 15 years to drink their wines. Even the last bastion of longevity, Vintage Port, is produced nowadays in a more forward, early maturing style.

In spite of the current trend to standardize the overall quality of wine to a common denominator—and the tragic loss of the terroir character of different wines from various regions, there are still islands of hope. Most producers in Burgundy (of both red and white varietals), several châteaux in Bordeaux—notably Figeac, Palmer, Domaine de Chevalier, and Ausone (until the tragic dismissal of winemaker Pascal Delbeck, in 1996)—and the leading Northern Rhône producers, such as Gerard Chave and the house of Jaboulet, insist on producing classic wines—true to their terroir character. These are the gifted traditionalists who, I believe, will prevail in the end, because the vast majority of wine lovers will understand and value the importance of the character of a region and its indigenous wines.

Not all apples taste the same; not all strawberries taste the same—nor should all wines taste the same. We have reached a very dangerous level of commonality, with too many students learning under too few masters—and with gurus who convince winemakers and owners of noble properties to start producing uniform, early maturing wines. This, in my opinion, is a tragedy—especially if one accepts the fact that wine is an art form. One must remember, however, that each generation has its critics.

Wine Author Ian Maxwell Campbell

In *Wayward Tendrils of the Vine*, first published in 1940, author Ian Maxwell Campbell describes the Bordeaux vintages of the 1920s: "I always maintained that Clarets of recent years, however fine they are, fail when compared with the older vintages, and I ask myself if this is due to modern methods of vinification or to a global change in climatic condition or what?"

It is interesting to note that today, we offer the same arguments about modern wines, compared to wines from the 1970s, 1960s, and 1950s. In another part of the book, Campbell wonders about another phenomenon of modern life—"modern" meaning 1940. Describing his generation's wine-producing methods, he writes: "It is possible that the hustling mode of life in these present days, the exiguousness of flat accommodation, and the anxiety to ensure sales for quick consumption with a minimum of trouble have produced a demand for wine that can be served at tables, immediately and undecanted. It cannot be denied that these light beverages are, as a rule, much more pleasant to drink when they are young and fresh than when they have acquired a mawkish bottle-taste, or as more often happens, have developed an obvious but elusive deposit that may cloud the wine and vitiate its flavours.

"The fact remains, however, that the slogans of the 'quick turnover,' the nimble sixpence, make hay, and *carpe diem* have or should have no place in the aesthetic domain of any art, and certainly not in what Mr. André Simon has rightfully called the 'Art of Wine.' I cannot but feel convinced that my Bordeaux friends, not lacking in human wisdom, must realize that Claret, the wine that has won for them a warm place in the hearts of wine lovers, will for ages to come maintain them in that secure and well-merited haven."

Another quote from Campbell—still relevant today—concerns the high taxation and high price of wines: "The connoisseur does not create an art or make it a luxury, but he keeps the cultural fit alive, and, though he himself indulges in the best his means permit and his taste allows, he encourages, by his example and precept, a wider interest in the particular branch of art which appeals to him. So it is with wine." This has been my goal during my many years of studying, educating, and lecturing on wine.

My Diaries

Between 1974—the time I started seriously collecting wine—and 1977, all the wines I tasted were entered in my Cellar Books. From 1977 onward, I have maintained a system of Diaries that include various tastings, important events, and trips to the wine-producing regions of the world, interspersed with historical events. In parallel, I have maintained Cellar Books that contain entries about wines tasted at home from my own cellar. This book is comprised of selected notes from my Diaries and Cellar Books.

Over the years, there has been an evolution in my style of writing and in my experience with wines. There has been one constant, though—my desire to learn about and to discover new wines. I have also tried to do my best as a consumer in our part of the world—to bring to the fore the fact that we have had liquor monopolies for so many decades in Canada—without input from and access to free enterprise—with anonymous bureaucrats determining which wines will be offered to the public.

My Friendship with Harry Waugh

Harry Waugh, my dear old friend and first wine mentor—whose wine diaries I read avidly in my early years of wine appreciation—celebrated his 95th birthday in June 1999. Harry once told me how fortunate he was to have met so many charming people who share his passion for wine. He maintains that people who are interested in, and who collect wines, are generous, kind, and friendly.

I have always admired Harry's ability to taste wines and assess them in their youth, and to predict their ageing potential—and ultimately, their future quality when they have reached their peak. This is a gift one cannot develop. One can develop expertise, but one must have the natural ability to taste wines blind. Many of today's leading and most prominent wine connoisseurs and wine authors do not have this gift. They may use technical or flowery terms, in very professional English or French or German, but they do not have the ability to taste young wines blind and truly predict their future potential and quality—let alone identify the varietal, vintage, region, and producer. Harry is one of the few people who had this ability when he was in his prime.

Wine Collectors

Where I disagree with Harry is in his belief that all wine collectors are kind and generous people. I agree with him in general that, yes indeed, I have met many kind and interesting people with a *joie de vie* and a generosity of spirit— after all, wine is meant to be shared with fellow wine lovers—but unfortunately, I have also met many wine collectors who are anything but kind and generous.

Collectors who have recently acquired the taste for fine wines or the wealth to acquire them know little about wine or its history, and have very little background or understanding of how wine is made and how it should taste. They use wine as one would use a fancy car or a 12-bedroom house or any other luxury object—in other words, they show it off, blindly following the "score" numbers affixed to wines by the "super wine writers" of today. For such people, if and when they open a fine bottle, it is to impress others—not necessarily to enjoy or to share. There are also many (too many!) speculators out there with no passionate attachment to wine. Even among the "well established" wine experts and collectors, I have encountered a great deal of wine snobbery and inflated egos.

A Quarter of a Century of Wine Tasting

In these volumes, which span a quarter of a century of wine experiences, the reader will note that sometimes I have rated the wines—and sometimes not. Most wines tasted at organized tastings were rated, but wines tasted individually or at friends' homes were not. Occasionally, however, I have indicated a score for extraordinary wines.

My most extensive experience has been with the wines of France in general—and of Bordeaux, in particular. I have tasted most of the great châteaux of Bordeaux, going back to the early part of this century, and several dozen going back to the mid- or even early 19th century; I have had the opportunity, over the years, to assess the style and the consistency, or lack thereof, of most châteaux. This is also true of other wine-producing regions of the world, notably Burgundy (both whites and reds), California Cabernets, and Chardonnays, Champagne, Piedmont, Vintage Port, et cetera.

I trust that the reader will enjoy this book—and that my passion and my experiences will add to the reader's knowledge and appreciation of the great world of wines.

Albert Givton
Vancouver, Canada
Summer 1999

The Author's Wine Titles, Awards, and Achievements

- Member, Marin County Branch of IW&FS, since 1985
- Maître, Commanderie de Bordeaux à Vancouver, 1988-1997
- Founder and Chairman, Le Tastevin Wine Club, 1976-1996
- Founding Member and Cellarmaster, Vancouver Chapter, Confrérie des Chevaliers du Tastevin
- Founding Member, Vancouver Branch of IW&FS
- Founding Council Member, Chevaliers des Vins de France
- Conseiller du Vin de Bordeaux, 1993
- Chevalier de l'Ordre du Mérite Agricole, 1991
- Cellarmaster, Chaîne des Rôtisseurs, 1980-1984
- Organizer and speaker at numerous charity wine auctions, wine festivals, and rare wine tastings

DIARIES 1-19

Diary 1

February 4, 1980

Tasting of 1974 California Cabernet Sauvignons at Sid Cross's. An excellent vintage.

1. Mount Eden, Santa Clara:

Darkest of flight. Big, sweet nose. Lots of tannin, high acidity, high alcohol; massive. Hard to judge at this stage. Needs time. (15)

2. Mount Veeder Vineyards:

Dark; open, herbaceous nose. High tannin, medium body, on dry side. Although I liked it best, I changed my mind. A bit short and dry, but still good. Lacks extract for such a fine vintage. May improve in three to five years. (16)

3. Stag's Leap, Napa Valley:

Dark; lovely, stemmy, spicy nose; fruity flavours. Well balanced. Not too high tannin. Enjoyable now, but a fine future ahead. (17)

4. Mayacamas, Napa Mountain:

Dark, sweet, fruity nose; still closed. Packed with tannin, still very closed. Hard to judge. (14) The low score is a bit unfair. This is a big, chunky wine that needs many years to evolve. I am certain that in a few years, this will be very good.

5. Robert Mondavi "Reserve," Napa Valley:

Very dark. Lovely, big, open, herbaceous, spicy nose. Tiny bit of volatile acidity on nose. Lots of tannin, good fruit, medium body. Very fine. Needs time. (17)

6. Arroyo, Sonoma Valley:

Very dark. Open, green, sweet nose. High tannin, good acid-fruit balance. Big wine. Lovely aftertaste, but lacks complexity. (15)

7. Beaulieu Vineyards Georges de Latour "Private Reserve," Napa Valley:

Dark. Closed nose, slowly opened up a bit into a lovely, sweet nose. Hint of vanilla and American oak. Very sweet on palate; spicy, big wine. Some tannin. Warm, rich wine. (16.5)

8. Robert Mondavi (Regular), Napa Valley:

Lightest, most elegant wine of flight; clean, fruity nose. Lovely flavour, some tannin, fruity, good aftertaste. Most approachable. (16.5)

9. Sterling "Reserve," Napa Valley:

Dark. Sweet, Port-like nose. Loaded with tannin, very closed. A very substantial wine with great potential. Uncanny resemblance to Château Ducru-Beaucaillou 1970 when it was a baby. (17.5)

The group ratings

All the wines were big, massive, dark, closed, and hard to judge. The worst was still good. This is an excellent vintage. One to buy.

#1: sixth; #2: ninth; #3: seventh; #4: eighth #5: second; #6: fifth; #7: first; #8: fourth; #9: third. I am convinced that this order of preference will change once the wines evolve and develop more personality and character. A fine assessment tasting.

May 27, 1980

Heubelein pre-auction tasting, in San Francisco.

1949 Château Latour:

Dried out, big, hard, murky. A poor sample.

1955 Château Margaux:

Good, deep colour for a 25-year-old wine. Fruity, well balanced. Nice fruit and aftertaste. Elegant. Lots of class here, but soft and evolved. Most 1955s are, by now.

1947 Château Lafite:

Medium-pale colour. Aged nose. Dried out, yet some delicate flavours and complexity. Surprisingly evolved.

1945 Château Latour:

Fruity, sweet nose; medium colour, lots of tannin, almost dried out. Tired. This is a pity, because this should be an extraordinary wine. Poor storage?

1943 Château Latour:

Not unlike the 1945, but a little lighter. Hard, some sweetness, old flavour. Good, Cabernet, cedary nose. Soft fruit, but tight finish. Best on nose.

1924 Château Leoville-Lascases, in magnum:

Lovely nose, fruity, holding well. Some tannin, slightly acidic. Nice fruit; soft, round. Has held extremely well—thanks obviously to the fact that it was a magnum.

1924 Château Latour:

Dark colour. Good, chocolate-sugar and cedar on nose. Holding very well. A bit dry, some tannin. Very well "put together." Very good.

1905 Château Gruaud-Larose:

Not too much on nose. Medium-light colour. Quite dry and watery, but drinkable. Not too much complexity. Well past its prime.

1870 Lafite, "Ten Boek" Collection:

Low shoulder-fill, long cork. Good, sweet, delicate nose. Orangy-brick colour. Dry and a bit thin, but still had the delicate bouquet of Lafite. Round, soft, elegant, with hint of the depth that this wine must have had 50 years ago. This is my first (and hopefully not last) experience with this legendary vintage.

1966 BEAULIEU VINEYARDS GEORGES DE LATOUR "PRIVATE RESERVE" CABERNET SAUVIGNON, NAPA VALLEY:

Lovely, dark colour. Good Cabernet Sauvignon characteristics. Ready, a bit thin, high acidity. Good fruit, vanilla, and American oak.

1973 LE MONTRACHET, BOUCHARD PÈRE ET FILS:

Butterscotch nose and flavour. A bit flat, but delicate. High acidity, a bit low in fruit; "watered down." Should have been better.

1959 CHÂTEAU MARGAUX:

Medium colour, a bit thin, woody. Hard to judge. I got some leftover from another participant as there was none left to taste.

The place was a zoo, with hundreds of people mingling around, going from table to table to taste the wines. I did not stay for the auction itself, which was held later that afternoon.

June 1980

Château l'Arrosée tasting.

Organized by Dr. Allan Tobe, who is an allergist, but who also owns a wine agency representing, among others, Château l'Arrosée in St. Emilion. Allan is also the founder and the present Maître of the Commanderie de Bordeaux in Vancouver.

1961:

Darkest. Big, closed, sweet nose. Rich flavour and body. A bit too high in acidity; excellent concentration and weight. Lovely bouquet. A sleeper, even at 18 years of age. (18)

1962:

Medium-light. Open, pleasant nose. A bit chaptalized, but delicate. Starting to dry out, but pleasant. Tasted well. (15)

1966:

Dark. Sweet, vanilla nose. Big and austere. Very well balanced. I preferred it to the 1961. It will last for a long time. Good concentration of fruit. Serious wine. (18.5)

L'Arrosée has a high proportion of Cabernet Sauvignon in the blend. This is unusual for a St. Emilion.

1967:

Medium light, palest of flight. Delicate nose, a bit grassy. A bit watery, high acidity. Short on palate. Needs drinking. (13.5)

1970:

Very dark. Just behind the 1961 in intensity. Closed nose; big, herbaceous, St. Emilion style. Still backward, but will make an excellent bottle. Well balanced. Later, opened and became velvety. (17.5)

1971:

Dark colour. Very weedy, big nose. Peppery. Monterey Peninsula style. A bit watery and off balance. (14)

Château l'Arrosée is made from two-thirds Cabernet Sauvignon and Cabernet Franc, and one-third Merlot. All six wines were opened and decanted at the same time, one hour before the tasting.

Later, at the same tasting

1975 BELLE GRAVE, PAUILLAC:

Simple, no complexity, but has some depth and fruit. (13)

1975 BEAULIEU VINEYARDS GEORGES DE LATOUR "PRIVATE RESERVE" NAPA CABERNET SAUVIGNON:

Very deep colour. Sweet, coconut nose. Not as big and classic as the 1974, but good, nevertheless. More forward. (16)

July 1980

Tasting of Château St. Jean Single Vineyard Chardonnays, of the 1977 and 1978 vintages.

1. 1978 "MCRAE":

Light gold. Moderate, green nose. Some sweetness. High acidity, a bit harsh at this stage. Clean and crisp; powerful. (15)

2. 1977 "LES PIERRES":

Closed nose, some sweetness. Big, flavourful wine, but not very complex. Throws itself at you. Good extract; dull, short finish. (14.5)

3. 1978 "ROBERT YOUNG":

Lovely, open nose; its lemony-greenness is characteristic of Château St. Jean. A rich middle. Good aftertaste and flavour; sweet, ripe fruit. Very good potential. (17.5)

4. 1977 "WILDWOOD":

Dark gold; lovely, rounded, sweet, relatively mature nose. Not too flavourful, a bit simple. (14.5)

5. 1978 "LES PIERRES":

Bright gold; good, sweet, oaky nose. Not as lemony-green as some. High acidity, big wine, high alcohol. (16.5)

6. 1978 "HUNTER":

Dark gold. Round, sweet, oaky nose. Not too fresh-smelling. Lovely flavour, intense, round, full. Very good. Surprisingly evolved for such a young wine. (16)

7. 1978 "BELLE TERRE":

Light colour; elegant, expansive nose. Very flavourful, excellent. Round, fruity, good balance. An impressive bottle. (17)

8. 1978 "WILDWOOD":

Rich, fruity nose; sweet, oaky, but a bit closed. Flavourful wine. Intense aftertaste. (17)

9. 1977 "ROBERT YOUNG":

Darkish colour. Big, clean, crisp nose. As lovely as #8, but even more impressive. Lots of substance, good balance, long aftertaste. (17.5)

10. 1977 "MCRAE":

Sweet, almost toasty nose; not very open. Quite closed, actually. Simple, not much complexity. A bit harsh. (15)

All above wines seem immature. They need more time, but this tasting is giving a rough indication of their potential and stage of development. The "Robert Young" 1978 is the overall favourite.

August 1980

Dinner at a friend's home.

1966 POL ROGER CHARDONNAY:

Rich nose. Still quite fizzy, creamy, elegant. Very good.

HEITZ CELLARS CHARDONNAYS, NAPA VALLEY, LOT Z-21 (1972), LOT Z-32 (1973), AND LOT Z-41 (1974):

Comparative tasting of three Chardonnays. They were typically California, and had something in common. Very similar, yet in different stages of development.

The 1972 was the driest; still-pleasant nose, but a bit short and dry.

The 1973 had the most complex and elegant nose, but a bit "hidden" (closed) and tight at this stage.

The 1974 was the most typical California Chardonnay. At its prime. My favourite, although in retrospect, the 1973 had a bit more class. Actually, I feel that given an extra two to four years of bottle-age, the 1973 (Lot Z-32) will be a very fine wine.

CHÂTEAU L'EGLISE-CLINET 1961:

Spicy bouquet, some iron. Very intense, dark colour. Lovely flavour and aftertaste. Lacking a bit in complexity. Very good, though, with the ripeness of that fine vintage.

August 16, 1980

First Dinner at home, of the "Group of Ten."

The Levines, the Sid Crosses, the Dr. Allan Tobe, the Ken Crosses, and Carol and me. Each couple brought a course and one bottle of wine—and we shared three special bottles bought for our group at Draper and Esquin's, in San Francisco.

CHAMPAGNE KRUG N/V BRUT:

Lovely, toasty, big nose. Tiny bubbles. Purchased in 1975. A bit acidic at finish, but holding well. Actually, the acidity gives this wine its longevity.

1972 MAYACAMAS CHARDONNAY

AND

1972 STERLING CHARDONNAY:

The Mayacamas was more buttery; more California in its bouquet. Good fruit, well balanced, a bit sweeter.

The Sterling had higher acidity, was lighter, and had a shorter finish. Both very good, with the Mayacamas having the upper hand. Both lasted very well.

MONTRACHET "MARQUIS DE LAGUICHE" 1969, JOSEPH DROUHIN:

Complex, big, toasty nose. Real aristocratic bouquet. Good flavour. A bit short aftertaste, but good fruit and acidity. Really fine.

CHÂTEAU TROTANOY 1964

AND

CHÂTEAU PETRUS 1955:

The Trotanoy was opened a bit too early (two and one-half hours,) but showed better than the Petrus (which cost US$150!) Rich, ripe fruit, some tannin. Good, fruity nose; a bit less intense than the Petrus, which was more elegant on nose and more complex.

After 30 minutes in the glass, however, the Petrus thinned out. A bit of a short finish; a bit light for a great wine from a good year. I thought that it would hold and show better. At first, lovely, complex delicate nose. For the price and the fame, a bit disappointing. The Petrus was also quite a bit lighter in colour than the Trotanoy, and finished a bit drier, too.

CHÂTEAU CHEVAL-BLANC 1947, CHÂTEAU-BOTTLED:

The king of the evening. Port-like nose; lovely, deep colour. Cork disintegrated. Most of the sediment was crusted, and I decanted it carefully! Sweetish, rich wine; full, perfectly balanced, and intense. High alcohol, lingering aftertaste. The greatest Cheval-Blanc this century (to date). I heard and read so much about this wine, and I wasn't disappointed at all. It cost us a small fortune (US$300!) Definitely one of the greatest experiences in winetasting, as far as I'm concerned. Maybe lacks a bit in complexity as compared to a Haut-Médoc, but nevertheless a perfect wine.

CHÂTEAU CLIMENS 1949:

Dark-gold colour; lovely, elegant nose. Not too sweet, but perfectly balanced. Clean, nice acidity. For a 31-year-old Barsac, this is the finest I've tasted to date. Lovely aftertaste. Unanimously great. Cost: US$50 for that bottle.

What an experience this evening has been!

September 4, 1980

Commanderie de Bordeaux tasting of Château Bouscaut, Graves, at "La Belle Auberge" restaurant, in Ladner, BC.

1923, IN MAGNUM:

Very light colour, brownish. Oxidized nose. Quite acidic. Flat, but drinkable. Sweet, woody. Started to fall apart after ten minutes. An experience. (14)

1964:

Surprisingly dark colour (close to 1975), and quite young-looking. Clean, toasty nose. Not too herbaceous. Medium light-bodied. A bit acidic. Ready. A bit flat. Not too much on nose. (13.5)

1966:

(I contributed this bottle.) Very dark colour. Good, earthy, gravelly nose. Good flavour. Has middle and good aftertaste. Good fruit. Unfortunately, it fell apart and dried out after 15 minutes in glass. (14)

1967:

Quite dark for a 1967. High acidity; a bit thin, but sound. Not too much fruit. Some tannin. Dull, mediocre nose. Opened up and improved after a while. Drink up. (13.5)

1969:

Watery, dull nose. Medium-brownish colour. Flat, lean. High acidity. Well past its prime—if it ever had one. (12)

1970:

Tight, closed nose, vegetal, stemmy. Very high acidity. Dark colour. Too dry and hard. May improve with age. (14)

1971:

Medium-dark colour. Dull, unyielding nose. Better flavour and more fruit than the 1970. Some tannin. (14.5)

1973:

Medium colour, orange tinge. Good nose. Easy to drink. Open, gravelly flavour and a bit too acidic. Good for a 1973. (13)

1974:

Colour similar to the 1975. Closed nose. Very thin, short. (10)

1975:

Medium-dark colour, a touch of brown. Good fruit. Solid backbone typical of the vintage, but backed by enough fruit. I liked it best. (16)

1976:

Light, watery, vegetal, thin, acidic, pale colour. Ordinary. (11)

Overall impressions

Hard, acidic, tannic wines that are too dry, lacking charm, class, or complexity. It seems that this property is doing a better job with its white wine than with the red. Apparently, they don't have the right soil required to produce fine red Graves at Bouscaut.

September 8 to October 31, 1980

Two-month trip to the Vineyards of France. We took our kids along: Michael, age five, and Orly, two-and-a-half.

September 8, 1980

Problems in the morning with the brand new, leased Renault 18TS.

Radiator perforated. Steaming! Took them two and one-half hours to fix it. Proceeded to Champagne. Stayed at Le Champagne in downtown Epernay. Nice modern little hotel. Pleasant and comfortable.

Grapes look really tiny. They expect the vintage to start around October 10 to 15. Very late. It has been a fairly rainy and cool summer this year. Does not augur well.

September 11, 1980

We had a little sunshine today. In the afternoon, we visited Reims, the cathedral, and the downtown area.

Then we walked through Pinot Noir-planted vineyards near our hotel in Champillon. Chalky soil; many shrunken and tiny grapes. Vintage not expected before October 10.

In the morning

Visit with Mr. de Bellinex at Roederer.

Moira Fitzpatrick and Bud Kanke from Vancouver were there and we visited the chais together. Tasted their Vintage Brut 1975. Delicate and a bit sweet for a Brut. Apparently, this is a characteristic of Roederer. They did not know that at Pol Roger, they pick Pinot Noir at night for their Rosé so the grapes are cool and therefore will not release red pigments too fast during fermentation.

Currently, Roederer are selling the 1976 vintage in France and the 1975 in North America. I spoke to their oenologist. He said that they were the only house to declare the 1974 and they think very highly of it. As for the 1975 and 1976 vintages: light, elegant; will mature early. They do not use any Pinot Meunier and think it is too low in quality. They own 80% of the grapes, a very high proportion. The rest is purchased. Approximately 60% Chardonnay in their blends, therefore they make elegant Champagnes.

They actually do add some crystal in their bottles of "Cristal" to strengthen the bottles (flat bottom, at 15 pounds pressure). They do not feel threatened by California sparkling wines, but said that Alsace (which produces sparkling wines) definitely feels threatened by the "new and improved" quality of California Rieslings.

At Roederer, they use a computerized system of putting the exact amount of liqueur and yeast in the wine. They also use, in the vineyards, a Japanese product that can fight mildew; therefore late vintages are not as dangerous as they used to be. André Rouzeau retired in July, but drops by once in a while.

Later that day

We visited Christian Pol Roger.

Tasted several fine Champagnes. Christian is a nice man and a generous host.

September 12, 1980

Drove to Colmar.

Out of Reims to Metz, it was raining, then it turned sunny and warm. Péage was $20! And gas (super) is $4.25 per gallon! What are we complaining about in Canada?

Drove through the "route des vins" into Colmar; through lovely vineyards and small towns and villages. Checked into Park hotel: noisy, with a crummy bed and a rather nasty, unintelligent, frustrated female receptionist. Drove 445 kilometres today. Phoned and made an appointment to see Jean ("Johnny") Hugel tomorrow.

September 13, 1980

Visit at Hugel's.

We all drove to Riquewihr. Bought two bottles of Dopff & Irion Late Harvest 1976: one Gewürztraminer and one Riesling. Met "Johnny" (Jean) Hugel and we went on a two-hour tour of the winery. Visited the whole process. The 1979 was a large but good vintage. Best since 1976, but not nearly as great. No Late Harvest or Grains Nobles in 1979.

About the 1980 vintage

Early flowering, frost almost disastrous. It will be late into October before they harvest. Quantity will be small. Quality? Too early to tell, but not very promising. Soon, the Réserve Personnelle 1979 Riesling will be listed in Vancouver. For botrytis, they need fog in the morning and sun in the afternoon, accompanied by a warm wind—same as in Sauternes.

Tasted various 1978s and 1979s, notably Rieslings and Gewürztraminers "Réserve Personnelle"—but I lost the tasting sheet and comments.

At the end of the tasting, he brought up one of his greatest wines.

1976 RIESLING "SÉLECTION DE GRAINS NOBLES":

Beerenauslese style. Really great. Luscious, ripe fruit; exotic on both nose and palate. Very young, of course, but this will be great. Must get some!

We discussed quality control, regulations, BCLDB, etc. He is probably coming to Vancouver in May 1981.

They own 100% of their vineyards and no purchased juice comes into their winery, only whole grapes. They use wooden barrels because of a tartrate crust that sets all around and coats the inside of the barrels. In stainless steel and glass (cement), the tartrates rot after two to three weeks; while in wood, tartrates create a crust over many (80 to 100) years! They export wines to 112 countries.

September 14, 1980

Today we drove by a few lovely small towns ("route des vins") including Trois-Epis, Roufach, Château d'Issanbourg, etc.

In the evening, we went to the Auberge de l'Ill, in Illhausern. We walked around the town: barns, lovely flowers, with tobacco leaves hanging to dry everywhere. Before dinner, we walked around the river Ill.

Dinner at the Michelin three-star restaurant "Auberge de l'Ill."

Tasted the following wines.

RIESLING "LES MURAILLES" 1978, DOPFF ET IRION, IN HALF-BOTTLE:

Good, clean wine. Spicy, round, good, crisp fruit.

1978 CHINON "VIEILLES VIGNES," CHARLES JOGUET, LOIRE:

Made from Cabernet Franc grapes. Young, youthful, yet solid. Very good, fruity wine. Long, rich, and spicy.

Incredible brioche with fresh goose liver. Carol had salmon in "mille feuilles" dough and heavenly sauce, superb slice of mixed fish terrine in a lovely sauce. I had tenderloin of baby deer (chevreuil). Very good.

Besides a lovely dessert dish (various little cakes of great quality), we had fresh strawberries and raspberries au gratin with sabayon sauce and ice cream. Looked and tasted like a work of art. Same as at "Boyer," but Boyer's was a bit better. Really great experience, pleasant atmosphere, and very interesting marble washroom and washbasins.

September 15, 1980

Departed for Lyon.

The trip to Alsace was a success and the weather was great. Pleasant trip to Lyon on highway. Cannot get over the price of gas in France. Mrs. Lefèvre's house turned out to be a pleasant surprise. Nice suite and lovely garden. She is the lady from whom we are renting two furnished rooms for a month. She lives near the centre of Lyon.

September 16, 1980

Menashe arrived from Israel, as planned.

He spent one night with us, then he moved to the Val de Sâone hotel next door.

September 17, 1980

Menashe and I visited Lyon, including Vieux Lyon, where we had a fine lunch.

In the evening, we all went out together for dinner to an Italian restaurant.

September 18, 1980

Made a reservation at "Paul Bocuse" for Sunday, September 21.

Lovely day. We left the kids all day with the landlady for the first time (9 a.m. to 5 p.m.), and went to visit the Beaujolais. The Gamay grape looks quite decent; quantity is below average, but not the catastrophe of Champagne or Alsace. We tasted and bought a few bottles of Chenas, Moulin-à-Vent, and Fleurie (all 1979). 1979 seems to be very similar in style to 1978, but a bit softer and richer.

We all had a lovely lunch at "Chez Robin," in Chenas.

Fixed menu with a bottle of 1978 Chenas and a half-bottle of 1976 Moulin-à-Vent. Both excellent. Food was plentiful. A very good atmosphere and the view was just perfect; so was the weather.

Menashe really seemed to enjoy himself. We all had poulet de Bresse, lovely duck liver pâté, excellent cheeses, and beautiful fresh fruit for dessert. In the evening, we had a light dinner in the Vieux Lyon.

September 20, 1980

Left the kids with Mme. Lefèvre, and the three of us went to Grenoble, up in the cablecars, and drove all day through the French Alps. Lovely view and countryside.

In the evening
We ate at Mme. Lefèvre's, and opened the Champagne Pol Roger "Réserve" 1975 that Christian Pol Roger had given me when we visited him in Champagne.

CHAMPAGNE POL ROGER "RÉSERVE" 1975:

Excellent bottle. Rich, round; good yeast, ripe fruit, with the good acidity and backbone typical of the 1975s.

September 21, 1980

Dinner at "Paul Bocuse."

Very fancy, lovely setting. Excellent food (we all had fixed menus); a lovely bottle of 1979 Pouilly-Fuissé; and a disappointing bottle of 1961 Hermitage "La Chapelle" (Jaboulet), which I sent back (very dark, pruny colour, corked smell, thin and acidy). Instead, we had a pleasant Chambolle-Musigny 1971 (Joseph Drouhin). Atmosphere was a bit strict. Our waiter did not seem to give a damn (bad attitude, and dirty ashtrays as coasters for the water carafe). Also, very expensive. Food not any better than at "Boyer" or "Auberge de l'Il," but prices were 30% to 40% higher.

Bocuse definitely thinks that he is a "god." His picture hangs everywhere and his name is on every item. Even the rolls of toilet paper in the washrooms have the letter "B" printed on them!

About the bottle of 1961 Hermitage "La Chapelle" that I sent back

I had just tasted a great bottle of that wine for lunch with Gerard Jaboulet, yet the waiter at "Bocuse" had the temerity of arguing with me that his oxidized bottle of 1961 "La Chapelle" was "une excellente bouteille en bon état." I actually requested that he bring me another bottle, but he refused, saying that "les autres bouteilles sont toutes les mêmes!" I think that Bocuse has a "slight" problem with his staff.

Rained all day. Went to the Musée de l'Automobile where we had a clash with some nasty French clerks who wanted to kick us out. We had arrived at 3:40 p.m., purchased our tickets, walked in, only to be told that they close at 4:00 p.m. and that we had to leave. Menashe and Carol wanted to leave, but as I am almost as stubborn as the French, I proceeded to visit the museum. They did not dare kick us out. Then on to the cathedral by tram, overlooking Lyon.

September 22, 1980

Last night, we had the most fantastic thunderstorm I have ever heard.

Menashe thought that we were "under attack." We all went to the airport and, as usual, it was a "sad" send-off to see Menashe fly back to Israel.

September 24, 1980

Morning visit to Maison Drouhin in Beaune.

Met Robert Drouhin and tasted the following wines.

1979 La Forêt-Mâcon Villages Blanc:

Good, crisp, fresh, young fruit. Pleasant commercial wine.

1978 Puligny-Montrachet Premier Cru "Folatières":

Toasty, lovely nose. Good acidity, good fruit. Needs two to three years of bottle-age, but already showing very well. Excellent backbone and extract.

1978 Beaune "Clos des Mouches" Blanc:

A bit more austere and sweeter, but lacks the youth of the "Folatières." Quite serious. Tight at this stage. Good fruit extract. Needs three to four years, or more.

1978 Chorey-lès-Beaune Rouge:

Simple, pleasant. Chorey is the only Appellation Contrôlée with vineyards on the "wrong side of the road." Nice, clean fruit. Almost ready.

1977 Beaune "Clos des Mouches" Rouge:

Surprisingly good for the vintage. Clean, spicy nose. Complex and pleasant. Needs one to two years. Well made. Fermented at low temperature of 27° to 28° C for 28 to 30 days. Only the healthiest grapes were used. Fine effort.

1976 Chambolle-Musigny:

Elegant, but not great. A bit too baked and clumsy; a problem with many 1976s. Needs more time. Lacks the elegance of Chambolle.

Had an interesting talk with their young technical manager, Jean-Paul Cropsal, and later talked with sales director Gerald Uhlen. They are represented in Canada by Schenley's. They feel, overall, that 1978 is better than 1979, but 1976 is the best. I disagree. Surely 1978 red Burgundies are better balanced than the 1976s.

Afternoon visit to Doudet-Naudin.

Met Yves Doudet-Naudin and gave him a bottle of 1976 Beaulieu Vineyards Pinot Noir "Reserve." He gave me a bottle of his 1961 Corton. Pleasant man. By the end of the visit, he'd had a bit too much to drink, and when he walked us to our car, he proceeded to show us how British Sergeant-Majors salute! His 80-year-old father still supervises the business. Yves is married and has a six-year-old daughter. Tasted his 1978 whites, Savigny-lès-Beaune and Meursault, both in casks and both disappointing. They were flat and tasteless. They do not do business at all with North America, except for ordinary table wines (to Québec).

Tasted the following red wines.

1978 Savigny-lès-Beaune:

Pleasant, good body. Spicy Pinot Noir. Almost ready, yet it has been in bottle for only a few months.

1978 Chambolle-Musigny:

Elegant, ripe berries; good balance. Good fruit extract. Still very youthful. Drink around 1982.

1978 Gevrey-Chambertin:

Big, robust, a bit rustic. Good potential. We are fortunate to be able to taste 1978s now (just bottled); the best vintage for red Burgundies since 1971.

1978 Corton:

Big, massive wine. Impressive. My idea of how a red Burgundy should be made. Lots of fruit extract, backed by solid tannins. A bit rustic, though.

Doudet-Naudin thinks that his wines need ten to 20 years to reach their peak. He does not use egg whites at all. Uses old casks, leaves stems in, clears rot by submerging grapes in water. According to Yves, they throw everything in the vats, including red spiders!

He also ships wines under the label of "Albert Broulot" and is interested in contacts in BC.

About the 1980 vintage

If the weather stays sunny, they may produce decent wines in Burgundy. Picking will start on October 12.

September 25, 1980

Morning visit to Maison Jaffelin.

Went to see Mr. Barriaux at Jaffelin at 10:20 a.m.; he made us wait until 11:00 a.m. Then we decided to leave without meeting him. He had a very disappointing attitude. His secretary told us to "go for a walk" for a few minutes!

Jaffelin's wines are not that good that they can afford to treat visitors—who come from afar, and make appointments to visit them—in this manner. Even if their wines were great—or good, at least—this kind of attitude would be bad for their image.

Drove instead around the vineyards of Puligny, Chassagne, and Montrachet, then had lunch at a restaurant, in Meursault.

Afternoon visit to Pierre Ponnelle.

We met Terry Price, who is Welsh and manages the business. Very friendly. We tasted a lovely, big, full 1978 Corton-Charlemagne (Ponnelle). Excellent quality. I also bought a few bottles of good wine to drink while we are in Lyon, including some fine 1964s. He then introduced us to their cellarmaster, Monsieur Jean-Pierre Escano, who took us to their various cellars where we tasted a range of wines in barrel (1978 and 1979) of excellent quality. Many were from Hospices auctions.

WHITES

1978 PERNAND-VERGELESSES, FROM CASK:

Clean, crisp, well rounded. Nice fruit, hint of oak, good extract.

1978 AUXEY-DURESSES, FROM CASK:

Lovely, full, very good. Bigger, richer than the above; requiring an extra two to three years of bottle-age.

1978 MEURSAULT-CHARMES, FROM CASK:

Great elegance and intensity on both nose and palate. Still very youthful, but already displaying great intensity, oak, almonds, and ripe fruit.

1978 MEURSAULT, FROM CASK:

Clean, simple; good depth. Overshadowed, however, by the "Charmes."

1978 PULIGNY-MONTRACHET, FROM CASK:

Crisp, clean, fresh fruit. Very good extract. Leaner, tighter than the Meursaults. Fine effort for a simple Village wine.

All the whites are well balanced and intense, with lovely fruit; will last a long time. Very well made. Mr. Escano thought that the 1978 whites will be even better than the 1976s (especially Chablis). He prefers the 1978 reds over the 1976s (more complete), and compared the 1979s to the 1973s (softer, rounder, and more forward).

REDS

1978 MONTHÉLIE

AND

1978 VOLNAY, BOTH FROM CASK:

Both are good. Quite tannic. Rich, round; good backbone and tannins. They will fine them later, before shipping. What a pity, because this robs the wines of their depth and character.

1978 POMMARD, FROM CASK:

Lovely and big. Really good. He thinks that a good Pommard should be ready in ten to 15 years. Solid, full, serious. Needs five to seven years. Doesn't have the class of a Premier Cru, though.

1979 VOLNAY

AND

1979 BEAUNE, BOTH HOSPICES DE BEAUNE, BOTH FROM CASK:

Both have a lovely nose, a bit toasty-spicy. Dark colour. Very good fruit. Very fine potential.

CORTON 1978, FROM CASK:

A winner. Really great; full, lively, and complex. Why don't these wines show well at home in bottles? Maybe because they are overfiltered?

Then, we tasted these wines.

1979 NUITS-ST.-GEORGES VILLAGES,

1979 NUITS-ST.-GEORGES PREMIER CRU "LES PORRETS,"

AND

1979 NUITS-ST.-GEORGES PREMIER CRU "LES ST. GEORGES":

All three were fabulous; the last one was really lovely. All were Hospices purchases. Very little was made, only two casks of each.

This was a very pleasant and informative visit.

September 26, 1980

Visit with Paul Bouchard and his assistant Simon Alper of Bouchard Aîné et Fils.

Lasted from 10:30 a.m. until 4:00 p.m., including a fabulous lunch at the "Auberge" in Beaune, where we tasted a lovely Mercurey 1975 Blanc, a Fixin Tasteviné 1973 (which was surprisingly full), and a 1971 Chambertin "Clos de Bèze" (which was excellent).

Before lunch
We tasted several wines from casks. Frankly, I was not overimpressed. The less said about these wines, the better. Simon offered me to taste a lovely bottle marked "AU-1," which is a 1963 Meursault-Genevrières. It was lovely, with an intense nose. A bit dry, but really great, with a lovely, clean, dark-gold colour. What a success for 1963!

After lunch
We tried a nutty tasting liqueur of very good quality. It was a delicate Amaretto-like liqueur called Prunelle de Bourgogne. We drove back to Beaune at record speed, and in a very good and merry mood. We had a great time.

September 29, 1980

Visit to Maison Jaboulet Aîné et Fils.

Gerard Jaboulet plans to come to Vancouver next year. His agent in Vancouver is Featherstone. Tasted a whole range of wines. Overall, reds are fuller in 1978, but less elegant than in 1979. They have great extract and potential, however. Whites are better in 1979, at least they are more accessible. The 1978s were bottled only a few months ago.

GIGONDAS 1978 AND 1979:

The 1978 is ripe, luscious. Deep colour. Still a bit tannic.

The 1979 is rounder, even fatter at this stage. Spicy, rich, long. Both very good.

TAVEL "L'ESPIÈGLE" 1979:

Quite a deep colour for a Rosé. Fruity, crisp, clean. Nice ripe fruit. Tavel is considered to be the best still-Rosé wine produced in France.

CROZES-HERMITAGE "THALABERT" 1979:

This is the Crozes made entirely from their own grapes. They also produce a "regular" Crozes from purchased grapes. Deep colour. Bigger, spicier, peppery, and riper than both the 1978 and 1979 Gigondas. Lots of extract. Try around 1984 to 1987. Made from 100% Syrah.

CÔTE-RÔTIE "LES JUMELLES" 1979:

Gerard says that it is better in 1979 than in 1978, but we did not taste the 1978 because it is going through an "upset" phase (bottled recently). Approximately 8% white juice added to the blend. "Jumelles" means twins: a blend of Côte Blonde and Côte Brune. A rich, full wine. Still closed, peppery, yet has some elegance. Needs at least seven years to be drinkable.

CORNAS 1979:

Excellent. Masculine, solid, unyielding wine. 100% Syrah. Lots of extract here.

HERMITAGE BLANC "CHEVALIER DE STERIMBERG" 1979:

A blend of Marsanne and Roussanne. Bright-gold colour. Luscious, ripe, exotic fruit. Full, round. Very enjoyable. This wine used to be called "La Chapelle Blanc" before World War II. Caspar de Sterimberg was a knight who, upon returning from the Crusades, became a hermit and settled on the two hills near Tain and planted grapes there. Thus, the name "Hermitage."

HERMITAGE "LA CHAPELLE" 1979:

26 hectolitres per hectare. A good, full wine; but it needs ten years to mature, and is comparable to the 1971, according to Gerard. Spicy, rich, tight. Excellent ripe fruit.

HERMITAGE "LA CHAPELLE" 1978:

A bigger and fuller wine that needs 20 years of bottle-age. Nine hectolitres per hectare! The same as in 1961! A monumental wine. One has to go back to 1961, or even as far back as 1911, to get such quality. Essence of Syrah. Very big, massive. Great extract; luscious fruit. A "new-born genius." Must get some!

Gerard told me that the BC liquor monopoly was offered this wine, replacing the 1974 vintage. They turned it down, asking for more 1974(!) instead, because a new vintage requires a new submission, new code number, etc. There is no limit to bureaucratic stupidity! Gerard had to contact his Hamburg agent to get some 1974 for British Columbia, and sent him, in exchange, some 1978! The liquor monopolies in Canada must be dismantled. They are a disgrace for anyone who cares about wine.

MUSCAT DE BEAUMES-DE-VENISE 1978:

A lovely, fresh, delicate, young wine that does not age well. Sweet, yet not cloying. Good, spicy Muscat flavour.

Then we went back to Gerard's office and tasted the following great wine.

1961 HERMITAGE "LA CHAPELLE":

A sensational wine! Perfection now. Almost 1959 Lafite complexity, but with extra weight and extract—and peppery, too, of course. Layers of complex fruit; ripe, round, very long. A great bottle. Sells at auction for £50 per bottle!

If the 1978s are ever shipped to Vancouver, I must buy some. A most enjoyable visit. Gerard Jaboulet is a very friendly, lively man. He was very generous in opening a bottle of 1961 "La Chapelle."

Afternoon visit to Gerard Chave.

We met the father (Jean-Louis Chave) and son (Gerard), who is the boss now. They make only Hermitage white and red and they think that 1979, overall, was excellent; not as big as 1978, but more complete. Gerard Chave likes California wines and likes salmon fishing. A very small operation. They are sold out of red Hermitage 1978. I ordered five cases of red and five cases of white Hermitage 1979. Both superb wines. They will be shipped next year. Gerard Chave is a soft-spoken, kind, quiet, and very gifted winemaker.

First, we tasted the whites, which are made mostly from Marsanne, and 20% to 25% Roussanne, which is more delicate, but shorter-lived

HERMITAGE BLANC 1979:

Fabulous. Great extract; exotic, rich fruit. Quite fat, long, rich. Great potential. Chave's whites can age well for 20 years, or longer.

HERMITAGE BLANC 1978:

Good, but not as intense as the 1979. Very tight, subdued, unyielding. Needs many years to open up. Hard to judge.

HERMITAGE BLANC 1969:

Deep, golden colour. A lovely, rounded, beautiful wine. Will live for a long time. Exotic, ripe fruit. Mouthfilling. Serious white wine.

Then we tasted the reds.

HERMITAGE ROUGE 1979:

Deep colour and full-bodied. It needs at least ten years of ageing. Rich, peppery; some oak, loads of ripe fruit. Not too tannic for such a young wine, still in cask.

HERMITAGE ROUGE 1978:

A wine that is massive, with lots of tannin. Tight, solid. Great fruit extract. Only 14 hectolitres per hectare. Essence of Syrah. Will be a great wine in 15 or more years. Released at Ffr35 per bottle! A great buy.

HERMITAGE ROUGE 1977:

Elegant, full, lovely wine. Very well made. Good fruit extract in a difficult year. It is in vintages like these that one can separate the men from the boys.

HERMITAGE ROUGE 1975:

Tiglio flavour; elegant and fruity. Very good. Again, a fine effort in a difficult vintage. Ready now, but no rush.

HERMITAGE ROUGE 1969:

Very big, yet full of flavour. Still tannic at 11 years of age. Excellent fruit, even quite ripe. Approachable, but not quite ready.

Gerard is very fond of Vintage Ports. We talked about Quinta do Noval Nacional. The Chaves are very traditional and own vineyards all over Hermitage. They have been involved with wine in the Rhône since the 1490s! Five centuries, and there was always a male to keep the name Chave alive.

At the end of the visit, I mentioned to Gerard that our daughter Orly was born in 1978, and that I would dearly love to acquire a case of his 1978 red Hermitage. He told me that he would ship a case for me to his US agent, Kermit Lynch, in Berkeley. Later, I found out that it was a gift! He did not charge me for it; what a generous present. Gerard shipped this case from his private stock.

September 30, 1980

Visit to Château Grillet.

A lovely, sunny day. Old M. Neiret-Gachet was waiting for us. He opened a bottle of 1978 Château Grillet, which Carol and I drank with cheese and crackers. We walked around the vineyard and ate a few fabulous pears from his pear trees, and some mature 1980 Viognier grapes. All vines are set in "méthode (coupe) Guillot simple." He was reserved, but friendly. He sold me three bottles of Château Grillet 1978 at Ffr65 per bottle. Lovely wine. Elegant. It is ready, yet could use another two years to age. We agreed that I will write to him to place an order for his 1979, of which 500 cases were produced. I ordered five cases.

Afternoon visit to Condrieu.

Visited Georges Vernay in Condrieu. His son Daniel received us. We tasted their Condrieu 1979. It was good, but simple; not enough complexity. He kindly gave me a bottle. In 1978, they produced nine hectolitres per hectare! In 1979, they got 23 hectolitres per hectare. The 1978 is a masterpiece. Essence of Viognier.

Then, he took us on a drive to their vineyards. We also tasted their finest Condrieu from old vines, called "Côteau de Vernon," situated on a nearby hill. Vernay leases this plot from an old lady. This 1979 is a beauty. It is heavy, full, fruity, with great, exotic fruit extract, but lacks the delicacy of Château Grillet. In any event, it was a revelation. Tiny production.

October 2, 1980

Visited the Vineyard of Château Rayas in the morning.

They were pressing the whites (Grenache Blanc) for their Clos Pignan. Mr. Reynaud died in August and his son is taking over. He seems to be in his late 40s or early 50s. We tasted the separate 1979 cépages for Château Rayas (before the blend): Cinsault, Grenache, and Syrah. Then a sample of the 1978 blend. It had a deep colour; was closed, but very good potential.

The surprise was his Côte du Rhône A/C "Château de Fonsalette." The 1976 is shipped presently. It has all the characteristics of a Châteauneuf. It consists of 70% Grenache, 20% Cinsault, and 10% Syrah. His Château Rayas is almost exclusively Grenache. We also tasted some lovely Syrah grapes. They will start to pick their reds next week. Everywhere, 1980 is a late vintage.

October 9, 1980

Left Avalon in the morning, stopped in Beaune.

Bought some more 1964 Côte de Nuits 1964 (Ponnelle) and some Puligny-Montrachet 1966 (Ponnelle) from Terry Price. In the afternoon, we drove through the Côte de Nuits and Aloxe, and tasted some Corton and Chambertin grapes. They were really tiny; some were sweet and some were sour. It is already October 9, and some growers haven't even started picking yet; 1980 will be a difficult vintage.

Terry said that picking is starting in two days because of the poor weather and the grapes are starting to rot in the Mercurey and white Burgundies. In the Côte de Nuits, they will start picking in two to four days and they seem to be faring better than the Côte de Beaune, because of better exposure to the east.

Afternoon visit to Domaine de la Romanée-Conti.

Mr. Noblet looked older, but was still as friendly as ever, and we had an even better time than in 1977. He has had heart problems, and likes salmon fishing. He thinks highly of the 1978s. The 1979s are softer than the 1978s. First we went to the cellar and tasted the following 1979s.

1979 Echézeaux, from cask:

Luscious, intense Pinot Noir. Very fresh, rich, yet already mellow. Hint of oak. Nice, peppery aftertaste. These wines will spend another eight to ten months in oak casks before bottling.

1979 Grands Echézeaux, from cask:

Bigger, more tannic, and more depth than the Echézeaux. Superb fruit. Very dark colour. Lots of class here.

1979 Romanée-St.-Vivant, from cask:

Even bigger and more masculine. More closed, tighter on both nose and palate. Hard to assess. Unyielding at this stage.

1979 Richebourg, from cask:

Lovely bouquet and flavour; elegant and complex. Great class, yet a bit stemmy. They are starting to uproot the vines and replant in Richebourg (after the 1978 vintage).

1979 La Tâche, from cask:

As big as the St. Vivant, but with more style. More depth. Superb ripe raspberries on both nose and palate. A very "individual wine." Will be very good in ten years.

1979 Romanée-Conti, from cask:

A blend of all five. Perfect, complex, noble, great. Very dark, luscious. A mouthful of great Pinot Noir extract—and it will gain even more depth in cask, as will, of course, all of the above.

Then, we went to the second cellar and tasted the following wines from bottle.

1977 Richebourg:

Lovely, intense, complex; big yet elegant wine, considering the year. A bit green (stemmy), but already enjoyable. Fine effort.

1963 Richebourg:

Almost ready. Great, complex. Long-lasting, peppery, fruity aftertaste. Again, a superb effort in a miserable vintage.

1970 Le Montrachet:

Great, intense; best white Burgundy I have ever tasted. Unbelievable! Essence of Chardonnay with fruit, oak, vanilla, acidity, and tannins all in perfect harmony. A masterpiece.

During the harvest and fermentation, Noblet sleeps in a chair, right beside the cuves. That is dedication, and it shows in the wines.

Domaine de la Romanée-Conti's production in 1979

Echézeaux and Grands Echézeaux: 15 hectolitres per hectare.

La Tâche, Richebourg, and Romanée-Conti: ten hectolitres per hectare.

There was very little La Tâche due to hail. New barrels from the Vosges each year. They purchase them for Ffr1,000 and resell them at Ffr700 after one year's use.

We were almost drunk when we left, and desperately had to pee! What a great afternoon. We spent three hours at the Domaine de la Romanée-Conti. Noblet is a very gifted winemaker. We spoke French, as he speaks no English. What a great advantage it is to be fluent in French when visiting Burgundy.

October 10, 1980

Lunch at "Lameloise" in Chagny. Competes with "Auberge de l'Ill" as our favourite three-star restaurant.

It is great all round. Lovely pigeon with fresh pasta, truffles, and duck liver bits. We had a fine bottle of Pol Roger N/V Champagne.

Michel Veniat of Louis Latour was there with their Australian agent, and offered us the following wines to taste.

1971 Corton-Grancey, Latour:

Good, dark colour to rim. Open, herbaceous, yet ripe Pinot Noir on nose. Nice fruit. Still fairly sturdy, but long, clean finish. Needs two extra years of bottle-age. Had this wine travelled, maybe it would have been softer. When tasted last year in Vancouver, it was softer and rounder.

1959 Corton "Bressandes," Latour:

Incredible depth of colour. Lovely nose and flavour. Great chocolaty extract. Big, fine wine.

The 1980 Bordeaux Report from the Australian agent is bad news: rot, rain, and cold. 1979 turning out to be better than 1978 for the reds. Their depth is similar to the 1970s, according to him. The good news is that there is a lot of wine made in Bordeaux in 1979.

Afternoon visit and tasting, at Domaine Louis Latour.

We tasted from the 1979 vintage reds. One year in cask. All wines below will develop more body and tannins, of course, as they spend more time in oak barrels.

1979 ILE DE VERGELESSES:

Elegant, fruity, pleasant. Nice Pinot Noir fruit.

ALOXE-CORTON:

Light colour. Already has lots of tannin. Good fruit; fairly solid.

ALOXE-CORTON "LES CHAILLOTS":

Elegant. Good acidity. Good fruit, too, but less tannic than the above at this stage.

CORTON "VIGNE AU SAINT":

Beautiful balance. Big, already solid, powerful wine. Fairly tannic. Promising. This Grand Cru "lieu dit" belongs wholly to Latour.

BEAUNE "VIGNE FRANCHE":

More elegant than the "Vigne au Saint." Paler colour. Elegant. Nice, complex fruit.

CORTON "POUGETS":

Deep, big, powerful, solid. Already displaying the character of a big Corton. Needs racking and a bit of sulphuring. Lovely flavour.

CORTON "PERRIÈRES":

Elegant, well balanced; the best. Softer at this stage than most Cortons tasted, but has the most class and elegance. Sold in Britain, Germany, etc.

Latour also produces some Corton-Charlemagne Red and Meursault Red, which is sold as Volnay "Santenots."

Old copper cuves with a double bottom are used to encourage fermentation, producing wines with style rather than depth or power.

October 11, 1980

Drove to Mâcon and Fuissé areas.

Picking has started, but a real downpour forced us back to Lyon. Had dinner at home.

CÔTE DE NUITS VILLAGES 1964, PIERRE PONNELLE:

What a lovely bottle of wine. Elegance, class, and finesse. Consistently fine, and only a minor Village wine.

Also had a lovely pear we picked at Château Grillet. It was really fabulous. It has been rainy and cold the last three or four days, a bad sign for the vintage. There is no hope for a large production in Burgundy this year, but at least for a good vintage, as it was a lovely September, but everything is turning bad in the last four or five days: rain, fog, and cold weather.

October 12, 1980

It rained all day. Bad news for the vintage in Burgundy.

We went to the Parc de la Tête d'Or (zoo) with the kids. In two days, it will be goodbye to Lyon, as we proceed across the Massif Central to Bordeaux.

October 13, 1980

Three days ago, I called Maison Mommessin and spoke to old Mr. Mommessin.

We set up an appointment for today, to visit, taste, and have lunch with Isabelle Mommessin and her father. Just as I was asking for directions, I was told by an old lady that Mr. Mommessin passed away on Friday night, just a few hours after we had spoken on the phone!. Indeed, when I got there, Isabelle told me that her father had died. We did not go out for lunch, of course. Mr. Mommessin was a very nice man and a generous host.

Drove back toward Lyon and stopped at "Au Chapon Fin" in Thoisey for lunch.

Fresh goose liver en bloc, lovely turbot filet with white sauce, small crêpes with sugar, and a lovely half-bottle of 1979 Mâcon Blanc.

Later, I visited the Georges Duboeuf vineyard at Romanèche-Thorin.

Tasted the whole range of the 1979s, but I did not write down any notes. The overall impression is that the wines are clean and very well made.

In the evening
We packed and got ready to depart. Good-bye Mme. Lefèvre (Dumb Fève, as the kids called her). She managed to rip us off with an extra Ffr500, but what the heck! We did what we wanted and had a good time.

Later, we found out from the kids that on several occasions during our stay in Lyon, when we went on long day trips to visit the vineyards, Mme. Lefèvre had left the kids alone for the whole day; she went out to do her errands. With kids aged five and two, that was not a very safe thing to do.

It has been raining and cold for three weeks now. Bad news for the vintage.

October 17, 1980

Made a few phone calls and appointments for next week, including Gruaud-Larose, Talbot, Ducru, Palmer, and La Mission. In the afternoon, I went to see the general manager of the Grand Conseil de Bordeaux, and he set up appointments for me at Haut-Brion, Trotanoy, Petrus, and three vineyards in Sauternes. Maybe it will include d'Yquem. I have been a member of the Commanderie de Bordeaux in Vancouver since 1978.

October 18, 1980

Sunny! We drove to Soulac.

Decided that Carol and the kids would leave to go home in a week. Everyone is getting on everybody else's nerves. Actually, the kids have been well behaved, but two months of constant travelling and poor weather is all that we could take together in a small Renault. I will stay in Bordeaux for an extra week and then fly home.

October 20, 1980

Visit to Château Talbot.

40% of 1980 harvest is already picked. A sunny day, but the sun should (and must) last for another week! They have acquired a new round steel fermenting vat that is experimental, using the concrete mix principle. 1978 has just been bottled. They replace half of their casks yearly. Yield of 40 hectolitres per hectare on average; 44 hectolitres per hectare in 1979. 30% Merlot, 2% Petit Verdot, and 68% Cabernet Sauvignon and Cabernet Franc.

In the opinion of Pottier (the cellarmaster), the 1978 versus the 1979 is the same as 1970 versus 1971.

1979, FROM CASK:

(Before egg white collage) Big, dark colour. Massive, powerful, well balanced, but overwhelming tannin. A wine to watch.

1978:

Bottled recently. Powerful, tannic; quite stemmy and herbaceous. There wasn't much Merlot in 1978, so most red Bordeaux are quite vegetal, lacking the roundness and ripeness imparted by this grape varietal.

Visit to Gruaud-Larose.

Met Mr. Moreau, Maître de Chais, and saw Cabernet Sauvignon being pressed. Similar blend this year as at Talbot: 80% Cabernet Sauvignon, and balance of other varietals. Little Merlot this year. 40% of harvest picked already.

Tasted the 1979

The 1978 just bottled and suffering from bottle-sickness. He compares 1979 and 1978 to 1962 and 1961. (Frankly, I cannot see how Moreau can compare 1978 to 1961.) He's really excited about his 1978 and 1979. The 1979 has a good, very dark colour, lots of fruit, lots of tannin (before collage). There is no gray rot in 1980.

That afternoon

We moved to a flat on a farm in the northern Médoc.

With dinner, on the farm

1976 CHABLIS "LES CLOS," PIERRE PONNELLE:

Woody, oaky, and a bit lacking in fruit. Improved later, but not up to par with the other fine Ponnelle wines we have tasted recently.

October 21, 1980

Visit to Ducru-Beaucaillou, Haut-Batailley, and Grand-Puy-Lacoste.

We met Jean-Eugene Borie and his son Bruno. Bruno was in California and is in the army now, but he is helping out with the vintage. M. Luceau has been the Maître de Chais at both Haut-Batailley and Ducru-Beaucaillou since 1978. They also own the excellent Château Grand-Puy-Lacoste in Pauillac.

Another lovely, sunny day.

Mr. Borie has picked 50% of the 1980 crop, 70% of which is Cabernet Sauvignon. He said that Michael Broadbent is very knowledgeable, but that he is not a very good taster when he tastes blind. He also said that Eddie Penning-Rowsell likes to see the labels before he tastes. Why are these renowned wine experts so afraid to taste blind? Mr. Borie showed us the grounds and the salon and then his son took us over to visit the chais, concrete cuves, and the cellars.

1979 DUCRU IN CASK:

Big, but soft and fruity. Also tasted the 1979 Haut-Batailley, which was a bit drier. Bruno's opinion is that the 1978 is better at Ducru, but the 1979 is better at Haut-Batailley. They produced 40 hectolitres per hectare in 1978 and 42 hectolitres per hectare in 1979.

Drove to Haut-Batailley and Grand-Puy-Lacoste.

At Haut-Batailley, Mr. Borie designed new cuves. On top and under them are the holding tanks. His sister owns this property. Since 1978, when Mr. Dupuis (the then-owner of Grand-Puy-Lacoste) died, they have owned Grand-Puy-Lacoste wholly. Old wooden cuves; they will change that. Tasted the 1979: lovely, big, intense, yet fruity. Must buy some.

Afternoon visit to Châteaux Palmer and d'Angludet.

We met Peter Sichel at Palmer. We also saw Pierre and Yves Chardon, the winemaker and régisseur. Fairly large production in 1979; 20% more than in 1978. Approximately 60% Cabernet Sauvignon in the blend now, at the expense of the Merlot.

1979 PALMER:

Deep colour. Elegant, fleshy, but tight at this stage. Very good potential.

1978 PALMER, FROM BOTTLE:

Deeper, bigger. Great extract. A bit stemmy due to the lack of Merlot that year—a varietal that plays a major role in Palmer's style.

Peter said that he would compare them to 1966 and 1967, with 1979 being a bit better and richer than the 1967. We talked about the liquor control boards and his agents in Canada (for all Sichel wines), including possible orders for my wine club, Le Tastevin.

Weather improved this week and those who picked early are sorry.

Palmer will finish picking on Saturday. There is very little Merlot this year, mostly Cabernet Sauvignon. We saw them bringing in the grapes and crushing them. Peter is planning to come to British Columbia in 1982. Then he invited us to d'Angludet. It is a lovely place, very "English," with tennis court and pool. He raises ponies. He has five sons and a three-and-one-half-year-old girl! The grapes were coming in at 12% sugar. Very good. We saw the whole process, including crushing, etc.

I climbed on top of a cuve and saw the fermentation. Everywhere there are problems with fermentation because of the cool (but sunny) weather. They are quite optimistic for 1980, but they do not expect a miracle. Too late for that.

We tasted the 1979 d'Angludet in barrel and the 1978 in bottle. Both were lovely and well made. Elegant, fruity. 1978 was bigger… but too stemmy for my taste.

Last week, in the rain, the first batch of grapes was coming in at 9.5% sugar, so the three to four days of sunshine have helped dramatically. Peter purchased d'Angludet in 1961, and only in the 1970s did they start to produce quality and quantity. Peter was very friendly and suggested that we have lunch next week.

That night, back at the farm, we had lovely cassoulet provençal.

1970 CHÂTEAU TALBOT:

(In Chablis, we paid Ffr68 for this wine, while in Bordeaux it costs Ffr130!) Good, deep colour. A bit too high in acidity. Hard yet fruity wine. Good flavour. Later, softened and became elegant.

October 22, 1980

All day at Maison Borie-Manoux.

We met Philippe Casteja and we talked for two hours. He will be in Vancouver in early November. We talked politics, investments in BC, the liquor monopoly, PAL wines (their BC agents), special orders, wine shops, etc. Then I had a tasting of their 1978 and 1979 wines with their North American export manager Charles Brossier. The 1979 Batailley was very good.

Carol and I had lunch with Charles in a bistro.

We drove to Batailley where we visited the chais. We met Mr. Becker, Maître de Chais. The 1980 is coming in now at approximately 11.5% to 12.5% sugar. Everybody has problems starting fermentation because the chais are cold. Drank the juice; it was sweet and good.

I met Mrs. Casteja, Philippe's mother, a nice, friendly lady. Charles is a very nice young man. He will be in Vancouver in January 1981. He will try to arrange an appointment for me at Château Latour next week. Then we drove to Beau-Site in St. Estèphe. It is an old-style operation; looks quite poor. A "poor relative" of Batailley. Had some nice 1980 juice there, too. They were in the process of chaptalizing. Bags of sugar everywhere. A very nice, interesting day.

In the evening, we had a bottle of this wine.

POUILLY-FUMÉ 1978, LADOUCETTE:

Light colour, but lovely bouquet and flavour. Lots of fruit, Very good, but not as big as the 1976.

October 23, 1980

Morning visit to Château La Mission Haut-Brion.

We ate some Cabernet Sauvignon grapes off the vine. They were uneven, but no rot; small, but thick-skinned and sweet. Charles Dodson, a public relations person from England, met us and we tasted some 1979 La Mission Haut-Brion and La Tour-Haut-Brion from cask. La Mission was a lot bigger with a better bouquet. He said that the 1978 was richer and bigger than the 1979.

In 1980, the Merlot suffered a lot; there was hardly any. Laville-Haut-Brion had good Semillon and Sauvignon Blanc this year, but not as good as in 1978 and 1979. Another sunny day. It rained last night, but it has not hurt the grapes. They are very busy and Monsieur La Gardère was not there. Originally, we were supposed to meet him, but he is busy running around the various vineyards. These are hectic, heart-throbbing days.

Lunched at the "St. James" (two stars, Michelin).

The entrance was dirty, but the service was good, and the food was very good. Carol had sole with white sauce and I had a lovely tenderloin in bordelaise sauce.

1970 Château Ormes de Pez, in half-bottle:

It was lovely; round, soft, fruity, and flavourful. Very good. A mini-version of the excellent (but too young) 1970 Lynch-Bages.

1970 Château Lynch-Bages, in half-bottle:

Very dark colour; molasses and black currant nose. Lovely big flavour and aftertaste. Really fabulous. Very good. One of the finest 1970s. Massive and intense. In full-bottle, it will last for a long time. A great wine.

Afternoon visit to Château Haut-Brion.

We met Mme. Darracq, the friendly public relations person at Château Haut-Brion. She was very knowledgeable. They finished picking on Monday. Their Merlot and Cabernet Franc are good. The quality of the Cabernet Sauvignon is as yet unknown. 1978 is bigger than 1979; very similar to 1970. 1979 will be more successful in St. Emilion than in the Médoc; lots of tannin and fruit, according to her. She likes Lafite more than Haut-Brion in 1978.

We tasted the 1979

It was not as deep in colour, fairly forward, and not impressive at this early stage. The 1978, according to her description, is definitely better. 500 cases of 1979 white Haut-Brion were produced. They finished picking almost a week earlier than at La Mission. In 1978, 12,000 cases; in 1979, 15,000 cases; 1980 is as yet unknown and everything depends on the quality of the Cabernet Sauvignon. Haut-Brion is one of the few châteaux that produced decent Merlot in 1980.

Before leaving, I retasted the

1979 Haut-Brion:

Seemed a bit bigger and richer than half-an-hour earlier. Really hard to assess these barrel samples.

Then we drove past d'Angludet and I left a bottle of Mayacamas 1974 Cabernet Sauvignon for Peter Sichel. Later, Charles Brossier of Borie-Manoux phoned. He has arranged a visit at Château Latour for next week. Another lovely day.

October 24, 1980

Morning visit at Château Coutet in Barsac.

With Mr. Mike Conroy, the Maître de Chais since 1978. It has been raining all day. They have already picked the Sauvignon Blanc, Muscadelle, and about 40% to 50% of the Semillon. 1980 is still a question mark. Not too much botrytis. His opinion is that potentially, 1971 and 1975 are their best wines in the 1970s, with the edge going to 1971. Lichine is sole distributor; this wine sells well on the Australian market. 1976 had lots of sun but not enough humidity. The wines were sweet, good, but light and fruity, with little rot. In 1978, they had a late harvest (at the end of November), but had the same problem as in 1976. The 1979 was too early, but should be good; maybe without enough botrytis.

The skins are not removed during fermentation at Coutet. The wine ferments completely in casks, usually racked three times a year. It is bottled after 23 or 26 months. They do collage with a very light fishbone mix.

I tasted a sample of the 1979

Big, alcoholic, clean, good fruit. Very pleasant, but little botrytis. It poured all day; at 10:00 a.m. they had to stop picking.

He also opened a lovely bottle of this wine.

1975 Château Coutet:

This is superb. Still very tight. Lots of fruit, botrytis, and excellent acidity and balance. I must get some of this when I get back home. This will be a long-term ager.

They also make a dry white wine. Not tasted.

Afternoon visit to Clos Haut-Peyraguey.

High grounds, very good small property. Dourthe Frères are their agents in BC. The 1979 was the best wine tasted at that property: some botrytis, good flavour, fairly big. 1977 was fat, sweet, ready; much better than one would expect from a 1977. They have already picked the Sauvignon Blanc and Muscadelle, but only 15% of the Semillon. Mr. Pauly is the owner. Average production is 100 barrels per year. Château Haut-Bommes is another property he owns. Less complex, but good in 1978 and 1979, according to Mr. Pauly. Not tasted.

Later, visit to d'Yquem.

D'Yquem will produce nine to ten hectolitres per hectare in 1980, using the same kind of presses as at Coutet. Vintage picking lasted 50 to 60 days. There was a group of French Canadians there, too, and we visited as a group. The second and third pressing is most important and sweetest. If they have leftover

Sauvignon Blanc, they will make d'Yquem's dry wine, called: "Y," Vin Sec du Château d'Yquem.

1976 D'YQUEM:

A soft, creamy, fat wine. Not too acidic, but enough backbone. Mr. Lafon (Maître de Chais) said that although they usually pick last, they did not do so in 1976. (Rieussec picked too late, according to them, and the grapes there were overripe.) The 1975 has more acidity and should live longer than the 1976. Both wines are superb. The 1976 will be excellent and ready around 1987 to 1990. The 1975 is superb. Best vintage since the great 1967! Will last well for 30 or more years. I must acquire some of this. Michael was born in 1975; lucky kid!

In the evening

CHAMPAGNE PIPER-HEIDSIECK 1973 BRUT:

Simple, good, very dry. Not great, but sound. Too acidic.

October 25, 1980

Left Moulin de Saussac today.

This is the farm where we spent the last week. Pigs and chickens all over the place. No heat. We were freezing. It was, however a nice experience for all of us. One very large pig followed Carol everywhere.

A lovely sunny day. Had a lovely bath at Hôtel Normandie, where we are staying before Carol's return to Vancouver. At the farm, all we had was a tiny, unheated shower with no curtain or door, and tiny towels.

October 27, 1980

This morning Carol and the kids left for Amsterdam.

Tomorrow, they will continue on to Vancouver. A hectic morning. I was one hour late for lunch with Monsieur André Cazes, the mayor of Pauillac and owner of Châteaux Lynch-Bages and Ormes de Pez. I spent four-and-one-half lovely hours with him and his 25-year-old daughter Sylvie. His son Jean-Michel was not there. Jean-Michel lives behind Mr. Cazes's house until the château is refurbished, at which time he will move to Lynch-Bages with his family.

Information on other châteaux

Mr. Cazes made appointments for me with Jean-Louis Mandreau at Latour and with Mr. Ruelle, Maître de Chais at Beychevelle Last week, Château Cantemerle was sold to Cordier. The former owner, Clauzel, had 12 kids who could not make up their minds as to how to run the property. Mr. André Cazes's wife was killed in a car-train accident in 1975; what a tragedy. He has been mayor of Pauillac for 33 years. He gave me a nice souvenir plate as a gift. Boutellier, owner of Pichon-Baron, died of cancer at 44 years of age in 1974, and his kids had to sell Grand-Puy-Ducasse to pay the estate taxes.

Mr. Cazes said that Château Lanessan (also owned by the Bouteillers) is well made because younger people with modern ideas work there. Lots of replanting at Pichon-Baron and soon they should be making very good wine again, hopefully. They are better situated than Pichon-Lalande. D'Yquem is losing money, because it costs so much to produce. Lynch-Bages finished picking the 1980 this morning. It is a lovely warm day. He is sort of sorry that he did not wait a bit longer. They use 20% new oak barrels each year at Lynch-Bages.

He knows Henri Martin well and Mr. Lemelletier of the Grand Conseil de Bordeaux. He can help me organize a visit to Bordeaux for members of our Commanderie in Vancouver.

At lunch

CHAMPAGNE AYALA BRUT 1971, IN HALF-BOTTLE:

Big nose, lovely fruit. Ready. Round, yeasty, long.

Then, with a simple but nice lunch, Monsieur Cazes, Sylvie, and I had the following.

1967 LES ORMES DE PEZ:

Browning, round, lovely sweet nose. Still has good fruit and not too acidic.

Then he served a masterpiece.

1959 LYNCH-BAGES:

A real beauty. 11 years older than the 1970. Round, sweet, cedary nose. Long aftertaste. Really great. Classic Pauillac from a fine vintage.

Afterward, we enjoyed a cigar and coffee. Mr. André Cazes is keeping some 1955 Lynch-Bages for Sylvie's wedding; she was born that year. Then we drove to Château Lynch-Bages (75% Cabernet Sauvignon, the rest Merlot and Petit Verdot). His father, Jean-Michel's grandfather, used to plant Malbec, but they do not like it as it produces watery, simple juice. Met the Maître de Chais and tasted the following.

1979 LYNCH-BAGES, FROM CASK:

Not as tannic as some, but nice, deep colour, good fruit. One of the four best 1979 Haut-Médocs at a tasting of owners, held last week.

1978 LYNCH-BAGES:

Bigger, yet a bit too herbaceous and skinny. Somehow it lacks the ripeness and depth typical of this property. Hopefully, it will develop more extract as it ages.

Mr. André Cazes told me that he "gave away" his 1975 at a time of financial crisis. 1980 will be fairly good, better than expected, but not great. Saw the cuves fermenting. I visited the whole chais. Wet cloth wrapped around red metal vats to cool them off; they swear by it at Lynch-Bages.

A great afternoon and a great experience. Mr. André Cazes is a generous, informative, and pleasant host.

October 28, 1980

Visit to Château l'Evangile in Pomerol.

I met Mr. Ducasse. He is at least 75 or 76. Fermentation has just finished; they had problems starting it this year. They started picking late, on October 14. Two-thirds Merlot and one-third Cabernet Franc (Bouchet). Only 20 hectolitres per hectare this year; 14 hectares under vines. They must eliminate all sugar in the wine, otherwise it may start fermenting again in the bottle and "picure" may occur.

We talked about my last visit there in 1977. A château I would love to own! We tasted the 1979 against the 1978. The 1978 was more closed and harder. The 1979 was softer and more elegant. Ducasse thinks that 1979 will be a more complete wine than 1978 and loves his 1975. 1978 and 1979 both have a big, dark colour at this early stage.

Then he opened a half-bottle of 1975. It had a lovely big, complex nose. It was big, flavourful, lots of tannin; really great potential, needs at least five to seven more years. Then he went to the cellar and brought back a bottle of 1975 as a gift for me.

Mr. Ducasse said that in early May 1980, there was lovely flowering, but it was very cold at night and there was lots of coulure.

He sells to the trade in Bordeaux, especially Duclos and J. P. Moueix. A short, but informative visit.

Lunch by myself, at hotel-restaurant "Loubat," in Libourne.

They have 1947 Cheval-Blanc in bottles for Ffr1,000 and in magnums for Ffr2,000 on their wine list. I did something crazy. I ordered a bottle of 1947 Cheval-Blanc! The waiter looked at me with a funny expression, but he brought me a bottle, decanted it, and poured it carefully.

1947 CHEVAL-BLANC:

What a magnificent bottle! Inky colour. Luscious, ripe, rich. Full and unctuous. Great fruit extract. Very long. Fireworks on palate. A great, but very unusual wine. Almost sweet; lots of extract. I poured a glass for the waiter and offered it to him. He suddenly became very friendly. Drank the rest of the bottle by myself. What an olfactory orgy!

Visit to La Grave, Trotanoy, and Petrus, with Christian Moueix.

At 3:00 p.m., I met Christian Moueix and we talked briefly about the BCLDB and its new policies. I should keep him informed. He introduced me to Mr. Bernard Montouroy, who lives at Château La Grave (Trigant-de-Boisset). He is responsible for export to Germany and his father owned La Fleur-Petrus. Taillefer is owned by a cousin. Christian's brother, Jean-François, owns Duclos in Bordeaux.

We went to La Grave, then to Trotanoy, where they produced 20 hectolitres per hectare in 1980. Very small. Overall, 1979 in Pomerol and St. Emilion is better than 1978. (1970s style; well made, more complete than in 1978, and larger production.)

Visited the chais at Trotanoy.

They had to use heat to start fermentation. We saw the vineyards of La Fleur-Petrus and the soil is much more gravelly than Petrus, therefore more tannic and more Médoc-like wines. At Petrus, we visited the expanded chais. We tasted the 1979 Petrus, which had a deep, rich, lovely bouquet. Lovely, intense aftertaste. It should be ready in ten to 12 years.

Christian told me that at Vieux Château Certan, they have replanted a lot, therefore they are having problems with quality. The vines need to age. 1979 produced 20% more wine than 1978. I tasted a few Merlot grapes left for the birds. They had very thick skins, sweet juice, but small quantity. Of 11 cuves each at Petrus and Trotanoy, only four are full. The quality may be good, but the quantity of the 1980 will be small. Merlot suffered everywhere in Bordeaux in 1980 because of the coulure in May.

Another lovely sunny day, good for Sauternes. It is really warm in the evening, too. Some growers are sorry that they picked too soon.

October 29, 1980

Visit to Ausone and Belair.

Pascal Delbeck is the Maître de Chais of both properties. Both 1978 and 1979 Ausone are very fine, with the 1979 being slightly better, riper, with more extract. Pascal has been there since 1975. He is 27 years old and looks like a hermit, with a big, black, bushy beard. A gifted winemaker, who has turned this underachieving property around.

Tasted the 1980 while it was still fermenting.

Found it unpleasant. They produced as much in 1980 as they did in 1978. The average age of the vines is 45 years. 55% Merlot and 45% Bouchet. Seven hectares under vines, of which one-half hectare is replanted every five to six years. They use 100% new barrels each year. Chalky soil. Because of the steps and the high ground, they use a horse to plough the vineyard—an old, white, reliable beast.

Visit to Vieux Château Certan.

I met Mr. Thienpont. He has seven children. I saw the fermenting vats. In 1980, the yield was 38 hectolitres per hectare; 13 hectares. 50% Cabernet Sauvignon and Cabernet Franc, 45% Merlot, and 5% Malbec. He is not sure yet, but thinks that he will make more wine in 1980 than in 1978. The 1979 from cask seemed a bit thin; I preferred the 1978, which was bottled last month. The 1978 is bigger and more tannic than the 1979, which is soft and round.

Then we went to the château and tasted the 1971. Big, tannic, good. Quite elegant nose. New wooden cuves installed in 1972. Mr. Thienpont said that Château Certan-de-May has been producing very good wines since 1975.

Visit to Château Figeac.

Then I drove to Figeac for lunch, after first driving to Château La Grace Dieu with Thierry Manoncourt to borrow a heater for one of his vats. I gave him a bottle of 1975 Sterling Merlot, Napa Valley. Thierry has four daughters. I saw the pressing of Cabernet Sauvignon. Figeac is the last château still picking in 1980. They finished this morning.

Then he, his wife, and I had lunch with Thierry's 94-year-old mother.

We had a 1976 Figeac with the main course. It needs one to three more years, but is already elegant. Then we tasted the 1961: lovely, dark, cedary, and very ripe fruit. It needs three to five more years, yet it is already an excellent wine.

We talked a lot about the vintage, wine trade, and life in general. Thierry is pleased with both the 1978 and the 1979. The 1979 is rounder, more elegant. 30% new oak casks. 55% Cabernet Sauvignon and Cabernet Franc, 45% Merlot. We had coffee and his wife gave me a can of foie gras en bloc to take home. They are very busy these days. I met two of their daughters. Thierry is head of the Jurade de St. Emilion, and a supplier of wines for Commanderie branches (younger vintages). His younger daughter has been working in the vineyard since the age of 14. The Manoncourts lost their only son, who drowned when he was still a young boy. What a tragedy this must be.

Visit to La Gaffelière.

An anticlimax for the day, and compared to my last visit there in 1977. The owner, Count de Mallet-Roquefort, has also owned Château Tertre Dauguay since 1978; he also produces Château Roquefort. They use 25% new barrels. 65% Merlot, 35% Cabernet Sauvignon and Cabernet Franc.

I tasted the 1979 Tertre Dauguay, which he thought was a 1979 La Gaffelière! He seemed mixed up. Then we tasted a 1978 La Gaffelière in bottle and a 1979 La Gaffelière from the barrel. Both were deep, complex, and dark. The 1979 was slightly better balanced. Was the 1978 going through bottle sickness?

The Count was accompanied by a sexy blond secretary who I thought was his daughter. Somehow, I had some doubts about that. Maybe he had forgotten about my prearranged visit or maybe he had just had a "fight" with his "secretary." Anyway, the visit was disappointing and short.

October 30, 1980

Visit to Château Malescot-St.-Exupéry in Margaux.

I met Roger Zuger. His younger brother owns Marquis d'Alesme-Becker, and Roger owns Malescot separately now. Paul, the father, is still active. Roger likes fishing. He was born in 1931 and has two children: a boy and a girl, born in 1964 and 1966, respectively. His agent for the US is Almaden, working out of their Chicago office.

Cépage is 55% Cabernet Sauvignon, 10% Cabernet Franc, 30% Merlot, and 5% Petit Verdot. This year Petit Verdot still has not been picked. He does not know if he will use it at all. Old vines, nice chais. I tasted the 1979 in barrel. It was deep, elegant, good on both nose and palate. The 1978 was bigger and better. Overall, the 1978s and 1979s are good, yet they lack the sheer extract this property is capable of producing, such as the excellent 1959 and 1961.

Yield was 48 hectolitres per hectare in 1978. They use 25% new casks each year. He does not make a second wine, nor does he have a representative in Canada. He does not deal through the Bordeaux trade, but ships directly to customers and suppliers abroad. Frankly, I think that after the fine 1959 and 1961, Malescot has been an underachiever. The potential is great.

Visit to Château Beychevelle.

I met Madame Achille-Fould, the owner, who took me to the manager, Mr. Ruelle, who sent me to the Maître de Chais, Mr. Soussotte. Musical chairs! Large production; 70 acres, which produce 70% Cabernet Sauvignon and 30% Merlot. They have just replanted some Petit Verdot (one hectare). Shenley buys 30% of the production annually for the US. Robert Mondavi is there often. I think that a problem with this property is overproduction.

1979, FROM BARREL:

Elegant, with good colour and nice fruit. Soft and round, even at this early stage.

1978:

Just bottled. Bigger, darker colour at this stage. Herbaceous, even lean and short on palate. May improve in bottle—I hope.

The 1979 is more elegant and fruity St. Julien in style. No rot in 1980. They are pleased with it, but it will not be a very good year. They use 25% new barrels, but in 1977, there were no new barrels. They sell the 1975 at the château for Ffr120. Average production is 1,200 barrels. 1978 yielded 44 hectolitres per hectare, and 1979 yielded 50 hectolitres per hectare. Too much!

Visit to Château Coufran.

I met Jean Miailhe. The Canadian flag was flying in my honour. Visited the chais and château, also Château Verdignan. Château Citran, in a family split, belongs to his brothers and a sister. At Coufran, varietal proportions are 85% Merlot, 10% Cabernet Sauvignon, and 5% Petit Verdot. Jean Miailhe lives at Verdignan, while his daughter lives at Coufran. We had a nice lunch with some lovely Citran 1970; also some good 1976 Coufran.

Joining us for lunch, was the young owner of Château Moulin-à-Vent, Haut-Médoc, a friend of Jean-Louis Mandreau of Château Latour. They showed me the chais. Coufran has a large production of 300,000 bottles. At Verdignan, as an aperitif, we shared a lovely bottle of 1970 Rayne-Vigneau, Sauternes. They use 25% new barrels; 75% older barrels (second year) are purchased from Mouton.

Afternoon visit to Château Latour.

With Jean-Louis Mandreau. He told me that the 1979 Margaux will be the best Médoc of the vintage. Overall, 1979 was excellent, if not overproduced. He is not too optimistic about 1980: little Merlot, average production. We tasted the 1979 Latour. Big, dark, and well balanced. He said that in the 1970s, 1970 was the hardest, then 1975, then 1978, and 1979. Overall, the 1978 Haut-Médocs were better than the 1979s, but well-made 1979s are excellent. Jean-Louis was born in 1946 and has been with Latour since 1974. Professor Emile Peynaud was his mentor. Jean-Louis likes Grand-Puy-Lacoste and Domaine de Chevalier Blanc; he also likes Château St. Jean Sonoma Chardonnays and Robert Mondavi 's 1974 Cabernet Sauvignon "Reserve."

They use pneumatic presses at Latour. In 1979, 80 barriques of Les-Forts-de-Latour and approximately 950 of Latour were produced. The third wine is sold as Pauillac Appellation Contrôlée. They have 70 permanent employees. We visited the cellars of the château. Mandreau likes the 1962 and the 1964, and thinks that the 1966 is starting to open up. The 1970 is very hard, massive, but with great potential. He likes 1952 better than 1953 at Latour. I agree.

The final visit to a vineyard on this two-month trip, a very pleasant and informative day.

October 31, 1980

Peter Sichel phoned me at the hotel this morning; we made an appointment for lunch.

He has problems with his car and I have to return mine, so instead of lunch at Château Palmer, we will go to a restaurant in Bordeaux. I returned the car to Renault with no problems. We drove a total of 8,300 kilometres from September 8, 1980, to October 30, 1980.

Later, met Peter and we went for lunch to a nice restaurant in Bordeaux, and spent two-and-one-half hours together. We talked about politics, Palmer, various vintages, etc.

With lunch we tried these wines.

1979 "R," DRY WINE OF RIEUSSEC:

Lovely, crisp, clean, and complex. Needs two to three years. Peter said that he will buy a case for himself.

1973 CHÂTEAU D'ANGLUDET:

Ready, yet has depth. An elegant, soft wine.

Peter is a very nice man. He thanked me for the bottle of Mayacamas 1974 Cabernet Sauvignon. He likes travelling by train and bicycle in the city. According to Peter, Gruaud-Larose may be put up for sale because the Cordier couple are splitting; he thinks that Cordier are acting on behalf of someone else regarding the purchase of Château Cantemerle.

He admires Lucien Lurton, but does not know how Lurton can pull it off—managing in eight châteaux! He likes Nick Clark (the arrogant, ignorant purchasing manager of the BC liquor monopoly), and is sympathetic to them. I should contact their agent in Vancouver on my return regarding purchasing some d'Angludet!

Peter's kind words about the liquor monopoly are the only thing about which he and I disagree, wine-wise. As a consumer, I just cannot accept the totalitarian notion of a wine and liquor monopoly. Nor do I have tolerance for bureaucratic incompetence.

Peter said that both the 1978 and 1979 Haut-Brions are very good, the best First Growth. I certainly agree about the potential of the 1979, but I think that 1978 Latour and Margaux are better.

Peter cannot sell in the US under the name of Sichel, as a cousin on the German side of the family uses that name. (Sichel Sohne, shippers of Blue Nun Liebfraumilch: a flat, alcoholic gingerale, sometimes described as "wine.")

Production in 1979 is greater than in 1973 in the Médoc, but it is a much finer year. Peter likes the quality of 1979 Merlot, too.

November 22, 1980

Back in Vancouver. Dinner of the "Group of Ten."

CHAMPAGNE HENRIOT, 1969:

Lovely, elegant Champagne. Medium-gold colour, delicate, complex, flavourful, long finish. Excellent. Ripe and rich, yet well balanced, with good acidity backing the ripe fruit. (17.5)

DOMAINE DE CHEVALIER BLANC 1976:

Elegant, lovely, almond nose; clean, crisp, well rounded. Finished a bit harsh; fairly high acidity. Overall, very good and delicate. A good white Graves. (17)

PULIGNY-MONTRACHET "FOLATIÈRES" 1976, JOSEPH DROUHIN:

The nose was the greatest thing about this wine. Lovely, toasty, complex, rich, clean. Good flavour on palate, but seemed a bit tired and flabby. Good, but not great. Was better two years ago. Drouhin's whites usually mature fairly early. Rated (17.5) for bouquet and (16) for flavour.

CHÂTEAU MONTELENA CHARDONNAY 1973, NAPA VALLEY:

After tasting this wine, it became clear why the French judges, in 1976, thought it to be a great French Burgundy. Lovely, oaky, toasty nose. Brilliant gold colour. Complex bouquet. Good fruit. Held very well. Quite high acidity (the only fault), but maybe this is what kept this wine young. Very long, complex aftertaste. (18)

CHÂTEAU LA LAGUNE 1926

AND

CHÂTEAU HAUT-BRION 1926:

La Lagune travelled that day and was a bit cloudy. Recorked in 1978. Medium colour, orange-brown. Lovely, cedary Médoc nose. Very elegant, but tired. Drinkable, though. (16)

The Haut-Brion was quite a bit darker. Mocha-coffee nose and flavour. Intense. Very dry, lots of tannin, but not too much fruit. Will last for many years, but has nowhere to go but downhill. Lovely experience. More "put together" than the La Lagune. This bottle came originally from the cellars of Clarence Dillon, the owner of Haut-Brion. (18)

CHÂTEAU GUIRAUD 1967, SAUTERNES:

To me, a bit disappointing this time. Lovely colour and botrytis nose, but a bit too dry, and drying fast. In the past, it seemed more buttery and sweet. May be past its prime. (15)

GRAHAM'S 1945 VINTAGE PORT:

Dark colour, loaded with alcohol and exotic fruit. Powerful, yet the fruit is complex behind that power. Long finish. Will live for many years. An outstanding Port. (18.5)

December 1980

Dinner and blind tasting of 1966 Clarets, at Dr. Allan Tobe's, celebrating Allan's 50th birthday.

1. CHÂTEAU CARBONNIEUX:

Not too much bouquet. Some tannin. Dark, touch of brick. Lacks a bit in the middle; hard, low fruit. (14)

2. CHÂTEAU MALARTIC-LAGRAVIÈRE:

Earthy, sweet nose. Dark-brownish colour. Good fruit; more complexity on nose than on palate. (16)

3. CHÂTEAU CALON-SÉGUR:

Medium colour. Fruity, sweet, cedary nose. Good flavour, good fruit/acidity balance. Lovely aftertaste. Oaky. Smoky. Surprise! First time I've liked this. (17) In the past, I found this wine to be too soft and dull.

4. CHÂTEAU MONTROSE:

Darkish colour. Some tannin. Big, dry wine. Good flavour; St. Estèphe style. Dry finish. (17)

5. CHÂTEAU BRANE-CANTENAC:

Medium colour, good depth. Lovely, open bouquet. Sweet, earthy-oak mix. Intense, open nose. Good fruit. Quite complex and elegant. Best 1966 Brane Cantenac to date. Lovely aftertaste. (17.5)

6. CHÂTEAU LEOVILLE-BARTON:

Dark colour. Grassy, spicy, open nose. Lovely mouthful, long aftertaste. A bit burnt-oak. Spearmint. Lovely bouquet. Very good, but starting to lose its fruit. (17)

7. CHÂTEAU LEOVILLE-LASCASES:

Sweet, fruity nose. Quite high acidity, little tannin. "Warm," alcoholic wine. A bit short aftertaste. Simple, but big. Needs time. (15) This, and the Ducru (see #8), should have been the best wines of the evening. They both disappointed.

8. CHÂTEAU DUCRU-BEAUCAILLOU:

Similar to #7, but a bit harsher, woody. Some fruit. Good, but a bit high acidity. Lean. (15)

9. BEYCHEVELLE:

Delicate, baked, sweet nose. Dark colour. Good mouthful. Warm, rich, fruity, sweet wine. (16)

I had a lucky evening: I guessed them as being Haut-Médocs and 1966s. The only person to do so. This tasting was followed by an excellent meal (lovely moose roast), with the following wines.

MEURSAULT 1971, REMOISSENET:

Very young-smelling, tasting, and looking for a 1971 white Burgundy. Well balanced. Good fruit/acidity balance. Hard to guess as Meursault, but definitely French Burgundy. Lacked that extra dimension, nuttiness, and buttery flavour of good Meursaults.

CHÂTEAU LATOUR 1969:

At first, I thought it was a Montrose, but when told Pauillac, I said "Latour." But surely fine for 1969. Dark colour, big, simple, but solid; no doubt about it. Not too complex, but enough depth, fruit, and body to last three to five years. No one guessed the vintage correctly. I actually thought that it was the 1967.

CHÂTEAU DE FARGUES 1971:

I said "d'Yquem or de Fargues." Lovely, darkish-golden colour; good botrytis nose; nice, full. Excellent.

A great tasting night for me. Just a lucky day!

March 19, 1981

Tasting of 1974 and 1975 California Cabernet Sauvignons, with several friends, and members of the Commanderie de Bordeaux.

All wines served blind. Wines decanted at 6:15 p.m. Tasting started at 7:00 p.m. I guessed the vintages correctly, and #6 immediately.

FLIGHT #1
1975s

1. MAYACAMAS 1975, NAPA VALLEY:

Very dark. Good, spicy nose. Some volatile acidity, too. A bit thin middle. Not too much flavour at this stage. Lots of tannin. Quite acidic, hot. (15)

2. ROBERT MONDAVI 1975 "RESERVE," NAPA VALLEY:

Evolved colour. Herbaceous, yet ripe nose. Good spices, elegant, quite a bit of tannin. Very good aftertaste, but a bit thin in the middle. (16.5)

3. CUVAISON 1975 "SIGNATURE," NAPA VALLEY:

Very dark. Sweet, elegant, open, spicy nose; complex. Lovely mouthful of power. Loaded with tannin. Good flavour, good spice, long aftertaste. Philip Togni (the winemaker) thinks this wine needs 15 to 20 years. Made from 100% Cabernet Sauvignon. Very promising. (17)

4. RIDGE "MONTE BELLO" 1975, CALIFORNIA:

Lighter colour. Sweet, vegetal nose. Lovely flavours, elegant, some tannin; new oak, vanilla flavours. A bit acidic, but tasted good. Buttery. Reserve judgement. (16)

5. BEAULIEU VINEYARDS GEORGES DE LATOUR "PRIVATE RESERVE" 1975, NAPA VALLEY:

Closed nose. Hard. Lovely mouthful of fruit and flavour. Some tannin. Not too complex, but very pleasant. Better on palate than on nose. (15.5)

6. HEITZ CELLARS "MARTHA'S VINEYARD" 1975, NAPA VALLEY:

Open, complex, cedar-eucalyptus nose. Minty, cigar-box, too. Lots of tannin. Good balance. Long aftertaste. Very good. Slightly bitter aftertaste. Needs time. (17)

7. STERLING VINEYARDS "RESERVE" 1975, NAPA VALLEY:

Good nose, sweetish; delicate, yet full. Fairly high acidity. Not too much tannin. Evolved fruit, but lacks the extract of the fine 1974. (16)

FLIGHT #2
1974s

1. MAYACAMAS 1974, NAPA VALLEY:

Very dark; closed nose. Similar to their 1975, but more body, more flavour, and a better aftertaste. Very good potential. (17)

2. ROBERT MONDAVI "RESERVE" 1974, NAPA VALLEY:

Intense nose; lovely, minty, spicy. New oak, lots of tannin, rich, good fruit. Very good. This should make a very fine bottle in five years. (18)

3. STAG'S LEAP 1974, NAPA VALLEY:

Lovely, spicy, cedary nose. Typical California Cabernet Sauvignon. Elegant, good flavours, but not big. The lightest wine of the evening. In retrospect, I may have been a bit tough toward this wine because of its elegance, but the quality overall was impressive. (16.5)

4. RIDGE "MONTE BELLO" 1974, CALIFORNIA:

Not too much on nose at this stage. Some sweetness. Same style as their 1975; but harder, bigger, and more backward. Lovely rich flavour. Again, very good potential. (17.5)

5. BEAULIEU VINEYARDS GEORGES DE LATOUR "PRIVATE RESERVE" 1974, NAPA VALLEY:

Lovely cedary nose; soupy. Bigger than the 1975. Rich, big, fruity wine. Good aftertaste. Lots of tannin. Excellent. Typical sweeter, riper, American oak-vanilla. (17)

6. HEITZ CELLARS "MARTHA'S VINEYARD" 1974, NAPA VALLEY:

Intense, minty-eucalyptus nose. Clearly bigger and more intense than the 1975. Lots of tannin, body, flavour, and aftertaste. Very good. Will be a great bottle (if you like the style, which I do). (18.5)

7. STERLING "RESERVE" 1974, NAPA VALLEY:

Elegant, sweet nose. Good flavour. Much better than the 1975. Hot, lots of tannin, but not very complex at this stage. Massive. Great fruit extract. Needs time. (17)

Overall

Two things were obvious. The 1974s are bigger and more intense than the 1975s, and, #6 in each flight is the obvious "Martha's Vineyard." Also, the worst wine of both flights is quite lovely. This is a very fine range of wines.

WITH DINNER

ROBERT MONDAVI 1978 CHARDONNAY "RESERVE," NAPA VALLEY:

Bright-golden colour. Lovely flavour, good fruit/acidity balance. Well made. Oak, vanilla, and fruit all in harmony.

ROBERT MONDAVI 1975 CABERNET SAUVIGNON "RESERVE," NAPA VALLEY:

See tasting comments above.

The group favourites for the 1974 wines

Heitz "Martha's Vineyard," Ridge "Monte Bello," and Robert Mondavi "Reserve."

The group favourites for the 1975 wines

Heitz "Martha's Vineyard," Cuvaison's "Signature," and Ridge "Monte Bello."

Philip Togni (President and Winemaker of Cuvaison) was a student of Professor Emile Peynaud. Peynaud visited him at Cuvaison in 1976.

March 28, 1981

Special Dinner of "Group of Ten," at home.

CHAMPAGNE ROEDERER "CRISTAL" BRUT 1975:

Delicate nose, very tiny bubbles. Good flavour. Good acidity. More style and elegance than weight. An elegant wine.

CHÂTEAU GRILLET 1978

AND

CONDRIEU 1976, DELAS:

Not served together; Château Grillet served first.

Château Grillet was lighter in colour; more delicate and elegant; more subdued in flavour. Should be tried in a couple of years.

The Condrieu was darker-gold, with a bigger nose and more intense flavour; but it didn't have the elegance of the Château Grillet.

1959 CHÂTEAU MARGAUX,

CHÂTEAU HAUT-BRION,

AND

CHÂTEAU LAFITE:

Served in that order, at my suggestion.

The Margaux was the most elegant, and the lightest in colour, but still a dark deep colour. Lovely nose, elegant bouquet. Lovely flavour. After one hour, it started to dry out. It is probably two to three years past its peak, but still a great wine. Right now, it is my favourite among the three wines.

The Haut-Brion was darker than the Margaux. Good, but not-too-intense Graves nose, "goût de terroir." Some tannin left; a bit high in acidity; the driest of all. The least favourite wine among all three, yet great!

The Lafite was the most intense wine. Elegant, intense, sweet nose. Dark colour. Held the best. Has lots of life left in it. Lovely wine, great flavour. Almost unready. Young-looking and young-tasting. Excellent balance. Truly a great wine.

CHÂTEAU SUDUIRAUT 1959:

Dark golden colour. Great, exotic nose. Complex, fruity wine. Excellent balance. Slightly dry, but really great, with lots of ripe fruit and botrytis.

A fabulous evening. Could one ask for more?

April 2, 1981

A tasting of premium Australian wines, organized by the Australian Consulate and the Australian wine board.

WHITE WINES

1. MILDARA FINO SHERRY "WINEMAKER'S SELECTION":

Pleasant. Dry, but not too dry. Delicate. Nice nutty overtones on both nose and palate. (15)

2. LINDEMAN'S "NURSERY VINEYARD" COONAWARRA RHINE RIESLING 1979:

Grown in South Australia. A bit sulphury nose. Good acidity. Pleasant, not great. Decent fruit, but not complex enough. Decent commercial wine. (13.5)

3. Petaluma Chardonnay 1978:

Very slow cold fermentation (up to six or nine months!). Not too much on nose. Sweet on nose. Good fruit and acidity, but not enough complexity. Simple and pleasant, with light colour; decent, but not at $9 a bottle. (13.5)

4. The Rothbury Estate Individual Vineyard Semillon 1976:

The best Australian Semillon comes from the Hunter Valley. (Rothbury is divided into four lots; Murray Tyrrell is a partner.) Semillon grown in Australia as "Hunter Riesling," but it is not a true Riesling. Spritzy, pleasant, flowery. Quite sweetish. Pale, light colour. Decent fruit. Easy sipping wine. (14)

5. Kaiser Stuhl "Bin U31" Auslese Rhine Riesling 1976, Eden Valley:

Not botrytis-affected. Has not been produced again since 1976. Bright-gold colour. Spritzy, light, elegant. Low alcohol and acidity. Quite sweet. A bit short at finish. Too sweet to be served with a meal. Serve with a light dessert. (14.5)

6. Brown Bros. Milawa Spätlese Rhine Riesling 1970:

Botrytis-affected. Much sweeter than a German Spätlese. Darkish gold. Subtle, delicate nose. Not as open as the Kaiser Stuhl, and not much sweeter, but more elegant. (15)

RED WINES

1. Tyrrell's Pinot Hermitage 1978:

Peppery, good fruit, elegant. Fairly high acidity. Good with a clean, fruity nose. Soft, forward, pleasant. (14)

2. Wynn's Coonawarra Cabernet Sauvignon 1978:

Grassy nose. Bright, dark colour. Sweet grape flavour. Elegant, young, yet soft. OK, but not very exciting. (13.5)

3. Yalumba "Chairman's Selection" Cabernet Sauvignon 1976:

(Not released yet) Dark colour. Great depth with some tannin left, yet almost ready. Good, long aftertaste. Nice fruit; spicy Cabernet. Fleshy. (15)

4. Penfold's Grange Hermitage 1975:

Needs ten to 15 extra years of ageing time. Black colour! Lots of tannin. Massive, but not complex. Good peppery, spicy flavour. A big, powerful wine. Great fruit extract. A "brooding monster." (17.5)

5. Seppelt Great Western Hermitage "GW115" 1967:

(Not released) Fairly dark colour. Slight sulphur on nose; sweet on palate. Good acidity, but flat on palate. Little flavour. Getting tired. (14.5)

6. Morris Premium Liqueur Muscat:

1908-base wine. That is the oldest base wine (vintage) in this Solera-style dessert wine. Cloying, sweet, full, creamy; very long nutty-raisiny flavours. A good Muscat. (17)

Other comments on Murray Tyrrell's Chardonnays

1973:

Great potential. First made in 1971.

1977:

Bottled cold and had carbon dioxide (spritz) when bottled. I agree, having tasted this wine on several occasions.

1979:

Very good. Tyrrell produced a cask of special big Chardonnay. Huge wine. The "Regular" is very fine, very "French" toasty style, rather than the honeyed style of California Chardonnay.

1980:

Very good. Elegant, lots of fruit, good acid. Similar to the 1979.

May 14, 1981

Commanderie de Bordeaux vertical-blind tasting of Château Latour.

1. 1964:

Good, dark, evolved colour; orangy-brick rim. Slight earthy-chocolaty nose. A bit stemmy. High acidity, sharp. Woody, oaky flavour. No tannin left. Very good. Rich, long aftertaste. Actually quite ripe. Ready, but no rush. (17.5)

2. 1967:

Dark colour. Good depth; full, elegant, oaky nose. Green and sharp on palate. High acidity, typical for the vintage. Pleasant, long aftertaste. A bit chaptalized. (15)

3. 1959:

Dark colour; deep, rich-looking. Elegant, lovely, tea leaves, cedary nose. Rich tasting; medium-high acidity; some tannin left. Lovely aftertaste. A winner! Good now, but will get even better in five years. Obviously a ripe vintage. (18.5)

4. 1966:

Medium-dark colour. Fairly closed, oaky nose. A bit tight, high acidity. Some tannin. Closed and unyielding. Woody, tea-leaves flavour. A disappointing bottle. (14) This can be excellent. Obviously, a poor example.

5. 1971:

Medium-dark colour. Big, rich, oaky, cedary nose. Medium body, lots of tannin. Good fruit/acidity balance. Dry finish. I liked this wine more than other tasters. (15.5)

6. 1969:

Medium-dark colour. Touch of orange. Wet, earthy nose; big, sweet, chaptalized. Good aftertaste. Not too complex. Fine effort for the vintage. (14)

7. 1955:

Very good, dark colour, deep-looking. Intense, oaky, cedary bouquet. Lots of flavour. Fairly young-tasting, yet very much alive. Lovely complexity. Great. (18) This is the best 1955 Latour I have tasted to date, and it is surprisingly full and rich.

8. 1970:

Darkest wine of flight. No trace of age. Obviously the 1970! Very deep colour. Closed, intense, fruity nose. Some purple. Loaded with tannin. A great mouthful of perfection! Lovely aftertaste. Needs many, many years! (20)

9. 1961:

Dark, some orange at rim. Lovely, big, oaky, cedary, and ripe, fruity nose. Sweet. Very intense and ripe on palate. Woody, oaky aftertaste. Lovely concentration. Will last forever. A great classic! (19.5)

Although I have many of these wines in my cellar, I haven't tasted several of them before. A great experience! I correctly identified wines #2, 3, 7, 8, 9. Wine #4 (the 1966) was the most disappointing overall; I expected more. Everyone raved about the 1961 (lovely); personally, I slightly preferred the 1970, although it is still a baby.

WITH DINNER

1978 CHÂTEAU CARBONNIEUX BLANC:

Fruity, pleasant, crisp, clean. Some oak and vanilla, a bit stemmy, but long on palate.

1975 CHÂTEAU SUDUIRAUT:

Somehow drier than expected. Good, rich, botrytis nose. Medium colour. Needs time. Not sweet enough? Yet has good acidity and fruit extract.

May 16, 1980

Dinner at Ken Cross's, featuring a vertical tasting of Château Trotanoy (Pomerol).

Wines served double-blind. We had absolutely no idea what the wines were. All wines had impressive dark colours.

1. CHÂTEAU LATOUR-À-POMEROL 1971:

Medium-dark colour; touch of orange. Good depth. Good, fruity nose, stemmy. High alcohol, not too much tannin. Very dry. Opened up later; elegant nose and flavour. (16.5) This may have been added by our host in order to show a different style of Pomerol—or just to mix us up?

2. TROTANOY 1971:

Medium colour; lightest of flight, yet good depth. Closed nose, sweet. Very little tannin; fairly high acidity. Dry. A bit bigger than #1, but just as elegant. (16.5)

3. TROTANOY 1970:

Very dark, lovely colour. Sweet, ripe nose. Similar to #2 at first. Fairly high acidity, slightly volatile. A bit short. Later, opened up, with good fruit concentration. Needs another three to five years of bottle-age. Very promising. (17.5)

4. TROTANOY 1967:

Very dark, lovely colour, a bit orangy. Elegant, tea, cigar-box, spicy nose. Delicate. Some tannin, good balance, dry, fairly hot. Later, developed beautifully. (17)

5. TROTANOY 1964:

Darkest wine of flight; beautiful colour. Intense, open, fruity, ripe nose. Lots of tannin, not too complex, but has a rich middle. Good aftertaste. Remained hard and dry. Lots of body. Not a clean bottle; slight hint of mustiness. Can be excellent. (15) In the past, I rated this wine (17.5).

6. TROTANOY 1961:

Very dark, very deep. Earthy, ripe, big nose. Later, fruity, lovely open nose. Oak, lots of tannin, fruit/acidity balance. Great wine. Sweet complexity. Will last well. (18.5)

Comments were written after the wines were opened for 20 minutes.

Very difficult tasting. Some wines seemed to lack complexity. My first impressions: Pomerols, metallic, but since they didn't have too much complexity, I thought maybe California or Italian. (Barolos?) In hindsight, I didn't have a very good tasting. The best wines were the 1961 and 1970. The 1964 should have been a lot better.

June 9, 1981

Le Tastevin Wine Club, blind tasting of 1975 Clarets and 1974 California Cabernet Sauvignons.

We knew what the wines were, but not the order in which they were served.

1. Heitz Cellars "Martha's Vineyard" 1974, Napa Valley:

Very dark colour, slightly orangy at rim. Minty-eucalyptus nose. Very much "Martha's Vineyard." Lots of tannin and fruit; massive, long. A great wine. Needs another five to seven years. (18)

2. Mayacamas 1974, Napa Valley:

Massively dark-purple colour. Big, massive wine. Very dry. Mayacamas? This will either dry out or become a great bottle someday. (16)

3. Robert Mondavi 1974, Napa Valley:

Orangier than #1 and #2, and slightly lighter. Elegant, some tannin; a bit thin in middle, but well made. Long, spicy-cedary aftertaste. (15) This was the "Regular." The "Reserve" is a far superior wine.

4. Château Haut-Batailley 1975:

Bright, medium-dark colour; a bit watery at rim. Fairly high acidity, oaky, French style. A bit short aftertaste, and a bit simple. Not too much tannin. Ready, but lacks ripe fruit. (14)

5. Château Leoville-Lascases 1975:

Medium-dark colour, lots of tannin; hard, lovely fruit/acidity balance. Toasty, cedary bouquet. Great wine, but needs years to mature. (17)

6. Château Palmer 1975:

Very, very dark. Lots of tannin. Great fruit/acidity balance (heaps of fruit). Needs ten to 15 years. Good middle; long aftertaste. This should be a classic bottle by 1990 or beyond. (18)

DESSERT WINE

J. W. Morris 1978 Port, Sonoma County:

20% alcohol by volume. Very dark, very sweet. Black currant flavour. Needs lots of time. Lacks the spicy complexity of true Ports, but not a bad effort. Time will tell.

September 12, 1981

Dinner of "Group of Ten," at Dr. Allan Tobe's.

1970 Dom Pérignon Champagne:

Round, flavourful, and rich. Ready. Very elegant, well balanced. Good Champagne. (17.5)

1975 Mayacamas Chardonnay:

Bright gold, clean, elegant, lovely nose. Good fruit/acidity balance. Ready. Very good. (16.5)

Mount Veeder 1975 Chardonnay:

Dark-gold colour, lovely nose. No trace of madeirization; fresh, exotic fruit; good flavour, good aftertaste. Really fine wine. (17.5) This could compete with the best Chardonnays France has to offer.

Sterling Vineyards 1975 Chardonnay:

Good nose, a bit hot, a bit volatile acidity; fair amount of alcohol. Otherwise very good. Not in the same class as the top two. (15)

1920 Château Ausone:

(Group-bottle) Good ullage. Light colour, orange-brown. Bottle recorked in 1979. Cork and bottle smelled of stewed prunes. Quite sweet, but holding well after 61 years! Very pleasant. Cork very dry. Decanted and drunk within 20 minutes. Later, dried out. Good flavour, though, and lingering aftertaste. (17.5)

1928 Château Ausone:

(Group-bottle) Mid shoulder fill. Deep colour, browning. Similar bouquet to the 1920, but more lively. More body and complexity. The best wine of the evening. Still has lots of life in it. Quite a bit of acidity, expansive aftertaste. "Only" 53 years old! Good flavour, well balanced, stylish. A great bottle. (18.5)

1961 Château Ausone, in magnum:

Dark colour. Good, elegant, concentrated nose. Some tannin; hard and dry. This wine will last for a long time, but may not improve. Long on palate. Similar to l'Arrosée 1961. Sweeter on nose than on palate. Nevertheless, very good, but starting to lose its fruit. (17)

Château Rieussec 1970:

Medium gold, good botrytis. High acidity. Elegant, not very intense. Good flavour. Will improve. Not big, but lovely. Not too sweet or cloying. Typical elegance for the vintage.

The Château Ausone 1928 was very special!

September 16, 1981

A quiet dinner with Philip and Begita Togni, at "Miramonte" restaurant, in St. Helena.

Only Carol joined me. The rest of the group went somewhere else for dinner.

Joseph Phelps Sauvignon Blanc 1980:

Good character, pale gold; flowery, crisp, clean. Well balanced. A bit herbaceous.

1978 Cuvaison Chardonnay "Reserve":

("Ernie's" restaurant insignia) 3,000 bottles made. Lovely, elegant nose. Dark gold. Good on palate, but a bit short. Philip said that he preferred the nose to the palate. Togni is the vineyard manager and winemaker at Cuvaison.

1975 CUVAISON "SIGNATURE" CABERNET SAUVIGNON "RESERVE":

Opened and decanted before we left for the restaurant (at Philip's house). Made from 100% Cabernet Sauvignon grapes. Lovely, dark colour. Great spicy, minty nose. Fabulous on palate. Good balance, long aftertaste. Intense. Quite some tannin left. Philip expects this wine to be ready in 20 years. A great experience.

We also had lovely roasted duck. I tried sea urchins (yecch!) and fresh figs in Cabernet Sauvignon picked from a fig tree growing in the courtyard of the restaurant.

October 21, 1981

Comparative tasting of Robert Mondavi wines and French Equivalents, with John Lawson (Marketing Director of Robert Mondavi).

ROBERT MONDAVI 1979 FUMÉ BLANC:

Made from 90% Sauvignon Blanc, 10% Semillon. Light colour, fairly high acidity. Good aftertaste. Well made, but not as intense and complex as the 1978. (15.5)

1979 POUILLY-FUMÉ, LADOUCETTE:

High acidity. Some sulphur, vegetal nose. Intense. Quite similar on nose to the 1979 Fumé "Reserve" but, again, not as intense and complex as this producer's 1978. (16)

ROBERT MONDAVI 1978 FUMÉ BLANC "RESERVE":

Most complex of all three. Good flavour (three months longer in oak, and more bottle-age). Good acidity, well balanced, a touch of sweetness. Rich, long finish. (17)

ROBERT MONDAVI 1978 PINOT NOIR "RESERVE":

Lightish in colour, grapey, fruity, some oak. Forward on palate, not unlike a good Volnay. (16)

1976 CORTON HOSPICES DE BEAUNE "CUVÉE DR. PERTE," BOUCHARD AÎNÉ ET FILS:

Harder, darker, more tannic, closed; a bit bitter, stemmy. Slightly volatile acidity. A solid, masculine wine made in a ripe, sunny vintage. (15.5)

ROBERT MONDAVI 1979 PINOT NOIR:

Barrel sample. Pleasant, some tannin, sweetish, flowery, simple. (No score)

ROBERT MONDAVI CABERNET SAUVIGNON 1978 (REGULAR):

Medium-dark colour; sweet, minty nose. Pleasant, some middle, little tannin. Drinkable now. (15.)

ROBERT MONDAVI CABERNET SAUVIGNON 1976 "RESERVE":

Darker colour; minty, more tannic, more intensity, more complexity. Good now, but should last for a few more years. (16.5)

1976 CHÂTEAU MOUTON-ROTHSCHILD:

Deep red. Closed nose. Not as much tannin as the Mondavi Cabernet "Reserve," but not as open, either. Oak, cedar nose. Good flavour; not massive, but very good and complex. (17)

October 23, 1981

Tasting with John Lawson of Robert Mondavi Winery, featuring "oak components" on various wines produced or experimented by the Robert Mondavi winery.

The first two wines aged in Nevers Oak (Demptos).

1. 1978 CHARDONNAY, 14 MONTHS IN BARREL:

Light toast, fire only. Less oak-toast nose. Slightly more bitter, yet more vanilla, too.

2. 1979 CHARDONNAY, IN NEW BARREL:

Heavy toast, fire only. More toast-oak on nose. Smokier nose. More similar to white Burgundy. Darker and more brilliant colour. Traditionally, white Burgundy is aged in barrel style #2, California in #I.

The following are all new oak barrel samples in which Mondavi's 1978 Cabernet Sauvignons were aged for 20 months.

1. NEVERS (DEMPTOS):

Fire only, light toast. Open, pleasant, clean, producing a gentler wine style.

2. LIMOUSIN (DEMPTOS):

Fire only, light toast. Harder, more tannic. Not as pleasant as #1; more astringent, yet seems more mature. Oddly, this wine finishes too soft.

3. LIMOUSIN (FRANÇOIS FRÈRES):

Fire only, heavy toast. More body. The #1 is closer to #3 than to #2. Limousin needs heavier toasting to be similar to Nevers. European oak imparts more tannins. American oak imparts more vanillin to the wines.

4. NEVERS (FRANÇOIS FRÈRES):

Fire only, heavy toast, French oak. (Just different oak from #3.) Seems to be more forward than #1.

5. NEVERS (DEMPTOS):

Same as #1, but a barrel that is five years older (1974). Fire only, light toast. Not as clean, and not as much oak character as #1. At Mondavi, they prefer #1 overall. (Nevers from Demptos, light toast.)

6. 1975 AMERICAN OAK BARREL (COOPERED IN KENTUCKY):

No toast. Seems less toasty, more fruity than #5. But not too much character or complexity. Similar to a Louis Martini Cabernet Sauvignon. Very little tannin.

7. 1979 AMERICAN OAK:

New oak, no toast. Better than #6. Has tannin, a bit bitter, some greenness. Has lost the fruit character. Less vanillin than in the French oak barrels, which are fired.

Overall

A very educational tasting. Obviously, the choice of oak, of toasting the oak, and the length of time the wine spends in barrel are all factors of crucial importance in creating the final wine.

Later that night, we had the following wines with dinner.

1979 ROBERT MONDAVI CHARDONNAY "RESERVE":

Fully fermented in small oak barrels. Grapes picked at between 23 to 24 brix. A very clean, elegant, lovely wine. Well balanced, good complexity, good aftertaste. Will reach its peak in one to two years.

1976 ROBERT MONDAVI CABERNET SAUVIGNON "RESERVE":

Comments: see previous evening's notes.

1975 CHÂTEAU FILHOT:

(Donated by Bud Kanke, host of our evening at "Viva" restaurant) Never a favourite of mine. On the light side, pleasant. Lacks depth, not enough botrytis on nose. Lemon-green colour. Short finish. Filhot used to make fine Sauternes in the 1940s and 1950s.

October 30, 1981

Dinner at Sid and Joan Cross's, with Peter Sichel of Château Palmer.

It was lovely to see Peter again. Peter thinks highly of the 1978 Palmer. He compares it to the 1966. He's not too keen on the 1975s, including Palmer, but I tend to disagree. I hope to see him in Bordeaux next September. We had the following wines.

CHAMPAGNE POL ROGER 1973 "CHARDONNAY":

Evolved, sweet nose; elegant, well balanced. Clean, mature. Very good.

1974 HANZELL CHARDONNAY, SONOMA COUNTY:

A rare wine. Very little is made and it is hard to get. Clean, subdued nose. Elegant, well balanced. Lovely flavour and aftertaste. California, for sure, but with the elegance of a fine white Burgundy.

1968 HEITZ CELLARS CABERNET SAUVIGNON, NAPA VALLEY

AND

1968 HEITZ "MARTHA'S VINEYARD" CABERNET SAUVIGNON, NAPA VALLEY:

The regular Napa Cabernet was lighter in colour; more open, mint-eucalyptus nose. More forward, higher acidity, but shorter finish.

The "Martha's Vineyard" was very dark and deep, with a lovely nose, so typical of "Martha's Vineyard." This is a rare and fine wine that is very famous and highly rated. Lovely wine, plummy nose and flavour. Will last for a long time, but may not improve. I knew right away that they were Heitz, but I thought that both were "Martha's Vineyard" of different vintages, say 1970 and 1971, or 1966 and 1968. (All wines were served double-blind, of course.)

1952 BODEGAS BERBERANA "GRAN RESERVA" RIOJA:

This wine fooled me. Lightish colour; nice, spicy, sweet nose. Good, clean, sweet flavour; a bit short and acidic. I was sure that this was a red Burgundy, maybe the 1964 or 1966 vintage. A real experience. This bottle had no label. It was given to our host by the owner.

1970 D'YQUEM:

I guessed it as d'Yquem, but I thought that it was the 1966. In retrospect, the 1966 is darker, harder, and bigger. I knew it couldn't be the 1967 or 1971; just not great enough. Yet it was lovely. Long flavour. Medium-gold colour. Quite sweet. Slight dryness at finish; made me think more of a Barsac than a Sauternes, yet it had the style of d'Yquem. A bit buttery. Not one of the great d'Yquems, but a lovely wine nevertheless.

Peter stresses the soil factor rather than the microclimates, the weather, method of vinification, etc. This is the opposite view of the California growers, who put the soil low on their list of important factors. His favourite Palmer vintages in the past 20 years are 1961, 1966, 1962, 1978 (in that order). I tend to disagree because I think that the 1970 and 1975 are fabulous years. Peter prefers at this stage the 1971 to the 1970, which is surprising. He thinks that Château Margaux is improving, now that it is under new ownership.

Peter's favourite Haut-Médocs are Leoville-Lascases, Lafite, and Grand-Puy-Lacoste. Peter will be 50 this year. He has four sons, ages 14 to 19 (including 16-year-old twins), and a three-and-a-half-year-old girl. Her arrival must have been a surprise for both Peter and Diana!

March 6, 1982

Dinner of "Group of Ten" at Dr. Allan Tobe's, in honour of Harry Waugh, our guest.

Harry is staying with us. My daughter Orly, who is four years old, goes down to Harry's room every morning at 6:00 a.m. and wakes him up! She calls him "The Guy."

MAYACAMAS CHARDONNAY 1973:

Dark colour. Subtle, restrained nose. Good flavour, a bit hot, not bad. Slightly drying out. Quite big. (14)

MAYACAMAS CHARDONNAY 1974:

Fairly high acidity, subdued nose, not bad. A fine wine, although the least good of the three. Mayacamas is a reliable winery. One of the few that makes a Chardonnay that lasts. (15.5)

MAYACAMAS CHARDONNAY 1975:

Lovely bouquet and flavour. Good acidity, good balance. Toasty, oaky nose. Lovely. Everybody, including Harry Waugh, liked the 1975 best. (17)

WITH DINNER

Ridge "Monte Bello" Cabernet Sauvignon vertical tasting

1. 1977:

(11.7% alcohol) Medium-dark colour. Older-looking than the 1976. Vegetal, spicy Cabernet nose. Some tannin, medium body, on the dry side. Good. Well balanced, with 3% Merlot. Harry Waugh's comment: "Needs more time." (15)

2. 1976:

(12.7% alcohol) Darkest of the first group of four. Good, spicy, open, vegetal nose. Not as complex as the 1977. Softer, a bit high acidity. Harry's comment: "Elegant, but too forward." (14.5)

3. 1975:

(11.9% alcohol) Lightest. Complex, spicy nose. Sweet, good fruit on palate. Soft, elegant, least acidic. 5% Merlot in blend. (15)

4. 1973:

(12.8% alcohol) Medium to light colour. Least pleasant nose of the first four; vegetal, stemmy. High acidity. (13)

5. 1974:

(12.9% alcohol) Lovely, dark colour. Closed nose; elegant, complex, but tight. Good flavour, fair acidity, sweet. Acidity taking over. Later, improved, great depth, well balanced. (17.5) Will make a fine bottle some day.

6. 1968:

(12.7% alcohol) Very dark. Odd, unpleasant nose. Lots of tannin. Hard, woody flavour. Massive. Volatile acidity, too tannic. Must have been a bad bottle. (10)

7. 1970:

(13.5% alcohol) Very dark colour. Massive. Minty, spicy nose. Fabulous on palate; fruity, intense. Still a fair amount of acidity. An excellent, very serious Cabernet. Rare and expensive. (18)

8. 1974 RUBY CABERNET:

(13.4% alcohol) Medium light. Forward, open, vegetal nose. Very pleasant. Forward, elegant, but not in the same class as the others. This wine is a blend of 90% Carignan and 10% Cabernet. They only have one acre planted in Carignan and bottle it rarely (only in 1972 and 1974). (15)

Comments

The lightest wine was still very dark; the description of lightness is relative. The tasting was set the way Paul Draper suggested. He's the winemaker and part-owner. All wines were made by Paul Draper, except the 1968, which was made by Dave Bennion. All smelled very similar. Vines planted in 1945 and replanted in 1967. All 100% Cabernet Sauvignon, except 1977 and 1975, as detailed. My favourites were the 1970 and 1974. Harry Waugh preferred the 1973 (Bordeaux, elegant style) and 1974. The 1970 was terrific!

DESSERT WINE

CHÂTEAU RIEUSSEC 1976:

(I brought it along.) Good acidity, good balance, lovely. Harry Waugh is worried about the dark-gold colour, but it is surely a lovely wine right now. Unusually soft, rich, early maturing, but then, this is Rieussec's style.

March 9, 1982

Special Le Tastevin Wine Club tasting, in honour of Harry Waugh, at the Park Royal hotel, featuring 1966 Clarets.

1. CHÂTEAU L'ARROSÉE 1966:

Sweet, complex nose. Sweetest of the bunch. Rich flavour, not very complex, quite big. Well balanced. No tannin left. Good, clean, but not very complex aftertaste. Solid wine. (16.5)

2. CHÂTEAU BATAILLEY 1966:

Vegetal, closed nose; a bit chaptalized, chocolaty, toasty. Good flavour. Big, dry, very pleasant, but not very complex, a soft Pauillac style. (15)

3. CHÂTEAU CALON-SÉGUR 1966:

Medium colour. Hot, fairly stemmy Cabernet Sauvignon nose. Simple, rather watery, some tannin, too high acidity. Not complex enough. (14.5)

4. LES-FORTS-DE-LATOUR 1966:

Dark. Vegetal, deep, fruity, cedary Cabernet Sauvignon nose. Best bouquet. Lovely flavour, intense. Ready, yet big enough to last. Good, long aftertaste. Well made Pauillac. Surprisingly rich. (16.5) 1966 was the first vintage of this second wine of Château Latour.

5. CHÂTEAU GISCOURS 1966:

Dark; good, deep colour. Vegetal, alcoholic, tight nose. Hard wine, some tannin left, hot. Good fruit, yet quite hard. More of a combination of St. Julien and Pauillac than Margaux. (15)

6. CHÂTEAU GRUAUD-LAROSE 1966:

Medium-dark colour. Closed, tight nose; spicy, fruity. Nose opened up later, good complexity. Full, good flavour. Best potential so far, say around 1987 to 1992. Very promising, but not nearly ready. (17)

7. CHÂTEAU LA LAGUNE 1966:

Dark colour. Good, sweet, slightly vegetal, chocolaty nose. Luscious on palate, well balanced. Big, yet elegant. Long aftertaste. Very pleasant, well made. Fabulous ripe fruit. (18)

8. CHÂTEAU LEOVILLE-BARTON 1966:

Dark colour. Odd nose; berry-like, yet stewed fruit. Nose cleaned up a little later. Hard, high acidity, some tannin, some stewed flavour. Sour; tastes off. (12)

I knew the order of the wines beforehand. They were served blind. All had a maturing, deepish-brown colour. Harry Waugh found them very forward, except for #7. In retrospect, I enjoyed #1 better than I marked it.

March 10, 1982

Lunch at the Royal Vancouver Yacht Club.

Host: Judge Norm Collingwood. Participants: Harry Waugh, Brother Timothy (Christian Brothers), Brian St. Pierre (California Wine Institute), Darrell Corti (Wine Merchant in Sacramento), Sid Cross, John Levine, and myself.

CHAMPAGNE ROEDERER "CRISTAL" 1976 BRUT:

Elegant, soft, almost sweet; long, good flavour. Not very intense, but complex and well made.

CORTON-CHARLEMAGNE 1978, LOUIS LATOUR AND MEURSAULT PERRIÈRES 1978, DOMAINE JACQUES PRIEUR:

The Corton was more obvious: open, big, toasty nose. Good flavour. Youthful. Great potential.

The Meursault was more subdued, more forward and mature, yet with good potential. Well balanced, well made.

VOLNAY "CLOS DES SANTENOTS" 1976, DOMAINE JACQUES PRIEUR:

Surprisingly deep, dark, young, purple colour for a Volnay. Fair amount of tannin. Big, full; will improve in two to three years. Most participants liked it, including Harry. I'm glad I have recommended this wine to friends and members of our club. I purchased the wines for this event. They were all available in the specialty shop in British Columbia.

March 10, 1982

Dinner at "Le Pavillon" at the Four Seasons hotel, Vancouver, after the Wine Festival.

Marcena Levine, Harry Waugh, Brother Timothy of Christian Brothers Winery, and myself.

CHABLIS PREMIER CRU 1979, LOUIS LATOUR:

Clean, crisp, good nose, well balanced, well made. Not very complex, though.

CHÂTEAU MONTROSE 1976:

Too young, of course, but a lovely, deep, dark colour. Clean, cedary, complex nose. Montrose style, big St. Estèphe. Long, needs four to five years. Very good. Cork a bit short. Surprisingly rich for a 1976.

March 11, 1982

Special Commanderie de Bordeaux blind tasting of 1970 Bordeaux and Dinner, in honour of Harry Waugh, at the "Beach House" restaurant, in Stanley Park.

1. CHÂTEAU DUCRU-BEAUCAILLOU 1970:

Deep colour; good, clean, cedary-fruity nose. Very fruity. Quite dry on palate, hard, a bit too high acidity, but overall very good. Excellent potential, but needs time. This is now, and will certainly be in the future, the best St. Julien of the 1970 vintage. (17.5)

2. CHÂTEAU LEOVILLE-BARTON 1970:

Medium colour. Sweet, berry nose; slightly stemmy, oaky. Thin middle. Hard, high acidity, not very fruity, but good aftertaste. Later, improved, good flavour, but vegetal. Lacks the depth and weight of the Ducru. (15)

3. Château Beychevelle 1970:

Medium-dark colour. Good, fruity, berry, sweet nose. Good complexity. Similar to #2, but with a nicer ending. Later, complex, lovely flavour, vastly improved. A softer, but very elegant 1970. (16.5)

4. Château Haut-Brion 1970:

Medium colour. Closed nose; slightly toasty, oaky. Some tannin, fair acidity, good fruit; good, earthy, pleasant aftertaste. Later, beautiful, round, elegant, caramel complexity. (17)

5. Château Montrose 1970:

Darkest of flight. Deep, dark, huge Cabernet nose; berries and fruit. Hard, loaded with tannin; big, hot. Pauillac or St. Estèphe style. Latour or Montrose? Lovely fruity nose, palate, and flavour. Long aftertaste. Needs at least ten more years! (18.5)

6. Château Margaux 1970:

Good dark colour. Sweet, round, toasty nose. Good flavour, big, fair amount of fruit, well balanced, but sharp, acidic finish. (16)

7. Château Palmer 1970:

Medium dark; good ripe berry nose, slightly vegetal. Lovely flavour, intense, lots of tannin, big, well balanced. Needs a long time. Lovely flavour, very good. Needs five to ten more years. (18) As with the Montrose and Ducru, one of the great 1970s.

8. Château Lafite 1970:

Medium-light colour, good depth throughout. Smells more forward and older than the others. Prunes, caramel nose. Soft flavours; some tannin, slightly high acidity, good aftertaste. Elegant, but light. Lafite? (16)

9. Château Lynch-Bages 1970:

Very dark, deep colour. Minty-eucalyptus nose of Mouton (or Lynch-Bages?) Big, full, lots of tannin, easy to like. Great fruit extract. Not very complex at this stage, but really lovely. (18)

10. Château Latour 1970:

Very dark. Massive, rich, but very tight nose. Hard, big, lots of tannin, very powerful. Complex, cedary, but totally unyielding. (19) Possibly a perfect (20) in 20 years! A pity to open this too soon. Must be the Latour!

11. Harry Waugh Selection 1970 Bordeaux Supérieur:

Lightest colour; toasty, oaky nose. Light, simple, no contest against the other ten great wines, but fairly well made. (No score)

Latour easily won this contest; it is just too hard and unyielding at this stage, but in two decades, it will be a formidable wine!

Following the tasting, we sat down to dinner with the following wines.

1979 Château Laville-Haut-Brion:

Round, good flavour, long. Needs lots of time. Seems more forward than the tighter 1978, but really lovely. Jacques Barrière said that the 1978 (of which I have six bottles) is the best they ever made at Laville. I'm not sure of that. Fine it is, but what about the superb 1970, 1953, or 1945?

1961 Château Petrus:

A dream come true! I finally got to taste this wine, which I've been chasing for such a long time. Very dark, deep colour. Heavenly, rich, intense bouquet; long, big, full flavour. Needs five to ten years. 100% Merlot. Great. Power, sweetness, tannin, licorice, all in harmony! (19.5)

This was the last official event for Harry Waugh during his eight-day visit. He came to participate as a speaker at the Vancouver Wine Festival. Harry stayed with us and we had a great time. I learned a lot about him, and about wine, during his visit.

Harry Waugh has been my mentor since my early days of wine discovery. This visit by him has been a "historical event." A great Ridge Monte Bello tasting, then the great 1970s and 1961 Petrus with dinner, and on top of it all, Harry Waugh as guest speaker! What a lovely week.

March 1982

Tasting at the offices of Vintage Consultants, featuring the wines of Domaine Louis Latour, with Louis Latour.

WHITE WINES

1. 1974 Chevalier-Montrachet "Les Demoiselles":

Toasty, mature nose; darkish gold. Rich, complex, smoky, toasty on palate. Quite high acidity. Les Demoiselles plot owned by Latour since about 1902. The remainder of this particular vineyard belongs to Jadot. Not great, but not bad at all. Latour compared 1974 to 1973, but not as powerful. Frankly, I fail to see how any 1974 can be anywhere as good as 1973 for white Burgundies. (15)

2. 1973 Meursault-Genevrières:

Odd, metallic nose. Not too deep or complex. Unusually hard and acidic for a nine-year-old. Not the nutty flavour typical of Meursaults. Volatile acidity. Later, improved a bit, but not much. I didn't like it. (13.5)

3. 1978 Corton-Charlemagne:

Big, toasty, true Corton-Charlemagne. Austere, rich, powerful. Needs years. Latour said that it is a very big and an unusually rich wine. Superb quality and a keeper. (18)

4. 1971 Corton-Charlemagne:

Louis Latour mentioned that 1971 was very low in acidity, yet it has held very well. Medium deep-gold colour. Lovely, intense, complex, elegant wine. Rich, typical Corton-Charlemagne. Well balanced. Will hold. Superb quality, but, as expected, quite a bit more evolved than the 1978. (17.5)

In response to my question, Latour said that 1976 was a very odd year for reds as well as whites, due to drought, producing ripe wines with unusual balances and complements of acidity.

The 1971s and 1978s (both reds and whites) are the best vintages of the decade, followed by 1972 for reds and 1973 for whites. Frankly, most 1976s don't turn me on.

RED WINES

1. 1969 Corton-Grancey:

Fairly high acidity. Sweet, spicy nose; seems upset. Later, a bit forthcoming, good extract. Good colour; lovely, spicy nose. Not quite opened up. Latour said that it needed another three to four years. (16) Only 15 hectares (38 acres).

Since 1964, the best vintage for red burgundies is 1978, according to Latour. The 1972 is good, but too high acidity. (Even some producers are underrating the 1972s. I think that those that are well made will last for 15 or 20 years and that the acidity is what will keep them fresh.)

2. 1964 Romanée-St.-Vivant "Les Quatre Journaux":

Big, intense, tea-leaves nose. Lovely, flavourful. Still quite big. Good, dark colour. A classic. Latour own the whole vineyard of "Quatre Journaux." (18)

3. 1959 Chambertin "Cuvée des Héritiers Latour":

Big, intense wine. Dark, good depth, well balanced. Fairly high acidity, some tannin. Complex; soft, elegant, yet ripe. A true classic. Latour said, "We cannot do better; our greatest vintage to date." (18.5)

All three reds have been decanted in France, where the sediment was siphoned off and the bottles topped before shipping, specifically for this tasting. According to Latour, old Chardonnays lose the fresh fruit taste and develop a nutty, buttery flavour. Obviously. He thinks that 1979 whites may turn out to be as good as the 1973 whites, both being elegant vintages.

Louis Latour added that with white Burgundies, the nose/bouquet is important only during the first six to eight years. Later, it is the palate that counts. They buy a lot of Meursault-Genevrières from a grower who is also called Latour (no family connection).

His great grandfather started the Corton-Charlemagne (Chardonnay) planting on the hill of Corton. The vines produce alcoholic wines, like 1971 (almost 15% alcohol), making big wines with a lot of character. In ripe years, such as 1959, they had to add water because the wine was so big and concentrated. 1971 produced a very small quantity, both reds and whites. Harvest started very early (September 9) and the musts had low acidity.

Latour said that the 1978 Corton-Charlemagne was a late vintage (mid-October), high acidity, big, like 1969. Slow-maturing vintage. The 1971 and 1978 are opposite styles. Usually 13 to 14% alcohol (1978 is 13%), but in some years it is much higher. New oak casks every year for Chevalier-Montrachet and Corton-Charlemagne. Latour said that he prefers the 1979 to 1978 Corton-Charlemagne. (Maybe for drinking around 1984 to 1987, but for the long haul, I think that he is mistaken. The 1978 is in a class all by itself!) Grancey is the name of the previous owners of the vineyards, until about 100 years ago.

After the tasting, we sat down for dinner and had the following wines.

1979 Meursault-Genevrières, Louis Latour:

Elegant, well balanced, crisp, clean, very well made. Fruity-nutty character.

Vosne-Romanée 1976, Latour:

Good, dark colour; open, spicy Pinot Noir nose. Good acidity, flavourful. After 15 minutes, opened up; good complexity. But unfair against such tough and great competition tasted before the dinner.

Latour compared 1972 reds to 1957s: edgy, but lacking in charm, with high acidity. He said that the 1971 Corton-Grancey is ready, while the 1979 needs more time. The reds were very similar in style; all were quite powerful.

June 1, 1982

Commanderie de Bordeaux tasting of 1978 red Bordeaux, at "La Belle Auberge" restaurant, in Ladner.

Prepared by chef (and fellow Commandeur) Bruno Marti.

1. Château Kirwan:

Evolved colour, lightish rim; vegetal, Margaux nose. Forward on palate, elegant, very little tannin, excessive acidity, lacks concentration. Rather disappointing. (13.5)

2. CHÂTEAU PALMER:

Dark colour, good depth, concentrated fruit on nose. At first, bouquet not forthcoming; later, bouquet opened a bit. Spicy, herbaceous fruit, some tannin, good depth, good fruit, quite concentrated, sweet. Needs seven to ten years. One to buy! (17.5)

3. CHÂTEAU LYNCH-BAGES:

Medium colour. Open, herbal Cabernet nose. Elegant, some fruit, lacking middle. Soft. Very different from #2 in style. In the context of Lynch-Bages 1970 or 1975, this is a failure. (14)

4. CHÂTEAU BATAILLEY:

Medium dark; vegetal, not very complex nose; stemmy on palate. Fair amount of acidity (too much). Not bad, but not great. (14)

5. CHÂTEAU PICHON-LALANDE:

Darkest of flight, good depth to rim. Concentrated Cabernet nose. Has lots of class. Lovely flavour, very well balanced. More forward than the Palmer, yet has a fair amount of tannin. Long aftertaste. Really good. Cedary. Too young! This will make a fine bottle around 1990 to 1995. One to buy. (18)

6. CHÂTEAU MOUTON-ROTHSCHILD:

Medium colour, forward-looking, orange-brown rim. Sweet, not very complex nose. Good flavour, some soft fruit. A bit cedary. Somehow lacks extract and depth, especially for a Premier Grand Cru. Disappointing. Too loosely knit. (16.5)

7. CHÂTEAU LA LAGUNE:

Lightish colour. Sweet, jammy, toasty nose; not very complex. Noticeable acidity. Lacks middle. Rubbery. I didn't get enough wine due to poor pouring; the level in the glass was the lowest. La Lagune is the only non-First Growth Médoc to use 100% new oak barrels each vintage. Maybe in 1978, that was a mistake because of lack of ripeness in the fruit. (15)

8. CHÂTEAU LEOVILLE-LASCASES:

Medium colour; watery edge. Good, spicy-oaky nose. Good fruit, little tannin, but quite long. Good, but needs ten years to achieve more complexity. (17)

9. CHÂTEAU LEOVILLE-POYFERRÉ:

Medium, evolved colour. Clean, forward, lightish. Some tannin, well balanced, but not very complex. Too loosely knit, lacking extract. (15)

10. CHÂTEAU BEYCHEVELLE:

Lightest colour, orangy rim. Vegetal, sharp, open nose of an older wine. Bad bottle. The other bottle (across the table): darker, purplish colour; good fruit, medium concentration. Better on palate than on nose. (14)

This wine, together with Lynch-Bages and Mouton, should have made better wines in 1978. They are pleasant rather than fine, and lack concentration.

Clearly, the top wines were the Pichon-Lalande and Palmer, followed closely by the Lascases. All three would make a fine addition to any cellar.

WITH DINNER

CHÂTEAU CARBONNIEUX, GRAVES BLANC 1979:

Pale gold; fresh and crisp. Needs time. Complex nose. Will improve with age. Well balanced. Drink over the next four years.

CHÂTEAU D'YQUEM 1961:

Dark gold; "old" botrytis nose. Quite long on palate. Showing quite a bit of age and not very sweet, but has class. Will hold, but past its peak. Slightly madeirized on palate. A rare experience nevertheless. The 1962 is much better and livelier.

Spectacular dinner, organized by the owner/chef and member of our Commanderie, Bruno Marti. Lovely quenelle of scampi, great duck, and superb strawberry bavaroise dessert.

A note on the 1978s tasted

Most had a noticeable herbaceous character. 1978 was called "the miracle vintage" by Harry Waugh, saved at the last moment by a burst of fine weather. Alas, while the Cabernets improved, the fine weather came too late for the Merlots. Oddly, the two "winners" at our tasting, Pichon-Lalande and Palmer, depend on the Merlot heavily, yet both managed to make fine wines nevertheless.

1970 CHÂTEAU SUDUIRAUT, SAUTERNES:

The star of the evening. Lovely, deep, gold colour. Great botrytis, complex, elegant, peach-apricot nose. Long, sweet, thick on palate. A classic Sauternes, very well balanced. Will last for many years. Surprisingly good for a 1970. In general terms, Sauternes performed in an opposite way to red Bordeaux in terms of quality through the 1960s and early 1970s. While overall the reds were better in 1961 than in 1962, better in 1966 than in 1967, and better in 1970 than 1971, Sauternes turned things upside down, producing better 1962s, 1967s, and 1971s than 1961s, 1966s, and 1970s.

June 1982

International Wine and Food Society Black Tie Dinner, before my departure for Spain and the World Cup soccer games, in Madrid and Barcelona.

The Freemans and Jim Fitzgibbons, general manager of the Four Seasons hotel, were at our table. Each participant was to bring his/her own bottle; each table of six had therefore six different wines.

1973 HENRIOT BRUT CHAMPAGNE:

Lovely texture, well balanced, good weight; complex, toasty nose; long on palate. Very good, smooth, rich in the Roederer "Cristal" style.

1976 PULIGNY-MONTRACHET PREMIER CRU "COMBETTES," REMOISSENET:

Big, complex, toasty nose. Lovely bouquet. Good colour, big on palate, long aftertaste, complex. At its peak, but will hold. A fine bottle.

1964 MUSIGNY

AND

1961 CHARMES-CHAMBERTIN, BOTH PRODUCED BY JOSEPH DROUHIN:

Both excellent red Burgundies; "the way they used to make them."

The Musigny was deeper in colour and younger-looking. It was straightforward, easy to like, with a lovely Pinot Noir spicy nose. Good velvety fruit on palate.

The Charmes was a bit lighter, orangy colour, with more age. It was more intense on nose and palate, more complex, and fuller-bodied, but a bit too high in acidity. It had more sediment. Both fabulous wines; the Musigny was made in a more feminine, velvety style (the "Margaux" of Burgundy, as I like to call it), and the Chambertin deeper, more solid, more masculine.

1961 CHÂTEAU COS D'ESTOURNEL:

The king of the evening—at least at our table. Very dark, deep colour; didn't show its age at all. Needs more time. Lovely, big, intense, masculine, cedary Cabernet Sauvignon nose. Long, full on palate. Well balanced, some tannin left. Needs two to three more years. Marvellous St. Estèphe! This is a serious bottle of Claret.

1976 CHÂTEAU ST. JEAN "BELLE TERRE" JOHANNISBERG RIESLING "SELECT LATE HARVEST," SONOMA VALLEY, IN HALF-BOTTLE:

15.4% residual sugar. Very deep, orange-gold colour. Intense, apricot-peaches bouquet. Sweet, good acidity, big, well balanced, long. Will hold for a long time. Almost overwhelming.

Also tasted from other tables
(At these events where each table has different wines, we tend to offer samples of our wines in exchange for samples from other tables.)

RENÉ LALOU MUMM'S 1975 CHAMPAGNE:

Stemmy, rather disappointing. Nowhere near the complexity of the Henriot. Sharp, acidic, low fruit. Mumm's should do better than this. Fancy bottle, though.

1966 AND 1967 CHÂTEAU CHEVAL-BLANC:

Both had very good noses.

The 1967 more forward, ready, soft, good herbaceous nose, medium colour and body. The 1966 is a favourite of mine; darker colour; complex, long, open, sweet, jammy nose. Very good. Almost ready, but will hold. Lots of rich fruit here.

1961 CHÂTEAU LA GAFFELIÈRE-NAUDES:

Dark colour, no sign of age (21 years old). Sweet, forward, not very complex, easy to drink and enjoy. Enough fruit to hold. Smooth, round, chocolaty. The best La Gaffelière to date.

1970 CHÂTEAU D'YQUEM:

A bit disappointing. Medium-gold colour. Closed, delicate nose; not very complex or deep, but good botrytis. A bit forward and "weak"; however, I had tasted our Château St. Jean Sonoma beforehand, and that was a bit unfair. What is certain is that the 1971 and especially the 1967 and 1975 d'Yquems are far superior to this.

1976 RIESLING BEERENAUSLESE RHEINPFALTZ:

Shipper unknown. Lighter by far in colour and texture to our Château St. Jean, yet easier to drink. Good acidity; good botrytis on nose. Elegant fruit, lovely.

1976 CÔTE-RÔTIE "LES JUMELLES," PAUL JABOULET:

Deep colour, great, spicy nose. Long, very rich, ripe fruit. Will hold.

I should also mention the food. Michel Clavelin, the chef at the Four Seasons hotel, who has prepared great meals for us in the past, has outdone himself.

A most enjoyable evening.

The World Cup soccer games turned out to be quite a mess. This was supposed to be a childhood "dream come true" for my good friend Menashe and myself. Menashe practices law in Jerusalem. I purchased sets of two tickets to all the games held in Barcelona and for the final in Madrid. I also booked as a package, two rooms at our hotel. Just before the games started, Israel embarked on its "Peace in Gallilee" operation to oust the PLO from Lebanon. As Menashe is a paratrooper (airborne artillery) in the Reserves, he was called up, of course, and spent the World Cup games watching it on TV from battered Beirut. while I was stuck in Barcelona for two weeks with no one with whom to share the experience.

July 30, 1982

Blind tasting of 1978 and 1979 red Bordeaux Classed Growths at Dr. Allan Tobe's.

It turned out that we were tasting five châteaux as pairs: each of the 1978 and 1979 vintages.

1A. CHÂTEAU LA LAGUNE 1978:

Full, purple colour; lovely, fruity, spicy nose. Fairly hard wine, a bit thin, austere, tight, and herbaceous. 1978? (16.5)

1B. CHÂTEAU LA LAGUNE 1979:

More purple than #1A, a bit watery at rim. Good, spicy nose. Harder than #1A; more new oak on palate. Looks younger than #1A; 1979? OK, but not great. Wet cardboard? (15) Difficult to judge at this stage. (These 1979s were just bottled and shipped a few months ago.)

2A. CHÂTEAU MARGAUX 1979:

Good, dark colour; lovely, sweet, fruity nose. More open nose than #2B. Fruitier nose than #1A and #1B. Some tannin. Sweet, vanilla bouquet. 1979? But what? Slightly tight, hard, but very promising. Hard to judge the final quality in ten years' time, but I think #2B will be better. (17.5)

2B. CHÂTEAU MARGAUX 1978:

Darker than #2A, but very close in appearance. More open, sweeter, jammy nose. Lovely flavour, lots of tannin. 1978? Whatever it is, this is magnificent. Needs ten or even 15 years. (19)

3A. CHÂTEAU LEOVILLE-LASCASES 1979:

Darker-looking than #3B, more purple. Younger? Lovely, fruity, jammy, vanilla bouquet. Good flavour, easy to enjoy, good acidity and tannin. 1979? Very good "Cabernet" style. (17)

3B. CHÂTEAU LEOVILLE-LASCASES 1978:

A bit watery at rim; more closed nose. Hard, lots of tannin, Pauillac-like, lovely, long flavour. A bit stemmy. 1978? Very good, though, but really needs lots of time. (17.5)

4A. CHÂTEAU COS D'ESTOURNEL 1978:

More mature-looking than #4B, yet very dark. More open nose; oak, vanilla. Vegetal, Margaux-like. Elegant, good middle, some tannin, fairly high acidity. A bit short on palate. 1978? If so, probably Palmer. (17)

4B. CHÂTEAU COS D'ESTOURNEL 1979:

More purple than #4A, younger-looking, dark. More pungent, potent, closed, concentrated fruit nose. Hard. Lots of tannin. Not similar to #4A; lacks the elegance. Too hard for me. May improve with time. (16)

5A. CHÂTEAU PICHON-LALANDE 1978:

Touch of purple, dark. Lovely, jammy, vanilla, sweet nose. 1978? Herbaceous, perfumy, yet rich and plummy. Is this the Palmer? Anyway, a lovely bottle. (18)

5B. CHÂTEAU PICHON-LALANDE 1979:

Looks slightly more mature than #5A. Dark. Fuller flavour than #5A. Lovely, big. 1979? Quite cedary, not at all like #5A. Riper, less elegant, but more chocolaty/coffee beans. Very good. (17)

Overall

I was right about all the vintages, but I was wrong about the actual châteaux. I had a bad cold, so it was very difficult to smell or taste. Overall, the 1979s have a fair amount of acidity, and not as much depth as the 1978s, yet they're quite good. Anyway, all these wines are so young! We will all be much smarter in seven to ten years when these lovely wines develop some maturity. Two good, but different, vintages nevertheless. We are lucky.

We had the following wines with dinner, following the tasting.

1979 CHALONE CHARDONNAY:

Good fruit, acidity, flavour. Full-bodied, typical California. Well made, maturing fast.

1979 BACIGALUPI PINOT NOIR, SONOMA VALLEY:

(The Bacigalupi kids were there: John and his new wife.) Finally, a French-style Pinot Noir from California! Good flavour; spicy nose. Good flavour, light-bodied. Very French-like. Very forward Volnay style.

HEITZ CELLARS 1978 "FAY VINEYARD" CABERNET SAUVIGNON, NAPA VALLEY:

Spicy, good flavour, but quite forward for a 1978 Cabernet Sauvignon. Good fruit, straightforward. Not in the class of the 1978 or 1979 Clarets, tasted before the meal, of course.

CHÂTEAU D'YQUEM 1967:

A masterpiece. Great, intense, honey, botrytis nose. Superb fruit/acidity balance. I was half-drunk! Great wine! This surely helped me fight my cold. This is not wine; it is making love! Perfect (20).

August 1982

Dinner and tasting at "La Belle Auberge" restaurant.

With S. Crosses, K. Crosses, Levines, Tobes, Mottersheads, Freemans. Our friend, chef/owner Bruno Marti, was there to cook for us.

First we sat down to taste Chardonnays from two California (Napa) leading estates: St. Clement and Robert Mondavi.

1980 St. Clement Chardonnay, Napa Valley:

Youthful, good acidity, green-yellow colour. Good nose; fresh, oak-honey, vegetal but good. Fine quality. Needs two to three years. (15.5)

1979 St. Clement Chardonnay, Napa Valley:

Nice complexity, good depth, quite high acidity. Raw, needs time. More age and complexity than the 1980. Well balanced. (16.5)

1979 Robert Mondavi "Reserve" Chardonnay, Napa Valley:

Lovely, elegant, good acidity, not overwhelming, oaky. Classy. This is really a fine effort by Mondavi. Maybe not a keeper, but boy, is it good! (17.5)

1978 Robert Mondavi Chardonnay (Regular), Napa Valley:

Good acidity, well balanced, but not very complex. The "Reserve" is a better wine. (14.5)

1978 Robert Mondavi "Reserve" Chardonnay, Napa Valley:

Darker than the 1978 Regular; a bit higher oak. Good, a bit short in fruit. Drink soon. (15)

1976 Robert Mondavi "Reserve" Chardonnay, Napa Valley:

Unfiltered. Lightish colour; lovely, elegant nose; good acidity. A modest wine. Not overwhelming. Elegant, well balanced. Ready now. (15.5)

Overall

The group preferred the Robert Mondavi to the St. Clements. While I agreed that the 1979 "Reserve" was superb, I thought that the St. Clement samples were as good as the Mondavi.

Then it was time for dinner.

1973 Mirassou Champagne:

"Late disgorged." The texture and bubbles of a French Champagne. However: closed nose; sharp; dry; no texture or complexity; not very yeasty. Rather simple.

1969 Charmes-Chambertin, Faiveley:

Medium-dark colour, orangy rim. Spicy, typical Pinot Noir bouquet. High acidity on palate overwhelmed the fruit. Good flavour, though a bit short. Good, but didn't stand a chance against the 1961 and 1929! (15.5)

1961 Echézeaux, Joseph Drouhin:

Lighter than the 1969 Charmes; orangy colour. Earthy, slightly edgy nose. Good balance, long aftertaste, good backbone. Will keep, but will not improve. Excellent fruit. This is a fine bottle. (17)

1929 Charmes-Chambertin, Joseph Drouhin:

The star of the evening! It is 53-years-old; similar in colour to the 1961 Echézeaux! Lovely, elegant nose. Good on palate; intense, complex, clean. Better than the 1961 Echézeaux. A great wine. Fruit has kept well. I wish they made such Burgundies today. The first 1929 red Burgundy I've tasted to date, and a great one at that. (19)

1966 Château L'Arrosée:

I was the only one to guess this wine, although I thought it was the 1961. Hard, dark, ripe fruit; unusually hard for a St. Emilion, yet so typical of this property, which has an unusually high proportion of Cabernet Sauvignon in its blend for a St. Emilion. (17)

1961 Château Coutet:

A bottle that I brought along. I purchased it seven years ago and waited for a special occasion. Very dark gold. Much better than expected. Good botrytis nose. Not very sweet, clean, well balanced, not overwhelming. Easy to drink, and greatly enjoyable. Having said that, it is not as good as Coutet's 1962. (15.5)

September 1982

Dinner of "Group of Ten," at home.

Champagne Krug "Grande Cuvée" Brut N/V:

Not the usual Krug. Elegant, nice, very well made, but without the extract, depth, and intensity of the older style of Krug. Pity they changed their winemaking procedure. They seem to want their nonvintage cuvée to be more accessible, softer. (16.5)

Puligny-Montrachet "Pucelles" 1978, Leflaive:

The greenest-gold of the three whites. Needs much more time. Good depth. Good oaky, lemony nose. Should have a very good future. Clean, oak bouquet. Fabulous, yet tight, like so many great 1978 white Burgundies. Too young. (17.5)

Puligny-Montrachet "Pucelles" 1978, Henry Boillot:

More forward. Some sulphur on nose. Well balanced. Vanilla, oak, and truffles on nose and palate. Very good. Needs three more years. Lovely. (17)

Corton-Charlemagne 1978, Remoissenet:

After 30 minutes, it developed a toasty, nutty nose. Good depth, well balanced, clean. Needs three to five more years. Very good—actually will be really excellent. Give it time. (18)

All three are fine white Burgundies!

CHÂTEAU MARGAUX 1953:

(Group-bottle) Low shoulder, dried cork. Brownish colour, orangy rim. A bit excessive acidity, needs drinking. Lovely, elegant, typical "aged" Médoc. Lovely bouquet. Previous bottle tasted with this group was better. (16.5)

CHÂTEAU MARGAUX 1961:

(Group-bottle) Good level. Great colour for a 1961. Good depth of flavour, some acidity. Should hold. Lovely, elegant, classic Margaux. Rich, long, cedary-chocolaty; magnificent fruit. A beauty! (19)

1906 CHÂTEAU MONTROSE:

(Group-bottle) A 76-year-old wine! Fairly deep colour, orangy-brick rim, but amazingly deep for the vintage. Lovely, sweet bouquet. Good flavour, fairly high acidity, long on palate. Vanilla aftertaste. What a great experience! (18.5)

Comments on the 1906 Montrose Special Bordeaux Label

Imported by Collectors' Cellar, Riverside, California. Recorked on August 10, 1979 (Whitwham and Co. Wines Ltd., Altringham, England). Label on back read: Gilis and Co, Bordeaux, Château Montrose 1906 A/C St. Estèphe. We must have been fortunate, because I have earned that Whitwham's recorkings are not very reliable. This was a great bottle.

1970 CHÂTEAU GUIRAUD, SAUTERNES:

Unusually deep, gold colour; more like a Madeira. Woody, Spanish-like, even some fizz (secondary fermentation in bottle). A disappointing finale for an otherwise great dinner. (13)

September 1982

Les Compagnons des Vins de France tasting, at the Four Seasons hotel.

With Jean Hugel as our guest speaker, featuring Hugel's wines from Alsace, listed locally.

1. SYLVANER 1980:

Crisp, clean, nice bouquet. Good, everyday wine. Rather simple. (13)

2. PINOT BLANC 1979, BLANC DE BLANCS:

Too much acidity and sulphur; a bit fizzy; very dry. I preferred the Sylvaner.

Later, sulphur disappeared. (12.5)

3. RIESLING 1978:

More character than above two. This is their regular Riesling. Clean, crisp, good aftertaste. Quite high acidity. (14) 1978 was not a particularly good year for Alsace. Their best vintages of the decade are 1971, 1975, and 1976, with the latter producing magnificent late harvest wines.

4. RIESLING "CUVÉE TRADITION" 1977:

Well rounded, pleasant. Rich for a lean year. Good, toasty flavour. Fine effort. Actually, it is amazing that "Johnny" made any decent wines in 1977. (15.5)

5. RIESLING 1976 "VENDANGE TARDIVE" (LATE HARVEST):

Petroleum nose, typical of ripe Riesling. Auslese-style; full, rich, good acidity, intense; drier than I remember from previous tastings. Residual sugar, 9 grams. 14% potential alcohol. Lovely length, concentration. This is really nice. (17)

6. MUSCAT "CUVÉE TRADITION," 1979:

Good Muscat aftertaste. Crisp, pleasant, well balanced, good acidity. Johnny Hugel said that the very ripe 1976 Muscat didn't taste like Muscat. Too much ripeness eliminates the Muscat bouquet. (15.5)

7. GEWÜRZTRAMINER "CUVÉE TRADITION" 1979:

Very flavourful, apples-peaches. Not my style, but quite good and clean. (15)

8. GEWÜRZTRAMINER 1979 "RÉSERVE PERSONNELLE":

Not as open as #7, but more delicate and complex. Not as forward. Closed. Needs more time. Good potential. (15.5)

9. GEWÜRZTRAMINER 1976 "SÉLECTION DE GRAINS NOBLES":

Only produced in 1921, 1929, 1945, 1959, 1961, 1967, 1971, and 1976! 40 grams of sugar left unfermented. Good with sorbets (strawberries or raspberries). Three fûts made. A very great, very rare wine—in 25 years! (19)

Hugel said about the Riesling "Sélection de Grains Nobles" that the 1976 was the first time this grade of Riesling was made since 1865! Actually, there has been no Riesling Hugel Sélection de Grains Nobles since that year, over a century ago.

September 1982

Le Tastevin Wine Club, vertical tasting of Château l'Arrosée, St. Emilion Grand Cru Classé.

Blend of approximately 35% Cabernet Sauvignon, 55% Merlot, and 10% Cabernet Franc. Mr. Rodin, the owner, is an odd, eccentric man trying (and often succeeding) to produce solid "Haut-Médoc-like" wines in St. Emilion.

FLIGHT #1

1. 1976:

Light colour, orangy rim. Dull nose. Lacks depth, sweetish, fairly high acidity, but pleasant. (13.5)

2. 1973:

Lightest, weak-looking, orangy rim. Sweet, herbaceous nose. Lacks body, short. (13)

3. 1971:

Medium to pale colour, orangy rim; oaky, woody, mature nose. Mature, long on palate. Better than expected. Finishes slightly acidic. Best nose of #1 to #4. (15)

4. 1967:

Medium colour, orange-brown rim. Good depth on nose; tight, some berries, sweet. A straightforward wine. Not pretentious and not complex. A bit volatile on nose. (14)

FLIGHT #2

5. 1961:

Medium dark, orangy rim. Intense, complex; mature, long, leathery nose. Very complex on palate. Quite some tannin. Starting to show signs of maturity, but no rush. Very good. Fairly high acidity. Tobacco bouquet. (17.5)

6. 1970:

Darkest; deep, purple-red-brick appearance to rim. Unyielding bouquet, concentrated, clean; needs time. Young on palate. Good flavours, intense, lots of tannin. Well balanced. Needs four to six years. Pepper, mint. A solid wine. (17.5)

7. 1966:

Dark, very similar in colour to #6, but more orange at rim. Closed, tight nose. Dark, hard, fruity, lots of tannin; needs time. This wine has excellent potential. (17.5)

The 1970, 1966, and 1961 are all fine, serious wines. They are actually quite similar in style. It is really only a matter of level of maturity.

October 1982

Côtes de Buzet tasting, in my office, with Walter Van Vloten and Tony Gismondi.

BUZET 1979 REGULAR:

Light, pale red; simple, short, rather uninteresting. (12)

BUZET 1980 REGULAR:

Better than the 1979. More colour, more fruit. Simple, but well balanced. Good everyday wine. (13)

BUZET 1978 "CUVÉE NAPOLEON":

This is their "Reserve" wine. Good depth, pleasant, dark colour, well balanced. The best of all three. Concentrated, fruity, fairly rich. (15)

All are produced by co-op Vignerons Réunis des Côtes de Buzet.

October 1982

Tasting and dinner at Joe Heitz's.

Also Sid and Joan Cross, Alice and Kathleen Heitz, and a young South African winemaker, who is doing his apprenticeship at Heitz Cellars. (Twelve years later, this young man is the winemaker at Thelema Winery in South Africa.)

1980 HEITZ CELLARS CHARDONNAY, NAPA VALLEY:

Just released. Good, clean, oak nose. Medium acidity, pineapple, not very intense. Hot. Too alcoholic for me. Lacks a bit in middle.

Then we tasted his four just-released 1977 Cabernets.

1977 HEITZ CELLARS CABERNET SAUVIGNON, NAPA VALLEY:

Medium colour; good, minty nose. Harsh, hot, a bit high acidity, long on palate. Needs one to two years. 1977 was a hot, drought year in the Napa Valley, as was the previous (1976) vintage. (15)

1977 HEITZ CELLARS "FAY VINEYARD," NAPA VALLEY:

Sweeter than the above, more elegant nose, slightly darker; forward, some tannin, well balanced. A bit short aftertaste. Good, but not great. (16)

1977 HEITZ CELLARS "BELLA OAKS," NAPA VALLEY:

Lovely, cedary nose. Not overwhelming; very dark, intense, rich, good fruit, complex. Needs a few more years. My favourite for drinking now. (17)

1977 HEITZ CELLARS "MARTHA'S VINEYARD," NAPA VALLEY:

Very deep colour, lovely bouquet, quite similar to Bella Oaks, but more pronounced eucalyptus. Right now, Joe prefers the Bella Oaks, but potentially, in four to five years, he thinks the "Martha's" will be better. Harder and coarser on palate than the Bella Oaks at this stage. (17)

1979 HEITZ CELLARS PINOT NOIR, NAPA VALLEY:

Grapes purchased from a single source. Good Pinot Noir character. A bit hard, not bad. Easy to drink. Quite evolved, spicy, round. (14.5)

I told Joe that I considered the 1974 Cabernets to be the equivalent of the great 1961 Bordeaux, in the context of California Cabernets. He agreed and said that 1974 put California's Cabernets on the map.

At dinner, we had the following wines.

SCHRAMSBERG 1976 CALIFORNIA CHAMPAGNE "RESERVE":

Joe Heitz received a case of this wine from Jack Davies in exchange for a case of his Cabernets. Lovely, elegant nose. Soft, creamy. Not very complex, but very good. One of the best California sparkling wines I've had to date.

HEITZ CELLARS PINOT CHARDONNAY 1973 "CASK Z-32," NAPA VALLEY:

A masterpiece. Lovely wine. Dark gold; lovely, oak nose. Soft, round, at its peak. Great, long aftertaste. Like a dry Sauternes. I wish Joe produced more Chardonnays like this in recent vintages.

1969 HEITZ CELLARS CABERNET SAUVIGNON "LOT C-91"

AND

1969 HEITZ "MARTHA'S VINEYARD," NAPA VALLEY:

The C-91 is a blend of 45% "Martha' Vineyard" grapes and 55% other Cabernet Sauvignon grapes. Heitz made this blend for financial reasons. He needed the money, so he "stretched" some "Martha's."

The 1969 "Martha's" is Joe's all-time favourite! This was a lovely, big wine; bigger than the C-91, and bigger than his 1968 "Martha's." Not as delicate. Great complexity, typical eucalyptus and mint.

The C-91 was more forward and an excellent wine on its own, but had a bit of a hard time against the "Martha's."

1974 HEITZ CELLARS "MARTHA'S VINEYARD" ANNIVERSARY LABEL, NAPA VALLEY:

A great Cabernet Sauvignon. My favourite. I own eight bottles. Fabulous, big, very dark, intense, mint-eucalyptus. Great future.

1968 ROBERT MONDAVI PINOT NOIR, NAPA VALLEY:

Disappointing. Light, sugared, over-the-hill. Joe was very disappointed because he had fine bottles of the same wine previously. Not too bad actually, but to serve this after the great 1969 and 1974 "Martha's"?!

JOSEPH PHELPS JOHANNISBERG RIESLING 1978, "SELECT LATE HARVEST" TBA, NAPA VALLEY:

(30% residual sugar) Full-size bottle. Served at room temperature, which made it even sweeter; Joe gave us ice cubes to put in the wine, and that helped. A masterpiece of intensity, colour, bouquet, and concentration; apricot-peach nose and flavour. A great evening and quite an experience!

The following day

Visit to Caymus Winery, with Sid Cross.

We met Charlie Wagner, his son Chuck, and Randy Dunn, the young winemaker who will be starting his own winery shortly, called Dunn Vineyards. He will start with the 1979 Cabernet Sauvignon; he has planted six acres in Cabernet Sauvignon up above Burgess, on Howell Mountain.

OEIL DE PERDRIX 1980:

Made from Pinot Noir grapes. Sweetish on nose, but dry on palate. Pleasant summer sipping wine, made in the Tavel Rosé style. (14)

LIBERTY SCHOOL 1979 CHARDONNAY:

Caymus's second label. Sells for $7 retail. Not much Chardonnay character. Quite stemmy, a bit short, but for the price, this is a decent everyday wine. (13)

1980 CAYMUS CHARDONNAY:

Sold only at the winery. Honey-oak nose, lean, quite high acidity, oak aftertaste. I did not like this wine. Not enough ripe fruit and too much wood. Clearly, Caymus's forte is their reds. (13.5)

1981 FUMÉ BLANC, SAUVIGNON, NAPA VALLEY:

Good, varietal nose. Clean, crisp, nice fruit. Pleasant. (14)

1979 PINOT NOIR, NAPA VALLEY:

($8) Medium-lightish colour. Good Pinot Noir character on nose. Hard and tannic on palate. This is a contradiction between appearance and taste. (13.5)

1979 ZINFANDEL, NAPA VALLEY:

Good nose, light body, lacks middle, yet hard (tannic). OK, but not special. (13)

1979 CABERNET SAUVIGNON, NAPA VALLEY:

($12.50) Good, elegant, cedary nose; unusual for Caymus. Needs two to three years. Quite a bit of tannin, but soft and lacks middle. Not very concentrated. (15)

Randy let us taste the 1982 Cabernet Sauvignon in barrel while it was still fermenting and had 5% residual sugar. He said that the 1982 will not be quite as concentrated as some people say.

Charlie Wagner has the reputation of being a grumpy old man. Rumour has it that he shot at someone once for trespassing on his property. He also doesn't like people who criticize his wines. I didn't dare offend him, so I actually swallowed all the wines he gave me to taste. Sid Cross, on the other hand, knowing that we had a long tasting and eating day ahead of us, very politely, and supposedly unnoticed, stepped outside to spit (no spittoons in the tasting room).

This went on for a while until Wagner noticed it and followed Sid outside. When asked if he didn't like the wines, Sid replied that he did so, very much, actually, but could taste better when spitting. Somehow he got away with it (Sid usually does), but from that moment onward, he swallowed.

Lunch at Domaine Chandon (after the visit to Caymus).

DOMAINE CHANDON "BLANC DE BLANCS" BRUT:

Well made, well balanced, clean. Crisp fruit, good flavour.

1975 CUVAISON CABERNET SAUVIGNON "SIGNATURE," NAPA VALLEY:

Philip Togni's "Reserve" wine. Sells for $40 at winery, and we paid only $35 at the restaurant. Very dark, big colour. Concentrated wine. Lots of fruit, some tannin. Not very much sediment. A lovely, big, excellent, and rare wine. Needs at least ten more years.

Later that day

At Draper and Esquin's Wine Shop, in San Francisco.

We tasted the following.

1964 BONNES MARES, PIERRE PONNELLE:

Sells for $75 per bottle! Very soft, lightish, orange-brown colour. Tired, lacks fruit. After 15 minutes, it started to fall apart. My experience with Ponnelle's older wines is that most of them are great in Beaune, but they are too delicate to travel, especially long distances.

October 1982

Dinner at "Chez Panisse" in Berkeley, Alice Water's restaurant.

Alsatian evening, very good food. We brought our own wines.

1978 WHITE CORTON-VERGENNES, CHÂTEAU DE BLIGNY, PIERRE-YVES MASSON:

Costs $15 on sale, instead of $27. Steely, crisp, Chablis-like, but with good character. Well made, but a bit thin. Good value, however. With age, this wine should improve.

1962 CHÂTEAU LA MISSION HAUT-BRION:

Purchased from Draper and Esquin's that day for $78; rather expensive. A fabulous wine. Great character and style. Dark colour; younger than its age would indicate. At its peak. Lovely, sweet, earthy, complex nose. Full, lingering aftertaste. Cannot fault that wine at all; wish we had more of it. Ready, soft, yet full. A great bottle!

November 1982

Double-blind tasting, at a Le Tastevin member's home.

1. GRANDS ECHÉZEAUX 1972, DOMAINE DE LA ROMANÉE-CONTI:

Orangy brick colour. Spicy, sweet nose. High acidity; a bit thin, sharp, but good fruit extract. Later, softened up a bit. Sweet, ripe fruit. Very long, yet still tight. Needs an extra five years. (17.5)

2. BEAUNE, HOSPICES BEAUNE "GUIGONE DE SALINS" 1972, BEYERMANN:

Darkest of flight. Delicate, yet concentrated, spicy Pinot Noir nose. Better fruit than #1 at this stage, but again, high acidity. More forward. Charming wine. (16.5)

3. CORTON-GRANCEY 1972, LATOUR:

Medium colour, orange-brick rim. Slight sulphury nose. Buttery. Not as intense as #1 or #2, but softer. Fair acidity, a bit short. (15.5)

4. GEVREY-CHAMBERTIN "COMBES AUX MOINES" 1972, GESWEILER:

Medium-light brick-orange colour. Beet-sugar, toasty, spicy nose. Similar to #1. Very sharp; high acidity. (14) Gesweiler is a négociant house located in Nuits-St.-Georges.

5. NUITS-ST.-GEORGES "CLOS DES FORÊTS" 1972, JULES BELIN:

Medium-dark. Good depth of colour. Best appearance. Good, clean, sweet, spicy nose. Good flavour, well balanced. Some tannin, excessive acidity; long, flavourful. (16.5)

6. VOLNAY "SANTENOTS" "HOSPICES DE BEAUNE-CUVÉE GAUVIN" 1972,BEYERMANN:

Lightest colour. Orange-brown watery rim. Sweet Pinot Noir nose. Smooth; similar to #3. Quite elegant, without excessive acidity. Drinking well now. (16)

Comments

Wines very similar in style, appearance, and flavour, with slight variations. I would guess 1972 red Burgundies; they show the maturity and the acidity typical of the 1972s. (I guessed them all correctly!)

After the tasting, we learned that the subject wines were 1972 red Burgundies. These wines are now ten years old.

DESSERT WINE

AUREO "RESERVA ESPECIAL PRIVADO," MUY VIEJO, TARRAGONA:

20% alcohol. Solera system. Similar to a Solera or a Madeira/Muscatel/Málaga; Tarragona/Barcelona area. Not bad. Amber colour. Rich, nutty, and ripe raisins flavours.

November 1982

Trip to Israel and France.

In Israel

MURFATLAR 1978:

A Romanian wine similar to an Auslese or Spätlese, but not as complex; higher alcohol. Rather simple, but elegant and light. An "afternoon" drink.

CARMEL CABERNET SAUVIGNON"SELECT" 1978 AND 1979:

Both had good Cabernet Sauvignon noses; ready to drink. Pleasant and clean; good colours. The 1978 (decanted) was a bit acidic and mature, but still enjoyable.

CARMEL PETITE SYRAH N/V:

Had it twice. Dark colour. Good depth, good fruit; very pleasant, ready. Quite rich and peppery.

CHAMPAGNE VEUVE CLICQUOT BRUT N/V:

As usual, reliable, full, good nose. Very good yeasty, fruity flavours. Purchased it in a wine shop in Jerusalem. It cost almost as much as in Vancouver—high taxes on imported goods.

In France, at the "Tour d'Argent" in Paris.

With Renate and Annick, two lady friends from Vancouver who are spending a few weeks in France, Spain, and Majorca.

CHAMPAGNE PERRIER-JOUËT BRUT N/V:

Good nose. Elegant, easy to drink; a bit sweeter than usual, more like an "extra dry." Well made.

CHAMBOLLE-MUSIGNY "CHARMES" 1971, CHANSON PÈRE ET FILS:

Pale and dead! We had to send it back. The sommelier at the "Tour d'Argent" was not amused—but that's his problem

SANTENAY 1969, CHANSON PÈRE ET FILS:

Good, mature Burgundy nose; good colour. Little sediment. Nice, soft fruit. Not very complex, but pleasant.

November 22, 1982

In Bordeaux. Lunch at "La Chamade," with Mr. Lemelletier of the Grand Conseil de Bordeaux.

CHÂTEAU HAUT-BAGES-LIBÉRAL 1976:

A wine in which the younger grapes from vines of Château Lynch-Bages are used as a "second" wine, according to my host. Good, dark colour for a 1976;

bright, deep red. Not quite ready. Good, clean Pauillac nose. Good fruit, well made. Very enjoyable. Later, I found out that Lemelletier was wrong. The second wine of Lynch-Bages is called Haut-Bages-Avéroux.

Visit to Figeac.

Visited with Thierry Manoncourt. In his opinion, the 1982 will be better and bigger than 1979; maybe better than the 1978, but hard to judge at this point. We tasted separately the Cabernet Sauvignon, Cabernet Franc, and Merlot; all 1982s before the blending—only two months old. They all have a fair amount of tannin, good depth, colour etc. Then we blended the Cabernet Sauvignon and the Merlot. That gave the wine more complexity, but still way too young.

The problem with some 1982s is that the grapes came in too warm at 30º to 32ºC and those who were not careful or did not have cooling equipment made vinegar. Then we tasted the 1981 in barrel, not yet fined with egg white. His 1982 is in 80% new oak barrels, instead of 100%, because the wine has enough ripe natural tannins. The separate cuves of 1982 seem to all be very ripe, very sweet. The acidity is low and the tannins are round and ripe. Another 1959? Maybe.

FIGEAC 1981, FROM BARREL:

Dark, fairly big, and very promising. Similar to 1978? Quite stemmy, herbaceous. Figeac has an unusually high proportion of Cabernets, about two-thirds, and only one-third Merlot.

In 1832, they sold six hectares from which Cheval-Blanc was created; in 1840, another eight hectares, and in 1930, another 15 hectares, and then six more to make a total of 35 hectares. Cheval-Blanc is now only slightly smaller than Figeac. Two-thirds of Figeac and Cheval-Blanc are planted in gravelly soil. All other châteaux that have the name Figeac added to them are 95% to 100% in the sables (sandy soil).

1970 FIGEAC, IN HALF-BOTTLE:

Good colour. Elegant. Softening up, not very big. Slightly high acidity, good fruit. Just about ready.

Then came a real surprise. I had mentioned to him that my daughter Orly was born in 1978, so he took me down to their private cellar and gave me a double-magnum of Figeac 1978! What a lovely present.

Today, I found out that Mr. Ducasse of l'Evangile had passed away last month, at the age of 85. A dedicated winemaker. I have enjoyed visiting his château and tasting his wines with him. He was quite a character.

November 23, 1982

Visit to Château Leoville-Lascases.

Michel Delon, the owner, could not meet me as he was away on urgent business, so my host was the winemaker Michel Rolland. We tasted the 1981, before the fining, as they were in the process of fining when I got there. 40% new oak barrels in 1981. Good colour, well-balanced; a very good wine, but my impression is that it is not as good as the 1982. He said that the 1981 should be bigger than the 1979, but maybe not quite like the 1978. It is difficult to know at this stage.

Tasted the 1982 (only one month old).

They produced 48 hectolitres per hectare in 1982 (50% new oak for the 1982). Very good colour, lots of ripe tannins, very well structured. Impressive. Rolland thinks very highly of the 1982. An excellent year? Everybody had the same problem in 1982 in that the grapes were coming in at 30º to 32º C and those who were not equipped to cool the juice off had problems. In his opinion, Talbot has the poorest soil of all the great St. Juliens, yet they usually make good wine. I must try and get some of the 1982 Leoville-Lascases when it is offered "en primeur" next spring.

Michel Rolland's opinion of Pichon-Lalande.

Very good property. Elegant wines, but not made in the big Pauillac style, and not a very good keeper. Too much Merlot (yet at one point, Michel Delon was managing Pichon-Lalande and he replaced some of the Merlot with Cabernet Sauvignon). Delon made the 1975 and 1976 Pichon-Lalande until May de Lencquesaing took over the management of that fine property from her brother in 1978.

Michel Rolland likes the 1959 Lascases better than the 1961—I do, too—but admits that there is a lot of bottle variation. Lascases uses all three types of cuvée: wood, cement, and stainless steel. He loves 1978 Palmer, but thinks that the 1979 is a bit too soft. He is one of those who are worried about the 1975s; will they be too hard and will the fruit last? He said (and I agree) that Beychevelle is producing too much wine and therefore the wine lacks concentration; the same problem occurs at Brane-Cantenac and even at Mouton, in some vintages.

In regards to Leoville-Barton, Michel said that Ronald Barton is a believer in less alcohol (11% to 11.5%) and that produces lean, lighter wines. He thinks highly of Ducru Beaucaillou.

Their second wine, "Clos du Marquis," represents approximately 20% of the total production. He thinks that Rausan-Ségla has finally made a very good 1982 after decades of producing indifferent wines. He confirmed that Henri Martin (of Château Gloria) has purchased the name, château, and part of the vineyard of St. Pierre. The rest of the vineyard went to Cordier, owners of Talbot and Gruaud-Larose, among others.

Visit to Château Palmer.

Lunch with Peter Sichel and a group of English businessmen, including Jeremy Roberts, who wrote a book on Bordeaux wines. Peter said that they produced a fair bit of 1982, yet the quality will be excellent. With lunch, we had the 1971 and 1964 Palmer (served blind).

Peter likes the 1971 better. I found them very similar in appearance and maybe the 1964 had a more complex nose. I thought the 1971 was the 1967, but I guessed the 1964 correctly. Then he served the 1962 with cheese. I was the only one who guessed this one. The maturity and softness, yet depth of colour, gave it away.

Before lunch, I met the manager, Claude Chardon.

Yves Chardon, the winemaker, is his brother. Claude likes their 1982. May be another 1961 or 1966. He thinks that the 1970s are a bit too lean. He thinks very highly of the 1978 and said that the 1979 may be another 1962. They managed to cool the 1982s when the grapes came in at 30° to 32° C and that picking only lasted one week.

Those who picked after October 4, 1982, had rain problems as did those who did not have the equipment to cool the juice. Palmer finished picking on October 3! About his comment that the 1970s are too lean: maybe some are, but who can describe the 1970 Latour, Palmer, Montrose, Lynch-Bages, Ducru Beaucaillou, or Grand-Puy-Lacoste as too lean?!

Afternoon visit to Château Pichon-Lalande.

We met the son of General de Lencquesaing. His parents were on a trip to the United States. Pichon-Lalande uses about 40% new oak. He likes the 1982s very much; promising vintage. We tasted the 1981 before fining. It was good, with a dark, deep purple colour. Excellent, lovely elegance, surprisingly forward. Too much Merlot? That seems to confirm what I have been told at Lascases.

He said that Beychevelle has family problems and that they are negotiating with Rothschild (Mouton or Lafite?) about a possible partnership or outright sale. He said that Bruno Prats of Cos d'Estournel is experimenting with all sorts of new methods, and not using too much new oak, yet the end result is very good. All in all, a very exciting and informative day.

November 24, 1982

In the morning, I visited Frank Mähler-Besse, part-owner of Palmer and consul of the Netherlands.

I also met his father. They also sell Cheval Noir (St. Emilion) and Château du Vieux Moulin (Appellation Contrôlée Bordeaux).

They have a large stock of old wines, including dozens of cases of the great 1929 Mouton-Rothschild and 1929 Leoville-Poyferré. He likes Palmer 1979 better than the 1978, and thinks the 1979s are like the 1959 (?). He said that next time I am in Bordeaux, we should have dinner at Palmer. They own everything, including 50% of Palmer, clear title. He has an uncle by the name of Mähler working in the forest industry in Vancouver.

Then Frank gave me a lift to the home of Bruno Prats, owner of Cos d'Estournel. Bruno said that Château La Mission Haut-Brion is for sale for 80 million francs, which is $12 to $13 million Canadian dollars. He wants me to send him information about the BCLDB. He likes his 1978 better than the 1979 Cos d'Estournel.

Then he drove me back to my hotel. On the way, we stopped at his new restaurant, "Au Chapon Fin," which will be inaugurated next week. He showed me the old cellar there.

In the afternoon I drove to Libourne.

Lunch at Hôtel Loubat, in Libourne.

CHÂTEAU LATOUR MUSSET 1970, PARSAC ST. EMILION, IN HALF-BOTTLE:

(Now the name has been changed to Latour St. Christophe, but it is still owned by a Henri Guiter.) Very good colour; good fruity nose. Mature, ready, nice fruit. Well made and very enjoyable.

Afternoon visit to Châteaux Ausone and Belair.

With the new cellarmaster/manager Pascal Delbeck. I also met the part-owner, Mme. Dubois-Chalon. We started with a visit to Château Belair (exclusively owned by Mme. Dubois-Chalon), and tasted the 1982 Cabernet Franc (Boucher) and Merlot, as well as their single cuvée of Cabernet Sauvignon (all from individual casks). The wine is promising. Good colour, quite tannic.

This and Ausone are good in 1982. They produced 56 hectolitres per hectare at Belair; only 48 at Ausone. Relatively large production at Ausone in 1982; 2,300 cases, as opposed to only 1,600 cases in 1981. While Ausone is roughly 50% Cabernet Franc and 50% Merlot, Belair has more Merlot (approximately 65%). At Ausone, they replant one-half hectare every year, out of a total of only seven hectares under vine.

Pascal told me that many growers in Bordeaux have had serious problems with their 1982s, for four reasons.

1. Overproduction. Some châteaux have produced as much as 70 hectolitres per hectare.
2. The intense heat during the picking. The grapes were coming in at 30° to 32°C and those who did not have cooling equipment were in trouble.
3. The 1982s lack a bit in acidity. In 1982, there was very little chaptalization.
4. Some grapes, especially in the Médoc, were picked after October 4, when it started to rain seriously. At Ausone and Belair, they picked their 1982s in three days, in late September.

Apparently, a grower in Bordeaux and another in Beaujolais (same weather problems) committed suicide when they realized that their whole crop was wiped out ("Piqué").

Pascal likes the 1979 Ausone better than the 1978s because it is rounder. Better balanced. Having tasted both on several occasions. I concur.

We tasted the 1980, 1979, and 1976 Ausone.

1980:

Lightish colour. Because of the lack of depth and fruit, the acidity is obvious and the wine is marked significantly by the nose and flavour of new oak barrels (which they buy from Demptos). Yet, it definitely shows elegance and class. Drink now to 1990. (14)

1979:

Lovely wine; complex, opening up, elegant, well balanced. Should make a very fine bottle in seven to ten years. Rich, ripe, round fruit. Long on palate. Oak, ripe fruit, all in harmony. A silky yet full wine. (18)

1976:

Incredibly dark and tannic! Hard as nails; very unusual for a 1976. Lovely, warm, complex nose (lots of heat in 1976), but on palate, a mouthful of tannin. Will need a very long time to mature. Yet it is backed with good fruit. (17.5)

1976 was the first vintage in which Pascal was involved in all the stages of vinification at Ausone: from vineyard management to the ultimate product—and he had an immediate impact. This is obvious when one tastes the 1976, as compared to earlier vintages in the 1970s.

He likes the 1971 Ausone better than the 1970, but, in reality, both are failures in the context of the respective vintages and of a Premier Grand Cru. We also visited the private cellar of very old bottles (back to 1843). Very interesting and informative visit, as usual.

November 25, 1982

Visit to Château La Lagune.

I met Mme. Boirie, the winemaker and régisseur. The same setup as during my last visit there in 1977. They use 100% new oak barrels every year (the only non First Growth Médoc to do so). They picked before the rain in 1982. They did not overproduce in 1982. She likes her 1978 and 1981 better than the 1979. She said, and I agree, that her 1966 is excellent. 1970 is hard, but will come around. She does not think that the acidity in the 1982s is too low. Mme. Boirie has already sold all of her 1980 and 1981 yield. At La Lagune, they believe in selling the whole production at once, rather than "playing the market" and releasing wines gradually in "tranches" (literally, in slices). Therefore, from a consumer's point of view, this wine represents excellent value.

Tasted the 1981 from cask before fining.

Deep-purple colour. Quite elegant; good depth and fruit. Will make a lovely, well-balanced wine in eight to ten years.

Short, but interesting visit.

Visit to Château Cissac.

Met Jacques Viallard, the son, and had lunch at the Château with him and his mother and sister. Jacques is a nice man, about my age (has two kids, too). We discussed possible business in BC. Then we tasted a range of young wines that they represent, and three separate cépages of the 1982 Château Cissac: Merlot, Cabernet Sauvignon and Petit Verdot. They are firm believers in Petit Verdot. The various components of the 1982 had great colour and good balance, but, of course, are way too young. It was interesting to taste the Petit Verdot by itself; lots of body, extract and tannins.

Château Cissac

1977:

Hard, green, lean, yet well made. Better on nose than on palate. Typical of the year. (13)

1980:

Light, elegant, lacks middle, but quite good. The rain has damaged this vintage. (13.5)

1978/1979:

The 1978 is leaner and harder than the 1979. The 1979 is better balanced with good concentration of fruit. A wine to watch. Rated the 1978 (15) and the 1979 (16.5).

We then sat down for lunch with the following wines.

1981 CHABLIS:

Made by Albert Pic, whom they represent. Good flavour, well balanced. A bit young, but well structured. A "serious" Chablis. Very good, crisp, flinty; backed by nice fruit. (16.5)

1973 CISSAC:

Far better than I would have expected. Almost ready. Lovely nose. Good fruit, well balanced. Very good quality. Elegant. (16.5)

1966 CISSAC, SERVED DOUBLE-BLIND:

Guessed this wine correctly by the dark, yet maturing colour. At its peak. Opened up. Lovely wine of fine quality. A true Haut-Médoc at its prime. (17)

1969 CÔTEAU DU LAYON, CO-OP:

Represented by Viallard. It is an interesting wine made in the Loire (Tourraine) of botrytized Chenin Blanc grapes. Like an Auslese, without the complexity of Johannisberg Riesling. Pleasant sipping wine. (16)

Visit to Château Cos d'Estournel.

Met their oenologist, Mr. Robert Hallay. Visited the château and the chais and saw an interesting slide show. They will do the collage (egg whites) only next April, while most other châteaux I have visited are doing their 1981 vintage collage about now. About 40% of the barrels are new every year (Seguin-Moreau of Cognac, Limousin oak). Tasted their white Maître d'Estournel 1981 (Entre-Deux-Mers) and the 1979 red Maître d'Estournel (Appellation Contrôlée Bordeaux, mainly Castillon and Blaye). Both clean, honest, well-made, everyday wines.

The Prats family owned Château Margaux through Ginestet (Bruno's mother is a Ginestet), and they have extensive old stocks of Château Margaux. Other than their house in Bordeaux, they also live at Château Marbuzet. Cos is only used as a winery and not as a residence.

Tasted the following wines

1982 COS D'ESTOURNEL:

A special blend with at least 80% Merlot (for tasting purposes only). A massive Pomerol! Very good colour, fruit, and balance. If the Cabernet is as ripe, this wine is very promising. The potential of this 1982 is excellent.

1981 COS D'ESTOURNEL:

Before collage. Lovely, elegant wine. Definitely new style. Concentrated, good fruit. Will make an excellent wine. The charm and fruit of a St. Julien, rather than the solid backbone of a St. Estèphe. The increase of Merlot in the blend is becoming obvious.

1971:

The smell of oak is blended nicely in the wine. Tannic, needing five to six more years, Hard, typical St. Estèphe, yet lovely nose. Good colour. Mr. Hallay said that the 1970 is very similar to the 1971, but with more class and concentration. From personal experience, however, I find both their 1970 and 1971 too lean and lacking fruit. The 1970 Montrose is far superior to the 1970 Cos d'Estournel.

A disturbing fact is that during my meeting with Frank Mähler-Besse a few days ago, he told me that the only thing they have in common with Peter Sichel is joint ownership at Palmer. Otherwise, "we insist on making wines of quality." (While Sichel does not make wines of quality!?)

November 26, 1982

Visit with Christian Moueix, at their offices in Libourne.

A very nice visit with Christian Moueix who invited Carol and myself to dinner the next time we are in Bordeaux. As a whole, the 1982 vintage in Pomerol has similar characteristics to the 1947, but it is really too early to tell. He gave me a bottle of 1979 Petrus. Christian thinks that their 1981s will be like the 1979s, but more concentrated. They made a lot of 1982. One of the largest crops ever, but picked only in the afternoons (no water on the grapes), and finished picking on September 29, well before the rains.

He is a good friend of Bernard Portet of Clos du Val in the Napa Valley, and he recently purchased 1,200 acres of land and vines across from the Napa Valley Lodge in Yountville, between Domaine Chandon and Mondavi. He told Robert Mondavi that the Americans do not know how to cut the grapes off the vines (cheap Mexican labour rather than trained people). His new vineyard is called "Napanook," and is owned by him and by the two daughters of the late Mr. John Daniel, who used to be the owner of Inglenook. Various varietals are planted there. Christian's share is 50%, and the two sisters hold 25% of the shares each.

Then his manager at La Grave Trigant-de-Boisset, Mr. Bernard Montouroy, took me to Petrus where we tasted these wines.

1982 PETRUS:

It has just finished the secondary (malolactic) fermentation. Good, deep, dark, colour. Lively, fruity bouquet, yet lots of tannin. Should be an excellent wine some day, maybe in 12 years' time.

1981 PETRUS:

They have just finished the collage and will rack two more times before bottling next May to July. Lovely wine. Great colour and nose. Rich, deep, yet elegant. Another 1971? But it does not have the massive, ripe fruit of the 1982.

Then we drove around Trotanoy, La Fleur-Petrus, Lafleur, and La Grave. Christian is now deeply involved (investment-wise) in Lafleur. I learned first-hand the cutting of the vine (Guyot simple; seven or eight buds) and that was very exciting. We went out into the Petrus vineyard, and I did a little pruning. Christian likes Certan-de-May very much and likes l'Evangile, too, but thinks that the potential is greater than the wines produced there so far. Lots of cooling was necessary in 1982, because of the excessive heat.

All in all, a very exciting and interesting trip. I was fortunate to be in Bordeaux just as the excellent 1982 vintage was being made. Overall, it looks like 1982 will be an excellent vintage on both sides of the Gironde.

November 30, 1982

Black Tie Dinner and blind tasting of 12 vintages of Château Mouton-Rothschild, at the Four Seasons hotel, in Vancouver, organized by our Commanderie de Bordeaux.

The vintages were 1943, 1945, 1947, 1952, 1959, 1961, 1966, 1970, 1971, 1975, 1978, and the 1981 barrel sample.

APERITIF

CHAMPAGNE HENRIOT (ROTHSCHILD) 1973:

A bit lean; high acidity, good nose, tea-like on palate. Over the hill.

Château Mouton-Rothschild vertical tasting

1943:

Lightest colour of flight; orangy-brown. Decanted at the last minute. Sweet, caramel nose. Minty, thin, woody. High acidity. Some tannin, very cedary. Past its prime, but still showing some class. (15)

1945:

Lovely, dark, mature colour. Big, minty, cedary, cigar-box nose. Still hard, tannic. Will last for a long time. Like Heitz's "Martha's Vineyard." Great fruit extract, luscious fruit. Rich, very long. The tannic backbone so typical of this vintage, but backed by great fruit extract. (19)

1947:

Dark colour; slightly deeper than the 1945. Similar nose to the 1945, but not as intense. Lovely, round, elegant, just great. Hard to fail it in any way. Long, long aftertaste. Great bottle. (19)

1952:

Deep, dark, orange colour. Lovely cedar on nose. Not as intense as the 1945 or the 1947; oak on palate, but similar minty, cigar-box characteristics. Dry, lean; drying up. (17)

1959:

Deep, mature colour. Lovely, elegant, chocolaty Mouton nose. Slightly high acidity. Definitely ready. Very pleasant, but I have tasted greater examples of this wine. These samples were merely good. (17)

1961:

Very deep colour to rim. Closed nose. Lots of fruit, well balanced. Best so far. Intense, big; will last for a long time. Superb fruit extract and great concentration. Superb bottle. (19.5)

1966:

Similar colour to the 1959. Nose opening; lacks a bit of middle. Lean, high acidity. Should have been better. Leanness of the 1966s, but really too lean for its own good. (15.5)

1970:

Nice, medium-dark brick colour. Prefer this to the 1966, by far. Rounder, better balanced, longer on palate, and not too acidic. Elegant, very good now, yet with enough body and tannin to last for some time. Cedar, complexity, and ripe fruit, all in harmony here. Drink 1985 to 1997. (18)

1971:

A bit more age in colour than the 1970. Green, stemmy, yet pleasant; sharp, high acidity, but good fruit. Not very impressive. (15)

1975:

Medium-dark colour. Closed, tight on nose, yet typical Mouton coming through. Lots of fruit, tannin. Well balanced, hard, young. Will be a lovely wine in ten years. Top class. (18.5)

1978:

Slight touch of purple. Sweeter than the 1975 on nose; a bit stemmy. Will be an elegant wine in five to seven years. Good tannins, but I do not think that it is a great sleeper. Tannic, quite dry. (16)

1981:

Barrel sample brought for this event. Young, deep colour. Good, young, fruity nose. Well balanced; new oak/vanilla. Wait and see. Good, but not great.

Met Charles McConville, president of Featherstone (the local agency representing Mouton).

Mouton is composed of 95% Cabernet Sauvignon and Cabernet Franc, and 5% Merlot. All the wines had the minty, cedary, cigar-box nose so typical of Mouton. All the wines were shipped directly from the Château. Xavier d'Ezaguire, their North American export manager, was our guest. I gave our members a background speech on the 1982 vintage in Bordeaux as I just got back from there.

With dinner we had the same wines, as well as this one.

1979 CHÂTEAU LAVILLE-HAUT-BRION:

Lovely flavour. This property is always a favourite of mine. Clean nose; not too fruity, flowery, or intense. Just perfect. Will mature relatively early. (17)

DESSERT WINE

1975 CHÂTEAU COUTET, IN MAGNUMS:

Lovely wine; very good botrytis nose, great fruit. Good depth, well balanced, long. Very good future. (18)

February 1983

Dinner of "Group of Ten" at John Levine's.

CHAMPAGNE AYALA BRUT "RESERVE" 1973:

Elegant, relatively sweet, yeasty, mature; finish a bit bitter. Good, clean. Had it been fuller, it would have been a great Champagne.

1976 PULIGNY-MONTRACHET "PUCELLES" LEFLAIVE,

1976 PULIGNY-MONTRACHET "FOLATIÈRES," JOSEPH DROUHIN,

AND

1976 MONTRACHET "MARQUIS DE LAGUICHE," JOSEPH DROUHIN:

Overall, the Leflaive was the finest. Luscious, great complexity; intense, big, open nose. Long on palate. Ready and needs drinking.

The "Folatières" was the least good; rather ordinary and vegetal compared to the other two.

The Montrachet was long, complex, good acidity, but not as open, full, or intense as the "Pucelles." Not bad, but not classic either. Very good, though.

1945 CHÂTEAU BÂLESTARD-LA-TONNELLE, ST. EMILION:

I purchased it for the group at Draper & Esquin's in San Francisco for $80. Very dark colour, almost Zinfandel-like. Full all the way to rim. Spicy, sweet, woody, mature nose. Some tannin left; a fair amount, actually. Big, full, fair amount of fruit. Tea leaves, cedar. Long on palate. Lovely wine. Will last for a very long time. Decanted for 30 minutes. Fair amount of sediment. Short and unbranded cork. A solid wine from a solid vintage.

1961 LA TÂCHE

AND

1961 ROMANÉE-CONTI,

both Domaine de la Romanée-Conti:

La Tâche shipped by Cruse. La Tâche label stuck on a 1961 Mâcon-Cruse label! Maybe illegally shipped to the United States and then the original label added? These are two of the most expensive wines our group has ever owned. I only paid $100 per bottle, but replacement cost today is easily $500 for the Romanée-Conti and $300 for the La Tâche. Very rare wines. Medium-dark, mature colours. Pale compared to the Bâlestard-La-Tonnelle.

The Romanée-Conti was very slightly darker than the La Tâche. Both had fabulous noses. Complex, sweet, spicy Pinot Noir. On palate, the Romanée-Conti was less tired and a bit better balanced, with more fruit. Both had some tannin. Allan thought that they both had too much acidity at the end, but I did not taste that at all.

La Tâche was better five years ago. Romanée-Conti is at its peak. However, these wines cost four to five times as much as the Bâlestard. Poor value! But what an experience. I have one bottle of each of these three wines in my cellar.

1963 CROFT'S VINTAGE PORT, BOTTLED BY CHARLES KINLOCH:

After all the wine we'd had, we could not concentrate on this one. However, typical Croft's 1963. Forward, good nose, very well balanced. Long on palate, good flavour, and very enjoyable.

A great wine evening.

Late March 1983

Vancouver's Annual Playhouse Theatre International Wine Festival, Black Tie Tasting and Dinner, at "L'Orangerie."

Guest Speaker: Robert Mondavi. All the wines featured were produced by the Robert Mondavi winery. We started with a vertical tasting of their Pinot Noir "Reserve," followed by a dinner.

1976 PINOT NOIR "RESERVE":

Darkest of all five Pinot Noirs. Some tannin, concentrated. (Hot, very little rainfall in 1976; very small crop.) No new barrels used. Good Pinot Noir on nose, but slightly baked and stemmy. Similar impressions on palate. Not bad, but not special. (14)

1977 PINOT NOIR "RESERVE":

Medium-orange colour, pale rim. 40% of stems retained. Slightly bitter, more tannic than the 1976. Second and driest drought year in a row. 1976 richer than 1977, but the 1977 is more complex. No new barrels. (15)

1978 PINOT NOIR "RESERVE":

Similar in colour to the 1977. Too much contact with new oak. Pronounced character of new oak. 25° Brix; too much sugar. 40% stems retained. 30% new barrels. 1° higher alcohol than the 1977. (14.5)

1979 PINOT NOIR "RESERVE":

Similar in colour to the 1977 and 1978, but a bit more purple. Sweet, lightish oak flavour. Also too sweet for me. Milder, better balanced than the 1977 and 1978. New Nevers barrels. After tasting the 1979, it made the 1976 seem flabby. (16.5)

1980 PINOT NOIR "RESERVE":

Deep, medium-dark colour, with a touch of purple. Some tannin, good fruit, well balanced, very pleasant. Needs two to three years. Good quality. Lots of rain, cool growing season. 40% retention of stems. 86% new barrels. Alcohol slightly higher than in 1979. Unfiltered. Potentially the best. (17)

WITH DINNER

1978 AND 1979 CHARDONNAY "RESERVE," NAPA VALLEY:

The 1978 was oakier, heavier, more Californian than French Burgundy in style. Quite intense, buttery. (16)

The 1979 was more pleasant with food, more acidity, lighter, yet elegant and with a lot of character. Approachable and very good. (17)

1975 AND 1978 CABERNET SAUVIGNON "RESERVE":

The 1975 has 85% Cabernet Sauvignon, 10% Cabernet Franc, and 5% Merlot in the blend. 25% new oak barrels. The 1978 was served from magnums, yet was more forward, almost drinkable.

The 1975 was darker in colour, more concentrated on nose and palate. Needs two to three more years. Mondavi thinks that his 1978 is better balanced, but I prefer the bigger style of the 1975. Both well made; good concentration of fruit, good bouquet. The glasses had a smell of cardboard—most unfortunate! I rated the 1975 (17) and the 1978 (16).

DESSERT WINE

1978 SAUVIGNON BLANC "BOTRYTIZED," NAPA VALLEY:

43° Brix at harvest. Had this wine in half-bottle at the winery with John Lawson (their export manager). This wine has never been released for sale. The closest thing to a fine Sauternes, without the butteriness. Leaner, more acidic, but a fabulous botrytized nose, and clean. Lovely on palate. For me, the star of the evening. Lovely dessert wine. 100% Sauvignon Blanc from one of their finest vineyards. (17.5)

March 1983

Trip to England and Israel with Carol, Michael, and Orly.

Dinner at Harry and Prue Waugh's.

Their young kids, Harriet and Jamie, were there, too.

MUMM'S N/V BLANC DE BLANCS "CRÉMANT DE CRÉMANT":

With an unusual simple, typed "sample" label, and thick metal strap holding the cork. Good, complex, yet delicate nose. Clean on palate. Good, long, yeasty. Lacked a bit in fizz.

1967 CHÂTEAU LATOUR:

Intense Cabernet and cedar on nose; new oak. Lovely now. Ready and very enjoyable. Clean, slightly acidic (again, the good old 1967s). However, it was overshadowed by a lovely 1955 Château Haut-Brion.

1955 CHÂTEAU HAUT-BRION:

Harry's last bottle of this fine wine. Complex, earthy, woody, caramel nose. Dark colour, but lighter and less youthful-looking than the 1967 Latour. Clean, long, soft, elegant on palate. Showing a lot better than the same wine I had with the "Group of Ten" against the 1955 Ausone a few months ago. Ready, very enjoyable. A good , stylish wine of a vintage that is getting rather tired.

We finished with a glass of Champagne.

GRANDE CHAMPAGNE COGNAC "GRANDE RÉSERVE":

Bottled by Woltner Frères who are the owners of Château La Mission Haut-Brion. Given to Harry by Henri Woltner before his death in 1974. A lovely 40-year-old Cognac. It is one of the loveliest Cognacs I have had to date. Dark, sweet, fruity, complex nose. Smooth, yet full on palate. A classic!

An enjoyable evening. Harry is really a very nice man. He is 79 years old and has nine-and-a-half-year-old twins! I always enjoy visiting him and talking about wines. He thinks that the 1982 vintage in Bordeaux will be very similar to the 1959s or even the 1947s. This is very good news. I will buy some futures of this vintage. He thinks that Latour and La Mission Haut-Brion are an absolute must to acquire in 1982. He was very pleased that Feret's 13th edition, Bordeaux et Ses Vins, *has placed Latour above Lafite!*

June 7, 1983

1961 Bordeaux blind tasting, at home, with 12 participants.

Wines known but not the order. All the wines, except for the 1961 l'Eglise-Clinet, are from my cellar. These wines are from a great vintage and, at 22 years old, should be fully mature.

APERITIF

1972 ARBOIS-VIN JAUNE, DOMAINE DE LA PINTE:

From the Jura region of France. Medium-dark gold colour. Fine Sherry-style delicate nose. Not as rich or nutty as Sherry on palate, but more acidity and easier to drink. Clean, oaky, good. An unusual and rare wine aged in wood for six to eight years. Made from the Savagnin grape. Aged well.

1. CHÂTEAU LA GAFFELIÈRE-NAUDES:

Good, dark colour; orangy rim. Sweet, spicy nose. Warm. Some tannin, good fruit, slightly high acidity. Long on palate. Sweet Merlot base. Quite big. A bit one-dimensional. A bit vegetal; not unusual for a St. Emilion. (17)

2. CHÂTEAU LYNCH-BAGES:

Darkish colour (not as dark as #1), orangy rim. Spicy, subdued nose; ripe berries, cedar too, as well as oaky Cabernet. Some tannin left. Good fruit/acidity balance. Long on palate. Classic Claret. Forward and elegant. Minty, cedary. Lynch-Bages? (17.5)

3. CHÂTEAU FOURCAS-HOSTEN:

Colour similar to #2, but more orangy rim. Warm, mature, woody nose of old Claret. Good fruit, still quite hard, some tannins to lose. Slightly high acidity. Long aftertaste. Rich and hefty. (16.5)

4. CHÂTEAU HAUT-BAGES-AVÉROUX:

This is the second wine of Château Lynch-Bages. Quite dark (less than the above, though); showing age. Fairly acidic, lean, rather simple nose of ageing Claret. Not very complex, quite hard. Too high acidity. A bit one-dimensional; more like a 1966 Cru Bourgeois. (15)

5. CHÂTEAU L'EGLISE-CLINET:

Fullish, medium-dark, mature colour. Elegant Merlot nose. Lovely, big mouthful. Some tannin, lots of fruit. Long. So far, the biggest and fullest wine. Good aftertaste. A bit caramelly on nose. Hint of cedar on both nose and palate. (16.5)

6. CHÂTEAU DUCRU-BEAUCAILLOU:

Similar colour to #5. Mature Claret nose. Elegant, soft wine. Too high acidity, but very elegant, with a lot of class. Later, opened up. Best classic Cabernet nose so far. Surprisingly soft. (17.5) On previous occasions, this wine showed superbly. Can be great.

7. CHÂTEAU BRANE-CANTENAC:

Medium colour, orangy rim. Rich, complex nose of mature Claret. A bit herbaceous. Lovely, full, round; perfect balance. Some acidity, some fruit, some tannin. Lasted well on palate. A fine mouthful. Slight hint of dill on palate. Lovely. (18) This surprised us all. We did not expect Brane-Cantenac to show so well. I wish they would produce this quality nowadays.

8. CHÂTEAU LASCOMBES:

Medium colour, orangy rim. I find that these 1961s are very close in colour and appearance. Rich, fruity wine; well balanced. Not as complex as #7, but big and rich. A typical 1961. (17.5)

9. CHÂTEAU GRUAUD-LAROSE:

Good, dark colour; orangy rim. Rich, sweet wine. Good Cabernet flavour; long on palate. Very well balanced. No rush. Quite complex, yet not as complex as #5 or #7. St. Julien? Big and dark. Great ripe fruit extract. Needs time. Potentially (18.5).

DESSERT WINE

1933 MOULIN TOUCHAIS, ANJOU:

Made from Chenin Blanc. Purchased in Amsterdam a few months ago for $30. Amber colour, like a Tokay Aszú (5 or 6 Puttonyos). Madeira-Tokay nose. Good acidity. Not very sweet, yet sweet enough to be a light dessert wine. Perfectly sound. Ullage was about two-and-one-half inches from the cork and that worried me. (16) as a wine and (18) for what it is and how it has lasted.

Overall

A special and informative tasting.

June 11, 1983

Dinner of "Group of Ten" at the Tobes'.

CHAMPAGNE KRUG BRUT 1971, IN MAGNUM:

Young-looking, smelling, and tasting. Good acidity, good nose. Still youthful and needs another four to five years. Lovely balance, excellent quality. Good, yeasty nose and clean on palate. Soft, yet good acidity. This wine is 12 years old, yet it is still fresh.

1974 MAYACAMAS CHARDONNAY, NAPA MOUNTAIN, IN MAGNUM:

Medium-dark gold colour. Complex, concentrated, pineapple, oaky nose. Full wine, good concentration, good flavour. Not too hot; held well and reconfirmed my trust in Mayacamas Chardonnays.

Then, with the main course, we were served four vintages of Château Lafite (vintages unknown until after the tasting). We were told by our host that all four wines were Lafites.

1. 1970 CHÂTEAU LAFITE:

Evolved colour. Soft, elegant nose: a bit vegetal. Hard, lean; not nearly as complex or opulent as #2 or #4. Not enough length; weak effort. 1966? A bit short on finish. (15.5)

2. 1959 CHÂTEAU LAFITE:

Dark colour. Lovely concentration, lots of tannin. The "size" and concentration of a 1961. Rich, Cassis, chocolaty nose. Great mouthful of lovely, ripe Cabernet. Great complexity and extract. No rush, yet after one hour, it started to dry out a bit. (19)

3. 1966 CHÂTEAU LAFITE:

Lightest colour, watery rim. Cigar-box on nose. Elegant, long, sweet nose. Fairly high acidity. A bit thin. Very similar to the 1970. Turned out to be the 1966. Lafite should have done better, both in 1970 and 1966. (16)

4. 1961 CHÂTEAU LAFITE:

Dark colour, showing some age. 1959? Fabulous wine, great concentration; elegant, yet has depth and great intensity. Complex, meaty, long, beautiful. Magnificent. My favourite. (19.5) This really surprised me, because in the past I have always preferred the 1959 over the 1961.

1978 DIAMOND CREEK "VOLCANIC HILL" CABERNET SAUVIGNON, NAPA VALLEY:

Deep, dark, purplish. Concentrated Cabernet without being too herbaceous. Well balanced, lovely wine. High pH. Intense, spicy, ripe fruit. (18) I wonder why our host served this wine after the four Lafites.

DESSERT WINES

1959 CHÂTEAU DES COULINATS, STE. CROIX-DU-MONT:

(My bottle. Purchased last month in San Francisco. I served it double-blind.) Dark-golden colour. Good botrytis nose. Big on palate without being overly sweet. Lovely quality and a great value. Most participants thought that it was a top class Sauternes.

1979 CHÂTEAU GUIRAUD, IN HALF-BOTTLE:

Clean, crisp, sweet. Hardly any botrytis, but elegant, pleasant; good lemony-acidity. At $9.50 per bottle, not a bad wine, but not luscious. 1979 was not a particularly fine vintage for Sauternes. The 1980s promise to be superior; this is the opposite of the quality of the reds.

Comments

Excellent dinner. Very good food; each couple produced a course. The 1959 and 1961 Lafites were excellent, but very misleading in that the 1959 showed like a 1961 and the 1961 more in the 1959 style. Both were markedly darker, more intense, and more opulent than the 1966 or the 1970, with the 1970 being short and disappointing. The Ste. Croix-du-Mont was a lovely wine. Great quality at a reasonable price. The Krug Champagne was lovely and so was the Mayacamas Chardonnay.

August 1983

Barrel Sample tasting of 1982 Clarets.

Organized by Vintage Consultants, local wine agents. These wines have only spent about nine months in oak, so far.

1. CHÂTEAU GLORIA:

Bright red colour. Clean, spicy, elegant, sweet nose. Fairly open on nose. Lean, quite acidic; lacks middle and not enough fruit at this stage. Not representative of the vintage.

2. CHÂTEAU CHASSE-SPLEEN:

Deeper, more concentrated on nose. Spicy, fruity, lovely bouquet. New oak on palate. Concentrated, big, complex. Good tannin. Medium body. A wine to watch.

3. CHÂTEAU PHÉLAN-SEGUR:

Similar in colour to #2. More vegetal on nose. Leaner, sharper on both nose and palate. Hard wine; grassy, vegetal. Lacks fat. A bit too high in acidity. Not very promising.

4. CHÂTEAU MALARTIC-LAGRAVIÈRE:

Similar in appearance to #2 and #3. Fruity, hint of caramel on nose; not forthcoming. Oaky, powerful, yet not really big or concentrated. Later, improved dramatically. Quite concentrated. Hard to taste. Long. Very good. These are all barrel samples that will spend at least another year in wood before bottling.

5. CHÂTEAU GRAND-PUY-LACOSTE:

Darkest colour, fantastic depth. Great concentration of sweet berries and tobacco on nose. Big, intense, concentrated; a true 1982! Lovely depth and length. I am glad that I have ordered some of this as a "future" purchase. The price was very reasonable, US$120. per case.

6. CHÂTEAU LA LAGUNE:

Very closed on nose. Dark purplish colour. Concentrated, ripe berry, fruit on palate. Long, tannic, medium-bodied. New oak. Good style. Have purchased a couple of cases of this for US$86. per case.

7. CHÂTEAU LYNCH-BAGES:

Good, dark colour. Very good appearance. Lovely, sweet nose. Slightly vegetal, but good depth and elegance. Lovely mouthful on palate. Round, long, clean; oak-fruit-vanilla. Clean aftertaste. Almost California style. Lacks a bit in acidity. Very good potential. This wine is offered as "future" for US$145 per case. Must get some.

8. CHÂTEAU FIGEAC:

Colour as above, but slightly more mature-looking. A bit vegetal, spicy. Slightly volatile acidity. Lovely wine. Great finesse, yet very concentrated. Long on palate, intense, very well made. Purchased a case of this at US$190. This is quite expensive, but I think that it is well worth it, as it is going to be an excellent wine some day.

9. CHÂTEAU DUCRU-BEAUCAILLOU:

Lovely, deep purple colour. Closed nose; some fruit coming through. Almost drinkable now! Lovely, fruity, intense, yet delicate. I only faulted it because of being so soft (at least at this stage). A case of six magnums of this wine cost me US$165 last June.

10. CHÂTEAU LEOVILLE-LASCASES:

Deep, dark colour. Intense, fruity, yet austere nose. Good fruit; clean, lovely, and dark. Concentrated, but not as intense as #5 at this stage. Yet in the same class. Good tannic backbone. Long, spicy, ripe aftertaste. Should become a lovely bottle in ten years. Bigger and more concentrated than the Ducru. Last June, I acquired two cases of this wine for US$190 per case. It has already increased to US$245 per case—in just a few months!

11. CHÂTEAU HAUT-BRION:

Lightest colour; almost the colour of a bright Beaujolais! Closed, sweet, complex nose, but not deep or concentrated. Hard, tannic, yet delicate. True Haut-Brion style, but not very concentrated in terms of depth. Smoky, lovely, elegant. Another year in oak will make a lot of difference.

All the above wines are barrel samples and have not been fined yet. They will spend another year in oak. These wines have not picked up enough oak yet (one more year to go in wood), have not been racked enough.

Overall

I liked the Grand-Puy-Lacoste and the Leoville-Lascases best overall—true Clarets of the 1982 vintage. For elegance, the Figeac. For concentration of fruit and "California style early maturity," the Lynch-Bages. And for traditional big, hard Haut-Médoc, the Lascases.

August 1983

Dinner and tasting of the Portet Brothers' wines, at the Four Seasons hotel, in Vancouver.

First, we tasted wines from Bernard Portet's Napa Valley winery, Clos du Val.

1. 1977 CLOS DU VAL CABERNET SAUVIGNON, NAPA VALLEY:

15% Merlot. Slightly browning colour. Elegant, toasty, spicy nose. Slightly high acidity. Some tannin, lean, lacks some depth. Good aftertaste. More impressive on nose and visually than on palate. (15.5)

2. 1978 CLOS DU VAL CABERNET SAUVIGNON, NAPA VALLEY:

15% Merlot. Slightly paler colour than #1, #3, and #4. Similar nose to #1, but a bit tighter. Rounder than the 1977 on palate, but not as intense. (15)

3. 1979 CLOS DU VAL CABERNET SAUVIGNON, NAPA VALLEY:

13% Merlot. Rich, intense wine. Better put together than the 1978 or 1977. Good fruit, some tannin; still tight, yet elegant. Needs three to four more years. (16.5)

4. 1980 CLOS DU VAL CABERNET SAUVIGNON, NAPA VALLEY:

8% Merlot. The 1979 and 1980 are more subdued and more French in style. 1978, and especially 1977 are more California in style. Did not rate the 1980 as it was too young. Bell pepper nose, slightly stemmy, like a young St. Emilion, yet it has good fruit, and promises to be a fine bottle by 1987.

Bernard likes his 1979. Narrower base than the 1978, but better put together. 1978 was the year with the highest alcohol to date (13.5°).

This small vertical was followed by a tasting of wines made by Dominique Portet, Bernard's younger brother, who produces the Taltarni range of wines in Australia.

Taltarni Cabernets, Australia

1. 1978 TALTARNI CABERNET SAUVIGNON:

Intense, sweet, "sweaty-saddle" nose. Quite similar in colour to the 1978 Clos du Val. Round. Needs one to two years, but not as rich as I expected. Good acidity, fairly lean. 12.9° alcohol. (16)

2. 1979 TALTARNI CABERNET SAUVIGNON:

Similar to the 1978, slightly deeper in colour. More depth than the 1978; cleaner wine. Elegant, well balanced. 12.8° alcohol. (16.5)

3. 1980 TALTARNI CABERNET SAUVIGNON:

Purplish colour. Good fruit, quite tannic. Very young on nose and palate. Well balanced, long on palate. A wine to buy. Difficult year, very hot. Forthcoming, more forward than the 1978 or the 1979. 12.1° alcohol (lowest of all three years). Fairly light year. (16.5)

All three above wines have the baked, "sweaty-saddle" nose typical of Australian reds. Taltarni has 290 acres under vine (out of 2,000 acres), 120 miles north-west of Melbourne in Moonambel. Average production is 35,000 cases. Taltarni was the name of the property before the winery was built. "Taltarni" means "red earth." They produce a Pinot Chardonnay sparkling wine, too.

The Taltarni wines were overall darker than the Clos du Val, because of the soil.

Taltarni Cabernets need a bit more ageing time. Both wineries use Nevers oak barrels and both have the same owner. Dominique Portet thinks that his 1978 is still austere. 1979 was a dry year in Australia, producing a small crop. According to Dominique, these Australian Cabernets should be drunk between 1986 and 1990. 1978 should be drunk in four to six years.

Overall impression of the Taltarni wines tasted

Although they taste a bit "hot," as Australian wines do, they have good acidity and complexity. All three vintages are made up of 90% Cabernet Sauvignon, 3% Cabernet Franc, and 7% Malbec.

They are starting to grow Merlot, too, at Taltarni. 1980 was the first year with some Merlot in it. They are trying to make (like the 1979 and 1980) rounder wines, more elegant and earlier maturing, yet they aim for the wine to have a long plateau. 1978 and earlier vintages were bigger wines. I agree with these comments overall, but I was surprised at how quickly the 1978 has softened up. Last year, this wine was really massive, not unlike a young Château Latour.

Clos du Val "Réserve" is aged for six to eight months longer in wood than the regular Cabernets, and a bit more press wine is added (but not too much, because it will unbalance the wine).

With dinner (a fabulous and artistic dinner, top quality as usual, at the Four Seasons hotel), we tasted the following wines.

1981 CLOS DU VAL CHARDONNAY, NAPA VALLEY:

Crisp, good acidity, clean, and lean. A good wine to accompany food. (Bernard likes leaner wines in the French style, rather than the California "heavyweight" style.)

1978 TALTARNI SHIRAZ:

A full, meaty, dark, intense wine; but rather simpler than Dominique Portet's Cabernet Sauvignon.

With cheese, we had a wine made by their father, who was the régisseur at Lafite in the 1960s.

1961 CHÂTEAU LAFITE, IN MAGNUM:

I had this wine at Alan Tobe's earlier this year and, although this was in a magnum, it was very similar. Medium colour. Intense, yet elegant and perfumed caramel nose so typical of Lafite. Slightly high acidity and a bit lean on palate. Long, elegant, lovely aftertaste. I personally prefer the style of the 1959 Lafite as it has more depth, colour, and fruit, but how can one complain about such a masterpiece?!

Very informative evening, overall. Bernard likes fishing and I have invited him up to Turnagain Island when he comes back to visit us in Vancouver.

Visit to Diamond Creek Winery near Calistoga.

They only produce Cabernet Sauvignon. Met the owner, Al Brounstein, but not the winemaker, Jerry Luper. They usually pick well into October and sometimes even early November. Al would not let us taste, but he said that he will send us an invitation to one of the six days of picnics and tastings at the winery next year. Al is not known for his generosity. In style, he compares his "Volcanic Hill" to Château Latour, the "Gravelly Meadow" to Haut-Brion, and the "Red Rock Terrace" to Margaux.

We visited the winery and the three vineyards, which are close to each other.

The Volcanic Hill Vineyard is grayish in colour, volcanic residue from the Mount St. Helens eruption. The Red Rock vineyard has red soil with lots of rocks. Each one of the three vineyards is facing the sun from a different direction.

Red Rock is eight acres, Volcanic Hill is seven acres, and Gravelly Meadow is five acres in size. Total production is 2,200 to 2,500 cases. They allocate 200 cases to restaurants and sell the balance all over the world.

88% Cabernet Sauvignon, 3% Cabernet Franc, 8% Merlot, and 1% Malbec. Petit Verdot and Malbec do not grow well there. Planted and mixed together, and crushed together. 50% new barrels every year. Only one month in new oak in the first year, then wine is transferred to previous year's barrels.

In 1982, they produced 3,000 cases, their largest production to date. First crush was in 1972 with 135 cases. The winery was purchased in 1965.

Cabernet

1978:

Very fine year. Needs time.

1979:

Relatively light (all three vineyards), ready soon. However, having tasted them recently, I think that the 1979s will need at least ten more years to reach the plateau of drinkability.

1980:

Excellent, big year. Needs more time.

1981:

Rather similar to 1979.

1982:

Very big wines, but not as intense as the 1980.

All three vineyards' wines sold for the same price ($20 per bottle, 1981 vintage). Al Brounstein thinks that they do not differ in quality, only in style. He likes to compare his vineyard to Romanée-Conti (single dominant varietal, small vineyards). Quite an interesting visit. Too bad we couldn't taste any wine.

Alice and Joe Heitz came over to see our new townhouse and we had a bottle of this Champagne.

CHAMPAGNE BILLECART-SALMON 1976 BRUT:

(From Kermit Lynch at $24) Good, yeasty nose. Well balanced, long, complex, very elegant. Ready.

Joe is in the middle of the 1983 crush. They stopped crushing today because of a sudden drop in temperature and sugar content in the grapes. He thinks the quantity will be average this year, lower than last year's very large crop. He had problems with his new Chardonnay from his own vineyard. The 1982 is still in cask, and the 1981 had too many tartrate deposits and the wine supplied to restaurants had to be returned to the winery for re-fining. He brought over a magnum of 1976 Cabernet Sauvignon "Martha's Vineyard" as a gift. We spent some time on our patio.

Lunch at Robert Mondavi's winery, with John and Renée Lawson.

They will have dinner at our home in Vancouver next week as part of the IW&FS convention.

1981 ROBERT MONDAVI WHITE:

Blend of Sauvignon Blanc, Chenin Blanc, and Semillon. Pleasant, good fruit.

1981 FUMÉ BLANC REGULAR AND "RÉSERVE":

The "Réserve" (not yet released) has more complexity, more depth. Needs another year. Both have good noses; clean, fruity Sauvignon Blanc. Both are 90% Sauvignon Blanc and 10% Semillon. The "Réserve" is barrel-fermented and aged and they both come from separate parts of the vineyard.

1977, 1978, 1979, AND 1980 PINOT NOIR "RESERVE":

All released now, all very similar in colour (the 1980 is a bit darker), and all fairly light colour (like a Volnay). The 1977 and 1978 are showing a bit of age. The 1978 has an odd nose and volatile acidity. The 1977 is good, but rather simple. The 1979 is nice, too. The 1980 has some tannin and needs extra two years of bottle-age. The 1977 is the only wine that was de-stemmed.

With lunch

1981 CHARDONNAY "RESERVE" AND 1975 CHARDONNAY "RESERVE":

The 1981 is not released yet. The 1975 had more depth of colour, with a complex, elegant nose, but starting to lose its fruit. The 1981 is a departure from the old style in that it is leaner, more acidic, and more suitable with food. Both aged in oak. Very nice wines.

1979 AND 1975 CABERNET SAUVIGNON "RESERVE," NAPA VALLEY:

Good, dark, bright colour on both wines. The 1975 has a cedary, spicy nose. Elegant, good fruit, but a bit more forward than I expected.

The 1979 is brighter, and has a younger Cabernet nose, yet the Mondavi style seems to be changing. Almost ready to drink. Needs two more years to get rounder and more complex, but not a big, tannic, or hard wine.

1982 "SPECIAL SELECTION" JOHANNISBERG RIESLING:

(9° alcohol, 4° residual sugar) Not yet released. Slightly spritzy, very pleasant; somewhere between an Auslese and a Beerenauslese in style. Good acidity, flowery. Should go well with fruit desserts.

1978 SAUVIGNON BLANC BOTRYTIZED, IN HALF-BOTTLE:

Had this wine before, once at Mondavi's last October, and once last March in Vancouver at a reception/tasting/dinner of Mondavi's Pinot Noirs. Lovely, dark-gold colour. Rich, botrytized nose. Sweet, intense. Great complexity. They did not make this wine in 1979 or 1980, but made some 1981 and 1982. This Sauvignon Blanc comes from a vineyard off the Silverado Trail near Bob Mondavi's home toward Yountville. It sells for $25 per half-bottle.

Later that week

Tasted in Yountville.

RODDIS CELLAR 1981 CABERNET SAUVIGNON, NAPA VALLEY:

(12% alcohol, $7 per half-bottle, just released) My curiosity was aroused after visiting Diamond Hill Winery. Al Brounstein showed me a vineyard right next to his which he thought was promising. Apparently, Mr. Roddis has multiple sclerosis and has worked hard himself to start this winery. The wine is, of course, too young and has just been released, but it has a lovely, deep-purple colour and a lovely, oak, cedar, spicy, complex nose. Good depth and structure. Needs five to six years. I may buy some bottles.

BURGESS 1981 CHARDONNAY, NAPA VALLEY, N HALF-BOTTLE:

(13.7 ° alcohol) Typical big, complex Napa Chardonnay of good quality. Not my style; too big, but very good, a bit too high in alcohol. Should hold well for two more years.

Visit to Roddis Cellar Vineyard near Diamond Creek.

Bill Roddis has been producing only Cabernet for three years now. (500 cases or 20 barrels, 3.5 acres under vines) He is preparing another 6.5 acres which will triple his production to 1,500 cases by 1990. 50% new oak barrels every year (ten barrels!). He gave me a bottle of his 1980 Cabernet and we tasted the 1982 in barrel. André Tchelischtcheff is his consultant.

Bill is partly paralyzed and has his winery for sale. He is asking $1.5 million, which ended my dreams of owning a winery in the Napa Valley. He is a very nice man, and a dedicated winemaker. What a tragedy that he is inflicted by this terrible disease. Bill loves 1970 Château Latour—my kind of wine, too!

Dinner at "Miramonte" restaurant, in St. Helena.

So far this has been the finest and most pleasant meal we have had in the Napa Valley. We had dinner there before, two years ago with Phillip Togni, the then winemaker at Cuvaison. At that time Phillip brought a bottle of his lovely 1975 Cuvaison Cabernet Sauvignon "Signature," made from Spring Mountain grapes. This time we had the same wine which I brought along.

1975 CUVAISON CABERNET SAUVIGNON "SIGNATURE," NAPA VALLEY:

Lovely wine; one of the finest California Cabernet Sauvignons I have tasted. Deep, dark colour; lovely, oaky, spicy, complex, nose. Full, fruity, long on palate. Some tannin left. Needs at least five more years to become accessible.

The dinner was lovely, too. Excellent Maine lobster and great sauce. Lovely duck, with great, dark Cabernet and pear sauce and poached pear. Then superb three-flavour sorbet and figs (from a fig tree in the restaurant's courtyard), loaded in Cabernet and ice cream. Great wine and a great meal.

October 4, 1983

A Four-day International Wine and Food Society 50th Anniversary Convention, in Vancouver.

FIRST EVENT
1979 First Growth Claret tasting

1. CHÂTEAU CHEVAL-BLANC:

Dark colour, orangy rim; mature-looking. Stemmy, vegetal nose typical of St. Emilion. Sweet, forward, high acidity, lacking middle. Elegant, but does not have the concentration of a big St. Emilion. Very soft, even at this young age. (17)

2. CHÂTEAU AUSONE:

Better depth of colour and youth than the Cheval-Blanc. Similar on nose, but more concentration. Bell pepper. More backbone and more tannin and fruit. Long on palate. An excellent wine. (18.5)

3. CHÂTEAU PETRUS, IN IMPERIAL:

Darker, deeper-looking than the first two wines. In fact, most wines at this tasting were quite a bit darker than numbers 1 or 2. Full, concentrated, vanilla, lots of tannin, new oak, but not as complex as some of the others. Powerful, big wine. (18)

4. CHÂTEAU HAUT-BRION:

Deep, dark colour. Lovely, caramel, sweet nose; typical Haut-Brion (resembles Lafite on nose). Elegant, long, vanilla and fruit on palate, some tannin. Complex, round. Ripe and elegant fruit. A lovely bottle. (18)

5. CHÂTEAU LAFITE:

Deep colour. Lovely, elegant, chocolaty, cedary nose. Concentrated fruit; very elegant on palate. Not too hard. Will reach its peak in three to four years, but as it has good fruit, it should hold for quite some time. (18.5)

6. CHÂTEAU MARGAUX:

Deep colour. Stemmy, vegetal nose. Concentrated bell pepper compared to Lafite. Deeper and bigger, which is surprising, Margaux being traditionally a more elegant wine. Somehow seems a bit too hard for its own good. (17.5)

7. CHÂTEAU LATOUR:

Deep colour. Odd nose; cheesy. A bad bottle? Big, hard, concentrated wine, but lacks a bit in ripeness.

Would make a nice bottle (someday) by itself, but not against such competition! (17)

8. CHÂTEAU MOUTON-ROTHSCHILD:

Very dark colour. Cedar, tobacco nose. Harder even than the Latour, but with more fruit. Noticeable acidity, though. Good complexity. I hope that the fruit will outlast the tannins. Based on reports about this wine, I was pleasantly surprised. (17.5)

I was one of the two guest speakers at the above event.

October 1983

SECOND EVENT

Robert Mondavi Barrel (component) tasting of 1978 Cabernet Sauvignon "Reserve," Napa Valley

Conducted by John Lawson of Mondavi's.

1. DEMPTOS:

Nevers Oak. Light toast, more open on nose. Cleaner, more complex. Nice, understated fruit.

2. DEMPTOS:

Limousin Oak. Light toast, tighter on nose than #1. Leaner, a bit harder.

3. FRANÇOIS FRÈRES (BURGUNDY):

Limousin oak. Heavy toast; more toasty on nose, but more open and elegant, and better intense bouquet. Bigger on palate, too; almost too tannic, with a touch of bitterness.

4. FRANÇOIS FRÈRES, TRONÇAIS:

Heavy toast. More new oak and vanilla on palate. Resembling #1, but harder.

5. DEMPTOS:

Old barrel, Nevers oak. True fruit, elegance, but very little tannin or oak imparted to the wine.

6. AMERICAN OAK:

Old barrel-steamed. More open, rounder than #5. Prefer it to #5. More complex.

7. AMERICAN OAK:

New barrel-steamed. Odd nose, almost sulphury. Herbaceous, sharp, good tannins, but short on palate and too woody.

8. ROBERT MONDAVI CABERNET SAUVIGNON 1978 "RESERVE":

87% new French oak, light and average toast (Nevers). (The final blend is 92% Cabernet Sauvignon, 5% Merlot, 3% Cabernet Franc.) The darker the toast, the darker the wine after it is taken out of the barrel; especially noticeable with white wines. This final product resembles #4 quite a bit on nose.

I tried a blend of #1 and #4 and I got a wine that resembled the final product, yet with more body and tannin. Also, the final product is the only blend, the others being 100% Cabernet Sauvignon.

This was a fascinating tasting. The importance of the provenance and quality of the oak, the amount of toasting and the length of barrel-ageing, cannot be stressed enough.

October 1983

Dinner at home, as part of the International Wine and Food Society Convention.

Several local members hosted a dinner for the out-of-town guests. Each host was allocated specific wines by our organizing committee. Our guests were John and Renée Lawson (Robert Mondavi Winery), Bob Grath (Washington, DC), Mr. and Mrs. Frank Procter (Baltimore), and Chris and Linda Barnes (Australia).

CHAMPAGNE PERRIER-JOUËT GRAND BRUT N/V:

Lovely wine. Yeasty, complex, long; like a fine vintage Champagne of good quality. Well balanced. My style of Champagne.

CORTON-CHARLEMAGNE 1979, REINE PEDAUQUE:

A shadow of what a Corton-Charlemagne should be. Some nuttiness and complexity on nose and palate, but thin, too acidic, rather ordinary. Like an average Meursault. I wonder why our committee chose this particular wine.

1964 BAROLO "BUSSIA SOPRANA" ALDO CONTERNO,

1964 BAROLO "RISERVA," GIACOMO BORGOGNO,

AND

1967 BAROLO "RISERVA," GIACOMO BORGOGNO:

Three fine Italian red wines. Compared to the two 1964s, the 1967 was rather lean and simple with a more mature orangy-brown rim to it.

Of the two 1964s, the Conterno was more elegant, softer, with a lovely complex nose.

The Borgogno was better structured, more body. Both lovely. All three smelled like dry Port! Decanted hours before dinner. Quite an experience.

1959 CORTON, DOUDET-NAUDIN:

Held very well after three Barolos! Lovely, dark colour. Mature, complex Pinot Noir nose. Great depth on palate. My type of big, mature, lovely, red Burgundy. Backed by good fruit concentration. Not too rustic, thankfully.

1970 CHÂTEAU RIEUSSEC:

Bright golden colour. Nice botrytis on nose. Round, soft, elegant, and forward.

A very pleasant evening.

The following day, at noon

1970 red Bordeaux tasting

Guest speaker was Michael Broadbent, introduced by me. There were 220 participants. Michael Broadbent decided to serve the wines in the following illogical order! The opposite of what it should have been. He does not believe in opening the wines too soon; he is not too hot on decanting!? He insisted that we serve the bigger wines first, and the elegant Right Bank wines last. Also, because of his insistence on not decanting the wines, many participants were quite upset with the amount of sediment in their glasses.

1. CHÂTEAU LYNCH-BAGES 1970:

Lovely dark colour. Spicy, cedary, intense nose. Rich, full. long. My type of Claret. (18)

2. CHÂTEAU DUCRU-BEAUCAILLOU 1970:

Elegant, harmonious, gentle, well structured. Not as concentrated as #1. Complex, lovely on nose and palate. Slightly more age on colour. Understated, broad, elegant. (17.5)

3. CHÂTEAU LEOVILLE-LASCASES 1970, IN MAGNUMS:

Not as dark as the Ducru or the Lynch-Bages. Complex nose. Long, cedary, fruity, intense on palate. A bit stemmy and leaner than the Palmer or the two preceding wines. (16.5)

4. CHÂTEAU PALMER 1970:

Deep colour; fairly young-looking. Rich, lovely chocolaty, ripe nose. Flowery, elegant, long. Gorgeous wine. Clear winner at this event. Just gorgeous. In 1970, Palmer made a much finer wine than Château Margaux. (19)

5. CHÂTEAU LA FLEUR-PETRUS 1970, IN MAGNUMS:

Vegetal, light, sweet on nose. Big, yet round and soft on palate. Rich, meaty Pomerol. Ready and lovely. (17)

6. CHÂTEAU FIGEAC 1970:

Typical St. Emilion. Medium colour, orangy rim. Stemmy, vegetal, open nose. Soft, forward, round, lovely on palate. Ready, soft. Good characteristics. Quite light for a 1970. (16.5)

Comments

Very poorly organized! Michael Broadbent gave us blow after blow. First, he did not want the wines to be served blind. Then, he chose the oddest order, with the bigger wines first, and the softer, more forward wines last. Then, he wanted them served one glass at a time (for 220 people!) with waiters running all over the place. And finally, he did not want the wines to be decanted. Many people got sediment in their glasses and cloudy wine. Very poorly organized and conducted.

We tried to talk him out of it, but he and his wife were adamant. His wife (Daphne) called me "PSSST"—I gave her a blast! She whispered to me that maybe Michael had made a mistake and that the remaining wines should be decanted after all. I replied by saying that first, my name was not PSSST, and, second, that now that she and her famous expert husband had made a mess of it, it was up to them to decant. I proceeded to sit down and enjoy the wines. Many participants were angry. At the end of the tasting, "His Majesty" left the podium without a question-and-answer opportunity, because he had to catch a flight to Seattle. Bon Voyage!

Sid Cross, the Chairman of our branch, and the organizer of this event, was very diplomatic—as usual—so it was up to me to straighten things up with the "Broadbent Twins."

That night

André Simon Black Tie Dinner, at the Hotel Vancouver (300 Attending).

CHAMPAGNE BOLLINGER "RD" TRADITION BRUT 1973, IN DOUBLE-MAGNUMS:

This wine was on its lees for ten years and was disgorged for our event a month earlier. Fabulous, complex, yeasty nose. Long on palate. Complex, full, and rich. Great Champagne.

MEURSAULT-GENEVRIÈRES 1979, LOUIS LATOUR:

Still young, but good complexity, well structured, long on palate. Elegant. very good.

CHABLIS GRAND CRU "GRENOUILLES" 1966 "TÊTE DE CUVÉE," REMOISSENET:

A 17-year-old Chablis and what a fabulous wine! Long, complex, beautifully balanced. Lovely, big, flinty, yet rich, sweet nose. Great intensity; still full of life. Unbelievably rich for a 17-year-old. The hit of the night as far as I am concerned.

CHÂTEAU PICHON-LALANDE 1964:

Soft, forward, fragrant, beautiful, long nose. Soft, forward on palate too. Elegant, delicate wine. At its peak. We opened 72 bottles of this wine!

CORTON 1961, DOUDET-NAUDIN:

Last night we had his 1959, and tonight the 1961. Very similar to the 1959 on both nose and palate, with the 1961 having slightly more depth to it. Both lovely wines. Ready.

1933 MOULIN TOUCHAIS, ANJOU:

Made from sweet Chenin Blanc grapes. 1933 was the year the IW&FS was created and we were celebrating its 50th Anniversary. Fragrant nose. Extremely young on nose and palate, and in appearance; like a 1975. Not very deep or full. (I had tasted a bottle purchased in Amsterdam earlier this year and it was darker, more mature-looking and tasting.) We purchased the last three cases of this wine from the grower, Monsieur Touchais, and chances are that we shall never see this wine again.

1955 TAYLOR'S VINTAGE PORT, LONDON-BOTTLED BY BRITISH INTERNATIONAL HOTELS:

A disappointment to me. I must have had it from a mediocre bottle. Soft, forward, rather simple. Not bad, but not what 1955 Taylor's should be. Quite spirity.

The following day

Luncheon and tasting of young white Burgundies of Maison Joseph Drouhin.

Tasting conducted by Ed Lazarus of Los Angeles, an experienced wine taster and contributing writer for The Underground Wine Letter.

1. 1982 PULIGNY-MONTRACHET:

Crisp nose; not very complex. Still young fruit. Good acidity, good body, but lacks complexity. Buttery, apples. (15.5)

2. 1982 PULIGNY-MONTRACHET "FOLATIÈRES":

More depth and complexity than #1. Good intensity. Rounder, bigger, than #1. Long, toasty, quite ripe, with a fair bit of alcohol. (16.5)

3. 1982 PULIGNY-MONTRACHET "CLOS DU CAILLERET":

Warmer, rounder wine than the above; similar, yet not as pungent on nose. Definitely more intense, rounder, great depth. Lovely, fruity, rich wine. (17.5)

4. 1982 BÂTARD-MONTRACHET:

Lovely depth; round bouquet. Beautiful. Similar description to #3, yet has less acidity and depth, but lovely complexity. Almost too sweet and soft. I am a bit worried about the low acidity. Rich intensity of fruit. Very good but not a keeper. (17.5)

5. 1978 PULIGNY-MONTRACHET "CLOS DU CAILLERET":

Darkest colour, of course, because of the four years of extra age. Toasty, oak-vanilla nose. Complex, round, mature, well balanced, good acidity. Long on palate. Enjoyable now, but no rush drinking it. Lovely, smoky wine. (18)

Overall

Better acidity than I thought. Quite hot, rich wines. But not really agers. 1978 is still the year to buy. These 1982s are almost ready now and only need one to three years to develop completely. This is particularly true Drouhin's whites, which are early maturing anyway.

That night

Canadian Game Dinner, at the Bayshore Inn hotel.

APERITIF

CHAMPAGNE LOUIS ROEDERER 1971 BRUT, IN MAGNUMS:

Intense, rich, yeasty nose. Long, complex; a bit heavyweight. Mature Champagne, yet full of life. Similar in weight, structure, and on nose to a Krug.

AUXEY-DURESSES BLANC 1978, LOUIS LATOUR:

A wine not often seen here. Nice white Burgundy. Complex, long, lovely, fruity, toasty nose. Very well structured. Complex. Very good.

1978 MEURSAULT "CUVÉE LOPPIN," HOSPICES DE BEAUNE, BOUCHARD AÎNÉ ET FILS, IN MAGNUMS:

Very little of this wine was made and it was great. Big, oaky, toasty, nutty on nose and palate. Rich, full, intense. A lovely, big, powerful wine. In structure (but not in flavour), similar to a big California Chardonnay.

SPANNA "MONTALBANO" 1966, ANTONIO VALLANA:

Deep, dark wine. Similar in colour to a big 1970 Bordeaux. Spicy, ripe berries on nose, almost an intense Bordeaux, but on palate, definitely Italian. Big, fruity, woody. A lovely bottle. Lots of sediment and required decanting two hours before dinner.

1971 LATRICIÈRES-CHAMBERTIN "TASTEVINAGE," FAIVELEY:

Excellent, medium-deep colour. Spicy, complex Pinot Noir nose. Fair amount of sediment. Good flavour, delicate, yet with enough stuffing; typical of a Côte de Nuits. Should have been served before the Spanna. Very good anyway.

1959 CHÂTEAU PALMER:

A fine, mature Margaux. Unbelievably fragrant bouquet. Delicate on palate. Fair bit of sediment. Good fruit; complex, round, soft. Ultimate elegance. (19.5) on nose, (19) on palate.

GEWÜRZTRAMINER 1976 VENDANGE TARDIVE "SÉLECTION DES GRAINS NOBLES," JEAN HUGEL:

Lovely, spicy, sweet, complex nose. Not too rich, yet with a fruit dessert it was just perfect. Long, sweet, complex. Very unusual and rare.

A creepy member (guest from out of town) of IW&FS stole a bottle of dregs (sediment) of 1959 Palmer that I had worked so hard to collect!

Pleasant dinner, but not outstanding.

On Sunday

"Farewell" luncheon of the International Wine and Food Society, "Great Chefs Lunch."

Fabulous luncheon. Every famous chef from Vancouver prepared one course; artistic and great presentation.

We served the following wines.

CHAMPAGNE KRUG 1969 BRUT "COLLECTION," IN MAGNUMS:

Magnificent Champagne! Complex, lots of depth; long on nose and palate. One of the finest Champagnes I have ever tasted. Great concentration, still full of life.

CHÂTEAU DE L'HÔPITAL 1982, GRAVES BLANC:

A rare wine; only 25 cases arrived on the West Coast. I purchased some for this convention. Delicate, crisp, complex nose. Fairly light, but nice fruit. Perfect with lunch.

1978 SANCERRE "LES PERRIÈRES," HIPPOLYTE REVERDY:

Richer, darker colour than the above. Flinty, vegetal, fruity wine. Ready.

CARMIGNANO 1975 "RISERVA," VILLA DI CAPEZZANO:

Medium-dark brick colour. Spicy, almost sweet, delicate nose. Fruity, soft, long on palate. Ready. The only red wine served at this farewell lunch.

1982 CHÂTEAU DOISY-DAËNE:

Flowery, elegant; a bit too delicate and sweet for me. Not bad, but lacked botrytis and depth. Too young, of course.

Most members' comments were very positive. Even the Broadbent fiasco was saved by the sheer quality of the great 1970s tasted.

November 1, 1983

Dinner at Dave and Alice Spurrell's.

With Bruce Guimaraens of Oporto, part-owner of Fonseca's and Taylor's. Bruce is a good friend of ours, and he has met Dave Spurrell on several occasions, both in Vancouver and Oporto. All wines served double-blind.

1974 MIRASSOU CHAMPAGNE, SONOMA VALLEY:

Disgorged in 1980. Quite dry and delicate, almost like a good sparkling Loire. Good acidity, but lacking the depth or complexity of real Champagne. Not bad and a new experience for both Bruce and myself.

1979 ROBERT MONDAVI CHARDONNAY "RESERVE," NAPA VALLEY

AND

1979 CHÂTEAU ST. JEAN CHARDONNAY "ROBERT YOUNG," SONOMA VALLEY:

The St. Jean was quite forward, delicate. Not as massive as the 1978 and a bit flabby. Should be drunk up.

The Mondavi had more acidity and fruit concentration. Both delicate, complex, fine wines. Basically, both are ready and will not improve.

1970 CHÂTEAU L'ARROSÉE

AND

1970 CHÂTEAU L'ANGÉLUS:

L'Arrosée had the classic deep red, bright colour of the 1970s. Big wine; intense, complex, a lot of flavour, depth, and potential. Very good.

The L'Angélus looked brown, tired, duller nose, high acidity, (I thought it was a 1967 l'Arrosée). Rather disappointing.

1975 ROBERT MONDAVI CABERNET SAUVIGNON "RESERVE," NAPA VALLEY:

Deep, 1970-like colour. Delicate, minty-eucalyptus, cedar nose. At first I thought it was a Lynch-Bages, but because of colour I figured it was a fine California Cabernet. I actually mentioned Mondavi "Reserve." Good structure, but quite forward and delicate. Very fine wine.

1978 QUADY PORT "LOT II,"

1975 TAYLOR'S VINTAGE PORT,

1967 TAYLOR'S QUINTA DO VARGELLAS,

AND

1970 TAYLOR'S VINTAGE PORT:

The Quady was deep-purplish in colour. Some tannin, needs time. Rather fruity on nose. For me, quite a surprise and better than expected. Needs another four to five years or more. (Served in half-bottle)

The 1967 and 1975 Taylor's were both soft, quite forward, showing age on both colour and palate. Bruce said that Taylor's has a long plateau and the 1975 will stay good for many years.

The 1970 was a winner. Big, dark, lovely nose, long on palate. A classic Port. No rush; needs time.

Bruce Guimaraens said that they have reactivated Quinta do Terrafeita and may bottle this single Quinta shortly. Some of this Quinta, as well as the "Vargellas," goes into Taylor's Late-Bottled Vintage as well as into the true vintage port. We drank lots of wine and it was an interesting evening. As far as the 1983 vintage is concerned, it is too early to say who will declare, but the vintage looks very promising.

Possibly the best vintage since 1977, producing bigger wines than in 1980.

November 1983

Dinner at Sid Cross's home.

All wines served double-blind. Guests were Alan Tobe, Ken and Barb Cross, and Peter Adams, the official London buyer for the BC and Ontario liquor monopolies. Peter has been in the trade for 50 years, and is quite a knowledgeable man, yet the specialty shop in Vancouver is very poor in terms of the selection of wines! Peter lives in Surrey, England. He should have made an extra effort to get us decent wines in this province.

CHAMPAGNE KRUG "SPECIAL RESERVE" 1961:

Great, complex, and yeasty nose, yet too dry for my taste. Almost bitter-almonds aftertaste; woody-oaky flavour. Has lost its fruit, but not its power. Most other participants liked it more than I did. I am usually very fond of Krug Champagnes, but this one did not appeal to me.

1973 MOUNT EDEN VINEYARDS CHARDONNAY, SANTA CLARA, CALIFORNIA

AND

1973 STONY HILL CHARDONNAY, NAPA VALLEY:

Both are hard-to-find ten-year-old California Chardonnays.

The former had a darker gold colour, good toasty nose, good fruit; an elegant, mature Chardonnay. (Both Ken and I thought it was French!)

The latter was paler in colour, softer, more delicate, maybe more complex. Both have held very well and both very individual. A rare experience.

Three 1961 St. Emilions followed.

CHÂTEAU TROTTEVIEILLE, (IN MAGNUM),

CHÂTEAU L'ARROSÉE,

AND

CHÂTEAU LA GAFFELIÈRE-NAUDES:

I actually thought they were 1961 or 1966 Haut-Médocs (St. Juliens).

The Trottevieille, although served from a magnum, was the softest, roundest, and most elegant.

The l'Arrosée had a slight minty-cedary nose, great depth and concentration, some tannin. For me, the best of the lot.

The La Gaffelière was a bit dry, complex, elegant wine; some tannin. All three had mature, yet deep colours, and were lovely. What a fine vintage 1961 has turned out to be.

1933 SEPPELT PARA LIQUEUR PORT, SEPPELTSFIELD, AUSTRALIA:

Quite an experience. A 50-year-old Australian wine similar to a dark, concentrated Málaga. Deep, dark, brown-yellow (yet red) colour. Sweet, intense nose. Long on palate.

November 1983

Tasting of Inglenook's Napa Valley red wines.

Guest speaker was Inglenook's sales manager, Bill Uren.

1978 "LIMITED CASK" CABERNET SAUVIGNON:

Hot, Spanish-style wine. Spicy, peppery. Some tannin to lose. Dark colour, yet browning for a young wine. Not a keeper. Made from 100% Cabernet Sauvignon. Later, opened up, elegant, soft, rather simple. (14.5)

1974 "LIMITED CASK" CABERNET SAUVIGNON "CASK A-17":

25% Merlot. Evolved colour, similar to the 1978, but browner. Dark, mature Cabernet nose. Pleasant on palate, but soft and forward. Leafy-tobacco aroma and flavour. At its peak, unusually soft for a 1974. (16)

1973 "LIMITED CASK" CABERNET SAUVIGNON "CASK A-7":

11% Merlot. Dark colour, similar to the 1974, yet a bit more depth and youth. Better, more complex nose. Elegant. Forward; acidity showing signs of taking over (a warning). At its peak now. Fruity, forward on palate. Retails in the US for $40. Quite good. (16.5)

1970 "LIMITED CASK" CABERNET SAUVIGNON "CASK F-31":

Retails for US$50. Nice colour; dark, good depth, browning. Lovely, spicy, round bouquet. The best of the bunch. Soft, yet full. Rich, well balanced. Not too acidic. Long, elegant, mature wine. Should hold at its peak for some time. Slightly tannic. This wine came from the winery's library. (17)

1980 MERLOT "LIMITED BOTTLING":

Would retail in Vancouver for $24.50. Ridiculous! Dark, purplish, young colour. Open, fruity, berry nose. Needs two to three years. A bit too sweet for me. (13.5)

1978 NAPA CHARBONO, NAPA VALLEY:

Apparently, the source of this grape is in the Jura (Charbonneaux). Dark, fruity, elegant, simple, yet sturdy, beefy red wine. Good, but landed in Vancouver for $18. Very overpriced for the quality. (14)

November 1983

Chevaliers du Tastevin Dinner, at "La Cachette" restaurant, Vancouver.

At this event, I received my diploma of "Chevalier du Tastevin."

CHAMPAGNE POL ROGER "CHARDONNAY" 1975:

Yeasty, clean nose. Well balanced; good fruit and acidity. Delicate, yet had stuffing. Better than the 1973. (17.5)

1978 CORTON-CHARLEMAGNE, LOUIS LATOUR:

Lovely, intense, toasty, nutty nose. Great balance and complexity. Excellent fruit. Will be ready in two to three years and hold for many more. This is a truly fine wine of great class and extract. I know it well, having tasted it on six previous occasions. (18.5)

1969 MEURSAULT-CHARMES, REMOISSENET:

Elegant, buttery, toasty wine of great finesse and complexity. Delicate. At its peak at 14 years of age. Very long, classy. (18)

1971 CORTON "POUGETS," REINE PEDAUQUE:

An undistinguished wine (I never thought much of Reine Pedauque). Bright colour. Spicy, sweet Pinot Noir nose, but lean, hard, high acidity, and short. Rather simple. May have been better four to five years ago. (14.5)

1964 CLOS DE VOUGEOT, REMOISSENET:

A very nice wine. Some age at rim. Subdued, delicate Pinot Noir nose. Round, soft; very pleasant and complex on palate. Easy to drink and most enjoyable. (17)

1978 CHÂTEAU ROUMIEU, BARSAC:

Nutty, clean, buttery, fat wine; more like a good Ste. Croix-du-Mont. No botrytis (reflecting the vintage). Pleasant. (15)

November 1983

Australian Wine Society tasting at the Maritime Museum. Subject: Penfold's Grange Hermitage "Bin 95."

Made from 100% Hermitage/Syrah grapes.

1974:

Mature, deep-brown colour. Lovely, complex, "sweaty saddle" nose. Almost "Tawny." Well balanced. Oddly, needs more time. Massive wine. (17)

1973:

Cleanest and fruitiest-smelling of flight. Good colour, showing a bit more youth than the 1974. Better fruit/acidity balance. Big, tannic; needs at least two to three more years. (17.5)

1972:

Ageing colour. Almost minty-eucalyptus on nose. Soft on palate, yet tannic finish. A bit too acidic, but lovely, complex; hot, long wine on palate. The leanest of all four. (17)

1968:

The 1968 is a very famous wine. "Sweaty saddle" on both nose and palate. Long, complex, soft, yet powerful and tannic underneath. Almost too overpowering on palate; leathery. An unusual wine; starting to get tired. (17)

November 1983

Le Tastevin Wine Club vertical tasting of Château St. Jean Cabernets.

APERITIF

CHÂTEAU ST. JEAN CHARDONNAY 1978, SONOMA VALLEY:

(13.9° alcohol) Clean, bright gold; oaky nose. Complex; good fruit/acidity balance. Ready.

CHÂTEAU ST. JEAN CABERNET SAUVIGNONS:

All wines dark and purplish, with the single Merlot being slightly lighter. All are made from 100% Cabernet Sauvignon grapes.

1. 1978 "WILDWOOD" CABERNET SAUVIGNON, SONOMA VALLEY:

Tight, clean Cabernet nose. 1978 was the last year that this 100-year-old vineyard (Wildwood) has produced Cabernet. In 1979, the vines were uprooted. 15.9° alcohol—unbelievable! Hot, very spirity; volatile alcohol. Undrinkable at this stage. May never be good, as the excessive alcohol will not disappear with time. (13.5)

2. 1977 "WILDWOOD" CABERNET SAUVIGNON, SONOMA VALLEY:

Closed nose. Rounder and more mature than the 1978. Hard, lean, very tannic; the hardness masks any fruit that might be there. (14)

3. 1977 "GLEN ELLEN" CABERNET SAUVIGNON:

Very vegetal and stemmy on nose. Bell peppers. Better balance and better fruit than the 1977 "Wildwood." Tastes better than it smells. (15)

4. 1977 "LAUREL GLEN" CABERNET SAUVIGNON:

Deep, closed, full Cabernet nose. Rounder than #2 or #3, but still very hard. Nice and spicy, but too high alcohol. (14.5)

5. 1977 "JACK LONDON" CABERNET SAUVIGNON:

Slightly vegetal, grassy; a combination of #2 and #3. A bit leaner than #4, but not as lean as #2 or #3. Reasonably forward, but still needs a few years. (14.5)

6. 1977 MERLOT, SONOMA VALLEY, IN MAGNUM:

Merlot nose, all right! Vanilla-oak, stemmy, sweet, slightly vegetal. Very oaky on palate; new oak. A bit lean, very tannic. Nose better than flavour. (14)

7. 1976 "WILDWOOD" CABERNET SAUVIGNON:

Nice, elegant nose; a bit closed. Good fruit, a bit mellower, still very tannic. Needs four to five years. Quite fruity. (16)

8. 1976 "GLEN ELLEN" CABERNET SAUVIGNON:

Slightly more herbaceous on nose. Elegant. Same comments on palate. A bit more acidic; some tannins, good fruit, but quite dry. Quite pleasant. As it breathed, it improved. (15.5)

9. 1975 "WILDWOOD" CABERNET SAUVIGNON:

The first Cabernet that Dick Arrowood and Château St. Jean have ever made. Sweet, alcoholic, closed, tight nose. Big, hard. Good acidity, good fruit. Needs years. Later (after two hours), it opened up; long on the nose, quite complex. I hope that the fruit will outlive the tannins. (16)

DESSERT WINE

CHÂTEAU ST. JEAN JOHANNISBERG RIESLING "BELLE TERRE" 1978 TBA, IN HALF-BOTTLES:

(28.3° residual sugar) Dark amber-gold colour. Apricot-peach jam nose. Good acidity. Sweet, cloying, intense, big, and very rich. Needs years. Almost too much of a good thing!

Overall

An interesting tasting. These red wines are not made any more. Frankly, I am pleased. This was not an impressive range of wines. St. Jean should concentrate on their whites, which are far superior to these red wines.

December 1983

Dinner at the Tobes'.

All wines served double-blind.

1978 CORTON-CHARLEMAGNES, LOUIS LATOUR AND REMOISSENET:

The Latour was darker, more toasty-oak on nose and palate, more intense; almost seemed older.

The Remoissenet was a bit leaner; needs more time. Later, opened up. The Latour was more opulent, but the Remoissenet seems to age well. Wait and see. Both excellent.

Four vintages of Château Ducru-Beaucaillou

1970:

Darkest, youngest-looking. Intense, deep, dark colour; youthful-looking. Needs time. Well balanced. Almost Pauillac in style. (At first, I thought all four were Pauillacs.) Lovely wine with a promising future.

1966:

Some age in appearance. Good nose. A bit earthy; round, mature, well balanced, lovely flavour. Elegant Claret. Good fruit.

1964:

At first, odd corked nose; cleared later on. Soft, forward; the softest and simplest of the bunch, but still elegant and easy to enjoy. A bit short.

1961:

Fabulous, elegant, complex, beautiful chocolaty nose. Elegant and long on palate. Age at rim; orange-brown. Ready. Some cedar; long aftertaste. Superb bottle.

Last, the "pièce de résistance."

1927 TAYLOR'S VINTAGE PORT:

The best Port of that famous vintage. Recently purchased from the Wine Warehouse in Los Angeles for US$200 per bottle. Fabulous wine. Aged, browning, medium-light colour. Spicy, long nose. Complex. Good alcohol and fruit on palate. Holding very well. Long aftertaste. A lovely bottle and a great experience. Decanted 15 minutes before serving. Allan is a very generous host.

February 1984

"Group of Ten" Dinner.

The Tobes, K. Crosses, S. Cross, Mottersheads, and Carol and myself. Each couple contributed a wine and prepared some of the food.

1964 AYALA BRUT CHAMPAGNE, IN MAGNUM:

(Sid Cross's bottle) This wine was served at the International Wine and Food Society dinner convention in October 1983. I purchased six cases of magnums for the convention from Draper & Esquin's in San Francisco. A lovely, mature Champagne. Elegant, yeasty Chardonnay nose. Tiny bubbles. Long, complex, yet very delicate. Fabulous bottle. (18)

Three Corton-Charlemagnes followed, served blind. We all guessed them right. We knew what the wines were, but not the order in which they were served.

1. 1978 CORTON-CHARLEMAGNE "DIAMOND JUBILEE," REMOISSENET:

Closed, oaky, toasty nose. A leaner wine, quite high acidity but has fruit. Good future; needs two to three more years. Very good. (18)

2. 1978 CORTON-CHARLEMAGNE, LOUIS LATOUR:

Darker, deep, bright gold. Big, complex, nutty, oaky nose. Intense. Rich, full, and long on palate. Very well structured. Needs a few more years and will hold. Fabulous. (18.5)

3. 1979 CORTON-CHARLEMAGNE, TOLLOT-BEAUT:

(I brought this bottle along.) Lovely, complex; unusual eucalyptus and sage on nose. Excellent flavour; long, well balanced, not as lean as #1 or as intense as #2, but flavourful. All three were great bottles! (18) Tollot-Beaut produces only four barrels (100 cases) of this fine wine.

1949 CHÂTEAU LAFITE, IN MAGNUM

AND

1945 CHÂTEAU LAFITE, IN BOTTLE:

(These were our group-bottles.) Both wines had a fair bit of sediment. Both had similar dark colours; younger-looking than their age, the 1949 slightly paler and more brown at rim.

On nose, the 1949 was open, delicate, lovely complex; so typical of Lafite. Great delicate nose. The 1945 was similar yet more concentrated and a bit more intense on nose. On palate, the 1949 was softer, more forward, at its peak (even from a magnum). Needs drinking. Delicate, long, and complex. Fabulous.

The 1945 was a bit harder and tighter-structured; long, intense, well balanced, yet the unmistakable elegance of Lafite. A magnificent and memorable bottle, and from my birth year. Both rated (18.5). I have previously tasted several examples of 1945 Lafite. Each previous time, it was soft, pale, and disappointing.

DESSERT WINE

1966 CHÂTEAU D'YQUEM:

Deep, almost amber-gold. Good body. Nose a bit tired. Lacks the depth and intensity of the 1967 and the youth of the 1971, yet it was still a lovely bottle. Ready. (18)

February 1984

Tasting of 1963 Ports, at "Hawthornes" restaurant, in Point Roberts, Washington State.

I was the guest speaker. 24 participants. We started with some unusual Ports, and other wines, as follows.

SHENANDOAH VINEYARDS ZINFANDEL PORT "LOT 2" N/V, AMADOR COUNTY, IN HALF-BOTTLE:

Deep, yet maturing colour. Closed nose; not a spicy Zinfandel nose at all. Very sweet, lacking concentration, high alcohol; pleasant, but rather simple.

1973 PRIMITIVO, AZIENDA VINICOLA AMANDA, ROSSO DI SAVA, ITALY:

17% alcohol by volume. The forefather of Zinfandel? Late harvest grapes. No Brandy added. Very dark, still-youthful colour; spicy, subdued nose. Very sweet, intense. Similar to a California Port rather than the Portuguese variety, but for a ten-year-old, it is young-looking and tasting. Needs another ten years. (16.5)

1964 DOW'S LATE-BOTTLED VINTAGE PORT:

Palish, browning colour; subdued, delicate nose. Sweet on palate, delicate, forward. Pleasant. (16)

1960 TAYLOR'S VINTAGE PORT:

Medium-browning colour; very little on nose. Pleasant on palate; soft, forward, well structured, stylish. Needs drinking. (16.5)

Then came the turn of the 1963s. These wines are now fully 20 years old, approaching their peak.

AVERY'S OF BRISTOL:

Medium-dark colour. Good depth. Concentrated yet delicate. Forward for a 1963; better structure than the 1960 Taylor's. Rather sweet. Vanilla on nose. (16.5)

SANDEMAN'S:

A little more depth in appearance. Clean, not very intense nose. Sweet; quite forward, too. At its peak. A bit sweeter than the Avery's. (16.5)

CROFT'S:

Similar colour to Sandeman's. Lovely nose, delicate complexity, but an explosion of fruit on palate. Long, complex; forward, yet well structured. A classic. (18)

DOW'S, LONDON-BOTTLED, ST. JAMES:

A bit more depth than the Croft's. Not as complex on nose as Croft's at this stage. Deeper, harder, tighter. Very well structured. Needs five more years. (17.5)

DOW'S, OPORTO-BOTTLED:

Similar nose to the above: similar colour, similar on palate. Flowery, although I have detected a bit more sweetness and depth in this Oporto bottling, and more extract, too. Still a bit tight. Very promising in five years. (17.5) Possibly (18).

FONSECA'S:

Deeper colour than any of the above. Intense, spicy, ripe nose. Generous and round. Sweet, rich, complex; almost a blend of the Croft's and the Dow's. Beautiful wine. (18.5)

TAYLOR'S FLADGATE:

Not as dark as Fonseca's. Pronounced vanilla on nose. Harder and better structured than the Croft's, but not as fruity as the Fonseca's. (18.5)

We ended this "spirity" evening with a bottle of Cognac.

1929 PRUNIER GRANDE CHAMPAGNE COGNAC, A/C:

Palish, intense, long, oaky; lovely Cognac. Complex nose; dry and very smooth.

Group rating of the 1963s

Fonseca's: first
Croft's: second
Taylor's: third
Dow's: fourth

My rating

Croft's: first
Taylor's: second
Fonseca's: third
Dow's: fourth

We rated them according to drinkability rather than future potential. Sandeman's and Avery's both rated fifth.

February 1984

"Pink" Dinner at the Mottersheads', on the occasion of Valentine's Day.

Everyone had to wear something pink, and there had to be some pink in the food and wines.

CHAMPAGNE POL ROGER "ROSÉ" 1975:

Pleasant, elegant, lively, but lacking the yeasty, toasty complexity of really classic Champagne. Rosés are not my favourite Champagnes.

DOMAINE CHANDON "BLANC DE NOIR" CHAMPAGNE N/V, NAPA VALLEY:

Slight salmon-pink colour. Pleasant, better structured than the Blanc de Blancs. Not bad, but not the "real" thing.

CHAMPAGNE VEUVE CLICQUOT 1978 "LA GRANDE DAME" BRUT:

Ian served me this wine a few months ago, too. Lovely, elegant nose. Complex, yeasty, long. Quite forward, but well structured. Very good.

1970 GONZALES-BIAS VINTAGE PORT:

I have never tasted this house's Port before. Surprisingly forward for a 1970 (13 years old). Good, spicy nose. Pleasant; good depth, but rather sweet and simple. I thought it was a Sandeman's.

The food was good, too, with the exception of a beet sorbet. Even our hostess had to admit that it was "rather unpleasant." Besides, I happen to hate beets.

February 26, 1984

Commanderie de Bordeaux and Chevaliers du Tastevin Joint Compound white Burgundy tasting and lunch, at the Four Seasons hotel.

I was the speaker for wines #1 through #8, Group A.

GROUP A

1A. 1979 CHASSAGNE-MONTRACHET "LES CAILLERETS," DELAGRANGE-BACHELET:

Medium-gold colour. Elegant, toasty, flowery nose. Intense flavour. Good fruit, long, vanilla-oak on palate. Very good fruit/acidity balance. Lovely. (17.5)

2A. 1979 PULIGNY-MONTRACHET "LES CHALUMEAUX," ROPITEAU-MIGNON:

Slightly lighter colour than #1 and more subdued nose. Leaner, higher fruit/acidity concentration. Long, steely, masculine. (17)

3A. 1979 MEURSAULT-GENEVRIÈRES, LOUIS LATOUR:

Nutty on nose. Round, elegant, nutty on palate, too. Long, round, fat, and softer than #1 or #2. A true Meursault. Well made. (17.5)

4A. 1979 CHABLIS GRAND CRU "LES CLOS," JOSEPH DROUHIN:

Leaner, more simple than the previous three wines. Not as flinty or as smoky as it should be. Pleasant, long, hot wine. Not great. (15.5)

5A. 1979 CORTON-CHARLEMAGNE, LOUIS LATOUR:

True Corton. Nose similar to, but not as open as, #3 and the structure of #2. Lovely wine, well made, long and very pleasant. (17.5)

6A. 1979 CRIOTS-BÂTARD-MONTRACHET, P. DE MARCILLY:

Similar to #1, yet much more intense. Dark colour. Toasty, oaky, intense on palate, but ends a bit short. More mature-tasting than #7 or #8. (16.5)

7A. 1979 BÂTARD-MONTRACHET, ROPITEAU:

Medium-gold colour; slightly lighter than #6. More elegant, subdued nose than the Criots. Overall more elegant and softer aftertaste. (17)

8A. 1979 CHEVALIER-MONTRACHET, JOSEPH DROUHIN:

A delicate wine. Complex, but not as good as it could be. Better balanced than #7 and more elegant. Quite good. (17.5)

The overall quality of Group A was very good. At four years old, these wines are showing very well.

GROUP B

1B. 1979 CHASSAGNE-MONTRACHET "BOUDRIOTTE," GAGNARD-DELAGRANGE:

Similar in style, colour, and structure to #1A, but a bit more toasty. Very good, full, complex wine. (17.5)

2B. 1979 PULIGNY-MONTRACHET "LES REFERTS," LATOUR:

Rich, round, intense; beautiful balance. Steely, well structured, and long. Very good. (17.5)

3B. MEURSAULT-PERRIÈRES 1979, GUYON:

Leaner and a bit more volatile acidity than #3A, yet similar flavours. Leaner and not as round as #3A. (17)

4B. 1979 CORTON-CHARLEMAGNE, A. RODET:

Not tasting at all like a Corton; lacking intensity or complexity. Simple, acidic. Egg-yolk nose. (14)

5B. 1979 BÂTARD-MONTRACHET, A. RODET:

Rather closed nose; lean, acidic, vegetal, herbaceous nose. Lean, not very pleasant. Mâcon-like. Ordinary. (14) The Rodet wines showed poorly.

6B. 1979 CORTON-CHARLEMAGNE, REINE PEDAUQUE:

Good, characteristic Corton. Nutty nose. More forward and less intense than Latour's (#5A), but much better than Rodet's (#4B). (16)

7B. 1978 CORTON-CHARLEMAGNE, LOUIS LATOUR:

One of the two 1978s at this tasting. Lovely, round, intense on both nose and palate. Intense, round, long; needs time. Probably the finest wine of the whole tasting. Great fruit extract, balance, depth, and complexity. Marvellous bottle. (18.5)

8B. 1978 MONTRACHET, THÉVENIN:

Dark-gold colour; herbaceous nose. Round, some greenness on palate. Long, very nice wine; quite intense in structure, but not in complexity. Needs more time. Improved later. Thévenin's half-acre of Montrachet was sold recently to Domaine de la Romanée-Conti. (17.5)

With lunch (after the tasting)

MEURSAULT-CHARMES "CHARMES DESSUS" 1979, DOMAINE DE LA GUYOMIÈRE:

Odd, oxidized nose. Steely, vegetal, herbaceous, rubbery. Not very impressive. (14)

Comments

All in all, a very extensive and complex tasting. Most people were not up to it, but I found it very interesting. Except for the Rodet wines, which were well below average, and the Romaine Guyomière, which could have been better, the other wines were very good to excellent.

February 1984

Le Tastevin "Group B" Inaugural blind tasting of 1979 Bordeaux within Le Tastevin Wine Club (which I created in 1977).

A group of members asked me to help them organize into a small-tasting group. We created that group in 1982. Now, a second group of members of Le Tastevin wants to do the same thing. So we have designated this as "Group #2" or "Group B."

1. 1979 CHÂTEAU LANGOA-BARTON:

Medium-dark colour; slightly watery, orange rim. Spicy, subdued, elegant, not very intense nose. Slightly high acidity and a bit thin. Short, metallic finish. Lacks ripeness. (13.5)

2. 1979 CHÂTEAU SOCIANDO-MALLET:

Purplish, dark, youthful-looking to rim. Good appearance. Closed nose; sweet, spicy Cabernet. Later, opened up. Oaky, intense flavour. Some tannins. Very well structured, long on palate; not very complex, but a solid wine. Best structured of the bunch. (16.5)

3. 1979 CHÂTEAU BATAILLEY:

Medium colour, lighter rim. Toasty, slightly vegetal nose. Elegant, but not intense. Delicate, well balanced, a bit tannic. Good fruit. Early maturing (in two to three years). Pleasant, clean aftertaste. After the Sociando-Mallet, this wine seems soft. (14.5)

4. 1979 CHÂTEAU KIRWAN:

Dark colour; young, purplish-looking. Baked Cabernet nose; toast, hay. Flavourful, round, forward, soft, and enjoyable. Vegetal, yet hint of caramel. (15)

5. 1979 CHÂTEAU LA CONSEILLANTE:

Medium-dark colour, orangy hue. Slightly spirity nose. Sweet fruit. A bit lean, well structured, elegant, not very big. Needs two to three years. Has class, breed, elegance, and long aftertaste. (17)

6. 1979 CHÂTEAU LEOVILLE-BARTON:

Dark colour; good depth. Vegetal, stemmy nose. Spicy, but not as round and ripe as some of the others. Solid on palate, yet rather lean. Better than #1; more concentrated, but not as rich as it should be. True Leoville-Barton in style. (16)

In retrospect, #5 and #6 were finer wines than #2, with more complexity and class, but considering the fact #5 and #6 are top-classified wines—while the Sociando is a relatively "unknown wine"—it certainly deserves the high rating given to it. Most tasters liked the Kirwan best; I thought it was pleasant but rather simple.

March 1984

Le Tastevin small-group tasting, at the Carruthers'.

Wines served double-blind. Three whites and three reds.

1. 1977 Corton-Charlemagne, Louis Latour:

Toasty Chardonnay nose; French. A bit lean on palate, woody. Slightly lemony. Could be Rhône. Hard; lacks ripe fruit yet has a fair bit of oak. Maybe leaner-style Puligny? (15) In retrospect, not bad for such a poor vintage.

2. 1978 Nuits-St.-Georges "Clos de l'Arlot" Blanc, Jules Belin:

Sauvignon Blanc? Could be Bordeaux or Loire? Hint of Chardonnay, though. Quite tight, unyielding, some oak; good intensity. (16.5) I had a hard time figuring this one out. Quite rare to taste a white Côte de Nuits.

3. Grgich Hills 1977 Chardonnay, Napa Valley:

Typical oak-honey nose of California Chardonnay. Quite rich on palate. Intense, yet only medium-bodied. Must be a Napa Chardonnay. (16.5)

4. 1979 Acacia Pinot Noir "Lund Vineyard":

Herbaceous, dill nose. Too lean to be California or Australia. Quite big structure, though. Rhône? Medium-dark colour. May be a big Pinot Noir. Too stemmy for my taste. (15)

5. 1980 Acacia Pinot Noir "Lund Vineyard":

Darker than #4. Herbaceous Cabernet Franc on both nose and palate, like a Chinon or a Bourgueil. A bit more elegant and more complex than #4. (16)

6. 1978 Nuits-St.-Georges "Clos de l'Arlot," Jules Belin:

Medium colour, similar to #4. Same herbaceous nose as #5 and same dill as #4. A mystery, maybe a St. Emilion? Cabernet Franc? Unusual, very hard to guess. Yet, this has a hint of Pinot Noir. (15.5)

I'm afraid that I wasn't even close with these three reds.

DESSERT WINE
1969 Château Suduiraut:

Botrytis on nose. Dark-gold colour. A bit short; finishes lean and short. Prematurely old or poor vintage? Obviously Sauternes. (15) No wonder. 1969 was not a good year.

Late March 1984

Chevaliers du Tastevin Dinner at the "William Tell" restaurant, Georgian Court Hotel, Vancouver.

Champagne Pol Roger "Blanc de Chardonnay" 1975:

Well structured, fairly hard and lean. Needs more time. 1975 was a very good year in Champagne. Bigger and harder than the 1973. Very good fruit and flavour. (17.5)

1978 Corton-Charlemagne, Louis Latour:

I have been fortunate to have tasted this wine numerous times in the past. A lovely, big, oaky, toasty, intense wine which will be long-lived. Well structured, very well balanced, and great fruit extract. (18.5)

1971 Corton "Pougets," Reine Pedauque:

Good colour. Spicy Pinot Noir nose, but too lean and hard on palate. Too dry and losing its fruit. Dull, short finish. (14)

1952 Clos Vougeot, Remoissenet:

Unbelievable youthful colour for a 1952. Looked more like a 1971 or 1976. Elegant, spicy nose. Long, complex; quite big on palate. Very good and quite an experience. Will last for a long time. Odd that older red Grands Crus of this producer have little or no sediment. It almost seems as if they have been filtered or pasteurized. Very good, nevertheless. (18)

March 1984

Lunch at "Le Gavroche," with Hugh Johnson.

Hugh is in Vancouver as a guest speaker at the 1984 Vancouver Wine Festival. Also: Gary Bannerman and Jarvis Whitney (both journalists), John Lawson (Robert Mondavi Winery), Alan Hemphill (Château St. Jean), Harry McWatters (Sumac Ridge Winery in the Okanagan Valley), Sid Cross, and John Levine. We tasted (blind) six white wines. Easily guessed them as being California Chardonnays. They turned out to be 1978 California Chardonnays; five from Napa and one from Sonoma.

1. 1978 Clos du Val Chardonnay, Napa Valley:

Typical California Chardonnay. Elegant, oaky, butter nose. Round, delicate, ready; drying up a bit. Needs drinking. (15)

2. 1978 VILLA MOUNT EDEN CHARDONNAY, NAPA VALLEY:

Leaner than #1. Tea-leaves flavour. Better acidity than #1, but not as round. For me, the least impressive of the group. (13.5)

3. 1978 ROBERT MONDAVI CHARDONNAY (REGULAR), NAPA VALLEY:

Elegant; rounder and more complex on both nose and palate than either #1 or #2. At its peak and enjoyable. Drink up! (16)

4. 1978 ST. CLEMENT CHARDONNAY, NAPA VALLEY:

Beautifully balanced with better structure than above three wines. Has breed. Nice vanilla-oak and ripe fruit/acidity balance. Ready, but no rush. (17)

5. 1978 CHÂTEAU ST. JEAN "MCRAE VINEYARD" CHARDONNAY, SONOMA VALLEY:

Lovely nose, good acidity; intense, well balanced, still youthful. Good, ripe, exotic fruit. Fine quality. (16.5)

6. 1978 KEENAN CHARDONNAY, NAPA VALLEY:

Very California style. Good fruit, slightly volatile, but overall good, if a bit coarse. A bit heavy-handed, low acidity. Drink up. (15.5)

Hugh Johnson's favourite was the St. Clement. I liked both St. Jean and St. Clement very much. Later tonight, Hugh Johnson will be a guest speaker at the Vancouver Wine Festival.

Early April 1984

Le Tastevin small-group blind tasting of 1970 First Growths, at Bob Sinclair's.

I organized it and supplied most of the wines. The order was unknown to us.

1. CHÂTEAU LATOUR:

Darkest of the bunch; touch of purple. Deep colour to rim. Lovely, cedary, fruity, intense nose; still a bit closed. Rich, full, fair bit of tannin to lose. Great Cabernet extract. Impressive wine. Needs another ten years. Must be Latour! (19)

2. CHÂTEAU MARGAUX:

Medium, ageing colour; orangy rim. Lightest colour together with #6 and #8. Stemmy, spicy nose. Hard, unyielding, some tannins to lose. Not very open or opulent at this stage, yet delicate underneath. Could be Margaux? Slightly vegetal. Noticeably high acidity. (16)

3. CHÂTEAU HAUT-BRION:

Medium colour, orange rim. Elegant, sweet, fruity yet earthy nose. Round, spicy wine on palate. Good intensity, depth, some tannin to lose. Long, clean, still a bit hard. Well balanced. Could be Margaux, yet rounder than Margaux 1970 as I remember it. Maybe Haut-Brion? (17)

4. CHÂTEAU AUSONE:

Very similar in appearance to #3; orangy rim. Sweet, open nose. Big, spicy Cabernet Franc on palate. Round, well balanced. Cedar, even ripe nose; herbaceous. Margaux? A surprise! Turned out to be Ausone, and a good bottle! (17.5) I do not like 1970 Ausone, but I must admit that this was surprisingly good.

5. CHÂTEAU PETRUS:

Similar orangy rim to #4, but much more depth. Magnificent, unusual vanilla, oak, and sweet fruit. Yet dry, hard, some tannins to lose. Big, rich wine. Concentrated. Licorice. Could be Petrus? Some dill on nose. Very long. Great future in ten years. (19)

6. CHÂTEAU CHEVAL-BLANC:

Lighter than #5, orangy rim. Slight wet wood on nose. Some tannin, fair bit of acidity. Good fruit, yet lacks depth and ripeness. Pleasant, sweet aftertaste. Forward. Could be Lafite or Haut-Brion? Too acidic. (17) I was wrong here!

7. CHÂTEAU MOUTON-ROTHSCHILD:

Lovely dark colour; wet-wood nose. Magnificent big mouthful. Tannins to lose. Beautifully balanced. A bit hard, cedary Cabernet character. Could be Latour. Long vanilla-oak on palate. Fabulous, intense. (At first, I thought Latour, but once I identified #1 as Latour, there was no doubt that this was Mouton.) (18.5)

8. CHÂTEAU LAFITE:

Light, orangy colour. Caramel, wet-earth nose. Rather sweet on nose. Lafite 1970? Elegant in mouth, good finish, but noticeably high acidity. Long and elegant, but a lightweight. Similar impression on palate as on nose. (16.5)

The three darkest wines (#1, #5, and #7) were also the best wines.

DESSERT WINE

1955 MOULIN TOUCHAIS, ANJOU:

Chenin Blanc from the Loire Valley. Well balanced, good acidity, not very sweet or cloying, easy to drink, youthful. No rush. A bit earthy, "wet cement" aftertaste.

Overall

A great evening! I am very fortunate to have purchased some Latour 1970, as well as a few bottles of Mouton and Petrus 1970. I acquired the Latour 1970 in Seattle in 1976 for US$216 per case. Sells now for US$900 to $1,000 per case!

Next day, April 1984

Le Tastevin "Group B" blind tasting of 1970 red Bordeaux.

Two days in a row, tasting 1970s. But today they are not First Growths, with one exception.

1. 1970 CHÂTEAU CLOS RENÉ:

Lovely, deep colour; orangy rim. Fairly closed nose. Hard on palate. High acidity; metallic and short. Little tannin. Not very long on palate. Rather lean. Could be a Pomerol? Odd; could even be St. Emilion. Too big, though. (14)

2. 1970 CHÂTEAU HAUT-BATAILLEY:

Beautiful dark colour to rim; younger-looking than #1. Fruity, sweet cedary nose. Round wine, good fruit, some tannins to lose. Pauillac? Not very complex. Tea leaves. Cabernet and some cedar on palate. Rather woody nose, but good round fruit. (15.5)

3. 1970 CHÂTEAU MARGAUX:

Colour similar to #2. Elegant, toasty, delicate nose. Lacks complexity and depth, yet has some fruit. Too sharp and tight. Charmless. Will last for some time, but will not improve. Cabernet. Pauillac? (15.5) Later: This is the Margaux. How disappointing. I have read recently that Michael Broadbent gives this wine a potential five stars out of five. I frankly don't know which cask at Margaux he has been tasting from! Or does he own a case of "special" bottling of this wine?

4. 1970 CHÂTEAU LE PRIEURÉ, ST. EMILION:

Similar to #2 and #3, but darker to rim. Sweet, yet tannic; hard, not very complex. Easy to drink, simple on palate. Lacks complexity, but pleasant and well balanced. Merlot? Could be a Pomerol, yet too elegant and not big enough to be one. (15)

5. 1970 CHÂTEAU LEOVILLE-LASCASES:

Sweet, herbaceous, complex nose. Deep colour. Complex, but noticeable acidity. Has class; long, elegant, yet solid. No rush, but a bit too acidic. Better on nose than on palate. Lascases? (17)

6. CHÂTEAU BELGRAVE, HAUT-MÉDOC:

Darkest wine of flight. Still youthful. Good, chocolaty Cabernet nose, but a bit tight. Some tannins to lose. Good fruit, but high acidity. Long on palate, a nice wine. Riper fruit than #5, but less complex. (16.5)

Ratings

The group rated the Lascases first and Clos René second. Margaux was fourth. Château Margaux was disappointing and I definitely think that the group was wrong about the Clos René. It is a mediocre wine and rather disappointing. This was the first opportunity I have had to taste Château Belgrave, a Fifth Growth. Colour-wise, all wines had the deep appearance so typical of this lovely vintage.

DESSERT WINE

1970 FEUERHEERD VINTAGE PORT:

Medium, youthful colour. Good nose. Not very intense or complex; rather simple, but very sweet. Pleasant, Sandeman's style, but lighter.

April 1984

"Group of Ten" Dinner, at our home.

CHAMPAGNE MERCIER BRUT RÉSERVE N/V:

Round, pleasant; rather simple and commercial. Not bad, but not fine or complex.

CHAMPAGNE PAUL BARA BRUT 1979:

100% Grand Cru grapes. Lovely Champagne. Fine, complex, yeasty bouquet. Tiny, fine bubbles. Long, well balanced. No rush drinking it. Had it with fine Romanian Black Sea caviar. (Both Champagnes were my contribution.)

1979 AND 1978 HERMITAGE BLANC, CHAVE

AND

1970 CHANTE ALOUETTE, HERMITAGE BLANC, CHAPOUTIER:

The Chante Alouette had some sediment. Soft, flowery, spicy bouquet. Rather delicate, but a bit tired and short.

Of the two Chaves, the 1979 was a bit more forthcoming; lovely chalky, fruity nose. Big, long, round; needs three to five years. Will be excellent.

The 1978 was tighter, harder, much bigger, powerful. Has hidden fruit. This wine will need at least five to seven more years, but should be a classic. Tonight I preferred the 1979.

1961 CHÂTEAU AUSONE, IN MAGNUM:

A lovely bottle. Lively, round, mature, delicate nose. Long. Good, deep, maturing colour. Full, round, forward, spicy on palate. A fine bottle. Better than previous magnum of this wine tasted (with the same group) in September 1981.

1928 CHÂTEAU AUSONE:

Good level in bottle; soft, crumbling cork, medium sediment. Decanted ten minutes. Medium-dark colour. More like a 1966! Lovely, long, open, spicy, very complex nose. Fabulous. However, on palate it did not deliver. Perfectly drinkable, but drying out. Lean and acidic. We had both above wines in September 1981, and at that time, the 1961 wasn't as good, but the 1928 was superb—the opposite of today.

1963 DALVA VINTAGE PORT:

A disappointment. Medium, palish colour. Very spirity. Brandy on nose; lean and short on palate. Rather simple. I have not tasted a good bottle of Dalva Port of any vintage to date.

April 18 to May 4, 1984

Trip with Carol to London, Eugenie-Les-Bains, Bordeaux, and Oporto.

On the same day as we arrived in London, we had dinner at Harry and Prue Waugh's. Their twin children (born in 1973) Harriet and Jamie were there, too, as well as an elderly couple from London, Lena and George Rainbird. Both are publishers. Mr. Rainbird is Harry's age (80) and has just published a book called Wine, *a nice coffee-table book with maps, pictures, etc. Mr. Rainbird is the past chairman of the International Wine and Food Society (took over from André Simon).*

CHAMPAGNE BOLLINGER BRUT 1976:

Two bottles. Having had the 1975 only last week in Vancouver, I could compare both vintages. The 1976 was more forward, softer, pleasant, but without the complexity and fresh fruit of the 1975. However, it was rich, long, and most enjoyable.

1979 PULIGNY-MONTRACHET "LES COMBETTES," ETIENNE SAUZET:

Two bottles. A lovely, complex, fairly big wine for the vintage. Lovely depth and length; well balanced. No rush drinking it. Very fine quality. Good fruit extract; oak and fruit in harmony. This property produces superb Pulignys.

1955 CHÂTEAU PICHON-LONGUEVILLE-BARON:

Deep, dark colour. Round, complex, cigar-box, Cabernet nose. Sweet, spicy, long; very well balanced. Great Claret. At its peak. Classic, cedary Pauillac. A lovely bottle of wine. This wine, together with Pichon-Baron's 1959, 1961, and 1952, shows the potential of this Château. However, it has been making disappointing wines over the past two decades.

1945 CHÂTEAU GRUAUD-LAROSE:

I helped Harry pull out the cork (the cork disintegrated). Dark colour. Lovely nose; not as intense as the 1955 Pichon-Baron, but rather delicate and complex. Typical structure of the 1945s. Still hard, some tannin to lose; but has enough fruit. Opened up in the glass. Complex, round, long. A lovely bottle of classic Claret of the great 1945 vintage… my birth year!

1963 FONSECA'S VINTAGE PORT:

Harry's favourite. Still a bit young, but perfectly balanced. Deep, dark, spicy, round, long; a lovely bottle of Port. By 1988 to 1995, this will be a great Port.

By then we were very tired, not having slept for 38 hours (jet lag et al.). A great wine experience. How nice to see Harry again. He is amazingly active for an octogenarian.

Comments

After Harry's bad car accident in Burgundy a year ago, he has lost his sense of smell completely, but can still taste a bit. He is lucky to be alive, though. Harry is fortunately able to assess the structure of wines. He has so much experience that, between his structural assessment and my description to him of the bouquet and taste, he can describe a wine accurately.

On Eddy Penning-Rowsell, I learned the following: he has built himself a cellar of "gifted" wines.

On Château Mouton

Harry is worried that when Philippine de Rothschild takes over from her father, the quality may decline. I am not sure of that. Time will tell.

Of course, Baron Philippe and his cellarmaster, Raoul Blondin, (and Blondin's father), have been making the wines at Mouton for almost 60 years, so changes are bound to occur when they retire. Besides, Mouton may have been consistent in its management team, but not in the wines produced. For instance, after 1962 and until 1975, what great vintages has Mouton produced? Even recent vintages, such as 1978, 1979, and 1981, are disappointing. The 1982 is very promising, however.

On Ronald Barton (Leoville-Barton and Langoa-Barton)

Harry likes the man very much, but not his wines, which are too lean. I agree, yet I love the Leoville-Barton 1945, 1959, and even the 1970. When Ronald's nephew, Anthony Barton, takes over, maybe things will change for the better.

On the sale of La Mission et al. to Haut-Brion

Harry Waugh is worried that the style of La Mission will change and not for the better. I definitely agree. The competition is over. Jean Delmas may say that "nothing will change." Things always change when a new team (especially the competition) takes over. I will try to acquire as much La Mission as I can find (pre-1983), especially 1982, 1978, 1975, and 1966.

On Michael Broadbent

We discussed the painful International Wine and Food Society Convention in Vancouver, in October 1983, and the 1970 Bordeaux-tasting fiasco.

On the 1983 vintage in Bordeaux

A very good and promising vintage, producing Clarets; fairly similar to 1981, but bigger, better structured, especially in Margaux and the southern Médoc.

As usual, we had a great time with Harry. He is still a member of Boodles Club and is the wine buyer for the Ritz hotel and other clubs.

Friday, April 21, 1984

At Michel Guerard's "Capmartin" restaurant, in Eugenie-Les-Bains, where we spent two nights.

CHABLIS GRAND CRU "GRENOUILLES" 1979, CHÂTEAU DE GRENOUILLES:

Complex, round nose. Long, very full and flavourful for a Chablis. Round rather than lean; the structure of a Meursault, yet the nose and flavour of a very good Chablis.

MADIRAN 1981:

Even in a three-star restaurant, this wine cost only 65 francs ($10). Young, purplish, deep colour. On nose, similar to a rich California Merlot, but on palate, leaner and more tannic. Rich, full, very good value.

We had the "Menu Gastronomique," a selection of the finest and most typical of Michel Guerard's dishes. Food, service, and decor were excellent.

Saturday, April 22, 1984

Second Dinner at Michel Guerard's.

Now, this was a let-down from the previous night! Service was very slow and disorganized. My main course (tenderloin) wasn't tender. My foie gras (warm) was in tiny bits; a very small portion and very salty. (Later, as I complained about it, they reduced my bill by an appropriate amount.)

Overall, a disappointing evening. We were made to wait for 45 minutes before being seated (yet we had a reservation). No one explained anything or apologized. I also had to ask for water three times before I got any. How can a fine three-star restaurant be so great one night and so disappointing the next? How can a fine three-star restaurant be so inconsistent?

1976 GEVREY-CHAMBERTIN PREMIER CRU, ARMAND ROUSSEAU:

1976 was a drought year; consequently, I expected a big, solid wine. Also, Rousseau makes big, traditional Gevreys. Well, this was neither. Medium-light colour. Elegant, well balanced. Spicy, fruity nose of Pinot Noir, but not what it should be. Lacks depth and structure.

We stayed in Eugenie-Les-Bains two nights. We had a lovely room ("Potirons"—each room has a name rather than a number), lovely balcony, great weather. Breakfast was simple, disappointing, and a rip-off.

April 24, 1984

Lunch at Château Latour.

Thanks to Harry Waugh, who organized it for us. We met the winemaker, Jean-Louis Mandreau (whom I met back in 1980). The Canadian flag was raised for us. We went straight to the elegant small château for lunch.

Before lunch, I tasted a sample of this.

1983 LATOUR:

Tight, cedary; purple colour. A bit diluted for Latour. Does not have the great extract of the 1982.

APERITIF

CHAMPAGNE POL ROGER PR "PRIVATE RESERVE" 1975:

A lovely, complex, rich Champagne in the style of Bollinger, rather than the elegance of Pol Roger. Yeasty, complex, big; very good.

WITH THE FIRST COURSE

1976 LES-FORTS-DE-LATOUR:

Light, elegant, spicy Cabernet nose. A "little" Latour. Forward and very drinkable now.

WITH THE MAIN COURSE

1962 CHÂTEAU LATOUR:

Dark, mature Claret. Complex, beautiful nose. Long, round, at its peak; elegant, yet fruity. Some acidity, but overall very good. A fine, mature Claret.

WITH THE CHEESE

1949 CHÂTEAU LATOUR:

A magnificent, classic Latour at its peak. Jean-Louis Mandreau said that this wine was more successful than their 1947. (I agree.) Full, mature colour. Great, mature, complex, classic, cedary Cabernet nose. Magnificent. Well balanced, soft, very good structure; at its absolute peak.

WITH DESSERT

1976 CHÂTEAU CLIMENS, BARSAC:

A wine that I have in my cellar. Not very big, yet buttery, long, lovely nose; rich on palate. Complex, elegant. A lovely Barsac. Full of life. Will age beautifully.

WITH COFFEE

1961 FINS BOIS COGNAC (BOTTLED 1979):

From a local grower in Cognac. Very dark, dry, complex. A real traditional Cognac. Quite an experience.

We spent three-and-a-half hours at Latour for lunch, and were late for our visit to Pichon-Lalande.

Jean-Louis told me that his father is a grower at Entre-Deux-Mers. Jean-Louis has been to California once. He knows Tim Mondavi well, as well as Warren Winiarski, the owner of Stag's Leap. Jean-Louis said that stocks of vintages older than 1961 are very low at Latour; the previous owners sold most of them. He doesn't believe in Petit Verdot: too inconsistent. Doesn't like Cabernet Franc; replants with Cabernet Sauvignon where possible.

They produce 18,000 to 22,000 cases of the Grand Vin annually, on average. He said that Cheval-Blanc's problem was too much Cabernet Franc. He likes the 1970 and 1975 Latour. Said that 1978 will need another ten years, but will last well, especially in magnums.

1981 will be classic, like the 1978s or better. (Frankly, I find this hard to believe, especially for Latour.) 1982s are absolutely magnificent, probably better than 1975 and 1970, yet not quite in the class of the 1961s. 1983: too early to tell but may be like the 1979.

It is quite hot in Bordeaux for late April, (80° F!) and they were spraying in the vineyards.

Other comments

In Jean-Louis's opinion, the best St. Julien properties (soil-wise) are Leoville-Lascases, Leoville-Barton, and Gruaud-Larose. Château Cantemerle still belongs to Cordier. Branaire belongs to Tari of Château Giscours. He also said that Pichon-Lalande makes lovely wines, but that it is not a long distance runner.

He advised Pascal Delbeck (winemaker at Ausone) that Cheval-Blanc has too much Cabernet Franc in the blend, and that he (Pascal) should resist the temptation to increase the Cabernet Franc content at Ausone. Frankly, I like Cheval-Blanc, even if it has too much Cabernet Franc.

That afternoon

Visit to Château Pichon-Lalande.

Next door to Latour. I have visited this property twice before. This time I met the young winemaker, Mr. Lopez. We tasted the 1982 and the 1983 (both still in cask). They aim at, and produce, feminine wines. Blend of 45% Cabernet Sauvignon, 35% Merlot (high proportion), 12% Cabernet Franc, and 8% Petit Verdot.

1983, FROM CASK:

A more classical Pauillac. A bit tight, yet very good depth and fruit. A wine to buy. Great, solid fruit extract. Excellent potential. From cask, this is more impressive than the 1983 Latour tasted earlier today.

1982, FROM CASK:

Fabulous. Lots of depth, very concentrated. Round, long, and lovely. I am glad to have purchased a case (futures) of this superb wine. I paid US$160 per case. By now, it has increased to US$260 (in less than a year).

That evening

Dinner at Château d'Angludet, with Peter and Diana Sichel.

They are also part-owners of Château Palmer. D'Angludet is a lovely estate: horses, ponies, swans, etc. A rustic, lived-in château. We ate in the kitchen—a beautiful, large kitchen.

APERITIF

CHAMPAGNE ALFRED GRATIEN 1976 BRUT:

A lively, round Champagne. Very well made; long and elegant. I have never tasted it before.

1979 CHABLIS GRAND CRU "BLANCHOTS," RAVENEAU:

(With a grilled local fish called Shad) Green-gold. Intense, long, yet flinty. A very good Chablis that ages very well. Well balanced, classy. Raveneau is an excellent producer.

1971 CHÂTEAU D'ANGLUDET:

A bit herbaceous, round, forward, a bit lean. Very pleasant. Good colour and nose. Slightly high acidity.

Peter purchased d'Angludet in 1961 and moved there in 1962. They have five sons (ages 17 to 21) and a six-year-old daughter, Rebecca, for whom I brought a pair of Indian moccasins (also a pair for Diana). They can use them on cold winter nights.

Then Peter opened a bottle of wine for me that I have read and heard a lot about, but never tasted it (other than a rather disappointing London-bottling by Berry Brothers). During his dinner at our home in Vancouver last month, I opened a 1961 Château Margaux for Peter and hinted that I had never tasted the 1961 Palmer. Well, that is what he served next.

1961 CHÂTEAU PALMER:

Essence of Cabernet! Very dark colour to rim. Intense, complex, delicate, elegant, unmistakable Palmer nose. Full, rich, long, perfectly balanced on palate, very long aftertaste. This wine is a classic and can compete against most First Growths in 1961 in quality. (Peter likes the 1961 Gruaud-Larose and so do I. I still have some 1961 Gruaud in my cellar.) This 1961 Palmer was beyond description. At its peak, but so concentrated that it will hold for another ten to 20 years without any problem. A great experience and a lovely evening. Perfect score. (20)

Peter and Diana are a very nice, down-to-earth couple. Carol felt very comfortable with them—always a good sign.

Next day

Visit to Château Lafite.

With Guy Schÿler. Interesting visit and movie; no tasting, though! Guy is a good friend of Harry Waugh's. His firm, Alfred Schÿler & Co., is not connected to the Schroeder & Schÿler firm (Kirwan), but they are related (cousins). Guy is about 70, and has been Public Relations Manager at Lafite since 1961.

He told me about how the "Reserve" wines were salvaged from the Germans in WW II, and spared. Somehow, a visit to a famous vineyard—even if it is interesting and informative—remains hollow if the main purpose of the visit, tasting the wine, turns out not to be part of the visit. This is the second time that I have had this experience at Lafite. Maybe the Rothschilds of Lafite have lost a lot of money recently, and they cannot afford to allow visitors to taste.

Visit to Mouton-Rothschild.

We met the young Assistant Manager, Dominique Alba, a nice young man from Dijon. He assists Xavier d'Ezaguire in exports. We had a light lunch with him in Pauillac before our visit to Château de Pez. At Mouton, we met the 72-year-old winemaker Raoul Blondin, who has been at Mouton for 58 years. He will probably retire when old Baron Philippe does (he is 83). We tasted the 1982 and 1983 from cask.

1983 MOUTON-ROTHSCHILD, FROM CASK:

Will be very good; a bit lean, like a 1966, but with better fruit concentration. Blondin agreed with me about that.

He said that in 1982, there were seven rainless months, so the roots had to go deep to get their nutrition. They got the best out of the soil in 1982. At a depth of 70 feet, the water is yellow and rich with minerals. Baron Philippe tried to build a pool near the château, but the water was yellow from all the minerals in it.

Blondin also said that Margaux made better wine in 1981 and 1983 than in 1982. Apparently, in 1982 at Margaux, they made too much wine and had storage problems.

1982 MOUTON-ROTHSCHILD, FROM CASK:

Magnificent. Deep, rich, round, concentrated, long. Blondin said that it is a combination of the fruit and concentration of the great 1929 and the body and tannins of the 1945! The greatest wine he has ever made or tasted at Mouton. A lovely wine needing 20 years to mature. I am glad to have acquired several cases of this wine (as futures) last year. A case purchased in Napa cost me US$395 and the two cases acquired in Seattle cost me US$365 each.

He said that J. P. Gardère of Latour has admitted that Mouton is greater than Latour in 1982! He also said that the 1978 Mouton is very good (1975, too). I disagree with him about the 1978 Mouton. It is a thin, vegetal, disappointing wine, in the context of a Premier Grand Cru.

A very interesting visit and very educational.

Later that afternoon

Visit to Château de Pez.

The winemaker has been there since 1954 and hopes that his sons will take over after him. He said that the 1970 de Pez is variable but likes the 1971. (I disagree about the 1970. It is a fine wine.) He thinks the 1975s are very good. The reason the 1978s have more Merlot than usual (usually 70% Cabernet Sauvignon, 20% Merlot, 10% Cabernet Franc) was that after the frost of 1977, it took the Cabernets two years to reach their previous standard of productivity. This is odd, because in other Médoc properties, 1978 lacked Merlot.

We tasted the 1983 (six months old) and the 1982, just after the collage (egg whites, six per barrel, no filtering). He said that filtering takes away the glycerine, richness, etc. from the wine.

1983, FROM CASK:

Leaner and simpler, but not bad at all. Well balanced, but forward.

1982, FROM CASK:

Darker, bigger, more concentrated and intense, yet not a giant. Needs four to six years.

Two-thirds of the production sold through Gilbey's at Château Loudenne; one-third is sold by the château directly to the public.

Dinner in a Nice restaurant, in Bordeaux.

1982 CHÂTEAU DE BELLEGARDE, GRAVES BLANC, IN HALF-BOTTLE:

Good Sauvignon Blanc. Full, rich, long, typical 1982.

1981 CUVÉE NAPOLÉON "CÔTES DE BUZET," CAVE CO-OP, IN HALF-BOTTLE:

Rich, round, smooth; easy to drink. Pleasant.

Thursday, April 26, 1984

Morning visit to Châteaux Ausone and Belair.

With Pascal Delbeck, the young winemaker. He lives at Belair and he suggested that next time, I have lunch with the owner, Mme. Dubois Chalon. Blend of 50% Cabernet Franc and 50% Merlot usually. Average age of vines at Ausone is 45 years. We tasted various Demptos barrels of Ausone 1982 and 1983.

1982, FROM CASK:

Light toast, stemmy; bigger, fuller; has more tannin, which is, however, hidden behind the fruit. Lovely.

1983, FROM CASK:

Will be very good. Rich, yet a bit lean, long, complex. More typical Ausone than the 1982. I think that in the long run, the 1983 will surpass the 1982 at Ausone.

Production: 2,000 to 2,400 cases. We saw the old 12-year-old white horse working the fields. In 1983, they had problems starting the fermentation because of a lot of heat and no rain; the natural yeast was killed. Their wines are cut "Guyot simple" (one branch only). I gave Pascal a bottle of 1980 Rutherford Hill Napa Merlot.

From there, we went to Château Belair, across from Ausone.

We blended the 1983 Merlot and Boucher. The Boucher was very rich. (Boucher is the name of Cabernet Franc in St. Emilion.) Both 1982 and 1983 are very promising. At Belair, they add 5% Cabernet Sauvignon, too. They also make a second wine from young vines. The 1982 is beautiful. A wine to buy. Production is double that of Ausone (4,000 to 5,000 cases). At Belair, they use one-third new barrels yearly, all from Demptos, but with steel rims (rather than the more expensive wood, as at Ausone). As usual, a lovely and informative visit.

Visit to Château Petit-Village, in Pomerol.

The property of Bruno Prats of Cos d'Estournel; he has two brothers as partners. Their mother is a Ginestet, the former owners of Château Margaux. Production of 5,000 cases; about 80% Merlot, 10% Cabernet Sauvignon, and 10% Cabernet Franc. They filter early and use 50% to 100% new oak barrels.

1983, FROM CASK:

Good, but a bit light. (I don't like the idea of filtering.)

1982, FROM CASK:

Very good; a full, rich, long, ripe Merlot. A wine to buy.

Visit and lunch at Château Figeac.

Carol and I were received by Thierry Manoncourt, his wife Marie-France, and her sister Mathilde. Mr. and Mrs. Roger Lemelletier of the Grand Conseil de Bordeaux joined us there. As I am a member of the Council of our Commanderie in Vancouver, we discussed several matters that concern our branch. Both the Manoncourts and the Lemelletiers will be in Vancouver in early June as part of a delegation of the Commanderie visit across Canada.

1982 AND 1983 FIGEAC, FROM CASK:

Both dark, intense wine.

The 1983 is more traditional, herbaceous, spicy, with good fruit concentration, even at this early stage.

The 1982 is much more concentrated, yet not really massive. Deep, dark colour. Great fruit extract. Ripe. Will be excellent.

With lunch, we tasted the following wines.

1980 FIGEAC:

Soft and forward, but round and elegant. I thought it was the 1976, as this wine was served blind.

1975 FIGEAC:

Lovely, dark, big. Not quite ready yet, but a marvellous, long bouquet and flavour. In four to five years, it will be a classic. Has that all-important fruit that many 1975s lack.

1971 FIGEAC:

Much softer and more forward. Elegant. Needs drinking. Browning and very soft. Pleasant.

1964 FIGEAC:

Magnificent! A favourite of mine for many years. Like a 1961. Deep, dark, concentrated; mature, long, full, and round on palate. At its peak. A lovely bottle; spicy, complex, and a classic, by any yardstick.

Visit to Château Canon.

A château I have never visited before. We were met by the owner, Mr. Eric Fournier, a man around our age. His wife is a cousin of Philippe Casteja of Borie-Manoux (Batailley, etc.). Eric has been managing the Château since 1975 (his father died in 1974). They also own Château Broustet in Barsac (since the 1880s). Château Canon is very close to Ausone. They use a blend of 55% Merlot, 40% Cabernet Franc, and 5% Cabernet Sauvignon and Malbec. They have about 18 hectares and produce on average 8,000 cases annually. 50% new oak barrels annually. Traditional chais with Cognac-region oak cuves. No filtering; egg-white fining.

We tasted these wines.

1983, FROM CASK:

Good fruit, pleasant; a bit on the lean side, but already showing some class.

1982, from cask:

Bigger, more concentrated, with more fruit, but not massive.

Wines of very good quality, elegant rather than big. In earlier days, Canon made fairly big, hefty wines. But since Eric took over, the wines have become more complex, more delicate, and classier. A fine property and a most pleasant host.

Friday, April 27

Last day in Bordeaux and visit, with Christian Moueix, in Libourne.

We met Christian and his public relations manager, Monsieur Montouroy (he lives near Château La Grave). We started at 11:00 a.m. by visiting the chais of La Grave, then a tour by car of the various properties owned and managed by the Moueixes, including Trotanoy, Petrus, and La Fleur-Petrus.

We also visited Château Magdelaine, their St. Emilion property.

Nobody lives there. The plateau (above) is planted with Merlot (approximately 60%). The bottom level is Cabernet Franc and Cabernet Sauvignon. Average age of vines is 35 to 40 years. They also have a horse to work the vines (same as at Ausone).

From there, we drove back to the offices.

Moueix act as advisors to Château Certan-de-May, but they do not actually make the wine. One of the two old sisters (Mesdemoiselles Robin) who owned Lafleur and Le Gay had died three weeks previously. Christian produces the wine there and markets it on their behalf.

We went back to the offices in Libourne for a small tasting of the 1983s, from cask. These wines are, of course, still in their infancy and will develop more depth with an extra year of oak-ageing.

1983 Château Leydet-Figeac, St. Emilion:

Lean, tannic, medium-bodied. Dark-purple colour. Good fruit; simple but pleasant. A bit vegetal on nose.

1983 Château Plince, Pomerol:

Not impressive. Leaner than above. Lighter, tannic, not enough fruit.

Château Bourgneuf, Pomerol:

Very dark. Hearty, meaty, big, and rich. Good fruit. Not bad. One to watch.

Château La Grave Trigant-de-Boisset:

From Christian Moueix's own property in Pomerol. Wine not as big as above; more complex and stylish. Elegant and good.

Château Trotanoy:

Darkest colour; deep and purplish. Rich, intense; well balanced. Not as ripe as the 1982, but very good, yet somehow seemed a bit diluted at the end. As it develops in cask, maybe it will increase in concentration.

Then we tasted some 1982s, also from cask.

Château Fonroque:

This property was purchased in 1930 by Christian's grandfather. This was the family's first property. Big, concentrated, slightly herbaceous (Cabernet Franc). Long, quite good.

Château La Grave Trigant-de-Boisset:

Big, fruity, concentrated; promising 1982.

After the tasting, we drove to Christian's house for lunch.

Mr. Montouroy and an Austrian wine merchant from Innsbrük by the name of Bruno Gottardi joined us. There we met Christian's wife Marie-Laure and his two kids, ages five and eight. (We brought along some moccasins for the kids.) Lovely house, pool, yard, and garden in the suburb of Libourne, on the bank of the Gironde.

Christian has purchased recently a property of 125 acres called Napanook, across from Yountville in the Napa Valley, from the two daughters of the previous owners of Inglenook. Actually, he purchased a 50% share in the property. The sisters own the other 50%. Planted mostly in Cabernet Sauvignon. He hopes to open a winery there in 1986 and call it "Dominus." Christian is a friend of Bernard Portet of Clos du Val. I told him that we will now be neighbours, as I have purchased a summer residence in the Napa Valley (in Yountville).

At lunch (in the garden)

Champagne Dom Pérignon 1976 Rosé:

Elegant, round, fairly rich, but not very intense. Very pleasant but not great.

1975 Château Trotanoy:

(Two bottles) Lovely, dark colour, showing some age. Rich, sweet nose. Long, full, rich, big on palate. Not very tannic, yet very long, intense, and complex. Magnificent bottle. Drink now (a bit young) to 1995, or beyond. Christian thinks that this wine is better than their 1975 Petrus. I have tasted the 1975 Petrus recently. It is very tight and unyielding; unusually hard for Petrus and for a wine made almost exclusively from Merlot grapes—even for a hard year like 1975.

1952 Château Petrus:

A real classic. Christian said that in Pomerol, the 1952s were more successful than the 1953s. This wine is dark, maturing, with a lovely, magnificent, complex nose. Rich, full, mature on palate. A once-in-a-lifetime experience. Classic, but much more forward than the 1961 Petrus, which I have had the good fortune of tasting on three occasions to date.

Then, although it was hot, he served us an unusual vintage Port (given to him by Mr. Bronfman of Seagram's), as a prelude to our upcoming trip to Oporto.

1957 SANDEMAN'S VINTAGE PORT:

A rarely seen vintage. Light, yet good fruit. Lovely, complex on both nose and palate. This wine showed much better than other Sandeman's vintages, such as 1960 or 1966. Like a very good 1960. Very pleasant surprise.

We spent four-and-a-half hours with Christian, and then drove to Merignac to catch a flight to Madrid. A lovely afternoon.

April 28, 1984

A day in Vigo, then drove on to Oporto.

April 30, 1984

Lunch at Taylor's Lodge, in Villa Nova de Gaja, with Bruce Guimaraens and associates.

Had a white Port, a local Dão, and a Tawny. We finished lunch with a fine bottle.

1966 TAYLOR'S VINTAGE PORT:

Good but evolved appearance. Medium, lightish colour. Lovely, complex, spicy nose. Not a big or very fruity Port, fairly alcoholic. Good backbone.

Later that day

Visit to Croft's Lodge.

Croft's also own Morgan and Delaforce. Croft's best quinta is called "Da Roeda." We met Dr. John Burnett (about my age), the quality control manager. His boss is Robin Reid, whom we haven't met yet. We visited the various cellars, including their private cellar. Their pipes (barrels) are about two-and-a-half times the size of Bordeaux or Burgundy barrels, and some are kept for as many as 50 to 60 years.

Large ageing vats are made of mahogany. They store true vintage Port in large containers (140 pipes). Their recently declared 1980 vintage is compared to the 1966 or 1975 vintages, which I find odd because 1966 was much finer than 1975. Here, 1977 is considered the finest vintage since 1963. Vintage Port is made up of 100% red grapes (four to five kinds, although many more varietals are allowed). We tasted the 1982, 1980, 1979, 1978, 1977, and 1970 vintages, which will go into the Tawny blend.

Among other spirits, they also make Bailey's Irish Cream. They are owned by a large British conglomerate. Croft's have declared their 1982 Quinta do Roeda (single quinta). John gave us a bottle of very good 20-year-old Croft's Tawny. A very interesting first experience with the Oporto Lodges.

Tuesday, May 1, 1984

A Holiday in Portugal.

We drove up the Douro with Bruce Guimaraens. Bruce is a very big, very nice, gentle man, who drives up the Douro like a nut. Apparently, car rental companies refuse to lease him any cars, so he had to buy a Volvo. It is still a practically new car, but it already looks like, and feels like, the armoured half-tracks we used to drive in the Israeli army!

We drove to their guest house and storage facility in Pinhào, in the heart of the Douro Country.

Part of the Quinta do Sibio has gone into Taylor's Port, until 1975. In the afternoon (after lunch at Taylor's and a rest), we visited their newly acquired quinta "Terra Feita" and visited the house of the keeper, and tasted some of the new 1983 vintage. "Terra Feita" will shortly become larger than their Quinta do Vargellas, in terms of planted acreage.

We saw new grafted vines, 85 cm-wide tractors (used to work the narrow rows of vines), and the lovely country around the Douro. Martinez is part of the Cockburn group. Bruce likes Martinez and it is good value, too. He likes the idea of picking grapes at night (cooler grapes, Pol Roger Champagne system). He is a friend of Andrew Quady.

The pruning of the vines in the Douro is "Guyot double," with three buds on each shoot, rather than "Guyot simple" (one shoot with six to eight buds). They call their large storage vats "Ginas," after Gina Lollobrigida; the Ginas are shaped like her gorgeous breasts, the nipples facing skyward.

That evening, Carol, Bruce, and I had a quiet dinner at the Taylor's guest house in the Douro. At the end of the meal, Bruce offered us Port.

1948 FONSECA'S VINTAGE PORT:

Fabulous! At 36 years of age, this is sheer perfection. Great complexity and fruit extract. Very long, superb Port.

Wednesday, May 2, 1984

After Breakfast, we took the train back to Oporto.

A very interesting two-and-a-half-hour journey back to Oporto. Bruce stayed in the Douro as he had a lot of work to do there.

Wednesday, May 2

Second visit to Taylor's.

Had a tasting of a few young vintages as well as the following.

1967 TAYLOR'S "QUINTA DO VARGELLAS":

Medium colour; round, complex, fairly forward and soft. Good.

1970 TAYLOR'S VINTAGE PORT:

Deep colour; rich, round, long, spicy nose. Intense, fairly young on palate. Needs five more years. Quite concentrated. Very good potential.

1948 FONSECA'S VINTAGE PORT:

Fabulous bottle. Tasted twice in three days! Almost the intensity and youth of a 1963. Browning rim. Rich, round. Very good depth. Long on palate, fruity, youthful. Very good. No rush drinking this wine. (Of course, if tasted in North America, this wine would be more forward because of travel and storage.)

1934 FONSECA'S VINTAGE PORT:

Ageing colour, medium brown. Opened the previous evening. Unpleasant, raisiny bouquet; same on palate. Well structured, but something wrong. Reserve judgement.

From there, we went for lunch to the "Factory House."

On the Oporto side of town (men only; lunches every Wednesday). We were 32 in all. Pleasant lunch; stuffy English people. Warren Wilson of Vancouver, a friend and fellow Commandeur de Bordeaux, was there, too. At the end of the meal, a Port was served blind, chosen by the chairman (Treasurer) for 1984, Mr. Richard Delaforce. (His firm is now associated with Croft's.)

1963 DELAFORCE:

Dark, intense, youthful, yet shows age. Very fruity and very sweet. Has class. To my right and left, people thought it was a 1960 or 1966, probably Graham's. I thought that it had to be a 1963 because of its structure and colour. I thought Graham's, too. It turned out to be a 1963 (good guess!), but a Delaforce—a Port house whose wines I have never tasted before. A lovely Port.

In the afternoon

Visit with James and Amos Symington at Warre's, Graham's, and Dow's.

Quite an interesting visit. Overall, an exciting and very interesting three days in Oporto and the Douro, thanks mostly to Bruce Guimaraens, our generous host.

On the last night there, I had—as it turned out later—an attack of pleurisy (water around my left lung). I thought that it was all over for me! I was taken to a rather dirty-looking hospital in Oporto. They gave me some oxygen and a muscle relaxant medication, as I had difficulty breathing. Not a very pleasant evening for Carol or myself.

Mid-May 1984

Council meeting of Le Tastevin Wine Club, at home.

1. 1981 MERCUREY BLANC, CHÂTEAU DE CHAMIREY, JOUENNE D'HERVILLE:

Appley, delicate; hard to guess it as a Chardonnay. Rather disappointing. (13.5)

2. POUILLY-FUISSÉ "TASTEVINAGE" 1981, DUFOULEUR:

Flat, woody; too much sulphur on nose. Not very good; practically dead. (12)

Both of the above are new listings at the BC liquor monopoly stores. Both sell for $16.50. This is what happens when ignorant bureaucrats are entrusted with the task of purchasing wines for the public.

May 1984

International Wine and Food Society Black Tie Dinner, at the "William Tell" restaurant.

It was a BYOW event. Each couple brought along two bottles. We sat with the Crosses.

1969 HENRIOT BRUT CHAMPAGNE, ROTHSCHILD:

(My bottle) Cork hard to get off, had to use a corkscrew. Bottle disintegrated halfway, but we managed to salvage the bottom-half of the bottle. Elegant, complex, tiny bubbles. Mature, classy, elegant Champagne. There must have been a hair-thin crack in the glass.

1978 BIENVENUES BÂTARD-MONTRACHET, LEFLAIVE AND 1978 BÂTARD-MONTRACHET, LEFLAIVE:

Both magnificent bottles, probably the stars of the evening. Both had a lovely, toasty, oaky, complex nose.

The Bienvenues was more forward, more open, round, long, well balanced; a classic!

The Bâtard was more intense, a little more closed, and had better acidity, needing two to three more years. Both great classic white Burgundies. Rated both (19).

1964 CHÂTEAU PETRUS,

1964 CHÂTEAU TROTANOY,

AND

1964 VIEUX CHÂTEAU CERTAN:

(The Petrus was jointly owned by Ken Cross and myself, and the Trotanoy and Certan were Sid Cross's bottles.) All three are now 20 years old.

The Vieux Château Certan had a medium colour (lightest). Open, complex, delicate on nose and palate. At its peak, well balanced, and very enjoyable. Made from 25% Cabernet Sauvignon, 25% Cabernet Franc, and 50% Merlot. (17)

The Trotanoy was much darker. A wine I know well. Loveliest nose of all three Pomerols. Ripe Merlot (95%, same as at Petrus). Complex nose; long, beautiful, mature bouquet. Ripe, big, and hard finish. Powerful wine, dry finish. Overall, a lovely bottle. (18)

The Petrus is selling (in 1984) for US$175, or Can$220—a small fortune and not worth it. Dark colour; closed nose. Opened up after an hour, but not as complex or as rich as the Trotanoy. A bit lean and simple. A bit short. Good bottle and an experience, but not the magnificent classic one would expect, based on its reputation or price! (17.5)

1978 CHÂTEAU ST. JEAN "BELLE TERRE," JOHANNISBERG RIESLING "SELECT LATE HARVEST," SONOMA, IN HALF-BOTTLE:

28.4% residual sugar. Low alcohol (8%). Liquid honey; very sweet, cloying, apricot-peaches on nose and palate. No rush!

I also tried other tables' wines, including the following.

1961 CHÂTEAU GRAND-PUY-LACOSTE:

Better than the three 1964 Pomerols at our table. Complex, long, beautiful Haut-Médoc. Long on palate; elegant, yet with excellent backbone. Fabulous wine. Classic ripeness and intensity of this great vintage. (18.5)

1961 CHÂTEAU LYNCH-BAGES, LONDON-BOTTLED BY ARMY AND NAVY:

Australian style; old, mature Shiraz nose and flavour. New cork, no sediment. Recorked? Very poor and no Claret character! Château-bottled versions of this wine can be excellent. (14)

1970 CHÂTEAU RIEUSSEC, SAUTERNES:

Elegant, soft; not too sweet or too dark. Ready. Not very complex. (16)

1971 CHÂTEAU SUDUIRAUT, SAUTERNES:

Even lighter than the above, but more elegant. Good botrytis. Stylish. (16.5)

1967 CHÂTEAU SUDUIRAUT, SAUTERNES:

Fabulous bottle! True classic style, yet not as fat or rich as 1967 d'Yquem. More elegant. Long, perfectly balanced. Great fruit and botrytis extract. Very long. Honeyed overtones. Very fine wine. (18)

1971 VINO LIQUOROSO "VECCHIO SOLIENTO BIANCO," CROCE D'ORO (GOLDEN CROSS), RUFFINO, ITALY:

16% alcohol. Dark colour. Madeira-Tokay-like on both nose and palate; sweet, high alcohol. A new experience. Not bad, but nothing special.

June 5, 1984

Commanderie de Bordeaux Events.

In honour of the visit to Vancouver of 25 members and spouses of the Grand Conseil de Bordeaux.

FIRST EVENT

Lunch and reception at the Four Seasons hotel.

1976 CHÂTEAU LATOUR:

Medium colour, quite forward for Latour. Spicy, cedary nose. Medium body. Typical, yet very good 1976; fairly forward. Good drinking now through 1990.

CHÂTEAU LYNCH-BAGES 1979:

The cedar and mint nose typical of Lynch-Bages, yet a bit too lean for a 1979 and too high in acidity. I feel that this estate hasn't produced wines in 1978 and 1979 vintages at the level of which they are capable. Is it because the son of André Cazes, Jean-Michel, had at that time just taken over the management of this fine estate? Maybe they are going through a "fine-tuning" period. The 1982 and 1983 tasted from cask are very promising, though.

1979 CHÂTEAU GRUAUD-LAROSE:

The best Claret of the evening. Lovely, deep colour. Intense, long fruity nose. Relatively big for a 1979. Good fruit extract; classic, fruity St. Julien. Very good future. Needs five years.

1955 CHÂTEAU GILETTE "CRÈME DE TÊTE," SAUTERNES:

Surprisingly fruity and youthful, yet the depth of colour of an older Sauternes. Not too fat, tired, or cloying. The owners, Mr. and Mrs. Medeville, told me that this 1955 will be dedicated to a good friend who died recently, Jean Troisgros (the famous chef), a great supporter of Sauternes.

Comments

Had a long chat with Marie-France and Thierry Manoncourt, friends and owners of Château Figeac. Also, Mr. Roger Lemelletier of the Grand Counseil de Bordeaux, whom I know well. Also, Mr. André Cazes, owner of Château Lynch-Bages and Mayor of Pauillac. I met him, and had lunch with him (and his daughter Sylvie) in Pauillac in October 1980. Nice old gentleman. Also: Mr. Pauli, general manager of the Cordier estates (Gruaud-Larose, Talbot, etc.). They have recently sold most of their estates except the two above.

Andrée and Christian Medeville, owners of Château Gilette in Sauternes, age their wines in concrete vats for 20 years or more, and yet their wines retain their youth. I have, however, sometimes noticed an aftertaste of wet cement in their wines.

An interesting chat with Mr. Jean Paul Gardère, until his retirement a few months ago, the régisseur of Château Latour and a close friend of Harry Waugh. He has known Harry for 32 years and thinks that Harry is both an excellent taster and "a man who doesn't know how to hurt other people or make enemies." How true. In spite of Harry's accident in Beaune a year ago, in which he lost his sense of smell, he has so much experience that his palate alone can help him judge the quality and structure of wines.

SECOND EVENT

Dinner at the Four Seasons hotel.

I sat with Mr. Pauli and Mr. and Mrs. Medeville. We started with two white Graves. I purchased both for our Commanderie in San Francisco.

CHÂTEAU DE L'HÔPITAL 1982

AND

CHÂTEAU MALARTIC-LAGRAVIÈRE 1981:

L'Hôpital was a bit too young; needs two to three more years. Good nose, very well balanced. A cousin of Christian Medeville runs it for the owner. Well structured, good fruit. Fine wine.

The Malartic was a bit more open, yet a hard and fairly steely wine, needing two to four more years. Made exclusively from Sauvignon Blanc.

CHÂTEAU CARBONNIEUX BLANC, 1981:

More elegant and maybe better balanced than the Malartic.

CHÂTEAU TALBOT 1976

AND

CHÂTEAU CANON-LA GAFFELIÈRE 1975:

The Talbot was more elegant, more complex, rounder, softer: a better dinner wine. Ready.

The Canon-La Gaffelière was darker, harder, simpler; closed, needing three to four more years. A typical 1975.

1970 MÉDOC A/C CUVÉE DE LA COMMANDERIE DU BONTEMPS:

Typical, if not a great 1970. Good, dark colour; complex nose. Long; still a bit hard and closed. Needs two to four more years. Not great, but good.

CHÂTEAU CLIMENS 1976:

Medium-light colour. Atypical for a 1976 (most are soft, fat, rich, dark golden wines). Perfect balance. Elegant, long, lovely nose. Good fruit, very good botrytis. A lovely bottle that has excellent potential.

I translated Dr. Allan Tobe's speech, welcoming the delegation. Allan is the founding Maître of our Commanderie. Overall, a successful and interesting evening.

June 1984

Trip to Yountville and San Francisco.

(Including an IW&FS dinner on the occasion of Harry Waugh's 80th birthday.)

MEURSAULT-PORUZOTS 1981, FRANÇOIS JOBARD, IN HALF-BOTTLE:

(Tasted at Singer & Foy) Round, open, nutty, complex Meursault nose. Fairly lean and alcoholic on palate, but good fruit and complexity. These 1981s are not as rich or fat as the 1982s. Needs one to two more years. Good.

Saturday, June 9, 1984

International Wine and Food Society (Marin County) Tasting and Dinner, in honour of Harry Waugh's 80th birthday, at the Stanford Court hotel, in San Francisco.

THE MAIN TASTING

There are 16 vintages of Château Latour (in magnums) from 1970 back to 1929!

I met Dr. Haskell Norman, the chairman of the branch, and we had a nice chat. The food was very good and suited the wines. It was nice to see Harry and Prue Waugh again. I also met Warren Winiarski, owner of Stag's Leap Vineyards, and Ed Lazarus, wine taster and writer for The Underground Wineletter.

Other tasters included Dr. Brad Klein; Dr. Bipin Desai, a nuclear physicist and famous wine collector and taster; and Mr. Toufiq Khouri, who has one of the most impressive wine collections in the world. I was also introduced to Dr. and Mrs. Rhodes, long-time friends of Harry Waugh. Barney Rhodes is the owner of Bella Oaks vineyard, from which Joe Heitz produces one of his two famous Cabernets.

THE WINES

CHAMPAGNE DEUTZ BRUT N/V, IN MAGNUMS:

Good complexity and fruit; youthful, fresh, good aftertaste.

CHAMPAGNE DOM PÉRIGNON 1971:

Delicate nose; complex and long. On palate: getting tired, a bit soft and flabby. Pleasant. Needs drinking.

With two seafood courses, we had two mature Chardonnays.

MOUNT EDEN VINEYARD CHARDONNAY 1974, NAPA VALLEY:

Deep-gold colour; mature nose. Some fruit left, but starting to madeirize. Getting tired. (15)

1969 CHEVALIER-MONTRACHET, GEORGES DELEGER:

Finer wine than the 1974 Mount Eden; better balanced, still lively. Lovely, long, mature, toasty nose. Good, long, complex wine on palate. At the end of its peak. Will not improve. A fine bottle. (17.5)

The main event of the evening, other than giving Harry Waugh a special award, was a tasting of 16 vintages of Château Latour (Harry is a director at Latour), from 1970 back to 1929.

FLIGHT #1

1970, 1967, 1966, 1964, and 1962

Overall, I found this flight to be the most consistent, with all wines showing both the style of Latour and the overall quality of the vintages tasted.

1970:

Dark, big, fairly hard and closed wine, with that lovely harmony and intensity of fruit and colour of the 1970s. Needs another ten to 15 years. Massive; great fruit extract. Lots of depth; cedar, ripe fruit, tannins, all in harmony. (19)

1967:

We got lots of it—we had two magnums instead of one. A fine 1967, probably the best. Dark colour, open, complex, cedary nose. Some tannins to lose. Rich, round; drinking very well now. No sign of the high acidity for which this vintage is renowned. (17)

1966:

Most participants found this wine to be the best of the flight. I disagree. Big, fine, lovely, complex nose. Dark, concentrated. May need ten more years to round up. Typical leanness of the 1966s, but a very fine bottle, yet I prefer the 1970. (Harry preferred the 1966.) (18.5)

1964:

A softer, rounder wine; not as lean as the 1966. Round, mature, chocolaty, open nose. A bit short at the end. Harry found it to have a bit too much acidity. I didn't think so, although it ended a bit short. Lovely bottle, nevertheless. (18)

1962:

Typical colour and structure of this overlooked vintage. Deep, bright-red colour. Soft, rich, round, yet still a bit tannic. No rush drinking it (in magnums); slightly acidic. Very enjoyable wine. (18)

FLIGHT #2

1961, 1959, 1955, 1953, and 1952

In this group, the wines that showed the best tonight were the first and last, namely the 1961 and 1952—the 1952 probably the best drinking bottle now in this flight.

1961:

Well. What can I say? A true, classic 1961! Dark, deep colour. Still closed; needs five to ten more years. Magnificent, round, intense nose. Tannic. Luscious, ripe, cedary fruit. An experience. Perfection. (20)

1959:

Dark colour, orangy rim. Round, soft, very long, complex, Cabernet-cedar nose. Yet on palate, a bit dry at the end. Not the best example of this wine that I have tasted. Good, nevertheless. (17.5)

1955:

The first disappointing wine of the evening so far. A hard, lean, dry, acidic wine. Not enough fruit. (The wines came from various sources and were collected over the years. Poor storage was evident with some of the older bottles.) (15.5)

1953:

Latour is not famous for its 1953. Too much second-rate wine was added to increase production. Orangy rim. Lean, hard wine. Acidic, yet fine complexity; open, soft. After 30 minutes, it started to dry out. (16.5)

1952:

Good, deep colour. Well balanced; complex, round wine on both nose and palate. Finally approachable after being hard for many years. Lovely bottle. Ready. Classic, masculine, cedary, spicy Cabernet wine. I am glad to own several bottles of this wine.(18)

FLIGHT #3

1949, 1948, 1947, 1945, 1934, and 1929

The 1945 was the only wine served in bottle, rather than magnum. Nobody could find it in magnums, and the château doesn't own any.

1949:

Deep, dark colour. Very good complex nose. Round, chocolate-caramel nose. A bit tannic, ended a bit short, its only fault. Good, though. (17.5)

1948:

Dill, spicy nose; dark colour; weedy on palate. Not one of my favourites, but sound. Drink up! (16)

1947:

Brownish colour, orangy rim. A bit weedy; drying out and a bit acidic. Lean, yet still enjoyable. Had a better bottle three years ago. Harry thought that all these older bottles would have shown better if they had been tasted in England or at the château. He may have a point there. In any case, 1947 is not one of Latour's "finest hours." (16.5)

1945:

Some people weren't too impressed. I loved it! Deep, mature Claret colour. Concentrated nose; typical wet wood nose of the 1945s. Hard, big, tannic wine; sweet aftertaste. Classic Latour; will it ever come around? Great! (19.5)

1934:

The poorest wine of the evening; practically undrinkable. Dark, cloudy colour; dusty drawer on nose and palate. Old rotten wood with vegetal overtones. Like smelling an empty jar of pickles. (No score)

1929:

Similar appearance to the 1934; a bit cloudy (poor decanting?). Pleasant old-Claret nose. Not showing at its best. Past glory. Fading, yet an experience, nevertheless. (15)

Overall

A great experience and an unforgettable evening. In the third flight, the 1945 was by far the best wine. For me, the three giants of this particular evening were the 1961, 1945, and 1970.

DESSERT WINE

Louis Roederer Carte Blanche N/V Champagne (Demi Sec):

Pleasant, slightly sweet; a palate-cleanser.

In honour of Harry's birth year (1904)

1904 Grande Fine Champagne Cognac, Gaston Briand:

Very dark colour; young, caramel nose (of a much younger Cognac), but very dry and woody on palate. Almost bitter.

A memorable evening, and I met very interesting and knowledgeable people.

June 1984

Father's Day Dinner, at the Tobes'.

All wines served double-blind.

1971 Bâtard-Montrachet, Joseph Drouhin:

I guessed this one right away as a fine 1969 or 1971 Puligny or Chassagne Premier or Grand Cru. Deep, bright gold. Lovely, complex, toasty, mature nose of great older Burgundy. Very long on palate, good complexity. Classy. At the end of its peak. Perfect now for lovers of older white Burgundies. I would have preferred it two years ago. Very fine, nevertheless. (18)

This was followed by a vertical tasting of four vintages of Château Lynch-Bages (also served double-blind).

At first, smelling them, I thought that they were California Cabernets (cedary, minty noses). But as I tasted them (good acidity, showing some maturity; one, the 1970, was very deep-purplish colour), I thought they were all 1975 (!) Pauillacs—Mouton and/or Lynch-Bages (because of the cedary nose). All four (1959, 1961, 1966, 1970) were fairly serious, hard wines; some tannin, fairly high acidity, but with fine and ripe fruit extract.

1959:

For drinking now, the 1959 is the finest, most forward, most complex on nose and palate. Rich, chocolaty, round, with that unmistakable minty-eucalyptus nose so typical of both Mouton and Lynch-Bages. (18)

1961:

The 1961 is harder. Similar in colour to the 1959. Closed nose, yet it had a lovely, rich, ripe flavour. Very concentrated. Drink from now till 1995 or beyond. (18)

1966:

The 1966 is slightly lighter. Similar nose to the 1961. A bit leaner, but lovely, cedary; good fruit and long finish. (17.5)

1970:

The 1970 very dark, purplish, intense, hard. Needs five to ten years. A California-lover's Claret, loaded with ripe fruit. Excellent potential. (18.5)

A great experience. Fine wines and great food.

June 1984

Dinner at John and Renée Lawson's, in Napa.

With Marcia and Pete Fredericks, the US Trade Commissioner to Vancouver, and also with the lawyer for the Robert Mondavi Winery and his wife.

1980 PIPER-SONOMA CHAMPAGNE

AND

1975 DEUTZ "CUVÉE WILLIAM DEUTZ" BRUT CHAMPAGNE:

The Piper-Sonoma was as good as on the previous day; nose similar to a good Spanish sparkling wine.

The Deutz was unmistakably French: yeasty, toasty, good acidity; elegant, yet fairly lean, like a Taittinger. Will last.

1981 AND 1977 ROBERT MONDAVI CHARDONNAYS "RESERVE":

Both served at room temperature. Too warm, especially on a hot summer day; hard to judge.

1980 AND 1977 ROBERT MONDAVI PINOT NOIR "RESERVE":

The 1980 was more French in style, elegant, well structured. The 1977 was harder, bigger (yet had good acidity); almost the structure of an older Cabernet.

1975 AND 1979 ROBERT MONDAVI CABERNET SAUVIGNON "RESERVE":

Both had a classy, complex, eucalyptus nose.

The 1979 still hard, a bit simpler at this stage.

The 1975 was round, complex, long, a fine Cabernet. Well made.

1982 ROBERT MONDAVI MUSCAT D'ORO:

(5.5% residual sugar) Muscat nose. Light, fruity, elegant, a bit spritzy. Pleasant.

July 21, 1984

Dinner of "Group of Ten."

We started with a tasting of three Lanson Champagnes

CHAMPAGNE LANSON "BLACK LABEL" BRUT N/V:

Lacks complexity on nose; crisp, fruity, but sharp. Fairly high dosage, maybe as much as 2%? Simple.

CHAMPAGNE LANSON "RED LABEL" 1976:

High acidity, needs one to two years. Good nose, good structure and complexity. A bit light.

CHAMPAGNE LANSON "CUVÉE NOBLE" N/V:

Their top-of-the-line Champagne. Complex yeasty nose. On palate: a bit oxidized (like an old white Burgundy); thick, rich, fizzy, yet delicate.

Then, with the fish course, we had an extraordinary tasting.

CHÂTEAU GRILLET (VIOGNIER) 1978, 1979, AND 1980:

The 1980 and 1978 were my bottles. This wine is fermented and left on the lees for a while (until winter), then it spends 18 months in oak.

1978:

Richest, darkest gold, most concentrated; small production. Some apricot on nose; intense. Long, complex, yet elegant. In a class of its own. Fabulous bottle. (17.5)

1979:

The structure of a Chablis. Lighter than the 1978, but needs one to two years. Slightly high sulphur. Somehow lacks ripeness and exotic fruit extract at this stage. (16)

1980:

The lightest, but may need more time. Almost bitter, perfumy, floral nose, yet dry. Nice wine, good potential. (16.5)

1949 CHÂTEAU LA MISSION HAUT-BRION, IN MAGNUM:

Purchased for our group from Corti Bros. in Sacramento in 1981 for US$250. Now the wine is worth $850 per magnum! Extraordinary, chocolaty, intense, earthy Graves nose. Deep-red colour to rim for a 35-year-old wine! Earthy, tobacco, leather character. Fantastic nose and flavour; one of the finest Clarets I've ever tasted. An outstanding bottle. Perfectly balanced, long, complex. Later, earthiness was replaced by tobacco nose. Outstanding. They don't come any better!!! (20)

1947 CHÂTEAU CHEVAL-BLANC, LONDON-BOTTLED BY CORNEY AND BARROW:

A bit closed, elegant nose. Not as fresh and concentrated ripe fruit as the château-bottled. A bit tough, spirity, powerful, tannic, Port-like. The château-bottled (tasted on several previous occasions) is richer, more concentrated. Not bad at all, but overshadowed by the magnificent 1949 La Mission. (18)

DESSERT WINE

1967 Château Suduiraut:

Medium dark-gold colour. Lovely, long, complex, botrytized nose. Surprisingly dry (relatively speaking) on palate. The dessert was too sweet for it. I've had this wine previously and it has been sweeter. Good balance. Very good, but a bit too lean. (17)

This was a memorable tasting and dinner. I will remember the magnum of La Mission 1949 for as long as I live.

July 1984

Dinner at the Freemans'.

All wines served double-blind.

Champagne Pol Roger Brut N/V "Cuvée Réserve," in magnum:

Pleasant, elegant Pol Roger style. Crisp; good acidity and fruit; has some complexity.

1966 Corton-Charlemagne, Joseph Drouhin:

Medium dark-gold colour. Nutty, mature Chardonnay nose. Mature on palate, too. Good acidity (which is why this wine has held this long), but losing its fruit and getting tired. Still very pleasant. An experience. Must have been very good five years ago.

1969 Clos des Mouches Rouge, Joseph Drouhin:

I thought it was a 1964 or a 1969. Deep, dark colour. Complex, typical Drouhin. Spicy Pinot Noir and strawberries on nose. Long on palate. Good fruit; some tannin left. Unusually big for a Côte de Beaune. Very nice.

1961 Château Pontet-Canet, Cruse, Bordeaux-bottled:

I guessed this one as being a 1961 or 1966 Pauillac. In retrospect, it couldn't have been a 1966 because it wasn't dry or hard. Very dark colour. Spicy, complex, mature Cabernet nose; very long. Full, rich, round on palate; well balanced, some tannin left. What a great year 1961 is in Bordeaux! And what fine wines Pontet-Canet has produced in 1945, 1947, 1949, 1952, 1955, 1959, 1961, and 1966, compared to the dull wines they produce nowadays. It is now owned by the Tesserons of Château Lafon-Rochet. They must improve the quality of both properties… soon!

1967 Château Bel Air, Sauternes, Larronde Frères, château-bottled:

Dark, rich gold colour. Good botrytis nose at first; lost it later. Pleasant, round, but a bit simple.

August 1984

Double-blind tasting of various wines, at home.

With Allan Tobe, John Levine, Doug Spence, Ian Weir-Jones, Dave Spurrell, Ian Mottershead, Sid Cross, Bill Murray, Tony Gismondi, Walter Van Vloten, and myself.

APERITIF

Cotnari N/V, Monimpex, Roumania:

Purchased in Israel in 1982; probably a 1980 or 1981. Bright, deepish-gold colour. Slightly flowery-Riesling on nose. Elegant, warm, slightly sweet (Spätlese style) on palate. Good acidity, if not as flowery as a German wine. Quite good.

1978 Corton-Charlemagne, Labouré-Roi, Maldant Père et Fils, in magnum:

Amber colour. Nutty nose; tea-leaves. A bit acidic, flat, woody. Some nutty resemblance to a Corton-Charlemagne, but very disappointing; already over the hill. Sulphur nose, poor handling? (10)

The following six wines were served together, also double-blind.

1. Oksamit Ukrainy 1976:

A wine from the Vorontsov, Ukraine. Terribly herbaceous, burnt-tire nose. Medium-deep colour. Sour, lean, thin on palate; dill, too. Bad! (0)

2. 1969 Château Musar, Lebanon:

Medium-light colour, showing some age. Warm, open, slightly toasty, oaky "old-barrel" nose. Good complexity and fruit. (16)

3. 1968 Inglenook "Estate-Bottled" Cabernet Sauvignon, Napa Valley:

Closed, yet jammy nose. High acidity; lean yet fruity on palate. Some semblance to Cabernet. Leathery, ageing, has good fruit. Hint of eucalyptus. (15)

4. 1967 Lindeman's Nyrang Hermitage "Bin 3610," Australia:

Wet saddle, leathery nose. Lean and drying out; getting tired, but not bad. (13.5)

5. 1963 Vin Nakad-Jdida Chtoura, Lebanon:

Similar to #2, but more acidity and less complexity. Some fruit left, but tired. (13)

6. 1959 Chianti Classico "Riserva," Fossi:

Spicy Chianti on both nose and palate. Very obviously Italian. High acidity, good depth, sweetish. Peppery nose. (15.5)

1955 Côte-Rôtie "Côtes Brune et Blonde," Chapoutier:

Palish, old colour. Open, round, spicy nose of Pinot Noir rather than Syrah. Evolved on palate; very mature, quite elegant, good fruit. (16.5)

1945 "Côteaux de l' Aubance" Botrytized Chenin Blanc:

Made from prephylloxera grapes in an area that does not exist any more—now there is an Anger-Cholat highway there. Used to be owned by Mr. Sarazin. The vineyard was located at Denée near Pont-de-Cé. Bottled in an old Vittel bottle (shortage of bottles during WW II). Delicate botrytized nose. Not very sweet, good acidity, some fruit left, well balanced. Quite good and still youthful. An experience. (17)

An unusual tasting, with unusual wines. None of the participants came even close to guessing correctly what the wines were.

September 4, 1984

Le Tastevin small-group tasting of St. Estèphes (Montrose, Cos d'Estournel, and Calon-Ségur) of the 1961, 1966, and 1970 Vintages.

Blind tasting. Wines known, but not the order.

1. 1966 Château Montrose:

Dark, concentrated colour. Delicate, subdued, toasty nose; closed. Lean, spicy, good fruit, long aftertaste. A bit high in acidity. Austere. Hint of caramel, chaptalized nose. Tannic. The leanness of a 1966. (16.5)

2. 1961 Château Cos d'Estournel:

Similar colour to #1. Slightly more mature, orangy colour. More open nose than #1. Classic Claret. Slight vegetal smell that improved later. Mouthful of lovely, ripe wine. Still tannic, very well balanced, good fruit. Sturdy and solid; typical St. Estèphe. No rush. Must be a 1961. Montrose? (18)

3. 1961 Château Calon-Ségur:

Similar colour to #2. Orangy, mature colour. Closed, spicy, berry-like nose. Leaner and harder than #2, but fruitier, caramel-herbaceous nose. Good fruit, still young. Not too impressive. Tannic. (16.5)

4. 1970 Château Calon-Ségur:

Good, dark, mature colour. Still some youth. Lovely, classic nose. Complex, mature, vegetal, lean, hard wine. Slightly acidic. Similar to #3 (1970?), but better balanced and better fruit. (17)

5. 1970 Château Montrose:

Darkest colour; deep purplish colour. Closed nose; great fruit extract. Big 1961 or 1970 concentration; massive fruit, essence of Cabernet! 1970 Montrose? (19)

6. 1966 Château Calon-Ségur:

Lightest colour, orangy-brick, watery rim. Delicate, open, herbaceous nose. Light, acidic, open, elegant, cedary, sweet. Calon 1970? or even 1961? Not in the same class as the others, yet elegant. (15.5)

7. 1970 Château Cos d'Estournel:

Good, dark colour; youthful, some purple. Delicate, open, sweet, complex nose. Fruity, round, long, typical 1970, yet hard and dry finish. Cos 1970? Needs five to ten years. Will be a fine bottle, but low fruit is worrisome. (17)

8. 1961 Château Montrose:

Dark, solid colour to rim. Mature, yet good concentration and lovely colour. Sweet, rich, complex, classic cedary nose. Excellent bottle; elegant, mature. Great quality. Fairly tannic. Possibly 1961, maybe Cos? (18.5)

9. 1966 Château Cos d'Estournel:

Dark, mature colour, but not as concentrated as #8 or #5. Good fruit and tannins. Rich, almost sweet, on entry, but dry, lean finish. Could be 1966 or 1970 Cos. (17)

Group rating

1961 Montrose: first
1961 Cos: second
1970 Montrose: third.
The 1961 Calon-Ségur was voted last.

DESSERT WINE

1976 Château Rieussec:

As usual for this property and vintage: deep, dark-gold colour. Big, rich, botrytized nose. Intense. Rich, round, forward, luscious. Yet seemed not as fat as in the past. Fairly hot and alcoholic. Needs drinking.

A great tasting.

Election Night in Canada.

After the tasting, we watched the election results on TV. After 16 disastrous years of socialist-style Trudeau "Liberal" government, the "Liberals" have been kicked out of office. It will take us at least two generations to repair the damage—if we can recover at all. I do not know if the new Conservative government will be any better, but at least they are not doctrinaires.

They may turn out to be corrupt and greedy, but Trudeau was a doctrinaire—and wealthy, the most dangerous kind. Such people do not steal. They change things because they believe. Lenin, Mao, Trotsky, et al. were believers—not crooks. Yet look at the results. The economy is in shambles. The Canadian dollar is a weak shadow of itself. Our youth have been brought up to demand from, not give to, the country. Quebec has been alienated, possibly permanently. The deficit is disastrous. Thank you, Pierre!

September 1984

Dinner at Sid Cross's.

All wines served double-blind.

CHAMPAGNE KRUG N/V "CUVÉE SPÉCIALE":

Stylish, classy Champagne. Elegant, yeasty, complex, long, well balanced. Elegant and round. Very good quality. (18)

1976 BEAUNE CLOS DES MOUCHES BLANC, DROUHIN:

I never liked the 1976 vintage of this wine. Hardly any Chardonnay on nose; none on palate. Like an old, tired Rhône. Lean, acidic, alcoholic, but no fruit. Gone. Drouhin must have had problems with their whites in the 1976 drought year. (12)

1966 AND 1970 CHÂTEAU GRAND-PUY-LACOSTE:

Just by the colour, I guessed the vintages right away.

The 1970 was bright, deep, dark; still purplish. The 1966 was dark, too, but showed more age.

The 1970 had a "neutral," deep, closed, yet lovely Cabernet nose; undoubtedly a Pauillac or St. Estèphe.

The 1966 was more vegetal and stemmy. The 1970 was rounder, fruitier, needing five to ten more years.

The 1966 was hard, herbaceous, forward, yet should last for quite some time. By elimination, I guessed Pichon-Baron or Grand-Puy-Lacoste (too hard and not complex enough to be anything else… if they are Pauillacs). Both very good. The 1970 excellent! Rated the 1966 (17) and the 1970 (18).

1947 MUSIGNY, FAIVELEY, IN HALF-BOTTLE:

I identified it immediately as a fine, delicate, mature Burgundy. Well balanced. Long on nose and palate; complex, round, well structured. I thought it was a 1969 or 1964, but a 1947!? Has held extremely well, especially in half-bottle. Lovely wine. Excellent. True delicacy of Musigny. (18)

1963 CROFT'S VINTAGE PORT, CHARLES KINLOCH:

Typical Croft's. No doubt 1963. Good depth, complexity, and structure, yet fairly forward, round, delicate (for a 1963). Fine quality. Ready, but no rush.

October 1984

Le Tastevin "Group A" blind tasting.

Group wines purchased jointly: three whites, three reds, and two dessert wines.

THE WHITES

1. 1978 CORTON-CHARLEMAGNE, LOUIS LATOUR:

Nutty, complex, intense nose. Undoubtedly Louis Latour's Corton! Luscious. New oak, vanilla; great intensity, superb fruit. Outstanding, and a keeper. (18.5) Postscript: Having tasted this wine on at least two dozen occasions to date, I cannot remember a single time where this wine was less than outstanding.

2. 1978 MEURSAULT-PERRIÈRES, J. PRIEUR:

Subdued, fruity, herbaceous nose. Rich flavour, fairly high acidity. Complex, but seems to be maturing early. Slightly lemony. Must be the Meursault. (16.5)

3. 1978 CORTON-CHARLEMAGNE "DIAMOND JUBILEE," REMOISSENET:

Nutty Corton nose; not as intense as #1, leaner style. Remoissenet? Rich, elegant, long; very well balanced. Not as intense or luscious as #1, but very fine wine. Ready, but will hold. (17.5)

Group rating on 1978 whites

Latour's: first
Remoissenet's: second

THE REDS

The reds were opened and decanted one hour before tasting. Only our host knew the order in which the wines were served.

1. 1961 CHÂTEAU PICHON-LALANDE:

Medium-dark, maturing colour; browning. Good depth. Lovely, sweet, complex, open nose. Drying out a bit on palate, but still well balanced. Soft, yet some leftover tannin. Very elegant, long. Lacks a bit in depth. Pichon-Lalande? (17.5)

2. 1961 CHÂTEAU AUSONE:

Slightly lighter colour than #1. Less browning than #1. Open, elegant nose; a bit stemmy. Similar impression on palate; longer and better balanced than #1. Very St. Emilion in style. Ausone! (18)

3. 1961 CHÂTEAU MOUTON-ROTHSCHILD:

Darkest of group. Intense, full, rich, deep; still some tannins to lose. Fairly hard, cedary, spicy Cabernet. Long, complex, luscious. In a class all by itself; without the massive weight of the 1961 Latour, Palmer, or Petrus. Surely must be Mouton! (19)

I correctly identified all of the above six wines.

DESSERT WINES

1976 CHÂTEAU CLIMENS, BARSAC:

Elegant rather than big. Perfectly balanced, complex, clean, botrytized, buttery. Lovely wine. Very well balanced. Will age well. (18)

1963 DOW'S VINTAGE PORT:

Typical 1963. Big, dark, intense. Relatively hard style. No rush; will hold for many years. Needs time to round up. Great potential. (18)

This was a fabulous tasting, featuring some treasures.

October 1984, Napa Valley

Visit with Joe Heitz.

Visited the winery, followed by a small tasting. After 1978, they stopped producing the "Fay Vineyard" because it was variable in quality, and other wineries used to purchase and bottle Cabernet under "Fay Vineyard." On the other hand, they produce 100% of both "Bella Oaks" and "Martha's Vineyard." New oak barrels' proportion varies from year to year.

1981 HEITZ CELLARS CHARDONNAY "HEITZ VINEYARD," NAPA VALLEY:

From their own property. (They also produce a regular Chardonnay, from purchased grapes.) 13.5% alcohol. Too alcoholic for me; noticeable because this wine is fairly delicate. 2,500 cases produced.

1981 HEITZ CELLARS ZINFANDEL:

Grapes purchased from the Coppola vineyard. Light, elegant; some tannin to lose. Older-looking than its age would indicate. Pleasant, but not special. Will not age well, in my opinion.

1979 NAPA CABERNET SAUVIGNON:

Medium colour. Elegant, complex, some mint-eucalyptus. Needs two to three more years. This wine sells for $11 and includes the entire production of 1979 "Bella Oaks." No 1979 "Bella Oaks" declared.

1982 HEITZ CELLARS PINOT NOIR, NAPA VALLEY:

Light colour. Bottled only two months ago. Good Pinot Noir character; delicate, elegant. In two years, will make a very nice bottle.

Later we went into the house with Alice and Joe's daughter Kathleen, and we had a bottle of this wine.

1973 HEITZ CELLARS CABERNET SAUVIGNON "MARTHA'S VINEYARD," NAPA VALLEY:

The colour of a 1966 Claret. Fine, delicate, typical "Martha's" nose. Not a massive giant like the 1974, but well structured. Good length, some tannin to lose. Ready, but can hold for four to five more years.

We had a nice talk and spent two-and-a half hours together. I hope that I'll be back in December to visit them again.

Also tasted in Yountville.

1983 FRENCH COLOMBARD, NAPA VALLEY:

Opened by our neighbour in Yountville, Dr. Bob Stone. Made by Dr. Wermuth, a colleague of Dr. Stone's at the Yountville Veterans' Hospital. He makes wine during his free time; also makes Sauvignon Blanc. This wine, at the age of one year, is elegant, crisp, well balanced, delicate. 13% alcohol. Enjoyable and excellent value at $30 to $40 per case.

1961 CHÂTEAU BEAU-RIVAGE, MACAU, A/C BORDEAUX SUPÉRIEUR:

At that time, the owner was a certain Mr. H. Barateau, although Borie-Manoux had the monopoly. Today this wine is produced by the Castejas Borie-Manoux and is a rather ordinary, everyday wine. Purchased from the Oakville grocery for $40. Good depth, some age at rim, but excellent appearance and level. Decanted 20 minutes. Complex, elegant nose of an old Margaux-type wine. The nose was far superior to what one would expect from a simple wine like this. Round, soft, yet well balanced on palate. Clean. At its absolute peak. What a pleasant surprise. Some sediment. For its classification and price, and the quality it has delivered at 23 years of age, this wine deserves at least (18).

Visit and lunch at Robert Mondavi's, with John and Renée Lawson.

A vertical tasting of "Reserve" Chardonnays of the 1976, 1977, 1978, 1979, 1980, 1981, and 1982 vintages.

1976:

Elegant, buttery nose. Delicate, lemony; slight almond bitterness at finish. Good fruit extract. At its peak. (16)

1977:

Deeper gold; looks and smells older, more evolved. Delicate, long nose. Richer, fatter, higher alcohol on palate. Both 1976 and 1977 were drought years, yet the 1976 was fresher, livelier. Almost tasted like a dry, light Barsac. (15.5)

1978:

As deep in colour as the 1977. Nose more closed than above two. More acidity and more fruit than in the 1977. A blend in style between 1977 and 1976. (16)

1979:

Darker gold than the 1976, but not as dark as the 1978 or the 1977. Best fruit so far. Rich, lemony, round, well balanced; very good. Best complexity, too (more barrel fermentation). (17)

1979 MEURSAULT-GENEVRIÈRES, FRANÇOIS JOBARD:

This wine was included to show the differences and similarities between Mondavi's style and fine French

Burgundy. Colour of the 1976 Robert Mondavi, but lovely, nutty, complex, typical French Burgundy. Well balanced, oak-straw flavour; intense, big, long, lovely Burgundy. Round, perfectly balanced. Drinking very well now. (17.5)

1980:

Similar bright-golden colour of the 1979. Complex, oak-vanilla, exotic nose: similar to the 1979. Richer than the 1979, higher alcohol, more oak on palate. Classier. 14.2% alcohol; that is its drawback—too spirity.

1981:

Closest to the Meursault in style. Very French! Well balanced, round, leaner, good acidity, complex, lighter in colour, similar to the 1979 Meursault. The 1981 has the best balance. 100% barrel-fermented. This wine would mislead anyone who prefers white Burgundies. (17.5)

1982:

Similar appearance to the 1981, although back to California style. Rich, luscious, round, long. Only two-thirds of the production was barrel-fermented. Much more volume was produced in 1982—almost double the 1981 production. I prefer the 1981. (16.5)

Most informative tasting, showing the change in style and winemaking philosophy at Mondavi's. Obviously, they are experimenting, trying to fine-tune a final house style of Chardonnay. They are doing the same thing with their Pinot Noir. I hope that Tim Mondavi will decide soon on a final style for both because, as a consumer, I never know what to expect with this winery's Pinot Noirs and Chardonnays.

Also tasted

1980 PINOT NOIR "RESERVE":

Lovely, spicy, complex California Pinot Noir. Elegant style. Fine, long, well made; clean, fresh fruit. Hint of toasted (charred) barrel. Excellent value. (17)

1980 AND 1981 CABERNET SAUVIGNON "RESERVE":

The 1980 has more depth, complexity, elegance, and mintiness. Made from 90% Cabernet Sauvignon and 10% Merlot. A bit harder. Good depth of flavour. Very elegant. (17)

The 1981 is a bit simpler. Higher acidity, but nice. Forward. Soft fruit; somehow less extract or ripe fruit. (16)

The final wine of this informative, generous tasting was a special treat.

1974 ROBERT MONDAVI "RESERVE" CABERNET SAUVIGNON:

Deep, dark colour to rim. Complex, Latour-like in colour and cedary nose. Great, classic Cabernet nose; maturing, fabulous! Reaching its peak, but well balanced and some tannin to lose. Will last for a long time. Nice, classic wine. No new oak was used in 1974. 1975 was the first year in which new oak barrels were used. John said that the 1974 is excellent, but doesn't have enough length. I disagree. A great effort. (18)

Interesting information

John told us that Mondavi is now abstaining from watering their vines (except the young ones), and they are planting both whites and reds closer together (same as in France). Around August, they also cut the branches, leaves, and shoots that are excessive, to allow more sun exposure on the grapes. However, volume is 300% per acre more than in Bordeaux!

October 1984

Double-blind comparative tasting of Robert Mondavi wines and approximate French equivalents (in their opinion) with John Lawson, in Vancouver.

1981 ROBERT MONDAVI FUMÉ BLANC "RESERVE":

Stemmy Sauvignon Blanc on nose. Well balanced, rich, pleasant. (15)

1982 LA DOUCETTE FUMÉ BLANC, LOIRE VALLEY:

Closed, toasty, lightly fruity nose. Lean, acidic, stemmy wine. Too lean—or is it because it was tasted after #1? French! Maybe Graves? (14)

1976 ROBERT MONDAVI FUMÉ BLANC (REGULAR), NAPA VALLEY:

Richer and darker than #1 and #2; rounder. Like a Chardonnay on nose. Elegant on palate, yet lacks middle. Good entry, elegant finish; watery, short middle. Mondavi? (12)

1981 MEURSAULT, JAFFELIN:

White Burgundy. Toasty, elegant. Good fruit/acidity balance. A 1979 or 1981 Puligny? Could be a 1982, but a leaner one, which is unusual. (15)

1975 ROBERT MONDAVI "RESERVE" PINOT NOIR, NAPA VALLEY:

Closed, slightly herbaceous nose. Darker colour than #4. Musty and declining. (14)

1981 ROBERT MONDAVI "RESERVE" PINOT NOIR, NAPA VALLEY:

Elegant, rich, long. Well balanced. Good, long aftertaste. Probably Robert Mondavi "Reserve." (16)

1976 ROBERT MONDAVI "RESERVE" PINOT NOIR, NAPA VALLEY:

Medium colour, some age. Elegant, subdued, spicy nose. On palate: a bit bitter and ageing. Some oak-vanilla. Pleasant, but drying out a bit. Possibly French? (13.5)

1980 La Tâche, Domaine de la Romanée-Conti:

Spicier, more forward nose, but deeper, younger colour. Young, fruity raspberries on palate; elegant rather than intense. Good acidity. Needs time. Very good potential. (17)

1980 Robert Mondavi "Reserve" Pinot Noir, Napa Valley:

Similar to the previous wine in style, but more elegant and evolved on nose, with fuller colour. Slightly stemmy. Quite good complexity. (16)

1979 Château Mouton-Rothschild:

Got it right! French Cabernet! 1978 or 1979. Complex, long, elegant, cedary. Mouton? Needs four to five more years. Classy. Oak and cedar, but lacks ripeness. (17)

1979 Robert Mondavi "Reserve" Cabernet Sauvignon, Napa Valley:

Young Mondavi Cabernet. Spicy, complex, minty. Good length. A bit too obvious. Made from 90% Cabernet Sauvignon, 4% Cabernet Franc, and 6% Merlot. 24 months in barrel. (16.5)

1975 Robert Mondavi "Reserve" Cabernet Sauvignon, Napa Valley:

Older-looking than the 1979. Showing some age, but better balanced than the 1979. More elegant and stylish. Very good wine. Made with 10% Cabernet Franc and 5% Merlot in blend. 33 months in barrels; 25% new oak barrels. (17)

October 30, 1984

Le Tastevin small-group tasting of 1979 Pomerols.

1. Château La Fleur-Petrus:

Darker than #2. Bright colour, good depth. Closed, sweet, "fresh baked bread" on nose. On palate: full, fairly forward, no tannin left, long, very enjoyable. Good quality, slightly stemmy. Rich, sweet, fine bottle, needing two to three more years. (16.5)

2. Château Clos René:

Lightest colour, yet fairly deep, purplish; touch of orange at rim. Open, vegetal, sweet nose; slightly sulphuric. Pleasant on palate; one-dimensional. Fairly high acidity. More St. Emilion than Pomerol. This wine is suffering from the high quality of the other five wines. (14)

3. Château Certan-de-May:

Very deep, purplish colour; darkest of bunch. Very sweet, ripe, almost exotic nose. Intense, fruity. Essence of Merlot. Lovely, rich, intense, full, long. Well balanced. Little tannin, but very full. Lovely wine; needs three to four more years. Excellent backbone and extract. (18) The Pomerol of the vintage?

4. Vieux Château Certan:

Very dark, but not quite as dark as #3. Delicate, elegant, flowery, complex nose; complex and intense, but not as rich as the Certan-de-May. Both lovely, long wines. This one more austere, slightly acidic finish, but classy. (17)

5. Château L'Evangile:

Similar colour to #1, but a little paler at rim. Spicy, slightly stemmy, rich, chocolaty. More austere than #3 and #4; leaner, but nearly as complex. Needs two to three more years. Stylish. (16.5)

6. Château Trotanoy:

Quite dark, deep colour; slightly orangy rim. Elegant, deep, ripe berries on nose; spicy, long, and slightly minty. Rich, fruity Merlot flavour. (17.5)

Most participants rated the Trotanoy first, and the Certan-de-May second. While the Trotanoy was very good, I still feel that the Certan-de-May is the greater of the two.

The final wine of the evening was a real treat.

1961 Château Petrus:

One of the classic wines of the century. Opened and decanted very carefully. This wine retails today for US$600 to $700! Our small group purchased it a year ago from a private cellar in Portland for US$200. Deep, maturing colour. Complex, sweet, intense, incredibly long, cedar-wood, yet ripe fruit on nose. Mature on palate, at its peak. Will not improve and is starting to show slight hint of acidity, but at this stage, it is barely noticeable. Incredibly intense, complex, long nose. Great, ripe Merlot on palate. Very ripe, yet perfectly balanced. A lovely bottle of classic, mature Claret and a great way to finish this notebook! (19.5)

November 1984

Dinner of "Group of Ten."

CHAMPAGNE CANARD-DUCHÊNE CHARLES VII BRUT N/V:

Delicate. Good yeast, complex, forward; similar to Roederer's style.

Three 1979 white Burgundies were tasted blind. We knew the wines, but not the order.

1979 CRIOTS-BÂTARD-MONTRACHET, DOMAINE DE MARCILLY:

Darkest, but a bit oxidized. I have had it previously and it was better. This tasted more like a 1969 or 1973. Very old for its age. Disappointing. (14)

CHASSAGNE-MONTRACHET PREMIER CRU "LA ROMANÉE," LABOURÉ-ROI:

Medium-golden colour. Good nose, fruit, but a bit too lemony. Sharp, citric finish. (13.5)

CHASSAGNE-MONTRACHET PREMIER CRU "LES VERGERS," MICHEL NIELLON:

Palest colour. Complex, elegant, well balanced. Clearly the best of the three. Lovely fruit. Long finish. (17.5)

1961 CHASSAGNE-MONTRACHET "MORGEOT" PREMIER CRU, MARQUIS DE LAGUICHE:

I purchased this bottle for our group in San Francisco (at Draper and Esquin's). Deep, dark gold. A bit Sherry-like, with a bitter finish. Austere, but clean, well made, well balanced. Lasted quite well, but lost its fruit. (Sid and Allan didn't like it. Ken and I did.)

1947 CHÂTEAU CHEVAL-BLANC, BOTTLED BY CHRISTOPHER AND CO., LONDON, AND SHIPPED BY CALVET

AND

1947 CHÂTEAU CALON-SÉGUR, ENGLISH-BOTTLED BY WILLIAMS AND STANDRING:

Both incredible, deep colours to rim. The Cheval-Blanc was much deeper in colour.

The Calon-Ségur had a lovely, cedary, complex nose. Big, austere, tannic, but had good fruit. Enough tannin to last for some time (five to ten more years), but the fruit is soft. Lovely, classic bottle. Very fine. One of the last great vintages produced by this property. (18)

The Cheval-Blanc was true of its fame. Port-like on nose. Incredible dark colour, tannic, hard, full, and rich. Luscious. Will last for many years. Top quality. Port-like on palate, too. Long, full, incredibly rich. Quite alcoholic. (19)

1955 TAYLOR'S VINTAGE PORT:

From leftovers of a year ago at the IW&FS convention that Ken Cross topped up and recorked. Elegant, older, sweet, pleasant; good quality but not the real thing.

This evening, I tasted a 1947 Cheval-Blanc for the third time (all with the same group and all within the past two years). Both the château-bottling and the latest one (Christopher and Co.) have been typical of this wine. The Berry Bros.-bottling was a bit disappointing: leaner, lighter, and not quite what one would expect from this wine. Overall, I am very fortunate to have had these three great experiences.

November 1984

Port tasting, at "Hawthornes" restaurant, in Point Roberts.

I was the guest speaker.

DOW'S EXTRA DRY WHITE PORT N/V:

Full, like a dry Madeira. Rich. Nice aperitif wine.

DOW'S BOARDROOM TAWNY N/V:

Tawny, dark wood, gold colour. Sweet, luscious nose. Nutty, clean, long on palate.

GRAHAM'S FINE RUBY PORT N/V:

Dryish, big, fruity, quite pleasant, but seemed a bit tired.

1980 DOW'S VINTAGE PORT:

Very dark colour, closed nose, soft middle. A wine for the mid-term. Based on this wine, 1980 will be a useful, but not a great vintage. Time will tell, as they are only four years old.

1977 WARRE'S VINTAGE PORT:

Not as dark as the Dow's 1980. Complex, round, elegant, yet full of flavour. Needs ten or more years, but surprisingly soft for a 1977.

1975 TAYLOR'S VINTAGE PORT:

Deep colour. Rich, long, fruity. Good quality. Complex. This fine Port needs another five years. One of the best 1975s.

1970 FONSECA'S VINTAGE PORT:

Rich, deep, fruity. Needing another five years. Sweet, well balanced. Good. Lovely on nose and palate, if not in the class of 1963. Very promising, but not quite ready.

1966 SANDEMAN'S VINTAGE PORT:

Soft, getting ready, round, sweet, rather simple. One-dimensional. A beginner's Port.

1963 FONSECA'S VINTAGE PORT:

Deep colour. Lovely, intense, rich, fruity. Great concentration. Spicy, sweet. Perfect. Needs five more years. Great potential. These 1963s are becoming quite expensive. The 1963 Fonseca's retails now for $35 per bottle! Seven years ago, I purchased it in Vancouver for $7.50 per bottle.

1955 QUITA DO NOVAL VINTAGE PORT, (RECORKED BY WHITWHAM AND CO. BUT ORIGINAL PORTUGUESE-BOTTLING):

Good, darkish colour; browning, orangy rim. Sweet, toasty, complex nose. Elegant, forward, spicy, but not very deep. Lovely balance. Fine bottle at its peak.

1948 TAYLOR'S VINTAGE PORT:

Similar colour to the 1955 Noval, more spirity on nose, Chunky, fleshy, heady. Not as elegant on the nose as the 1955 Noval, but long aftertaste and well structured.

1917 CROFT'S VINTAGE PORT:

Looks like a Tawny. Sweet, slightly spicy nose (cantaloupe). Sweet, forward. It is 67 years old! Still has Port character, but soft and elegant. Lovely! Recorked in 1979 by Whitwham and Co. Wines Ltd., Altrincham, Cheshire, England.

As an experience, the 1917 showed best. For drinking tonight, the 1955 Noval was the finest. In the future, the 1963 Fonseca's will be great. The 1970 Fonseca's and 1975 Taylor's are very promising, and the 1977 Warre's has excellent potential. The 1980 Dow's is typical of the vintage and the 1966 Sandeman's is disappointing, especially against such competition.

November 1984

Commanderie de Bordeaux Dinner and Tasting, featuring 1981 Clarets, at "Jean-Pierre's" restaurant, in Vancouver.

This was a second-assessment tasting of this young, promising vintage. The wines were tasted blind.

1. DOMAINE DE CHEVALIER 1981:

Medium-dark, purplish, slightly watery rim. Slightly herbaceous, stemmy nose. Elegant, mature-berry fruit. Medium body. Good fruit, oak. Soft, lacks a bit in depth. Graves? (16.5)

2. CHÂTEAU HAUT-BRION 1981:

Slightly lighter colour than #1. More open, round nose, but still slightly herbaceous, chocolaty, complex. Bigger than #1 on palate. More intense. More tannic, but not by much. Good fruit and length. Medium-bodied. Graves? (17.5)

3. CHÂTEAU LA MISSION HAUT-BRION 1981:

Darker than #1 or #2. Full colour to rim. Purplish. Fruity, sweet, slightly herbaceous nose. Long, intense, rich, but not very tannic. Not as long on palate as nose would indicate. La Mission! A bit alcoholic. Biggest and richest so far. (17)

4. CHÂTEAU LA LAGUNE 1981:

Medium-dark, purplish colour to rim. Good depth. Rich, herbaceous, complex, long, open nose. Jammy, fruity, rich wine. Round, some tannin, well balanced. More fruit than #1 to #3 but not too complex; very good, though. La Lagune? (16.5)

5. CHÂTEAU PALMER 1981:

Lighter than #1 to #4, but still has good depth. Fruity, toasty. Medium-bodied, fairly forward. Good acidity, some tannin. Needs three to four years. Elegant, classy, but forward. (17)

6. CHÂTEAU MARGAUX 1981:

Very dark, intense colour to rim. Very concentrated. Darker than all the other wines. Lovely, intense, spicy, slightly stemmy, oak-vanilla, beautiful, complex nose. Rich, big, intense, new oak-vanilla on palate. Long. Margaux? Great extract and balance. Needs lots of time. (18.5)

7. CHÂTEAU DUCRU-BEAUCAILLOU 1981:

Medium colour, fading a bit at rim. Rich, fruity, sweet nose. Open on palate. Round, forward, elegant. Good fruit, well balanced. Try in five years. A bit lean. (15.5)

8. CHÂTEAU LEOVILLE-LASCASES 1981:

Slightly darker than #7. Purplish. Rich, round, toasty. Similar nose to #7, but a bit more open. Harder, more masculine than above. Pauillac or St. Julien? Tannic. Full, intense Cabernet. Vanilla-oak. Try this in six to eight years. (16.5)

9. CHÂTEAU TALBOT 1981:

Medium-dark colour to rim. Complex, open, intense Cabernet nose. Round, slightly spicy, stemmy. Full, rich, straightforward, luscious. (16.5)

10. CHÂTEAU GRUAUD-LAROSE 1981:

Very similar colour to #6; even darker! Opaque, full, thick colour to rim. Touch of purple. Rich, intense, sweet Cabernet nose. Concentrated. Ripe raisins. Full, rich, very impressive. A mouthful of lovely wine. Incredible intensity. Well balanced. Lots of fruit. Lascases or Gruaud? (17.5)

11. CHÂTEAU MOUTON-ROTHSCHILD 1981:

Open, sweet, elegant, spicy, herbaceous nose. Medium colour. Good depth to rim. Enjoyable cedary nose. Elegant, complex, quite tannic, yet only medium fruit. Lacks extract. Pichon-Lalande? (16.5) Surprise: Mouton!

12. CHÂTEAU PICHON-LALANDE 1981:

Good, medium-dark colour to rim. Rich, sweet, cedary nose. Chocolate, round, beautiful. Sweet, elegant, yet quite tannic. Cedar, vanilla, very long. Top class. Mouton? (17.5)

These are very good wines. The Margaux, Pichon-Lalande, and Gruaud-Larose have great potential. I must buy some more of these.

I guessed all communes right and most châteaux, but I mixed Mouton and Pichon-Lalande. The Mouton is disappointing.

WITH DINNER

Pavillon Blanc du Château Margaux 1981:

The white wine of Château Margaux. Made from 100% Sauvignon Blanc grapes and aged in 100% new oak casks. At first, slightly sulphury nose; later, complex, fruity, very elegant, well balanced Sauvignon Blanc. Yet without the sharpness this grape varietal can possess and which I don't like. Elegant, long, very pleasant, but at $50 per bottle?! Nice balance, delicate, very enjoyable. New oak. (17.5)

DESSERT WINE

1981 Château Rieussec:

Medium gold. Good botrytis on nose. Sweet, complex, quite long, pleasant. Almost ready. Fine effort for the vintage. (16.5)

Overall impressions of the 1981s

Better than expected. Excellent potential. Re-taste in three to four years. Château Margaux must be the wine of the vintage.

December 1984

Chevaliers du Tastevin Black Tie Dinner at the Hyatt Regency hotel.

Our guest of honour was François Faiveley.

APERITIF

Champagne Pol Roger "Blanc de Chardonnay" 1975:

Softer than expected. Elegant, round, complex. François thought the style resembled Krug. Frankly, while this is a very nice Champagne, I think that the weight of Krug (and the depth) would overpower this.

1982 Puligny-Montrachet "Folatières," René Monnier:

Very 1982 in style. Round, soft, complex, good vanilla-oak on both nose and palate. Long. Very well made. Will mature early.

1973 Meursault-Perrières, Boillot-Buthiau:

Controversial. We had a corked bottle; others had better bottles, which had a fine, complex, nutty, but elegant rather than heavy Meursault nose. Fuller, more mature, of course, than the "Folatières."

1979 Nuits-St.-Georges "Clos des Porrets St. Georges" Tasteviné, Faiveley:

Good, deep colour. Not very tannic, but good concentration of fruit. Fermentation of up to 28 days extracted a lot of colour. Needs three to five more years. Good wine.

1966 Richebourg, Remoissenet:

Deep, bright yet mature colour. Complex, delicate nose; hint of truffles. Long, slightly acidic finish, but overall very fine. François loved it.

1970 Graham's Vintage Port:

Very deep, very dark, very fruity wine. Typical Graham's style. Needs five to ten extra years. Will be a fine Port by 1992-1996.

The food was excellent, as was the service. I was the senior host and organizer of this event.

January 1985

Trip to Napa Valley and San Francisco with Sid Cross.

Dinner at "Mustard's" in Yountville.

1983 Puligny-Montrachet "Folatières," Roux Père et Fils:

Bottle purchased at Draper and Esquin's for US$15. Our first 1983 white Burgundy tasted from bottle. These wines are being released now. Very young nose. Good, fresh fruit. Some complexity, well balanced, good acidity. Needs two to four more years, but should make a good bottle. 1983 seems to be better balanced and not as soft and flabby as many 1982s.

Apparently, many 1983 white Burgundies are too alcoholic. Time will tell.

Visit to Stag's Leap Wine Cellars.

Warren Winiarski, a friend and a very gifted winemaker in the Napa Valley, met us. We tasted the following wines.

Stag's Leap Cabernet Sauvignon 1982 "Lot 23":

75% of the grapes come from the Stag's Leap vineyard, up the hill, just north of Clos du Val. We tasted it just after the fining. Delicate, quite sweet, yet herbaceous. Some harshness due to youth. Somehow upset at this stage. Will be bottled soon.

1983 Merlot, also from cask:

Dark, deep, purplish colour. Spicy, sweet, complex Merlot nose. Delivers same impressions on palate. Promising.

Warren has also produced a Chardonnay 1982 "Marriage" from a blend of various vineyards. He partially barrel-ferments his Chardonnays.

The winery is across the street from Robert Mondavi's home and Robert Mondavi 's Sauvignon Blanc vineyard, from which they produce their lovely, botrytized Sauvignon Blanc.

Dinner at Joe and Alice Heitz's.

Joe invited me and I took Sid Cross along. We had a problem getting Sid into the house; the Heitzes have two large, very tame dogs, but Sid is scared to death of dogs. He sat in the car until the dogs were taken away.

Kathleen Ryan (Joe's daughter), Rolly (Joe's younger son), and his new bride Sally and their four-month-old son Ryan also joined us. Joe is very proud of his new grandson. (Joe was born in 1919.) I hope the Heitzes will come to visit us in Vancouver in July or August, as they will be in Seattle on a business trip.

APERITIF

MEYER'S BRUT, MÉTHODE CHAMPENOISE N/V:

An interesting "Champagne" from Texas (Pinot Noir and Chardonnay), but none of us was sure what exactly went into the bottle. Neutral, clean nose. Good bubbles (went flat after a few minutes). Dull, no complexity, yet clean and crisp. Good acidity. An experience.

WITH DINNER

1971 PINOT BLANC HEITZ CELLARS "LYN CREST VINEYARD":

Joe's last bottle! Deep golden colour. Lovely, complex, mature nose. Long, creamy, slightly woody. Slightly madeirized on palate, but after 20 minutes, the fruit came through. At the end of its useful life, yet still quite good. This was quite an experience. Surprising how well this wine has held, but then, good Pinot Blanc ages very well and, if well made, it can last for a decade or more.

1969 HEITZ CELLARS CABERNET SAUVIGNON "C-91":

Two bottles. Joe went through hard financial times in the 1960s and had to blend 45% of his "Martha's Vineyard" with 55% of his regular Cabernet (Code: C-91). Very deep, mature colour. Some eucalyptus on nose, but not as pronounced as the true "Martha's." Good depth, complexity, and aftertaste. Has held very well. Very fine wine. Long, good fruit extract.

Then, Joe served us a red wine, double-blind. At a previous dinner, I had mentioned to him that I had never tasted any 1946 California wines and that 1946 was Carol's birth year. He remembered! Unfortunately Carol wasn't there to enjoy it. Joe was really kind to remember this.

BEAULIEU VINEYARDS GEORGES LATOUR "PRIVATE RESERVE" 1946 NAPA CABERNET SAUVIGNON:

Made by André Tchelischtcheff. Joe's last bottle. Fabulous, complex, long, chocolaty nose. Rich, full, still alive, and well balanced. Very complex and well structured. Possibly the best California Cabernet Sauvignon I have tasted to date, and certainly the oldest. What an experience! Long aftertaste. Similar label to today's Beaulieu Vineyards.

Sid thought it was a 1954 or older Beaulieu Vineyards, or maybe an old Inglenook. I guessed, because of the spicy, herbaceous and chocolate character of this wine, that it was a 1946 Beaulieu Vineyards Pinot Noir. We were both pretty close.

With this wine, we had some lovely lamb shanks cooked by Rolly, Joe's son.

DESSERT WINE

HEITZ CELLARS NAPA VALLEY PORT N/V, POSSIBLY 1973:

Made from very ripe grapes. Dark, luscious, jammy; not my style of Port, but nevertheless quite fine.

A very enjoyable evening. Joe Heitz and I get along well in spite of the age and background differences between us. Joe has the reputation of being a grouchy, unfriendly person. This has not been my experience. He has always been friendly and hospitable to me, as have Alice and Kathleen. I guess that the chemistry is right.

Lunch at "Mustard's."

Second meal there in three days. With Bill Uren, export manager of Inglenook, and Ric Forman, who used to be the winemaker at Sterling in the 1970s, then winemaker at Newlan. He is now starting his own winery on Howell Mountain (just below Randy Dunn's winery) and will make Cabernets and Chardonnays.

Ric has also planted some Petit Verdot. He likes the 1973 Sterling "Reserve" Cabernet Sauvignon, but doesn't like the Sterling 1970 Cabernet Sauvignon because it tastes barbecued! He said that the oak in which it was stored in 1970 and 1971 was too green and too toasted.

Ric also likes the Sterling 1971 Pinot Blanc, which is the true Pinot Blanc rather than the Melon grape which we had the previous night at Joe Heitz's. Bill Uren will be in Vancouver in March 1985 for the Four Seasons Barrel Sample Dinner, and he will bring along Inglenook's 1978 Cabernet Sauvignon "Reserve" (selected cask) and 1983 barrel samples. This event forms part of Vancouver's Playhouse Theatre charity wine festival.

First, we tried a 1980 Merlot, Inglenook, but it was corked, so we ordered this.

1982 DUCKHORN NAPA MERLOT "THREE PALM VINEYARD":

Good colour, lovely nose, good fruit and tannin, very well balanced. In two to four years, this will be a fine Merlot. Well made. Classy.

Visit with Sid Cross to Caymus Vineyards.

We met Charlie Wagner, his son Chuck, and their winemaker, Randy Dunn. By the way, Randy thinks that his 1981 Dunn Vineyard Cabernet Sauvignon is his best effort so far. His first vintage was 1979. Charlie Wagner showed us a signed photograph of Ronald Reagan. He sent Reagan a case of wine through a secret agent of the president who lives in Los Angeles. Charlie's favourite red Burgundy is a 1964 Chambertin he had in 1979 at the Hotel St. Louis near Autun in Burgundy. He did not remember the name of the grower.

Sid broke one of the tasting glasses just before the tasting. Old Charlie Wagner gave him a dirty look!

1983 "Oeil de Perdrix" Pinot Blanc:

Touch of orange colour. Clean, crisp, good fruit, delicate. Very enjoyable.

1983 Sauvignon Blanc, Napa Valley:

Crisp, clean, easy to drink, but oddly, tasted like an Alsace Riesling; little varietal character. (Charlie likes Alsace Gewürztraminer very much.)

1983 Chardonnay, Napa Valley:

Served from the bottom of a bottle. I didn't like it. Dull, vegetal, uninteresting. Maybe opened too long.

1980 Pinot Noir, Napa Valley:

Light colour, good depth. Similar in colour, nose, and flavour to a decent Santenay or Volnay. Clean and well made.

1982 "Special Selection" Pinot Noir, Napa Valley:

Much darker, bigger, spicier, like a big, old-style Côte de Nuits. Well structured, French-like, rich. Needs three to four years; some tannins to lose.

1980 Zinfandel, Napa Valley:

Bordeaux-like. Leaner than most Zinfandels. Good nose, medium depth, tannic. Needs three to four years of ageing. Quite complex.

1982 "Liberty House" Cabernet Sauvignon:

(Their second label) For $6, good value. Round, spicy, elegant. Well structured, full, and clean. Touch of green; a bit stemmy. Young vines?

1981 Cabernet Sauvignon, Napa Valley:

Rich, deep colour. Well balanced, tannic, long, spicy, clean. Complex. Needs four to five years, but a wine to buy. Will be very good.

January 1985

Lunch at "Chez Panisse."

With Sid Cross, John Tilson (of The Underground Wineletter*) and his wife Laurie, Ed Lazarus, Dr. Brad Klein, Dr. Arnold Christiansen and his wife.*

Champagne Pommery N/V Brut:

Crisp, quite yeasty, complex, good fruit, well made. (16.5)

Sancerre 1976, Chavignol, Cotat:

Medium gold colour. Held together well. Well balanced, good acidity, tight and hiding its fruit. Long, rich. Later, the fruit seemed to be there and still lively. (17) This Loire Valley wine is made from 100% Sauvignon Blanc.

Château La Grange 1964, Graves Supérieur Blanc:

Deep gold. Round, Semillon nose. Full, rich, like a dry old Sauternes. Mature, austere, slightly musty nose. Better on palate. (15)

Then, we tried Avery's older red Burgundies.

1964 Mazis-Chambertin, Avery's:

Medium colour, good depth, orangy rim. Elegant, delicate, mature, spicy Pinot Noir nose. Good complexity, forward, delicate. Second-best of tasting. (17)

1955 Nuits-St.-Georges, Avery's:

Deeper, better colour than the 1964. Incredible depth, slight touch of orange at rim. Sweet, "fortified" nose. Leather and wet wood. Sharp, fruity, leathery, intense. Lacks class. (16)

1955 Gevrey-Chambertin Premier Cru "Clos du la Justice," Avery's:

Darkish colour. Sweet, vegetal, musty-cellar nose. Acidic, stinky on palate. (13)

1955 Chambertin, Avery's:

Low fill. Light-orange colour. Elegant, sweet, complex nose. Almost as good as the 1964 Mazis. Soft, forward, round, elegant. I enjoyed it quite a bit. Showing well, but getting tired. (16.5)

1949 Charmes-Chambertin, Avery's:

The most expensive at $160. Good depth, good fill, good cedary taste, good complexity and depth. Has held very well. Long, complex, without being great. Very good, though. (17.5)

January 1985

International Wine and Food Society Black Tie Dinner, featuring 1959 Château Lafite in various-sized bottles, at the Stanford Court hotel, in San Francisco.

Same participants as for lunch at "Chez Panisse." Plus Bipin Desai, Barney Rhodes, Haskell Norman (our Chairman), Dennis Foley, George Linton, etc.

APERITIF

CHAMPAGNE KRUG "GRANDE CUVÉE" N/V, IN MAGNUMS:

Elegant, round, yet austere. Fairly hard and powerful Champagne of fine quality, probably requiring another two to five years of bottle-age. Obviously coming from a fresh, young batch. (17.5)

Through the first two courses, we tasted Champagne.

CHAMPAGNE KRUG "CUVÉE RÉSERVE" 1976:

This Champagne had a lovely, complex, toasty, yeasty nose. Full, rich, round on palate. Perfectly balanced; great. (18.5)

WITH DINNER

We tasted Château Lafite 1959 in two flights. First, from bottles and magnums; later, we tasted the double-magnum and a jeroboam. A total of six bottles, three magnums, one double-magnum, and one jeroboam.

CHÂTEAU LAFITE 1959, IN BOTTLES:

At first, the most elegant, open, and lovely. Later, it faded a bit. It was also, relatively, the one showing the most age. Deep, mature, lovely colour. Great nose. Long, complex, and incredibly fine. Very Cabernet-like in spite of 14% to 15% Merlot in the blend. Ripe, chocolaty, exotic, yet the unmistakable elegance and class of Lafite. (18)

CHÂTEAU LAFITE 1959, IN MAGNUMS:

The magnums were my favourites. Deeper, lovely intensity and complexity, which lasted for a long time. Beautiful wine. It was also the majority's favourite, but some liked the jeroboam best. (19)

CHÂTEAU LAFITE 1959, IN DOUBLE-MAGNUM:

I liked it least. Hard, steely, metallic, and tannic, yet it was still a fine wine. Somehow lacked the ripeness and fruit intensity of the magnums. (17.5)

CHÂTEAU LAFITE 1959, IN JEROBOAM:

Deep, concentrated, fruity. Needing another ten years, and will last well into the next century. (18.5)

What a magnificent experience. Until and including 1961, Lafite wasn't equipped for blending, so the wine was bottled from individual casks over a period of several months. As a result, there is some bottle variation, yet all four samples were very good to magnificent.

Barney Rhodes told us about his importing days, when he and George Linton imported 1962 Lafite (vintage indicated on box and label), yet the cork was branded 1961! A pleasant surprise.

These 1959s were so good that little attention was paid to one of the most superb Sauternes I have ever tasted.

1959 CHÂTEAU SUDUIRAUT:

Sheer perfection. Deep gold. Creamy, rich, lovely botrytis on nose. Perfect balance, long. Good fruit, acidity, complexity. Surely, one of the finest Sauternes. (19)

We ended with an excellent glass of
RÉMY MARTIN LOUIS XIII COGNAC:

(The average age of the blend being 75 to 80 years). Great length and complexity.

At this event, two people sponsored me, and I will hopefully join the Marin County branch of the International Wine and Food Society very shortly.
A lovely, successful evening.

January 1985

Vertical tasting of Quinta do Noval Vintage Ports (Regular and Nacional), from 1960 to 1970.

Note

Two extensive tastings were held, a year apart, of Quinta do Noval Vintage Ports. The second session, January 1986, featured the 1931 to 1960 vintages. *(See January 1986 for comments.)*

Both events were organized by Dr. Haskell Norman, chairman of the Marin County branch of The International Wine and Food Society. Dr. Barney Rhodes, a contributing member, and an acknowledged authority on Port, conducted both events.

It is always fascinating and educational to participate in vertical tastings, because they enable one to really get to know the style and overall performance of a specific vineyard or winery over a period of several years or decades. In this particular case, we were able to taste both the regular Noval Vintage Port and their special (and very small) production of ungrafted Nacional vines.

By planting vines without American rootstocks, one runs the almost certain risk of the vines being attacked by the phylloxera louse. However, when successful, wines that are produced from ungrafted vines are unusually concentrated and rich. While the regular

Noval Ports are made from a blend of various grape varietals, as is the case with the other Port houses, their tiny production of "Nacional" is made solely from the Tourriga Nacional grape varietal.

These wines are rare and expensive. The 1931, both Regular and Nacional, have become a legend among wine connoisseurs. These wines sell for $500 to $600 per bottle for the regular, and practically limitless sums for the Nacional. In terms of its structure, Quinta do Noval Port is usually early maturing and is made in a more delicate style, not unlike Croft's. The Nacional, however, is much more concentrated, fuller-bodied, and intense. The scores are my own. I have indicated where my comments were different from the majority of the other participants.

1960:

Palish colour; elegant, forthcoming nose, soft and forward. Showing signs of drying up a bit. At its peak. Typical of the vintage and of Noval. (16)

1960 NACIONAL:

Much darker and more concentrated than the regular. Full, long on palate with a distinct smoky, perfumy aftertaste. Ready, but holding very well. (17.5)

1962 NACIONAL:

Intense, dark colour. Tighter and more closed than the 1960 Nacional and as concentrated. At 23 years of age, this Port isn't quite ready yet. Great quality. (18.5)

1963:

Darker than the 1960 regular, but paler than either the 1960 or 1962 Nacional. Good concentration of fruit on nose. Full, fruity, and rich on palate. At its peak now. I have experienced bottle variation with this Port. Sometimes it can be soft, forward, and rather thin. This fine example does not fit any of these descriptions. Very good. (17.5)

1963 NACIONAL:

Very dark, youthful colour. Superb intensity of ripe fruit on palate; perfectly balanced with great length. Truly a great bottle requiring five to ten extra years of bottle-age. (19)

1966:

Dark colour with palish rim. A rich, jammy, sweet wine. Full, fruity but somehow one-dimensional. A good wine, nevertheless. (16)

1966 NACIONAL:

Medium depth, but slightly cloudy. Rich, good concentration of fruit, but didn't have the complexity of the 1960, 1962, or 1963 Nacionals. (16.5)

1970:

Elegant, sweet, soft, and surprisingly forward for its age. Good but straightforward and simple. (15)

Only six to eight pipes of the Nacional are produced, and it is declared only twice or three times per decade. An interesting comment made by Dr. Rhodes. There are two schools of thought about "rousing" Port. Some producers shake the barrels before bottling to spread the sediment, therefore adding structure and depth, to the Port. Others prefer a clearer wine, if a bit lighter and, therefore, do not rouse.

February 1985

Dinner of "Group of Ten."

CHAMPAGNE PERRIER-JOUËT "FLEUR DE CHAMPAGNE" BRUT 1973:

Medium gold. Elegant, complex nose. Good entry, but bitter almond finish.

Four white wines (three known, and one mystery wine) followed.

MONTRACHET "MARQUIS DE LAGUICHE" 1976:

Deep-gold colour. Closed nose. Clean, slightly toasty. Tired on palate. Mature, woody, fairly hot. Some acidity. Losing its fruit. Disappointing. (15)

CHABLIS GRAND CRU 1976 "VAUDÉSIR," MOREAU:

Deep colour, lacking any green hue. Lemony, toasty nose; pineapple. Similar on palate. Tired, slightly musty. Going flat. Losing its fruit. (14)

PULIGNY-MONTRACHET "COMBETTES" 1976, REMOISSENET:

Bright gold. Forthcoming, intense nose. Slight hint of sulphur, but not enough to bother. Rich, fruity, intense, yet soft. Luscious, round, long, complex. Needs drinking. Top class. (17.5)

PULIGNY-MONTRACHET "PUCELLES" 1976, LEFLAIVE:

Youngest-looking. Bright, light gold. Tight, closed nose. Fruity, austere, rather lean. Well balanced. Lovely flavour. Younger-looking and tasting than all above. Lovely nose, but later, dried out. (16.5)

1976 was a drought year in Burgundy, and the above wines told the story. Heavy-handed, clumsy, overmature, getting tired, and several were unbalanced. No sense keeping them any longer.

Then we tasted two magnificent red Bordeaux, which I purchased for our group last June in San Francisco, at Draper and Esquin's.

1926 CHÂTEAU MONTROSE

AND

1928 CHÂTEAU DURFORT-VIVENS:

Both had good, dark colours, like 1966s. Orange rim. Both had excellent appearances. The sediment in both bottles was crusted, so we could extract almost all the wine.

The Durfort had a brilliant colour and a lovely, buttered-popcorn nose. Elegant, delicate, round, and lovely. On palate, it was round, still had very good backbone, a bit lean (as 1928s have been for so many years), yet very well structured, long, and fabulous. Has held incredibly well. (18)

The Montrose was a bit denser-looking. Rounder, more depth. Fabulous, mature, complex cedary nose. Very long on palate. Excellent structure and superb aftertaste. (18.5)

At almost 60 years old, these two wines were magnificent indeed, some of the finest Clarets I have tasted. Montrose was château-bottled. Durfort was Bordeaux-bottled by Delors. A great experience; unforgettable.

1963 TAYLOR'S VINTAGE PORT, LONDON-BOTTLED:

Lovely, deep colour. Fabulous spicy nose, still a bit closed. Long on palate, full, almost austere. Very well balanced. One of the finest 1963s. Needs another decade to reach its peak, and will hold for many years beyond that. (18)

February 1985

Tasting at "Le Magazin," featuring Château Musar (Lebanon).

Organized by Schenley's, the agents for Château Musar.

1. 1977 CHÂTEAU MUSAR:

Made with 70% Cabernet Sauvignon in blend; 12% alcohol. Medium, mature colour. Slightly watery at rim. Leathery, spicy nose. Round, almost sweet. Good fruit, some tannins. Some noticeable acidity. (16.5)

2. 1980 SASSICAIA (BOLGHERI), ANTINORI:

This was included as a ringer, which is odd, because it is obviously such a different wine. Darker than #1; touch of purple at rim. Oak, vanilla, sweet nose. Spicier, more concentrated, tannic, acidic (but not in a negative sense). Intense, spicy, oaky nose. Quite long and clean. Needs time. Very different, less leathery, more elegant style. (17)

3. 1975 CHÂTEAU MUSAR:

About 40% Cinsault in blend. Mature-looking, similar to #1, but lighter. Mature, toasty, spicy nose. Soft, forward, fairly high acidity. Spicy, lean, hard finish. Harder at finish than on entry. (15)

4. 1972 CHÂTEAU MUSAR:

With 60% Cabernet Sauvignon in blend. Mature colour, medium depth. Open, spicy, leathery nose, like a mature Australian Cabernet Sauvignon or a ripe Chianti. Sweet candy, evolved on palate. Again, slightly bitter finish. Nice wine. Well balanced. Forward and elegant. (16.5)

5. 1969 CHÂTEAU MUSAR:

Dark but evolving colour. Barolo-like on nose. Mature, wet wood. High acidity. Hard, tannic, yet low fruit. Like a 1964 Barolo. (15)

6. 1966 CHÂTEAU MUSAR:

Approximately 70% Cabernet Sauvignon in the blend. Lightest, most mature colour; browning. Open, bright, elegant nose. Elegant, flowery, long, yet high acidity and almost lemony. Drink up. (14.5)

All wines had the same style on nose (except for the Sassicaia): warm, open, spicy, stemmy, like a mature Cabernet Franc/Cinsault.

Château Musar is made from a blend of Cabernet Sauvignon, Cinsault, Syrah, etc. 1959 was their first vintage. Usually 60% to 70% Cabernet Sauvignon. 140 hectares planted on Mt. Lebanon and Eastern Bek'a Valley. Up to 18 months in Nevers oak barrels. Released after five years of storage and ageing. Very mature northern Italian (Piedmont) in style, with unmistakably high acidity and slightly sweet finish.

February 1985

Commanderie de Bordeaux Dinner and Tasting, at Bruno Marti's "La Belle Auberge" restaurant, in Ladner.

I was the organizer and guest speaker at this event.

Vertical tasting of Moulin Touchais, Anjou, Loire Valley.

Technically, these are not, of course, Bordeaux wines, but it was a convenient forum to hold this event.

1928:

Deep-gold colour. Clean, crisp, fresh nose. Rich, round, mature, yet not cloying. Excellent acidity. "Moelleux mais pas liquoreux." 2.5 bommé. Not overwhelmingly sweet. Later, thinned out a bit. (16)

1933:

Deep gold, slightly lighter than the 1928. More open than the 1928 on nose. Clean. Good acidity. Well balanced. The best of the first three. Not as luscious as the 1928 or 1937, but younger and fresher-tasting. (17)

1937:

Lighter than the 1928 or 1933. Medium gold. Slightly musty. Slightly drier, well balanced. Mature on palate, good aftertaste. Earthy, cement on palate. (15)

There was a little bottle variation.

(We tasted two bottles of each vintage.) According to Alex Wilbrensinck, the general manager of "La

Française d'Exportation" (sole agents of Moulin Touchais around the world), these wines, once opened, oxidize quickly and should be drunk soon. When picked, the grapes have some mould on them.

The varietal used to produce this wine is the Chenin Blanc. These wines have little or no botrytis. What helps them last this long is the relatively high acidity.

1945:

Similar deep-gold colour of the 1928; clear and bright. Better balanced, more concentrated. Lovely length, sweet, almost candy-sweet, yet very well balanced. The best of all the oldest wines. Later, caramel-taffy on both nose and palate. (17.5)

1947:

Bright, medium-gold colour. Light, crisp, well balanced. Good fruit/acidity balance. Amazing youth for its age. A bit musty nose. Quite good. (16)

1949:

Deeper colour than the 1947, but not as deep as the 1945. Well balanced. Good fruit/acidity balance. Particularly high acidity. (16.5)

1955:

Medium-deep gold. Clean, sweet nose. Intense, perfectly balanced. Crisp, acidic, long, complex. (17)

1959:

A bit more luscious, sweeter, richer than the 1955, but not quite as well balanced. Good acidity and fruit. (16.5)

1962:

One of the darkest, yet watery. Thin and a bit woody. Drying out. The driest wine of all ten vintages. Tired. (13.5)

1964:

Medium-pale gold. Sweet, good acidity, well balanced. Will hold for quite some time without declining. Candy-sweet aftertaste. (15)

An interesting and unusual tasting, but it has not made me a fan of this wine.

WITH THE MAIN COURSE

CHÂTEAU LAFITE 1961, IN DOUBLE-MAGNUM:

Deep colour to rim; maturing. Incredibly complex, long, elegant nose. Full, round, slightly green, well structured. Fabulous length. Great complexity. Great wine; a classic. They don't come much better. Slightly tannic. Made with 11% Merlot and 20% Cabernet Franc in the blend, which gives it a bit of a green, stemmy flavour. Apparently, at the time, Lafite also used some Malbec (5% to 10%). Lovely bottle. Best 1961 Lafite tasted so far. It can be variable. (19)

A very educational and interesting evening. Chef Bruno Marti did an excellent job as usual, and in this case, he had to match food with an unusual range of wines.

March 1985

Vancouver Wine Festival Black Tie "Barrel Sample Dinner," at the Four Seasons hotel.

Hopefully this wine festival will become a yearly affair. I was the organizer and moderator of this event. The participating wineries brought along both barrel samples and bottled, recently released samples of their wines, as follows.

The name in parentheses is the name of the winemaker, owner, or manager who joined us for this event.

1. CHÂTEAU ST. JEAN CHAMPAGNE, 1980 AND 1981 PRERELEASED, SONOMA VALLEY (PETE DOWNS):

1980: 75% Pinot Noir, 25% Chardonnay. 1981: two-thirds Pinot Noir and one-third Chardonnay. Cold-fermented. I preferred the 1981. Better balanced, better acidity, better fruit. The 1980 was a bit flat and uninteresting. Both were slightly too sweet for me.

2. RAYMOND VINEYARDS JOHANNISBERG RIESLING, 1983 AND 1984 BARREL SAMPLES, NAPA VALLEY (KEN VIGODA):

Pleasant, well balanced. Flowery, a bit too sweet for the rabbit course that accompanied it, but elegant and spicy.

3. COLUMBIA WINES WASHINGTON STATE SEMILLON, 1982 AND 1983 PRERELEASED (DAVID LAKE, MW):

Aged in stainless steel only. Crisp, fresh, lean, fruity. Pleasant but simple wines.

4. KALIN CELLARS SEMILLON 1982 AND 1984 BARREL SAMPLES, LIVERMORE VALLEY (DR. TERRY LEIGHTON):

Aged in wood. Complex, long, well balanced. Not unlike a Puligny-Montrachet in style! Good fruit, oak, vanilla. Crisp. Needs time. Oddly, tastes like a Chardonnay. Maybe barrel samples play tricks on the palate.

5. GRGICH CELLARS 1982 CHARDONNAY AND 1983 PRERELEASED CHARDONNAY, NAPA VALLEY (JOY KAGELE):

The 1982 was more complex at this early stage, well balanced, long, elegant. A fine Chardonnay.

The 1983 was a bit unbalanced and needs a year or two of bottle-age. Both serious wines. I am certain that the 1983 will improve once it has had a chance to "get its act together" in bottle.

6. CHALONE VINEYARDS CALIFORNIA PINOT NOIR 1980 REGULAR (RECENTLY BOTTLED) AND 1983 PINOT NOIR BARREL SAMPLE (PHIL WOODWARD):

They did not show the "Reserve" wines. The regular was clean, pleasant, spicy Pinot Noir; French style (new oak barrels). Like a Monthélie or Volnay.

The 1983 barrel sample was purple, with very clean, spicy, fresh fruit. Hint of fizz, but some Pinot Noir and vanilla in evidence.

7. RUTHERFORD HILL MERLOT 1981 (RECENTLY RELEASED)AND 1983 BARREL SAMPLE, NAPA VALLEY (TARY SALINGER):

Made with 15% to 25% Cabernet Sauvignon in the blend.

The 1983 was bottled last Friday.

The 1981 was made with 17% Cabernet Sauvignon in the blend, aged in Nevers oak, and bottled in May 1983. Both disappointing. Not nearly as big and rich as the 1979 or 1980. Vegetal, slightly bitter finish. Too lean. Hard to judge the 1983, as it is clearly upset.

8. DE LOACH ESTATE ZINFANDEL "RUSSIAN RIVER" 1981 (FROM BOTTLE) AND 1983 BARREL SAMPLE (MIKE DE LOACH):

The 1981 was dark, very big, hot, high alcohol (14.5°). Well made and intense, but too big for me.

The 1983 was, at this stage, fresh, crisp grape juice.

9. INGLENOOK VINEYARD CABERNET SAUVIGNON "LIMITED CASK RESERVE SELECTION" 1978 AND 1983 BARREL SAMPLE, NAPA VALLEY (BILL WREN):

The 1983 was spicy, purplish, very fruity.

The 1978 is at its peak now. Complex, soft, lovely nose. Long, well made. Cedar, American oak-vanilla. Nice fruit. Not very intense; rather understated. Bill has recently changed the spelling of his last name from Uren to Wren, because of pronunciation problems.

10. ROBERT MONDAVI BOTRYTIZED SAUVIGNON BLANC 1981 AND 1983 BARREL SAMPLE (JOHN LAWSON):

Both disappointing when compared to Mondavi's very fine 1978.

The 1981 was leaner, lighter, and simpler. Not as full. Good, but not great.

The 1983 will spend another ten months in oak. Time will tell.

11. QUADY WINERY VINTAGE PORT 1979 AND 1983 BARREL SAMPLE (ANDREW QUADY):

The 1979 was rich, round, and not as big as the 1978, but very pleasant. Needs two to four years.

The 1983 barrel sample will be bottled in a few months. Deep, purplish colour. Ripe raisins, spicy, fresh fruit on nose. Quite sweet. Will be good in eight to ten years.

March 16, 1985

International Wine and Food Society Black Tie Dinner and tasting, featuring 1959 Domaine de la Romanée-Conti wines in imperials, at the San Diego Sheraton hotel.

Host: Toufiq Khoury. All Domaine de la Romanée-Contis and Montrachets were contributed by Toufiq.

APERITIF

CHAMPAGNE BILLECART-SALMON BRUT 1966 "CUVÉE NF BILLECART":

Has held surprisingly well. Complex, yeasty nose. Long, fairly dry. Well balanced. Still full of life, but at its peak. Very good. (18)

1959 MONTRACHET, BOURGOGNE BLANC, LEBEGUE-BICHOT:

Medium-deep gold. Lovely, mature nose. Slightly woody. Well balanced. Good acidity. Mature, toasty, long on palate. Still lively, but certainly at its mature best. Very good. Full, rich. (18) I wonder why the words "Bourgogne Blanc" are indicated on the label? (Lebegue-Bichot have been the UK agents of Domaine de la Romanée-Conti and d'Yquem for many years.)

1959 MONTRACHET, MARQUIS DE LAGUICHE, DROUHIN, IN MAGNUMS:

While the Lebegue Montrachet was excellent, this was even greater. More depth, more complexity, more length. Still good fruit. Not as woody as the Lebegue, but fabulous. A noble, complex, generous wine. Younger-tasting than the above. (18.5)

Both Montrachets were purchased from Avery's. Some bottles of the Lebegue were a bit more oxidized than others. Overall, both wines were fabulous and have held very well.

1959 RICHEBOURG, DOMAINE DE LA ROMANÉE-CONTI, IN IMPERIAL:

Medium-deep colour, slightly orangy rim. Delicate, spicy Pinot Noir nose. Soft, forward, slightly acidic, a bit short. Surprisingly forward for an imperial. Bottles of this wine are far superior to this large format. (17)

1959 La Tâche, Domaine de la Romanée-Conti, in imperial:

Similar colour and appearance to the Richebourg. More intense flavours, better balanced and longer. Spicier, more intense Pinot Noir character than the Richebourg. Classy, with raspberries on nose (a trademark of La Tâche), yet even this is clearly finer in regular-size bottles. Does Domaine de la Romanée-Conti have a problem with the corks in some large-format bottles? (17.5)

1959 Romanée-Conti, in imperial:

Slightly darker than both the Richebourg and La Tâche. Intense, full, rich, incredibly long. One of only four imperials of Romanée-Conti 1959 made, and the last one to be tasted! A once-in-a-lifetime experience. Good fruit, complex, long, fabulous. Delicious. (19)

Later, the Richebourg opened up into lovely complexity, spicy fruit, while the La Tâche stayed closed and slightly dull. The La Tâche was the most disappointing. All three wines were surprisingly forward. They are probably fetching now $2,500 per imperial, yet Richebourg and La Tâche did not quite deliver.

1967 d'Yquem:

Contributed by the ever-generous Paul Pinski. At 18 years old, this wine is not quite ready. Needs another ten years. Almost creamy texture. Intense, complex botrytis on nose. Deep, bright-gold colour. Full, very long, very good fruit and acidity. This wine will last for at least another 20 years. A classic. (19.5)

Cognac Delamain "Réserve de la Famille":

True Delamain: elegant, palish colour; lovely nose; long, fabulous Cognac.

Overall

The stars of the evening were the Montrachets, the Romanée-Conti 1959, and the d'Yquem 1967. The other Domaine de la Romanée-Conti wines were disappointing. A great experience, nevertheless.

March 1985

Commanderie de Bordeaux Dinner, featuring the Olympic Chefs, at "La Belle Auberge" restaurant, in Ladner.

Bruno Marti, owner of "La Belle Auberge," is leading the Canadian team at the Culinary Olympics, to be held in Frankfurt, West Germany.

APERITIF

Champagne Lanson "Black Label" N/V:

Simple and pleasant, on the lean side. Lanson has never been a favourite of mine, yet sometimes it can be good. Variable.

Château Malartic-Lagravière Blanc 1982:

Made from 100% Sauvignon Blanc. This wine is never aged in wood. Pale gold colour. Light, flowery nose. Clean and round on palate, fairly rich, but lacks complexity. (16)

Corton-Charlemagne 1978, Louis Latour:

Deep gold, with lovely, intense, nutty Chardonnay nose. Oaky, intense, full, very long and rich. Very long aftertaste. Well balanced. A classic. (18.5)

Château l'Arrosée 1966

and

1970 Grand Cru, St. Emilion:

Both had very dark, deep colours and a fair bit of sediment.

The 1966 had more age, while the 1970 still had an intense colour with purplish rim. The 1966 had a lovely, complex, warm nose. Slightly stemmy, austere, a bit lean. Typical 1966.

The 1970 was rounder, fruitier, softer, and very enjoyable. Both fine, both typical of their vintages, with the 1966 maybe being slightly classier, but the 1970 more youthful. Serious wines. Rated both (17.5)

Château Montrose 1970:

Very deep, dark colour. Tight, closed, spicy Cabernet nose. Big, hard, tannic on palate; more so than usual. Great length, but needs a lot of time. A brooding giant. Excellent potential (five to ten years). (18.5)

Château Coutet 1975, Barsac, in magnums:

Still too young, especially in magnums. Light to medium gold. Lovely, long, complex, botrytis nose. Full, long on palate, but not a heavy wine. Great length and very well balanced. Will last for many years. (18)

Bruno and his team produced a fine meal and a fabulous dessert.

April 1995

Dinner at the Freemans'.

All wines served double-blind.

Champagne Canard-Duchêne Brut N/V:

Medium gold. Elegant, yeasty, complex nose. Solid, yet elegant on palate. Firm, good fruit. Fairly high acidity and lemony. Will age for another two to three years. Quite nice.

1957 Chante Alouette, Chapoutier; (Hermitage Blanc):

Two bottles opened, both identical. Deep-gold colour; clean and bright, yet very dark. Complex, long, clean, lemony, yet woody; very slightly oxidized. Full, rich, some fruit left, and good acidity. A very mature, yet round and lovely flavoured wine. At 28 years old, it has held fantastically well! A great experience. Why can't Chapoutier produce such wines nowadays?

1971 CHABLIS GRAND CRU "LES CLOS," JOSEPH DROUHIN:

Deep-gold colour. Round, old-Chardonnay nose. Soft, forward, woody, but sound. Much older-tasting than its age would indicate. Absolutely no hint of Chablis, though. I thought it was a 1966 or 1964 (or older) Meursault. Good for a wine, but disappointing for a Chablis Grand Cru.

1959 CHÂTEAU PONTET-CANET:

I guessed this wine right away as being a Pauillac and a 1959! Deep, dark colour. Lovely, complex, cedar, mature chocolaty Cabernet nose. Perfectly rounded; full, long, rich on palate. These old Pontet-Canets (1959, 1961, 1966, and even older vintages) are fabulous wines. A classic. At its peak, but no rush.

1956 CHÂTEAU LAFITE:

I thought it was a 1952 or 1957 Pauillac, so I was pretty close there, too. Lighter colour than the 1959 Pontet-Canet. Elegant, cedary, old-Cabernet, complex rosewater nose. Light-bodied and fairly high acidity. Soft, good flavour, and not really as bad as this vintage's reputation. The nose was the best part. I have never tasted a 1956 Claret before, and this was quite an experience.

1958 CHÂTEAU D'YQUEM:

Very deep-old colour. Lovely botrytis; mature, long, complex nose of apricots. Great length. Full, rich, well balanced. Sid, Ken, and I thought it was a 1953 or 1959 d'Yquem. Again, I have never tasted a 1958 Sauternes before, and this was a great revelation. A magnificent bottle at its peak, but no rush!

A lovely evening with great wines. I learned a lot.

April 20, 1985

Vertical tasting of Château Lynch-Bages 1928 to 1984, at the Century Plaza hotel, in Los Angeles.

Organized by Bipin Desai. 50 participants, including Jean-Michel Cazes, the owner of Château Lynch-Bages, and our old and dear friend from London, Harry Waugh.

Château Lynch-Bages

FLIGHT #1

1984:

(Barrel sample flown in) Dark, purplish colour. Slightly volatile, berry nose. Fruity, tannic, yet hard, acidic, and not very full. A success for the vintage. Obvious lack of Merlot. Harry liked it. Will be bottled next year. (14)

1983:

Deep, dark, purplish colour to rim. Clean, spicy, fruity, closed, concentrated nose. Well structured. Good fruit, cedar, oak, long flavour. Typical austere wine of the vintage. Very good potential. Harry Waugh's comment: "Good, classic vintage." (17)

1982:

Darker than the 1983. Similar nose, yet a bit more baked. Great concentration of fruit, good acidity, lovely flavour. Long, full, rich. Will live for many years. Excellent potential in seven to ten years. Harry Waugh's comment: "Exceptional—all on its own. Great depth of flavour, but no long wait." (18)

1981:

Very good, dark colour. Slightly lighter than the 1982. Spicy, cedary nose. Opening up a bit. Very well balanced. Well structured. Long. Slightly herbaceous. Not as charming as the 1982, but not bad at all. Needs four to five years. (15.5)

1980:

Medium-deep, purplish colour; showing slight age at rim. Closed Cabernet nose. Acidic, lacks middle. Hard. A bit tannic. Needs two years. Not bad at all for the vintage. (13.5)

1979:

Medium-dark colour. Good, spicy nose. Needs another three to four years, but not a keeper. Medium-bodied, clean, elegant, typical 1979, with good depth. Harry Waugh's comment: "Good acidity, well balanced." (17)

1978:

Slightly older and paler-looking than the 1979. Not too much on nose. Vegetal, a bit lean, but not bad. Good quality without too much concentration. Some tannin to lose. Needs three to four years. The 1979 is clearly a better wine. (15) Jean-Michel thinks it's a classic. I disagree. Harry Waugh liked it. "Splendid?!?" I disagree here, too. Am I missing something? I have never been impressed by this wine.

1977:

Medium-dark colour; slightly orangy rim. Toasty nose. A bit green and lean. Clearly chaptalized. Short, acidic, but clean and not bad for the vintage. Drinking well now. (13)

1976:

Deep, mature colour. Spicy, herbaceous nose. Forward, round, elegant. Slightly high acidity. Similar in style and structure to the 1977 and 1980, but slightly riper. I prefer the 1979, by far. Useful for drinking now. Do not expect much. (14.5)

1975:

Dark colour to rim. Cedar starting to come through. Full, rich, tannic, hard, typical 1975, yet with enough fruit to last. Loaded with tannin; needing another five to seven years. Very good potential. Will hold for many years. Bottle variations; ours was good. Harry Waugh's comment: "Massive. Long time to come around." (17)

FLIGHT #2

1973:

Palish, maturing colour. Open, warm, cedar nose. Thin, soft, a bit skunky. High acidity, lacks middle. Ordinary. May taste better with food. (12)

1972, IN MAGNUMS:

Good depth; mature, orangy rim. Open, spicy, cedary nose. Green, sharp. Lean, hard, very high acidity—almost citrus! Short; even chaptalizing it didn't help. Thin and sharp. Useless, even in magnum. (11)

1971:

Mature colour, orange-brown rim. Vegetal, complex, cedary nose. Round, forward, very soft. Slightly acidic. Woody and lacks middle. Getting tired, but still sound. Drink up. Better on nose than on palate. Chocolaty, chaptalized nose. (14.5)

1970:

Deep, dark colour to rim. Touch of orange. Lovely, cedary, spicy, rich nose. Full, rich, round, still tannic. Well put together. Cedar-oak aftertaste. Needs at least four to five years, or a lot more. Fabulous quality and excellent potential. (18.5) Jean-Michel Cazes didn't like it. "Unusual and too California in style," he said. I told him to try and produce more such "California" wines!

1969, IN MAGNUMS:

Medium-deep colour. Palish rim. Toasty, vegetal nose. Acidic, hard. A bit short, sharp finish. Clearly chaptalized. Better than the 1972, but not by much. (12)

1967, IN MAGNUMS:

Medium, mature colour. Spicy, herbaceous, open nose. Acidic, soft, very forward. Like the 1971, but more acidic. Needs drinking and declining. (13)

1966:

Good, deep colour; slight sign of maturity at rim. Lovely, cedar, spices, complex nose. Mature, complex. Long aftertaste, but still quite hard and tannic. Ready, yet tannic! Good quality. (17)

1964, IN MAGNUMS:

Medium-light orangy colour; mature-looking. Open, cedar, cigar-box nose. Soft, forward, round. A bit high in acidity, but firm. Elegant, long. At its peak. If one waits, one will lose the fruit and be left with a dried-out wine. Probably better than in bottles. (14.5)

With the exception of Latour, and to a lesser degree the softer Pichon-Lalande, most Pauillacs are to be avoided in 1964. St. Juliens, on the other hand, are another story altogether.

1962:

Darker colour than the 1964 (typical of the vintage). Good depth. Lovely, spicy, elegant nose. Complex and long. Beautiful. Round, mature, well structured. At its absolute peak and perfection! The best so far for current drinking. (17)

FLIGHT #3

1961:

Beautiful, deep, dark colour. Lovely, spicy, cigar-box nose. Big, full, rich, mature. Perfectly balanced, yet with enough depth, tannin, and backbone to last for many years. Classic. Mature raisins and fruit. Long finish. (18.5)

1961, IN MAGNUMS:

Slightly darker-looking than the 1961 in regular bottles. Similar lovely, deep, classic nose. As big and beautiful. Even a bit harder and more closed. Both are lovely, classic bottles. Bigger and more backward in magnums. (18.5)

1960, IN MAGNUMS:

Medium colour, orange rim. Vegetal Cabernet nose. Soft, forward, still sound, but drying out. Has seen better days. In bottles, it is probably gone. (13)

1959:

Medium-dark, mature colour. Slightly lighter than the 1961. Elegant, round, some tannin, slightly high acidity. Well made, but overall I prefer the 1961. Starting to dry out. Needs drinking. (17) I have tasted better samples of this; much riper.

1959, IN MAGNUMS:

Same comments as for the regular bottles, but harder and clearly more tannic. Lovely flavour. Velvet over an iron fist! (17.5) Harry Waugh preferred the bottles. Most disagreed, myself included.

1957:

Deep, dark, maturing colour. Lovely, cedary, complex nose. Good flavour. Round, complex, firm, good backbone. One of the best 1957s around. Long, complex, excellent; mature, yet firm quality. Power. (17) or better.

1955:

Very similar colour to the magnum. Medium-deep, orange rim, good depth. Similar on nose; spicy, cedar, open, complex, elegant. Soft, mature. Some tannin, but still fruity. Lovely complexity. Long and very fine. Ready, enjoyable, and a classic. (17.5)

1955, in magnums:

On the palate, the difference was clear. Bigger, deeper, better structured; long, fabulous, well put together. No rush. A classic. Fabulous, long, full, hard, yet round. Great quality. No rush. (18.5)

1954:

Mature brown-orange colour; good depth. Open nose; some wood. Round, soft, surprisingly well balanced, elegant. Similar structure to the 1962, but lighter and slightly leaner. At its peak. Drink up. (15) A fine effort in an undistinguished vintage.

FLIGHT #4

1953, in magnums:

Deep, intense colour. Mature, but rich. Complex, cedary nose. Cedar and oak; mature fruit. Well balanced, long. Cedar and ripe fruit on palate. Lots of fruit. Excellent. No rush. Regular bottles probably more forward. (18)

1952:

Deep, dark, mature colour. Closed, more herbaceous on nose than the 1953. Good flavour. Well put together. Slightly high acidity, but good length. Firmer and more masculine than the 1953. Leaner, too; typical 1952. Long, cedar, spices. Finally made it there! (17) The 1952s took a long time to come around.

1950:

Medium, mature orange colour. Good depth. Soft, forward, elegant. Slightly dry at the end, and short, but overall has held very well. Beautiful minty/cedary flavour, typical of the château. Soft and forward. (15.5)

1949:

Good, deep, mature colour. Lovely cedar, mature nose. Similar to 1947 in many ways, but clearly drier and leaner, with a bit higher acidity. Still a classic. (17.5)

1948:

Good, dark colour; orangy rim. Open, elegant, old Claret nose. Dry, acidic, lean, tannic. Lost its fruit. Very hard and unpleasant finish. Sour. Excessive malic acid. (12)

1947:

Very good, deep, dark colour; like the 1961 or 1966. Fantastic appearance. Lovely, complex, spicy, cedary, old Cabernet, ripe nose. What can I say—they do not come much better. Fabulous, long, complex. Absolutely great. Full of life. Well balanced. A great classic. After 30 minutes, acidity starting slightly to take over, but still great. (19)

1945, in magnums:

Beautiful, deep, dark colour to rim; similar to the 1961. Round, complex, masculine, youthful, full of fruit. Much younger-tasting than its age would indicate. Long, still tannins to lose, good fruit, yet lacking a bit in complexity.

Overall, the 1947 was better. Those were also my comments to the audience. It just didn't have the depth and complexity of the 1947, yet still very fine. (17.5) Jean-Michel likes best the Schröder and Schÿler-bottling, which we did not taste at this event. Harry Waugh thought the 1945 lacked complexity, too.

FLIGHT #5

1937:

Deep, mature colour. Lovely, cedar-wood, fruit on nose. Clean, round, and complex. Long, elegant. Still sound, but slightly drying out. Clean finish. Well balanced. (17)

1936:

Vegetal, herbaceous Cabernet Franc nose. Clean, elegant, round on palate. Slightly higher acidity. Like (or better than) a good 1966 or 1970 St. Emilion or Margaux. (16) Surprisingly fine for the vintage.

1934:

Good depth, mature colour. Round, elegant, long, flavourful. Long finish. Overall, stemmier, more Cabernet Franc in style. Later, dried out. (15)

1929, in magnum:

Very good depth. Lovely, rich, tannic, yet well balanced. Healthy, long, complex. A bit harder than expected. Lovely length. Good fruit. This magnum came from the estate. The previous owners forgot nine magnums at the château; we had one of them. (18)

1928:

Pruny, apricots on nose. Hard, lean, not as concentrated or well balanced as the 1929. Drying out and hard at the end, but held very well. The hard structure typical of the vintage. Unfortunately, it has outlasted the fruit. (15)

We finished with bottle of the following.

Champagne Taittinger "Comtes de Champagne" Rosé 1976:

After all these Lynch-Bages, this unfortunate Champagne didn't stand a chance and couldn't really be appreciated. Why do some people insist on serving

Champagne at the end of a big tasting or long dinner? It seems such a waste!

I gave the closing summary. It was an honour and a pleasure. With very few glitches (notably the 1978), this property deserves its reputation of being a "Super Second."

April 21, 1985

Château Lynch-Bages (1955 to 1982) vertical tasting and Dinner, a Marin County branch of the International Wine and Food Society Event at the "St. Tropez" restaurant, in San Francisco.

Two verticals of Lynch-Bages in two days! Jean-Michel Cazes and his wife Theresa were there, as well. (I met them the previous day in Los Angeles). No wines were served in magnums at today's tasting.

We started with the following white wines.

1977 "Y," DRY WINE OF CHÂTEAU D'YQUEM:

Elegant botrytis, oak, round vanilla on nose. Fairly alcoholic, nicely balanced. Not as luscious as the 1979, but long, oaky. Hint of Sauternes on nose, yet quite dry on palate.

1978 MEURSAULT-CHARMES, RENÉ MONNIER:

Elegant, toasty, almond nose. Round, fairly high acidity. Not a big or luscious wine, but elegant and well made.

Château Lynch-Bages

1955:

Medium-dark colour. Good depth. Spicy, mature, cedar nose. Some fruit, but starting to dry out. Elegant, long, metallic finish, yet flavourful. True Pauillac. Needs drinking. This wine is better in magnums. (17)

1959:

Metallic, iron nose; some complexity. Better on palate than on nose. A bit thin and seems tired. Complex, classy flavours, though. Later, nose became more concentrated, more fruity, and lost some of its metallic impressions. Good quality but not as great as it can be. (17)

1961:

Beautiful, dark, concentrated colour. Tannic, perfectly balanced. Very good fruit, still a bit hard and closed. Long, complex. No rush. This wine will live for many years. Later, opened up in glass. Lovely, long, cedar, cigar-box nose. (18.5) As great as when tasted 24 hours ago!

1962:

Lighter than all above, but still good depth. Open, mature, round nose. Light, elegant, slightly acidic. Very nice drinking now. Not much future. Later, nose dried out. (16.5)

1964:

Mature, browning colour. Open, soft, forward, cedar nose. Acidic, thin, hard. Over-the-hill. (12)

1966:

Deep colour. Complex, long; tannic, yet mature. Similar to last night's tasting. Typical, austere 1966: hard, yet mature. I found the 1961 better. The 1966 is slightly high in acidity. (16.5)

1970:

Very deep, dark, purplish colour. Closed, spicy, concentrated nose. Full, rich, tannic, loaded with ripe fruit. Well balanced. Lovely bottle, needing another five to ten years. Will be great by 1990 to 1995. (18.5)

1971:

Chaptalized nose; sweet and closed. Medium, mature colour; orangy-brown rim. Soft, forward. High acidity. Similar to last night's experience, but even shorter and disappointing. (13.5)

1975:

Very dark, deep colour. Concentrated, young, fruity nose. Full, well-balanced; good, ripe fruit. Tannic, needing ten years. Will be a very good wine. Promising. (17.5)

1979:

Dark colour. Vegetal, cedary, spicy on nose. Young and fruity. Fairly tannic. Needs five to seven years. Well structured. (16.5)

1981:

Slightly stemmy, vegetal. Lean, medium-bodied. Well balanced. Drink from 1989 onward. Fruit, spices in harmony. (16.5)

1982:

Full, rich, round. Good depth, acidity, ripe tannins. Well balanced. Needs seven to ten years. Very promising. Luscious, youthful. (18)

Two vertical tastings of Château Lynch-Bages in two days!! Harry Waugh and Bipin Desai suggested I write a book on Lynch-Bages.

April 24, 1985

Lunch and dinner with Joe Heitz in Yountville.

First, we met at the winery and tasted his 1980 Cabernets with Alice, his son David, and daughter Kathleen.

1980 HEITZ CELLARS CABERNET SAUVIGNON, NAPA VALLEY:

Light colour. Pleasant, spicy, minty nose. Medium-bodied. A bit thin, but pleasant, clean, and almost ready. (15.5)

1980 HEITZ CELLARS "BELLA OAKS," NAPA VALLEY:

The most complex and elegant at this stage. Medium-deep colour. Lovely, complex, sweet, cedary, open nose. Medium-bodied, elegant, well balanced. Needs three more years, but enjoyable now. Fine wine. (17)

1980 HEITZ CELLARS "MARTHA'S VINEYARD," NAPA VALLEY:

Much darker, deeper-looking. Closed, spicy, sweet nose. Big, hard, tannic, and needs at least four to six more years. Dry, hard, masculine wine. Promising. (17.5)

Later that day

Lunch at "La Belle Helène" in St. Helena, with Joe, Alice, and Kathleen.

HEITZ CELLARS 1975 PINOT CHARDONNAY, NAPA VALLEY:

At its peak. Deep gold. Complex, lovely, oaky, fruity, mature nose. Thick, creamy, good acidity, but showing signs of getting tired. Still very good and complex.

1980 ST. CLEMENT CABERNET SAUVIGNON, NAPA VALLEY:

(I chose this from the wine list.) Deep colour. Long, austere. Needs two to four more years. Very good quality. St. Clement belongs to Dr. Casey, whom I met Sunday night at the Lynch-Bages dinner in San Francisco.

That evening

Dinner with Joe and Alice Heitz.

I brought cheeses and lovely chocolate truffles. We spent a quiet evening together. Joe opened two fabulous 1970 Cabernets: Heitz Cellars "Martha's Vineyard" and Beaulieu Vineyards Georges de Latour "Private Reserve." Two great classics. Served double-blind. Joe had a mischievous grin on his face when he poured them, but not for long. After a few minutes, and after tasting the wines, I told him that they were Beaulieu Vineyard and "Martha's Vineyard," possibly 1968 or 1970. He wasn't amused!

1970 BEAULIEU VINEYARDS GEORGES DE LATOUR "PRIVATE RESERVE" CABERNET SAUVIGNON, NAPA VALLEY:

Dark, deep colour. Showed more maturity, great depth, complexity. Well balanced. Long, complex, ready, but no rush. Good length, Chocolaty, spicy on both nose and palate. Elegant, fine wine, with the classic American oak/vanilla character so typical of this property. (18.5)

1970 HEITZ CELLARS "MARTHA'S VINEYARD," CABERNET SAUVIGNON, NAPA VALLEY:

A bit more edgy. Spicy, eucalyptus nose that is typical of this wine. Sharper, harder, younger-looking, needing three to four more years to round up a bit. Very fine, but tonight I preferred the Beaulieu Vineyards. (18)

Joe talked me into trying these Cabernets with chocolate truffles; it wasn't bad, but still isn't a very good match! Then, he served (also double-blind) the most fabulous scotch I have ever tasted; actually, I thought it was a fine Cognac. When I told him that I thought it was a very fine Cognac, he exclaimed: "Goddamn it. I finally got you!"

MACALLAN SINGLE MALT SCOTCH WHISKY

(25 years old): Deep, dark colour. Lovely oak. Fine Cognac complexity. Full, rich, long, great creamy concentration. A fabulous drink. A memorable experience.

The evening was very enjoyable.

May 1985

At Dr. Allan Tobe's on the occasion of Sally Tobe's 50th birthday.

Their son Stuart was there, too.

1961 CHÂTEAU LA LAGUNE:

(Served double-blind) Medium colour. Mature, spicy, complex, slightly green nose (Cabernet Franc). Even a hint of Pinot Noir! Medium, a bit thin, and a bit high in acidity. I thought it was a 1967 or 1964 Haut-Médoc. Allan agreed it was not a typical 1961, (which should be deep, full, jammy, and rich). Sound wine, but not what it should be. The severe frost of 1956 destroyed most of the vineyard of this château. The vines were young in 1961, explaining why the wine was a bit green. Also, as the saying goes, "If it is not a Burgundy, then it must be the 1961 La Lagune!"

1935 COCKBURN'S VINTAGE PORT:

50 years old; 1935 is Sally's birth year. Medium colour, still youthful, like a 1955 or 1958! Lovely, elegant, complex wine on both nose and palate. Round, long, improved in the glass. Elegant and very good; this Port has held very well.

May 23, 1985

Special tasting of rare wines, at my residence.

All wines came from my cellar; 12 participants.

APERITIF

CHAMPAGNE VEUVE CLICQUOT N/V BRUT, IN MAGNUM:

Round, long, complex; good yeast and bubbles. Mature and well balanced. Fine, consistent wine. Has aged in my cellar for three years.

CHÂTEAU PAPE CLÉMENT BLANC 1979:

An extremely rare wine. Only a minute quantity is made. Only 100 cases produced, and not shipped commercially. Clean, crisp, obvious new oak-vanilla. Good acidity, but a bit soft. Long, yet the oak overwhelmed it. Buttery popcorn. Clean Sauvignon Blanc character. An unusual and rare wine.

CLOS DE VOUGEOT BLANC 1978, HÉRITIERS-GUYOT:

Medium-gold colour. Nutty, oaky, Meursault-like. Round, ready, mature, toasty. Still good acidity (almost too high) at the end. A rare experience. Not a great white Burgundy, but actually not bad.

1972 GRANDS ECHÉZEAUX, DOMAINE DE LA ROMANÉE-CONTI:

Medium colour. Mature, orange rim. Lovely, spicy, open, complex nose. Toasty, high acidity, typical 1972. Complex. Ready. Good depth. Very nice wine.

1972 ROMANÉE-ST.-VIVANT, DOMAINE DE LA ROMANÉE-CONTI:

Lightest of the three Domaine de la Romanée-Contis. Complex, elegant, spicy nose. Clean, spicy, mature; rich, toasty oak and fruit. Elegant on palate. High acidity is characteristic of the 1972 vintage.

1972 LA TÂCHE, DOMAINE DE LA ROMANÉE-CONTI:

Darkest of the bunch, yet not too dark. Beautiful balance. Great complexity and length. Will last for a few years. Classic raspberries and toasty oak on both nose and palate.

These 1972s are turning out to be beautiful wines. Of the three, the La Tâche was the most outstanding. The Romanée-St.-Vivant was the most disappointing in the context and the softest. Overall, the quality was high and the La Tâche was outstanding.

1955 CHÂTEAU PICHON-LALANDE:

Elegant, cedary, mature nose. Forward, elegant on palate, too. A bit herbaceous, very soft, forward. A bit too soft, but good length and complexity. Typical style of the vintage.

1955 CHÂTEAU CANTEMERLE:

A bit darker, deeper, more concentrated and solid than the Pichon-Lalande. Not as elegant as the above, but deeper, bigger, and better structured. Both classy and lovely wines.

1952 CHÂTEAU LATOUR:

Deep, yet mature colour. Complex, intense, mature Cabernet and cedar on nose. Full, rich, round on palate. Finally, this wine is coming around! Great complexity, length, and class. Very fine quality, but still has the leanness of this slow-maturing vintage.

1937 CHÂTEAU CAILLOU, SAUTERNES:

Very good level well into neck. Deep-gold colour. Some sediment. Lovely botrytis nose. Full, round, mature, perfectly balanced. Lovely fruit, acidity, and length. Great complexity, not unlike a 1959. A rare and most enjoyable experience. Good fruit, yet obviously mature. At 48 years, this wine has held very well.

1963 DOW'S VINTAGE PORT:

Being opened at the last minute, this wine was a bit hard, yet it had good complexity, length, and spicy character. Very enjoyable, but not ready. Try around 1992 to 2000.

May 27, 1985

Dinner at home with Bruce Guimaraens, part-owner and winemaker at Fonseca's and Taylor's Ports, who stayed with us.

In the afternoon, Bruce and I tried the following wines.

1977 BURGESS CHARDONNAY "WINERY LAKE VINEYARD," NAPA VALLEY:

Very disappointing and over-the-hill. Deep brown-gold colour. Madeirized, dried out, and woody. Dead!

1977 ZD CHARDONNAY, CALIFORNIA:

Medium-deep golden colour. Complex, buttery, slightly vegetal on nose. Long, round, elegant on palate. At its peak; this wine has rounded up very nicely over the years. Very good. In its youth, it was very harsh and herbaceous, but it has improved tremendously.

With dinner, we had the following.

CHAMPAGNE RENÉ LALOU BRUT 1973:

Elegant, complex, mature, yeasty nose. Tiny bubbles. Creamy, soft, but getting tired and showing signs of oxidation. Complex, but losing its fruit. Needs drinking.

1979 CHÂTEAU GRILLET:

Bruce had never heard of this wine or the grape varietal (Viognier) before. Delicate, complex nose. Crisp, yet round, slightly lemony (typical of northern Rhône whites). Delicate, long, and elegant. At its peak.

1978 Corton-Charlemagne "Diamond Jubilee," Remoissenet:

Typical of this shipper. Elegant, complex, nutty, long, and reaching its peak. Very well balanced, no rush. Fine quality. A classic wine.

1978 Merlot "Three Palms Vineyard," Napa Valley:

The first Merlot released by Duckhorn, and a prizewinner. Rare and expensive. Deep, maturing colour. Complex, sweet Merlot nose. Full, round, long on palate. Some sediment. A bit tannic. Almost at its peak, but will hold there for two to four more years. Fine bottle.

1971 Château Beychevelle:

One of the more successful 1971 Clarets. Round, mature, soft, at its peak. Good Cabernet spice and complexity. Delicate. Very good wine.

1966 Spanna "Montalbano," Vallana:

Made in Piedmont from the Nebbiolo grape. Deep, mature colour. Fair bit of sediment. Rich, full, heavy. Good, mature, full, rich, Barolo style. A new experience for Bruce.

Robert Mondavi 1978 Johannisberg Riesling "Botrytis" TBA, Napa Valley, in half-bottle:

(20° residual sugar) Deep-gold colour. Lovely, delicate, peaches, botrytis, fruity nose. Good acidity. Delicate, round, long, and exquisite.

A very entertaining evening. I tried to serve wines that I knew Bruce wasn't familiar with. I think that he has enjoyed himself.

June 20, 1985

Commanderie de Bordeaux vertical tasting of Château Lynch-Bages 1953 to 1982, at the Engineers Club, in Vancouver.

The third vertical tasting of the fine property I have participated in, in the past six months! I was the guest speaker.

1982:

Very deep, intense colour. Lovely, warm, round, mature, ripe nose. Full, round, rich on palate. Good length; not too tannic. Great fruit extract and concentration. Very fine potential. Just bottled last year. Drink in ten to 15 years. (18)

1981:

Dark colour, but lighter than the 1982. Herbaceous, vegetal nose. Some spice and depth. Leaner, greener style, a bit raw at this stage. Needs time. High acidity. Good aftertaste. Try around 1990 to 1995. (16.5)

1979:

Good, dark colour. Closed nose. Some spice; touch of green. Pleasant round wine, typical of the year. A bit one-dimensional, but nice. Needs three to five years. Clean aftertaste.(16)

1978:

Similar appearance to the 1979, yet without the depth of the above. Leaner, more vegetal on nose. Sharper, leaner, higher acidity, without the ripe fruit of the 1979. Harder, more tannic, too. Short, acidic finish. Needs five years. Not sure about its future. Lacks ripe fruit. Certainly not one of the better efforts of this fine property. (14.5)

1975:

Deepish, maturing colour; pale rim. Ripe, chocolaty, toasty nose. Typical hardness and tannins of the 1975 but backed by ripe fruit. No excessive acidity (as opposed to the 1978). Good length. Needs six to eight years. (17.5)

1970:

Deeper colour than the 1975, almost to rim. Fabulous, intense, ripe fruit on nose. Spices, cedar, and length. Still very tannic. Full, rich, round. Big, yet perfectly balanced. No rush. A luscious wine. (18.5)

1966:

Austere, mature Cabernet; classy, elegant, and round. Cedary, full, austere, masculine. Typical 1966. Fairly hard, but excellent length. At its peak; will not improve. Fairly high acidity. (17)

1962:

Deeper colour with a touch of bright red; typical of the 1962s. Lovely, open, chocolaty nose. Complex, elegant, round, soft, forward. Low fruit, high acidity. At its peak. Actually declining. Was better when tasted earlier this year. (15)

1961:

Brighter red, but has same deep colour as the 1966. Intense, concentrated, cedary nose. Great length. Solid, closed, concentrated, hard, tannic. Well balanced with lots of ripe fruit. Needs three to five years. Excellent quality. (18)

1959:

Deep, maturing colour. Plummy, rich nose. Ripe fruit: prunes and raisins. More forthcoming than the 1961. Lovely complexity. Ripe, rich, great length. Fabulous; at its peak. (18.5) I hope that, some day, the 1982 will turn out like this. This 1959 was far superior to the examples tasted last January.

1957:

Austere, toasty nose; similar to the 1966. Dark, mature colour. Round, elegant on entry, but hard finish, tannic, and some acidity. Good length; clean, well structured, if a bit on the hard side. One of the successes of the vintage. (17)

1953, LONDON-BOTTLED BY BARTON ET GUESTIER:

Dark, evolved colour, excellent for the vintage. Mature rim. Complex, ripe, round nose. Round, chocolaty. Soft and ready. High acidity. Drink up. Good length and aftertaste. (18)

June 1985

1982 red Bordeaux tasting, at the Liberty Wine Shop, in Bellingham, Washington State.

These wines have just arrived, and have been in bottle for only a few months.

1. 1982 CHÂTEAU GLORIA, IN MAGNUM:

Dark, purplish colour; palish rim. Slightly stemmy, herbaceous nose. Hot, rich. Too herbaceous. A bit thin. Lacks the ripeness typical of this vintage. (14)

2. 1982 CHÂTEAU HAUT-BATAILLEY:

Deep colour, purplish rim. Oak, spice flavours. Middle-weight. Good length. Clean, good aftertaste. Flavourful. Needs five to seven years. (16.5)

3. 1982 CHÂTEAU HAUT-BAGES-LIBÉRAL:

Very deep, purplish colour to rim; slight hint of maturity. Full, rich, long; quite tannic and intense. A mouthful. Not very complex, but great concentration. A bit edgy at this stage. Loaded with fruit. Needs ten years. (17)

4. 1982 CHÂTEAU GRAND-PUY-LACOSTE:

Dark purplish colour. Lovely, young ripe, complex Cabernet and cedar on nose. Hard, very tannic, intense. Unyielding at this stage. Great potential, but needs 15 years or more. Rich, long, powerful aftertaste. Great fruit underneath. One to buy! (18.5)

5. 1982 CHÂTEAU LYNCH-BAGES:

Dark, dense, purplish colour. Lovely, spicy, cedary, complex, long nose. Not as massive at #4, but full, round, riper tannins. Elegant, very good length. Needs ten years. (18)

6. 1982 CHÂTEAU PICHON-BARON:

Deep colour, slight maturity at rim. Unyielding, ripe nose. Very nice flavours. Medium-deep, open, elegant. Complex, not massive, but very well structured and has great length. Needs eight to ten years. (17)

7. 1982 CHÂTEAU LANGOA-BARTON:

Deep, intense colour; purplish tint. Ripe fruit, round. Closed. A bit green, but good fruit. Quite high acidity, well structured, but simple at this stage. Lacks the complexity of the Pichon-Baron. A bit sharp with a green finish. May improve. (15.5)

8. 1982 CHÂTEAU FIGEAC:

Deep colour, slightly mature rim. Complex, delicate, spicy, vegetal St. Emilion nose. A mouthful of flavours. Well balanced, full, round, long; great complexity. Good ripe tannins. Needs seven to ten years. Fabulous. (18.5)

9. 1982 VIEUX CHÂTEAU CERTAN:

Medium-dark colour; lighter than all above, yet still quite dark. Closed, toasty nose. Rather leaner, greener wine, without the depth of the Figeac. Short finish. Green, acidic. Not bad. May improve with a few years of bottle-ageing. Drink 1989 to 1994. (16.5)

10. 1982 CHÂTEAU LA CONSEILLANTE:

Medium-deep colour, similar to the Vieux Château Certan. Concentrated, closed, ripe nose. Big, rich, round, austere, tannic. A bit tight finish at this stage. Should improve. Later, opened up a bit. Fabulous potential. (18)

11. 1982 CHÂTEAU MONTROSE:

Medium-dark colour. Spicy, tight Cabernet nose. Spirity. Very good, austere wine. Full, hard, tannic, rich, big, unyielding. Needs ten to 12 years, or more. Very good potential. (17)

12. 1982 CHÂTEAU COS D'ESTOURNEL:

Deep, purplish colour to rim. Lovely, complex, ripe Cabernet nose. New oak. Great length, yet full, hard, tannic. A great sleeper. Opulent, even at this early stage. Great potential. (18.5)

13. 1982 CHÂTEAU HAUT-BRION:

Medium-deep, purplish colour. Lovely, complex, rich, ripe nose. Fabulous. Delicate complexity. Elegant new oak-vanilla. Perfectly balanced. An elegant mid-term wine. Great length. Drink 1992 to 1998. (18.5)

14. 1982 CHÂTEAU CHEVAL-BLANC:

Medium-deep, purplish colour; slightly lighter than #13. Baked, rich nose; hint of dill (Cabernet Franc). New oak flavours. Warm, rich, very full mouthful. High alcohol. Like the 1947! Rich, complex, great length. Needs at least ten to 12 years. Great future. (19.5)

15. 1982 CHÂTEAU MARGAUX:

Darker colour than #13 or #14. More depth. Incredible, ripe, mature, complex, long nose. Fabulous mouthful. New oak-vanilla. Delicacy, very good length. Great complexity and potential. Needs ten to 15 years. Absolutely fabulous. (19.5)

16. 1982 CHÂTEAU LAFITE:

Even deeper colour than the Margaux! Ripe, intense, yet elegant Cabernet cedary nose; touch of greenness, but ripe. Great nose! (Not quite as nice as the Margaux, though.) Lovely new oak and great length on palate. Rich, round, complex, delicate (above all). What a wine! Needs ten to 15 years. (19.5)

17. CHÂTEAU LATOUR:

Deeper than #15 or 16! Surprisingly open nose for Latour; chocolaty, spicy, masculine, though. Not quite the classy nose (at this stage) of #13 to #16. Needs time. Full, rich, long, ripe, chocolaty on palate. Good tannins. Great length. Needs ten years, but not as massive as the 1970 was in its youth. Not quite as complex as the other First Growths at this stage, but great potential. (19)

18. 1982 CHÂTEAU MOUTON-ROTHSCHILD:

Lovely, spicy, exotic, ripe nose. Very dark colour, but not quite as dark as the Latour. Essence of Cabernet. Full, very intense, great length, lovely structure. Needs 20 years, or more. Fabulous, with new oak, vanilla, and ripe fruit in harmony. An absolute classic! (20)

Overall impression of these 1982s

Deep colours; ripe, intense fruit and tannins. Maybe low acidity, but the fruit may hide good acidity. At least as good as 1970, and maybe like 1959 or 1947. Lovely wines. How great will they really be? Time will tell. If they turn out to be as good as the 1959s, I will dance in the streets!

July 17, 1985

Back in Vancouver, a "surprise" tasting, at Tony Gismondi's, on the occasion of my 40th birthday.

With Sid Cross, Allan Tobe, Kostie Killas, Alastair Carruthers, John Levine, Ian Mottershead, Bill Murray, and Stuart Tobe. I was really surprised and did not suspect anything until I got there. Each participant brought a bottle along. All wines were served double-blind.

1952 CORTON-CHARLEMAGNE, REINE PEDAUQUE:

(Sid Cross's bottle) Deep-gold colour. Slightly madeirized. Dry, over-the-hill, tired. High acidity, no fruit. Lemony (like an old white Rhône, which is what I thought it was at first). Later, I said: "Maybe a very old Corton-Charlemagne that has lost its fruit." Poor and dead.

1970 ROBERT MONDAVI "UNFILTERED" NAPA CABERNET SAUVIGNON:

(John's bottle) Deep colour; slightly orangy rim. At first, obviously California Cabernet. Minty, eucalyptus. Later, spicy, straw, and dill. Good fruit. A bit short at the end. Still lovely and an experience. Good ripeness. This was Robert Mondavi's fourth vintage.

1972 GRAND ECHÉZEAUX, DOMAINE DE LA ROMANÉE-CONTI:

(Allan and Tony's bottle) Mature red colour. Complex, spicy Pinot Noir nose with hint of beet sugar. Round, complex, forward, with the acidity of the 1972s. Classy Pinot Noir; black fruit, hint of oak. Will last well, at least until 1995.

1961 BARBARESCO, ANGELO GAJA:

(Allan's bottle) The nose of a mature Pauillac or St. Estèphe. Like a 1955 or 1957, yet hot, alcoholic, tannic (surprising for the palish colour). I thought that it was an old Claret. Yet, I wondered about the tannins being there. Complex, lovely nose. I guessed the origin and right age of the Mondavi and the Grand Echézeaux, but I was totally wrong about the Gaja.

1945 CHÂTEAU HAUT-BAILLY, GRAVES,SHIPPED BY BARTON ET GUESTIER:

Cork read: "Mise au Château." Purchased by Tony and Bill. Clean, bright colour. Complex, classy nose. Round, full, tannic; great complexity. No rush drinking it. I thought that it was a 1961 Pauillac! Lovely bottle of Claret. Very well balanced and fabulous. My birth year, of course.

1945 CHÂTEAU LEOVILLE-LASCASES, CHÂTEAU-BOTTLED:

(Ian's bottle) A bit dense, cloudy colour; it was shaken a bit before it got there. Lovely, fruity complex nose. Good fruit, great depth, and absolutely loaded with tannin. Because of that, I said "1945." I also said that it was a Pauillac or St. Estèphe or St. Julien, with high proportion of Cabernet Sauvignon. Lovely bottle, but I preferred the Haut-Bailly, which had more class.

CHÂTEAU SUDUIRAUT 1962:

(Alastair's bottle) Deep-gold colour. Lovely, delicate, complex, mature Sauternes on nose. At first, I thought it was d'Yquem, but it wasn't intense enough for that. Later, I said: "a 1955 or 1962." Great length and complexity. At its absolute peak and very flavourful. Lovely botrytis.

1945 SANDEMAN'S VINTAGE PORT, OPORTO-BOTTLED:

(Kostie's bottle) Glossy, bright, medium-red colour. Good depth. Spirity, elegant, leaner rather than sweeter style. Complex, but not the Sandeman's style. Fairly high alcohol.

Overall

A very pleasant surprise and great wines (except for Sid's 1952 Corton-Charlemagne).

Late July 1985

International Wine and Food Society Dinner, celebrating Haskell Norman's 70th Birthday, at the Stanford Court hotel, in San Francisco.

APERITIF

CHAMPAGNE BOLLINGER BRUT "RD" 1975, IN DOUBLE-MAGNUMS:

Disgorged only three months ago. 70% Pinot Noir and 30% Chardonnay in the blend. Elegant, yeasty, complex, long. Very good, although some bottles seemed more flat than others. The best bottles were fruity, rich, with fine fruit extract and acidity, typical of this fine vintage.

In Champagne, as in Burgundy, double-magnums are actually called jeroboams. In Bordeaux, on the other hand, a double-magnum is just that, while a jeroboam is the equivalent of six bottles. This mixes some people up, especially when buying at auction.

1977 "Y," DRY WINE OF CHÂTEAU D'YQUEM:

Seemed slightly sweeter than the 1979 tasted several times recently. Complex, rich, long bouquet of sauternes. Much drier, yet with a touch of sweetness and botrytis. Quite complex, but too rich for me.

1971 MONTRACHET "BARON THENARD," REMOISSENET:

First bottle was corked and musty. Second bottle better: complex, but a bit tired and not as rich or full as this wine should be. OK, but not great.

1971 CHABLIS GRAND CRU "LES CLOS," DOMAINE ROBERT VOCORET:

Complex, long, full, good fruit/acidity balance, but lost its Chablis crispness and character. Overall, I disagree with the French as to when to drink their wines, but as far as Chablis is concerned, I think that waiting too long regardless as to how good it is, Chablis tends to lose its flinty character and crispness. Having said that, the French (in general) drink their wines, and especially their Champagnes, too young.

1961, 1962, 1964, 1971, and 1976 La Tâche, Domaine de la Romanée-Conti, in jeroboams.

A jeroboam is equivalent to four regular-size bottles. Rare and very expensive. Each of these bottles today costs $1,500 or more, each!!!

1961:

Medium colour. Complex, spicy, fairly hard, full. Needs another four to five years to mature. Not too dark, showing some maturity. While very good, it doesn't have the sheer extract, concentration, and class of this wine's 1959, 1962, or 1964 vintage. (17.5)

1962:

Complex, open, round, elegant, spicy, nose. Classic raspberries, too. Sweet ripe fruit. At its peak. Bright colour. Very nice; actually a lovely bottle. (18)

1964:

A bit cloudy and dense colour (some sediment got into the wine). Medium colour. More brown than the 1961 or 1962. Forward, elegant, yet simple. Not bad. I rated this wine (16.5), but it can be great. Regular-size bottles are a lot better than this.

1971:

Definitely the best of all five. Deep, bright, young-looking colour. Full, spicy. Long, rich, and tannic on palate. Needs ten years in jeroboam. Full, luscious Pinot Noir; long and lovely. A classic. (19)

1976:

Lighter and more tired-looking than the 1971; brown-orange. Sweet, baked nose. Open. Soft, sharp, short, and the simplest of the bunch. Disappointing. (16)

Then we tasted one of my all-time favourite Sauternes.

CHÂTEAU SUDUIRAUT 1959:

Deep gold colour. Full, rich, yet not overwhelming on either nose or palate. Great length, lovely balance, good fruit and acidity. Fabulous botrytis. A great classic! Not as cloying as a 1967 d'Yquem, but as good, if not better. (19)

1934 ARMAGNAC "AVERY'S SPECIAL SELECTION":

Deep gold, wood colour. Complex, woody nose. Sharper and harder than a fine Cognac, but long and complex. Very smooth.

All in all

A great evening. As is so often the case, Dr. Haskell Norman, our chairman, pulled it off again.

August 1985

Vertical tasting of Corton-Charlemagne, Louis Latour, at home.

15 participants. All the wines for tonight's tasting are from my cellar.

1. 1982:

Medium-gold colour. Buttery, oaky, toasty nose. A bit closed, yet round. Forward, high alcohol, but pleasant fruit. Disappointing for such a fine wine. (15.5)

2. 1976:

A bit sharper and more alcoholic than the 1982. Similar colour, if slightly darker. Slightly oxidized. Getting tired. Low fruit. High alcohol. A tired, overripe 1976. (15)

3. 1971:

Deep, bright-gold colour. Complex, concentrated, maturing, long nose. Open and very elegant. Good toast, nutty-oak. Slight touch of sulphur. Round, long, very well structured. However, I was the only taster who placed it first. (18)

4. 1981:

Medium-gold colour, pale rim. Fairly closed, unyielding nose. Appley. Round, delicate, good young fruit, but not nutty. Very different from the others. (15.5)

5. EDNA VALLEY VINEYARD 1980 CHARDONNAY, SAN LUIS OBISPO:

The ringer. Darkest of the lot. Deep, bright gold. Spicy, oaky, nutty, and herbaceous. Some toast. Round, full, rich, long. Not quite as complex as the others at this stage, but promising. Very big and full. Ready. Uncanny nutty complexity, very similar to a Corton-Charlemagne. (17)

Back to the Corton-Charlemagne.

6. 1973:

Medium gold. Lemony, nutty, oak-toast nose. Lovely length. Very well balanced. No rush. Needs one to two extra years, but enjoyable now. Very fine quality. (17.5)

7. 1979:

Medium gold. Nose of fine, mature white Burgundy. Long, complex, delicate. Very typical nose. Good length; full, long. Lovely. Good fruit, acidity. Perfect now. (17.5)

8. 1978:

Touch of sulphur. Citrusy, complex, but a bit closed. Young, rich, powerful, very long. Needs time. Great potential. Needs three to four years. (18)

The difference between 1978 and 1979 was the state of maturity and overall elegance (1979) as opposed to power and concentration (1978).

The Edna Valley Vineyard fooled them all! It was as close to a Corton-Charlemagne as one could get. Each taster, without exception, thought it was a Corton-Charlemagne, and that #4 (the 1981) was the odd-man-out!

September 20 to 23, 1985

A four-day tasting and dinner marathon, in San Francisco.

Drinking "history." Imagine tasting a great bottle of wine that was produced when George Washington was a toddler!

A dream came true in September 1985 when I was invited to participate in a four-day tasting marathon that culminated in a tasting of prephylloxera wines. The tastings were organized jointly by California and German wine collectors and connoisseurs. Most participants (about 30 in number) contributed one or more wines for the occasion.

September 20, 1985

First tasting and dinner, at the Four Seasons Clift hotel, in San Francisco.

APERITIF

CHAMPAGNE PHILIPPONAT "TAILLEVENT" BLANC DE BLANCS 1980:

A lovely bottle. Clean fruit on nose. Elegant, crisp, long; some yeastiness. (17.5)

1976 BÂTARD-MONTRACHET, CORON PÈRE ET FILS:

Tired, lacking fruit, showing signs of oxidation. Disappointing. (14)

FLIGHT #1

A sample tasting of 1920 Clarets (all château-bottled)

1921 CHÂTEAU GRUAUD-LAROSE, IN MAGNUM:

Deep, mature colour with orange rim. Much younger-looking than its age would indicate. Complex, delicate, yet slightly musty on nose. Long, round, and soft on palate; a bit woody. Some fruit left, and surprisingly, some tannin, too. Finished a bit sharp, but quite long. Later, it lost its mustiness and developed a lovely complex nose. Needs drinking, even from magnums. (17.5)

1924 CHÂTEAU LEOVILLE-LASCASES, IN MAGNUM:

Similar in appearance to the 1921 Gruaud-Larose, with slightly paler rim. Delicate, sweet, mushroomy nose. Rounder and not as austere as the Gruaud. Long, complex, and delicate on palate, yet finished a bit oxidized. An elegant wine. A bottle tasted in 1980 at a Heubelein preauction tasting was much better. (16)

1926 CHÂTEAU HAUT-BRION, IN MAGNUM:

Deep, mature colour, not unlike a 1959 or 1961. Buttery-truffles nose. Hard, full, and still tannic on palate, finishing sharp and woody. Prunes and Madeira. Its structure indicates that this wine will last for many years, but will not improve. As with the 1924 Lascases, a bottle tasted in Vancouver in 1983 was much finer and livelier. (16)

1928 CHÂTEAU CALON-SÉGUR, IN BOTTLES:

Darker yet than the 1926 Haut-Brion. Lovely, complex, full nose, typical of fine mature Claret. Fruity, clean, and complex on palate, with very good depth. Elegant, long, yet finished a bit hard. The best "drinking" wine of the flight. Some tasters found it to be a bit too dry and hard, but that is typical of the structure of the 1928s. A classic bottle. (18.5)

1929 CHÂTEAU HAUT-BRION, IN MAGNUM:

Dark, mature colour. Slightly medicinal, woody nose. Hard, full, and tannic on palate, but losing its fruit. A solid wine that will last for a long time, but will dry out. Bigger than the 1926. (17)

The Calon-Ségur, a Third Growth and the only wine served in bottles, was my overall favourite of this flight. This property produced great wines in the 1920s, 1930s, and 1940s.

FLIGHT #2

A sample tasting of the 1940s (all château-bottled)

1945 CHÂTEAU PETRUS, IN MAGNUM:

This magnum was purchased recently at auction at a cost of about US$2,000! Very deep, pruny, thick colour. Sour, spoiled nose, reminiscent of rotting vegetables. Similar impressions on palate. (No score.) How disappointing!

1945 CHÂTEAU TALBOT, IN MAGNUM:

Structured more like a soft 1953, this wine was delicate, round, forward, with a palish colour, but well balanced. Long, clean finish. At its peak and needs drinking. Most enjoyable. (17)

1947 CHÂTEAU CHEVAL-BLANC, LONDON-BOTTLED BY CHRISTOPHER AND CO., IN MAGNUM:

Having tasted this legend three times previously (one château and two London-bottlings), I was able to compare it to my previous experiences. Deep colour. Lead-pencil, iron nose. Sweet, Port-like on palate. Rich, full, big, and intense, even a bit tannic. Fairly high alcohol. Long finish. A star in its own right. Almost too much of a good thing; this wine should be enjoyed by itself rather than accompanied by food. (19)

1947 CHÂTEAU LATOUR, IN MAGNUM:

Vegetal, sharp nose. Volatile and still a bit tannic, with sweet aftertaste. Short and tired, with some sharpness. Disappointing. I have never tasted a really good 1947 Latour. Has anybody? (15)

1947 CHÂTEAU CLOS FOURTET, IN MAGNUM:

Together with the 1947 Cheval-Blanc, the darkest wine of the flight. Complex, clean, long, and well-balanced. At its peak. A lovely bottle and, in my opinion, the best wine of the flight with the exception of the Cheval-Blanc. (18)

This flight was followed by a dinner accompanied by the following wines.

1949 CHÂTEAU LAFITE:

In Marie-Jeanne (equivalent to three bottles and rarely seen). Surprisingly forward, brick-red colour. Delicate, caramel, spicy nose. A bit short and thin, with high acidity. A magnum of this wine tasted in Vancouver last year showed much better. (16.5)

1961 CHÂTEAU AUSONE, IN DOUBLE-MAGNUM:

Fairly deep colour, with the spicy nose of a rich Burgundy or a California Cabernet. Fruity, slightly stemmy, yet typical St. Emilion; the stemminess imparted by the relatively high proportion of Cabernet Franc. Complex, long, well balanced, and surprisingly good for a wine that did not distinguish itself since the mid-1940s and until 1976. One of the best wines of the evening. Better than when tasted numerous times over the years from both bottles and magnums. (18)

1961 CHÂTEAU LATOUR, IN DOUBLE-MAGNUM:

Pity to have opened this wine so early in its life, especially in double-magnum! Not nearly ready. This wine needs at least another decade to reach its peak. Spicy, complex, rich nose. Fairly high alcohol and unyielding at this stage. Closed and chunky. Massive concentration of fruit. Great potential. (19.5)

1961 LA TÂCHE, DOMAINE DE LA ROMANÉE-CONTI, IN MAGNUM:

Medium-mature browning colour. Spicy, open, complex nose. High alcohol, short and somewhat unbalanced. Lacking depth or length. Disappointing. (16)

As years go by, and I experience 1959 and 1961 red Burgundies, it is becoming quite obvious that 1959 was a much finer vintage there than 1961.

WITH DESSERT

1961 TOKAY ASZÚ 5 PUTTONYOS:

Amber colour, madeirized nose. Deep, full, and rich. After the great wines tasted tonight, it was a bit unfair to expect this wine to stand out. It did not. (16)

Saturday Afternoon, September 21, 1985

At Draper and Esquin's, Wine Merchants, with Sid Cross, Paul Pinski, and Bipin Desai.

1959 SCHLOSS VOLLRAD'S RIESLING KABINETT, RHEINGAU:

Very bright, green-gold. Elegant, clean, mature nose. Creamy on entry, but fairly dry finish. Low fruit, but very enjoyable. Has held very well.

Saturday Evening, September 21, 1985

Second tasting and dinner session, at the Stanford Court hotel, in San Francisco.

The subject was 1953, 1959, and 1961 vintages of Châteaux Haut-Brion, Lafite, Margaux, and Petrus (in magnums).

APERITIF

CHAMPAGNE PERRIER JOUËT 1976 "BLASON DE FRANCE," IN MAGNUMS:

Delicate, complex, and yeasty on nose. A bit flabby and mature, with a short finish. Quite nice, but not outstanding. (16.5)

1975 CHÂTEAU HAUT-BRION BLANC:

Buttery, rich, woody nose. Older-looking and tasting than its age would indicate. Buttery, oaky on palate, but low fruit. A few tasters said that this wine needs more time. I disagree. If anything, it has seen better days. There was also some bottle variation, with a few samples a bit livelier, but not by much. (16.5)

FLIGHT #1

The 1953s

1953 CHÂTEAU HAUT-BRION, IN MAGNUM:

Medium-dark, mature colour. Complex, earthy, lead pencil nose. Austere, dry, with touch of acidity. Round and complex, with long tobacco finish. At its peak. Spicy and very enjoyable. (18)

1953 CHÂTEAU LAFITE, IN MAGNUM:

Similar appearance to the Haut-Brion, but slightly paler. Expansive, open, complex, with fine mature fruit on nose. Round, long, elegant, and complex. Very long finish. An elegant wine of great class. At its peak. (19) Lafite really only produced two stars to date (in the first seven decades of the 20th century): the 1953 and the 1959.

1953 CHÂTEAU MARGAUX, IN MAGNUM:

Having tasted this wine several times previously, I expected a great experience. I was not disappointed. Similar appearance to Lafite. At first it had an unyielding, closed nose. Bigger, better structure and more depth than the Lafite. Later, it opened up into an explosion of great complexity. Open, rich, round. Absolutely fabulous. Everything a great Margaux should be. This wine is clearly more forward in bottles, but there is no rush drinking it from magnums. (19)

1953 CHÂTEAU PETRUS, IN MAGNUM:

The darkest of all 1953s tonight. Very good depth. Mature rim. Intense, lead-pencil, spicy Merlot nose. Full, rich, still a bit tannic. Good length and complexity. A solid, beefy wine. Straightforward rather than elegant complexity. Spicy and rich. Essence of Merlot, yet compared to the above three wines, a bit one-dimensional. I prefer the 1952. (18)

FLIGHT #2

The 1959s

1959 CHÂTEAU HAUT-BRION, IN MAGNUM:

Dark colour. Vanilla, complex, elegant, earthy nose. Rich, round, full, and complex on palate. Great length and aftertaste. Chocolate and truffles. At its peak and actually betraying signs of getting tired (slightly sharp finish with hint of excessive acidity). Needs drinking. (18.5)

1959 CHÂTEAU LAFITE, IN MAGNUM:

Elegant, open, complex nose. Spicy, full, very well balanced. Solid and some tannin. This wine is ready in bottles, but needs another four to five years in magnums. A majestic wine. The last great Lafite until 1982. Most backward of all 1959s tasted. (19.5)

1959 CHÂTEAU MARGAUX, IN MAGNUM:

Elegant, open, perfumy Margaux nose. Round, forward, and soft, even in magnums. Showing signs of drying up a bit. Great class and complexity, so typical of this fine property. If you own any, drink it now, or miss the boat! (18)

1959 CHÂTEAU PETRUS, IN MAGNUM:

Deep, mature colour. Spicy, sweet Merlot nose. Full, rich, hard, and a bit tannic. Masculine and austere. Lacks the elegance of above three wines, but it is solid and has great concentration and power. Enjoyable now, but no rush (especially in magnums). (19)

After an hour in the glass, the Margaux clearly showed its age and became sharper. The Lafite developed great concentration and depth. Choosing a winner in this flight was no easy task.

This was followed by a tasting of the same properties, but of the 1961 vintage. This flight was served blind (we knew the wines but not the order in which they were served).

FLIGHT #3

The 1961s

1961 CHÂTEAU LAFITE, IN MAGNUM:

Medium colour, mature-looking. Flowery, caramel, complex nose. Round and elegant on palate, with some tannin. Great length and delicacy, yet structured to last for a few more years. Fabulous bottle. I have tasted this wine several times and have always preferred the 1959, but this 1961 was very good indeed. (18.5)

1961 CHÂTEAU HAUT-BRION, IN MAGNUM:

Deep, dark colour. Concentrated, ripe nose. Classic Claret, with smells of truffles and freshly baked bread. Great depth and concentration. Long and rich on palate. Some tannin. Hints of truffles and chocolate. "Latour" structure. Absolutely magnificent. My favourite of all four 1961s. Ready in bottles, but could use another three to five years and beyond in magnums. (19.5)

1961 CHÂTEAU MARGAUX, IN MAGNUM:

Medium-deep, mature colour with orangy rim. Slightly vegetal, open nose which cleared after a few minutes in the glass. Fairly high acidity, the lightest and most forward of the flight. Elegant, complex finish with very good length. I have tasted better examples of this fine wine. (18)

1961 CHÂTEAU PETRUS, IN MAGNUM:

Darkest of the lot. Rich, big, jammy nose. Round, full, and a bit tannic on palate. Obviously Petrus! 1947 Cheval-Blanc's "cousin." Slight touch of oxidation and very ripe. A few tasters liked it. Others thought it was faulty. Hard to decide on a score for this wine. (18) would be appropriate on this occasion.

I identified the Haut-Brion and the Petrus, but mistook the Margaux for the Lafite. Overall, top quality wines.

WITH THE CHEESE COURSE

1955 ROMANÉE-CONTI, DOMAINE DE LA ROMANÉE-CONTI, IN MAGNUM:

Browning, tired colour. Dry, low fruit, acidic and slightly oxidized. This was disappointing. (15.5)

WITH DESSERT

1955 MOULIN TOUCHAIS, ANJOU:

Made from Chenin Blanc. An elegant, mature dessert wine. Surprisingly fresh. Not much botrytis on nose, but crisp and well balanced. Chenin Blancs from the Loire are quite acidic and require many years to reach their peak. Moulin Touchais 1945, 1947, and even older vintages are drinking very well now. But frankly, this is not my style of wine. (16.5)

WITH COFFEE

COGNAC "RESERVE LAFITE-ROTHSCHILD":

Mature, long nose, but rather sharp on palate. Long, clean finish. A bit too sweet. Not bad.

Sunday Afternoon, September 22, 1985

That afternoon, I moved from my hotel to Paul Pinski's residence.

We had a tasting of various Rödel sardines for lunch and a bottle of the following.

1971 CABERNET SAUVIGNON "OAK CREST VINEYARDS," NAPA VALLEY:

(Produced by Peter and Joan Avenali) Medium-mature colour. Delicate, spicy, mature Cabernet nose. Simple, soft, forward, well balanced and slightly sweet. (16)

Then, I tried some lovely 1934 Armagnac, bottled by Avery's.

Sunday Evening, September 22, 1985

Third tasting and dinner at the Mark Hopkins hotel, featuring a vertical tasting of Château Mouton-Rothschild, from 1962 back to 1928.

APERITIF

CHAMPAGNE LAURENT-PERRIER "GRAND SIÈCLE" 1978:

Elegant, crisp, slightly bitter finish and showing some age. Quite pleasant. (17)

This was followed by one of Louis Latour's masterpieces.

1978 CORTON-CHARLEMAGNE "COMTES DE GRANCEY":

A "king" of Burgundy. Deep, bright gold. Complex oak-toast-nutty nose, so typical of this property. Perfectly balanced. Intense, full, and very long. Not quite ready. Needs another two to three years and will last for a long time.

This was, in my opinion, the best white dinner wine of all four evenings. I recently organized a vertical tasting of this lovely wine (1971 to 1982). The 1978 was the clear winner, followed by the 1979 and the 1971. The 1973 was very good, too but needs drinking. The 1976 was flabby and tired. The 1982 heavy and clumsy and the 1981 disappointing. This 1978 rated (18.5).

This was followed by the vertical Château Mouton-Rothschild tasting.

FLIGHT #1

1962, 1961, and 1959

1962, IN MAGNUM:

Deep-red colour (typical of the 1962s), with hint of maturity at rim. Spicy, minty, complex, open nose. On palate: more concentrated than its appearance and bouquet would indicate. Slightly dry, but lovely, complex, long finish. Fine length and class. (17.5) In their youth, the fine 1962s were practically being given away. With lots of excellent 1961s and 1959s around, nobody really noticed this "supposedly" early maturing, "useful," and abundant vintage. How good they have turned out to be.

1961, IN MAGNUM:

Slightly darker than the 1962. Concentrated, intense, spicy Cabernet and cedar nose. Full, rich, and long, yet quite hard and a bit unyielding. Needs another four to six years to reach its peak (in magnums) and will last for many more. (18.5) I have rated this wine higher on previous occasions.

1959, IN MAGNUM:

Deep colour, mature orangy-brown at rim. Very complex, long nose with hint of eucalyptus and mint. Bordeaux's "Martha's Vineyard." Full, rich, and round on palate. Long, spicy, minty aftertaste. An unusual Claret, but familiar to lovers of fine California Cabernets. A great wine. (19.5)

FLIGHT #2

1955, 1953, 1952

1955, IN MAGNUM:

A more delicate version of the 1959. Good, dark, mature colour and delicate, complex nose. Full and soft, with slightly high acidic finish. Very elegant wine. Magnums may hold for a few more years, but bottles should be drunk up. After a few minutes in the glass, it showed signs of drying up. (17.5)

1953, IN MAGNUM:

Medium, mature-brick colour. Lovely, delicate, complex, long nose. Beautifully balanced. Soft, forward. Rounder and cleaner finish than the 1955. A delicate, feminine, and lovely wine as befits this vintage. Classic. (18.5)

1952, IN MAGNUM:

Medium-dark colour. Rich, warm nose; spicy Cabernet. Harder on palate, with obvious acidity. Sharper finish than the 1955 or 1953. Very enjoyable and typical structure of the 1952 vintage, which produced hard, slow-maturing wines. (17.5)

The three above wines were true examples of their respective vintages and were consistently very good. The 1953 was my favourite.

FLIGHT #3

The 1940s

This flight was served blind (order unknown).

1949, IN MAGNUM:

Deep, mature colour. Lovely, spicy Cabernet nose. Subdued, yet elegant and mature on palate. Clean, round, forward, rich, with good fruit. At its absolute peak. Lovely complexity, yet slightly high acidity. Sweet, ripe, classic Claret. (18.5)

1948, IN MAGNUM:

Good, dark colour. Spicy, cigar-box nose. Round, full, but a bit harsh and tannic. Dry finish, but good flavours and length. Its only fault was obvious sharpness at finish. Again, true to the vintage. (17.5)

1947:

Deep, mature colour. Hard, tannic, yet full and very long. Round, ageing, slightly pruny on palate, with great length. Structured like a solid 1945, which is what I thought this wine was. Enjoyable now or over the next decade. Excellent. (18.5)

1945:

I could not figure out what this wine was. Slightly cloudy, old-looking Claret. Pruny, "off" nose. Similar impressions on palate. Sweet, short, and slightly oxidized. High acidity and hard finish. Seemed tired. This wine was one of the two major disappointments of this four-day event. The other was the magnum of 1945 Petrus. (No score)

One of the German guests, Mr. Hardy Rodenstock, who "discovers" mysterious cellars and rare bottles of wine going back to the 18th century, guessed this wine as being the 1945. Mr. Rodenstock was accompanied by his young sommelier, who did most of the decanting and often whispered into Mr. Rodenstock's ear. How could he have known that this poor bottle was the 1945? Anyway, this German wine collector makes me nervous. I can't quite figure him out. He seems too sleek.

FLIGHT #4

The 1920s

1929, IN MAGNUM:

A historic wine which can sometimes be disappointing at this age, but not this great magnum! Having tasted this wine on two previous occasions, I was needlessly worried. Lovely, mature colour with good depth. Sweet, long mature nose of incredible elegance. Round, fruity, and very long. Slight acidity, which did not take a thing away from this magnificent nectar. A memorable bottle (19.5)

1928, IN BOTTLE:

Lighter colour than the 1929. Pale-orangy rim. Elegant, open, mature nose. Typical 1928 on palate. Fairly hard, still tannic, and acidity at finish. Very good flavour and lingering aftertaste. A very good wine. (18.5)

1924, IN MAGNUM:

Darker than both the 1928 and 1929. Mature, deep brown colour and slightly cloudy. Elegant, delicate, but getting a bit tired. Fairly high acidity. Good length and complexity. This was the first vintage produced by Baron Philippe. Hint of dill and slight oxidation, but still very good. (17)

Other than the disappointing 1945, the wines were of excellent quality, and had the typical Mouton characteristics and were true to the structure of the respective vintages. A great experience.

This tasting was followed by a dinner where the following wines were served.

1959 CHÂTEAU PETRUS, IN DOUBLE-MAGNUM:

Very deep colour with purplish rim. The appearance of a 1978 or even a 1982! On nose: fruity, ripe, very young essence of Merlot. Very well balanced. An outstanding wine requiring another 15 to 20 years (in double-magnums). In fact, it was so young-looking and young-tasting for a 26-year-old wine that some cynics commented that what was in the bottle, while outstanding, could not possibly be 1959! An incredibly great, very young, wine. (19.5) If it is an authentic bottle, it deserves a perfect (20).

1921 CHAMBERTIN "COLLECTION DU DOCTEUR BAROLET," IN MAGNUM:

Brilliant colour of a 1961 or 1966, slightly orangy rim. Full, spicy, earthy nose with touch of sweetness and showing signs of oxidation. Better on palate than on nose. Round, well balanced, long finish. At 64 years of age, this fine Burgundy has held very well. (17)

DESSERT WINE

1976 RAUENTHALER BAIKEN RIESLING TROCKENBEERENAUSLESE, SCHLOSS ELTZ:

Deep, brilliant-golden colour. Complex peaches-apricots on nose. Round, full, forward, with low acidity. At its peak. Very enjoyable, but not a keeper. (17.5)

Monday Afternoon, September 23, 1985

Visit to Dr. Ben Ichinose's home.

The final day's event started with an afternoon visit at the home and cellar of Dr. Ben Ichinose, a renowned wine collector, where we tasted two lovely Champagnes.

CHAMPAGNE BOLLINGER "RD," 1961 AND 1964, IN MAGNUMS:

Both had the wonderful depth, yeasty nose, great complexity and length typical of the Bollinger style.

The 1961 was more mature and forward, but still alive and kicking.

The 1964 was lovely, long, and perfect now.

September 23, 1985

Fourth and final tasting and dinner, at the Bankers' Club, 51st floor Boardroom.

Later that afternoon, we met for our final event which was the "Jewel in the Crown." An extensive tasting of prephylloxera wines. It was an eight-hour affair, divided equally between a tasting and a memorable dinner.

APERITIFS

1904 DORFJOHANNISBERGER, A. KOCH SOHNE, MAINZ:

Deep-amber colour. Sweet, lemon-tea nose. Well balanced and starting to taste like a light Tokai. After a few minutes in the glass, it opened up and developed a lovely flowery nose with some Riesling character. Very enjoyable and quite elegant. (17)

1878 "FINE OLD BROWN SHERRY" (SHIPPER UNKNOWN):

Deep, bright-gold colour. Elegant, clean, Sherry nose. Similar on nose and palate to an amontillado. Full, round, rich, and very long. Great quality. Will last forever. (18)

Then came the oldest wine of the whole event, and the oldest wine I have tasted to date (or will probably ever taste).

1735 TOKAY ESSENCIA:

Formerly owned by the princely family of Bretzenheim (now extinct); the cellar was walled during the Hungarian Revolution of 1849 and rediscovered in 1929. The bottle was full, wide, and had a long, crooked neck. The cork was original, short, narrow, and black. Deep-brown colour; clear and bright. Caramel, spicy nose, with some grapiness. Sweet, with good acidity. Round and rich, not unlike a fine Madeira. Incredible at almost 250 years of age. George Washington was two years old when this wine was produced! The oldest wine I have ever tasted and an unforgettable experience. (20)

1792 MADEIRA (SHIPPER UNKNOWN):

Similar in appearance to the Tokay, but older-smelling, slightly rancid nose. High alcohol, clean aftertaste of mushrooms and truffles. Finished long and nutty. (18)

1832 HERMITAGE (PRODUCER OR SHIPPER UNKNOWN):

Tired tea colour, slightly rancid nose. Smell of a very old Pinot Noir. Flat and no life left in it. No fruit. Dried out and sour. Like chewing old leather. (No score.)

Then came the turn of the Clarets.

1869 CHÂTEAU MONTROSE:

Mature, pale-red colour with orange-brick rim. Nose of very old, delicate Claret. Quite dry on palate, yet it had a sweet aftertaste. A fragile wine, getting tired but still sound. This must have been a fine wine 40 years ago. (17)

1870 CHÂTEAU GRUAUD-LAROSE:

Deeper colour than the Montrose; similar in colour to a 1940s or 1950s Claret. Pleasant, complex, fruity, mature nose. Good length and structure on palate. More lively and younger-tasting than the 1869 Montrose, but a bit sharper and harder. Incredible for a wine that is 115 years old. (17.5) How can one rate history?

1881 CHÂTEAU LATOUR

AND

1874 CHÂTEAU LAFITE:

Both wines have seen better days.

The Latour was produced when the phylloxera was at its peak. Deep-brown colour. Pruny and oxidized on palate. Dried out and very tired. Still drinkable, but just. Must have been a deep, rich wine half-a-century ago. (15)

The Lafite was a brownish, cloudy colour. Madeirized nose. Sour and thin on palate. Delicate finish with cold lemon-tea overtones. Passé. (13)

1887 CHÂTEAU LAFITE:

Pale brown colour. Definitely dead. This wine was made at the height of the phylloxera, too. (No score)

These wines were followed by six masterpieces, all prephylloxera.

1848 CHÂTEAU BELAIR, MARQUIS D'ALIGRE, MARGAUX:

We were fortunate to taste two bottles of this wine. Bright colour of a wine that is a century younger. Spicy complex Cabernet nose; round and elegant. A bit short on palate and slightly high acidity, not unlike a good 1928 or 1957. Solid; lead, iron, and some fruit. May last for another 50 years, but will not improve. After 20 minutes in the glass, it dried out. (17)

1865 CHÂTEAU GRUAUD-LAROSE:

Beautiful, deep, dark colour with incredible depth. Lovely, full, intense, rich, ripe nose. Rich, round, jammy on palate, with great intensity. Very long, ripe, and elegant. Absolutely marvellous. At 120 years of age, this is Claret perfection. Made from good, ripe grapes. An amazing wine. Maximum marks and a memorable experience. (20)

1965 CHÂTEAU LAFITE-ROTHSCHILD:

Mature colour with some orange-brown at rim. Light caramel and sealing wax nose typical of old Lafites. Soft, forward, and elegant on palate, with very good length and complexity. Unfortunately, it was overshadowed by the superb 1865 Gruaud. (18.5)

1858 CHÂTEAU HAUT-BRION:

The colour and appearance of a wine a century younger! Rich, sealing-wax nose typical of prephylloxera Clarets. Mature, leathery Cabernet, with overtones of earth and peat. Well structured and quite intense. Slightly bitter but incredible intensity. This was a controversial wine. Some tasters liked it very much. Others, including myself, found the earthiness and peat flavours overwhelming. (17.5)

Having committed myself to an absolute score of (20)/(20) for the 1865 Gruaud-Larose, I was faced with two wines which were even more extraordinary, almost indescribable.

1878 CHÂTEAU MOUTON-ROTHSCHILD, IN MAGNUM:

Lovely, dark, deep colour, not unlike a 1945 or a 1949. Intense, complex nose; essence of Cabernet. Full, rich, and beautifully balanced. Great length and full of life. Cigar-box and spicy-mint so typical of this property, even at 107 years of age. Absolute perfection. Great, great wine. (20+) out of (20)

1870 CHÂTEAU LAFITE, IN MAGNUM:

From the Glamis Castle Collection. I tasted the 1870 Lafite at a Heubelein preauction tasting in San Francisco in 1980. It was forward, delicate, with caramel on both nose and palate. Long, complex and elegant, but getting tired. This wine, served from a magnum, had a very good deep colour with brown rim (lighter than the 1878 Mouton). Brilliant, lovely, elegant. Ripe, rich nose with marvellous complexity. Full, round, long, and fabulous on palate. What a wine! A perfect masterpiece. (21) out of (20), whether mathematically possible or not!

This wine ended the first portion of the prephylloxera tasting. We then had a short break with this glass.

CHAMPAGNE ROEDERER "CRISTAL" 1979:

Elegant, yeasty, round, and long. Very fine Champagne. (18)

To accompany a lovely dinner, we enjoyed the following wines.

1959 CHÂTEAU LATOUR,

CHÂTEAU LAFITE-ROTHSCHILD,

AND

CHÂTEAU MOUTON-ROTHSCHILD,

all in double-magnums:

All three were superb wines. They varied in style and individual character of the particular châteaux, but all three were great bottles.

1959 CHÂTEAU LATOUR, IN DOUBLE-MAGNUM:

Deep colour, with great cedary, chocolate Cabernet concentration on nose. Tannic, big, and hard, yet very well balanced. A giant of a wine. Needs 15 to 20 years in double-magnums, but how good it will be when it will finally reach its peak! (19.5)

1959 CHÂTEAU LAFITE-ROTHSCHILD,IN DOUBLE-MAGNUM:

The Lafite had a brilliant, deep colour and a very, complex nose. A wine which is both complex and long, with great finesse, and yet is full, powerful, and has a long life ahead of it, especially in large bottles. Touch of cedar, slightly herbaceous. A wine I know very well, and that is as great as it is described by just about anyone who has tasted it. (19.5)

1959 CHÂTEAU MOUTON-ROTHSCHILD, IN DOUBLE-MAGNUM:

The Mouton was just that—Mouton. Brilliant, dark colour. Spicy, minty, cedary, eucalyptus nose. Full, fruity, rich, and round, yet needs another decade to reach its peak. Another very great bottle. (19.5)

WITH THE CHEESE COURSE

1971 LA TÂCHE, DOMAINE DE LA ROMANÉE-CONTI, IN MAGNUM:

Much, much better than the disappointing 1955 Romanée-Conti served on the previous night. Medium-dark colour; orangy, mature rim. Lovely, elegant, complex, spicy Pinot Noir nose. Long, spicy raspberries, elegant, and very complex on palate. On the rare occasions that red Burgundies are great, they are very great. Ready in bottles. No rush drinking it in magnums. (19.5)

Until 1935, "Les Gaudichots" was a vineyard surrounding the original "La Tâche," which was then only one-and-a-half acres in size. In 1935, de Villaine purchased "Les Gaudichots" vineyard, and now it forms an integral part of "La Tâche."

DESSERT WINES

1973 FREEMARK ABBEY RIESLING EDELWEIN TBA, NAPA VALLEY:

The only California wine at these events. Deep, bright-gold colour. Fragrant long nose, peaches and apricots, but not overwhelming. Very good balance, fruit, and acidity. Surprisingly fresh for its age. Great length. Fabulous flavours. No rush drinking this. The best California dessert wine I have tasted in a long time. (18)

1959 CHÂTEAU D'YQUEM:

Deep-gold colour, darker than the 1973 Freemark. Great nose of complex Sauternes, with good botrytis. At its peak. Very well balanced and long aftertaste. D'Yquem, as it should be. (19)

These two great wines were followed by prephylloxera Ports and Madeira.

CIRCA 1750 PORT (SHIPPER UNKNOWN):

Mature Madeira colour, slightly cloudy. Very soft, but still had the unmistakable smell and taste of a Port, even at 235 years of age! Still alive, elegant, and very sound. A bottle of 1908 Cockburn's and a 1917 Croft's tasted recently seemed older than this. (15) as a wine, and (18) for the experience.

1863 FENTON'S PORT:

Bright, deep-gold Madeira colour, yet on palate, it had the spice and complexity typical of old Port. Higher alcohol than the 1750. A bit woody and on the dry side, yet with enough sweetness there. It finished a bit short and alcoholic, not unlike an old Tawny. (17.5)

1851 MADEIRA, SHIPPER UNKNOWN:

Bright, clear Tawny colour. Drier than the two Ports tasted earlier. Cherry-wood-like with very good character. Burnt wood flavours. Good complexity and nutty style. Very fine quality. (18.5)

This flight was followed by two old and rare liqueurs.

1780 HOLLAND GIN:

Bottled in a narrow, tall, square bottle (narrowed at the base), with a tiny cork. Yellow-orange colour. Incredibly long, juniper nose. Complex, round, long, and marvellous. Not at all like present-day gin. Fabulous, long, with a great flavour. If all gin tasted like this, I could become a gin addict! Perfect score. (20) By this time, most of the participants were exhausted and many hardly touched their 1780 gin! So I went from table to table and filled a wine glass with this fabulous liqueur. I had a great time!

1880 BENEDICTINE:

Bottled in a similarly shaped container as modern Benedictine, but with a regular wine cork, thick lead capsule, and ornamental lead leaves around the neck. Light, bright, browning colour. Spicy, unmistakable Benedictine flavours. Not unlike a Chartreuse. Spices, good flavour and length, slightly minty. Very good. (18)

At the last minute, the organizers added a Port.

1945 SANDEMAN'S PORT:

Dark, deep colour. Good length and complexity. Youthful and fresh for its age. A solid Port, but at that stage of the evening, and having tasted irreplaceable masterpieces, nobody really took any time to consider this last wine seriously. (17.5)

Thus ended what was, at least for me, the greatest wine experience to date. Looking out of the window from the 51st floor of the Bankers' Club, I contemplated what I had just experienced. I was very happy to have been fortunate enough to participate at such a memorable event and—at the same time—saddened by the fact that it was over.

Upon my return to Vancouver and after giving my battered liver 48 hours of rest, I had a quiet dinner at home with a bottle of Château Chasse-Spleen 1970. It was very good. It brought me back to earth.

November 11 to 23, 1985

A two-week trip to Bordeaux.

Visit to Château Suduiraut, in Sauternes.

With the régisseur, Mr. Pierre Pascaud. He, too, loves their 1959 and 1967. According to him, the 1975 is ready now. Overall, low opinion on the 1976s. All are ready; not keepers. Sole North American (US) representative is Cobran's.

Pascaud's comments

1984 was a very mediocre vintage. In 1985, there was lots of wine, but no botrytis, like the 1970s. Grapes loaded with fruit. (80% Semillon, 20% Sauvignon Blanc) Alas, a rather straightforward vintage. Ironically, a fine, even a great year for the reds, if elegant and early maturing. On November 12, they were still picking in Sauternes.

We tasted the following.

1983 SUDUIRAUT, FROM BARREL:

Fairly high alcohol, medium-body, medium-pale gold. Good acidity, but not thick or intense enough. He agrees overall about the lack of botrytis in the 1982 Sauternes, but says their 1982 is very good! (better than the 1983). This is turning out to be correct. 1982 Suduiraut is clearly better than their 1983, one of the very top 1982 Sauternes, if not the best.

1982:

Better depth and colour, better nose than 1983. Longer, more typical. Very good. They picked early. Lovely botrytis; rich, complex. Excellent potential.

1982 "CUVÉE MADAME," FROM BARREL:

Made rarely (once in every decade or so). Even bigger than the regular 1982. Deep gold. Long, complex. Lovely, rare wine needing ten-or-more years. There were 25 cases to be shipped to the USA (Cobran's). Château Coutet also produces a "Cuvée Madame."

Pascaud thinks highly of Clos Haut-Peyraguey. He owns his own little vineyard in Barsac, near Climens. Somehow, I can't get excited over Clos Haut-Peyraguey. The 1975 and 1976 are not bad, though.

Afternoon visit to Château Climens, in Barsac.

With Mrs. Janin, we tasted the following wines.

1983:

Will be bottled in late 1986, one-third new barrels. Complex, full, creamy wine. Good length and acidity. Green-gold colour. Promising to be very good.

Their second wine is Château Doisy-Dubroca. They do not make a dry wine. In her opinion, it is atypical of Barsac. Also, now they use 100% Semillon (she said that Sauvignon Blanc loses its character when attacked by botrytis, so what's the use). She raved about the 1985 (contrary to Suduiraut). She said 1985 was as good or better than 1983. I find this hard to believe. Good botrytis, yet good, big, healthy golden grapes, too. 1982 is OK; she compared it to 1975. She likes 1921 and especially 1929 and 1976 Climens. No wonder; these were great years for Climens, as was 1949. It is clearly my favourite Barsac. Very reliable.

November 13, 1985

Visit to Château Malartic-Lagravière, with Jacques Marly.

I spent three hours with him. He lives alone. His wife, a Ricard (Domaine de Chevalier), died a few years ago. He has ten children. One of his granddaughters lives in Israel. Two of his kids lived in Quebec until recently. Marly used to live in Algeria when it was a French Colony. He had a mirror factory there. Several older vintages of Malartic show, on the label, the name of the Château as a reflection, a mirror image.

We tasted the 1984, 1983, and 1982 reds.

1984 BARREL SAMPLE:

Medium-body, elegant, well structured. Four to six years. Not bad, especially for the vintage. A bit hollow and vegetal, though.

1983:

Typical of the property (quite perfumed) and a good 1983. Ten years. Well balanced, long, complex. Good depth, earthy. (16)

1982:

Darker, heavier, thicker. Very good. Ten years. Quite long. The ripeness of the vintage. (17)

Then we tried the 1983 and 1984 whites.

1984:

Very elegant; good acidity, complex. Very good 1984.

1983:

Darker gold, more serious, long, complex.

All his whites are 100% Sauvignon Blanc and see no oak ageing. Very good gravely soil. His Merlot (25%) suffered a lot during the frost of 1985. 25% Cabernet Franc and 50% Cabernet Sauvignon in the blend. He admires Petit Verdot, but there is the usual problem. It's rarely successful because this varietal needs hot and sunny Octobers to ripen properly. He was surprised that I had tasted Château Pape Clément White. He said that the 1980 was great. One-third new barrels for reds, 10% for whites.

1966 Red:

Deep, mature colour. Round, elegant, and long. Well balanced. Not as hard as most 1966s. Very long and enjoyable. (17)

Then we went to the chais, where we tasted these wines.

1985 Cabernet Franc, from barrel:

Promising. He said that they made a very good 1985. Fresh, spicy nose. Good, purplish colour. The elegance, delicate texture of the vintage, yet a bit coarse. About 25% of the 1985 will be Cabernet Franc.

1985 white, from barrel:

I was the first person ever to taste it in barrel, other than himself and the winemaker. Not as forward and flowery as the 1984. More serious. Complex and long. It will be an excellent white. Very good, ripe fruit. Tight, solid. Needs five years. He hopes that his youngest son will take over.

Then we went to the private cellar. He gave me a 1961 and a 1962 Malartic red and a rare bottle of Pape Clément Blanc 1980. He only had five bottles!!

Interesting visit. I learned a lot. In 1983, there was a new label showing a sailing ship, the "Marie-Elizabeth," of which his great grandfather was the captain. Mr. Marly's parrot died recently at age 35. An autopsy showed he died of cirrhosis of the liver; he liked whisky and wine before falling asleep at night! Now, that's a parrot!

Afternoon visit to Domaine de Chevalier.

With Mr. Claude Ricard, (his grandfather owned also Malartic, Lagravière, and Fieuzal), who sold his property to Mr. Olivier and is acting as a manager for another year. (Sold in 1983.) They also suffered a lot from the spring frost, and had to pull up a lot of Merlot vines. Claude Ricard is also an excellent pianist.

1985 (not tasted):

Has almost no Merlot in it.

1984 barrel sample:

Medium colour, quite tannic, medium-bodied, flowery nose. Ready 1989 to 1990. Not bad for the vintage. Domaine de Chevalier usually make elegant, understated reds, not unlike their neighbours at Château Haut-Bailly.

1983, 1982, and 1981

1981:

The lightest (needs four to five years). Medium-body, a bit herbaceous, complex, good finish, but clearly lacks middle. An elegant wine for mid-term drinking. (16)

1982:

Bigger, more austere, closed at this point. Should be very good. (Ricard prefers his 1983 to the 1982.) Rich, full, yet without the intense ripeness of the 1982 Haut-Médocs. (17)

1983:

Excellent wine. Masculine, big, long, complex. Very good future. Needs ten years, but will be excellent. This is clearly better than the 1982. As with the commune of Margaux, it seems that in Graves, the 1983s are more successful than the 1982s, with La Mission Haut-Brion perhaps being the exception. (18)

1984 and 1983 whites:

Made from 70% Sauvignon Blanc and 30% Semillon. As at Malartic, the 1984 was young, elegant, flowery, complex, and will be ready fairly soon. (16) The 1983 white will be a great bottle! Austere, unyielding, great depth. Needs ten years. A must buy! (Whites: 30% new barrels, reds: 50% new barrels.) (18)

Next day

Drove to St. Emilion to visit Château Bâlestard-La-Tonnelle.

Visit with Mr. Jacques Capdemourlin at Château Bâlestard-La-Tonnelle (also owner of Château Cap de Mourlin and Château Rodia, A/C Montagne St. Emilion). A very nice man. He moved in 1964 to the Château (Bâlestard is a beautiful property worth buying). Jacques is the winemaker, too. Presently they are not selling in Canada at all. I tasted all three properties (all 1982, 1983, and 1984).

I also tasted the 1985 Bâlestard, just vinified. Very good potential. All three properties have a high percentage of Merlot (60 to 65%). One-third new barrels yearly.

Jacques has two boys in their teens. His offices are at Cap de Mourlin. His father died in 1981 and he is now the sole owner of the property.

Château Rodier 1984, 1983, 1982:

The 1984 was the simplest of the three. A bit green and vegetal, quite pleasant, and reasonable. The 1983 had good colour; better depth and fruit than the 1984. The 1982: ripe fruit, rich, full-bodied. Ready soon.

Château Cap de Mourlin 1984, 1983, 1982:

The 1984 was the lightest. Needs three to four years. Quite long and pleasant. The 1983 was typical. Complex, long, well structured. The 1982 was fuller, tighter, and of very good quality.

CHÂTEAU BÂLESTARD-LA-TONNELLE:

The 1984 was elegant and nice. (Bâlestard tastes, looks, and is structured more like a Pomerol than a St. Emilion.) Needs four to five years.

Their Merlot did not suffer too much during the frost of 1985. Jacques is worried about the nationalization of properties by the socialist government. The 1983 and 1982 were both excellent, especially the 1982, which was lush, very long, full-bodied, and loaded with ripe fruit. Still quite tannic. Will last well for 15 years.

1983:

A bit more open, yet big and tannic. Both typical of the respective vintages.

I have recently tasted this wine.

BÂLESTARD 1945:

A truly impressive wine that, while tannic, is dark, rich, packed with ripe fruit, and impressively youthful. (18)

Lunch at Château Figeac.

With Thierry and Marie-France Manoncourt and three of their four daughters. First I went for a long walk with Blondie, one of their daughters. One of the hills is called "L'Enfer" (Hell): gravely soil, very hot in summer and workers used to work there barefoot!

The reason rose bushes are planted at end of rows of vines is that roses are prone to the same diseases as the vines, but roses are infected earlier; thus they warn the grower!

With lunch

1983 FIGEAC:

Typical Figeac, complex nose, new oak, not very big, but beautifully balanced, spicy, and herbaceous. Promising. (16.5)

1975 FIGEAC:

Similar comments to my own bottles. Ready now and lovely. This is one of the better 1975s, and together with Cheval-Blanc, the best St. Emilion of that hard vintage. The tannins are softening up; the fruit is lush and lovely. Long, cedar, and spicy fruit on palate. (17.5)

Then he offered a Cognac, which was given to him in Normandy.

COGNAC CIRCA 1850:

Surprisingly young, lovely bouquet, quite round. Not as dry as some old Cognacs.

Afternoon visit to Château La Conseillante.

With the Maître de Chais. He compared the 1985 to 1947.

1985:

Full, rich, and round. Excellent depth. Well balanced, long and quite good. Full, typical Pomerol. (17.5)

1984:

Quite good, but leaner and lighter. Needs four years. Good, but not great. (15)

La Conseillante and Vieux Château Certan make leaner, more herbaceous Pomerols, as the proportion of Cabernet Franc is quite high. In most other top Pomerol properties (l'Evangile, Lafleur, Petrus, and Trotanoy, for example), Merlot is the dominant varietal, producing lush, fat, richer wines.

November 15, 1985

Visit to Château l'Evangile, where I met old Mrs. Ducasse, the widow of Mr. Ducasse.

They had two robberies in September: over 200 cases (mostly 1975s) were stolen from their cellars. Pity. l'Evangile 1975 is a great wine. As elsewhere, the 1985 is very good (I did not taste it). We tasted the 1982 and 1983.

1982:

Excellent. Typical structure of the 1982s: deep, full, long, great potential. Needs ten to 15 years. Will be great. (18.5)

1983:

Slightly lighter, quite tannic, similar structure as the 1975. Also excellent and great future. Leaner style of the 1983s. Possibly the best Pomerol in 1983. (17.5)

Both the 1982 and the 1983 are "must buys" for lovers of Pomerol. They produced very little 1984. She told me that Mr. Thienpont, owner of Vieux Château Certan, died recently, and that his gifted nephew Alexandre had taken over the management of that estate. The family is originally from Belgium.

Visit to Château Canon.

Eric Fournier was out of town. I met Mr. Cazenaves, maître de chais (his first vintage there was 1947 and he also worked for a while for Moueix). As elsewhere, 1985s matured late. What everyone thought would be a small harvest turned out to be as large as 1983. Also, very good quality. As good, if not better, than the 1983. Usually they have 45% to 60% new oak barrels, depending on the vintage.

Mr. Cazenaves knows John Carpenter (the Wine House). He asked Eric what to open for me. Eric told him: "Whatever, he's tasted them all!"

I tasted the following Canon wines.

1982:

Outstanding. Typical depth, length and concentration. (18)

1981:

A bit lighter, elegant, quite long. Typical St. Emilion (predominantly Cabernet Franc) rather than the 1982, which, in St. Emilion, behaves more like a Pomerol.

1983:

The elegance rather than truffles/mushroom taste of the 1982. More herbaceous, but it worried me a little. Too light. Elegant, perfumy, flowery, well balanced. Reserve judgement. (16.5)

1984:

Not a failure. Quite good, for early drinking.

Upon my request, he opened this wine.

CHÂTEAU CANON 1961, IN HALF-BOTTLE:

Better than the 1961 in full-bottles tasted last Thursday in Vancouver. This half-bottle had good colour, concentration, and fine bouquet. Finished a bit nervous. Needed more time airing. Would have been excellent a bit warmer or with food. (17.5)

Cazenaves thinks that various St. Emilion wines should be tasted separately, based on the composition of the soil (area tastings). He likes vintage Port. Says that Belgian-bottlings are especially tricky and unreliable.

Lunch and tasting at Château Pavie.

With Mr. and Mrs. Valette. I spent over four hours there. They also own Château Pavie-Decesse (since 1971) and Château Cluzeau (also a St. Emilion).

Old vines. At Pavie, the average age of the vines is 40 years. A plot of Merlots is over 100 years old and still producing. Very good drainage, some gravel and soil, but mostly rock. Yet some roots grow very deep. They have very impressive cellars dug deep in the rock (same as at Ausone). Definitely worth visiting. I had lunch with his wife (who has a wine shop in St. Emilion) and daughter and son.

With lunch, we tasted the following wines.

PAVIE-DECESSE 1981 AND 1966

AND

PAVIE 1971:

All were quite good.

The Pavie 1971 is soft and forward. Perfect now. (17)

The 1981 Pavie-Decesse needs three to four years and the 1966 is as good as the 1971 Pavie.

Later, we tasted the 1983, 1982, 1981, 1980 Pavie and Pavie-Decesse. All typical to the vintages. Pavie 1982 very good. 1983 quite good. They think that their 1985 is very promising.

Before I left, Mr. Valette (who started managing the property in 1971 after a few years in Chile where he was in the wood industry), gave me a magnum of 1966 Pavie to take back to Vancouver. A very generous gift and a most pleasant visit.

Saturday, November 16, 1985

Visit to Château Gilette.

In the evening, I drove to Preygnac in Sauternes for dinner with Christian and Andrée Medeville, owners of Château Gilette, Château Les Justices, and a recently acquired red Graves property (some white made, too) called Château Respides-Medeville. I arrived early for a tasting and visit of the chais. We were later joined by Mr. and Mrs. Le Melletier of the Grand Conseil du Vin de Bordeaux, and Chantal and Albert Vuillier, owners of Château Rieussec.

In the chais (and a very nice tasting-reception room), we tasted the following.

LES JUSTICES 1982:

Moelleux; long, full and rich. A very good "lesser" Sauternes. Will be bottled shortly. Bright-gold; good nose; some botrytis.

1979:

Lighter, more flowery, elegant style. Not my type. More like a simple Sauternes. (14)

1975:

Still young-looking, good acidity and nose. Not as "moelleux" as the 1982. A harder-style Sauternes. Will hold well, but may be short in fruit. (15)

1950 LES JUSTICES "DOUX" (THE OLD LABEL):

Deep, mature gold. Structured like the 1975. Not very sweet, but well balanced and long. A collector's item. Good complexity, developing a bit the flavour of earth of an older wine. An experience. (16.5)

Then we tasted four old vintages of Château Gilette. (They age their Gilette for 20 or more years and only then do they release it. Now, at 26 years of age, they are selling their 1959.)

1959 "CRÈME DE TÊTE":

Very deep, bright, gold colour of a mature Sauternes. Lovely, long, complex nose. Full, moelleux, long, rich, and sweet. Very long finish. Rich, luscious wine. The best of the flight and one to buy! (18)

1955 "CRÈME DE TÊTE":

Lighter than the 1959 in appearance and body. A bit steely, drier style, medium-body, quite long and well balanced. Can be enjoyed now or in ten years. (17)

1953 "CRÈME DE TÊTE":

Paler, yet much younger-looking than its age would indicate. Not as complex as the 1955 (and nowhere near the complexity or the length of the 1959). Similarly structured to the 1955, but not as hard. Softer and more elegant. (16.5)

1950 "CRÈME DE TÊTE":

Deep gold, similar to the 1959, but a bit leaner. Definitely ready. Mature, long wine. Drier style and tastes a bit of earth-cement (since it has been stored for 20 or more years in cement vats). (16.5) Maybe it is a mistake to keep this wine for so long in cement vats?

Christian is known as "L'Antiquaire de Sauternes," because of his large supplies of older wines.

Andrée is a very lively, nice lady. They have three daughters (aged 24, 17, and 11). She's pretty young to be a grandmother. Christian does his assemblage at night and wakes her up to ask her opinion. If she agrees, it's OK; if not, he tells her that she knows nothing.

We also tasted this wine.

RESPIDES-MEDEVILLE RED GRAVES 1984:

100% new casks yearly. Elegant, complex and quite long. Obviously new oak. Well balanced. They only started to make it in 1982. (16)

With dinner, we started with fabulous whole fresh foie gras and this wine.

1929 CHÂTEAU GILETTE:

Very deep gold. Incredible length, nose, and complexity. This wine may have converted me to serving Sauternes with foie gras! Incredible depth and length. A true classic. A very rare and great Sauternes. (He opened two bottles!) (18.5)

Christian did not decant any of the wines served. Also, the French definitely serve their wines, both reds and whites, much cooler than at home in Canada.

1966 CHÂTEAU BRANE-CANTENAC:

(Two bottles) Typical structure of the 1966s. Good depth, complex, slightly herbaceous, but mature nose. Quite hard and lean on palate. Will not improve. Needs drinking. Not great, but certainly better than what this property has been producing since then. (16.5)

Then he served one of my all-time favourites. Christian is a fan of Lascases; so am I.

1959 CHÂTEAU LEOVILLE-LASCASES:

Deep, rich colour of the 1959s. Full, round; very long and complex. Great length and class. A true classic Cabernet. At its peak, but no rush. Very well balanced. Fabulous wine. Rich, chocolaty, cedary fruit. Better by far than Lascases 1961. (18.5) Grand Vin!

DESSERT WINE

CHÂTEAU GILETTE 1949 "CRÈME DE TÊTE":

Same deep, mature gold colour and nose as the 1929, but not the length and class of the 1929. A very good 1949, at its peak and a bit drier; lovely, but it is not the 1929! (17.5)

We finished with a lovely old grande Champagne Cognac. A very enjoyable (if long) evening, and a great wine experience. Then came the long drive back to Bordeaux.

Monday, November 18

Visit to Château Leoville-Lascases, with Mr. Michel Delon.

He is also an advisor to Suntori for Lagrange and to Pichon-Lalande

He doesn't like to ship the wines before they have spent six months in the bottle. That way, the cork has time to settle in the neck. He also said that 1985 will be excellent, but harder, like their 1975. That is odd; my impression of the 1985s that I tasted from barrel is that they will be rather elegant wines.

One-third new barrels in the Grand Vin (up to 50% in some vintages). Clos du Marquis has only 10% new barrels. Wood, cement, and stainless steel vats (all three!). Good production in 1984. Their Merlot didn't suffer much.

Château Leoville-Lascases 1985: A bit less volume than 1983, but not by much.

Potensac, Clos du Marquis, and Lascases 1984, 1983, and 1982: Overall, the 1984 is much better than expected. Only 2% Merlot in the blend! 1983 is more masculine; 1982 is full and massive.

We talked about Ducru Beaucaillou, about the 1976 vintage (which I thought disappointing). When asked, I told him that I would like to taste the 1975 and 1978 Lascases.

LASCASES 1978 AND 1975:

The 1978 is lovely, rich, starting to show complexity, needs ten years.

But it paled against the 1975: incredibly big, dark, tannic. A massive wine. Delon said ten years. I think much longer. I rated the 1978 (17) and the 1975 (18).

Very interesting visit. Delon wants me to send him a letter expressing my opinion of the change of the label of Château Lagrange. He agrees with me that it should be changed. He said that 1984 Lagrange is quite good and that as of the 1985 vintage, it will be very good.

It has been so long since Lagrange has made a decent wine. The reason for the letter he suggests I send is that he wants to convince the Suntori management that they must change the weird old label and that consumers, such as myself, support such a change.

Visit to Château Gruaud-Larose.

From Leoville-Lascases, we drove to Château Gruaud-Larose. (Very cold and locked gates everywhere.) The winemaker (Mr. Moreau) and the régisseur of both Gruaud and Talbot (as well as Cantemerle), Mr. Pauli, met us there.

First we tasted the 1985, just assembled. Even Mr. Cordier, the owner, hasn't tasted it yet and Moreau and Pauli had just tasted it half-an-hour before us.

GRUAUD-LAROSE 1985:

Will be an incredibly intense, full, rich ripe wine. (25% Merlot, one-third new barrels.) A great wine, possibly as good as the 1983 or even the 1982!

1984:

Medium-body, quite good, a bit green and sharp. Only 8% Merlot, or even less. (15)

The 1983 and 1982 had each about 25 to 30% Merlot. Both excellent. The 1982 deeper, according to Moreau, like 1959 or even 1929. But alas, we did not taste them during this visit.

At Gruaud, the production is very large. In 1983 and 1985, 40,000 cases of each vintage were produced!

Mr. Delon of Lascases said that 1967 d'Yquem is a great wine, but that it is starting to decline. Apparently Lur Saluces agreed. He also likes Gilette, but not much else in Sauternes. I also noticed that only at Pichon-Lalande, Latour, and Lascases, there were still green leaves. In most properties, the leaves have shrivelled by now. It is very cold (freezing), and pruning has started (especially at La Lagune).

Tuesday, November 19

Visit to Château Latour.

(Cold and some snow) With the winemaker, Jean-Louis Mandreau. He said the 1985 will be very good and quite tannic, a bit like the 1975. Very promising. Again, this puzzles me. I am really not convinced that 1985 can be compared to 1975. They are such different vintages.

MERLOT:

Very good. Their vines are old; the deep roots did not suffer from the summer and fall drought. Younger vines with short roots suffered a bit.

LES FORTS:

The vines have reached 20 years of age so they are maturing. At Les Forts, 10% to 30% new oak, depending on the vintage. The wines are produced from a vineyard called "Petit Batailley" and an area behind Pichon-Lalande.

Latour is made only from the best vineyards around the château. He is not worried about the style of La Mission now that Haut-Brion has acquired this great property from the Woltner-Dewarvins. Mandreau thinks it will keep its style, now that Haut-Brion owns it. He said that Raoul Blondin, the old winemaker of Mouton, was mistaken when he thought that 1985 would be like the 1976. He thinks Laville is much better than Haut-Brion Blanc. He said that Robert Parker (Wine Advocate) *is OK, but lacks the experience Harry Waugh has. How can Parker know if and how young Latours will turn out? And how will they age? Especially in view of the fact that Parker was either a child or not even born when the great (now mature) wines of Latour were made.*

Personally, I feel a sad loss now that La Mission is under the management of its arch-rival. Time will tell, but I am going to buy as much older La Mission (pre-1983) as I can lay my hands on, just in case.

We tasted the following wines.

1984 LATOUR:

Typical of vintage. Hard, tannic yet lighter colour; not enough flesh, and finishes a bit green. Drink now to 1991.(15)

1983 LATOUR:

Dry, complex, austere, masculine. Very good, but hard. Jean-Louis definitely prefers the 1982 and says the 1982 will need even longer than 1983 to mature. I think that they overproduced in 1983. The wine is good, but not nearly as concentrated as Mouton or the great Margaux. (17)

1976 LES FORTS:

Elegant, complex, round. A good 1976. Ready now. (16)

1978 LATOUR:

Still closed and very hard. Needs ten more years. Complex, big, tannic. Medium, dark colour, medium-body. Very masculine and very Latour. Very good potential. (18)

I gave him a tin of maple syrup, as a gift from Vancouver.

A secret

Later, May de Lencquesaing of Pichon-Lalande told me that apparently, the bosses at Latour will let Jean-Louis Mandreau go in the spring. The reason is still unknown. Maybe it is because in 1983 and possibly in 1985, Latours are not quite up to the standard we have grown accustomed to? Pity. He seems like a nice man, He also has Parker on his back, downgrading Latour 1983 and 1985. Parker is becoming the Nero of Bordeaux. Thumbs up—and you live. Thumbs down—and the music (career) is over!

Visit to Château Haut-Bages-Libéral.

Recently purchased by the group headed by Bernadette Villars (Chasse-Spleen in Moulis and La Gurgue in Margaux) in 1982. They purchased it from the Cruse group; the property is in very poor shape. Priority is given to vinification and new barrels (one-third). 20% Merlot, very little Cabernet Franc (she doesn't like it), and some Petit Verdot. She thinks Pontet-Canet and Lafon-Rochet are a disgrace (I agree). They should do better, especially Pontet-Canet, which used to make such lovely wines in the 1940s, 1950s, and up to the mid-1960s.

1984 Haut-Bages-Libéral:

Typical 1984, medium-body, some tannin, medium colour. Not as sharp as some 1984s. Good oak flavours. Needs three to four years. (14.5)

Bernadette likes the Jean-Eugene Borie properties. Borie vinifies and manages Grand-Puy-Lacoste, which is also one of my favourite Pauillacs, and a reasonably priced, reliable wine. Borie also owns Château Haut-Batailley and, of course, Ducru-Beaucaillou.

After lunch at Pichon-Lalande, I met Bernadette again at Chasse-Spleen. We tasted the 1984 (typical, but well made), then the 1984 Château La Gurgue (Margaux), which they manage. The oak barrels are Demptos, which she prefers. Soon she'll experiment with Yugoslav oak (handmade).

Lunch at Pichon-Lalande.

With Mme. de Lencquesaing. Roger Lemelletier of the Grand Conseil of the Commanderie de Bordeaux joined us. Mme. had the Canadian flag flying for me. She is also involved with the development of Lagrange (owned now by Suntori).

She agrees about Beychevelle, Rausan-Ségla, etc., overproducing. She bought her sister out and now owns the whole stock of Pichon-Lalande. They are expanding the chais. She told me about Mandreau leaving Latour. She told me that next time I came, she would let me choose any vintage I wanted. She was impressed by the prephylloxera tasting in which I participated last September in Los Angeles, and will send me notes of their records of the era (late 19th century).

With lunch

1976 and 1964 Pichon-Lalande:

The 1976 was better than when tasted in North America. So was the 1964. Both did not travel well. I told her that the 1964 was very good, but ready. May last six to eight more years but it will not improve.

We visited the private chais. She may visit Vancouver in November 1986.

November 20

Morning visit with Pascal Delbeck at Ausone and Belair.

I gave Pascal a bottle of 1980 Château St. Jean Johannisberg Riesling "Belle Terre" Select Late Harvest. When I left, he gave me two bottles of Château Ausone (1981 and 1983), and the labels separately. We tasted the 1982 and 1983 Belair and the 1981,1982, 1983 Ausone. Only a tiny amount of 1984 was made.

General impressions

They make hard wines requiring many years of bottle-age.

Belair 1982 and 1983:

The 1983 Belair is leaner than the 1982, but both are hard and unyielding. 1982 is a bit bigger and harder. Both need at least a decade. About 50% new oak. Made from 50% each Merlot and Cabernet Franc (at Ausone, too, but there they age the Grand Vin in 100% new barrels).

1983 Ausone:

Big, hard, tannic; fairly lean, yet good fruit underneath. For the long haul; this wine should approach its peak around 1996 to 1998, or beyond. (18).

1982 Ausone:

Similar to the 1983, but darker, fuller, and even harder. Yet somehow it seems that the 1983 is better balanced. (17.5)

1981 Ausone:

The most forward, complex and elegant, but even so, quite hard and needs a full decade. One of the better 1981s. (17.5)

Very good potential for all three. Overall, Pascal likes the 1985s, but says that reporters are getting too excited about that vintage. He thinks that it will be an elegant, complex, early maturing vintage.

About the 1975s
After three mediocre vintages, people were happy to have a good year. They were worried about the weather and picked overall a week too soon in St. Emilion. Some properties produced very good wines; others lack fruit.

A few general comments about Ausone
They have old vines with deep roots. They did not suffer from the drought and frost in 1985. Their vineyard is quite elevated, more so than most vineyards in St. Emilion.

I told Pascal about Jean-Louis Mandreau leaving Latour. He was surprised. I showed him my notes on the prephylloxera tasting of last September. He was quite impressed. This was my fourth visit to Ausone; I like Pascal and what he has done there. He has certainly turned this property around since his arrival in 1976.

One final comment
I mentioned to him that I preferred the 1979 Ausone to the 1978. He agreed. The 1979 is lush, rich, and long. Together with Haut-Brion, Pichon-Lalande, Palmer, and Certan-de-May, one of the best wines of that vintage.

Visit to Château Petrus.

Visited with Madeleine Cloverie (the guide of Château Petrus) and the winemaker of Newton Vineyard, John Kongsgrood at Petrus. Quite a few Merlot vines suffered from the frost earlier this year, but the roots survived, so they regrafted shoots on the existing rootstock ("regrafage").

Then we went inside and had a tasting of three different cuves of Merlot 1985 at Petrus. (The little Cabernet Franc made was not tasted.)

CUVE #4:

Round, elegant, not very intense, but quite flavourful with very good depth.

CUVE #7:

Darker, deeper, and richer. Quite intense, but not in a California sense. Very long.

CUVE #9:

Darker yet; sharper and a bit herbaceous.

I thought that cuve #9 was the Cabernet Franc. It turned out to be a lesser quality Merlot from the gravelly boundaries, which will not be used in the Petrus wine. Then we drove to a small restaurant in St. Emilion, where we were joined by Christian Moueix and Jean-Claude Berrouet, the manager and principal winemaker (for 20 years) of the Moueix properties. They were also impressed by all the prephylloxera wines I had tasted last September, including Petrus 1945, 1959, and 1961.

With lunch
1975 TROTANOY:

(Two bottles, brought over by Christian) One was a bit hard yet forward, quite complex. Slightly sharp finish, but lovely nose. The other was fuller, richer, darker, with more fat and body.

Berrouet explained that the corks are what made the difference. The first bottle had a harder cork that did not expand when pulled out. The second (better) did! The length of the cork may determine how long the wine will age. Standard Bordeaux-length corks are useful for about 20 to 25 years of ageing. The longer the cork (as a rule), the longer the wine should be able to age.

At Petrus, most of the soil (including the five best hectares purchased from Gazin in 1969) is clay (and clay soil produces fat, rich, deep Merlots). There is a tiny bit of gravel, producing leaner, harder wines, not always included in Petrus.

They buy (for all Moueix properties) oak staves from Demptos, but have their own cooper. Berrouet is against the use of glass tops for barrels because it doesn't seal the barrel perfectly and some bacteria develops. (Delbeck at Ausone has the same philosophy.)

Moisture is not very important in a wine cellar, but for the sake of long-term ageing, 80 to 85% moisture is ideal. The crucial factors of a good cellar are low temperatures (ideally 55° F), darkness, and no vibrations

We had a long lunch and an interesting technical discussion on soil, grafting (phylloxera problems in Monterey where the vines are not grafted), casks, oenology, vintages, etc.

Then I revisited Ausone.

(Pascal Delbeck was surprised to see me twice at Ausone in one day!) They have there an old church with dry human bones and skulls, and a graveyard. The bones are stored in bags. I also saw their old white horse. We tasted a few cuves of Merlot and Cabernet Franc before the assemblage. The 1985 is promising.

By the way, Berrouet said that careful buying is important and that 1985 was a better year for Merlot than for Cabernets. While very good overall, the Médocs will be fairly early maturing wines.

Then we drove to Canon-Fronsac in Fronsac to have a look at Christian's recent acquisitions of Canon de Brem and La Dauphine.

He also makes "Dominus," part of Inglenook (Napanook) vineyard in Napa.

Thursday, November 21

Morning visit to Château Sociando-Mallet, North of St. Estèphe.

An impressive modern operation making solid, masculine, long-ageing wines. I tasted the various cuves of the 1985 vintage. It will be very good and a long-ager. 50% new oak, sometimes even more. The 1984 in barrel is one of the best; medium-body, a bit hard, not as dark as other vintages. A typical 1984, but a good one. Drink from 1990 to 1994.

Mr. Gautreau agrees with me about Montrose being excellent in 1982, but an atypical St. Estèphe (a bit too soft). He doesn't think that most wine writers know what they are doing. Mr. Gautreau has a daughter, no other children. We tasted the 1982 and 1983.

1982:

A monster, needing at least 20 years. Deep, inky colour. Intense ripe fruit and tannins on palate. (18)

1983:

Very good, complex, long, new oak. Good potential. One to buy. (17)

Gautreau said that Haut-Marbuzet and Cos d'Estournel are excellent, but earlier-maturing wines. He would like an agent in Canada. I tasted the 1984 from a new barrel and from a second-year barrel. They made more Merlot than usual in 1985; their vineyards did not suffer from the frost. They also make a second wine, Lartigues de Brochon. I tasted four different cuves before the assemblage. This is an excellent property worth watching.

Visit and lunch at Château Lynch-Bages.

With Jean-Michel Cazes and his wife Marie-Therèse (whose family is from Mozambique, but they live presently in Portugal). He is going to Oporto and I told him to contact Bruce Guimaraens, a dear friend of mine and winemaker of Fonseca's Port. I took them some Indian artwork and he gave me three very nice books on Bordeaux.

First, we visited the chais and complex where extensive renovation work is being done.

We tasted the 1984, 1983, and 1982 vintages of Ormes de Pez, Haut-Bages-Avéroux, and Lynch-Bages.

My general impression is that with Ormes de Pez they are not doing a good job. The wine seems lighter and stemmier than it should be, yet older vintages (notably the 1970) can be very good.

The Haut-Bages-Avéroux is the second wine of Lynch-Bages. They have been producing it since 1971. The wines are not bad for their class and the 1984 is, surprisingly, quite good and full. Certainly better than the Ormes. Lynch-Bages 1983 is quite nice, but not great (a bit lean), yet I feel that it will have a good future by 1992. The 1984 is typical of that vintage (some greenness and acidic finish but not bad). The 1982 is very nice and well known to me. Not a massive 1982, but good, with rich, ripe, cedary fruit. Lots of potential there. (18)

Then we had lunch with Marie-Therèse and Jean-Michel's sister Sylvie's husband, who is a young doctor in Pauillac (a radiologist).

They have a very modern bottling and labelling machine (the first of its kind in Pauillac). Soon they will have guest rooms at the château and I am invited to stay there. Bipin Desai will be in Bordeaux in two weeks; Jean-Michel will be in Los Angeles in February 1986 for the extensive tasting of 1945 Clarets (so will I).

Jean-Michel likes vintage Port very much. He was impressed with the prephylloxera wines I tasted. I'll send him photocopies of the article I wrote on the subject. He said that Cordier and his partners are doing a lot of replanting at Cantemerle and that in ten years, the wine will be of top quality, as it used to be in the 1940s, 1950s, and early 1960s.

With lunch

CHAMPAGNE ROEDERER "CRISTAL" 1979:

Creamy, complex, long, and elegant.

1979 ORMES DE PEZ:

Quite a nice 1979, fairly rich and dark. Spicy Cabernet and long. Ready by 1987 to 1990.

1970 LYNCH-BAGES:

A favourite of mine. (At that time, they were bottling from separate barrels and not as an "assemblage.") Typical of the wine: full, rich, dark, a bit closed. Mint-eucalyptus, long and rich. Needs three to five years. Excellent. (18)

1983 LYNCH-BAGES BLANC:

Made from 70% Semillon and 30% Sauvignon Blanc. Produced for their own use. Quite nice, typical white Bordeaux, soft and ready.

1945 CHÂTEAU CANTEMERLE, CHÂTEAU-BOTTLED:

Jean-Michel knew that I was born in 1945 so he surprised me by opening this bottle (of which he has a case, but never tasted it). Full, complex, rich, mature Claret. The tannins of 1945, yet quite full and soft. Long. No rush drinking it. Dark, mature colour. A lovely bottle. (18)

1969 Quart de Chaume, Château de Sarronde, Loire:

(Served blind) By elimination, I guessed it to be a Loire and a Quart de Chaume. I have only tasted it once before. He was impressed! Typical acidity of Loire sweet whites. Palish gold, quite nice. Not very sweet or thick and no botrytis. OK, but nothing special. I cannot get excited over this wine or even over Moulin Touchais (Anjou). Give me a fine Sauternes instead—any day.

1945 Taylor's Port:

(Opened the previous day for other friends.) Deep, mature colour. Long, yet masculine; a bit hard. Lovely length. Has held very well. No rush drinking it. Typical Taylor's (leaner style) structure. Very good. Was probably even better the previous day. (17.5)

I had a very nice three-hour visit. Marie-Therèse is a very nice, lively lady.

Visit to Château Cabannieux in Graves.

In the evening, I met Jacques Barrières in Bordeaux. He runs a wine export business. We drove to the house of his sister and brother-in-law at Château Cabannieux in Graves. We tasted various vintages of both whites and reds. They have mostly Merlot (75%) and the rest is Cabernet. The soil there is much better for Merlot. The 1985, tasted from separate cuves, is quite good in Merlot (full, round, and rich). The Cabernet was disappointing. With dinner we had 1983, 1981, 1978 and 1975 Cabannieux. A decent wine. The whites are mostly Semillon and some Sauvignon Blanc. The 1984 is dull. The 1985 quite nice. It was a pleasant, simple family dinner with very nice down to earth people.

All in all, a successful and very informative two-week trip. I visited a total of 19 properties and one négociant.

November 28, 1985

Commanderie de Bordeaux 1961 Haut-Médoc and Graves tasting, at "Le Pavillon," the Four Seasons hotel, Vancouver.

Champagne Charles Heidsieck Brut 1976:

Fully mature. Yeasty, rich, long. Good fruit/acidity balance. Ready.

1. 1961 Château Calon-Ségur:

Medium-mature colour, orangy rim. Ripe, subdued, complex nose. A bit sweet and vegetal. A bit acidic, too short, quite hot, unflavourful. Tired. A disappointing wine. (15)

Up to the early 1950s, Calon-Ségur made superb wines, notably the 1928, 1945, 1947, 1948, and 1949.

2. 1961 Château Ducru-Beaucaillou:

Medium-dark, mature colour. Lovely, complex, long nose. Very opulent and elegant. Complex, round, long. Just a bit of tannin. A masculine wine (more so on palate than on nose). In retrospect, a bit disappointing and too acidic. I have had many better bottles. Maybe it is starting to dry out? Can be superb. (16)

3. 1961 Château Brane-Cantenac:

(Two bottles. One château-bottled. The other a Nicolas-bottling. I had the Nicolas.) Lightest of the bunch. Old-looking, brown-brick (orange). A bit fruitier, sharper on nose. Slightly vegetal, light, acidic finish. Elegant Margaux structure. Finishes a bit short. Lovely nose, though. (16)

4. 1961 Château Cos d'Estournel:

Good, dark, solid colour. Orangy rim. A bigger, more masculine version of #2. Big, rich, fruity, ripe nose. Tannic, hard, yet fruity; very fine quality. No rush. Austere. Typical St. Estèphe structure. I liked it more than most. (17.5)

5. 1961 Château Pape Clément:

Similar impressive colour to #4. Open, sweet, ripe, fruity nose. Without the complexity of #2 or #4, but better than #1 or #3. Elegant, fruity, slightly tannic, without the concentration of #4. Earthy, tobacco. Lovely bottle. Later, improved. Full, long, very well balanced. A lovely bottle, probably the last good year of Pape Clément to date. (18)

6. 1961 Château Leoville-Poyferré:

Similar colour to #2. Open, fruity, spicy nose. Forthcoming and elegant, slightly candy-smelling. Minty, spicy. Lacks middle. Some tannin, but losing its fruit. Delicate. Was better three to five years ago. (15)

7. 1961 Château Beychevelle:

Medium-palish brown-orange rim. Not as light as #3, though. Subdued, very elegant nose. Earthy, hard, a bit citric; lovely complex nose. A very elegant and well-made wine. Drink up soon. (17)

8. 1961 Château Mouton-Rothschild:

Darkest in appearance of flight. Good, deep colour to rim. One bottle more closed than the other. Both very hard, unyielding. Cedar; very intense and ripe wine. Still closed. Hard; needs three to five years or longer. Will be a classic. Drink 1990 to beyond 2000, if well cellared. (19)

WITH THE FIRST COURSE

1981 Château Carbonnieux White:

Lightish gold. Spicy Sauvignon Blanc nose. Crisp, clean, complex.

DESSERT WINE

1961 CHÂTEAU D'YQUEM:

Deep-gold colour. Complex nose; not as rich, deep, or botrytized as the 1967. A bit thinner and not luscious. Very nice, but not great. Anyway, Sauternes were better in 1962 and 1967 than in 1961 and 1966.

The Mouton was the clear winner and Pape Clément second. The Calon-Ségur and Brane-Cantenac were last.

The 1961 Lafite (in magnum) which we were supposed to have with the dinner did not show up. Our cellerier, Sid Cross, somehow failed to bring it back across the border in time for this event.

Overall

The wines were true to their fame. The only surprise was the lack of depth and a bit short finish of the Ducru. I have had many better bottles. The Pape Clément was surprisingly good and a revelation.

November 29, 1985

Lunch with Dr. Brad Klein in Los Angeles.

APERITIF

CHAMPAGNE VEUVE CLICQUOT "LA GRANDE DAME" 1979:

Lovely, elegant, yeasty, toasty. With beluga caviar.

1926 CHÂTEAU COS D'ESTOURNEL, CHÂTEAU-BOTTLED:

Low neck level. Lovely, deep, bright colour of mature Claret. Elegant, very open, complex nose. Ripe fruit. On palate: soft, round, very sound, very long. Round and rich. A magnificent bottle, full of elegance. Not as hard as the 1928s or as jammy as the 1929s. Structured like a great 1953!! A lovely bottle and a great experience. (18)

November 29 to 30, 1985

Two-day event, tasting and dinner, at "Valentino's," in Los Angeles. Subject: Brunello di Montalcino Biondi-Santi 1891 to 1980.

A group of wine collectors met in late November 1985, for a two-day event featuring the rare and expensive Brunellos of Biondi-Santi. Our guest of honour was Dr. Franco Biondi-Santi. This tasting was organized by Bipin Desai of Los Angeles, with the help and participation of the principals of Wilson and Daniels Ltd., a wine-importing company located in St. Helena, CA. Wilson and Daniels are the agents for Biondi-Santi and also for Domaine de la Romanée-Conti. The tastings (dinner on November 29 and lunch on November 30) were held at "Valentino's" Italian restaurant, in Santa Monica, CA. The owner, Piero Selvaggio, served us two outstanding meals to accompany these fine and rare wines.

The wines of Biondi-Santi are produced from the family-owned "Il Greco" vineyard. No purchased grapes are used to produce this wine, which is marketed as "Anata," made from ten to 25-year-old vines, and "Riserva," produced only in exceptional vintages from the oldest and best vines, up to 100-years-old. Lesser wines are not sold as Brunello and are declassified. All Biondi-Santi Brunellos are vinified, aged, and bottled in the same way. The bottles were opened, and the older wine decanted up to five to six hours before the tasting, by Dr. Franco Biondi-Santi.

The average production of the "Riserva" (roughly 30% of the vintage, when declared) is 7,000 to 10,000 bottles, and "Anata" from 40,000 to 50,000 bottles. The wines had an average of 12.8% to 12.9% alcohol. Biondi-Santi sells his wines approximately ten months after bottling, usually in the month of September of the fourth year after the vintage. Ideal maturity dates indicated are those of Dr. Biondi-Santi. The scores, out of (20), are my own.

APERITIF

CHAMPAGNE ALFRED GRATIEN 1979 BRUT:

Elegant, long, and clean.

The tasting

FLIGHT #1

1980 ANATA:

This was the first year of the new DOCG classification. No "Riserva" was produced. Age 20 to 30 years (potentially). Good, dark colour; closed and unyielding nose at this stage. Hard, tannic, fairly high acidity and low fruit, but showed some ripeness. Needs time. (15)

1979 ANATA:

No "Riserva" declared. Potential ageing 20 to 25 years. Fairly dark, purplish colour. Spicy, ripe, fruity nose. Showing more maturity than the 1980, but still hard and unyielding. More personality and fruit showing, though. I liked it better than the 1980. Biondi-Santi thought otherwise. (15.5)

1978 ANATA:

Age for another 20 to 30 years. Palest colour of flight, watery rim. Metallic nose, light, soft, with low fruit but good acidity. A bit sharp. (14.5)

FLIGHT #2

1977 ANATA:

Age 20 to 30 years. Medium-red young colour. Ripe, slightly pruny nose, typical of mature Italian wines.

Hard and steely on palate, but has good fruit. Needs time. (15.5)

1977 "RISERVA":

Ageing potential 50 to 60 years. Darker than the 1977 Anata and quite similar on nose. Slightly better concentration of fruit. (16)

1975 ANATA:

1975 was an exceptional vintage for Brunellos. Ageing potential: 20 to 35 years. Good, dark colour to rim. Fairly lean with acidity. Quite good, but clearly inferior to the 1975 "Riserva." (15.5)

1975 "RISERVA":

Very long ageing potential of up to 100 years. Deep, dark, intense colour, showing slight signs of maturity. Intense, ripe nose. Lovely, full, rich wine, with excellent complexity and concentration of fruit. Well balanced. Needs many years to reach its peak. The difference between the 1975 Anata and "Riserva" was more obvious than that of the 1977 Anata versus 1977 "Riserva." (17.5)

FLIGHT #3

1971 ANATA:

Ageing potential: 20 to 30 years. Medium-dark colour. Clean, young, fruity nose. Elegant, spicy, round, with good length, yet finished a bit hard. Had more backbone and class than the 1973 that followed. (16)

1973 ANATA:

Ageing potential: 20 years. Deep, mature colour. Toasty, fruity nose, but fairly alcoholic, too. Harder and leaner than the 1971. Needs another three to five years. Quite good. (15)

1970 "RISERVA":

An exceptional year. Potential ageing: up to 80 years. Medium-dark colour with orangy-brick rim. Lovely, ripe, pruny, leathery nose with hint of tar. Very good fruit, high acidity, and little tannin. Long on palate, with great complexity. A lovely wine. (18.5)

I had only tasted Biondi-Santi's Brunellos twice before and found it hard to understand how wines with such low tannins could last for so many years. Biondi-Santi's explanation was that the tannins found in their wines are "soft" tannins and that the acidity is what keeps these wines for so many decades.

1971 "RISERVA":

Long-ageing, up to 80 years. Spicier, younger-tasting than the 1970. Good fruit, well structured and medium-bodied. Needs five to seven years. Very good. (17)

This flight showed more class and better overall structure than the younger wines.

DESSERT WINE

BIONDI-SANTI MOSCATELLO 1969:

Made from lightly dried grapes of Muscat di Montalcino and not produced anymore. 1969 was the last time they produced this rare and unusual wine. Rich, luscious, quite alcoholic, not unlike an old Sauternes, but spicier and more alcoholic. Buttery, caramel, Muscat nose. The grapes were late-picked, 20 days after normal vintage time. After 1969, the vines were uprooted (a total of one acre) because there was no market or interest for this wine.

Lunch, November 30

FLIGHT #1

1969 "RISERVA":

Excellent vintage. Ageing potential: 30 to 50 years. Dark, mature-looking. Leather, tar, and fruit on nose. Full on palate but still hard with good fruit. Needs at least seven to ten extra years of bottle-age. (16.5)

1968 "RISERVA":

Described as "great vintage, long-ageing, up to 50 years." Similar appearance to the 1969, but closed, unyielding, and leaner style. Lacking the ripeness and depth of the 1969, in my opinion. (15.5)

1967 "RISERVA":

Age: 30 to 40 years. Deeper colour than either the 1968 or 1969. Mature "Claret" nose. Similar impressions on palate. Complex, long; a bit lean, but elegant. Typical high acidity. Ready. (16.5)

1964 "RISERVA":

Exceptional vintage. Recorked September 1985. Potentially very long-lived, up to 100 years. Dark, deep colour. Ripe, fruity nose with good complexity. Full, fruity, long, and well balanced. An ager and a very good wine. (17.5)

1961 "RISERVA":

Ageing potential: 30 to 40 years. Deep brick-red mature colour. So far, the most mature on both palate and nose. Round, leathery, complex, a bit austere. Ready and very enjoyable. (17)

While I do not doubt the staying power of most of these wines, I feel that the recommended ageing potential indicated by Franco Biondi-Santi is exaggerated. Biondi-Santi's Brunello vineyard is situated fairly high and has good exposure in all four directions. The best vines are those planted at the upper part of the hill.

FLIGHT #2

1958 "RISERVA":

Deep, mature colour. Sturdy, fruity, and well balanced. Good backbone and should hold well for at least another decade. (17)

1957 "RISERVA":

Mature colour with good depth. Tar, prunes, and ripe fruit on both nose and palate. Round, elegant, complex. Great length. A lovely bottle. (18)

1955 "RISERVA":

Exceptional vintage. Recorked in Spring 1978. Potential ageing: 100 years. Dark, mature colour; darkest of the flight. Ripe, Claret-like nose. Concentrated, full, and rich wine. An outstanding bottle of great length and complexity. The finest of the flight. (18.5)

1951 "RISERVA":

Age 50 to 60 years (?). Paler and older-looking. Open, soft, and forward. Seemed a bit corked and sour. This bottle was purchased in Wisconsin. Biondi-Santi said he had tasted better examples of this wine. Poor. Not ranked.

FLIGHT #3

1946 "RISERVA":

Great vintage. Age 50 to 60 years. Mature brown-orange colour. Open, complex, tarry, and fruity nose. Delicate, round on palate. A fine bottle at its peak, but its good structure indicates there is no rush drinking it. (18)

1945 "RISERVA":

Exceptional vintage. Recorked in spring 1970 and again in September 1985. Very long-ageing, up to 80 years. Livelier and fruitier than the 1946 on both nose and palate. Great length and complexity. A bit tannic, and loaded with ripe fruit. A great bottle. (19)

1925 "RISERVA":

Recorked spring 1970 and again in September 1985. Very long ageing potential, up to 100 years. Similar appearance to the 1945. Delicate, long, and subdued nose. Prunier than the 1945, yet had great concentration of fruit, length, leather, and tar. Incredible intensity for such an old wine, yet acidity becoming obvious. Any further ageing may see this wine losing its fruit, and the acidity and pruny character may take over, to the detriment of this fine winc. (18)

Biondi-Santi is, in principle, against decanting wine, unless it is absolutely necessary when very young, to allow the wine to breathe, or if it has unusually high sediment. He feels that decanting shocks the wine and accelerates the oxidation process. He is not the only wine producer who thinks so. I have encountered the same argument with various producers in Bordeaux and Burgundy. I personally feel that decanting is not harmful if properly done. Timing is of the essence here. It's a matter of different philosophies and as yet, nobody has come up with concrete evidence one way or the other.

1891 "RISERVA":

Recorked in 1927, 1970, and September 1985. When available, this rare and exceptional wine sells for over US$5,000 per bottle. This amazing wine has held extremely well. Good, dark colour for age, with orange-brown rim. Not unlike a fine Brunello 40 or 50 years younger! Subdued, elegant nose. Long, delicate, not as acidic as most. A bit dry, but still has good fruit. Fruity, clean, and long finish with a trace of high alcohol. An outstanding wine, especially for its age and a once-in-a-lifetime experience. (18.5)

It is obvious that what keeps these wines for so many years is the high level of acidity and alcohol, and not the tannin. Being a Bordeaux fan, this was a great learning experience for me. Until this tasting, I thought that a balance of concentrated fruit, good levels of acidity, and a large dose of tannins was a prerequisite for longevity.

One of the guests at this event was a young wine writer, representing The Wine Spectator *magazine, by the name of Jim Gordon. He sat beside me and copied many of my notes, because he said that he had never tasted a Biondi-Santi or any other Brunello before, and didn't know anything about this wine. While I was more than pleased to help him out, I found it odd that this popular wine magazine wouldn't send a wine writer who at least would have some experience with these wines. How does the publisher of* The Wine Spectator *expect this young man to write about these wines, with no previous experience?*

January 1986

International Wine and Food Society Dinner at "Modesto Lanzone's" in San Francisco.

CHAMPAGNE LOUIS ROEDERER BRUT 1973, IN MAGNUMS:

Well structured, long, mature, but not over-the-hill. Good bubbles. Fine quality.

CHAMPAGNE CHARLES HEIDSIECK 1962 EXTRA DRY, IN MAGNUMS:

Both magnums mature, but sound; the sugar helped them hold this long without deteriorating too much.

One magnum was a bit madeirized. The other was better. Old, but complex and fine.

1962 MEURSAULT-PERRIÈRES, POTINET-AMPEAU:

Excellent appearance, nose, and palate. Round, long, complex, nutty, with good fruit. Much better than expected.

This was paired, oddly, with

1982 CONDRIEU, CHÂTEAU DU ROZAY, P. MULTIER:

Light, delicate, flowery. Very elegant and fresh. Good fruit and well balanced. Spicy and not too hot, as some Condrieus can be.

THE REDS

The subject of the dinner was 1962 First Growths in magnums, served in two flights.

FLIGHT #1

Ausone, Petrus, Cheval-Blanc, and Margaux

This flight was lighter in colour and disappointing.

PETRUS:

The best, good depth, fruit, and structure.

AUSONE:

Nice, open, complex nose, but was dried out.

CHEVAL-BLANC:

Leaner, harder, and losing its fruit, which surprised me. Should have been better.

MARGAUX:

Drying out, too. Except for the Petrus, they all had excessive acidity. Ratings were as follows: Petrus (17), Ausone (15.5), Cheval-Blanc(15), and Margaux (15).

FLIGHT #2

The second flight was much better, deeper, riper, and more complex

HAUT-BRION:

Deep colour; spicy, mature, cigar-box nose. More backbone than La Mission. Mature and at its peak. (17.5)

LA MISSION HAUT-BRION:

Softer than the Haut-Brion. Complex, good length, earthy, ready. Nice chocolaty overtones. (16.5)

LAFITE:

Deepest of the flight. Rich, deep colour. Complex, long, spicy, oak-Cabernet nose. Full, fruity, round, and rich on palate. Ripe. Ready, but no rush. (18) Lafite produced a fine 1962.

LATOUR:

Surprisingly, lighter and leaner than Lafite. Dry, a bit hard, older-tasting. (17)

I have definitely had better examples of this wine in the past.

MOUTON-ROTHSCHILD:

Deep colour. Full, round, well balanced. Straightforward. Not a star, but good Mouton. Spicy, cedar. Really nice. (17.5)

DESSERT WINE

1962 CHÂTEAU D'YQUEM, IN MAGNUMS:

Lovely Sauternes, better than 1961. Medium-gold. Delicate on nose and palate. Long, complex, not overwhelming. "Delicacy." Very good. (18.5)

Overall

The wines have seen better days, yet they should have shown better, especially in magnums. Poor storage?

January 1986

A rare tasting of Quinta do Noval Regular and Nacional, 1931 to 1955.

This tasting included some of the rarest Ports anywhere in the world. The first part of this tasting was held in January 1985.

APERITIF

CHAMPAGNE LOUIS ROEDERER BRUT N/V:

Delicate, long, complex. Very fine.

1. 1931:

Dark colour, showing quite a bit of maturity at rim. Ripe, complex nose. Full, concentrated, and rich. Surprisingly, it had more depth and fruit than the 1931 Nacional. Complex, finishing with very good length and elegance. Yet, dare I say this, not as memorable as one would expect from such a legend. (17.5)

2. 1931 NACIONAL:

Surprisingly, more forward and paler than the regular 1931. Open, rich, and long on palate. Mature and ripe. A perfumy, elegant wine. Expansive. I detected a hint of madeirization on nose. A bit woody. Very good? Yes. Great? No. (17)

3. 1934:

Deep, dark colour. Concentrated ripe fruit, rich and long. Surprisingly youthful for a 50-year-old wine. Not unlike a great 1963! Ready, but has a great future ahead of it. Clearly, at least at this event, superior to both 1931s. A superb bottle. (19)

4. 1934 NACIONAL:

Mature and lighter colour than the regular 1934. Slightly cloudy. Delicate, soft, forward. Easy to drink and at its peak. Lacking the concentration of the regular wine of that vintage. (16.5)

5. 1945:

Showing maturity on both nose and palate. Excellent balance and breed. Long, rich, and complex, if without the concentration of the 1934. A delicate wine that is fully mature now. Doesn't have the power of 1945 Taylor's or Graham's, but very good nevertheless. (18)

6. 1947:

Similar colour to the 1945, but a bit cloudy. Open, spicy, sweet Port, finishing a bit hot and spirity. Needs drinking. (16.5)

7. 1947 NACIONAL:

Clearer, brighter colour than the 1947 regular. Mature, concentrated nose. Full, round, quite solid. Rich with good fruit and depth. Not unlike a very good 1963. Lovely. (18)

8. 1955:

Mature colour with orangy rim. A well made, mature Port finishing a bit sharp, yet had good fruit. Similar structure to the 1945, but a bit fruitier (ten years younger) and simpler finish. (17)

9. 1955 NACIONAL:

Another superb bottle and, together with the 1934, my favourite of these two events. Dark, bright colour with a slight touch of orange at rim. Rich, spicy nose. Superb length and concentrated ripe fruit. A huge, lovely wine. Vintage Ports come much better than this. (19)

The Regular is mostly made of Tourriga grapes (producing deep, tannic juice). Nacional is made exclusively from Tourriga, not a blend of four to five varietals as the Regular. Ungrafted, therefore susceptible to attack by the phylloxera louse.

Overall

1934 Regular was the best wine, followed by 1947 and 1955 (both Nacional).

February 14 to 15, 1986

A two-day marathon, at the Century Plaza hotel, in Los Angeles.

Bordeaux 1945: A Retrospective

A group of wine collectors met last February 14 at the Century Plaza hotel in Los Angeles for an extensive two-day tasting of 1945 red Bordeaux. The organizer of this event was Bipin Desai, who has organized many a great and rare tasting in the past. Our guests of honour were Harry Waugh, a dear friend and mentor; Michael Broadbent of Christie's; and Jean-Michel Cazes, owner of Château Lynch-Bages.

What started in the planning stages as a 40-châteaux, three-day event ended up as a 60-châteaux, two-day marathon! As it was pouring rain in Los Angeles, we had the extra excitement of rain pouring in through the candelabras and onto the buffet table, an event that did not take a thing away from the wines, other than some difficulty in concentrating.

Each session, we tasted approximately 30 wines in four and three flights, respectively. The wines came from various sources, mostly château-bottled, with some Bordeaux or London-bottlings. Most were regular-size bottles; others were magnums (as indicated in the notes on the individual châteaux tasted). Each session lasted about three-and-a-half hours, a bit short and a rushed time span, especially when tasting 30 of the rarest wines from a great vintage. It therefore took a lot of concentration and effort. Fortunately, most participants had good and trained palates.

The wines were not tasted blind. Since the wines were 40 years of age and from various sources in the United States and Europe, one would find it hard to have a fair blind tasting. The levels varied, too. I have indicated the level of the wine in the bottle only when particularly low, or unusually good, or if wines were served from magnums. We had two bottles of most of these wines and experienced some (sometimes substantial) bottle variations.

Overall impression

There are still a lot of very fine and even some great Clarets of this vintage that have held surprisingly well. Most, however, have seen better days. It seems to me that they were better seven to ten years ago, at least the ones I have tasted previously. There is nothing to be gained in keeping them much longer. They have either seen better days or are at their peak now. Many were true to the vintage, with very good concentration of fruit; classic, complex, mature noses; and the hard tannins so typical of 1945. The notes and scores are my own. I have indicated where I differed from most other tasters.

Friday Evening, February 14, 1986

FLIGHT #1

1945 St. Estèphes

CHÂTEAU MONTROSE:

Mature, orange-brick colour. Slightly "piqué" sharp nose and sour. Forward, short, and a bit weedy. After a few minutes in the glass, it developed some complexity, but the fruit declined fast and it dried up. Some tannin left. A second bottle was corked. (14.5)

CHÂTEAU LAFON-ROCHET:

Darker than the Montrose, with good depth and mature brick-colour to rim. Rich, chocolate nose, but herbaceous, too. Hard, dry, and acidic on palate. Has seen better days. Lacked fat or depth, and a bit decayed. Disappointing. As with the Montrose, it dried out after 15 minutes in the glass. (14)

CHÂTEAU COS D'ESTOURNEL:

Orangy, mature colour; surprisingly pale for a 1945. Slightly fruity, mature nose. Drying out. Hard, St. Estèphe style, with hint of fruit. Masculine, still tannic, yet one-dimensional. May last for a few more years, but if by now it hasn't developed complexity, when will it? (15.5)

CHÂTEAU CALON-SÉGUR, IN MAGNUM:

Excellent level. Darkest colour of the flight, not unlike a rich 1959 or a 1961. Rich, ripe raisins on nose. Round, full, but hard and tannic; typical of the 1945s. Best balance of flight. A sturdy, hard wine, with ripe fruit and good length. A lovely, austere, old-style St. Estèphe. Ready, but no rush, especially from magnums. (18)

With the exception of the Calon-Ségur, this flight was disappointing. The wines were paler, drier, more acidic, and not as well balanced as expected.

FLIGHT #2
1945 Graves

CHÂTEAU HAUT-BAILLY, IN MAGNUM:

Excellent, deep colour; like a 1961. Complex, long, slightly earthy nose. Round and rich on palate, with good backbone, yet elegant. Mature, round, and long finish. An excellent wine that has held very well, in magnums as well as bottles. (A bottle tasted last July was very good, but more forward than this magnum.) (17.5)

CHÂTEAU HAUT-BRION, IN MAGNUM:

A bit darker than the Haut-Bailly, with a warm, yet delicate tobacco-vanilla nose. Expansive, elegant, and very well balanced. Lots of class. The backbone of the 1945s and the elegance of Haut-Brion. Superb wine. (18.5)

CHÂTEAU LA MISSION HAUT-BRION:

Slightly darker than the Haut-Brion. Intense, tobacco-earthy, ripe nose. Full, round, long, and solid, but marred by some acidity. Lacking the elegance of Haut-Brion, but true in style to both the 1945 vintage and to this property. Some volatility. (17) The second bottle was better balanced than ours and would rate at least (18).

DOMAINE DE CHEVALIER:

Good, deep colour with mature, orange-brick rim. Vanilla-oak nose, slightly green (stemmy), with earth overtones and hints of chocolate. Dry and hard on palate. Tannic and lacking depth or complexity. Most people rated this wine higher, yet their comments were similar to mine. (17)

The flight was consistent and very good. The disagreements were in terms of which were the favourites.

FLIGHT #3
1945 St. Emilions

CHÂTEAU AUSONE:

Deep, mature colour. Ripe, slightly herbaceous nose. Hard and tannic, lacking fruit. Solid wine. This wine developed some complexity and even a hint of fruit after a few minutes in the glass. Will last a while longer, but the fruit is disappearing fast. (17)

CHÂTEAU CHEVAL-BLANC:

Similar appearance to Ausone, if a bit lighter. Open, ripe, earthy-herbaceous nose. Good depth. Round, elegant, complex, and forward. Tobacco and ripe fruit. Lovely, long finish. An excellent bottle. Picking started on the same day as in 1982; September 13. A hint of things to come? (18.5)

CHÂTEAU LA GAFFELIÈRE-NAUDES:

Delicate, open, clean, mature nose. Round and soft on palate, with a slightly sharp finish. A very elegant, stylish wine. (17)

CHÂTEAU GRAND CORBIN D'ESPAGNE:

We only had one bottle and therefore only got a tiny amount in each glass. Deep, impressive colour. Slightly rubbery nose. Rich, solid, sweet, and fruity. Hard, tannic finish. A good and solid wine, lacking maybe in complexity. (16.5)

CHÂTEAU CLOS FOURTET:

Mature, dark colour, with orangy rim. Open, slightly medicinal nose. Raisiny, soft, and a bit sharp finish, but still had some fruit. Otherwise quite delicate. Hint of madeirization. Drink up. (15) I have tasted finer samples of this in the past.

FLIGHT #4
1945 Pomerols

CHÂTEAU LA CROIX DE GAY, LONDON-BOTTLED BY HARVEY AND CO. IN 1947:

Deep, mature colour. Ripe, lead-pencil nose, with some greenness. Slightly sharp and acidic, yet still tannic. Opened up into an elegant, complex wine after a few minutes in the glass. Has seen better days. (16)

CHÂTEAU L'ENCLOS, BORDEAUX-BOTTLED BY CRUSE, SECOND BOTTLE LONDON-BOTTLED:

Fairly pale, mature colour. One bottle had an odd, medicinal, fluoride nose; short and ordinary. The second bottle was rounder, had an elegant nose, and was rich, with clean finish. (12) and (15.5) respectively.

CHÂTEAU LAFLEUR, ENGLISH-BOTTLED, SHIPPED BY CRUSE:

Big, dark, thick wine. Port-like. Closed, ripe, baked nose. Very intense, full, and rich. Tannic. One bottle was a bit pruny. Some tasters thought this wine was "doctored" (alcohol added). Others, and I agree with this version, said that Lafleur is always a richer, alcoholic wine. Michael Broadbent thought it was "sweaty and unpleasant." A matter of taste. (17)

CHÂTEAU LA FLEUR-PETRUS, IN MAGNUM:

Medium-dark colour. Some fruit and complexity on nose, but not very distinguished. A bit sharp. Leaner style, with some elegance. Not unlike La Conseillante. After a few minutes in the glass, it improved into a round, elegant wine. (17)

CHÂTEAU LAFLEUR-GAZIN, ENGLISH-BOTTLED:

One bottle only. Low shoulder level. Pale colour, showing a lot of age. Mature, slightly oxidized nose. A bit sharp, but still enjoyable. Pleasant, but simple. (14)

CHÂTEAU LA POINTE:

Very good, deep colour. Full, rich, round, and well balanced. Lots of fruit. Long life ahead and a true Pomerol. Lead-pencil, iron, and spices. Has it all. Outstanding quality. This surprised me. La Pointe is usually a mediocre Pomerol, not unlike Gazin or de Sales. Simple, straightforward, and uninspiring. This bottle was superb. Whoever made this wine knew what he was doing. (18.5)

CHÂTEAU NENIN:

Good, deep, mature colour. Leathery, ripe nose. Round, elegant, with good fruit. Doesn't have great depth, but well balanced. Hint of barnyard, not unlike a mature red Burgundy. Very enjoyable. I liked it more than most. (17)

CHÂTEAU PETRUS, BOTTLED BY CALVET:

Dark, deep colour to rim. Lovely, spicy, rich Merlot nose. Concentrated, full, and very rich. An impressive wine. Still full of life. Broadbent described it as the "1931 Quinta do Noval" of Pomerol. (19)

CHÂTEAU TROTANOY:

Mature colour, with good depth. Open, spicy nose, with hints of dill. Odd, pruny flavour. Short, hard finish. Disappointing. A second bottle was much better. Solid, but not outstanding. Lacking charm. Most tasters rated it higher than I did. (16) Having tasted this wine twice previously, I know Trotanoy 1945 can be outstanding.

CHÂTEAU CLOS L'EGLISE, BORDEAUX-BOTTLED BY HANNAPIER, IN MAGNUM:

Deep colour. Full, rich, and round. Solid, loads of fruit, and tannic. Great concentration. No rush drinking it, especially from magnums. (17.5)

CHÂTEAU CLOS RENÉ, ENGLISH-BOTTLED:

Deep colour. Ripe and solid on palate, but one-dimensional. Similar structure to Clos l'Eglise, but with bitter finish. The nose was the best part of this wine. (16.5)

VIEUX CHÂTEAU CERTAN:

Very good, deep colour. Vanilla-sweet nose. Full, yet very tannic and hard. Some fruit and a bit pruny, but way too tannic. Oak and molasses. (15)

This flight was quite extensive. Jean-Michel Cazes said that he found a lot of variation and inconsistency in this flight. I agree.

Overall impression

Simple wines, lacking overall the finesse of the Graves and St. Emilions.

Saturday, February 15, 1986

We met at noon for our second session, comprising the Haut-Médocs (except for the St. Estèphes, tasted the previous night).

FLIGHT #1
1945 Margaux and Haut-Médocs

CHÂTEAU BRANE-CANTENAC:

Deep, mature colour. Open, spicy, herbaceous, elegant nose. Full, rich wine. Good length and well balanced. The lovely bouquet lasted forever. Very good. The second bottle seemed a bit tired. Why can't this property produce this quality nowadays? (18)

CHÂTEAU CANTENAC-BROWN:

Slightly paler colour than the Brane. Herbaceous nose and a bit oxidized. Dry and hard, yet had a little fruit. Faded fast. (15)

CHÂTEAU KIRWAN, BORDEAUX-BOTTLED BY SCHRÖDER AND SCHŸLER:

Dark colour. Clean, elegant, spicy nose. Round and elegant on palate. Without the depth of Brane or the hard structure of the Cantenac-Brown. Long, clean finish, with some tannin. Very nice bottle. (17)

CHÂTEAU MALESCOT-ST.-EXUPÉRY:

Deep colour. Concentrated, rich, mature nose of fine old Claret. Minty, spicy flavour. Harder style, typical of both the vintage and this property. Solid wine. Very good. (17)

CHÂTEAUX MARGAUX:

One bottle was flat, oxidized, and dead. Pale, cloudy-tea colour, not unlike an old Sherry. The second bottle was much better. Elegant, round, and soft, yet it was a bit tannic. Forward, needs drinking. (16.5) I have definitely tasted better examples of this wine in the past.

CHÂTEAU PALMER:

Dark amber colour. Closed, unyielding nose. Hard, acidic, not well balanced. Solid structure, but the fruit has almost disappeared. Delicate finish. An unusual 1945. Disappointing. (15) Having tasted this wine previously, it can be better, but not great.

CHÂTEAU RAUZAN-GASSIES:

Dark, mature colour. Clean, aristocratic, ripe nose. Full, flavourful, long, and solid. Some tannins and good length. A lovely bottle. Great quality. (17.5) Probably the last good wine made by this property to date.

CHÂTEAU RAUSAN-SÉGLA:

Very deep colour to rim. Excellent appearance. Full, solid wine, with hints of oak and vanilla. Good fruit. Fabulous, long nose. A superb bottle; much younger-looking and tasting than its age would indicate. Why can't Rausan-Ségla make such wines these days? (18)

CHÂTEAU LA TOUR DE MONS, IN MAGNUM:

Elegant, open, mature nose. Soft on palate, with some tannin. Pleasant and round. It has got it all, but showing signs of age. Needs drinking. (16)

CHÂTEAU CANTEMERLE:

Dark colour with mature, orange rim. Well balanced, long, still tannic, with excellent fruit. Great length and structure. Superb quality. Fine all-round Claret. A classic wine. Last November, I had the pleasure of sharing a bottle of this great wine with Jean-Michel Cazes at Château Lynch-Bages. It was as great as this one. (18.5)

CHÂTEAU GRAND LA LAGUNE, ENGLISH-BOTTLED:

In the old days, the world "Grand" appeared before the now-familiar "La Lagune." Deep, rich-looking colour. Round, full, rich, and long on palate. Straightforward, beefy wine. Typical La Lagune. Very good. (17)

CHÂTEAU LA TOUR CARNET:

Top shoulder level. Medium, mature colour. Dill, herbaceous nose. Similar impressions on palate. Solid, with good fruit, but a bit sharp and acidic. A second bottle was slightly better, but it still had the obvious dill flavours. (15.5)

Brane-Cantenac, Kirwan, Rauzan-Gassies, and Rausan-Ségla were among the finest wines of the flight. How times have changed!

FLIGHT #2

1945 St. Juliens

CHÂTEAU BEYCHEVELLE:

Dark colour to rim. Clean, fruity, elegant nose. High acidity on palate, but otherwise soft and elegant. Drink up. Lacks complexity. Did not hold very well in glass. The second bottle was corked. (16)

CHÂTEAU BRANAIRE-DUCRU, CHÂTEAU-BOTTLED:

Deep, mature colour. Lovely, complex nose. Round, fruity, rich. An elegant wine. Beautiful bouquet, with hints of coffee beans. A charmer. Needs drinking. I liked it more than most. (17.5)

CHÂTEAU DUCRU-BEAUCAILLOU, IN MAGNUM:

Very low fill. Dark colour. Oxidized nose. Similar impressions on palate. Acidic and tired. After a few minutes in the glass, it improved slightly but not by much. (13)

CHÂTEAU DUCRU-BEAUCAILLOU, IN BOTTLE:

Deep colour, mature rim. Lovely, long, complex, elegant nose. Fruity St. Julien. Round and well balanced. Similar to the 1961 and without the excessive tannins so typical of the 1945 vintage. Long, clean finish. (17)

CHÂTEAU GRUAUD-LAROSE:

Very deep, impressive colour. Rich, jammy, and solid. Full, chewy, rich. Superb wine, loaded with fruit and incredible intensity. Not unlike 1945 Latour. (19)

CHÂTEAU LANGOA-BARTON, BORDEAUX-BOTTLED BY BARTON ET GUESTIER, IN MAGNUM:

Good, dark colour. A bit acidic, but solid wine, with good fruit and length. A masculine wine, with good fruit. Rich, complex nose. (17)

CHÂTEAU LEOVILLE-BARTON, LONDON-BOTTLED BY CORNEY AND BARROW:

Medium, mature colour. Full and long. Odd, "off" nose. Opened up and became more elegant after 20 minutes. Quite good. (16)

CHÂTEAU LEOVILLE-BARTON, LONDON-BOTTLED BY COCKBURN AND CAMPBELL:

Cloudy colour showing age. Madeirized, sour, and tired, but had some tannin. Drying out. My previous experiences with this wine (château-bottled as well as London-bottlings by Block, Gray and Block, Justerini and Brooks, and Berry Bros.) were much better. Can be a superb wine. The two London-bottlings tasted tonight were disappointing. (13)

CHÂTEAU LEOVILLE-LASCASES:

Good, dark, mature colour. Not much on nose. Solid, dry, and hard. Unyielding, austere, yet well balanced. Powerful Cabernet. Not unlike Latour, but with less complexity. (17)

CHÂTEAU LEOVILLE-POYFERRÉ:

Mature colour, with good depth. Round, elegant, forward. Good length and complexity. Needs drinking. (17)

CHÂTEAU TALBOT:

Surprisingly good. Round, fruity, well balanced, and forward. Good fruit and length. Spicy, mature Cabernet nose. A lovely, faultless bottle. (18)

Gruaud-Larose and Talbot stood out. They were Harry Waugh's favourites of this flight. I expected more from the other St. Juliens tasted. Tasting so many wines together, however, one tends to be a bit too critical.

FLIGHT #3:

1945 Pauillacs

CHÂTEAU BATAILLEY:

Very good, almost purplish colour. Spicy, cigar-box nose. Rich, round, and full. Well balanced, with excellent fruit. Top quality. A plummy, rich wine, with very slight hint of acidity. Lovely and a surprise. (18)

CHÂTEAU GRAND-PUY-LACOSTE, IN MAGNUM:

Even darker and more purplish-looking than the Batailley! Intense and much younger-looking than its age would indicate. Spicy, rich, ripe nose. A bit herbaceous. Full, tannic, and massive. Dry and quite hard. Will last for many more years, especially in magnums. A solid, typical 1945. I liked it more than other tasters, who found it to have some volatile acidity and a bit too lean. (18)

CHÂTEAU LAFITE-ROTHSCHILD:

Mature colour, with orange rim and good depth. Paler than most Pauillacs. Elegant, caramel, cigar nose. Long, elegant, with some tannins, but a bit acidic. Good, long finish. Disappointing for Lafite. Michael Broadbent tried to defend Lafite. The usual excuse is that it is unfair to compare Lafite with big, hard, and powerful wines such as Latour and Mouton. This is nonsense. Lafite is a Pauillac, too, and costs as much, if not more, than the other two First Growths. It should deliver accordingly. It did not. (16.5)

CHÂTEAU LATOUR:

Deep, full colour. Excellent appearance. Not as dark as Grand-Puy-Lacoste, though. Complex, spicy, minty nose. Long and rich. Essence of Cabernet. No rush drinking it. A big, solid wine. Superb. (19.5)

CHÂTEAU LYNCH-BAGES:

Beautiful, dark colour; mature rim. Spicy, baked bread, herbal nose. Hard, tannic, and masculine, yet had some elegance underneath. Very good length. Spicy Cabernet nose, with hint of mushrooms. The second bottle wasn't quite as good. (17.5)

CHÂTEAU MOUTON-D'ARMAILHACQ (BETTER KNOWN THESE DAYS AS MOUTON-BARON-PHILIPPE):

Dark colour. Open, elegant, slightly oxidized nose showing age. Round, elegant, and complex on palate, with hint of crème-brûlée. Very enjoyable long finish. An elegant wine. (17)

CHÂTEAU MOUTON-ROTHSCHILD:

Mature, deep colour, with orange rim. Excellent depth. Spicy, eucalyptus nose typical of this property. Huge cedar and mint. Great intensity and length. Superb long finish. A perfect wine. The second bottle had a hint of cork, but was still very good. Classic. (19.5)

CHÂTEAU PICHON-LONGUEVILLE-BARON:

Good depth. Slightly cooked, medicinal nose. Solid, hard, and tannic, with earthy overtones. Good, but not great. A bottle tasted in 1984 was superb. (16.5)

CHÂTEAU PICHON-LALANDE:

Deep, mature colour. Hint of coffee beans on nose. Similar impressions on palate. Odd. Solid wine lacking finesse, depth, or Cabernet character (a trademark of the great wines this property has been producing in recent vintages). (16)

CHÂTEAU PONTET-CANET:

(Three bottlings: one Bordeaux-bottled by Cruse; one château-bottled, the property was owned by Cruse at the time; the third Bordeaux-bottled by another négociant.)

The two Cruse-bottlings were similar in appearance and style. They had a good, dark colour, and a delicate, long, complex nose. Round and forward, with very good fruit and length. Clean finish.

The château-bottled wine was slightly bigger. Both lovely. (17.5)

The Bordeaux-bottled (other shipper) wine was darker in appearance, with an earthy, burnt nose. Sharper and not as well balanced as above two examples, as well as having an acidic finish, with pricked-sharp impressions. (15)

Overall

The Pauillacs, with their share of disappointing wines, were overall the most outstanding flight. Some wines were clearly better a decade ago. One veteran taster noted that great vintages grow in quality in the mind, but not necessarily in the bottle!

One could not hope for a more extensive or educational tasting than this, especially of wines from one of the greatest vintages this century. We were a bit rushed and it was, maybe, a bit too much of a good thing, but I learned a lot and enjoyed myself.

Saturday, February 15

Quiet dinner at Brad Klein's home.

CHAMPAGNE LOUIS ROEDERER BRUT N/V:

(Selling in Los Angeles for an unbelievable $8.99/bottle!) With fresh Sevruga caviar. Elegant, fresh, long, complex. Will improve if allowed to age for a year or so. Great quality, especially for the price.

1928 CHÂTEAU LA GAFFELIÈRE-NAUDES:

Leaking cork, very old. Low level, almost to top of label. Undrinkable. The deepest wine I have ever seen. Molasses, thick, madeirized nose. The colour and texture of Tia Maria coffee liqueur, even darker. Couldn't see a thing through it. I am sure that other, sound, bottles are still drinkable.

1948 CHÂTEAU LEOVILLE-LASCASES:

Low neck level. An elegant wine. Good depth of colour. Delicate, spicy, mature nose. Round, forward, yet very well structured. Clean aftertaste. Good length. A lovely, very enjoyable bottle. (17.5)

1945 MUSIGNY, MORIN PÈRE ET FILS:

Heavy, old-style bottle; deep punt. Very good level. Excellent colour; like a good 1966 Claret. Nose closed at first, but later, opened up into a good, classy, spicy Pinot Noir nose. Long and lovely. Full, rich, round, with the elegance of Musigny and the power of 1945. A lovely, very, very good bottle; full of life! (18)

A very enjoyable evening.

February 1986

Vertical tasting of Warre's Vintage Port, at the Four Seasons hotel.

Organized by Vintage Consultants (agents for this Symington Port). Guests: Mr. Paul Symington of Oporto and Dr. Valadas, Consul General of Portugal. Paul Symington is fourth-generation (young man). Tourriga Nacional, Tourriga Francesa, Roriz, and Barroca are the varietals used in the blend. Before bottling vintage Port, they stir up the barrels.

1945 WARRE'S:

Medium, mature colour. Orangy rim. Flowery, spicy, complex nose. Quite perfumy. Beautiful, elegant (not nearly as massive as Graham's 1945). Long, complex, very fine. Drinking very well now. Great balance and class. A good "Lafite" of Oporto. (18)

1958 WARRE'S:

Similar colour to the 1945, but not as expansive or complex nose. Fairly alcoholic. Elegant, long, soft, forward, drier style. (17)

1960 WARRE'S:

A bit darker than above. Very similar nose and obvious high alcohol as the 1958. Not as fruity, complex, and long as the 1958. Quite nice. Simpler style. Round, forward. Typical. A bit sharper on nose. (16)

1963 WARRE'S:

Good, deep, maturing colour. Rich, concentrated, still-closed nose. Not jammy, excellent depth. Full, long, not quite ready. Beautiful complexity. Great length. Drink 1986 to 2000. Medium-bodied. An elegant Port. At Oporto, they feel it'll be as good as the 1945. (17.5)

1966 WARRE'S:

A bit lighter in appearance than the 1963. Still youthful, with touch of pink at rim. Sweet, pleasant, forward nose. Round, elegant, sweet, forward. Very clean, long, and complex. (17)

1970 WARRE'S:

Very good, deep colour to rim. Closed, yet lovely, sweet, intense, concentrated nose. Very long, full wine. Rich, intense, jammy, excellent intensity. Great potential. Like a Graham's or Fonseca's. One to buy. (18)

1974 WARRE'S LATE-BOTTLED VINTAGE PORT, BOTTLED IN 1978:

Very good, deep colour, not as intense as the 1970. Open, spicy, elegant, fruity nose; a bit dusty. Old, traditionally made (only four years in cask, no filtering). Surprisingly good. Full, rich, round, complex. Excellent, clean, good fruit. Very close to a vintage Port, like 1966. (17)

1975 WARRE'S:

Light, evolved colour, maturing rim. Open, sweet, simple, spicy nose. Simple and not very concentrated. Surprisingly forward. Round, elegant, yet soft. Ready now to 1990. (15.5)

1977 WARRE'S:

Very good, deep, dense colour. Intense, ripe, young nose. Full, rich, ripe fruit, very long. Great quality. Needs ten to 15 years. Like the 1970 or 1963. (18)

1980 WARRE'S:

Deep, bright colour. Fresh, open, sweet, fruity nose. Not as ripe as the 1977, but very nice. Round, forward, elegant. Mid-term, ready 1990 to 1995. (17)

1983 WARRE'S:

Deep, purplish, intense colour. Fresh-pressed juice. Similar structure to 1980, but obviously younger, richer, and fruitier. Quite similar potential. (17)

WARRE'S WARRIOR, FINEST VINTAGE CHARACTER:

Palish, mature, brown colour. Open, sweet, nutty nose, with elegant complexity. Soft, forward, easy to drink. Blended to produce an easy to drink wine. Five to six years of age. Similar to other late-bottled vintages.

Symington agreed with the description that Graham's is jammy and rich. Dow's is leaner, with more aggressive tannins, and Warre's is complex and elegant, yet long and has breed.

February 24, 1986

Tasting of rare 1947 St. Emilions, at home.

This turned out to be one of the more memorable tastings I have organized. The 1947 vintage was very successful in St. Emilion and Pomerol, producing rich, ripe, concentrated wines, not unlike the 1982s.

APERITIF

CHAMPAGNE VEUVE CLICQUOT N/V BRUT, IN MAGNUM:

(Purchased five years ago) Round, yeasty, complex, long, and classy. At its peak.

Preceding the tasting, a small vertical of Condrieu.
Château du Rozay, 1981, 1982, 1983, P. Multier

1981:

Medium-deep gold. Flowery, almost-elegant Riesling nose. Fruity, round, good length. Clean, yet without the freshness of the two younger wines. Stylish. (16)

1982:

Lightest, palish gold. Fresher, yet higher alcohol, hot finish. A bit leaner and thinner. More delicate. Elegant, fine, fresh. Touch of sweetness. Quite nice. (16.5)

1983:

Similar colour to the 1981. Round, full, rich, long, flowery (lilacs). Fairly alcoholic finish. Long aftertaste. Rich in an elegant way. Slightly cardboardy. Full, fruity, obviously youngest. Exotic. (17)

The 1947 St. Emilions

1947 CHÂTEAU PAVIE, LONDON-BOTTLED BY AVERY'S:

Good, deep, mature colour. Orangy rim. Warm, complex, open, round, mature nose. Great length. Round, mature, with earthy flavours. Long and clean. Very elegant. The only negative comment: after 20 minutes in glass, it thinned out a bit and became stemmy. (18)

1947 CHÂTEAU TROPLONG-MONDOT, CHÂTEAU-BOTTLED:

Similar appearance to the Pavie. Fresher nose. Mature, yet a bit more herbaceous and not as open or ripe as Pavie. Rich, full, a bit sharp and acidic finish. Not as complex, elegant, or well balanced as the Pavie. (17)

1947 CHÂTEAU PIN-DE-FLEURS, CHÂTEAU-BOTTLED:

Lighter colour and paler-orange rim than above two. Open, round, mature nose. Elegant, clean, and sound. Round, ripe, mature fruit. Clean, long finish. Great effort. Elegant. What a pleasant surprise. (17.5)

1947 CHÂTEAU CROQUE-MICHOTTE, CHÂTEAU-BOTTLED:

Good, deep, mature colour. A bit jammy, rancid nose. Still rich, spicy, elegant. Similar structure, toasty, elegant, round, fruity, good length. Has held extremely well. Long. Burnt cream, rich nose. (17)

1947 CHÂTEAU CANON, CHÂTEAU-BOTTLED:

Medium-dark, mature colour. Orangy rim. Closed, unyielding nose at first, but one could find fresh, elegant fruit underneath. Quite pleasant. Full, beefy, well balanced, some tannins. Toasty, ripe nose. Flowery aftertaste. An austere, noble wine. Nowadays, Canon makes more elegant wines. (17.5)

1947 CHÂTEAU CHEVAL-BLANC, LONDON-BOTTLED BY CHRISTOPHER AND CO., SHIPPED BY CALVET:

Darkest, deep colour. Mature rim. Chocolate, ripe fruit (so typical nose). Rich, full, tannic, massive. Long, rich, and chocolaty. Port-like. A giant by itself. Almost a pity to have it with anything else. (19)

The overall quality of these St. Emilions was outstanding!

1947 MOULIN TOUCHAIS, ANJOU:

Bright gold. Clean, well balanced, elegant, long. Good complexity and style. Has held extremely well. 1947 was a great year in the Loire valley. (17.5)

1934 TAYLOR'S WOOD PORT, BOTTLED IN 1985:

This bottle was given to me by Bruce Guimaraens, principal of Fonseca's and Taylor's, who brought it over last year when he stayed with us in Vancouver. This wood Port was like a fine cream Sherry, but with a lot more depth, length, and complexity. Fairly high degree of brandy. Great and rare quality. (18)

March 22, 1986

Group of "Ten" dinner at the Tobes'.

CHAMPAGNE POL ROGER BRUT 1976

AND

CHAMPAGNE KRUG "GRANDE CUVÉE" N/V:

The Pol Roger was a bit sugary on nose and slightly sweet on palate. Odd, bitter finish. Seemed tired, yet typical ripeness of the 1976s.

The Krug was fresher, crisp, lovely complexity, well balanced, and long; still fresh.

1982 CHASSAGNE-MONTRACHET PREMIER CRU "MORGEOTS," ALBERT MOREY

AND

1982 CHASSAGNE-MONTRACHET PREMIER CRU "LES CHAUMÉES," MICHEL COLIN DELEGER:

The "Morgeots" was deeper gold, open, complex, oak-toast. A bit flabby. Ready. Full, rich, good length. (16)

The "Chaumées" was paler gold. Apples, elegant nose. Crisp, delicate, well balanced. Needs two to three years. Most people liked it best. Perfumy and elegant. (17.5)

1961 AND 1970 CHÂTEAU BEYCHEVELLE:

The 1961 was a bit lighter, more brown and evolved in colour. It had a lovely, open, complex, mature-tobacco nose. Great length. Round, complex, long, ripe, mature. A fine bottle, at its peak and will not improve. (17.5)

The 1970 had a spicy, rich, tobacco, slightly herbaceous bouquet. Deeper colour. Concentrated. (17)

1961 CHÂTEAU LATOUR

AND

1961 CHÂTEAU MOUTON-ROTHSCHILD:

Latour a bit darker and younger-looking. Mouton a bit more age at rim. Both great depth.

Latour: essence of Cabernet, ripe, rich nose. Great depth. Both very backward.

Mouton: cedary, concentrated nose. Rich, round, full, well balanced, and long. Slightly high acidity. The Latour was ripe, big, rich, solid.

Mouton needs five to ten years; Latour needs ten to 20 years. Latour a perfect (20), Mouton (19.5)! Two magnificent, classic Clarets, by any standard.

Although these two wines have great potential, the 1961 Beychevelle was more enjoyable as a dinner wine tonight. Great delicacy, length, and complexity.

DESSERT WINE

1971 CHÂTEAU DE FARGUES:

Deep bright-gold. Lovely, long, complex, botrytis nose. Full, rich, luscious, and well balanced. Top quality and at its peak. Very slight bitter finish. (18)

May 1986

Dinner and double-blind vertical tasting of Leoville-Lascases, at Sid Cross's.

APERITIF

CHAMPAGNE POL ROGER BRUT 1976, IN DOUBLE-MAGNUM:

Lovely, yeasty, rich, complex. Well balanced and long. Very nice.

THE TASTING

I thought they were 1966 or 1967 (or maybe 1971s, too) from Haut-Médoc, with lots of Cabernet, yet I never thought it would turn out to be a vertical.

Leoville-Lascases

1. 1980:

Dark to rim. Spicy, pleasant, with good depth, but a bit leathery (getting tired?). Low tannins, high acidity, and green. Needs drinking. (14)

2. 1973:

Lighter than the 1980. Vegetal on both nose and palate (stemmy). High acidity, not unlike a simple St. Emilion. Was better five to six years ago. (14)

3. 1971:

Good, dark, mature colour to rim. Hard tannins like a 1966! Short on palate, lacking complexity and depth. Slightly corked. I have tasted better examples of this wine. (14.5)

4. 1970:

Good, dark colour to rim. Dull nose, high acidity. Some tannin, short finish. I never liked the 1970 Lascases. (14.5) The best 1970 St. Julien is Ducru Beaucaillou. Far superior to Lascases.

5. 1967:

Mature colour, orange rim. Complex nose. A bit watery and tannic. Fair bit of acidity. I knew this was a 1967. (15)

6. 1966:

I guessed 1966, but I thought it was a Pauillac. Good, deep, mature colour. Mature, complex nose. Round, spicy, complex, hard tannic finish. Good length and depth. (17)

7. 1978:

Deep, youthful colour. Full, rich, spicy, and complex. Has class. A bit acidic. Seemed unbalanced. Needs time. Good potential. Drink 1990 to 1998. (17)

8. 1975:

Tannic, hard, lots of class and fruit. A big, solid wine. Classy, complex nose, and good, long finish. Promising. My favourite. Must be a 1975! Will last well until the end of the millennium. (17.5)

Group preference

1978: first; 1975: second; 1966: third. I cannot argue with that order. All three were fine wines.

The 1980, 1971 (surprisingly), and 1973 were the most disappointing. It seems that between 1967 and 1974, Lascases didn't make any outstanding wines (even the 1970 is disappointing).

May 1986

Lunch and tasting of Opus One, at the BC liquor monopoly specialty store, Cambie Street, Vancouver.

With Philippine de Rothschild, Xavier d'Ezaguire (Mouton-Rothschild's export manager), Tim Mondavi (winemaker and younger son of Robert Mondavi), the liquor monopoly brass, and the press.

1982 Opus One:

Deep, purplish colour to rim. Young, fresh, spicy, elegant nose. Spicy Cabernet, with hints of oak and vanilla. Lovely flavours. Great length and complexity, but not a big wine. Ready 1990 to 1995. (17)

1981 Opus One:

More mature colour, slightly purplish rim. Not as deep as the 1982. Less obvious oak-vanilla and a bit leaner style, with slightly bitter, yet complex finish. More elegant and less overblown than the 1982. Ready 1987 to 1990. My favourite. The most complex and French-like. (17.5)

1980 Opus One:

Very dark, deep colour. Big, solid colour showing some age. Fairly tannic, a bit leathery. A serious, big wine. Not as luscious as the 1982 or as elegant as the 1981, but intense, dry finish. Drink 1990 to 1995; will the fruit hold? Australian-like, rich, leathery. Tim Mondavi's favourite. All three are very different. They are obviously experimenting. (17)

1982: 82% Cabernet Sauvignon, 16% Cabernet Franc, 2% Merlot

1981: 97% Cabernet Sauvignon, 3% Cabernet Franc

1980: 94% Cabernet Sauvignon, 6% Cabernet Franc

"Fine de Mouton":

Only one barrel is produced per year. Aged in old barrels (about 15 years old). Deep gold, with a touch of green. Complex, elegant; good character and depth; maybe lacking a bit in Cognac complexity.

Baronesse Philippine de Rothschild and Tim Mondavi explained about Opus One being "not French and not California, but different." I disagree. It is a very well-made, complex, elegant California Cabernet, produced with Mondavi grapes and selling at a ridiculous $70 per bottle. Unmistakably Californian in style.

June 1986

Trip to Napa Valley (Yountville)

Visit to Napanook (Christian Moueix's Vineyard).

With Daniel Baron, the manager, and Harry Waugh, whom I picked up from Barney Rhodes's residence. We also met the retired vineyard manager who has been with the John Daniel family at Inglenook since 1942. He said that after Mr. Daniel died in the early 1970s, his widow, a Mormon, sold the whole wine collection and library for a mere $10,000 to Heubelein (who purchased Inglenook).

We walked through the vineyard and saw the various varietals, including an old Cabernet Franc that produces wine very similar to Merlot. The old vineyard manager's name is Joe Baranzini, who is retired now. Harry was happy and thankful that I took him there to visit the vineyard and taste the wine.

We drove to Rombauer Vineyards.

Met Koerner Rombauer, the owner. Harry had met him earlier in the week. Rombauer has an agreement with Moueix. He leases part of his premises to Christian so that Christian can produce the wine there.

They will release the 1983 Dominus First Vintage next November 10 in New York. For the 1983, they used second-year barrels from Château Cheval-Blanc (total production will be 2,500 cases). The 1984 and 1985 (4,000 cases each year) are ageing in 20% new oak; the rest, as in 1983, are in Cheval-Blanc's second-year barrels. They put a tiny bit of Malbec in their wine. The rest is 75% Cabernet Sauvignon and 25% Cabernet Franc from old vines, producing a juice that is very similar to Merlot. All grapes are from their own Napanook vineyard. Harry let me smell the wine for him because he still hasn't regained his sense of smell. I also described them to him. Harry had a bad car accident in Burgundy last year, and he has never regained his sense of taste or smell.

We tried barrel samples of the 1985 and 1984 vintages.

1985 DOMINUS:

In cask since February and just racked. The best of all three. Deep, purplish colour. Lovely, spicy, fruity, young nose, but not overwhelming. Great depth and balance. Long, solid, complex. A superb wine. Excellent potential.

1984 DOMINUS:

16 months in cask so far. Similar colour to the 1985, but just a bit less depth. Well balanced. All these wines have good natural acid. Daniel told me that they do not add acid at all (acidify), as do many Californian producers. This wine needs six to eight years to mature. Very good to excellent potential. They were fortunate to start producing (and release) three very good vintages in a row!

1983 DOMINUS:

Bottled earlier this year. A bit of age at rim. Charming wine. At first, all three reminded me of a serious St. Julien; later, similar to a solid Pomerol. The 1983 will be lovely in eight years or so. Daniel is setting aside some of it for me, including magnums, of which they bottled only 120.

Lunch at Meadowood hotel/resort.

Managed by Robin Lail, a daughter of the late Mr. Daniels. She is Christian Moueix's partner at Napanook. Very nice lady. The other partner is Marcia Smith, Daniel's other daughter. Both own 50% of Napanook and Christian owns the other 50%. Mondavi wanted to buy her property but she preferred to keep an interest there.

The food and beverage manager at Meadowood prepared lovely lamb for us, with a sauce made with 1983 Dominus! He took a glass out of the open bottle we brought along, and made a superb sauce. Went perfectly with both the lunch and the wine. Surely, this must be the first time anywhere that the first vintage of Dominus has been used to produce a fine sauce!

1984 GRGICH CHARDONNAY, NAPA VALLEY:

Full, big, rich, yet very well balanced. Needs two to three years and will be of top quality. Hint of oak backed by fine fruit.

Harry told me that the new winemaker at Château Latour (replacing Jean-Louis Mandreau) is Christian Le Sommer. Daniel Baron told me that Moueix is having problems with the surviving sister at Château Lafleur and Le Gay. She is selling some Lafleur behind his back while he has exclusivity!

Christian Moueix's father, Jean-Pierre, will be in New York for the launching of Dominus. First time he's been to North America. Harry thinks that the 1985 Château Pichon-Lalande is a great wine. He blames the négociants and wine merchants, rather than the producers, for hiking the opening price of the 1985 red Bordeaux.

Back to the Dominus.

If I had to rate them, I would give the 1985 the highest marks (great concentration). Second would be the 1983, and third, but still very good, the 1984 because of its slightly lesser depth.

Dinner at "La Rose et Favour" in St. Helena.

With Ed Lazarus (who stayed with me in Yountville), Brad Klein, and his friend, Nancy. I brought along two bottles.

CHAMPAGNE LECLERC-BRIANT BRUT 1978

Mature, complex. Good, yeasty nose. Full, round, and pleasant. (17)

1978 CORTON-CHARLEMAGNE "DIAMOND JUBILEE," REMOISSENET:

Medium-gold. Complex, toasty, oaky nose; typical of Corton-Charlemagne. Well balanced, at its peak. Long, elegant, and flavourful. A very nice, white Burgundy from a top vineyard and from a great vintage. (18)

Then we tasted two superb red Burgundies.

1971 CHAMBOLLE-MUSIGNY "LES AMOUREUSES," COMTE DE VOGÜÉ

AND

1971 ROMANÉE-ST.-VIVANT, DOMAINE DE LA ROMANÉE-CONTI:

(The Chambolle was Brad's bottle; the Romanée was Ed's bottle.)

Both had very good mature colours, with good depth.

The Romanée-St.-Vivant was a bit darker. The "Amoureuses" had a lovely, complex nose. Great elegance, spice, and length. The St.-Vivant was a bit spicier and less elegant. Both superb wines. On palate: The "Amoureuses" was rounder, more elegant; great depth and elegance. At its peak and a lovely bottle. The St.-Vivant was spicier, a bit bigger, long, superb. Both were at their peak, but no rush. Top-quality wines. I rated both (18).

We unfortunately entered into a political discussion about South Africa, etc. It did something to spoil the evening. C'est la vie! The food was excellent and the wines were great. Why mix wine and politics?

June 22, 1986

Lunch and tasting of Inglenook Cabernet Sauvignons 1941 to 1983.

Members of the Marin County Branch of the International Wine and Food Society met at Inglenook Vineyards in the Napa Valley for a rare and extensive tasting of their Cabernet Sauvignons, going back to 1941. Our guest speaker was Harry Waugh, the well-known wine taster and author.

APERITIF

INGLENOOK SAUVIGNON BLANC "RESERVE" 1984:

Fresh, spicy, well balanced. Good depth, herbaceous and crisp.

After the aperitif, we started with the tasting and luncheon.

FLIGHT #1

1941:

Mature colour with good depth. Slightly stemmy, open, and complex nose of mature Cabernet. Round on palate, with surprising amount of fruit. Well balanced, long, with very good flavours and ripeness. It softened after a few minutes in the glass, but developed great complexity. At 45 years of age, this wine has held amazingly well. (18)

1943:

Slightly darker than the 1941. Claret-like nose. Mature, delicate, with lovely complexity. Fuller on palate than the 1941; rich, round, and long. A ripe, well-balanced, and impressive wine. My favourite of the flight, yet the decision wasn't an easy one because they were all very good. (18.5)

1946:

Good, mature colour. Complex, older nose of mature Cabernet. Not as ripe as the 1943 or the 1949, and higher acidity with some sharpness at finish. This wine is getting tired and is not as voluptuous as its peers in this flight. Not bad though, for a 40-year-old wine. (17)

1949 "CASK J-46":

Similar appearance to the 1946. Ripe, rich, and complex nose, with hint of sugar and wet straw. Good fruit, a bit acidic finish. At first, it seemed less outstanding than the 1941 or 1943, yet as it opened up in the glass, it improved quite a bit. A very good wine. (17.5)

FLIGHT #2

1955:

Dark, mature colour; orangy rim. Round, fruity, elegant, and ripe. Not as voluptuous on nose as the wines of the 1940s, but ripe and clean. A bit Port-like. Soft and forward on palate, with trace of acidity. Needs drinking. (16)

1958:

Similar colour and appearance to the 1946, with a fruitier, riper nose resembling the 1949. A bit leaner on palate, though. Leathery, Port-like, rich, and fruity. Very nice wine that should be consumed now. (17)

1959 "CASK J-6":

Darkest of the lot so far. Excellent appearance with some age at rim. Ripe, rich nose. Full, solid, and still a bit tannic. A great bottle that is enjoyable now, but should hold well for some time. (18)

With the first course, we had a glass of Chardonnay.

INGLENOOK CHARDONNAY "SPECIAL RESERVE" 1984, NAPA VALLEY:

About 80% barrel-fermented, this wine is made from grapes grown in a Carneros and a Stag's Leap vineyard. Bright-gold colour. Ripe, fruity nose with hint of oak and vanilla. Buttery, flowery, with good acidity and fruit. A bit too alcoholic for my taste, but I was in the minority there. Most participants seemed to like it better than I did. (16)

FLIGHT #3

1961:

Good, dark, mature colour. Rich, ripe, and complex nose. Full, intense, and well balanced. Ripe and fruity on palate. Finished long, with hint of tobacco and some tannins. An outstanding wine and, in my opinion, the best of the flight. (18)

1963 "CASK F-19":

Excellent appearance to rim. Wet straw and mature fruit on nose. Big, rich, and solid—even bigger than the 1961, but marred by too much acidity. Quite hot and alcoholic, too. A bit edgy. Quite good, but needs drinking. (16.5)

1966 "CASK G-28":

Medium-dark colour with mature, brown rim. Clean, open, complex nose. Round, elegant, and well balanced, with clean finish. Soft and elegant, but holding well. Some tasters, including Harry Waugh, preferred this wine to the 1961. (17)

WITH THE MAIN COURSE

1981 CABERNET SAUVIGNON "RESERVE" INGLENOOK, NAPA VALLEY:

A wine that is now being released and available for sale in the US and highly recommended. It retails for around US$13.50 to $15. Deep, young colour with purplish rim. Spicy, rich nose. Well balanced and long, needing four to six years of extra bottle-age. Clean, spicy finish. Very promising. (17)

We then continued with the tasting.

FLIGHT #4

1974 "CASK A-17":

Dark colour with brown-orange rim. Subdued, elegant nose, with hint of wet straw and spices. Rich, long, and well balanced. Concentrated, yet showing signs of maturity. The 1974 "A" series limited cask wines are drinking very well now. (17)

1970 "CASK F-31":

Similar appearance to the 1974, but a bit more age showing. Elegant, open nose. Round, rich, complex, and long on palate. Rich and full. This wine, like the 1974, was lovely. Best wine of the flight, followed closely by the 1974. (17.5)

1978 "LIMITED CASK":

Dark colour, with touch of orange at rim. Ripe, rich nose. Seemed to have a touch of residual sugar. Full, rich, and finishing clean. Some people liked this wine better than the 1974. (16.5)

1980 "LIMITED CASK":

Medium-deep colour. Clean, fresh fruit on nose, with hint of wet straw. Fruity, tannic, and not ready. Needs four to five extra years of bottle-age. (16)

1983 "LIMITED CASK," BARREL SAMPLE:

Deep, purplish colour. Spicy, rich, young fruit on nose, with hint of dill. Tannic, rich, and well balanced. This wine is to be bottled in two weeks. In 1983, and for the first time in 30 years, grapes from all three of Inglenook's Cabernet vineyards were used in the blend. A very promising wine. Potentially (17).

We finished with a glass of this wine.

INGLENOOK GEWÜRZTRAMINER 1985, IN MAGNUMS:

(Magnums had long, flowery designs on them.) Fresh, spicy, crispy, and fruity. Made from grapes grown in their own vineyards.

While I have tasted older California Cabernet Sauvignons on previous occasions, this was my first experience with an extensive vertical tasting of Cabernets of such an outstanding and consistent quality.

August 1986

A rare tasting of mature South African wines.

The concept was born last spring, during a discussion on South African wines that I had with a few wine-collector friends from Vancouver. We decided to deplete our cellars of some of the old South African wines and try them, side by side, during one extensive tasting and dinner. All participants (ten collectors and their spouses) contributed wines to this event. Three of the participants contributed most of the red wines that they have been cellaring since the mid- and late 1960s.

The tasting was held at my residence on a sunny early-August afternoon. After an aperitif (Champagne Gosset "Grand Millésime" 1976) and a pleasant Chablis (1982 "Valmur" Grand Cru, J. M. Raveneau), we started with the red wines.

FLIGHT #1

Pinotage

Pinotage has been cultivated in South Africa since the 1920s. It is a cross between Hermitage (Syrah) and Pinot Noir.

1970 PAARL "SELECTED" PINOTAGE, KWV:

Deep colour, showing some maturity at rim. Ripe, spicy on both nose and palate, not unlike a rich Hermitage. Tannic, with good fruit and hint of tar. A big, ripe wine holding very well. (16)

1966 PAARL "SELECTED" PINOTAGE, KWV:

Dark colour, showing more maturity than the 1970. Different style. More delicate, open, complex nose, reminiscent of mature Claret. Good depth, some spice. More class and elegance than the 1970; drier, too. Long, clean, and complex finish. Very good. (16.5)

1964 PAARL "SELECTED" PINOTAGE, KWV:

Deep, mature colour to rim. Ripe, raisiny nose with hint of prunes. Tannic, with fairly high acidity but low fruit. A hard, ageing wine, but impressive appearance (colour). (14.5)

1962 PINOTAGE LANZERAC:

Palest of the flight. Medium, mature red colour. Mature, complex nose, reminiscent of toast and buttered popcorn. Round, complex, and spicy on palate, not unlike a mature California Cabernet. Elegance and style. Has held surprisingly well. (16.5)

At the last minute, a younger wine was added to this tasting.

1978 CINSAULT LANDSKROON, LANDGOEDWYN:

Medium, maturing colour. Stemmy, herbaceous nose resembling a Cabernet Franc. Round and pleasant, with good fruit but fairly high alcohol. Simple, one-dimensional finish. (13)

FLIGHT #2

Nederburg Cabernet Sauvignons

As we managed to gather five Cabernets of this winery, we decided to taste them as a vertical, and taste the other Cabernets in a third flight.

1976 CABERNET SAUVIGNON:

Mature colour with good depth. Slightly medicinal nose with some sharpness. Round, forward, and soft on palate, with good fruit. A bit too acidic at finish. (14)

1971 CABERNET SAUVIGNON:

Ageing colour, brick-brown rim. Round, spicy, open nose. Soft, elegant, and well balanced. Good fruit and fairly alcoholic. Needs drinking. (15)

1969 "SELECT" CABERNET SAUVIGNON:

Medium-dark, mature colour; orange rim. Subdued nose. Medium-bodied, round, forward. Well structured, with good acidity and fruit. Some tannin there, yet needs drinking. Better on palate than on nose. Drink up. (15.5)

1968 "SELECT" CABERNET SAUVIGNON:

Very good, dark, mature colour. Lovely, complex, Bordeaux-like nose. Ripe, round, forward, and elegant. Well structured. Lovely, long finish. At its peak, but no rush. (17)

1962 "SELECT" CABERNET SAUVIGNON:

Spicy, elegant, open nose, with hint of mint and eucalyptus, not unlike a fine California Cabernet. Full, round, yet still solid with very good fruit extract. A lovely wine of top quality, matured for about two years in large American oak barrels. This is an extremely rare wine, fetching at auction over US$500 per bottle. (18)

These Nederburg Cabernets receive little or no small oak-cask ageing. The older "Select" Cabernets have a larger proportion of Cabernet Sauvignon in the blend. The younger regular Cabernets have a lesser proportion of Cabernet Sauvignon in the blend, the rest being made up of Syrah.

FLIGHT #3

Other mature South African Cabernet Sauvignons

1978 SIMONSIG CABERNET SAUVIGNON:

Youthful colour. Spicy, fruity, vegetal nose. Acidic, sharp, and stemmy on palate; lacking ripeness. (13.5)

1971 BACKSBERG ESTATE CABERNET SAUVIGNON:

Deep, mature colour. Rich, fruity, ripe nose with hint of straw. A big, solid, and jammy wine. Heavy and one-dimensional. Good, but not great. (14.5)

1970 VERGENOEGD CABERNET SAUVIGNON:

Medium, red colour, mature at rim. Elegant, herbaceous nose. Lighter than the Backsberg, but much more complex and elegant, with good depth. Clean, long finish. Lots of class there. (17)

1969 BACKSBERG ESTATE CABERNET SAUVIGNON:

Dark colour. Elegant, subdued nose. More complex than the 1971. Well structured, finishing a bit short. Needs drinking before it loses its fruit. (15.5)

1969 ALTO CABERNET SAUVIGNON:

Dark colour to rim. Spicy, ripe Cabernet nose. Complex, well balanced, with a lovely long finish and firm structure. A very good wine. (16.5)

1968 Groot Constantia Cabernet Sauvignon:

Dark colour. Stemmy, herbaceous nose, with hint of dill. Sharp on palate with dill overtones. Peppery, little fruit, and tired. A poor bottle. (11)

1965 Alto "Select" Cabernet Sauvignon:

Medium colour with palish rim. Elegant, yet rich nose with hint of coffee and mocha. Ripe on palate. Tannic, solid wine. Long finish, with some volatile acidity. Impressive for its age. (16) Alto usually produce big, intense wines.

Paarl Cabernet Sauvignon N/V, KWV, in half-bottles:

This wine was purchased by one of our contributing tasters, and has been cellared since the mid-1960s. Possibly a 1962 or 1963. Round, elegant, full-bodied wine. Slight hint of iodine. Considering its age and being in half-bottles, this wine has held very well. (15.5)

One interesting thing about these wines is the almost total lack of oak on either nose or palate. Also, most of the corks were surprisingly short and of poor quality.

DESSERT WINES

1978 Edelkeur, Wine of Origin, Nederburg, in half-bottle:

Made from Steen grapes (Chenin Blanc) and occasionally blended with some Johannisberg Riesling, this wine had a deep, bright-gold colour. Rich, ripe nose, with hint of peaches, oak, and botrytis. Should last for a few more years. A rare and very enjoyable experience. Not unlike a fine California BA or TBA. This wine is usually released (and sold through) the now-famous Nederburg auction. (17.5)

1930 Muscadel, Wine of Origin, "Boberg Superior" Bin B14, KWV:

Deep amber colour, turning to olive-green at rim. Rich Muscat, ripe, complex nose. Full, long, and very flavourful on palate. An ageless wine. Top quality. (17.5)

Thus ended a unique experience. To my knowledge, such an extensive tasting of rare mature South African wines has never been held before in Canada or the USA.

August 21, 1986

Tasting of Angelo Gaja wines, with Angelo Gaja. Sponsored by English-Gunn, his agents in Western Canada.

1. 1984 Chardonnay, Gaya & Rey:

Made from 100% Chardonnay. Production of 1,000 cases per year. Aged in new small oak barrels. Palish green-gold. Clean, crisp, complex nose, with some oak and slight touch of sulphur or cheese. Full, rich, round, intense, oaky. Lovely, complex, rich wine. Good acidity. Slightly high alcohol. Otherwise top quality. (18)

In 1964, they decided to go it alone and produce all their wines from their own vineyards. Gaja also decided not to produce Barolo (they had never owned vineyards there). Their goal: 60% of 17,500 cases to be Barbaresco; 20% unusual varietals for the area (such as Cabernet Sauvignon); and 20% traditional varietals (Barbera, etc.).

Chardonnay is planted in the Traiso area. Vineyards are now planted vertically rather than horizontally because they were afraid to cause or precipitate erosion of the soil in that steep vineyard.

"Sori San Lorenzo" vineyard clones were selected by Angelo's grandfather, also named Angelo. First vintage for Chardonnay was 1983 (planted in 1979). Density: 7,000 vines per hectare—double the average density. This lowers production—vines fighting for nutrition. Production of 17.4 hectolitres per hectare in 1984 was very low.

The Cabernet Sauvignon is planted at 6,200 vines per hectare. Rey is the name of his grandmother's family. Stainless steel vats are used for fermentation. Oak barrels are purchased from all over France, Italy, Yugoslavia, Romania, etc. Angelo has two daughters, born in 1979 and 1981. (I am writing all these details down as Angelo is speaking and answering questions from participants.)

The Chardonnay 1984 we tasted was picked at 21 brix; total acidity 10.5 grams/litre; pH 2.9. Now 7.5 grams/litre acidity and pH 3.2. The 1983 Chardonnay didn't go through malo. Acidity higher. Alcohol 13%. Then the Chardonnay was aged for five months in new oak and five months in stainless steel. Fermentation lasted 55 to 56 days (cold, at 14° to 15° C). 1984 Chardonnay harvested September 8 to 10. 1985 Chardonnay harvested September 3 to 5.

1983 Darmagi:

100% Cabernet Sauvignon. Medium-deep colour to rim. Full, ripe, fruity Cabernet nose. Spicy, still a bit stemmy (young vines). 1983 is the second harvest. A bit sharp, medium-bodied, good tannins, not very complex. Good potential. Vines should be allowed to age a few more years. "Darmagi" is the name of the vineyard. It means "pity," because his dad was against his planting Cabernet Sauvignon and said "Pity!" Planted in 1978. Production of 1,000 cases. Interesting Bordeaux-shaped bottles with a deep punt and a very long, unusual neck—used to be traditional southern-Swiss bottles, before World War II.

First and only Cabernet Sauvignon planted in Piedmont. Yield of 26 hectolitres per hectare: 14 months in oak, mostly new. Fining with fish gelatine, no filtering. Cabernet Sauvignon vines from Bordeaux; Chardonnay clones from Savoie. Angelo selected low-yield clones. Cabernet Sauvignon racked four times. He is a friend of Zelma Long, and they exchange experiment information.

1983 BARBARESCO:

Production of 8,500 cases. 100% Nebbiolo. Medium colour, bright red, not very deep. Spicy, fruity, open nose. Fairly forward. Round, full, needs two to three years. Not a massive wine. Fermented at 29° C to get colour and extract out of the Nebbiolo. Same problem as Pinot Noir: low extract and needs heated fermentation. 22 days fermentation. The 1983 is elegant, in Gaja's opinion, like the 1979, which is already accessible. (16)

1983 BARBARESCO "COSTA RUSSI":

Deeper colour than the regular Barbaresco. Vines 19 years old. Elegant, complex, a bit hard. Needs ten years. Not massive but good. Well balanced. A bit leaner than the San Lorenzo. (17)

1983 BARBARESCO "SORI SAN LORENZO":

Vines 26 years old. Even deeper colour, purplish, deep. Soil has a vein of sand, unusual in the area. (Only in "San Lorenzo.") Helps dry the soil faster. Concentrated, full, rich, round. Needs ten to 12 years. Flavourful, rich wine. (18)

1958, 1947, 1961 are very good years for Barbaresco, with excellent ageing potential, as are the 1978 and the 1982 vintages.

According to Gaja, "Sori Tildin" will mature in between the "Costa Russi" (earlier maturing) and the "San Lorenzo" (later maturing). Age of "Sori Tildin" vines is about 20 years. "Sori" means "South Exposure." When the vines reach around 30 years of age, they like to replant.

Regular Barbaresco yield: 35 to 42 hectolitres per hectare. Single vineyard yield: 25 to 32 hectolitres per hectare.

The first vintage produced in each of the three individual vineyards is as follows: Sori San Lorenzo, 1967; Sori Tildin, 1970; Costa Russi, 1978.

1961 BARBARESCO:

Made by Angelo's father. The wine has high sugar content. After three years in large barrels, they bottled some, but it started to re-ferment. They left the rest of the 1961 in large vats for 48 months. Therefore, they released it late. Medium colour, pale-orange rim. Lovely, complex, Pinot Noir style on nose. Like a mature, red Burgundy. Fuller, though, on palate. Big, complex, long, mature. A lovely wine. Hint of residual sugar. Superb finish. (18.5)

Until 1970, they sold all their wines in Italy. They aren't planning to expand. Total production is 20,000 to 22,000 cases yearly.

September 17 to October 1, 1986

Trip to London, Burgundy, and the Northern Rhône Valley.

September 22

Visit to Domaine Jacques Prieur.

With the son, Martin. They will bottle their Volnay and red Meursault in March, and the Côte de Nuits in May. We tasted the following from cask.

1985 MEURSAULT ROUGE "CLOS DE MAZEREY," MONOPOLE:

Lots of oak. Round, elegant. Well structured but a bit too oaky.

1985 VOLNAY "CLOS DES SANTENOTS":

By law, red Meursault Premier Crus must be called Volnay. Great balance. Good fruit, well balanced. This 1985 will be bottled in March 1987.

Then, I met the father. He used to sell wine to "La Cachette," a restaurant in Vancouver. Now he is selling to the Ontario liquor monopoly. Used to deal with Calvet. They deal with Cobrand and Parliament Imports now.

1985 BEAUNE "CLOS DE LA FEGUINE":

Lovely, flowery, elegant nose. Nice structure, well balanced. Quite good. Some new oak (François Frères). All their Grand Cru 1985s are matured in new oak.

1985 CLOS VOUGEOT:

Bigger, more intense. Full, round, but a bit acidic. Long, elegant. Quite good. Good balance. Only 15 barrels, partly in new or one-year-old barrels.

1985 CHAMBERTIN:

Good depth, more tannic and more body, yet slightly too acidic. Good balance, though. Somehow, lacks the concentration, extract, and class of this famous vineyard. Time will tell.

1985 MUSIGNY:

Closed nose, unyielding. Buttery, yet tannic. Will be bottled in March or September 1987. They're starting to experiment with different kinds of oak. Good, but not great at this early stage.

All wines tasted above are from their own vineyards.

Overall impressions: the wines seemed a bit too light and lacked distinction, especially for a fine, fruity vintage (1985).

Everywhere I went, people were getting ready to pick.

1986 is a rather late vintage. Lots of fruit on the vines, but not quite concentrated enough. They absolutely need warm weather for the next week to ten days. Some are starting to pick as early as Saturday, September 27. Maybe this will turn out to be a softer, more diluted year than 1985. The whites, however, are very promising.

Visit to Maison Louis Trapet in Gevrey.

Met Jean Trapet. Friendly visit. An interesting and friendly man. He starts picking his 1986s on Monday (employing 50 vendangeurs). They use a fair bit of new barrels, 50% in 1984, more in better years.

Trapet thinks that the 1986s will possibly be like the 1979s (I actually said that, and he agreed). Fairly large production, but not very big wines. The 1984s were bottled in May and June. Since 1980, their US agent is Robert Haas. Before, for 30 years, it was Alexis Lichine. All the wines he produces are from his own vineyards.

First we tried Trapet's 1984s.

GEVREY-CHAMBERTIN:

Pale, typical 1984. Clean nose. Pleasant, but a bit acidic and too green. (14.5)

CHAPELLE-CHAMBERTIN:

A bit darker. Vanilla-oak. Elegant. Much better than the above. Round, elegant, mid-term. Some tannin. Nice. (16)

LATRICIÈRES-CHAMBERTIN:

Medium colour. Ripe, round, elegant nose. Very good. Better balanced. Hard, tannic. A bit green. Quite good. (17)

CHAMBERTIN:

Just bottled last month. Good colour for a 1984, which are usually pale. Tannic, quite hard with oak and good fruit. Trapet thinks that it will be ready in about six years. (17)

Then came the turn of the 1985s.

GEVREY-CHAMBERTIN, FROM FIRST CASK:

Good colour, darker than any of the 1984s, but odd nose. Needed airing. These 1985s haven't been fined yet and have been racked only once. They'll be racked again in October. Good fruit. This cask came from grapes picked toward Morey-St.-Denis (south).

GEVREY-CHAMBERTIN, FROM SECOND CASK:

Grapes from farther north, near Blochon. No Grands Crus there, so commune wines planted in better soils. More concentrated than above. Ripe, darker. Fruity. Very good.

All the casks of Gevrey will be blended.

Cuvaison is 14 to 15 days. Natural alcohol for the 1985s is 12.5%, very good! They renew planting by row, rather than single vines. Trapet said that "Mazoyères" is very similar in style to "Charmes" near Morey-St.-Denis (very close to each other).

CHAPELLE-CHAMBERTIN FROM CASK:

Lovely, dark colour to rim. No collage, or very little needed, because these 1985s are so naturally bright. Ripe, round. Excellent quality. Well balanced. Not nearly as hard as the 1983s; tannins are softer and blend better in the wine.

LATRICIÈRES-CHAMBERTIN FROM CASK:

More serious and less feminine than the Chapelle. Ripe. Concentrated and big. Needs lots of time.

Trapet told Sid Cross and me (I took Sid along to visit both Trapet and Roumier) that Roumier's brother Alain does not make the Vogüé wines any more. His wife died and he retired. The son-in-law of Ladoucette replaced him at Vogüé.

(Sid Cross happened to be in Burgundy at the same time as I was, but because he speaks no French, he has to stick with the négociants, such as Latour, Jadot, and Drouhin, where people speak English. He found it advantageous to join me in visiting smaller producers, and I translated for him.)

CHAMBERTIN 1985 (FROM 30-YEAR-OLD VINES) FROM CASK:

Medium-dark. Complex, unyielding nose. Touch of sulphur. Big. Very good length. Not as fruity as the Latricières, but still very good.

CHAMBERTIN "VIEILLES VIGNES" 1985 FROM CASK:

Superb. Great wine. Dark, deep, perfect balance. Fruity, concentrated. Will be great some day.

I noticed that he had a code on his casks.

"A" means old vines, 80 years old! They will probably make some in 1985 (only in selected vintages). Then he gave Sid and me one bottle each of his 1983 Chambertin "Vieille Vignes." A most enjoyable visit.

Visit to Domaine Georges Roumier.

They're starting to pick on Monday. We tasted the 1985s (from cask, no collage yet and only one racking so far).

SIMPLE BOURGOGNE ROUGE:

Medium colour. Clean, spicy, elegant. Forward. Without faults. Ripe tannins (typical 1985).

Mr. Roumier said that Ted Lehman, winemaker at Woltner (Howell Mountain, Napa), worked at

Roumier previously. Ted is a friend of Roumier's son Christophe, whom we met, too. He said that the nights in September were too cold this year. Agrees with me that 1986 will be, maybe, like the 1979s.

Chambolle-Musigny (from the flats):

Darker, sweet, elegant, a bit simple, but good character.

Chambolle-Musigny (from the hills):

Better soil and exposure. Better and darker than the above. Spicier, rounder, bigger. Ripe tannins. More harmonious in his opinion than the 1983s. He'll blend both and produce a single Chambolle.

Roumier said that what saved the 1983s was good weather in early October (sunny). Powerful tannins in 1983, producing sharper wines. The major problem with many 1983s is the widespread gray rot, imparting mustiness to the wines that will never go away, contrary to what several wine "experts" think and write.

Morey-St.-Denis "Clos de la Bussière" Premier Cru 1985, Monopole:

Deep, lovely concentration. Ripe tannins; long, fine wine. One to buy! Spicy, oak-vanilla.

Roumier compared the 1985s to the 1978s and the 1983s to the 1926s. I don't know enough about the 1926s. I think, however, that while the 1985s are the best vintage for reds since 1978, the 1978s are more solid, more powerful. The 1985s will be more elegant charmers.

Chambolle-Musigny "Les Amoureuses" 1985:

Dark, harmonious, long. Beautiful fruit, yet finishes hard. Needs a few years yet. Will be excellent.

Bonnes Mares Grand Cru 1985:

Loaded with ripe fruit. Dark, complex, superb. Misleading because it seems elegant, yet it is very big. A serious wine (my comment, he liked this expression). Definitely a must-buy!

Musigny 1985:

A bit lighter colour than the Bonnes Mares. More forward (relatively). Cinnamon, elegant, lovely. Easy to like. Yet Roumier thinks that he'll leave it in wood as long or longer than the Bonnes Mares. He said delicacy doesn't mean "forward." Long on palate, loaded with nuances. One to buy!

His agent in the USA is Château and Estate. No Ruchottes sold in the USA (very little made).

Then he opened two 1983s.

Chambolle-Musigny 1983, in half-bottle:

Dark, full, hard tannins. Touch of rot. Touch of mustiness. Careful picking in 1983 was a must. Backward, hard, needs time.

1983 Ruchottes-Chambertin 1983, in full-bottle:

Very dark, ripe fruit. Hard tannins. Needs at least ten years! Slight touch of mustiness. Loaded with fruit, though.

This was a very interesting visit, too.

Visit to the Domaine de la Romanée-Conti.

We joined a small group there, with the young winemaker Hervé de Ferrer. Hervé is a serious and capable young man. I found out that the old winemaker, André Noblet, died last March (retired in 1983). He had a heart attack while visiting Moscow. I had two great visits with Noblet in 1977 and 1980. The 1984s were bottled very recently.

1984 La Tâche:

Forward. Palish colour. Well balanced. Spicy. Complex. Better than most 1984s. (17)

1982 Richebourg:

Elegant, forward, better structure than the 1984. Long on palate. Quite good. Ready soon, as so many 1982s are, yet lovely complexity and toasty oak, even rich. (17.5)

1981 La Tâche:

Good colour. Not as long and complex as the 1982 Richebourg, but more backward. A bit hard, needing four to six years. Tannic. Fruit a bit low, though. (16.5)

1980 La Tâche:

Darker than the 1981. Complex, spicy. Oak-vanilla. Ripe fruit. A bit leathery. Some wood. Long finish. Not too aggressive. (17)

1979 Grands Echézeaux:

Ripe, obviously leathery. Mature, long, well balanced. Fairly alcoholic. A very good wine. Drink from 1989 to 1995. (17.5)

1975 La Tâche:

Very pale. Orange-brown. Chaptalized. No fruit. Tired. Acidic. Disappointing. (Hervé knows that. It was just for the experience to taste a really poor vintage.) (12)

All their new barrels are acquired from François Frères. They're starting to pick late this year, on October 6, a week after most other growers.

Then we went to the cellar and tasted all the 1985 reds from cask. The wines are not scored as they have not yet been bottled.

Echézeaux:

Good, dark colour. Medium body, soft tannins. Complex, well balanced. Round. Very good.

GRANDS ECHÉZEAUX:

More spicy and closed, but less fruit on nose at this stage. More pronounced tannins. More complex, very good. Good balance. Very promising.

ROMANÉE-ST.-VIVANT:

Less tannic than the above. Rounder and a bit softer, fewer spices. More forward. Vanilla. I like the Grands Echézeaux better, yet this will be very fine indeed.

RICHEBOURG:

Fantastic, elegant, complex, on both nose and palate. Hervé's favourite; mine, too, at this stage. Will be ready in ten years. A great wine. A "must-buy" at just about any price. These wines will not be cheap!

LA TÂCHE:

Big, deep, dark. Unyielding, concentrated, tannic. Sweet and serious. Needs time, yet softer than the 1983. Classic raspberry nose, so typical of this property even at this early stage.

ROMANÉE-CONTI:

Mocha, chocolate, coffee on nose; very pronounced. Deep, spicy, concentrated, tannic. Fabulous balance. Someday this will be a great bottle. A most enjoyable and interesting visit. We were fortunate to taste these great 1985 "babies."

Wednesday, September 24, 1986

Morning visit to Domaine Tollot-Beaut (Chorey-lès-Beaune), with Sid Cross.

Clean, modern offices and bottling facilities. Lovely old cellars. In 1985, small production. Oak 30% to 50% new, from François Frères. In 1986, large production of 50 hectolitres per hectare. In my opinion, too much volume to make great, concentrated wines. But then, 1986s will probably be soft, early maturing wines anyway. A "useful" vintage.

Their agent in the USA is Château and Estate. They ship 25 cases per year of Corton-Charlemagne to the USA out of a total production of 100 cases. Corton-Charlemagne: 30 hectolitres per hectare average. They only produce four barrels of this great wine!

Mrs. Tollot-Beaut has three brothers (Tollot). Beaut is the maiden name of their grandmother.

In 1985, small production of 25 hectolitres per hectare. In 1986, large production of 50 hectolitres per hectare. What a difference!

They picked their first Corton-Charlemagne in 1969; 55-year-old vines. Their Charlemagne is from a vineyard above Ladoix. All the wines (both reds and whites) come from their own 50 acres of vineyards.

First, we tasted the 1984s, in bottle.

CHOREY-LÈS-BEAUNE:

Light, palish. Vanilla, good fruit, no greenness. Pleasant and clean. (15)

SAVIGNY "CHAMP CHEVREY" PREMIER CRU, MONOPOLE:

A bit darker. Solid, more body and tannin. More acidic, too, and a bit edgy. (14)

SAVIGNY "LAVIÈRE" PREMIER CRU:

Made across the road from Champ Chevrey. More concentration and fruit. Needs more time. Riper, too. (15)

They waited a long time to pick their 1984s, but they picked the 1985s early.

BEAUNE "CLOS DU ROI" PREMIER CRU:

Concentrated, ripe, yet hard and edgy. Bottle sickness? Wait five to six years. Touch of oak. Good for 1984. (15)

ALOXE-CORTON:

Closed nose. Ripe berries. Premier Cru vines. Harder than previous wine. I like the Beaune "Clos du Roi" better. Needs time. (14)

CORTON "BRESSANDES":

Perfume, class, complex. Tannic. All these 1984s were surprisingly good and clean for the vintage. (15.5)

Then we tasted the 1985s from cask. These wines have only been in oak for eight to ten months. They have a long way to go until final evolution and bottling.

CHOREY-LÈS-BEAUNE:

Good colour, fruit, balance. As expected, a very pleasant 1985. They have two lots of Chorey. Near Ladoix and near Beaune (the latter is the best, but they blend them).

SAVIGNY "CHAMP CHEVREY":

Elegant, round, lighter style.

SAVIGNY "LAVIÈRE":

More smoky, more oak, more class, good balance.

BEAUNE "CLOS DU ROI":

Racked in July. Closed, very good fruit. Concentrated, lovely. Vines planted in sandy soil. Very promising.

BEAUNE "GRÈVES" PREMIER CRU:

Hard, tannic, yet lovely flavours. Not as much ripe fruit as the "Clos du Roi." Vines planted in calcareous argillite soil. More masculine. Very good.

CORTON GRAND CRU:

Planted just under Daniel Senard's clos. Very good, rich fruit. Good, yet soft tannins. Well balanced. Needs time, but easy to like now. Only 1,200 bottles produced!

CORTON "BRESSANDES":

Concentrated, intense, solid, loaded with fruit. Similar to the Beaune "Clos du Roi," while Grèves resembled the Corton—more serious, harder wines.

All these 1985s will be bottled in January and February 1987.

THE WHITE

1984 CORTON-CHARLEMAGNE:

Honey, flowers, delicate yet big underneath. Alcoholic, rich, full. Good acidity and will hold. Not as nutty as Latour's. Will be bottled January/February 1987 (same as the reds).

1985 CORTON-CHARLEMAGNE, FROM BARREL:

Four barrels. Two new and two older. Total production is only 1,200 bottles. That is 100 cases for the whole world. Why do great things come in small packages?

1. SECOND YEAR BARREL:

Almost ready. Rounder, richer, delicate, long oak, flowers. Harmonious, with a hint of honey. Lovely intensity.

2. NEW BARREL:

Vanilla on nose. Livelier and more backward. More bite and acidity. Fresher. More backbone. A blend will make their usual great Corton-Charlemagne.

Sid Cross was very fortunate to join me on this fascinating visit. With his zero knowledge of French, he would have been lost, as nobody at Tollot-Beaut speaks a word of English.

Their wines are charming, elegant, clean, round. Not edgy or unbalanced. Impressive, honest operation.

Visit to Coche-Dury.

Sid and I drove in pouring rain to Meursault to visit one of the greatest producers of Meursault: Jean-François Coche-Dury. A very pleasant and friendly young man. Clean compact operation. Again, no English spoken here. Maybe someday Jean-François will learn English, as time goes by and his wines become known in America. Unfortunately, this is bound to drive the price up!

First, he let us taste his reds, except for the Monthélie, which he pulled out and will start to produce again in six years. He is replanting his Monthélie vineyard now.

All 1985, from cask.

MONTHÉLIE:

Last vintage before uprooting the vineyard. Palish, pretty red. Soft, round, delicate. Well structured. Fresh, not unlike carbonic maceration (which it did not go through). He buys new barrels each year: from François Frères for his reds and Damy for his whites.

MEURSAULT ROUGE:

Lovely Pinot Noir varietal. Sweet, round, long, and clean. Made from two parcels, one, near Caillerets, which will be ripped out soon and replanted with Chardonnay for Appellation Contrôlée Meursault "Caillerets." The other parcel only has the right to Appellation Contrôlée Meursault, so he's leaving it alone. No sense planting white there.

AUXEY-DURESSES:

Needs to be racked soon. Very good, dark colour. This is his first crop, no greenness (in spite of the fact that the vines are only four years old!). Round, long, sweet, and rich. He said that he pruned severely in 1985.

They're starting to pick on Friday.

Today (Wednesday, September 24), it rained and there are some signs of gray rot. Large crop. As for quality—not clear yet, but not great.

VOLNAY PREMIER CRU:

Blend of "Clos des Chênes" and "Taillepieds." Not as dark as the Auxey. Round, complex, long, well balanced, elegant. Feminine. Typical Volnay. His reds are great, too!

In 1986, they will produce Corton-Charlemagne for the first time, from a 25-year lease he signed with a lady who used to lease her land to Louis Latour. From one hectare, he gets to produce and pick one-third. Jean-François hopes to produce 120 to 150 cases annually. Judging by his other wines, this Corton-Charlemagne should be great!

Then we tasted his whites, all 1985s, all from cask.

BOURGOGNE ALIGOTÉ:

Elegant, well balanced; flowers and perfume. Very nice, especially for such a simple wine. Really lovely.

BOURGOGNE CHARDONNAY:

Planted one-half kilometre toward Volnay. Lovely, round, rich. 12.5% natural alcohol. Honey and flowers. Beautiful. If this is everyday wine, what is a great wine?!

MEURSAULT "LA BARRE-NARVAUX":

13% natural alcohol. Delicate, round, well balanced. Harmony. Some oak. Complex. Very good.

MEURSAULT "LES CASSE TÊTE":

Sweeter, richer, more concentrated. A bit harder. Very good.

MEURSAULT "LES ROUGEOTS":

Yield of 50 hectolitres per hectare. Lovely, long, delicate, easy to like. Perfume, almonds, oak on nose. Superb quality. After swallowing, bigger, seems to have bottle-age! Toasty. Great potential, in spite of relatively large yield per hectare.

MEURSAULT-PERRIÈRES:

Even better balance than above! Toast, oak, lower acidity. Superb quality. Richer. Thicker. This is his only Meursault Premier Cru. Jean-François refuses to add acidity to his whites, but sometimes he does acidify his reds. He doesn't filter his whites at all (his reds, occasionally).

1982 MEURSAULT "CUVÉE LA BARRE-NARVAUX," FROM BOTTLE:

Deep, bright gold. Lovely, long, nutty-oak nose. Lots of fruit. Soft. Elegant. Complex. Toasty. Ready, with very good acidity. (18)

This was a very informative visit with a great winemaker!

Visit to Robert Chevillon.

I drove to meet François Faiveley for lunch. François knows Bruce Guimaraens well. After lunch, he joined me for a visit to Robert Chevillon, also in Nuits-St.-Georges. I drove François back to his winery after the visit to Robert Chevillon. Chevillon uses Servrugues oak barrels.

François and I tasted the following Chevillon wines from barrel.

1985 NUITS-ST.-GEORGES:

Light, elegant; violets, complexity. Clean. Good, concentrated fruit. Lovely juice, even at this early stage.

1985 NUITS-ST.-GEORGES "RONCIÈRES":

Darker, soft, supple. Well balanced. Good fruit extract, yet not a big or powerful wine.

1985 NUITS-ST.-GEORGES "PERRIÈRES":

A bit sharper, darker, and spicier. Perfumed and lovely. Soft tannins. Again, very promising.

Chevillon seemed a bit worried about the relatively low acids of the 1985s. I think, however, that the fruit is so intense that while these wines may not be very long-agers, they will be very good, with rich fruit and they will last well until at least 1997 to 2000.

1985 NUITS-ST.-GEORGES "LES CAILLES":

From 60-year-old vines. Superb! Long, round, spicy, excellent balance. Concentrated. A splendid bottle. Faiveley loved it, too. Definitely one to buy.

1985 NUITS-ST.-GEORGES "VAUCRAINS":

Touch of residual sugar. Sweeter, bigger style. Also made from 60-year-old vines. This wine was slightly spritzy and more nervous because it has been racked only once so far. Masculine, solid, good potential. Chevillon thinks that he'll manage to get rid of the sugar. He had fermentation problems with this wine. It rained during picking. Rain washed yeast off the grapes so it caused starting difficulties in the fermentation.

1984 NUITS-ST.-GEORGES "LES CAILLES":

Incredible for 1984! Dark, long, beautiful depth and complexity. Sweet, round, fruity, very clean. Touch of oak. Ready soon. Worth buying!

Then he opened this bottle.

1979 NUITS-ST.-GEORGES "VAUCRAINS":

Deep, full, big, round, and long. Leathery. A gold medal winner and top quality. He really makes excellent Nuits-St.-Georges. François Faiveley enjoyed them very much, too.

Tasting at Lalou Brize-Leroy.

That evening, I drove with Sid and Joan Cross for a tasting and dinner at Lalou Brize-Leroy. Lalou received a "Personality of the Year" award. It was an extensive tasting of 1966 red Burgundies of Maison Leroy to celebrate that vintage's 20th anniversary. Foggy, rainy day. About 60 people at tables of four. Mostly writers, wine producers, and restaurateurs (Pierre Trois Gros, Eberlin, Georges Duboeuf, etc.). Michael Broadbent was supposed to fly in from London, but his plane could not take off because of the fog, so he missed this fine event.

All wines were from the Leroy estate, and all were 1966s. All wines were served blind.

FLIGHT #1

1. POMMARD "GRANDS EPENOTS":

Deep colour to rim. Concentrated, spicy, big nose. Solid, a bit simple. A sturdy, big wine. Good fruit. A bit short. Pommard? (15)

2. BEAUNE:

Similar appearance to #1, yet a bit more age at rim. Spicy, sweet nose. Better than #1. Fruity, pleasant, round. Not very complex, but good character. (15.5)

3. BEAUNE "CENT VIGNES":

Darker than #1 or #2. Most forthcoming of the three, yet still very intense and rich. Richest of #1 to #3. Full, fruity, sweet. Long, best character and complexity. Good length. Very good. (17.5)

4. BEAUNE PREMIER CRU:

A bit paler than #1 to #3. More age at rim. Slightly skunky, vegetal. Round, elegant, flowery. Simple, but good and clean. Long. Good fruit. (15.5)

5. HOSPICES DE BEAUNE, BEAUNE "CUVÉE ESTIENNE":

A bit darker than #4 (which was quite dark anyway). Toast, delicate, complex, slightly leathery (hardly noticeable). Full, rich, round, yet still tannic. Hard, ripe fruit. A bit too acidic at end. Pommard? (15.5)

6. POMMARD:

Closed nose. Good colour. Ripe fruit. Clean (as others were, too). Delicate, round, forward. Well balanced. Not too deep but long, delicate finish. Touch of chocolate-mocha. Beaune or Volnay? (16.5)

7. POMMARD "CLOS MICAULT":

Lovely, elegant nose. Most open of bunch so far. A bit lighter than #1 to #6, but not by much. Round, sweet on palate. Forward. A bit of a sharp finish. Quite nice. Delicate. Another Volnay? (16.5)

8. HOSPICES DE BEAUNE, BEAUNE "CUVÉE GUIGONE DE SALINS":

Palest of bunch. Light. Complex, open, spicy, and forward. A bit sharp. Some tannins. Round, a bit short finish. Not as good as #6 or #7, but good quality. (15.5)

9. BEAUNE "CHAMPIMONTS":

Dark, maturing colour. Not as dark as #1 to #3, but darker than #6 to #8. Open, elegant nose. Rich, fruity, round. Well balanced and long. Very good. (17.5)

10. BEAUNE "BRESSANDES":

Lightish red. Mature. Open, toasty, fruity, forward, elegant. Not as long as #9. Complex, but a bit shorter. Not as intense. (15.5)

11. HOSPICES DE BEAUNE, BEAUNE "CUVÉE NICOLAS ROLIN":

Darker than the "Bressandes." Still-closed nose. Spicy, round. Quite rich. Full, round on surface, yet hard underneath. Quite intense. (16.5)

Very difficult flight of 11 wines.

FLIGHT #2

1. CORTON "PERRIÈRES":

Dark colour. Complex, spicy nose. Rich, round, yet underneath solid, hard. Clean, long finish. Top quality. (17)

2. CORTON:

Unyielding nose. Not as complex as #1. Ripe, rich, dark. Solid. Concentrated. Very ripe, yet a bit simple. Heavy. A bit short. (15.5)

3. ALOXE-CORTON:

Medium-dark. Very good depth. Solid, big, round, but not very complex (relatively speaking). Later, sweeter, longer, cleaner. Oak. Good finish. (16.5)

4. CORTON "RENARDES":

Very dark, dense colour. Solid, big, hard. Ripe, jammy, yet tannic. Must be a Corton. (17)

5. SAVIGNY-LÈS-BEAUNE:

Long. Complex. Elegant. A bit tannic, but a lot of class. Round. Very long on palate. (17.5) Surprise! The simplest appellation, yet the best in this flight!

I was very close in this flight. I guessed Cortons, but I was wrong about the Savigny. I thought that it was a Corton, too.

FLIGHT #3

In this flight, the wines were lighter in appearance

1. CHAMBOLLE-MUSIGNY:

Medium depth. Open, sweet, complex nose. Round, delicate. Complex on palate, good depth and length. Very nice wine. Lovely. Spicy. (17)

2. ECHÉZEAUX:

Lighter than #1. Not as open or complex. Soft. Higher acidity. Getting tired. Not bad, though. Some spices. (15.5)

3. MUSIGNY:

Similar in appearance to #1. Good depth. Closed, unyielding nose. Solid, deep. Serious wine. Loaded with fruit. Very good quality. No rush. Lots of life, but lacks the elegance of a true Musigny, in retrospect. (17)

4. GRANDS ECHÉZEAUX:

Medium-dark. Deep. Spicy, masculine nose. Slightly earthy. Ripe, round, full, long, solid. Fruitier than #3. Not as hard as #3, yet powerful and with lots of fruit. Outstanding wine. (18.5)

5. CHAMBOLLE-MUSIGNY "LES AMOUREUSES":

Medium colour. Delicate, open nose. Round. Hard on palate. Tannins, some acidity. Surprising tannins for colour. A spicier, richer version of #3. (17.5)

6. CLOS DE VOUGEOT:

Good, deep colour. Closed, unyielding nose. Big, well balanced, fruity, long. Rich. Masculine, lovely, long, delicate nose. Long, forward. Great, elegant finish. Musigny? Superb. Complete. A star. (19)

FLIGHT #4

1. MOREY-ST.-DENIS:

Very deep, dark colour. Very ripe, rich nose. Long, intense, loaded with ripe fruit. Surprisingly good for a simple commune wine. (17)

2. CHAPELLE-CHAMBERTIN:

Palish. Mature colour. Elegant, soft nose. Round, forward, elegant on palate. (17)

3. GEVREY-CHAMBERTIN "CLOS ST. JACQUES":

Medium-dark colour. Solid, serious nose. Big, mature, long, intense. (17)

4. Charmes-Chambertin:

Good, dark colour. Round, complex, solid, serious, but a bit too acidic. Not much "Charm." (16.5)

5. Gevrey-Chambertin "Les Cazetiers":

Very deep, dark colour. Hard, solid, not too complex, yet long. Rich, round, full of life. (17)

6. Chambertin:

Good, dark colour; mature rim. Elegant, complex, lots of class here. Super quality. Rich, full, solid, almost hot. A big wine. Still tannic. Obviously Chambertin! Outstanding. (18.5)

7. Mazis-Chambertin:

Medium colour. Mature, orange rim. Round, simple, not much nose. Morey? Short, disappointing. The Mazis! Very disappointing. (14.5)

A great evening, yet too much of a good thing! After a while it was difficult to notice the difference. Also, some of the wines were atypical of their respective communes. These wines will be released for sale shortly. They will fetch a lot of money… not always justified.

At this tasting and dinner, I shared a table with Mme. François, wife of the Tonnelier François (barrel maker), a Norwegian wine writer, and the purchasing agent for the Swedish liquor monopoly.

Friday, September 26, 1986

Morning visit to Louis Latour with Menashe.

Our guide was Justin Crawford.

Drove to Corton-Grancey.

Visited chais, old cellar, and tasted some wines. Tasted some grapes, too, off the vines. A bit watery. Also, there are already signs of gray rot! Too cold at night and rained for quite a while. The weather is not collaborating. Looks like 1986s will be soft, diluted wines.

The Domaine Louis Latour wines tasted are as follows.

WHITES

1984 Chassagne-Montrachet:

Pleasant, crisp, good acidity. Not much depth.

1983 Corton-Charlemagne:

Fabulous, long, oak, big, round, elegant. Not as alcoholic as expected. Great in three to five years. (18)

REDS

1982 Savigny-lès-Beaune:

Light, elegant, simple, and too acidic. (14)

1982 Aloxe-Corton "Les Chaillots":

Medium depth. Flowery, spicy, elegant 1982. Well balanced. Ready in two to three years. (15)

1979 Morey-St.-Denis Premier Cru:

A bit sharp at finish and too acidic. Not as soft or round as 1979s should be. (14.5)

1979 Corton-Grancey:

Elegant, complex, good depth. Quite dark. Ready around 1988 to 1990. Quite good. (16)

So far, the visit to Latour was a low on this trip.

They treated us too much like tourists—they should have known better! Yet, I had written to Louis Latour in advance, as I usually do before a trip, and in the past I have had most enjoyable visits with him. Well, we can't win them all.

Afternoon visit to Domaine Armand Rousseau in Gevrey-Chambertin.

An exciting three-hour visit. Charles Rousseau is a very friendly man. His agent in the USA is Wildman (Hiram Walker). He deals a bit with Ontario. He knows J.-M. Cazes. He likes Domaine de Chevalier and de Pez, especially the 1967 (an odd vintage to like). At first, he said that although he was expecting us, he had "only 20 minutes" for the visit. Three hours later, we were still tasting!

About the 1986 Vintage

Large crop. Starting to pick on Monday. Unfortunately, not enough northern wind to dry grapes after rains, therefore some gray rot. About 1983s: like 1971s, he says, the early signs of rot in the wine will disappear but he says one must wait for a few years. I tend, however, to disagree with him about the gray rot of the 1983s. I think that this will never go away.

The 1985s are just afterracking, and they don't show too well. He knows Harry Waugh quite well. Harry saw him recently and gave him a bottle of Château Latour 1970. Rousseau likes 1972 red Burgundies more than the 1971s, which he says, are too soft. He thinks that most 1959s are finished, yet 1957s (high acidity) are excellent. He also said that the 1976s were not too successful in the Côte de Beaune, but the Côte-de-Nuits need time—"not to worry, be patient." Personally, while I like the 1972s, I think that 1971 was much more consistent and better overall for the reds. And to call the 1959s "finished" is a bit of an exaggeration, to put it mildly.

We went to the cellars to taste the 1985s from cask.

GEVREY-CHAMBERTIN:

Deepish colour, fruity nose. Soft tannins, elegant, with good depth. 1985s (Charles says) are fat, round, luscious.

GEVREY-CHAMBERTIN "LES CAZETIERS":

Round, long, and on the dry side. More masculine. Very good fruit extract, colour, and depth.

His Grands Crus are aged in 100% new oak; Premier Crus in 50% new oak or less. His regular Gevrey sees no new oak. Rousseau uses Alier (from François Frères).

MAZIS-CHAMBERTIN:

Dark, closed, concentrated. Rich. Fair bit of acidity. Fatter, richer style. He will bottle the 1985s between June and September 1987. Very fine quality here.

CHARMES-CHAMBERTIN:

Seemed a bit upset after racking. Elegant, softer than the Mazis. Not as dark. A charmer. Needs seven to ten years, though.

CLOS DE LA ROCHE:

Big, rich, dark; masculine, hard, tannic, closed. A solid wine needing many years.

Charles said that most of these 1985s will pick up more colour in barrel.

RUCHOTTES-CHAMBERTIN "CLOS DES RUCHOTTES," MONOPOLE:

(Purchased in 1977 from Thomas Bassot, a firm that does not exist anymore) Much more elegant than the Clos de la Roche. Very complex, fabulous nose. A great wine. Length, class, elegance, complexity. Only 25 hectolitres per hectare produced and only 15 hectolitres per hectare in 1984! This monopole is made up of three-quarters old vines (about 60-years-old) and one-quarter younger vines planted by Bassot.

GEVREY-CHAMBERTIN "CLOS ST. JACQUES":

Contrary to what wine "authorities" say, this is not Charles Rousseau's favourite, but he likes it very much. Made from old vines (60-years-old or older). Round, forward, soft, some oak. Very good depth. Elegance and harmony. Soft tannins, but they're there.

CHAMBERTIN "CLOS DE BÈZE":

Dark, oak-vanilla, very long. Great class. Will be a superb bottle some day.

CHAMBERTIN:

Wine seemed a bit upset, but Rousseau said that because it is always bigger than the "Clos de Bèze," the oak and vanilla are not that obvious. (Both wines matured in 100% new oak.) Bitter, slightly spritzy. Needs a lot of time.

Then we opened this bottle.

1982 CHAMBERTIN "CLOS DE BÈZE":

Soft, round, lots of depth, though. Needs another five to seven years. Great length. Very good. Excellent extract for a 1982. (17.5)

He asked me what I wanted to taste. I said "a 1983," so he opened this one.

GEVREY-CHAMBERTIN "LAVAUX ST. JACQUES" 1983:

Dark, brilliant colour. Complex, ripe nose. Hard, very tannic, typical 1983, with a touch of rot in aftertaste, "goût de grêle." He said that with time, the taste of rot will go away. Needs ten to 15 years. Of course, I could have requested a finer wine from a finer vintage, but I intentionally wanted to taste a 1983. And, yes, the rot was there!

We ended up talking in his office for over an hour, and Charles generously opened this great bottle.

1972 CHAMBERTIN "CLOS DE BÈZE":

What great depth and complexity! Medium-body. Medium-dark colour, showing its age. Round, well balanced. Clean nose and long, spicy, complex character of great red Burgundy. Excellent backbone. A superb bottle! (18.5)

We talked about the problems he had with his 1977s, 1978s, and partially with his 1979s, which he called "la tournée." He said that it started around 1972, but became really bad in 1977 and 1978. He also had bad experiences with pasteurization, which he says makes all wines even, losing their individual character.

"Tournée" occurs when certain bacteria attack the citric acid in the wine (in bottle) and turn it into malic acid, not unlike a second malolactic fermentation, and causes deposits and cloudiness in the bottle. He finally learned how to control it.

Starting with his 1980, his methods were as follows.

1. After the secondary fermentation around mid-December, he drops the temperature in his cellar (turns off heat). Then in February, he racks, thus getting rid of all bacteria. (In the past, he used to leave the wines on their lees too long.)
2. Follows the pH balance very closely, never allowing it to go beyond 3.5 (usually 3.4 to 3.45). That way, with lower pH, the bacteria cannot grow, especially in a cold wine (the same principle as in a swimming pool).
3. He stopped feeding potash to the vines, a practice that his father and others used to do, because potash lowers the pH!

Charles said that he vinified his first vintage in 1946, as a very young man, when his father passed away. This was indeed a most enjoyable and educational visit. Menashe had fun, too. It is nice that Rousseau spent three hours with us during such a busy time of the year.

That evening

Dinner at "La Meloise" in Chagny, with Menashe.

My third visit to this fine restaurant. The food was a masterpiece and the service was impeccable. This three-star Michelin restaurant is excellent. It has never let me down, yet I know of someone who had a less-than-enjoyable lunch there.

1982 MEURSAULT "LE LIMOZIN," MICHELOT BUISSON, IN HALF-BOTTLE:

Full, round, forward, long, serious. Nutty-oak-fruit. Very good and ready.

All in all, a very good day. Nice weather, too, for a change.

Saturday, September 27, 1986

Visit to Mercurey in the Côte Chalonnaise.

We met Michel Juillot. His daughter showed us around, but I spoke to him, too. They were busy picking and vinifying. They produce mostly reds (24 hectares planted) and only two hectares of white Mercurey. The reds spend eight to 12 months in new oak. They only vinify juice from their own grapes.

I also found out that in 1986, they will start to produce a Corton-Charlemagne (about 4,000 bottles) from a parcel that was leased until recently by Louis Latour. Two other producers are leasing from the same lady. Coche-Dury (as indicated earlier) and Belland. Juillot has leased double the area that Coche-Dury got.

They have a few single-vineyard Mercurey reds, including two Premier Crus ("Tonnerre" and "Barrault"). Also, "Champ Martin" (red and white), "Clos L'Evêque," and "Clos du Roi."

We tasted the following.

1985 MERCUREY BLANC:

Already bottled. Light, crisp, elegant, long. Quite nice.

Then we tasted most of the Mercurey reds from large vats where the wines have already been assembled, but not yet bottled.

1985 "CLOS TONNERRE":

Deep colour, round, elegant, complex, and spicy. Very nice. Ready around 1988 to 1990.

1985 MERCUREY (GENERIC):

A bit thinner, simpler, with higher acidity, but not bad.

1985 "CLOS OUDIN":

Much darker and deeper. Big, masculine, solid, concentrated. Tannic, oak-vanilla. Needs five to seven years.

1985 "CHAMP MARTIN":

Still in 100% new oak. Feminine, elegant, oak, vanilla, good length, lovely nose. Lighter colour and structure than the "Clos Oudin."

1985 "CLOS BARRAULT":

Good, deep colour. Structured halfway between "Oudin" and "Champ Martin." Touch of fizz. Tannic, yet elegant. Finishes hard and a bit hot. "Champ Martin" was my favourite in terms of complexity.

A pleasant visit. We saw them crush the grapes. That was a new experience for me as I have never visited the Côte Chalonnaise before.

Sunday, September 28, 1986

Drive from Beaune to Vienne, and lunch at "Alain Chapel," in Mionnay.

A lovely lunch, accompanied by two wines.

1983 SANCERRE "CLOS DU CHÊNE MARCHAND," LUCIEN CROCHET, IN HALF-BOTTLE:

Lovely. Typical spicy, stemmy, rich nose of good Sauvignon Blanc. Round, long, full, very well balanced. A lovely bottle. Good fruit; long, rich finish. (16.5)

1978 CHÂTEAU DUCRU-BEAUCAILLOU, IN HALF-BOTTLE:

Decanted 45 minutes. Deep, dark colour, still youthful. Starting to show a lovely, complex, rich nose. Full, well balanced, long. If it is so good (but not ready) in half-bottle, the full bottles will be great—in five to ten years! Great potential. (18)

Monday, September 29

Morning visit to Jaboulet.

I was disappointed when I found out that Gerard was in Copenhagen and could not meet us, but we met his father, Paul, who turned out to be a very friendly man. We talked for a while in his office, then went to the tasting room where he had samples (in bottles) of the 1985s. In his letter to me, Gerard definitely said that he would meet us. I guess he had urgent business in Denmark.

Mr. Jaboulet Sr. talked a lot about French politics.

Then we switched to the Middle East, when he found out that both Menashe and I had fought in the Six Day War, both of us on the Jerusalem front, but in different brigades—Menashe in the 55th Airborne, and me in the 16th Infantry.

At Jaboulet, they started picking last week. The harvest will last for two weeks. The weather is nice, warm, and sunny. Maybe 1986 will produce rich, dense Hermitages.

We tried the following 1985 white wines.

CROZES-HERMITAGE "LA MÛLE BLANCHE":

Rich, big, alcoholic. Perfumed nose, good acidity. A bit too alcoholic for me (14%). They got 30 hectolitres per hectare. This wine is made from 50% Marsanne and 50% Roussanne.

Their whites are stored in stainless steel vats, no wood, and bottled in February after the vintage. Paul Jaboulet said that this way, he gets lots of fruit into the bottle "and it lasts longer." I am not so sure!

HERMITAGE BLANC "CHEVALIER DE STERIMBERG":

This wine is made up of 70% Marsanne and 30% Roussanne, but they are aiming for a 50-50 balance in future vintages. They produced 45 hectolitres per hectare in 1985, fairly large production. Finer, better balanced, much more complex than the "Mûle Blanche." Very good.

Then we tried the 1985 reds.

ST. JOSEPH "LE GRAND POMPÉE":

Medium-deep red; purplish rim. Fresh, spicy nose, on the dry side. A bit stemmy with good length. Ready in three to five years.

CROZES-HERMITAGE:

(From purchased grapes) Deep, dark, purplish colour. Black currant and Cassis nose. Heavier, tannic, hard, and finishes a bit sharp. Needs four to five years.

CROZES-HERMITAGE "THALABERT":

(Their own domaine) Very dark, deep, purplish. More harmony on nose, finer, rounder, better balanced. Hard and tannic. Ripe fruit. Needs at least ten years, but very good potential.

CÔTE-RÔTIE "LES JUMELLES":

They do not put any Viognier (white) in their Côte-Rôtie because the Viognier is good when young and fresh, so why put it into a red wine that needs age? Maybe he's right, but the whole idea of Côte-Rôtie is to make a rounder and more elegant wine than Hermitage. Very dark. A bit leathery on nose. Ripe fruit. Perfumed, elegant, with a touch of oak. 35 hectolitres per hectare. Needs eight to ten years.

CORNAS:

They purchased the grapes for this wine from up to 12 different suppliers. Very dark, almost black. Ripe, rich nose. Sweet. Rich, ripe, tannic. Very big. Clean finish. Needs at least ten years.

HERMITAGE "LA CHAPELLE":

Very dark. Tobacco, leather, ripe fruit on nose. Tannic, hard, yet complex and elegant. Top class. Good acidity, well balanced. Needs 15 years or more! Loaded with fruit.

Then we went back to his office and Mr. Jaboulet Sr. opened this bottle.

1971 HERMITAGE "LA CHAPELLE":

Mature colour, orange-brown rim, but still good depth. Lovely, complex, open, long nose, not unlike a fine Claret. He said that good old Hermitage is often mistaken for fine Claret at blind tastings. Still had some tannin. Long, very complex. Ready but no rush. Lots of class. I was hoping for the 1970 or the 1961 but this wasn't bad, either. (17)

He apologized that he couldn't come for lunch with us but phoned hotel-restaurant "Du Château" in Tournon and told them that our lunch was at his expense.

With a very nice lunch, we had a half-bottle of this wine.

1979 HERMITAGE "LA CHAPELLE," JABOULET:

Not ready. Dark, deep colour, not showing any sign of maturity yet. Lovely, leathery, ripe, rich, and round. Long and excellent. Needs another five to six years.

Mr. Jaboulet, Sr.'s views on politics are similar to mine. A pleasant man and a nice visit.

Afternoon visit with Gerard Chave.

I brought Gerard a bottle of 1975 Graham's Vintage Port. He likes Port. He knows Christian Moueix and J.-M. Cazes (Lynch-Bages) very well. He remembered me from my last visit there in 1980. He likes Kermit Lynch and thinks journalists generalize and speculate too much about vintages.

He said that the French drink their wines too young and that restaurants in France charge too much for their wines.

Also, he sends cheques back to people who want his wine because he doesn't have enough and can't supply "the whole world." He likes Zinfandel very much, especially Joseph Swan's.

Gerard said that in 1985, there was no need to chaptalize. In 1984, yes, but he said that only enough sugar should be added to increase the alcohol level by 1%; otherwise one can taste the sugar in the wine. He keeps his whites mostly in older oak barrels for up to

18 months in order to produce his style, which is heavier and fuller.

1985 Hermitage Blanc:

Old cask. Full, rich, long. Thick (has glycerine). A big wine requiring a decade.

1984 Hermitage Blanc:

Not as rich as the 1985 (this wine is already in bottle). Spicy, crisp, ready in four to five years. Round, ripe peaches. Touch of oak.

1983 Hermitage Blanc:

Fat, rich, loaded with fruit. Long, yet a bit unyielding. Needs ten years. Hint of honey and tiglio. Will be exquisite by 1992 to 1995 or beyond.

Then we tasted his reds. He starts with seven different vineyards (single-vineyard designates) then blends them until he gets three different cuves. He then narrows it to a single final blend. What doesn't go into the blend and is eliminated is sold in bulk to other people. No "second wine" is produced here. He uses four egg whites per barrel to clarify the wine.

We tasted from cask the following single vineyards of red Hermitage (before blending).

1985 "Beaumes":

Very dark, round, elegant. Flowery and long.

1985 "Le Meal":

Darker, much more fruit extract. Impressive. Full, big, long. Great quality.

1985 "L'Hermite":

Lovely, open, spicy, complex nose (violets). Superior acidity than above two. In terms of weight, halfway between "Beaumes" and "Le Meal" (my comments, and he agreed).

1985 "Les Dionières":

Rounder, sweeter, tannic, and without the elegance of the above wines.

1985 "Peleat":

Chave is the sole owner of this "climat" (stored in eight to ten-year-old casks, like most others). A bit green, spicy, leaner style.

1985 "Roucoules" Cask A:

Tannic, long, sweeter, a bit simpler, shorter finish but not bad.

1985 "Roucoules" Cask B:

Better balanced than the above. Richer, longer, with more elegance.

1985 "Bessard":

Very dark, intense, spicy, rich. Massive and tannic. Very concentrated. Like a young, big Château Latour!

He is experimenting with a little new oak—Limousin from Seguin-Moreau.

Then we tasted several Hermitages from bottle.

1984 Hermitage Rouge:

Medium colour and body. Elegant, spicy nose. Medium weight yet still quite tannic. Needs four to five years. (16.5)

1983 Hermitage Rouge:

Massive, big, long, complex, closed, and unyielding. This wine needs at least ten years. Gerard said that his 1985 will probably be as good. (18)

1982 Hermitage Rouge:

Very dark. Hotter, jammier, rich, warm, and powerful. Typical of this hot vintage. Will be a lovely bottle in eight to ten years. (17.5)

1981 Hermitage Rouge:

Medium-deep colour. Baked, leathery nose. Rich, too. Jammy, tannic. Medium body with very good fruit. Needs five to six years. Better than most 1981s. (17)

Then we tasted some reds and whites (1985s) in new oak barrels. He is against excessive new oak because it takes away from the character of the wine. He said that oak hides defects in wine. He doesn't want to use much new oak or single vineyard designates (as opposed to Guigal), even though he knows he could make more money. All he wants is true character in his wines!

1985 Hermitage Blanc:

In new oak. Made from 90% Marsanne and 10% Roussanne. This wine smelled and tasted like a big Montrachet. Massive, toast, oak, vanilla, rich, long. Incredible length, but it had lost its Hermitage character and that is what Gerard is against!

1985 Hermitage Rouge "Les Roucoules"

and

"Bessards":

Both in new oak barrels since last March.

The Roucoules tasted better than in old cask "A," but not as good as old cask "B." Exotic, round, complex.

Bessards had formidable concentration. As good as in old cask, but with an extra dimension. Richer, more complex, bigger. Oak-vanilla, Cassis. A superb bottle. If he were to bottle it by itself, it would be a very great success! However, Gerard refuses to fall into this trap. He buys two to three new casks when he needs them and blends everything into one wine.

Then he opened two great bottles for us.

1978 HERMITAGE ROUGE:

Wow! Deep, dark, not showing its age. Great complexity on nose. Finesse and power. Long, long wine. Tannic, hard, concentrated. An absolutely great bottle of wine for the year 2000. (19)

1967 HERMITAGE ROUGE:

Much lighter colour, showing age (but still very good depth, from a relatively mediocre year). Round, open, long, complex, leathery. Mature, Claret-like. Very clean, long finish. Perfect now. (17)

Chave is a believer in decanting older wines and letting them breathe. He is upset that many French people don't bother to decant.

This was a very successful visit that lasted two hours. Gerard Chave is a gentle man and a great winemaker, not unlike Coche-Dury in Meursault.

They are having lovely weather in the northern Rhône valley these days, and this is very promising for the vintage. The quantities will be large. I think that 1986 will be a fine year for Hermitage.

Tuesday, September 30

Visits to Maison E. Guigal and to Albert Dervieux.

We visited two growers in Ampuis (Côte-Rôtie) who have completely different methods and attitudes in winemaking.

At Maison E. Guigal, where we met the father (Etienne) and the son (Marcel). They are believers in new oak and make a wide range of wines: Côte-Rôtie and Condrieu from their own vineyards, as well as Hermitage red and white, Gigondas, Châteauneuf, Côtes du Rhône red and white, etc., from purchased juice and grapes. Modern operation. They also own now the house of Vidal-Fleury. They start picking next Thursday, same day as Chave, and pick for ten days. No rot this year. The weather has really improved and it is warmer and sunny.

1985 CÔTES DU RHÔNE WHITE:

Made from good grapes (Marsanne, Roussanne, and some Clairette). Round, spicy, full, rich, long. Very good for what it is. (15.5)

1985 CONDRIEU:

Marcel said that it must be drunk young when fresh, peachy, and flowery. Traditionally (this one, too) high alcohol, 14.8%! Intense peaches and apricots on nose and palate. Long and very good, but doesn't have the depth of Georges Vernay's "Côteau de Vernon." Matured for six months in oak (about one-third new barrels). (17)

1983 HERMITAGE BLANC:

Hard, tannic, full, rich, and spicy. No new oak (one to three-year-old wood). Six months in oak. (17)

They never sell their wine before it is three years old or older.

1983 CÔTES DU RHÔNE RED:

Made from Mourvèdre, Syrah, and 8% Cournoise. Matured in one-quarter new and three-quarter older oak barrels (fine treatment and good grape varietals for a simple Côtes du Rhône). Full, rich, masculine. This 1983 needs two to four years of bottle-age. Tannic. Marcel likes his 1983s very much. (16.5)

1983 CÔTE-RÔTIE "CÔTES BRUNE ET BLONDE":

Produced 30 to 35 hectolitres per hectare. Only 4% Viognier added. Leathery, rich, ripe prunes. Very tannic. Needs seven to ten years. Guigal said that it may last for 30 years. (17.5)

1983 HERMITAGE ROUGE:

Very dark. More elegant than the Côte-Rôtie. Complex, hard tannins underneath. No new oak in this. Needs eight to ten years or more. (17)

1983 GIGONDAS:

Lighter, rounder. Good fruit. Needs three to four years. (16)

1982 CHÂTEAUNEUF-DU-PAPE ROUGE:

Big, dark, jammy, pruny, touch of age on colour, like a very big Rioja. 14.5% alcohol! Leathery. Too ripe for me. Hot. This wine, as well as his Gigondas, are aged in used, very large vats—never in oak barrels. (16)

All his single-vineyard reds are aged from 24 to 42 months (very long!) in 100% new oak barrels, purchased from all over, including François Frères.

1982 CÔTE-RÔTIE "LA MOULINE":

From the Côte Blonde. 14% Viognier in this blend. This is a large proportion. Very ripe, typical 1982 (a hot year). Deep, dark, a bit leathery. Long and solid. Concentrated. Needs ten years, but will it become too pruny? (17.5)

1982 CÔTE-RÔTIE "LA LANDONNE":

From the Côte Brune. Traditionally, the bigger of the two, coming from darker soil. No Viognier here. Unyielding, closed nose at this stage. Dark, deep; bigger and harsher than the "La Mouline," requiring ten to 15 years. Tannic, powerful, masculine, yet seemed less "baked" than the "La Mouline." I prefer this. (18)

Guigal said that 1986 will produce a large crop. As for quality: fair to good. He explained that at this time of year, an extra week of sunshine and warm weather means an extra 1.5° natural alcohol. Guigal will bottle his 1983s in February 1987, after 42 months in wood!

1983 CÔTE-RÔTIE "LA MOULINE":

Also 14% Viognier in the blend. Deep colour, long, elegant, complex. Lovely quality, touch of oak. Needs eight to ten years. Not a powerful or overwhelming wine. (17.5)

Guigal said that they usually rack their wines four to six times before bottling. He also added that he liked the 1985s very much, but that they had softer tannins than the 1983s. This structural difference is similar to red Burgundies in both vintages.

1985 CÔTE-RÔTIE "LA MOULINE," FROM CASK:

Purple. Oak-vanilla. Elegant. Tannic, long, not overwhelming. Well balanced. Will be in oak for another 24 months. A lovely wine.

1985 CÔTE-RÔTIE "LA TURQUE":

A masterpiece. From the Côte Brune. Very little Viognier (4%) added. Last time this wine was made (before 1985) was in 1932! Framboises (raspberries), ripe, long, dark, full, rich, superb. No sign of leather as in most others. Like a young Petrus! Very ripe, perfectly balanced. Great extract and fruit intensity. Only 4,000 to 5,000 bottles. A gorgeous wine with character of both Côte Brune and Côte Blonde.

The vineyard used to belong to Mr. Dervieux, the uncle of Albert Dervieux.

This man refused to comply with appellation controlée regulations and went crazy. He was locked up in 1933 and eventually Vidal-Fleury purchased this vineyard, but never replanted it. When Guigal purchased it recently, he replanted it. The vineyard is strategically located on a round hill, getting both morning and afternoon sun.

"La Landonne":

12,000 bottles. "La Mouline" (a monopole, same as "La Turque"): 6,000 bottles. "La Landonne," however, is also produced by others.

A very interesting visit, but Marcel Guigal seems arrogant. A practical businessman. Smart, shrewd, but not the peasant/gentleman-farmer type. The man makes good wines, however.

Then we visited old Mr. Albert Dervieux. Totally different operation. Very small; no new oak. Very old oak barrels and casks, similar to the ones seen in Oporto, and large old wooden vats. A tiny place. He deals occasionally with an agent in Montreal (Provinoma Inc.). He buys three to four-year-old barrels from Bordeaux and Burgundy. Dervieux has started picking at Gentaz (his brother-in-law's vineyard). He will start harvesting his own vineyard tomorrow (only 7.5 acres).

Dervieux adds about 7% of his own Viognier in his Côte Blonde, but no Condrieu is produced, as he has too little of it. There is no Viognier in his Côte Brune "Viaillère." Aged 18 to 24 months in old wood, depending on the vintage. Blonde is bottled earlier, Brune bottled later. Average production 40 hectolitres per hectare, about 1,300 cases per year on average. He likes the 1983s and 1985s very much.

1984 CÔTE-RÔTIE CÔTE BLONDE "LA GRANDE":

Good depth, leathery, baked. Like a rich 1982. Finished a bit hot. Impressive concentration for 1984, but not my style. (15.5)

1984 CÔTE-RÔTIE "CÔTE BRUNE" "LA VIAILLÈRE":

This vineyard has 50- to 60-year-old vines. More masculine. Fuller, richer, harder. No Viognier. Well balanced. Impressive. (17)

1983 CÔTE-RÔTIE "CÔTE BRUNE" "FONT GENT":

Oddly, lighter and more elegant than above two 1984s! Complex, delicate, but a bit short. (16)

1983 CÔTE-RÔTIE "CÔTE BRUNE" "LA VIAILLÈRE":

Dark, unyielding, big, closed. Rich and intense. This is absolutely top-quality wine. No faults. Lovely, long finish. Needs ten to 15 years. A "must-buy." (18)

1979 LA "VIAILLÈRE":

Ageing, deep, dark colour. Open, spicy nose. Prunes and leather. Almost ready. Long and elegant. (17)

1978 "LA VIAILLÈRE":

Extremely dark, yet showing some age. Long, rich, majestic. Ripe, clean, and long. A lovely bottle needing more time (four to five years). Still tannic, but already enjoyable. (18)

A very enjoyable visit and an interesting finish to an informative ten-day trip.

October 5, 1986

Commanderie de Bordeaux Dinner and blind tasting of 1983 red Bordeaux, at the Vancouver Museum.

1. CHÂTEAU D'ANGLUDET:

Deep colour, paler rim. Ripe, spicy nose. Rich, solid, tannic, well balanced. Slightly bitter finish. Needs eight to ten years. Powerful. Good potential. Classy. (16.5)

2. CHÂTEAU BRANE-CANTENAC:

Lighter colour. Palish rim. Stemmy nose with some fruit. Vegetal, spicy, medium bodied, less depth than #1. Ready in five to seven years. Not enough depth for a 1983, but then Brane-Cantenac has been an underachiever for so long. (16)

3. CHÂTEAU FOURCAS-HOSTEN, IN MAGNUM:

Medium-dark colour. Ripe, slightly spicy nose. Closed, hard, tannic, unyielding. A solid wine, but without the elegance and complexity of most. Steely ending. Simple, but good. (15.5)

4. CHÂTEAU LA LAGUNE:

Medium colour. Paler than most. Fruity nose, lacking intensity or complexity at this stage. Tannic. High acidity, without enough depth. Quite good, though. A hard wine requiring at least ten years. Odd for La Lagune, which is usually jammy. Time will tell. (16.5)

5. CHÂTEAU MALARTIC-LAGRAVIÈRE:

Medium colour, good depth. Elegant, classy, sweet wine. Leathery, rich, new oak. Tannic. Powerful wine. Unyielding at this stage. Earthy. A serious wine requiring eight years. (16.5)

6. CHÂTEAU PRIEURÉ-LICHINE:

Good, dark colour; older at rim than its age would indicate. Ripe fruit, hint of spices and herbs. Not very intense or complex. Lighter on entry, yet tannic. Good fruit, some oak. (16)

7. CHÂTEAU RAUSAN-SÉGLA:

Deep, dark colour. Perfumy, elegant, complex nose. Good ripe fruit. A serious wine. Solid, hard, very tannic. Needs ten years or more, yet stylish. (17) How nice to see that this property is finally starting to produce fine wines once again.

8. CHÂTEAU COS D'ESTOURNEL:

Medium colour. Good depth. Ripe, complex, long nose. Rich, sweeter, long. Fairly forward. Drink from 1992 onward. A bit too forward for a top-quality wine. (16.5)

9. CHÂTEAU GRUAUD-LAROSE:

Very deep, dark colour. Intense, ripe nose. A bit animal. Rich, spicy Cabernet. Solid. Big, powerful. Tannic, great intensity. This is very promising. (17.5)

10. CHÂTEAU GRAND-PUY-LACOSTE:

Medium-dark colour. Herbaceous, elegant nose. Hard, tannic, serious. Without the ripe fruit of #9, but good balance. Needs eight years. (16.5)

11. CHÂTEAU HAUT-BRION:

Medium-dark colour. Long, oaky, complex, elegant. Great class. Lighter than most, but very fine. New oak, vanilla. Typical elegant structure of Haut-Brion. I liked it more than most. (18)

12. CHÂTEAU MARGAUX:

Dark, deep, intense colour. Ripe, rich nose. Big, exotic wine. Great length and complexity. New oak. Sensational. An absolute "must-buy." (19) If this is not the wine of the vintage, I don't know what is.

13. CHÂTEAU MOUTON-ROTHSCHILD:

Deep, dark, purplish colour. Cigar-box, cedar nose. Long, complex. Fine ripe character. Full, rich, round. Perfectly balanced. Long, complex wine. Easy to like and easily recognizable. Drink from 1994 onward. (18)

14. CHÂTEAU PALMER:

Dark, purplish colour. Ripe nose. Unyielding, yet elegant; great ripeness, lots of Merlot. Will mature relatively quickly. Drink from 1992 onward. Superb wine. (18.5)

This tasting made it quite clear that the 1983 Margaux (especially Château Margaux itself and the beautiful Palmer) are great wines, better than the Margaux commune's 1982s overall.

October 23, 1986

Dinner and tasting of Krug Champagnes with Rémy Krug, at the Four Seasons hotel, in Vancouver.

Three hours after my return from a trip to Peru with my 11-year-old son, Michael.

CHAMPAGNE KRUG "GRANDE CUVÉE" N/V:

Still young, complex; long, fine bubbles, very well structured. Unfortunately, it was overshadowed by the great quality of the Champagnes that followed. (17.5)

CHAMPAGNE KRUG VINTAGE 1979:

Great length and complexity. Fabulous nose. Long, round, full bodied. Great balance. Needs five years and will be excellent. Has an unusually steely backbone. A sleeper. (18)

CHAMPAGNE KRUG "CLOS DU MESNIL" 1979:

100% Chardonnay. Crisp, spicy, touch of greenness (young vines). Contrary to most Blanc de Blancs, this needs time, but will be very good in three years. Lots of class here. (18)

CHAMPAGNE KRUG "COLLECTION" 1961:

Deep gold, yeasty, toasty, nutty nose of mature Meursault! Has held extremely well; very long and full. Still has good bubbles, yet it seems a bit too old for my taste. Top quality nevertheless. (18)

CHAMPAGNE KRUG "COLLECTION" 1969, IN MAGNUM:

This, for me, was the greatest wine of the evening. Full, long, round, at its absolute peak. Magnificent nose. Full on palate. A great Champagne! Yeast, ripe fruit, toasty-oak, all in harmony. (19)

CHAMPAGNE KRUG ROSÉ N/V:

Pale salmon colour. Elegant, soft, not as hard as other rosés. Fruity, lovely now. Made from Pinot Noir (both black juice with skins and white juice) and Chardonnay, but no Meunier (which is used in their other blends). (17.5)

The Grande Cuvée, because of a blend of older vintages, seemed sweeter than the steely and crisp 1979 vintage. A most enjoyable experience. It was nice to see Rémy Krug again.

October 28, 1986

Vertical tasting of three decades of Château Montrose 1953 to 1983, at my residence, with 18 participants.

All wines were from my cellar.

APERITIF

CHAMPAGNE PAUL BARA BRUT 1979, BOUZY:

100% Grand Cru. Good complexity; still fairly hard, with some bitterness. Well balanced, quite rich. Needs two to three years. Fine potential.

FLIGHT #1

Château Montrose 1983 to 1978

1983:

Medium colour. Paler than the 1982. Closed, oak, elegant, a touch of herbaceousness on nose. Sharp, stemmy, but good fruit, too. Not as big as one would expect. Needs five to seven years. A bit herbaceous at finish. Has character, complexity; agreeable. (16.5)

1982:

Darkest of flight. Deep colour. Closed, yet ripe berries, concentrated nose. Big, solid, hard, tannic. Well balanced, long, serious; my idea of a St. Estèphe. (17.5)

1981:

Medium colour. Palish rim. Open, spicy, herbaceous, tobacco nose. Touch of greenness, leaner, higher acidity. Not well balanced. Too sharp. Lightweight, lean, and green. (15)

1979:

Good, deep colour. Touch of orange at rim. Spicy, open, ripe, herbaceous nose. Tobacco. As acidic as the 1981, but more tannic, better balanced, fuller. A bit short and lacking fruit. (15.5)

1978:

Medium colour, good depth. Stemmy, spicy nose. Open, but still not ready. Starting to show some bouquet. Herbaceous, hard, a bit tannic, lacking a bit in fruit. A hard wine needing more time, but should be good. (16)

Overall

This period produced no truly great Montroses.

FLIGHT #2

Château Montrose 1976 to 1970

1976:

Medium-dark colour, good depth. Complex, long, spicy, forward, elegant, classic Claret nose. Chocolate, too; later, a bit skunky. Sharp, getting thin, was better two years ago. Needs drinking. In my opinion, not a good bottle. Can be fine. (14.5)

1975:

Good, deep colour to rim. Deep, young, fruity nose. Beautiful length. Big, tannic, well balanced, long, solid. Very good potential from 1992 onward. Very tannic, but backed by ripe fruit. (17.5)

1973:

Medium-dark colour, evolved at rim. Touch of caramel and oxidation. A bit stemmy, coffee, chocolate. Hard, oxidizing, sharp. Has seen better days. Drink up. Bigger than most 1973s. Sweet finish. (14)

1971:

Ageing at rim. Medium-dark colour. Hint of chocolate, not very open nose. Elegant, forward, a bit tannic, long. Surprisingly good. Fully developed on both nose and palate. (15.5)

1970:

Dark colour. Complex, cedar and ripe fruit on nose. Big, full, tannic, well balanced, long. Massive. Needs ten years, or more. A great wine with a great future. Tobacco. Loaded with ripe tannins and fruit. (18.5) Should be ready by 1995, and last well into the 21st century.

1953, LONDON-BOTTLED BY IECWS:

(Tasted on its own) Medium colour. Lovely, complex, classic Montrose. Great length. Lovely wine. Mature, yet still has excellent backbone (some tannins). Great classic mature Claret. At 33 years of age, it has held very well. This bottle was a gift from Brad Klein of Los Angeles. (19)

FLIGHT #3

Château Montrose 1966 to 1959

1966:

Mature nose and colour. Complex, elegant, long. Pity it does not deliver on palate. Sharp, hard, sour, acidic, lean. Montrose is usually hard, but this is too hard and acidic for its own good, without enough fruit. (15.5) Having said this, I did taste a pretty good bottle of this wine last year.

1962:

Good, deep colour; mature rim. Soft, forward, elegant nose. Has seen better days. Acidic, sour, yet still elegant and clean finish. Quite nice, and better with food. Needs drinking. (16)

1961:

Dark, complex, serious, hard, tannic, cedary, spicy. Needs time. Long, complex, big St. Estèphe. Lovely, long, serious. At 25 years, it is still not quite ready. Needs five more years. (18.5)

1959:

Chocolate. Ripe, dark, long, big for 1959. Long, complex, ripe. Ready, yet big. No rush. Riper than the 1961, yet as full and no rush drinking this. (18.5)

DESSERT WINE

1976 CLOS HAUT-PEYRAGUEY, SAUTERNES:

Deep gold. Good botrytis nose. Full, forward, but well balanced and long. Drier style; not as sweet as the bigger, richer Sauternes. (16.5)

Overall

A very interesting, educational, and successful tasting. All 18 participants liked it. The 1953, 1970, 1959, and 1961 were the clear favourites, with the 1975 and 1982 close behind.

November 1986

Blind tasting of 1982 First Growths and 1982 La Mission Haut-Brion, at the Liberty Wine Company, in Point Roberts, Washington State.

These 1982s are now two years in bottle—a good time to taste them before they close up. Three ringers included.

1. 1980 GRGICH ZINFANDEL, NAPA VALLEY:

Medium purplish-red colour. Eucalyptus on nose. Very California. Sweet, ripe fruit nose. Later, seemed even sweeter, but with less complexity. Hard, thin, edgy, fairly alcoholic. Acidic finish. Italian or Californian? Or is it something else? Did the organizers add this to throw us off? (14)

2. 1982 CHÂTEAU CHEVAL-BLANC:

Medium-dark colour. Delicate, French oak-vanilla nose. Lovely length and complexity. Hard, tannic, herbaceous. Serious, solid, ripe wine, yet not as ripe as some, but needs many years. Margaux? Or Cheval-Blanc? Lots of breed there and great potential. (18.5) to (19)

3. 1983 CHÂTEAU MARGAUX:

Deep, purplish colour. Ripe fruit on nose. Not as much oak-vanilla as #2, but more ripe fruit. Lovely depth, great intensity and power. Hard, tannic, serious, big. Pauillac? Closed, unyielding. Possibly La Mission? A bit earthy, gravelly. Tighter than most. Needs 15 or more years! (19) This superb 1983 is bigger and better than many 1982s!

4. 1982 CHÂTEAU MARGAUX:

Good, deep colour. Closed, unyielding nose with hint of new oak and vanilla. Ripe, lovely length. Rich, full, well balanced, tannic finish. Great length and lots of new oak. Needs ten years, but has great future. Margaux? (18.5) or (19)

5. 1982 CHÂTEAU AUSONE:

Medium-dark colour. Spicy, closed nose. Hint of new oak, leaner style, some vegetal character. Lighter-bodied, elegant, yet solid, tannic finish. Lacks somehow in the depth and ripe fruit of most, but still very good potential. Haut-Brion? Or possibly Ausone? Lovely length and elegance, though. (17.5) In retrospect, maybe a bit diluted.

6. 1982 CHÂTEAU LAFITE:

Intense, dark colour. Ripe, cedary nose. Tighter than the above at this stage, but lovely, ripe fruit. Full, solid, big, massive. Oak, vanilla, great fruit extract. Great concentration of ripe fruit and tannins. Lafite? (19)

7. 1982 CHÂTEAU LA MISSION HAUT-BRION:

Deep colour. Ripe fruit. Not as massive or rich as most on nose, yet ripe, vegetal nose. Hard, tannic, alcoholic, yet a bit thin in middle. Powerful, alcoholic finish. Earthy. Classy wine. Needs ten to 15 years, or more. (18.5)

8. 1982 CHÂTEAU HAUT-BRION:

Medium-dark, good depth to rim. Closed, unyielding nose, yet obvious ripe fruit. Hard, serious, unyielding. Great class and depth. Pauillac? Lafite style. Great length. Oak, tannins, ripe fruit. (18)

9. 1982 CHÂTEAU MOUTON-ROTHSCHILD:

Very impressive, deep colour to rim. Ripe nose, but unyielding at this stage. Later, great length and style. Mouton? Complex, fabulous, vanilla-oak, cedar, and ripe berries. Open, yet solid. Lots of power. Maybe Mouton or Latour. (19.5)

10. 1982 CHÂTEAU LATOUR:

Very good, deep, young colour. Very ripe Merlot, fruity nose. Intense, spicy, long, lovely. Incredible ripe fruit. Full, rich, long, ripe Merlot. Petrus or Cheval-Blanc? Possibly Petrus. Excellent ripeness. In retrospect, I was totally "off" in terms of the property, but oh! how fine this wine is. (20)

11. 1982 CHÂTEAU PETRUS:

Dark colour, but not as purplish as most. Big, full, solid, masculine. Fruity, tannic, fairly high acidity. Different, powerful. Needs ten to 12 years. Mas de Daumas Gassac? Yet Bordeaux nose. Somehow, while

1925: Father as a young man in Alexandria.

1944: Mother on the eve of her wedding in Cairo.

In the 1920s: Notre Dame de France, Jerusalem. A pilgrim's hostel. Between 1948 and 1967, the left wing was occupied by Israeli troops as an observation post. The building faced the Old City walls, only 50 yards away.

October 1964: Basic Training. Learning to operate the indigenous Uzi submachine gun.

1965: Signal Corps, 16th ("Jerusalem") Infantry Brigade.

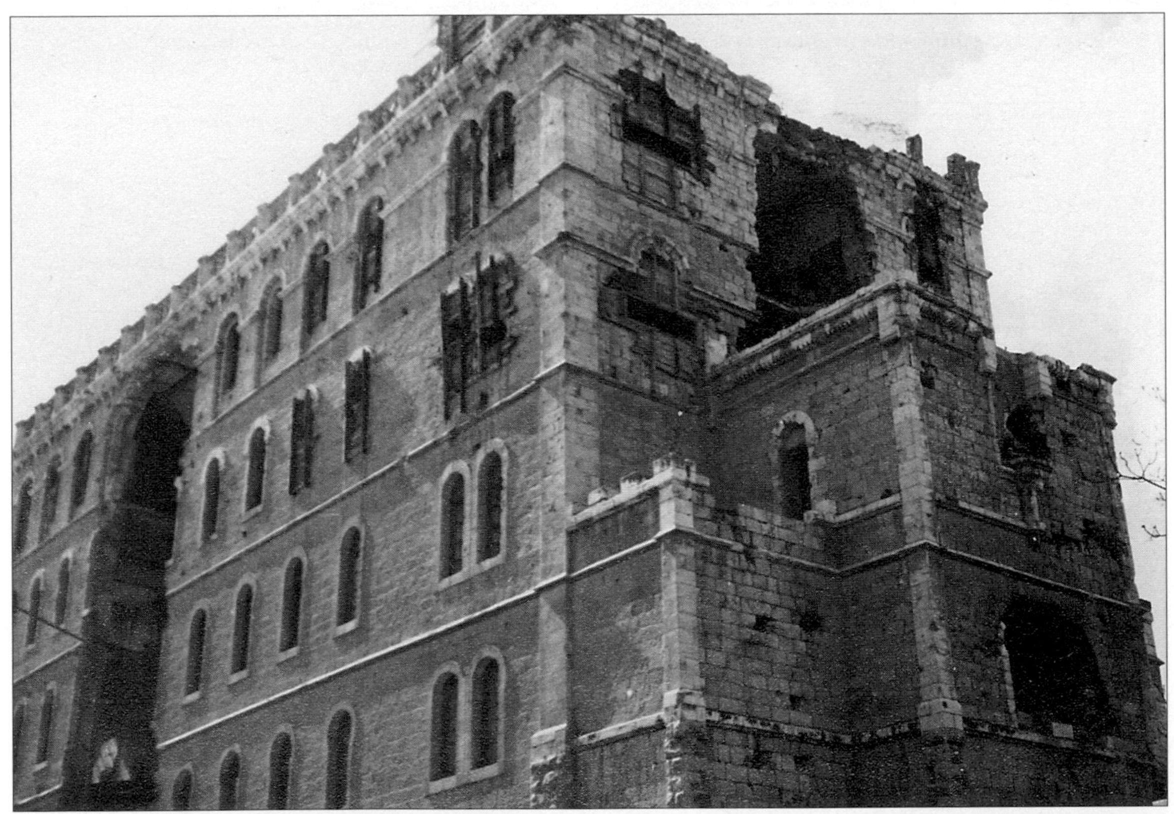

1967: Notre Dame de France, Jerusalem. The left wing is an Army post. Note machine gun and observation windows on upper floors. Spent the first 48 hours of the Six Day War in that post, while my parents were sheltered in the basement.

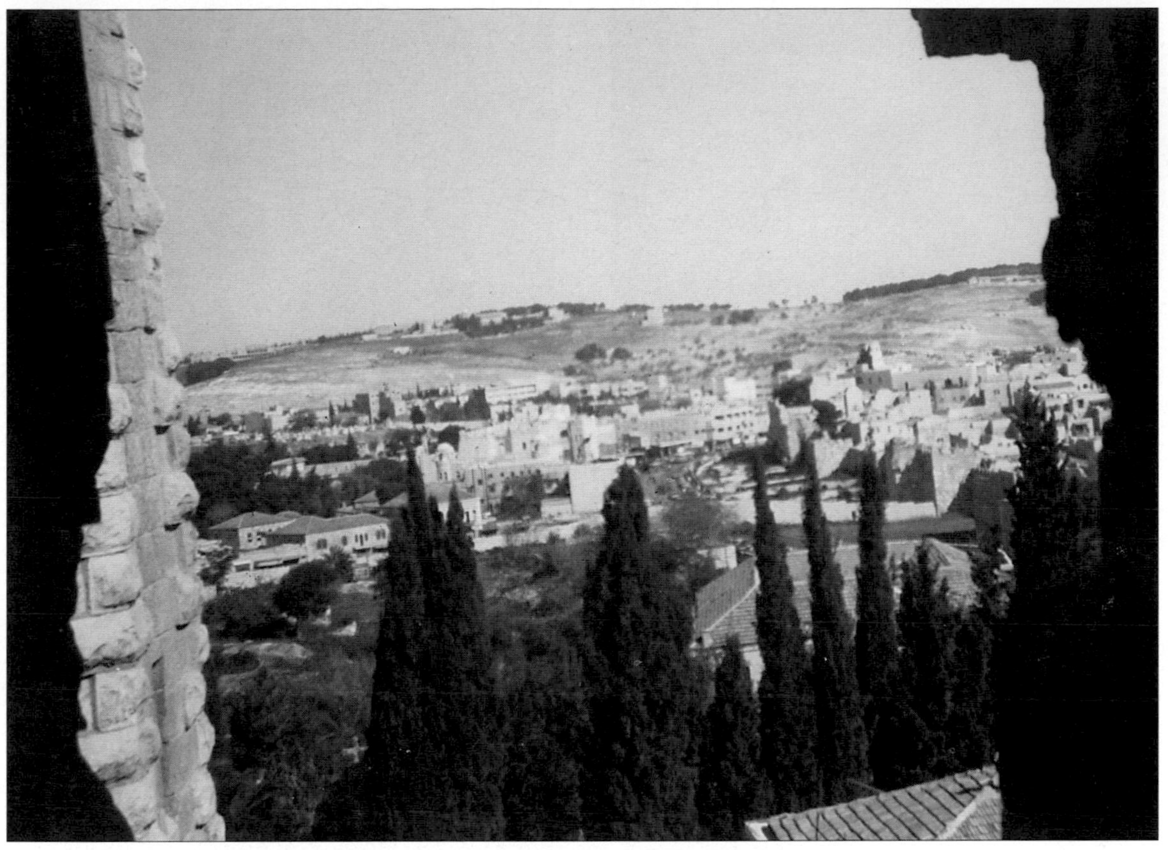

June 1967: Notre Dame, Jerusalem. View of Mount Scopus and part of Mount of Olives, from the Army post.

June 1967: Six Day War, on road to Hebron. Armoured half-track of 86th Signal Company, 16th ("Jerusalem") Brigade, carrying a cypher room.

Winter 1968-1969: Security duty at Israeli Consulate General, on McGregor Street, Montreal, Canada.

September 1969: Practising the cello while living at the Israeli Consulate General, Montreal.

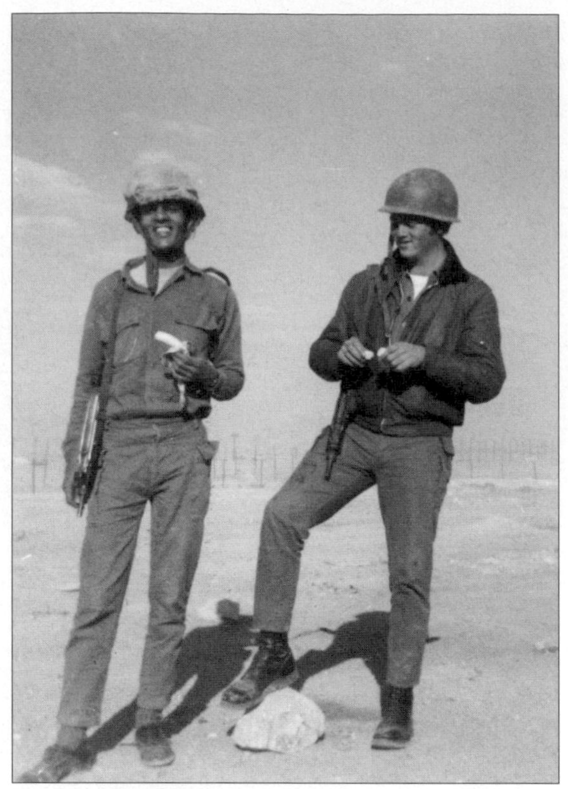

Fall, 1970: Sharing a banana with a fellow Reservist, during War of Attrition, in Bir Gifgafa (Sinai Desert), near Suez Canal.

August 1973: London. My parents on their way to settle in Vancouver, Canada.

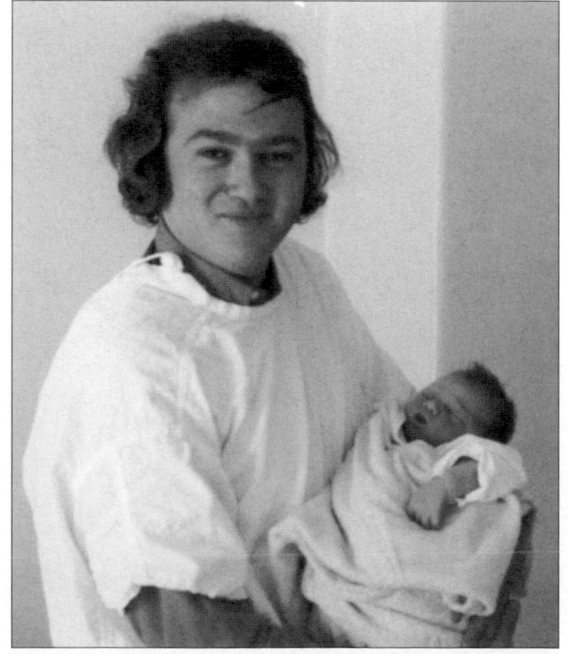

June 30, 1975: Proud father with newborn son. "A great vintage."

1978 to 1985: Cellar on Adera Street, Vancouver.

1980: "Cellar treasures."

1981: "Cellar treasures."

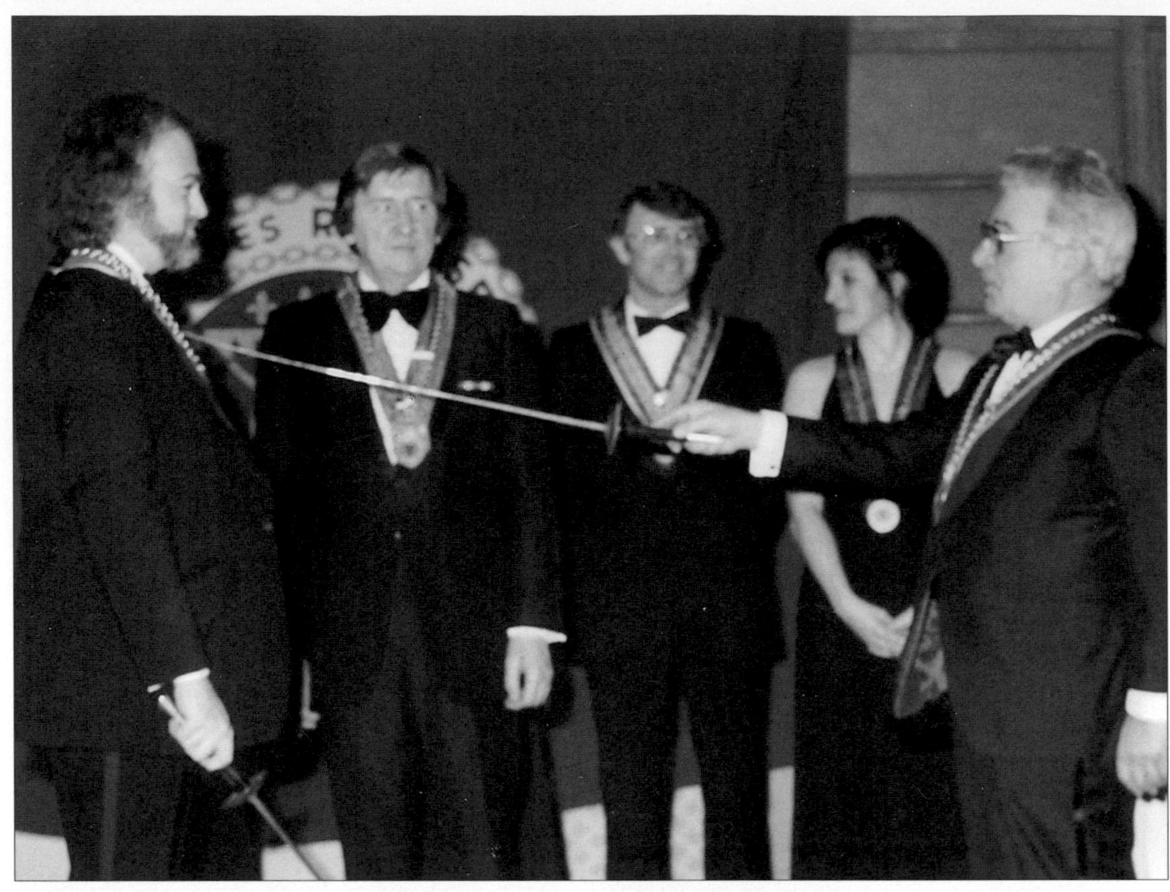

1980: Induction into the Chaîne des Rôtisseurs, in Vancouver.

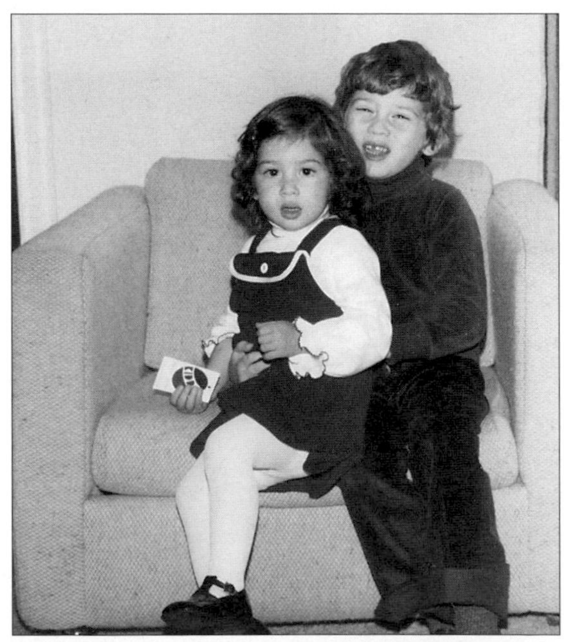

1980: The Givton Kids–Orly (two) and Michael (five).

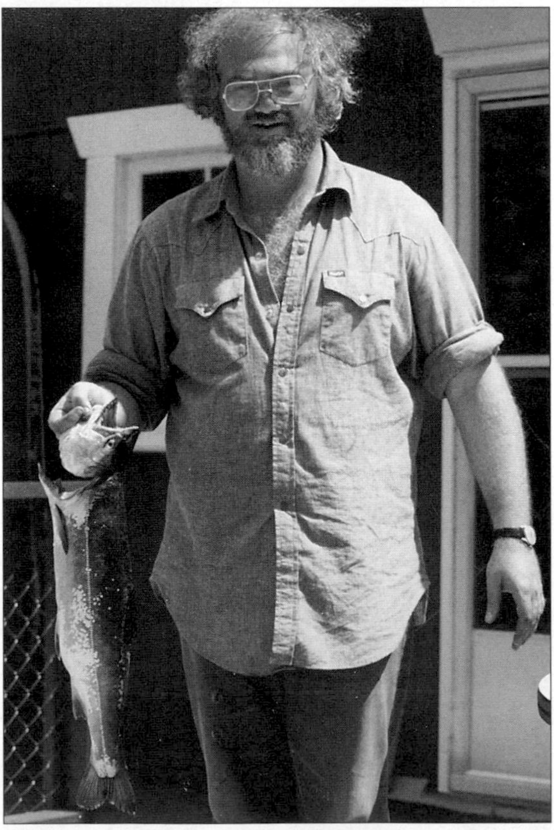

Summer 1981: On Turnagain Island. Tonight: a Meursault with fresh Coho salmon!

Summer 1981: Tasting of white Burgundies and California Chardonnays, on Turnagain Island.

1982: Commanderie de Bordeaux tasting of 1970 First Growths, in honour of Harry Waugh.

1982: Commanderie de Bordeaux tasting of 1970 First Growths. "1970 Latour or Petrus . . . the two top Clarets of the vintage" . . . discussing merits of each with guest speaker Harry Waugh.

1982: Ridge Vineyards "Monte Bello" Cabernet Sauvignon vertical tasting, Vancouver. We put guest of honour Harry Waugh to work.

1982: With Harry Waugh, at Ridge Vineyards "Monte Bello" Cabernet Sauvignon vertical tasting.

March 24, 1984: With Carol, at the Vancouver Wine Festival Gala charity auction dinner, Four Seasons hotel. I organized and chaired the event.

it has the power, it lacks class at this stage. (17) Disappointing for Petrus!

12. 1982 SASSICAIA:

Deep, purplish colour. Spicy, herbaceous nose, yet doesn't seem as ripe or intense as most. Tannic, hard, more acidic. Possibly Latour? Very tannic aftertaste. Something unusual here, yet certainly a fine wine. This was the third ringer. (17.5)

DESSERT WINE

1982 RIEUSSEC:

Round, complex, elegant. Forward. Needs two to three years. Not as massive or as intense as the 1983 or 1976, but very nice. (16.5)

I didn't guess too many wines right, but the overall quality of these 1982s was outstanding. The Sassicaia and the Margaux 1983 threw me off. Also, the less-than-great performance of the Petrus was odd. Maybe it is closing up faster than the others.

November 13, 1986

Special Commanderie de Bordeaux Dinner and vertical tasting, featuring Château Pichon-Lalande, at the Four Seasons hotel, in Vancouver. In honour of Mme. Eliane de Lencquesaing and her husband, Général de Lencquesaing.

All wines generously contributed by Eliane de Lencquesaing. Her friends call her "May." The Général was late because he had misplaced his passport and had a hard time getting past Canada Customs and Immigration at the airport. Other guests included Peter Sichel of Châteaux Palmer and d'Angludet.

APERITIF

CHAMPAGNE GOSSET "GRAND MILLÉSIME" BRUT 1976:

The agent (Mark Anthony Wines) contributed a case of this wine for this event. Their sales representative, Craig Hanson, and his wife were our guests. As on previous occasions, an elegant, very smooth Champagne. At its peak.

Château Pichon-Lalande

1983:

Medium-dark, bright colour. Spicy, ripe, complex nose. Touch herbaceous. New oak-vanilla. Tannic, medium-bodied. Very long, lovely. Not a very big wine, but has lovely fruit and elegance. Ready in eight years. Quite tannic at this stage. Very fine potential around 1995 to 1998. (18)

1982:

Deep, dark colour. Green olives. More herbaceous, spicier than the 1983. Closing up. Bigger, fuller, riper than the 1983. Great depth and concentration. A rich, big wine. I preferred it to the 1983 at this stage, but both are excellent. (18.5)

1981:

Medium to dark red colour. Not as concentrated as either the 1982 or the 1983, but still very good depth. Closed nose, some flowers (lilacs). More forward, lovely structure, elegance. Clean, long aftertaste. Five to seven years. Not as tannic as the 1983 or as rich as the 1982, but very good. Lovely complexity; classic and elegant. Much smaller crop than the huge 1979 crop. (17.5)

1979:

Similar appearance to the 1981, but showing some age at rim. Closed, ripe, mature, spicy nose. A bit vegetal (high Merlot proportion). Rounder than the 1981, yet seemed fuller and softer (but quite tannic for a 1979). Full, rich, very successful. (17)

1978:

Deep, dark colour. Slight maturity at rim. Spicy, herbaceous Cabernet nose. Great elegance and length. Rich, still tannic, needs five or more years. Full, rich, slightly stemmy, yet almost sweet. Ripe, but in a Cabernet sense, not Merlot. The nose was a bit musty. Also, slight taste of cork. Second bottle much better and a lovely wine. (18)

1975:

Deep colour. Lovely, yet closed on both nose and palate. Well balanced, tannic, typical 1975. A solid, well-balanced wine requiring seven to ten years of extra bottle-age. Top quality. Excellent. (18.5) This wine was made by Michel Delon of Leoville-Lascases, before May took over the management of the estate in 1978.

1970:

Deep, mature colour, typical of the 1970 vintage. Mature rim. Lovely, open, cedary nose. First wine so far that is definitely ready. Complex, open, ripe, round, soft, a bit leathery, slightly high acidity. Tobacco, leather nose. Like velvet. Elegance, yet solid structure. At its peak. Drink soon. (18)

1966:

Mature colour, good depth. Tobacco, complex, elegant nose. Ripe and forward. Hard, dry, but has enough fruit; better than many 1966s, yet obvious hard tannins. Ready, but will hold. Long, complex, elegant. Fine quality. (17.5)

1964:

Even deeper colour than the 1966. Deep, mature red. Not as complex on nose as the 1966 but clean, sweet, and elegant. Round, soft, forward. Needs drinking. Not as intense as the 1966, nor as complex. (16.5)

This tasting was followed by a dinner (other guests included John Carpenter of the Winehouse in San Francisco and my friends, Dr. Mark and Tracy Schonfeld). The dinner, prepared by Chef Mark Baker, was innovative and excellent.

1982 CHÂTEAU LARRIVET-HAUT-BRION, GRAVES BLANC:

Crisp, round, spicy Sauvignon Blanc character. Pleasant, without having too much depth or complexity.

Château Pichon-Lalande 1962 and 1953

Both in Marie-Jeanne (an unusual size bottle, equivalent to three 25-oz. bottles).

THE 1962:

Deep colour; charming, expansive nose. Complex, soft, elegant, and at its peak, even in such a large format. Well balanced, complex, fruity, with no sharp edges. Rounder and more complete than the 1964. (17.5)

THE 1953:

Surprising backbone for a 1953. Sturdy, cedary, earthy, with tobacco overtones. Essence of Cabernet. Full, round, yet solid. Ready, but no rush. Opened up beautifully in the glass. (18.5) Of the three Marie-Jeannes of 1953, one was clearly sharper, drier, and a bit musty. The other two were fine.

Then came the turn of the oldest Pichon-Lalande tasted at this event.

1934 CHÂTEAU PICHON-LALANDE, IN MAGNUMS:

Deep, mature colour. Leathery, spicy nose of old Claret. Some sharpness, but still very much alive. Powerful, sturdy, fairly high acidity, which helped the wine last this long. Very slight hint of oxidation. Needs drinking soon. (16.5)

DESSERT WINE

CHÂTEAU DE FARGUES 1976, SAUTERNES:

Bright, deep-golden colour. Subdued, buttery, oaky botrytis on nose. Not overly sweet or cloying; almost Barsac-like. Lovely class and elegance here. (17.5)

A memorable vertical tasting. May has done an excellent job with this property. I hope, that some day, its "relative" from across the street, Château Pichon-Longueville-Baron, will start to produce serious Pauillacs once again.

November 14, 1986

Lunch with Général and Mme. de Lencquesaing at Sid Cross's Residence.

I picked them up from the Hotel Le Meridien, where they were staying. May gave me a lovely silver Tastevin Bordelais. She said that she is in favour of increasing the planting of Petit Verdot, which now represents 8% of the vineyard of Pichon-Lalande. When successful, usually when the weather is dry and warm well into October, it adds an extra dimension of great depth to the wine (as was the case in 1982, 1983, and 1985).

Sid and I prepared an array of California wines to give May an opportunity to taste New World wines.

DOMAIN CHANDON BRUT "TENTH ANNIVERSARY," CALIFORNIA CHAMPAGNE:

I purchased this bottle at the winery two years ago. A very pleasant surprise. To date, this is one of the best California sparkling wines I have tasted. Good yeast and ripe fruit on nose. Complex, quite dry, well balanced. Long, clean aftertaste. Fine mousse. (17)

1976 CHARDONNAY "UNFILTERED," ROBERT MONDAVI, NAPA VALLEY:

In the old days, Mondavi indicated "Unfiltered" instead of "Reserve" on their labels. Bright green-gold colour, not unlike a Chablis. Complex, vanilla, mature fruit on nose. Spicy, round, elegant, with good acidity. At its peak and has held very well. (17)

1974 BEAULIEU VINEYARDS GEORGES DE LATOUR "PRIVATE RESERVE" CABERNET SAUVIGNON, NAPA VALLEY

AND

1974 ROBERT MONDAVI CABERNET SAUVIGNON "RESERVE," NAPA VALLEY:

Beaulieu Vineyards looked more mature; deep, browning colour. Nose of American oak, vanilla, and hint of Tawny Port, like older-style California Cabernet Sauvignons. Round, forward, complex, ripe, and ready. Very nice wine; yet not quite as good as it can be. (17)

The Robert Mondavi was brighter, younger-looking, more elegant in style. Vanilla, oak, eucalyptus, spicy Cabernet. Well balanced, long, fruity. Ready, but no rush. This is a very fine Cabernet. (18)

1977 CHÂTEAU ST. JEAN JOHANNISBERG RIESLING "ROBERT YOUNG VINEYARD" "INDIVIDUAL BUNCH, SELECTED LATE HARVEST," SONOMA, IN HALF-BOTTLE:

(28.2% residual sugar) Deep, dark gold. Lovely, complex nose. Good acidity. Sweet, yet not cloying.

Lovely length and complexity. Essence of apricots. Excellent. (18)

Same night, November 14, 1986

Tasting of Château Palmer and Château d'Angludet.

Conducted by Peter Sichel. May de Lencquesaing was there, too. How odd: Last night Peter participated as a guest at May's event. Tonight, she is a guest at a tasting that Peter is conducting. How fortunate we are to have these two gifted owners/winemakers here in Vancouver simultaneously, and two nights in a row!

THE TASTING

1983 CHÂTEAU D'ANGLUDET:

Medium-dark, young colour. Ripe, closed nose, slightly vegetal. Fuller, more tannic than the Palmer. Big, well structured, good fruit, and well balanced. Needs seven to ten years. (16.5) D'Angludet is made up of 55% Cabernet Sauvignon, 8% Cabernet Franc, 35% Merlot, and 2% Petit Verdot. Palmer, on the other hand, is planted with approximately 40% Cabernet Sauvignon, 45% Merlot, and 15% Cabernet Franc and Petit Verdot.

1983 CHÂTEAU PALMER:

Deeper, darker than the 1983 d'Angludet. Lovely, complex, delicate, vanilla-spices-oak nose. Perfumy. Round, medium-bodied, good acidity. The main obvious difference between these two 1983s is the more extensive use of new barrels at Palmer and the sheer elegance and class of the latter. Not as heavy or rustic as d'Angludet, but more complexity. Needs eight to ten years. Great potential. (18.5)

Peter says that they plan not to replant Cabernet Franc at Palmer. He says that this grape varietal, planted in typical light gravelly soil, does not produce rich-enough wines. They're replanting with Cabernet Sauvignon, when the Cabernet Franc is uprooted. No 1963 or 1968 Palmer or d'Angludet was ever sold under their label.

About Petit Verdot

Peter indicated that this varietal is compatible with light soils and they get from it colour and alcohol, just what lighter Margaux wines need. Proportion of grape varietal doesn't concern them at Palmer, just the overall quality.

About the 1983 vintage

Not too hot, good acidity and complexity. Wines from the commune of Margaux are going to be excellent in 1983, possibly better than in 1982.

May de Lencquesaing thought that Palmer 1982 and 1983 were a bit disappointing, not bright or clear enough. Maybe because they have been shipped so recently? Also, the 1982s were actually barrel samples that had been shipped to Peter's agent in Vancouver two years ago.

1982 CHÂTEAU D'ANGLUDET:

As deep in colour as the 1983, but less purple (more age). Ripe, closed nose. Not as perfumy as the 1983. Hard, tannic, closed. Leave alone for five to seven years. (16)

1982 CHÂTEAU PALMER:

Deeper colour than the 1983. Tighter, richer, riper, but not as elegant on nose as the 1983. Big, solid, rich, unyielding. Not very complex at this stage. Needs time. (17.5)

Overall, Peter compares the 1982s to the 1970s (good news!).

1981 CHÂTEAU D'ANGLUDET:

Clearly less depth than the 1982 or 1983. Spicy, stemmy, elegant nose. Good, solid structure, without being too big. Hint of barnyard. Later, nose cleared. Very good potential. Needs six years. (16.5)

1981 CHÂTEAU PALMER:

Bright, clean, but lighter colour than the 1982 or 1983. Lovely, long, ripe nose. Perfumy elegance and style. Ready soon, around 1989 to 1992. (17)

1980 CHÂTEAU PALMER:

Similar depth to the 1981 (surprising) yet more age. Simple, clean, (yet slightly dusty) nose. Soft, forward, elegant, a bit acidic. Ready. Quite good for the vintage, but should be consumed soon. Diluted. (14.5)

1979 CHÂTEAU D'ANGLUDET:

Good, deep colour for a 1979. Open, ripe nose, developing quite a bit of complexity. Still fairly hard and tannic, with some greenness. Young vines? A nice wine nevertheless. (15)

1979 CHÂTEAU PALMER:

Darker colour than the d'Angludet. Not as open, either. Not as solid on palate as the d'Angludet, but more elegant, complex, good depth. Needs three to five years or more. Chocolaty, ripe fruit. 1979 was a cool, dry summer, producing a large crop. 1979 Palmer is closing up more and more, yet has very good potential. (17.5) Possibly (18).

1978 CHÂTEAU PALMER:

Medium-deep colour. Some maturity at rim. Starting to open up a bit. Lovely, complex, long nose. Fabulous. Hard, solid, tannic, yet great complexity and style. Needs five to ten years, but will be great. Compact. Concentrated. Slightly vegetal. Very little

Merlot ripened that year. This is a problem, because Palmer depends so much on this varietal. (18)

1967 CHÂTEAU PALMER:

Medium-palish colour with orange, mature rim. Open, caramel nose. Round, elegant, some obvious acidity. A bit short; fragile and needs drinking. (15.5)

These days, about one-third new oak barrels are used yearly at both Palmer and d'Angludet. Peter commented that the 1978 Palmer had more extract and was more solid than either the 1982 or the 1983. I tried two samples of the 1978. One was more open than the other.

Later, I drove May de Lencquesaing back to her hotel. A long and tiring— but exciting—24 hours. Next morning, Carol and I left for San Francisco and the Napa Valley.

November 16, 1986

International Wine and Food Society (Marin County) event, lunch at "Fleur de Lys" restaurant, in San Francisco, featuring a vertical tasting of Montrachets from the Domaine de la Romanée-Conti, 1964 to 1984.

APERITIF

CHAMPAGNE SALON "LE MESNIL" BRUT 1971:

A rare Champagne, produced from 100% Chardonnay grapes and declared only in successful vintages. While this Champagne ages well, this particular wine seemed a bit tired, yet it had good length and complexity. When tasted from a magnum about a year ago, it was superb.

Montrachet is one of the rarest and possibly the finest white wine made anywhere in the world. It is always expensive and hard to find. As the production of the Domaine de la Romanée-Conti is limited to about 1,000 bottles per year, little wonder that this wine retails for upwards of US$275 per bottle nowadays—if one can find it.

We tasted all the vintages produced by the Domaine to date, from 1964 (their first vintage) to 1984, with the exception of the 1980, which was not produced—and the 1973, which did not arrive in time for this event, but was tasted separately. I had the good fortune, however, of tasting the excellent 1973 Montrachet DRC with the late Maître de Chais, André Noblet. It was a lovely bottle, at its peak now, with great length, complexity, and elegance.

The wines were tasted in several flights, the oldest first, ending with the youngest and freshest samples.

FLIGHT #1

1964:

Caramel and popcorn on nose; mature, yet clean. A bit flat, soft, with hint of wood taking over. Losing its fruit and low in acidity. After 30 minutes, the wine went flat and lifeless. Needs drinking. (14.5)

1965:

Elegant, open nose with touch of sulphur which dissipated after a few minutes. Good acidity, spicy, leaner style. Later, this wine softened quite a bit and showed signs of ageing. Remarkable for such a poor vintage, but even the Domaine de la Romanée-Conti couldn't make a great wine under such miserable weather conditions. (15.5)

1966:

Deep, gold colour. Ripe, mature nose of older Burgundy. Acidic, fairly oaky on palate, yet rich and long. For lovers of old white Burgundies. Past its prime. (16.5)

1967:

Spicy, crisp, green, yet mature on nose. Good acidity, while being obviously old. Better structured and a bit livelier than the 1966, but it lacked the depth and weight of the former. (15)

FLIGHT #2

1968:

This was the first vintage Domaine de la Romanée-Conti Montrachet that I had ever tasted, back in 1977 during a visit to the Domaine. The nose of a lovely, mature white Burgundy, with hint of apricots, honey, and oak. Good acidity, rich and long on palate. How they managed to pull it off in such a poor year is beyond me. I can well imagine the severe selection and the tiny amount produced. (16)

1969:

Long, complex, rich nose, with hint of oak and touch of sulphur. Spicy and complex, yet this wasn't followed by a similar impression on palate. Soft, round, not as lively as the 1968. It did improve a bit after a few minutes, but started to show its age. Disappointing for the vintage. (16)

1970:

Mature, elegant, and long nose, with touch of oak and buttered popcorn. Soft, forward, at its peak. Great elegance and complexity on palate. Excellent balance. An outstanding bottle. (18.5)

1971:

Odd resin on nose, reminiscent of ageing Chardonnay. Deep, gold colour. Had some fruit, but seemed tired. This wine has seen better days. Poor storage? (16)

Based on the reputation of the respective vintages, the 1969 and 1971 should have been the best wines of the flight. They were clearly outclassed by the fabulous 1970.

FLIGHT #3

1972:

Deep, mature-gold colour. Lively, complex nose with good ripeness for that difficult vintage. Rich, round, and full on palate. As time went by, the high alcohol and acidity took over and the wine seemed tired. Originally, I rated it (17) but downgraded it to (16).

1974:

Medium-gold colour. Subdued, ripe, slightly raisiny nose. Full, forward, and rich on palate, with low acidity. A bit yeasty with hint of cardboard. Good nevertheless, especially for such a mediocre year. (15)

1975:

An elegant wine on both nose and palate. Round, crisp, fairly acidic, with good fruit. Finished clean with hint of oak. Later, the fruit seemed to fade, but another successful effort in a poor vintage. (16)

FLIGHT #4

1976:

With few exceptions, white Burgundies of this vintage have become tired by now. The wines are flabby, flat, and most are over-the-hill. Deep gold. Rich honey-oak on nose. Typical structure of the 1976s, with fairly high alcohol and low acidity, yet it had good concentration of fruit and flavours. Has held well for a 1976, but not an outstanding wine. (17)

1977:

Medium to dark gold colour. Oaky, complex nose. High acidity and low fruit, again typical of this lean vintage. Getting tired and too sharp. (15)

1978:

What a wine and what a vintage! Subdued, still-closed nose, yet clean with a lot of class. Full, rich, long. A serious wine of great concentration and balance. Great length and potential, but it must be left alone for at least another three to four years. A superb wine. (19) Based on my experience, I think I can safely say that 1978 was the finest vintage for white Burgundies in the past 20 years, with 1973 not too far behind.

1979:

A prolific, mid-term vintage. Deep-gold colour. Rich, full, soft, and forward. At its peak now and should not be left to age too much longer. On the sweeter side with, oddly enough, a hint of botrytis. Some tasters commented that they have experienced some bottle variation. (17)

FLIGHT #5

1981:

Brilliant gold colour. Clean honey-oak and ripe Chardonnay on nose. Rich, long, very well balanced. Luscious wine of great quality. Excellent potential. Should be ready around 1989 to 1992. (18) A small and, unfortunately, overlooked vintage that produced some fine white Burgundies.

1982:

More age on both nose and palate than the 1981. Rich, full, big, and alcoholic; typical of a hot year. Ready around 1989, but in my opinion, lacking the acidic backbone to be a long-ager. Similar structure to the 1976. Most participants seemed to like it better than I did. (17)

1983:

Full, rich, big wine, with better balance, acidity, and depth than the 1982. A big, serious wine, requiring many years of bottle-age. A bit too alcoholic, but then I'm not a fan of the 1983 vintage for white Burgundies. Great potential nevertheless. (18)

1984:

Very fresh, young, spicy fruit on both nose and palate. Almost "barrel sample grape juice" at this early stage. Well balanced, clean, long, with good acidity. Difficult to assess at this early stage, but potentially a very good bottle. (17)

One tends to be overly critical at comparative or vertical tastings. My overall impression is, however, that because of severe pruning and meticulous winemaking, this is an outstanding wine. As for the cost of these wines, it reflects their rarity and prestige rather than the actual quality. The 1970 and 1978 were superb, though.

We ended this rare and outstanding event with this bottle.

1976 CHÂTEAU D'YQUEM:

Ripe, full, rich, and long. Reaching its peak. Exotic fruit, complex botrytis and hint of new oak and vanilla on both nose and palate. Should reach its peak around 1989 to 1993. (18.5)

The food and presentation were outstanding—a work of art rather than "plain good food."

After the Montrachet, Domaine de la Romanée-Conti event, we drove up to our home in Yountville.

Barney Rhodes, whom we saw yesterday at the "Fleur de Lys" restaurant, phoned us. Before going out for dinner, we went to Barney and Belle Rhodes' house.

We tried a bottle of champagne.

1979 Deutz "Blanc de Blancs" Champagne:

Elegant, complex, soft, delicate, typical Blanc de Blancs. Lots of class there and clearly an elegant "Chardonnay" Champagne.

Then we drove to "Mama Nina's" for dinner. Barney brought along two bottles of "Bella Oaks" (owned by the Rhodes: they sell the grapes to Joe Heitz). Barney decanted the wines before we left for the restaurant.

1977 and 1980 Heitz Cellars "Bella Oaks," Napa Cabernet Sauvignon:

The 1977 was typical for that drought year. Dark, big, rich, some mint-eucalyptus. Soft and forward. Drinking well now.

The 1980 was a bit lighter in colour, crisper, leaner, more elegant, yet still tannic, requiring four to five extra years of bottle-age (Barney agreed). The 1980 definitely had more class.

We had a very nice dinner. Then we drove the Rhodes back to their home, and Barney served a Port (of which he had purchased a pipe). (Barney knows Bruce Guimaraens well; Bruce is a dear friend of ours, too.)

1970 Messias "Quinta do Cachao" Vintage Port:

Used in the blend of Taylor's Vintage Port. Has the structure of Graham's or Fonseca's. Deep, rich, sweet, complex, round, yet more forward than the two above Ports. Very nice and almost at its peak.

I told Barney that in 1984, I had tasted, at the Factory House in Oporto, a lovely bottle of 1963 Delaforce. He likes it, too, and knows Mr. Victor Delaforce well (as does Joe Heitz).

Barney also loves 1962 Macallan single malt. I'll try to get some older vintages of this whiskey. All in all, a very enjoyable evening. Belle and Barney are planning to bequeath their extensive cellar to the wine library at UC Davis.

Tuesday, November 18

Visit to Napanook, and lunch at "Mustard's."

Napanook is Christian Moueix's property. We met his manager, Daniel Baron. We went up to Rombauer and tasted the 1985 Dominus, which was being racked for a third time (it will be racked two more times before bottling). A lovely wine of excellent potential. It will probably be released in early 1989.

They postponed the release of the 1983 until March 1988 and will release it at the same time as the 1984. They seem to be a bit nervous about the quality of the 1983.

Then we drove to "Mustard's" where we had lunch.

1961 Château Mouton-Baron-Philippe:

(I brought it along.) Ullage mid shoulder. A fine wine that is at its peak. Complex, mature, elegant, full, rich, and long. In the old days, Mouton-Baron used to make lovely wines. We enjoyed it thoroughly.

Daniel told me that for the 1985 Dominus, they use 20% new Demptos barrels and 80% older Demptos and Seguin-Moreau barrels from Château Cheval-Blanc. We also tasted Cabernet Sauvignon and Cabernet Franc (young vines) of the 1986 vintage, which were elegant but not very big or concentrated. Certainly not as good as the 1985 at this stage. Time will tell.

December 9, 1986

Le Tastevin Wine Club tasting of 1975 Vintage Ports, at Hotel Le Meridien, in Vancouver.

These Ports are only 11 years old, but they are turning out to be quite soft and early maturing.

1. Warre's:

Palish colour, mature rim. Spicy, alcoholic nose. A bit lean and unyielding. A touch vegetal. Soft, forward, a bit thin and a bit short, but clean and pleasant. Ready. (15.5)

2. Cockburn's:

Similar colour to #1, but more youthful. Riper, fruitier, and sweeter than the Warre's. More body, too. Clean, long finish. Ready, but no rush. Good fruit. (16)

3. Dow's:

Medium, mature colour to rim. Good depth. Elegant, subdued nose. Sweet, yet not overly so. Good backbone. A bit hard and masculine. Ready but no rush. Good fruit. Not heavy. (16)

4. Fonseca's:

Deep, dark colour to rim, showing some maturity. Sweet, ripe fruit and prunes on nose. Full, rich, ripe, loaded with fruit. Big, rich; not ready. (17.5)

5. Graham's:

Medium colour, browning rim. Odd, alcoholic nose. Hint of cardboard. Later, opened up a bit. Harsher, leaner style. A bit sharp, yet soft fruit and forward. Unbalanced. (14.5)

6. Quinta do Noval:

Good, dark colour. Mature rim. Unyielding, vegetal nose. Later, riper and richer. Watery, yet good fruit. Fairly sharp, but finished sweet. Lacking breed but quite pleasant. (15.5)

7. Taylor's:

Deep colour to rim, similar to Fonseca's. Rich, ripe, spicy, intense nose. Like the Fonseca's, but more youthful. Full, fruity, well balanced. Lots of class. Great depth, length, and complexity, yet has the softness of the 1975s. (17.5)

Fonseca's and Taylor's were clearly the best, as expected. Graham's was disappointing. In retrospect, maybe they should not have declared the 1975s, but 1970 was followed by four undistinguished years, so I guess they had to declare the 1975s.

January 17, 1987

Tasting at Singer and Foy Wine Shop, in San Francisco.

A wine shop that usually carries Kermit Lynch's line, including Jean-François Coche-Dury's recently released 1983 Meursaults. The wines are in short supply, and most are gone by now. I purchased the "Narvaux" and the "Casse-Tête" last week.

1983 Coche-Dury Meursaults

"Les Narvaux":

Bright green-gold. Complex, Chardonnay nose, oak, vanilla. Fruit, acidity. Great length and structure. Not too alcoholic (a fault of many 1983s). Rich, intense, promising. Very good potential. Drink 1990 to 1995. (17.5)

"Les Rougeots":

Similar appearance to Les Narvaux. Not as rich on nose or palate as the Narvaux. Leaner, harder wine, requiring two to three years of extra bottle-age (1991 to 1994). Less fruit. Very good potential. (17)

"Les Casse-Tête":

Rounder, more elegant, subdued nose. Riper fruit than above. Great class and length. Needs two to three years. A lovely bottle. (18)

"Les Charmes":

Oddly, what this wine lacked, at least at this stage, is charm! Closed nose, not as opulent or pronounced as the Casse-Tête. Unyielding, hard, fairly alcoholic. Powerful. At this stage, seems to lack ripeness and finesse, but should improve if allowed to age. (17) Potentially (18).

"Les Perrières":

Intense, ripe, rich, luscious nose. Ripe, full, long, oak-vanilla, honey, ripe Chardonnay. Not unlike a great Montrachet. The greatest and most expensive. For the price, the Casse-Tête is a better buy (half the price). (19) This is Coche-Dury's only Premier Cru Meursault.

Then we tried a bottle of

Viejo (Burgos) Fino, Vinos Finos Sancho:

Produced around 1935 to 1938. Amber, rich, Madeira-like. Complex, slightly sweet. Very good depth and not dried out.

January 17, 1987

International Wine and Food Society Dinner, featuring 1949 Cheval-Blancs, at Clift Four Seasons hotel, in San Francisco

APERITIF

Champagne Lasalle "Imperial Preference" Brut N/V:

Pleasant, crisp, well balanced, simple, but sound. Good, but nothing "imperial" here.

This was followed by two white Burgundies.

1979 Corton-Charlemagne, Bonneau du Martray:

I tried it from three different bottles. One was deep gold, oxidized. A second was corked. The third was very good, lively, complex, long, nutty. At its peak.

1973 Montrachet, Domaine de la Romanée-Conti:

This is the wine we missed at our Domaine de la Romanée-Conti Montrachet vertical tasting last November. We opened four bottles of this wine. One was superb (apparently), but I didn't taste it. Our bottle was very good, new oak, very well structured, long, good acidity, and youthful for its age. Very good, but not great.

Then, we enjoyed 1949 Château Cheval-Blanc, in imperial, magnums, and bottles.

Imperial:

The wine was cloudy. Lovely complexity, especially on nose. Great length of mature Claret, yet it seemed a bit astringent. It was probably better ten years ago.

Three magnums:

One was a bit leaner and more tired than the other two. Darker than the imperial, yet, again, all three magnums were cloudy. Lovely, long nose. Elegant. Clearly more complex than the bigger bottle, but again, needs drinking.

BOTTLE-SIZE:

A surprise. Darkest, brightest, and clearest, as well as liveliest. At its peak now. Somehow I preferred the complexity on the nose of the magnums. Rich, chocolaty, fruity. Round, with hint of herbaceous aftertaste.

Then we tasted one of my favourite Sauternes.

1959 CHÂTEAU SUDUIRAUT:

Deep, brilliant-gold colour. Superb, lovely nose of ripe peaches and apricots with lovely botrytis. Superbly balanced, mature, yet lively. Great length, fruit, ripeness. A superb bottle of Sauternes and no rush. Perfect. (20)

January 18, 1987

Lunch and tasting of Graham's Vintage Ports 1887 to 1945, at Haskell Norman's in Ross, California.

APERITIF

MARTÍNEZ-GASSIOT WHITE PORTO XSR 120:

Deep gold. Sweet, nutty, rich. Well made and long. Solera-like Port. Very enjoyable. #120 is a batch. (Corti Brothers Importers)

Graham's Vintage Ports

1945:

Second darkest, after the 1927. Good, dark, mature colour. Lovely, complex, ripe, round nose. Long and superb. Softer than when tasted three years ago. The structure of the 1927. Great depth. Oddly, slightly more forward than the 1927, but great class. (19)

1942:

Surprisingly good colour for the vintage. Not as ripe on nose as the 1945. A bit metallic. Softer, less complex than the 1935, but has held very well. Clean, forward, soft. Needs drinking. Good fruit. (18)

1935:

Palish brown-yellow. Ageing, woody on nose. A bit leathery. Round, forward; a softer, more elegant style. Needs drinking. Not nearly as alive as the 1927, but good. Not unlike a Madeira. The nose is its main fault, but it tasted pretty good. Tired, slightly oxidized. (15)

1927:

Darkest of the lot. Very good, dark, youthful colour. Charming, fruity, young nose. Full, rich, lovely, fruity, complex. Superb. One could not hope for much better. No rush. (20)

1920:

Mature colour, palish, orange rim, yet more colour than the 1935. Clean, ripe nose, slightly leathery and woody. Round, rich fruit, a bit shorter, yet richer than the older wines. Very good fruit. (18)

1912:

Pale colour to rim. Elegant, open, clean, sweet nose. Slightly medicinal, but not really a fault. Rich, thick, round, a bit sharper, but more fruit than 1908 or 1887. Long, fruity finish. Delightful. (18)

1908:

Palish orange-brown. Sweet, forward, clean nose, elegant and open. While it doesn't have the class of the 1887, it is alive, rich, long, with a very good finish. Still retained Port character, if a bit alcoholic. (18)

1887:

Similar appearance to the 1908, but sweeter, richer, more open nose. Round, forward, yet lively, rich, well balanced. At 100-years-old, surprisingly lively. Drying out at the end, but still excellent, with lovely length and complexity. The bottle was slightly bigger and heavier than the others. Top quality. Later, opened up on nose. Great intensity, ripe fruit, yet a bit drying on palate. A bit spirity, but no sign of getting tired. Amazing at 100 years old. (18.5)

The 1927 and 1945 were clearly the two winners.

The 1912, 1908, and 1887 were stunning for their age. The 1935 was the loser, a bad bottle. The white Port was richer than an aperitif should be, but it was lovely. There seemed to be a cut-off at the 1927 level. Older wines (maybe with the exception of the 1920) seemed more spirity and had a hint of Tawny. The younger wines were more obviously vintage Port.

February 7, 1987

A small Champagne and caviar tasting with Dr. Haskell Norman, in his hotel room at the Four Seasons, Newport Beach.

Paul Pinski brought along some fine Beluga caviar.

CHAMPAGNE BILLECART-SALMON "CUVÉE NF BILLECART" 1979:

Complex, long, delicate, rich. Lots of class and style, depth, complexity. A very fine Champagne. (17.5)

CHAMPAGNE LOUIS ROEDERER BRUT PREMIER N/V:

Lean, harsh, acidic, lacking depth. I've had better examples. A poor bottle. (14)

CHAMPAGNE LOUIS ROEDERER BRUT N/V:

Elegant, with good yeast and complexity. Clean, crisp, and quite full. (16)

LOUIS ROEDERER "CUVÉE MARC MENEAU" BRUT N/V:

The most elegant of the three Roederers. Complex, soft, elegant, well balanced. Nice, clean fruit. (17)

CHAMPAGNE WILLIAM DEUTZ BRUT N/V:

Well balanced, crisp, quite full, but too much sulphur and rotten vegetables on nose. Fine on palate, but nose spoils this. (14.5)

February 7, 1987

International Wine and Food Society Dinner at the Pacific Club, Los Angeles, featuring 1953 Lafite.

Most wines were contributed by Toufiq Khouri.

CHAMPAGNE BILLECART-SALMON BRUT 1976, IN MAGNUMS:

Quite lively, yet soft, elegant nose as Billecart usually has. Complex, round, soft. At its peak.

1979 "Y," DRY WINE OF D'YQUEM:

The previous night, we had the 1977 (see earlier comments). This had a similar appearance, if a bit less dark. Softer, leaner, less luscious than the 1977, yet better with food. Needs drinking. (16)

1982 CORTON-CHARLEMAGNE, BONNEAU DU MARTRAY:

There was some bottle variation, but ours was very good. Elegant structure, typical of 1982. Green-gold, young colour. Nutty, yet fruity, young nose. Crisp, well balanced. Good fruit and clean finish. Will probably improve over the next two years, but it will not be a long-term ager. Very good nevertheless. (17.5)

1953 CHÂTEAU LAFITE, IN BOTTLE, MAGNUM, AND DOUBLE-MAGNUM:

(All decanted by Dennis Foley and myself)

Bottles

The bottles were the most forward, as expected. Lovely, open, forward, elegant nose. Lighter colour, showing some age and the elegant structure so typical of the 1953s. Forward, soft, long, complex, yet seemed a bit tired and drying out. Excellent nevertheless. (18)

Magnums

The magnums were superb, and were the favourites of most participants. Deeper, richer-looking. Lovely, fruity, mature nose of butterscotch and caramel, so typical of mature Lafite. Round, full, rich, great fruit. At its absolute perfection and a lovely wine of great quality and class. One knowledgeable taster said that the 1953 Lafite, together with the great 1959, are the two best Lafites of this century; certainly between 1900 and 1975. (19)

Double-magnums

The double-magnum had the same lovely appearance as the magnums, with a lovely nose. It was full, rich, and elegant, yet it was a bit harsher, with higher acidity, and without the lovely balance of the magnums. Some of the participants liked it better than the magnums, though. All in all, 1953 Lafite is a great wine. (18.5)

1962 CHÂTEAU CLIMENS, BARSAC:

Some tasters who know this wine well said that it was better ten years ago. Medium-dark gold colour. Paler, though, than its age would indicate. (Climens is usually paler than most Sauternes.) Nose reminiscent of coconut with good, mature botrytis. Full, long, rich, yet leaner Barsac style and seemed to be drying out at the end. Needs drinking, but very good. (17)

We finished this tasting with a glass of

COGNAC RÉSERVE CHÂTEAU LAFITE-ROTHSCHILD:

Dark, a bit simple on nose and harsher style, similar to Courvoisier. Good, but not great, and overpriced.

All in all, a very enjoyable evening.

Sunday February 8, 1987

International Wine and Food Society Lunch, in Newport Beach, at the Four Seasons hotel, featuring Musigny 1949.

Most of today's wines were contributed by Toufiq Khouri. Chef Monte Derksen learned his profession at the Four Seasons in Vancouver, and prepared an excellent meal.

APERITIFS

CHAMPAGNE PERRIER-JOUËT "BLASON DE FRANCE" 1976, IN MAGNUMS:

Not very fizzy, but rich, well balanced, long, full, elegant. Ready. Clean, yeasty finish. Quite good. (16.5)

HARVEY'S "VERY FINE OLD AMONTILLADO" SHERRY, BOTTLED IN BRISTOL IN 1951:

Dr. Haskell Norman has had this wine in his cellar for over 15 years. Amber colour; nutty, raisiny nose. Full, rich, creamy, with a touch of sweetness. Dry, yet sweeter and richer than Spanish-bottlings. (17.5)

WITH DINNER

MUSIGNY BLANC, COMTE DE VOGÜÉ 1982:

A rare and expensive white Burgundy. Bright, green-gold colour. Nutty nose, reminiscent of Pinot Blanc or a rich white Graves. Good acidity and balance. Crisp, fresh; after half-an-hour in the glass, it opened up and showed quite a bit more class and complexity. Leave it alone for five years or more. Good potential. Probably made from Pinot Blanc grapes (blended with some Chardonnay?). (17)

MUSIGNY 1966, COMTE DE VOGÜÉ, CORON PÈRE ET FILS:

We were a bit worried as to this inconsistent shipper and bottler, but while this wine was clearly doctored (chaptalized), it was quite good. Dark, mature rim; spices and black pepper on nose. Good fruit. Not a great bottle and certainly the price is not justified, but good nevertheless. Ready now. (16.5)

MUSIGNY 1949, COMTE DE VOGÜÉ, IN DOUBLE-MAGNUM:

Originally, we thought we were getting an imperial, but even a double-magnum retails today in Los Angeles for close to $8,000! There was no indication on the label of "Vieilles Vignes." Much better than the 1966. Impressive, dark colour. Complex, open, elegant, mature, Pinot Noir nose. Great Musigny class and elegance, yet surprisingly youthful for a 38-year-old wine. Great length, lovely balance and fruit. Long, clean finish. No sign of getting tired. Very fine. (18)

1967 CHÂTEAU CLIMENS, BARSAC, IN MAGNUMS:

Climens, being a Barsac, is usually paler in colour and slightly lighter. This was no exception. Surprisingly bright, gold colour; light for its age, but brilliant. Lovely, buttery, fruity, botrytis nose. Elegant, still fresh, spicy. Well balanced, good fruit. Ready, but no rush, especially in magnums. (17.5)

We were rushed, and had to catch a flight back to Vancouver so we didn't have time to stay for dessert. Sid Cross grabbed a glass of Barsac on his way out, so I tasted the Climens in the car on the way to the airport. Overall, an exciting, busy, and interesting weekend.

February 25, 1977

Le Tastevin 1976 Cabernet Sauvignon tasting.

Dr. Allan Tobe was guest speaker. We knew what the wines were, but not the order (blind tasting).

CHÂTEAU ST. JEAN "WILDWOOD" CABERNET SAUVIGNON 1976, SONOMA VALLEY:

Very dark, deep colour. Sweet, ripe, rich, mature nose. Very good colour to rim. Sweet nose, Port-like, tobacco. Full, thick, yet high acidity and drying out. Losing its fruit. Sharp, acidic finish. Over-the-hill. I liked it less than most. (13)

RIDGE "YORK CREEK" CABERNET SAUVIGNON 1976, CALIFORNIA:

Medium-dark colour. Good depth, orangy rim, slightly stemmy, open, complex. Some hard tannins, but good fruit. Leaner style. Clean, long finish. Well balanced. Ready and will not improve. (16.5)

MARTIN RAY CABERNET SAUVIGNON 1976, CALIFORNIA:

Similar colour to the "York Creek," but more maturity. Volatile, odd nose. Rotting vegetable soup. Sour garbage. Acidic, sharp, very unpleasant. (0)

CUVAISON CABERNET SAUVIGNON 1976, NAPA VALLEY:

Medium colour. Good depth, showing some maturity. Open, elegant, stemmy, Sonoma-like. Open, soft, yet good fruit. Long finish. Good intensity. Not showing signs of age. Later, acidity took over. Drink up. (15)

SPRING MOUNTAIN "TROIS CUVÉES" CABERNET SAUVIGNON, NAPA VALLEY:

A blend of the 1975, 1976, and 1977 vintages. Medium colour. Mature, orange rim. Touch of cork, but still pleasant. Vegetal, round, open. Another bottle was more elegant. Open, clean, leaner style, hard, tannic. Hard and hot (high alcohol). Too much bottle variation. (15)

ROBERT MONDAVI CABERNET SAUVIGNON 1976, NAPA VALLEY:

Lightest of the lot. Open, forward elegant nose. Good length, pleasant. Well balanced. Still some tannin, but not massive. Round, complex, good fruit; more elegant Napa style. (16)

CHAPPELLET 1976 CABERNET SAUVIGNON, NAPA VALLEY:

Dark, browning colour to rim. Not much nose. Some vegetal overtones, but still too tight. Big, tannic, powerful, lots of fruit, but high acidity, too. Structure says "wait," but fruit is mature. Ridge? (14.5)

The "York Creek" was the clear winner, and the Martin Ray was the most disliked.

DESSERT WINE

1983 QUADY BLACK MUSCAT, CALIFORNIA:

Light-red colour; spicy Muscat on nose. Not very sweet, but some sweetness there. OK. Not my style of wine. A bit too spirity. Somehow Muscat doesn't turn me on unless it is a really old Setúbal or Madeira. (15)

March 3, 1987

Commanderie de Bordeaux Dinner and blind tasting, at "Café Splash."

Subject: 1966 Classed Growths Haut-Médocs.
I organized this event.

1. CHÂTEAU BRANE-CANTENAC 1966:

Medium colour, orangy rim. Slightly leathery, medicinal nose. Later, a bit chocolaty, round, elegant. Forward, soft; some sharpness (acidic), but quite pleasant. Needs drinking. Later, it became thin, acidic, and sharp. I've tasted better examples of this wine in the past. (14.5)

2. CHÂTEAU BEYCHEVELLE 1966:

Medium-dark colour, good depth. Palish, mature rim. Rich nose; full, fruity, ripe. Still young. Full, rich, round on palate, yet getting a bit astringent. Needs drinking. Good solid middle. Good nose, but finishes sharp. (16)

3. CHÂTEAU DUHART-MILON 1966:

Medium-light colour. Orangy, mature rim. Round, elegant, yet tannic, mature nose. Drying out a bit. Leaner. Still has class. High acidity, but good complexity. Drink up. (15)

4. CHÂTEAU GISCOURS 1966:

Medium colour, good depth; mature, orangy rim. Fairly tannic, some fruit, but high acidity. Getting lean and hard; was better a few years ago. Later, opened up. Quite elegant. Chocolaty nose, but fruit disappearing. (15.5)

5. CHÂTEAU GRUAUD-LAROSE 1966:

Impressive dark colour. Lovely, round, rich, sweet nose. Appealing. Full, tannic, yet loaded with fruit. Needs five years or longer. The biggest, best balanced, and most youthful of the bunch. Not necessarily finesse, but excellent quality. (17.5)

6. CHÂTEAU LA LAGUNE 1966:

Good, dark colour to rim. Slightly green, stemmy nose, yet elegant, open. Chocolaty. Rich, round, elegant, well balanced. At its optimum. Hint of acidity at the end. Lovely. (17) Having said that, I have tasted even better—truly exceptional—examples of this fine wine.

7. CHÂTEAU LEOVILLE-LASCASES 1966, LONDON-BOTTLED BY ARMY AND NAVY STORES, IN MAGNUM:

Very good, dark colour to rim; good depth. A solid, big, hard wine. A bit metallic (steely); good fruit, though. Seemed a bit corked. Later, it was acidic, lean, sharp. Needs retasting (preferably château-bottled). (No score)

8. CHÂTEAU LYNCH-BAGES 1966:

Good, dark, mature colour to rim; good depth. Chocolaty, rich nose. Full, rich, cedary, eucalyptus. Typical Lynch-Bages. Hard, tannic, yet good fruit. Round, rich, big, "sweet." Very good, better than expected. Best nose of the bunch, but leaner, tannic style. (17)

9. CHÂTEAU MONTROSE 1966:

Good, dark colour; mature, orangy rim. Steely, hard nose. Austere, hard, tannic, low fruit. A lean, mean wine; not enough fruit. A tannic monster. (15) The 1970 is far superior, with great fruit extract.

10. CHÂTEAU PICHON-LONGUEVILLE-BARON 1966:

Dark, brick colour; good depth. Slightly cedary nose. Lean, hard, acidic. A solid, serious wine. Lean, acidic, and losing its fruit. (14.5) After 1961, Pichon-Baron ceased to be a serious contender for a reputed second Classed Growth—to this day. Pity. The owners (Bouteillers) better clean up their act soon.

11. CHÂTEAU PONTET-CANET 1966:

Medium colour, a bit lighter than the three previous wines. Mature, orange rim. Elegance on nose and palate. Round, complex, elegant, slightly acidic, but lovely length. Holding well. A very good wine. (17) Alas, after 1966, Pontet-Canet's quality has come down hard and fast. Obviously, the Cruses (and now the Tesserons) seem to have problems turning this fine property around.

12. CHÂTEAU TALBOT 1966:

Medium colour, good depth, orange rim. Mature, ripe nose. Not very complex. Leaner, drying out on palate. Later, became softer, but still lean and acidic. Some people liked this wine more than I did. (15)

Overall

The group's favourite wines were the Lynch-Bages and Pontet-Canet. The least favourite wines were the Brane-Cantenac, Pichon-Longueville-Baron. The Lascases was corked, unfortunately. Later we had the same wines with dinner. Some opened up nicely. The Gruaud-Larose was the liveliest, freshest, and has a good future, even if it lacks at present some complexity. The rest need drinking or are past their prime. After all, these wines are 20 years old.

WITH DINNER

1982 CHÂTEAU CARBONNIEUX BLANC:

Bright-gold, mature colour. Rich, round, spicy Sauvignon Blanc. Round, with good length. At its peak and quite pleasant. (16.5)

1981 PULIGNY-MONTRACHET PREMIER CRU "LES REFERTS," LOUIS JADOT:

Round, elegant, forward, fairly alcoholic, but with good complexity. Quite good, but not outstanding. A fine effort for the vintage nevertheless. (16.5)

CHÂTEAU GILETTE "CRÈME DE TÊTE" 1953, SAUTERNES:

Bright, young gold colour for age. A bit earthy, with smells of concrete and earth (because of very long storage in cement vats). Not much complexity, lacking botrytis and sweetness. Not very interesting. (15.5)

March 1987

One-week trip to Napa Valley (Yountville) with Carol and the kids.

Dinner at Belle and Barney Rhodes' home.

Other guests included Dr. Stan and Helene Schwartz, Joe and Alice Heitz, and Mrs. Winiarski (Warren's wife, from Stag's Leap). Warren was ill and couldn't make it.

DEUTZ CALIFORNIA BRUT CHAMPAGNE N/V, NAPA VALLEY:

Their first, limited release, made from purchased grapes with a fair bit of Pinot Noir in the blend. They are planting 100 acres of vines but it will take a few years to grow. Quite good California Champagne. Complex, fresh nose with some yeastiness. Round, elegant, young. Fine mousse and bubbles. Slight hint of dosage (syrup added). (16.5)

SONOMA-CUTRER 1984 CHARDONNAY, RUSSIAN RIVER:

Fresh, slightly sweet, elegant, not overly alcoholic or ripe. Well balanced, lacking a bit in weight and concentration, but not bad. (15)

1977 AND 1976 HEITZ CELLARS "BELLA OAKS" CABERNET SAUVIGNON, NAPA VALLEY:

Joe made the wine and Barney sold him the grapes. (Barney Rhodes is the owner of Bella Oaks vineyard.) 1976 was the first vintage in which "Bella Oaks" was produced. Both 1976 and 1977 were drought years; the 1977 was obviously so. Rich, dark, round, full, fruity, at its peak. Both had some hint of mint. The 1976 was more Claret-like, leaner, more tannic, more serious, and had more class. It will also last longer. Barney and Joe preferred the 1977. Carol, Alice Heitz, Stan Schwartz, and myself preferred the 1976. I rated the 1977 (15.5) and the 1976 (17).

1979 ZINFANDEL "MONTE ROSSO," SONOMA VALLEY, SAM SEBASTIANI:

Fairly dark, solid, red oak-barrel nose, spicy. Not very complex, but nice. (15) Joe Heitz told me that at a blind tasting, the way to know if a wine is Zinfandel or Pinot Noir is by keeping it in your mouth, swallowing it, and then noticing if the taste comes from the two sides of the tongue; if so, then it is a Zinfandel. If you can taste it from the tip of your tongue, then it is a Pinot Noir. I'm not sure if he was serious or joking.

DESSERT WINE

1982 SANTINO "EL DORADO" RIESLING "DRY BERRY SELECT HARVEST," SHENANDOAH VALLEY, IN HALF-BOTTLE:

Probably the sweetest dessert wine I've ever tasted. Acid 0.99; sugar 57 brix at harvest! Residual sugar: an incredible 42%. Dark, deep-gold colour. Peaches, very ripe, botrytized nose. Liquid honey; full, creamy, thick, rich, luscious. Yet it had good acidity and clean finish. Quite good. (17)

1979 QUARLES HARRIS LATE-BOTTLED VINTAGE PORT, CORNEY AND BARROW:

Imported by Warren Winiarski of Stag's Leap. Leaner style, elegant, complex, quite nice. Good fruit, fairly long finish. (16)

Visits to Joseph Phelps.

Visited with Joe Phelps. I had met him previously at IW&FS functions. Joe will send me a poster of the detailed vineyards of the Napa Valley. He showed me where all the good vineyards were on his map. We also had a talk about Canadian liquor monopolies. Then, he took me around the winery. After visiting the winery and installations, we tasted the following.

1985 SAUVIGNON BLANC, NAPA VALLEY:

Made with 12% Semillon. Hard, lean, low fruit. I didn't care for it too much. It had a pale colour with a touch of pink-gold. (13.5)

1983 CHARDONNAY "SAN GIACOMO VINEYARD," NAPA VALLEY, CARNEROS DISTRICT:

Barrel-fermented for six months. Their regular Chardonnay is fermented in steel tanks. Made from their own grapes; some of their top Cabernets come from purchased grapes (Eisele, for instance). Leaner style, crisp, touch of oak, low fruit, but not bad. (14.5)

1982 SYRAH, NAPA VALLEY:

Their Syrah is the true French varietal, but they don't have much success in selling it. Appearance and nose of an elegant Pinot Noir, light red. Yet on palate, it is quite hard. Good fruit, though. Needs two to three years. (15)

1984 Cabernet Sauvignon "Backus Vineyard," Napa Valley:

Located near Oakville on seven acres. Red soil, terraced, rich in iron. Dark, ripe nose with hint of mint, eucalyptus, and oak. Hard, tannic, leaner, masculine style. Complex. Needs seven to eight years. Blended with 5% Merlot. Typical style of this vineyard. Very good. (17)

1984 Cabernet Sauvignon "Eisele Vineyard," Napa Valley:

Purchased grapes from Milt Eisele. Darker than the Backus. Spicy, ripe, fruity nose. Some oak-vanilla, no mint. Fresh, complex, and concentrated flavours. Medium-bodied. Médoc-like, high tannins. Needs eight to ten years. Very good potential. (17.5)

We couldn't taste the 1985s because they are being blended right now (March 1987).

1983 Cabernet Sauvignon "Insignia," Napa Valley:

This is their traditional "Reserve" wine, made from a blend of 60% Cabernet Sauvignon, 20% Cabernet Franc, and 20% Merlot. Hint of eucalyptus; rich, complex, round, tannic, leaner style. Very good concentration. Needs five to seven years. A very good wine. (17.5) My impression is that Phelp's clear forté is their fine single-vineyard Cabernets and Late Harvest Rieslings.

Visit to Duckhorn's.

I visited with Dan Duckhorn. His winemaker is Tom Rinaldi. Dan likes Château Palmer because of the high proportion of Merlot. His daughter worked for a while with Peter Sichel.

Duckhorn is a compact, modern winery. We tasted the whole range of Merlots and Cabernets of the prolific 1986 vintage. They purchase most of their grapes and use a fair bit of new oak, about 30% annually on average.

About the Sauvignon Blanc

(Blended with 20% Semillon) Dan said he's not very happy with Semillon. He thinks it is too flabby and that he'll try to blend Pinot Blanc instead in the future.

We tasted five separate cuvées of Merlot (all 1986).

1. Merlot grown on clay soil:

It has a burnt-coffee nose because of new toasted barrels. Bright colour, leaner- style, quite fruity.

2. Merlot from a vineyard located in the south of the Napa Valley:

Cooler vineyard. Blended with 25% Cabernet Sauvignon. Fruity, rich, cleaner on nose, high pH, a bit flabby. Dan Duckhorn said that 1986 was a very prolific year and high pH is a general problem. He thinks his 1986s will needs more barrel-ageing and more racking than usual.

He uses mostly Nadalié (Bordeaux) barrels. His favourite white Graves is Domaine de Chevalier. He is trying to find out why Semillon is so much more successful in Bordeaux than in California.

3. 100% Merlot from a vineyard near the town of Napa:

Good, drained, gravely soil. Young vines. Touch of greenness, hint of sulphur. Good, dark colour. Young. In 1986, because of mildew, grape growers had to use a fair bit of sulphur and some of it ended up in the wine.

4. 100% Merlot from the Stag's Leap area:

Older vines. Sweet, elegant, full, rich, round, and tannic. Dan said that 1986 produced the largest crop in Napa's history! What will be needed is careful vinification. He likes the 1985s very much, especially the Cabernets from the Napa Valley. I tend to agree with him. Must look into purchasing some of the top 1985 Cabernets.

5. 100% Merlot from the "Three Palms Vineyard":

This is their choicest vineyard source and they usually bottle it unblended as a separate bottling. Superb quality! Rich, full, round, spicy, and ripe. Perfectly balanced. Since 1981, he's been blending 20% to 25% Cabernet Sauvignon in this "Three Palms" Merlot. Their first vintage was 1978, which is becoming a collector's item.

Dan said that most of the juice from young vines goes into new barrels to give them more complexity.

Then, we tasted various samples (unblended) of Cabernet Sauvignons.

1. Cabernet Sauvignon 1986:

From a vineyard at the peak of Mount Veeder. Leaner, complex (new wood helped), tight. 1986 produced an average of six tons of grapes per acre instead of the usual four to five tons.

2. 100% Cabernet Sauvignon from Spottswoode:

Spottswoode is at the foot of Spring Mountain. Dan is very impressed by the quality of Spottswoode's Cabernet Sauvignon. He has a long-term contract with them. Incredibly dark, deep intense colour. Sweet, concentrated; lovely, rich fruit. Some oak, but predominantly ripe fruit. Incredible concentration in view of very large crop.

3. 100% Cabernet Sauvignon from Howell Mountain, near Randy Dunn's vineyard:

Intense berries on nose and palate. Leaner, classy style. This will be added to his Cabernet Sauvignon blend.

All samples tasted came from new, identical, French oak barrels. Duckhorn usually also uses some American new oak barrels.

4. 100% Cabernet Sauvignon from an area called Dry Creek

(not to be confused with Sonoma's Dry Creek), near Trefethen's vineyard:

Deep, dark, leaner style. Promising. He's even decided to give up some of the Spottswoode Cabernet for some of this Dry Creek, which he thinks has excellent potential.

5. 100% Cabernet Sauvignon from Mount St. John, south of St. Helena:

Fresh, good acidity, great balance. Very good for the blend. Not too rich. Well balanced. This vineyard of four acres was picked twice. The bottom part was picked ten days after the top part, to allow grapes there to mature better.

All the above Cabernets will go into the 1986 blend, eventually. A very interesting and informative visit.

March 20, 1987

At the Heitz's home.

I spent the whole day with the Heitz family at their home near the winery, helping Joe reorganize his cellar. We worked all day and a little more on the following day. We removed close to 1,500 bottles from his cellar and sorted everything out. That evening, Joe Heitz gave me a few rare old bottles of Port and Madeira, and a magnum of 1974 Heitz Cellars "Martha's Vineyard" Cabernet Sauvignon "Anniversary Label."

During lunch (with Alice, Kathleen David, and Rolly), we tried the following wines.

"London Port," California-bottled by Goldberg and Owen:

Low shoulder. Shipped and bottled before the introduction of prohibition in 1919, so it is at least 75 years old. Madeira, deep-gold colour. Woody, elegant, slightly sweet nose. Round, very good, like an old Tawny. I opened a second bottle, but that one was dried out (loose cork).

Heitz Cellars Sherry N/V:

Produced in 1968. Made from juice purchased from Sebastiani. Nutty, elegant, deep-gold, long, slightly creamy. Quite good.

1964 Beaulieu Vineyards Burgundy, Napa Valley

and

1966 Beaune "Clos du Roi" Premier Cru Coron:

The Beaulieu was made from a blend of Gamay and Mondeuse grapes. It was darker, with a more open nose. Complex, oddly Burgundy-like on palate. Tired, drying out, lean, but still alive. Past its prime.

The Beaune had a less open, less complex nose, but better fruit and cleaner colour. Spicy, still lively, well structured. Good, but not great. Needs drinking.

"Port Wine" (shipper and provenance unknown):

Joe Heitz said that all eight bottles he owned (he later gave me one) were originally beer bottles. The Port was made between 1911 and 1919, according to Joe. Very mature, but still some red colour. Woody, raisiny nose. Round, mature, elegant. Not bad at all. Not unlike a very old late-bottled Vintage Port.

After all that, we went back to sorting out his cellar. The next day (Saturday), I went back to the Heitz's for three hours, to finish sorting out the cellar.

March 21, 1987

Dinner at Joe and Alice Heitz's.

Bob and Mary Travers (owners of Mayacamas Vineyard) joined us, as did Father Don (a local Catholic priest who helped us a bit with cleaning the cellar and in the process, broke a bottle of 1975 Angelica), his mother, and an elderly couple called Romy and Philip.

APERITIF

1933 Pandora "Old Sherry," New York-bottled by William H. Fearing:

In glass for 40 years. Joe purchased this and many other old treasures in 1975 from the Crocker Cellar. (Crocker, whose family owns the Crocker Bank, was known as the "King of Silver.") Amber, incredibly brilliant colour. Lovely, nutty, Sherry nose. Great length, structure, slightly creamy, complex. An excellent drink. Slightly sweet. I had never heard of this Sherry previously.

1978 Meursault "Les Narvaux," Michelot-Buisson:

Medium gold. Nutty, some sulphur, flinty nose; cleared later. Flowery, slightly sweet, complex on palate. Good but not great. Needs drinking.

1980 Monterey Cabernet Sauvignon, Maryland:

Given to Joe by the winemaker. Deep-red; spicy, clean, complex Cabernet nose. Didn't sing on palate. Lean, acidic, lacking ripe fruit and body.

Casa di Sonoma N/V "California Cabernet," Napa Valley:

Made by El Gavilan winery in Sonoma, bottled in 1947. Joe said possibly a 1941 or 1942. In those days, wines were left in large vats for six to seven years. Sebastiani sold it commercially in the late 1940s and early 1950s. Mature, medium colour; brick-brown-orange. Surprisingly like an old Claret on both nose and palate. Woody, complex, tired, losing its fruit. Like an old Claret from the 1920s or earlier. Better than expected. Finished old, slightly woody, and leathery. Very unusual and one of the oldest California Cabernets I've tasted.

Beaulieu Vineyards Georges de Latour "Private Reserve" Cabernet Sauvignon, Napa Valley:

Vintage unknown, label fell off, but based on the shape of the bottle and cork, Joe thought it was early to mid-1950s. Deep, mature colour. Ripe, mature, spicy, California Cabernet nose. Slightly leathery. Similar impressions on palate. Rich, long, complex. Very good. Mature. A true old Beaulieu Vineyards wine. Obvious American oak.

Château dY'Quem N/V "Mountain Crest," Napa Valley, Livermore, Sonoma Valley:

This is not the French d'Yquem, but a California imitation. Note the odd spelling: dY'Quem! In the old days, California producers were imitating French names. Joe said that it was definitely pre-Prohibition, probably made around 1915 to 1920, and (he guessed) probably made with Wente's Semillon. Low shoulder level.

Like black molasses. This was deep gold, not unlike an older Sauternes. Incredible appearance for such an old wine. Earthy nose, touch of Muscat, earthy on palate, almost dry, yet some sweetness. Very little botrytis there. Woody, bright colour. Unusual and quite good. Tasted like a Sauternes from the 1930s or 1940s. Definitely drinking history.

1951 Ficklin's California Port:

Bottled in 1954 and given to Joe by old Walter Ficklin. It has 5.5 brix, 20% alcohol. 1951 was the very first of only three declared vintages of this house. They usually (to date) do not sell their Port as a vintage. Medium, palish colour. Leathery, odd, medicinal nose. Not very good. Fairly alcoholic, low fruit. Still alive, but has probably seen better days.

Then, I tasted an old Cognac that Joe had hidden in a cupboard.

Ehrmann Frères Grande Champagne Vieux Cognac:

Old-Bordeaux bottle, deep punt. Probably bottled in the late 1930s. At least 30 (or more) years in wood. Green-amber colour. Lovely nose, rich and dry, as true Cognac is; smooth, lovely. Slightly herbal.

So ended an evening of historic wines and we heard history from the oldtimers around the table. An exciting week in the Napa Valley.

March 26, 1987

Le Tastevin Wine Club's tenth anniversary, at the Four Seasons hotel, Vancouver.

Le Tastevin is a club I established with 22 members in 1977, which has grown to 100 members at present.

APERITIF

Champagne Bollinger Brut 1973, in salmanazar:

(Equivalent to 11 bottles, 8 litres) Superb, yeasty, complex, long. Great fruit. A lovely wine.

Subject: Vertical tasting of Château Palmer 1970 to 1980.

1980:

Medium-light red colour. Stemmy, spicy, open nose. Herbaceous, soft, a bit lean, but round, forward, ready. Quite good, though. Pleasant. Drink now. (14)

1977:

Medium-dark colour. Stemmy, herbaceous, green nose, typical of the vintage. High acidity, sharp, lean, but some fruit and complexity, too. Not bad for the year. Not as round as the 1980. (13)

1976:

Round, ripe nose. Good depth with orange, mature rim. A bit astringent on palate. Baked (drought year), losing its fruit. I've had better bottles. Ripe, complex nose. Later, improved. Good but needs drinking. (15)

1979:

Good, dark colour to rim. Round, complex, delicate, well balanced, fruity. Still a bit tannic, but generous. Drink from 1989 onward. Flavourful, round, very enjoyable. Margaux complexity. Promises to be a fine wine. (17.5)

1978:

Good depth, palish rim. Spicy, herbaceous Cabernet nose. Round, complex, very long. Elegant, yet Cabernet spiciness. Great depth and complexity. A lovely wine. No rush. Drink 1990 to 1995 or beyond. More tannins and complexity than the 1979. (18)

1975:

Deep, dark colour, palish rim. Superb, ripe fruit on nose. Hint of licorice. Chocolaty. Very tannic, big, powerful; backed by excellent fruit. A big, serious wine. Needs ten to 15 years. (18.5)

1970:

Fabulous, open, complex nose. Nuances of delicate, ripe fruit. Good, dark, maturing colour. Round, complex, reaching it peak. Well balanced. Great length. Superb! A great bottle. Ready, but no rush. (19)

1953 Château Gilette "Crème de Tête," Sauternes:

Bright gold; young-looking for its age. A bit earthy, sweet, not much botrytis. Clean, crisp, pleasant. (16)

April 7, 1987

Commanderie de Bordeaux Dinner and vertical tasting of Château Palmer and Château d'Angludet, at the Vancouver Club.

Two Palmer verticals in two months! I'm getting spoiled. Peter Sichel was our guest speaker. He came along with his son James. I invited Peter to come; he very generously contributed most of the older wines, as well as barrel samples of the 1985 vintage.

We started with two of Peter's wines.

Bordeaux Prestige White and Red, both 1985s:

The white is made up of 100% Semillon, aged in new oak casks. Bottled in May 1986. To me, it tasted more like a Sauvignon Blanc: pleasant, crisp, fresh, with decent fruit.

The red had 20% juice made with carbonic maceration from 55% Merlot, 30% Cabernet Franc, and only 15% Cabernet Sauvignon. Matured nine months in new oak. Pleasant, fresh, spicy, herbaceous. Almost ready, yet still had a little tannin and good structure. If they're not expensive, they're worth it. Small production: 28,000 bottles of red and 16,000 bottles of white.

Palmer and d'Angludet 1985 to 1978

d'Angludet 1985, barrel sample:

Deep, purplish colour. Subdued, clean berries on nose. Ripe fruit, elegant, well balanced. Good depth. Promising.

Palmer 1985, barrel sample:

Deep, bright purple. Spicier than above and more intense nose. New oak. Lovely complexity. Elegant, long, vanilla, complex. Excellent potential. No score because it is not in bottle yet, but promising. Tannins a bit more aggressive. Great potential.

d'Angludet 1984:

Medium-colour for a 1984. Good balance. Pruny nose. Slightly leathery, off. Leaner. Acidic, sharp. Not a winner. (12.5)

Palmer 1984:

Good depth for a 1984. Clean, elegant, open nose. Not much ripeness, though. Much more class than the d'Angludet. Clean, oak-vanilla, but a bit sharp and acidic at end. Needs three to four years to reach maturity. (14)

Both 1984s aged in 25% to 30% new oak, and both bottled in June, 1986.

d'Angludet 1983:

Very impressive dark colour to rim. Ripe, rich, yet unyielding nose. Fine balance, depth, and tannins. Good potential. Drink 1993 to 1998. (16.5)

Palmer 1983:

Similar appearance to d'Angludet, but much more elegance and class on nose. Lovely complexity, but starting to close up. Solid, serious, riper, harder tannins than the 1985. Needs many years but will be excellent. I cannot help but feel that this could be another 1970. Superb potential. (18.5)

d'Angludet 1982:

Slightly more mature-looking than the 1983. Beefy, ripe nose. Surprisingly, more elegant than the 1983 on palate. Clearly at d'Angludet, the 1983 is the better of the two. The 1983 is better structured. (15) Peter compares 1982 to 1970. I think that, in the Commune of Margaux at least, the 1983s will be better than the 1982s. This includes Château Palmer itself.

Palmer 1982:

Similar appearance to the 1983, but rather riper, more leathery nose. Full, rich fruit, quite tannic, starting to close in. Drink from 1992 and beyond. Very good. (17)

d'Angludet 1981:

A bit darker than the Palmer 1981. Some maturity at rim. Sweet, elegant, yet closed nose. Leaner than the 1982. Elegance rather than power. Good fruit. Relatively early maturing. Small crop, poor flowering. Opening up. (16)

Palmer 1981:

Surprisingly, more evolved colour than the d'Angludet 1981. Dull, some straw on nose. Elegance rather than power. Good fruit. Relatively early maturing. Small crop, as at d'Angludet. Already approachable. (16.5)

Palmer 1980:

Paler, watery rim. Clean, elegant, open nose with Margaux complexity. Slightly stemmy (rain, immature grapes). Elegant, forward, some aggressive acidity. Enjoyable now. Scored low in context but overall, quite pleasing. (14.5)

D'ANGLUDET 1979:

Medium-dark colour, still young-looking. Similar appearance to the Palmer. Closed, unyielding nose. Leaner, yet soft. Good fruit, but closed. Give it two to three years to open up. Some tannin. Not much complexity. A serious, yet not very complex, wine. Needs time. (15)

PALMER 1979:

Rich, ripe, complex, lovely quality. Good open, complex nose. No rush, three to five years and longer. True Margaux elegance. Well balanced. Good acidity and fruit; excellent character. (17.5)

D'ANGLUDET 1978:

Dark, maturing colour. Toasty, still closed nose. A bit green on palate, but good ripeness, too. Better than expected. Finishes a bit acidic and sharp. Needs three to five years. (15)

PALMER 1978:

Good, dark colour to rim. Closed, tough, solid, serious. Will be great, but needs time. Great complexity, but very backward. Give it eight more years. This, together with the 1985 and 1983, are the outstanding wines of this tasting. (18)

Overall

Palmer is more of a true Margaux. Elegance and class, new oak, great complexity. D'Angludet is chunkier, almost like a St. Julien. Big, rich, solid.

Later, we went into the dining room for dinner. With a well-prepared dinner, we had the following.

PALMER 1976 AND 1975:

The 1976 was obviously paler, soft, open, ripe on nose (drought year), a trace of acidity at the end. Pleasant, but needs drinking. (15)

The 1975 was much darker, still closed on nose with some Cabernet spiciness, but not much Palmer elegance at this stage. Typical, but good 1975 structure. Still tannic, closed, hard, but has the all-important fruit. Needs five to eight years. While 1975 has its detractors, with some justification, this is certainly one of the successes of this vintage. (18)

1971 AND 1970 PALMER:

The 1971 showing more age, orange-brown. Leaner on palate than in past experiences. Drying up, a bit lean. Still enjoyable, but needs drinking. Good complexity. Peter said that it is getting tired and was better two to three years ago. (15)

The 1970 was much darker and younger-looking. Still solid. Lovely, complex, elegant nose. Spicy, ripe, and long. Full on palate. About ready, but no rush. Excellent fruit. A great wine. Drink 1987 to 1995 or beyond. (18.5)

PALMER 1966 AND 1961:

Masterpieces! Both had very similar appearance to mature Claret, with good depth.

PALMER 1966:

Lovely, open nose of mature Claret at is peak. Full, round, long, well balanced, without the hard structure and low fruit of many 1966s. Long, complex. Excellent, chocolaty, cedar, classy aftertaste. Unfortunately, it had to compete with one of the all-time masterpieces in Bordeaux. (18.5)

PALMER 1961:

Slightly deeper colour. A magnificent, open, ripe, nose of intense fruit. Great length and class here. Full, fruity, complex, long, rich, perfect balance. Ready, but should hold. Superb. (19.5) These older wines matured to perfection at the château.

DESSERT WINE

1980 CHÂTEAU D'YQUEM:

Bright-gold, still young-looking. Young, fresh fruit, some botrytis. Not overwhelming or very rich, honeyed botrytis wine, but well balanced with excellent fruit. Needs three to five extra years of bottle-age. (18)

A memorable tasting. The next day, Carol and I had lunch with Peter Sichel and his son James at a Chinese restaurant, in Vancouver. From there, Peter flew to Edmonton for a wine festival.

The following day, I invited Peter (who had just come back from Edmonton) and his son, as well as a few members of the panel of The Wine Consumer, *for lunch at "Tsui Hang," a Chinese restaurant. From there, I drove Peter to the airport.*

May 2, 1987

Dinner at Drs. Alastair and Jean Carruthers'.

CHAMPAGNE LECHÈRE "ORIENT EXPRESS" BRUT N/V PREMIER CRU:

Round, soft, forward, elegant, but a bit flat and showing signs of age. Quite pleasant. A bit too much "dosage." (16.5)

CHAMPAGNE ROEDERER "CRISTAL" 1976 BRUT:

A lovely, elegant, very well-balanced wine. Long, complex, flavourful. Good fruit and acidity; quite lively for a 1976. Very good. A ripe vintage. (18)

NUITS-ST.-GEORGES BLANC "CLOS DE L'ARLOT" PREMIER CRU, JULES BELIN 1978:

It had an uncanny resemblance on both nose and palate to a fine white Graves or rich Pouilly-Fumé or a mature, big Chablis. More like Sauvignon Blanc than anything else. Deep, bright-gold colour. When told that it was a Côte d'Or (all wines were served blind), I said that it had to be Pinot Blanc, which it was!

1961, 1962, and 1964 Château Canon Grand Cru, St. Emilion:

The 1962 and 1964 were château-bottled; the 1961 London-bottled by Grants of St. James. I guessed right away that there was a lot of similarity in the style and said that it was possibly a vertical. I also said Bordeaux. I thought (as did Sid Cross) that they were Pauillacs or St. Estèphes. Later, Sid said "maybe Pomerol." We were all wrong. We also thought that the 1962 was 1961, 1964 was 1966, and 1961 was 1970. Canon produces big, austere St. Emilions and that's why we were wrong as far as the commune was concerned. Anyway, we didn't do too well. At least we guessed the general region correctly.

1962:

More age. (All had good depth of colour, though.) Lovely, forthcoming Claret nose. Great elegance, complexity. Well balanced. Long, excellent, and at its peak. My favourite. (17.5)

1964:

Sturdier than the 1962. Good fruit, serious, but not as delicate or complex, and a bit sharp at the end. (16)

1961:

Darkest, deep colour, young-looking for its age. Solid, big, excellent structure, but lacking finesse and complexity. Will live on for many years, but will not improve. I thought it was a 1970. (17)

1970 Château Suduiraut:

Deep, bright-gold colour. I knew it had to be older than 1975 or 1976, and not as complex as 1967 or 1971, so I said "this is 1970." But I couldn't tell which property. Rich, solid, mature, but lacking botrytis and complexity, and a bit too alcoholic at the end. Not too sweet either. Quite good, though. (16)

1955 Graham's Vintage Port:

I guessed Graham's or Fonseca's because of the depth and sweetness, and I said 1966 or 1955. Round, full, rich, but a bit too sharp and spirity at the end. A very good Port nevertheless. (17.5)

May 7, 1987

Small Tastevin group, vertical tasting of Château Leoville-Lascases.

Champagne Dom Ruinart 1979 Brut:

Complex, elegant, yeasty, long. Well balanced. Good, creamy fruit. A very good Champagne. (17.5)

Château Leoville-Lascases 1982 to 1961

1982:

Intense, dark, deep colour to rim. Excellent fruit extract. Ripe, full, rich, long, quite tannic. Very rich fruit. Excellent balance. Will be a great wine in ten to 15 years. Great concentration. Will be a classic some day. (19) A "must buy," but it already retails for US$350 per case across the border!

1981:

Good, dark colour, but lighter than the 1982. Charming, perfumy, elegant, fruity nose. Spices. Good body, some tannin, lovely balance. Complex, fruity. Mid-term; drink from 1990 onward. Not big, but good elegance and balance. A charmer, yet it has some tannins, too. (17)

1979:

More age, but also better depth than the 1981. Closed nose, yet ripe. Unyielding. Big, solid, quite tannic. More serious and more depth than the 1981. Good structure. Needs seven to ten years. Leaner style, but good fruit. Later, softened a bit, but retained moderate tannins. (17)

1978:

Good, dark colour, yet lighter than the 1979. Big, rich nose, a bit vegetal. More Cabernet, less Merlot richness. Very good, though. Solid, well balanced, still tannic. No rush. Will be excellent. Lovely structure. More appealing than the 1975 at this stage. (17.5)

1975:

Similar colour to the 1978, but showing a little more age. Similar nose to the 1978, yet better concentration and a bit closed. Tannic, solid, excellent. Typical 1975, but very good fruit, too. Drink from 1990 to 2000. (17.5)

1973:

Surprisingly dark colour; mature, orange rim. Dusty, sweet, beet-sugar nose. Vegetal, thin, showing slight signs of oxidation, but still quite pleasant and has good complexity. Needs drinking. A bit too acidic. (13.5)

1971:

Surprisingly good colour. Rich, toasty, mature nose. Perfumy and delicate. Round, still a bit tannic, yet some excessive acidity. Rich, tannic, good depth, solid. Maybe losing some fruit. Drink up, but quite enjoyable. Better than the 1970. (15.5)

1970:

Similar colour to the 1971, yet without the depth of the 1971. A bit more closed, austere, and dusty, too. Acidic, harder, citric. Too sharp. Not as fruity as the 1971. It is a mystery why Lascases failed to make a good 1970. (15)

1966:

Complex, open nose of ripe, mature Claret. Lovely length. Good dark colour, orange-brown rim. Elegant, forward, delicate, at it peak. Complex, forward. Very good. Hint of earth and barnyard (rustic). (17.5)

1961:

A bit darker than the 1966, mature rim. Ripe, fruity, complex, lovely nose. Surprising fruit, yet not quite the elegance of the 1966. Good concentration, backbone. At its peak, yet no rush drinking it. A fine bottle. Better than expected because this property produced a 1959 that is consistently better than the 1961. (18)

DESSERT WINE

1976 WINZERHEIMER ROSENHEER RIESLING BEERENAUSLESE, VON PLATTENBERG:

Delicate, not massive. Good (almost high) acidity, typical of Nahe. Medium body, palish gold. Pleasant, delicate, leaner style. Quite pleasant, but not intense enough for me. (16)

May 11, 1987

Vertical tasting of Château Grand-Puy-Lacoste Pauillac 1983 to 1945.

I organized this blind tasting for 16 people. It was held at our home. All wines were from my cellar. It took me almost ten years to collect all the wines for this tasting.

APERITIF

VIN JAUNE 1972, ARBOIS "DOMAINE DE LA PINTE":

In "Clavelin" bottle (640 mL). Deep gold. Fine, Sherry-like, but richer and higher alcohol. Quite good and unusual. Nutty, long; oxidized, but not in a negative sense. A rare treat. Made from the Savagnin grapes in the Jura.

CHÂTEAU GRAND-PUY-LACOSTE 1983 TO 1945:

Made from about 75% Cabernet Sauvignon and 25% Merlot. This is a solid, classic, consistent, and reliable property. If you cannot afford Latour, this will definitely do.

The tasting

FLIGHT #1

1983 to 1978

1978:

Good depth of colour. Closed nose with hint of vegetal Cabernet. (Little Merlot in 1978.) A big, serious wine, but a touch too green and acidic. I hope that it will round out with age. Tannic. Drink 1991 to 1995. (16)

1982:

Darkest of the flight, as expected. Deep, purplish colour to rim. Rich, spicy, fruity nose, but starting to close in. Rich, big, jammy. Loaded with ripe fruit. Very well balanced. Needs seven to ten years, or more. Lovely. (18)

1979:

Good, dark colour, purplish rim. Sweet, spicy, forthcoming nose. Big, rich, jammy. More forward and rounder than the 1978, but a bit more spirity. Good flavours. Still powerful. Ready around 1990 to 1994. Very good structure. Well balanced. (16.5)

1981:

Similar appearance to the 1979. Sweet, elegant, fruity, toasty nose. Most elegant of flight, yet still powerful and tannic. Medium-bodied, good fruit. Ready by 1990 to 1994. Not very rich, but good. (16.5)

1983:

Purplish, young colour. Spicy, fruity, young nose. Vegetal, elegant, classic style. Like a young 1978, but with riper fruit. Classic Pauillac. (17)

FLIGHT #2

1975, 1970, 1966

1975:

Good, dark colour to rim. Rubbery. Very good fruit. Tannic, big, solid, typical 1975, but with good fruit. Needs five to ten years to reach its peak. Drink 1992 to 2000. Hopefully, the fruit will hold. Other tasters had their doubts as to whether the fruit will hold and rated it lower. (17)

1970:

Darkest of flight. Deep colour. Ripe, complex, intense. No rush. Needs three to five more years. Still tannic, but not as hard as the 1975. Ripe, round, full. Very good, concentrated fruit. Lovely. (18) I read Robert Parker's recent negative notes about this wine. I hope that he continues to dislike this wine, otherwise the price will soar up in no time!

1966:

Mature colour with elegant, tobacco ripe nose. Spicy, earthy, smoky. Sweet on palate. Rich, hard (typical 1966) yet mature, round, and long. At its peak. (17.5)

FLIGHT #2

1961, 1955, 1945

1945:

Deep, dark colour. Earthy, yet fruity. Mature, chocolate nose. Earth and wet wood. Tannic, solid, austere. Surprisingly, still some fruit. I preferred the 1955, but this 1945 has held so well. Besides, 1945 is my birth year, so I am a little prejudiced. (18)

1955:

The 1955 was added at the last minute. I purchased it recently in San Francisco. Medium, palish colour. Mature. Lovely, elegant, opulent wine. Complex, elegant, a charmer. Still fruity. A stylish, classy wine that has held very well. Still quite rich. (18.5) I may be going a bit overboard with my high score on this wine, but in the context of this vertical, it was fabulous.

1961:

Dark colour, yet not as dark as the 1945. A bit closed on nose. Closed, hard, not bad, but not great. A bit sweaty, yet tannic and quite intense. I've had better examples. Can be very good. (17)

The 1945 and 1955 were outstanding. The 1966 and 1970 were close behind. Overall, consistent serious style and a very reliable property.

DESSERT WINES

1966 QUINTA DO NOVAL AND 1966 QUINTA DO NOVAL "NACIONAL" VINTAGE PORTS:

Bottled by Army & Navy Stores, celebrating their 100th anniversary "Centenary" 1871 to 1971.

THE REGULAR:

A bit lighter, complex, elegant, good depth. Well put together, complete. Elegant, a fine wine. At its peak, but no rush. (17)

THE NACIONAL:

Concentrated, darker colour. Spirity, spicy, very concentrated. Lovely, spicy nose. Great extract. A lovely wine. Needs five to ten more years. (18.5)

May 1987

Dinner and blind tasting, at Sid Cross's.

CHAMPAGNE KRUG "GRANDE CUVÉE" N/V:

First released and purchased in 1979. Complex, round, good acidity, length. A lovely Champagne that improves in the bottle with age. Great finesse. Toast, fruit, good acidity. (18)

WHITE WINES

Served double-blind.

All Mayacamas Chardonnays, Napa Mountain, as we later found out.

MAYACAMAS CHARDONNAY 1974:

Darkest of flight, bright gold, good depth. Toasty, complex nose. Mature oak on nose and palate. Excellent structure. Great depth, alcohol, rich, round. White Burgundy? Structure of 1978 or older. If California Chardonnay, then impressive. Best of the lot. (17.5)

MAYACAMAS CHARDONNAY 1975:

Medium-gold. Popcorn, mature nose. Good fruit. Elegant, complex, evolved. Good fruit. Softest of bunch. (16.5)

MAYACAMAS CHARDONNAY 1976:

Medium-gold. Sharper, more acidic than #1. Older-smelling and tasting. Good fruit, though. Not much on nose. A bit buttery, popcorn. Quite rich. A bit hot. California? (15.5)

MAYACAMAS CHARDONNAY 1977:

Medium-gold, slightly musty nose. Hint of sulphur. Tea leaves (camomile), just slightly). Round, least acidic. Complex. Good fruit, but less intense than above three. Clean, long, mature Chardonnay. Rich, full. Later, lost some fruit. Fairly hot finish. Hint of cork. Became leaner. (14.5) Chardonnay. If California, then good acidity.

When we found out what they were, I was pleasantly surprised. Bob Travers produces fine Chardonnays. The 1977 was a weak effort, though.

DINNER WINE

ROBERT MONDAVI "REGULAR" CHARDONNAY 1983, NAPA VALLEY:

Similar to first four, but fresher, more youthful, more acidic and not as well balanced, but quite good. Mayacamas 1978 or a younger wine. Maybe Mondavi?

RED WINES

Served double-blind. A vertical tasting of Château Ducru-Beaucaillou (as we later found out). All had good, dark colours and all had an open, intense, herbaceous nose, not unlike St. Emilion or Margaux.

1. CHÂTEAU DUCRU-BEAUCAILLOU 1982:

Darkest and youngest-looking. Purplish rim. Intense, ripe, cinnamon nose, with great intensity of young, ripe fruit. Rich, ripe, soft tannins, herbaceous. Lovely. Needs eight to ten years. Superb. (18.5)

2. CHÂTEAU DUCRU-BEAUCAILLOU 1981:

Deep, purplish colour. Not as intense as #1. Spicy, complex nose. Elegant, open, herbaceous, leaner, sharper than #1. A bit higher acidity. Clean, long finish. (16.5)

3. CHÂTEAU DUCRU-BEAUCAILLOU 1978:

Delicate, elegant nose. Deep colour, but more mature than #2. Subdued, delicate, flowery, stemmy. Very good. A bit acidic. Good length. Very good Cabernet. Stemmy, cedary. Lovely. Typical 1978, if that is what it is. (17.5)

4. CHÂTEAU DUCRU-BEAUCAILLOU 1975:

More mature, yet elegant, sweet, tobacco nose. Ripe. Sharper, harder, more intense than #3. Tannic, steely, but backed by great fruit. Needs years. I liked it more than most. (17) to (17.5) My notes describe simultaneously "soft" and "hard," but that is how it tasted.

5. CHÂTEAU DUCRU-BEAUCAILLOU 1973:

Mature colour. Not nearly as dark as the others. Round, elegant. Forward. My guess is 1976, but it is too soft. Needs drinking. (13.5)

6. CHÂTEAU DUCRU-BEAUCAILLOU 1970:

Are we having a vertical here? Dark colour to rim. Mature, yet deep. 1970? Slightly sulphuric, rich, fruity, open nose. Full, round, slightly sweet. Long, superb. No rush, though. Loaded with good, ripe fruit. An excellent wine. (18)

7. CHÂTEAU DUCRU-BEAUCAILLOU 1967:

Paler than above, more mature. Medium-red, brown-orange. Open, chocolate nose. Delicate, woody, good length. On palate: tea, sweet, slightly hard, acidic. Good length, vegetal. A bit sharp, but good. Forward, but holding well. Surprisingly good. (16)

8. CHÂTEAU DUCRU-BEAUCAILLOU 1966:

Deep, mature, browning colour. Lovely tobacco nose. Open, complex, spicy, long. Like a ripe 1961. Elegant, forward, sweet, good acidity. Length, complexity. At its peak. (18)

During the tasting, I said that if it is not a Margaux or St. Emilion, then the class and style are possibly Ducru-Beaucaillou or Beychevelle. As we neared the end of the tasting, it became obvious to me that we were faced with a vertical, and a fine Haut-Médoc.

June 6 to 20, 1987

Trip to Bordeaux and Paris, with my assistant, Tony Gismondi.

We landed in Amsterdam, rented a car, and drove to Bordeaux. This is Tony's first trip to Bordeaux, or anywhere else, as a matter of fact—other than destinations in Canada or the USA. He has been employed by one of my companies since 1981. I have taught him a lot about wine and have introduced him to the Commanderie de Bordeaux. He has a good palate and has learned well.

Monday, June 8, 1987

Visit to Château Prieuré Lichine.

We met Sacha Sichel (Alexis's son) at Prieuré-Lichine. We tasted the 1986 from four different casks. Variation in colour, nose, and body. Overall, typical Margaux, yet typical 1986. Dark, ripe, round, fairly tannic. Already seven months in cask. Ripe fruit, oak. We tried Seguin-Moreau and Demptos casks. A promising wine—and vintage.

Yesterday, there was a sudden, unexpected tornado in Bordeaux: four dead, many injured. Flowering has started, but weather through May was poor and raining. In a way, producers like the rain because it hasn't rained too much this year, but rain now, during flowering, doesn't help!

Lunch at "Relais."

Sacha reserved a table for us. A nice place and a good lunch.

CHASSAGNE-MONTRACHET PREMIER CRU 1983 "LES CHAUMÉES," BOUZEREAU-GRUERE:

Odd to have a white Burgundy in Bordeaux, but there wasn't an interesting Bordeaux on the list. Deep gold. Lovely, complex nose. Full, well balanced, round, lots of fruit, not too alcoholic. A well-made Chassagne.

On our way out, we saw Jean-Michel Cazes, who confirmed lunch for Wednesday at Lynch-Bages.

Tuesday, June 9, 1987

Visit to Chasse-Spleen, with Bernadette Villars.

It was pouring rain over Moulis, yet fairly dry in Margaux. It has been rainy in May and early June. Bernadette said that she's worried about the Merlot. Early flowering. This is bad news. Cabernet still flowering, so hopefully weather will improve soon. If this continues, maybe it will hurt the quality of the 1987s. Certainly the quantity will be reduced.

Bernadette usually uses 50% new oak; in 1986 it was 60%. Maury (the local tonnelier) is best for Chasse-Spleen this year (it varies from vintage to vintage), then Demptos and Seguin-Moreau. At Haut-Bages-Libéral, Demptos seem to be the best barrels this year. Nadalié good, too. Coulure in Merlot this year! (Rain and tornado). Bernadette doesn't like Cabernet Franc and uses very little of it, but she likes Petit Verdot. This year, they start steaming barrels and not just filling them with water. At Haut-Bages-Libéral, they're introducing the system of Chasse-Spleen.

Haut-Bages-Libéral, according to Bernadette, has a style that is a blend of Grand-Puy-Lacoste and Pichon-Lalande (they have vineyards near both properties).

In the chais, we tasted the following.

1986 CHASSE-SPLEEN:

Six months in wood. Very deep, dark colour. Hard, tannic, fairly acidic at this stage, concentrated fruit. Drier, serious style, like a Pauillac. Ripe tannins. In 1986, the blend is made from 70% Cabernet Sauvignon, 25% Merlot, and 5% Petit Verdot. In 1985, more Merlot (35%). Bernadette agreed with me that 1986 is similar in style to 1983 at Chasse-Spleen. She (and I) preferred the 1986 to the 1985.

1985 CHASSE-SPLEEN:

A bit lighter in colour. Just bottled. Good fruit-oak. Elegant. Seven to ten years. Softer tannins. She has already sold all her 1985 and 1986 (1985 at Ffr42, 1986 at Ffr40).

1986 Haut-Bages-Libéral:

Mostly Cabernet Sauvignon, some Petit Verdot, very little Merlot. Dark, ripe fruit. Lovely nose. Full, rich, round; still tannic, though. I told her that at a blind tasting, one could confuse them, thinking that Chasse-Spleen was the Haut-Bages-Libéral. The oenologist of Haut-Bages-Libéral, Mr. Couasnon, tasted with us; he agreed with me about the style of the two wines. At Haut-Bages-Libéral, they use only one-third new oak casks. They both swear by Grand-Puy-Lacoste and try to emulate that style. They said it represents the essence of true Pauillac.

Tony has been sick all day. We didn't go to Branaire-Ducru in the afternoon and didn't visit Palmer. We went directly to d'Angludet for lunch with Peter and Diana Sichel. (Tony lay down in the living room and didn't have anything to eat or drink.)

Chablis Premier Cru 1985 "Vaudevay," Domaine de la Maladière:

Pleasant, elegant, round. A well-made Chablis. Good fruit and fairly forward.

1978 Château d'Angludet:

Served blind. I thought it was a 1975, maybe d'Angludet. In retrospect, not as lean as a 1975, but high Cabernet content nevertheless. Complex, spicy, good fruit. A bit edgy and acidic, but otherwise a good wine. Not quite ready. Needs two to three years.

1950 Château Lafite:

Also served blind. That was really a surprise. Not unlike a good, mature 1955, which is what I thought it was. I said "1955 Palmer or other Margaux." Mature, medium colour. Lots of orange. Open, sweet nose; delicate, wood and earth. Delicate, round, well structured, with good acidity, which probably helped it last this long. Quite classy and a surprise. Lovely, complex aftertaste. It also held quite well in the glass.

Then, we went into the chais and tasted the 1986 and 1985 d'Angludet which is being bottled right now.

1986 d'Angludet:

Made from 55% Cabernet Sauvignon, 40% Merlot, 5% Petit Verdot. (Peter isn't very fond of Cabernet Franc and has very little of it. Like Bernadette Villars at Chasse-Spleen, Peter likes Château Grand-Puy-Lacoste very much.) Fairly hard, dark, not quite concentrated. Tannic, but because of rain during the vintage, a bit diluted. It will be a keeper, though. Peter said that the 1986, while hard and tannic, is not as concentrated as the 1983. I agree. (We also talked about Michael Broadbent. Peter said that the problem with Michael is that he has no sense of humour.)

1985 d'Angludet:

He gave me a sample from a barrel being bottled (from the source, just before bottling). Much rounder, fruitier, and more elegant than the 1986; better balanced, too. It's all there. Round, ripe, complex, dark. Good fruit on nose and palate. Will mature around 1992 to 1994. More Cabernet Sauvignon than 1986, and less Merlot. Made from 70% Cabernet Sauvignon, 25% Merlot, and 5% Petit Verdot: a complete wine.

Peter recommended that we try "Chapon Fin" (Mr. Garcia runs it now; it used to belong to Bruno Prats of Cos d'Estournel); and also "Jean Ramet's." He said that Château Citran (Jean Miailhe) was sold to a Japanese company that plans to have a vacation home there for tourists and businessmen. He also said that now that Pichon-Longueville-Baron was sold by the Bouteillers for an astronomical amount (300 million francs) to the AXA group, Michel Delon will manage it. (The owner of Lascases, Delon also manages Château Lagrange for the Japanese firm Suntori.)

Peter said that for tax purposes, this is not good (high prices for properties) because it increases values and, therefore, taxes. (AXA is an insurance company from Paris and J.-M. Cazes of Lynch-Bages coordinated the sale. The president of AXA and Jean-Michel Cazes are childhood friends.) Peter bought a new corking machine for d'Angludet and had some problems with corks that didn't have even lengths. He likes oak barrels from Maury and some from Radoux.

His swans at d'Angludet had four little chicks that were chewed up by rats! As usual, a most enjoyable visit. Peter Sichel is a very friendly, knowledgeable, and modest man.

Wednesday, June 10, 1987

Visit to Cos d'Estournel.

Tony is really sick. He stayed in bed all day and I went to the Médoc by myself. This is my fifth visit to this château. Bruno Prats was busy in town and his régisseur showed me the modern operation and a nice slide show. They hoisted the Canadian flag on the occasion of my visit. Pity Tony missed this day. In 1986, they used 75% new oak (half Seguin-Moreau, the rest from six other suppliers, including Nadalié, Demptos, Taranceau, Radoux, etc.).

After many experiments, they decided to use Alier-oak casks; light toast, sun-dried for three years, cleaned with water, sulphur, and some old wine. They don't like steaming. We also visited the old private cellar of the Prats family, where one can find Cos going back to 1865, and lots of Château Margaux (from the

Ginestet era), and from exchanges with other châteaux.

Then we went to the modern tasting room.

MAÎTRE D'ESTOURNEL BLANC 1986 A/C BORDEAUX:

Grapes from Entre-Deux-Mers, purchased each year from different growers. Made from 90% Sauvignon Blanc, 5% Muscat, and 5% Semillon. Round, elegant, good acidity and fruit. Will improve. Not aged in wood.

The 1985s will be bottled in July, over two weeks. They are a bit worried because of the cool weather and rain, but do not know yet definitely if there'll be a lot of coulure in 1987.

MAÎTRE D'ESTOURNEL ROUGE 1985 A/C BORDEAUX:

Grapes vary yearly, mostly Blaye, Bourg, Première Côtes de Bordeaux, etc. Made mostly from Merlot. Six months in used oak (second-year Cos-oak barrels). Elegant, round, fruity, well made. Not quite ready. Drink around 1989 to 1990.

CHÂTEAU DE MARBUZET 1985, ST. ESTÈPHE:

This is the second wine of Cos d'Estournel. Medium-red, good depth, not bottled yet. Elegant, round, forward, well balanced. Made from 65% Cabernet Sauvignon, 35% Merlot. Ripeness and fruit on nose. Vanilla, a bit tannic, but not an ager. Drink 1990 to 1992.

CHÂTEAU DE MARBUZET 1986:

Only six months in oak so far. Lovely, ripe, big nose, oak, vanilla. Bigger, darker than 1985. Lots of fruit. Very good. Made from 60% Cabernet Sauvignon, 40% Merlot. Impressive colour. Drink 1992 to 1995. Definitely better than the 1985.

CHÂTEAU COS D'ESTOURNEL 1985:

Aged in 80% new oak. Deep purplish colour; lovely, complex nose of ripe fruit. New oak, vanilla. Lots of class. Tannic, but not massive, well balanced. Merlot on nose and palate; since 1978 the maceration period is shorter. A more elegant wine. Very good. Drink from 1994. This is going to be one of the best 1985s. One to buy!

CHÂTEAU COS D'ESTOURNEL 1986:

Made from 58% Cabernet Sauvignon, 2% Cabernet Franc, 40% Merlot; aged in 95% new oak. Essence of wine! Only six months in wood, so far. Very deep, purple colour. Impressive! Incredible concentration of fruit, not unlike Mouton 1982, which I tasted from barrel in 1984. Ripe, concentrated, full, lots of ripe tannins. Perfect balance. A wine to absolutely buy! By 1998, it will be superb. Unusually high proportion of Merlot, especially for a St. Estèphe.

Lunch at Château Lynch-Bages.

I drove to Château Lynch-Bages for lunch with Jean-Michel Cazes. His wife Marie-Therèse is in Turkey (shopping), coming back tonight. This is much to Jean-Michel's distress, because he has to pick her up at the airport and tonight is the Championship Cup soccer game between Marseilles and Bordeaux. (Bordeaux won, 2 to 0) The chais and offices were renovated recently. The guest house will be ready next year. I told him that I had recently tasted Haut-Bages-Avéroux 1961. He said that his grandfather made this wine. Avéroux is the second wine of Lynch-Bages.

Tasting the 1985s from cask

1. ORMES DE PEZ:

No new oak. Light, elegant, a bit sharp. Elegant, but simple. Not bottled yet.

2. HAUT-BAGES-AVÉROUX:

No new oak. Made at Lynch-Bages. Darker, fuller than the Ormes. Full, beefy, solid, ripe. Good fruit. Will be quite good in 1992 to 1994.

3. LYNCH-BAGES:

Lovely, dark-purplish colour. Not bottled yet. Big, round, ripe tannins. New wood, spicier, tannic, long. Very well made. One to buy. This will surely be one of the finest wines of the 1985 vintage. As impressive at this stage as Cos d'Estournel 1985 tasted from barrel earlier today.

Tasting the 1986s (only a few months in cask so far)

1. ORMES DE PEZ:

Much better than the 1985. Darker, riper, fruitier, more body and tannins. Good fruit.

2. HAUT-BAGES-AVÉROUX:

Even darker and bigger than the 1985. Big, rich, full, tannic. Needs seven to ten years. Promising.

3. LYNCH-BAGES:

A bit more Merlot than in 1985. Very dark, very fruity, good tannins, new oak. Rich and long. Very good wine. Will not be ready for at least ten years. It will remain in oak for another year.

From there, we went into the living room and had a nice lunch with the following wines.

CHAMPAGNE LOUIS ROEDERER N/V:

Round, pleasant, a bit too much dosage and not enough complexity.

1979 CHÂTEAU ORMES DE PEZ, ST. ESTÈPHE:

Surprisingly good. Dark, mature rim. Round, some age on nose and palate. Well balanced, long, ripe fruit. Ready, but no rush.

1975 CHÂTEAU LYNCH-BAGES:

Special labelling in honour of Michel's very good Astronaut friend, J. Baudry, who flew in the space shuttle "Discovery." Baudry is based in Toulouse and flies low over Lynch-Bages in his Jaguar jet fighter, shaking the whole château—especially when he knows that Jean-Michel has guests over for lunch! The wine was more forward than expected, better balanced, softer than most 1975s. Round, full, soft, hardly any tannins left. A very good 1975, backed by good, ripe fruit.

1953 CHÂTEAU PICHON-LONGUEVILLE-BARON:

Classic, old-style Pichon-Baron. Good colour, mature, browning, good depth. Complex, very long on nose. Full, round, soft; a lovely mouthful of classic Claret. We had it because Jean-Michel Cazes will start to manage this property soon. He bought a share with a group of Insurance companies from Paris (friends of his—the AXA group), who bought Pichon-Baron and will take possession next Monday from the 14 Bouteiller family members.

The Bouteillers have owned this property since 1920. The Bouteillers also own Château Lanessan, but aren't selling it. J-M also has an interest now in Château Franc-Mayne in St. Emilion, and plans to open a hotel/winery in the Médoc called Château Cordeillan-Bages. Yesterday, Peter Sichel told me that Michel Delon of Lascases would manage Pichon-Baron. Maybe I misunderstood him.

We talked about my problems with Michael Broadbent, and my letter to Decanter *magazine concerning Michael Broadbent and the Château Lafite 1945 tasted in Los Angeles recently. He will send a letter to* Decanter. *Cazes took part in that tasting, too. His comments overall are similar to mine concerning all the wines at that tasting. We also talked about and finalized his planned trip to Vancouver, hopefully in early September. A very enjoyable visit.*

The following is an exchange of open "Letters to the Editor" between Michael Broadbent and myself, as well as other contributors.

May 1987

DECANTER MAGAZINE

Impossible Perfection.

"I would like to make a few remarks about Michael Broadbent's comments in 'Bordeaux—1961 vs. 1945' (August 1987), or more specifically, to his comments on page 22 regarding Château Lafite 1945. He describes the wine as being 'not as intense or deep as Latour or Mouton, relatively light-weight but with delicious flavour, exceptional length, and crisp, dry finish. (20) out of (20)'

"Wine is a subjective commodity. However, under controlled conditions, and in association with experienced tasters, there are certain criteria to judge and rank specific wines. I attended that particular 1945 Claret tasting, as did another three dozen people, including Harry Waugh, Jean-Michel Cazes of Château Lynch-Bages, Raoul Salama of Revue du Vin de France, Bipin Desai (who organized the event), and other experienced tasters from the US, Germany, and Vancouver. None of the people I spoke to rated the Lafite 1945 any higher than (16) or (17). Furthermore, these particular samples of Lafite had a hard time struggling against fine examples of Batailley or Lynch-Bages 1945.

"Michael Broadbent is an experienced taster. Few people have accumulated his experience and knowledge of wine. Yet, how could he award that wine (Château Lafite 1945) a perfect score? Following the tasting, Michael apologized for Lafite's performance against Mouton and Latour, using the now-familiar argument that Lafite is lighter and more elegant in style than the other two Pauillac First Growths, and therefore it is 'unfair' to taste them side by side.

"Unfortunately, other participants did not buy this argument. One taster said that Lafite, being a Pauillac First Growth and fetching as much as the other two (if not more) at auction, should have delivered accordingly. It did not. There were a few people there who have tasted Lafite 1945 (in any size bottle imaginable) more often than Michael or I will ever taste it in our lifetimes, and none saw fit to rave about this disappointing wine.

"Certain responsibilities come with fame and status. Many people read his (Michael's) comments and base their purchases on them. It might be to the advantage of wine enthusiasts all over the world that in future, tastings of this importance be conducted anonymously. Inevitably in such tastings, we all make mistakes from time to time, but in the long run, the truth comes out. In any case, Michael is entrenched enough to carry off the occasional mistake—none of us is perfect."

Albert Givton
The Wine Consumer *Magazine*
Vancouver, BC

May 1987

DECANTER MAGAZINE

Broadbent replies.

"Mr. Givton is perfectly entitled to express his own opinion about any wine he tastes. So am I. He chooses to question my rating of Lafite in Bipin Desai's remarkable tasting of 1945s. Having re-read the notes I made at the tasting itself, here is my reply.

"It was perhaps unwise, and inconsistent, of me to have quoted the points I made at the time. I should either have published scores for all the wines in the 1961 and 1945 tastings, or none at all.

"As a matter of interest, I use a 20-point system at most comparative tastings, to supplement and qualify my descriptive notes. They help me, looking back months or years later, to pinpoint those wines I rated at that moment the most highly. But, as David Peppercorn cogently stated in the January issue of *Decanter*, numerical scoring is misleading. The same points might not apply to the same wine on a different occasion.

"Having said this, I personally found great beauty in the Lafite 1945 and subtract not a word or a point. The colour was correct; it had an exquisitely scented bouquet, delicacy, lovely flavour, great length, and fragrant aftertaste—all symptomatic of Lafite at its best.

"Latour 1945 is a great wine, but at this tasting, neither bottle was up to its best. Indeed, one showed excess volatile acidity and was positively sharp on the palate.

"Givton refers to Batailley and Lynch-Bages. I agree they were showing well, and I gave them appropriate marks. But in the final analysis, both lacked that extra ounce of finesse—the hallmark of a First Growth.

"He refers to other tasters. I happened to sit between our host Bipin Desai and Michel Cazes. Michel and I not only agreed closely on virtually all the wines in the tasting, we even found ourselves using precisely the same adjective.

"I do not recall apologizing after the tasting for Lafite's performance, but would certainly have defended the wine against snipers and detractors.

"Which brings me to the core of the problem, one I have noticed over the many years—nearly 20—that I have been travelling in North America. Coincidentally, it was discussed quite recently over Lafite 1955, Cheval-Blanc 1966, and Petrus 1949—all contrasting but outstanding wines—at a dinner of the Bordeaux Club. (The Club, founded in 1947, and whose membership includes Harry Waugh, comprises some of the most experienced and refined Claret palates that I know.) In effect, it is that the North American palate, with notable exceptions like Dr. Bernard Rhodes, has a built-in preference for the obvious, which accounts for the appeal of Mouton, Palmer at its best, La Mission Haut-Brion, and Latour of almost any vintage, and leaving aside supply and price, that arch flesh-pot Petrus. All the foregoing have a readily noticeable depth of colour, a positive—sometimes overwhelming—bouquet, loads of fruit, and fairly blatant component parts; whereas the distinctly different style and flavour of Haut-Brion, with its subtlety and finesse, and the less deep appearance, the delicacy, fragrance, and lingering qualities of Lafite, are less eye-catching, less mouthfilling, less strident.

"It is for the same reason that at comparative tastings, much to the irritation of the Bordelaise, California Cabernet Sauvignons do so well.

"And this is why, with missionary zeal, I try to preach the gospel of finesse and delicacy: concentration of mind not of fruit. Not to keep up the price of Lafite at auction, not to ingratiate myself with the proprietors.

"Looking back through my tasting books, I see that I have had Lafite 1945 on 13 occasions over the past 20 years, just once from a magnum. It is a great wine. Sheer perfection at a Bordeaux Club dinner in 1983. Excellent—from a deceased American-collector's cellar—at a presale tasting in Chicago in 1985. And so on. At its best, a lovely drink, a perfect table wine; not a blockbuster, but sensible (in the French sense).

"That some of Mr. Givton's acquaintances have tasted the wine many more times is irrelevant. One is not necessarily a consummate authority or the final arbiter merely because one attends a lot of tastings, or writes about wine—I do both—or, heaven forbid, presumes to publish a wine buyers' guide."

Michael Broadbent

August 1987

DECANTER MAGAZINE
In favour of blind tasting.

"I was most interested to read the letters of Albert Givton and Michael Broadbent in the May issue. Unfortunately, I have not tasted many 1945 Clarets so I am not going to join the debate about the Lafite 1945. Nonetheless, a number of good points were made on both sides.

"First, I agree with Givton's argument that tasting should be blind. If you are aware of the identity of the wine one is tasting (rather than drinking), then all your previous experience of that wine, other vintages of the same wine, the château or domaine and its owners, and other tasting sessions, will affect your judgement. This is rather like reading out the accused's record in a court of law before the trial, a practice which is forbidden in British legal trials (but obviously not vinous ones). Of course the record is read out before the sentencing, but after the judgement. I think that tasters should make a judgement on the quality of that bottle on that day in that company before adding in their previous experience.

"The second interesting point is made by Broadbent in his comments about the difference between the European-trained and American-trained palate. My initial acquaintance with wine was in the UK and I did not come to North America until ten years ago at the age of 32. I would agree with Broadbent's assessment that many people brought up on California wines do seem to have a fundamental perceptive difference from my own assessment of some wines. This difference disappears, however, at the more experienced tasting levels. In other words, as with many education courses, there are differences in approach between the two sides of the Atlantic, although the end result may be very similar. Interestingly, although I am sure Broadbent's remarks were not meant to refer to Givton, he did not come to North America until 1973.

"Finally, Broadbent's last comment… or, heaven forbid, presumes to publish a wine buyers' guide,' was beneath him. I have bought a number of lots of wine at Christie's, London, in the past few years and have found *The Great Vintage Wine Book* to be most useful when going through the catalogue. I now find that Broadbent does not consider it as an aid for consumers, or I presume so, considering his disparaging remark about Givton. Perhaps it is intended as bedtime reading for gray-haired oenophiles to relive some of the glorious bottles of their youth? Does Broadbent intend to criticize similarly others such as Clive Coates and surely even the editor of *Decanter* magazine, a wine buyers' guide if ever there was one?

"*The Great Vintage Wine Book, The Wine Consumer, The Vine*, and *Decanter* are all, it seems to me, designed to give pleasure and information to wine lovers and also to help them purchase wines more knowledgeably. Whatever Broadbent's intentions, *The Great Vintage Wine Book* is to me, and many others, a wine buyers' guide which he has written, if not published.

"My admiration of Broadbent and my appreciation of his achievements remain intact. However, as Givton points out, neither he nor any of us is perfect."

Dr. Alastair Carruthers
Vancouver, BC

October 1987

DECANTER MAGAZINE

"In saying that 'the North American palate with notable exceptions has a built-in preference for the obvious which accounts for the appeal of Mouton, Palmer at its best, La Mission Haut-Brion, Latour, and Petrus,' Mr. Broadbent (May issue) accomplishes the neat trick of giving every impression of demeaning the above wines as well as people's ability to taste nuances in any country other than his own.

"Come off it, Mr. Broadbent! Haut-Brion, one of the wines described as being more subtle, is American-owned, and a significant part of its production goes to that country. Americans and Canadians don't need fancy preaching about finesse and delicacy and wines being 'sensible' (whatever happened to the use of English?). Wines of this category are already being made in, and imported into, North America, where there is a market for them. Mr. Broadbent's self-styled 'missionary zeal' is not so much misplaced as superfluous.

"It also seems like a very pious wish for Mr. Broadbent to give his scores out of (20) and expect consumers not to look at them independently of his full written descriptions. Is this not inevitable? Not everyone has the time or inclination to go into the verbal gymnastics of Mr. Broadbent. Like so many of us in the wine trade, he has fallen into the trap of losing touch with the average wine consumer. He forgets that the common run of mortals, price being equal, will simply choose a wine rated (16) over one rated (14), in Chicago or in Tunbridge Wells.

"I don't believe that any of the discussion surrounding Robert Parker in *Decanter* mentioned the fact that he too is against commercial exploitation of his evaluations by score alone and is finding out what legal action he can take.

"Meanwhile, one cannot sidestep the issue by pretending it doesn't exist because it ought not to exist… ."

Alex Rychlewski
Bordeaux, France

October 1987

DECANTER MAGAZINE
Tasting notes.

"Might I respond briefly to a couple of letters in the August issue?

"Under most circumstances I, like Dr. Carruthers, am also in favour of blind tastings, believing that knowing what the wine is tends to undermine one's critical faculties and introduce bias, one way or the other. On the other hand, in mammoth vertical or horizontal tastings, I find that tasters spend too much time trying to work out what the wine is called rather than observing and noting deeply what the wine is like. Moreover, an element of competition creeps in between tasters.

"I must take up one major point about *The Great Vintage Book*. It was quite definitely not written as a buyers' guide. It was intended to be a guide to vintages, what made them good or less good, what the wines of each vintage were like, are like, and might develop into, using many years of tasting notes to illustrate this. The fact that it has been used as a sort of buyers' guide, though flattering, is one of the reasons I have been reluctant to update it.

"Lastly, I should have resisted a dig at Albert Givton, but like practised orators at Speaker's Corner who can always put down the heckler, one is sorely tempted always to have the last word!"

Michael Broadbent
Christie's

Back to the trip

Visit to Gruaud-Larose.

The General Manager, Georges Pauli, wasn't there, but I spoke to Philippe Carmagnac, the young winemaker who used to work at Clos des Jacobins in St. Emilion (another Cordier property), and who has replaced the retired Mr. Moreau as winemaker at Gruaud. A nice young man. He's been at this château since June 1986.

GRUAUD-LAROSE 1985, FROM CASK:

Will be bottled next month. Gruaud is aged in approximately 35% new oak. Made from 68% Cabernet Sauvignon, 25% Merlot, and the balance is Cabernet Franc. Purplish, subdued, closed, rich, solid, austere. Will be excellent and concentrated, but needs many years. Very promising.

GRUAUD-LAROSE 1986, FROM CASK:

Smaller grapes, thicker skins, even more concentrated colour and tannins than the 1985. Very promising. Massive, dark, loaded with ripe fruit and tannin. One to buy!

GRUAUD-LAROSE 1979, IN BOTTLE:

Dark, slight maturity at rim. Rich, tannic; needs three to five years or more. Lacks the ripeness of 1985 or especially of 1986. Tannic, yet lacks a bit in depth. Evolved, a bit sharp at the edge. Not quite well balanced, yet good. (16)

GRUAUD-LAROSE 1981, IN BOTTLE:

A favourite of mine and one of the very best 1981s (an underrated year). Very dark, intense, no sign of maturity. Mint and eucalyptus. Spices, ripe fruit, lots of tannin. Rich, needs ten years, but will be excellent. Very concentrated. A very good, maybe great, wine. (17.5)

Thursday, June 11, 1987

Visit to St. Emilion and Pomerol.

Tony finally felt a bit better and joined me for this long, exciting, and tiring day.

Visit to Château Cheval-Blanc.

With the owner/manager Jacques Hebrard. (Mr. Ducasse of Château l'Evangile, who died in 1982, was his uncle.) Mr. Hebrard is a very pleasant man who speaks English fairly well. We talked about the German wine collectors (Hardy Rodenstock, etc.) and their "mysterious" old bottles, and about various vintages of Cheval-Blanc I have tasted.

He likes sailing and salmon fishing, and would like to visit BC.

Some of his clients want cases of six bottles and 12 half-bottles (unusual size cases). He is a bit worried about the cool weather during flowering and the rain in 1987. He complained about Parker, Clive Coates, and other wine writers who jump to conclusions too early, decide on the quality and potential of vintages and individual wines too soon, and going by one barrel sample, decide the fate of a wine. They use 100% new-oak casks each vintage. This is of course the case for all Premier Grands Crus Classés.

The 1985 was just fined, some sulphur added, and will be bottled shortly (in July).

1985 BARREL SAMPLE:

Lovely, elegant, good depth of colour; fruit, medium tannins. Both 1985 and 1986 are made from one-third Merlot and two-thirds Cabernet Franc. Quite rich, very good potential.

1986 BARREL SAMPLE:

Six months in wood so far. A bit lighter in colour than the 1985 at this stage. More elegant, yet good tannins. At this stage, I prefer the 1985, but it is still too early to tell. The average age of the vines is 32 years (some 18, some as old as 60 years, especially the Merlots). The 60-year-old vines are tired and more susceptible to suffer from frost. They went through the frost of 1956, 1977, 1984, and 1985. A nice, modern, well-kept property.

Hebrard agreed that most London-bottlings of Cheval-Blanc 1947 are very good, but warned me about the Belgian-bottlings. He had several bad samples.

Visit to Château Figeac.

We met the owner, Thierry Manoncourt, and his wife Marie-France. They are rebuilding and renovating the château. Marie-France took us around, showed us the property, and we tasted the 1986, 1985, and 1975.

Their eldest daughter, who is 30, is getting married this summer.

CHÂTEAU FIGEAC 1986 AND 1985:

At this stage, the 1985 seems better, more complete, stylish.

The 1986 was a bit harder, more tannic. They use 100% new oak in both vintages.

Both 1985 and 1986 are not blockbusters. Both are about 30% Merlot, and 35% each Cabernet Sauvignon and Cabernet Franc.

CHÂTEAU FIGEAC 1975, IN HALF-BOTTLES:

Lovely, medium-dark, complex, good depth. At its peak, but no rush. Lots of class, well balanced, and long.

A rushed visit, but that was OK as we had a busy day. My previous visits to Figeac were longer, more interesting, and we usually had lunch.

Visit to Château Ausone and Belair.

Visited my good friend Pascal Delbeck. Since my last visit, Pascal married Madeleine Claverie, a nice girl who used to work for Christian Moueix. They have a two-month-old baby girl, Marie-Amandine. I met Madeleine twice before at Petrus. Pascal is a good friend of Charles Joguet (from Chinon in the Loire Valley), whose wines I know well.

Tony and I visited the chais at Ausone. We tasted Belair and Ausone 1985 and 1986, from cask.

CHÂTEAU BELAIR 1985, FROM CASK:

Good, dark colour. Purplish rim. Spicy, Cabernet Franc nose. Some oak. Medium-bodied, good depth, a bit tannic. Needs seven to eight years. Will be bottled next month.

CHÂTEAU BELAIR 1986, FROM CASK:

Only four months in wood. Harder, more obvious tannins at this stage. Good fruit, good colour. Harder than the 1985, but less flesh at this stage.

CHÂTEAU AUSONE 1985, FROM CASK:

A lovely, elegant wine. Good depth. Rich, round, and luscious. Lots of class, spices, and wood. Needs ten years to evolve, but I don't think that it will be a blockbuster. Typical, softer elegance of the vintage.

CHÂTEAU AUSONE 1986, FROM CASK:

A bit leaner, harder at this stage than the 1985. Solid, big, powerful. Needs even longer than the 1985 to mature. Typical, hard Ausone structure in its youth. Very good potential. Over the long haul, it will probably be better and more serious than the 1985.

CHÂTEAU AUSONE 1985, FROM EXPERIMENTAL OAK CASK:

Made in a more popular style. Atypical of Ausone. Richer, rounder, spicier, more modern Médoc style. Rich, forward, elegant. Pascal tried to make it as an experiment, but he says it is not the Ausone style. Appealing early maybe, but not what Ausone is, or should be.

Pascal agreed with me that in Bordeaux, there is a tendency for uniformity these days. Too many fine wines taste the same. We discussed this problem in depth. I said that there's no more true St. Estèphe. Too charming when young; too much Merlot, too much oak, too forward. Producers are starting to try to appeal to consumers and wine writers, and damaging tradition and style; and, most important of all, many wines are losing their "terroir" character in the process.

Also, because so many producers seek the advice of Professor Peynaud, many wines start to taste like each other, and even the clones of Merlot start to be the same in every vineyard. Pascal suggested that I do something about it (write an article, etc.), which I might do.

Then we met Mme. Dubois-Chalon, the co-owner of Ausone and sole proprietor of Belair, a nice, lively, and very talkative woman. We had a good lunch, but Tony ate and drank little because he was still feeling a bit sick.

We tried the following wine with lunch.

1973 CHÂTEAU AUSONE:

Browning, but with good depth. Earthy, soft, round. Truffles, mushrooms on nose and palate. Getting tired and needs drinking. A trace of acidity. Not bad, though, for the vintage.

Then, Pascal served us two wines from vintages that represent the beginning of both World Wars. The wines were served blind.

1939 CHÂTEAU BELAIR:

Good, dark, mature colour. Good depth for this fairly abundant and mediocre vintage. Truffles, earth, wet wood, touch of oxidation, but still alive. Flavourful. Old, but sound and rare wine. A good effort; has held very well.

1914 CHÂTEAU AUSONE:

A lovely wine that, instead of falling apart in the glass, improved after half-an-hour. Good, mature colour. Lovely complex nose of Graves, soil, truffles, mushrooms, and spices. Round, very elegant, good backbone, slightly acidic, but lots of class. Incredible for the vintage. Mrs. Dubois-Chalon said that they opened it in my honour because Pascal spoke so highly of me. They only have five bottles left. A nice gesture, which I appreciate very much.

Pascal told me that in the old days (before the Russian Revolution), they used Russian oak at Ausone, the best in those days. Mme. Dubois-Chalon likes the Ausone

1847 very much, but has little left of it. She also likes the 1849, which has held well and is still available. We spoke about our planned Ausone tasting (going back to the 1849) in Los Angeles next year; she and Pascal may be able to attend. Pascal likes fine white Burgundies, but hasn't heard of J. F. Coche-Dury. I'll send him some information on this fine Meursault producer.

Mme. Dubois-Chalon knows well the Commander of the French air force base in the area, and complained to him that his jets were flying too low over Ausone and scaring her cats. The overflights ceased immediately. A memorable lunch and visit.

Visit to Château Canon.

We met the owner, Eric Fournier, whom I had met previously. They are modernizing the whole château and chais. Lots of renovations going on everywhere (both in the Médoc and St. Emilion). We discussed a possible trip to Vancouver by the Jurade of St. Emilion.

Since 1979, they have been using closed vats, therefore allowing longer maceration, and they get more colour and extract. Eric likes Canon 1979 very much: concentrated, only 32 hectolitres per hectare and aged in 65% new oak.

We tasted the following wines.

CHÂTEAU CANON 1985, FROM CASK:

Made from 70% Merlot and 30% Cabernet Franc, aged in 55% new oak barrels. Leaner style, quite tannic, hard; good Merlot nose, though. Leaner than 1986, but of course, one more year in oak at this stage. Will become elegant as it ages. Fine potential.

CHÂTEAU CANON 1986, FROM CASK:

Made from 50% Merlot and 50% Cabernet Franc, and in 65% new oak barrels. The Cabernet Franc was so rich that it was too good to declassify. Roughly same quantity made as in 1985. Soft, mellower tannins than 1985. Dark, full, rich, ripe, intense. Great, long finish. Fine potential. Definitely one to buy. Will be a very good wine.

Visit to Libourne.

We visited with Christian Moueix. A young assistant of his drove us to Petrus, where we tasted the Petrus 1985 and 1986.

PETRUS 1985, FROM CASK:

183 barrels produced. Ready for bottling. (Half-bottles already bottled.) A bit nervous and upset because of handling, etc., before bottling. Because it is relatively soft, it is being bottled now instead of in September. Classy, elegant, good depth, good colour. Very long, spicy; not as fat or rich as the 1986.

PETRUS 1986, FROM CASK:

Made from 100% Merlot (no Cabernet Franc at all). Intense, deep colour. Rich, ripe, full, intense. Very big, rich wine. Essence of Merlot at this stage.

Then, we drove back to Libourne where Christian had prepared for us a tasting of various 1986s.

We also met the winemaker responsible for all of Moueix's properties, François Veyssière, and the charming and very gifted Jean-Claude Berrouet, the general manager, whom I know well.

We tasted the 1986s (four to five months in wood)

CHÂTEAU CANON DE BREM, CANON-FRONSAC:

Grapey, young fruit. Spicy, quite rich, well balanced. Good fruit, a bit herbaceous. Merlot-Cabernet Franc-like. Quite good.

CHÂTEAU FONROQUE, GRANDE CRU CLASSÉ, ST. EMILION:

Deep, dark colour. Subdued nose. Tannic, hard, unyielding, powerful; will be very good, but needs time.

CHÂTEAU MAGDELAINE, PREMIER GRAND CRU CLASSÉ, ST. EMILION:

Ripe nose, very mature, ripe grapes. Very deep, dark colour. Loaded with fruit. Impressive. Big, not unlike a great 1982! Very fine. One to buy.

CHÂTEAU LA GRAVE, TRIGANT-DE-BOISSET:

Deep, dark colour. Subdued nose at this stage. Fruity, hard, tannic; ends ripe and rich, if without the depth and ripeness of the Magdelaine.

CHÂTEAU TROTANOY:

Deep, dark colour. Tannic, hard, leaner style. Good fruit, but much leaner than Magdelaine. The opposite of what it should be! A serious, hard, austere wine needing many years. I said Ausone and not Cheval-Blanc in style and Jean-Claude agreed; so did Christian. Maybe too lean for its own good?

Tasted again in the tasting room.

PETRUS AND TROTANOY 1986:

Petrus seemed sweeter, riper, fruitier, yet powerful and tannic. Excellent complexity, depth, and ripe flavours. Magdelaine had some similarity to Petrus, even richer.

Trotanoy was the opposite: tighter, leaner. Petrus, of course, has this extra dimension and depth.

Then we drove to Christian's house, where we had dinner with his wife Marie-Laure, the two kids, and an old nanny.

They will be in Yountville in early July, but we will miss them by a few hours. Christian told me that there is a crisis on the horizon and that American importers are cancelling orders. Prices will have to come down.

About his La Grave Trigant-de-Boisset

He wanted to call it La Grave. I told him that there is such a château in Graves, and that "La Grave-Pomerol" would be a better idea. The Chinese architect, Day, who is designing a pyramid at the Louvre in Paris, has agreed in principle to design a new winery for "Dominus," but Christian has not, so far, decided to go ahead.

We tasted the following wines with dinner.

CHAMPAGNE AYALA 1979 BRUT:

A lovely, elegant Champagne. At its peak. Smooth, elegant, round. Taittinger or Pol Roger style.

1975 CHÂTEAU TROTANOY, IN MAGNUM:

Bigger, darker, fuller than in regular bottles. A rich, round, big wine, typical of the better Pomerols of that vintage. Lovely wine. Great, ripe Merlot concentration; lovely, sweet fruit. This, together with l'Evangile and Lafleur, made a better 1975 than Petrus, in my opinion.

A very long, tiring, but enjoyable day.

Friday June 12

Visit to Château Palmer in Margaux.

A short visit—we were expected there on Tuesday, but Tony was sick and had to be taken back to the hotel. Yves Chardon, the maître-de-chais, showed us around and then we tasted the 1985 and 1986. Since 1983, there is a second wine made at Palmer, called "Réserve du Général."

CHÂTEAU PALMER 1986:

Lovely, dark-purplish colour. Full, long, racey, fairly tannic. Good fruit. Very promising, solid backbone. Made from 50% to 55% Cabernet Sauvignon, 40% Merlot, and a little Malbec, Petit Verdot, and Cabernet Franc. Chardon said that 1986 will not have the finesse of the 1985, same as 1979 doesn't have the class of the 1978. I tend to disagree with him about the 1979. I think that it will be a lovely, ripe, mellow, and chocolaty wine in four to six years, and maybe become more enjoyable than the 1978. Time will tell. Of course, the 1978 is a very fine wine, too.

CHÂTEAU PALMER 1985:

Similar cépage and quantity as 1986, but not quite as dark as the 1986. Lovely, ripe fruit, elegant, complex. A very charming wine. Fine, long, superb style. Optimum Palmer, great potential.

Chardon said about the Palmer 1961 that it should be tasted by itself and never with other vintages of Palmer, not unlike 1947 Cheval-Blanc. Not too many wines can compete with 1961 Palmer anyway.

Both 1985 and 1986 were fermented for one week. They rack every three months. In both vintages, they eliminated 200 to 225 barrels! In both vintages, they used 50% new oak. They used mostly Nadalié, very little Demptos or Seguin-Moreau.

1983 was the first vintage in which everything was done automatically at Palmer; the last great château to embrace automation.

Chardon compared the 1975 Palmer to 1945. He said that both 1978 and 1983 are atypical of the property. He compares 1970 to 1985, but 1985 has more finesse. 1979 is heavier and more concentrated than 1981, 1981 almost ready, and he agreed that 1981 was not a great success at Palmer. Oddly, he said that one shouldn't count out the 1976 and that it will hold longer than people think, yet I find this wine very soft already.

Visit to Châteaux Leoville and Langoa-Barton.

We met with Anthony Barton. Lots of renovations and restorations going on there (as everywhere else in Bordeaux). The producers made a lot of money in the past few years and the value of the properties has soared into the stratosphere; recent very important sales include Pichon-Baron, Citran, and others. Anthony said that three years ago, the Spanish owner of Lagrange sold to Suntori of Japan for 50 million francs. Today it's worth 150 to 160 million francs!! He mentioned Terry Robarts, who is wined and dined well in Bordeaux, and then writes articles criticizing their wealth and the high price of Bordeaux wine. Anthony has a brother who lives in New Zealand.

We tasted these wines.

1985 AND 1986 LEOVILLE

AND

LANGOA-BARTON, FROM CASK.

In 1985, his Merlot matured better than in 1986. Cépage is similar in both vintages. In 1986, the rain before the harvest was beneficial. In both 1985 and 1986, he eliminated about 20% of the crop. They used about one-third new barrels in 1985. Cépage: 70% Cabernet Sauvignon, 15% Merlot, and the rest Cabernet Franc and Petit Verdot. In 1986, 60% in new oak barrels (new trends among many leading châteaux). They are also in the process of increasing the Merlot by 5% to an average of 20%.

1985 LANGOA, FROM CASK:

Dark, purplish colour. Elegant, ripe, well balanced. Very good fruit and length. A wine for mid-term drinking (seven to ten years).

1985 LEOVILLE-BARTON, FROM CASK:

Analytically similar to Langoa, yet different because of the soil. Harder, closed, serious, better concentration than Langoa. Darker, too. A bit stemmier with more class. Needs ten years. Overall, there was 20% less tannin in 1985 than in 1986, according to his analysis. A lovely wine and well worth cellaring.

1986 LANGOA, FROM CASK:

Darker than the 1985. Tannic, solid; this wine will need more time to mature than the 1985. Very promising. Fairly chunky.

1986 LEOVILLE-BARTON, FROM CASK:

Very dark, deep colour. Powerful, big, long, solid. A sleeper. Lots of fruit; ripeness, too. Hard, tannic. This is an excellent bottle with an outstanding future ahead. One to buy! How this property has improved since Anthony took over the reins from his late uncle Ronald!

Visit to Château Latour.

Visit, tasting, and lunch with Jean-Paul Gardère, the general manager. We also met John Kolasa, his assistant and sales manager, who has been at Latour since April and before that, lived in St. Emilion and worked there. He is from the UK, of Polish origin. Gardère is a "living history" who was born in Margaux and spent the last 30 years in Pauillac. When I said that the three best soils in St. Julien are Lascases, Gruaud, and Leoville-Barton, he agreed. At Ducru, he said, it is the man (Jean-Eugene Borie) who makes its fame, not the soil. He loves Grand-Puy-Lacoste, a traditional wine. He said that Mouton 1945 is one of the greatest wines of all time, and agreed with me that Lafite 1945 is no big deal. He said that Lafite can be great, notably in 1953 and 1959, for some odd reason, it missed in other fine vintages, such as 1945, 1961, and 1970.

About Michael Broadbent

He's becoming too famous for his own good. Gardère likes Raoul Salama, the taster from Paris who writes for the Revue du Vin de France, *and thinks that Raoul is a good taster. He said that Pichon-Lalande is very good, but Pichon-Baron has greater potential (same soil as Latour). He said that May de Lencquesaing is sometimes a pain, but she helps the whole Médoc, through her publicity and outspokenness. This may be unkind, because she produces an excellent wine and has contributed a lot to Bordeaux's present fame and fortune.*

The best soils in Pauillac, according to Gardère, are Latour, Grand-Puy-Lacoste, and Pichon-Longueville-Baron.

Gardère is also a négociant in Bordeaux running the firm of "Ulysse Cazabonne," and is the treasurer of the Grand Conseil du Vin de Bordeaux, under Henri Martin of Château Gloria (who used to work with him at Latour). He's sorry that the British owners of Latour didn't purchase Grand-Puy-Lacoste from Mr. Dupin in 1978. He also makes and vinifies the "Cuvée de la Commanderie de Médoc."

He agreed with me that Ausone is the true great wine of St. Emilion for the real connoisseur.

He described the two round hills where the vineyards of Latour and Lascases meet as "the most beautiful pair of buttocks in the world!"

Gardère likes my dear friend Harry Waugh very much, and says that Harry cannot say anything negative about anyone. Harry has been a director at Latour for quite some time now.

He said that in his opinion, the three greatest events in history are: the discovery of fire, Christ (debatable), and the landing on the moon, and said that man takes too many things for granted. About the bad weather these weeks: the flowering at Latour is just starting and the next two to three days are important (by the way, in the next three days, they expect poor weather: cold and rain). He said that cool weather is worse during flowering than rain. It is beginning to look like the 1987 vintage will have quite a few problems. Anyway, it is still too early to tell.

When we sat down for lunch, Jean-Paul said that he is the only survivor of the people who sat around the same table in 1971 to decide about Mouton becoming a First Growth. He said that Baron Philippe, a real "personality and giant" of the Médoc Ginestet of Margaux, objected to Mouton being made a First Growth (for business considerations). Lafite objected for family competition reasoning, and Haut-Brion was indifferent. But, he and Henri Martin said that they had to be objective and they had to agree that in great years, Mouton makes great wine. A historic event. Eventually Mouton became a Premier Grand Cru Classé two years later, in 1973.

About the failure of many Pauillacs in 1964

(But not Latour, because Gardère decided against advice to pick early because the grapes were mature.) It is a consequence of the rivalry between Mouton and Lafite, both trying to be the last to pick, and both were caught before picking when the rains started on October 6.

In 1977, a well-known lady wine writer from London wrote incorrect things about Bordeaux people. No fault of hers, he said; she was misled by some Bordeaux people spreading false rumours. Gardère told her that one must live all the time in Bordeaux in order to know the "inside, true story" of what is happening there. He said that this was why "bassets know best what is happening under a woman's dress, and that even bassets are fooled these days because women wear slacks!"

About Latour 1984

A bit like 1974 (hard, acidic) yet a bit rounder than 74, and more class.

About Latour 1982

A blend of 1929, 1945, and 1961! A once-in-a-lifetime vintage. When Cuvées #7 and #8 (which had Merlot in them) achieved 13.1° and 13.2° of natural alcohol, he called the young men at Latour and told them to watch this carefully, because never in their lifetime would they see this again.

About Latour 1983, 1985, and 1986

A gradual but constant improvement, with 1983 very good, 1985 even better, and 1986 better than both—true solid Latour. I cannot help but sense, however, that Latour has had a minicrisis from 1983 to 1986. Rumours abound about the fate of the winemaker, Jean-Louis Mandreau.

Gardère described 1970 Latour as "Charles de Gaulle" because "it looks down on you!" About 1970 Latour, we agreed completely. A great wine with a great future. Unusual because the quantity was large, yet it is such a massive wine.

About Latour 1975

Like 1945; wait for many years. He also agreed with me that Montrose made a great wine in 1970.

Les-Forts-de-Latour is partly made from young vines, up to eight or nine years old. The vines are marked and they use their full-time, experienced staff rather than seasonal pickers to pick those, because they know what goes into the second wine. Also made from grapes from a lesser soil in areas called "Petit Batailley" and "Comtesse de Lalande." About 25% new oak (up to 50% in some vintages). A third vineyard from which Les Forts is produced is called "Santa Anna."

When we arrived at Latour, they had the Canadian flag flying in our honour. Tony was impressed and was very fortunate to be there with me. He is learning a lot—and from the top players!

We went to the tasting room, where they organized a tasting for us before lunch.

Les-Forts-de-Latour

1981:

Medium colour, palish rim. Subdued, clean nose, good fruit, spices elegance. Early maturing, good flavours, and well balanced. (15.5)

1979:

Darker, deeper than the 1978. Bigger, too. (Originally Gardère through that 1978 was bigger but he has changed his mind.) Closed nose. Ripe, lovely fruit. Round, complex, good depth. Promising. They will release it next year. Now they're offering the 1978. I prefer the 1979 to the 1978. We agreed that the best would be a blend of 1978 and 1979. (16.5)

1978:

Lighter, showing more age than the 1979. Open, spicy herbal nose. Spices and oak. Round, forward, a bit sharp, but still very good. Typical stemmy Cabernet. Will be ready before the 1979. (16)

1975:

Nice, dark, mature colour. Subdued, but maturing nose. Typical 1975, hard, tannic, but good fruit behind. Clean, cedary finish. Needs five to seven years. Better than when tasted last in Vancouver in 1985. (16.5)

Château Latour

1986, FROM BARREL:

Very dark purple. Serious, complex, very tannic, typical Latour. Very good concentration of fruit. One to watch. It has only spent six months in oak so far.

1985, FROM BARREL:

Dark, purplish colour, but not as deep as 1986. Subdued, elegant nose. It is being bottled now and seemed a bit upset. Must return to taste after it has had a chance to rest. Oddly, I found the structure unusually light for Latour.

1984:

Good, dark colour. Slightly leathery-skunky nose. Good for a 1984. Hint of leather, sugar, solid for the year. Gardère thinks it resembles 1957. Hint of fresh bread on nose. Try by 1990. (15.5)

1983:

Very good depth. Subdued, cedary nose. Classic Pauillac. Tannic, hard, good fruit. Needs 12 to 15 years, at least. Good length and clean, long finish. Not tarry or enormous but certainly very good. Finishes a bit short, though. One wishes it had a little more depth. (17)

1982:

Oh, what a wine! Black, ripe nose. A great classic. If 1970 is serious, classical Pauillac, then 1982 is Marilyn Monroe, Brigitte Bardot, and Sophia Loren all in one! Essence of wine. Super. Gardère said: "Drink it in ten-or-50 years!" (20)

From there, we went into the château for lunch.

CHAMPAGNE ROEDERER BRUT 1979:

Gardère agreed with me that the dark gold, the ripe nose, roundness, fullness, low acidity, toast and hint of oxidation resembled more a 1976 than a 1979. 1976 was a hot drought year in France.

1974 Les-Forts-de-Latour:

Forward, good depth of colour, but showing lots of maturity. A bit sharp. Pleasant, but not very good. A bit woody. (14)

1970 Château Latour:

As superb as ever. Not ready yet. Big, dark, solid, perfect balance. Full, fruity; a serious, big master. Great potential ahead! Almost a sin to open this wine now. (19) or (20)

1964 Château Latour:

Probably the best 1964 around and still full of life. Dark, mature-looking. Nose of truffles, mushrooms, spices, classic Latour. Round, full, long, rich, complex. (18.5) A great ending to a great visit.

Visit to Leoville-Lascases.

Michel Delon was tired, so Michel Roland, the régisseur (who looks a lot like Dr. Allan Tobe), showed us around. They're working and expanding and renovating everywhere. Lascases is now a big, modern operation.

1986 Clos du Marquis, barrel sample:

The second wine of Lascases. Intense, dark colour. Ripe fruit and lots of it. Sweet, rich on palate. Will be very good in six to seven years. If this is so dense, one can only imagine how concentrated the Grand Vin will be.

1986 Château Leoville-Lascases, barrel sample:

Very deep, dark colour. Almost perfection. Fruit, depth, balance, class, tannic, oak, all in harmony. It is all there.

Roland said that the difficulty in 1986 was to make rich wines without aggressive tannins. According to rumours and my personal experience, the wines to watch very carefully in 1986 are Cos d'Estournel, Lascases, Mouton-Rothschild, Margaux, Pichon-Lalande, Leoville-Barton—among others.

1985 Clos du Marquis, barrel sample:

Slightly lighter than the 1986, but very good depth. Less richness, more finesse than 1986. Touch of greenness (young vines?) and a bit sharper. Will mature before the 1986. Some sharpness at the end. I prefer the 1986.

1985 Leoville-Lascases, barrel sample:

Very dark, but again, not as intense as the 1986. More elegance, lovely balance. Complex, long, rich. More delicate than 1986. Very, very good quality. Potentially great. A charmer.

All over the Médoc, it is becoming obvious that 1985 will be an elegant, relatively early maturing vintage. On the other hand, the best properties will produce solid, long-ageing wines in 1986. Maybe not as ripe as the 1982s, but really serious stuff.

Monday June 15, 1987

Visit to Château Pichon-Lalande.

Weather still cold and rainy. Looks like the Merlot's flowering is really suffering. Instead of Sauternes, we decided to visit Pichon-Lalande (with Mme. de Lencquesaing). Her husband, the Général, showed us around and we tasted Pichon-Lalande 1985 and 1986. Cépage: about 50% Cabernet Sauvignon, 10% Cabernet Franc, 30% to 35% Merlot (high for Pauillac), 5% to 8% Petit Verdot.

They use 50% new oak barrels on average; because their wines are more delicate, they want to avoid too much new-oak tannins. We also saw the régisseur, Mr. Godin.

1985 Pichon-Lalande, Barrel Sample:

Medium-dark colour. Lovely, elegant nose. Complex, delicate, feminine. Typical of both the vintage and the style of this property. Yet, I detected a trace of greenness and some high acidity. The wine is being bottled right now and may be upset.

1986 Pichon-Lalande, from cask:

Much darker, bigger, more tannic, more concentrated fruit than the 1985. More Pauillac-like than 1985. A very promising wine. Godin agreed that it needs much more ageing than the 1985 (like 1975). The Général disagreed, but he is not the winemaker.

Then we had tea and pastries and visited the old cellar. They had the Canadian flag up in our honour. Mme. de Lencquesaing's birthday is on May 17, the same day as J. P. Gardère's of Latour. She is five years younger. She said that Latour has union problems and needs twice as many employees to do the same job as she does. Pichon-Lalande is really increasing its planted acreage and production. That worries me in the long run.

June 17 to 20, 1987

Four-day visit in Paris (where I met my friend Menashe).

Lunch at "Tan-Dinh."

With Menashe and the Lebanese owner and winemaker of Château Musar, Serge Hochar. This Vietnamese restaurant is reputed to have an excellent wine list. Indeed, they had a very good wine list and the food was excellent, but the two are not compatible. We had a very enjoyable, long lunch and got along together quite well. We tried the following wines.

Château Magence 1983, Graves Blanc, in half-bottle:

Crisp, round, elegant, well balanced. Very good Graves. (16)

Meursault "Les Narvaux" 1983, Michelot, in half-bottle:

A typical 1983 white Burgundy. Bright, deep gold. Oaky, nutty, big, rich nose. Full, big, powerful, quite alcoholic. Impressive, but not my type of wine. Too alcoholic. (16.5)

1970 Château Le Gay, Pomerol:

My choice, and as expected, an excellent wine. Deep, dark, full, earthy, mature. Long and full, typical style. Together with Lafleur, one of my favourite Pomerols. Both Serge Hocher and Menashe enjoyed it very much.

A most enjoyable and interesting lunch. After a glass of 1972 Armagnac, we parted company with Serge inviting me to Beirut to visit his winery. He even promised me protection, but with the civil war going on there, I would rather have a peaceful lunch with him when we're both in Paris again.

All three of us grew up in the Middle East so we talked politics through the meal. While I only fought in the June 1967 "Six Day War," Menashe also participated in the "War of Attrition" along the Suez Canal (1969 to 1970), the "Yom Kippur" war of 1973, and the "Peace in Galilee" operation in Lebanon, in June 1982.

July 18, 1987

International Wine & Food Society (Marin County) Dinner, at the Stanford Court hotel, in San Francisco. The subject of the tasting is 1955 First Growths, in magnums.

APERITIF

Champagne Billecart-Salmon N/V Rosé Brut, in magnums:

Pink-salmon colour. Delicate nose. Delicate on palate. Round, soft, easy drinking. A very elegant Champagne.

1955 Château d'Yquem:

Bright deep-gold colour. Lovely nose. Elegant, hint of wet cement and earth (like 1953 Château Gilette). Elegant, long, not too sweet. Lovely complexity. Not cloying. Very good acidity. Good fruit. Clean, long finish. At its peak, but the lovely fruit and acidity will make it a keeper. (18.5) We had this, and the following, with excellent fresh foie gras.

1955 Château Doisy-Védrines:

A bit deeper, darker gold than the d'Yquem. Sweet, crisp, elegant. Good botrytis. Rich, yet without the lusciousness or complexity of the d'Yquem. Very good, though. Held well in glass even after three hours. (17)

1978 Meursault-Genevrières, François Jobart:

Lacks depth of both 1978 and of this fine vineyard. Bright gold, young-looking. Herbal on nose. Touch of sulphur. Fairly high acidity, slight touch of oxidation, low fruit. Was better three years ago. Quite lean. Some nuttiness but finishes sharp. Hard act to follow the lovely 1955 Sauternes, but I expected more from this gifted winemaker. (16)

1978 Corton-Charlemagne, Bonneau du Martray:

Deeper-gold colour. Typical 1978. Lovely nose. Full, round, forward, toasty. Good fruit/acidity balance. Soft fruit. Corton-character. Long, round, at its peak. Needs drinking; if not, will become lemony and oxidized. (17) A second bottle tried was flat. A third bottle was more alive, but too much sulphur on nose. A sample tasted later was quite a bit better. Too much bottle variation.

1955 First Growths, in magnums

FLIGHT #1

Château Ausone:

Good depth, orange rim. Delicate subdued nose. Mushrooms, a bit dusty. A bit lean. High acidity, hard, serious. Good fruit, but not ripe enough. I liked it more than most. Later, developed some complexity and style. At its peak. Finishes clean and round, if a bit less complex than the others. (17)

Château Cheval-Blanc:

Slightly darker than Ausone. Sweeter, richer on nose, chocolaty. Full, rich, chunky, good fruit, solid. No rush. Ripe, long, like the 1949. Hint of Cabernet Franc stemminess. A very good bottle. Some tasters chose this as their favourite. (18)

Château Petrus:

More orange at rim than Cheval-Blanc. Less depth than Ausone. Lovely, subdued nose. Mushrooms, smells a bit old but delicate. Delicate, round, sweet, complex on palate. Long, superb Merlot at its peak. Well balanced. My favourite of the flight. No rush. An excellent bottle. (19)

Château Haut-Brion:

Deep, mature colour. Sharper nose than above three. Peat on nose. Earthy, truffles. Very different than above. Rich, full, leathery, peaty. Fairly chunky. Almost charred. The most unusual tasting of the brunch. A bit sharp and acidic. Some tasters liked it more than I did. (17)

CHÂTEAU MARGAUX:

Palish, mature colour. Delicate elegant nose. Soft, forward, good fruit. At its peak, even in magnums. A bit dry, but lovely. (18)

FLIGHT #2

CHÂTEAU LATOUR:

Impressive deep colour. Spicy, complex, clean nose. Still fresh. Full, round, rich, fruity. Big, serious, solid. A fine classic. No rush in magnums. Bottles should be ready now. (18) This was far better than expected. On previous occasions, the 1955 Latour showed less than outstanding.

CHÂTEAU LAFITE:

Surprisingly pale colour. Caramel and cigar-box nose. Open, elegant, round, crisp, fair bit of acidity taking over. Still long and elegant. Classy, but finishes slightly sharp. Lovely nevertheless. A bit lean. (17) Does not have the class of the great Lafite 1953 or 1959.

CHÂTEAU MOUTON-ROTHSCHILD:

Almost as deep in colour as the Latour. Some cedar on nose. Round, rich, ripe. Beautiful balance. More forward than the Latour. Round, gorgeous fruit, balance: it's got it all. Hard to find a favourite, but I slightly preferred Mouton. (18.5)

CHÂTEAU LYNCH-BAGES:

Medium colour, good depth. More obvious open cedar nose. Some mint (typical) round, rich, complex. Delicate. Without the concentration of Latour or class of Mouton, but challenging Lafite! (17) This wine is holding its own against the First Growths.

In the first flight, Petrus was my favourite, with Cheval-Blanc a close second, and Margaux third. In the second flight, Mouton first, Latour second, Lynch-Bages third. Overall Mouton first, but in my opinion, Petrus, Latour, d'Yquem, and Cheval-Blanc were close behind—until we tasted the Krug!

Can you imagine?

At the end of a tasting of this class, tasting a Champagne that leaves all other wines of the evening behind? Well, that is exactly what happened!

CHAMPAGNE KRUG VINTAGE 1955, IN MAGNUMS:

First magnum: Fabulous nose, rich, complex, classic. Still alive after all those years. Great class, complexity, and depth. Hard to imagine a better Champagne. Magnificent. Great length. A classic. (20)

Second magnum: Amazingly even livelier than the first magnum. Superb. Rich, long, round, yeast; complexity. A magnificent bottle. Young colour, amazing, youthful. Classic! Touch of ripeness and sweetness. Incredible how it has held well after all the great reds. A magnificent Champagne! (20)

We ended this evening with more Champagne.

CHAMPAGNE KRUG "GRANDE CUVÉE" N/V, IN MAGNUMS:

Lovely, classy Champagne. Complex, long, elegant. A very well-made Champagne. (18)

The order of serving the wines at this event puzzles me. The food was a bit disappointing, but the wines were excellent. Dr. Haskell Norman asked me to speak about the two white Burgundies. I must admit that later on in the evening, the Corton-Charlemagne improved and developed more balance and class, but overall, these two wines were the "lows" of the evening.

July 1987

In Yountville.

Dinner at "Tre Vigne," in St. Helena.

First we visited with Belle and Barney Rhodes at their home. Joe and Alice Heitz joined us. Before going out for dinner, we had this bottle.

1979 DEUTZ "CUVÉE WILLIAM DEUTZ" CHAMPAGNE:

I had this Champagne at Barney's previously. Crisp, elegant, still lively with a fair bit of acidity. Good fruit. Quite good.

I brought along two half-bottles of 1959 Château Pontet-Canet. I opened them, decanted them, and as they were very similar, we blended them together. Barney decanted a mystery wine, and the six of us drove to a new restaurant in St. Helena (which used to be the old "St. Georges," called "Tre Vigne," meaning "among the vines"), opened just a month ago. It featured excellent northern Italian food and is owned by the same people who own "Mustard's" (between Yountville and Rutherford, CA). The food was excellent.

CABREO "VIGNETO LA PIETRA" 1984 CHARDONNAY, RUFFINO, TUSCANY:

Interestingly, the back label describes it as a 1983 and the front label as 1984!! (Joe was the first to notice it.) Pale gold, sulphur, and some oak on nose, but resembled Sauvignon Blanc rather than Chardonnay. Lean, acidic, sharp. Not very good. (13.5)

Then, we had the 1959 Pontet-Canet, which I brought along, and also a mystery wine.

1959 PONTET-CANET, IN HALF-BOTTLES:

Good, dark, mature colour. Complex, elegant nose of mature, rich Claret. Well balanced, long. A bit acidic, but good body. Lots of class and depth. How good old Pontet Canets are: much better than wines they've been making since 1967. Even in half-bottles, still good. (17.5)

When Barney served the mystery wine, Joe and I said "Bordeaux." I added: "the mint and cedar of Mouton; if not, then Lynch-Bages." We were both wrong! It was Spring Mountain Napa Cabernet, the wine being produced by Joe Heitz! The label read "Lot H-68/69-LN." Joe told us that H = HEITZ; 68/69 = 1968 and 1969 blend; LN = aged in Limousin and Nevers oak. He had sold the juice to Spring Mountain during the "old, difficult days." The wine was great! Deep, dark, mature. Mint and cedar on nose. Round, rich, full, soft, and classy. A lovely Cabernet at its peak. An experience for all of us. Made not only from a blend of both vintages, but 50% "Martha's Vineyard" and 50% Regular Napa Cabernet.

I also learned that Bill Casey sold St. Clement to a Japanese firm recently.

Then we polished off a bottle of Port.

FICKLIN CALIFORNIA PORT:

Ruby style, excellent, well made, and reasonable.

Joe used to study oenology with David Ficklin, old Walter Ficklin's son. Joe said they use only traditional Portuguese grape varietals and no Zinfandel. Joe and Alice invited us for lunch on Thursday. A most enjoyable evening.

Also tasted in Yountville.

DOMAINE DE ST. JEAN DE BEBIAN 1981, VIN DE PAYS DE L'HERAULT, ALAIN ROUX:

Purchased a while ago from Kermit Lynch; some sediment. Deep, bright-red colour. Spicy, Cabernet nose with hint of Syrah or Cinsault. Full, rich, fruity, not very complex, but a solid, fruity wine. Ready but youthful and no rush, and at $4.25/bottle, a very good buy (comes in a Claret-shaped bottle). (16)

Thursday, July 23, 1987

Lunch at Joe and Alice Heitz's.

Picked up Belle Rhodes (Barney couldn't make it) and we drove to Joe and Alice Heitz's for lunch. Joe's sons (Rolly and David) and daughter Kathleen were there, as well as the two daughters-in-law and all three grandchildren. We had a nice buffet lunch and tried the following wines.

MARKKO VINEYARDS 1983 CHARDONNAY, CONNEAUT, OHIO:

The only wine served blind and one Rolly brought back from Ohio. Deep gold, touch of sulphur on nose, but good Chardonnay varietal: a blend of Burgundy and California. Thick, good acidity, soft, fairly alcoholic. Quite good and unusual. Seemed to age fast. Both Belle and I and Joe's son David thought that it was a ten to 15-year-old Chardonnay or rich Pinot Blanc. Then we tried four wines from Joe's cellar, which I told him to start drinking last March when I helped him reorganize his cellar.

1967 CHÂTEAU GISCOURS:

Palish, mature colour, good depth. Round, soft, elegant, good fruit. Clean, complex nose. Better than expected but definitely needs drinking. Quite good. (16)

1955 CHÂTEAU MARGAUX "HARVEY'S SELECTION":

Selected by Harry Waugh when he was working at Harvey's. Paler colour than the Giscours. Subdued, elegant, soft nose. Astringent, soft, lacking fruit. Drinkable, but very tired. The magnum tasted Saturday night was much livelier. Should have been consumed ten years ago. Disappointing. (14)

1964 AND 1966 CHÂTEAU HAUT-BRION:

Both typical Haut-Brion and true to the respective vintages, both at their peak. The 1964 was darker, rich, complex, chocolaty, ripe, and slightly charred nose. Full, round, rich, and long. Very good. (17.5)

The 1966 was lighter, yet more tannic, typical 1966. A bit more vegetal, but with good fruit and elegance. Quite long on palate, too. A fine wine. (17.5)

Then, we tried two of Joe's own wines.

1976 HEITZ CELLARS "BELLA OAKS" CABERNET SAUVIGNON, NAPA VALLEY:

Deep colour; elegant, complex, spicy Cabernet nose. At its peak. Good fruit, rich, long, well balanced. Not baked or pruny as most 1976s are (a drought year in California). (16.5) This was the first vintage for "Bella Oaks."

1979 HEITZ "MARTHA'S VINEYARD"CABERNET SAUVIGNON, NAPA VALLEY:

Typical "Martha's"; minty, eucalyptus, spicy, very individual nose. Rich, round, forward, drinking well now. Loads of fruit, oak, spices. Well balanced. A very good wine. Drink from 1987 to 1992 or even beyond, but I can't see how it can get any better. (17.5)

Belle Rhodes asked me if I would like to help Barney organize his cellar, too. I said "Why not"?!

August 6, 1987

Lunch at Pierre Dubrulle's Cooking School, in Vancouver.

Our host was Jean Hugel from Alsace, whom I know well from both visits to Alsace and his many trips to Vancouver.

1983 GEWÜRZTRAMINER VENDANGE TARDIVE "RÉSERVE PERSONNELLE," HUGEL:

It had 15.5% alcohol potential. Flowery, elegant, spicy. Lilacs on nose. Long, complex, fruity, classic. Late-harvest wine. Very good: 14% alcohol and 14%

residual sugar. 40% of the grapes picked had botrytis. His nephew made this wine. Jean would have liked to have more sugar and less alcohol. A bit too hot, but very good nevertheless. (17)

About the 1986 vintage in Alsace

Jean said that it was a large crop. Average of 90 hectolitres per hectare! Ripe grapes. He compared it to the useful 1979 vintage.

The Gewürztraminer "Sélection de Grains Nobles" 1976 had 26% potential alcohol! A good, but not great vintage.

About 1987

(I asked him to comment because of poor weather in June during flowering.) A year of ups and downs in weather. April was very hot and very cold. Rain. By the end of July, it had rained the yearly average! Flowering started June 22, ten days later than average. Very short flowering period, though; only five days. Irregular size of crop. At least 20% below 1986 in volume, but quality at this early stage is, of course, an unknown.

GEWÜRZTRAMINER "SÉLECTION DE GRAINS NOBLES" 1976:

Three fûts (casks) made.

CASK #67:

Higher temperature, warmer fermentation; therefore, a bit higher alcohol and drier than the other two.

CASK #28:

Best now. Forward, elegant.

CASK #20:

Best barrel. Richest, deepest, longest-lived. Two brix higher than casks #28 or #67.

I am fortunate to own a couple of bottles of each of the three individual casks of Hugel's Gewürztraminer "Sélection de Grains Nobles" 1976. Maybe someday I will organize an interesting tasting with them.

August 16, 1987

Blind tasting of 1974 California Cabernet Sauvignons, at Dr. Allan Tobe's.

Joe and Alice Heitz joined us, and Joe brought along two bottles of 1969 "Martha's Vineyard." On a previous visit to the Napa Valley, I suggested to Joe that he come up for this event and spend two or three days with us. I was very pleased when he accepted the invitation.

I contributed several wines for this event. All wines were served blind. We knew what the wines were, but not the order.

APERITIF

CHAMPAGNE KRUG N/V ROSÉ:

Lovely, elegant, but without the complexity and yeast of the regular Krug. Salmon-pink colour. Nice, rich fruit. I prefer the Grande Cuvée, but this is probably one of the finest Rosé Champagnes I've tasted.

The 1974s

1. ARROYO CABERNET SAUVIGNON 1974, SONOMA VALLEY:

Medium dark. Good depth. Flowery nose of green grapes. Vegetal and oaky. Wet straw, too. A bit sour and thin. Tired. Some fruit, fairly acidic; cold tea. Has seen better days or was a poor bottle. Very disappointing. (13)

2. MAYACAMAS CABERNET SAUVIGNON 1974, NAPA MOUNTAIN:

Much darker than #1. Young-looking for its age. Elegant, black-currant nose. Fresh for its age. Full, rich, still young. A bit tannic. Good fruit. Well structured, sweet, fruity, yet lots of extract. Not quite ready. Very good. (17)

3. BEAULIEU VINEYARDS GEORGES DE LATOUR "PRIVATE RESERVE" CABERNET SAUVIGNON 1974, NAPA VALLEY:

Mature-looking, orange-brown, good depth. Herbal nose. Wet straw and ripe fruit. A bit medicinal and flat; sweet lemon-tea, yet more lively than #1. I have had several finer examples of this wine and it can be very fine. On this occasion, it did not deliver. A variable wine. (14.5)

4. MOUNT EDEN VINEYARD CABERNET SAUVIGNON 1974, NAPA VALLEY:

Deep, dark colour. Impressive; slight touch of age. Ripe, spicy, vegetal. Some straw and oak. Intense nose. Full, rich, long, serious. Well balanced. Lovely fruit. Ready but no rush. Lots of class here. (18)

5. CHÂTEAU MONTELENA CABERNET SAUVIGNON 1974, SONOMA VALLEY:

Medium colour, good depth, and youthful. Candied, sweet nose. Young on nose. Good fruit, but lacks class. Later, opened up. Quite complex. A bit minty. Full, solid, still tannic, but too acidic. Otherwise very good. (16.5)

6. HEITZ CELLARS "MARTHA'S VINEYARD" CABERNET SAUVIGNON 1974, NAPA VALLEY:

Impressive colour, yet not as dark as #4. Mint, eucalyptus, cedar, Cassis nose. Full, rich, long, intense, well balanced; long life ahead. Lovely "Martha's!" Very good. Very special. (18)

7. STAG'S LEAP CABERNET SAUVIGNON 1974 REGULAR "LOT 1," NAPA VALLEY:

Medium colour, good depth. Tight nose. Good fruit. A bit pruny. Round, soft, lacking class, but pleasant. Hint of oxidation. Drink up! Stag's Leap also made "Lot II" and "Cask 23" in 1974, but we didn't taste them on this occasion. (15)

8. STERLING VINEYARD 1974 CABERNET SAUVIGNON "RESERVE," NAPA VALLEY:

Medium colour. Palish rim. Slightly rubbery nose (new rubber). Later, nose cleared. Full, round, a bit tannic at end but backed by good fruit. Long, serious, very good. In spite of high tannins, soft fruit. Start drinking now to 1995. (17)

9. MOUNT VEEDER VINEYARD CABERNET SAUVIGNON 1974, NAPA VALLEY:

Impressive dark colour. Spicy, fruit nose of Cassis. Complex, a bit herbaceous. Sonoma? Very big, youthful, tannic, unready, but has enough fruit to last. Very good. Classy. (17)

10. ROBERT MONDAVI CABERNET SAUVIGNON 1974 "RESERVE," NAPA VALLEY, IN MAGNUM:

Colour cloudy, palish. Something wrong here. Sour, acidic, yet I can tell it has some class. Pity. Later, cleared a bit. Some complexity. Bad bottle. Even so: (16.5). This can be very fine indeed, especially from magnums. In the past, I have rated this wine (18).

11. JOSEPH PHELPS CABERNET SAUVIGNON "INSIGNIA" 1974, NAPA VALLEY:

Good, dark colour. Ripe, rich, complex. Serious. A bit stemmy on nose. Classy, full, rich, sweet. Very California. Some residual sugar. Very ripe grapes. Mayacamas? Tannic, yet luscious. Very good if you like that style. Controversial. Certainly well made, but not my style at all. Too sweet and too ripe. (17)

12. CLOS DU VAL CABERNET SAUVIGNON 1974, NAPA VALLEY, IN MAGNUM:

Medium-dark colour. Clean nose of Cabernet, straw, oak. Slightly rubbery. Full, rich, solid. Not ready. Good acidity and fruit. Not very ripe fruit. A bit herbaceous, but still very good. Another Sonoma style? (17)

Then came three Chardonnays (all in magnums), also served blind.
All colours were excellent.

1. MAYACAMAS 1979 CHARDONNAY, CALIFORNIA, IN MAGNUM:

Medium-gold colour. Herbaceous. Good acidity. Complex, good fruit. Well balanced. Still fresh and lovely. Round and elegant. (17)

2. CHÂTEAU ST. JEAN "ROBERT YOUNG" 1978 CHARDONNAY, SONOMA VALLEY, IN MAGNUM:

Bright, deep gold. Touch of sulphur. Richer, rounder, riper than #1. A bit stemmy grassy, but intense. Well balanced. Some new oak. Well made. (17)

3. MAYACAMAS 1976 CHARDONNAY, NAPA MOUNTAIN, IN MAGNUM:

Similar appearance to #2, if not as deep. Slightly rubbery. Rich, round. Solid, big, too alcoholic. Good fruit. Mature, ripe. At its peak. All three Chardonnays were of good quality. (16)

WITH THE CHEESE COURSE
HEITZ CELLARS "MARTHA'S VINEYARD" 1969 CABERNET SAUVIGNON, NAPA VALLEY:

(Joe brought along two bottles of this wine.) The wine had just travelled, but was very good nevertheless. Similar nose to his 1974. Unmistakable "Martha's!" Deep colour. Fruity, big, rich, a bit steely. Lots of character. Excellent. (18)

Later that evening, Allan opened a single bottle of ROBERT MONDAVI'S 1974 CABERNET SAUVIGNON "RESERVE," NAPA VALLEY:

Much better and cleaner than the magnum. Full, a bit minty, dark, rich. Very slight metallic smell. Lively and ripe fruit. Very good. No rush! (17.5)

September 1987

Le Tastevin small-group vertical tasting of Château La Lagune, 1961 to 1983. The tasting was double-blind. Later, we discovered that it was a vertical tasting of Château La Lagune, Haut-Médoc.

1. 1981 LA LAGUNE:

Very good depth, but not as intense as the 1982. Spicy, unyielding Cabernet nose with some spice. Serious. Full, tannic, rich. Hard. Well balanced. Very good, leaner style. Drink from 1991 onward. (16.5)

2. 1983 LA LAGUNE:

A bit paler than #1. Good depth, young-looking. Open nose of oak, spices, toast, Cabernet fruit. Softer on palate yet some tannins to lose. Three to five years. Good finish. Clean, elegant; new oak. 1981? (16.5)

3. 1980 LA LAGUNE:

Palest of bunch, yet bright-red colour; palish rim. A bit stemmy, some Cabernet; clean, open nose. Dry and lean on palate. Soft, a bit too acidic. Needs drinking, but too sharp. (13) These are definitely Médocs, but what?

4. 1982 LA LAGUNE:

Very deep, dark colour, not unlike 1982. Closed nose with hint of very ripe fruit. perfumy. Rich, full, luscious. New oak, vanilla. Ripe Cabernet. Superb length. A lovely, great wine. Great intensity at finish. Ready by 1994 to 1996. (18)

5. 1979 LA LAGUNE:

Good, dark, mature colour, but lots of red, too. Closed nose, a bit vegetal. Round, forward, fairly soft, slightly high acidity but elegant. 1979? Still some tannin, but not much. Ready in one to two years. (15.5) This is definitely a vertical of the same property.

6. 1975 LA LAGUNE:

Good, deep, but mature colour. Complex nose of mature Claret. Wet wood, raisins. Soft, forward. A bit hard, yet has age. 1970? If so, not ripe enough, but quite good. Quite dry and needs drinking. Some barnyard on nose. (15.5)

7. 1970 LA LAGUNE:

Deep colour. Palish rim. A bit woody, complex, yet vegetal. Lovely ripe fruit. Concentrated. Long, elegant nose. Possibly 1978 or 1975. Evolved yet serious. Ripe fruit. Needs four to five years. (16.5)

8. 1978 LA LAGUNE:

Maybe 1978, younger-looking (more purple than #7). Deep, dark colour to rim. Weedy, vegetal nose but good fruit. Hard, tannic; typical 1978. Ripe fruit, too. Will be excellent but needs time. Big, serious wine. Some leanness. Needs eight to ten years. Very good. (17.5) Low Merlot year.

9. 1966 LA LAGUNE:

Lovely complex nose of mature wine. A bit stemmy. Lovely length. Round, complex, rich chocolaty aftertaste. At its peak. Long, complex, ripe. Superb. Great tobacco nose. This must be La Lagune. I have tasted this wine at least 18 times previously and I know it by heart! (18.5)

10. 1961 LA LAGUNE:

Mature, complex nose. Elegant, yet vegetal. Spicy, almost Pinot Noir nose. Sweet, a bit green (very young vines, after the frost of 1956). Intense. A bit vegetal, lean, yet almost sweet. Odd but very good, especially considering the conditions after the frost. Vegetal, green, yet has some ripeness. (17)

It should be noted that this property is the only one in the Médoc (with the exception of the First Growths, of course) that ages its whole production in 100% new oak barrels.

DESSERT WINE

1976 CHÂTEAU RIEUSSEC:

Very impressive; typical dark, deep gold. Almost amber. Lovely, impressive, ripe botrytis nose. Full, rich, long. Great length; honey, full, rich. Essence of Sauternes. Superb. Great balance. Ready, but no rush. (18)

September 1987

Trip to Napa Valley (Yountville) Dinner with Christian Moueix, at the "California Café."

We had a nice quiet dinner and chat. He's supervising the 1987 harvest at Napanook (Dominus) and next week, he is flying back to France to supervise the picking in Pomerol, etc.

We ordered a bottle of Merlot.

RUTHERFORD RANCH MERLOT 1983, NAPA VALLEY:

Christian said that it was an imitation, probably made from Cabernet Franc. Acidic, lean, vegetal, slightly corked. We didn't bother to drink it (and we weren't charged for it).

Then, we ordered this bottle.

JORDAN CABERNET SAUVIGNON 1983, NAPA VALLEY:

Spicy, round, well balanced; good fruit and flavour. Good, but not great.

Christian said that he watched the first pick of Opus One 1987 (Mondavi-Rothschild) from their own vineyards. Mondavi pay their pickers per hour, so the pickers work slowly. Christian pays his Mexican pickers per ton, so they work fast but aren't always very careful, and need close supervision. I'll meet him on Wednesday to watch the picking. He said that at Napanook, they have finally identified the old "Cabernet Franc" as being actually Merlot (which they suspected all along), and found proof that the owner, late in the 19th century, ordered and planted Merlot at what is today Napanook.

They also have some old Chardonnay grapes, which they sell to Inglenook. Christian said that l'Evangile is for sale but the price is ridiculous (160 million francs for seven hectares). He said it is much wiser to buy land now (in 1987) in Napa than in France.

He confirmed my suspicions about the 1987 vintage in Bordeaux. Average at best, but a respectable 35 to 40 hectolitres per hectare. Lots of "coulure." They cut the green bunches at Petrus. Lots of green grapes take away the nutrition of the ripe grapes so they cut them off, and that has boosted up the sugar level in the riper grapes.

His agents in the USA were Almaden. Now it is Hubelein, including Christian's own property, La Grave. They'll change the label in 1986 and will call it "La Grave-à-Pomerol" with maybe a hint in small print "Trigant-de-Boisset."

He said that the top 1984 Bordeaux should have been declassified and that the excessive price increase for the 1987s was a mistake. Many importers were stuck with the 1984s.

The 1986 vintage sales are slow.

Down by 60% from 1985! He expects a crisis. He tried several times to do business with the Canadian liquor monopolies, but it is not worth it. Bureaucratic incompetence.

About the sluggish sales of the 1986s: this is odd because it is going to be a great vintage, especially in the Médoc. People are so taken in with the 1982s that they are going to miss the boat on the 1986s.

His kids are going to school in Bordeaux now, and Marie-Laure (his wife) has rented a small flat in Bordeaux for weeknights. I have a feeling that things are not going well between Christian and Marie-Laure. We had a nice meal and chatted about politics, travel, etc.

October 3, 1987

Dinner at the Levines', after Kippur.

Also Joan and Sam Fromowitz, the US Consul General to Vancouver.

As we were finishing our dinner, Sam received a phone call from Washington, DC, telling him that Canada and the USA have reached a tentative agreement on Free Trade. This may mean eventually a much lower markup on imported wines. If so, it is a major change. However, knowing bureaucrats and the fanatical addiction of Canada's provincial governments to the income from wine, beer, and liquor sales, I am convinced that roadblocks will be raised to delay implementation. I hope and pray, for the sake of Canadian consumers, that the Americans hold firm and don't give in. Free Trade must mean just that—free trade.

October 4, 1987

Tasting of 1982 Pomerols, at Liberty Wine Co. in Point Roberts, Washington State.

The 1982s

1. LA CROIX DE GAY:

80% Cabernet Sauvignon, 15% Merlot, and 5% Cabernet Franc. Medium, palish colour. Herbal, clean, a bit sharp. Light-bodied for a 1982. Some fruit. Touch of acidity. OK, but nothing special. (13.5)

2. DOMAINE DE L'EGLISE:

75% Merlot, 25% Cabernet Franc. Similar appearance to #1, but more depth. Riper nose, a bit stemmy. More fruit, medium-bodied. Touch of tannins; almost ready. A pleasant wine for early drinking. (14) Before Borie-Manoux took it over, this property used to produce rich, hefty, well-made wines.

3. LA PROVIDENCE:

55% Merlot, 45% Cabernet Franc. More depth than #1 and #2 to rim. Unyielding, a little leather on nose. Metallic, acidic, sharp, lacking ripe fruit. A bit tannic and bitter finish. (13)

4. LA LOUBIÈRE:

55% Merlot, 45% Cabernet Franc. Good, dark colour to rim. Dusty on nose and palate. Lead capsule. A corked bottle. Metallic, musty. Not rated.

5. FEYTIT-CLINET:

70% Merlot, 30% Cabernet Franc. Medium depth. Delicate fruit and oak overtones. Charming nose. Round, delicate, forward. Good fruit. Slightly tannic, but almost ready. Touch of bitter tannins at end. Overall, a pleasant wine. Drink 1989 to 1992. (15)

6. LA POINTE:

80% Merlot, 15% Cabernet Franc, 5% Malbec. Medium depth. Pleasant fruity nose. Perfumy. Good backbone and concentration of fruit. Simple, but so far the best structure, but without the complexity of #5. (14)

7. LA CROIX:

60% Merlot, 20% Cabernet Franc, 20% Cabernet Sauvignon. Medium depth to rim. Too acidic, but good fruit. Ripe berries. Medium-bodied. A pleasant, fruity wine. (14)

8. CLOS L'EGLISE:

60% Merlot, 20% Cabernet Franc, 10% Cabernet Sauvignon, 10% Malbec. Medium depth. Short and dull on nose and palate, yet has some pleasant aftertaste. Needs one to two years. Some tannins and hint of oak. Later, some class. (14.5)

9. CLOS RENÉ:

70% Merlot, 30% Cabernet Franc. Good deep, dark colour to rim. Good nose of ripe fruit. Rich, full, ripe, long, good concentration. One-dimensional, almost ready. Best so far, showing the ripeness of the vintage. (15.5)

10. LE GAY:

50% Merlot, 50% Cabernet Franc. Lovely, scented nose of ripe fruit and oak. Classy, full, ripe, long, complex, rich. True Pomerol. Good concentration. Soft tannins. Good backbone. Very long. Lovely, ripe raspberries. (17)

Wines #1 to #10 are clearly the "second class" wines of Pomerol, as was made plainly obvious when tasting wines #11 to #17.

11. VIEUX CHÂTEAU CERTAN:

50% Merlot, 25% Cabernet Franc, 20% Cabernet Sauvignon, 5% Malbec. Good, deep colour. Palish rim, more herbal, stemmy than Le Gay (less Merlot). Elegant, subdued nose. Ripe, round, long. A lot of class in a delicate way. Some tannin. Not aggressive. Medium-bodied. Stylish. (18)

12. LA CONSEILLANTE:

45% Merlot, 45% Cabernet Franc, 10% Pressac. Medium-dark colour. Subdued, delicate nose of ripe fruit. Leaner, lovely body, class, elegance. A great bottle. Not too jammy or fat, but elegant, long. Drink 1992 to 2000, or beyond. Very good potential. Lovely. (18.5)

The above two wines, Vieux Château Certan and La Conseillante, produce a rather more elegant Pomerol because of their higher proportion of Cabernets in the blend rather than the heftier, predominantly Merlot-based Pomerols, such as Lafleur, l'Evangile, or Petrus.

13. LA FLEUR-PETRUS:

About 80% Merlot, 10% to 20% Cabernet Franc. Good, deep, dark colour to rim. Riper on nose than #12. More like #11. New oak, lovely fruit, yet leaner, harder, more serious wine; not quite as complex as #11 or #12. A leaner #10. Hard, tannic. Drink 1993 to 1998. (17.5)

14. LATOUR-À-POMEROL:

Made from approximately 80% Merlot, 20% Cabernet Franc. Very good, dark colour. Lovely, ripe Merlot nose and oak. Full-bodied, round, perfect balance. Ripe, long, fruity. Clean, intense finish. Great quality. Needs four to five years. Superb. (18.5)

15. L'EVANGILE:

Made from two-thirds Merlot, one-third Cabernet Franc. Very dark. Lovely ripeness on nose and palate. Round, long, perfect balance. Rich, very ripe fruit.

Long finish. Perfect roundness. Great. Drink 1994 to 1997 or beyond. (19)

16. Trotanoy:

Made from 85% Merlot, 15% Cabernet Franc. Good, dark colour. Slightly lighter than #15. Delicate, perfumy nose. Sweeter, yet more delicate than the l'Evangile. Complex, long. Almost ready. Surprisingly elegant style. Very good, but lacks the intensity of Merlot of #15. Very good, nevertheless. May be going through a "dumb" phase. Will surely improve. At this tasting: (17.5).

17. Petrus:

95% Merlot, 5% Cabernet Franc. By far darkest of all above. Deep, concentrated colour. Lovely, intense nose of ripe fruit. Oak, mint (just a bit). Very tannic, very ripe. Very fruity. Essence of magnificent Merlot. Great! Superb length and ripe fruit and new oak. Needs ten years or more. A masterpiece. (19.5)

DESSERT WINE

1982 Château Rieussec:

Deep, bright-gold colour. Creamy, good botrytis, complex. Fine length, balance, elegance. Very good potential. Good acidity. Better than expected, but not as great or as intense as the 1983. (15.5)

October 17, 1987

Dinner at "La Belle Auberge," in Ladner (Vancouver), with a group of friends.

Chef Bruno Marti prepared an artistic, fabulous nine-course meal. Superb food.

Champagne Bollinger "RD" 1975:

(Two bottles) The bottle disgorged September 19, 1984, was richer, more yeasty, a bit older-tasting, but had great length and complexity. The bottle disgorged five months later (February 1985) was as good, but a bit fruitier and fresher.

Then we tasted three great white Burgundies from the fabulous 1978 vintage.

Chevalier-Montrachet 1978, Remoissenet,

Bâtard-Montrachet 1978, Leflaive,

and

Puligny-Montrachet Premier Cru "Clos du Cailleret" 1978, Joseph Drouhin:

The Chevalier was the greenest-gold, spiciest (some cabbage on nose), crispest, with excellent acidity and no rush drinking it. It will last for another decade. Great complexity, length, balance, and class. (18)

The Bâtard had the deepest-gold colour. Expansive, long, complex nose. The fullest, richest of all three. At its peak; rich, long, more forward and less acidic than the Chevalier. Superb length and complexity. A very great bottle. (19)

The Puligny "Cailleret" was the most delicate. Subdued, complex nose; lovely length and delicacy; not as intense as the first two and less rich, but nevertheless, a lovely bottle. (17.5)

1949 Château Pontet-Canet, Cruse:

Excellent level. The greatest red wine of the evening! Incredibly dark colour to rim for a 38-year-old Claret. Rich, open, long nose of mature Claret and wet earth. Great complexity. Soft, full, long, and rich on palate. At its absolute peak and a superb bottle. In the old days, Pontet-Canet made great wines. (18.5)

Château St. Pierre 1961 and Château Gruaud-Larose 1961:

Two fine, sturdy St. Juliens from a great vintage.

The St. Pierre had a darker, deep colour. Subdued nose, some rubber and fruit. Hard, tannic, full, chunky, and solid with a clean, cedary finish. Not as complex, though, as the Gruaud-Larose, which wasn't quite as dark. Complex, rich nose. Full, soft, round, and long on palate. Definitely one of the top 1961s and no rush drinking it. Rated the St. Pierre (17.5) and the Gruaud (18), although this can be truly great on occasion.

1929 Charmes-Chambertin, Joseph Drouhin:

David Freeman brought two bottles "just in case." We opened the one with the lower fill, two inches below the cork. Dave said that he had received this wine from Robert Drouhin in 1970 and that it had been recorked in the mid-1960s. Medium-red colour, pale rim. Spicy, complex, youthful nose of Pinot Noir and cherries. Alcoholic, long, rich, complex. This wine has held incredibly well for a 58-year-old wine! An experience. (18)

Château Suduiraut 1959, Sauternes:

One of my favourite Sauternes, other than some vintages of d'Yquem! This bottle did not disappoint. Deep, dark, bright gold, almost orange. Rich, yet complex and delicate nose of botrytis and ripe fruit. Full, rich, superb balance and length. A masterpiece and the ultimate Sauternes. (19)

Overall, great food, great wines, and a lovely evening.

October 30, 1987

Dinner of "Group of Ten," at home.

Champagne Pol Roger "Private Reserve" 1975:

Lovely Champagne; elegance, length, and complexity. At its peak. Well balanced. Subdued yet long nose. Fine oak and Chardonnay. A lovely Champagne.

1981 PAVILLON BLANC DU CHÂTEAU MARGAUX:

Bright green-gold colour. Delicate, complex nose of Sauvignon Blanc, hint of oak. Round, well balanced, good fruit on palate and some oak. An elegant wine. Due to its balance and good acidity, this wine will keep for quite some time.

1978 AND 1982 CHÂTEAU LAVILLE-HAUT-BRION:

Oddly, the 1982 was deeper gold, older-looking. A bit clumsy. Hint of oxidation. Getting tired, a bit flat, yet good complexity. Sweeter, thicker, richer. Good, but not great. (16).

The 1978 was younger-looking, pale green-gold. Lovely, spicy, yet subdued nose. Tight, excellent balance, fresh and long. Not nearly ready. Try around 1992 to 1996 and beyond. Very good. (18)

1961 CHÂTEAU LAFITE, IN MAGNUM:

(Group wine) The star of the evening. Excellent level, decanted 45 minutes. Some sediment. Good, dark colour to rim, showing a little age but excellent appearance. An explosion on nose of smells of spring. Lilacs, flowery, lovely, long, and elegant; great finesse. Medium-bodied, elegant on palate. Well balanced; long finish. A superb magnum and a great wine. Having said that, it did not have the depth and ripe fruit intensity of the magnificent 1959. Great, nevertheless. (18.5) The 1961 Lafite can be variable. In those days, they used to bottle each barrel separately, rather than as an assemblage. This is the finest 1961 Lafite that I have tasted to date.

1934 CHÂTEAU MOUTON-ROTHSCHILD, IN HALF-BOTTLES:

(Group wine) Both excellent, low neck levels. Very good, dark colour, not unlike a 1966. The similarity ended there.

One bottle was a bit too sharp. Some dill, lean, yet had some fruit too.

The second half-bottle had much better fruit, a cleaner nose, and more complexity. This wine must have been very sturdy in its youth. Has held very well for a 53-year-old wine. Sturdiness rather than complexity. Rated one (15.5) and the other (17).

LONDON DOCK PORT "SUPERIOR" N/V:

Bottled in San Francisco by Goldberg, Bowen and Co. Produced around 1918. Discovered by Joe Heitz at Mr. Crocker's cellar (of Crocker Bank fame) in 1975. Given to me by Joe Heitz. Pre-Prohibition. Tawny. Almonds, coconut on nose. Full, rich, quite alcoholic, still lively. Very good. A rare treat.

1963 CROFT'S VINTAGE PORT:

Bottled in London by Charles Kinloch. Good, dark colour. A bit simple, yet good depth and solid. Not as elegant as Croft's 1963 usually is. Needs five to eight years. Quite good but not great. I have definitely tasted better bottles of this fine, elegant Port.

November 2, 1987

Pol Roger Club Inaugural Event and Dinner, at Hotel Le Meridien, in Vancouver.

This group was established to meet twice a year to taste Champagnes from the house of Pol Roger. Christian Pol Roger was our guest. The food was OK, but nothing special.

APERITIF

CHAMPAGNE POL ROGER "BRUT EXTRA CUVÉE DE RÉSERVE" N/V:

Pleasant, round; some yeast and class. Good. Lively. (16)

CHAMPAGNE POL ROGER "BLANC DE CHARDONNAY" BRUT 1979:

A familiar Champagne. Round, silky, delicate, well balanced. Still fresh and lively. (17.5)

CHAMPAGNE POL ROGER ROSÉ BRUT 1979:

Pinker than usual. Earlier vintages were paler, salmon colour. Sweeter on palate than previous vintages. Not as hard or dry. Not very complex, but pleasant. (17)

CHAMPAGNE POL ROGER "CUVÉE SIR WINSTON CHURCHILL" 1979:

Real class. Complex, long, yeasty, not ready. Full, rich, still a bit closed. A solid, stylish Champagne with lots of class and potential. (18)

CHAMPAGNE POL ROGER BRUT "RESERVE" 1921:

We opened five bottles of this wine, one per table of six guests. They were all different. This wine has spent 65 years on its lees and was disgorged last week, before shipment to Vancouver! There was no dosage added. Christian Pol Roger said that the blend is made up of 80% Pinot Noir and 20% Chardonnay.

Our bottle: Deep, mature, gold colour. Still some very tiny bubbles. Very obvious mushrooms on nose. (Christian called it "champignons de Paris.") Hint of oxidation, some damp wood, not unlike very mature, old Claret. Delicate, round, rich, yet getting tired. Another bottle was cheesy and odd, yet paler and crisper than ours. The other three bottles were fresher, more delicate, with lots of toast, yeast, and length. Overall, a great and unusual experience. Pity our bottle wasn't the best but I would not and should not complain. A great experience. The best bottle should rate (18) for complexity and (19) for longevity.

November 6 and 7, 1987

Tasting of Château Mouton-Rothschild 1985 to 1853, at the Beverly Wiltshire hotel, in Los Angeles.

There were 28 participants. Organized by Jeffrey Troy of New York and Ed Lazarus of Los Angeles. 1853 was the first year that the Rothschilds have owned this property.

Friday, November 6

FIRST SESSION

CHAMPAGNE MUMM'S CORDON ROUGE BRUT N/V:

With fine Beluga caviar and smoked salmon. Rather ordinary Champagne. Pleasant, fresh, but large bubbles and not much complexity.

FLIGHT #1

1985:

Good, dark, purplish colour to rim. New oak on nose. Spicy, complex, elegant, vanilla. Lovely nose. Full, rich, long, complex. Lovely balance and length. Good intensity. Needs 12 to 15 years. Great class. Lots of fruit. Excellent potential. Drink 1995 to 2005. (18) Yet not the blockbuster the 1986 will turn out to be. True to the elegance of the 1985s.

1984:

Medium red, already showing some orange at rim. Subdued, unyielding nose. Fairly acidic on palate, yet good fruit and oak-vanilla. Citric finish. Needs two to three years. (14)

1983:

As dark as the 1985. Restrained, subdued nose at this stage. Full, serious, tannic wine, going through a "dumb" phase. Good balance and very good potential. Will be a fine Claret around 1995 to 2000. (17.5)

1982:

Impressive, deep, dense colour, typical of this vintage. Subdued, yet rich, ripe nose. Full, solid, very big, intense, tannic, massive, loaded with ripe fruit. Needs at least 15 years. A giant. Amazingly, because of its ripe fruit, it can be enjoyed now! (19)

1981:

Medium colour, good depth, touch of orange at rim. Leaner than the 1982 and more forward than the 1983, yet has good backbone, some tannin. Try around 1991 or 1992. Good fruit, clean, slight acidity at finish. (15.5) It seems that both Latour and Mouton "missed" this vintage. Lafite is more complex, but Margaux is the wine of the vintage.

1980:

Palish-red colour, orange rim. Open, fruity, delicate, slightly pruny nose of mature Claret. Soft, lean, yet some new wood. Quite stylish. More enjoyable now than the 1984, with less acidity. At its peak. (14)

FLIGHT #2

1969:

Tired, browning colour, some depth, orange-brown rim. Delicate nose of very mature Claret, wet wood, leather, yet round and clean. Acidic, lean, quite sharp on palate, yet some concentration, too, and in spite of the high acidity, good length. Drink up before what's left of the fruit disappears. Pleasant surprise. (14)

1968:

Brown, murky colour. Yellow-green edge, not unlike very old Port or Madeira. Madeirized, leathery nose. Lemon, cold-tea, oxidized, sour. Very poor. (0) Why did our hosts include this wine? What were they trying to prove?

1967:

Mature, light-red colour; pale, orangy rim. Herbaceous, stemmy nose. Hint of sulphur. Typical of so many 1967s: excessive acidity, lean, mean. Some body and fruit but too much acidity. (13.5)

1966, IN MAGNUM:

Metallic, hard, evolved. Good, dark, mature colour. Has depth and concentration. Minty, spicy nose so typical of Mouton. After 1961, this is the best vintage of the 1960s and a magnum to boot. Fairly hard, usual 1966 structure. A leaner, harder-style wine, yet has length and some complexity. Needs three to five years in magnums, but beyond that, fruit will disappear. In the context of a First Growth, not a great effort. (16)

1965:

Palish colour, orangy-brown rim. Hint of oxidation on nose, but much better than the 1968. Acidic, sharp, thin, little fruit. Passé, yet bearable. Rare label, though! (11)

1964:

Not a successful year for Mouton. Tired, caramel nose. Palish colour; mature, orange. Thin, fairly hard and tannic; some fruit, even some oak-vanilla noticeable in the background, but unfortunately lean, hard, and drying up. (13)

Overall

Disappointing flight. Most were obviously chaptalized yet that was what made them (barely) drinkable.

FLIGHT #3

1958:

Palish, red colour, orange rim. Delicate, open nose. Lean, fairly hard, yet had some fruit. Pleasant, round, drinking well now. Better than expected. Drink up. (14)

1957:

Medium colour, some depth. Mature rim. Young-looking for its age. Spicy, open, forthcoming, minty nose. Hard, tannic, yet good fruit, some acidity. Very enjoyable. Sweet, solid. (15.5) Some of these 1957s, notably Latour and Lynch-Bages, made wines that were not bad at all, but hard and masculine.

1956:

Very low fill. Mature colour. Thin, acidic, sharp, yet drinkable. Some fruit. Needs drinking. Acidity may keep this wine, though. We tasted it in a "spare" half-bottle because the full bottle was fizzy. (13)

1955:

Low fill. Good, dark colour, yet very mature, orange rim. Spicy, minty, elegant nose. Rich, elegant, long. A bit sharp, but lots of class, depth, ripeness, and power. Would have been better had the bottle been sounder. Much better when tasted previously. (15)

1954:

Surprising colour for age and vintage. Mature rim. Clean nose, some complexity. Minty on entry, typical Mouton, yet acidic, lean, and hard, but good fruit and classy Mouton finish. A pleasant surprise but not great. (14)

Overall impression of this flight

Not very impressive. Most are tired wines. The 1957 had the best structure.

FLIGHT #4

Made during the War under difficult conditions. Actually, the owners being Jewish and the property being under German control, it is amazing that they made any wine at all.

1944:

Deep, very mature colour. Minty (typical Mouton), leathery, woody. Lean, hard, medicinal. Very acidic. Not good. (12)

1943:

Mature-looking; brown-orange. Delicate, sweet nose. Round, forward, elegant, still alive. Frail, but can still give pleasure. Best of the War vintages. (14.5)

1942:

Deep, tired-looking. Leathery, oxidized nose. Sour, acidic, cold-tea. (10)

1940:

Palish, tired-looking. Dull on nose. Sour, a bit tannic, acidic. Drink up! Soft. Better than 1942 or 1944. (12)

Observation

Obviously they ran out of sugar, oak, and everything else during the War.

FLIGHT #5

"The Golden Age of Bordeaux" 1920 to 1929

It was interesting to see how these wines have held after 60 or more years in bottle.

1929:

Surprisingly pale colour. Mature rim. Sweet, almost ripe figs on palate. Odd. Hint of oxidation, yet the intensity is there. High alcohol. Better on palate than on nose. I've had better examples of this wine. Getting tired. A bit too sweet. This sample is giving up. (16.5)

1928:

Similar appearance to the 1929, yet more depth. Subdued, cedary nose; typical Pauillac. Typical 1928 and characteristic Mouton. Leaner, more tannic than the 1929. Solid, serious wine. Holding well. Good but not great. (17.5)

1926:

Some tasters found this to be volatile; I disagree; I didn't smell that. Good, dark, mature colour. Very yellow-orange rim. Clean, pleasant, delicate, subdued nose. Tobacco. Lovely fruit, length, balance. Fine quality. (17)

1925:

Very pale colour. Stemmy nose. Thin, dill, acidic. Dull, oxidized. (10)

1924, IN MAGNUM:

Good, dark colour. Dill on nose. Hard, acidic, citric, tannic, powerful. Must have been a giant of a wine in its youth. Tannins still there, yet getting tired. Good fruit but citric and sharp. Intense. Hint of saltiness. Unusual. (16.5)

1921, IN MAGNUM:

Impressive colour. Good, deep, mature colour. Elegant, ripe, mature nose; cigar-box, mint, etc. Lovely, ripe fruit. A bit sharp. Fairly hard, hint of mustiness. Has held well. Still big and tannic. Some tasters said that it had a short finish. I didn't find that to be so. (16.5)

1920:

Pale, tired-looking. Open, forward, sweet. Elegant nose of very mature Claret. Hint of oxidation, a bit acidic, yet tannic backbone. Past its prime. Sweet/sour. (13.5)

Overall impression of flight

This final flight was really disappointing. Poor provenance? The 1929 and 1928 should have been so much better!

Saturday, November 7, 1987

11:00 A.M. SECOND SESSION

We met at the same location for the morning session.

FLIGHT #1
1979 to 1975

1979:

Medium colour, good depth, touch of purple. Cedar, mint, subdued nose. Round, fairly forward, hint of prunes (oxidation). A bit sharp, but good. Not a keeper, though. A ripe, forward wine. A bit short. (15) If you must buy a 1979 First Growth, try to find Lafite, Haut-Brion, or Ausone. All three are head-and-shoulders above this, as are Palmer, Pichon-Lalande, and Certain de May.

1978, IN MAGNUM:

Medium colour, good depth, orange rim. Mature-looking for its age. Stemmy, closed nose. A bit metallic and herbaceous. Leaner style, quite acidic. Clean, good length, but lacks a bit in ripe fruit concentration. Drink from 1988 (bottles), 1992 onward (magnums). Not charming. 1978 was a year of very low Merlot yields, but Mouton should have done better. (16.5)

1977:

Medium brown-orange colour. Herbaceous nose (green). A bit sharp and acidic, thin. Some fruit; too lean, though. Not very good. (13)

1976, IN MAGNUM:

Good, dark colour to rim. Clean Cabernet nose. Fairly tannic, but good fruit. Forward, but no rush because of ripe tannins. One of the best 1976s. Ripe fruit. Clean, long finish. Very enjoyable. (16.5)

1975:

Good, deep, dark colour, not showing much sign of maturity. Closed nose, yet hint of cedar, oak, Cabernet spiciness. Very Pauillac nose. Tannic, hard, concentrated fruit. Very solid, big; typical 1975. Very good concentration. Needs at least ten years. A very good, all-round classic Claret. (18) Some tasters said that because of the hard tannins, this wine would never come around. Maybe. "Qui vivra, verra!"

FLIGHT #2
1953 to 1945

1953:

Mature-looking, good depth, orange rim. Dull, unyielding nose. Sharp, acidic, lean. Usually I prefer Mouton 1953 to 1952, but not today. Too sharp, acidic. Drying out. Some of the 1953 elegance. I've tasted far better samples. Poor storage? (16)

1952:

Good, dark, mature colour to rim. Lovely, tobacco-cedar nose. Subdued, elegant, sweet. Soft on palate. A bit dusty, cigar-box. Complex, long. Leaner 1952 style. (17)

1951:

Similar appearance to the 1953. Pleasant surprise. Very little nose, some sweetness. Quite tannic, some fruit. Pleasant for an off vintage. Some ripeness. (14.5) The label is worth a lot of money.

1950:

Medium depth; mature, orange-red, brick colour. Nose of older wine. Obvious oxidation on palate. Sharp, hard, dry. Going fast. (11)

1949:

Mid shoulder level. Similar appearance to the 1950. Ripe, delicate, complex nose. Round, very elegant, and long. Mint, eucalyptus. Very forward, very soft, yet lots of class. I've had better examples. Getting tired. This could and should have been great. (17)

1948:

Low fill. Good depth, darker colour than the 1949. Subdued nose. A bit sharper, harder, more acidic than the 1949. Best part of this wine was the nose. Considering the low fill, however, pretty good. (16)

1947, IN MAGNUM:

Very good, dark colour for a 40-year-old wine. Excellent appearance. Dark to rim. Delicate, minty, cigar-box nose. Full, rich, long, ripe, mature; still a bit tannic. Lots of class, length, character. Very good. Top quality. Great character. Velvety, smooth, intense. Best 1947 Mouton I've ever tried. (18.5) Finally, a fine bottle!

1945:

Very impressive, dark colour. Obvious mint on nose. Great concentration. Great intensity. Very tannic, big, solid, Superb concentration, lovely long finish. Ripe fruit, hint of leather and astringency due to lots of tannin, but great length and power. Superb quality. Minty, spicy, long. Will last forever. If I could fault this wine at all, maybe it had a bit of leanness at the end. Some people thought that the magnum of 1947 was the best wine of the flight. While I agree that it is great, I think that this sample of 1945 was the top wine of the flight. 1945 Mouton was bottled over a long period. Much longer than any other vintage. (19)

Overall, a good flight. The best so far.

FLIGHT #3
1938 to 1933
A difficult period for Bordeaux, and for business in general, and a disastrous era for international politics.

1938:

Subdued, delicate nose with very little Mouton character coming through. Dry, hard, tannic, sharp, citric, yet some backbone, too. Surprisingly good. (14)

1937:

Good depth, orangy rim. Ripe, leathery, minty nose. Sharp on palate. Acidic, good fruit, though. This was most people's favourite of flight. Held very well. Sweet, chaptalized, ripe, some cedar. Trace of acidity at end. Good, but not great. Too sweet. Best of flight. (15.5)

1934:

(I had this wine from half-bottles only two weeks ago!) Medium red; pale orange-brown rim. Subdued, delicate, clean nose. Delicate, round, very mature; very frail, yet still alive. Elegant finish. (14.5)

1933, IN MAGNUM:

Oddly, a few of the tasters liked this wine best of the flight, maybe because of nose, but surely not later. Good appearance. Clean nose. Fairly acidic and sharp, but some fruit and concentration, too. Has seen better days, yet for a "mediocre" vintage, this has held pretty well. Too lemony and citric. Too sour. Disintegrated fast. (13)

FLIGHT #4

1919 to 1911

1919, IN MAGNUM:

A disaster. Dead. Milky, yellow-brown colour. Rotten. (0)

1912:

Almost a Rosé. Vinegary nose. Some rotten wood. Sour vinegar, citric, sharp. Dill. One to forget. (0)

1918:

Pale colour, yet still some depth. Touch of sulphur, sturdy nose. Delicate, a bit acidic, thin, some sweetness, yet drinkable. Some fruit, actual drinkable. (12) Some 1918s can be great.

1911:

Very pale, Rosé colour. Rotten vegetables on nose. Earthy, sour, rotting vinegar. Awful. (0)

A disastrous flight.

FLIGHT #5

1900 to 1889

1900:

Rotting, flat Mateus Rosé. Unbearable. Liquid manure. (0) Should have been great, or at least drinkable.

1899:

Good colour, some orange rim. A bit vegetal on nose. Sour, acidic, sharp. Very tired and ordinary, but at least drinkable. (13) Another wine that should have been much better.

What a disappointment! By this stage, I am certain that our hosts, Jeffrey and Ed, must feel pretty awful. We have all paid a small fortune to participate in this event. I cannot help but feel that they were not very careful in their acquisition of these wines. They are both fine, experienced tasters. They should have known better.

1893:

Muddy brown-yellow-green colour. Caramel and rot on nose. Dead. Whitwham-bottling. (0)

1889:

Sweet, mildly unpleasant, some tannins, little fruit left. Very tired but drinkable. (11)

Overall impressions

A very disappointing flight. The 1900 and 1899 were recorked at the château.

I find it incomprehensible that wines recorked in 1984 were this poor. Something is very odd here! Surely the proprietors must have realized (when they recorked the wine) that it was dead!

Later, eight of us went back to Brad Klein's house and had an old bottle of Champagne purchased as a mixed lot at auction.

CHAMPAGNE KRUG VINTAGE 1955:

Good ullage. Deep, gold, mature colour. Old nose, Chardonnay, a bit of oxidation. Tiny bubbles, but soft. Only 0.75 dosage, yet it was sweet because of the age. Very old-style Champagne, yet quite sound.

THEOPHILE ROEDERER "JAMIN" BRUT CHAMPAGNE N/V:

Cheap ($10). Flowery, light, quite sweet for a "Brut." A bit foamy. More like an elegant Spumante than a true Champagne. Grapey and lacks character.

Saturday, November 7

7:00 P.M. THIRD SESSION

APERITIF

CHAMPAGNE PERRIER-JOUËT BRUT N/V:

Better than last night's Mumm's. Complex, delicate, round; good length and fruit.

FLIGHT #1

1974 to 1970

1974:

Medium red, good depth. Tobacco-cedar nose. A bit herbaceous. Fairly tannic. Bitter, lacking ripe fruit. Finishes lean, noticeable acidity. (13.5)

1973:

More forward-looking that the 1974. Delicate, tobacco nose. Some herbaceousness. Soft, round, spicy. A lightweight that is at its peak and needs drinking soon! (13) This is the year Mouton was reclassified as a Premier Grand Cru Classé. Pity the vintage wasn't better. Nice Picasso label.

1972:

Palish, mature colour. Orange rim. Herbaceous Cabernet Sauvignon nose. Dill, harsh, acidic, lean, low fruit. Finishes sour. (12)

1971:

Best colour of the flight so far. Good depth and concentration. Herbaceous nose. Some oak, too lean, acidic, low fruit, no tannins. Not very good and will get worse. Drink up. Finished short and vegetal. (13.5)

1970:

Impressive, dark, still youthful colour. Subdued, delicate, yet ripe and concentrated nose. Closed, still a bit hard. Not an overwhelming wine, rather elegant. Finishes slightly lean, but lots of class. Some cedar on nose. Overall, nose better than palate. A good, but not great, 1970. Drink between now and 1992. (16.5) Best wine of a very ordinary flight.

Overall impressions of this flight

1974, 1973, and 1972 tasted as expected. 1971 was very disappointing, 1970 was the best of the flight, but I can name at least half-dozen better 1970s.

FLIGHT #2

1963 to 1959

1963:

Tired, browning colour. Oxidizing nose. Sour, acidic; lots of sugar added, but it didn't help; gone. (0) Rare label!

1962, IN MAGNUM:

Good, dark colour to rim. Subdued, elegant nose. Deep, red colour, typical of the vintage. Round, forward, very enjoyable. Magnums will last, but from bottles, drink up! Lovely finish, round, delicate. Excellent food wine. Ready and delicious. (17.5)

1961:

Impressive, very dark colour to rim. Incredible nose! Intense mint, cedar, oak, Cabernet spiciness, cigar-box, you name it. Typical Mouton! Full, rich, long, ripe, almost at its peak, but no rush. Great length and concentration. Still a bit tannic. Drink 1987 to 1999 (19)

1960:

High shoulder fill. Medium colour, good depth, pale orange rim. Tobacco nose. Round, yet lean, but some elegance, class. Mouton character. A bit acidic. Getting tired, but not bad. A pleasant surprise. (14)

1959:

Very deep, mature colour to rim. Spicy, minty nose. Very Mouton! More vegetal, leaner, and more forward than the 1961. Good, but a bit edgy. The 1961 is more concentrated and nobler. Too much dill and veggies. Having said that, it was very enjoyable. (16.5) Clearly, not as good as it can be. Having tasted this wine twice last year, and several times before, I know how great it can be.

Surprising that many tasters thought that the 1962 was as good as, if not better than, the 1961.

FLIGHT #3

1909 to 1904

1909 and 1908 had high fills, but that didn't help.

1909:

Very pale, browning colour. Madeirized nose. Some sweetness on palate. Very tired, sour. Alive, buy barely. Some hint of what it once was. (11)

1908:

Orangy colour, good depth. Oxidized, sharp, medicinal nose. Acidic, wet, cold tea with lemon juice. Gone. (0)

1907:

Mid shoulder level. Very pale yellow-orange colour. Off, medicinal nose. Rotten compost. Awful. Dead. (0)

1906:

Good depth, very mature colour. Clean nose. Some class, yet oxidizing (slightly). Some mint, sweetness; elegant finish. Very soft, acidic at end, but alive. Good, clean wine. Enjoyable. (13)

1905:

Similar colour to the 1906, but more red. Round, vegetal, dill, acidic. Drying and dying, but better by far than 1908 or 1907. A bit short, lemony, but hint of what it used to be. (11.5)

1904:

Similar appearance to 1905. Good, spicy, Cabernet nose. Some cedar, even Mouton character. Full, solid, round, rich. still a bit tannic. Good fruit. Has held surprisingly well. Very good, especially for the age and the vintage! (14)

Overall

Many of the wines had volatile acidity. These are museum pieces overall. 1904 had more structure, 1906 more elegance. Overall, a flight to forget.

FLIGHTS #4 AND #5

Prephylloxera

FLIGHT #4

1878:

Very low fill, lower-than-low shoulder. Deep, yet very brown-orange colour. Leathery, oxidized nose. How disappointing after the magnum of 1878 tasted in September 1985 in San Francisco as part of the prephylloxera tasting. Full, jammy, leathery, like molasses. Must have been something great. The intensity is there, but the poor level obviously finished this wine off. A shadow of itself. (12) Can be absolutely superb! In September 1985, I tasted a great example of this wine.

1874:

Brighter and lighter colour than the 1878. Some fruit on nose. Some dill, too, and a hint of oxidation. Fairly acidic, citric, yet some fruit, too. Quite pleasant. Still some life in it. (14)

1867:

Pale orange-Rosé. Like an old Sauternes. Dead. No use commenting on this wine. (0)

1859:

Very pale-red colour. Recorked in 1964. Almost orange. Some tobacco on nose. Some spice, but very tired. Very sharp, citric, sour, yet still alive with a hint of ripeness. Drying fast, yet drinkable. (11.5)

Another very disappointing flight.

FLIGHT #5

1870:

Very good fill. Very impressive, dark colour. Orange rim, perfume on nose. Ripe fruit, a bit sweaty at first, but opened up nicely. Flowery and delicate. Round, full, tannic, solid, still concentrated at 117 years of age! Full, ripe, a bit dry. Has held incredibly well. Touch of volatile acidity. More aged than when tasted previously. (17)

1869:

Much paler than the 1870. Tired-looking. Again: oxidized, rotten wood, medicinal nose. Sour, acidic, sharp. No life left there. (0)

1865:

The year the Civil War ended and Abraham Lincoln was assassinated. Tasted young, yet old. Phoney? Cabernet Franc added? Darkest of the flight. Incredibly spicy, intense, ripe, vegetal nose. Full, soft, a bit sharp and acidic. Not as well balanced as the 1870, but alive and kicking. Elegant, complex, delicate. Very Cabernet Franc on nose and palate (herbaceous, vegetal). Possibly doctored. (16.5)

About the 1865

The cork was odd, as was the wine. An odd cork that had a classic Mouton brand on it, yet the date, 1865, was obviously stamped with an ink substance (rather than branded). This brings me to suspect a fake, a fraud, or otherwise a very intriguing mystery. Also, the cork looked relatively young, yet stated: "Mis en bouteilles au château"! Contributed by a European collector. Be aware of fakes! Other old vintages that were recorked said "rebouché en 1980" or "1964," etc. This 1865 didn't even indicate that.

1853:

The year Baron de Rothschild purchased Mouton. Browning, deep colour. Not clear. Cloudy, mint on nose and on palate. Drying out. Getting tired, yet some resemblance of the real thing. (15)

Overall impressions

A disappointing experience. Never before have I had so many poor wines at a tasting, especially when it cost "a large fortune." The people at Mouton didn't want to contribute wines or help in the event. I wonder if they had good reasons; maybe they were afraid to threaten their remaining stock of old wine. Mouton, it seems, made a great 1870, and great wines in the 1920s, the 1940s, and 1959, 1961, 1962. Otherwise, until 1975 and 1982, this château is not reliable. The "Dr. Jekyll and Mr. Hyde" of the First Growths.

Many of the wines were purchased at auction at Christie's.

Mostly good fills. Can't really blame the auction house because they are an intermediary and if the appearance and fill are right, what else can they do? Buyer beware. As the price of rare wine is going up, it is tempting to rip off unsuspecting collectors.

Latour has been consistently good and reliable, with a minor glitch from 1983 to 1985. Otherwise, a great property.

Margaux and Lafite have gone through stages of different owners and/or winemakers. Mouton has had the same team since the early 1920s, yet it is a wine of "Boom or Bust." Either they make great wine or they screw it up completely!!

❧ November 10, 1987

Dinner and tasting of 1970 red Bordeaux, at the Four Seasons hotel, in Vancouver.

Harry Waugh was our guest speaker, accompanied by his wife Prue. I organized the wines for this event. We knew what the wines were, but not the order.

CLASSIFIED GROWTHS

1. Château Leoville-Lascases 1970:

Excellent depth. Browning rim. Spicy, herbaceous. Open, complex nose. Fruity, forward, elegant. A bit short, but some class there. Rich, ripe nose. Full, almost ready. Better than when tasted previously, but overall, Lascases should have been better—and bigger. (16)

2. CHÂTEAU LEOVILLE-BARTON 1970:

Good, dark, deep colour. Closed nose, but quite a bit of class. Needs more time. Yet, a bit volatile and excessive acidity. Not well balanced. (15)

3. CHÂTEAU DUCRU-BEAUCAILLOU 1970:

Excellent, dark colour. A bit hard yet lots of fruit. Very closed. Needs much time. Serious, solid, five to seven years. Leaner at this stage, but intense, fruity St. Julien. Full, lovely balance. The best St. Julien of the vintage. (18)

4. CHÂTEAU LATOUR 1970:

Very deep, dark, youthful colour. Cedary, ripe, complex nose. Rich, full, very tannic. Very big. Closed. Needs many years. Grande Année quality. Lovely balance. Rich, massive, concentrated. Wait ten to 20 years, but will be great. (19)

5. CHÂTEAU MONTROSE 1970:

Good, dark colour, but orange-brown, too. Closed, serious, rich, big. A bit hard on palate, but tannic. Needs ten more years! Very solid. Quite tannic. Some sharpness but great extract. (18)

6. DOMAINE DE CHEVALIER 1970:

Deep, but mature colour. Ripe, a bit acidic, forward, touch of leather. Lovely nose. Big, rich complex. Lots of breeding, richness. (18) This wine was more elegant and complex than the Montrose, true to the style of this fine property. A fine 1970.

7. CHÂTEAU FIGEAC 1970:

Lovely, open, vegetal nose. Very St. Emilion. Herbaceous, some acidity, forward, charming, elegant. Figeac? Ready, at its peak. A bit acidic. Fragrant. Needs drinking. Most forward of the lot. (17)

Overall

The wines had the depth of colour of the 1970s. Some showed maturity. Many have good tannins. Others need more time to reach their peak, especially the Latour and the Montrose. Harry Waugh is 84 years old, and is amazing in his energy and exuberance.

November 14 and 15, 1987

An extensive tasting of Château Pichon-Lalande, from 1986 back to 1875, at the Beverly Wiltshire hotel in Los Angeles.

Harry Waugh was our guest of honour and Bipin Desai organized this event. There were two sessions. May de Lencquesaing was a guest, too, and she supplied several vintages from Château Pichon-Lalande's cellars. We started right away with the tasting. We had two bottles or one magnum of most of the wines.

FLIGHT #1
1967 to 1961

1967:

Good depth of colour, tailing a bit at rim. Toast, some greenness, open, fresh, elegant nose. Very slight volatility, but open and complex, too. Thin, fairly acidic, sharp, some class, but lacking ripeness and fruit. Too stemmy and light. (13.5)

1966:

More depth than the 1967. Better colour to rim, some brown. More concentrated, riper nose, yet some stemminess here, too. Evolved bouquet. Briny. Richer than the 1967. More concentrated but a lean hard wine. Very 1966, a bit too citric finish. Should be better with food. Cabernet Franc too obvious. Some tasters commented that they liked 1967 better than 1966 (we had two bottles of each). (15)

1964, IN MAGNUM:

Very similar colour to the 1966. Better bouquet than 1966 or 1967. More chocolate, ripeness. Less greenness and stemminess. Elegant, not as expansive on nose. Subdued. Round, well put together. Good balance. Very soft, even from magnums. A most enjoyable bottle. (16.5)

1962:

Even darker than the 1964. (The 1962 vintage is renowned for its colour.) Lovely, open, perfumy nose. Flowery, no greenness. Very elegant. Round, fruity. A bit astringent, but good fruit. Has held surprisingly well, yet better on nose than on palate. A bit simple. Slight bitterness at finish and leaner than the 1964. (16)

1961, IN MAGNUM:

High shoulder fill. Good, dark colour, a bit musty. Another sample was brighter, cleaner. Classic Claret nose. Intense, ripe, rich, mature. Great class. Tannic on entry, yet lacks middle. A bit short at finish (poor decanting). Having said that, quite complex, elegant, and stylish. Needs drinking. (18)

May said that most of the 1987 was picked under rainy conditions. Also, she said that in the old days (before her time), they picked too early.

FLIGHT #2
1959 to 1950

1959:

Deep colour to rim. Excellent appearance. Soft, odd nose, some toast, delicate, flowery. Short on palate, losing its fruit. Drying out a bit and getting tired. The good colour is misleading. Some mustiness. A disappointing bottle. Second bottle: same conclusion. I've had far better examples. Can be very good. (14.5)

1958:

Medium red, pale-orange rim, showing quite a bit of orange. Sweet, beet-sugar nose, ripe, a bit stemmy underneath. Light, slightly acidic, but charming. Soft, forward, elegant. (14.5)

1957, IN MAGNUM:

Impressive, dark colour; mature rim. Some stemminess on nose. Some acidity. Good fruit. Still fresh, a bit lean, but backed by fruit. The 1957s are turning out to be much better than expected. (16)

1955:

Very good appearance (similar to the 1953, but a bit younger). Ripe, serious, mature Pauillac nose. Lovely nose. Round, fresh, fruity; touch of acidity at the end, but nevertheless very, very good. Second bottle was corked. (17.5)

1953, IN MAGNUM:

Mature, ripe, elegant, expansive nose. Delicate. Old cedar-wood. Mature red-brown colour. Soft, round, delicate, very forward. Getting tired. Good fruit, though. Most enjoyable now, but very evolved, even when tasted from a magnum. (18)

1952:

Good depth, mature rim. Riper nose than the 1953 (surprising). A bit short on palate. Good flavour. Round, fruity, like the 1955. Serious. Very Pauillac-like. Lovely wine; not great on nose, but good fruit. (17)

1950:

Evolved red colour, orange rim. Astringent, soft, but good for a 1950. Still fruity. Delicate nose; a bit green (stemmy). Has held extremely well. Good fruit. (16)

The majority preferred the 1953 to any other vintage in this flight. Very good and consistent flight overall. The 1959 was disappointing.

FLIGHT #3
1949 to 1931

1949:

Excellent appearance for such an old wine. Good depth; lovely, open, ripe, tobacco nose. Sweet, elegant, subdued, yet intense. Classic old-Claret nose, but again, the stemminess of the older vintages. A bit acidic, fairly hard, a bit sharp. Getting tired; later, I liked it better than the 1947. (17)

1947, IN MAGNUM:

Excellent, dark, impressive colour. Ripe, roasty nose; hint of truffles, wet wood. Big, solid, serious, a bit acidic, and still tannic. Tarry, losing its fruit. Ends a bit sharp. A bit earthy nose; later, developed "goût de capsule." (16)

1945:

Very good, in spite of an odd, metallic nose. Dirty barrels? Even darker than the 1947. Deep colour to rim. Lovely rich, ripe, earthy nose. Full, rich, ripe, tannic, fabulous body. Very impressive, obvious 1945. Lots of life ahead. (Another bottle was a bit vinegary and sharp and paler-looking.) (18) Not at all the coffee-bean taste I had experienced of a year ago. (Later, it developed "gôut de capsule.") Lowered score from (18) to (17) because of that.

1942:

Impressive, dark colour; mature, orange rim. A bit stemmy, yet sweet nose. Fruity, but sharp and acidic. Needs drinking. Later, nose became stemmier, but good fruit. Too green, though. (14)

1937:

Dark, mature colour, orangy rim. Dry tannins and some bitterness. Sweet (chaptalized) nose; later, mint-eucalyptus, too. Like Mouton. Sweet, yet sharp, but good fruit and even some tannin. Has held extremely well. A serious wine. Starting to dry out a bit, but very good. Held well in glass, while the 1934 got tired. (17.5)

1934:

Very similar appearance to the 1937, but a bit lighter. Minty-eucalyptus nose, like Mouton and like the 1937. Some sweetness. Full, rich, long, round, elegant. Not too tannic, slight bitterness at finish, but good ripe fruit. Later, austere and getting dry. (17)

1931:

Brown, cloudy, dirty-looking. Raisins and prunes on nose. (Another bottle was much cleaner-looking and similar nose.) Tired, pruny, acidic; has seen better days, yet alive and drinkable. Even the better bottle wasn't too pleasant, but better than ours. (13)

FLIGHT #4
1918 to 1875

1918:

Impressive depth, orangy, old-looking rim. Vegetal, yet elegant. Hint of dill. Drying, yet tannic! Some fruit, elegance, long finish. Some sweetness. Surprisingly good. (18)

1917:

Paler colour, orange-brown rim: Old wood on nose. Delicate, a bit stemmy. Made during a War year. Good fruit, not as tannic as the 1918 but more elegant. Very enjoyable. Clean, fruity, surprisingly fresh for its age. A bit paler than the 1918, more fruit and less tannic. Some decay. Both 1917 and 1918 were surprisingly good. (17)

The 1900 and 1899 were purchased by Hardy Rodenstock in Belgium. Hardy is the famous German discoverer of rare and old wines. He took part in this tasting. Sometimes I am not so sure as to how truly "old and rare" these wines really are.

1900, IN MAGNUM:

Chocolate, mocha nose. Mature, clear colour. Similar cork and smell to the 1865 Mouton tasted earlier this year. Also, printed date on cork is unusual. It is obvious that the date was printed on the cork later rather than its being branded. Orange-brown. Similar impressions on palate. Oak, some fruit. A bit acidic. Very individual, very unusual. Hard to describe. Incredible length, as if chocolate liqueur was added. Hard to rank this. Buy a box of chocolates instead! I decided not to give this wine a score, as I have suspicions that it may have been tampered with.

1899, IN MAGNUM:

Very small crop. Frost in April, half-average harvest. Picked from September 20 to 29. Pale, but clear, brown-orange colour. Slightly vinegary nose. Madeirized, acidic, sharp. Tired, but alive. Later, buttery nose. (14)

1893, IN DOUBLE-MAGNUM:

The source of this rare double-magnum is Hardy Rodenstock. Apparently Rodenstock found this in a mysterious wine cellar in Venezuela. Excellent, deep colour to rim for the age. Oak-chocolate, ripe nose. Hint of mint, similar impressions on palate. Full, dark, rich, big, chewy, lots of fruit. Incredible structure. Very impressive. Very good, but unusual. Chocolate again! Take the score with a grain of chocolate (!) because this is very unusual. Attractive; later, chocolate with a hint of oak. (17)

1892:

Palish, orange-red colour. Dull on nose. Some fruit. Hint of leather, cold tea, getting tired. Sharp, acidic, short, but alive. Some fruit. Elegant, well structured. Amazing for such an old wine. Almost too fresh. A fake? A bit spirity and artificial chocolate liqueur. Hard to judge. (17)

1875:

Hermitagé? Impressive, dark, deep colour, if a bit cloudy. Vegetal, rich nose. Full, rich, tannic, loaded with fruit, but hint of oxidation; yet impressive for its age. Biggest of flight! The only prephylloxera wine of the evening. Concentrated prephylloxera wine. (17)

The 1875 was made under the supervision of the first Comtesse de Lalande. Later, the second Comtesse de Lalande made the wine. She died in 1916. Her son was killed in the Great War. In 1920, a new generation (two nephews) took over. So we tasted wines made under diverse winemakers and heirs.

Sunday Noon, November 15, 1987

At the Beverly Wiltshire hotel.

SECOND SESSION

Château Pichon-Lalande 1875 to 1986

FLIGHT #1

Réserve de la Comtesse 1985 to 1982

This is the second wine of Pichon-Lalande.

1985:

Very dense, deep, dark colour to rim. Fresh, toasty nose. Hint of greenness. Elegant, fresh, medium tannins, well balanced, obviously young vines (lacking ripeness), but top quality if sold at reasonable price. Complexity is there. Drink 1992 to 1998. (15)

1984:

Made from 100% Cabernet. The little Merlot that was available went into the Grand Vin. Impressive, dark colour for a 1984. Even darker than the 1985 with more purple, but not quite as dark as the 1983 or 1982. Touch of volatility on nose. Obviously chaptalized. Quite solid, but lacking the fruit of the 1985. Fairly alcoholic. Solid for 1984. Drink 1990 to 1993.

1983:

Very good, purplish colour to rim. Delicate nose. Slightly herbaceous, vegetal (young vines). Obvious wood coming through. Tannic, leaner, more classic-style Pauillac. Good fruit. Needs at least five years. Very good! (16.5)

1982:

Dark colour, yet surprisingly, not as dark as the 1983 at this tasting. Still young and youthful. Round, elegant nose. No sharp edges. Full, rich, serious. Great extract and backbone. Needs seven to ten years. I was in a minority there. Most tasters preferred the 1983. (17)

Réserve de la Comtesse goes through the same treatment and vinification as the Grand Vin, but made from the fruit of younger vines.

Another comment on last night's session

Most of the vineyard of Pichon-Lalande was pulled out gradually after the attack of phylloxera and replanting was gradual, so that some of the wines of the late 1880 to 1910s were made with partly prephylloxera ungrafted vines and partly with grafted vines.

FLIGHT #2

Pichon-Lalande 1986 to 1979

1986 BARREL SAMPLE:

Very deep, dense, dark colour (will be bottled in the summer of 1988). Very ripe, tannic, rich, masculine, serious Pauillac. Closed and unyielding. Full, rich, tannic, serious. Great potential. Even Petit Verdot was great in 1986! (8% Petit Verdot.) Incredible fruit extract, balance, and tannins. Ripe, classic, raspberries, great future. Definitely one to buy! No score; barrel sample.

1985:

Much more elegant than the 1986. Medium red-purple; good depth. Herbal, elegant, oak-vanilla. Great charm but surprisingly forward. Lovely balance, style, and class. Drink from 1993 to 1998. Quite soft, and developed. (17) Other tasters liked it more and said that 1985 is an elegant vintage. I agree. 1985 was a fine vintage, but the wines will become accessible relatively early, around 1993 to 1995. The 1986 is definitely more serious.

1984:

Good depth for a 1984; like 1985, but a bit more maturity at rim. Clean nose, a bit green, yet ripe, leaner, more tannic. Good body. Good effort for the vintage. Drink 1990 to 1994. (15)

1983:

Excellent, deep colour. Unyielding, closed nose. Full, tannic, serious, long, oak-vanilla and fruit extract. Big, rich. Great potential; superb. Needs ten or more years, though. Great balance. Classic Pauillac. Should be great around 1995 to 1998 and beyond. (18) A lot of dampness in 1983; tropical summer. Chemicals helped control the red spider and rot.

1982:

Typical, very dark, intense colour of the 1982s. Almost black to rim. Ripe, rich, fruit with hint of oak-vanilla. No stemminess. Full, rich, big, tannic, solid, very ripe. Superb. Needs ten to 15 years. Very great in 1982. Having modern technology and temperature control was crucial in this vintage. (18.5)

1981:

Good, deep, dark colour, lighter than above (1982) and showing some age. Similar to 1983. Spicy, lovely minty nose. Resemblance to Mouton or Lynch-Bages. Round, elegant, yet still solid. Sweet, fruity, slightly shorter and more acidic than above, but very good. Elegant, but not a weakling. Needs five to seven years. Very good; lots of class. (17.5)

1980:

Soft, elegant nose. Impressive dark colour for vintage. Soft, sweet, forward, ready. Fruity. Drink it while at its peak. Very good effort for the vintage. (14.5)

1979:

Very similar appearance to 1981 (colour). Closed, unyielding nose, yet ripe. Some greenness. Full, rich, soft, forward. Almost ready (drink 1988 to 1998). Full, round, well balanced. Very 1979 style. Very good quality. Lots of ripe fruit. A bit stemmy. (17.5)

Great flight and great potential! This is the modern "golden era" of Château Pichon-Longueville, Comtesse de Lalande.

FLIGHT #3

1978 to 1970

The 1976 and 1975 were made by Michel Delon of Château Leoville-Lascases, at a time when the heirs of Pichon-Lalande were having some problems as to how the property should be run, and by whom.

1978:

A bit stemmy, lots of Cabernet Sauvignon. Deep, mature colour. Lovely, ripe nose. Complex, round, very Cabernet spiciness. Surprisingly ripe for a big Cabernet year. Serious, solid, well balanced. Less obvious oak-vanilla. More fruit extract. Excellent potential by 1992. (18) This property uses a fairly large proportion of Merlot for a Pauillac. The lack of Merlot in 1978 has changed the style of this wine. Fine effort nevertheless.

1976:

Mature, medium-red colour; orange rim. Soft, forward, open, sweet. Needs drinking while it is still alive. Finishes a bit short. Drink up. Good for the vintage. (15)

1975:

Similar appearance to the 1978. Less stemmy on nose. More subdued and unyielding. Big, full, serious, tannic, very 1975, but with lots of ripe fruit backing it up. Needs ten more years. Great balance. Second bottle had a touch of volatility. Ours was great. (18) As in 1978, the Merlot suffered from coulure.

1970:

Good, deep, mature colour. Forthcoming, classic nose of fine, mature Claret. A touch leathery. Rich, ripe, full, long, and not tannic any more. At its peak. Ripe fruit. Lovely now. Great fragrance. The only wine of the flight that is truly ready to be drunk. The second bottle was a bit metallic and not quite as good. (18)

An excellent flight.

FLIGHT #4
1929 to 1920

1929:

Very mature, orange colour. Good depth and bright. Tea leaves on nose. Touch of leather and oxidation. Spicy, round, a bit short, some acidity. Tired, but sound. Honeydew aftertaste. Perfumy. Some good fruit left. (15.5)

1928:

Better depth of colour than the 1929. Younger-looking, touch of sulphur on nose. Good fruit, lively, quite tannic. Very 1928; solid structure. Lovely wine, holding better than the 1929. Overall, the 1929 had a more complex nose than the 1928, but the 1928 was better structured. (17)

1926:

Paler than the 1928, similar to 1929. Delicate, hint of tobacco. Charming nose. Round, soft, not as elegant as the 1929, or as big as the 1928, but quite pleasant. At the end of its life. Later, it became a bit medicinal. (14.5)

1924:

Appearance similar to the 1926. Drying out. Wet, rotting wood; a bit pruny and medicinal. Very dry. Acidic; still alive, but barely. A bit corked. Second bottle was better, cleaner. (13)

1921:

Surprisingly bright, dark, mature colour. Lovely, elegant, flowery nose. Lots of class here and fresh for its age. Fruity, round, well balanced. Still very much alive. A superb wine. My favourite of the flight. Incredible! Elegance, charm, yet has body and structure. The star of the two-day event. (19.5) Unfortunately, the second bottle was corked.

1923:

Similar colour to 1924 and 1926. Some dill. Odd, medicinal, leathery nose. Tired, sweet, short, but still drinkable. A bit astringent at end. Drying out and acidic. (13)

1920:

Similar colour to 1923, 1924, and 1926 (very consistent). Clean, mature nose. A bit herbaceous. A bit astringent, acidic, and short at end. Later, rotting wood and earth on nose; yet good fruit. Has lasted well. (15.5)

The two outstanding wines of the flight: 1928 and 1921. The 1929 was lovely, but faded too fast. Overall, an outstanding tasting; we tasted history here.

The 1920, 1924, and 1926 were recorked at the château, but not our bottles, which had the original cork. Both bottles of the 1923 came from the château. The other older vintages were acquired at auction or from several collectors.

It was nice to see my friends again, including Harry Waugh, who visited us in Vancouver last week.

Later that day, I went to Dr. Brad Klein's residence, where Harry and Prue Waugh were staying.

We tried a bottle of this Champagne.

Tarlant Père et Fils Brut Tradition N/V Champagne Oeuilly, Près Epernay:

Not bad at all for a very reasonably priced N/V Champagne. Crisp, elegant, round, toasty. Not very intense, but quite good. Some sweetness and decent fruit. (15.5)

Then Prue, Harry, Brad, and I went out to a new restaurant in Los Angeles called "Champagne," where we had a lovely meal and some fine wines.

1982 Meursault-Genevrières, Louis Jadot:

A lovely wine. Rich, round, nutty, well balanced, and long. Very good. Ready and holding well. (17)

1966 and 1916 Château La Conseillante, Pomerol:

The 1966 had a good, dark colour, showing some maturity at rim, but bright red, too. Good fruit, yet a bit metallic on nose and a leaner-style wine, with noticeable acidity on palate. Good but not "very" good. (15)

The 1916 was something else. Produced by female workers in the middle of World War I (the men were at the Front), the level was excellent; the cork indicates that this wine must have been recorked at the Château in the last ten years or so. I decanted the wine, showing an interested young waiter how decanting should be done. On the label was printed in small letters "fait entièrement par nos femmes."

Very good, dark colour for such an old wine, obviously more brown and orange than its fruity complex cigar-box nose of mature Claret would indicate. Well balanced, full, rich, long. Clean finish. Lots of class here. Very impressive for such an old wine. Much better than the 1966. An extremely rare wine and a great experience. (18) Harry Waugh was impressed, too. He has never tasted a 1916 La Conseillante before.

Winston Churchill

Harry told us an interesting story about his encounter with Winston Churchill and Sir Bernard Baruch while Harry was an officer in the Welsh Guards during World War II.

During the War, Harry was a company commander in the Welsh guards. One weekend, their company was assigned the task of protecting the Prime Minister at his weekend residence in Chequers. One morning, while Churchill was taking a walk in the gardens, he approached Harry and his second-in-command and asked them if they would like to have dinner with him that night. Of course, they agreed. At dinner, there was a fourth person present, Sir Bernard Baruch, President Roosevelt's personal envoy.

Harry and his comrade feasted on steak and kidney pie, Champagne, coffee, Cognac, and cigars—unheard of luxuries during the War years in Britain. At the end of the meal, Sir Bernard asked Churchill about rumours that there was a tendency in the British Officers Corps to vote Labour in general elections. Harry Waugh's colleague, under the influence of the relaxed atmosphere no doubt, replied that indeed it was so! Churchill raised his eyes, looked at the two young officers and said: "Young men, dismissed!" Harry and the second officer got up and politely left the dining room.

November 24 to 29, 1987

Trip to Napa Valley and San Francisco.

November 24, 1987

Dinner at Joe and Alice Heitz's.

We tasted three decent, but less than impressive, Chardonnays from New Zealand.

KUMEU RIVER WINES 1986 CHARDONNAY:

A gift to Joe by the owner Mr. Brajkovich. Good, deep-gold colour. Rich oak on nose, but good Chardonnay character. Fairly full, rich, a bit unbalanced (too much alcohol) and prematurely tired. Pleasant on entry, but dull finish. Best of the bunch, though. (14)

COOKS PRIVATE BIN 1986 CHARDONNAY:

A noncommercial sample given to Joe. A bit lighter in colour. Greener, stemmier nose. Fresher than the Kumeu and fruitier on nose, but flabby, too much wood, and not enough varietal character on palate. Finished short and dull. (13)

CORBANS PRIVATE BIN 1984 CHARDONNAY:

Thick, alcoholic, little nose. Tired, flat. Spent five months in oak. Fair bit of acidity. Disappointing but drinkable. (12.5)

Maybe in the future, New Zealand will produce fine white wines. These three were not impressive.

Then we tried Joe Heitz's own Chardonnay.

1983 HEITZ CELLARS CHARDONNAY, NAPA VALLEY:

From a lot that was returned by a mid-Western wholesaler who said the wine was no good! Well, it wasn't great (nor was it meant to be), but it had a good, rich colour and a good, buttery, Chardonnay nose. Fairly rich, thick, a bit too alcoholic. Overall, quite a good wine and I don't see what the fuss was all about. Clearly better than the three Kiwi Chardonnays. (15)

Then, we had this lovely bottle.

1961 CHÂTEAU MALESCOT-ST.-EXUPÉRY, MARGAUX:

Excellent level. I decanted it. A wine with a deserved reputation. Joe told me that I had told him a while back that the wine is ready and should be drunk. Well, it didn't disappoint us! Lovely, incredibly, young, dark colour. Rich, spicy, complex, ripe nose of great intensity. Full, rich, ripe, long on palate. Well balanced. A lovely wine from a great vintage. (18)

Before I left, Joe gave me a bottle of Alberta peach wine made by an ex-student of his. I recommended that they buy for their grandchildren (born in 1985 and 1986) some 1985 Graham's Vintage Port and 1986 Châteaux Margaux, Pichon-Lalande, and Mouton.

Friday, November 27, 1987

International Wine and Food Society Black Tie Dinner, in honour of Paul Pinski's 75th birthday, at the Clift Four Seasons hotel, in San Francisco.

APERITIFS

CHAMPAGNE BILLECART-SALMON 1975 "CUVÉE NF BILLECART" BRUT

AND

CHAMPAGNE BOLLINGER "RD" BRUT 1975:

The Billecart was a bit sweeter, rounder, with an odd peppery taste. At its peak, quite soft and pleasant. (17)

The Bollinger was more classic, yeast-toast nose. Good fruit/acidity balance, rich, long. Classic Champagne that is holding very well. (18)

1982 CORTON-CHARLEMAGNE, BONNEAU DU MARTRAY:

Fresh, nutty on nose and palate. A bit lean and steely, but good fruit, too. Well balanced, still youthful. Should peak around 1989 to 1990. Green-gold colour. (17)

1970 MONTRACHET, MARQUIS DE LAGUICHE, DROUHIN:

Deep gold, woody, oxidizing; a bit flat and flabby. Another bottle had better fruit on palate and was livelier, but old on nose. Has seen better days. Not nearly as good as the 1970 Montrachet of Domaine de la Romanée-Conti tasted just over a year ago. (15.5)

1974 Vosne-Romanée, Leroy:

Medium-light colour. Clean, spicy, round, forward. Good backbone. Very good for the year and for a simple Villages wine. (15.5)

Then, we had three rare jeroboams (in Burgundy, this is the equivalent of a double-magnum or four bottles) of Romanée-Conti 1961, 1964, and 1971.

These are extremely rare, very expensive wines, costing between $1,600 and $4,000 per jeroboam!

Romanée-Conti 1961, in jeroboam:

Medium colour, showing some maturity. Round, spicy, delicate, complex. At its peak, even in such a large format. This wine costs a small fortune these days. Somehow, 1961 red Burgundies lack the depth and richness of the 1959s. (16)

Romanée-Conti 1964, in jeroboam:

Very disappointing. Oxidized, pruny on both nose and palate. Tired, acidic, over-the-hill. 1964 is a fine vintage for red Burgundies, and Romanée-Conti is a famous vineyard. In this case, however, a total failure, and a very expensive one at that. (13)

Romanée-Conti 1971, in jeroboam:

By far, the best of all three. Darkest colour, liveliest. Good fruit, well balanced, rich, round, long. Not quite at its peak. Great raspberry complexity. (18.5)

1979 Château d'Yquem, in magnums:

Still very young, bright gold, medium intensity, impeccable balance, long, complex, crisp, still fresh. Needs four to five more years, especially in magnums. Nice botrytis and fruit. Fine effort for a 1979, but that is what a great property is expected to do. (18)

Saturday, November 28, 1987

Paul Pinski's 75th birthday, at the Stanford Court hotel, in San Francisco.

APERITIF

Champagne Roederer "Cristal" Brut 1981:

A lovely, long, complex, stylish Champagne. Tiny bubbles, classy, still fresh and young, fruity. Very well balanced. Very generous pours through the reception. (18)

1976 Corton-Charlemagne "Diamond Jubilee," Remoissenet and Avery's:

Most tables had the Avery's-bottling. Nutty, complex, rich, long, well balanced, and has held well for a 1976. (17.5) Most 1976s, including Latour's Corton-Charlemagne, are flabby now.

The Remoissenet-bottling (of which there were a few bottles) was even richer, spicier, and more intense. (18)

La Tâche 1971, Domaine de la Romanée-Conti, in magnums:

Paul was very generous, opening nine magnums of this wine! A superb (and consistent) wine, especially from magnums. Much better than any of the Romanée-Contis we had on the previous night (from jeroboams). Good depth of colour. Marvellous, complex, spicy-raspberries nose. Hint of barnyard, rich, long. Beautiful balance on palate. Great length and class. One of the greatest red Burgundies I have ever tasted. Ready but no rush, especially from magnums. (19)

1967 Château d'Yquem:

One of the great Sauternes of the century. Surprisingly deep-amber colour and forward, yet a superb bottle nevertheless. (I'm sure that it is a matter of proper storage, because my own bottles of 1967 d'Yquem are paler and fresher.) Great intensity on nose. Ripe botrytis and raisins. Mellow, long, full, forward, with great depth on palate, but these samples are getting tired. (18) The best would rate a perfect (20).

1912 Bas Armagnac "Château La Brise":

Bottled in 1985 (73 years in wood!); 1912 is Paul's birth year. Very good, deep, amber colour. Delicate, sweet, complex nose of fine Armagnac; mellow, long, very rich on palate. Great.

A lovely three-day event, marred by a nasty cold I had. Our host Paul Pinski is a very generous and kind man.

January 14 to 17, 1988

Four-day marathon tasting, featuring 1945 Bordeaux, at Dr. Brad Klein's residence, in Los Angeles.

A group of 14 wine aficionados met in Los Angeles at the home of Dr. Brad Klein, the organizer of this most extraordinary event: a three-day, five-session winetasting of the 1945 Bordeaux vintage. An incredible array—no fewer than 101 red Bordeaux, four dry white Bordeaux (Graves), and 11 Sauternes, as well as five Champagnes—was tasted and evaluated.

I do not know of a more extensive tasting of the 1945 vintage ever held anywhere!

It took Dr. Klein, with the help of other participants, several years to put this tasting together. The majority of the wines were contributed by Dr. Klein. For me, this is a particularly important, and fortunate, vintage; it is my birth year.

The 14 participants included Dr. Klein, Bipin Desai (who organized an earlier extensive tasting of the 1945 vintage Bordeaux); Ed Lazarus; John Tilson, founder and managing editor of The Underground Wine Journal, *formerly* The Underground Wineletter*); Nathan Chroman; Dr. Haskell Norman of San Francisco; Dr. Frank Robinson; Randy Sultan; and Dennis Overstreet (a wine merchant from Beverly Hills). From Chicago came John Hart (co-owner of The Chicago Wine Company), and from Massachusetts, Mr. George Buehler. Jeffrey Troy came from New York (as did his sister Alexandra Troy, who catered this extraordinary event). Sid Cross and I formed the Canadian contingent.*

At 42 years of age, these wines have spent an average of 40 years in bottle.

Based on my past experiences tasting old wines, I expected a lot of bottle variation. Some wines tasted better than on previous occasions; others were disappointing. This is, of course, to be expected with such old wines, coming from various sources and different storage conditions. The scores of each individual wine are my own. I have indicated where they differ substantially from the majority.

The wines were château-bottled, unless otherwise indicated. With only one exception, they were all regular-size bottles. Wines in larger bottles, such as magnums, age better and stay at their peak for several more years.

One of the most important factors in the maturity of a wine is the level of the wine in bottle. Therefore our host prepared a code that appears just behind the name of the individual château, indicating the level, as follows.

HF:	High fill
N:	Neck level
BN:	Bottom neck
TS:	Top shoulder
US:	Upper shoulder
MS:	Mid shoulder
LS:	Low shoulder

The wines were decanted by flights immediately prior to tasting. As expected, several of the wines were quite tannic (a characteristic of this great and long-lived vintage). The order of the wines was known to us in advance.

Thursday evening, January 14, 1988

FIRST SESSION

1945 St. Estèphes and St. Emilions

APERITIF

CHAMPAGNE KRUG "GRANDE CUVÉE" BRUT N/V, IN MAGNUMS:

Complex, yeasty, well structured. A big, rich Champagne. Classic Krug. Good depth, earthy, fairly fruity, yet obviously some age in bottle. Very good. (18)

Each session was preceded by a 1945 vintage Champagne.

MASSÉ 1945 BRUT CHAMPAGNE, MASSÉ PÈRE ET FILS, REIMS:

Very deep, gold colour. Nose slightly oxidized, not unlike a Sherry, mixed with wet earth overtones. Some fizz there. Good acidity, but very old-tasting, with hint of residual sugar. (14)

FLIGHT #1

1945 St. Emilions

CHÂTEAU L'ANGÉLUS (N):

Medium, mature-red colour with good depth and orangy rim. Earthy, mature, open nose with some complexity. Quite flavourful, rich, and round on palate. Well balanced and a bit tannic. Good fruit, slightly herbaceous. Typical (and good) St. Emilion. (17)

CHÂTEAU BÂLESTARD-LA-TONNELLE (BN):

Bâlestard's wines are big and chunky for St. Emilion, even in recent vintages. Darkest wine of flight. Deep red colour to rim. Mushrooms and oak on nose. Ripe fruit, too. A full, chunky wine on palate. Solid, hard, and concentrated. Not much complexity there, but no rush drinking it. I liked it more than most. (16.5)

CHÂTEAU GRAND-BARRAIL-LAMARZELLE-FIGEAC (BN):

Medium-red colour with good depth. A bit darker than the L'Angélus. Quite vegetal on nose, developing good complexity after a few minutes in glass. Round, elegant, earthy, and a bit tannic. Later, the wine got tired and dried up. Needs drinking. (15)

FLIGHT #2

1945 St. Emilions

CHÂTEAU CLOS FOURTET (TS):

Medium, mature red colour. Elegant, open, and sweet nose. Stylish, elegant, and round. After a few minutes in the glass, however, it dried out, with quite a bit of acidity coming through. The excessive acidity seemed to bother me more than it did other tasters. Needs drinking. I've had this wine twice before and both times, the wine was far superior to this bottle. (15)

Château Magdelaine (BN), Bordeaux-bottled by Hannapier-Peyrelongue:

Good, deep colour, showing some maturity at rim. Lovely intensity and bouquet. Full, rich, ripe, and long on palate. Ripe raisins, lots of extract. Excellent balance. Not unlike a super 1947 Pomerol. Unanimously, an excellent bottle. Best wine of flight. (18)

Château Trottevieille (MS):

Palish-red, orangy colour. Hint of oxidation on nose, but sweet, elegant fruit, too. On palate: slightly pruny, acidic, finishing short. Cracking up, yet tasted better than it smelled. Obviously the low level in bottle has damaged this wine. Can be very good. (14)

FLIGHT #3

1945 St. Emilions

Château Canon (TS):

Good appearance. Slightly minty, delicate nose. Elegance and perfume rather than ripe fruit. On palate: earthy, leathery, very dry. Hard and tannic, drying out. The finish, though, was complex. (15.5)

Château La Gaffelière (US):

Medium red, orangy rim. A bit musty on nose. Some mint on palate. Hard, lean, and acidic. Finished quite complex, but too dry. A controversial wine. Some found it round and elegant. Scored as low as 15 and as high as 18! (16.5)

Château Pavie (US):

Deep, brownish colour. Very ripe, sweet, pruny nose with some volatility. Quite tannic, pruny, and leathery. Not unlike a mature Syrah. Finished a bit medicinal. (14.5)

FLIGHT #4

1945 St. Emilions

Château Ausone (BN), London-bottled by Avery's of Bristol:

Good, dark colour to rim. Hint of cabbage on nose. Full, rich, and chunky on palate. Slightly metallic, concentrated fruit. A good wine. Most tasters preferred it to the château-bottling. While I liked it, I found it uncharacteristic for Ausone, which produces leaner, more austere wines. Maybe some "foreign agent" was added to this wine, such as brandy or a big Rhône wine? (16.5)

Château Ausone (TS), château-bottled:

Medium-red colour, showing quite a bit of maturity. Subdued, elegant nose. Tannic, dry, quite hard, classy, and complex. Finished clean. A serious wine. Ausone usually is. It requires many years to reach its peak. (17)

Château Ausone (US), London-bottled by Civil Service:

Similar appearance to the château-bottling. Oxidized, wet cardboard nose. Skunky, leathery, and oxidized on palate. Smells like the civil service—in any country! (12)

Château Cheval-Blanc (US), London-bottled by Berry Bros.:

Darker than the château-bottling, with orangy rim. Some volatility on nose. Sweet, yet simple on entry, finishing dry. Hard, tannic, and medicinal. The sturdiness of the 1945s, but lacking complexity or finesse. I have tasted much finer examples of this wine. (14.5)

Château Cheval-Blanc (BN), château-bottled:

Pleasant, subdued nose. Lighter colour than the London-bottling, orangy rim. Round and soft, without the tannic backbone of other 1945s. Later, it developed some complexity in the glass. I liked it more than most. Some tasters found it too spirity. (17)

Thus ended the St. Emilion group. The quality of the Magdelaine surprised us all; an outstanding wine.

FLIGHT #5

1945 St. Estèphes

Five different bottlings of Château Calon-Ségur, other than château-bottled.

Château Calon-Ségur (BN), London-bottled by Civil Service:

Good depth, orange rim. Cigar-box, open nose. Elegant, mature Claret at entry, but a bit medicinal. Dry, acidic, showing some fruit, but too hard. Lacks class and drying out. Later, it smelled unclean, too. (13)

Château Calon-Ségur (N), London-bottled by Cockburn and Co.:

Similar appearance to the Civil Service bottle. Closed, unyielding nose. Dry, hard, tannic, no fruit. A very lean wine. (14)

Château Calon-Ségur (BN), Belgian-bottled by Demets and Lyssens:

Darker colour, medicinal, oxidizing nose. Sour, acidic, sharp, and pruny. Very unpleasant. (11)

Château Calon-Ségur (BN), Scottish-bottled by Matthew Gloag:

Bright-red colour with orange-brown overtones. Open, toasty, elegant nose. Slightly herbaceous. Some fruit but hard St. Estèphe style. However, backed by reasonable fruit. Finished clean, with hint of coffee beans. This wine was a bit controversial. I liked it more than most did. (15)

CHÂTEAU CALON-SÉGUR (TS), LONDON-BOTTLED BY JOHN HARVEY'S:

Odd, skunky nose. Vegetables and barnyard. Drying out. Too hard and no fruit. (12)

FLIGHT #6

1945 St. Estèphes

CHÂTEAU CALON-SÉGUR (BN), CHÂTEAU-BOTTLED:

Clearly the best of all six bottlings of Calon that night. Good, dark colour. Nose was a bit unclean at first, but cleared after a while. Round, fruity, well balanced, tannic. Serious stuff. I have tasted superb samples of this wine on two occasions over the past four years. (16.5) Can easily rate (18), if from a good source.

CHÂTEAU COS D'ESTOURNEL (BN):

Palish, brick-red colour. Clean, elegant, and slightly sweet smell. Dry, hard, and tannic on palate, lacking fruit. I was kinder to this wine than other tasters. (15)

CHÂTEAU MONTROSE (US):

Medium-red colour with good depth. Palish rim. Slightly pruny, spicy nose. Full, quite rich, and fruity. Solid and masculine. Best example of 1945 Montrose I have ever tasted. On both previous occasions, it was dried out. (16.5)

Overall

The St. Estèphes were disappointing. Granted, they had that commune's characteristics of hard, serious wines, but most lacked fruit.

DESSERT WINES

1945 CHÂTEAU DOISY-DAËNE (TS):

Bright, deep-gold colour with a green hue. Fresh, clean, and crisp nose with a very slight hint of sulphur. Delicate on palate; long, clean, and complex. Honeyed and fruity with good botrytis. Much younger-tasting than its age would indicate. Very good. (17)

1945 CHÂTEAU DOISY-VÉDRINES (TS):

Brilliant, deep-golden colour. Nose of mature Sauternes with hint of wood. Thick, heavy wine, yet fruit drying out. A bit earthy. Has seen better days. If you own any, try it with foie gras or as an aperitif. (15)

WHITE CHARTREUSE:

The first session ended with a rare gem. Old, very rare, white Chartreuse liqueur, made in the 1878 to 1903 period, before the Chartreux monks were expelled from France to Tarragona, Spain (1903). From a one-litre bottle. Very pale, almost water colour. Thick, full, and spicy; this lovely, complex liqueur is made from over 100 different spices and herbs. The label read: "Liqueur fabriqué a la Grande Chartreuse, L. Garnier."

Friday, January 15, 1988

Lunch at "Citrus," in Los Angeles.

Six of us went for lunch to a new and fashionable restaurant called "Citrus," in Hollywood. Chef (and part-owner) Michel Richard is a friendly Frenchman. He is a great dessert chef (we tasted six different desserts, all fabulous, and lovely individual crème-brûlée tarts, bite-size).

Brad Klein brought along two bottles of red Burgundy.

1971 BONNES MARES, DROUHIN-LAROSE:

Excellent fill, little sediment. Surprisingly pale-orangy colour. Open, complex nose of Pinot Noir, barnyard, and some dill that cleared after a while. Quite flowery and soft. Surprisingly forward for such a young wine. Pleasant, but disappointing for what it was. (16)

1959 RICHEBOURG, AVERY'S:

Ullage one inch from cork. Much darker, fuller, and fruitier than the much younger Bonnes Mares. Fruity, meaty, rich, round. Not as complex as the Bonnes Mares, but very good. (17)

These two red Burgundies were purchased at Christie's London and shipped last month to Los Angeles.

Friday, January 15, 1988

SECOND SESSION

1945 white and red Graves and St. Juliens.

APERITIF

CHAMPAGNE POL ROGER BRUT "CUVÉE WINSTON CHURCHILL" 1979, IN MAGNUM:

Toasty, complex nose. Masculine, hard, and steely, but backed by enough fruit. Needs two to four extra years of bottle-age. Promising. (18)

CHAMPAGNE CHARLES HEIDSIECK 1945 "EXTRA DRY":

Deep-gold colour, not unlike old Sauternes. Flat, sour, bitter, and oxidized. May it rest in peace. (No score.)

FLIGHT #1

1945 White Graves

CHÂTEAU BOUSCAUT BLANC "EXTRA SEC" (TS):

Brilliant, bright-gold colour. Earthy, subdued nose, with slight hint of botrytis. Soft, round, rich, and full. Lovely balance. Rich, with a hint of residual sugar on palate. Ripe Semillon-like. Some tasters wondered if this wine actually began its life in bottle as a semisweet wine. Great quality. (18)

CHÂTEAU HAUT-BRION BLANC (MS):

Deep, golden colour. Lighter-bodied than the Bouscaut. Earthy nose with lovely perfume. Quite thick and rich on palate, with hint of cabbage.

Finished a bit steely. Great balance and class here. Intense, long, and stylish. Hint of oak at finish. Some tasters weren't as excited as I was about this wine. (17.5)

CHÂTEAU LAVILLE-HAUT-BRION (US):

Bright, deep-gold colour. Young-looking for its age. Delicate, perfumy nose. Subdued and elegant. Round, soft, and rich, if not as intense as the Haut-Brion. Still lively, crisp, with good fruit/acidity balance. Hint of lilacs on nose. Very good. (17)

CHÂTEAU LAVILLE-HAUT-BRION "CRÈME DE TÊTE" (HF):

Extremely rare. A single barrel (25 cases) was produced in 1945! Deepest, darkest of the lot. Slight hint of botrytis on nose. Full, rich, and long with incredible depth and balance. Made from very ripe grapes, not unlike a fine "Y" (dry wine of d'Yquem). An outstanding bottle and a great "once in a lifetime" experience. A revelation. (19)

A great flight! This was one of the three top (and consistent) flights of the whole event. Who said that dry white wines cannot age?

FLIGHT #2

1945 St. Juliens

CHÂTEAU BEYCHEVELLE (BN):

Medium, mature colour with good depth. Open, forthcoming, flowery, toasty, complex nose. Slightly leathery, but no sign of oxidation. Full and rich on palate, long and complex. Made with very ripe grapes. Lovely fruit, without the hard tannins of so many 1945s. At this tasting, the most outstanding St. Julien. (18)

CHÂTEAU BRANAIRE-DUCRU (BN):

Similar appearance to the Beychevelle. Subdued nose, slightly vegetal. Hard, acidic, with some sharpness. A leaner wine, showing signs of drying up. Earthy and hard. Needs drinking. Had some fruit, though. Some tasters gave this wine a lower score. (16)

CHÂTEAU TALBOT (HF):

Very high fill, like a wine that had just been bottled. Not recorked; original cork. Lighter colour than the above. Oxidized nose. Sweet on palate; thin and tired. (13) Pity, because Talbot has produced an outstanding 1945; tasted twice previously and on both occasions rated (18).

FLIGHT #3

1945 St. Juliens

CHÂTEAU LANGOA-BARTON (N), BORDEAUX-BOTTLED BY BARTON ET GUESTIER:

Excellent appearance. Deep, impressive colour. Delicate, subdued nose of mature Claret, but a bit pruny. Woody and medicinal, too. Hard, acidic, lead-pencil on palate. Leathery and unusual. Hint of barnyard, too. (Poor storage in old barrels?) (13)

This was followed by four different bottlings of Château Leoville-Barton.

CHÂTEAU LEOVILLE-BARTON (N), LONDON-BOTTLED BY BLOCK, GRAY, AND BLOCK:

Good, dark, mature colour. Rich and ripe on nose; full and youthful. Round, well balanced, with good backbone and tannins. Fruity with lots of depth. Ending a bit tired. Needs drinking. I liked it more than most. (16.5)

CHÂTEAU LEOVILLE-BARTON (US), CHÂTEAU-BOTTLED:

Mature colour with quite a bit of orange and brown. Pale rim. Open, round, forward nose, a bit stewed. Some complexity, but a bit too dry. Tannic, lean, and losing its fruit. Needs drinking. Leoville-Barton can be outstanding in 1945, but not at this tasting. (16)

CHÂTEAU LEOVILLE-BARTON (TS), LONDON-BOTTLED BY COCKBURN AND CAMPBELL:

Medium, red colour, orangy rim. Ripe, sweet nose. On palate: dry, medicinal, leathery, and very tannic. Lacks fruit. (14.5)

CHÂTEAU LEOVILLE-BARTON (BN), LONDON-BOTTLED BY CORNEY AND BARROW:

Paler than the Cockburn-bottling. Delicate, perfumy nose. Round and delicate on palate; complex, but excessive acidity and short finish. A solid 1945; some tannin left but getting tired. Enjoyable nevertheless. (15.5)

FLIGHT #4

1945 St. Juliens

CHÂTEAU DUCRU-BEAUCAILLOU (US):

My fifth experience with this property of the 1945 vintage, and my fifth disappointment. Mature colour. Oxidized, musty nose. Sour, acidic, and a bit corked. Has anyone tasted a good bottle of 1945 Ducru? (12)

CHÂTEAU GRUAUD-LAROSE (BN):

Impressive, dark colour. Impressive on palate. Full, rich, chunky wine. Unyielding, closed nose. Solid, hard, but backed by enough ripe fruit to last. I liked it more than other tasters. Having said that, the wine was not quite as great as it can be. A bottle tasted last year was superb. Can be very great. (17)

CHÂTEAU LEOVILLE-LASCASES (MS):

Medium-brick colour, old-looking. Open, delicate nose with hint of cardboard. Subdued and elegant on palate; earthy, leathery, and delicate, yet underneath it had the hard structure of the 1945s. A bit musty at finish, but considering the low ullage, not bad. (15.5)

CHÂTEAU LEOVILLE-POYFERRÉ (TS):

Good appearance, bright colour with good depth. Off nose, a bit skunky, but ripe fruit, too. Hard, tannic on palate with good fruit to back it up. Better on palate than on nose. (16.5)

CHÂTEAU LEOVILLE-POYFERRÉ (US), LONDON-BOTTLED BY STOKES AND HARVEY:

Dark colour to rim. Complex, subdued nose of fine old Claret. Fruity and round on palate with good balance. Spoiled by sharp, acidic finish. (15.5)

FLIGHT #5
1945 red Graves

CHÂTEAU CARBONNIEUX (US):

Pale orange-brown colour. Oxidized. May it rest in peace. (No score)

DOMAINE DE CHEVALIER (TS):

Dark, mature colour with good depth. Subdued, toasty, earthy nose. Aristocratic. Very "Graves" on palate. Earthy, spicy, with hint of oak and popcorn. Dry and austere. A serious wine that has held well. Can be a great bottle. (16)

CHÂTEAU HAUT-BAILLY (TS):

Good, mature colour, orangy rim. Elegant, forthcoming nose of old Claret, a bit vegetal and earthy. Supple, well balanced. Most enjoyable. Typical elegance of this property. Classy. (17)

CHÂTEAU SMITH-HAUT-LAFITTE (US):

Deep, dark colour, showing maturity at rim. Ripe, rich nose. Full, big, tannic wine, but a bit musty and too austere, lacking in complexity. A big, sturdy, straightforward wine. A bit vegetal. No rush drinking this wine. (15)

FLIGHT #6
1945 red Graves

CHÂTEAU HAUT-BRION (TS):

Bad bottle. Deep-brown colour. Tired, skunky, rotting vegetables on nose and hint of manure. This wine was purchased at auction in London three years ago. Good fill, clean label, awful wine! Can be very good. Last tasted in 1986 and scored (18). (No score)

CHÂTEAU LA MISSION HAUT-BRION (TS):

Good appearance; deep, dark colour. Vegetal, stemmy nose with hint of cold tea. Some fruit on palate, earthy, a bit steely and hard. Lots of extract, though. A solid, serious wine lacking elegance. Excellent when tasted in 1981 and again in 1986. Can be superb. (16.5)

CHÂTEAU LA TOUR-HAUT-BRION (TS):

Dark colour, similar hue as La Mission, but cleaner, more brilliant colour. Hint of game (gibier) on nose. The elegance and complexity of this wine is spoiled by too much acidity. Having said that, this wine had a lot of class and complexity. Controversial. Some liked it, others didn't. I did. (17)

Then we tasted two 1985 red Burgundies that one of the participants brought along. As if we didn't have enough wine!

1985 BONNES MARES, GEORGES LIGNIER:

Medium light-red bottle. Fresh, fruity, charming, elegant, open nose. Complex, round, some oak, delicate. Very good length. Almost ready. (17)

1985 CLOS DE LA ROCHE, GEORGES LIGNIER:

Perfumy, lovely, complex nose. Good depth, spice, fruit, ripe, elegant, cherries, cloves. Intense, complex, very good. A bit darker than the Bonnes Mares. Both, though, are very forward. Drink from 1991 to 1998. Good, clean, fruity extract. (17.5)

FLIGHT #7
1945 Sauternes

CHÂTEAU CAILLOU (BN):

This Barsac had a deep-gold colour, almost copper. Subdued nose. Round, sweet, long with good intensity. Full, rich, complex, and most enjoyable. (17)

CHÂTEAU FILHOT (BN):

Impressive, deep-gold colour. Ripe, rich raisins on nose, yet not much botrytis. Full, but old, fairly alcoholic. Rich, but lacked in complexity. Finished a bit dry and bitter. Good nevertheless. (15.5)

CHÂTEAU RABAUD, P. ROTHSCHILD (BN):

Special label for Baron Philippe de Rothschild. Impressive, dark-gold colour. Complex, rich, fairly thick, yet not cloying. Great balance and class here. Intense, good length. The subdued nose misled us into thinking that this would be a soft, simple wine, until we tasted it. Superb! (18.5)

We ended this session with another litre bottle of
YELLOW CHARTREUSE PRE-1903:

This time a yellow Chartreuse. Pale green-gold colour. Intense, spicy, herbal nose. Full, rich, complex on palate. Rich with lots of extract. Creamy and thick. Much thicker and heavier than the white Chartreuse tasted the previous night. This is so much finer than modern-day Chartreuse!

Saturday, January 16, 1988, Noon

THIRD SESSION

1945 Haut-Médocs and Margaux.

APERITIFS

CHAMPAGNE LAURENT-PERRIER "CUVÉE GRAND SIÈCLE" 1979, IN MAGNUMS:

Lovely, creamy, complex. A sweeter, delicate Champagne. Round, with fresh fruit. Lighter style. Elegant and classy. (17.5)

CHAMPAGNE BOLLINGER BRUT 1945:

Very deep-gold colour, not unlike an old Sauternes. Cork and oxidation on nose. Some fizz there with obvious acidity and quite intense. Many years ago, this must have been a full, rich, and big wine. Finished nutty and rich. (16)

The actual tasting started with two Sauternes, both 1945s, of course.

CHÂTEAU LA TOUR BLANCHE "PROPRIÉTÉ D'ÉTAT, MR. OSIRIS" (US):

Very deep colour, not unlike light tea. Orange-yellow rim. Amber. Very ripe, intense nose of exotic fruit and honey. Full, rich, and fruity on palate. Lovely intensity. Slightly earthy with botrytis and length. An excellent, classic wine. (18.5) La Tour Blanche has not made such a great wine since!

CHÂTEAU RABAUD (BN):

Dark, deep-gold colour, but not quite as dark as La Tour Blanche. Shipped by Bouchard Père of Burgundy (sic), yet château-bottled. Subdued, earthy nose with some hint of botrytis. A bit drier with less extract than La Tour Blanche, but with lovely balance. Clean, long finish with intense botrytis. (18)

Between the early 1920s and late 1940s, Sigalas-Rabaud and Rabaud Promis were briefly reunited, calling the wine Rabaud.

A great effort by both properties in 1945.

FLIGHT #1

1945 Haut-Médocs

CHÂTEAU BELGRAVE (M/US):

Medium red with good depth and orange rim. A bit skunky, cabbage on nose. Unpleasant on palate, too. Sharp, lemony, citric, tannic, and dried out. No fruit there. Nose worse than palate. (10)

CHÂTEAU LA TOUR-CARNET (N):

Deep, mature colour. Vegetal nose with some sulphur. Stemmy, green, and acidic on palate. Sharp and green, lacking fruit. (13)

CHÂTEAU SENEJAC (BN):

Good depth of colour. Spicy, vegetal nose (stemmy), with good complexity. Tannic, but with some fruit there. Rich, solid, straightforward. Fairly hard. Not much complexity on palate, but no rush drinking this. I have tasted better examples of this wine. (15.5)

FLIGHT #2

1945 Haut-Médocs

CHÂTEAU CANTEMERLE (US):

Excellent appearance. Deep, lively colour. Delicate, forthcoming nose. Very "old Claret." Sweet, rich, with lots of depth that is drying out a bit at the end. Better on entry than at finish. Previously, this was a great wine. (16) Last tasted with Jean-Michel Cazes at Lynch-Bages in 1986, it was superb; I rated that bottle (18).

CHÂTEAU GRAND LA LAGUNE (N), LONDON-BOTTLED BY COCKBURN AND CAMPBELL:

Good depth, palish-orange rim. Fruity, intense nose of ripe old Claret. Full, big, and fruity on palate. Very tannic, though. Lots of extract, but finishes dry and hard. (16.5)

FLIGHT #3

1945 Margaux

CHÂTEAU CANTENAC-BROWN (TS):

Dark, yet mature colour. Oxidized on nose. Leathery, wet earth on palate. Sour, sharp, and bitter. (11.5)

CHÂTEAU GISCOURS (HF):

This bottle was purchased from the château. Good appearance, deep colour. Vegetal and starting to oxidize. Unpleasant on palate. Madeirized, sour, and sharp. May have been good 15 to 20 years ago. (12)

CHÂTEAU KIRWAN (N), LONDON-BOTTLED BY LYONS:

Light, palish-red colour. Dull, slightly toasty nose with hint of tobacco. Lightweight, green, and tannic on palate. Vegetal, not unlike a dried-out St. Emilion. (13) Most tasters scored this wine even lower than I did. (Another bottle tasted at the Bipin Desai tasting two years ago was excellent and lively.)

CHÂTEAU KIRWAN (N), BOTTLED BY SCHROËDER AND SCHŸLER (THE OWNERS):

Medium red with good depth. Attractive fruit, delicate nose. Fairly full and tannic. Some fruit. Not bad at all, but not great. Lacks complexity. (16) Most tasters liked it less than I did. Some tasters rated it a low (13). I feel that this was unjust.

CHÂTEAU MALESCOT-ST.-EXUPÉRY (US):

Mature colour with good depth. On nose, starting to oxidize. Smells like red Cinzano. Woody, hard, and tannic, with signs of oxidation. Disappointing. (13)

Again, I tried this wine three years ago, and it was impressive.

FLIGHT #4

1945 Margaux

CHÂTEAU BRANE-CANTENAC (TS):

Medium red, orangy rim. elegant, open nose with the complexity so typical of the commune of Margaux. Classy, feminine, and delicate on palate. Well balanced, stylish. This was the fourth time I have tasted this wine. It has always been a fine wine. (17.5) *Why can't this property produce such wines today?*

CHÂTEAU RAUZAN-GASSIES (BN):

Sweaty, leathery nose. Hard, tannic, dry, lean, and acidic on palate. Too dry. Unbalanced. Later, nose cleared a bit, but this wine didn't show nearly as well as when tasted previous in the fall of 1985. (13.5)

CHÂTEAU RAUSAN-SÉGLA (US):

Very dark colour, but cloudy. Oxidized. Gone. (10)

CHÂTEAU RAUSAN-SÉGLA (BN), BORDEAUX-BOTTLED BY CRUSE:

Dark, lively colour. Nose of ripe fruit, tobacco, and mocha. Lots of fruit; rich, ripe, and tannic. A sturdy, chunky wine. Young-looking and -tasting for its age. While very good, this wine does not have the delicate Margaux complexity that it had when tasted in September 1985. (16.5)

FLIGHT #5

1945 Margaux

CHÂTEAU MARGAUX (US):

Slightly cloudy; may have travelled very recently. Medium, mature colour of old Claret. Elegant, stylish nose. Lean on palate, but with some fruit, too. Not unlike cold tea. Opened up and showed better after a few minutes, with better complexity. Good, but not First Growth quality. Can be very fine. (16.5)

CHÂTEAU PALMER (BN):

A very pleasant surprise, and the best 1945 Palmer I have ever tasted. Mature colour with palish rim. Subdued, delicate nose. Full and concentrated on palate, but delicate, too. Good fruit. Opened up into a lovely bouquet. Classy Margaux. Excellent wine. (18)

CHÂTEAU PALMER (TS), BORDEAUX-BOTTLED BY MÄHLER-BESSE:

Impressive appearance. Deep, bright-red colour. Oxidizing, hard, tannic, dried out. A beefy, hard, and unpleasant wine. Passé. (12.5)

Saturday evening, January 16, 1988

FOURTH SESSION

1945 Pauillacs

APERITIF

CHAMPAGNE HEIDSIECK "DIAMANT BLEU" 1979 MONOPOLE, IN MAGNUM:

Lovely, complex, round, great length, and classy. My favourite Champagne so far of the ones tasted at this event. (18.5)

CHAMPAGNE POMMERY ET GRENO 1945 ROSÉ:

Amber colour, no hint of Rosé in colour. Oxidized, madeirized nose. Sweetish on palate. Flat. Like a very old Tavel with hint of residual sugar. (13)

FLIGHT #1

1945 Pauillacs

CHÂTEAU BATAILLEY (HF), BOTTLER UNKNOWN:

Good depth of colour and extract. Earthy, yet complex Cabernet nose. Round, well balanced, but lacking complexity. A pleasant drinking wine that had a hint of mustiness at finish. (15)

CHÂTEAU BATAILLEY (BN), CHÂTEAU-BOTTLED:

Fairly light, mature-looking. Spicy, open, forthcoming on nose. Slightly vegetal. Good extract and complexity with some fruit here. A very good wine that is well balanced. (17) Improved in the glass after 30 minutes.

CHÂTEAU GRAND-PUY-LACOSTE (M/US):

Impressive, dark colour. Classic, toasty, earthy, and spicy nose. Very Cabernet. Full, round, rich, loaded with fruit. An outstanding wine that has held extremely well. The best example of this vintage of Grand-Puy-Lacoste I have ever tasted. Previously, the wine, while very good, seemed tough and tannic. (18)

CHÂTEAU HAUT-BATAILLEY (TS):

Toasty, attractive, herbaceous nose. Stemmy and lean on palate. Fairly hard with excessive acidity. Finishes austere and too hard, yet a sound wine. (15)

FLIGHT #2

1945 Pauillacs

CHÂTEAU DUHART-MILON (TS):

Smell of straw. Open, sweet, attractive nose, but with hint of oxidation. Good complexity, though. Fruity, fairly rich. Tobacco and spices. A well-balanced, elegant wine with good concentration. Most enjoyable. (17) The style of Lafite, its senior partner, is obvious here.

CHÂTEAU MOUTON-BARON-PHILIPPE (BN):

Earthy, complex nose of mature Claret. Sweeter, slightly minty on palate. Cigar-box and tobacco. Trying to be a "real" Mouton! Great length and class here. Well balanced, without excessive tannins or acidity. Lovely wine. (18)

Château Mouton-d'Armailhacq (TS):

This is, of course, the previous name of Château Mouton-Baron-Philippe. Interestingly, the corks were branded according to the name on the label. Maybe the winery had old stocks of corks and labels and bottled the 1945 vintage with both labels in separate batches. Even better than the previous bottle. Good dark colour, orangy rim. Clean, spicy Cabernet nose. Classy on both nose and palate. Full, round, fruity with excellent balance. Hint of mint, too. Great bottle. (18.5)

FLIGHT #3

1945 Pauillacs

Three different bottlings of Pontet-Canet. This can be a very good wine, yet all three bottlings disappointed this time.

Château Pontet-Canet (BN), London-bottled by Berry Bros.:

Light, pale, orangy colour. Sweet, beet-sugar nose. Tired, acidic, sweet tea. Over-the-hill. (12.5)

Château Pontet-Canet (TS), London-bottled by Block, Gray and Block:

This bottling is well known to me (tasted on at least six previous occasions), yet this was a poor bottle. Darkest of flight. Oxidized, caramel nose. Sharp, citric, and sour. Very disappointing. Can be quite good. (11)

Château Pontet-Canet (TS), Bordeaux-bottled by Cruse:

(Cruse were the owners of Pontet-Canet at the time, until 1973, and bottled most of this wine in Bordeaux.) Medium, mature-red colour. Hint of oxidation on nose. Sweet and sour on palate. Too tannic with excessive acidity. I've tasted far better examples of this wine. (13)

FLIGHT #4

1945 Pauillacs

Château Croizet-Bages (TS):

Good mature colour. Herbaceous, open nose. Full, quite tannic, but low fruit and too sharp. Still drinkable and sound, though. (14)

Château Lynch-Bages (TS):

As good as when tasted twice previously. Dark colour, mature rim. Minty, cedary, typical Lynch-Bages on nose. Round, fruity, and chunky. Well balanced with good fruit and clean finish. Its only fault was that it fell apart in the glass after 15 minutes and dried out. (17)

Château Lynch-Bages (BN), Burgundy-bottled by Lebegue:

Even darker than the above. Skunky, sweaty nose. Vegetal, compost heap. Sour, acidic. Passé. (11)

Château Lynch-Moussas (TS):

Better than recent vintages of this property. Dark, mature colour to rim. Subdued, flowery nose. Round, sweet fruitiness on palate. Well balanced, but on the thin side. A perfectly acceptable wine. (15)

FLIGHT #5

1945 Pauillacs

Château Pichon-Longueville-Baron (TS):

Deep, mature colour. Subdued, delicate nose. Sweet and leathery on entry, finishing hard and oxidizing. Sweet and sour; musty, too. Some volatility. I've had better examples of this wine. Other tasters liked this wine, and rated it higher. (14.5)

Château Pichon-Lalande (TS):

Similar appearance to the Pichon-Baron, if a bit lighter. Toasty, fresh-baked bread on nose. Complex on palate with excessive acidity and fairly tannic. Lacks the class or style of present-day Pichon-Lalande. On two previous occasions, this wine had an uncanny smell of mocha. (16.5)

FLIGHT #6

Haut-Médoc First Growths

Château Lafite-Rothschild (N):

Palest of flight. Palish red, orangy rim. Subdued, elegant nose. Round, soft, fruity, and well balanced. Quite sweet, finishing a bit short. Good, but not great. (17). The average score was (16.5).

I have now tasted this wine on eight occasions over the past ten years. Once in Vancouver, once each in London and Bordeaux, and five times in the USA. It has never been a great wine, and the price it fetches is a sales gimmick of auction houses. Until the early 1960s, the wine was bottled directly from individual barrels; one Bordeaux château owner whose palate I respect told me that he has tasted a lovely bottle of this wine. That makes it one out of nine! Good luck.

Château Latour (BN):

Deep, impressive colour to rim. Slightly musty on nose, with hint of spices and mint. Hint of cork, too. What a pity! This can be a great wine. Hard, tannic, rich, and fruity on palate. Rich and ripe with lots of extract. In this particular instance, the cork has defeated what could have been a great bottle. Scored widely from (14) to (17.5). After a show of hands, our host kindly opened a second bottle: high shoulder level. Vegetal, stemmy nose. Cleaner on nose than the first bottle, but thinner and sharper on palate. Hint of oxidation, too. This wasn't Latour 1945's day. (15)

CHÂTEAU MOUTON-ROTHSCHILD (N):

Another wine that can disappoint at times, yet when it's great, it has very few rivals. This was a super bottle! Dark colour with mature, orange rim. Typical Mouton nose. Mint-eucalyptus and cedar. Beautifully ripe, rich, and intense on palate. Solid, full, masculine Pauillac. Perfect balance, too, loaded with ripe fruit. This wine overwhelmed all others in this flight. A faultless wine. (19.5)

CHÂTEAU MARGAUX (N):

This bottle was kindly added by one of our participants to not miss this golden opportunity of tasting all four First Growth 1945s together. Medium to dark mature colour. Clean, subdued nose that opened up and developed quite a bit of complexity later on in the glass. Earth, gravel, and caramel on nose. Round and elegant on palate. Velvety, yet spoiled by hard tannins. Somehow lacks the harmony for which Margaux is so famous. (16.5)

Then we tasted two red Burgundies of the 1985 vintage

MAZIS-CHAMBERTIN 1985 HOSPICES DE BEAUNE, LEROY

AND

CHAMBERTIN 1985, LEROY:

Very rare and expensive wines.

CHAMBERTIN:

Dark, purplish colour to rim. Very young-looking, lots of colour and extract. Lovely, intense nose. Complex, great class and extract. Elegant, very long. Outstanding, ripe, intense cherries. Six to ten years. Enough acidity to keep it for several more. Raspberries; incredible varietal character. (19)

MAZIS-CHAMBERTIN:

Even darker, more intense than the Chambertin. Even bigger. Great intensity, depth. Fabulous, sweet fruit. Lovely, great extract and length. A superb wine. Drink in ten years. Very ripe, lovely balance. Super wine! One of the best young red Burgundies I've ever tasted. More oak than in the Chambertin, too. Black cherries. (19.5) These are two great Burgundies. Cost US$150 to $250!

I disagreed with most tasters, not in terms of the quality of these great 1985s, but in terms of longevity. Sid Cross and John Tilson said they'll last for 20 to 25 years. I said 12 to 15 years. In any event, essence of raspberries! I guess that it comes down to a matter of taste.

CLOS DE VOUGEOT 1985, GEORGES MUGNERET:

Blackberries on nose. Medium-dark colour, purplish rim. Not quite as dark as the Leroy wines. More acidity than in the two above. Lots of extract, if not as ripe as the two Chambertins. Nevertheless, an outstanding wine. Lovely, clean, complex; very fresh, ripe, perfumy fruit. Drink in ten years. (18.5)

FLIGHT #7

1945 Sauternes

CHÂTEAU DE FARGUES (BN):

Bright, deep-gold colour, green-yellow rim. This is an extremely rare and great wine. Complex, elegant nose of ripe fruit and botrytis. Great depth and concentration. Fabulous extract and fruit. Together with 1959 Suduiraut, and 1959 and 1967 d'Yquem, this is the most memorable Sauternes I have ever tasted. (19.5)

CHÂTEAU RIEUSSEC (BN):

Excellent, deep-gold colour with lovely depth. A bit earthy, too, on nose. Full, rich, round, and ripe. Thicker texture than the de Fargues, yet a bit older-tasting, without the liveliness of the above. Full, rich, and long on palate. A very fine bottle. (18) I liked this more than most.

CHÂTEAU D'YQUEM (TS):

Bright-amber colour. Earth and ripe fruit on nose. Very good extract; sweeter than both above Sauternes. Slight hint of oxidation and a bit musty, too. Can be great. (16.5) What a pity. This can be a "perfect 20/20" wine.

After a short night's "rest," we all assembled for the fifth and final session of this marathon.

Sunday, January 17, 1988, Noon

FIFTH SESSION

1945 Pomerols

APERITIF

CHAMPAGNE CHARBAUT ET FILS BRUT ROSÉ N/V:

Pale-salmon colour gave the impression of an older wine. Similar impressions on palate. Slightly sweet and simple. Must have been better a few years ago. (16)

CHAMPAGNE BILLECART-SALMON BRUT ROSÉ N/V:

Better, fresher, and livelier. Light-pink colour. Lively, tiny bubbles, and good complexity. (17)

This was followed by a future classic.

CHAMPAGNE KRUG VINTAGE 1979 BRUT:

Lively, crisp, intense, solid, with excellent depth. Needs three to four extra years of bottle-age. Top quality. (18.5)

CHAMPAGNE BOLLINGER BRUT 1945:

This can be great. I've tasted it once before, and it was a wine of great depth and complexity. This bottle had a deep-gold colour; skunky, vegetal nose. Oxidized, yet had the structure and depth of what must have been a fine bottle, many years ago. (12)

FLIGHT #1
1945 Pomerols

CHÂTEAU CLOS L'EGLISE (M/US):

Dark, old colour. Madeirized nose. Leather, tar, and burnt wood. Full, rich, big wine. A beefy wine, spoiled by the nose. (13)

CHÂTEAU L'EGLISE CLINET (MS):

Even darker than the above. Totally oxidized. Big, heavy, and tannic; prune juice. Gone. (10)

CHÂTEAU MAZEYRES (BN):

Lightest colour of flight with orange rim. Elegant, subdued nose. Quite sweet and delicate on palate, with hint of mustiness. Pleasant, though. Was better when tasted previously in the spring of 1985. (15)

CHÂTEAU ROUGET (BN):

Impressive, dark colour showing maturity at rim. Lovely, ripe, intense nose. Clean, full, long, and ripe on palate with good fruit extract and backbone. Very ripe and long. An excellent wine. Will the 1982 Pomerols turn out like this? Best wine of the flight by far, and an excellent bottle. (18)

FLIGHT #2
1945 Pomerols

CHÂTEAU CLOS RENÉ (TS), BORDEAUX-BOTTLED BY CRUSE:

Deep, red colour. Classy, elegant nose. Round, fruity, and rich on palate. Made from ripe grapes. The sweetness is almost too much of a good thing. A bit tannic and finishes short. (15.5)

CHÂTEAU LA CROIX DE GAY (BN), LONDON-BOTTLED BY HARVEY'S:

Paler, more mature colour than the Clos René. Stemmy, perfumed nose, with spices and good complexity. Full, rich, and solid on palate. A bit too acidic. A rich, fruity wine of good quality. Some tasters liked it, others didn't. (16.5)

CHÂTEAU L'ENCLOS (BN), BORDEAUX-BOTTLED BY CRUSE:

Dark, mature colour, orange rim. Metallic nose. Smells like raw meat. Very sweet on palate, quite hard and tannic, but backed by ripe fruit, too. Other tasters liked this better than I did. (15.5)

CHÂTEAU NENIN (BN), LONDON-BOTTLED BY ARMY AND NAVY:

Very dark. Alcoholic, medicinal, and barnyardy on nose. A big, hard, and tannic wine. Finished acidic and short. (14)

The four wines of this flight improved a bit after a few minutes in the glass. However, they all lacked the extra depth and complexity to make them really good.

FLIGHT #3
1945 Pomerols

CHÂTEAU GAZIN (BN):

Bright-red, mature colour. Lovely elegance and complexity on nose. Delicate and complex on palate, too. Lots of class here. Has breed and is well balanced. Not a big wine, but quite stylish. (17)

CHÂTEAU LA POINTE (L/MS):

Tired, pale-orange colour. Oxidized, off nose. Sour, acidic, and short. (10) The last time I tasted this wine from a magnum in the fall of 1985, it was a great bottle, rated (18)! In the case of older wines, provenance is everything!

CHÂTEAU LATOUR-À-POMEROL (BN):

Impressive, dark colour to rim. Corked, musty, mushrooms on nose. Fungus and mushrooms on palate. A good example of a badly corked bottle. (10)

CHÂTEAU PETIT-VILLAGE (BN):

Dark colour, orange rim. Rich extract on nose. Lead pencil, metallic, and meaty on palate. Very rich, full, sweet. A simple wine, but big and ripe. (15.5)

FLIGHT #4
1945 Pomerols

CHÂTEAU LAFLEUR (BN), BORDEAUX-BOTTLED BY CRUSE:

Excellent appearance to rim. Dark and impressive. Lovely, rich, ripe nose. Superb intensity and ripe, clean fruit on palate. Great extract, good length, depth, and lively, ripe fruit. Long finish. Still tannic. No rush drinking this lovely bottle. (18.5)

CHÂTEAU LAFLEUR-GAZIN (L/MS):

Dark, browning colour. Oxidized prune juice. (10)

CHÂTEAU LA FLEUR-PETRUS (N), IN MAGNUM:

The only 1945 served from a magnum. Impressive, dark, youthful colour. Full, fruity, and rich, but not overly ripe. Excellent balance. Long, clean finish. Leaner than the Lafleur (even in recent vintages, these two wines are different in style and weight); softer tannins. A lovely, balanced, classy wine. (18)

CHÂTEAU LA CONSEILLANTE (BN):

A controversial wine, rated (14) to (18). Medium-dark colour, mature at rim. Cigar-box, tobacco, delicate nose. Complex and long. In the old days, the winemakers used to add a softer grape varietal to the blend, to give this wine more elegance. Round, delicate, slightly sweet. Spicy, yet subdued. (17.5)

Château l'Evangile (N):

Dark colour, mature rim. Very slightly cloudy. At first, unyielding nose. Cold tea, but spicy fruit and wood, too. Later, the nose opened up quite a bit. Tannic, yet fruity and rich. Somehow did not have the delicate complexity of the La Conseillante at this tasting. Nevertheless a very good wine. (17.5)

Vieux Château Certan (N):

Very good appearance. Deep, dark colour. Complex, delicate nose. Full, round, mocha-coffee on palate. Intense, good backbone, rich, and fruity. Lots of depth and class here. Finishes a bit dry. A serious wine. Excellent. (18)

FLIGHT #6
1945 Pomerols

Château Petrus (BN):

Darkest wine of flight. Lovely, delicate, yet an intense, clean, ripe nose. One of the few very dark wines of this session that wasn't oxidized! Marvellous bouquet. Superb intensity on palate and incredible concentration of fruit. Great balance and extract. The greatest wine of the whole event? Most tasters thought so. So did I. Perfect. (20)

Château Petrus (BN), English-bottled, bottler unknown:

Dark colour to rim. Subdued, clean, and delicate nose. Not as intense as the château-bottling, but very good. Great intensity on nose after 15 minutes. Full, balanced, with lots of extract. A noble wine. Hint of coffee and finishes slightly dry. A lovely bottling. (18.5) The cork was unbranded. Label similar to the château-bottling, but without the words "Mise en bouteilles au château."

Château Trotanoy (BN):

The best Trotanoy 1945 I've ever tasted (tasted twice previously). Medium red, mature orangy rim. Spicy, forthcoming, elegant nose. Round, classy, and delicate on palate. Good extract. Cassis fruit. A leaner, more delicate wine. A fine bottle that was unfortunately overshadowed by the great Petrus. Perfume and elegance. (18.5)

FLIGHT #7
1945 Sauternes
Another great flight. Any of the following Sauternes would be memorable.

Château Lafaurie-Peyraguey (N):

Deep, bright-gold colour. Green-gold at rim. Intense, ripe, clean nose of peaches, apricots. Delicious wine. Great length and concentration of fruit. Perfect balance and superb depth. Outstanding. Has there ever been, consistently, a greater vintage for Sauternes since these marvellous 1945s? I don't think so. (19)

Château Rayne-Vigneau (N):

Similar appearance to the Lafaurie. Closed, subdued nose. Leaner, lighter on palate. Good ripe fruit and quite classy, too. Slightly high alcohol. Otherwise an excellent bottle. (17.5)

Château Suduiraut (BN):

Another superb bottle of rare nectar! Ripe, intense nose of botrytis and exotic fruit. Richest wine of the flight. Apricots and very ripe peaches. Superb length and balance. Essence of Sauternes. A richer, thicker wine. Great extract. Syrupy liqueur of Sauternes. How does one choose? (19.5)

Just as we thought that it was all over, our host opened and decanted a rare bottle.

1931 Dow's Vintage Port, Oporto-bottled in 1934 by Silva-Cosens:

Pale-red colour with touch of orange. Open, spicy, elegant nose. Soft, forward, still tasted like Vintage Port (very old Ports sometimes taste more like Tawnies than like true Vintage Ports). Round, sweet, forward; finishes a bit harsh and spirity. (17)

The most extensive tasting of 1945s ever held? Probably. Judging by the masterpieces we tasted (as if we didn't know it!), 1945 was a great vintage. There was a lot of bottle variation, though.

Overall impressions

Many of the wines are past their peak. There is absolutely nothing to be gained by keeping them any longer. Pick a special occasion—or just an average Tuesday night—and enjoy! And, by the way, I'm free for the rest of the year, so please do call me first!

January 24, 1988

Liberty Wine Company tasting of 1985 red Bordeaux, in Point Roberts, Washington State.

APERITIF

Château La Louvière 1985, Graves Blanc:

Green-gold. Toasty, complex nose. Some oak. Fairly full, rich, clean, crisp, good structure, well balanced. Lovely intensity. Very Sauvignon Blanc, but ripe! (16.5)

1. Château Sociando-Mallet, Haut-Médoc:

Bright, deep, cherry-red colour. Buttery, complex nose. New oak. A bit hard, tannic, bitter, green. Needs many years. A serious wine even in an elegant vintage. (17)

2. Château Larmande, St. Emilion:

Subdued nose. Clean, neutral. Good, dark colour. Sweeter, yet fairly tannic. Hard, drier style (leaner). Needs five years. Quite good. Not much ripe fruit. (15)

3. Château Pavie, St. Emilion:

Very good, deep colour to rim. Closed nose. Some sweetness. Round, sweet, delicate. Some new oak, but a bit astringent, acidic. Finishes short and too hot. OK, but not great. (15.5)

4. Château L'Arrosée, St. Emilion:

Medium dark; not as dark as Pavie. More vegetal, obvious St. Emilion. Clean, complex, long, solid, medium-bodied. New oak. Lots of class. Elegant, yet fairly big, tannic, serious. Excellent potential. (17)

5. Château Canon, St. Emilion:

Very good, dark colour to rim. Lots of class on nose. Perfumy, complex, vanilla, oak, ripe fruit. A bit tannic, hard, yet delicate. Most classy so far. Has breed. Oak, vanilla, fruit. Needs seven to eight years. Not very big. (17.5) to (18).

6. Château Cheval-Blanc, St. Emilion:

Colour worrisome! Medium colour, less cherry-red than above, hint of brown. Herbal, flowery, oak, vegetal. Expansive nose. Quite tannic (more than Canon), yet leaner middle. Hard, tannic, serious. Needs ten years. Less fruit than Canon. Reserve judgement. (17.5)

7. Château d'Issan, Margaux:

Cherry-red colour. Elegant, complex, perfumy. Lots of elegance. A bit hard, finishing acidic, but lovely nevertheless. I'm a bit worried about the balance. Clean, complex finish. Delicate. Needs six years. (16)

8. Pavillon Rouge du Château, Margaux:

Deep colour. Ripe nose, classy. Green, hard, young vines. Some sweetness. Pleasant. (15) This is the second wine of Château Margaux.

9. Château Clos René, Pomerol:

Good, deep colour. Sweet, ripe, rich nose. Slightly musty. Full, rich, round, a bit bitter at finish. Simple. (14.5)

10. Château Bon-Pasteur, Pomerol:

Medium cherry-red. Closed, subdued nose. Hard, tannic, low fruit, acidic; finishing bitter. (14)

11. Château Certan-Giraud, Pomerol:

Medium red. Flowery, perfumy, elegant nose. Full, fruity, rich, round. Good intensity and balance. Needs eight years. Very good depth. (17)

12. Château L'Evangile, Pomerol:

Excellent, deep, dark colour. Rich, luscious nose. Excellent extract. Full; lovely balance, extract, and depth of fruit. Clean, long, serious. Needs eight to ten years. (18)

13. Château La Conseillante, Pomerol:

Very good, deep colour. Lovely nose. Great extract, fruit, and perfume. Great length, depth, and complexity. Superb class. Much more forthcoming than l'Evangile. Earlier maturing. Super! (18.5)

14. Château Pichon-Lalande, Pauillac:

Very good depth, cherry-red. Sweet, perfumy nose. Charming. Herbal, grassy, elegant, sweet, complex. This tastes like a Margaux, not a Pauillac! (17.5)

15. Château La Mission Haut-Brion, Graves:

Very good, deep, dark colour. Slightly earthy nose. Big, serious, tannic, green tannins. Great length; very tight, hard. Biggest, most serious of bunch. Needs 15 years. (18)

January 29, 1988

Chevaliers du Tastevin Black Tie Dinner and tasting, at the "William Tell" restaurant, in Vancouver. Dinner was preceded by a tasting of mature vintages of Louis Latour's red wines.

I was the host, organizer, and speaker at this event. There were 19 participants.

1979 Corton-Grancey:

Medium-deep colour; watery rim. Unyielding nose, a bit volatile. Some fruit and barnyard. Acidic, metallic, hard, tannic. Too much acidity. Lean. Finished short. A bit too sharp. (14)

1969 Corton-Grancey:

Medium colour; orangy, mature rim. Delicate, clean, forthcoming nose. Perfumy, delicate, round, complex, too. Yet on palate, it is hard, full, masculine. Lacks that extra complexity to be great. (16.5)

1961 Corton "Clos de la Vigne au Saint":

Better depth to rim than the 1969 Corton-Grancey. Rich, fruity nose. Complex, sweet, rich, ripe. Quite young-tasting. Lively, round, rich; not great, but very good. This is a monopole of the house of Latour. (17.5)

1966 Chambertin "Cuvée des Héritiers Latour":

Complex, delicate, clean nose. Great depth, complex, rich, full, long. Lots of class here. Clean, long finish. Slightly vegetal. An excellent wine; at its peak. (18)

1964 Chambertin "Cuvée des Héritiers Latour":

Very good depth of colour. Closed, unyielding nose. A bit volatile. Better on palate. Round, soft, rich, big. Finishes a bit sweet. Not as great as a 1964 can be. A bit sharp, but good fruit. The only real problem is lack of complexity. (17)

1959 CHAMBERTIN "CUVÉE DES HÉRITIERS LATOUR":

Very good, deep, impressive colour. Lovely, rich, long, complex, fruity; fabulous depth and class. Great quality. A great wine from a great vintage. Outstanding. Taste and complexity lasted forever on palate. (19)

I purchased all the above wines from Draper and Esquin's in San Francisco.

Overall impressions

The three Chambertins had more class, depth, and complexity than the three Cortons. as for Latour's habit of pasteurizing their reds, I cannot see how it has hurt the wines. They were all big, rich, complex with lots of life. Most also had a fair bit of sediment. Also, as we used the same wines for the food, they held very well for over two hours in the glass!

The dinner and service were superb and flawless! After the tasting, we had a caviar and Champagne reception with fresh Sevruga caviar (on a lovely ice carving of a sturgeon) and this Champagne.

CHAMPAGNE BOLLINGER "GRANDE ANNÉE" 1976, IN JEROBOAM:

Has held very well in large bottle. Yeasty, rich, full, long, with very good complexity. At its peak. (18)

February 5, 1988

A special Black Tie Dinner, for our Commanderie de Bordeaux.

I was inducted as the new Maître, replacing Maître David Freeman, QC.

CHAMPAGNE VEUVE CLICQUOT "CARTE OR" 1982:

Full-bodied, yet soft and early maturing. Complex, tiny bubbles, lovely structure. Ready, with good fruit. Should last well. (17.5)

"R" 1983, DRY WINE OF CHÂTEAU RIEUSSEC:

Medium-gold colour, some oak and hint of Sauternes on nose. Quite dry, soft, at its peak. (15.5)

CHÂTEAU LAVILLE-HAUT-BRION 1981:

Palish gold. A delicate wine, not typical for Laville. Delicate, subdued, flowery nose. Soft, delicate on palate. Not much depth but well balanced. Ready. (16.5)

1975 CHÂTEAU LEOVILLE-POYFERRÉ:

Good, dark colour. Spicy, herbal, stemmy nose. Surprisingly soft for a 1975, but quite pleasant, fruity, forward. Best 1975 Poyferré I've tasted to date. Previous bottles were lean and uninspiring. (16.5)

1970 CHÂTEAU LAFON-ROCHET:

A wine I purchased for the Commanderie in Chicago, at auction. Quite a bit of bottle variation. Very good, deep colour, so typical of the 1970s. Earthy, slightly minty, complex, solid, very St. Estèphe style, yet well balanced and backed by enough ripe fruit. Some bottles were leaner and earthier, but our bottle was excellent.

1970 CHÂTEAU D'YQUEM:

Light-golden colour. Delicate, clean botrytis nose with some new oak and vanilla. Elegant, impeccably made, long, and complex. Ready, but no rush. (17.5)

I sat at the table with the two former Maîtres of our Commanderie: Dr. Allan Tobe and Dave Freeman, as well as with Ruy Paes-Braga, General Manager of the Four Seasons hotel, where this excellent event was held. The food and presentation were superb, as usual, at this fine establishment.

February 10, 1988

Tasting of Burgundies, at the residence of Dr. David Allan.

I conducted this tasting for a group of 16 doctors.

1983 BEAUNE, HOSPICES DE BEAUNE "CUVÉE NICOLAS ROLIN," MOMMESSIN:

Very good depth of colour to rim. Touch of purple. Ripe, round, rich on nose. Full, fruity, tannic. Round, very good quality. Drink 1990 to 1995. Very good, but doesn't have the extra dimension of the Hospices de Nuits. (17)

1983 HOSPICES DE NUITS "LES ST. GEORGES," "CUVÉE JOSEPH FAIVELEY":

Medium depth. Orangy rim. Spicier, greener than the Beaune. Complex, but good depth of flavour. Lovely length. Great complexity. Very good. Drink 1990 to 1995. (17.5) Thankfully, no rot here—a problem with so many 1983s.

1983 ECHÉZEAUX, FAIVELEY:

Good depth of colour, mature rim. Full, rich, tannic. Solid, great length. Power, but good balance and fruit. Excellent. Drink 1992 to 1998. (18)

At the end, we opened a rare bottle.

CLOS DES LAMBRAYS 1934:

Level was two inches below cork. Excellent appearance. Medium red. Good depth. Fair bit of sediment. I decanted it. Great complexity on nose. Barnyard and spices. Complex, long, elegant. Has held extremely well. Surprisingly good. (17.5)

February 16, 1988

Tasting of Mähler-Besse wines, at the Four Seasons hotel, in Vancouver.

After a tasting of their commercial wines, we proceeded with a vertical tasting of Château Palmer, of which the above firm controls 50%.

Château Palmer

1983:

Medium-dark colour, good depth to rim, yet not brilliant. Thick, glycerol, herbal, complex nose; hint of oak. Lovely nose. Loads of ripe fruit. Needs seven to eight years. Great depth, length, and complexity, yet has the elegance of Margaux. (18.5)

1982:

Less wine in glass because one bottle had "disappeared"! Hint of sulphur on nose. Not as much depth as the 1983. Some purple. Not as intense as the 1983. Leaner, less complex, but still very good. Doesn't have the ripeness of the great 1982s, though. (17)

1976:

Evolved, mature colour; palish rim. Herbal, ripe fruit on nose. Slight smell of barnyard. Round, soft, at its peak. (15.5)

1975:

Dark, colour. Very good depth. Starting to show lovely complexity on nose. Still a bit closed. Layers of fruit, but with the hard tannins of the 1975s. A spicy wine that has a promising future. Good balance. Try from 1992. (18)

1967:

Medium red, brownish, old-looking. Slightly pruny on nose. Elegant, slight acidity, but soft. At its absolute peak. Good complexity; more so than the 1976. Surprisingly good. (16.5)

1966:

Dark, yet maturing colour; orangy-brown rim. Cedary, expansive, elegant chocolaty bouquet. Superb complexity. Hint of leather. Classic Médoc. Lovely balance. Great wine. Everything one could want from a wine. At its absolute peak. (19)

February 24, 1988

Dinner at "Le Gavroche" restaurant, in Vancouver.

With Terry Leighton and his wife Frances, owners of California's Kalin Cellars. Carol and I were their guests for dinner. We brought the following wines along.

Champagne Veuve Clicquot Brut N/V:

Solid and reliable. Spicy, rich, lively, tiny bubbles. I like to age my Veuve Clicquot N/V for one to two years. Very good.

1980 "Y," dry wine of d'Yquem:

Medium gold, full, rich, but with good balance and finesse. Complex, long, hint of new oak and ripe raisins. Good fruit. Most enjoyable.

Chambertin 1982, Joseph Drouhin:

Well structured for a 1982. Spicy, complex, rich. Needs two to three years. Very good, dark for a 1982. Terry said that this wine resembled Louis Trapet's Chambertin in style, and that it is probably from them that Drouhin has purchased the juice. In any event, an excellent 1982 Chambertin.

I gave Terry a copy of my book, Wine Wise, *published last month.*

February 25, 1988

Le Tastevin Wine Club tasting of 1978 red Bordeaux, at Park Royal hotel.

Guest speaker: Ian Mottershead. These wines are now entering into their tenth year. 1978 is characterized in high Cabernet proportion, low Merlot (a varietal that suffered from a wet summer and early fall), and a vintage that was kinder to the Médoc than to St. Emilion and Pomerol.

1. Château Certan Guiraud, Pomerol:

Medium-red colour, mature rim. A bit musty on nose. Some ripe fruit, too; stemmy. Light-bodied, fairly alcoholic, some sweet fruit. On the sweet side. Well balanced. Almost ready. (14.5)

2. Château L'Evangile, Pomerol:

More depth than #1. Riper, more intense fruit on nose. A bit stemmy. Medium-bodied, some tannin, noticeable acidity. Better complexity than #1. Not as luscious as it can be and nowhere near the quality or intensity of the 1975 or the 1982 that this property has produced. (16)

3. Château La Lagune, Haut-Médoc:

Very good, deep, dark colour; purplish rim. Spicy, herbal nose. New oak. Complex and stylish. Full, rich, tannic, well balanced. Needs three to five years. (17.5)

4. Château de Fieuzal, Graves:

Medium-red colour, palish rim. Earthy, herbaceous nose; open and forward. Round, elegant, good fruit, slightly tannic, but clean finish. (15.5)

5. Château Beychevelle, St. Julien:

Medium-red colour, mature rim. Pronounced stemmy, green, bell-pepper nose. A bit tannic, hard, yet only light-bodied. Some bitterness at finish.

Finishes a bit sharp and chaptalized. This wine has never impressed me. it is too diluted. (14.5)

6. Château Leoville-Poyferré, St. Julien:

Good depth of colour, with orange hue. Straw, toasty, closed nose. Old wood. Acidic, sharp, hard, not much class here. Disappointing, finishes short. Lacks ripe fruit. (14)

7. Château Clerc-Milon, Pauillac:

Good depth of colour; palish rim. Ripe, subdued Cabernet nose. Slightly stemmy, but good, ripe fruit underneath. Slightly minty. Full-bodied, stemmy, rich. Finishes clean, if a bit simple. (16)

8. Château Lynch-Bages, Pauillac:

Medium-red colour; palish rim. Delicate, perfumy nose. Subdued and elegant. Too bitter and acidic on palate. Lean, tannic, lacking ripe fruit. Acidic finish. Masculine, unyielding wine. (14) This is the only disappointing vintage for this property between 1975 and 1985.

9. Château Giscours, Margaux:

As dark as #3 but more mature rim. Intense, stemmy nose. Not complex, just big. Full, chunky, rich, heavy, well balanced. Serious, yet lacks the charm of #3. (16)

10. Château Boyd-Cantenac, Margaux:

Medium red, good depth to rim. Subdued, slightly perfumy, but vegetal on nose. Not much there. Similar impressions on palate. A bit acidic, but some fruit, too. Pleasant; just lacks that extra complex dimension. (15)

11. Château d'Angludet, Margaux:

Good depth, slight maturity at rim. Spicy Cabernet nose, some earth; a bit leathery. Similar impressions on palate. Old wood, leather, rich, chunky, straightforward. (15)

12. Château Kirwan:

Dark purplish colour, yet pale rim. Open, stemmy nose. Some elegance, but quite vegetal. Good complexity, medium-bodied. A bit too acidic, but tannic, serious, very Cabernet. Needs two to four years. (15)

DESSERT WINE

KWV Boberg Superior 1956 Tawny Port, South Africa:

Pale amber, green tinge. Medium, complex nose. Some Madeira character. Fruity, well balanced, complex, elegant, and stylish. Very fine. Ready.

February 1988

Dinner of the "Group of Ten."

Champagne Krug Vintage 1979:

Still very lively and fresh. Crisp, lots of depth. A steely Champagne, requiring three to five extra years of bottle-age. Lovely structure. Fairly lean and acidic at this stage. Needs time. Excellent balance.

Champagne Krug "Grande Cuvée" N/V:

The Champagne was acquired five years ago. Smooth, rich, complex, with layers of fruit, tiny bubbles, and persistent mousse. Very long, rich, excellent quality... as usual.

Chassagne-Montrachet Premier Cru "Morgeot" 1983, Bernard Morey

and

Puligny Montrachet Premier Cru "Folatières" 1983, Monnier-Vaivrand:

Both identical, bright-gold colours.

The Chassagne was softer, richer, more oaky, more alcoholic. Ready.

The Puligny was a bit spicier, leaner; soft, but more lively. Overall, I think that the "Morgeot" has more depth and oak.

1953 Château Gruaud-Larose, in magnum:

(Our group bottle) Bottom neck level. Impressive, dark colour; like a 1961. Mature rim. Lovely, complex, long, open, charming nose of mature Claret. At its peak. Earthy, a bit austere, lovely length. Very good. Bottles need drinking. Magnums should be perfect now.

1966 Château Gruaud-Larose:

Impressive, deep, still youthful colour. Lovely, rich, complex nose. Full, fruity, excellent balance. Needs four to five extra years. Earthy, rich Cabernet. Full, hard, fruity, solid. Excellent. This is one of the better 1966s, and it has lots of fruit backing up the tannins.

1963 Dow's Vintage Port, London-bottled by Charles Kinloch:

Not quite ready. Decanted four-and-a-half hours. Spirity, dark, hard, but backed by good fruit. Still very young. Needs five to ten more years. Very good potential.

Visit and lunch with Joe and Alice Heitz.

A nice lunch. Michael and Orly were well behaved. Other guests included David and Diana Berkley, and Barb and Milt Eisele. David Berkley is a wine merchant from Sacramento, and is also the official purveyor of wines for the White House and President Reagan. Milt Eisele is the owner of the famous Eisele vineyard near Calistoga. He sells his Cabernet grapes to Joseph Phelps. They are a nice elderly couple.

We tasted the following.

S. ANDERSON "BLANC DE NOIR" 1984 SPARKLING WINE, NAPA VALLEY:

This is their first vintage, made from Pinot Noir grapes. The winery is very close to our townhouse in Yountville. Surprisingly good. Clean, fresh, complex nose. Round, good mousse, well balanced. A pleasant Champagne-style wine.

EISELE 1974 CABERNET SAUVIGNON, NAPA VALLEY:

Made from 100% Cabernet Sauvignon. Milt Eisele never sold this wine commercially. He gave this bottle to Joe Heitz exactly ten years ago, in March 1978. A typical, excellent 1974 Napa Cabernet Sauvignon. Dark, maturing colour. Intense, complex nose of ripe Cabernet. Mint, chocolate. Full, round, rich, smooth, excellent balance. Reaching its peak. This is a lovely bottle!

1974 NEDERBURG CABERNET SAUVIGNON "SUPERIOR," SOUTH AFRICA:

Good, dark colour. Totally different in style and weight from the Eisele. More subdued, more elegant. Smooth, well balanced, delicate. Touch of American oak, slightly leathery, good complexity. A very good wine. At its peak.

1979 JOSEPH PHELPS "EISELE VINEYARD" CABERNET SAUVIGNON, NAPA VALLEY:

Nowhere near the quality of the super 1974 Eisele. Quite dark. Subdued nose, hint of mint and spice. Quite dry, hard, low fruit, and finishes short. A pleasant wine that was overshadowed by the two stars above.

These wines were followed by two fine red Burgundies Joe asked me to decant. When I helped him reorganize his cellar last year, I told him to drink these wines soon as they were at, or past, their prime.

1973 ROMANÉE-CONTI, DOMAINE DE LA ROMANÉE-CONTI:

No sediment at all. Pale, mature colour, typical of the soft 1973s. Open, complex, spicy nose of Pinot Noir. Lovely elegance on both nose and palate. Round, soft, still alive, fruity. Great length. True Grand Cru quality.

1972 CLOS DE LA ROCHE, DOMAINE DUJAC:

Some sediment. Sharper nose, a bit green, intense, spicy. Typical Pinot Noir of a good producer. Full, rich, round, obvious acidity of the 1972s, but excellent fruit. Spicy, round, fruity, long. Another lovely bottle that is at its peak. This was a lovely, enjoyable lunch.

April 1988

Tasting of 1985 red Burgundies from the House of Faiveley, at "Wines and Things" Wine Shop, in Vancouver.

Tasting conducted by Christophe Voisin, Export Manager for Faiveley. We started with two white wines of the 1986 vintage:

François Faiveley believes in cold fermentation in order to give the wine longevity; Grand and Premier Crus are aged in new oak for six months, then in older oak for an extra 12 to 16 months. They use egg whites for fining.

1985 RULLY ROUGE:

Made from 85% of their own grapes; the rest are purchased. Palish, cherry-red, purplish rim. Subdued, delicate nose, with hint of licorice. Clean and charming. Good fruit, leaner-style wine. Some tannin. Good backbone, finishing a bit bitter. Needs two to three years. Quite good. (15)

1985 AUXEY-DURESSES:

Made from purchased grapes. Similar appearance to the Rully, with a little more depth. Fresh, spicy nose. Hint of oak, some tannins, good fruit. Good Pinot Noir character. Drink from 1990 to 1995. (15.5)

1985 FIXIN:

A little more depth than the previous two, but still fairly light in colour. Flowery, spicy nose; hint of ripe cherries. Another fairly solid wine. Noticeable alcohol, good fruit and backbone. Drink from 1990 to 1994. More masculine than the previous two. Too spirity. (14.5)

1985 GEVREY-CHAMBERTIN PREMIER CRU "LA COMBE AUX MOINES":

Much darker than the above three reds. Medium-dark colour; purplish rim. Fine quality here. Delicate, lovely, subdued nose. Some oak, fresh fruit, spicy, yet elegant. Full, rich, round, good balance, ripe fruit. Everything blends perfectly. Almost enjoyable now. Drink 1992 to 1995. Very good! (17)

1985 ECHÉZEAUX:

Similar appearance to the Gevrey. New oak, closed, needs time. Harder, leaner, and more alcoholic than the Gevrey. Lacks the charm of the Gevrey or the ripe fruit. Closed, or just doesn't have it? Noticeable acidity. Try from 1993. Some sharpness, greenness. (16.5) May improve with age.

1985 CLOS DE VOUGEOT:

Made 100% from their own grapes, from two-and-a-half hectares. Darker than the previous two wines. Some wood, mushrooms, quite closed. Full, rich, solid, good tannins and backbone. Top class here.

Long, full, powerful, rich, well balanced. Very good potential. Drink from 1995. (18)

1985 CLOS DE LA ROCHE:

Similar appearance to the Clos de Vougeot. Lovely, spicy, expansive, fresh berries on nose. Intense and long. Sweeter, fuller, richer style. Good backbone. Quite soft; some feminine elegance, too. Drink from 1993 to 1998. (17.5)

1985 LATRICIÈRES-CHAMBERTIN:

Best deep colour of flight. Dark, cherry-red. Most closed, most unyielding nose; cleared later. Very slightly musty on entry. Hard, tannic, solid, biggest so far. Hardest, but good, ripe fruit underneath. Needs a long time. Try around 1995 to 1998, or beyond. A sleeper. Will be very good. (18)

1985 MAZIS-CHAMBERTIN:

Very good, deep, purplish colour. Subdued nose. Ripe, some varietal character on nose. Hard, leaner, a bit noticeable acidity on palate. Somehow lacks the depth of some of the other wines. More elegant. Doesn't have the weight, at this stage, of the Latricières. A bit too acidic. Later, elegance improved, as did the balance. (17)

1985 CHAMBERTIN "CLOS DE BÈZE":

Paler colour than the Latricières, but very good depth. Not as purplish as the others. Closed, unyielding nose. Full, big, solid, lovely depth and class. New oak, great extract. A noble wine of great complexity. Needs seven to ten years. Later, nose opened, with an explosion of ripe fruit. (19)

April 1988

Vertical tasting of Château Ducru-Beaucaillou, at Alastair Carruthers'.

Property was known to us in advance, but not the order or the vintages.

FLIGHT #1
1983 to 1975

1. 1978:

Medium-dark colour; slightly orangy rim. Open, spicy Cabernet and oak nose. A bit herbaceous. Soft, forward, touch of green. Medium-bodied. Clean finish, but a bit short. 1978? Quite Cabernet, vegetal. Good complexity. Drink from 1990 onward. (16.5)

2. 1976:

Paler than #1, more orange, but good depth. Riper, more sugary on nose. Less elegant fruit. Full, solid, a bit tannic, slightly green. Leaner-style. 1981? (16)

3. 1983:

Good depth of colour. Fairly young appearance, purplish rim. Lovely, intense ripe fruit; hint of oak. Full, rich, tannic, long, youthful. New oak. Needs time. 1983? Or the hard tannins of 1975, yet seems too young for that. (17.5)

4. 1982:

Very dark, deep colour to rim. Impressive. Ripe nose, yet closed at this stage. Full, rich, fat, tannic, young, new oak, ripe fruit. Very 1982 structure. Drink from 1995. (18)

5. 1975:

Medium depth, quite a bit of orange at rim. Ripe, open, slightly leathery, hot nose. Not unlike 1979. A bit watery. Possible 1976? Just about ready. (16) When I found out what it was, it worried me a bit. Poor bottle? I have definitely tasted better examples of this. Should have been more solid.

6. 1979:

Dark colour to rim, showing a little maturity. Closed, yet green nose. Unyielding. A bit earthy. Hard, a bit tannic, yet acidic, too. Medium to light-bodied. Fresh, vegetal, elegant. A bit acidic finish. Could it be 1975? A bit too weedy for that. (15.5)

7. 1981:

Very good, dark colour to rim. Not quite as dark as #4. Ripe, young fruit. Rich, fruity, long, spicy. Excellent balance. Top quality. Well put together, leaner, and less tannic than #4. Possibly 1978 or 1981? Very Cabernet. (17)

FLIGHT #2
1970 to 1959

1. 1966:

Medium-dark, good depth; quite bright red; mature rim. Stemmy, elegant nose. Sweet, soft, forward. Tobacco, lovely, classy. Later, hint of dill on nose. 1964 or 1966? Some people didn't like it; too vegetal. (17)

2. 1959:

Mature, yet bright red. Like a 1962. Ripe nose, sweet. Full, rich, round. Later finishes a bit thin, but lots of charm and elegance. Forward, sweet. Lovely drinking now. 1962? (17)

3. 1964:

Medium red, mature rim. Lovely, forthcoming, tobacco, oak, vanilla nose. Lots of elegance. Harder, more 1966 structure. A bit more acidic and leaner. Quite vegetal. Finishes a bit too lean. Nose is best part. (16)

4. 1961:

Quite mature-looking. Ripe, rich, yet youthful nose. Fruity, slightly astringent. Forward, elegant, classy. 1959 or 1961, possibly 1961? Yet softer, like 1959. I have tasted better examples of this. (18)

5. 1970:

Darkest, very young-looking; deep, purplish, impressive. Rich, ripe, lovely nose. Liveliest, best of flight. Full, rich, tannic, big. No rush. Lots of tannins and extract. 1970? Backward. Drink from 1992 to 2000. Great wine! (18.5)

6. 1962:

Medium colour, good depth, mature. Rich, complex nose. Soft, forward, yet backed by tannin. Excellent length. Lovely complexity. Great quality, superb complexity. (18.5) This has got to be the surprise of the whole evening!

DESSERT WINE

1934 FONSECA'S VINTAGE PORT:

Deep colour, palish rim, browning. Old-smelling. Some oak. A bit leathery, skunky. Decanted two hours. High alcohol, dry, sharp, spirity. Not much sweetness. Cleaner on palate than on nose, yet simple. I guessed pre-1945. It is a 1934 Fonseca's, which is surprising because Fonseca's 1934 should be better than this. Cork fell apart. Not a good bottle.

Overall impressions

The older Ducru-Beaucaillous seemed bigger, more complex. Some of the younger vintages seemed more diluted. Since 1975, the wine has less depth or weight than the equivalent wines of Lascases or Gruaud-Larose, with the exception of the excellent 1982.

April 7, 1988

Chevaliers du Tastevin tasting of 1985 red Burgundies, at the Bayshore hotel.

Most wines were purchased from the Wine House in San Francisco. They were bottled about one year ago.

1. GEVREY-CHAMBERTIN, PHILIPPE NADEFF:

Medium-dark, good depth. Closed nose at this stage. Clean, slightly toasty. Some oak, vanilla. Solid Gevrey. Lovely fruit. Rich, serious, masculine. Drink from 1993 to 2002. (17)

2. VOLNAY "CHAMPANS" PREMIER CRU, MONTHÉLIE-DOUHAIRET:

Dark, purplish colour. Flowery, elegant nose, yet closed. Some fruit coming through. Later, sweet, elegant fruit. Round, forward, charming. A bit of tannin, clean, long. Drink from 1991 to 1995. Lovely flavours. (17)

3. CORTON "CUVÉE CHARLOTTE DUMAY," HOSPICES DE BEAUNE:

Medium red, some purple. Noticeable new oak on nose. Complex, delicate. Good Pinot Noir character on nose. Full, rich, solid, good fruit coming through. Very good length and extract. Outstanding. Best overall. (18.5)

4. CLOS DE VOUGEOT, CHARLES MORTET:

Deep, purplish colour. Not much oak on nose, but lovely complexity. Very good Pinot Noir. Some leather, ripe fruit. Unyielding, rich, solid, masculine. Not much charm, but very good potential. (17.5)

5. CLOS DE LA ROCHE, P. AMIOT:

Medium colour, good depth. Closed, unyielding nose. Later, good ripe fruit and intensity. Slightly stemmy. Charming, forward, more feminine, lovely depth and complexity. Drink from 1992 to 1999. Very good. Top quality. (17.5)

6. NUITS-ST.-GEORGES "MURGERS" PREMIER CRU, MÉO-CAMUZET:

More evolved colour, some purple. Hint of burnt oak. Complex, delicate on nose. Harder, more solid, masculine; singed tannin, though. Very good, yet without the class of some. New toasty-oak predominates. A bit too sharp, too. Later, improved quite a bit. (17)

7. VOSNE-ROMANÉE "LES CHAUMES," MÉO-CAMUZET:

Open, spicy, elegant nose. Palish colour. Lovely elegance. Forward, very Vosne. Complex, long, delicate. Lots of class here. A lovely wine. (18)

Overall impressions

A very good, charming vintage. Soft tannins, very good balance, and lovely fruit. Almost tempted to drink them over the next two to three years, but the best have the staying power to last a decade or more.

April 14, 1988

Commanderie de Bordeaux blind tasting of 1970 red Bordeaux, at the Hotel Vancouver.

My first event as Maître of our Commanderie. I took over from David Freeman, QC, earlier this year. These wines are now almost 18 years old.

FLIGHT #1

1. CHÂTEAU L'ARROSÉE:

Very good dark colour to rim. Quite young-looking. Still closed, slightly stemmy, vegetal. Clean. Fairly hard, a bit tannic, medium-bodied. Finishes a bit green. Later, improved. Solid backbone. (17.5)

2. CHÂTEAU BOUSCAUT:

Good, dark colour to rim. Closed, unyielding nose at first. Later, ripe, still closed. Full, rich. Not much complexity, but big and solid. No rush. Well balanced. (16) This was a pleasant surprise.

3. CHÂTEAU LANESSAN:

Good, dark colour; orange rim. Closed, slightly spirity nose. Some herbaceousness. Later, ripe Cabernet.

Round, complex, full, forward. Ready. Well balanced. Charming. Best complexity so far. (17)

4. CHÂTEAU ORMES DE PEZ:

Dark, mature colour to rim. Unyielding, slightly earthy nose. Earthy on palate. Oddly, very "Graves." Solid, chunky. Full, one-dimensional, but big. No rush. Clean, yet simple finish. Ripe nose, good structure. (17)

5. CHÂTEAU CHASSE-SPLEEN:

Dark colour; orange rim. Open, sweet, spicy, slightly vegetal nose. Round, rich, long, smooth. Some oak. Not much complexity, but lovely drinking now. (16.5)

6. CHÂTEAU LA GAFFELIÈRE:

Medium to dark colour; orange, mature rim. Open, forthcoming, spicy, vegetal nose. Similar impressions on palate. Very Cabernet Franc (St. Emilion). Elegant, ripe, rich, yet ready and soft. Perfect drinking now. (16.5)

7. CHÂTEAU PAVIE:

Medium to dark; palish rim. Toasted bread, warm nose. A bit herbaceous. Elegant. Lovely on entry, but a bit tannic and hard at finish. Quite good. Ready, but no rush. (17)

8. CHÂTEAU D'ANGLUDET:

Dark colour; mature rim. Earthy, closed nose, some tar. Full, rich, solid, big, and fruity. Only fault (other than not much complexity at this stage) is high acidity at finish. (15)

Overall impressions

Colour and appearance are impressive. Consistent; no poor or disappointing wines. A toss-up between #3 and #7 as to which showed best in this flight tonight.

FLIGHT #2

9. CHÂTEAU PALMER:

Very dark, impressive colour. Very youthful. Fabulous, ripe, rich chocolaty nose. Lovely length. Spicy, rich nose. Palmer! Superb. Full, rich, ripe, big, intense, lots of extract. Great bottle. No rush. (19)

10. CHÂTEAU BEYCHEVELLE:

Good, dark colour. Lighter than #9. Open, toasty, elegant nose. Slightly stemmy. Not as ripe as #9. Leaner, harder, greener, but complex and long. Very good. (17)

11. CHÂTEAU LAFON-ROCHET:

Medium-dark colour; mature, orange rim. Burnt oak, complex nose. A bit pruny, stemmy. Round, forward, ripe, yet a bit lean finish. (15)

12. CHÂTEAU LA LAGUNE:

Medium red, orange rim. Open, elegant nose. Delicate, slightly stemmy. Later, nose closed. Lean, hard, simple, a bit too acidic. Powerful, yet too lean. A bit musty. Good, but not great. (16) This can be a fine wine. Unfortunately, it did not show very well tonight.

13. CHÂTEAU LYNCH-BAGES:

Very impressive, very dark colour to rim. Minty, cedary nose. Ripe and rich. Must be Lynch-Bages. Fabulous intensity on palate. Mint, cedar, eucalyptus. It's all there. Rich, big, powerful, long, solid. Needs ten or more years. Lovely. (18.5)

14. CHÂTEAU COS D'ESTOURNEL:

Very good, dark colour. Open, hint of straw on nose. A bit pruny. Slight sign of oxidation. Lean, fairly acidic, some sharpness, hint of oak. Complex, but lean. (17)

15. CHÂTEAU GRAND-PUY-LACOSTE:

Very good, dark colour. Subdued, unyielding nose. Later, opened into rich, ripe nose. Full, rich, long, tannic, solid. Has to be Grand-Puy-Lacoste. Very Cabernet! Big Pauillac. Lovely. No rush. Lots of life. (18)

Overall impressions

The Palmer and Lynch Bages are very deep, and impressive. Most participants liked the Grand-Puy-Lacoste best, with the Lynch Bages second, and the Palmer third. I was in the minority placing the Palmer first, the Lynch Bages second, and the Lacoste third. All three wines were best of flight, and great bottles by any yardstick.

April 15, 1988

Dinner at Dave Spurrell's, also with the Freemans and the Sid Crosses.

All wines served double-blind, as usual.

CHAMPAGNE DE VENOGE 1975 CORDON BLEU "CHAMPAGNE DES PRINCES":

Beautiful decanter-shaped bottle with stopper. Some complexity on nose, but not much yeast. Fairly hard, yet sweet, caramel on both nose and palate. Good bubbles, still lively, but lacking complexity. I thought it was a California sparkling wine. Rather disappointing.

CHAMPAGNE KRUG VINTAGE 1979:

Lots of class and depth here. Complex, long, rich, yet elegant and quite forward. I thought it was a Pol Roger Chardonnay. Surprising, because two months ago this wine was bigger and harder, requiring three to four extra years. In any case, excellent.

1982 BÂTARD-MONTRACHET, LEFLAIVE

AND

1982 CHASSAGNE-MONTRACHET "LES CAILLERETS," JEAN-MARC MOREY (SON OF ALBERT MOREY):

I guessed white Burgundies and 1982s right away! I also said the Bâtard had to be a Bâtard or Chevalier, but I thought it was Drouhin's. Soft, rich, round, very intense, luscious, ripe fruit, lovely balance. Very good.

The Chassagne Caillerets was very good, too, but a bit too sulphuric on nose, leaner, and simpler on palate, without the depth of the Bâtard. Very good nevertheless. At its peak, while the Bâtard will last three to four more years.

1955, 1967, AND 1977 BAROLOS "RISERVA," BORGOGNO:

I guessed Italy and Barolo right away. (I had a good evening. Lucky!)

The 1967 and 1977 were decanted four hours earlier.

The 1977 had an odd, leathery, slightly oxidized nose. Fairly hard, tannic, and lean, yet good fruit, too. Improved in the glass. Good, but not great.

The 1967 had a nose of iodine, lead, and raw meat. Later, rich, chocolaty. Full, luscious, still a bit tannic, long, noticeable acidity. No rush. Very good.

The 1955 was very pale, but had a complex, delicate, clean nose. Round, soft, a bit woody and leathery, but stylish. Has held extremely well. I assume that the relatively high acidity is what keeps these wines alive for so long.

1971 CHÂTEAU SUDUIRAUT:

Bright gold. Delicate, subdued nose; some botrytis, but not very intense. Clean, buttery, soft, decent acidity. Enjoyable. I thought a it was a light 1976 Sauternes.

Then we tasted a mystery: an old wine, probably Madeira (Malmsey?). Amber olive-green at rim. Delicate, yet intense nutty nose. Off-dry, but not sweet. Quite good. No vintage, no label; short, unbranded cork. Purchased at Heublein's Chicago Wine Auction, May 24, 1979. I think this wine is at least from the 1920s or even older.

April 17 to 20, 1988

German-American "Rarities" group tastings in Los Angeles.

This was our third yearly event with this group.

April 17, 1988

FIRST EVENT

Black Tie dinner, at "Michael's."

APERITIF

CHAMPAGNE CHARBAUT BRUT ROSÉ N/V:

Salmon-pink; fruity, fresh nose. Round, soft, fairly sweet. Decent, but no great complexity.

1982 AND 1983 CHÂTEAU LAVILLE-HAUT-BRION:

1983: Lilacs, delicate nose; more intensity than the 1982; riper. Both had a hint of sulphur. The 1983 was rich, a hint of new oak, clean, ripe, long, and intense.

The 1982:

Leaner, harder, a bit too soft; finished short, too. 1983: better and more intense; quite good. Rated the 1983 (17.5) and the 1982 (16.5).

1983 AND 1982 CHÂTEAU HAUT-BRION BLANC:

1983: closed nose, softer, less obvious oak; more delicate. Very good, but needs time; subdued, yet complex and long. (17.5)

1982: darker than the 1983. Intense, rich nose; full, rich, long, obviously lots of new oak. Darkest of all four; richest, too. (18)

1945 Meursault-Charmes, Leroy, and 1945 Meursault-Perrières, Leroy:

CHARMES:

Deep yet bright gold, like a 1976 or 1978; good depth. Subdued, delicate nose. Some oak. Luscious, dry, but intense on palate. Rich, big year. Lovely and surprisingly lively for a 43-year-old white wine! More elegant, cleaner nose. (17.5)

THE PERRIÈRES:

Slightly darker, but excellent appearance. Some cardboard on nose, but some oak, too. Thicker, heavier, more Meursault (nutty), but not as lively as the Charmes. More intense, though. Richer, and slightly darker. After 20 minutes in glass, the Perrières got better and more intense overall. (18)

Both amazingly alive, intense, and classy for such 43-year-old white Burgundies.

CHAMPAGNE TAITTINGER "COLLECTION" 1981:

(Served as a "break.") Unusually rich for Taittinger. Complex, long, full, sweet, great depth. A lovely Champagne.

1945 Pomerols.

CHÂTEAU GAZIN, IN MAGNUM:

Good, dark, slightly mature colour. Delicate, complex, youthful Merlot nose. Slightly herbal. Quite sweet, delicate, slightly tannic. Ripe, a bit leathery. Held very well in magnum. (16.5)

CHÂTEAU LA POINTE:

Deeper, darker colour than the above. Impressive. Ripe, slightly rubbery nose. Hint of vanilla, oak. Lovely, ripe fruit. Very well balanced. Much younger-tasting than its age would indicate. Like a ripe 1970! Very good. (17.5)

CHÂTEAU LAFLEUR:

Another impressive, dark wine. Ripe, expansive nose of very mature Merlot. Slightly minty. Full, fruity, rich, long. Like a great 1961. This is great quality. Good length and structure. Superb. Loads of lively fresh fruit and great extract. (18.5)

CHÂTEAU PETRUS:

Darkest of the bunch. Ripest, most intense on nose. Big, solid, yet drier and not as ripe as the Lafleur. On this occasion, the Lafleur is the better wine. Later, as the wine evolved in the glass, they were about even, Petrus having more class, but less extract. Yet later, Petrus had the edge. (18.5) The 1945 Petrus was better when tasted at Brad Klein's residence in January 1988, however.

CHÂTEAU TROTANOY:

Good, dark colour; mature rim. Unyielding, slightly pruny nose. Sweet, slightly pruny on palate, too. Leathery, as well. Oxidizing, but still elegant and charming. Needs drinking. (16) Second bottle much better! Livelier, richer, more complex, and better structured. (17.5)

VIEUX CHÂTEAU CERTAN:

Good, dark colour. Slightly minty nose. Fairly hard and dry. Good tannic backbone typical of the 1945s, but too dry. Later, hint of tar, but finished lean. (17)

1945 red Burgundies

FLIGHT #1

CHAMBERTIN, RODET:

Dark colour; orange rim. Best colour of flight; darkest, too. Spicy, masculine Chambertin nose. Serious. Ripe, mature fruit. Hint of new oak. Lovely balance. Full, rich, round, slightly tannic. A bit vegetal. Very good fruit. (17.5)

CHARMES-CHAMBERTIN, PROSPER MOFOUX:

Good depth, orange rim. Surprisingly fresh. New oak, spicy Pinot Noir nose. Expansive, elegant, good structure, fairly full. Long on palate, some new oak. Lovely, complex flavours. Like a 1969! Very good. Finished a bit off (skunky). (17)

CLOS DE LA ROCHE, RÉMY:

Palest, most mature-looking of flight. Orange-red, clean. Delicate, complex Pinot Noir nose. Soft, elegant, spicy, very long. Lots of class. Lovely drinking. Good backbone. Very good! (17.5)

GRANDS ECHÉZEAUX, RENÉ ENGEL:

Good, dark colour. Not as clean a nose as the Clos de la Roche. A bit vegetal, sulphury, skunky. Fairly lean, hard, acidic. Burnt oak, high acidity. Needs drinking, but still alive. (16) Second bottle much better, livelier, rich, fruity. Great length. (18)

FLIGHT #2

Also 1945 red Burgundies

MUSIGNY, MORIN:

Much darker than the Vogüé. Intense, complex, spicy. Rich, open, long. Good fruit, a bit raisiny. Pleasant, but not great. (16.5)

MUSIGNY "VIEILLES VIGNES," VOGÜÉ:

Medium colour, good depth, mature rim. A bit rubbery. Not as complex as the Morin. More subdued, dull nose but better on palate; fruity, a bit lean at finish. Not bad but certainly not great. Disappointing. Costs a fortune! (16)

RICHEBOURG, DOMAINE DE LA ROMANÉE-CONTI:

Mid shoulder level. Good, dark colour; mature rim; not as dark as Morin's Musigny. Rubbery, pruny, slightly oxidizing nose, quite ripe. Similar impressions on palate. Solid, sweet, ripe. Not much complexity. Getting tired. (15) Obviously a poor bottle. This can be great.

LA TÂCHE, DOMAINE DE LA ROMANÉE-CONTI:

Low level. Similar appearance to the Vogüé. Spicy, complex nose. Quite classy. Round, a bit spicy and acidic, but complex and long. (17.5) Again, while certainly good, nowhere near as great as it can be.

Some of these 1945 red Burgundies were very good, but overall I expected more, much more, especially from the last three. Obviously, with such old wines, storage and provenance are a major concern.

Château d'Yquem 1945 and 1949:

1945:

Darker; brilliant, deep, gold colour. Lovely, ripe, complex nose of luscious, ripe, old Sauternes. Full, rich, long, luscious. Lovely balance. One of the great wines of the evening. Much better than when tasted earlier this year, in January 1988. (19)

1949:

Not as luscious on nose as the 1945. Some mint. Better on palate. Sweeter, richer, intense, and long. Good acidity. Still holding well. Hint of caramel. (18)

The evening ended with Champagne.

CHAMPAGNE LAURENT-PERRIER "GRAND SIÈCLE" 1970, IN MAGNUMS:

Still incredibly lively, rich, creamy. Excellent balance and fruit. A very good Champagne—18 years old.

Overall impressions

The Pomerols were very good, as expected, but not great—as were the red Burgundies, from which I expected at least one or two "super stars." It wasn't the case. The two d'Yquems were outstanding.

April 18, 1988

SECOND EVENT

At the "St. Estèphe" restaurant. Subject: California Wines.

Our hosts and organizers decided on a California motif, in honour of our European (mostly German) guests, who do not have the opportunity to taste rare California wines. The food was unusual: Mexican motif. Spicy, very fine, and imaginative.

1966 AND 1970 STONY HILL VINEYARD GEWÜRZTRAMINER:

The 1970: fresher, rounder, lychees, soft; finishes a bit fruity.

The 1966: heavier, more austere, but drying out and hint of oxidation. Rated the 1970 (17) and the 1966 (15).

Six California sparkling wines followed.

1. DOMAINE CHANDON "BLANC DE NOIR," N/V NAPA VALLEY, IN MAGNUMS:

As expected, quite good. Rich, generous on both nose and palate. (17)

2. DOMAINE MUMM N/V NAPA VALLEY:

Pleasant, round, complex; OK, but not special. (15)

3. MAISON DEUTZ N/V CALIFORNIA:

Foamy, bitter, dull. (13)

4. MICHEL TRIBANT N/V CALIFORNIA:

Foamy, ordinary. (11)

5. PIPER SONOMA N/V:

Foamy, ordinary. (13)

6. SCHRAMSBERG BRUT N/V NAPA VALLEY:

My favourite. Complex, long, elegant. Quite enjoyable. Tiny bubbles, good fruit. (17)

These sparkling wines were followed by a flight of Stony Hill Napa Chardonnays that had a surprising consistency of colour.

1978:

Clean, crisp, elegant, soft, forward. Lacks complexity and depth. (16)

1976:

Closed nose; hint of sulphur. Fruitier, more complex than the 1978. Bigger, richer but hot, too; a drought year. Better wine overall. (17)

1975:

Closed nose; hint of corn. Quite lean, acidic, some fruit. Complex Chardonnay. Very good. (17.5)

1974:

Dull, unyielding nose. Stylish, elegant, lots of class on palate. Best so far. Long, elegant finish. After 15 minutes in glass, however, getting tired; poorest! This wine really went downhill fast. (14.5)

1973:

Soft, rich, oaky, good acidity. Good flavour. Slightly hot finish. (16)

1964:

Most intense nose. Incredibly lively for its age. Fabulous flavour, great intensity. Like a superb white Burgundy. The best by far. Very unusual California Chardonnay, and very rare. The 1964 is a collector's item, costing over $200 per bottle! A superb California Chardonnay. Great! (18)

Overall impressions

The 1964 is one of the most outstanding—if not the greatest—California Chardonnay I have ever tasted. It seems, however, that more recent vintages of Stony Hill are not quite up to the standard of the older vintages.

Flight of various California Chardonnays

BERINGER "PRIVATE RESERVE" 1986, NAPA VALLEY:

Some wine writers rave about this wine, saying it is one of the greatest California Chardonnays ever! Medium gold. Elegant, complex, delicate nose. Rich, long, complex. Good fruit/acidity balance. Very good. (17.5)

RITCHIE CREEK VINEYARD 1985, NAPA VALLEY:

Palest of the bunch. Pale gold. Subdued, slight hint of paper, cardboard, petroleum on nose. Leaner, sharper, fairly acidic, but good fruit. Ready. Not a distance runner. (15)

MOUNT EDEN VINEYARDS 1983, NAPA VALLEY:

Bright gold. Not much on nose, but some elegance. Dry, clean, a bit too acidic. Quite good, but too green. Later, improved quite a bit. Held very well. Very nice Chardonnay, at its peak. (16)

MOUNT EDEN VINEYARDS 1978, NAPA VALLEY:

Brilliant gold. Lovely, buttery nose. Popcorn, classic, mature Chardonnay. Rich, a bit herbal. Complex. Sweet, rich on palate. Delicious. Very intense and rich. The oak on nose is almost too much of a good thing! Otherwise very good. (17.5)

HANZELL VINEYARDS 1974, NAPA VALLEY:

Colour similar to the 1978 Mount Eden Vineyards. Dull, unyielding, slightly medicinal nose. Harder, more closed, fairly alcoholic. Dry, bitter finish. Getting tired. Too alcoholic. Too weedy and dry. (14.5)

HEITZ CELLARS 1973 "LOT Z-32," NAPA VALLEY:

Bright, deep-gold colour. Ripe, oak, Chardonnay, herbaceous nose; almost hint of botrytis. Softer on palate, a bit short finish. Was better three to four years ago. Still rich. It has seen better days. Slightly minty. An old warrior. (16.5)

The Chardonnay flight was followed by a flight of Inglenook mature Cabernet Sauvignons

1960 "CASK A-1":

Impressive colour. Mature but dark. Rich, complex, spicy nose. American oak, vanilla. Soft, forward, delicate. Finishes a bit short. Slightly stemmy, smoky. (16.5)

1959 "CASK F-9":

Deeper than the 1960, but as old-looking. Fuller, richer, sweeter, more concentrated, too. Slightly leathery finish. (17)

1958:

Similar appearance, if slightly lighter than the 1959. Rubbery on nose. Minty, a bit tart, some sharpness, high acidity, good fruit. Not as ripe as the 1959 or the 1960, but livelier. Quite good. (15.5)

1954 "CASK J-3":

Mature, brown-orange rim. Older-looking than any other in the flight. Oxidizing on nose. Similar impressions on palate. Oxidized, pruny, sweet. Has seen better days. Drinkable, but just! (12)

1949:

Very good, dark colour to rim. Lovely, delicate, subdued nose of a much younger wine. Leaner, quite tannic, lively fruit. Very good and still very much alive. A bit cedary, rich. An impressive bottle. Top quality. Best, most complex wine of flight. (18)

The Inglenook flight was like drinking history. Old style, American oak, ripe Cabernets. With these wines, we had superb milk-fed veal (chops) marinated in red chilli pesto. A great course.

This was followed by a vertical tasting of mature Heitz Cellars "Martha's Vineyard" Cabernet Sauvignons, Napa Valley.

1974 "ANNIVERSARY LABEL":

Big, rich, sweet, ripe, intense. Long and luscious. So unusual. To love or to leave; I loved it! Big, rich, superb concentration of ripe fruity, eucalyptus, cedary flavours. Great wine. (18.5) If well stored, this wine should last well into the late 1990s.

1970:

Impressive, dark, young-looking. Even younger-looking than the 1974. Delicate, minty, fruity on palate. Quite acidic, not as rich or ripe as the 1974. Finishes a bit sharp. Very good, yet not as great as it can be. (17)

1969:

Quite minty on nose. Spicy, rich, round, complex, ripe fruit. Better fruit and balance than this 1970; better concentration, too. Lovely extract and fruit. Sweeter, heavier, fruitier, yet less complex than the 1968. Later, developed extra complexity, depth, and length. Superb. Good as the 1968 was, this 1969 surpassed it. Superb! (19) Joe Heitz prefers this wine to both his 1968 and 1970.

1968:

Slightly rubbery, mature nose. More subdued than the others. Soft, delicate, forward, complex, long. Lighter colour than the other three wines. Good fruit. Excellent. A bit hard at the end, but solid, complex, too. Lovely bottle. (18)

All four wines had the "Martha's Vineyard" trademark of mint-eucalyptus, intense nose.

This was followed by two Zinfandels.

1970 RIDGE "GIMSOMARE" ZINFANDEL:

Contributed by Brad Klein. Dark, mature colour. Slightly cloudy (shaken; it travelled recently). A rare bottle. Clean, elegant nose. Fruity, rich, ripe, long. Like a Cabernet. Dry, yet hint of sweetness. Good fruit. Soft, easy to drink. Very good and unusual. Subdued, not much Zinfandel spice. (17)

1968 RIDGE ZINFANDEL "ESSENCE":

Very dark, mature-looking; olive green rim. Sweet, ripe, mature fruit on nose. Sweet, yet not cloying. Elegant, almost Muscat-like. Complex, delicate, easy to drink. Well balanced. Very good. (17)

This was an interesting dinner, with very unusual and some excellent wines, but the food was a bit too spicy.

April 20, 1988

THE FINAL EVENT

Black Tie Dinner, at the Regency Club, in Los Angeles.

CHAMPAGNE BILLECART-SALMON BRUT 1982 "BLANC DE BLANCS":

Crisp, spicy, complex, and lively. Well balanced with good depth. Not ready, though. A bit too sharp and citrusy. Needs two to three extra years.

FLIGHT #1

1978 white Burgundies

1978 is my favourite vintage for white Burgundies. A great year. The best over the past 20 years.

1978 MEURSAULT-GENEVRIÈRES, LOUIS LATOUR:

Flowery, elegant nose. Not much oak. Getting tired. Better on palate. Quite rich, nutty, but a bit acidic and sharp. Outclassed by the next three wines. (16)

1978 CORTON-CHARLEMAGNE, LOUIS LATOUR:

Bright, deep gold. Typical, toasty, rich, long nose. Full, rich, luscious on palate. Great depth and ripe fruit. Hint of oak, fabulous balance. My favourite of the flight. (18)

CHEVALIER-MONTRACHET 1978, LEFLAIVE:

Very slight hint of oak. Fresh, complex fruit, too. Richer and softer on palate but a bit flabbier. Quite elegant and long. Too steely. (17) My bottles of this wine are far superior. Storage problems?

1978 MONTRACHET, PIERRE MOREY:

Deep, bright gold. Toasty, complex nose. Not very ripe. Full, rich, long, complex, quite oaky. Concentrated, yet more delicate than the Corton-Charlemagne. Quite fresh and lively, yet a bit too thin for a Montrachet. (17.5)

FLIGHT #2

1973, 1978, and 1982 Montrachets Domaine de la Romanée-Conti.

1982:

Youngest, yet deepest colour; bright gold. Lovely, intense, rich, superb nose. Quite subdued. Very 1982. Soft, forward, rich, long. Fabulous intensity! Great class. Almost at its peak. Perfect harmony. Perfect now. (19)

1978:

Hint of cabbage, but beautiful fruit, too. Rich, full, livelier, higher acidity than the 1982. More staying power. Superb balance. Rich, lively, long. Spicier than the 1982; steelier, too. Potentially a (20). Ripe, yet masculine, fruity, long. Not quite ready. A masterpiece. (19.5)

1973:

Fresh butter on nose. Delicate, at its perfect peak. Superb length, balance, elegance, class. Magnificent. Finishes long and clean. How can any wine get any better than this! Perfect (20). This is my third experience with this great wine (the 1973), and each time, it has shown extremely well.

BREAK

CHAMPAGNE TAITTINGER "COMTES DE CHAMPAGNE" BRUT 1975, IN MAGNUMS:

Complex, delicate, quite lively. Held well in magnums. Tiny bubbles; fresh, almost sweeter style. Very good.

This was followed by songs from a Broadway musical show, performed by a couple of gifted singers.

Back to the wines.

FLIGHT #3

1955 Red Bordeaux, in magnums

CHÂTEAU AUSONE:

Tobacco, spicy nose, slightly herbal, complex, some cedar. Delicate, soft, round. At its peak. Held well in magnums. Elegant, lovely drinking now. (17)

CHÂTEAU CALON-SÉGUR:

Slightly vegetal, dill. A bit hard, lean, and finishes sour. Too sharp, yet some sweet fruit, too. Has seen better days. (14)

CHÂTEAU LATOUR:

Darkest of flight. Ripe, intense nose; slightly overcooked, baked, leathery. Oxidized, pity. Hard, tannic, but a bad bottle. (No score)

CHÂTEAU PONTET-CANET:

Lightest colour of flight, good depth. Subdued, delicate nose; good, spicy Cabernet. Best nose of flight. Clean, complex, yet delicate. Good backbone. Good fruit. Long, clean finish. Trace of acidity. Needs drinking. Most classic of flight. (17)

CHÂTEAU MONTROSE:

Low shoulder fill. Good, dark colour. Clean, perfumy, delicate Cabernet nose. Not much age on nose. Very St. Estèphe on palate. Big, tannic, hard. Good fruit. Very lively, in spite of low level. (16.5)

Overall, a disappointing flight in the context of the vintage, and because of the fact that they were all magnums.

FLIGHT #4

Châteaux Gruaud-Larose and Mouton-Rothschild 1955, in jeroboam

CHÂTEAU GRUAUD-LAROSE:

Very good, dark colour. Mature, palish rim. Spicy, rich, classic St. Julien and classic Gruaud nose. Spicy, ripe, rich. Full, long, sweet fruit, well balanced. Good backbone, cedar. Rounder and at its peak. Velvety. (17.5)

CHÂTEAU MOUTON-ROTHSCHILD:

Even darker than the Gruaud, to rim. Spicy, slightly minty Mouton nose, some cedar, too. Full, rich, still tannic. Great concentration of fruit and extract. Harder than the Gruaud. A distance runner in large bottles. (18)

Some participants were less impressed than I was by these two jeroboams.

FLIGHT #5
1926 Clarets, in magnums

CHÂTEAU AUSONE:

Dark, mature colour. Totally oxidized nose. Sour. Dead. (0) When tasted on a previous occasion, this was a fine bottle.

CHÂTEAU CHEVAL-BLANC:

Paler, orange rim, old-looking. Oxidized, sour, leathery. Gone. (0)

CHÂTEAU LAFITE:

Pale-red colour, good appearance. Slightly stemmy, a bit sweet, some sharpness at finish, but some depth and complexity, too. Too tired, but drinkable. (15)

CHÂTEAU LATOUR:

Darkest of flight, but quite mature-looking. Slightly pruny nose. Oxidized. Hard, tannic, leathery, dirty wood. Gone! Latour is usually a dependable property, but lately I've had poor bottles of various vintages. (0)

CHÂTEAU MARGAUX:

Tired, old-looking. Undrinkable. Sour, leathery. Gone. Unacceptable. (0)

CHÂTEAU MOUTON-ROTHSCHILD:

Best of flight by far. Good appearance. Vegetal, Cabernet Franc on nose. Sweet on palate. Well structured. More Right-Bank nose. Good fruit, lively, complex. Has held quite well. Cedar and a little mint, typical Mouton characteristics. (17)

Overall impressions of the flight of 1926s

All in magnums and all purchased at auction at Christie's (London). I wonder if our hosts were not very cautious in selecting the wines for this event. Obviously, when tasting many old wines, it is expected that the odd bottle will disappoint. This time, an unacceptable number were poor. In fact, the whole flight was a total failure. Also, there were no spare—or replacement—bottles.

Also tasted

1927 TAYLOR'S VINTAGE PORT AND 1931 QUINTA DO NOVAL VINTAGE PORT:

The Taylor's was paler, quite tired-looking. Hint of oxidation on nose. Soft, forward, elegant, feminine. Quite pleasant, but not nearly as good as on previous occasions. (16.5)

The Noval 1931, a very famous and rare Port, fetching $600 per bottle, was darker, livelier and spicier, and better overall. Good fruit, not very concentrated, but complex. Better than when tasted previously, but at $600 per bottle? (17.5)

Overall impressions of this special weekend

The food was superb. The organization of the event seemed quite flawed. The overall quality of the wines was disappointing, and the 1926s were terrible, yet it can be an excellent vintage. I'm sure our German friends were very disappointed. So was I. A costly affair at US$2,500 per participant.

May 1988

Champagne Krug tasting, with Rémy Krug, at Hotel Le Meridien, in Vancouver.

Sponsored by Vintage Consultants, Krug's local agents. This was a repeat of a similar event held in Vancouver in the fall of 1986.

CHAMPAGNE KRUG "GRANDE CUVÉE" N/V:

Complex, round, forward. Good backbone. Lovely length. Full, with good acidity. Ready. Of course, being a nonvintage, one does not know how old this particular bottle is. Aged for six years before its release. (17.5)

CHAMPAGNE KRUG VINTAGE 1979:

Fresher, livelier than the Grande Cuvée; also leaner, longer, more depth, and higher acidity. A serious Champagne. Loads of fruit. No rush. (18.5)

CHAMPAGNE KRUG "CLOS DU MESNIL" 1979:

Production of 1,300 cases. Made from 100% Chardonnay. Clos du Mesnil is a five-acre vineyard, and 1979 is their first vintage. More delicate, yet more intense than the 1979 blend. Fermented in cask. Hint of oak and residual sugar; lovely elegance and balance. Finish not quite as intense as the 1979 blend. Dosage (1%) same as the 1979 blend. (18)

CHAMPAGNE KRUG "COLLECTION" 1969, IN MAGNUMS:

Fabulous. Lively, long, intense, complex bouquet; hint of mushrooms and earth; amazingly, lots of life, fruit, and acidity. A great bottle of Champagne! Magnificent. Has it all and still lively. Hardly any bubbles visible, but they're there. (19.5)

CHAMPAGNE KRUG "COLLECTION" 1962:

Skins on grapes were very rich and hard; long fermentation. This gave a slight colour "taché" (stained) to the wine. A fruity, seductive vintage. Darker gold than the 1969. Hint of mushrooms. Quite rich and fruity, but old. Low fizz. Caramel, hint of oxidation, earthy, and mushrooms. A heavy, rich Champagne. Good depth. Was better five or six years ago. (17.5)

CHAMPAGNE KRUG ROSÉ BRUT N/V:

Made from Pinot Noir grapes from Aÿ. Pale salmon colour. Some Pinot Noir on nose. Tight, full, rich, solid, yet not very complex. Has the weight and depth of Krug, but not the length or complexity of a great Champagne. (17.5)

Rémy Krug believes in ageing in oak barrels. Also, he said that Krug Champagnes have very few bubbles;

they are felt in the mouth but are not obvious to the eye (more subtle). At Krug, they ferment in wood, (October to May) in old barrels; they do not age in oak, however.

His brother Henri is the winemaker/blender. The Krugs like the Meuniers. They say that Pinot Meunier has a different personality in each village, while Pinot Noir has its own personality, no matter where it is grown. They say that Meunier does age well; the proof is in the quality of the older vintages of Krug.

Henri likes the 1981 (small crop), and especially the 1985 (to be released in 1991).

"Clos du Mesnil" is their Monopole, but in Le Mesnil, there are other growers and producers of Chardonnay, notably Salon.

May 17, 1988

Commanderie de Bordeaux Dinner and vertical tasting of Château Lafite-Rothschild, at the Delta Place hotel.

The food was prepared by Chef Bruno Marti and the culinary team going to the Frankfurt Culinary Olympics in October, where they will represent Canada.

CHAMPAGNE BOLLINGER BRUT 1975, IN METHUSELAH:

Full, rich, yeasty, forward. Typical, mature Bollinger. At its peak. Better than in regular bottle size, and more consistent. We had this with fresh Beluga caviar and blinis.

CORTON-CHARLEMAGNE 1983, LOUIS LATOUR:

Medium bright-gold. Oak, nutty, rich on nose and palate. Fairly alcoholic. Typical 1983 and typical Corton-Charlemagne of Latour's. Full, rich, long. Slightly low acidity. Lovely wine. Drinking very well now. (17.5)

FLIGHT #1

Château Lafite 1985 to 1978 and Moulin des Carruades de Château Lafite 1981 to 1979

Château Lafite

1985:

Bottle embossed with a comet—"Year of Comet," 1985. Deep purplish colour. Spicy, peppery nose, like the 1978s when they were young, but with riper, rounder fruit. Hint of oak. The lovely structure of the 1985s. Elegance rather than power. Oak, delicate, long, complex. Very promising. Surprisingly forward. Drink from 1994 to 2000. (18.5)

1984:

Impressive colour for the vintage. Almost as dark (if a bit more mature and paler rim) as the 1985. Delicate, subdued, perfumed nose; some straw and oak. Round, some tannin, medium-bodied, quite acidic. Quite good for the vintage. Finishes a bit short. (16) Drink now to 1995.

1983:

Very good, dark colour to rim. More mature than the 1985. Ripe, closed nose. Tannic, rich, yet typical Lafite elegance, too. Going through the closed phase. Tight. Needs seven to ten years. Elegance of Lafite, and lean, tannic structure of the 1983s. Very promising. (18)

1982:

Deep, dark colour typical of the 1982s. Ripe, rich, leathery nose. Clean, long, and lovely. Full, rich, ripe, tannic. Loaded with ripe fruit. Excellent balance. Outstanding. (19.5) Drink from 1996 to 2010.

1981:

Dark colour; palish rim. Open, spicy, the elegance of Lafite and of the vintage. Round, soft, forward, but with just enough backbone to hold well for five to ten more years. Very pleasant. (17.5)

1980:

Open, straw, vegetal nose; delicate. Palish, mature, orange rim. Spicy and vegetal on palate. Complex, long, delicate. At is peak now. Quite good. (16)

1979:

Much deeper-looking than the 1980; mature rim. Rich, ripe, spicy. Typical for the vintage. Pruny, fruity, rich. Almost ready. Very good, clean, long, ripe finish. Second bottle was livelier, spicier, but not as ripe on nose. (17.5)

1978:

Good depth, but quite mature colour. Woody, spicy, open nose. Slightly stemmy, vegetal. Leaner, harder on palate; quite acidic. Needs three to five years. Later, developed lovely complexity. Very good. (18) Drink now to 1998. Typical high Cabernet, vegetal overtones of the vintage.

Moulin des Carruades de Lafite

1979:

Riper, yet vegetal on nose; pruny, too. Good fruit. Pleasant. A bit musty. (15)

1981:

Medium depth. Complex, delicate, spicy. Elegance and class. Quite pleasant. Almost ready. (16.5)

Back to Château Lafite.

The following more mature wines, were served through the meal.

FLIGHT #1

1976:

Medium to dark colour; mature, orange rim. Lovely, intense, rich nose. Ripe, long. Lovely complexity. Full, rich, long, spicy, perfumy. At its peak. Superb bottle. Probably the top 1976 Claret. (17.5)

1975:

Darkest of flight, deep colour, orange rim. Spicy, stemmy nose. Hard, tannic, rich, solid. One of the better balanced 1975s. Tannic, yet soft enough. Leathery, tobacco nose. Needs time. Drink from 1992 to 1995 or beyond. Not unlike Haut-Brion in that vintage. A very good 1975, heralding the return of Lafite to top class, after underperforming between 1963 and 1974. (17.5)

1970:

Pale for a 1970. Light, vegetal, caramel, delicate. High acidity at finish. Pleasant, delicate, a bit too light, lacking the depth and the colour of the 1970s. Some caramel. Soft. Too acidic at finish. Cedar and mushrooms on nose. Controversial; some liked it. Most didn't. Can be charming, especially on nose. (16.5)

1966:

Palish, orangy rim; deeper than the 1970, though. Typical, herbaceous, leaner 1966. Quite stemmy, with Lafite elegance. Needs drinking. Hint of acidity at finish. (16.5)

1956:

The third time I've tasted this wine, all from the same source: David Freeman. Excellent for the vintage. Palish, tobacco, complex, delicate, spicy, round; a bit acidic and green, but excellent for the vintage. Very good! Rare and impressive. (17)

FLIGHT #2

Château Lafite 1962 to 1959

1962:

Lightest of flight, which is surprising, because 1962s are known to have a bright-red colour. Medium red, good depth. Perfumy, flowery, complex; sweet, cedary, forward. Lovely balance. At its peak. Lovely fruit. An excellent effort. Has the most elegance of the whole range tasted. (18)

1961, IN MAGNUM:

Deep colour, mature rim; actually medium depth. Harder, better backbone than the 1962. More serious. Lovely length, balance, and complexity. Slightly higher acidity. A very good wine, no doubt, but not quite great, as many 1961s are, especially from magnums. (18.5)

1959:

Bottle variation. One bottle not quite as rich; the other richer, rounder, fuller, with the intensity of the famous 1959, yet somehow just short of how great this 1959 can be. One bottle (17); other (18). Can be a perfect (20).

1961 CHÂTEAU D'YQUEM:

Deep, bright-gold, mature colour. Complex, botrytis, mature, yet subdued nose. Leaner than the rich 1962 or the opulent 1967; drier, too, but good length and complexity. Held well in glass. Very good. (17.5)

Overall, an outstanding event. Great wines, lovely food, intelligent and knowledgeable discussion by all participants.

May 26, 1988

Reception and lunch, at Featherstone, for Gerard Jaboulet.

We have many friends in common: Gerard Chave, Christian Moueix, and David Dougdale of O. W. Loeb and Co. of London. Gerard likes Tollot-Beaut's Corton-Charlemagnes as much as I do. I'll probably see Gerard again in Los Angeles, on October 30, when Bipin Desai will be organizing a vertical tasting of Hermitage "La Chapelle." Dougdale's allocation of Corton-Charlemagne of Tollot-Beaut is 28 magnums and ten cases of fifths—that's all! Mind you, the total average yearly production is four barrels, the equivalent of 100 dozen bottles.

June 1988

Tasting of 1985 red Bordeaux, at the Liberty Wine Co., in Point Roberts.

We started with a white wine

CHÂTEAU LAVILLE-HAUT-BRION 1985:

Palish-gold colour. Subdued, delicate, spicy nose; some new oak. Elegant and clean. A bit buttery. Rich, ripe on palate. Fairly alcoholic. Oak and honey. Intense and long. Lovely. Not too acidic, but good backbone. (17.5)

1985 red Bordeaux

CHÂTEAU DUCRU-BEAUCAILLOU:

Medium-red colour. Good depth, purplish overtones. Typical Ducru. Spicy, elegant, leafy, stemmy nose. Some new oak. Spicy, medium-bodied, clean. Oak, vanilla. Charming wine, charming vintage. Drink from 1993 to 1998. Low tannins. Hint of acidity at finish. (17)

CHÂTEAU PICHON-LALANDE:

Slightly more depth of colour than the Ducru. Tighter, riper nose. Hint of straw and ripe fruit. Subdued. Round, elegant, medium depth. Fruity, clean, impeccable. Quite complex. Finishes slightly bitter. Very good mid-term. Later, more ripeness and complexity. Very good. (17.5)

CHÂTEAU COS D'ESTOURNEL:

Much darker than the previous two wines. Ripe, yet closed, intense nose. Not much bouquet, just essence of Cabernet. Bigger, more intense, more tannic than above. Rich, big, ripe, great balance. Lovely concentration of ripe fruit. Clean, long, well-balanced finish. Needs ten years or more. Fleshy, very St. Estèphe. (18)

CHÂTEAU LA MISSION HAUT-BRION:

Medium colour, good depth. Surprisingly, lighter than all above, even than the Ducru. Elegant, subdued nose; some oak. Very clean. Leaner, greener, more acidic, not as ripe as the Cos. Structured like Ducru, if a bit more backbone. Somehow, not enough extract at this stage. Needs seven to eight years. Pity that the style is changing here. (17)

This property is now under the ownership of Haut-Brion. I pray and hope that Delmas will not tamper with this great property. Wishful thinking?

CHÂTEAU HAUT-BRION:

Similar appearance to the Ducru; a bit more depth than La Mission. Lovely, perfumy, classy, elegant nose. New oak, yet subdued. A classy, elegant wine. Very 1985 and very Haut-Brion. Flattering, complex, long, delicate. Needs eight years. (18)

CHÂTEAU AUSONE:

Lightest of flight, so far. Somehow doesn't sing. Delicate, subdued, odd nose; a bit cheesy? Soft, elegant, but lacks backbone. Not too impressive. Some ripeness, but noticeable acidity at finish. Good, but not great. Ready by 1993 to 1995. Much better on nose than on palate. Disappointing for a First Growth, especially at that price! Second bottle: similar appearance, but cleaner nose. Still a bit cheesy, sweaty. The 1983 and 1986 Ausones are better. (16.5)

CHÂTEAU CHEVAL-BLANC:

Impressive, deep colour; almost as deep as the Cos d'Estournel. Lovely, ripe, tobacco, smoky, leathery, stemmy, complex nose. New oak. Fabulous intensity and vanilla. Full, chewy, rich, long, solid. Excellent balance. Great future. Top quality. Drink from 1994 to 2000. (18.5)

CHÂTEAU MARGAUX:

This and the next three wines were noticeably darker than all previous wines with the exception of Cos d'Estournel. Lovely, deep, purplish colour to rim. Great, intense, ripe nose of fine Claret. Young, oak, vanilla, long, complex. Silky, round, beautiful wine. Great length. Fabulous fruit. Elegant and classy. Drink 1995 to 2002. (19)

CHÂTEAU MOUTON-ROTHSCHILD:

As dark as, if not darker, than the Margaux. Riper, richer nose; essence of Cabernet. Ripe, cedar, lovely intensity. Full, lots of tannins and backbone. Intense, long, serious. Very individual nose and taste. Fabulous bottle. Cigar-box, spicy, toasty, sweet, peppery, spicy. Totally different from the others. Needs ten years. (19)

CHÂTEAU LAFITE:

Superb, deep, brilliant colour. Subdued, delicate nose. Great length, structure, and class. Superb intensity. Long, oozing with ripe fruit. Fabulous intensity. Great ripeness. Unbelievable depth. One of the greatest young wines I've ever tasted! Iron fist in velvet glove. Great future, around 1997 to 2002. (19.5)

CHÂTEAU LATOUR:

Deep, dark colour to rim. Odd, slightly cheesy, sulphuric, leathery nose. Harder, a bit greener, manly, but without the class of the above four. Good extract, bell pepper, but high acidity, too. Very good, but not great. Somehow unbalanced and edgy. Needs time? (17.5)

Overall impressions

A softer, less intense vintage than 1983. Less ripe than 1982, but lovely, elegant wines of great charm. The best will last two decades or more. The majority should be ready by 1993 to 1996. Among the First Growths, Ausone and Latour (two favourites of mine) worry me.

July 9, 1988

Dinner of the "Group of Ten."

CHAMPAGNE KRUG "GRANDE CUVÉE" N/V:

As usual, complex, excellent structure. Some age, though. Hint of earth and mushrooms. Very enjoyable.

Three 1983 Grand Crus white Burgundies

1. BIENVENUE-BÂTARD-MONTRACHET, REMOISSENET:

Buttery nose. Rich, good intensity. Biggest of all three. Lots of weight, alcohol, extract. Big, fat wine. More California, but better acidity. Most intense, richest. Slightly too spirity for me, but excellent nevertheless. (18)

2. BÂTARD-MONTRACHET, REMOISSENET:

Rich, complex nose. Some oak; less sharp than #3. Full, rich, long, alcoholic. Great intensity. Lovely fruit. A big, rich wine. (17.5)

3. BÂTARD-MONTRACHET, LOUIS LATOUR:

Toasty, oaky, vanilla nose. Intense at entry and finish; a bit lighter middle. Leanest, lightest, yet still rich and full. Slightly more lemony and less hot than #1 or #2. (17.5)

All three had similar appearance. Bright, deep, gold colour. All smelled rich, hot; typical for this vintage. 1983 was a rich, fat vintage. The 1983 white Burgundies are not my favourites. Most are too spirity.

CHÂTEAU GRUAUD-LAROSE 1949, IN MAGNUM:

(Group bottle) Neck level. Excellent appearance. Very deep, dark colour to rim. Brownish, mature appearance. Perfumy, ripe nose. Lovely fruit and intensity. Soft, yet chocolaty; rich, long finish. (18)

CHÂTEAU LA TOUR CARNET 1934:

(Served double-blind) Purchased in London by Sid Cross in 1977. Excellent. Impressive appearance. Deep, brilliant colour; mature rim. Surprisingly deep for its age. Tobacco, complex, old nose, yet still lively. Noticeable acidity. I knew it was an old wine and said 1957, simply because of the acidity; I couldn't believe that because of the appearance, it could be older. Other participants guessed 1962, 1966, and 1967. Solid backbone. Better on nose than on palate. This is a Fourth Growth A/C St. Laurent. The capsule read "Calvet." The hand-cut cork was branded 1934, but nothing else.

PORTO "SPECIAL RESERVE 1897," BARROS:

Bottled in the early 1950s. Deep, mature, Tawny colour. Excellent appearance. At least 50 years in wood. Nutty, mature, oak nose of old Tawny. Rich, spirity, raisiny. Has held extremely well. Still lively and rich.

August 31, 1988

Dinner at Barney and Belle Rhode's.

Ten other guests included Bill Collins and his wife (the owners of Conn Creek winery); Barb and Milt Eisele (owner of Eisele vineyard, that sells grapes to Joseph Phelps; Milt has put his vineyard up for sale); Barney's friend from Atlanta; a young lawyer called Buck Goldstein; and Cathy and Chuck Ball (who started their own vineyard in Oakville near Vichon).

DOMAINE CHANDON NAPA BRUT "RÉSERVE" N/V:

Complex, round, rich, quite French style, but slightly too frothy for me. Good nevertheless. (16)

CONN CREEK CHARDONNAY 1983, NAPA VALLEY, IN MAGNUM:

Buttery nose, some oak. Round, at its peak. Not very intense, but well balanced. (15.5)

1975 RUTHERFORD HILL CABERNET SAUVIGNON, NAPA VALLEY:

Actually, this was Barney's "Bella Oaks" vineyard's first Cabernet, bottled at Rutherford Hill. Made from three-year-old vines. In 1976, Barney started to sell his grapes to Joe Heitz, who bottles it under his own label. A "historic" wine. Medium dark, maturing colour. Complex, tobacco, delicate nose. Medium-bodied, round, forward, good fruit, but noticeable greenness and acidity at finish (young vines). A fine effort. Has held well. (16.5)

1977 "EISELE VINEYARD" CABERNET SAUVIGNON, NAPA VALLEY:

Bottled by Milt Eisele under his own label. Best wine of the evening. Deep, mature colour. Lovely, intense, spicy, minty nose. Full, chunky, long, soft, yet complex. At its peak. A very good Cabernet and typical Eisele style. (17.5)

1985 "JUDGE'S ZINFANDEL" "KONSGAARD VINEYARDS," NAPA VALLEY:

(Tom Konsgaard, a judge, and his wife were guests, too. Their son is the winemaker at Newton Vineyards.) Very Gamay-like, structured like a fuller Morgon or Moulin-a-Vent. Round, fruity, well balanced; not too fat, heavy, or alcoholic. Well made. (16)

BELLATORE "GRAN SPUMANTE" N/V, MODESTO, CALIFORNIA, J. & E. GALLO:

Retails for around $5.50 per bottle. Better than most Italian Spumantes. Clean, fruity, spicy nose of Muscat. Round, semisweet; fresh, good bubbles, quite pleasant. (15)

Later that week, in Yountville

1934 CLOS DE LA ROCHE GRAND CRU, SOCIÉTÉ CIVILE DU CLOS VOUGEOT:

I purchased four bottles of this wine at auction earlier this year at Butterfield and Butterfield in San Francisco. Paid $225 for all four bottles! An excellent price for such a rare and old wine. I opened the bottle that had the lowest fill. It was shaken four days ago, travelling by car to Yountville, yet it was a lovely wine. Lots of sediment. Improved for over an hour in the glass. Fairly dark colour, very mature-looking, lots of brown. Unmistakable nose of very mature Burgundy. Barnyard, tea leaves, spices on nose. Full, round, slightly acidic, some wet wood and slight sweetness. Has held extremely well. (17.5)

September 2, 1988

Dinner, at our condo, with Joe Heitz.

Joe Heitz came by himself as Alice is away for a few days. We ate on the patio. A lovely evening.

CHAMPAGNE BOLLINGER BRUT "RÉSERVE CUVÉE" N/V:

Complex, yeasty, round, full, lively. Typical Bollinger, bigger style, and holding well.

1982 ST. CLEMENT SAUVIGNON BLANC, NAPA VALLEY:

Medium-gold, bright, yet maturing colour. Spicy, herbaceous Sauvignon Blanc nose. Full, round on palate, with very slight hint of madeirization. Good, but needs drinking.

1978 CÔTE-RÔTIE "CÔTES BRUNE ET BLONDE," E. GUIGAL, IN HALF-BOTTLE:

Can be excellent, but alas, a poor bottle (bad cork). Steely, sharp, and a musty, "off" nose.

1964 CHÂTEAU CANTEMERLE:

I purchased this wine a few days ago at Draper and Esquin's in San Francisco for $40; excellent value. Joe was very impressed, so were we. Excellent neck level. Deep, mature, red colour. Good depth. Elegant, complex nose of cigar-box and perfume. Just beautiful. Round, elegant, soft on palate. Joe admitted that while California wines may have more depth and riper fruit, they never have this magnificent nose. Last time I had this wine was also with Carol, in Amsterdam, in 1976. The last great Cantemerle until 1983. Great experience. Joe brought over a lovely present, a bottle of his Heitz "Martha's Vineyard" of the great 1970 vintage.

September 27, 1988

Commanderie de Bordeaux tasting of 1985 red Bordeaux, at the "Prow" restaurant.

As the 1985s are now appearing in our government monopoly stores, I decided to have this tasting to give our Commandeurs a feel for the vintage, and to assist them in choosing their favourites. I tried to find representatives of all communes, and from Crus Bourgeois to top classed growths. We knew the wines, but not the order in which they were served.

APERITIF

CHAMPAGNE VEUVE CLICQUOT BRUT "GOLD LABEL" 1982:

Elegant, complex, delicate, well balanced. Good length, ripe fruit and class. Ready, but no rush. These 1982s are turning out to be excellent Champagnes.

FLIGHT #1

1. CHÂTEAU SOCIANDO-MALLET 1985, HAUT-MÉDOC:

Open, spicy, herbal nose; hint of oak. Medium-bodied, complex, perfumy. Clean, pleasant finish. Solid backbone. Needs five to ten years. (16.5)

2. CHÂTEAU BATAILLEY 1985, PAUILLAC:

Fairly pale colour, medium depth. Not much on nose. Some spiciness, but no new oak and little ripe fruit. Some elegance. Softer on palate. Light, almost ready. Quite pleasant. Hint of bitterness at finish. (15)

3. CHÂTEAU D'ANGLUDET 1985, MARGAUX:

Dark colour to rim; purplish overtones. Herbaceous nose, flowery, hint of ripe berries. Fairly solid on palate. Chunky, new oak, medium-bodied. Finishes a bit short. Not quite put together yet, but rich and pleasant. (16)

4. CHÂTEAU TALBOT 1985, ST. JULIEN:

Good, dark colour to rim. Herbal, spicy nose. Hint of ripe fruit, some oak. Medium-bodied, surprisingly soft, good fruit, medium intensity. Well balanced. Clean, long finish. Serious, well made. Drink from 1992 to 1999. (17)

5. CHÂTEAU SOUTARD 1985, ST. EMILION:

Dark colour to rim. Subdued nose. Hint of raw meat, spices, some ripeness. Full, serious, more tannic than #1 to #4. Very good structure. Solid, big, rich, oak, fruit. Well put together. (17)

6. CHÂTEAU L'ARROSÉE 1985, ST. EMILION:

Fairly pale colour, medium depth. Baked bread, herbaceous nose. Open and forthcoming. Lacks middle. A bit hollow. Some tannin; bitter finish. Not enough ripe fruit. Needs four to six years. This wine didn't show too well. (14.5)

7. CHÂTEAU HAUT-BAGES-LIBÉRAL 1985, PAUILLAC:

Dark colour; purplish overtones. Spicy, rich, complex nose. Hint of mustiness; old barrels? Medium-bodied, good depth. Finishes a bit bitter, lean, and hard. Somehow not as clean as the others. (15)

FLIGHT #2

1. CHÂTEAU LEOVILLE-POYFERRÉ 1985, ST. JULIEN:

Good, dark colour. Clean, complex nose. Quite a bit of new oak on palate. Good backbone, fruit, length, and class. Perfumy. Needs five to seven years. Not fat, but very good. (17)

2. CHÂTEAU GRUAUD-LAROSE 1985, ST. JULIEN:

Darkest of flight. Deep, impressive colour. Hard, dull, unyielding nose. Hint of leather and ripe fruit. Full, solid, tannic, loads of ripe fruit. Rich, big. Gruaud? Needs ten years. Very good potential. (17.5)

3. CHÂTEAU LA LAGUNE 1985, HAUT MÉDOC:

Good, dark colour to rim. Tobacco, elegant nose. Complex, smoky, open, new oak. Medium-bodied, leaner, serious wine. Needs five to seven years. Promising, if the fruit will last. (16.5)

4. CHÂTEAU CANTEMERLE 1985, HAUT MÉDOC:

Palest of flight. Medium depth, palish rim. Perfumy, open nose. Merlot-like. Soft, round, classy, elegant, clean, long finish. Pomerol? Conseillante? Very pleasant. Well made. (17)

5. CHÂTEAU LYNCH-BAGES 1985, PAUILLAC:

Very good, dark colour to rim. Impressive depth. Straw, clean, ripe nose. Rich, ripe, long, full, loads of ripe fruit. Great potential. Top quality. Soft, rich. Great extract. (18.5)

6. CHÂTEAU LA CONSEILLANTE 1985, POMEROL:

Medium-dark colour, good depth. Perfumy, open, candied nose. Leaner, perfumy, delicate, yet tannic. Well made. Mid-term. Rich, long. Needs five years. Very good. (17.5)

7. CHÂTEAU L'EVANGILE 1985, POMEROL:

Medium to deep, dark colour. Subdued, yet ripe nose. Big, rich, alcoholic, tannic, full, long. Needs ten years. Lovely fruit extract. Very good potential. (18)

This tasting was followed by dinner with the following wines.

CHÂTEAU LA LOUVIÈRE 1985, GRAVES BLANC:

Excellent wine. Good depth, complex, ripe fruit, long, clean, fairly intense and well balanced. Clean, crisp, flowery, yet rich. Very good future. Surprisingly good. (17.5)

CHÂTEAU GRAND-PUY-LACOSTE 1961, PAUILLAC:

Good, dark colour; mature-looking, but very good depth. Rich, cigar-box, complex, ripe, mature Claret nose. Full, round, soft, yet very good backbone. Still has excellent fruit. What a lovely vintage 1961 is! (18)

1971 CHÂTEAU COUTET, BARSAC:

Medium gold; mature-looking, yet not deep gold. Complex, delicate, ripe, mature, botrytized nose. Superb length and balance. Lovely flavour, rich fruit. An excellent dessert wine. (17.5)

October 1988

Trip to Napa. Visit to "Groezinger Wine Shop," in Yountville.

A new owner just took over, by the name of Martin Blumberg, originally from South Africa. As it was a quiet morning, he organized a small tasting for me.

Martin told me that two Japanese firms have recently acquired two Napa Valley wineries: Raymond Vineyards and White Hall Lane. He also said that back in 1973, he had purchased, in London, 20 cases (!) of Château Palmer 1970, which he still owns. Lucky chap!

He also said that about 20 years ago, he used to work for Gilbey's, and that the only way to have wines and liquors listed in Canadian liquor monopolies was to bribe with hard cash! I'm hearing this rumour too often, and from various sources. There must be some truth to it.

Visit with Bob Travers at Mayacamas.

We didn't taste any wine, but he gave me a rare bottle of his 1971 Cabernet. Overall, he prefers his 1984 and 1985 reds and whites over his 1986s and 1987s. 1988 is a very small crop, half the average for both whites and reds. He does not produce his Late Harvest Zinfandel any more. It used to be made from purchased grapes. He puts some Semillon (10%) in his Sauvignon Blanc.

About his Chardonnays and Cabernets

He uses 10% new oak for both and 10% shaved barrels. His Chardonnay is aged for six months in large American oak casks, and then one year in small barrels. He has just released his 1984 Cabernet. His 1985 will be released next year. Bob is a an old friend of Harry Waugh.

Lunch with Joe and Alice Heitz.

About 16 other people were there, including his three kids, Kathleen, David, and Rolly (who cooked a Mexican lunch for us), and all the staff. This was the yearly "end of vintage" staff lunch.

First we tasted various wines outdoors.

WHITCRAFT WINERY CHARDONNAY 1985, SANTA BARBARA:

Excellent nose. Oak, ripe Chardonnay; not unlike a Corton-Charlemagne. Nutty, complex; marred, however, by too much alcohol (over 14%). Unbalanced, heavy, hot. (15.5)

1986 MUSCADET, MARQUIS DE GOULAINE:

Pale colour. Spicy, fresh, crisp, clean. Drink now. Imported by Christian Brothers. (15)

MARKKO CABERNET SAUVIGNON 1983, OHIO:

Pale red. Oaky, spicy nose. Quite thin, acidic, and sharp on palate. Unripe fruit. (13.5)

ARGER CELLARS NAPA CABERNET SAUVIGNON 1985 "FAY VINEYARD":

Good, deep colour. Spicy, very oaky nose. Fairly lean on palate. Well balanced, but overpowered by oak. (14)

We had the following wines with lunch.

HEITZ CELLARS NAPA CHARDONNAY"HEITZ VINEYARD" 1983:

Bright-gold colour. Clean, long Chardonnay nose. Round, rich, complex, long. At its peak. A well-made wine. (15.5)

1976 AND 1977 HEITZ CELLARS "BELLA OAKS" CABERNET SAUVIGNONS:

The 1976 was leaner, more delicate, round, complex.

The 1977 was richer, softer, more chocolate with ripe fruit. Both very good. Both rated (16.5). The 1976 was the very first vintage of this wine.

1979 HEITZ CELLARS "MARTHA'S VINEYARD" CABERNET SAUVIGNON:

Richer, spicier than above two. Better backbone and structure. Full, long, solid, yet quite ready. Very good. (17)

We also tasted these wines.

1980 HEITZ CELLARS "BELLA OAKS" AND 1980 HEITZ CELLARS "MARTHA'S VINEYARD":

Bella Oaks: Softer, rounder, more elegant. (17)

"MARTHA'S VINEYARD":

Bigger, spicier, richer, and with more depth. (18)

Both need at least five more years of bottle-age. The "Martha's" has excellent potential.

Visit With Philip Togni of Togni Vineyards on Spring Mountain.

Philip has planted ten acres, seven with Cabernet Sauvignon and some Merlot, and the rest with Sauvignon Blanc. His vineyard is located next to Keenan's. We tasted his 1987 and recently racked 1988. In 1988, his production is down to half. Many wineries reported they had small harvests in 1988.

Togni uses 100% new oak (Nadalié) for each vintage. His Sauvignon Blanc is 100% (no Semillon), planted at 2,000 ft. altitude. Crisp, green, spicy, cooler-weather wines, not unlike Sancerre.

1987 CABERNET SAUVIGNON, FROM CASK:

Round, a bit powerful, quite ripe, but not overwhelming. Clean, long. Needs six to seven years.

1988 CABERNET SAUVIGNON, FROM CASK:

A bit greener and leaner, but clean, backed by good fruit.

October 28, 1988

Dinner at "Piano-Zinc" restaurant, in San Francisco.

I was a guest of Dr. and Mrs. Schwartz (Stan and Helene). Also attending: their friend Joanne, Dr. Ron Light and his wife, and Harry Waugh, who is staying with the Lights. It was nice to see Harry again. The last time I saw him was two months ago in Vancouver, where he spent a week with us (together with Prue, Harriet, and Jamie). With a very nice (and late) meal that lasted past midnight, we had the following wines, brought along by both Stan and Ron.

1977 AND 1978 GRGICH HILLS NAPA CHARDONNAY:

The 1977 was complex, delicate, a bit lean, but still fresh.

It was overshadowed, however, by the excellent 1978, which at ten years of age, has held extremely well. Deep gold. Complex, long nose of clean Chardonnay; mature, yet lively, with some oak. Classy on palate, with excellent balance and depth. Great fruit concentration, too. This is a lovely Chardonnay. One of my two favourite wines of the evening.

1979 CHÂTEAU GRILLET, RHÔNE:

Past its prime. Lean, acidic, lacking fruit. Starting to oxidize. Has seen better days. I know this wine very well. Was much better at five years old.

1974 and 1978 Beaulieu Vineyard Georges de Latour "Private Reserve" Cabernet Sauvignon, Napa Valley

THE 1974:

Rich, leathery, American oak on nose. Full, round, at its peak. Rich and long. Lovely, rich, ripe wine.

THE 1978:

Livelier, more Bordeaux style. Leaner, complex, delicate, well balanced. Ready, but no rush. Both very good.

1970 HERMITAGE ROUGE, JABOULET-ISNARD:

Deep colour. Spicy nose, hint of dark chocolate. Round, complex, good backbone. At its peak, but no rush. Good fruit. Clean, long finish. My second-favourite wine of the evening. Stylish. Very good.

A most enjoyable evening that ended at 1 a.m.!

October 30, 1988

Two events: lunch and dinner, both at "Citrus" restaurant, in Beverly Hills, Los Angeles.

These events were organized by Bipin Desai, featuring the wines of Jaboulet, and in particular, a vertical of Hermitage "La Chapelle" 1986 back to 1937, with the participation of Gerard Jaboulet. All wines were in sets of two bottles per vintage, or one magnum, where indicated.

FIRST SESSION, LUNCH

GIGONDAS 1967 AND 1966, JABOULET:

Grenache represents about 95% of the blend. The rest is Cinsault and Syrah.

THE 1967:

Much darker and younger-looking. Leathery, spicy, rich nose; tea leaves and straw. Full, rich, and hefty. Almost chocolate and coffee on palate. No rush. Fairly alcoholic. Much better, richer, and bigger. (16.5)

THE 1966:

Older, lighter, more orange. Leaner, more acidic, losing its fruit. Over-the-hill. (13.5) The 1967 was very impressive, especially for a 19-year-old wine.

FLIGHT #1
Châteauneuf-du-Pape "Les Cèdres" 1969, 1967, 1966, 1962, and 1957

1969:

Medium, bright colour; good depth. Spicy, slightly baked nose. Sweet, round, forward, toasty; a bit thin at end; starting to oxidize. A bit diluted, finishing lean. (14.5)

1967:

A very good vintage in the Southern Rhône. Made from 70% Grenache and 30% Syrah. Best appearance of flight, by far. Deep, dark colour to rim. Intense, ripe, spicy nose. Full, rich, chocolaty, tobacco, truffles. Very good length and depth. (17)

1966:

Similar appearance to the 1969. Sweeter on palate. Round, soft, not quite as concentrated. Starting to decline. More diluted than the 1969. Drink up. (14.5)

1962:

Made from 65% Grenache, the rest being Mourvèdre and Syrah. Cloudy. Still sound. Better on palate than appearance. A bit woody, mushrooms, sweet, round, soft. Odd bottle, yet had some elegance. (14)

1957:

Similar appearance to the 1969. Delicate, leathery nose. Drier, harder on palate, yet well balanced, good fruit, and depth. Still solid. Finishes spicy, slightly bitter. A manly wine. Not unlike 1957 red Bordeaux. (16)

Overall a pleasant flight, with the 1967 clearly better than the others.

FLIGHT #2
Hermitage "La Chapelle"
1984, 1982, 1980, 1975, 1974, 1973.
(The 1974 from a magnum. Only one bottle of the 1973.)

For "La Chapelle," Gerard Jaboulet only use grapes from two of seven vineyards; "Bessard" and "Meal." It is made from vines at least 15 years old. The average production is 9,000 cases yearly.

1984:

Clean, perfumy, young. A bit lean, not enough ripe fruit, yet impeccably made. Clean, spicy, some oak. A bit green overall. (15)

1982:

Aged in 35% new oak. Darker, riper, sweet. Almost overripe. Typical of the vintage. Almost residual sugar. Rich, good acidity, but overripe for me. (16.5) Some tasters rated this quite a bit higher.

1980:

Very good colour for the vintage; pale rim. Dull nose, some straw. More depth than the 1984; richer, fuller. Still a bit hard. Fairly acidic. Overall, very good effort. Some greenness. (15.5)

1975:

Good, dark colour. Straw and ripe fruit on nose. Almost chaptalized. Quite fruity, yet obvious chaptalization. Some greenness. (14)

1974, in magnum:

Even darker, but more mature-looking than the 1975. Clean, leathery, subdued nose. Round, a bit diluted, but good fruit, too. Clean, rich, long. Ready. (15.5) Surprisingly good for a 1974.

1973:

Good colour for year. Sweet, chaptalized, spicy, leathery nose. Tobacco. A bit acidic, but good fruit. Rich, spicy. Still alive. Hint of oxidation. Complex, elegant. More Claret-like than the other wines. (16)

FLIGHT #3
Hermitage "La Chapelle"
1986, 1985, 1983, 1979, 1978, and 1976.
This flight featured the "big guns," the best recent vintages of "La Chapelle."

1986:

Barrel sample shipped in July. Very dark, purplish colour. Fairly hard, tannic, well balanced. Ripe fruit. Needs seven to ten years. Will be very good. More extract than the 1985. Shouldn't really score a barrel sample. Very promising. (No score)

1985:

Similar appearance to the 1986, but paler rim. Softer, rounder, complex, delicate. Early maturing. Lovely. Soft, round; almost enjoyable now. Much more elegant than the 1986. (17)

There is a parallel between the Rhône Valley and Bordeaux in 1985 and 1986, with the former being more elegant, looser knit, and the 1986 being richer, harder, more hefty.

1983:

Good, dark colour; maturing rim. A more serious wine than the 1985. Better balanced than the 1986 at this stage. Spicy, long. Needs seven years, or more. Tight and withdrawn. Great extract and potential. (18)

1979:

Good, dark colour, but lighter than the above. Spicy, vanilla on nose. Open, perfumy, forward, ripe. At its peak. Actually, surprisingly soft. (16.5)

1978:

Impressive appearance and structure. Darker than the 1979, and even darker than the 1983! Deep, rich nose of very ripe berries, but without the baked, annoying smell of the 1982. Long, perfect balance, full, rich. Great concentration. A giant of a wine. Needs ten more years. Outstanding. If well stored, this wine will last forever. Only 14 hectolitres per hectare produced. No wonder this wine has such great concentration. Grand Vin! (19)

1976:

Dark colour; palish rim, yet purple, too, at 12 years of age. Open, forthcoming nose. Soft, round, but better balanced than the 1979. Better backbone and acidity. Lovely flavour. (17)

DESSERT WINE

MUSCAT DE BEAUMES-DE-VENISE 1986, JABOULET:

Medium to deep gold. Lively, spicy Muscat nose. Rich, cloying, long, round, great depth. A very good Muscat. Worth buying. (17)

EVENING SESSION

HERMITAGE "LA CHAPELLE" BLANC:

Before World War II, they produced a "La Chapelle" white. After 1948, they reintroduced the old, pre-World War l "Chevalier de Sterimberg" label. Before World War II, they used 50% Marsanne and 50% Roussanne. After World War II, they used very little Roussanne because it's prone to disease. Since the mid-1970s, however, they use 45% Roussanne in the blend. This wine is fermented in stainless steel, then in new oak for three months.

1937 HERMITAGE BLANC:

Deep, bright gold, like an older Sauternes. Nose of mushrooms, old wood, and slight hint of oxidation. Full, rich, good (even high) acidity. Fairly alcoholic. Rich, not unlike dry Sauternes. Rich, big, full, and long. Opened up and went on and on in the glass. (18)

1973 HERMITAGE BLANC:

Medium gold. Some sulphur on nose; hint of rubber, too. Quite dry, high acidity, lemony, solid, but lacks ripe fruit. Will not improve. (14)

1975 HERMITAGE BLANC:

Slightly darker than the 1973. Some oak on nose; some ripe fruit, too. Higher acidity than the 1973, but less depth. Clean finish. A bit lemony. (15)

1985 CHEVALIER DE STERIMBERG:

Bright, green gold. Fruity, young nose. Good fruit, depth, and balance. Clean finish. (17.5)

From 1937 to 1985, typical characteristics: high alcoholic, high acidity, and fairly thick texture.

FLIGHT #1

Hermitage Rouge "La Chapelle" 1972, 1971, 1970, 1967, 1962, and 1944

1972:

Livelier colour than the 1971, but not as dark as the 1970. Rich, meaty nose. Full, ripe, long, rich, very good length. Voluptuous, well balanced. Surprisingly good. Young, fruity, rich, lovely. (17)

1971:

Medium, mature colour. Coffee beans, chocolate nose of older wine. Older-tasting than the 1972. Some stemminess. A bit sharp, high alcohol, but some fruit there, too. Fairly rich, but finishes high in acidity. Too green. (14.5)

1970:

Closed, yet clean nose. Hard, solid, still tannic. Structured like the 1978, if without the ripe fruit of the 1978. Needs a few years. Serious, big, chunky, masculine. No rush, but will the fruit hold? (17.5), possibly (18). Bottles of this in my cellar taste better.

1967:

Dark, maturing colour. Open, elegant, tar, spicy, almost Barolo nose. Hard, tannic, even more so than the 1970. Solid, but low fruit. Clean, yet hard finish. Not bad. Drink up. (16)

1962, IN MAGNUM:

Browning, unclean colour, but not cloudy. Toasty nose. Round, fairly hard, low fruit. Like the 1967, yet not as "mean and lean." Tobacco and leather, some sweetness. Fruit weakening. Quite elegant. (17)

1944:

Gerard never tasted this before. They have 16 bottles of this 1944 at the property, but it is his brother's birth year. As expected, lightest of flight; palish, orangy, yet unmistakable character of "La Chapelle." Leathery, meaty nose. Soft, elegant, yet quite rich and alcoholic. Has held extremely well! (16)

I liked the 1971 less than most other tasters did.

FLIGHT #2

Hermitage "La Chapelle" 1969, 1964, 1953, 1952, and 1937

1969:

Medium, mature colour. Lovely, ripe, subdued, delicate nose. Full, rich, long, powerful. Biggest, richest wine of flight. No rush. Very good balance. (17.5)

1964:

Mature colour. Mature nose, some oxidation. Clean, subdued nose. Leathery, slightly sweet, solid, rich. Long on palate. Round, soft, yet holding well. (17)

1953:

Similar colour to the 1964, but more brown. A bit dusty on nose. Drying out. A bit sharp, metallic. A bit lean. Finishes dry. Much better with food. Needs drinking. Later, opened up. Complex, long, lovely finish. (17) This wine needed time in the glass to express itself.

1952:

Paler colour than the 1953. Mature, elegant nose of tea leaves and chocolate. Round on entry, but a bit dry, yet finishes clean. Holding very well. Elegant, tobacco, spices, sweetness. I preferred it to the 1953. (17.5)

1937:

Browning, pale colour. Oxidized nose. Still drinkable. Still fruity. Amazing, after all these years. Rich, round, long. Good depth. Slight hint of dill at finish. (16)

Overall, an outstanding flight. These old wines have held surprisingly well.

FLIGHT #3

Hermitage "La Chapelle"
1966, 1961, 1959, 1955, and 1949.

1966:

Medium to dark colour. Intense, complex, leathery, spicy nose. Full, round, rich, complex. Fruity, mature, yet still at its peak. In terms of fragrance, this wine belongs to the previous group. (18)

1961:

Deep, impressive colour to rim. Great depth on palate. Rich, full, long, essence of Syrah. Solid, masculine, fruity, great length. What a great Hermitage is all about! This is a lovely bottle with a great future. (19.5) Only the 1978 expressed the potential of becoming another 1961.

1959:

Palish, mature colour; orangy rim. Open, spicy, dill nose. Round, soft, forward, almost sweet. Long, clean, and delicate on palate. Dill, too. At its peak. Drink up. (17.5)

1955:

Light, mature colour. Complex, long nose. Perfume, leather, spices. Great length and class. A bit drier on palate than the 1959, but clean, long, and delicate. Later, weakened a bit, but very good! (18)

1949:

Palish, mature, orangy colour. Subdued, delicate nose. Softer, a bit tired, but still drinkable and enjoyable. Flavourful. Some dryness, but overall very good. Has held very well. Not unlike a fine old Claret. (17.5)

Overall

An outstanding event with impressive wines. Hardly any poor wines here. A real treat, and a testament to the potential of Hermitage and to the house of Jaboulet.

November 8, 1988

Chevaliers des Vins de France, vertical tasting of Château Margaux, "The Mentzelopoulos Era," 1978 to 1985.

Sid Cross and I conducted this event. All wines served blind.

1. 1984:

Medium-dark colour; palish rim. Spicy, elegant, fruity, open nose. Not very intense or ripe, but fruity. Slight hint of oak. Clean, fresh, green, spicy. Fairly young, yet fairly acidic. Mid-term. Some oak. Elegant. 1984? (16.5)

2. 1982:

More depth than #1 and more mature at rim. Riper, richer, more leathery (baked), and closed, yet perfumy, too. Rich, ripe, full, fairly solid. Great depth, ripe tannins. Needs eight to ten years. Lovely, perfumy nose. Almost Californian. Typical 1982. (19)

3. 1985:

Most obvious purple of the lot. Spicy, young, fresh fruit. Rich, round, charming. Young, youthful, new oak, vanilla. 1985? Lovely length and complexity. Very good potential. Needs eight years. (18.5)

4. 1983:

Very good, dark colour to rim. Very good depth. Intense, rich, ripe nose, yet subdued. Big, rich, hard, tannic, solid. Great concentration of fruit. Superb wine. Needs ten to 15 years. Exquisite balance. 1983? (19) This surely must be the wine of the vintage.

5. 1979:

Very closed, unyielding nose. Not quite as dark as the 1983. Slight hint of coffee beans and vegetables. Later, opened up a bit. Full, rich, round, less complex than most. Quite forward. Little tannin. Very good overall, just not complex enough. (17)

6. 1978:

Most mature-looking; hint of orange at rim. Spicy, expansive, a bit vegetal on nose. 1978? Hard, tannic, yet complex, lovely, and long. Good fruit. Serious. Needs five to seven years. Top class. (18.5)

7. 1981:

Good, dark colour. Herbaceous, open nose. Round, rich, complex, medium depth. Clean, long finish. Good backbone. Still a bit tannic, concentrated. Will be very good in five years. (17.5), possibly (18).

Overall appearance

Very good, dark colours, with excellent depth. I had a good tasting and guessed them all right! The group favourite was #6, the 1978. The least favoured was #5, the 1979. Personally, however, I found the 1982 and 1983 to be the top wines, with the 1978 close behind.

One taster brought a bottle of 1980 along, giving some of us the opportunity to complete the vertical tasting.

1980:

Sweet, spicy, soft, elegant, yet vegetal. Quite sweet, not unlike a Monterey or Sonoma Cabernet, yet more complex. Needs drinking. (15)

November 1988

In Israel. Visit to the Yarden Winery in the Golan Heights (Quatzrin) in northern Israel.

Modern, up-to-date winery. The winemaker, American Kenneth Greene, told me that 1988 was the hottest vintage in Israel in 50 years! This will probably produce rich, ripe (too alcoholic?) wines. After visiting the modern facilities, we went to the tasting room. They also bottle under the "Golan" and "Gamla" brands.

Yarden "Galil" Sauvignon Blanc 1987:

Has 20% Semillon in the blend. Clean, spicy nose. Quite Graves-like. Medium fruit. This wine has spent only six to seven weeks in one to two-year-old barrels. Good acidity.

The winemaker said that their forté is their reds, and that their whites need some improvement. I agree. Even their whites are far superior to most other Israeli wineries' wines, however.

Yarden "Galil" Chardonnay 1987 "First Release":

First commercial release of Chardonnay. Made from five to six-year-old vines. The first crop (1986) was never commercially released. Four to five months in oak. No malo fermentation. Medium gold. Obvious oak on palate, yet good fruit, too. Crisp, slightly riper fruit is wanting. They should pick at one degree brix higher. Some tropical fruit and pleasant varietal character.

Yarden "Galil" Merlot 1986:

Vines grafted on other varietal root stocks, including Chenin Blanc. Aged in two to three-year-old French oak for eight months. Production of only 750 cases. Medium depth, purplish rim. Fruity, spicy, fresh nose. Good, leaner-style Merlot character. Soft, forward, easy to drink. Ready, clean, and complex, with hint of oak and raspberries. Quite good. (15.5)

Yarden "Galil" Cabernet Sauvignon 1986:

Aged in one to two-year-old barrels. Made from 100% Cabernet Sauvignon. Spicy, complex, cedary nose, with hint of new oak. Softer, rounder than the 1985 tasted recently in Vancouver; less intense, but better balanced. Good pH (3.5). According to the winemaker, the 1987 will be the best Cabernet Sauvignon since it was first produced in 1983. Not too big or tannic, but good acidity, medium-ripe fruit. A very pleasant surprise. (16.5)

Next year, or in 1990, they plan to produce their first sparkling wine made from 75% Chardonnay and 25% Pinot Noir. It will spend three years on its lees.

Yarden "Galil" White Riesling 1987 "Special Release":

This is their first release and "special" is misleading as there is no "regular." Palish gold. Spicy, sweet nose. 5% residual sugar. Auslese style. Good balance and varietal character. Round, soft, complex, delicate. A fine effort. (15.5)

Overall impressions

Promising future for the winery. Prices, however, especially on the domestic market, are very excessive, costing $15 to $35 per bottle!

December 18 to 30, 1988

Trip to Maui, with Carol and the kids.

Château de Pez 1982:

The colour, depth, and rich fruit typical of the 1982s. Fullish, fruity, rich, straightforward, good complexity, ripe fruit. Drink 1990 to 1995, yet I must admit that it is enjoyable even now.

With Paul and Sara Pinski, our old friends from San Francisco.

Paul and Sara are in their mid-70s.

Hanzell California Chardonnay 1984:

A superb bottle of Chardonnay. Full, rich; magnificent depth and intensity. Loaded with ripe fruit, yet excellent balance. Long. Not quite ready. Hanzell's Chardonnays need five to eight years, or more, to reach their peak. Top quality.

Also tasted on Maui:
Wines I brought along from Vancouver.

Champagne Pol Roger Chardonnay 1979:

Complex, delicate, long, at its peak. Lots of class on nose and palate. A very fine Champagne.

1978 Corton-Charlemagne "Diamond Jubilee," Remoissenet:

Great Corton-Charlemagne and great 1978. Full, nutty, long, classy nose. Full, rich, excellent balance. Went on and on, on the palate. What a superb year 1978 was for white Burgundies! At ten years of age, no rush.

December 29, 1988

Bad news.

At 8 a.m., we found out that Carol's father had passed away. Carol arranged to get a flight out. The kids and I couldn't get seats until New Year's Eve.

I took off with the kids back to Vancouver exactly at midnight, New Year's Eve 1988 (12:03 a.m., January 1, 1989, to be exact). A new experience. I hope that 1989 will be a good year. The plane was almost empty. The stewardess offered me a glass of Mumm's Cordon Rouge N/V. Then, she looked at me and asked, "Would you like me to leave you the bottle?" I smiled.

Late January 1989

Dinner of "Group of Ten."

CHAMPAGNE VEUVE CLICQUOT "LA GRANDE DAME" 1979 BRUT:

Elegant, delicate, complex, hint of sweetness. Was better two years ago. Hint of peaches, yeast, very slight oxidation. Still very good but needs drinking. With the exception of Krug 1979 and Bollinger "Vieilles Vignes Françaises" 1979, it seems that most 1979s are soft, forward, and have peaked at eight or nine years. (16.5)

Three great 1978 white Burgundies followed

CORTON-CHARLEMAGNE "DIAMOND JUBILEE," REMOISSENET:

Bright green-gold. Subdued, delicate, lovely nose. Crisp, full, rich, excellent balance, acidity, length, charm. Ready, but no rush. Excellent bottle. (18)

Remoissenet's white Burgundies are usually slower maturing and last for a long time. That also includes their Chablis Grands Crus.

CORTON-CHARLEMAGNE, LOUIS LATOUR:

This bottle wasn't as good as on past occasions. Deep gold. Full, nutty, rich, oaky, soft, and long. A big, rich wine. Getting soft. Good, but needs drinking. Can be great. (17)

CHEVALIER-MONTRACHET, REMOISSENET:

Delicate, long; not as intense as their Corton-Charlemagne and less full than Latour's Corton-Charlemagne. Great length. No rush. Well balanced. Nutty, classy. Even tight and still youthful. (18.5)

Overall impressions

All three very good, but if they need ranking: Chevalier first; Corton-Charlemagne Remoissenet second; and Corton-Charlemagne Louis Latour third.

1962 CHÂTEAU LAFITE, IN MAGNUM:

(Group bottle) Bright-red colour. Good depth; typical 1962. Slight maturity at rim, yet younger-looking than the 1961 Côte-Rôtie that followed. Open, delicate, complex vanilla nose; tea leaves, tobacco. Forthcoming, long, lovely perfume. Later, still complex on nose, but acidic, lean on palate. At or past its peak. Lafite has produced a fine 1962. (17.5)

CÔTE-RÔTIE 1961, JABOULET-ISNARD:

Impressive, deep colour to rim—for its age. Gerard Jaboulet told me that it is the same wine as his Côte-Rôtie "Les Jumelles." Still closed, rich, ripe, spicy nose. Full, powerful, ripe raisins. Good intensity, length, and weight. Will last for many years. Maybe a bit simple, but quite big for a 28-year-old Côte-Rôtie, and holding well. Some sharpness; straightforward. (17)

1963 CROFT'S VINTAGE PORT, LONDON-BOTTLED BY HEDGES AND BUTLER:

Medium depth, still youthful colour of the good 1963s. Rich, yet the elegance of Croft's. This is a familiar wine. Somehow this bottle was a bit harder and not as elegant as on past experiences. A bit too spirity, with a harsh finish. Overall quite good, though. (17)

January 30, 1989

Small Tastevin vertical tasting, with friends, of Château Gruaud-Larose 1961 to 1985.

FLIGHT #1
1985 to 1978

1. CHÂTEAU GRUAUD-LAROSE 1979:

Deep colour. Slightly orangy rim. Delicate nose of maturing Claret. Leathery, herbaceous, tea leaves. Some sharpness on palate. A short finish. Needs four to five years. Good breed. Smoky on nose and palate. Hard, unyielding. (16.5)

2. CHÂTEAU GRUAUD-LAROSE 1980:

Similar colour to #1, but quite a bit more brown (maturity) at rim. Also, less depth. More herbal, vegetal, open, mature nose. A bit metallic. Harder than #1. A bit simpler and green. Drink up. (15)

3. CHÂTEAU GRUAUD-LAROSE 1985:

Very deep-purplish colour. Opaque; together with #7, darkest of flight. Rich, ripe, roasted on nose. New oak. Youngest-looking and smelling. Vanilla. Full, rich, yet stylish. Typical for the vintage. Very good depth. Should approach its peak around 1995 to 2000. (17)

4. CHÂTEAU GRUAUD-LAROSE 1982:

Deep, maturing colour; leathery, ripe nose. More mature, sweeter, less vegetal than the 1985. Full, solid, still a bit tannic. Good length, complexity, and class. Needs five to six years or more. Lovely, rich wine. (18.5)

5. CHÂTEAU GRUAUD-LAROSE 1978:

Quite a bit of brown, good depth. Open, vegetal nose like the 1980, but cleaner, less metallic. Developing complex nose. Classy. Round, yet tannic. Drink over next four to six years. Good structure. Hard, serious. Very good potential. (17)

6. CHÂTEAU GRUAUD-LAROSE 1983:

Deep colour. Palish rim. Closed, unyielding nose. Good spiciness, some leather. Sweeter, riper, richer, higher alcohol than all above. Very good length and complexity. Drink from 1994. Excellent potential. (18)

Gruaud-Larose has produced a fine 1983. It also sells for a very reasonable price. Definitely one to buy.

7. Château Gruaud-Larose 1981:

Very good, deep colour. Touch of purple. Closed, classic Cabernet; spicy, oaky, serious nose. Not as ripe as #3. Big, full, tannic, sweet, loaded with ripe fruit. 1982 style. What a surprise! (18) Together with Château Margaux (the wine of the vintage), this is one of the very best 1981s. Certainly the best St. Julien in 1981.

FLIGHT #2
1976 to 1961

1. Château Gruaud-Larose 1976:

Medium to light maturing colour. Orange-brown. Dull nose; clean, though. Sweet, then acidic; soft, yet clear and sound. Pleasant. At its peak. Not as diluted as other 1976s. Some ripeness. Quite pleasant. Drying out; not much substance. (14.5)

2. Château Gruaud-Larose 1975:

Darkest of flight. Some maturity at rim. A bit vegetal on nose. Ripe, concentrated. Lovely depth. Spicy, full, loads of tannin and ripe fruit. Leathery, rich. Maturing, serious. Very good. About ready, but no rush. Drink from 1995 or beyond. Very 1975 and very good! (17)

3. Château Gruaud-Larose 1973:

Similar appearance to the 1976. Spicy, elegant nose. Better balance than the 1976. Spicy, clean, surprisingly good for a 1973. Good complexity. Long finish. Quite good, but needs drinking. (15)

4. Château Gruaud-Larose 1970:

Medium, mature colour. Good depth. Sweet, doctored nose. Chaptalized. Not a good example of the vintage. Sweet on entry. Sharp, acidic. Can be much better. (13)

5. Château Gruaud-Larose 1966:

Medium dark. Ripe, complex, rich nose. Full, loads of tannin; ripe, rich, complex, long. Tobacco nose. No rush. Ready, but will hold well. Superb bottle. Classic Claret. Now to 1997. Someday, hopefully, the 1982 and 1983 will be as good as this. (18.5)

6. Château Gruaud-Larose 1961:

Low neck level. "Old bones." This is too bad. Can be superb. Like a wine from the late 1940s or 1930s. Green-orange rim. Very old. Some delicate perfume on nose, but a tired bottle. Having tasted this wine on many occasions, I have no doubt that better-stored bottles are superb. (16)

DESSERT WINE

1925 Château La Montagne, Sauternes, Milleret Prop., shipped by Montac and Bourbon:

(I brought this bottle along.) Good cork. Very deep, green-gold colour. Mature, ripe, crème-brûlée nose. Complex, delicate. Some sediment. Rich, long, very mature. Still very much alive. Good acidity. Real treat. Like drinking history. (17)

Saturday, February 4, 1989

In the afternoon, vertical tastings of Croft's Vintage Port, at Dr. Haskell Norman's home, in Marin, California.

Dr. Barney Rhodes conducted both events.

APERITIF

White Porto "Very Finest" XSR 120, Martinez and Gassiot:

Deep gold. Nutty, complex, some sweetness, unusually similar nose to red Port. Lovely nutty length.

Croft's

First of two sessions

1985 to 1950

1985:

Youthful purplish colour. Rich, ripe nose. A bit metallic. Medium-bodied, sweet, not big. Almost too soft. Ready around 1995. Surprisingly forward (like the Croft's 1977). Too leathery. Something wrong. A bit dusty. Barney Rhodes liked it. (15)

1977:

Good dark colour; palish, browning rim. Very ripe, leathery nose. Full, rich, yet surprisingly forward and approachable. Lacking the backbone of other 1977s. Prematurely ageing? (16.5)

1970:

Good youthful colour. Medium depth. Leathery ripe nose. Smoky, rich, a bit sharp. Medium depth. Quite good, still youthful, yet sharpness at finish. Drink from 1990 to 1995. (17)

1966:

(I contributed this bottle.) Deeper colour than the 1963. Sweeter, more raisiny nose, less spice. Round, delicate, sweet, soft. Ready. Quite good, yet the 1960 had more backbone. Needs drinking, but good. (16.5)

1963:

Medium red, mature-looking. Soft, round, spicy, good depth, very good overall. Not as intense as others, but typical Croft's style. (17.5)

1960:

Surprising colour for a 1960. Still a bit youthful, less brown than the 1963. Sweet, charming, pleasant, delicate. Without the complexity of the 1955, but good. Not quite as sweet as the 1963, 1966, or 1970, but very good for the vintage. (16.5)

1955:

A little more depth than the 1950. More subdued; delicate, mature nose. Clean, long, soft, delicate. Good length, complex, lovely now. (17.5)

1950:

Palish red (lightest of flight), mature rim. Raisiny, mature nose. Sweet, soft, delicate, a bit leathery. Needs drinking. Much softer than the 1955. Most 1950s are. Good for the vintage. Starting to dry out. (16.5)

The 1985 was liked the least, together with the 1977. The 1963 came second, and the 1955 scored first overall.

Following the afternoon Croft's tasting, an International Wine and Food Society Dinner, at "Emilio's" restaurant, in San Francisco, featuring several 1870 and 1970 red Bordeaux (same properties)

CHAMPAGNE BILLECART-SALMON BRUT N/V:

Crisp, fruity, fresh, good acidity, a bit steely. Needs one to two years. Fine mousse. Long on palate. A fine Champagne. (17)

The 1870s came from the Ononaga Collection, originally from a Bordeaux cellar, possibly Lafite's. Sold at Christie's Chicago. Most have been recorked over the past 20 years at Lafite, and new labels added.

1970 BÂTARD-MONTRACHET, HENRI CLERC, AVERY'S, IN JEROBOAM:

Very rare in jeroboam. Beautiful, mature, medium golden colour. Lovely oak; classic, nutty, buttery, complex Chardonnay nose. Mature, but not over-the-hill. Long, complex. Great length and classic Chardonnay. (18)

Noëllat information

Martine Saunier, who represents many Burgundian properties in Northern California, including Leroy, was seated beside me. We had a nice chat all evening. Martine told me that Lalou Brize-Leroy has recently purchased Domaine Noëllat from the two sisters (their father died in 1980, and mediocre wine has been produced there since). The 1988 will be the first Leroy vintage of the Noëllat properties. Should be great. New vinification methods. There are 14 hectares of old vines. Côte de Nuits, Romanée-St.-Vivant, etc. Leroy system: ferment in large oak vats; break "chapeau" with special plunger that has a cooling device in it, instead of stainless steel cold-water belts around vats.

FLIGHT #1

The 1970s

1970 LANESSAN, ONE CHÂTEAU-BOTTLED AND ONE LONDON-BOTTLED BY CORNEY AND BARROW:

(I brought along the London-bottling.) Both similar appearance. The château-bottled was a little more closed on nose; both very similar on palate. Good, dark, maturing colours. Perfumy, spicy, still tight, slightly acidic. Good fruit. The London-bottling a bit more complex. Very good depth. Lovely. The château-bottling was a bit drier and simpler. Later, the London-bottled Lanessan improved, while the Château-bottled dried up. Ratings: Château-bottled (15.5), London-bottled (16.5).

1970 COS D'ESTOURNEL:

Good deep colour. A bit dusty, tannic. Lacks fruit, very hard, unyielding, too lean and acidic. A hard, mean wine. Montrose has made a much finer 1970 than Cos. (15)

1970 GRUAUD-LAROSE:

Not quite as dark as the Cos. Spicy, complex, ripe fruit, a bit too acidic. Good backbone. Not as hard as Cos, and more fruit. Serious, quite good. Needs five years. Complex aftertaste. Showing better than when tasted recently in Vancouver. (16.5)

1970 MONTROSE:

Deepest, best appearance of flight. Purplish rim. Lovely, ripe, young nose. Intense, sweet fruit. Loads of fruit, very tannic, massive, rich, long, excellent balance. Needs ten to 15 years. Excellent potential. Miles ahead of any other 1970 tasted tonight. Superb! Buy more of it!!! (18.5)

FLIGHT #2

The 1870s

COS D'ESTOURNEL 1870:

Excellent level, well into neck. Medium red, mature colour, like a wine from the 1940s. Barnyardy, sweet nose. Ripe, tobacco; lively; excellent length, sealing-wax nose. Fruity, delicious. For its age—a masterpiece. Has held extremely well. (1870 was a hot, rich, massive year.) After 15 minutes, it started to fall apart. (18)

GRUAUD-LAROSE 1870:

Low shoulder, worrisome. Browning. Sour, oxidized. Gone! Sharp, acidic. (No score)

LANESSAN 1870:

High shoulder level. Excellent appearance, like a wine from the 1950s! Slightly leathery, earthy. Lovely, ripe fruit. Rich, a bit sharp, but good fruit. Has held extremely well, better than some Lanessan 1955s (that is 1955) tasted recently. Lovely. Surprise! (17.5)

MONTROSE 1870:

Sealing-wax nose. Lovely, long. The star! Full, rich, sweet, clean, mature, good backbone. Lively, solid. Serious. Very good wine. A classic. Rich, fruity, long. What a wonderful year and a wonderful wine. Great, great! Still a bit tannic. Hint of new leather, lovely bouquet. A complete wine. (19.5)

Three good 1870s out of four—incredible. Not just good, but truly classic wines. A lovely, memorable impression. Lanessan: cost $450. The Cos and Montrose were $1,320 per bottle. The Gruaud-Larose cost $1,100. (These wines were purchased last year.)

1870 was a great vintage of classic proportions. Many wines needed 50 to 75 years to reach maturity. They were made for two, even three, generations later. My excitement with these 120-year-old wines was not only because of the rarity of the wines and the reputation of the 1870s—the wines were simply exquisite, especially the Montrose. A great experience. I liked the food, too. Artistic, very good, but very tiny "sample portions" instead of a meal.

DESSERT WINE

1870 MOSCATEL, OSBOURNE:

Deep-amber colour; green-orange rim. It is actually a Solera, around $17 a bottle from Darrell Corti in Sacramento. Rich, ripe Muscat nose. Creamy, round, complex; very good length.

The 1870

The overall favourite was Montrose. Lanessan was surprisingly good and Cos was lovely, too. We also had, at the beginning of this event, a Champagne Billecart-Salmon Rosé Brut N/V, a bit simple, almost tired wine, and a Champagne Bollinger "RD" 1970 Brut (disgorged in 1978) that had seen better days. Bollinger had an original gold label for its "RDs." Mushrooms, earthy nose with hint of oxidation. Poor storage? The Billecart Rosé can be lovely. Probably poor storage.

February 5, 1989

Brunch at the Pinskis'.

MONTRACHET 1983, RENÉ MONNIER:

(Tasted with Paul and Sid Cross) Label indicated 12% alcohol. Baloney! Tasted more like 13.9%. Deep, bright green-gold. Rich, oak, intensely thick. Like a big California Chardonnay. Low acidity, ready. Good, but not great. I've had better. (16.5)

Sunday, February 5,1989

SECOND SESSION

Croft's 1945 to 1912

1912:

Very pale, almost Rosé. Mushrooms, delicate nose. Soft, still has Vintage Port character. Rich, spirity, lovely, perfumy nose. Long, complex, delicate. Still alive and quite good. Slightly spirity, but fine. A classic year. An "old man" that has held well. (17)

1917:

Darker than the 1912, pale brown. Clean, spicy, elegant nose. Sweet, no sharp edge. Velvety, lovely, long. All class, and stylish. Clean finish. Has lasted extremely well. (18)

1920, LONDON-BOTTLED BY G. F. GRANT AND CO.:

Darker brown yet than the 1917. Smells a bit rancid, leathery, old. Earthy, still sweet. Slightly sharp finish. Complex, hint of raspberries on nose. Old-smelling. (16)

1922:

Good, dark, oldish colour. Little nose. Spirity. Fairly sharp, harsh. Leaner style. Atypical for Croft's. Hard, bitter finish, yet sweet, too. (16)

1924:

Medium brown, maturing colour. Cleaner nose than the 1922. A bit medicinal, though. Sweet on entry. Round, forward, a bit sharp at end, but better than the 1922. Good backbone. Clean finish. Not as complex as the 1917. (17)

1927:

Similar appearance to the 1924. Clean, delicate nose of very mature Port. Leather, earth, roses. Round, soft, forward, a bit earthy. Elegant. True Croft's style, yet not quite as complex as it could be. A bit short at finish. Peculiar woody nose. (17)

1935:

Darker, deeper than most, except the 1922. Candied, caramel nose. Round, delicate, soft. More classy than the 1927. Lovely length and balance. Complete mature Port. Still at its peak. Classy, delicate, complex. All there. (18)

1945:

Best colour of flight. Deep, mature appearance. True Port character. Spicy, rich, big, yet subtle nose. Full, elegant, complex. Still youthful. Drink to 2000! The liveliest by far. A fine Port from a great vintage. (18.5)

I rated the 1945 first, 1935 second, 1917 third.

1900 and 1896 in half-bottles, recorked by Whitwham's, a firm whose bottlings I do not trust, as a rule.

1900:

Very pale Tawny; smells like a Tawny. Tastes like a light, elegant, youthful Solera Sherry rather than a Port. Excellent Tawny, but alas, no Vintage Port character. (15.5)

1896:

Colour similar to the 1917. A bit vegetal, spicy nose. Very soft. Good fruit, clean finish, better structure than the 1912, more grip. It has held very well—yet remembering the 1870 red Bordeaux we had last night, we wondered why these Ports are not holding better! 1896 was a great year. I wonder if Whitwham doctored this with younger wine. Barney Rhodes, who conducted this tasting, commented that it is one of those rare occasions in which Whitwham's did not ruin a wine—but actually may have improved it. (17)

Overall impressions

This was an excellent tasting with only a few disappointing wines. It also clearly expressed the style of Croft's, one of the more elegant Ports.

February 6 and 7, 1989

Spent the next two days in Yountville, in bed with fever and a bad cold.

Had to cancel a luncheon and meeting with Italian winemakers, including Angelo Gaja at Joe Heitz's. C'est la vie!

March 8, 1989

Le Tastevin vertical tasting of Château Musar (Lebanon)

CHAMPAGNE LANSON "BLACK LABEL" N/V:

Yeasty, complex nose. Round, well balanced, long. Creamy. Lanson is variable. It can be very good or disappointing.

CHÂTEAU MUSAR 1978:

Aged-looking and smelling. Prematurely old. Medium depth. Nose of Cabernet, and Rhône-like. Cinsault and Cabernet Sauvignon in the blend. Fairly lean, yet some fruit, but leathery, light, and sharp finish. Drink up. (13)

CHÂTEAU MUSAR 1977:

Better depth than the 1978. Riper, more intense fruit on nose. Spices and fruit. Tannic, no rush. Well balanced, hard St. Estèphe-style wine. (Almost all Musars are like that, to one degree or another.) Needs two to four years. Quite good. (14.5)

CHÂTEAU MUSAR 1975:

Lightest of flight. Pale red. Open, vegetal, sweet nose. Light, watery, diluted, sharp acidity. Over-the-hill. Drink up. Disappointing. (12)

CHÂTEAU MUSAR 1972:

Similar appearance and structure as the 1977, yet harder and less fruit. Don't wait for it to soften, because the fruit is fading fast. (14)

CHÂTEAU MUSAR 1970:

Best wine of flight. Best appearance. Good dark colour to rim. Some maturity. Ripe, long complex fruit on nose. Claret-like. Full, sturdy. Very good fruit and backbone, fairly tannic. No rush. A well-made wine. (16.5)

CHÂTEAU MUSAR 1964:

Mature-looking. Medium depth. Little character on nose. Soft, a bit leathery. Low fruit. One bottle was starting to oxidize. A bit musty, too. Drink up. Has seen better days. (14)

Serge Hochar, the owner-winemaker of this property, is to be admired for his efforts to produce decent, even good, wines in the middle of a terrible civil war in his country.

DESSERT WINE

1955 MOULIN TOUCHAIS, ANJOU:

Variable. Two months ago: tired, oxidizing, very dark. Tonight, the bottles were very good. Earthy-concrete nose, but good finish, too. Clean, medium sweet, rich, long, well balanced. I'm not a fan of Moulin Touchais, though. (16)

March 19, 1989

Tasting of 1986 Clarets, at Liberty Wine Shop, in Point Roberts, Washington State.

These wines have just been shipped very recently, and have barely spent six months in bottle.

APERITIF

CHÂTEAU DE FIEUZAL BLANC 1986, GRAVES:

Green gold. Ripe nose, slight hint of rubber. Nice oak, ripe fruit, rich, long. Opulent. Fairly alcoholic. Wine from a hot year. Lots of depth. (16.5)

1. 1986 CHÂTEAU CHAMBERT-MARBUZET, ST. ESTÈPHE:

Palest colour of flight. Medium cherry colour. Delicate, forward nose, some oak. Medium-bodied, a bit astringent (green), but good fruit. Bitter tannins from oak. Not bad. Harder St. Estèphe style. Drink from 1993 to 1996. (14.5)

2. 1986 COS D'ESTOURNEL, ST. ESTÈPHE:

Great, deep, dark, purplish colour. Superb nose of ripe berries, vanilla, new oak. Warm, rich, and concentrated. Hard, tannic, rich, serious wine. Needs 15 years! Great length, complexity, and class. One to buy. (18.5)

3. CHÂTEAU LYNCH-BAGES 1986, PAUILLAC:

Similar appearance to the Cos, just slightly less concentrated. A little sweeter, less hard. Lovely perfume, oak-vanilla, fruit. Leaner, less concentrated on palate. Stemmier. Very good, but without the power and concentration of Cos. Needs eight to ten years. (17)

4. CHÂTEAU CANON 1986, ST. EMILION:

Good dark, deep colour, but less purple than #2 or #3. Refined, elegant, lovely nose. Oak, spicy, long, charming, feminine. Like a Margaux. New oak, quite tannic, but lovely, elegant fruit underneath. Not as hard as #2 or #3. Needs eight years. (17.5)

5. Château l'Evangile 1986, Pomerol:

Subdued nose, some straw, ripe fruit, little oak. Overall rounder, but less backbone or class than the Canon. A bit thin in middle. Clean, long. Somehow lacks the ripeness and richness of the 1983 or the great 1982 of this property. Good nevertheless. (16.5)

6. Château Cheval-Blanc 1986, St. Emilion:

More concentration, riper fruit, and elegance than the Canon. Medium-bodied, elegant, stylish. I prefer the 1985, but this is very good. Not a monster. Elegant, lovely finish with oak and fruit in harmony. Somehow not as ripe or concentrated as the others. (18)

7. Château La Mission Haut-Brion 1986, Graves:

Slightly more purplish than the Haut-Brion. Rubbery, straw on nose.

Fairly hard, masculine, tannic. A bit low in ripe fruit. Austere. Hard tannins, yet not as ripe as Cos. Needs ten years. (17)

8. Château Haut-Brion 1986, Graves:

Subdued, delicate, clean nose. Some fruit, hay, earthy, oak. Lovely length, balance, class, and fruit. A beauty. Typical structure of the property. Needs eight to ten years. Will be excellent. Not very ripe, but harmonious. Top class. (18.5)

9. Château Lafite 1986, Pauillac:

Good dark colour to rim. Lots of purple. Seductive, sweet, warm nose. Oak-vanilla, ripe berries. Superb classic length. Great intensity, complex, long, balanced, good depth, yet elegant. Marvellous. A very well-made wine. Very long on palate, yet not a blockbuster. Ten years. (18.5)

10. Château Mouton-Rothschild 1986, Pauillac:

Slightly more purple than the Lafite. Otherwise, similar appearance. Serious, closed nose. Some cedar, very ripe fruit. New oak not as apparent. Sweet, full, very rich. Ripest by far. Ripe tannins. "Fondu." Great concentration of fruit. Try in eight to ten years, but will last for a very long time (20 or more years). Very long, rich finish. (19)

11. Château Margaux 1986, Margaux:

Brilliant, deep-purplish colour. Very concentrated, big, tannic. A giant of a wine, yet elegant and classy. Hard, clean tannins, new oak. Great concentration of fruit. Much bigger than Lafite. Even harder than Mouton at this stage. A 50-year wine. Drink from 2000 to 2025. Great wine for the next generation. (19.5)

12. Château Latour 1986, Pauillac:

Even darker than the Margaux. Excellent deep-purple colour. Ripe, very Pauillac nose. Not much new oak or vanilla, but ripe fruit. Full, tannic, concentrated, yet not as ripe as Mouton or as hard as Cos! Serious, certainly top class. Very good, but showed better and was more concentrated when tasted from barrel in June 1987. (18)

13. Château Climens 1986, Barsac:

Typical medium green-gold colour. Lovely, clean, crisp nose. Elegant, botrytis. Full, rich, round, surprisingly soft. Lovely length. Quite sweet. Not as acidic/lean as Climens 1983 or 1976. I think that the 1983 is better. (17.5)

Comments

The great wines in this tasting were Margaux, Mouton, Lafite, Haut-Brion, Cos d'Estournel, and Cheval-Blanc. The good wines were Latour, Canon (very good), and Lynch-Bages. The wines that should have been better were Climens and La Mission. The real disappointment was l'Evangile, but then, 1986 is not a Pomerol year.

April 1989

Press tasting and lunch, at "Five Sails" restaurant, in the Pan Pacific hotel.

Organized by Vintage Consultants, the agents for Mondavi in British Columbia. Tim Mondavi was the guest speaker. We started with a comparative tasting of Robert Mondavi and French "equivalent" wines.

1. Robert Mondavi Fumé Blanc "Reserve" 1986, Napa Valley:

Green gold. Spicy, fresh, crisp on nose. Good varietal character. Some oak. A bit sharp on palate, but good fruit concentration. From Tokalon vineyard. Lively, fresh. Good length. We also had this wine with the luncheon. (15)

2. Ladoucette Pouilly-Fumé 1986, Loire Valley:

Similar appearance to Mondavi's. More sulphur on nose. Leaner, less rich. Higher acidity, less intense, but crisp, clean, spicy. Well made. Should have had a little more ripe fruit. A bit flintier, too. On nose, better varietal character than the Mondavi. (15.5)

3. Robert Mondavi Chardonnay "Reserve" 1986, Napa Valley:

Bright-golden colour. Clean, subdued nose. Not much oak or intensity. Rich, fairly thick on entry, but a bit short middle. Clean finish, with hint of new oak. Softer and a bit more forward. Drink now to 1990. (16)

4. Puligny-Montrachet Premier Cru "Les Pucelles" 1986, Joseph Drouhin:

Bright-golden colour; slightly less depth than the Mondavi Chardonnay. Slight hint of sulphur, toasty nose. Round, complex, delicate, yet rich. Good depth. Flavourful. Long, classy. Needs two to three years. More fragrant than the Mondavi. (17)

5. Robert Mondavi Pinot Noir "Reserve" 1986, Napa Valley:

Darker, younger-looking than the Dujac. Some purple, too. Subdued, clean, spicy nose. Very elegant. Quite nice on palate, but rich, big, tannic. Solid, quite concentrated. Good structure, clean finish. Drink now to 1994. Well balanced. We also had it with lunch. (15.5)

6. Clos de la Roche 1986, Domaine Dujac:

Pale colour, orange hue. Pale rim. Spicy, sweet, clean, warm nose. Open and forward. A bit stemmy. Dry, diluted, soft. A bit tannic, but no ripe fruit to back it up. Poor effort. Should never have been bottled as a Grand Cru. (13) I know that most 1986s are too soft, but this is really sad. In any event, the 1986 red Burgundies (with few exceptions) have never been favourites of mine.

7. Robert Mondavi Cabernet Sauvignon "Reserve" 1985, Napa Valley:

Young, bright, purplish colour, with good depth, but palish rim. Not as ripe as Robert Mondavi's Cabernets can be, nor as spicy-eucalyptus (hardly any). Subdued, clean oak-spices on nose; good class and elegance. Full, round, lovely. Concentrated, complex, long. Beautiful balance. Excellent structure. Top quality. Needs five to eight years. Made from 82% Cabernet Sauvignon, 12% Cabernet Franc, and 6% Merlot. (17.5)

8. Château Margaux 1985:

Less purple, nice colour to rim. Closed on nose. Big, rich, serious. Great depth and balance. Very good bottle. Harder tannins than the Mondavi's. Vanilla-oak finish. Long, complex. Lovely overall. Seven to ten years. When tasted side-by-side, the Margaux has more taste and less greenness, but overall, both wines are very good. (18)

DESSERT WINE

Robert Mondavi 1983 "Botrytized" Sauvignon Blanc, Napa Valley:

Deep bright-gold. Intense, rich-looking. Rich, ripe, herbal, clean nose. Quite long; good acidity, subdued botrytis, but very elegant. No rush. Very good. Made with 21% Semillon in the blend. (17)

April 18, 1989

Tasting at Dr. David Allan's in Coquitlam, with 20 other doctors from Royal Columbia Hospital.

I conducted the tasting. The main subject: a vertical tasting of Les-Forts-de-Latour (the second wine of Château Latour) made from young vines, lesser-quality wine of the Grand Vin, as well as from grapes picked in three plots called "Petit Batailley," "Comtesse de Lalande," and "Santa Anna."

Les-Forts-de-Latour 1979 to 1970, Château Latour 1980 and 1983

1979:

Typical 1979. Good, dark colour. Evolved nose. Fairly rich, round; not very complex but solid, yet without the backbone of the almost 100% Cabernet of the 1978. Ready but no rush. Good but not great. Clean finish. (16)

1978:

Spicier, cleaner, more complex nose than the 1979; more herbaceous, vegetal, too (typical 1978) Solid, long, still tannic, serious, and has class. Needs three to five more years. Potentially very good. (17)

1976:

Odd nose, a bit leathery, straw. Medium, mature colour. Fairly lean, short, simple, and dull on palate. A disappointing wine. No future. Drink up. (14)

1975:

Dark, maturing colour. Very 1975. Solid, hard, tannic, powerful, but backed by good fruit. Ripe, rich, serious. Needs ten years or more and has enough fruit to last. (17)

1973:

Surprisingly good and elegant. Light colour. Delicate, open, forthcoming nose. Elegant and long on palate. Round, clean, tobacco/cedar, complex. Lovely for current drinking. Very good for a 1973 and has held well. (16)

1970:

Super wine. Very deep, dark, impressive colour. Round, rich, all in harmony. Long on nose and palate. Rich, full, solid. Ready, but will last another decade or more; very impressive wine. Very Pauillac and very rich 1970 style. Top quality. (18) Trying desperately to mimic the Grand Vin (Latour) in 1970, which, to quote Jean-Paul Gardère, the manager of Château Latour, is a "Charles de Gaulle." We did not taste the 1966, the first vintage of Latour's second wine.

May 27, 1989

Commanderie de Bordeaux Dinner and tasting, at Four Seasons hotel, Vancouver, featuring four decades (1985 to 1945) of Château Gruaud-Larose, St. Julien.

This is my second year as Maître of our Commanderie.

FLIGHT #1
Château Gruaud-Larose 1985 to 1975
(Tasted blind)

1. 1983:

Medium dark, mature orange rim. Peppery, spicy, forthcoming nose. Sweet, rich, solid, yet elegant. Good length. Quite vegetal, spicy, 1978-like. Evolved, tobacco. When I found out it was the 1983, I was surprised as to how evolved it was. Something wrong here. 1983 Gruaud-Larose usually has great depth and concentration. (15.5) Can easily achieve a score of (17.5). It is an excellent wine.

2. 1978:

More depth than #1. More peppery, spicy, vegetal. Tighter, more concentrated. Slightly acidic at finish. A bit simple, but quite good. Lean and too acidic. (15.5)

3. 1979:

Dark colour. Palish rim. Spicy, complex, elegant. Younger, leaner, fair acidity, sharpness, but lots of fruit, too. Quite rich. Better than I remembered the 1979 to be. (16)

Between 1967 and 1980, this property did not produce wines up to its high standards.

4. 1981:

Deep colour to rim. Lovely, oak, spices, peppery. Full, solid, tannic. Very 1975-like, but with better fruit. Gruaud made one of the best 1981s. Promising future. Drink from 1994 onwards. (17.5)

5. 1982:

Very good, deep colour, some purple at rim. Closed, yet clean nose. Very rich, ripe, solid. Obviously 1982. Superb depth. Rich, long. Needs ten or more years. Will be excellent. (18.5)

6. 1975:

Medium red. More evolved. Good depth. Leathery, hot nose. Spices, pepper, open. Concentrated, rich, but a bit too tannic. 1979? I was really off there. I should have known better because it had the toughness of the 1975s. (16.5)

7. 1985:

Deep, purplish colour. Very young, fresh, ripe berries. Charming nose, yet not enough backbone—like many 1985s. Still has some bitter tannins. Lovely mid-term wine. True to the vintage. Will be very good by 1995 to 1997. (17.5)

FLIGHT #2
Château Gruaud-Larose 1973 to 1961
(Served through the meal)

1973:

Medium red, orangy rim. Elegant, delicate nose. Soft, elegant, forward, a bit acidic at finish, but certainly very good quality, better than expected. One of the better 1973s. Needs drinking. (14.5)

1967:

Medium dark, mature, orangy rim. Elegant nose. Acidic, lean, solid, too sharp. Not as good as the 1973. Yet a second bottle more intense, richer, fruitier, and much better overall; ripe. True to the vintage and a fine effort. Needs drinking. (14)

1971:

A bit tight, vegetal. Lean, a bit chaptalized. Simple and tannic. Harder, more solid than most 1971 Haut-Médocs, but lacks fruit. (14)

1970:

A tight 1970, not as charming as some. Solid, hard, lean, yet well balanced. Sweet fruit. One bottle was clearly better than the other. Overall, a serious 1970. Needs time, but will it lose its fruit? (16.5)

1962:

Very good dark colour. Orange rim. Sweet, subdued nose. Roasted, ripe fruit. Forward, spicy, peppery, rich, long, old style. Very good. Holding very well. Lovely bottle. At its peak. (18)

1966:

Very good intense colour to rim. Rich, ripe, solid; needs lots of time. Massive, ripe fruit, superb. Very impressive. Needs ten years! Better structure, depth, and fruit than most 1966s at this stage. (18)

1961:

What a nose! Tobacco, complex, superb length. Deep, rich, long; great bottle. Sweet, ripe. In my opinion, the best wine of the evening. Dark, complex, great!! Drinking well now, but will hold well until the end of the century. (19)

FLIGHT #3
Château Gruaud-Larose 1955 to 1945
(Served with cheese course)

1957 AND 1955:

Fairly hard, solid, ripe, leathery, earthy. Quite soft. Some sharpness at finish. It turned out that in our bottle, the cork read 1957 (!), and indeed, it was a 1957, yet the label clearly indicated 1955!

The other—a true 1955: softer, rounder, tobacco. Superb, long. Best of flight. More elegant and velvety than the 1957, but both very good. Rated the true 1955 (18). The 1957 was harder, leaner, as 1957s should be. Rated it (17).

1949, IN MAGNUM:

Ripe, earthy on both nose and palate. Rich, long, complex, soft, mushrooms, and earth. Starting to dry out a bit. Lovely, though. Needs drinking. A bit "rich tea"-like. In my opinion, a bit tired. I've tasted better examples of this wine. (17)

1945, IN DOUBLE-MAGNUM:

(A rare bottle worth today, in 1983, over $1,000!) Impressive dark colour. Still hard on palate. Lovely old mushrooms-truffles-earthy nose of mature Claret. Solid, not as fruity as at previous occasions, but nevertheless good. (17)

My overall favourites

The 1961, then 1962 and 1966, then 1955. For future drinking: the 1982 (of course), the 1981, the 1983, and the 1985.

A very successful, well-organized event. It took five years to put this one together, but it was well worth it. Chef Kerry Sears prepared an outstanding dinner.

Friday, June 16, 1989

Lunch at "Champagne" restaurant, in Los Angeles, with a group of friends.

Organized by Dr. Brad Klein. The person who brought the poorest bottle had to buy lunch for the person who brought along the winning wine. Our dear old friend from London, Harry Waugh, was there, too.

APERITIF

CHAMPAGNE PERRIER-JOUËT BRUT N/V:

With hors d'oeuvres. Round, some yeast and complexity. Not much depth. Medium to small bubbles; fruity and clean. Good length. (16.5)

Subject: 1968, 1969, and 1970 California Cabernet Sauvignons

Served blind—actually double-blind—because we knew the subject, but each participant only knew the identity of his own wine, but not the order. There were a couple of ringers. I brought a 1967 (see #3 below), and another person brought a 1985 Lynch-Bages (see #1 below). The food was very good.

1. LYNCH-BAGES 1985:

Very good dark colour, with even a hint of purple. Lovely, spicy, fruity, youthful nose. Hint of American oak. Quite woody, new oak, green and raw at this stage. Very young, concentrated, rich, and youthful-looking. Slight hint of barnyard. It was obviously the Bordeaux. Excellent potential. (17.5), possibly (18).

2. 1970 BEAULIEU VINEYARDS GEORGES DE LATOUR "PRIVATE RESERVE":

Quite a bit more brown and more mature than #1. Orange-brown rim, but good depth. Older, evolved nose. Slightly medicinal and herbal. Sweet nose. Round, soft, forward; some leather, tea. Soft, tired, still sound, but needs drinking. Delicate. Later, a bit acidic and falling apart. (14.5)

3. 1967 HEITZ CELLARS "MARTHA'S VINEYARD":

(My bottle) A bit darker than #2, but as mature-looking. Old leathery-woody yet slightly cedary nose. Lovely mint-eucalyptus. Rich, ripe, complex; good depth and long finish. Elegant and at its peak. Enjoyable. Hint of acidity at finish. Surprisingly good and has held well. (17) I didn't know, of course, that this was my bottle.

4. 1968 RIDGE "HOLLIWOOD CUVÉE," MONTE BELLO:

Nice, deep, mature colour; little maturity at rim. Lovely, complex, spicy, Bordeaux-like nose. Very slightly dusty. Quite forward, soft, yet acidic, Older-Bordeaux-like. Quite good. Complex finish. Very good balance. Chunky, not unlike Grand-Puy-Lacoste. Straightforward, solid, rich. A bit hard, but good. (16) (See also comments under #13.)

5. 1970 BEAULIEU VINEYARDS GEORGES DE LATOUR "PRIVATE RESERVE":

(A second bottle) Good dark colour to rim without much age showing. Mature, complex nose of cinnamon, spices, and oak. Mint and cedar, too. Round, full, rich, still a bit tannic. A bit astringent at finish. Good flavour, class, and style. Needs drinking. Better than #2. (16.5)

6. 1970 BEAULIEU VINEYARDS GEORGES DE LATOUR "PRIVATE RESERVE":

(A third sample!) Medium dark colour to rim. Subdued, delicate, spicy, ripe, mature nose. Hint of cedar. Round, elegant, complete, good backbone. Well balanced. Lovely, rich, mature finish. Soft, delicate. Classy. (17.5) Talk about bottle variation!

7. 1968 BEAULIEU VINEYARDS GEORGES DE LATOUR "PRIVATE RESERVE":

Very impressive deep-purple colour to rim. Earthy, metallic nose. Full, young, fruity, straightforward. Very good fruit. Lively, good depth. Full, generous. Lots of depth. (17.5)

8. 1969 BEAULIEU VINEYARDS GEORGES DE LATOUR "PRIVATE RESERVE":

Deep, dark colour; orangy rim. Earthy vegetal nose. Drier, hard, solid, round, yet powerful. (13.5) So far, I like this one the least. Finishes harsh. Later, softened a bit, but still uninteresting.

This was Sid Cross's bottle and unanimously the poorest. Sid lost and had to pay US$60 for the lunch of the person who brought #13, the overall winner.

9. 1970 MAYACAMAS:

Very dark-purplish colour to rim. Spicy, rich complex cedary nose. Full, still youthful. Powerful, tannic, a bit too dry and trace of acidity at finish. A bit murky, too harsh at finish. (15) Made in the big Mayacamas style.

10. 1970 MAYACAMAS:

(Second bottle) Very dark-purplish colour to rim. Subdued nose. Deep colour. Chunky, big, powerful, lacks charm. Solid, dry, yet has lots of fruit. Intense. Very good future. Both #9 and #10 are big wines, but #10 has more fruit and is better balanced. Must be Mayacamas or Ridge. (17)

11. 1969 HEITZ CELLARS "MARTHA'S VINEYARD," NAPA VALLEY:

Medium dark, maturing colour. Obvious minty, spicy, eucalyptus. Full, sweeter, complex, minty, rich, and long. Lovely depth. Superb. Needs drinking, a bit lean in middle, but still lovely. (17.5) Most tasters liked it (three didn't). Harry Waugh liked it. He rated it (18). Joe Heitz is very proud of this wine—with good reason.

12. 1968 SOUVERAIN:

Medium dark, mature colour. Good depth. Subdued, closed nose. Hint of cedar. Soft, forward, at its peak. Slightly sweet, rich, ripe, elegant. Easy to drink, but later not much depth. Good. (Lee Stuart's Souverain. Now it is called Burgess Vineyards.) (16)

13. RIDGE 1968 "HOLLIWOOD CUVÉE," MONTE BELLO, CALIFORNIA:

(A second bottle) Very deep, dark colour; some age at rim. Rich Bordeaux-like nose. Complex, long, and ripe. A bit earthy, but very good. Full, rich, elegant. Classy, long. Slightly green at finish. I liked it more than most. Good extract, depth. Fairly alcoholic. Leaner and controversial. Harry Waugh didn't like it. (Picked by Hollywood Wine and Food Society. This is the Monte Bello. Bottled in May 1971.) (18) Most rated it (16.5) to (17).

14. 1970 BEAULIEU VINEYARDS GEORGES DE LATOUR "PRIVATE RESERVE":

(Yet another bottle) Medium colour, mature rim. Good depth. Leathery, leaner, more American oak and vanilla, good depth. Fruity, slightly acidic finish, but rich, ripe, too. Very good. Clean and at its peak. A bit pruny, old-style, mature wine. Old Beaulieu Vineyards style. (16.5)

We also tasted the following two Late Harvest Zinfandels.

1970 RIDGE "JIMSOMARE" LATE HARVEST ZINFANDEL:

15.8% residual sugar. Medium colour, good depth, quite a bit of orange-brown. Almost salty, severe, hard, sour. Disappointing. Lost its sweetness. Not good. (12)

1968 MAYACAMAS LATE HARVEST ZINFANDEL:

Impressive, dark, mature colour. Harsh, tannic, sour, powerful. No charm or complexity. Just hard, disappointing wine. 17% residual sugar! (12) Anyway, Late Harvest Zinfandel is really not my style of wine.

The two Zinfandels were not officially included in the tasting. They were added as a curiosity, which is what they were.

Overall

At least five of the Cabernets were top notch. My favourites (in that order): #13, #11, #7, #1. My least favourites (in that order): #8, #2, #9. There were no fewer than four 1970 Georges de Latour "Private Reserve"—quite a bit of bottle variation.

Next day

Lunch and tasting at Dr. Brad Klein's home

The "main event," with Harry Waugh as guest; only 12 participants. Subject: 1928 Bordeaux—a great vintage and, when well stored, the wines can be superb.

APERITIF

CHAMPAGNE BILLECART-SALMON BRUT ROSÉ N/V, IN MAGNUM:

Very pale-salmon colour. Elegant, round, soft, small bubbles, not as dry as many Rosé Bruts. Softer, delicate. Not much complexity, but better than when tasted previously.

Harry spoke about his experience with the 1928s since 1934, when he entered the wine trade (at Block, Gray and Block, a London wine merchant firm).

All the wines were château-bottled, levels indicated.

CODE

US: Upper shoulder
BN: Bottom neck
(Very good for wines of this age)
MS: Mid shoulder
TS: Top shoulder
N: Neck

APERITIF

CHÂTEAU HAUT-BRION BLANC 1928 (MS):

Bright, deep yellow-gold, like a 1967 Sauternes. Delicate, subdued nose; some Sherry character. Very delicate, soft Sherry on palate. Even hint of oak and botrytis. Quite rich finish. Quite alcoholic. Sweeter on entry, but finishes dry. Later, developed honeyed-character. (17.5) Other tasters rated it (16) to (16.5).

FLIGHT #1
St. Emilions

CHÂTEAU CLOS FOURTET 1928 (BN):

Fairly light, mature colour. Orange rim. Tea and wood, herbaceous on nose. Delicate, soft, round, not much St. Emilion character, but still sweet, round. Good length and complexity. Delicate clean finish. (16.5)

CHÂTEAU LA GAFFELIÈRE-NAUDES 1928 (LS):

Very low shoulder level. Very deep, dark colour. Oxidized on nose. Almost black. Tar. Sharp, acidic, yet still drinkable. Pruny, stemmy. There must be a better bottle of this somewhere! (13.5)

FLIGHT #2
Pomerols

CHÂTEAU L'EVANGILE 1928 (TS):

Medium-to-pale colour; orange rim. Ripe, earthy, herbaceous nose. Sweet on palate, rounder. A charming wine. Complex, delicate. Most enjoyable. (17)

CHÂTEAU ROUGET 1928 (BN):

Good, medium dark colour. Corked on nose. Similar on palate. Good fruit intensity. Sharp and drying out. (13)

CHÂTEAU TROTANOY 1928 (N):

Medium red colour, orangy rim. Excellent appearance. Recorked in 1978 at the château. Lovely, subdued, ripe nose. Full, rich, young, round, fruity. Complex and long. Superb balance and length. A charming, lovely wine. (18)

FLIGHT #3
Margaux

CHÂTEAU BRANE-CANTENAC 1928 (TS):

Good depth, still deep red, palish rim. Rich, complex, open, fruity nose. Lovely fruit, rich. Impressive youth, like a 1962! Very long. In the old days, they used to make great wines at this château. Has held extremely well. (18)

CHÂTEAU DESMIRAIL 1928 (US):

Mature, palish red; orange rim. Delicate, subdued nose. A bit astringent, vegetal. Meaty nose. Definitely drinkable, but a bit tired and astringent; too dry. Drinking history. Desmirail was made at Palmer in the 1940s, 1950s, 1960s, and 1970s. (15)

CHÂTEAU PALMER 1928 (TS):

A wine of great reputation. Evolved, rich, cedary nose. Ripe, delicate, yet full. Lovely length. Slightly overly sweet and astringent, but good fruit. Rich, full wine. A lovely bottle, yet not quite as great as it can be. This wine and Brane-Cantenac are two great Margaux examples, yet very different from each other. Brane is livelier; Palmer more mature, rounder, and sweeter. Wonderful complexity later. (18.5) Nicolas-bottlings of this wine can easily score a perfect (20)!

CHÂTEAU LASCOMBES (BN):

Medium colour, good depth, but mature orange rim. Pleasant, mature, fruity nose. Still lively on palate. Round, complex, fresh, well balanced. Together with the 1961, this is the best Lascombes I've ever tasted. (16)

FLIGHT #4
St. Juliens

CHÂTEAU GRUAUD-LAROSE 1928 (BN):

Medium dark. Tea-like on nose. Slightly ripe. Full, rich, better on palate. Solid, intense, leathery, earthy backbone of Gruaud. Full, intense, but very individual. A bit edgy and raisiny. Very good concentration, though. Some tasters said that it was a bit volatile. A tougher wine, true to the vintage and to Gruaud's style. (17)

CHÂTEAU LEOVILLE-LASCASES 1928 (TS):

Good dark colour to rim. Mature orange. Fruity, beefy, coffee nose. Full, round, perfect balance on palate. Lovely depth, complexity. Slightly leathery. Later, a bit edgy at the end. Didn't last as long as the others in glass, but during first 15 minutes, great. Downgraded it to (17.5) from (18.5) because of its drying out. Can be a great bottle.

CHÂTEAU TALBOT 1928 (BN):

Very mature, a bit cloudy colour. Old nose. Leather, earth, dry; weak, lean, sharp, and odd. Not very good, yet still drinkable. Old and starting to oxidize. (13.5)

John Brincko (a fellow taster) told me that when he was in Burgundy recently (in 1986), he went to one of Lalou Bize-Leroy's famous blind tastings of older Burgundies. Apparently Brincko's wife did better than Robert Parker and, as usual, Michael Broadbent had a poor tasting and was among the last in terms of guessing the wines correctly. No wonder Broadbent doesn't like to taste blind. While I respect his vast knowledge of wines, he seems to have a problem at blind tastings. That is why he prefers to see the labels before he comments on the wines.

FLIGHT #5
Pauillacs

CHÂTEAU MOUTON-D'ARMAILHACQ 1928 (BN):

Medium, mature orange-brown colour. Bright and clean. Odd vegetal-dusty nose. Hard, musty, lean, sharp, some fruit, but, too acidic, too sharp, vinegary. Has some fruit, but too lean and dry; too musty, but drinkable. (14) I have tasted this wine only once previously. That example was far superior to today's bottle. Nowadays, this wine is called Mouton-Baron Philippe.

CHÂTEAU PICHON-LALANDE 1928 (TS):

Odd nose, a bit skunky. Stale. Hard, a bit fruity (better on palate), dry. Old, yet some fruit. Drinkable and certainly quite good, but a bit sharp. Lacks charm, yet still alive. Fairly alcoholic and acidic. (14.5)

A disappointing flight.

FLIGHT # 6
First Growths

CHÂTEAU LATOUR 1928 (US):

Impressive dark colour. Lovely, fruity, rich, complex nose. True classic Claret. Cedar, spices, mint. Great length. Great depth. Full, rich, long. Outstanding. Great bottle! Superb structure and youth. No rush! Spicy, rich, long, solid. Classic Latour and classic Pauillac. Drink now to 2000. Great wine. (19.5) This is a masterpiece.

CHÂTEAU MARGAUX (BN):

Good dark colour. Controversial wine. Some liked it; others said it was too dry and past its prime. Spicy, complex nose. Full, fruity, a bit hard and tannic; serious structure but backed by good fruit. Lovely wine. A bit sharp, but very good. (18)

CHÂTEAU MOUTON-ROTHSCHILD 1928 (TS):

Lightest of all three, but good depth, mature rim. Lovely, ripe, mature nose. Fruity, round, well balanced, long, complex, spicy. Hard to identify as Mouton, but a very good wine. Sweet, easy to drink. I've tasted better (see reference). Quite good. Ripe and sweet, but certainly without the intensity or structure of the Margaux. (17.5)

Theory about Château Petrus, according to John Tilson, editor of The Underground Wineletter, *who also participated at this tasting:*

John's theory, told to him by an anonymous producer in Pomerol, is that Petrus is not really Petrus, but the best cuvées from Trotanoy and other properties managed and owned by Moueix. This is nonsense, and I really do not believe it. This must be "sour grapes" by other producers. I find it very hard to believe this kind of "theory." I don't think John seriously believes it himself.

FLIGHT #7
Graves
A great flight!

CHÂTEAU HAUT-BAILLY 1928 (BN):

Medium, mature colour. Vegetal, spicy, open nose. Clean and complex. Round, sweet, elegant. Soft, stylish. Lovely length. As always, elegant, stylish, classy wine. Even good backbone. Superb drinking now. Fine, long finish. A real revelation and an outstanding wine. All class, suppleness, and elegance. (18)

CHÂTEAU LA MISSION HAUT-BRION 1928 (BN):

Very good, deep colour. Ripe, spicy, intense nose. Hard and unyielding. Solid (as always), serious, powerful, tannic, even at 60 years of age. A bit sharp, yet good depth and fruit. My score was a bit high. (17) Most rated it (16).

CHÂTEAU MALARTIC-LAGRAVIÈRE 1928 (TS):

Very dark colour to rim, like a 1961. Palish rim. Rich, chocolate nose. Full, youthful, very impressive. Great depth, length, and complexity. Coffee, chocolate, earthy. One of the best Malartics I've tasted. (17.5)

FLIGHT #8
St. Estèphes
An excellent flight!

CHÂTEAU CALON-SÉGUR 1928 (BN):

Most impressive dark, deep colour to rim of all the wines in this flight. Lovely, serious, ripe nose; intense, superb, clean. True St. Estèphe on palate. Hard, intense, loads of ripe fruit. Serious old-style St. Estèphe. Coffee beans. A bit astringent. Spicy, wonderful, long, lively. Excellent. Still young! (18) How great Calon-Ségur was in the 1920s and 1940s, notably the 1928, 1943, 1945, and 1947.

CHÂTEAU COS D'ESTOURNEL 1928 (BN):

Medium to dark mature colour. Much more evolved, riper nose. Leaner on palate, good depth, a bit acidic, hard, but some fruit there. Unfortunately, stuck between two great wines. A bit lean and tannic. Hard, sharp finish, but very good length and depth. Improved in glass. (17.5)

CHÂTEAU MONTROSE 1928 (TS):

Good, dark, mature colour. Clean, serious, fruity, mature nose. Solid, rich, deep, complex, long. A lovely, great, fruity St. Estèphe. Complete, superb bottle. Fruity, clean. This is more Cabernet, more serious. Calon-Ségur has more Merlot, riper. Both excellent. Held very well in glass for almost an hour. Grand Vin! (18.5)

The three St. Estèphes were outstanding wines. All three were true to their individual property styles, vintage, and commune.

FLIGHT #9
Sauternes

CHÂTEAU SUDUIRAUT 1928 (TS):

A little darker than the d'Yquem. Amber-gold colour. Lovely depth, honey, botrytis, and great all the way through. Superb balance. Great length, well balanced. Definitely one of the best wines of the event. (19)

Château d'Yquem 1928 (BN):

Excellent appearance. Very dark gold (pale-tea) colour. Not quite as dark as the Suduiraut. More subdued, closed nose. Great length, depth. Caramel, acidity, fruit, botrytis, length, and balance. Later, more depth, concentration; classic, magnificent wine! A superb "as-great-as-they-come" Sauternes. Slightly fresher than the Suduiraut. Grand Vin! (19.5)

These two Sauternes were absolutely superb.

Overall

In terms of the overall quality and consistency, this was an excellent tasting, with very few disappointing wines and many outstanding ones. Some flights were superb, and the two Sauternes were amazingly great! An excellent event. All 12 participants were very knowledgeable and the tasting was well paced.

At the end, Brad served some smooth Grande Champagne Cognac 1904, T. Hine and Co. (1904 being Harry Waugh's birth year), and 1959 vintage cigars from Cuba, the last batch (50,000!) taken out by Jeffrey Troy's father before Batista was ousted by Fidel Castro.

July 6, 1989

Chevaliers des Vins de France vertical tasting of Château Haut-Brion 1985 to 1964, in Vancouver.

I purchased the wines from the Wine House in San Francisco, and conducted the blind tasting with Sid Cross's assistance.

1. Château Haut-Brion 1981:

Medium colour. Mature rim. Elegant, open nose. Spicy, evolved, classy. Forward, some tannins. Medium-bodied; clean, long finish. Drink now to 1998. (16.5)

2. Château Haut-Brion 1985:

Deep, purplish, youthful colour to rim. Delicate, spicy, oaky nose. Typical elegance of the vintage. Full, yet not overly so. Round, long, ripe. Good concentration. Drink from 1995 to 2002. (17.5)

3. Château Haut-Brion 1983:

Dark maturing rim, but good depth. Closed nose, but classy and flowery. Fruity, powerful, tannic, hard, masculine, backed by good fruit. Clear finish. Excellent potential. Drink from 1996 to 2005. This wine is still undervalued at auction. (18)

4. Château Haut-Brion 1982, in magnum:

Very good, deep colour to rim. Lovely, ripe, spicy, concentrated nose. Forthcoming. Full, solid, very tannic, concentrated, yet the finish is not as nice as the 1983. Very good, though. Drink from 1995 to 2005. (18)

5. Château Haut-Brion 1978:

Dark, maturing colour. Stemmy, herbaceous nose. Similar impressions on palate. Solid, yet evolved. Complex, long, well balanced. Clean, stylish. Approaching its peak, but no rush. My favourite for drinking now to 1998. (17)

6. Château Haut-Brion 1976:

Medium depth; mature orange rim. Dull nose. Tannic, acidic, yet diluted. Some sharpness at finish. Good, but not great. Least favourite of the group. Lacks middle. Drink up. (15) Having said that, not a bad effort and one of the better 1976s.

7. Château Haut-Brion 1979:

Very good dark colour, some brown at rim. Lovely tobacco, earthy, ripe nose. Round, elegant, long, complex, delicate, forward. Very good length. Rich, long, complex, and popular. Drink now to 1999. This must surely be one of the best wines of the vintage, and the best Haut-Brion of the decade of the 1970s. (17.5)

8. Château Haut-Brion 1964:

This wine was served separately at the end, as a "bonne bouche." Consistent—all six bottles were good. Complex, round, long, a bit chocolaty, ripe. Very good wine that is at its peak. One of the successes of 1964, and a consistently complex wine. I'm glad I chose this over the 1966 or 1970, retailing for the same price. (18)

My favourites

Potentially 1983, 1982, 1985, and the 1986.

For drinking now or soon: 1978 and 1979, and of course, the 1964.

Overall impressions

The tasting was quite good, yet the overall quality of the wines was not, I felt, in the class of a First Growth. All wines were good, some were very good, but none were truly great. Also, the tasting didn't go as well as expected. My cohost kept interrupting me. This interfered with my concentration.

July 17

My birthday. In the evening, we went to Joe and Alice Heitz's place for some Champagne.

The other guests were Richard Danskin and his girlfriend Sherry Hatchet, both artists (painters) from Palm Springs, California. Richard is the artist whose painting is on Heitz's famous "Martha's Vineyard" 1974 label. Richard's painting will also be on the "Martha's Vineyard" 1985 Anniversary Cabernet.

We tried two Champagnes.

CHAMPAGNE JACQUART BRUT 1982:

Crisp, fresh, fruity, well balanced, with tiny bubbles. Better than expected and nice, clean finish.

CHAMPAGNE BOLLINGER "SPÉCIALE CUVÉE" BRUT N/V:

(I brought it along, together with some BC smoked salmon, for the Heitzes.) Deeper, richer, longer; more yeast, more complex. Very Bollinger style and very good length, balance, and character.

Then we all drove to the restaurant "Trilogy" (formerly "Le Rhône"), in St. Helena.

Excellent food and service, and an interesting, well-thought-out wine list. Joe asked me to choose the wines. Since he likes Gewürztraminer and Pinot Noir, I wanted him to try some fine French wines, which he usually does not try; I chose two wines that turned out to be excellent.

1986 GEWÜRZTRAMINER "CUVÉE LAURENCE," DOMAINE WEINBACH, ALSACE:

Superb Gewürztraminer. Rich, deep, bright-gold colour. Lovely, ripe, spicy lychee-nut nose. Full, long, intense; great depth and balance. Even Joe had to admit this was a super wine.

1985 POMMARD "EPENOTS" PREMIER CRU, DE COURCEL:

A really fine Burgundy from an excellent vintage. Medium red colour, not too deep. Still touch of youthful purple at rim. Lovely nose of fresh, young, ripe Pinot Noir and oak. Clean, long, and lovely on palate. Well balanced, good backbone. Drink from 1992 to 1996, or beyond. A lovely, classic Pinot Noir.

Then we tried a bottle Joe Heitz brought along.

1974 HEITZ CELLARS "MARTHA'S VINEYARD" CABERNET SAUVIGNON, NAPA VALLEY:

Carol and I tasted it with the man who made the wine (Joe Heitz) and the man who painted/designed the label (Richard Danskin)! Deep, dark, yet maturing colour. Lovely, mint-eucalyptus, intense nose so typical of "Martha's." (Joe doesn't like the term "mint"; he prefers "eucalyptus.") Big, rich, intense, approaching maturity, but good fruit, depth, and backbone to last for ten more years or longer. Excellent classic Cabernet.

July 22, 1989

International Wine and Food Society Dinner, featuring 1966 First Growths, as part of Dr. Haskell Norman's 74th birthday celebrations.

Guests included Jean-Claude Vrinat (owner of Taillevent in Paris).

1983 TAILLEVENT CHAMPAGNE "BLANC DE BLANCS" BRUT:

(Vineyard located east of Epernay in Verteuil) Delicate, round, complex nose. Fresh, well balanced with good depth. Will be very good in one to two years. Tiny bubbles; delicate and clean. (17)

1982 PULIGNY-MONTRACHET "FOLATIÈRES" PREMIER CRU, MONNIER-VAIVRAND:

Medium gold. Oak, complex Chardonnay nose. Delicate, round. A bit sharp at finish. Needs drinking. Quite complex and good, but too lean. (16)

1982 CORTON-CHARLEMAGNE, BONNEAU DU MARTRAY:

Slightly lighter colour. Lovely, delicate nose; round, fruity, intense. Oak and ripe Chardonnay in harmony. Soft, typical 1982; ripe and herbaceous. Later, as it warmed up, it was a bit sharp, but still had good length. (17.5)

CHAMPAGNE KRUG "COLLECTION" 1966, IN MAGNUMS:

(Two magnums kindly sent by Rémy Krug) Bright, deep, golden colour. Tiny bubbles. Earthy nose with hint of mushrooms. Quite rich, yet sharp, acidic, and starting to oxidize. Certainly has depth and character, but has seen better days. I have tasted better examples of this on previous occasions. (16.5)

CHAMPAGNE DOM PÉRIGNON 1966, IN BOTTLES:

Deep, golden, mature colour. Honeyed nose. Very ripe; starting to smell like Sauternes and yeast. Rich, ripe, intense, full, and fruity. Very mature. Not as lean or with as tough a backbone as the Krug, but more delicate and riper. Both good, but both have seen better days. The Dom was so sweet that it seemed to have too much dosage. (16.5) As with the Krug, I have previously tasted better examples of this Champagne.

1966 First Growths (All from magnums)

All had excellent neck levels.

FLIGHT #1

Pomerol and St. Emilions

CHÂTEAU AUSONE 1966:

Medium colour, showing some age at rim. Herbaceous, spicy, stemmy nose. Quite light, forward, elegant; a bit leathery. Showing age, even in magnums.

Oaky. A bit too lean and acidic. Bad period for Ausone. (15.5)

CHÂTEAU CHEVAL-BLANC 1966:

Very good, deep, slightly maturing colour. Lovely, intense cedar on nose. Full, ripe, classic Cheval. Full, rich, solid, slightly tannic. A bit hard, not unlike most 1966s and ending sharp, but overall, lots of depth and character. My favourite of the flight. (18)

CHÂTEAU PETRUS 1966:

Best colour of flight. Full, round, ripe nose. Quite good, yet not as complex as the Cheval. Round, easy to drink, no sharp edges. Still has some tannins. No rush drinking it. (17.5)

FLIGHT # 2

Graves and Margaux

CHÂTEAU HAUT-BRION 1966:

Good dark colour. Quite stemmy on nose. Herbaceous, spicy, quite lean on palate. Good fruit, spicy. Good complexity, but lacks depth. I have tasted better examples of this. (17)

CHÂTEAU LA MISSION HAUT-BRION 1966:

Superb wine. Best of the first five, so far. Complex, tobacco, leather, earthy nose. Ripe, round, warm. Great length. At its peak; superb balance, length, and class. Sweet, lovely fruit, tobacco, earthiness, all in harmony. (18.5)

CHÂTEAU MARGAUX 1966:

Medium, maturing colour. Subdued, tight nose; slightly herbal and green. Round on palate, delicate, complex. Trace of acidity at finish, otherwise quite elegant, no sharp edges. At its peak. Other bottles tasted previously have been superb. (17.5)

Château Palmer 1966 should have been included, too. Like the La Mission, not a First Growth, of course, but a great wine, especially in 1966.

FLIGHT #3

Pauillacs

CHÂTEAU LAFITE 1966:

Medium to light colour. Maturing. Delicate, charming, sweet nose. Round, delicate on palate. Noticeable acidity at finish, yet elegant and complex. Better than I remember it, yet made during a period (1963 to 1975) when Lafite was an underachiever. (17)

CHÂTEAU LATOUR 1966:

Dark, deep, youthful colour. Closed tight nose, yet unmistakable classic, ripe Cabernet. Big, solid, powerful, very youthful, no rush. Complex, fresh, great, and powerful. Lots of life ahead. (18.5)

CHÂTEAU MOUTON-ROTHSCHILD 1966:

Impressive dark colour. Typical spicy Cabernet nose. Some cedar; too sharp and acidic on palate. Harsh, lean, past its prime. This has never been a favourite of mine. (16) After the great 1961, Mouton has done very little until 1982. The 1970 and 1975 are good, but not great. As for the 1964, 1966, 1971, 1978, 1979, and 1981... the less said, the better, especially for a First Growth.

CHÂTEAU D'YQUEM 1966, ALSO IN MAGNUM:

Dark amber-gold colour. Spicy, elegant, delicate nose. Quite round, rich, yet not overpowering. Very good length, delicate, good acidity. I was pleasantly surprised because, in the past, when tasted from regular bottles, it tasted tired and clumsy. (17.5)

CHAMPAGNE TAILLEVENT N/V ROSÉ:

Made from 70% Chardonnay and 30% Pinot Noir (with 7% red wine in the blend). Delicate pink-salmon colour. Fresh on nose and palate; clean, crisp, and well balanced, with good fruit. (17)

TAILLEVENT FINE CHAMPAGNE COGNAC, "SÉLECTION OFFICIELLE BICENTENAIRE DE LA REVOLUTION FRANÇAISE 1789 - 1989," FIVE YEARS OF AGE:

Made from 70% Grande Champagne and 30% Petite Champagne. Dark, round, sweeter style; mellow, delicate, yet full. Easy to sip. Very good Cognac.

September 4, 1989

With panel of *The Wine Consumer*, at home.

CHÂTEAU LEOVILLE-LASCASES 1964:

Low neck level. Decanted 30 minutes. Fair bit of sediment. Good, dark, maturing colour. Tobacco, cedar, mature, open nose. Lots of class, soft, complex, with good depth on palate. This wine is at the last stages of its plateau and it will start to decline soon. Needs drinking. Long, complex on palate. Has style and depth. Obvious Cabernet predominates. (17)

Most St. Juliens were successful in 1964. This cannot be said about most St. Estèphes, Pauillacs, or Margaux (except for Latour, Grand-Puy-Lacoste and a handful of others).

1978 Heitz Cellars' Napa Valley Cabernets (Fay, Bella Oaks, and "Martha's Vineyard")

FAY VINEYARD 1978:

Dark, brilliant colour to rim. Good depth. Quite sweet. Evolved, yet stemmy and vegetal on nose; like a Merlot, yet hard on palate, intense, rich, spicy, straightforward. A bit too hot (alcoholic) and harsh lean finish. Good, but not great. (15)

BELLA OAKS 1978:

Subdued, but unyielding nose. Lightest colour. Medium depth. Soft on palate, but lean finish and too alcoholic. I've tasted this wine half-a-dozen times previously and all were delicate, complex, ready. This example poorest. Harsh, lean, tight; simple for what it is (15.5).

"MARTHA'S VINEYARD" 1978:

Similar colour to Fay, but a bit less brilliant. Typical minty-eucalyptus nose. Intense, rich, long, full. Best balance, but again, too lean, and a bit too alcoholic. Best style and intensity, though. Good, but not great. (17)

September 14, 15, 16, 1989

Mr. Gourmet 1989 (Sid Cross was inducted), Society of Bacchus America.

Because of previous engagements, I could not attend the September 14 and 15 events.

Saturday, September 16

At the Four Seasons hotel.

Great meal, great presentation, especially battery-lit dessert and migniardises. Bruno Marti was the supervising chef. An outstanding meal.

CHAMPAGNE KRUG "COLLECTION" 1969, IN MAGNUMS:

Rich, yeasty, complex, long. Some people thought that it was over-the-hill and a bit oxidizing. I thought it was great, intense, and fabulous. Served with Amur River and Russian beluga caviars. (18.5)

CORTON-CHARLEMAGNE 1986, CHANSON:

Bright green-gold. Some sulphur on nose. Acidic, some nuttiness, but too hard. Some greenness, too lean. Somehow unbalanced. Least favourite wine of the evening. (15)

CORTON-CHARLEMAGNE 1986, JOSEPH DROUHIN:

Lovely, nutty Chardonnay; concentrated. Good acidity. Best of all three Corton-Charlemagnes tonight. Long, complex, oak finish; almonds, all in harmony. Drink from 1989 to 1992. (18) Drouhin's whites tend to be early maturing.

CORTON-CHARLEMAGNE 1986, MOILLARD:

Most forward; round, buttery, rich. Delicate, complex. Well balanced. Not great, but certainly good. Drink now to 1992. (17)

Corton-Charlemagne, Louis Latour, 1983, 1985, and 1986

1983:

Most forward. Quite alcoholic, typical 1983. Full, rich, forward. Drink now to 1994. Long on palate with Latour's oak and nutty flavours. Somehow, too spirity for me, but not bad. (16.5)

1985:

The leanest and most backward. Medium-bodied, not as rich or intense as the 1983 or the 1986. Well balanced, but does not have Latour's usual concentration and intensity. Lack of ripe fruit puts the future of this wine in doubt. Good, but not great. (16.5)

1986:

Intense, rich, long. Needs two to three years. Best potential. Full, luscious, typical 1986. Promising. (17.5)

CHEVALIER-MONTRACHET 1978, REMOISSENET:

Typical leanness of Remoissenet (fairly high acidity), but evolved, rich, ripe nose. Long on palate. Beautiful balance. Very good. Ready, but no rush, although if one waits too much longer, acidity might predominate. Drink now. (17.5)

Château Palmer 1978, 1976, and 1975

1978:

Probably the most disappointing wine of the evening, as far as I am concerned. 1978 was a Cabernet year; little Merlot was made. Medium depth, open nose. Round, delicate, evolved, but too green and stemmy. Somehow lacks charm. Needs more ripe fruit and more Merlot; too bad. Maybe going through a phase and may improve—I hope, because I own three cases! (16.5) It was definitely better when tasted previously in 1980, 1982, and 1986.

1976:

Typical for the year. Warm, round, soft, forward. Good depth, but at its peak. Needs drinking. Ready and most enjoyable. (17)

1975:

Darkest, richest, best depth of the flight, and riper than most 1975s. Chocolate, ripe fruit. Long yet tight, solid; typical hard 1975. Will last another decade. Very good potential. Drink from 1991 to 1998, or beyond. (18) Some people don't like this wine. "A chacun son goût!"

Château Palmer 1970, 1966, and 1961

1970:

Darkest, most youthful and tight of flight. Full, rich, long. Not quite ready. Needs two to five more years. Loads of fruit; complex, spicy, rich, long. Excellent potential. A wine I know well. (18.5)

1966:

Maturing yet dark colour. Chocolate, ripe, evolved nose. Full, yet soft. Was better when tasted three years ago. Soft, velvety, round, long, delicate. Very complex, lovely. (18)

1961:

A masterpiece, yet more evolved than when tasted previously. Tobacco, cedar, ripe raisins, forthcoming, delicate. Robert Mondavi, in his comments, thought that if Palmer had used more new oak, it could have been great. I agree. Lovely length, velvety, intense, rich, yet soft. Quite evolved. No sense keeping it any longer. Super quality. (18.5)

1971 La Tâche and 1971 Romanée-St.-Vivant, (both Domaine de la Romanée-Conti), in magnums

Romanée-St.-Vivant:

Medium colour, good depth. Medium-bodied. Rich, spicy, a bit vegetal (green) on nose, with good Pinot Noir character. Round, trace of acidity at finish. Very fine. (17.5)

La Tâche:

The wine of the evening! A superb magnum! Deep colour to rim. Magnificent, rich, spicy, classy, open Pinot Noir and typical raspberries on nose. Full, intense, complex on palate. Great length and balance. No rush, especially in magnums. A wine I know well and love. Perfect balance and will hold. Superb. (19)

Château d'Yquem 1970:

Bright, deep-gold colour with orange hue. Lovely, open, mature botrytis nose. Long, rich, yet not cloying, with good acidity and length. At its peak. Showing, and holding, much better than expected. Very good. Rich finish with lingering aftertaste. (18)

Cognac "Réserve Lafite-Rothschild":

A lovely and mellow Cognac. Spices and oak in harmony. Smooth, delicate. Most enjoyable.

The dinner was outstanding, the "lit" dessert on a frozen transparent bowl was sensational. The migniardises (baskets around a chocolate wine press) were a masterpiece.

Sunday, September 17, 1989

At our home.

That afternoon, we entertained the Normans and Dr. Barney and Belle Rhodes at home, for some smoked salmon and a couple of wines.

Champagne Veuve Clicquot "La Grande Dame" 1979:

Barney likes older, richer Champagnes and this bottle fit the bill. Creamy, rich, long. Good mousse, tiny bubbles, yeasty. Lovely drinking now.

Condrieu "Côteau de Vernon" 1985, Georges Vernay:

Barney was really fond of this. Rich, long, fairly alcoholic. Flowery, lilacs and peaches. Complex, superb length, delicate. A great and rare wine. Only one cuvée made. Superb quality and at its peak. Barney has a source in England that supplies him with one bottle of this wine per year. He was really impressed by this. Vernay's "regular" Condrieu is very good, but the "Vernon" is his top Condrieu.

Sunday, September 17, 1989

Dinner at Val and Dick Bradshaw's, with Dr. Haskell Norman and his wife Rae.

Dick provided the Champagne and white wine. I provided the two reds and the dessert wine.

Champagne Krug "Grande Cuvée" N/V:

Leaner, typical of this producer. Complex, tight, serious, long. Very fine bubbles. A classic Champagne that will hold well for four to five more years. Krug is Krug. (18)

Bâtard-Montrachet 1982, Remoissenet:

Bright, palish gold. Oak and ripe Chardonnay on nose. Leaner style, typical Remoissenet, yet also typical for the vintage (well balanced, delicate, forward). At its peak. A classy, very good Burgundy. Fruit and oak in harmony. (17.5)

1978 Sassicaia "Bolgheri," Antinori:

Only 1,500 cases produced. Extremely rare and a fine bottle. Fair bit of sediment. Decanted one hour. Very impressive, deep, dark colour to rim. Subdued, ripe Cabernet nose. On palate: full, great balance, rich, ripe fruit. Superb long finish. One of the greatest Italian wines I've tasted to date! Everyone was impressed. Great future. Drink now to 1995, or beyond. (18.5)

1945 Château Pontet-Canet, English-bottled by Block, Gray and Block:

(Harry Waugh's old firm) High shoulder level. Cork disintegrated. Fair bit of sediment. Impressive dark, yet maturing colour, typical of the 1945s. Tobacco, cedar, and mature fruit on nose. Expansive. Full, good backbone, trace of tannins; typical of 1945s. Superb length and fruit extract. A lovely bottle. Haskell was happy to try it because once before, he missed the opportunity to taste it, because his waiters poured too much into some glasses at one of the International

Wine and Food Society events; Haskell gave his wine to an irate guest, so he didn't have a chance to try it then. (18)

FREEMARK ABBEY "EDELWEIN GOLD" 1982, BOTRYTIZED JOHANNISBERG RIESLING TBA, IN HALF-BOTTLE:

Deep orange-gold. Honey and ripe apricots on nose. Similar impressions on palate. Not cloying, but rich, long, concentrated. Quite sweet. (17.5)

A most enjoyable evening.

September 22, 1989

Dinner at Ian Mottershead's.

As is usual at Ian's home, the wines were served double-blind.

CHAMPAGNE KRUG ROSÉ N/V:

(Ian has cellared it for five years.) Barely a Rosé. Very pale salmon-pink colour. Delicate nose of mature Champagne. Not very complex, too much dosage (hint of sugar) on palate. A bit old and earthy, too. Not bad, but in the context of Krug, disappointing. Storage problem?

1970 CHÂTEAU LATOUR:

I guessed this right on! I said, "Must be Latour, and if it is, then it is 1970." Very deep, dark colour to rim. Some cedar, unyielding nose. Massive, powerful, tannic, excellent balance; good ripe fruit, but needs many years. Drink from 1997 to 2010, or beyond! Will be great, but nowhere near ready. (19)

OPPENHEIMER SACKTRAGER GEWÜRZTRAMINER TROCKENBEERENAUSLESE 1976, GUNTRUM, RHEINHESSEN:

Bright, deep gold. Spicy, ripe Gewürztraminer on nose and palate. Great extract. Creamy, rich, long; excellent acidity and fruit. Ready, but no rush. A lovely bottle. (18)

October 3, 1989

Commanderie de Bordeaux Dinner and tasting of 1986 Clarets.

Alice Spurrell prepared a heavy "Germanic" meal. Overall, the 1986s were very deep, dark, purplish, and quite tight. These wines have been bottled only 14 to 16 months ago.

1. CHÂTEAU CANON 1986:

Medium to deep colour. Evolved rim. Good depth. Forthcoming, sweet, ripe, medium tannins. Rich, long; six to eight years. Some green tannins. Later, ripe, rich, sweet. More elegant. Not nearly as powerful as the Left Bank wines. (17)

2. CHÂTEAU L'ARROSÉE 1986:

Good dark colour. Unyielding nose. Ripe raisins. Quite hard, noticeable acidity, but good backbone. Intense. Rich, well balanced. Ripe. Bigger than the Canon. Solid, big serious. Drink from 1995 to 2000. (17)

L'Arrosée, with its high proportion of Cabernets, makes long-lived, sturdy, Haut-Médoc-like wines.

3. VIEUX CHÂTEAU CERTAN 1986:

Very dark colour to rim. Slightly evolved. Spicy, grapey, green nose. Herbaceous and new oak. Very fresh. Tannic, yet fruity. Powerful. Oak, vanilla, yet elegant. Very "Right Bank." Promising; ten years. (17.5)

4. CHÂTEAU FIGEAC 1986:

Medium dark. Most evolved colour. Stemmy, green St. Emilion style. Forward, tannic, yet soft. Warm, round, classy, ripe aftertaste. Ready soon (three to six years). Obviously, a Cabernet-based wine. Spicy, vegetal. I wasn't too impressed when I tasted it at the château (from barrel) in June 1987. Good, but not great. (16)

5. CHÂTEAU LA MISSION HAUT-BRION 1986:

Dark purplish colour. Some sulphur on nose. Oddly, round, soft, some tannins. Very ripe. Medium-bodied. A bit diluted. Not bad. Elegant ripe finish. Four to six years. A bit too acidic (sharp). Lacks the solid structure of the vintage. (16)

Poor La Mission! It is becoming a thing of the past. Pity. What a tragedy that it belongs now to the Haut-Brion stable. The Woltners were great winemakers. Jean Delmas of Haut-Brion has declared, after the purchase of La Mission in 1983, that the style would not change. Really?!

6. CHÂTEAU PICHON-LALANDE 1986:

Deep, dark, purplish colour. Intense, ripe, rich nose. Full, solid, great length, balance, new oak. Lovely finish. Great wine. Needs 15 years. Noticeably high alcohol, but backed by great fruit extract and ripe tannins. (18.5) Usually, Pichon-Lalande makes a more elegant, Lafite-style Pauillac. This 1986 is very different. Almost Latour-like. Finally a true Pauillac from this property, instead of a "St. Julien."

7. CHÂTEAU D'ISSAN 1986:

Evolved colour. Orange rim. Herbaceous, vegetal. Soft, forward, elegant. Almost ready. Nice, but not typical 1986. A bit too green and diluted for me. I liked it less than other tasters. Those who liked it did so because it was more evolved. I think it just does not have the depth or structure of a true 1986. (15)

8. CHÂTEAU DUCRU-BEAUCAILLOU 1986:

Deep, dark colour to rim. Grape juice from a barrel! Full, massive, rich, yet simple at this stage. Jammy, intense, very big. Rich, ripe fruit, tannins in harmony. Needs time to "get it together." May become great. Try around 1996, or beyond. (17)

9. Château Sociando-Mallet 1986:

Inky blue-black colour. Young, ripe fruit. Big, powerful, rich, long, serious. Needs 15 to 20 years. Impressive wine. Great concentration of fruit. A bit sharper and greener than #6. Very intense ripe fruit, yet some greenness at finish. Needs time. Will be excellent. (18)

10. Château Leoville-Barton 1986:

Very deep, dark colour. Intense, ripe nose. Full, solid. Ripe fruit. Massive fruit. Superb balance and finish. Not as hot as #9, yet riper, richer, new oak. Fabulous; 12 to 15 years. Excellent wine and great value! (18) How nice to see Leoville-Barton making superb wines once again, now that Anthony Barton has taken over from his uncle. (The 1985 is very good, too.)

11. Château Latour 1986:

Grapey smell, like a barrel, or a winery. Very freshly crushed grapes. Full, intense, tannic backbone. Without the round ripeness of #10. Solid, powerful, big. Needs 15 years. Trace of acidity at finish. Not as ripe or just too young? Needs time, but will it be great? (17.5) or (18)

12. Château Mouton-Rothschild 1986:

Very deep, dark colour. Ripe grapes and oak on nose. Powerful, impressively rich. Long on palate. Great length. Ripe tannins. Needs 15 or more years. Great potential. (19)

October 15, 1989

Afternoon tasting of Gosset Champagnes, with Antoine Gosset, at the "Cannery" restaurant.

No malolactic fermentation at Gosset. Slower maturing, but longer life. They produce 40,000 cases yearly. They sell 80% of their production outside of France. Aiming for 50,000 cases. Because of lack of malolactic fermentation, the wines last longer in bottle. Six different cuvées. They own 12 hectares, representing only 20% (all Pinot Noir) of required grapes, from four villages; 80% of grapes are purchased. They also own a Loire property in Chinon; 100% Cabernet Franc bottled in their special Champagne bottles. About 30% to 40% of their harvest in Champagne is used to produce their Rosé.

Gosset Brut Rosé N/V:

Palish pink-salmon. Tiny bubbles. 10% to 12% of the blend is carbonic maceration. (The rest is blending red juice to obtain the colour.) Fresh, ripe, herbaceous nose. Quite dry on palate. Lean, a bit watery, but nice aftertaste. Made from 70% Chardonnay, 30% both Pinots (including 11% red wine). Drink young while fresh. This was a blend of 1983 and 1985 vintages. (16.5)

Gosset Brut "Réserve" N/V:

Tiny bubbles. Pale green-gold. Clean, buttery, herbaceous, fresh nose. Some yeast, a bit earthy. Some dosage. Quite light. Good length. Blend of eight villages. With 70% Chardonnay in blend, mostly 1983 and 1985. (Five years of reserves in stock; they age their Champagnes for five years before marketing.) (16.5) All of Gosset's wines are Brut, maximum 2% dosage.

Gosset "Grande Réserve" Brut N/V:

Vinous nose. Fresh, delicate, rich, long, complex. Good fruit, acidity. Long finish. Some yeast. Quite elegant and long. A bit yellower in colour, no green. Good quality. Made from 55% Pinot Noir/Meunier and 45% Chardonnay. Blend of 18 villages. Aged in magnums and poured back in vats for blending. (17.5)

Gosset Brut Vintage 1983:

Greener than the "Grande Réserve." Less dosage. Foamier. Quite good. Rich, ripe, typical 1983. Forward. Tiny bubbles. Made from 42% Chardonnay and 58% Pinot Noir/Meunier (half-each). (17.5)

Gosset "Grand Millésime" Brut 1982:

Lovely, perfumy, long, yeasty, fresh nose. Great complexity. Full, richer on entry, yet drier finish. Some was aged in oak barrels in order to achieve the "goût anglais." Creamy, rich, ripe, mature. Best of flight. Excellent quality. Made from 62% Chardonnay, 38% Pinot Noir. Blend of 28 villages, plus dosage made up of 1973, 1975, and 1978 reserves. (18)

Gosset "Grand Millésime" Rosé 1982:

Similar appearance to their regular Rosé (pink-salmon). Round, less vegetal. Quite sweet on palate. Lovely, round, elegant, stylish. Together with the 1983, my second favourite. Made from 100% Chardonnay and a little red juice from Bouzy. Blending of 18 villages including the top ones. All above 95% in rating scale. Liqueur (for dosage) is the 1979 reserve. (17.5)

Antoine Gosset is a good friend of François Faiveley. He is about my age, around 40 years old and a charming man.

October 10, 1989

WITH DINNER

CHAMPAGNE BOLLINGER "RÉSERVE SPÉCIALE" BRUT N/V:

Typical Bollinger. Yeasty, rich, good weight, length. Creamy, round. Very pleasant.

NUITS-ST.-GEORGES BLANC 1986, ROBERT CHEVILLON:

Surprisingly, the white had lots of new oak, something the reds lacked! Medium gold. Good intensity. Oak-vanilla, fairly alcoholic. A bit stemmy; hint of sulphur that dissipated after a while. Rich, intense, long, straightforward. Apparently made from Henri Gouges cuttings of Pinot Noir that produces white grapes!?! (16)

CLOS BLANC DE VOUGEOT 1983, HÉRITIERS-GUYOT:

Rare wine. Quite dark colour. Mature gold. Almost dry Sauternes-like on nose and palate. Starting to oxidize. Ripe, rich, quite alcoholic (like most 1983s). Getting tired. Unusual. (15)

1940 MASSANDRA COLLECTION MUSCAT, CRIMEA:

From the Massandra collection, sold recently at Sotheby's. In an old-style Burgundy bottle and wax top. Level: mid-neck. Fair bit of sediment. Deep amber colour, green-olive rim. Muscat, mature nose. I thought it was a 25-year-old Moscatel de Setúbal. Sweet, cloying, like a 25 to 35-year-old Muscat. Heavy, low acidity, intense, rich. Fine sipping wine. A bit cloudy (thin sediment). First time I've tried this Russian wine. A new experience.

November 9, 1989

Commanderie de Bordeaux 1979 tasting and dinner, at "Jean-Pierre's."

The day East Germany decided to tear down the Berlin Wall. Among the guests: the new French Consul General to Vancouver, Bernard Ledun, and the French Trade Commissioner, Jean-Yves Conte. All the red wines were served blind.

APERITIF

CHÂTEAU LA TOUR-MARTILLAC 1984, GRAVES BLANC:

Light, crisp, herbaceous. Starting to crack up a bit, but still pleasant and drinkable.

CHÂTEAU HAUT-BRION BLANC 1983:

Bright green-gold. Superb, long, oak nose. Full, vanilla, intense, round, great complexity. Long finish. Drink now or in 20 years! (19)

FLIGHT #1
WITH THE MAIN COURSE

1. CHÂTEAU D'ANGLUDET 1979:

Dark, mature rim. Good depth. Oaky, smoky, Cassis, earthy. Rich, powerful, good fruit. Good intensity. Good ripeness. Hard Cabernet style. Old barrels. (15.5)

2. CHÂTEAU BATAILLEY 1979:

Medium, subdued nose. Herbal, delicate. Lighter, more forward. Slightly astringent and sharp. Some fruit, but too lean. One bottle was corked. Later, improved. Fruity, complex. Good length. Ready. (15.5)

3. CHÂTEAU COS D'ESTOURNEL 1979:

Very dark colour. Unyielding nose. Some ripeness, pruny. Sweet, full, rich, tannic, but short finish and astringent. Better on entry than at finish. Second bottle was much better and not as baked. (16.5)

4. CHÂTEAU GRAND-PUY-LACOSTE 1979:

Good dark colour. Delicate, earthy Cabernet nose. Haut-Médoc/Pauillac. Rich, a bit rubbery. One-dimensional, tannic, solid. (14.5)

5. CHÂTEAU GRUAUD-LAROSE 1979:

Dark, mature colour. A bit rubbery, skunky. Acidic, sharp, unpleasant on palate, too citric; odd, rubbery, "unclean" flavours. St. Estèphe structure. Bad bottle? Good colour, though. (14.5)

6. CHÂTEAU HAUT-BAILLY 1979:

Fresh, herbaceous nose. Sweet on entry. Round, complex, delicate finish. Margaux-like; herbal. A bit oaky, smoky. Good complexity. Mature. Spicy. (16)

7. CHÂTEAU MONTROSE 1979:

Smoky, oaky, complex nose. Class here. Round, delicate. Not as tannic, rich, or ripe as most. Ready. Easy drinking. Well made. Very elegant, surprisingly so for Montrose. (17)

Overall

Good dark colour and better ripe fruit and tannins than expected, yet most were a bit ordinary.

FLIGHT #2
WITH THE CHEESE COURSE

1. CHÂTEAU HAUT-BRION 1979:

Good dark colour. Chocolate, coffee beans nose. Full, rich, complex, very good depth. Lovely ripe fruit. Top class. Excellent balance. Haut-Brion? (18.5)

2. CHÂTEAU LEOVILLE-LASCASES 1979:

Dark, maturing colour. Delicate, lovely, complex nose. Classic Cabernet-tobacco. Soft, ripe, long. Harmony, warmth, length, balance. Soft, sweet, velvety, Burgundian. Lascases? (17)

3. CHÂTEAU AUSONE 1979:

Dark. Good depth. Spicy Cabernet Franc nose. Rich, solid, ripe, long. A bit sharp. Not as well balanced as the Haut-Brion, but very good nevertheless. Spicy, herbal, Pichon-Lalande? Slightly herbaceous. (18)

4. CHÂTEAU PALMER 1979:

Very deep, dark colour. Subdued, clean, complex nose. Full, long, delicate, well balanced. Velvety. Palmer? Very good. No rush. Good purple colour. Best wine of both flights. (18.5)

5. CHÂTEAU PICHON-LALANDE 1979:

Subdued, chocolaty nose. Hint of mint. Complex, lots of depth and balance. Lighter, more evolved colour. Stemmy, tobacco. Ausone? Surprisingly light for the vintage. Not bad, but I've had better. (17)

Flight #2 was clearly better than flight #1.

CHÂTEAU COUTET 1962 BARSAC:

One bottle corked. Other two bottles were fine. Deep, dark-golden colour. Mature botrytis nose with earthy overtones. Drier; typical Barsac. Full, complex, mature, some botrytis; a bit earthy. Having said that, last time I tasted the 1962 Coutet, it was much more complex.

A successful evening.

November 11, 1989

Special double-blind tasting and dinner, at Allan Tobe's.

CHAMPAGNE KRUG VINTAGE 1979:

Superb, yeasty, round, long, complex. Approaching its peak. Superb depth and class. Great Champagne. Toasty, rich, long. (18.5)

FLIGHT #1

1. BÂTARD-MONTRACHET 1982, LEFLAIVE:

Rich, toasty. Very French. Full, buttery, long, yet not fat. Good acidity, intensity, and class. Slightly earthy. More evolved. Fabulous. Like a 1982 or 1983. (18)

2. BIENVENUES BÂTARD-MONTRACHET 1982, LEFLAIVE:

More closed and subdued than #1, yet similar. A bit sharper, leaner, more intense. No rush. More backward than #1. Fabulous intensity and class. Needs time. Elegant, superb. (18.5)

3. CHEVALIER-MONTRACHET 1982, LEFLAIVE:

Tightest of all three. Herbal, rich, full; oak and ripe fruit in harmony. Very similar to #1 and #2, yet richer. Great depth. Most complex and greatest length. Fabulous. (19)

I thought they were 1983, 1985, and 1986 Montrachets! No doubt, Leflaive is a master!

These fine white Burgundies were followed by red wines (also served double-blind).

FLIGHT #2

1. CHÂTEAU LA TOUR-HAUT-BRION 1978:

Very good, deep, maturing colour. Looks and smells like mature Claret with very good depth. 1970? Rich, full, leathery, little tannin. Mature, lots of extract. Slightly minty. A bit hard. Fairly acidic, but new oak. A bit cedary. Similar appearance to #2. Great depth and structure. Powerful. Mondavi? Tannic and acidic and minty. High alcohol. Very good. Five to seven years. (17)

2. CHÂTEAU LA MISSION HAUT-BRION 1978:

Deep, mature. Haut-Brion-like. Spicy, bigger than #1. Open, expansive nose. Cassis-tobacco. Full, concentrated, backed by lots of fruit. Like a great 1975. Both #1 and #2 have great depth. Unusual; #1 and #2 inky, powerful wines. This is bigger than #1. More tannic. Great depth. Needs ten years. Raw, intense, old-style Cabernet. Excellent. (18.5)

FLIGHT #3

1. CHÂTEAU LA TOUR-HAUT-BRION 1966:

Very good, deep, maturing colour. Hint of mint and cedar. Mouton, Lynch-Bages-like. 1970 Mouton? Great length and fruit. Mint-cedar. I was surprised when I found out what it was. Very good. Ready. Top class. Chocolaty-earthy, tobacco. (18)

2. CHÂTEAU LA MISSION HAUT-BRION 1966:

Excellent deep colour. Hint of rubber, but great depth. Sweet, ripe, long, earthy, complex. Beautiful extract. Powerful. Big, intense. Hard, long, very Pauillac-like. Solid, serious, tobacco-earth. Fabulous. Maybe Graves. (18.5)

3. CHÂTEAU HAUT-BRION 1966:

Excellent deep colour, slightly maturing rim. Full, rich, tannic, like a 1966. Great structure, ripe, mature, about ready. Great cedar, Cabernet nose. Serious. Good quality. More evolved. Without the depth and intensity of the La Mission. (16.5)

4. CHÂTEAU HAUT-BRION 1959:

Very deep. Most evolved nose. Mature. Oldest. A bit pruny. Great length and depth. Ripe, earthy, long, chocolaty. While very good, I've had better bottles. (17.5)

We were all fooled. We thought they were all Pauillacs or St. Estèphes. (Ken Cross, Sid Cross, and other guests were as "off" as I was.)

1945 GRAHAM'S VINTAGE PORT:

Lots of sediment. Good depth of colour. Lovely, flowery, velvety, rich, long wine. Lots of class and character. Yet not as big as when tasted on previous occasions (oddly, same bottling). More like a lovely 1955 or 1963. In any event, an excellent Port. (18)

A great evening, and a very generous host.

December 1 and 2, 1989

A two-day, three-session tasting of Château Latour, in Los Angeles, organized by Bipin Desai.

Two bottles of each wine; 40 participants. Harry Waugh and the president of Château Latour, Alan Hare, were there, as well as the Maître de Chais (technical director since 1986), Christian Le Sommer. He has replaced Jean-Louis Mandreau, who had the unfortunate bad luck to produce Latour's 1983 and 1985, both nice wines, but way too soft for Latour.

Friday, December 1, 1989

"Mabé" restaurant, in Los Angeles.

FIRST SESSION

APERITIF

CHAMPAGNE LECHÈRE "ORIENT EXPRESS" BRUT N/V:

Toasty, delicate, round, complex. Well balanced and most enjoyable.

FLIGHT #1

Château Latour 1987 to 1981

1987:

Bottled in July 1989, a few months ago. Medium red, pale at rim. Fresh, oak, spicy, clean nose. Slightly green. Delicate, a bit sharp, but clean new oak and Cabernet coming through. Needs three years. Lots of oak. A bit green. Difficult vintage. (15.5)

1986:

Dark, inky colour to rim. Subdued, ripe nose. Big, tannic, powerful, rich, intense. Trace of acidity at finish, but very good structure. Promising. Much darker than the 1987. Needs ten years. Oddly, bouquet of old, rather than new wood. (17.5)

1985:

Slightly darker than the 1986. Cleaner, oaky nose. More herbal, stemmier, not unlike the 1978s in their youth. 1986 smells riper. 1985 stemmier, more elegant. Complex, delicate, well balanced, yet atypical Latour lacking depth. Needs three to five years. Easy drinking. Most enjoyable. Most attractive wine of flight. (17) Not what Latour can and should achieve.

1983:

Deep colour, similar to the 1986, but more mature-looking. Closed, unyielding nose. Rich, full on entry, but too acidic and a bit green. Needs at least five more years. Later, wine opened up a bit and improved in glass. More oak-toast. Somehow, a bit hollow in middle. Overproduction? (16.5)

1982:

Very dark, deep, impressive colour. Slight maturity at rim. Clean, ripe, unyielding nose. Sweet, very ripe fruit on entry. Massive. Soft tannins (yet they're there). Great depth and length. The ripeness of the 1982s and the power of Latour. Great potential. Towers and overpowers all others in this flight. Ripe Cassis. Lovely. Drink from 1998 to 2015. (19)

1981:

Medium to dark colour. Actually, surprising depth for a 1981. Cedar, cigar-box nose. Unfortunately some cardboard, too (from the glass?) Lean, a bit acidic; less fruit than the 1983, but less acidity, too. One bottle was corked. I really cannot get excited over this wine. (15.5)

FLIGHT #2

Château Latour 1979 to 1970

1979:

Darker than the 1981, maturing rim. Spicy, toasty, delicate nose. A bit metallic. Not as ripe as expected. A bit gamey, smoky nose. Very good, though. Serious, sturdy, good depth. Clean finish. Drink now to 1997. (16.5)

1978:

Medium-to-dark colour, mature rim. Older-looking than the 1979. Rich, round nose. Full, long, ripe. Serious, old-style Latour. Powerful, solid, intense, and chunky. Earthy, tobacco, mushrooms. Great depth. I expected a vegetal Cabernet nose. Excellent. Needs five to ten years. Typical old-style Cabernet. More evolved than either the 1975 or the 1970. (18)

1976:

Medium-dark, maturing colour. Hint of cardboard (from the glass?) Fresh nose. Not as baked as most 1976s. Spicy Cabernet. Good on entry; a bit hard and lean at finish. (16)

1975:

Much darker than the 1976 to rim. No amber, very good appearance. Closed nose. Some Cabernet and a bit stemmy, but has ripeness, too. Big, powerful. Hard, tannic, serious. Classic Latour and classic 1975. Needs 15 years. Good colour and enough fruit to last. Yet, not as big as expected, but very good. (18)

1970:

Very impressive appearance. Deep, dark, opaque. Very ripe, complex, intense nose. Ripe mouthful of Cabernet. Big, powerful, rich, long. Very big, very rich, very special. Great potential and great future. Fruit, tannins in harmony. Great nose, too. The 1978 is very good, but ageing faster than the 1970. This 1970, as expected, is a great wine. Drink 1995 to 2015. (19) Jean-Paul Gardère, the long-time régisseur of Latour, likes to describe this wine as a "Charles de Gaulle."

Overall

1970 and 1982 were the two favourite wines of the first two flights. Actually, they were both stunning.

FLIGHT #3

Château Latour 1966 to 1960

1960:

Good, deep colour; paler appearance than the 1961; slightly lighter rim. Open, forthcoming, cedar nose. Impressive for a 1960. Good length, balance, depth. Very good fruit. Still alive and kicking. Obviously leaner than the other three in this flight, but successful for the vintage. Worth buying if price is right. Best 1960 Bordeaux made? (16)

1961:

Very good, deep, mature colour. Ripe raisins, intense nose. Great depth, intensity, Cassis, ripeness. Superb length. Cedar, tobacco. Essence of Cabernet. Near perfection. Not (20) out of (20) because it needs ten more years. (19.5)

1964:

Very good, dark colour. Chocolaty, ripe nose. Hard, tannic. Later: soft, elegant, ripe, complex. Perfect now. Lovely length and balance; dense, ripe. Cedar, Cassis, traditional. Excellent. At its peak. The best 1964 Haut-Médoc. (18)

1966:

Deep, maturing colour. Serious, big, tannic. Cedary bouquet, classic nose. Excellent balance, depth, and lots of fruit. Needs five to ten years. Serious, typical Latour. Definitely one of the top 1966s in the flight. (18)

Unfortunately, we did not taste the 1962—a very good wine (see comments in Session #3).

FLIGHT #4

Château Latour 1959 to 1950

1959:

Impressive dark colour. Outstanding, ripe, cedar-chocolate nose. Lovely ripe fruit; a bit leathery and starting to show signs of ripening and acidity. The 1961 is a more complete wine. Much better on nose than on palate. I like it, but not as much as other tasters. It just didn't deliver on the palate the promise of the nose. I have tasted much greater 1959 Latours. (17.5)

1957:

Browning, good depth. Ripe, mature nose. Some earth and cedar. Lean and hard, but acidity kept it fresh and alive. Not much charm, but not really poor either. Typical of this hard, lean vintage. Unfair to serve this after the superripe 1959. (15)

1955, IN MAGNUM:

Browning, good depth. Showing its age. Mellow, ripe, mature nose. Round, soft, almost sweet, yet ripe and even tannic. Quite supple, elegant, lots of style here. Good length, class, and elegance. Surprisingly good. Best 1955 Latour to date. (17)

1953:

Very good, dark colour; orangy rim. Odd nose. Hint of earth. Similar on palate. Sweet and sour. Quite sharp, acidic. Late picked? Rotting? Almost like sweet-and-sour Chinese food! Latour didn't make a great 1953, but this is really disappointing. (13.5)

1952:

Not quite as dark as the 1953, more orange at rim, but good depth. Our bottle was corked. The other bottle was much better. Rich, yet lean. Fruity, serious. Hard, but excellent fruit. Lots of character. Ready. Will not improve. Can be a solid (18) when at its best. (16.5)

Latour produced a better wine in 1952 than in 1953.

1950:

Medium-dark colour, orange rim. Clean, delicate, mature Cabernet nose. Sweet, round; tannins helped it last. Hard, but without the weight of the bigger vintages; has class and elegance. Very good for the vintage. Tannins slowly taking over. (17)

Overall

This first session went as expected. The wines were consistent and very good. The food was excellent, but it was too noisy and crowded… too many participants. Bipin Desai sure knows how to divide two bottles among 48 participants!

Saturday, December 2, 1989

At "Patina" restaurant, in Los Angeles, 12 noon.

SECOND SESSION

APERITIF

CHAMPAGNE BILLECART-SALMON BRUT N/V:

Richer than the "Orient Express" of the previous session. Creamy, good yeast and toast. Fine bubbles. Clean and fresh. Good. A reliable producer.

FLIGHT #1

Château Latour 1971 to 1936: the "lesser" vintages

I was asked by Bipin to talk about these wines. Why does he always pick me to speak about the poor vintages? I guess he trusts me not to make a mess of it.

1971:

Maturing, browning, good depth. Open, forthcoming nose. Fairly hard, tannic, serious, but touch of acidity. Not bad, but a bit green. Better with food. Better on nose than on palate. Best 1971 Pauillac, though. (16)

1967:

Better colour and depth than the 1971. Rounder, fuller, more complex, softer. Good length, spicy nose. Cedar, mushrooms. At its peak, but no rush. Better on palate than on nose. Yet a bit acidic. (16.5)

1965:

Palish, browning colour. Soft, sweet caramelized nose. Sweet and yet sour. Fairly acidic, hard, yet surprisingly drinkable, even quite good! Certainly not dead. (14)

1963:

Similar appearance to the 1965, but more brown. A bit pruny, sour, acidic, thin, sharp. Poor wine. Some lees of 1961 added into this 1963. An impossible vintage. Harry Waugh's comment: "What a poor vintage for the new owners of Latour to start with!" (12)

1958:

Browning, but impressive colour. Meaty, metallic nose. Starting to oxidize. Hard, tannic, leathery, lacks fruit. Powerful but charmless. More life than the 1963, but too acidic. (13)

1956:

Browning, mature colour. Hint of mint and cedar on nose. The year of the terrible frost. Hard, hint of oxidation, but some tannin and even some fruit; too acidic and volatile. (12.5)

1944:

Pruny "off" nose. Pale, browning colour. Sour, sharp, acidic, dead. (10)

1943:

Browning colour. Decent depth. Tea leaves, tobacco, cedar on nose. Hard on entry, yet soft finish. Tired, but still drinkable. Some fruit even. Sweet beets. I have tasted better examples of this wine in the past. (13.5)

1942:

Meaty, metallic nose. Brown. Surprising fruit. Hard, leathery, like an old Rioja. Still drinking well. Better than the 1943 this day. (14)

1940:

Similar appearance to the 1942; lots of brown. Nice toast, oak on nose. Hard, tannic, but not too acidic. A serious, yet hard and tired wine. Later, oxidized. (13)

Harry Waugh said that during the War years, there were no chemicals used, such as copper sulphate, and no bottles, either; the wine was left in wood for three or more years, so the wine is browning and tastes woody.

1936:

Browning, too acidic; woody nose. Has some fruit. Hard, tannic, unyielding. A bit sharp. (13)

This flight of "the difficult vintages" wines was better than expected. They were not totally decomposed, but sound and even drinkable. World War II was a difficult period for Latour, for France, and for the Free World.

FLIGHT #2

Château Latour 1949, 1948, 1947, and 1945

Colour of all four similar, with the 1947 and 1945 slightly darker. All have a fair bit of orange-brown, but good depth. The 1945 has excellent depth.

1949:

Subdued, delicate nose. Some oak, sweet fruit. Round, rich on palate. Good intensity, some ripe, sweet fruit. Trace of acidity, but good depth. Classy wine. Not as spectacular as it could be. A bit too lean at finish. Usually it is fat, richer. These two bottles were too weedy and lean. (17) Mouton and even Lafite are usually better than Latour in both 1949 and 1947.

1948:

Our bottle was cleaner than the other bottle. Hint of cedar, mint, and smoke. Hard, like many 1948s, but good depth and class. Fresh fruit, sweet. Much better than expected. Hint of chocolate. (16.5)

1947:

Coffee beans, chocolate. Ripe, rich, mature nose. Sweet "Australian." A bit baked, hard, tannic; too citric. Rich, loads of fruit, yet too severe. Some sharpness at finish. Latour 1947 is not a great success, yet this bottle was better than expected. (17.5)

1945:

Darkest of flight. Very ripe, yet subdued nose. Loads of ripe fruit and tannins. Great length, solid, ripe, and rich. Top quality and true to its reputation. Lovely wine. The second bottle was too lean and harder. I was lucky. (19.5).

In this flight, the 1947 was better than expected and the 1949 not quite as good.

FLIGHT # 3

1937, 1934, 1926, 1924, 1920, and 1918 Château Latour

1937:

Deep, mature colour. Minty, leathery nose. Still hard, tannic, excellent fruit. Mature, complex. Richer, riper than the 1934. At this tasting, the 1937 is clearly the better wine. (17)

1934:

Lighter than the 1937. Browning. Harder, leaner, more acidic than the 1937. Clean, a bit hard and citric, but has fruit. A bit minty. Later (30 minutes), became thin and lean. (16)

1926:

Surprisingly deep, mature colour to rim. Superb essence of ripe, mature Latour. Great quality. Great depth, class, and length. Outstanding. Coffee, chocolate, ripe Cabernet, cedar. Big mouthful. Superb length. Hard to fault this ripe, rich wine. Improved in glass! (19)

1924:

Very good, dark, mature colour. Full, rich. Even bigger and more backbone than the 1926. More typical Latour. True classic old-style Cabernet. Still hard. No rush. Great finish. Those who tasted the second bottle preferred the 1924, but everyone liked both. (18)

1920:

Dill, vegetal nose. Dark, mature colour. Too lean and acidic, quite sharp, yet ripe, leathery (1920 was a very ripe vintage). Second bottle: mouldy, earthy. Ripe, solid, rich. Still has depth and power. (17)

1918:

Browning quite a bit. Very mature, woody, sweet nose. Still has fruit. Ripe, sweet, a bit acidic, but clean. A bit pruny, though. At over 70 years of age, has held very well. Later, it fell apart. (15)

FLIGHT #4

Château Latour 1899 to 1874

1899:

Very mature, but good depth. Not very clear; a bit cloudy. Clean, buttery nose. Good fruit, round, a bit leathery, very sound. Most enjoyable. Delicate, like the 1943 or 1950, but with more class and elegance. Best of flight. Outstanding by any yardstick. (18)

1892:

Very dark, molasses colour; brown rim. Odd, old wood, old Port nose. Full, rich, a bit acidic, good fruit. Very good for a century-old wine. A bit hard and acidic, but certainly sound. Good fruit, but a little sharp. (16.5)

1875:

(Cruse-bottling) Deep colour, ripe, pruny, very old. Madeirized, oxidized. Gone. (0)

1874:

(Hardy Rodenstock's bottle) Toasty, youthful Cabernet Franc nose, but old-looking. Crème de Cacao and young Cabernet Franc. Strange. A controversial bottle, too artificial. Many of Hardy Rodenstock's wines seem to be controversial. The more I taste his wines, the more I feel that something is "fake" here. A blend of Robert Mondavi Cabernet and chocolate liqueur. (No score)

FLIGHT #5

Château Latour 1893, 1870, 1847

1893:

Very pale, tired Rosé colour. Undrinkable. (0)

1870:

Whitwham-bottling in a Port-like bottle. Pale, dead. (No score)

1870:

(Second bottle) Contributed by Hardy Rodenstock (or supplied by someone else who got it from him). Deep, dark colour. Coffee liqueur. A fake. (No score)

These two bottles of 1870 were so disappointing! I have been looking forward so much to tasting this great wine and great vintage. The fake bottle was particularly insulting.

1847:

(Bottled by Barton et Guestier) Clean, delicate nose. Palish, some orange. Quite long and pleasant. A great wine for its age. Tea, tobacco. A really nice 132-year-old wine!! Old Claret, but nothing artificial about it. (18)

"Patina" is a fabulous restaurant. Each course was top quality. Joachim Spichal (chef/owner) is a gifted chef.

Saturday evening, December 2, 1989

THIRD AND LAST SESSION

At "Michael's" restaurant, in Los Angeles.

APERITIF

Champagne Billecart-Salmon Brut N/V:

See comments under the previous session.

FLIGHT #1

Château Latour 1962, 1964, 1959

1959, in magnum:

Darkest of the lot. Rich, concentrated, ripe nose. Full, fruity, warm, lovely. Great depth. Round and ripe. True 1959. Rich fruit. Nice, long finish. Better on palate than when tasted from bottles, but not as good on nose. (18)

1962, in magnum:

Bright-red colour, typical of the 1962s. Lovely, cedar-toast, ripe nose. Fruity, full of life and more tannic than the 1959! No rush. Excellent balance. Long, rich, and fresh. Best of flight. Really nice wine. One of the best 1962s made. A revelation. (18.5)

1964, in magnum:

Lighter in colour than the 1962, but not by much (more brown). Nose a bit stemmy and dusty. Leaner, a bit hard. Was better in bottles at lunch. More fruit, ripe, chocolaty. Later, opened up. Quite good, but not the best example. (17)

FLIGHT # 2

Château Latour 1929 and 1928

1929, IN MAGNUM:

Unmarked capsule. Medium red, tired rim (browning). A bit chocolaty, sweet nose. Ripe raisins on palate. Has seen better days. Tired. Still alive, but on its way out. Hint of oxidation. Toffee, caramel. Odd, quite acidic. Later, a bit better, but definitely over-the-hill. Disappointing. Can be great. (16)

1928:

Two bottles. Better, brighter colour than the 1929. Good red colour to rim. Lovely, ripe, complex Cabernet nose. Full, intense, ripe. Great depth and intensity. Fabulous structure. One of the best wines of these events. Cedar, ripe fruit. A bit hard at finish; true 1928. Great quality. We were fortunate to taste this superb bottle. (19.5)

FLIGHT #3

Château Latour 1900, 1899, 1865, 1864

1900, IN MAGNUM:

Good colour for age. Ripe, clean nose. Full and rich. Much darker than the 1899. Leathery, quite hard, a bit acidic, but rich and long. Lovely, old-style, big Latour. Amazing fruit for an 89-year-old wine. An outstanding magnum. Really amazing. (19)

1899:

Browning. Petroleum, plastic, and leather. Awful! The bottles we had at lunch were so much better! (No score)

1865, IN MAGNUM:

Recorked at the Château in 1980. Spicy, stemmy, yet candied-sweet nose. Round, fruity, not unlike a much-younger St. Emilion. Tobacco, tea, nice finish. Drying out a bit, but nice. Has held well, but needs drinking. Atypical Latour. More like Ausone! (17)

A note about the 1865

It seemed odd, yet good, but atypical Latour. Another Hardy Rodenstock "special"?

1864:

Good, dark colour. One bottle poor. Our bottle (bottled by Brandenburg and Co., Bordeaux) was excellent. Hard, tannic, but good fruit and nice finish. Amazing wine that has held very well. (18) The second bottle was totally oxidized.

The food was excellent and the wines were overall consistently good. These tastings confirmed the reputation of Latour. My personal favourites at this event were: 1961, 1982, 1945, 1970, 1928, 1900, 1926, and 1924.

At midnight

John Hart (formerly a partner in the Chicago Wine Company), Harry Waugh, Brad Klein, and myself went back to Brad's place where we were staying and tried the following.

1921 CSOPAKI FURMINT, HUNGARY:

From the Royal Hungarian State Wine Co. Imported by A. Hartog and Co. Inc., Los Angeles. Colour of Madeira. Medium amber. German-type bottle. Low (three-inch) level. Unmistakable Furmint, yet Sherry-like. Quite dry, acidic, but sound with good length.

At 1:00 a.m.

We tried two pre-1903 Chartreuses (yellow and white) from one-litre bottles, L. Garnier, (produced before the Chartreux monks were expelled from France to Spain and Italy).

YELLOW CHARTREUSE:

Cloying, intense, rich, sweet, alcoholic. Lots of depth, extract. Excellent.

WHITE CHARTREUSE:

Very rare. Licorice and mint. Spicy, more refined, sweet, but less cloying than the yellow. Stylish. Really excellent. They do not make Chartreuse like this any more. Both bottles are real treasures.

By 2:30 a.m., we were all knocked out, except for Harry Waugh, who is almost double the age of Brad, John, or myself! This guy is like "Energizer" batteries: keeps going and going!

Sunday, December 3, 1989

Lunch at Brad's, with a few friends who participated at the Latour event.

1961 CHÂTEAU LA MISSION HAUT-BRION:

Brought over by Stephen Kaplan of Chicago. Excellent fill. Lovely, dark, deep colour to rim. Great, ripe, earthy Graves nose. Full, long, superb balance. Great depth. A superb wine from a great year. No rush drinking it. Harry Waugh loved it. Excellent. A fitting ending to a fine weekend. (19)

December 11, 1989

Le Tastevin Wine Club tasting of Torres Gran Coronas "Black Label" and Vega Sicilia wines from Spain. As usual, I was the speaker.

Vertical tasting of Vega Sicilia

1982 VALBUENA CINCO AÑOS (FIVE YEARS):

Ripe, fresh, fruity nose. Almost sweet berries. Medium to dark colour. Full, ripe, sweet, subdued oak. Elegant, long, complex, well balanced. Quite fresh. No rush. An understated wine. All the Vegas were more subdued than the Torres Gran Coronas "Black Label." (16.5)

1976 "UNICO" COSECHA:

Deep, maturing colour; orange rim. Ripe, subdued, elegant nose. Hint of oak and vanilla coming through. On palate: rich, intense; long and complex finish. Quite full and impressive. No rush. Drink now to 1996 or beyond, if well stored. (17.5)

1973 "UNICO" COSECHA :

Similar appearance to the 1976, but slightly lighter. Earthy, fuller, riper nose. A bit leaner. Harder, more forward. Elegant. Clean, long finish. 1976 quite a bit more powerful than this. Getting tired. No sense keeping it much longer. Hint of acidity at finish. (15.5)

1965 "UNICO" COSECHA:

Very deep, maturing colour. Subdued, ripe nose. These wines do not throw themselves at you. Rich, tannic, but backed by good fruit. Great intensity, tannins, backbone, and extract for a 24-year-old wine. Top quality by any yardstick. (18)

1962 "UNICO" COSECHA:

Deep, maturing colour. Closed nose, subdued. Sweet, forward, elegant, still hint of tannins. Not unlike a delicate, complex Rioja. Good length. At its peak and needs drinking. (17) In the past, I scored this wine (18.5); it can be great.

Overall impression on the Vega Sicilia

Subdued, elegant wine. Lots of class, stylish and well made. Very expensive and rare. While the wines are fine indeed, I doubt that the price can be justified, other than because of scarcity. (Unico: $70 to $160 per bottle in 1989!)

January 17, 1990

Blind tasting and dinner, featuring Mouton-Rothschild versus Lynch-Bages, at the Vancouver Club Organized by Ian Mottershead.

The wines were arranged in two rows. We didn't know the order of the vintages or which château was in front and which was behind. The meal consisted of nine small courses to fit the tasting, and was absolutely outstanding.

Front Row "A"
Back Row "B"

THE TASTING

1A. LYNCH-BAGES 1981:

Medium dark colour; maturing at rim. Herbaceous, stemmy nose. Some cedar. Soft, a bit lean, metallic. Later, softened a bit. Some bitterness at finish and mellow. More class than #1B. Mouton 1978 or 1981? (16)

1B. MOUTON-ROTHSCHILD 1981:

Darker, deeper than #1A. Mature colour to rim. Not as open as #1A, but similar nose. Fuller, more tannic, yet leaner finish. More stuffing than #1A but too acidic at finish. (16.5)

2A. LYNCH-BAGES 1982:

Deep, maturing colour to rim. Ripe, subdued, leathery nose. Earthy, some oak and leather. Full, round, very rich. Still tannic. Lots of extract. Big, ripe. 1982 Lynch-Bages? (18)

2B. MOUTON-ROTHSCHILD 1982:

Fresher, livelier, more herbaceous and cedary than #2A. Darker, too. Fuller, richer, riper. More depth. Seemed more evolved than #2A. Later closed up; great depth and extract. Needs time. Fabulous but tannic. Great potential. 1982 Mouton! (19.5)

3A. MOUTON-ROTHSCHILD 1978:

Brighter, slightly darker than #3B. Fresher, stemmier nose. Too lean, acidic, sharp. Some fruit, but lacks depth. Tannic, yet too lean. Not bad. (15.5)

3B. LYNCH-BAGES 1978:

Medium, mature colour; good depth. Open, warm, toasty nose. Cedar, too. A bit lean, some tannins. Too acidic. Hard finish. (15)

4A. MOUTON-ROTHSCHILD 1979:

Good, dark, still youthful. Cedary, spicy nose. Round, mellow on palate. Soft and elegant. (16.5)

4B. LYNCH-BAGES 1979:

Much deeper than #4A. Tighter nose than both #1s. Full, rich, solid. Good depth, ripe. Some mint. (17)

5A. LYNCH-BAGES 1970:

Deeper, darker than #5B. Brilliant, deep purplish, almost black colour. Great depth, ripe fruit, excellent balance. Tannic, but ripe. Needs ten years. Maybe 1970 Lynch-Bages? Ripe raisins. (18.5)

5B. MOUTON-ROTHSCHILD 1970:

More forthcoming than #5A. Good, dark colour. Cedar, mint. Leaner, less ripe. Too sharp at finish. Herbal and spicy. Quite elegant, but maybe not rich enough to be a great 1970. 1970 Mouton? (17.5)

6A. LYNCH-BAGES 1975:

Very good, dark colour. Spicy Cabernet nose. Still a bit hard. Needs five to seven years. Nice finish. Good length. Good fruit, ripe, old style, leathery. Very good. 1975 Lynch-Bages? (17.5)

6B. MOUTON-ROTHSCHILD 1975:

Very good, dark colour; slightly deeper than #6A. Riper on nose. Richer too. Full, long, excellent depth. Still fresh. Fabulous fruit. Lovely balance. Needs ten years. 1975 Mouton? (18.5)

Overall impressions

The 1982 Mouton (my contribution) and the 1970 Lynch-Bages were the two outstanding wines of the evening. The two 1975s, especially the Mouton, were excellent. Both 1978s were disappointing. Both 1979s were better than expected. The 1970 Mouton was very good, but overshadowed by the great 1970 Lynch-Bages. The 1982 Lynch-Bages, while very good, wasn't even close to the great 1982 Mouton. Eventually, I guessed all the vintages correctly. A successful evening.

January 23-28, 1990

Trip to Yountville and San Francisco. Visit with Joe Heitz.

We tasted the three 1985 Cabernets to be released next week.

HEITZ CELLARS CABERNET SAUVIGNON 1985, NAPA VALLEY:

Good, dark colour. Cedar and mint on nose. Round, fruity, good depth, and solid backbone. Very good. Needs three to four years. (16)

HEITZ CELLARS "BELLA OAKS" CABERNET SAUVIGNON 1985, NAPA VALLEY:

Darker than the Napa Valley. Riper, richer nose. Little oak or cedar. Full, yet surprisingly soft. The Napa Valley has more backbone, but less ripe fruit than this. (17)

HEITZ CELLARS "MARTHA'S VINEYARD" CABERNET SAUVIGNON 1985, NAPA VALLEY:

There is a lot of hype about this wine, and every merchant and wholesaler is getting it on strict allocation. The label is also a special anniversary edition. Very, deep, dark colour. Not as minty-eucalyptus as the 1974 in its youth. More class and elegance, but has power and depth. Great potential, and deserves its reputation. Joe and his daughter Kathleen were kind enough to sell me, "prerelease," three cases, including one case of magnums, at US$50 per bottle and $100 per magnum. This fine wine will require at least eight more years of bottle-age. As intense as the 1974, but more class. Joe thinks this will be better than the 1974. He compares it to the 1969, which is one of his favourites. (18.5)

Later, Joe and I went for lunch to "Trilogy," in St. Helena.

Lovely lunch. Their wine list is excellent. I chose a wine that Joe has never tasted before and didn't know much about.

Condrieu "Côteau de Vernon" 1987, Georges Vernay:

Made from a tiny parcel. The restaurant was only allocated six bottles. Not as ripe as the 1986, but elegant, ripe pears, fairly alcoholic (Condrieu usually is); perfumy and elegant. Very good. Joe was impressed, and it was a new experience for him. Vernay's "regular" Condrieu is very good and reliable, but his "Côteau de Vernon" is top class.

January 26, 1990

International Wine and Food Society (Marin County) Black Tie Dinner, at the Park Hyatt hotel, San Francisco, featuring 1945 Château Talbot.

APERITIF

Champagne Krug "Grande Cuvée" Brut N/V:

As usual, excellent length, balance and class. Tiny bubbles, yeasty, complex, long, with great depth.

Puligny-Montrachet "Les Pucelles" Premier Cru 1983, Leflaive:

Leflaive is a master of Puligny Premiers and Grand Crus. This 1983 is true to form. As a rule, I do not like 1983 white Burgundies (too alcoholic), but this is well balanced, long, complex; nothing excessive here. Very good fruit. At its peak. Good Chardonnay varietal. Clean, long finish.

1945 Château Talbot, in bottles, magnums, and a jeroboam:

By far the most popular was the jeroboam. Most youthful, deepest, youngest colour, best structure, still had fresh fruit. Will last for many years.

Personally, I preferred the magnums. More complex on nose; expansive, earthy, mature old Claret. Still-tannic backbone, still youthful, yet classy and complex. Some sharpness at finish, but very good.

The bottles were very good, too. Two were oxidized, however. As expected, more evolved colour. Lovely, sweet, mature nose of ripe Cabernet, chocolate, and mushrooms. Best during the first 15 minutes, but after that, became acidic and lean.

Overall

All sizes were good and true to the style of this chunky wine. Not very complex, but straightforward and reliable.

I had a nice chat with Bartholomew Broadbent, son of Michael Broadbent. He called me "the controversial chap," in view of my heated exchanges with his father regarding the 1945 Lafite tasted in 1988, and other "encounters" I have had with his father in the past.

January 27 and 28, 1990

Vertical tasting of Warre's Vintage Port: 1920 to 1985, at the residence of our Chairman, Dr. Haskell Norman, in Ross, California.

The guest speaker was Bill Warre, once associated with Warre's Port.

First session

FLIGHT #1
1985 back to 1958

1985:

Deep, purplish colour. Ripe, young raisins. Fresh, sweet, well balanced. Not too hot. Good fruit. Needs 15 years. Very good future. Lots of class. (17)

1983:

Good, dark colour. Slightly less purple than the 1985. Ripe, raisiny nose. Harder, drier, and riper raisins than the 1985. More serious. (17.5)

1980:

Lighter appearance than the above. Bright red. Not as much extract as the 1983. More forward. Not unlike a good 1975 or 1960. Very pleasant. Almost ready. (16)

1977:

More evolved yet than the 1980, and, surprisingly, less depth. Full, but not as powerful as expected. Quite sweet. Will mature sooner than most. Worrisome: this wine seems too evolved for a 1977. (17)

1975:

Quite light, mature colour. Sweet, pleasant, well balanced, forward, soft. (15)

1970:

Deeper, darker colour than the 1975. Maturing colour, but bright red, with good depth. Rich, ripe, fruity nose. Full, sweet, fruity, still youthful. No rush. (18)

This is very good—and underrated, judging by the reasonable price it fetches at auction.

1966:

Good depth, mature colour. More subdued on nose than the 1970, less opulent. Softer, round, good depth. Not as complex or as sweet as the 1970. The 1970 shows much better; more concentrated and livelier. (16)

1963:

Browning, good depth, palish rim. Tight, yet ripe, concentrated nose. Depth and extract typical of the 1963s. Full, rich, sweet, less lively and less spicy than the 1970, but much more depth and concentration than the 1966. (18)

For me, the disappointing wine was the 1966. Too lean, lacking fruit. The 1983 was a pleasant surprise.

FLIGHT #2
1962, 1960, 1958

1962:

Mature, orangy colour. Odd, fish-oil, cardboard nose. Harsher, more alcoholic than younger vintages. A bit lean and mean. Bottled in 1966 after four years. Over its peak. (14)

1960:

Surprising depth for a 1960. Mature nose. Fruity on palate. Nice, round, soft, complex. Surprisingly good and sweet. Lots of life. Ripe, rich, long. Very good. (17)

1958:

Mature, dark colour. Subdued nose. Round, softer than the 1960. Sweet, elegant. Most enjoyable. Not quite as lively as the 1960, but very good. This was an Avery's-bottling. (Dow's did not declare a 1958.) (16)

January 27, 1990

Dinner at Paul and Sarah Pinski's.

Also Sid and Joan Cross, Babette and Steve Pinski (Paul's son and daughter-in-law), and other guests. Fabulous veal, great red wines, and Port!

CHAMPAGNE BATISTE PERTOIS BRUT "BLANC DE BLANCS" 100% CRAMANT 1985:

Taittinger style. Delicate, young, fresh, good.

CHAMPAGNE J. LASALLE 1983 BLANC DE BLANCS "CHIGNY":

Green, delicate. Good yeast, complex, fresh. Well balanced. Soft.

1976 CORTON-CHARLEMAGNE "DIAMOND JUBILEE," REMOISSENET:

Deep, bright gold. Toasty, mature, woody, nutty. Soft, slightly ageing, hint of oxidation. A second bottle was much fresher. (17)

1959 CHÂTEAU LEOVILLE-LASCASES:

Low neck. Decanted 20 minutes. (I did the decanting.) Deep, maturing colour. Chocolate, earthy, classic Cabernet nose. Full, round, rich, ripe, concentrated. Lots of class, flesh, and elegance. A great bottle and one of my all-time favourite Clarets. (18.5) Better, in my opinion, than Lascases 1961.

1953 CHÂTEAU MOUTON-ROTHSCHILD:

High shoulder fill. Upside-down label! Cedary, elegant nose. Long, soft, round, complex. Great length and class. Superb balance and fruit. Soft, but all there. Cedar, cigar box. All class. A great bottle. Fabulous. (19.5)

1955 CHÂTEAU PETRUS:

Good neck level. Deepest, most youthful of all three. Amazingly young, fresh, round, sweet Merlot. Lots of flavour, but lacks the complexity of the 1953 Mouton. Incredible intensity and fruit. Obvious Merlot. Straightforward, youthful. (18)

1947 QUINTA DO NOVAL "NACIONAL," DA SILVA'S, OPORTO-BOTTLED IN 1949:

Medium colour, good depth, mature rim. Elegant, complex nose. Flowery, perfumy. Lots of class. Superb nose. Great balance. Fruit and spirit in harmony. (19)

Label read: "Produced from prephylloxera grapes." This is incorrect. Actually, this Port is not made from "prephylloxera" vines, but rather from ungrafted vines (original rootstocks).

Then we tried an oddity.

WEST INDIES RUM, BLEND OF THE CHOICEST "GROG AMERICANO PALIDO, RHUM FOUR PATHS," ARTUROS S.A., "HECHO EN MEXICO," T. NOIROT AND CO.:

In one-litre bottles. Probably produced in the late 1950s. Purchased in 1959 by Paul Pinski. Deep, amber colour. Green-olive rim. Sugary; full, rich, complex, ripe. Not unlike an old Armagnac (hint of wood). Quite hot on palate. Hint of vanilla, too. Unusual, rare old Rum. Straw around bottles.

January 28, 1990

SECOND SESSION

Warre's Vintage Port Vertical tasting

The 1920 and 1947 were contributed by Dr. Barney Rhodes. The 1945 to 1955 were purchased by Paul Pinski for this event.

FLIGHT #1
1920 to 1955

1955:

Maturing colour, good depth. Still fruity and youthful on nose. A bit spirity. Good fruit on entry, nice sweetness. A bit too spirity at finish. Still youthful, lively fruit. Maybe this wine should have been part of the first session because of its youth. (17)

1947, London-bottled by G. F. Grant and Co.:

Lighter colour than the 1955; pale rim. Subdued, more neutral on nose. Unyielding; hardly any bouquet. Quite sweet, clean, holding well. Good balance. Clean finish. Less spirity than the 1955. Nose is a letdown. (16)

1945, Portuguese-bottled, shipped by Avery's:

Mature, orangy rim; lovely, intense, classic, spicy nose. Fuller, richer, longer than either the 1955 or the 1947. Excellent depth. Lovely balance. Not very fat or rich. Fabulous bouquet. Hint of Tawny. Complete, mellow, at its absolute peak. (18.5)

1934, London-bottled by G. F. Grant and Co.:

Similar colour, but more brilliant than the 1945. Earthy, mushroomy nose. A bit stemmy. Similar impressions on palate. Quite hard, sharp, leaner, yet good fruit. A severe Port. Not unlike the combination of the 1947 and the 1955. Later, nose cleared a bit. (17)

1927, London-bottled by G. F. Grant and Co.:

Fearon and Block—later called Block, Gray and Block—actually bottled it. Deep, mature colour. Darkest of the 1947 to 1934 flight. Subdued, ripe raisins on nose. Good fruit and elegance on entry, but very spirity at finish. This helped this wine last, but it is too spirity at the end. (16.5)

1924 (1927), bottled by Cockburn and Campbell:

Purchased at Christie's in 1968. The label indicated "1924," but the cork was clearly branded "1927." The auctioneer made a mistake. So we had two 1927s and no 1924. Surprisingly youthful! Good colour for age. Neutral nose; some wood and smoke coming through. Later, opened up. Nice ripeness. One of the richest, most generous Ports of the flight. Rich, long, well balanced. Good backbone. Concentrated. Impressive. (18.5)

1922, London-bottled by G. F. Grant and Co.:

Maturing, orange-brown. An older, almost Tawny nose. Also rich and thick on palate, but noticeable spirit at finish. Too hot for me. Very good length and backbone. Livelier than the 1920, but sharper, hotter. Too spirity! True vintage- Port nose, though. (17)

1920, London-bottled by Hedges and Butler:

Similar appearance to the 1922. Slightly older-looking. Less intense, more subdued nose than the 1922. Good, ripe raisins. Unmistakable Vintage Port character on nose. Sweet, delicate, round, well balanced. Rich, long. Perfect finish. A lovely bottle. Nothing sharp or obtrusive here. Soft and delicious. Elegant. (18)

Surprisingly good second flight.

Better overall than first flight tasted yesterday. The group favourites were: 1945 (first), 1927 (second), 1920 (third). Overall, the second flight (the older wines) seemed more consistent than the first day's wines. My impression was that while the younger Warre's were (and are) very good, I prefer Dow's and Graham's (also owned by the Symingtons). The 1970, however, is delicious.

During the afternoon, the city of San Francisco was empty because of the 24th Super Bowl: San Francisco 49ers versus Denver Broncos. The 49ers won.

February 19 to March 10, 1990

Trip to Burgundy and Bordeaux, to assess the 1988 and 1989 vintages.

February 22, 1990

Lunch at "Brook's Club," in St. James's Street, with Harry Waugh and Simon Taylor.

Simon is a wine merchant importing fine Burgundies.

Harry had a nasty accident on the way to the club. A large board fell from a construction site and hit him. He fell, tore his coat and suit, but fortunately wasn't injured.

During the lunch, we discussed my trip and Simon gave me a few tips on properties to visit. I doubt that I'll have time to follow his advice, as all my visits were prearranged and organized before my departure from Vancouver.

February 25, 1990

Visit to Maison Jadot, in Beaune.

I had a nice chat with Pierre-Henri Gagey. Later, his Director of Export (Europe), Hubert Naus, a friendly man, took me to their cellars for a visit and tasting.

1988 whites

Pouilly-Fuissé:

Round, rich, quite soft, fairly alcoholic; some wood. Aged in 15% new oak. Complex, but lacks freshness. (15)

Meursault:

Just bottled. New oak and ripe fruit on nose. Complex; honey, toast, and wood in harmony. Good backbone and depth. Very good for a 1988. One to buy. (16.5)

PULIGNY-MONTRACHET:

Slight volatile acidity, but elegant, oaky, and long. It has in it some declassified Premier Crus. Well balanced. Not much weight or depth, but elegant. (16)

CHASSAGNE-MONTRACHET "MORGEOT" PREMIER CRU, DOMAINE DU DUC DE MAGENTA:

Just bottled. Still tight on nose. Clean, some oak. Pronounced oak on palate. Has body. Rich, but tight. Glycerine. Needs time. (17)

CORTON-CHARLEMAGNE:

Just bottled. Tight on nose. Full, rich, intense, and creamy. Medium-bodied, aggressive tannins at this stage. Will taste better in a year. I love this house's Corton-Charlemagnes. (18)

1989 whites

Not rated, as they are not bottled yet. All wines tasted below were tasted from cask.

CHABLIS PREMIER CRU "VAILLONS":

This is the first vintage of Chablis they have ever vinified. (The winemaker said that in 1989, the problem is having enough acidity in the whites.) Some oak, crisp, green Chablis. Rich, well balanced, but still closed. Hard to judge.

PERNAND-VERGELESSES:

Floral nose. Honeyed. A bit neutral at this early stage. Fatter and riper than in 1988, but not very complex.

MEURSAULT:

Still going through malolactic fermentation. Riper nose than the 1988. Only one month in wood so far. Has depth. Promising. Will be good. Worth buying.

PULIGNY-MONTRACHET "CLOS DE LA GARENNE," DOMAINE DU DUC DE MAGENTA:

Tasted from a new oak barrel. The blend will have 30% new oak. Ripe, rich, honeyed. Lovely depth. Vanilla. Deep, golden colour. Very promising.

PULIGNY-MONTRACHET "CLOS DE LA GARENNE," DOMAINE DU DUC DE MAGENTA:

From a two-year-old barrel. Green-gold colour. Fruit without wood impressions. Rich, lovely, complex. The blend should be very good.

BÂTARD-MONTRACHET:

Beautiful, bright green-gold colour. Fabulous, toasty, open nose. Intense, great depth, concentrated, great wine. True "heavier" Bâtard style. Very intense. Will be great! Worth buying.

CORTON-CHARLEMAGNE:

Tight, closed nose; same impressions on palate. Needs time. Hard to assess, but lingered and opened up in glass. Should be excellent.

They have a 20-year contract with the Duc de Magenta to produce their wine.

1988 reds

The winemaker said that overall, the 1985s (reds) are more consistent than the 1989s and more charming, too. The 1988s have a tougher backbone than the 1985s. They will be "vins de garde."

PINOT NOIR:

Medium red. Elegant, clean, spicy nose. Fruity, round. Very good. Worth buying if price is right. Delicate, not much depth, but well made.

MONTHÉLIE:

Medium red. Elegant nose. Wood, complex, sweet, delicate. Good depth.

POMMARD "EPENOTS" PREMIER CRU:

Typical Pommard; powerful, tannic. This is the first year that they have vinified it. Epenots is one of the most aggressive, masculine Pommards. Very good, deep colour. Needs eight to ten years.

BEAUNE "CLOS DES URSULES":

From their own Domaine. Fat, rich, concentrated. Will be bottled in two months. Very good depth. Ripe, expansive nose. A very promising wine. Worth buying.

Since 1985, Musigny has been produced from their own domaine, and they don't have to buy other people's grapes. Also, they think that their Bonnes Mares is the best wine that they have produced in 1985!

Back to the 1988s

VOSNE-ROMANÉE:

Lighter than the Beaune "Ursules." Elegant, delicate, some hard tannins in background. Not finished yet. Reserve judgement.

NUITS-ST.-GEORGES "CLOS DES CORVÉES":

Ripe nose, concentrated. Superb, elegant, classy. Very good balance, loads of ripe fruit. This has great potential. Finishes clean, long, and ripe, all in harmony. Worth buying!

GEVREY-CHAMBERTIN "LAVAUX ST. JACQUES":

From their own domaine. Sweeter, riper, richer, bigger than the "Clos des Corvées," but without the class of the above.

CHAMBERTIN "CLOS DE BÈZE":

Elegant, yet solid. Powerful backbone, new oak, leaner. Serious. Needs time. Great potential.

1989 reds

Very youthful. Only five months in oak casks so far.

GEVREY-CHAMBERTIN "CLOS ST. JACQUES":

From their own domaine. New wood. A young, fruity baby. Dark, good fruit, still fermenting.

BONNES MARES:

From the Morey-St.-Denis side. Feminine, elegant, some fizz, still fermenting. Lots of class and fruit. Will be very good.

CLOS DE VOUGEOT:

From the former Clair-Daü vineyard, which they now own. This is their first vintage. Only three-year-old vines. Young and fresh, lacking depth. Vines need to get older!

MUSIGNY:

Excellent depth, balance, and fruit. Lots of class here. Only four months old, yet a great wine in the making. Worth buying.

Before leaving, I tasted a half-bottle of this.

GEVREY-CHAMBERTIN "LAVAUX ST. JACQUES" 1985:

Beautiful, fruity, young. Lots of ripe, yet fresh, fruit. Super wine from a great vintage.

Visit to Domaine Albert Morot, in Beaune.

I drove to see Mlle. Choppin at Domaine Albert Morot in Beaune. They are the exclusive owners of Savigny-lès-Beaune "La Bataillère," and they own vines in Beaune (Premier Crus). All the wines are produced from their own domaine. Mlle. Choppin doesn't like too much new oak, and complains that her American agents insist on more new oak. She never uses more than 25% new oak. They have very cold cellars.

1989s, barrel samples

SAVIGNY "BATAILLÈRE":

Sulphured only last month. From one-year-old wood. Slightly acidified. Harmonious, round, rich, complex, ripe fruit. Good balance and depth. Will be very good. Worth buying.

BEAUNE "LES TOUSSAINTS":

From two-year-old barrel. Not as dark as the Savigny. Delicate, leaner style. Some aggressive tannins.

BEAUNE "CENT VIGNES":

Very good, dark colour. Beautiful nose. Long, rich, sweet fruit, complex. Licorice, spicy. Will be excellent. Worth buying.

BEAUNE "GRÈVES":

Old vines. Dark, rich, and full. Long, with great depth. Worth buying.

BEAUNE "BRESSANDES":

From new oak barrel. Lighter than all of the above. Fresh fruit. A bit stemmy. Long, complex, delicate. Solid, yet sweet. Some oak, vanilla.

BEAUNE "BRESSANDES":

From a two-year-old barrel. Rounder, less sharp, like a good Vosne. Good length. Lots of class and elegance. Eventually, will be blended with the above to produce the "finished" wine.

BEAUNE "MARCONNETS":

Marconnets is the most masculine of the Premier Crus of Beaune. Dark colour. Lovely, clean flowery nose. Solid, leaner on palate. Powerful, serious. More like a Corton. Maybe lacks ripe fruit a bit.

BEAUNE "TEURONS":

From one-year-old barrel. Lovely, complex, elegant, yet masculine, with lots of depth. Classy.

BEAUNE "TEURONS":

From three-year-old barrel. Fruitier, richer, tannic. Not as big as the 1988, and relatively more forward. Worth buying.

This was followed by a tasting of the 1988s.

All bottled in December 1989 to January 1990 (two months ago). Mlle. Choppin said that the 1988s are overall more complete wines than the 1989s. She thinks that her 1988s are better than the 1985, best since 1978!

SAVIGNY "BATAILLÈRE":

Very good, deep, dark, impressive colour. Great concentration, fruity nose. Full, rich, ripe wine. Will be very good. (17)

BEAUNE "TOUSSAINTS":

Ripe, a bit pruny, older-tasting. Good, but not great. (16.5)

BEAUNE "CENT VIGNES":

Great depth of colour to rim. Deep, well balanced, complex, and long. Very good potential. Worth buying. (17.5)

BEAUNE "BRESSANDES":

Old vines. Straw, oak, and fruit on nose. Elegant, yet ripe. Long, fruity, excellent depth. Worth buying. (17.5)

BEAUNE "MARCONNETS":

Masculine wine. Harder, leaner, more tannic, less complete. May develop well, but needs time. (17)

BEAUNE "TEURONS":

Dark, ripe, pruny. Very good colour to rim. Solid, ripe, and fruity. A bit austere, old style. Barnyardy, rustic flavours. (17)

Then we tasted the 1987s

SAVIGNY "BATAILLÈRE":

Good colour. Lighter, more elegant on palate than the excellent 1988. Leaner, greener, more acidic. Good, but not great. (16)

BEAUNE "TOUSSAINTS":

Medium cherry-red. Lovely, elegant nose. Complex. Had a late malolactic fermentation. Fruity, fresh, complex. Needs five to seven years. Long, clean, fruity finish. Very good. Worth buying. (17)

BEAUNE "GRÈVES":

More evolved colour. Too alcoholic, not enough fruit. Some bitterness at finish. (15.5)

BEAUNE "BRESSANDES":

Medium purple-red, pale rim. Hint of rubber. Closed, tight. Lacks a bit in ripe fruit. (16)

BEAUNE "TEURONS":

Nice, young, cherry-red colour. Slight rubber, perfume. Very good fruit. Tannic! Needs time, yet backed by ripe fruit. Worth buying. (17)

Then we tasted two 1983s, in half-bottles.

Mlle. Choppin said that she picked her 1983s without rot, and it shows.

1983 BEAUNE "TEURONS," IN HALF-BOTTLE:

Ripe, clean nose of fruit, oak, and barnyard. Sturdy, ripe raisins. Masculine, concentrated. Very good, ripe fruit. Lots of depth, class, even elegance. No sign of rot. Needs ten years. (17)

1983 BEAUNE "TOUSSAINTS," IN HALF-BOTTLE:

Similar colour to above, but leaner, harder, tannic. Good fruit, but not as concentrated as the above. Needs three years. (16.5)

Later, I ordered several 1987s, and especially 1988s, for the BC liquor monopoly, a total of 100 cases. I am not an agent and make no profit from these purchases. I offered my services (for this particular trip) to try to find some 1988 red Burgundies for British Columbia before it is too late, and the purchasing department has agreed to allow me to try and purchase some for our government liquor monopoly.

Visit with Gerard Potel, in Volnay.

That afternoon, I went to see Gerard Potel at Domaine de la Pousse d'Or, in Volnay. He has Australian partners. He produces mainly Volnay Premier Crus and a Santenay, and one Pommard (Jarollières) Premier Cru.

1989s, tasted from cask

SANTENAY "GRAVIÈRES" PREMIER CRU:

Still fermenting, fresh, fruity. Hard to assess.

VOLNAY "CAILLERETS":

Very good, dark colour. A bit sharp, acidic. Going through malolactic fermentation.

VOLNAY "CAILLERETS" "CLOS DES 60 OUVRÉES":

Made from young vines. Also going through malolactic fermentation. Fairly lean, hard to assess. Not very dark at this stage.

VOLNAY "CLOS DE LA BOUSSE D'OR":

Their monopole. Good, dark colour. Deepest, richest of the lot. Potel said that he did very little chaptalization in 1989

POMMARD "LES JAROLLIÈRES":

Still has some gas. Tannic, rich, powerful Pommard. This vineyard is close to Volnay and has some Volnay elegance, but combined with the power of Pommard.

1987s, from bottle

SANTENAY "GRAVIÈRES":

Lighter, medium-bodied, round, fruity, elegant. Ready in one to two years. Simple. (15)

VOLNAY "CAILLERETS" "CLOS DES 60 OUVRÉES":

Planted in 30% new vines, but as new vines are more productive, about 45% of the juice comes from these young vines. Very good, dark colour. Round, fruity, yet rich and powerful. Good length and balance. A bit edgy at this stage. (16)

VOLNAY "CLOS DE LA BOUSSE D'OR":

Complex, elegant, expansive. Very good length. Long, well-balanced. Worth buying. (17)

POMMARD "JAROLLIÈRES":

Very good, deep colour. Ripe nose, full, rich, some oak, all in harmony. Complex. (17.5)

1986s, from bottle

VOLNAY "CLOS DE LA BOUSSE D'OR":

More evolved colour. Lighter, leaner, noticeable acidity. Not as powerful as the 1987s. Greener acids. (15.5)

Potel said that wines can still be tasted ten to 14 days after bottling, but after that, they close up for a few months.

He also said that cigarettes and Sauternes don't go well together. A famous old sommelier from a fine restaurant in Paris told him that in the late 1930s, when women started smoking, they preferred Champagne to Sauternes at the end of a meal. He also thought that Sauternes should be bottled in 500 mL bottles as 750 mLs is too much and 350 mLs is too little.

Potel has fallen out of grace with Robert Parker, who didn't like his 1987s.

Yet, oddly, Potel never submitted his 1987 wines for Parker to taste when Parker tasted 150 different 1987s on his last trip to Burgundy. This is very strange. He wonders where Parker got "to taste my wines, which I never submitted." Also, a neighbour of Potel's says the same thing. That neighbour is Mussy. If this is true, it is a major scandal.

Then we tasted the 1988s.

An average of 30% new oak was used in these 1988s, but the Santenay never sees new oak.

SANTENAY "GRAVIÈRES":

Brilliant colour. Lovely fruit. Rich, lively, good structure. Very good balance. (16.5)

VOLNAY "CAILLERETS":

Fruity, rich, complex, good backbone. Acidity, fruit, and oak in harmony. Hard and tannic, but ripe, too. Very good potential. Worth buying. (17.5)

VOLNAY "BOUSSE D'OR":

Bottled last Friday! Full, serious, rich, and round. Very good balance, depth, and ripe fruit. Worth buying. (17.5)

POMMARD "JAROLLIÈRES":

Deep, rich, full, and powerful, Loads of ripe fruit. Very good tannins. Will be excellent. Worth buying. (18)

Usually, Potel does not destem, but he did so in 1989; there were too many thick stems, and that would have made the wines taste too stemmy. Potel thinks that while the 1985s are excellent, the 1988s are more powerful and will be longer lived.

1984 VOLNAY "CLOS DE LA BOUSSE D'OR":

Evolved, tobacco, and toast. Delicate, but of course without the depth of the 1988s. (16)

Later, he opened a bottle of this wine.

1972 VOLNAY "CAILLERETS":

(He likes the 1972s and so do I.) Evolved colour. Beautiful, open, ripe, mature tobacco on nose. Full, round, trace of acidity at finish. Typically 1972. (16.5)

I ordered a total of 60 cases, mostly 1988s, for the BC liquor monopoly. I am not a representative of the BC liquor monopoly. I am doing this on a purely voluntary basis: no commission or remuneration from either the producers or the liquor monopoly.

An enjoyable visit.

Weather

Today, the third wave of violent winds has hit north-western Europe, especially the UK, but also France, Holland, and Belgium. All in February 1990. In between, there was a stretch of unusually warm and mild weather.

February 27, 1990

Visit to Maison Georges Roumier, in Chambolle.

Pouring rain; a chilly, miserable morning. I met the father (Jean-Marie) and had a nice visit with his son Christophe, a nice young man and a gifted winemaker.

All the wines are made from their own vines. In 1989, it was a bit patchy in terms of acidity. They were surprised at how soft the 1989s turned out to be; like the 1979s, but with riper fruit. We tasted a few 1989s. Some were still going through their malo; others were over it, but sulphured.

1989s

MOREY-ST.-DENIS "CLOS DE LA BUSSIÈRE" PREMIER CRU:

Elegant, medium colour at this stage. Well balanced, good body and structure. This, and the Chambolle (below) have about 10% to 12% new oak. Grands Crus are matured in 30% new oak.

CHAMBOLLE-MUSIGNY:

Beautiful, deep, rich colour and nose. Very good intensity, ripe fruit. Less acidic, more elegant. Classy. Will need seven to eight years. Worth buying.

CHAMBOLLE-MUSIGNY "AMOUREUSES":

They just added sulphur to the wine so the colour seemed lighter. This is only a phase. Fine, elegant, complex, still has some gas. Nice finish and fruit.

BONNES MARES:

Made 100% from the Chambolle side. Only Clair Daü (now Jadot) have Bonnes Mares in Morey. Dark colour. Serious, tannic, very good depth, solid. Better acidity than the "Amoureuses." Clean, long finish. Will be excellent.

Then we tasted the 1988s.

These will be bottled next month. I tasted the 1988s from one to three-year-old casks, so that the fruit wouldn't be masked by new oak.

CHAMBOLLE-MUSIGNY:

Good, dark colour. Complex, oak and fruit in harmony. Delicate, yet powerful. Excellent complexity. Will be very good. Worth buying.

MOREY-ST.-DENIS "CLOS DE LA BUSSIÈRE":

Still going through egg-white collage. More austere, rich, tannic, powerful. Harder wine. More power and depth, but not as elegant as the Chambolle.

The following two wines, also 1988s, are produced personally by Christophe Roumier, under his own label. He produces these two wines "en metayage": the land is owned by someone else, and the owner gets half the production. His share is only 900 bottles of the Ruchottes and 600 bottles of the Charmes.

RUCHOTTES-CHAMBERTIN:

Superb depth of colour, nose, and palate. Rich, creamy, medium acidity, yet tannic, powerful, and elegant. Lots of character here. Racey wine. Great balance! Worth buying… if one can find any.

CHARMES-CHAMBERTIN:

More feminine, more forthcoming, lighter. Rounder, some bitter tannins at finish, and more noticeable acidity. Very good, though. Less depth than the Ruchottes.

Back to Domaine Roumier's 1988s

CHAMBOLLE-MUSIGNY "AMOUREUSES":

Great! Deep colour and body. Rich, fat, yet elegant; solid, yet soft. Complex, long, solid finish. Will be excellent. Worth buying. No wonder Roumier has the reputation of being one of the finest producers of Chambolle.

BONNES MARES:

Great extract, ripe tannins on entry, but hard finish. Will be excellent. Depth and superb bouquet. Worth buying.

BONNES MARES "VIEILLES VIGNES":

From 35 to 75-year-old vines. More massive than the Ruchottes; great depth, length, ripe tannins. Very solid. Lots of complexity. Fresh on nose and palate. Lovely. A must!

Christophe said that the wines change daily, while in cask, depending on the weather.

I managed to order a barrel (25 cases) of his Chambolle 1988, the only one he has left and was willing to sell. A very nice young man, and a nice visit. I hope that the BC liquor monopoly will hasten to send him an order and money soon, or else he will sell it elsewhere.

Visit to Philippe Nadeff, in Marsannay.

In the afternoon, I met Jeanne-Marie Deschamps, a nice lady who is a négociante in Beaune, supplying (among others) the "Wine House" in San Francisco.

We met in Gevrey and drove to Marsannay to visit young Philippe Nadeff.

He was busy, but his wife allowed us to taste. Their production is really tiny. The entire production is from their own vineyards, which Nadeff inherited from his mother. They use 100% new oak for their Premier and Grand Crus. They use second-year barrels for their village Gevrey, and third-year barrels for their Marsannay.

1988 MARSANNAY:

Just being bottled during our visit; 600 cases produced. Medium depth, fresh, crisp, elegant, good complexity and acidity. Retails in the US for about $15 to $16. Quite good, but not very big or concentrated.

1989s, from cask

MARSANNAY:

Medium red, hint of fizz, fresh, round, delicate. Very clean fruit and sweet, fruity finish.

GEVREY-CHAMBERTIN:

Nice, bright colour. Fresh, fruity, elegant. Good backbone. Some sharpness at this stage, fairly alcoholic. Solid. Will improve and get more complex, of course. This is very young.

GEVREY CHAMBERTIN "CHAMPEAUX":

Medium depth, perfumy, yet closed nose. Tight. Very promising.

All the above 1989s had just been sulphured, and therefore temporarily lost some colour. This is a natural process. Eventually they will regain their original darker colour.

Back to the 1989s

GEVREY CHAMBERTIN "CAZETIERS":

Produced from 40 to 50-year-old vines; tiny production. Much better colour than above. Brilliant colour. Sweet, ripe nose. Harmony between oak and ripe fruit. Long. Very good balance. Great and rare. This was the first wine to be treated with sulphur and its colour is back to normal. Worth buying.

MAZIS-CHAMBERTIN:

Tiny production from 70 to 80-year-old vines. Great, purple-red colour. Powerful, tannic, solid, serious. Not as ripe and sweet as the Cazetiers. More masculine. Hint of smoke, toast, and oak. I prefer the Cazetiers at this stage, but this is very good. Worth buying.

Then we tried some1988s.

BOURGOGNE ROUGE:

Coarse, lean, and green, yet good fruit and complexity. Not bad.

GEVREY-CHAMBERTIN:

Very good, cherry-red colour. Clean, perfumy, vanilla nose. Oaky, sharp, hard. Serious wine that needs time. Very good, but maybe too much oak?

BOURGOGNE BLANC:

Made from 100% Chardonnay. Smells and tastes more like a Pinot Blanc from the Côte de Nuits. Good acidity, but a bit lean. Lacks fruit, yet solid and big. Dull, short finish. Not very impressive.

Nadeff has a big dog that gets him in trouble. The dog runs away and goes to a neighbour's property where he kills the neighbour's ducks! That happened while I was there.

Deschamps said that she had problems with liquor monopolies in Canada. They're too slow ordering, and in general, do not know what they are doing. What else is new?

February 28, 1990

Visit to Domaine Bruno Clair, in Marsannay.

I had a short chat with Bruno (a very nice man in his mid-30s), and then I tasted with his winemaker, Philippe. All wines are made from grapes of their own domaine. Most whites are made from 100% Chardonnay, but his white Marsannay is a blend of Chardonnay and Pinot Blanc. In their Premier and Grand Crus, they use between 25% and 40% new oak, never more, depending on the year.

1989s, from cask

SAVIGNY-LÈS-BEAUNE "LA DOMINODE":

About one-and-a-half hectares from very old vines, most planted since 1902. Still has gas. Lively colour. Very good fruit. Hard to taste, but should be excellent. Fresh and full. Worth buying.

MOREY-ST.-DENIS:

Not as opulent as the Savigny. Leaner, more masculine. Still being made. Hard to assess.

GEVREY-CHAMBERTIN "CLOS ST. JACQUES" PREMIER CRU:

Very good colour. Still fermenting. (According to Bruno, the 1989s will be bigger, better than the 1979s, more concentrated, as a vintage.) Good acidity. Good colour. Complex, long, and clean. Worth buying.

All 1988s undergoing collage with egg-white at present. Softer wines will be bottled next month. The rest will be bottled next May. They have old "foudres," which they use for storage. They made more wine in 1989 than in 1988. This seems to be a general, worrisome trend.

1988s

ROSÉ DE MARSANNAY:

Salmon pink. Should be drunk young. Lively, lovely, fresh fruit on nose and palate. No wood at all. Excellent fruit. One of the very best still Rosés I've ever tasted. Worth buying.

MARSANNAY "VAUDEVELLES":

Bottled yesterday. Good, cherry-red colour. Opulent, round, soft, gentle on entry, yet solid finish. Very nice, clean, and long. Aged in two-year-old casks. Good backbone.

MARSANNAY "LANGEROIS":

Also bottled yesterday. More austere, harder; full, rich, ripe, more serious. Needs more time. Richer and bigger than the Vaudevelles. Excellent. Worth buying.

VOSNE-ROMANÉE "CHAMPS PERDRIX":

Not a Premier Cru. Only seven barrels made! Tiny production. All elegance, true Vosne. Feminine, delicate, complex. Perfumy. Oak blends nicely. Very classy and long. Will be really fine. Worth buying.

SAVIGNY "LA DOMINODE":

Only 20 hectolitres per hectare! The colour and depth of a great Côte de Nuits! Best Savigny I've ever tasted, by far. Great length, deep colour, lots of extract. Superb. All there. Will need ten years. Worth buying.

GEVREY-CHAMBERTIN "CLOS ST. JACQUES":

Oak and very ripe, charming fruit in harmony on nose. Lots of fruit, excellent backbone. Tight, rich, serious Gevrey. Tannic. Great length. Needs ten to 12 years, or more. Worth buying.

GEVREY-CHAMBERTIN "CAZETIERS":

Leaner, tighter, less extract than the "Clos St. Jacques," but Bruno said that this wine takes longer to come around. More pronounced oak. Assemblage already done.

CHAMBERTIN "CLOS DE BÈZE":

Great class here. Fabulous harmony and classic nose. Complex, good balance, long, fine. Racey. Not as fat as the "Clos St. Jacques," but lots of depth. Superb wine. Worth buying.

We then tasted a bottle of

1986 GEVREY CHAMBERTIN "CLOS ST. JACQUES":

Tasted from bottle. Leaner, tighter, quite solid. Not as much extract as the 1988s, but very good. Needs five years.

I ordered several wines, all 1988s, for the BC liquor monopoly. Bruno gave me two bottles: a Chambertin "Clos de Bèze" 1987 and a Marsannay. A short, but very instructive visit. He makes excellent, serious wines.

Visit to Domaine Daniel Rion.

During the early afternoon of the same day, I visited with Patrice Rion of Domaine Daniel Rion in Premeaux. He has been making the wines on his own there since 1980; he produced the 1977s, 1978s, and 1979s with the help of his father.

Villages wines age in 15% to 30% new oak. Premier Crus have 30% to 40% new oak. Grand Crus are aged in 50% to 55% new oak casks.

1989s

All the 1989s have finished their malo, but are still upset. They will be bottled in a year or so.

NUITS-ST.-GEORGES:

Nice colour, complex, delicate, still had gas.

NUITS-ST.-GEORGES PREMIER CRU "VIGNESRONDES":

Very deep colour. A round, ripe, fleshy wine. Not much acidity, but ripe tannins. Very nice, "round" wine, typical of this "climat," as its name indicates.

VOSNE-ROMANÉE:

Lighter than the Vignesrondes, but nice colour. Complex, delicate Vosne. Feminine. Better acidity. Straightforward. Very nice.

VOSNE-ROMANÉE PREMIER CRU "CHAUMES":

Sweet, perfumy, complex. Still has some gas. Should be very nice. Fair acidity.

Then came the turn of the 1988s

The 1988s were bottled very recently.

CÔTE DE NUITS VILLAGES:

Not from young vines, rather from vines grown on sandy soil. Fresh, acidic, nice colour, elegant. Not too deep or complex.

NUITS-ST.-GEORGES "LAVIÈRES":

Not a Premier Cru. Spicy, licorice, and mint on nose; subdued. Very deep, rich, ripe, and long. Concentrated. Soft tannins, but they're there. This is good.

VOSNE-ROMANÉE:

Medium-deep colour. Class and elegance on nose. Tannic finish. Will need seven years. Worth buying.

VOSNE-ROMANÉE "BEAUMONTS," PREMIER CRU:

Very elegant nose, oak and fruit. Complex, rich, but not heavy. Long on palate. Classy. Never a fat wine; Rion's Beaumonts are always racey. Worth buying.

NUITS-ST.-GEORGES "CLOS DES ARGILLIÈRES," PREMIER CRU:

They purchased this vineyard in 1984. It was planted in 1956, Patrick's birth year. Very ripe fruit on nose. Raspberries and Cassis. Lovely, ripe fruit on palate. Oak blends nicely. Full, rich, and solid. One to buy! Lots of class and extract.

VOSNE-ROMANÉE "VIGNESRONDES," PREMIER CRU:

Made from 35 to 40-year-old vines. Round, more like the Nuits (above), but the elegance of Vosne on palate. Big and rich, though. Very good potential. Fleshy and rich. Not as much class as their Beaumonts, but worth buying.

CLOS DE VOUGEOT, GRAND CRU:

Made from purchased grapes "en metayage." They keep half the production. From 45 to 50-year-old vines. They were making the wine even as far back as Daniel's grandfather. Like a young Premier Grand Cru Pauillac. Mouton-like! Made from very small grapes with very thick skins, and it shows! Incredible colour and depth. Very rich, big, tannic; superb balance and extract. A great wine. Needs 15 years. Grand Vin.

1987

VOSNE-ROMANÉE "VIGNERONDES," PREMIER CRU:

Only 22 to 28 hectolitres per hectare; less than in 1985, 1986, or 1988. Spicy, tobacco nose. More evolved. Complex, round, tannic finish, leaner style. Masculine, like so many other 1987s. Noticeable acidity, but good tannins and fruit. Promising.

1986s

NUITS-ST.-GEORGES:

Ripe, pruny on nose. Showing some age in the colour. Sweet, forward, leaner finish. Needs a bit more depth and extract. (16)

NUITS-ST.-GEORGES "CLOS DES ARGILLIÈRES":

Very good tannins, rich, long, full. Impressive for a 1986. Very good. Good backbone. Needs six to seven years. One to buy. (17)

VOSNE-ROMANÉE "BEAUMONTS":

As with the 1988, a classic Vosne. Elegant, complex, most marked by new oak. Good, dark colour. Oak and ripe fruit. Stylish. Leaner than the others, but lots of class and length. Worth buying. (17.5)

NB: He confirmed Potel's story (Domaine de la Pousse d'Or). Parker wrote about Potel's 1987s without having tasted them. This story about Robert Parker ("King Parker," as he is known in Burgundy), if true, is a real scandal!

We talked about 1945 Beaune "Montée Rouge," up the hill in Beaune.

The soil is red because of its high iron content. He knows that vineyard well. I asked him about this because I had recently acquired a couple of bottles of this 1945.

Rion refused to sell any 1988 to the BC liquor monopoly. He may send us quotes on his 1989s soon, but he has allocated all his 1988s already.

Visit to Domaine Méo-Camuzet.

From there, I went to visit the Domaine Méo-Camuzet in Vosne-Romanée, where I was received by young Jean-Nicolas Méo. They use 100% new oak in all their wines, even Villages wines. They work 11.5 hectares, of which 3.5 hectares are their own and the rest "en metayage." They keep half the production.

Méo Camuzet have taken back two Vosne vineyards (Cros-Parantoux and Brulées) from Henri Jayer, who worked them "en metayage." Méo appointed Jayer as consultant winemaker in 1986. Their western-US agent is Martine Saunier (Martine's Wines).

We started by tasting the 1988s, which will be bottled next April.

VOSNE-ROMANÉE:

Medium-bright colour. Elegance of Vosne on nose and palate, yet backbone and tannins typical of the 1988s. Lovely, balanced, complex. Worth buying.

VOSNE-ROMANÉE "CHAUMES," PREMIER CRU:

Better colour. Classy, complex, lots of charm. Nice balance and harmony. Definitely one to buy.

NUITS-ST.-GEORGES "LES MEURGERS," PREMIER CRU:

Sweet, ripe fruit. Concentrated, long, oak, vanilla. Typical of the appellation. Great extract. Worth buying.

NUITS-ST.-GEORGES "LES BOUDOTS," PREMIER CRU:

Made from 30 to 35-year-old vines, in part. The rest is 50 years old. More ripe fruit, less oak on nose. Ripe cherries and Cassis. Sweet on entry, yet later, long, tannic, powerful. Great, clean, impeccable fruit. This is a lovely bottle. Worth buying!

CORTON "CLOS REMIER," GRAND CRU:

Walled clos. Sweet, rich, ripe, and long. Solid. The intensity and depth of the Nuits-St.-Georges "Boudots." Very good.

VOSNE-ROMANÉE "LES BRULÉES," PREMIER CRU:

Deep, purple colour. Tight on nose, yet Cassis and ripe cherries coming through. Classy, super depth, good tannins. More harmony than the Nuits-St.-Georges "Boudots." This is really lovely. A "must" in any serious cellar.

CLOS DE VOUGEOT, GRAND CRU:

From their own vineyard, but vinified by someone else. Jayer? All 1988s were made by someone else, but supervised by them. In 1989, they vinified their own. This property is located right next to the Château du Clos de Vougeot; a good location, not too low. Lots of class and elegance here. Complex, tight, stylish. Very good depth. Solid, yet not massive. Worth buying.

They will bottle this wine directly from individual barrels.

VOSNE-ROMANÉE "CROS-PARANTOUX," PREMIER CRU:

Bright purple-red. Elegant on entry, yet hard, solid tannins. Not very ripe, but stylish. Classy, elegant wine. Delicate, but good backbone. Worth buying.

RICHEBOURG, GRAND CRU:

Floral, lovely nose. A beauty. All elegance and class. No sharp edges. Honey and flowers. Superb balance and length on palate. Very fruity, yet not massive. Everything in harmony. A classic. Great future. Buy—at any price!

Then we tasted the 1989s.

Many didn't have the "soustirage" done yet, but all have finished their malo very recently, and still had an odd smell.

NUITS-ST.-GEORGES "LES MEURGERS," PREMIER CRU:

Ripe fruit, sweet. Softer, fatter, rounder than the 1988s. Charming.

NUITS-ST.-GEORGES "CROS-PARANTOUX," PREMIER CRU:

A little sturdier than the Meurgers. Ripe, full, tannic. Will be very good.

Méo-Camuzet make excellent wines, no doubt. However, I'm not sure they should all be aged in 100% new oak, especially the Villages wines or the softer, more elegant Premiers Crus.

They are starting to plant some Chardonnay in the Hautes-Côtes; the first vintage will be commercially available in three years. As with Daniel Rion, Méo wouldn't sell any to the BC liquor monopoly. All his 1988s are for his good clients. He may offer the liquor monopoly some 1989s later this year.

March 19, 1990

In the evening, a visit in Meursault at the home and winery of Jean-François Coche-Dury.

We met as it was getting dark, at 6:30 p.m., on a cold but bright winter evening. Jean-François just got back from his share of a Corton-Charlemagne vineyard. (Part of that vineyard is leased to Adrien Belland and part to Michel Juillot of Mercurey.) See comments from my last visit there in the fall of 1986. Coche-Dury is a dedicated and very gifted winemaker.

1989s, tasted from cask

MEURSAULT:

Still going through malo. Fresh, spicy, some gas. Very good fruit. Ripe.

MEURSAULT "LES NARVAUX":

Some sulphur, malolactic fermentation. Lovely, ripe fruit. Very ripe, rich, long. Medium acidity. Easy to like. Charming wine.

MEURSAULT "LES VIREUILS":

Higher acidity, leaner, racier than the "Narvaux." Very good length. Clean, rich, complex. More class.

MEURSAULT "LES ROUGEOTS":

Still going through malo. A combination of the fat of the "Narvaux" and the nervous spiciness and acidity of the "Vireuils." Excellent. Some gas. Will be very, very good.

MEURSAULT-PERRIÈRES, PREMIER CRU:

Noticeable alcohol. Jean-François said that it had a half-degree alcohol higher than the village wines. Richer, riper, bigger, more intense. This Perrières has already finished its malo. Most serious, longest lived.

Will be excellent. Maybe even great! This is the only Premier Cru Meursault that he produces; the rest are either Villages wines or "lieu dit."

CORTON-CHARLEMAGNE:

Only three barrels produced as his share. That's 75 cases for the whole world! The vines are 28 years old. Rich, ripe, some noticeable alcohol. Full, sweet finish, blended with nuts, vanilla, and oak. Great length. The character of Corton; more toasty, almonds. Great extract, fruit, and overall quality. It will be impossible to get any of this!

Then we tasted the 1988s, from cask.

All 1988s will be bottled in May. Most 1988s are still undergoing the egg-white collage.

BOURGOGNE BLANC:

From 15-year-old vines. Full, solid, rich. Aged in three-year-old oak barrels. Better than many other producers' Meursaults!

MEURSAULT:

Tight, closed nose. Less fat than the 1989, leaner. Not my style, but very nice. Touch of oak, vanilla. Some acidity at finish.

Coche-Dury said that the 1988 whites are quite a bit leaner than the 1989s. He said that the 1989s that were well made will be great. There were problems in 1989 (as in 1982, when some produced clumsy wines), but he added that those who knew what they were doing, made great 1989s.

1989 reds, from cask

MEURSAULT ROUGE:

Made from a blend of ten to 15-year-old vines. No new oak. Malo finished, but not yet racked (soutiré). Flowery, spicy, elegant. Classy.

AUXEY-DURESSES:

Ripe cherries, sweet, expansive nose. Some gas still. Perfumy, lovely fruit.

VOLNAY "CLOS DES CHÊNES" PREMIER CRU:

Vines are 28 years old. A beauty! One of the best Volnays I've ever tasted. Great class, elegance, perfume, yet rich, ripe fruit. Medium-cherry colour. Finesse, balance, and backbone.

Back to 1988, both red and white

VOLNAY "CLOS DES CHÊNES" PREMIER CRU:

Aged in one to two-year-old oak casks. Still going through egg-white collage. Some oak influence is there, but not too much, because his Volnays are very elegant. Complete, soft, long, flowery, clean. Great breed. Coche-Dury said this should be drunk at three to five years of age.

MEURSAULT-PERRIÈRES, PREMIER CRU:

Still "sur colle"; going through egg-white collage. Coche-Dury said that as a rule he doesn't allow wines to be tasted when they are still being fined, but he made an exception. A solid, long-distance runner. Full, long, tight, serious. Needs a full ten years.

Jean-François said that many 1989s will be drunk too soon. He also said that 1988 was a cool, acidic season so there was no problem producing the wine, but 1989 was much more difficult and variable, with many greats but many failures, too.

As usual, a most enjoyable visit and tasting; no doubt Coche-Dury is a master at his task, and a nice man.

March 2, 1990

Last day in Burgundy. Visit to Domaine Etienne Sauzet, in Puligny-Montrachet.

An early morning visit with Gerard Boudot of Domaine Etienne Sauzet. Boudot is the great-son-in-law of Etienne Sauzet. He has worked with Sauzet since 1973, and has been making the wine himself since 1980. His agent for all of the United States is Robert Haas.

He uses Seguin-Moreau oak barrels; one-third new oak yearly for village and Premier Crus; and about 40% to 45% for Grands Crus. Gerard said that in Puligny, the water table is so high that no deep cellars can be dug, and therefore there is a lack of moisture. Thus, even two to three-year-old oak barrels look relatively new.

We tasted only 1989s. He didn't chaptalize at all in 1989.

1989s: All from cask, of course

BOURGOGNE BLANC A/C:

First vintage. Third-year vines. 12.6% natural alcohol. Quite intense, rich, and complex for a simple Bourgogne. Good fruit, acidity, and even complexity. Hint of oak and honey on nose.

Boudot said that his 1989 Premier and Grand Crus produced 13.2% to 13.6% natural alcohol. He also said that three-year-old vines had more fresh fruit and delicacy than a six to seven-year-old vine. At around ten years, vines start producing better fruit and complexity.

CHASSAGNE-MONTRACHET "ENSEIGNERS":

Not a Premier Cru. From 50-year-old vines, located just under Bâtard, straddling the corners of Puligny and Chassagne. Better than average Chassagne. Ripe fruit, long, lively, and rich; typical 1989. Medium acidity. Needs six to eight years. Very good. Acidity is four grams; less than ideal (four-and-a-half grams), but still good.

PULIGNY-MONTRACHET "LES MEIX":

A "lieu-dit." From 29-year-old vines, above the village, under Pucelles. More concentrated than the above. More subtle, excellent balance, good acidity. Long, complex, rich. Worth buying.

Gerard makes Puligny from seven different vineyards (lieus-dits), but he blends them all into a single Puligny assemblage.

The 1989s were all a bit cloudy, and had just finished their malo. He was heating the cellar a bit to encourage the malolactic fermentation. (Leflaive, on the other hand, objects to heating cellars, and allows longer malo.)

PULIGNY-MONTRACHET "PERRIÈRES," PREMIER CRU:

From young, seven-year-old vines. The old vines were getting diseased and had to be pulled out. Fruity, fresh, clean. Good length. Lacks a bit in extract. Vines are too young. Good, though.

PULIGNY-MONTRACHET "LES REFERTS," PREMIER CRU:

Located near Meursault, but retains the character of Puligny. Tannic, solid, serious, masculine wine. Quite concentrated. Will age well. Worth buying.

Boudot knows Gerard Jaboulet and he likes the wines of Gerard Chave. He does not like white Hermitage. He never heard of "Côteau de Vernon" of Georges Vernay in Condrieu. I told him to try to get some. He exchanges wines with Moueix, but has never met Christian Moueix. He likes red Bordeaux, and purchased a fair number of 1982s. He likes Pomerols very much (Château Certan-de-May, etc.). He likes Jaboulet's 1961 Hermitage "La Chapelle." Who doesn't?

PULIGNY-MONTRACHET "LES TRUFFIÈRES," PREMIER CRU:

Located between Folatières and Blagny. Only six-and-a-half barrels produced. Lean soil, lots of rocks. Only half the vineyard is planted. The rest has no soil at all, only rocks. The depth of the soil is only 25 cm! A subtle wine. Elegant, youthful, complex, delicate. Opposite in style to the Referts. Classy. Worth buying.

PULIGNY-MONTRACHET "CHAMPS CANET," PREMIER CRU:

Located near Meursault-Perrières. Highest alcohol; 13.5 to 13.6%, natural. Noticeable alcohol, but lots of fruit extract, too. Good acidity. Big and rich, but a bit too spirity for me.

PULIGNY-MONTRACHET "COMBETTES," PREMIER CRU:

Best acidic support of the lot. Just finished malo. Most complex, long, delicate, very good balance and intensity. This will be lovely. Worth buying!

BIENVENUES BÂTARD-MONTRACHET:

Only two-and-a-half barrels produced: 62 cases! He only keeps half of it. And, to make matters worse, the vines are starting to degenerate, and may have to be pulled out soon. Full, rich, long, complex, and fat. Honey, oak, and ripe fruit in harmony. Toast, too. Great stuff!

BÂTARD-MONTRACHET:

Leaner, more masculine, serious. Great depth. Long term. Drink in ten to 15 years. Great extract and depth. A lovely wine.

The total production of Sauzet's is planted on 11.5 hectares. Gerard likes the 1973 whites very much. He said that, oddly, in big years (large quantities), white Burgundies are usually very good. He likes the 1979 whites better than the 1978s. He said that the 1978s are too lean and drying out. He is in a minority there. Maybe some are drying out, but 1978 has been a great year for whites. He likes Château Palmer very much, and knows Yves Chardon well (winemaker at Palmer). Boudot was born in 1950. I told him to try Lafite 1950 or Latour 1950. He has been to California, and likes Paul Draper's (Ridge's) wine very much, both Cabernets and Zinfandels. Boudot is a nice, knowledgeable man.

March 3, 1990

Visit to Domaine Leflaive.

Vincent Leflaive, who is 79, was ill. I was received by his nephew, Olivier Leflaive. Olivier is about 50 years old. He said there was no hope of selling the wines of the domaine in British Columbia, but he is interested in selling wines from his firm, Olivier Leflaive, of which he produces 80 different appellations (about 85% whites, 15% reds). He said that his only "direct" Canadian customer is the Federal Minister of Labour.

He didn't allow any barrel tasting, a policy of their company. They only allow bottle tasting. This philosophy of tasting is the opposite of Sauzet. At Leflaive, they use 20% to 25% new oak barrels on average, 15% for Villages wine, and 40% for Grands Crus. Unit of measurement: one ouvrée produces on average one pièce (barrel) or 25 dozen bottles.

We tasted the following Vincent Leflaive wines from bottle.

PULIGNY-MONTRACHET 1986:

Twelve months in oak. Very good fruit. Rich, full, and long. Lovely complexity. Excellent depth. Mineral bouquet and aftertaste.

PULIGNY-MONTRACHET 1987:

Smaller production than in 1986. More earthy, mineral. Good acidity, backbone. Lively, complex, spicy. Very good balance. A fine effort in a difficult year. (16.5)

Leflaive likes the 1986 better because the wines are fatter, but I think that this particular 1987 is better than the 1986 tasted above.

PULIGNY-MONTRACHET "PUCELLES," PREMIER CRU 1987:

Lean, complex, tight, yet long. Very good body and acidity. Great length. A lovely bottle in five years. (17)

PULIGNY-MONTRACHET "PUCELLES," PREMIER CRU 1986:

Fatter, richer, fuller-bodied. Lots of depth. Medium acidity. Rich and long. Lovely. Better than the 1987. Worth buying. (17.5)

CHEVALIER-MONTRACHET 1987:

Great extract. Superb length. Very intense, big, serious. Gorgeous bottle. Very good acidity. Masculine. Long. One to buy! This must be one of the great successes in 1987. (18)

CHEVALIER-MONTRACHET 1986:

Riper, more intense nose than the 1987. Fatter, fuller. Great fruit extract. 13.4% natural alcohol. Superb length, backbone, and depth. A great bottle. (19)

Leflaive refuses to heat the cellar in order to encourage malolactic fermentation. He lets it take its own course and pace, the opposite of Sauzet.

In June and July following the vintage, they assemble the wine in cuves and leave it alone to rest. They filter lightly before bottling, and because the wine is rested, this filtering is done smoothly, without problems.

Visit to Michel Juillot in Mercurey.

The last call at the end of a successful week in Burgundy turned out to be disappointing. Michel Juillot forgot about my visit, and was away for a few days. His son-in-law (Mr. Laborde) received me, but wasn't much help. Juillot's daughter was rather arrogant and impatient. The place seemed disorganized. However, they produce some of the best white and red Mercureys.

1988 MERCUREY BLANC:

Full, rich, honeyed. Lots of extract, ripe fruit. Very fine. Oak and fruit in harmony. Rich and long. Excellent.

1986 MERCUREY ROUGE "CHAMP MARTIN":

A future Premier Cru. Palish colour. Spicy, sweet, clean Pinot Noir nose. Perfumy, complex, soft, and forward. Evolved. Ready now. Tannic backbone. Good depth. Ripe cherries. Very good! Worth buying.

1987 MERCUREY ROUGE "CLOS TONNERRES":

Brighter, cherry-red colour than the 1986 Champ Martin. Delicate, spicy, sweet nose. Leaner, more serious. Solid. Acidity of the 1987s. Needs two years. Very good structure. Very good.

Then we tasted two wines produced by the son-in-law at the same winery, but with separate vinification and labels

1988 GIVRY "CLOS MARCEAUX" MONOPOLE, LABORDE-JUILLOT:

Only a third is matured in oak, of which 15% is new oak. Bottled after 12 months in wood, same as the Rully. Deep, purple colour. Lovely fruit, extract, and tannins. Very good depth, ripe cherries, and spices. Promising.

1988 RULLY, LABORDE-JUILLOT:

Fairly alcoholic, acidic, lean finish. Paler colour. Aggressive on palate. A bit astringent. Laborde said that Rully usually produces more aggressive reds than Mercurey.

I left for Lyon a bit disappointed. I could have ordered a fair bit of Juillot's wines for the BC liquor monopoly. The previous visit in the fall of 1986 was much better, more educational, and more enjoyable.

Weather

After three waves of cold air and terrible winds in February, everybody was happy that the record heat wave in between storms was over and it was cold again, because they were afraid of early flowering, followed by frost. Growers all hope for cold weather through mid to late March. I wonder how the 1990s vintage will be?

March 4 to 10, 1990

Trip to Bordeaux, after a week in Burgundy.

March 5, 1990

Morning visit to Pichon-Baron and Lynch-Bages.

Jean-Michel Cazes was away in the US, so his assistant Malou Le Sommer was my hostess. She is an engineer in Agronomy, and the wife of Christian Le

Sommer, technical director of Château Latour. (I first met Christian in Los Angeles at the Latour 1847 to 1987 vertical tasting last year.)

Other than Pichon-Baron, the AXA insurance group have also acquired Petit-Villages in Pomerol (from Bruno Prats of Cos d'Estournel), Franc-Mayne in St. Emilion, and Cantenac-Brown in Margaux (through the purchase of a competing insurance company called MIDI).

We toured Pichon-Baron, where extensive work is going on. They hope to be ready for visitors in a year or so. From there we went to Lynch-Bages for a tasting of recent vintages.

1987s

ORMES DE PEZ:

Medium-dark, purplish. Fairly acidic, lean, typical of St. Estèphe and of the vintage. Tannic, solid. Good fruit. Needs three to four years.

HAUT-BAGES-AVÉROUX:

The second wine of Lynch-Bages. Rounder, sweeter, more elegant, and forward.

LES TOURELLES DE LONGUEVILLE:

The second wine of Pichon-Baron, formerly called "Baronet." Medium-red, maturing rim. Good on entry, but lean, hard finish.

CHÂTEAU PIBRAN:

Also owned by AXA. (J.-M. Cazes manages all these properties.) Located near Pontet-Canet and Mouton. Darker than the above. Spicy, concentrated nose. Green, stemmy, yet quite big. Rich finish too. Needs three to four years.

LYNCH-BAGES:

Deep, dark colour. Hard, tannic, big. Bitter tannins at finish. Like a young 1957?

PICHON-BARON:

Deeper, darker still. Very good balance, depth, and rich fruit. Riper tannins. Excellent depth and ripeness for a 1987. Better than Lynch-Bages. First vintage produced by the new team.

1988s, tasted from cask

No Ormes de Pez tasted because only 30% of production is left after the fire they had there.

HAUT-BAGES-AVÉROUX:

Rich on entry, warm, yet simple. Tannic finish. Nice colour, solid, yet short.

LES TOURELLES DE LONGUEVILLE:

Good, purplish colour. Elegant, rich, ripe, good complexity. Easy to drink. Charming. Needs three years.

CHÂTEAU PIBRAN:

Very good, dark colour to rim. Round, rich, ripe, full, spicy. Very nice nevertheless.

LYNCH-BAGES:

Very good, dark, purplish colour to rim. Ripe, concentrated, rich, yet round. Ripe tannins, like 1982, but less concentrated or fat. Very good.

PICHON-BARON:

Dark, harder, tannic, very concentrated. Lots of ripe fruit. Powerful. A rich, serious Pauillac. More class and depth than Lynch-Bages.

Lunch at "Le Relais de Margaux," with Malou Le Sommer.

This restaurant is now owned by the Japanese. I noticed that Malou liked Burgundies, so I ordered a bottle of white Burgundy.

PULIGNY-MONTRACHET PREMIER CRU "FOLATIÈRES" 1986, JADOT:

Big, rich, creamy, concentrated. Lots of depth, weight, ripe Chardonnay, and oak. Needs two years, but really very good!

After lunch, we went to visit Château Cantenac-Brown, one of AXA's newest acquisitions.

Lots of improvements and modernization there. This château should produce better wine now. 65% Cabernet Sauvignon, 25% Merlot, and 10% Cabernet Franc in the blend. They use 65% to 70% new oak; too much, in my opinion. 1988 was their first vintage. Expensive barrels; not the bulky "transport" type with all metal rims and 27 mm thickness of wood, but the fancier barrels with round edges, thinner oak, 21 mm thickness, allowing more contact between air and wine, and more oak influence, quicker maturation, and a shorter period in wood, only 14 months.

1988 CHÂTEAU LE CANUET:

Cru Bourgeois, 10 hectares, the second wine of Cantenac-Brown. Bright purple. Elegant, Margaux nose. Round, delicate, complex, but a bit lean and acidic. Made from a separate parcel and young vines.

1988 CHÂTEAU CANTENAC-BROWN:

Much improved from previous vintages. Very good, deep colour. Fairly lean, acidic, tannic, nice oak and fruit. A bit too oaky finish. I told the winemaker to reduce the amount of new oak. Will be bottled shortly.

I also found out that General de Lencquesaing (of Pichon-Lalande), age 69, is seriously ill with cancer of the pancreas. Also, the son of Anthony Barton of Leoville-Barton, Thomas, was killed last month in a car accident, at age 31. What a tragedy!

Afternoon visit to Chasse-Spleen, with Bernadette Villars.

Tasted the following from cask.

1988 L'Hermitage de Chasse-Spleen:

Their second wine. Medium-dark purple. Clean, spicy, vanilla, oak, complex nose. Delicate, sweet fruit. (Bernadette wants to imitate "Coste Borie," the second wine of Ducru, rather than "Clos du Marquis," the second wine of Lascases, which she thinks is too good for its class and too expensive.) She added less of Chasse-Spleen into this, as since 1983, no lees are added to Chasse-Spleen. But no press wine is added, (part of which goes into Chasse-Spleen).

1988 Chasse-Spleen:

Very good, dark colour. Riper fruit, intense, solid, tannic, and serious. Powerful wine, lots of depth. Needs seven to eight years, or more.

They use sterile equipment when they pump their wine, reducing the need for sulphuring.

1989 Haut-Bages-Libéral:

Malolactic fermentation ended in November; very early! Bernadette noticed that the yeast in the skins induces malo fermentation. Very nice, purple colour. Tannic, powerful, lots of masculine Pauillac power.

She likes the 1986s better than the 1985s, and the 1989s more than the 1988s. She likes bigger, more tannic wines. Bernadette said that 1989 was classic in Pauillac, but more variable in Margaux and St. Emilion, where the tannins are not backed by enough fruit, as a rule. (There are exceptions.)

They started picking the Merlot at Chasse-Spleen (in 1989) on September 3, with 80% of the Merlot picked by September 6! Early picking was important. At Haut-Bages-Libéral, they started the harvest on September 11. The 1989 was a great year for Petit Verdot, of which they have 10% (eight hectares) at Chasse-Spleen. Any vine that produces over 60 hectolitres per hectare is automatically put into the second wine.

Postscript

This was the last time I saw Bernadette. In early 1992, she was killed, together with her husband, during a hike in the Pyrenées. A sad and tragic loss!

March 6, 1990

All day in Pomerol and St. Emilion.

A very busy day! In the morning, I met Alexandre Thienpont at Vieux Château Certan. He is a dedicated, serious young man who has really improved the property since his uncle, Leon Thienpont, died. Alexandre "does his own thing" rather than following other people's opinions. They use about two-thirds new oak barrels annually. The second wine is called "La Gravette de Certan."

1989s: (from cask)

I tasted individual grape varietals, and different lots of the same varietal.

Merlot:

From 30-year-old vines. Dark, rich, sweet, straightforward Merlot. Lots of ripe fruit. 13.8% natural sugar! No chaptalization at all in 1989. Sweet and fat.

Merlot:

From vines planted in 1952, on a gravely, lighter soil. More serious, masculine, leaner. Very good fruit. Harder, more aggressive tannins.

Merlot:

From vines planted in 1932. Very ripe, yet subdued nose. Richer, sweeter, more concentrated. Very long, best complexity.

They produced a total of 34 barrels of each of the three Merlots in 1989, representing about 50% of the wine. Cabernet Franc represents 25% of the wine, and Cabernet Sauvignon 20%. The remainder is made up of Malbec and press wine.

Cabernet Franc:

Vines planted in 1958. Spicier nose, lovely colour. Stemmy, typical of this varietal, very good fruit. 12.5% natural alcohol. Complex.

Cabernet Franc:

Second barrel. Deeper, darker, more tannic. Just finished the sulphite treatment. Lots of body, fairly acidic, leaner. Will complement the fat, rich Merlots well.

Cabernet Sauvignon:

Only one lot produced. Ripe nose, sweet, solid. Vanilla and oak. Most serious. Very good.

1988s:

All the 1988 was in steel tanks after assemblage and before bottling. (Soustiré in May or June.) Superb nose of elegant, complex wine. Classy. The "Margaux" of Pomerol. Finesse, class. True Vieux Château Certan style. Very fine.

Overall impressions

The 1988 will be leaner, more classic than the 1989. The 1988 tastes like the 1983, and the 1989 resembles the 1982, but with less extract, although local people compare the 1989 Pomerols to 1947, as they did in 1982.

Visit to Château Canon, in St. Emilion, tasting and lunch.

The tasting was with the very experienced and knowledgeable Mr. Cazenave, Maître de Chais.

Canon is made up roughly of 55% Merlot, and 45% Cabernet Franc. The 1986 is made up of 50% Merlot and 50% Cabernet Franc, no Cabernet Sauvignon. Cazenave said that it is too hot in their vineyard to produce balanced Cabernet Sauvignon. The main vineyard of Canon is indeed called "Trop Chaud" (too hot!). Cazenave also said that many St. Emilion growers plant their Cabernet Sauvignon and Cabernet Franc too low, with Merlot higher (where it is warmer). Therefore, often the Cabernet Sauvignon and Cabernet Franc don't mature properly. Cabernet Sauvignon needs better, warmer exposure. Cazenave is experimenting with both Merlot and Cabernet Sauvignon planted in the lower parts of the vineyard. The Merlot was always riper, the Cabernet Sauvignon greener.

At Canon, they use 50% to 60% new oak casks yearly, 70% in very great years. 1989 was an early vintage. Cazenave agreed with me that in light years like 1987, First Growth shouldn't automatically use 100% new oak. The 1989 has a bit higher pH than usual, and it needs more oak to give the wine more backbone and tannins because the wine is a bit too soft. He said that 1989 is certainly not "the vintage of the century." Very good, yes; but "great," no. He said that journalists are too sensational.

1988:

Will be bottled in July. No filtering. Excellent depth and balance. Complex, virile wine. Rich, long. Very good, deep colour. Lots of class, too. Good representation of soil. Complex, Quinquina nose (wine with touch of orange peel). Ripe prunes on nose, too.

1987:

Lighter, leaner, spicier, greener. Typical 1987. Not great, but not bad at all. Spicy Cabernet Franc on both nose and palate. Less mature Merlot. Fair acidity. Clean fruit.

Cazenave agreed with me that the 1960 Canon was underrated, and said that Woltner of La Mission Haut-Brion bought everything Canon had produced that year that was available.

Comparing 1989 to 1982

His opinion is that the 1989 was too ripe, too soft, with low tannins and acidity. Cazenave said that they could have actually picked the Merlot in late August! They didn't because acidity and tannins were still too low, so they waited. Some 1989s will also be lighter in colour. There was overproduction and shorter fermentation because things happened too fast and producers needed the vats for grapes that were coming in, one load after another.

Later, Eric Fournier and I had a quiet lunch at the château.

We talked a lot about estate taxes, and the new, silly American health regulations about sulphites, "the danger of wine," etc. We had two reds and a white through lunch.

CHÂTEAU BROUSTET 1982:

Their Barsac. Clean, delicate, good acidity, typical Barsac. Not too much botrytis or honey, therefore easy to taste with salmon.

1979 CHÂTEAU CANON:

Like most 1979s, not quite ready, but getting there. Very good colour, ripe fruit on nose and palate, rich tannins, lots of life and depth. It seems that often the 1979s are gaining on the 1978s. Very good wine.

1970 CHÂTEAU CANON:

This should have been served before the 1979. (Eric agreed.) Much softer, chocolate and tobacco, delicate, long but lacks fat. Past its peak and needs drinking.

A very enjoyable visit, and Eric said he'd try to visit Vancouver for the Commanderie's convention in May 1991.

Afternoon visit with Pascal Delbeck, at Ausone and Belair.

Ausone: (100% new oak barrels)

1989 FIRST BARREL:

Fat, rich, concentrated, like the 1982. Long, complex, beautiful balance. Unusually rich for Ausone.

1989 SECOND BARREL:

More masculine, powerful, harder. More typical Ausone, but backed by ripe tannins and good acidity.

1989 THIRD BARREL:

Will not go into the Grand Vin. Leaner, harder, more vegetal, lacking volume. Higher acidity, yet classy.

1989 FOURTH BARREL:

Hard, aggressive tannins. Serious, solid, more noticeable oak and tannins.

1989 FIFTH BARREL:

This one made of oak from Charente. Cashew, licorice, spices. Too oaky, bitter tannins. Oak too predominant. Pascal doesn't like this, nor do I.

All of the above were tasted before the assemblage.

1988:

The final blend. Just finished egg-white collage yesterday! Powerful, classic Ausone. Great depth, ripe fruit, masculine, yet ripe tannins. Will be very good in 15 years.

Comments on the 1989 vintage

Grapes that were picked too late missed out. This is why Pascal was upset over the other half-owner's

(Mme. Dubois-Chalon's nephew, Mr. Vauthier) decision to delay picking. Pascal thinks that this was a big mistake. He left a little of the "late-picked" wine for comparison. It is fat, ripe, pruny, flabby. He said he feels like a doctor who knows his patient (the vines), and he tried to pick the grapes as early as he could. It is becoming obvious to me that there are problems at Ausone between the owners. This is too bad.

From there we went to Belair, where they are modernizing the extensive underground cellars and mechanizing the chais. It will be something fantastic when it is finished.

It seems to me that since the ownership problems at Ausone, Pascal and Mme. Dubois-Chalon, who owns Belair outright, are putting more money and effort into that property. The new underground tunnels will go right through to the centre of St. Emilion, with an opening (access) there!

1988 BELAIR:

Aged in one-third new oak. Made from 70% Merlot and 30% Cabernet Franc. Long, delicate, complex. Has stuffing. Clean, long, spicy finish. Needs 12 years. Oak blends nicely.

Then we had a fascinating experiment. We tasted Belair 1988 and 1989 from sample barrels made in the same method of vinification as in 1830. Pascal found documents of that period at Belair. They made the wine the following way.

1. No new oak.
2. Only five days of maceration.
3. Wine was put in oak at the end of the fermentation.
4. Only one "soustirage" (racking) before bottling.
5. Very long malolactic (cold) fermentation!

1989 (1830 METHOD):

Less wood on nose and palate. Fruitier, fresher; straightforward, honest fruit. Very Burgundy-like. Lighter colour.

1988 (1830 METHOD):

Finished fermentation in barrel; very long, at cool temperature. Fresh fruit, spicy, hint of barnyard. Could easily be mistaken for a Pinot Noir. Maybe this is why old-timers compared St. Emilions to Burgundy?

Fascinating experiment.

Then we tasted the modern version, from various casks.

1989 BELAIR:

Before assemblage. Pure Cabernet Franc barrel. Leaner, typical varietal. Herbaceous, hard, tannic. Lots of extract, but bitter finish.

1989 BELAIR:

Before assemblage. Pure Merlot barrel. Softer, darker, sweeter, round, elegant, some fat.

1989 BELAIR:

I made my own blend in the glass; 70% Merlot and 30% Cabernet Franc, approximately. Beautiful. Rich, complex, long, oak, vanilla. Warm and smooth. Needs ten years.

1989 BELAIR:

Final blend. Has only been in oak for five days, so little oak character yet. Breed, backbone, depth, and ripe fruit. Will be very good in 12 years.

Pascal gave me a bottle of Ausone 1976, his first vintage, to take home.

About Parker

Pascal said that Parker is often given a very "special" barrel to taste, and the owner "prepares" that special barrel in the style that Parker likes. Parker has "spies" locally, who taste and send him their comments, which he prints as if he had tasted them himself. This is not very honest. Parker is having a real (not always positive) influence on the French wine scene. They seem to fear him in Bordeaux. He's really made a success of himself. Nothing wrong there as long as he is honest. I do not know how trustworthy these rumours are. I hope, however, that they are only rumours, and not facts.

Later that afternoon, I visited Ets. J.-P. Moueix, in Libourne, with their gifted winemaker, Jean-Claude Berrouet, and the young winemaker of Dominus (Napanook), Chris Phelps. We tasted a whole range of 1989s. After a long tasting, we all joined Christian Moueix for dinner. He was busy all afternoon with a council of vignerons (a hearing) because they object to his buying out so many properties. He is trying to acquire a property in Lussac or Montagne St. Emilion, but he's getting fed up with their attitude. The four of us had a very interesting and most enjoyable dinner at Christian's house. His wife, Marie-Laure, and the children were in Bordeaux for the night.

Tasting barrel samples of 1989s, in the tasting lab: (Of which I ordered several lots of five, ten, and 25 cases for the BC liquor monopoly). I also told Christian that he should find himself a good agent in Vancouver.

1. CHÂTEAU DE LA DAUPHINE, FRONSAC:

Medium-dark. Ripe, baked nose. Sweet, rich, ripe. Like pure Merlot. Alcoholic. Low acidity. Concentrated. Low tannins. Needs three years.

2. CHÂTEAU MAZERIS, CANON-FRONSAC:

Deeper than the above. More perfumy, even riper nose. More tannic. Bigger, richer, powerful. Little oak. Concentrated. Needs five years. Low acidity. Solid.

3. Château Canon de Brem, Canon-Fronsac:

Similar to the above, deeper rim. More complex nose, some oak and vanilla. Solid, tannic, concentrated fruit. Very good depth and ripeness. Needs six years.

4. Château St. André Corbin, St. Georges-St. Emilion:

Colour like #1. Spicy, herbal Cabernet Franc. Leaner St. Emilion style, yet sweet, clean, quite tannic. Good fruit/acidity balance.

5. Château Puy-Blanquet, St. Emilion Grand Cru:

Deeper, purple colour. Lovely toast, oak, ripe berries on nose. Tannic, solid, big, rich. Medium acidity. Sweet, ripe finish.

6. Château Fonroque, St. Emilion Grand Cru Classé:

Very good colour, purple to rim. Spicy, stemmy, oak nose. More masculine than Puy-Blanquet; more solid, more aggressive tannins. Very good fruit. Needs seven to eight years.

7. Château Magdelaine, Premier Grand Cru Classé, St. Emilion:

Impressive, deep colour to rim. Lovely, complex, elegant, rich nose of ripe fruit. Subdued oak. Beautiful balance, depth, length, complexity. Very ripe tannins. Medium acidity. This wine is unusual in that it is made almost exclusively of Merlot. This is unusual for a St. Emilion, but then Merlot is what the firm of Moueix knows best. Who can argue with that?

8. Château Siaurauc, Lalande de Pomerol:

Sweet, Merlot nose. Straightforward, sweet, ripe, rich. Ripe tannins. Good acidity.

9. Château Plince, Pomerol:

Medium colour, purple rim. Sweet on entry, yet tannic. Solid. Needs time. Little oak yet. Not fat; leaner style. A bit diluted.

10. Château Lafleur-Gazin, Pomerol:

Very good, deep, purple colour. Ripe, herbaceous nose. Cabernet Franc predominates. Good backbone. Rich, solid. Pruny aftertaste. Later: good, big, complex finish.

11. Château Bourgneuf, Pomerol:

Deep, purple, dense colour. Complex, long, elegant nose; oak, vanilla, spices. Solid, tannic. Excellent ripe fruit; long finish. This is going to be very good.

12. Château La Fleur-Petrus, Pomerol:

Even darker than #11. Fabulous nose; extract, oak, spices. Hint of Cabernet Franc. Rich, ripe, very long. Ripe tannins. Medium acidity. Needs ten to 12 years.

13. Château Trotanoy, Pomerol:

Slightly deeper than #12. Perfumy. Lovely on nose and entry, but very hard, ripe, tannic finish. Needs at least 12 years. Lots of depth and extract here. Masculine. Austere, classic structure. Best Trotanoy since 1982.

14. Château Petrus, Pomerol:

Darkest, deepest, inky colour. Great, intense, rich nose. Concentrated, sweet, ripe fruit. Fabulous depth, power, and oak. Great wine. Lots of depth and extract. A superb wine. Very concentrated! Must buy!

Later, with dinner, we tasted the following.

Champagne Bollinger "Grande Année" 1983:

A bit earthy, leaner. Good character, body, and depth, but without the ripe fruit of the 1982. (17)

All the other wines were served double-blind, and I guessed them all! Berrouet was impressed, and he and Christian commented that very few people are as dedicated and knowledgeable as I am in the field of wine. Nice words from the experts!

1983 Bâtard-Montrachet, Domaine Henri Clerc:

Bright, deep gold. Incredible intensity on nose of ripe fruit, honey, toast, oak, all in harmony. Great length, balance, and acidity on palate. Superb, long finish. I am not a fan of the 1983s (too alcoholic), but this was superb. The best 1983 white Burgundy I've tasted to date, by far! (19)

1975 Château Trotanoy and Château 1975 Cheval-Blanc:

I guessed the vintage, I guessed the Trotanoy, and I said that the other must be Cheval-Blanc!

Trotanoy:

Very good, dark colour. Spicy, iron, complex, mature, old wood, old-style nose. Full, round tannins, approaching its peak. Great classic fruit extract, yet earthy, "old style" wine. Excellent. (18)

Cheval-Blanc:

Even darker, deeper. Spicy Cabernet Franc nose, yet sweet Merlot, too. Very good structure and backbone. Sturdier than the Trotanoy; bigger, more solid. (18) Both are excellent wines.

Berrouet said that 1975s, which he likes and thinks will become classics, had high acidity. He said that Ducasse at l'Evangile acidified his 1975, and damaged it! I disagree with Berrouet's comments on the 1975 l'Evangile, which I think is an excellent wine. Berrouet said that in 1975, there were already modern vinification methods, but the grapes themselves were "old style," very small grapes, very thick skins, like in 1945, and that accounts for the similarity of the two vintages, in terms of structure.

He and Christian don't like the Pomerols and St. Emilions in 1978, because Merlot suffered from rain, obviously.

They didn't know about Delbeck's experimentation with 1830s methods at Belair.

We discussed Harry Waugh and their participation in an event for him, to be organized in London shortly. We decided to start a tiny club (eight people) who would meet once a year (in London?) to taste "great wines through the night!"

Christian thinks that Hardy Rodenstock is a mystery, and doesn't know where that man is coming from. About Parker, I heard the usual comment; they worry about the man having too much power and too individual a taste. A most enjoyable evening and a long day.

March 7, 1990

I visited Château Margaux, with the régisseur, Mr. Paul Pontallier.

Pavillon Rouge sees 50% new oak. The 1988 vintage will be bottled in November. In 1988, 40% of the production went into the second wine.

1988 CHÂTEAU MARGAUX:

Very good, purplish colour to rim. Superb nose, complex, round. Oak, vanilla, spicy fruit in harmony. Excellent balance, ripe tannins. Aggressive, classic wine. Not as powerful as 1986. Harder than the 1983. More masculine than 1985, by far.

Noon visit to Château Pichon-Lalande.

May de Lencquesaing is with her husband in Paris. He is dying of cancer. I was received by the régisseur, Mr. Godin, whom I've met before.

We tasted the following vintages of Château Pichon-Lalande.

1987:

Medium-dark, nice colour. Spicy, stemmy, noticeable oak on nose. Elegant, subtle. Good tannins. Lacking depth of a good year, but classy, complex finish nevertheless. Drink now to 1993. (15.5)

1988:

Excellent, deep colour. Delicate, complex, typical Pichon-Lalande nose. Very good, ripe tannins and concentration. Lovely. Still undergoing egg-white collage. Classic style; aggressive, but not massive tannins. Reminds me of the 1983 in its youth, but maybe without that extra depth that the great 1983 has.

We talked a lot about 1975 and the mistake many people are making by underrating that vintage. He said the 1975 Pichon-Lalande is beautiful now.

Mr. Godin said that the 1989 is very good, but not as good as 1982. Those who waited and picked late produced another 1976! (in 1989).

1985:

Lively, ripe fruit. Very dark. The elegance of the vintage, and of Pichon-Lalande. Lovely length and concentration. Needs eight to ten years. Parker didn't review this 1985 well, and said that it was too herbaceous, but upon visiting Pichon-Lalande and tasting it again, he changed his mind. Godin, like many others, is afraid of Parker.

At Pichon Lalande, they seem to have a close relationship with Newton Wines in California, as does Christian Moueix. Godin produced four experimental barrels of pure Petit Verdot in 1989, two in new barrels and two in second year barrels. They have a total of 10% Petit Verdot planted, and a warm, long summer like 1989 can do fantastic things to that grape varietal.

1989 PURE PETIT VERDOT:

Unbelievably deep, inky colour. Dense, ripe, rich, powerful, fat, and concentrated. Perfect balance. A beauty by itself, without blending. After Mrs. Newton, I am apparently the first person in the world to taste this special experimental wine. This must surely be the greatest Petit Verdot that I have ever tasted. In Bordeaux, they are now realizing that it has been a mistake to uproot the Petit Verdot. Many owners are now replanting this varietal, which in late, warm summers, produces inky ripe juice.

Lunch and meeting with Roger Lemelletier, of the Grand Conseil de Bordeaux.

We discussed business and future events of our Commanderie de Bordeaux in Vancouver. This is now my third year as Maître. How time flies!

With lunch, we had a nice bottle.

1984 CHÂTEAU SOCIANDO-MALLET:

Medium colour. Spicy, oaky, fine fruit, good tannic structure. Most enjoyable. A successful 1984. Drink now to 1994. Spicy Cabernet; round, yet solid. This is a serious property.

March 8, 1990

Visit and lunch at Château Mouton-Rothschild.

1989s, tasted from barrel

CHÂTEAU MOUTON-BARONNE-PHILIPPE:

Surprisingly light for a 1989. Feminine. Medium-dark, purplish. Clean, spicy, herbaceous nose. Leaner, like a 1988. A bit short. Quite good. May develop more depth, colour, and body with an extra year of barrel-ageing.

Château Clerc-Milon:

Darker, deeper, tannic. True Pauillac. More concentration, masculine. Very good depth and personality. Promising.

Château Mouton-Rothschild:

Deep, dark colour, yet not as dark as the 1982 or the 1986 when tasted from cask. Closed nose. Tight, masculine. Not as ripe as expected. Surprisingly hard. Should improve in oak, hopefully. After all, this wine will spend the next 18 months in oak, so it is really difficult to judge.

1988s, also from cask

The 1988s have just finished the collage, and will be bottled later this year.

Château Mouton-Baronne-Philippe:

Very nice oak, vanilla, clean nose. Medium depth. Elegant, spicy. Trace of acidity at finish. Early maturing. Complex.

Château Clerc-Milon:

Ripe, closed nose. Serious, tannic, rich, big, and powerful. Lots of depth. Potentially very fine.

Château Mouton-Rothschild:

Typical nose. Lovely tobacco, cedar nose. Rich, tannic, classic, complex. Like the 1983, but better. Lots of class here. Excellent and serious. Needs 12 to 15 years. Not as hard as the 1986 or as elegant as the 1985. Less colour than the 1985. Lovely, spicy, cedary nose. Special.

With lunch

Mouton-Cadet White:

Ordinary.

Château Mouton-Baronne-Philippe 1981:

Typical 1981. Elegant, delicate, good fruit. Clean. Ready.

Château Mouton-Rothschild 1971:

Over-the-hill. Dirty nose of old barrels. Leathery, harsh, lean. I have never really cared much for Mouton 1971.

Comments

The food they served for lunch was much better than the wines. Mouton could have done better with the wines. On the way out, I saw Raoul Blondin, the old cellarmaster. He is retired now, about 85, and looking very old. He did remember me, though, from previous visits.

Visit to Château Branaire-Ducru in St. Julien.

This is my first visit to this property. New owners since 1988; the Tapie-Tari Group, have sold out to a sugar company and to a few other owners, including a gentleman named Mr. Soulasse.

In 1988, they used two-thirds new oak barrels; 75 to 80% Cabernets, mostly Cabernet Sauvignon, and 15% Merlot (very old vines). They are starting to replant Petit Verdot. In 1989, they used 50% new oak. They started picking the 1989 on August 31! In 1988, they started to pick on October 1, which is normal. In 1991, they will have a nice chais and modern installations. Two-thirds of the 1989 harvest will be Branaire. The rest will go into the second wine, Château Duluc. The 1988 will be bottled in May.

1988:

From new oak barrel. Elegant, classy, delicate. Well balanced. Press wine will be added later to give more structure.

1989:

The 1989 has already been assembled.

First barrel "Taransaud":

Made by a company that also supplies barrels to Cognac Moët-Hennessy. Made from Tronçais oak. Sweet, ripe nose. Elegant oak. Sweet, soft wine.

Second barrel "Lasserre":

More tannic, more aggressive. More powerful. Lots of depth. Masculine.

The barrels are the "transport" style, yet not thick (27 mm), but thinner (22 mm), allowing for more interaction between air and wine.

Barrel of Pure Merlot 1989:

Picked August 31, at 13.8% natural alcohol! Fairly high tannins. Lovely, complex, sweet Merlot. Very ripe, rich, well balanced. Classic. Like a fine Pomerol!

March 9, 1990

The last day of a long, interesting, and educational trip to Burgundy and Bordeaux.

Morning visit to Château Pape Clément (Graves) in Pessac Léognan.

My guide was the Maître de Chais. They have 30 hectares under vine: 40% Merlot and 60% Cabernet Sauvignon. The 1988 will be bottled in April and May. They used 80% new oak that year. They produce 10,000 to 12,000 cases yearly.

1989, from cask:

Very good, dark colour. Rich, ripe, powerful. Big, yet ripe and no hard tannins. Very good depth. Lovely length. Will be very good.

1988, from cask:

More classic than the 1989, less fat, more aggressive tannins. Complex, spicy, oak, vanilla, nice fruit. Well balanced. Will be very good. Definitely one to buy.

Since 1986, this property has been producing excellent wines. Nice to see them making a come-back.

Visit and lunch at Château Latour.

My last visit before leaving Bordeaux. With John Kolasa, and Christian Le Sommer, the technical director since 1987.

John and Christian agreed with me that 1989, while very good and ripe, is not a sensational vintage, not a "vintage of the century," and that overall, 1988 is more classic and traditional. There are some excellent 1989s, but some disappointing wines that are stretched (overproduction) and too soft. By the way, rumours have it that both Pichon-Baron and Haut-Brion have produced a great 1989. Two properties to watch closely that year.

First, we had a small tasting.

LES-FORTS-DE-LATOUR 1982:

Evolved, complex colour. Deep, ripe, mature nose. Solid tannins. Complex, spicy, tobacco and ripe fruit. Soft, ripe on entry, but powerful, tannic finish. Very good. Drink from 1993 to 2002.

CHÂTEAU LATOUR 1988:

Deep, dark colour to rim; one of the darkest 1988s I've tasted. Hasn't been cleared with egg-white yet. Concentrated, ripe tannins. As classic as the 1986, if not better. This is excellent.

CHÂTEAU LATOUR 1987:

Too much oak. Medium-red colour. Sweet, pruny nose. Leaner on palate, as expected. Fairly hard. After swallowing or spitting, too much obvious oak on palate. I still think that Latour, and other First Growths, shouldn't have used 100% new oak for a light vintage such as 1987.

We then went to the main building, the château, with Canada's flag raised in my honour, for a luncheon.

With lunch

1986 CUVÉE DE LA COMMANDERIE DU BONTEMPS, BLANC:

Ripe, some oak, good fruit. Not much complexity, but good depth and balance.

1975 LES-FORTS-DE-LATOUR:

Typical 1975; tannic, masculine, old-style nose of earth, wood, and ripe fruit. Has backbone and depth. Ready, but no rush. A serious wine.

1966 CHÂTEAU LATOUR:

Certainly one of the most successful 1966s. Deep, impressive colour. Cedary, oaky, ripe, classic, mature Cabernet nose. Full, serious; tannins and fruit in harmony. A classic wine. Getting ready, but no rush.

Latour will also try to participate in the May 1991 convention that I am trying to organize in Vancouver for the Commanderie de Bordeaux.

It seems that in Bordeaux, Robert Parker is much more feared than in Burgundy. I wouldn't be surprised if, one of these days, some of the leading Burgundy producers refuse to allow Parker to taste their wines from cask. Several producers are really annoyed with him.

March 21, 1990

Commanderie de Bordeaux tasting and dinner, at the Hotel Vancouver, featuring a vertical tasting of two decades of Château La Lagune, 1966 to 1986.

It was important for me to organize this tasting because I believe that this property has been very loyal to the consumer. Never achieving spectacular heights, but always producing very well-made, reliable wines that are reasonably priced.

CHAMPAGNE KRUG "GRANDE CUVÉE" BRUT N/V:

Masculine, steely. Complex and long. Not quite ready, but impeccably made. Very good future. Tiny bubbles, yeasty, complex, and well balanced. Serious Champagne from a lot purchased last year.

Château La Lagune

FLIGHT #1

1986:

Deep colour to rim. Tight on nose. Powerful, solid, hard, concentrated, serious. New oak. Clean, long finish. Complex. Excellent extract. Drink from 1996 to 2002. (17.5)

1985:

Similar appearance to the 1986, if a bit darker. Herbaceous nose. More elegant. Also new oak. Buttery, complex, long, well balanced. More delicate than the 1986, yet very good depth. Almost too much new singed-oak for its own good. Try around 1994 to 1997. (16)

1983:

More evolved colour. Closed nose. Spicy, earthy Cabernet. Solid. Tannic, yet backed by good fruit. Serious. Hard. Needs ten years. (17)

1982:

Very good, deep colour. Darkest of flight. Powerful, rich, ripe, complex. Lots of depth and class. Tight, hard, unyielding. Closed up. Needs ten years. This wine is closed tight. Going through a phase, as most fine Clarets do. (18)

FLIGHT #2

1981:

Medium-dark colour; good depth. Delicate, toasty nose; with some earth and spiciness. Complex, delicate, long, well balanced. Evolved. Almost ready. (16.5)

1978, in magnum:

Very good, deep colour to rim. Hard, solid, tannic, yet ripe fruit is there. Slightly musty on entry, but good clean finish. Earthy, Graves-like. Very good. Surprisingly tight, maybe because it is from a magnum. (17)

1975:

Cedary, complex nose; a bit earthy. Full, round, well balanced, long. Tobacco, good fruit. Fine quality. Some hard tannins at finish. Needs two to four years. Surprisingly good. Some 1975s are coming around. (17)

FLIGHT #3

1970:

Very good, deep colour. Sweet, rich, long. Very good fruit. Complex. Still youthful. This wine has improved a lot over the past few years. No rush. Lovely depth and rich fruit. Getting better and better. (17.5)

1966:

Good, dark colour; orangy rim. Mature. Herbs and chocolate on nose. Full, rich, round, long, old style, slightly leathery, but lovely length and depth. Well balanced. A favourite of mine. (18)

April 1990

A comparative tasting of Robert Mondavi reds and red Bordeaux, at the Four Seasons hotel, with Jay Hollowell of the Robert Mondavi Winery.

The wines were opened for one-and-a-half hours. All wines served blind.

1. Château Latour 1985:

Medium red, good depth. Toasty, straw, herbal nose. Elegant, green, Margaux elegance. Acidity of the 1987s. Toast, oak, good length. I was surprised to find out that it was Latour 1985! (16.5) Way too soft for Latour. What has happened here?!

2. Robert Mondavi Cabernet Sauvignon 1985 "Reserve":

Medium-dark, youthful, purplish colour. Fresher than #1. Spicy, clean Cabernet nose. Full, fruity, minty, spicy. Lots of length, oak. Very California. Classy. (17.5)

3. Robert Mondavi Cabernet Sauvignon 1986 "Reserve":

Purplish, deep colour. Ripe, rich, rubbery nose. Lots of ripe fruit. Clean, long, quite rich. Some eucalyptus. Harder, bigger than the 1985. More Cabernet. Made from 94.5% Cabernet Sauvignon, 5% Cabernet Franc, and only 0.5% Merlot. No wonder it is such a hard wine. (17)

4. Château Lafite 1986:

Impressive dark colour to rim. Subdued, new oak, vanilla, ripe and elegant nose. Hard, full, masculine for Lafite; typical of the vintage. Serious Pauillac. Great potential. Try around the year 2000. (18.5)

5. Robert Mondavi Cabernet Sauvignon 1987 "Reserve":

Impressive deep colour to rim, same as the 1986 Lafite. Fruity, clean nose. Mint, eucalyptus, exotic spices. Quite similar to the 1985, but, of course, less evolved. Made from 87% Cabernet Sauvignon, 8% Cabernet Franc, and 5% Merlot. Will be a very fine wine in seven to ten years. (17.5)

6. Château Margaux 1987:

As expected in a lighter vintage, more evolved colour than most, yet severe, tight, closed nose. Herbaceous, lighter, leaner on palate. Quite elegant and stylish. (16.5)

7. Robert Mondavi Cabernet Sauvignon 1989 "Reserve":

Barrel sample. Very purplish, young colour. Very fresh, ripe fruit. Soft, elegant, long, complex. Touch of oak. Lots of class. Complex, delicate, feminine. (no score)

May 1990

Trip to Prague, Budapest, and Tokay.

Tokaji: Vinum Regum, Rex Vinorum.

During a trip to Czechoslovakia and Hungary in May of this year, I had the opportunity to visit two of the leading wine-producing cooperatives in the famous Tokay region of Hungary. This region has always fascinated me. I like the wines and have had the good fortune to taste rare gems from Tokay, including several vintages from the 19th century and a superb and extremely rare Tokay Essencia 1735 in San Francisco in 1985. A 250-year-old wine, the oldest wine I have ever tasted.

In recent years, cooperatives and large wineries have been able to export wines on their own and are no longer dependent solely on "Monimpex," the export monopoly. Between 1945 and 1983, the Tokay vintages are generally categorized as follows in terms of quality.

VERY GOOD OR GREAT

1983, 1975, 1972 (vintage of the century, according to a leading winemaker in the area), 1968, 1964, 1963, 1959, 1957, 1956, 1952, 1950, 1949, and 1947.

GOOD

1982, 1981, 1979, 1976, 1973, 1971, 1969, 1966, 1962, 1961, 1958, 1955, 1953, 1948, and 1946.

My first of two extensive visits was in the cellars of the large co-op "Hungarovin," with their chief oenologist,

Mr. Daniel Szabo. 1964 was his first year with them, and the last year in which they crushed the grapes with their feet. From 1965, grapes have been crushed mechanically. According to Mr. Szabo, 1988 was a very good year for botrytized grapes, while 1989 had a higher sugar concentration in the grapes, but less botrytis. They filter their wine with gelatine and, if grapes contain too much iron or copper, an extraction process known as "blue process" is introduced to get rid of these chemicals.

At Hungarovin, they do not produce 6 Puttonyos, but rather a richer, sweeter, and more intense 5 Puttonyos and, if a truly great year is produced, they make Aszú Essencia. Other than their own vineyards, they buy grapes from various growers within the co-op. If, however, an individual grower/producer has produced particularly fine must or juice, they will actually purchase the end product (wine) and add it to their various blends.

The wines tasted at Hungarovin were as follows.

1989 FURMINT:

(13.1 alcohol, 1.1 grams sugar after fermentation, and 7.8% acidity per litre) Pale gold. Fresh, spicy nose. Noticeable acidity. Fermentation lasted six months. Hint of residual sugar, not unlike a delicate Barsac. This wine will spend at least three years in barrel before bottling.

1988 FURMINT:

(13.1 alcohol, 4 grams residual sugar, 7.2% acidity) Starting to oxidize—as it should, to make Tokay. Fatter, richer wine. Clean, quite acidic and lively, good depth. This wine fermented for three-and-a-half years.

The above Furmints are the base wine to make Szamorodny or Aszú.

1986 DRY SZAMORODNY:

(13.9° alcohol, 1 gram residual sugar, 7.4% acidity) Dry Sherry on nose. Fullish, well balanced, hint of oak. Quite dry on palate with a rich, complex, nutty finish. It is still in cask.

1983 DRY SZAMORODNY:

(14.2° alcohol, 1 gram residual sugar, 7.2% acidity) Already in bottle. Spicy, aromatic, dry, fairly acidic. Leaner than the 1986 and more refined at this stage. Quite good.

1989 MUSCAT LUNEL:

(12.6° alcohol, 6.8% acidity, and less than 1 gram residual sugar) Bright gold. Flowery, spicy, elegant, and soft. Noticeably lower acidity. A pleasant sipping wine.

This co-op has only 11 hectares planted with this varietal. Mr. Szabo said that the main difference between Muscat Lunel and the more traditional Muscat Otonel is that the Otonel is more forthcoming and obvious on nose, but tighter on palate. On the other hand, the Lunel is tighter and less open on nose, but longer on palate. Muscat Otonel is not legally allowed to be planted in the Tokay region.

This particular co-op also does not produce a sweet Tokay Szamorodny, simply because its staff and technical director believe in the more complex, drier style.

1988 TOKAY ASZÚ 3 PUTTONYOS:

(13.7° alcohol, 8.8% acidity, and 8.98 grams residual sugar) This borders on a 4 Puttonyos. In order to be legally a 4 Puttonyos, the juice has to have a 9% residual sugar content. This wine will require an extra two years of fermentation. Complex, ripe nose of raisins, nuts, and botrytis. Elegant on palate; not too sweet. Classy, long finish, with obvious botrytis and good acidity. Should be at its best between 1995 and 2005.

1986 TOKAY ASZÚ 4 PUTTONYOS:

(14.6° alcohol, 10.4 grams residual sugar, 9.7% acidity) Deeper, darker golden colour than the above. Thicker, richer on palate. Full, sweet, yet not cloying. Good acidity; long, complex. Nice botrytis and ripe raisins flavours. Smooth and easy to drink. Try around 1992 to 2005.

1986 TOKAY ASZÚ 5 PUTTONYOS:

(13.4° alcohol, 14 grams residual sugar, 9.5% acidity) This wine will be bottled in a couple of years. Tight on nose; quite sweet and rich on palate. Well balanced, but lacks character at this stage. Will be much better when ready to be bottled.

1983 TOKAY ASZÚ 5 PUTTONYOS:

(14.4° alcohol, 14 grams residual sugar, 8.6% acidity) Still in barrel, but will be bottled shortly. Brilliant, deep-gold colour. Ripe peaches and apricots on both nose and palate. Full, rich, big, and complex. Lovely wine. Ripe raisins and botrytis. Well balanced. Drink around 1993 to 2010 or beyond.

1979 TOKAY ASZÚ 5 PUTTONYOS:

(13.8° alcohol, 14.4 grams residual sugar. 8.4% acidity) Deep, almost amber colour. Delicate, complex nose. Lighter, less fat or freshness, but more classy and "finished" than the yet too young 1983. Well balanced, long, lovely dessert wine. Drink now to 2000.

This was followed by two wines that were, in themselves, an extraordinary experience. Mr. Szabo kindly served me two recent vintages of free run essence of botrytized Herslevelü grapes. The Aszú (or late harvest botrytized) grapes are left to stand in a tub, their own weight causing them to exude a dark, highly sugared juice (sometimes as much as 50% to 60% of the juice is sugar and it therefore never ferments and has little or no alcohol). After 15 to 20 years, it becomes a marvellous essence that can be used to improve Aszú wines. It is never commercially bottled and can actually last well in bottle for a century or more. The texture is that of maple syrup.

1988 PURE FREE RUN ESSENCIA:

Slightly cloudy. Deep-golden colour. Creamy, thick, very sweet peach syrup. Incredible intensity. No alcohol.

1989 PURE FREE RUN ESSENCIA:

Brilliant, deep-gold colour. Syrupy; as thick as the 1988, but fresher peaches and apricots nectar. Cloying, very thick. A great experience. Both "wines" have good acidity and excellent extract. A rare treat.

They were followed by these wines.

1986 MUSCAT ASZÚ 4 PUTTONYOS:

(13.1° alcohol, 10.8 grams residual sugar, 8.5% acidity) Deep gold. Flowery, spicy nose of ripe raisins and Muscat. Rich structure with subdued Muscat flavours. Long, clean finish. A lovely dessert wine.

1983 TOKAY DRY SZAMORODNY:

Made from grapes purchased in a remote area of Tokay. This was Mr. Szabo's favourite. Deep colour, low acidity. Good depth, not unlike medium-dry Sherry. Nutty, smooth, and complex. Better balanced than the other 1983 Szamorodny. This was the last wine tasted.

On the following morning, I visited the winery and vineyard of the Tokay Wine Trust, another large co-operative.

I was received by their export manager, Mr. Zoltan Hegedus, at their modern offices in Satoraljaujhely, in the Tokaji region.

During luncheon, several dry wines were served, as well as this one

TOKAY ASZÚ 1983 3 PUTTONYOS:

Deep gold, smooth, nutty, not too sweet, but complex and well balanced.

After lunch

We drove to one of their cellars/tasting rooms (with caves dug deep underneath the town, including small side caves in which they used to wall treasures that they wanted to save from various invaders over the centuries). Their winemaker opened the following wines.

1989 DRY FURMINT:

(14° alcohol, 8.0% acidity, 2 grams/litre residual sugar) Pale-golden colour. Creamy, rich, long, quite dry. No oxidation as yet and no hint of botrytis. This wine will be bottled in three to four years. Grapey, fresh, and young. After bottling, they allow the wines to rest for a few months before shipping.

1987 DRY FURMINT:

Not bottled yet. Hint of oxidation—this is achieved by not topping the barrels and even by removing some of the wine from the barrel to expose as much of the wine as possible to air and encourage oxidation. Dry, smooth, quite rich. Very good length and clean aftertaste. Slightly nutty.

1984 TOKAY DRY SZAMORODNY:

Bright, deep-golden colour. Earthy, nutty, some oxidation; complex and long. Leaner style. Good acidity and very little residual sugar, yet has depth and glycerine.

1983 TOKAY SZAMORODNY SWEET:

Still in barrel, with 3.8% residual sugar. Medium to deep golden colour. Raisins, ripe apricots and peaches on nose. Not cloying. Can be served as an aperitif or dessert wine. Well balanced, delicate. This would be the ideal base wine to make Puszta cocktail, a traditional aperitif which I experienced in a fine old restaurant in Budapest, called "Hungaria," but which will be renamed shortly "New York"—its original name before Socialism—a meeting place of reporters, writers, and artists in the 1920s and 1930s.

1983 TOKAY ASZÚ 3 PUTTONYOS:

Still in barrel and fermenting, having at this stage 7% to 7.5% residual sugar. Deep, bright-golden colour. Subdued nose. Very little oxidation at this stage; slight hint of gas. Sweet, delicate, and lively.

1981 TOKAY ASZÚ 4 PUTTONYOS:

Not bottled yet! Bright-gold colour. Spicy, raisiny nose. Long, deep, complex.

Unless the winemaker decides otherwise, the formula in terms of how long Aszú is allowed to stay in barrel before bottling is as follows: Add two years to the number of Aszús. Therefore, a 5 Aszú wine will have spent an average of seven years in barrel before bottling. Normally, for instance, a 1974 Aszú 4 Puttonyos will have been bottled in 1980.

1975 TOKAY ASZÚ 5 PUTTONYOS:

Deep, amber colour. Slightly earthy, raisiny nose. Mellow, smooth, long, and delicate on palate. Very well balanced. Oddly, seemed less sweet than the 1981 4 Puttonyos that is still in barrel. Ripe peaches and apricots aftertaste.

1972 TOKAY ASZÚ 6 PUTTONYOS:

Just one level below Essencia and from a great vintage; there are no higher Puttonyos designates than 6. Deep-amber colour. Concentrated raisins and unusual, slightly smoky nose. Lots of extract, depth;

hint of oxidation. Smooth, rich, fabulous. Excellent balance. A lovely drink.

1957 Tokay Aszú Essencia:

From their own "library." Darker than the 1972 6 Puttonyos. Brilliant colour. Noticeable acidity—11% acidity when in barrel. Concentrated, sweet, nectar of peaches. Very low alcohol. Great length. A rare experience. It should be noted that an Aszú Essencia is usually the equivalent of a 9 or 10 Puttonyos and it spends an average of 15 years in barrel before bottling.

We ended this fascinating tasting with another example of "nectar of the gods."

1983 Pure Free Run Essencia:

With over 50% residual sugar. Unfermented, slightly cloudy. Apricots and peaches nectar. Thick, cloying; cream rather than liquid. A truly great experience. Very good acidity and incredible extract. This liquid will be used to boost lesser wines, but will not be bottled as is.

The wines of the Tokay Wine Trust are available in Ontario and Quebec, but not in BC at present. The wines of Hungarovin Wine Co-Op are available in BC as follows (all in traditional 50 cl bottles; 16 oz):

1980 Tokay Aszú 3 Puttonyos:

Bright, medium golden colour. Nutty, raisiny nose. Slightly sweet; smooth and long. Drink now to 1995. An aperitif wine, rather than for dessert.

1979 Tokay Aszú 5 Puttonyos:

Deeper colour than the above. More extract on nose and sweeter on palate. Full, rich, delicate. A lovely dessert wine in its own right, but without quite the same concentration as the Essencia. Long, ripe finish. Price is a steal for such quality wine ($17 per bottle). Drink now to 2000.

1976 Tokay Aszú Essencia:

Still relatively light colour, but with good depth. Creamy, smooth extract; quite sweet, but not cloying. Good acidity. Has a long life ahead. Peach, raisiny aftertaste. Lovely. Drink from 1992 to 2000, or beyond. Sells in BC for $57 per bottle.

A few words of general interest

Nowadays, about 75% of Tokay grapes are Furmint; 20% to 24% are Herslevelü (Linden Leaf); only 1% to 2% are yellow Muskotaly (Muscat Lunel).

The original recipe for Aszú wines calls for one "gonci" barrel (approximately 30 gallons or 136 litres) of fermented, drinkable Tokay wine. These barrels are produced by the famed coopers of Gonc, a village in the Tokay-Hegyalja region. Next, "hods" (Puttony) of about 30 litres each of mashed Aszú berries or paste are added to the wine. This paste is prepared by hand (until the mid-1960s, by feet, too). Pounding will not do, as the seeds must remain intact. The two ingredients are mixed for several days, filtered slowly to remove the seeds, and after months of fermentation, the ageing process follows. The dough (paste) and wine mixture is put in wooden casks of 136 to 220 litres each, in a deep, cool cellar for as many years as the number of "hods" (Puttony) of grapes used, plus two or more years of further ageing, before bottling.

Tokay wine matures best when it meets the air on a large surface. About 20 or 30 litres are drawn off from these casks to allow Tokay to develop. When the wine has reached its optimum, the cask is then topped up to guarantee that Tokay reaches the consumer at its peak. The walls of the cellars of Tokay are covered with a dark, gray mould: a fungus. This mould is the reason why Tokay can be matured in the cellars in upright bottles. The mould keeps the humidity in the cellars high, which stops the corks from drying out. This mould also stops the reproduction of other harmful fungi.

It is suggested, however, that in private cellars, the wine be stored on its side. Also, most Tokay wines will last well for a few weeks (or in the case of Essencia—months) in a refrigerator, after uncorking.

Over the next few years, and as the last vestiges of Communism disappear, we will see a movement to privatize the Hungarian wine industry. They are desperately short of modern equipment and technology—and cash.

May 24, 1990

Commanderie de Bordeaux Dinner and comparative tasting of Châteaux Margaux and Pichon-Lalande 1978 to 1983, at the Pan Pacific hotel.

Champagne Taittinger Comtes de Champagne 1981 "Blanc de Blancs":

Delicate, round, smooth, complex. Quite forward. Long and clean. Yeasty nose, but with the delicacy of a 100% Chardonnay.

1983 to 1978 Châteaux Pichon-Lalande and Margaux

1983 Margaux:

Deep colour to rim. Superb nose of vanilla, oak, ripe fruit. Classy. Magnificent on palate. Great depth and length; complex, full, rich. Perfect balance. This is great. Concentrated, essence. Sensational. (19) Surely, the wine of the vintage.

1983 Pichon-Lalande:

Brighter, yet not as dark as the Margaux. More herbaceous, spicy nose. Lovely bouquet. Full, rich, intense, classic, not nearly ready. Tannic, but very good depth and complexity. A lot of promise. Needs ten years. May be longer-lived than the 1982! (18)

1982 MARGAUX:

Slightly more mature colour than the 1983. Sweet, ripe berries on nose. Lovely, clean. Full, rich, not very tight. Ripe, slightly leathery, complex, long. Very good depth. Ripe tannins, long finish. Needs five to eight years. (18.5)

1982 PICHON-LALANDE:

Very good, deep, dark colour. Toasty, smoky, herbal, complex, ripe, intense nose. Surprisingly sweeter, richer, longer, fatter than the 1982 Margaux, and as complex. Spicy. Great length and ripeness. Very ripe, sweet wine. (18.5)

1981 MARGAUX:

Almost as dark in colour as the 1982. Spicy, herbal, complex nose. Good backbone. More solid than the 1981 Pichon-Lalande. Very good depth. Power. No rush. Excellent fruit. Classy bouquet and flavour. Later, it was delicious, open, lovely. (18.5) As with the 1983, Margaux surely produced the best Haut Médoc in 1981.

1981 PICHON-LALANDE:

Good, medium-dark colour. Similar nose to the 1981 Margaux, but in a more obvious, forthcoming way. Herbaceous. Warm, sweet, round, fruity, elegant, complex. Lots of class and charm. Better balance than the 1979. Perfect now. Drink now to 1999. (17.5)

1979 MARGAUX:

Subdued, slightly stemmy nose. Good, dark colour. Little sign of age. Ripe raisins. Still a bit tannic. More concentration, depth, intensity, and structure than the 1979 Pichon-Lalande. More ripeness, too. A bit short at finish. (17.5)

1979 PICHON-LALANDE:

Lighter colour, but good depth. Open, herbaceous, forthcoming nose. Some oak and toast. Round, complex, nice length. Slight sharpness (acidity). A bit short at finish and metallic, but good flavours. Ready. Drink now to 1997. (17)

1978 MARGAUX:

Very good, dark colour. Still youthful. Closed, yet tobacco, spices, perfumy nose. Ripe raisins, too. Concentrated, full, rich, long. Slight hint of greenness. Great depth. Not as evolved or elegant as the Pichon-Lalande 1978, but more depth. Needs time. (18.5)

1978 PICHON-LALANDE:

Maturing colour, good depth. Herbaceous Cabernet nose. Complex, perfumy, long. Lovely, evolved nose. Full, long, complex, rich, especially for a Cabernet year. Great length, balance; stylish. Very good. Impressive. Drink until 2000. Lots of class. (18.5)

With dinner

CORTON-CHARLEMAGNE 1986, MOILLARD:

Bright, deep gold. Full nose of ripe, nutty, vegetal Chardonnay, and oak. Similar impressions on palate. Full, rich; but no excessive alcohol. Drink now to 1993. (16.5)

CHÂTEAU PICHON-LALANDE 1934, IN MAGNUMS:

Recorked at the château in 1981. I brought these magnums along for the 36 participants as a "bonne bouche." Both magnums were similar. Fair bit of sediment. Both slightly cloudy. Mature, old nose; earthy, herbaceous. Some acidity, but tired and drying out. Has seen better days. (15.5)

The reason I organized this tasting was to feature two properties which, in my opinion, have shown the most impressive improvement over the past decade.

June 12, 1990

Vertical tasting of Jaboulet's Hermitage "La Chapelle" 1971 to 1986, at the Four Seasons hotel.

Gerard Jaboulet was our guest speaker. John and Etienne Hugel came along as guests. The buffet was very good.

CONDRIEU 1985, JABOULET:

Medium gold. Some spice on nose, but a bit volatile, too. Quite hot, alcoholic, but not backed by enough fruit. Burning sensation at finish. (14)

Hermitage "La Chapelle"

1986:

Very good, deep colour, yet no purple. Ripe, tight, sweet, spicy nose. Very ripe, raisiny. Full, rich, complex. Too young. Some acidity at finish bothered me. Very good length. Solid, yet not massive. Drink from 1998 onward. (17.5)

1985:

More brilliant than the 1986; younger-looking. Closed, tight nose. Some spices. Rounder, riper, and richer than the 1986, yet softer. Not as hard or tight. Good fruit and length. Spicy. Very good balance. Rich, soft, elegant, not aggressive. More approachable than the 1986. Drink from 1995. (17.5)

1984:

Medium depth, pale, orangy rim. Herbaceous, open nose. Lean, harsh, tannic, sour. Tannins and acid; needs time, yet fruit is low! (14)

1983:

Very good, dark colour. Slightly pale rim. Tight nose, clean, some ripe fruit. Full, very powerful, totally closed. Needs ten years. Rich, solid; most serious of flight. Later, opened up a bit, but still tight. Very ripe. Excellent potential. Try around 1998. (18.5)

1982:

Similar appearance to the 1983, but more mature rim. More forthcoming on palate, ripe, generous, "hot year" wine. Very big, hefty, ripe raisins, rich. Lots of depth. Great concentration, but no elegance. A bit unbalanced. Will peak in three to four years, and may start to decline after 1998. (17.5)

1981:

Palish colour, orange rim. Tobacco, green leaves on nose. Acidic, lean, hard. Needs drinking. Needs food. Only 6,000 bottles made for collectors. Gerard wanted to declassify the whole crop. (13)

1980:

Pale, orangy colour. Candied, chaptalized nose. Very soft and easy. Sour, bitter finish. OK, but nothing special. Drink up. Losing its fruit. (13.5)

1979:

Medium, maturing colour. Open, spicy, herbal, elegant nose. Sweet fruit, round, complex, rich. Ready, but no rush. Well balanced. Gerard compares it to the 1986. (17)

1978:

Very deep colour to rim. No hint of maturity. Perfumy, complex, ripe, tight, concentrated. Spices and black olives. Superb depth, power, concentration, and length. Great potential. Needs ten to 15 years. Only 12 hectolitres per hectare produced that year! (19)

Jaboulet's "La Chapelle" is made up of two vineyards that they own exclusively: "Bessard" and "Meal." "Bessard" produces more aggressive juice, "Meal" more delicate. Average blend is made up of 40% "Bessard" and 60% "Meal." 22 hectares planted in red and seven hectares in white. They usually use one-third new oak barrels. In mediocre years, they use much less new oak. Their average production is 84,000 bottles of both red and white Hermitage.

1971 HERMITAGE "LA CHAPELLE":

This was supposed to be a mystery wine, but I blew it by inadvertently mentioning the vintage while thanking Gerard. Maturing colour, medium depth. Open, spicy, elegant, complex, sweet nose. Long, delicate, soft; getting a bit tired, but very good. Needs drinking. Tobacco, spices, etc. (17)

According to Gerard, the 1985 Côte-Rôtie is their best Côte-Rôtie since 1971, even better than the 1978.

June 22, 1990

Dinner with Stan and Helene Schwartz, in Danville, near Oakland.

Carol and I stayed with them overnight. Lovely home and a very nice dinner.

1982 MEURSAULT-PERRIÈRES, COCHE-DURY:

Bright gold. Nutty, toasty nose, with hint of oak, vanilla. Medium-bodied. Very good depth, but not fat. Long, complex. Good acidity-fruit balance. Long, oak, Chardonnay, vanilla finish. Excellent. (17.5)

1962 CHÂTEAU LYNCH-BAGES

AND

1962 CHÂTEAU LATOUR:

Both impressively dark red colours, typical of the 1962s, especially Latour: deep colour to rim, impressive depth. Cedary, sweet nose. Full, rich, complex. No rush. Ripe, tannic, excellent length and depth. Very good balance. Lovely wine. Classic. (18)

The Lynch-Bages was cedary, minty, spicy, complex, more forward, but no rush. Long, delicate, flowery, well balanced. (17.5)

Both excellent wines.

June 23, 1990

Presentation of the "Harry Waugh Fund" to Harry and Prue Waugh.

The fund is for their children's education (Harriet and Jamie). The hosts were Drs. Barney Rhodes, Brad Klein, Haskell Norman, Bipin Desai, and myself.

Among the guests were Joseph Phelps, Milt Eisele, Frank Robinson, and many other friends. We managed to collect about $28,000, far more than expected. Barney gave a short speech about Harry's contribution to wine in general, and to California wine in particular. The whole idea came up at my home in the fall of 1989, at a meeting with Haskell and Barney, who were in Vancouver for Sid Cross's "Mr. Gourmet" event. The one disappointment was that a leading Vancouver wine connoisseur, and apparently a friend of Harry Waugh, refused to donate to this cause. Most people contributed $500. I also wrote to Christian Moueix and Jean-Michel Cazes, and they kindly contributed.

July 12 to 23, 1990

Trip to Yountville with the family.

Visit and lunch at Far Niente Winery, in Oakville.

With owner Gil Nickel, arranged by Archie McLaren, who was there, too. (Archie and I met at various rare wine tastings in Los Angeles, usually organized by Bipin Desai.) Beautiful landscape, nice winery, and a rare car collection, including a "one and only" Ferrari 1951, worth five million dollars!

They use 100% new French oak barrels for their Cabernets, and about one-third new barrels for their Chardonnay. All their Cabernet is from their own vineyard, as is 90% of their Chardonnay. They use Champagne and Montrachet yeasts (proportions vary yearly) in their Chardonnays in order to get both the creaminess and the steely character. They dug new tunnels under the winery. Originally, their winery and land was owned by Doug Stelling, a doctor from Vancouver, whose parents died in a car accident in the early 1950s. The estate was left with 6,000 acres of prime vineyard land between Yountville and Rutherford. Most was sold cheaply in 1979 by the trustees, a fair bit being acquired by Mondavi! Some trustees are not to be trusted.

We tasted the 1989 red from barrels

Made from 74% Cabernet Sauvignon, 20% Cabernet Franc, and 4% Merlot. Very good, medium-dark colour. Complex, perfumy, oak, vanilla nose. Nice fruit. Medium-bodied. Needs six to seven years. Well balanced and stylish.

Then, in the reception and lunch room, we tasted the following Cabernet Sauvignons.

1987:

Relatively long maceration period of almost three weeks. 20% Cabernet Franc in the blend, but no Merlot. Medium colour, purplish. Herbaceous nose. Medium weight, elegant, softer than the 1986. Margaux-like, much more so than the 1985 and 1986, which are more like St. Julien or Pauillac. New style, although Nickel and Hampson (his winemaker) said that there was no change in winemaking in 1987, yet to me, the style of the 1987 (and the 1989) is more elegant and more refined than earlier vintages. (16.5)

Every vintage that we tasted, except for the 1984, had no Merlot in the blend.

1986:

Deep, dark colour. Rich, ripe, hefty, masculine wine. Powerful and solid. Well balanced. Needs seven to ten years. Concentrated. (16.5)

1985:

Even darker than the 1986. Stemmier, more complex nose than the 1986. Spicier. Excellent extract. Lovely length. My favourite of the flight. Lots of class here. Needs five to seven years. The 1986 and 1987 are still too young, and not showing their true potential. (17.5)

1984:

Hint of maturity at rim. Warm, elegant, perfumy, yet aggressive tannins on palate. Minty, oaky nose. A bit harsh. Smoky, too. (16)

1983:

Deep colour to rim. Sharp nose. Hard, tannic, powerful. Lots of depth. Powerful. Young vines, obviously; green tannins. (15)

1982:

Mature, round, complex, perfumy. Old wood, herbaceous. Austere, high acidity. Surprisingly complex for a wine made from four-year-old vines. (16)

Lunch

Winemaker Dirk Hampson had lunch with us. He is a gifted winemaker. We retasted the 1982 and 1985 with lunch.

FAR NIENTE CHARDONNAY 1985, NAPA VALLEY:

Impressive, deep, golden colour. Very mature visually and on nose. Honey and oak. Full, smooth, rich on palate. Very long. Needs drinking, but classy. Still has fruit. (16.5)

After the two reds (see above), we had a very good dessert wine.

1986 FAR NIENTE "DOLCE":

Made from two-thirds Semillon and one-third Sauvignon Blanc. Fully botrytized. Only seven barrels made. Not released commercially; 1989 was the first commercial release. Lovely, deep-golden colour. Complex botrytis. Well balanced. Full, rich, yet smooth and delicate. Excellent length. Climens-like, yet the sweetness of Rieussec. (17.5)

July 17, 1990

My birthday: lunch at "Piatti's."

Carol and I went down the road to Christian Moueix's townhouse (which I sold to him in 1985), and we had a glass of Champagne together.

CHAMPAGNE ROEDERER BRUT PREMIER N/V:

Smooth, complex, yeasty, heavier, masculine style.

Then, together with his winery's manager (John Daniel Society, Napanook), Daniel Baron, and his winemaker for Dominus, Chris Phelps, we all went to "Piatti's," a northern Italian-style restaurant at a walking distance from our homes. We were carrying a bottle each: Christian, a decanted bottle of 1975 Petrus; Chris, a magnum of 1985 Dominus; and I, a not-yet-decanted bottle of 1945 Clos de Vougeot (René Engel). As we were approaching the restaurant, an old man got off a parked bus, approached Christian, and asked if he could have some of "this Champagne," (pointing at Christian's bottle of Petrus). We were all amused. At the restaurant, we noticed that Belle and Barney Rhodes were seated at another table, and sent them a glass of the Petrus.

THE WINES

DOMINUS 1985, IN MAGNUM:

Obviously too young, but it held its own against the spicy first course. Deep, youthful colour, very St. Julien in structure and taste (as Harry Waugh had mentioned a few years earlier when we tasted it from cask at Rombauer's), full, sturdy, excellent extract. Should be a fine bottle in 1995 or beyond.

1945 CLOS DE VOUGEOT, RENÉ ENGEL:

Purchased the previous week, a two-bottle lot at a Butterfield and Butterfield wine auction. Ullage was one-and-a-half inches. Bad corkscrew, but I managed to pull out the long cork almost intact. We decided not to decant it, and poured it carefully into our five glasses. Old but good, dark colour. Lovely, earthy, chocolate, spicy Pinot Noir nose. Full, round, smooth, and complex. Not adulterated. The real thing. Held well in glass for at least 45 minutes. Much better than expected.

1975 CHÂTEAU PETRUS:

Decanted two hours before we tasted it. Still too young and tight. Needs five to ten more years. Very good, deep colour. Tight, concentrated nose. Very serious, as most fine 1975s are. Hard, concentrated; excellent balance and backbone. Complex, old-style wine. Lovely.

Not a bad way to spend my 45th birthday! Christian told us about how they couldn't sell the 1975 Château Petrus in 1976, and an English buyer purchased 100 cases at Ffr40 per bottle! He also said that the market could be in trouble with the 1990 vintage, regardless of quality, because of the sensational press over the 1989s. If not in 1990, then in 1991. There is just too much fine wine out there.

July 19, 1990

Dinner at the "French Laundry" restaurant.

Joe and Alice Heitz came over to our place for a visit, and then we went out for dinner. A nice meal. Alice is to have hip surgery in August. She can barely walk.

CHAMPAGNE LAURENT-PERRIER BRUT L.P. N/V:

Round, smooth, well made, good depth, tiny bubbles, creamy, and complex.

Last year, Joe purchased over 500 acres on Howell Mountain. They've planted about 200 acres, mostly with Cabernet and the rest Zinfandel. They'll start producing in 1992 or 1993.

With dinner

1987 RUTHERFORD HILL GEWÜRZTRAMINER, NAPA VALLEY:

Flowery, elegant, spicy, well balanced. Lychees, delicate, subdued. Nice wine.

1981 CHÂTEAU MARGAUX:

I brought this bottle along. Superb wine. Deep, youthful colour. Great, complex nose. Perfumy, long, oak, Cassis, lovely Cabernet. Full, velvety, yet still powerful. Great depth. This is very special, probably the best Bordeaux in 1981. Joe asked me if I could get him some, as well as the 1983 which I recommended to him. I said I'd try.

1989 HEITZ CELLARS ALICIA, NAPA VALLEY:

Named after Alice. Bottled December 19, 1989, shortly after production. Only 300 cases made. "A nectar of Chardonnay," with 7% residual sugar. The wine was not good enough to make regular Chardonnay because of the large amount of rain before the vintage. Not unlike a slightly sweet Loire wine. Perfumy, delicate, soft, elegant. Nice summer sipping wine. White peaches on nose. Good fruit. Fair acidity. A novelty.

September 14, 1990

Dinner at the "William Tell" restaurant, for the executive of the Chevaliers du Tastevin, from both the USA and Canada.

As cellerier, I chose the wines.

CHAMPAGNE ROEDERER "CRISTAL" 1983:

Complex, creamy, long, still lively and full of fruit. Very good length. Complex and very fine. No rush. (18)

CORTON-CHARLEMAGNE 1982, TOLLOT-BEAUT:

I purchased this at auction. The best wine of the evening! Medium gold, good depth. Expansive Chardonnay, ripe apples, and oak on nose. Only four barrels produced. Very rare and the favourite of the evening. Great intensity, length, and depth. Not as rich as Louis Latour's Bonneau du Martray or Louis Jadot's Corton-Charlemagnes. More stylish, elegant, yet ripe raisins. Superb balance and depth. A rare treat! (18.5)

CLOS DE VOUGEOT 1964, REMOISSENET:

Very little sediment, as is often the case with older red Remoissenets. Pasteurized or some brandy added? Delicate, flowery, mature nose. Round on palate. Delicate, yet trace of high alcohol at finish. Lacks the true class of and the velvety finish of other 1964s. These old Remoissenets have been at a plateau for ten years. (17)

September 20, 1990

Rosh Hashana dinner at John Levine's.

SIGNORELLO'S 1985 CHARDONNAY "FOUNDERS RESERVE," NAPA VALLEY:

Their first vintage. Medium gold. Crisp, subdued, elegant, even racey. Well balanced. Hint of oak and delicate Chardonnay, with good depth. (17)

DE LOACH 1985 CHARDONNAY, SONOMA COUNTY, RUSSIAN RIVER VALLEY:

Deep gold, too mature-looking. Heavy nose of old, rich Chardonnay. Oak, too. Over-the-hill. Heavy, tired, still drinkable, but too alcoholic. As with many "show" wines, it had a short orgasm! Drink up. (14)

HERMITAGE 1979, CHAVE:

The best wine of the evening. Deep, dark, excellent colour to rim. Expansive, lovely, spicy, rich, concentrated nose. Full, long; loads of ripe fruit; good, soft, ripe tannins. I thought it was a 1978. Great depth. Excellent. Gerard Chave is a master. (18)

KALLSTADTER SEINACKER SIERER-REBE BEERENAUSLESE 1971, RHEINPFALTZ-WEINGUT KARL UNCKRICH UND SOHNE:

One of the experimental blends of Riesling and Sylvaner. John's mother gave him this bottle in the early 1970s. Deep, bright, amber-gold colour. Elegant, spicy nose. Not much Riesling character, but rich, ripe raisins. Excellent balance. Very good acidity has helped this wine last. Full, yet not cloying. Easy to drink. Lovely, long finish. A very nice experience. (17)

September 24, 1990

Commanderie de Bordeaux council meeting.

CHAMPAGNE VEUVE CLICQUOT "CARTE OR" BRUT 1982:

A superb Champagne. Great bouquet, length, and balance. Lovely flavours, full, creamy, big, and rich. Top quality. At its peak. 1982 was a great year in Champagne. (18)

BURGWERBENER HERZOGSBERG 1989 GUTEDEL, DOGE WINZER GENOSSENSCHAFT:

An East German white wine. Absolutely disgusting, yet the East Germans are trying to list it here! (In a few days Germany will be united again… thank heaven!) Smells like cow manure and sulphur. Sour, bitter finish. Flavour very mediocre at best, nose disgusting. (0)

1984 DOMINUS, JOHN DANIEL SOCIETY, NAPANOOK:

Christian Moueix's California venture. First vintage released, before the "real" first vintage of 1983. Good, dark, youthful colour. Like a 1985 Claret. Rich, ripe, spicy Cabernet nose. Medium-bodied on palate. Complex, a bit minty, spicy, but some bitterness at finish. Needs time. (17.5)

October 2 to 7, 1990

Trip to Yountville.

Lunch at "Brava," with Alice and Joe Heitz.

The restaurant is located near the Freemark Abbey winery. Very good food, but inexperienced staff.

FREEMARK ABBEY CHARDONNAY 1987, NAPA VALLEY:

Crisp, round, complex, delicate. Well balanced and nice.

1966 CHÂTEAU BEYCHEVELLE:

I brought this bottle along. Purchased from Draper and Esquin's. Very good neck level. Oddly, Joe had a disappointing bottle of 1970 Beychevelle the previous week. This 1966 was very good. Dark, maturing colour. Complex, cedary, spicy, evolved Cabernet on nose. Mellow, full, round, and delicate on palate. Very long and complex. Delicacy is a characteristic of Beychevelle. Has held very well. Not harsh or tannic, and not drying out. Very good.

While at "Brava's," I met Hanns Kornell, who is in a wheelchair, after a stroke and a fall. Then we went back to Taplin Road, where I picked up a case of 1981 Château Margaux which I had stored at the Heitzes'. From there, Joe drove me up Howell Mountain, to a 500-acre property overlooking Pope Valley, which they purchased 18 months ago from the University of Washington. Rolly (Joe's younger son) has done an excellent job planting 200 acres of new vineyard, mostly Cabernet Sauvignon and some Zinfandel. They haven't decided yet if they'll produce and bottle themselves, or sell the grapes or juice.

I also ordered some Château Lafaurie-Peyraguey 1986 and some 1988 red Burgundies for Alice, from the Wine House. Joe will be coming to Vancouver next week to conduct a vertical tasting of "Bella Oaks" 1976 to 1985, as a guest of the American Wine Society's tenth anniversary. I talked Joe into coming up for this special event, and I got the wines from the winery for this event.

Joe said that now Warren Winiarski of Stag's Leap vinifies "Fay's Vineyard," all of it. He apparently replanted it because the vines were diseased and in poor shape.

October 11, 1990

American Wine Society's Tenth Anniversary Dinner, and vertical tasting of Heitz Cellars "Bella Oaks" Cabernet Sauvignons, 1976 to 1985.

Joe Heitz was guest speaker. He came for one day. About 116 people participated. I introduced Joe, and he conducted the tasting.

With an early dinner, before the tasting
SUMAC RIDGE 1988 GEWÜRZTRAMINER, OKANAGAN VALLEY, BC:

2% residual sugar. Nice Gewürztraminer. Slightly off-dry. Crisp, lychees, complex, delicate. Well balanced and nice fruit. This is Sumac Ridge's forte.

TIGNANELLO 1983, ANTINORI:

Not nearly as rich as the 1982, or as intense and well structured as the 1985. Some volatile acidity. Leaner. Some leathery spice. Typical Italian, but too lean and sharp. Not one of the finer efforts by Antinori.

THE TASTING
HEITZ CELLARS CHARDONNAY 1973 "LOT Z-32," NAPA VALLEY:

Dr. Larry Burr, one of the members, brought this bottle along. Bright, very deep, golden colour. Some botrytis, and intense, ripe Chardonnay and oak on nose. Full, creamy, rich. Losing some of its fruit and needs drinking, but fabulous intense nose. Was a great wine eight years ago.

Heitz Cellars "Bella Oaks" Cabernet Sauvignon 1976 to 1985, Napa Valley

1976:

Very good, dark, deep, maturing colour. Dense-looking. Lovely, minty, spicy, rich, cedary nose. Drought year; ripe and concentrated. Powerful, tannic, solid, yet leaner, acidic finish. Very ripe, almost sweet aftertaste. Soft, round, complex. Later, I preferred the 1977 to the 1976, because the 1976 became harsh at the end. A bit heavy, hearty, and coarse, but very nice nevertheless. (16) This was the first official vintage of "Bella Oaks." (The 1975, from three-year-old wines, was bottled by "Rutherford Hill.")

1977:

Less dense-looking than the 1976. Bright, youthful rim. Not as intense on nose as the 1976. More subdued. Eucalyptus, delicate, tobacco. Not as tannic as the 1976, more forward. Some sharpness at finish. Later, improved in glass. Lovely length. Rich. Another drought year. (16.5)

1978:

Lighter colour than both above. Palish orange rim. No mint or eucalyptus. More straightforward. Less powerful, too. Soft, forward, subdued, and delicate. Ready. Nice drinking now. (16)

In 1979, no Bella Oaks was made. Quality was not up to par. Some years they didn't make Fay either. Vines suffered from leaf disease and the fruit was unripe. Juice went into the regular Napa Valley Cabernet Sauvignon.

1980:

Medium-dark colour; slightly orange rim. Closed nose; some cigar-box and ripe raisins. Sweeter on entry, not unlike the 1978, but richer, fatter, and more intense. Will live longer than the 1978 as well. Some Cassis. Not classic Cabernet; more spicy Zinfandel. (16)

1981:

Slightly paler than the 1980, but similar appearance. Prunier, less individuality than all above. More straightforward Cabernet. Full, solid. A bit too hot, alcoholic; burning sensation. Sharper finish. (15.5)

1982:

Very nice, deep, slightly maturing colour. Spicy, herbaceous nose. More personality than the 1981 or 1980. Full, rich, ripe, nice fruit; eucalyptus and spices are there, too. Long, still a bit tannic. No rush. My favourite so far, with the 1976 and 1977. Cassis and raspberries. Lovely. (17)

1983:

Light cherry-red colour, slight hint of purple. A leaner wine. Some bitterness at finish. Quite herbaceous and stemmy. Too bitter for my taste. Lightest; less serious than most. (15)

1984:

Very nice, medium-dark, bright cherry colour. Subdued, closed nose. On palate: cedary, rich, yet elegant; full, yet subdued. Well balanced. Needs three to five more years. Not very intense, though. Nice bouquet. Typical "Bella Oaks." (16.5)

1985:

Good red, dense colour. Subdued, lovely, sweet Cabernet nose. Very slight hint of eucalyptus, with lovely, ripe, long fruit. Well balanced. Long, rich, complex. Needs four to six years. Not a blockbuster, but very nice. Some sweetness. (17)

November 13, 1990

Double-blind tasting.

After the tasting, we were told that the wines were 1983 red Burgundies.

APERITIF

CHAMPAGNE PAUL BARA BRUT 1982:

Nice, fruity, yeasty nose. Round, fresh, well balanced, long. Most enjoyable, and, in my opinion, the best wine of the evening. (17)

1. CORTON "RENARDES" 1983, REINE PEDAUQUE:

Herbaceous, sweet nose. Dill, too. Medium to light red, maturing rim. Sweet, artificial finish. Soft, prematurely tired. (14)

2. NUITS-ST.-GEORGES "LES PERRIÈRES" 1983, ROBERT CHEVILLON:

Similar appearance to #1, but a bit lighter. More subdued, less vegetal nose. Some fruit. Ageing, a bit dry and acidic finish. Lighter, less intense than #1. Another old-style Italian wine? (14)

3. ECHÉZEAUX 1983, JOSEPH DROUHIN:

Good dark colour. Richer, riper wine than above two. Less herbaceous, yet stemminess is there. Loads of tannins. High acidity, impressive depth and fruit. Very Italian. Stemmy, leathery, rich. Full, ripe tannins. Powerful. Needs time. Caramel. (16)

Is this a tasting of old Italian reds? If so, they are overall rustic, tired, and sharp. Several taste musty.

4. CLOS DE VOUGEOT 1983, ROBERT ARNOUX:

Medium-dark, maturing colour; leathery nose. Powerful, rich, sweet. Dill, solid, too much residual sugar. Trace of bitterness and mustiness at finish. Chaptalized. (14)

5. BONNE MARES 1983, CLAIR-DAÜ:

Very deep, dark colour. Darkest of flight. Subdued nose. Sweet fruit and slightly leathery. Full, rich, round, still tannic. Powerful. Good fruit. Well balanced and good length. Still has fresh fruit. Actually tastes like Pinot Noir. My favourite. Ready, but no rush. Best wine. (16)

6. GEVREY-CHAMBERTIN "CLOS ST. JACQUES" 1983, CLAIR-DAÜ:

Medium-mature, cloudy colour. Acidic, yet still kicking. Powerful. Very old-style Brunello. Sweet and sour. Has some class, though, and some rot, too. Falling apart at end. These must be old Italian wines, maybe from the 1960s? (13.5)

7. POMMARD "CLOS DES BOUCHEROTTES" 1983, DOMAINE COSTE-CAUMARTIN:

Dark, maturing colour. "Odd man out" on nose. Sweet, candied, pruny. Sweet on entry; round, too sweet. Residual sugar? Yet powerful, tannic, rich. Hint of oxidation and rot. Like a dry Port. Poor bottle. (12)

8. ELK COVE PINOT NOIR 1983 "WILLAMETTE VALLEY," OREGON:

Best colour. Fruity, nice Pinot Noir nose. Hint of sulphur. Fruity, round, but slightly metallic. Not as complex as #3, but at least cleaner and better fruit. Bell pepper. What is a young Pinot Noir doing in the midst of these old, tired, and musty Brunellos? (13.5)

Overall

Very unusual tasting. I thought the wines were Brunellos from 1970 or older. I was shocked when I found out what the wines were! How disappointing. In my wildest dreams I did not imagine that these reputable producers would bottle this stuff. These 1983s were really a humbling experience. Very disappointing. Most wines were old, brownish-looking, tired, musty. Have we been "had" with the 1983 red Burgundies?

November 1990

At home.

VEGA SICILIA "UNICO" 1962, RIBERA DEL DUERO:

Excellent level, little sediment. This wine is well known to me and it is magnificent. Impressive, medium-dark, youthful colour to rim, like a wine ten to 15 years younger. Lovely, delicate nose of maturing Cabernet; oak and straw. Silky, round, long, well balanced, smooth. Superb, complex wine. I cannot see how any other Spanish wine can even approach it in quality. Very good fruit, little tannin, but very good balance and depth. Lasts on palate forever! Great wine. (18.5)

December 3 to 8, 1990

Trip to Yountville and San Francisco.
Visit to Duckhorn Winery.

With Margaret Duckhorn. Her husband, Dan, was out hunting. I visited them once before, about two-and-a-half years ago, when I met Dan Duckhorn. According to his wife, Dan is still dreaming about producing that elusive Domaine de Chevalier white in California! He's now experimenting with adding some Viognier and 25% Semillon to his Sauvignon Blanc. He still hasn't found the formula. Margaret suggested that next time, I notify them and maybe we can have a "duck dinner" together.

They own the Sauvignon Blanc/Semillon vineyard around the winery, but buy most of the grape juice for their red wines. They stagger the contracts over three to five years, and have about 20 different suppliers. They pick and choose certain lots, or even rows, as the grapes are picked, including "Three Palm Vineyard." They hope to own 80% or more of vineyards that supply their juice in years to come, now that they know exactly what style of wine they want to produce.

Most of their oak barrels are Nevers, some Limousin. About 50% new barrels yearly for the reds, and 18 to 22 months in barrel. Whites spend only two to three months in wood.

Margaret told me that "Three Palm Vineyard" is planted mostly in Cabernet Sauvignon and not Merlot. They produce about 7,000 cases per year of Merlot and 9,000 cases of white wine. The rest is Cabernet Sauvignon. "Three Palm Vineyard" only produces 700 to 1,000 cases of Merlot yearly.

We tasted only 1989s, all from barrels (no whites).

MERLOT 1989 (A BLEND OF SEVEN DIFFERENT LOTS):

Spicy, round, elegant; good tannic backbone and berry fruit. Needs middle (which it will probably get when blended with 20% to 25% Cabernet Sauvignon and some Cabernet Franc, before bottling).

MERLOT 1989 (FROM TWO LOTS ON HOWELL MOUNTAIN):

Fatter, rounder, richer than the above; less tannic, and more forthcoming. Easy to drink. Ripe fruit. A bit simple. Will be a separate bottling.

MERLOT 1989 "THREE PALM VINEYARD":

Ripe, intense, rich; lots of depth and extract. Very Pomerol-like. Complex and long. Needs five to six years, or more.

CABERNET SAUVIGNON 1989:

Blended with some Merlot. Very serious "Sociando Mallet," St. Estèphe style. Dark, solid, tight. Very good balance, rich. Not very complex; will develop complexity with age. Needs seven to ten years. A good ringer for a blind tasting.

This was an enjoyable visit. With the exception of the first Merlot, the wines were richer than expected from a cool, rainy 1989 season. At Duckhorn, they picked before the rain.

December 6, 1990

Dinner at "Terra" restaurant, in St. Helena.

As the guest of Barney and Belle Rhodes. Also present were my good friends Joe and Alice Heitz, and Dr. Marvin and Sue Overton from Texas. The Overtons are here for Barney's 70th birthday celebration.

DOMAINE DEUTZ BRUT N/V, CALIFORNIA:

Technically very good. Good mousse. Small bubbles; nice, long, clean, crisp fruit. Well balanced. Lacking the yeast and extra depth of real Champagne, but quite enjoyable.

1987 BOUCHAINE "CARNEROS" CHARDONNAY, NAPA VALLEY:

Surprisingly dark gold for its age. Very slight hint of overripe fruit; even hint of oxidation. Round, full, pleasant, but lacks freshness.

1988 ZD "CALIFORNIA" CHARDONNAY:

Typical of this property. Light-golden colour. Spicy on nose and palate. Very well balanced. Tight, good acidity. Needs time. ZD wines age well. Very nice wine.

1988 ETUDE PINOT NOIR, NAPA VALLEY:

Bright, young, cherry-red colour. Impeccably made Pinot Noir. Clean, very fruity, soft, round. Elegant and easy drinking. Almost too "clean" (lacks the earthy, oaky, barnyardy flavours and smells of really good red Burgundy). Not unlike a fresh, well-made young Mercurey or Rully. Joe Heitz agreed. He commented that while nice and clean, this wine lacked extra dimension and complexity. A nice beginner's Pinot Noir.

After dinner, we drove back to Barney's home and tasted the following wines.

1970 QUINTA DO CACHAO VINTAGE PORT, MASSIAS:

This was Barney's last purchase of a "pipe" of Port. The producers bottled it for him and shipped it to him at the cost of $22 per case! Quinta do Cachao is close to Taylor's Quinta do Vargellas. Typical 1970. Deep colour, creamy, rich, smooth, lots of fruit. Very nice. Nose marred by residual detergent soap in glass.

December 7, 1990

A special dinner held on the occasion of Dr. Barney Rhodes's 70th birthday, at the Four Seasons Clift hotel, in San Francisco.

The first of two special dinners, this evening was organized by our friend from Chicago, Stephen Kaplan, who kindly contributed all the wines for this memorable dinner.

APERITIF

CHAMPAGNE KRUG VINTAGE 1976:

Two bottles. The first was clearly too old and past its prime. Butterscotch on nose, woody. Almost sweet on palate; soft, creamy. (15.5) The second bottle was livelier, with a fine mousse and tiny bubbles. Complex and yeasty on nose. Good backbone, racey, yet showing the ripeness of the 1976 vintage. At its peak. (17.5)

With dinner

MUSIGNY BLANC 1988, COMTE DE VOGÜÉ:

Only 125 cases (five barrels) of this wine are produced yearly, on average, from a "Pinot Blanc vrai" (apparently some white grapes grew out of what was believed to be Pinot Noir vines). Brilliant golden colour. Youthful, fresh, fruity nose, with hint of oak. Oak and fruit blend nicely on palate. Not a big wine, but two extra years of bottle-age will bring forth some more complexity. Expensive—because it is rare. (17)

MEURSAULT-CHARMES PREMIER CRU 1945, LEROY:

The two bottles tasted were completely different. These two bottles were more of a curiosity than a pleasure to drink. They cost a small fortune!

One bottle was dry, earthy, with little fruit left, but still drinkable. (14)

The second bottle was fresher, richer, and nuttier. Some caramel-butterscotch flavours. Too old, but still had some Meursault (nutty Chardonnay) character. (16)

CHÂTEAU LATOUR 1978 AND 1959, BOTH FROM MAGNUMS:

These two wines were served together because the organizers felt that some day, the 1978 would turn out to be like the 1959. I disagree. The two vintages are so different—the 1959s are ripe, rich, intense wines, while the 1978s are stemmier, drier, and leaner wines, suffering from a lack of Merlot, Médoc's "softening agent."

CHÂTEAU LATOUR 1978, IN MAGNUM:

Dark colour. Expansive, stemmy, herbaceous Cabernet nose; typical 1978. Needs more time, especially in magnums. Complex, long, very "Cabernet" wine. Hint of greenness at finish. Will be a fine bottle in five to seven years. (17.5)

CHÂTEAU LATOUR 1959, IN MAGNUM:

Maturing colour with good depth. Chocolaty, ripe nose. Soft, cedary, and ripe on palate. Deeper and richer than the 1978. Very good, yet I must admit that I have tasted better 1959 Latours in the past. Most enjoyable, though. (18)

CHÂTEAU LATOUR 1964, IN MAGNUM:

Latour is a star among Pauillacs in that difficult year for the northern Médoc. Far superior to both Lafite and Mouton. Dark colour to rim. Rich, ripe, chocolaty, cedary nose. Full on palate, loaded with ripe fruit, yet seemed a bit flabby at finish. Another 1964 Latour tasted from bottle two months ago was livelier and better balanced. (17)

CHÂTEAU LEOVILLE-LASCASES 1959, IN MAGNUM:

This is a wine I absolutely adore, and it can be magnificent. So I was very disappointed at the quality of this magnum. Similar appearance to the 1964 Latour, but drying out. Some cedary complexity, but dry and short finish. Where is the superb ripe Cabernet depth this wine can possess? (16)

CHÂTEAU GRUAUD-LAROSE 1928, IN MAGNUM:

Sweet, old fruit on nose. Forward, soft, yet had a solid backbone, typical of the 1928s. Finishes clean and complex, but showing signs of drying up. Some fruit there, but needs drinking—even in magnums. (17)

CHÂTEAU PALMER 1928:

Two bottles. Both had good neck levels and very lively red colour. Both bottles came originally from Caves Nicolas in Paris, a reliable source.

One bottle had some fruit, but was a bit musty, starting to dry out. (16.5)

The second bottle was superb and for me, the best wine of the evening. A memorable bottle. The tannic backbone was backed up by great fruit extract, intensity, and full, rich body. Lots of life in this great bottle. Still at its peak. Sweet, complex, long finish, with hint of tobacco and violets. (20)

CHÂTEAU LATOUR 1928:

Our guest produced a bottle of this fine and rare wine at the last minute. It had travelled recently and therefore it did not have the brilliant colour of the 1928 Palmer. Mature-looking. Smooth, a bit leathery, round, with lovely sweet fruit. Complex and long. A very fine wine that was a bit overshadowed by the great Palmer 1928. (18)

While the 1929 Clarets may have been greater wines in the 1950s and 1960s, it is clear that the 1928s have withstood the test of time better. I've tasted many more great 1928s than 1929s over the past 15 to 18 years.

CHÂTEAU FILHOT 1929:

One bottle was amber-brown, slightly oxidized, Hungarian Tokai-like on both nose and palate. Hint of Madeira, too. (15)

The second bottle had a deep, bright-golden colour. Botrytis/caramel nose. Long, complex, elegant, with good fruit and slightly tart. Butterscotch aftertaste. Has lasted extremely well. (17.5)

We ended the evening with two Ports of the celebrated 1920 vintage, Dr. Barney Rhodes's birth year.

1920 GRAHAM'S VINTAGE PORT:

Recorked by Whitwham's. I am always a bit suspicious when tasting wines that were handled by Whitwham's. As far as my personal experience is concerned, their track record of topping up and recorking rare wines is quite dismal, with few exceptions. Good Vintage Port character on nose. Spicy, flowery; delicate, too. Palish, evolved appearance. Soft, delicate on entry, but sharp, burning alcohol at finish. Too spirity. Unbalanced. (15.5)

1920 TAYLOR'S VINTAGE PORT:

Subdued nose, pale colour, little fruit, lean, drying out and, like the Graham's, too spirity. It had less charm than the Graham's. (15)

I've tasted far better examples of both Ports of the 1920 vintage.

Thus ended the first evening, with some great wines and others that should have been great, but weren't. The sensational 1928 Palmer more than made up for some of the disappointing wines.

Saturday, December 8, 1990

The official Black Tie Anniversary Dinner, in honour of Dr. Barney Rhodes's 70th birthday, at "Stars" restaurant in San Francisco.

This event was organized by Dr. Haskell Norman and the Marin County branch of the International Wine and Food Society. Barney kindly contributed his last magnum of 1870 Lafite.

CHAMPAGNE KRUG "GRANDE CUVÉE" BRUT N/V:

Complex, long, yeasty. Nice fruit, with solid backbone, yet creamy. Toasty on nose. Excellent fruit. (18)

BÂTARD-MONTRACHET 1983, LEFLAIVE:

Bright gold. Spicy, appley, complex nose with nuances of oak. Full, yet not overly fat or alcoholic—a problem with many 1983 white Burgundies. Long, rich on palate, with good acidity and fruit. May not have the extra depth and dimension of Leflaive's 1978 Bâtard, or the elegance of his 1982s, but very fine nevertheless. Later, it developed nuances of butterscotch and nutty flavours in glass. Very good wine. (18)

CHAMPAGNE KRUG VINTAGE 1961, IN BOTH MAGNUMS AND BOTTLES:

The magnums were superb. Much livelier than the 1976 Krug tasted the previous night. Tiny, lively bubbles and fine mousse. Long, complex, and smooth on palate. Superb balance and length. Hint of butterscotch at finish. Classic. (18.5) The bottles were sweeter, yet woody. Very old-tasting. Even lovers of "gôut anglais" would find this Champagne too old. A matter of storage? (16.5)

CHÂTEAU LAFITE 1953 AND 1959, BOTH IN MAGNUMS:

Both had good neck fills. To quote my friend Dr. Brad Klein: "Lafite owes its fame and reputation to the wines it produced in the 19th—rather than 20th—century." The 1953 and 1959 are possibly Lafite's only truly great successes this century, at least until the 1980s. The 1945 can be very fine, but more often than not, it is a rather disappointing wine.

1953:

Medium, mature colour. Expansive, sweet, ripe, Cassis nose, with hint of oak, tobacco, and smoky bacon. Silky, round, and long on palate. Round, mellow. Long finish and excellent balance. Drinking extremely well now (from magnums). I wish I had some of this in my cellar. (19)

1959:

Deeper, more intense colour than the 1953. After 30 minutes in glass, nose opened up with ripe, sweet fruit coming through. Intense ripe fruit, good backbone, rich and deep, full of life. This is another great Lafite that is definitely ready from bottles and can last well from magnums, if well stored. Lovely. (19)

This was followed by three vintages of prephylloxera Lafites.

CHÂTEAU LAFITE 1874, IN TWO BOTTLES AND ONE MAGNUM:

First bottle had an old Rosé colour, an unpleasant off nose; dried out on palate. Citric, with hint of wet, rotten wood. Dead. (No score.) The second bottle was the best of the three examples. Palish, mature colour. Smells of rosewater. Perfumy, delicate, soft, very forward. Hint of earth and mushrooms. (15)

These two bottles had no label, just a simple Christie's strip label.

The magnum had a pale orangy colour. Raisiny on nose. A little fruit left, but just. Sour, sharp finish. Very tired, but drinkable. (13.5)

CHÂTEAU LAFITE 1870, IN MAGNUM:

Contributed by Dr. Barney Rhodes. This magnum came from the famous cellars of Glamis Castle in Scotland. Good low neck level. The appearance of a 1955 or 1953! Nice depth, still lots of red there. Full, long, and fruity with excellent depth. Intense, even a bit tannic for this venerable 120-year-old wine! I tasted this great wine before (also from a magnum from Glamis Castle) in September 1985. This magnum was almost as great as the previous one. Very slight astringency at finish. Tobacco, earthy, mushrooms nose after 15 minutes in glass. Still lively, fruity, and elegant. Great bottle. (19.5)

Our dear friend Harry Waugh became ill in Los Angeles, and couldn't participate in these two events. Brad Klein, in whose home in Los Angeles Harry spent a few days, put some of the rare 1870 Lafite in a small test tube and brought this sample back for Harry to taste. Apparently the wine was still showing well the following day!

CHÂTEAU LAFITE 1864, IN MAGNUM:

High shoulder fill. Medium-red, mature colour. Earthy, mushroomy, beet-sugar nose. Soft and delicate on palate; a bit leathery. Still had some fruit and was much better than the three examples of the 1874 tasted above, but nowhere near the quality or depth of the great 1870. Drying out and some noticeable acidity at finish. Better on palate than on nose. (16.5)

CHÂTEAU D'YQUEM 1967:

Deep golden colour. Lovely, very ripe raisins and botrytis on nose. Full, long, creamy, and complex. Lots of depth. Slight bitterness at finish. Not as luscious as it used to be a few years ago. Still very fine, but don't wait much longer! (18)

This wine has the reputation (and price tag to go along with it) of being one of the greatest d'Yquems of this century. Yet, dare I say this, I think that it is past its prime. From personal experience, this wine was at its absolute peak five to ten years ago, and today the 1959—and even good examples of the 1945—taste livelier. Maybe there is some bottle variation here?

TAYLOR'S VINTAGE PORT 1920:

Much better than the 1920 Taylor's tasted the previous night, but not a great bottle. Light to medium-red colour. Open, forthcoming, spicy nose with good Vintage Port character. Elegant, round, clean, but noticeable spirit and drying out a bit. The 1927 Taylor's (from personal experience) is much better. Drink up. (16.5)

My stars for this evening were the magnums of Lafite 1870, 1953, 1959, and the magnums of Krug 1961.

January 12 to 13, 1991

Trip to Los Angeles for a two-event tasting of Musigny Blancs and 1945 red Burgundies.

Stayed with my friend, Dr. Brad Klein, in Belair.

At lunch

We tasted fresh Iranian Beluga caviar and three different kinds of smoked salmon (Norwegian, Scottish, and Nova Scotian) with these wines.

CHALONE PINOT BLANC 1981, CALIFORNIA:

Bright, deep golden colour. Honeyed, toasty nose. Hint of sulphur. Very Corton-Charlemagne-like nose. Rich, long, full. Very good fruit. Has held very well. Good balance, depth, and richness. (17)

1929 CHÂTEAU D'YQUEM:

Deep amber colour. Superb nose of crème-brûlée. Full, fat, creamy. Very intense, rich botrytis, crème-brûlée, and caramel on palate. Great concentration and depth. (18.5)

Brad opened some old Tokay a year ago. About one ounce was left at the bottom of the bottle. One year later, we tried it. Unbelievably, it was still lovely.

1889 TOKAY ESSENCIA, ZIMMERMAN LIPOT ES FIAI (16-OUNCE BOTTLE):

Label also read: "Bornagytermelök Tokaj-Hegyaljai Borvidek, Crescenz von den Ehemaligen Königl Kaiserl Weingarten, Messzela to in Erdöbenye." Deep amber. Raisins, ripe nose. Full, rich, fat Essencia. Luscious. Lots of flavour and depth at 100 years of age and left in open bottle for a whole year—incredible! (19)

January 12, 1991

Dinner at the Four Seasons hotel, in Los Angeles. Subject: Musigny Blanc 1935 to 1985, Comte Georges de Vogüé.

Host: Ed Lazarus. 14 participants.

APERITIF

CHAMPAGNE CHARBAUT "CERTIFICATE" BLANC DE BLANCS 1982:

Excellent, lively nose, entry, balance, and complexity. After a few minutes in glass, flat and bitter. Good nevertheless. (17)

MUSIGNY BLANC, COMTE DE VOGÜÉ

FLIGHT #1

1935, 1952, 1953

1935:

Deep gold, a bit cloudy. Low neck level. Old nose, almost Vermouth-like. Very dry, intense, fruity. A bit oxidized. Woody. Drinkable. Interesting. Not unlike a Fino Sherry. (15)

1952:

Low neck level. Bright, deep gold. Clean. Very dry, hint of dill pickle. Full, rich. Quite acidic. Some oak. Old, but alive. Nutty, too. Quite alcoholic. Almost like an old white Graves. Nice balance. (15.5)

1953:

Very deep, bright gold. Sweet, ripe nose. Earthy, rich, not unlike an old dry Moulin Touchais. Very mature, but still kicking. Most intense nose of flight. Rich, clean, long. (16.5)

FLIGHT #2

1969, 1970, 1973

1969:

Darkest of flight. Nice smoky-nutty nose. Complex, fruity. Full, rich, very ripe; lots of depth and complexity here. Old, madeirizing. Fat, rich, but not Burgundy! (15.5)

1970:

Surprisingly light colour for age. Medium gold. Slightly rubbery nose. Better on nose than on palate. Too sharp, acidic. Bitter finish. An hour later, improved dramatically. (16)

1973:

Bright yellow-gold colour, good depth; darker than the 1970, but really not old-looking. Elegant nose. Complex, round; good balance and depth. Has held very well. Best of both flights. Nice character, good complexity. Not great, but good. Best personality and closest to real white Burgundy. Half of the 14 tasters thought the 1970 was better. Odd!? (17)

FLIGHT #3

1976, 1978, 1979

All three very similar in appearance, with the 1979 slightly lighter.

1976:

Clean nose. Subdued, delicate. Hint of oak. Round, rich, complex, not too spirity. Clean finish. Well balanced. My favourite of first three flights so far. Buttery, rich, smooth, surprisingly good. (17.5)

1978:

Slightly old-smelling nose. Rich, straightforward, not very complex. Nice fruit. Lacks the balance and depth of the 1976, yet later, developed some complexity. (15.5)

1979:

Odd, earthy, unclean nose. Dull, simple on palate. Not bad, but merely a curiosity. Needs drinking. (14)

FLIGHT #4

1982, 1983, 1985

1982:

Darker than any in the last two flights (1976 onward). Deep, brilliant gold. Full, buttery, rich, vanilla, complex; a bit of oak. Very rich, round; very 1982-like. Ready. (17)

1983:

Austere, tight nose. Full, rich, serious, unyielding. The high alcohol of the 1983s. Buttery, oaky, rich. Impressive. Needs time. Good acidity for 1983. (16.5)

1985:

Tight nose. Tighter, leaner than the 1983. Too tight and acidic. Lacks depth. Needs time. Should improve in two to three years. (15.5)

1976 seemed to be most participants' favourite. Typical Pinot Blancs (or clones thereof), these wines were not "white Burgundies" in the Chardonnay-Beaune sense. Rather austere, solid, straightforward.

WITH CHEESE

LA TÂCHE 1971, DOMAINE DE LA ROMANÉE-CONTI, IN MAGNUM:

This was somehow a letdown. The wine was very good. Medium red, still young-looking. Spicy, lively cherries and herbs on nose. Sweet, intense fruit; clean, long finish. Very good, yet not as great as it can be. Somehow lacked the sheer size, depth, and weight (a bit too stemmy and lean) of previous 1971 La Tâche in magnums that I've experienced. Very good, but less depth or complexity than the superb magnums at Paul Pinski's birthday, and at "Mr. Gourmet" in Vancouver, last September. (17.5)

Sunday, January 13, 1991

Tasting of 1945 red Burgundies, at "Michael's" restaurant, in Los Angeles.

Tasting organized by our host, Ed Lazarus. No fewer than 23 different wines tasted, all Grand Crus, with the exception of one Premier Cru and one Villages wine. All from the Côte de Nuits.

APERITIF

CHAMPAGNE CHARBAUT "CERTIFICAT" ROSÉ 1982:

Lovely colour. Crisp, complex, fruity, fresh, and well balanced. Nice fruit. (17.5)

The wines were served in flights of three or four. They are described below in the order in which they were tasted. All wines are domaine-bottled and have good levels, unless otherwise indicated.

1. CLOS DE LA ROCHE 1945, RÉMY:

Mature-looking. Subdued, delicate, spicy, tobacco nose. Soft, round, and elegant, with some fruit. Some sharpness at finish, but good depth. Spicy, evolved Pinot Noir. Classic mature Burgundy with lots of personality. (17)

2. CLOS DES LAMBRAYS 1945, HÉRITIERS COSSON:

Deeper colour than the above. Buttery, delicate nose. Riper, richer, with more depth than #1 on entry, but odd, sweet finish. Losing its fruit. Obviously chaptalized. Not bad by itself, but not showing too well against such tough competition. (15)

3. NUITS-ST.-GEORGES "VAUCRAINS" 1945, HENRI GOUGES:

Paler, more evolved colour than either of the above. Subdued, mature nose. Some Pinot spiciness coming through. Light-bodied, yet tannic on palate. Herbaceous, fruity aftertaste. Good personality. Later, dried out in glass, showing sharpness. Needs drinking within 15 minutes of opening. (16)

4. MUSIGNY 1945, MORIN:

Excellent top neck level. Very good, deep colour. Slightly leathery. Good backbone, nice fruit, but little complexity. Almost too lively not to have been fortified or doctored. (16.5)

5. MUSIGNY 1945 "VIEILLES VIGNES," COMTE DE VOGÜÉ:

Clean, mature red colour with orange hue. Delicate, lovely Pinot Noir nose. Subdued, sweet, complex fruit. Round, very well balanced. Long, delicate, clean finish. A classy wine that is very soft and needs drinking. Best so far. (18)

6. CLOS DE VOUGEOT 1945, GRIVELET:

Good, mature, dark colour with orange rim. Nice, clean, spicy, evolved nose. Long and complex on entry. Good structure, nice sweet fruit. Spicy, long finish. Very enjoyable now. (17)

7. CLOS DE VOUGEOT 1945, CHÂTEAU DE LA TOUR:

Pale orange-yellow colour. Madeirized, with sour, acidic finish. Passé and barely drinkable. (12)

8. GEVREY-CHAMBERTIN 1945, FAIVELEY:

Lively, bright-red colour. Fresh and impressive on palate. Long and fruity. Very lively, nice ripe fruit and good backbone, marred by an aftertaste of unclean barrels. Pretty damn good for a 46-year-old Villages wine! (17)

9. CHARMES-CHAMBERTIN 1945, ARMAND ROUSSEAU:

Maturing red colour, orange rim, but good depth. Intense, leathery, fruity, sweet nose. Great class and length; lovely fruit. Excellent Pinot character. Very exciting wine. Best so far. (18.5)

10. CHARMES-CHAMBERTIN "TASTEVINÉ" 1945, GIROUX:

Palish colour; soft, sweet, forward. Too sugary and sharp finish, yet still drinkable. (15)

11. MAZIS-CHAMBERTIN 1945, GELIN:

Impressive dark colour, not unlike a wine 20 years younger. Musty, cardboard on nose. Much better on palate. Lots of ripe fruit, a bit chaptalized. Drying out, earthy, sharp overtones. Entry good, but nose and finish a letdown. (16)

12. CHAMBERTIN 1945, CAMUS:

Brownish, pale colour. Buttery, oaky nose. Oxidized, tired, acidic. Some fruit, but heavily chaptalized and over-the-hill. (13.5)

13. CHAMBERTIN 1945, FAIVELEY:

Nowhere near the quality of the ordinary village Gevrey of this producer, as described above. Palish red, orange rim. Clean, spicy, yet subdued nose. Has some fruit, but too sharp and drying out. With wines of that age, and coming from different sources, one can never be sure how the wine has been stored or how the wine will show. (14)

14. CHAMBERTIN 1945, RÉMY:

Madeira-like. Barely drinkable. (12)

15. CHAMBERTIN 1945, RODET:

Dark colour. Vegetal nose. Better on palate. Full and fruity. Smoky, too, but chaptalized (or blended with wine from "down south"?). A heavy-handed, beefy, old-style négociant wine. (13.5)

16. ECHÉZEAUX 1945, LUPÉ-CHOLET:

Bright red, maturing colour. Spicy, subdued Pinot nose. Round, complex. Nice ripe fruit. Good intensity. Very enjoyable and would have been much more impressive had it not been followed by some truly great wines. (16.5)

17. GRANDS ECHÉZEAUX 1945, RENÉ ENGEL:

Deep, impressive colour. Ripe, leathery, yet stemmy nose. Hard, dry, quite sharp. Has depth and a lot of masculine character, but pity that it doesn't have a little more fruit. (15.5)

René Engel's 1945 Clos de Vougeot tasted the following month in Vancouver was much better: smoky, toasty nose; full, rich, and long. Rated (17.5).

18. GRANDS ECHÉZEAUX 1945, LEROY:

Excellent dark colour. Clean, spicy, and long Pinot nose. Full, rich, long, and complex. Superb balance. Full of life. Best wine so far. A great classic. (19)

19. GRANDS ECHÉZEAUX 1945, DOMAINE DE LA ROMANÉE-CONTI:

Palish, mature colour. Perfumy, complex, lovely nose. Solid backbone is backed by nice, delicate fruit. Very classy, long, and elegant. Kept improving in glass. Needs drinking. (18)

20. RICHEBOURG 1945, CHARLES VIENOT:

Nice, quite evolved colour. Expansive, very long, perfumy, complex nose. Great length; sweet, clean fruit. Slightly smoky, oaky. This is really great! Superb length and class here. Hard to find a mature red Burgundy that can top this. Purchased by Ed in Switzerland a few years ago. My overall favourite of the whole event. (19.5)

21. RICHEBOURG 1945, DOMAINE DE LA ROMANÉE-CONTI:

Impressive, dark, mature colour. Odd, medicinal, dusty nose. Much better on palate. Full, solid, concentrated fruit. Much more powerful and richer than Vienot's Richebourg, but not nearly as complex. Very good extract, though. (17.5)

22. La Tâche 1945, Domaine de la Romanée-Conti:

Mature orange-red colour. Raisiny, slightly oxidized nose. Complex on palate, but aftertaste of beet sugar. Acidic, volatile. Some fruit, but a letdown overall. I have had the good fortune of tasting a great example of this wine in 1987. (16)

23. Romanée-Conti 1945, Domaine de la Romanée-Conti:

Clearly one of the very top wines of the whole tasting, although I had a slight preference for Vienot's great Richebourg. Only 50 cases of this treasure were produced. This was also the last vintage for Romanée-Conti for a few years, as the vines were uprooted and the vineyard was replanted. The very few remaining bottles sell for over $3,000 each! Subdued nose, elegant, hint of mint. Lots of depth here; backbone and fruit, too. Yet not quite as complex as Vienot's Richebourg. A serious, solid wine. Has character and power. A rare experience. (19)

As expected, there were some disappointing wines, but there were several great ones, too. Indeed, several were memorable bottles.

January 17, 1991

Chevaliers du Tastevin Dinner, at "Al Porto" restaurant, in Gastown, Vancouver. The war in Kuwait started 24 hours ago.

Just before the dinner, Israel was under SCUD missile attack! The dinner was good, but portions were too large and the food was too spicy and too heavy for the wines.

I hope and pray that the SCUDS that are landing on Israel do not have gas in them. The word "gas" is a psychological trigger in Israel. The retaliation could very possibly be nuclear!

January 29, 1991

Commanderie de Bordeaux Dinner and vertical tasting, featuring Domaine de Chevalier Rouge, at the "William Tell" restaurant.

This property produces some of the most elegant red wines in Graves. The limited production makes this wine hard to find, especially when one intends to put together a vertical tasting. It took me three years to put this event together. As an experience, it was well worth it.

APERITIF

Champagne Roederer "Cristal" Brut 1983:

Smooth, creamy, round, complex. Well balanced, long. Ready, but no rush. Fine bubbles.

Château Laville-Haut-Brion 1987:

Leaner style, typical 1987. Good acidity, subdued fruit; hint of apricots, oak and vanilla. Clean, long finish. Fine effort for the vintage. I should have served a white Domaine de Chevalier, but couldn't find any. An excellent, hard-to-find wine.

DOMAINE DE CHEVALIER

FLIGHT #1

1983 to 1975

1983

Medium-red colour with palish rim. Perfumy, oaky, spicy, earthy, herbaceous nose. Complex, round; nice fruit on palate. Hint of oak and vanilla. Elegance rather than power. Almost ready. (17.5)

1982:

Slightly darker than the 1983. Riper, richer, typical of the 1982 vintages, yet even in that context, quite elegant. Good extract. A bit short, with some aggressive tannins at finish that will disappear with two years of extra bottle-age. Nice wine, but not quite the class of the 1983. (16.5)

1981:

Similar appearance to the 1983. Oddly, less evolved on nose than either the 1982 or 1983. Herbaceous, hint of straw and earth. Round, good intensity, nice fruit, and well balanced. I preferred this slightly to the 1982. Almost ready. An underrated and overlooked wine and vintage. (16.5)

1979:

Medium-red colour, showing some age. Subdued, sweet, herbaceous nose. Rich, quite fat on palate. Finished a bit too dry and one-dimensional. Needs drinking. (16)

1978:

Similar, evolved colour as the 1979, but with more depth. Elegant, earthy, floral nose. Delicate, complex, well balanced. Nice fruit. It has it all. Ready now, but no rush. Very nice wine. (17)

1975:

Deeper colour than either the 1978 or 1979. Old-style, leathery, earthy nose. Baked, ripe, yet tannic and hard on palate, with overtones of wet earth. A serious, hard, tannic wine. Typical of the vintage, yet better balanced than many 1975s. Drink now to 1995. (16.5)

FLIGHT #2

1970 to 1964

1970:

Always a favourite of mine, this is one of the most elegant and complex 1970s. Sweet, earthy, complex nose. Forward, soft, drinking extremely well now. Classy and elegant. Well balanced with a long, clean finish. No excessive acidity. At its peak. Most enjoyable. (17.5)

1966:

(Tasted two months earlier) From personal experience, I've always preferred this property's 1964 to the 1966. This 1966 was lighter than the 1964, more open, a bit leaner, with some sharpness at finish. Drink up. (16)

1964:

There was some bottle variation here. Also, the wine was decanted one hour before drinking—too long for such a delicate wine. 1964 was a successful vintage for the early picked wines from Graves. Impressive, dark, mature colour. Earthy, complex nose. Tobacco, cedar, earthy. Nice balance and fruit. Rated (16.5).

The second bottle was leaner, drier, with an odd smell of old furniture and dust. Rated (15).

Here I blame myself for not watching the decanting staff more closely. They decanted this wine too soon.

FLIGHT #3

1962 to 1959

1962:

Medium-red colour with orange-brown overtones. Lovely, perfumy, sweet fruit on nose. Elegance and velvet here. Hint of wood and wet earth on palate, otherwise nice soft fruit. Stylish. If well stored, this wine should be most enjoyable now. As was the case with the 1964, the second bottle was harder and drying out. (17)

1961:

(Tasted separately a few days later, but comments inserted here) Typical, deep, rich, mature colour of the 1961s. Spicy, herbaceous, yet ripe and earthy nose. Fullish, quite sturdy. Finish is stylish and refined, but a bit dry. Nose is the best part. Needs drinking. (17.5)

1959:

Impressive, dark, mature colour, typical of this ripe vintage. Tight, austere, losing its charming ripe fruit. Flavourful on entry, but drying out at finish. A matter of storage? (15.5)

Overall impressions

The overall quality was very good. The style of this property is clearly elegance rather than power. The 1983, 1978, and 1970 showed best at this tasting.

DESSERT WINE

CHÂTEAU DE FARGUES 1980, SAUTERNES:

Bright golden colour. Spicy, subdued botrytis nose. Still fresh and lively. Well balanced, long. Very good. (17.5)

February 1, 1991

Farewell dinner to the panel members of *The Wine Consumer.*

After six years of publication, I have decided to stop publishing the wine newsletter. Each bottle tasted tonight was dedicated to an individual panel member, and several bottles were dedicated to the spouses.

CHAMPAGNE MICHEL NOIROT BRUT N/V "LES RICEYS":

Fine bubbles and mousse. Flowery nose. Quite lean, even metallic, yet nice fruit. Try it with food. (15.5)

CHAMPAGNE MICHEL NOIROT BRUT N/V "LES RICEYS, CUVÉE DU CLOS ST. ROCH":

Rounder, more complex than the above. Clean, fruity, and long. Refreshing. (16.5)

CHAMPAGNE KRUG "GRANDE CUVÉE" BRUT N/V:

Two bottles were tried. One purchased recently and the other five years ago. The younger Krug was quite masculine, even hard; tight and serious. Very good fruit underneath, with excellent balance. The older Krug had a more complex, flowery, yeasty nose. Rounder and longer on palate, with slight hint of oak and lovely finish. Both rated (18).

STERLING VINEYARD CHARDONNAY 1979, NAPA VALLEY:

Deep, mature, golden colour. Buttery, oaky, intense nose with nice, mature varietal coming through. Rich, full-bodied, and nicely balanced. Has good acidity and fruit at 12 years. Long, clean finish. (17)

PULIGNY-MONTRACHET PREMIER CRU "LES PUCELLES" 1978, HENRI BOILLOT:

Bright green-gold. Leafy, oak, slight hint of sulphur on nose. Delicate, spicy, green on palate; backed by nice fruit. The 1978 white Burgundies are holding up very well. Complex and long. Not unlike Remoissenet's whites, which are leaner, racier, and age well. (17)

CHEVALIER-MONTRACHET 1982, LEFLAIVE:

The class, depth, and weight of a Grand Cru, and the elegance of the 1982s are all here. Brilliant golden colour. Complex, round, long. At its peak. Oak and ripe fruit in harmony. Lots of class and character here. (18)

CHASSAGNE-MONTRACHET ROUGE "MORGEOT" 1970, JOSEPH DROUHIN:

Light red colour, evolved at rim. Open, spicy Pinot Noir on nose. Sweet fruit, even slightly tannic (surprising for a 1970 Burgundy). Has held very well for 20 years. Not unlike a Volnay. Drink up. (15.5)

CHÂTEAU GRUAUD-LAROSE 1958:

Poor vintage? Maybe, but this was a very good wine. Must be one of the best wines of this rarely seen vintage. Very good neck level. Deep colour reminiscent of the better 1966s. Spicy, minty, cedary nose. Still a bit tannic. Dry finish, but nice fruit. Complex, elegant, spicy Cabernet. At its peak. Very impressive effort. (17)

HANZELL CABERNET SAUVIGNON 1959, SONOMA VALLEY (BOTTLED BY HEITZ WINE CELLARS):

This was Hanzell's first Cabernet Sauvignon vintage. Good, dark, youthful colour. Subdued, spicy Cabernet nose. Quite austere and dry on palate, but still enjoyable. Full and solid, drying out. Nose was best part. A historic wine. Before starting his own winery, Joe Heitz was the winemaker at Hanzell's. (16)

CHÂTEAU LEOVILLE-LASCASES 1966 (SHIPPED BY DOURTHE FRÈRES, BORDEAUX, AND BOTTLED AT RIDGE VINEYARDS IN CUPERTINO, CALIFORNIA):

Drier, harder, and more youthful, but less complex than the elegant, mature, château-bottled Lascases 1966. Quite solid, powerful, beefy. Has it been "improved" with some Zinfandel or Cabernet? Old-style St. Estèphe, rather than elegant, fruity St. Julien. Quite good, though. (16.5)

DOMAINE DE CHEVALIER ROUGE 1961:

Typical, deep, rich, mature colour of the 1961s. Spicy, herbaceous, yet ripe and earthy nose. Fullish, quite sturdy. Finish is stylish and refined, if a bit dry. Nose is best part. Needs drinking. (17.5)

CLOS DE VOUGEOT 1945, RENÉ ENGEL:

This wine had a surprisingly dark colour and a toasty, smoky, "bacon bits" nose. Intense, full, and surprisingly rich. Powerful, beefy wine. More Rhône-like than Burgundy! Lots of depth and power here. Full of life. Oddly, I've experienced this smoky nose with younger vintages of Engel's Clos de Vougeot (1978, 1985). Impressive wine. (18)

CHÂTEAU SUDUIRAUT 1967:

Can be great. This bottle was merely "good," yet level was excellent, well into the neck. Dark, mature, golden colour; typical of the better 1967s. Subdued, elegant nose with nice botrytis. Soft, forward, low acidity. Creamy, soft, and long. This bottle rated (17).

A bottle tasted a month earlier was superb, with great depth, body, balance, and length, and was rated (18.5).

WARRE'S 1934 VINTAGE PORT "PROPRIETORS' RESERVE" (BOTTLED BY ARTHUR BELL AND CO., PERTH, SCOTLAND):

Good neck level. Decanted 30 minutes before serving. Delicate, silky Port. As mellow, round, and complex as one could hope for. Still lots of Vintage Port character. No sharp edges, not too spirity. Lovely balance, nice fruit. Long, lovely finish. Excellent Port. (18)

This dinner was a fitting ending to six enjoyable (and sometimes frustrating) years—publishing The Wine Consumer. *It may not have been a financial success, but it had a substantial impact on the local wine scene in British Columbia.*

February 11, 1991

Chevaliers des Vins de France vertical tasting of Château Mouton-Rothschild at the Four Seasons hotel, in Vancouver.

Conducted by Sid Cross and myself.

Château Mouton-Rothschild

1970:

Darker than the 1978, but lighter than the 1975. Cigar-box nose. Subdued, mature. Hard tannins at finish, a bit diluted. Good oak; sweet, mature, almost leathery fruit. At its peak. Somehow lacks concentration. Tea leaves, tobacco. While good, this wine is not in the class of the 1970 greats, such as Latour, Montrose, Palmer, or Lynch-Bages. (17)

1975:

Medium, mature red colour. Good depth. The stemmy herbaceousness of the 1975s. Full, tannic, hard, solid but backed by nice fruit. Better depth and extract than the 1970. Powerful, classic 1975. Excellent. Much better than the 1970, but dry and serious. (18)

1978:

Light-red colour. Orangy rim. Forward, herbaceous nose. Stemmy, fresh, spicy. High acidity, some oak. Medium to light bodied, yet hard finish. Mouton has not produced a memorable 1978. (16.5)

1987:

Medium to dark colour. Good extract for the vintage. Elegant, open, oaky, forward. Light, complex; not much depth, power, body, or tannins. But clean, spicy, cedary. (16)

1986:

Very deep, dense colour to rim. Almost black. Darkest of flight. Tight nose. What's there is very ripe, jammy, intense, luscious, tannic. Loads of ripe fruit. Oak. Concentrated. Powerful. Very long-lived. Try it in 15 years. Great balance and depth. (19)

1985, IN MAGNUMS:

Dark, ruby-red colour, but not nearly as dark as the 1986 or the 1983. Much more forthcoming than the 1986. Open, delicate, cedary, minty, oaky nose. Slightly smoky. Sweet, fuller, richer than expected. Lovely, elegant, complex. Great length and balance. Seven to ten years. (18)

1983:

Very deep, dark colour. Surprisingly, darker than the 1982 at this stage. Closed nose. Some chocolaty, ripe fruit. Surprisingly tight. Yet on palate, very 1983. Like the 1975, but less aggressive tannins. Needs seven years. Very good fruit, length, without the charm of the 1985 or the depth of the 1986. (17.5)

1982:

Very deep, dark colour. Dense. Third-darkest after the 1986 and 1983. Hint of maturity at rim. Ripe, jammy, rich nose. Full, powerful, ripe tannins. Lots of depth, class, and length here. Needs ten to 15 years. Very ripe, rich, intense. Like the 1986, but less severe, more ripe fruit. Quite tannic, but relatively low acidity. A bit leathery. (18.5)

Most tasters (96 participants in total) favoured the 1985, with the 1982 a close second. The 1986 was not very popular, yet it is outstanding. Too closed and tight at this stage. At this particular tasting, the 1986 is clearly the "serious grand man" of the bunch. I was not surprised by the popularity of the 1985: a charming, easy to like, and easy to understand vintage.

February 19, 1991

Black Tie Tasting and Dinner, at Dave Spurrell's.

(16 participants)

APERITIF

CHAMPAGNE LANSON "RED LABEL" 1982 BRUT:

Nice mousse, small bubbles. Complex, spicy, slightly earthy nose. Quite solid on palate. Good fruit, but earthy, "wet cement," sharp overtones. That's what made me guess that it is Lanson. Good fruit, but doesn't have the extra dimension of top Champagnes. (16.5)

Double-blind tasting of ten wines

At first, I thought that part was a vertical of Gruaud-Larose and part a 1982 tasting. Later, I decided that they were all 1982s, with one ringer (#9). I was pretty close.

1. CHÂTEAU LAFON-ROCHET 1982:

Deep, dark colour; one of the darkest of the flight. Tight, unyielding nose. Powerful, dry, tannic. A bit earthy, straightforward, and dull. Lacks complexity. Needs seven to eight years. (16)

2. CHÂTEAU DU TERTRE 1982:

Lightest of flight. Medium-red. Herbaceous, spicy, open, forward. A bit stemmy, yet beefy wine. Some sweetness, too. Noticeable acidity, low tannins, light fruit. Elegant and forward. (15.5)

3. CHÂTEAU GRAND-PUY-LACOSTE 1982:

Even darker than #1! Very deep red. Tight Cabernet nose. Very Pauillac/St. Estèphe, yet more complex and riper fruit than #1. Cigar-box, spicy, ripe. Powerful, rich, solid. Excellent extract. Needs lots of time. (18)

4. RIDGE VINEYARDS "HOWELL MOUNTAIN" CABERNET SAUVIGNON 1982:

Similar appearance to #1. Toasty, stemmy, ripe, rich. Biting. More evolved than #1 or #3. Sweet, straightforward, leathery, herbaceous. Lots of fruit extract, lower acidity. Needs two to four years. Quite good. This wine fooled me. I thought that it was a 1982 Claret. (17)

5. CHÂTEAU GRUAUD-LAROSE 1982:

Very deep colour, more evolved than #4, #3, or #1. Fat, ripe, spicy, evolved nose. Lower acidity, chocolaty fruit. Intense and powerful. Great depth, loads of ripe fruit and extract. This is excellent. Needs ten years. (18.5)

6. CHÂTEAU MONTROSE 1982:

Impressive, deep, youthful colour. Fruity, complex, lovely balance, sweet fruit. Lots of extract. Solid, powerful. Serious St. Estèphe? Excellent depth. Eight to ten years. (In retrospect, much better than expected.) (17.5)

7. CHÂTEAU LA LAGUNE 1982:

Good, dark colour, lighter than #6, though; slight maturity at rim. Sweet, subdued nose. Earthy, ripe fruit, less extract than #8, but lovely and rich. Four to six years. Very good. (17.5)

8. CHÂTEAU LYNCH-BAGES 1982:

Very good, deep colour. Stemmy, herbaceous, ripe, cedary Cabernet nose. A bit lean and sharp, but lovely extract, too. Medium body and tannins. Nice, spicy, rich fruit. Very good potential. Five to seven years. (18)

9. ROBERT MONDAVI CABERNET SAUVIGNON "RESERVE" 1982, NAPA VALLEY:

Deep, dark colour to rim. Very obvious nose; evolved, mint, eucalyptus, oak. Aggressive tannins, yet ripe fruit, too. Very Californian. Different from all others. Lovely long finish. Forward. Drink now to 1995. Is this a ringer? (17)

10. CHÂTEAU LEOVILLE-LASCASES 1982:

Very deep, dark colour to rim, not unlike #3. Superb, spicy Cabernet, oak, vanilla, chocolate nose. Full, loaded with ripe fruit. Perfect oak, fruit, tannins, acidity, and balance. Great complexity and ripe, spicy Cabernet. Great depth. A classic! Certainly one of the very top wines of the vintage. (19)

I had a very good tasting and was right on most of them (vintage and property). I thought #4 was

French, #9 very obviously Californian, and #10 obviously Lascases. Very good tasting.

Then we had an excellent dinner prepared by Alice, our hostess, with the following wines.

1983 AND 1985 BÂTARD-MONTRACHET, LOUIS LATOUR:

I thought they were both 1985s, but later, I guessed them right.

The 1983 was clearly better, fatter, richer. High alcohol, but very good fruit and extract. Better than expected. Ready, but good fruit and acidity. Long, oaky, complex. At first, excessive sulphur, which dissipated after ten minutes in glass. (17.5)

The 1985 was paler gold, more subdued nose, leaner on palate, higher alcohol (odd for a 1985), shorter, bitter finish. Good, but not great. (16.5)

1975 CHÂTEAU MOUTON-ROTHSCHILD:

Very deep colour, slightly maturing rim. Subdued, tight nose. Spicy Cabernet. Full, solid, powerful, ripe tannins. I thought it was a 1970, yet it has the hard tannins of a 1966. I didn't guess 1975, but thought "maybe Mouton." A serious, powerful wine that needs ten years. (18)

LA TÂCHE 1971, DOMAINE DE LA ROMANÉE-CONTI, IN MAGNUM:

Quite evolved red colour. Intense, open, luscious, spicy Pinot Noir nose, with hint of raspberries. Very sweet, much sweeter than expected. I thought 1969 or 1971, and having tasted the very same wine last month in Los Angeles (also from magnums), I guessed La Tâche 1971! (I also knew that Dave had a magnum of this wine, but I didn't think he'd open it. This magnum retails now for US$650!) Herbaceous, spicy, sweet, open. Very long. More forward than expected and without the extract of previous experiences. Classy, though. (18) Can easily achieve an almost perfect (19.5).

HERMITAGE "LA CHAPELLE" 1969, JABOULET:

I was completely wrong about this wine; my only poor guess of the night. Deep, mature colour. Lovely, chocolaty, warm, open; woody, spicy, vanilla, cinnamon nose. Round, full, great length, slightly short finish. I thought this was a 1961 Claret. I thought 1961 Grand-Puy-Lacoste or 1961 l'Arrosée. Very good. A surprise! (18) on nose and (17) on palate.

1975 CHÂTEAU D'YQUEM, IN TWO HALF-BOTTLES:

Really easy to guess! The acidity of the 1975s; the deep-gold colour, oak, botrytis, ripe fruit, and balance of d'Yquem. Not ready. Great depth and complexity. Superb balance. Great, rich nose. (19)

1967 TAYLOR'S "QUINTA DO VARGELLAS":

Mature, medium-red colour. Spicy, complex, subdued nose. Leaner on palate, without the depth of true great Vintage Port, but nice, spicy complexity. Drying out a bit. Needs drinking. Good. (17)

A nice evening with some memorable wines. Our host Dave Spurrell was very generous. Hard to replace these treasures, but then, aren't fine wines to be shared with friends who appreciate them?

Morning, February 28, 1991

Double-blind tasting of Pinot Noirs of the 1988 vintage, at Heitz Cellars.

When I arrived at the winery at 8:00 a.m., and sat down in the tasting room, I had absolutely no idea what was being tasted that morning. Other tasters included Joe Heitz, his two sons David and Rolly, his daughter Kathleen, and their technical team.

Later that day

Lunch at Joe and Alice Heitz's home, with their sons Rolly and David, and daughter Kathleen.

HEITZ CELLARS CHARDONNAY 1980, NAPA VALLEY:

Deep, mature gold. Earthy, rich Chardonnay nose. Full, yet soft. Some fruit and good intensity, but not very complex. Also, starting to show signs of cracking up. Pleasant, though. (15.5)

HEITZ CELLARS "MARTHA'S VINEYARD" 1986 CABERNET SAUVIGNON, NAPA VALLEY:

A much more subdued, different wine than the 1985 "Martha's." Not as spicy, more elegant. Excellent balance, good fruit. Medium tannins, good length. Not a blockbuster, but top quality and well made. Clean, long finish. Relatively early maturity (four to five years from now). Very good. Not easily recognizable as "Martha's" at a blind tasting. (17.5)

I brought along to taste a bottle of wine purchased at auction.

SPRING MOUNTAIN CABERNET SAUVIGNON LOT H 68/69 LN, NAPA VALLEY:

Dark, maturing colour. Fair bit of sediment. Spicy, open, mature Cabernet nose; some eucalyptus. Soft, forward, some acidity at finish. Needs drinking. Was better four to five years ago (according to Joe). (16)

History

Joe sold some of this wine (regular Cabernet Sauvignon and "Martha's") of the 1968 and 1969 vintages in cask because he needed cash in the late 1960s and early 1970s—and the banks wouldn't help him out. Lot H (H = Heitz), 1968/1969 (vintage blend), L = Limousin, and N = Nevers, in which it was aged at Spring Mountain.

HEITZ CELLARS "MARTHA'S VINEYARD" CABERNET SAUVIGNON 1984, NAPA VALLEY:

Structured like the 1986 rather than the 1985. Lovely, complex, elegant, long, ripe, soft tannins. Very good and long. Excellent balance. Not for long-ageing, though. (17.5)

We had lovely fresh asparagus picked by Joe from his garden, ten minutes before lunch.

March 8, 1991

Small tasting, at the home of Peter Henrikson.

With his friend Christiano Van Zeller (Quinta do Noval), Bartholomew Broadbent (Michael Broadbent's son), Nathan Maltz (a dentist and member of Le Tastevin, my wine club), and myself. An impromptu Friday afternoon event. All wines tasted were in half-bottles only. All were kindly contributed by Peter, except the 1983 d'Yquem, which was contributed by Nathan.

1945 MOUTON-ROTHSCHILD, IN HALF-BOTTLE:

Mid shoulder level. Dark, maturing colour. Cedary, minty, woody, very old Mouton nose. Hard, tannic, solid wine. Slightly pruny, showing hint of oxidation. Finishes a bit sharp, but very good intensity. After 30 minutes, became cleaner, but still hard, losing its fruit. Much better when tasted from full bottles and magnums. More intense than the 1952. (17)

1952 MOUTON-ROTHSCHILD, IN HALF-BOTTLE:

Similar colour to the 1945, but fresher. Good depth. Cedary, mature nose. Full, yet tannic and a bit sharp; typical 1952 style. Good fruit. Livelier than the 1945. Tannic, acidic finish. After 30 minutes, the 1945 seemed a bit bigger, more austere. Has held very well in half-bottle. (17.5)

1962 MOUTON-ROTHSCHILD, IN HALF-BOTTLE:

Bright-red colour, typical of the 1962s. Warm, charming, sweet, cedary nose. Round, delicate, complex, lovely balance. Good fruit. Best for drinking now. After 30 minutes, showed signs of drying up. (17)

1961 MOUTON-ROTHSCHILD, IN HALF-BOTTLE:

Best, intense, deep, dark, lively colour of flight. Subdued, yet ripe, rich, cedary nose. Great depth and intensity. Very ripe tannins, good acidity, lovely length. Still closed, even in half-bottles. No rush. Excellent. (19)

1978 MOUTON-ROTHSCHILD, IN HALF-BOTTLE:

Lightest colour of flight. Green, spicy, stemmy on nose and palate. Lacks character, depth, or intensity. Medium fruit. 1978 was not a great success at Mouton. (16.5)

We finished the tasting with this wine.

CHÂTEAU D'YQUEM 1983, IN HALF-BOTTLE:

Brilliant, deep, golden colour. Superb botrytis and fruit on nose. Full, rich, intense, long; great fruit and acidity balance, not cloying. About ready in half-bottles, but no rush. This is great! (19)

Christiano Van Zeller said that he doubts anyone will declare 1990 (that makes five years of no general declaration of Vintage Port). He said the 1990 crop was the largest ever in the Douro, double the average! Many diluted wines (overproduction). They will produce seven pipes of 1990 Nacional (double the average).

According to Christiano, the problem with the 1982 Noval was that they left it in wood too long (three years instead of two). The 1963 has a lot of variation and some bottles can be great, others light and soft (bottling from individual barrels took a long time). Mine are excellent. I reminded him that he and I corresponded via Decanter *Magazine on the subject. He tries to buy 1934 Noval, which he loves. Oddly, I think it is great, too, and I'm chasing after it, as well. My personal experience is that the regular Noval 1934 is better than the Nacional 1934.*

Other information Christiano volunteered

Cockburn is making better wines in the 1980s. Croft's is down and needs improvement, and too many mistakes were made there in recent years. Old vintages of Sandeman's are great, up to 1958, including "odd" vintages, such as 1957, 1947, etc. Smith Woodhouse is very underrated; they make great Port and excellent Late-Bottled Vintage (especially 1979 and 1981). I agree. The 1977 Smith Woodhouse is top quality.

Christiano said that he trades a lot with Bordeaux (Haut-Brion, Petrus, Figeac, Lynch-Bages, Cos, etc.). He is very fond of 1979 Clarets (especially Haut-Brion). He said that J. P. Moueix has decided that Petrus will go to his nephew and Christian Moueix will get the rest (Trotanoy, Lafleur, etc.), but Christian will continue to manage Petrus. I wonder if this is true.

Confidentially, he said that Fonseca's, Taylor's, and even the Symington Group blend, into their vintage, Port wines from other vintages, especially for LBVs, and true Vintage Ports, as well. (For example, Warre's 1985 has some 1986 in it!!!) If true, this is sensational news. Personally, I don't care, as long as the end-

product is great. But in terms of trust and reputation, this can become a real problem. Maybe his sources of information are not reliable, however.

Regarding Nacional

Christian said that, other than the use of ungrafted vines (they age well and are only occasionally attacked by phylloxera, with an average age of 25 to 30 years), the secret of the intensity of Nacional is the Sausal grape. It is not a "legal" or traditional grape, but rather a "provisionally permitted grape" since 1933. They put 15% to 16% of it in the Nacional blend, on average. The grapes are trodden and produce deep, black, intense juice.

Bartholomew Broadbent said that the German authorities are investigating the German "rare wine" collector Hardy Rodenstock, because of numerous fake wines. Bart's father, Michael Broadbent, is testifying on behalf of Rodenstock, saying that these rare wines are authentic. No wonder, since Rodenstock sold many of them through Christie's, and Michael Broadbent has stuck his neck out. If Rodenstock falls, so does Michael Broadbent—and Christie's! I think, however, that they will all get away with it, as it is so difficult to prove and the technology is not advanced enough... yet.

An interesting afternoon, and most enjoyable tasting.

March 27, 1991

Dinner at Sid and Joan Cross's home, on the occasion of a visit by our friend from Los Angeles, Dr. Brad Klein.

Also invited were the Spurrells. We were leaving next day for Yountville and therefore had to entertain Brad at the Crosses'. All wines were served double-blind. I had a fantastic evening and I guessed practically all the wines right on! Food was very good. Joan is a gifted cook.

CHAMPAGNE POL ROGER "PRIVATE RESERVE" 1982:

This is their top-of-the-line Champagne, made from a blend of six Grands Crus (three of Chardonnay and three of Pinot Noir). Usually excellent, this time it was disappointing. Superb mousse, tiny bubbles. Delicate subdued nose, but not enough yeast. Round, delicate, well balanced, but too sweet! Almost an extra dry. Not enough complexity. Odd. Apparently, Pol Roger's "Cuvée Sir Winston Churchill" is actually the "Private Reserve" bottled for the Anglo-Saxon countries.

CHEVALIER-MONTRACHET 1978, REMOISSENET:

Deep, mature, golden colour. Complex, toasty, round, ripe, fine Burgundy nose. Not nutty (as Meursaults or Corton-Charlemagnes are). Very good balance, long, complex. Much more forward than expected. Very good, but ready. I guessed the vintage and the producer, and by deduction, that it was the Chevalier. (18)

1970 AND 1966 CHÂTEAU PALMER:

1970 very deep, very dark to rim. Still youthful colour. Classic 1970 appearance and ripe structure. Closed, unyielding. Full, chunky, rich, ripe fruit. Superb balance. Will be great in five to seven years. Other examples tasted in California were more evolved. Will be great. (18.5).

1966:

Best red wine of the evening! More evolved colour than the 1970, rounder, softer. Perfect Margaux balance. Great nose of toast, ripe Cabernet, wood. Superb. At its absolute peak. (19)

I guessed both right on.

1961 Château Palmer and 1964 Château Gruaud-Larose

1961 CHÂTEAU PALMER:

Had a lovely, chocolaty, perfumy, mature nose. Very slight hint of pickle. Unmistakable ripe tannins and structure of the 1961s, but touch of acidity at finish. Very good, but not as great as it was five years ago or at Peter Sichel's (at d'Angludet), when Carol and I tasted it with Peter and Diana—one of the greatest Clarets I've ever tasted. Even so, I could tell that there was some family resemblance to the 1970 and 1966. I ventured to guess "1961 Palmer, possibly London-bottled." (17.5) to (18)

1964 CHÂTEAU GRUAUD-LAROSE:

Very deep, dense colour, yet maturing rim. Smoky, spicy, Cabernet nose; not as complex as the Palmer. They had a fire at Gruaud in 1965, and 60% of the 1964 vintage was destroyed. Maybe fire and smoke influenced some of the surviving casks of the 1964? Chunky, rich, solid, straightforward. I've had better examples. (16.5)

1967 CHÂTEAU SUDUIRAUT:

Deep, brilliant-golden colour. Superb botrytis; complex, long nose. Round, well balanced. Great acidity, ripe, complex, long finish. This is a great Sauternes, one of the best of the 1967s. Livelier than when last tasted at home (February 1, 1991). I guessed this right on, too! I knew it had to be 1967, but couldn't be d'Yquem or de Fargues (which are fatter). Great wine. (18.5) Together with the 1966 Palmer, best wine of the evening.

J. MONTEIRO VINHOS LDA, "MALMSEY SWEET" VINTAGE 1900 MADEIRA, FUNCHAL:

Imported by Kraus Bros. and Co., New York. A true vintage Madeira (not Solera). Brad brought this bottle along. Amber colour, olive-green rim. Ripe, nutty, woody, raisiny nose. Full, rich, long. Good acidity. Will last forever. Very good fruit. Lovely. (18)

A most enjoyable evening.

March 29 to April 7, 1991

Trip to Yountville with Carol and kids (Easter Break)

Passover Dinner with Carol and kids at the residence of Dr. Haskell Norman, in Ross, Marin County.

Haskell was very kind to invite us along to celebrate Passover with his family.

HOFFMANN MOUNTAIN RANCH "PASO ROBLES" PINOT NOIR 1976:

Haskell has several cases of this wine. The Hoffmanns sold the winery in 1976. They are related to Rae Norman, Haskell's wife. Deep, dense, maturing colour. Barnyardy, evolved, old-style Pinot Noir. Full, rich, a bit too sweet, but not bad. Too much dill. An experience.

Saturday, April 20, 1991

Dinner of "Group of Ten."

CHAMPAGNES KRUG VINTAGE 1982 AND 1979:

Both great, both complex and long, with tiny bubbles, yet completely different.

The 1982 had an incredibly complex nose, yeasty, oaky, elegant. Perfect balance, round, long. Superb. Ready, yet no rush.

The 1979 was more austere, more acidic, harder. The 1982 for sipping, the 1979 with food. Both great.

1978 CHEVALIER-MONTRACHET AND 1978 CORTON-CHARLEMAGNE, BOTH REMOISSENET:

The Corton was a bit corked and musty. Better on palate. Nutty, well balanced. Good, lively acidity. Bright green-gold. Smooth, sweet fruit. Good. (17)

The Chevalier had a taste of cabbage and toast. Round, long, soft, mellow. Rich. Very good. Both ready, but no rush (if well stored). Second time I've tasted this Chevalier in the past 30 days. (17.5)

1945 CHÂTEAU GRUAUD-LAROSE, IN MAGNUM:

(Group wine) Very good low neck level. Impressive, deep, youthful colour; even some purple. Very youthful-looking for a 1945! Lovely, spicy Cabernet nose. Tobacco, green leaves. Rich, leathery, quite dry, tannic; typical 1945 structure. Excellent, leathery, plummy. Pauillac-like. Cedary, rich. Seductive, opulent nose. Best 1945 Gruaud I've ever tasted. (18.5)

1961 CHÂTEAU L'ARROSÉE:

Dark, maturing colour; not as brilliant and lively as the 1945 Gruaud. Ripe, herbaceous, earthy Cabernet nose. Harder, concentrated, slightly acidic finish. Sid Cross thought it was a Graves. I guessed it right on! Good backbone, ripe tannins. At first, I thought it was a St. Julien (Leoville-Barton) or a St. Emilion 1961 with high proportion of Cabernet, "such as l'Arrosée." (17.5)

1963 CROFT'S VINTAGE PORT:

Served double-blind. Again, I said, "A nice soft 1955 or 1963 Croft's." Elegant, soft, round, complex. Very well balanced. Forward, perfect now. Very nice Port. Ready, but no rush. (17)

April 23, 1991

Tasting, at home, of white and red Rhône Wines of the great 1978 vintage.

18 guests. Tasting accompanied by a lovely meal of various crêpes of Brittany (seafood, ratatouille, cheese, and chicken fillings). For dessert, we had crêpes filled with strawberries or orange marmalades.

Even in a wine-producing region that is usually blessed with reliably good weather, vintages such as 1978 in the Rhône Valley are the exception. The main reason for the concentration and extract of these wines was the extremely low yields. Top Hermitage producers, such as Chave and Jaboulet, averaged 10 to 14 hectolitres per hectare, a ratio unheard of these days! Wine collectors who appreciated these wines in their youth were very few.

By today's standard, prices were unbelievably cheap. The famous and influential wine writers hadn't discovered this wine region as yet. The fad was yet to come. A range of no fewer than 19 different 1978 Rhône wines, both whites and reds, was tasted in my home in Vancouver, in April 1991. The wines were tasted blind in groups, as indicated below. Tasters knew which wines were in which flight, but not the order.

APERITIF

CHÂTEAU GRILLET 1978:

This tiny appellation has almost doubled its production over the past decade, from approximately 450 cases to about 800 cases or more, and it shows. These days, the wine is lighter and has less depth and less staying power—ending the big debate that went on in the 1960s and 1970s about whether Grillet should be consumed while young and fresh, or be allowed to age and be consumed after ten or even 15 years. Hint of Muscat and lychees on nose. Quite full for Grillet on palate. Long, well balanced. More serious on palate than the subdued, delicate nose would indicate. Drinking well now. (17)

FLIGHT #1
Hermitages Blancs 1978

Hermitage Blanc 1978 "Domaine de l'Hermite," Domaine Gray:

Deep golden, mature colour. Slight oxidation on nose. Earthy, with overtone of ripe raisins. Fat, rich, honeysuckle. Trace of acidity at finish. Drink up. (14.5)

Hermitage Blanc 1978, J. L. Chave:

Bright-golden colour. Honeyed, complex, rich nose. Good fruit on palate, full and rich. A serious wine that is still tight. Hopefully, it will come around in five to ten years. Chave's white Hermitages have a reputation for ageing very well. A 1952 tasted in 1980 was perfection. Score is conservative. Time will tell. (16.5)

Hermitage Blanc 1978, E. Guigal:

Palest of flight. Light golden colour. Fresh, flowery, charming wine. Complex, fruity, and rich. Full of life and most enjoyable. Hint of petroleum at finish detracted a bit, but otherwise very good. Should last well for another five to seven years. (17.5)

FLIGHT #2
1978 reds from the Southern Rhône Region

Château de Fonsalette 1978, AOC Côtes du Rhône, Paynaud:

Made by the owner of the famed Châteauneuf-du-Pape, Château Rayas. Bright, medium-red colour, with good depth. Clean, sweet fruit on nose, with hint of straw, spices, and oak. Full, peppery. Nice fruit. Good backbone, tannins. Has grip, yet is at its perfect peak now. Fine effort. (17)

Gigondas 1978, Paul Jaboulet Aîné:

Medium red, slightly browning colour. Tight on nose. Hint of caramel and coffee, too. Good fruit, but high acidity and some aggressive tannins reduced the enjoyment of this otherwise pleasant wine. Was better four to five years ago. Drink up. (14.5)

Vacqueyras 1978, AOC Côtes du Rhône, Paul Jaboulet Aîné:

Lively dark colour with palish rim. Nice, sweet fruit on nose disappeared after 15 minutes in glass. Good backbone, nice fruit. Straightforward and simple, yet good depth. Ready. (15)

Domaine du Vieux Télégraphe 1978, AOC Châteauneuf-du-Pape:

Deepest, darkest colour of flight. Concentrated, intense, yet slightly rubbery nose. Full, massive wine. Loads of fruit and ripe tannins. Too young. Pity to drink this wine before 1995 to 1998, or beyond. Great extract and depth. Several tasters disliked this wine because of its aggressive tannins, yet I can't help but believe that it has a great future ahead. (18)

Chante Perdrix 1978, AOC Châteauneuf-du-Pape, J. Nicolet:

Deep colour, showing slight maturity at rim. Sweet, elegant, spicy nose. Forthcoming. Complex and rich. Slightly metallic at first, but after a few minutes in glass, it developed nicely. Ripe fruit, peppery, elegant, and long. Best of flight for current drinking. (17)

FLIGHT #3
Various 1978 Northern Rhône reds

Cornas 1978, Delas Frères:

Medium-dark, maturing colour. Leathery, sweet, ripe nose. Full on palate, concentrated, slightly herbaceous. Quite hot and acidic at finish. Needs drinking. (15)

Crozes-Hermitage "Thalabert" 1978, Paul Jaboulet Aîné:

Best appearance of flight. Deep, dark colour to rim. Tar and ripe fruit on nose. Full, rich, concentrated on palate. Sweet, ripe fruit. Well balanced. Impressive and youthful. Classic, peppery Syrah. Enjoyable now, but no rush. (17)

Hermitage "La Sizeranne" 1978, Chapoutier:

Evolved, mature colour with pale, orangy rim. Herbaceous, peppery nose, with hint of straw. Light, delicate, nice complexity. Best for drinking now in this flight. Doesn't have the power and concentration one would expect from a 1978 Hermitage. Having said that, this bottle was far better and had more complexity than the five samples I've tasted previously between 1982 and 1990. (16)

FLIGHT #4
1978 Côte-Rôtie and Hermitage

Hermitage 1978, E. Guigal:

This wine introduced us to the flight of "what 1978 great Rhônes are all about." Impressive, dark, dense colour to rim. Long, spicy, complex, and clean nose of healthy, ripe berries. Full and rich on palate, with loads of ripe fruit. Well balanced. Good acidity and solid, fruity, long finish. Soft tannins blend nicely. Approachable now, but can only improve over the next four years. (17.5)

Côte-Rôtie 1978, André Drevon:

Dark colour, showing some maturity at rim. Expansive, spicy, slightly stemmy nose. Forward and elegant on palate. Fruit and spices blend together nicely. At its peak. Very good, but in the context of the vintage, the "iron fist" is not hidden behind the "velvet glove." (17)

HERMITAGE "LA CHAPELLE" 1978, PAUL JABOULET AÎNÉ:

Lovely, bright, deep, inky-purple colour. Impressive appearance for a 12-year-old wine. Still closed up, yet intense ripe fruit and peppery bouquet coming through. Excellent balance. Very intense on palate, very ripe, loaded with luscious fruit. Needs at least eight extra years of bottle-age. I do not believe in speculating in the wine trade, but for those who do—and being aware that this wine retails today for over $250 per bottle, with the original price in 1980 at $20 per bottle—this beats investing in real estate! (19)

CÔTE-RÔTIE 1978 "LA VIAILLÈRE," DERVIEUX-THÈZE:

Palest of flight, yet dark colour, nevertheless. Forward, sweet, spicy, flowery nose, marred by some mustiness. Noticeable, aggressive tannins that do not blend nicely. Quite intense, yet acidic sharpness at finish. Will not improve. Obviously aged in old (and not too clean) barrels. Not bad, but in the context of this flight, a poor effort. The wine smells like the winery used to when I visited this property several years ago. (15)

HERMITAGE 1978, J. L. CHAVE:

If "La Chapelle" wins in terms of sheer power and extract, this wine is the clear winner when it comes to class and structure. Excellent, deep-red colour to rim. Spicy, ripe, peppery nose. Classic Syrah. Full, long, superbly balanced. Lots of fine, intense, ripe fruit here. The balance and harmony in this wine is very impressive. Produced by a master. Needs five to eight extra years to reach its peak, and should hold for at least another decade. (19)

CÔTE-RÔTIE 1978 "CÔTES BRUNE ET BLONDE," E. GUIGAL:

Clearly the best of the three Côte-Rôties tasted. Good, deep-red colour. Complex nose with hint of chocolate, tobacco, coffee, and spices. Ripe, rich fruit. Excellent depth and balance. Approachable now, but no rush. The intensity of the best 1978s, yet the elegance of Côte-Rôtie. Fine wine. (18)

The group's scores rated Chave's Hermitage best, with La Chapelle close behind. We were all impressed by the quality and consistency of the Guigal wines—impeccably made.

A memorable vintage for red Rhône wines, especially at the top end.

May 4, 1991

Commanderie de Bordeaux blind tasting and luncheon, featuring 1982 and 1983 red Bordeaux, with John Kolasa of Château Latour.

We knew what the wines were, but not the order in which they were served. Most wines were shipped by producers. Others were from our cellar. The Latour 1982 and 1983 were from my cellar.

1. CHÂTEAU CANON 1982:

Medium-dark, maturing rim. Good depth. Ripe, rich, leathery nose. Full, solid, tannic, still a bit aggressive. Ripe finish. Deep, serious. Later, more approachable. Elegant, yet lacks the "gras" of the vintage. (17) Probably going through a phase.

2. CHÂTEAU CANON 1983:

Lightest of flight. More evolved. Sweet, perfumy, evolved nose. Clean and lovely. Round, delicate, elegant. Forward, classy, spicy. Later, slightly pruny nose. Ripe, rich, long. Oddly, more 1982 than 1983 style. Stemmy, herbaceous, but elegant and long. (17.5)

3. CHÂTEAU TALBOT 1982:

Very good, deep colour. Slight maturity at rim. Tobacco, cedar, rich Cabernet nose. Ripe, powerful, rich, tight, tannic. Solid, serious wine. Needs time. (17.5)

4. CHÂTEAU TALBOT 1983:

Very good, deep, evolved colour; less depth than the 1982. Subdued, cedary, earthy Cabernet nose. Not as intense or ripe as the 1982, but very nice; more evolved. Softer tannins, but needs time. Needs four extra years. (17)

5. CHÂTEAU COS D'ESTOURNEL 1982:

Dark colour. Evolved rim. Lovely, cedary, perfumy, spicy Cabernet nose. More complex than the two Talbots. Round, elegant, intense; ripe fruit and soft tannins. Very ripe, sweet. Nice, clean finish. Very good, but needs time. Tobacco, subtle. Still a bit tight. (18)

6. CHÂTEAU COS D'ESTOURNEL 1983:

Medium-red, evolved rim. Slightly dusty, metallic nose. Noticeable acidity on palate, but long, sweet finish, too. Very good length. Not fat. Straightforward. No rush. (16.5)

7. CHÂTEAU GRAND-PUY-LACOSTE 1982:

Intense, deep-red colour to rim. Youthful, elegant, perfumy nose. Cedar, oak. Loads of ripe fruit. Tannic. Needs time. Excellent balance. Great depth and ripeness. Cos 1982? Generous. Long. (18)

8. CHÂTEAU GRAND-PUY-LACOSTE 1983:

Quite evolved in colour, more so than the 1982. Pale, maturing rim. More evolved than the 1982 on palate, too. Toasty, ripe Cabernet, yet flowery, elegant nose. Round, soft. Hint of aggressive tannins, but almost ready. (16.5)

9. CHÂTEAU LYNCH-BAGES 1982, IN MAGNUM:

Very deep-red colour to rim. Intense, cedary nose; vanilla, wood. Full, rich, complex. A bit acidic finish, but lots of length and ripe fruit. Very good. Stemmy. Evolved, yet intense. (18)

10. CHÂTEAU LYNCH-BAGES 1983,IN MAGNUM:

Lighter colour than #9. More evolved on nose. Stemmy Cabernet Franc. Canon? Open, complex, classic St. Emilion nose. Sweet, ready. Elegant, long, complex. Best for drinking now. Was I ever wrong about this wine. Nobody said that blind tastings are easy! (18)

11. CHÂTEAU LATOUR 1982:

Deep-purple colour to rim. Great, oaky, spicy, ripe, cedary nose. Very ripe, sweet, very long. Great extract. Lots of depth here. Sweet, long finish. Needs 15 years. Grand Vin. (19)

12. CHÂTEAU LATOUR 1983:

Dark colour to rim, not as dark as #11. Herbaceous, spicy, open nose. Some new oak. Leaner, harder on palate, yet good intensity. Well balanced. Slightly soft in middle, but very good. Needs two to three years. Seems a bit diluted. (17)

All of the above red wines accompanied the buffet.

We also tasted the following.

WHITE WINE

CHÂTEAU LAVILLE-HAUT-BRION 1987:

As on previous occasions, complex, new oak, rich, surprisingly ripe for a 1987. Very good length and balance. Nutty—the "Meursault" of Bordeaux.

DESSERT WINE

CHÂTEAU CLIMENS 1983, BARSAC:

Outstanding Barsac! Bright, deep green-gold. Lovely botrytis nose. Clean, excellent balance, very long, lovely fruit. Needs ten years. Very good, but can only improve. Great potential. (18.5)

Overall favourite

1982 Château Latour—obviously! The 1982 Château Grand-Puy-Lacoste was excellent. Canon 1982 disappointed a bit. Going through a phase? Both Lynch-Bages were charming. The 1982 Cos was excellent.

Same evening, May 4, 1991

Commanderie de Bordeaux Gala Black Tie Dinner and Induction Ceremony, at the Four Seasons hotel.

At the end of the ceremony, the French Consul General to Vancouver, Mr. Bernard Ledun, awarded me the "Ordre du Mérite Agricole" medal. The food and wines were excellent, as usual.

THE WINES

CHÂTEAU LAVILLE-HAUT-BRION 1985:

Pale gold. Lovely nose; rich, vanilla, lots of new oak. Oak overwhelming, but the wine needs a few more years. Subdued, tight fruit. Odd wine. Some liked it. Others found it overoaked. A matter of taste. In my opinion, it just needs more time. Try around 1995 to 1999.

CHÂTEAU LYNCH-BAGES 1975 AND LES-FORTS-DE-LATOUR 1978:

Both very good and both typical of their respective vintages and of Pauillac.

Lynch-Bages was dark, had chunky, rich fruit, concentrated, without the hard, dry tannins of some 1975s. Long, complex, cedary. No rush, but drinking well now.

Les-Forts-de-Latour was spicy, herbaceous, long, very well balanced. Drinking well now (again, no rush). Good length, clean fruit. Nice cedary finish.

CHÂTEAU LATOUR 1971, IN MAGNUMS:

At its peak. Cedary, oaky, spicy nose. Earthy, rich, complex. Extra dimension and complexity than the two above. Bottles are declining (drying out), but these magnums are in good shape. Maturing colour, nice fruit. No aggressive tannins.

CHÂTEAU CLIMENS 1967:

(I purchased six bottles at auction at the Chicago Wine Co. as "1976." The vintage turned out to be a 1967!) Deep gold (for Climens), but lighter than most 1967s. Subdued botrytis, elegant nose. Not cloying. Lovely fruit, acidity, and length. Ready. Great balance. Best wine of the evening for me.

1961 COGNAC EXSHAW "FINS BOIS" (LANDED IN 1962, BOTTLED 1979 BY AVERY'S OF BRISTOL):

Amber, dry, complex, clean. Oak and fruit. No artificial flavours. Very long. Good.

May 7 to 21, 1991

Trip to Israel, Athens, and Vienna (by myself).

IN ISRAEL

1986 YARDEN CABERNET SAUVIGNON, GOLAN:

Full, elegant, French style. Complex, spicy; nice toast, oak, and fruit. Almost ready. Not as concentrated as the 1985, which I know well, having tasted it on several occasions.

IN ATHENS

Dinner at the home of my friends, Joan and Sam Fromowitz.

Sam is the political attaché at the US Embassy and deputy to the Mission Chief.

A very nice weekend with Sam and Joan. Visited Athens, Marathon, etc. We had a lovely Greek dinner at a very old Taverna. Sam is the third in command at the Embassy. Staff of 750! (500 Greeks and 250 US personnel.) He is very busy and stuck among the emotions of the Greeks, Turks, and Cypriots! In terms of "political dynamite," it doesn't get much more complicated than this.

IN VIENNA

Dinner at "Korso," a fine but very expensive restaurant.

1981 CHÂTEAU PICHON-LALANDE:

After two weeks of no really fine wines, I was glad to taste this. Good, dark colour. Lovely, cedary, spicy Cabernet nose. Still youthful, but very drinkable. Long, complex, good fruit. Clean, long finish. Very good structure for a 1981. Drink now to 1998. Classy. Cost 1,600 Schillings (Can$160). Very expensive!

My main purpose in Vienna was to visit the grave of my paternal grandmother Aurelie, who died in Vienna in 1916 at age 35, 29 years before I was born. My father was then only 13 years old.

June 2, 1991

International Wine and Food Society Dinner (BYOB), at "Windows on the Roof," Coast Plaza hotel, in Vancouver.

Each couple brought two bottles.

CHAMPAGNE DOM RUINART BLANC DE BLANCS 1981:

Still lively, fresh, crisp, and elegant, yet nice depth. Long, good backbone. Ready, but no rush. Classy. (17.5)

NUITS-ST.-GEORGES PREMIER CRU 1978 "CLOS DE L'ARLOT," JULES BELIN:

(My bottle) White wine made from Pinot Blanc grapes. Brilliant, deep green-gold. Oak, ripe raisins on nose, with hint of green apples. Full, solid; excellent balance and structure. Serious white wine that has held extremely well. (17.5)

1970 CHÂTEAU MONTROSE:

As expected, still very deep, very dark; solid, chunky, tight, classic Claret. Spicy, cedary Cabernet nose. Closed, tight. Needs ten years and will last for 30 or more years if well stored. A very serious wine. (18)

1971 CHÂTEAU DE FARGUES, SAUTERNES:

Deep, brilliant gold. Expansive, yet delicate botrytis nose. Long, creamy. Great balance, fruit, and length. At its peak, but no rush. Lovely Sauternes! (18.5)

Also tasted (from other tables)

1961 CHÂTEAU GRUAUD-LAROSE:

Classic Gruaud and classic 1961. Cedary, sweet, cigar-box, earthy 1961. Long, round, complex. Lovely balance and ripe, soft fruit. One of the best 1961s. At its peak, but no rush, if well stored.

Friday, July 26, 1991

Dinner at "The Prow" restaurant, for a group of friends from Los Angeles and Chicago.

Stephen Kaplan, Ed Lazarus, John and Laurie Tilson. John is the editor of The Underground Wineletter. *From town: The Crosses, Spurrells, Levines, Mottersheads, and ourselves. Everyone contributed wine, and the meal was excellent.*

CHAMPAGNE CHARBAUT "CERTIFICATE" BLANC DE BLANCS 1982:

(Ed's bottle) Flowery, spicy, elegant on nose and palate. Fruity, nice, long. Well balanced. Very enjoyable. (17)

CHAMPAGNE BOLLINGER "RD" 1969, IN MAGNUMS:

(Sid's bottle) Disgorged July 11, 1989. Bone dry, no dosage. Superb nose. Yeasty, serious, complex, long. Very dry, spicy. Great complexity. A "food" Champagne. A bit too dry for me, but very good, nevertheless. Serious. (18)

MEURSAULT-PERRIÈRES 1979 "TASTEVINÉ," J. F. COCHE-DURY:

(John Tilson's bottle) Brilliant, deep, mature gold. Superb, nutty, earthy nose. Classic Meursault. Great length, depth. Complex, long. Fabulous acidity, fruit. At its peak. Full, rich, complex. Excellent. (18.5)

BIENVENUES BÂTARD-MONTRACHET 1982, RAMONET:

(John Tilson's bottle) Lighter colour. Subdued, elegant wine on nose and palate. Classy, needs more time. Elegant. Lovely balance, but at this stage, lacks slightly in depth. Very good. (18)

1982 CHÂTEAU MARGAUX:

(Ian Mottershead's bottle) Excellent, deep colour. Ripe, spicy, yet elegant oak, ripe Cabernet nose. Full, rich, and long, yet finish is a bit tight. Very good, but not the great concentration of Mouton, Lascases, etc., in 1982. Nose is the best part. Needs five to eight more years. (18)

1988 LA TÂCHE, DOMAINE DE LA ROMANÉE-CONTI:

(Stephen Kaplan's bottle) Medium-red colour. Complex, lovely Pinot Noir nose. Long, fabulous fruit. Surprisingly evolved for such a young wine and a 1988! Very good even now. Lovely, long, complex. Super wine. Yet where are the depth and tannins of the 1988s? (18)

Château l'Arrosée 1970, 1966, and 1961

(1970 and 1966 were John Levine's; 1961 was Dave Spurrell's.)

1970:

Deep, youthful colour of the 1970s. Sweet, ripe, slightly herbaceous nose. Big St. Emilion. Straightforward. No rush. Loads of fruit. Simpler than the 1966 or 1961. (17)

1966:

Chocolate, maturing colour. Coffee on nose. Full, round, well balanced (not dry like many 1966s). At its peak. Like a Pauillac or St. Julien. Very fine. John Tilson said that it was a bit musty. I couldn't detect that. (17.5)

1961:

Similar appearance to the 1966, but slightly deeper. Superb nose of classic, intense, ripe, mature Claret. 1961 character. Long, full, rich, complex. Lovely balance. Ready, but no rush. Top quality. (18)

Our guests from out-of-town had never experienced these wines (only younger vintages of the 1980s) and they were impressed. Château l'Arrosée has been well known in Canada for many years. The Americans only discovered it when Robert Parker did, in the early 1980s.

CHÂTEAU LEOVILLE-BARTON 1945, LONDON-BOTTLED BY BLOCK, GRAY AND BLOCK:

(My bottle) Upper shoulder level. Decanted 15 minutes. Fair bit of sediment. Deep, very mature colour. Sweet, wet earth of Claret that is getting old on nose and palate. Not pruny, but tired. Full, rich, sweet, without the tannic backbone typical of the 1945s. I liked it more than most. (Prejudiced?) Still enjoyable. Having tasted this particular bottling on four previous occasions, I must admit that this did not show very well. (15)

CHÂTEAU CHEVAL-BLANC 1955, IN MAGNUM:

(Stephen Kaplan's bottle) Good low neck level. Decanted 30 minutes. Good, dark colour for a 36-year-old wine. Spicy, herbaceous, expansive St. Emilion nose. Long, complex, elegant, still quite lively. Fine quality. Personally, I preferred the complexity of the 1961 l'Arrosée, but this was very good. Needs drinking. (18)

CHÂTEAU SUDUIRAUT 1959:

(John Tilson brought two bottles along.) My favourite Sauternes. Very deep, mature, golden colour. Sweet, long, ripe, mature botrytis. Still has fruit and excellent acidity. Smooth, mellow, long. Fabulous botrytis aftertaste. Great stuff. (18.5)

TOKAY ESSENCIA 1988:

Pure Herslevelü. 65% sugar. Apricot cream! Thick, still fermenting (foam on top). Fat, rich. This was given to me in March 1990, during a trip to Tokay, by the winemaker. Can last 200 years in bottle. Not commercially produced. No score: an unusual rare experience. This is used to produce sweet Tokai, but never bottled "as is."

Food

Lovely lobster tail, duck timbale, and grilled veal chop. Very nice presentation.

Saturday, July 27, 1991

We went up to Turnagain Island.

With Laurie and John Tilson, their 13-year-old son Jeff, Ed Lazarus, and Stephen Kaplan. Everyone brought along some wine for dinner and for lunch on Sunday. Went for enjoyable Jeep rides, boat rides, walks, etc. Nice, fresh prawns and barbecued New York steaks.

CHAMPAGNE CHARBAUT "CERTIFICATE" 1982, BLANC DE BLANCS:

(Ed's bottle) Similar comments as on previous night. (17)

BÂTARD-MONTRACHET 1978, LOUIS LATOUR:

(Ed's bottle) Delicate green-gold colour. Spicy, leaner, racier style of the 1978s. Delicate, yet still lively, with good fruit. If well stored, no rush drinking this. Complex, spicy, long, very fine. Not as fat as some, but classy. (18)

MONTRACHET, DOMAINE DE LA ROMANÉE-CONTI 1978:

(Stephen Kaplan's bottle) Clearly the wine of the weekend. This retails now for over $500 a bottle!

Brilliant golden colour. Expansive nose of ripe, intense Chardonnay and new oak. Magnificent balance; loads of ripe fruit, acidity. Harmony, length. To be consumed by itself. Great stuff! No rush. The perfect balance and intense fruit will keep this wine alive for several more years. Memorable wine. I've had this wine (same vintage) on seven different occasions. Always great. (19.5)

LA TÂCHE 1988, DOMAINE DE LA ROMANÉE-CONTI:

(Stephen's bottle) Oddly, it was rounder, richer than on the previous night. See other comments above. (18)

ROBERT MONDAVI CABERNET SAUVIGNON "RESERVE" 1974, NAPA VALLEY:

(My bottle) Very good, deep colour. Expansive, sweet, spicy, Cabernet nose, with eucalyptus and oak in evidence. Full, round, at its peak. Holding very well. Lots of fruit, rich, very well balanced. Fine wine. (17.5)

CHÂTEAU PALMER 1970:

(My bottle) Top neck level. Deep, impressive, youthful colour. Great, complex nose of Margaux; ripe fruit, slightly earthy. Reaching its peak. Superb balance, length. Rich, ripe fruit, yet delicacy and length. One of the great Palmers. Together with the 1978 Montrachet Domaine de la Romanée-Conti, a star of the whole weekend. (19)

GEWÜRZTRAMINER "SÉLECTION DE GRAINS NOBLES" 1976, FÛT 28, JEAN HUGEL:

(My bottle) Cask #28 of three casks made: #20, #28, and #67. Medium to deep gold. Exotic, rich, sweet, spicy nose of mature Gewürztraminer. Surprisingly sweet, creamy, rich, and long. Medium acidity, approaching its peak. Petroleum on palate (more like Riesling), but spicy Gewürztraminer aftertaste. Lots of intensity, weight, and depth here. Top quality. (18)

PIESPORTER GÜNTHERSLAY RIESLING EISWEIN BEERENAUSLESE 1975, MARIENHOF, MOSEL:

(Ed's bottle) Very "Mosel." Delicate, subdued, flowery nose. Pale gold. The acidity of the 1975s. Surprisingly fresh. Spicy, yet delicate. Lighter than Hugel's Sélection de Grains Nobles 1976. Very nice balance. Fresh summer sipping wine. (17.5)

Sunday, July 28, 1991

Lunch on Turnagain Island.

We had lunch together before the group's departure for Vancouver.

BIENVENUE BÂTARD-MONTRACHET 1978, LOUIS LATOUR:

(Ed's bottle) More forward, deeper gold, softer than Louis Latour's Bâtard 1978 we had on the previous day. Evolved and needs drinking, but very nice, complex nose. Hint of acidity, astringency at finish, but complex. (17.5)

August 1991

During our stay in Yountville, Belle and Barney Rhodes came over for a visit. I opened the following Champagne.

CHARBAUT CHAMPAGNE BRUT N/V:

Crisp, clean, fresh nose. Quite lean, acidic, but with nice fruit. Crisp, but a bit too lean. Nice aperitif Champagne, though.

Then we went out for dinner at "Piatti's" in Yountville, and took our wines along.

FAR NIENTE CHARDONNAY 1986, NAPA VALLEY:

(Barney's bottle) Bright, deep gold. Intense, ripe Chardonnay and oak on nose. Rich, full, good depth. Went well with the spicy Italian food, but too big for me. Long, clean finish. Low acidity. Needs drinking.

1972 GRANDS ECHÉZEAUX, DOMAINE DE LA ROMANÉE-CONTI:

(My bottle) Part of a lot of seven bottles purchased at auction at Butterfield and Butterfield last June. This had the lowest fill (one-and-a-half inches from cork). Lots of sediment. I decided not to decant it because of the very forward, mature colour. (Other bottles with better levels should be more youthful.) Fabulous, spicy, sweet, open nose of classic Pinot Noir. Round, forward, soft, good length. Long, spicy, complex. This is very good, but very forward. Other bottles will be livelier.

The following day, Barney brought over a bottle of this wine.

GEMELLO CABERNET SAUVIGNON "GEMELLO SELECTION 35TH ANNIVERSARY," CALIFORNIA:

Probably a blend of the 1959 and the 1960 vintages. Very good level. Dark, yet forward, maturing. Nice, mature oak, chocolaty, herbaceous nose. Full, rich, soft, old-tasting. Not very complex, but has held well. Straightforward, mature, rich.

Barney told me that in the early days, Gemello didn't have any oak in which to age their wine, so Barney supplied them with a couple of oak barrels; eventually, he got some bottles out of those barrels, including the one we tasted.

Before our dinner at "Piatti's."

We bumped into Mike Grgich, a nice man still wearing his beret—very "European." This is a painful period for him. He is from Croatia and there is fighting going on in Yugoslavia between the Serbs and the Yugoslav army on one hand, and the Croats on the other. He seemed very upset. He has two older sisters (in their 80s) in Croatia.

Mike left Yugoslavia in 1954 (hated the Communists and saw no future there for himself). He waited in Germany for 18 months for his visa to the USA, got tired of waiting, and left for Vancouver. He lived in Vancouver for two-and-a-half years, still waiting for his visa to the USA, and worked as a dishwasher in restaurants on East Hastings Street, not a good area of town. Finally, in 1959 he was granted his visa and left for the Napa Valley, where he had some relatives. The rest is history. A charming, down-to-earth man, slight in build, and very lively for his age.

Wednesday, October 2, 1991

Dinner at Joe and Alice Heitz's home.

Other guests included his agent in Massachusetts (Boston), and a restaurateur from the Boston area, and their spouses.

One of the subjects we discussed was wine journalists and their comments, such as "How long are you going to keep the skin contact?" Joe quoted Mike Grgich, who once said: "The juice has been in contact with the skin for months on the vine! Just press the juice and start the fermentation!" I guess that some wine journalists try to sound "technical." It may give the reader the impression that these journalists are professionals, and know what they are talking about.

CHAMPAGNE DEUTZ N/V MONTANA, MARLBOROUGH, NEW ZEALAND:

A very pleasant surprise. Complex, clear, spicy, well balanced. Better than many commercial French Champagnes. Nice fruit and length. Little mousse, but nice small bubbles. (17)

HEITZ CELLARS 1986 CABERNET SAUVIGNON, NAPA VALLEY:

Nice, medium-red colour. Forward, ripe, round, more evolved with less extract and less lively than the very good 1985. (16)

HEITZ CELLARS 1986 "BELLA OAKS" CABERNET SAUVIGNON, NAPA VALLEY:

As above, but more classic, more complex, darker, more depth. Quite ripe and rich. Better than the 1985. Very good. (17)

HEITZ CELLARS 1986 "MARTHA'S VINEYARD" CABERNET SAUVIGNON, NAPA VALLEY:

Very dark, fabulous minty nose. Rich, full, long on palate. Excellent balance and depth. Lovely, long, ripe. No rush. This is top quality! Should peak around 1995 to 1998, and last well beyond. (18)

HEITZ CELLARS 1975 "MARTHA'S VINEYARD" CABERNET SAUVIGNON, NAPA VALLEY:

(Served blind) Opened at noon (!) for other guests. I thought it was the 1976 or 1977 (drought years). Hotter than expected, yet lovely fruit, maturity, length. Holding very well. Very good now, but no rush. Complex, well balanced, long. Slightly alcoholic. A fine bottle, with typical "Martha's" characteristics. (17.5)

HEITZ CELLARS 1974 ANGELICA:

Recently released in beautiful, long-necked bottles. Not unlike a Tawny with Bristol Cream smooth, mellow texture. Superb, spicy, nutty nose. Great length, balance. Fabulous fruit. Recently bottled. Lovely fruit. Great intensity. This is really very fine! (17.5)

Also tasted in Yountville

CHAMBOLLE-MUSIGNY PREMIER CRU "LES AMOUREUSES" 1969, DOMAINE GRIVELET:

I brought it along to the "California Café." Purchased from K and L Wines in Atherton on my way to Yountville. Very good top level, almost to cork. Mature, brick, orange-red colour with good depth. Some sediment, but less than expected. Mature, perfumy, yet barnyardy nose, typical of older Burgundies. Elegant, soft, yet still alive and complex. Very good length. I chilled the wine slightly and that made it taste much fresher. Very good bottle, but needs drinking. (17.5)

CHÂTEAU LA LAGUNE 1966:

Purchased from K and L Wines in Atherton. Good low neck level. Good, dark, maturing colour. Impressive, expansive, mature Cabernet and oak nose. Spicy, long, complex on palate. Well balanced. At its peak (since the early 1980s) and holding well, but will not improve. Surely one of the very best 1966s and a favourite of mine. Excellent wine. (18)

October 17, 1991

Commanderie de Bordeaux vertical tasting of Château La Mission Haut-Brion 1952 to 1982, at the "Centreboard" Room, Pan Pacific hotel.

The last three decades of the Woltner dynasty. Also that night: Provincial Elections and a new NDP government. That is all we needed now: a socialist government! At a time when in Eastern and Central Europe, the socialists and Communists have been kicked out.

We started with a tasting of Château La Mission Haut-Brion 1982 to 1975.

1. 1981:

Herbal, warm, stemmy, sweet, straw, earthy nose. Medium-red. Palish rim. Rich, round; trace of acidity at finish. Medium body, little tannins. Velvety, elegant. Ready. Not much depth, but very pleasant. (16.5)

2. 1979:

Similar appearance to #1, but slightly more evolved rim. More subdued on nose, too; tighter. Earthy, iron, metallic. Hard, unyielding. Sweet fruit, but tannic, high acidity. Stemmy. Needs time. (15.5) My score is conservative. Better bottles can easily achieve (17.5).

3. 1978:

Slightly darker than #2, but browner (ageing) rim. Lovely. Delicate, sweet, earthy, oak, ripe nose. Slightly leathery, sweet, evolved fruit. Cedar, cigar-box. Ready, but no rush. Nice oaky, smoky nose. (18)

4. 1982:

Very good, deep colour to rim. Youthful, sweet, subdued, young, ripe nose. Ripe fruit; rich, tannic, sweet cherries. Very ripe. Long, clean aftertaste. Needs ten years, or more. This is a classic vintage. (18.5)

5. 1975:

As dark in colour as the 1982, but much more evolved-looking. Superb, ripe, mature nose; loaded with ripe fruit. Great extract. Full, rich, long. Solid, tannic backbone typical of the 1975s. Great extract and fruit. Rich, long. Very good balance. Old style, great body, structure, depth. Lovely wine. Needs ten more years. (19)

Then we sat down for dinner and tasted the following.

Champagne Pol Roger "Chardonnay" 1982:

Tiny bubbles and fine mousse. Very nice fruit, elegance. Slightly sweet, complex. At its peak. A fine Champagne. (17.5)

Château Laville-Haut-Brion 1978:

Surprisingly green-gold. Good depth. Oak, herbal, ripe nose. Finally coming around. Full, rich, long, complex, very good fruit. Oak, long, delicate. Very fine wine. Ripe pears, beautiful! A couple of bottles were earthy, wet-cement, odd. Mine was lovely. At first, there was a hint of petroleum; later, it cleared. Ready, but will last for many years. (18)

Château La Mission Haut-Brion 1971, 1970, 1967

1. 1967:

Mature, palish colour. Earthy, musty nose. Ripe, chocolaty, soft, forward. I've had better bottles. This can be very good. In fact, it is possibly the best 1967 and the one that has lasted the longest. (15)

2. 1970:

Darkest of flight. Medium-dark, mature rim. Volatile acidity. Acidic, sharp, lean. Sauerkraut nose. Very good extract, but acidic. Nice ripe fruit, but too lean. Some people seem to like this wine. Maybe two batches were bottled? Personally, I have never tasted a truly fine 1970 La Mission. (14.5)

3. 1971:

Mature colour. Leathery, ripe nose. Sweet, ripe, elegant, surprisingly good. Better than the 1970. Complex, ripe, long. At its peak. Most enjoyable. (17)

All wines had excellent neck levels.

Château La Mission Haut-Brion 1966, 1964, 1955, 1952

The 1952 in magnum, bottled by Barton et Guestier. All other wines were single bottles, all château-bottled.

1966:

Good, dark, maturing colour; orange rim. Ripe, sweet, absolutely at its peak. Without the hardness of so many 1966s. Sweet, leathery, cedary, oaky elegance. Perfumy wine. Lovely. A classic. Great balance and elegance. (18.5)

1964:

Surprisingly, this was structured more like a 1966, and the 1966 like a 1964. Harder, darker than the 1966. Very good fruit, tobacco, earth, but a bit of hardness and acidity at finish. Very good, nevertheless. (17)

1955:

Impressive structure and appearance. Dark, not unlike a 1970! Cedary, earthy nose. Full, rich, even youthful for its age. Structured like the 1964, but with more fruit. Very good, long. No rush, but will not improve. (18)

1952, in magnum:

Excellent, dark colour. Riper, richer than the 1966, yet slightly less complex; but rounder and better balanced than the 1964 or 1955. Ripe, rich, full, long. Even a bit tannic (typical 1952); full, ripe fruit. An excellent magnum, at 39 years of age! (18.5)

Château La Mission Haut-Brion 1959 and 1961

1961:

Medium-dark colour. Magnificent nose, even richer than the 1966. Superb bouquet, earthy, ripe fruit, some oak. Complex. Magnificent flavours and length, and great balance. Very long aftertaste. Très Grand Vin! (19.5)

1959:

Surprisingly, even darker, richer, and bigger than the 1961! Harder, more tannic, like an "older" 1975. Superb depth, backbone, length. This and the 1961 are truly great, yet different styles. This is bigger, intense, no rush! Great fruit extract. (19.5)

Overall impressions

This was a great tasting, showing the consistency of this fine property. Four truly superb wines were tasted: the 1975, 1966, 1959, and 1961, with the 1982, 1955, and 1952 close behind. An outstanding property and a very successful event.

In 1983, the Woltners sold La Mission, Laville, and La Tour-Haut-Brion to the owners of Château Haut-Brion. A sad day. I am glad that the old Woltner brothers were not around to see this happen. Jean Delmas, régisseur of Haut-Brion, has promised that "nothing will change." This is bad news. It is rarely true.

The food and service were outstanding.

January 10 to 20, 1992

Trip to Los Angeles and Hawaii.

January 10, 1992

Dinner at "Citrus," in Los Angeles.

With Brad Klein (in whose house we stayed for the weekend), and his friends Beth and Russ Buchan, from Florida. Fabulous meal, as usual, at "Citrus."

CHAMPAGNE SALON "LE MESNIL" 1982, BLANC DE BLANCS:

Lovely, spicy Chardonnay nose. Steely, crisp, superb balance. Lean, backed by very good fruit. Needs two to three extra years. Excellent with food. Very stylish. (18)

CORTON-CHARLEMAGNE 1985, BONNEAU DU MARTRAY

AND

CHEVALIER-MONTRACHET "LES DEMOISELLES" 1985, LOUIS LATOUR:

The Corton-Charlemagne was more forward, nutty. Elegant, leaner style of the 1985s. Not quite ready, but nice fruit, long, smoky, oaky Chardonnay. (18)

The Chevalier was totally closed, tight, very little coming through. After one hour in the glass, it opened up a bit. Lovely, subdued complexity and power. Needs at least three to five extra years of bottle-age, but will be great! Excellent balance, grip, length. (18.5)

1926 CHÂTEAU GRAND LA LAGUNE, IN MAGNUM:

Brad purchased this at a Christie's auction in 1989. Excellent bottom neck level. We drank this without decanting, through main and cheese courses. Medium-red, mature colour. The cork broke, but was branded with the name of the château and vintage (original cork). Old Cabernet nose: sweet, earthy, tea leaves. Round, mellow, very nice balance. Sweet, old fruit, but very lively. Long, complex, silky. Most enjoyable. Better-tasting than many First Growths of that vintage. (18)

ROSEMOUNT ESTATE "NOBLE SEMILLON" HUNTER VALLEY 1985 "SHOW RESERVE," AUSTRALIA:

Bright, deep gold. Like Rieussec in structure and balance. Forward, intense; lovely sweet botrytis and fruit. Classy, elegant. No hint of wood. Very fine. Drink now through 1995.

January 1992

Tasting and buffet dinner, at Brad Klein's, featuring Château Calon-Ségur 1918 to 1962, château-bottled.

Unless otherwise indicated, all wines were in regular-size bottles. Brad, myself, John Tilson, Ed Lazarus, Frank Robinson, Randy Sultane, Stephen Kaplan, and two other guests participated. The six ladies with us spent the evening in the living room, sipping Champagne. No, this was not an all-male chauvinistic affair. Our group had planned this event and paid for it a long time ago. Inviting our ladies was an afterthought, and they did not object to the set-up.

CHAMPAGNE LAURENT-PERRIER "GRAND SIÈCLE" BRUT N/V, IN MAGNUMS:

Yeasty, evolved nose. Smooth, round, complex. Fresh, yet has age. Nice fruit.

THE TASTING

Château Calon-Ségur, 1962 to 1918, in flights

1962 and 1961

1962:

Very close in colour to the 1961. Brick rim. Evolved, yet slightly more youthful than the 1961. Harder, even a bit tannic. Some acidity. Drier than the 1961. Both surprisingly good. (16.5)

1961:

Slightly lighter than the 1962. Herbaceous, green-olives nose. Forward, complex, earthy, oaky, mature. Hint of acidity at finish. Mellow. Easy drinking, fruity. Later, nose opened up. Complex, classy. Chocolaty and caramelly. Very nice, soft, ready. Sweet finish. Somehow lacks the ripe extract of the great 1961s. (17)

1952 to 1955

All three had consistent, dark colours.

1952:

(From Christie's) Bottom neck fill. Very good, deep colour. Darker than 1961 or 1962. Mature, orange rim. Hint of mustiness. Excellent fruit, good backbone. Long. Much richer than the 1961 and livelier. Lots of depth. Very good. (17.5)

1953:

Bottom neck. Elegant, fruity nose. Very good depth. Sweet, silky, elegant, long. This and the 1952 are excellent. Chocolaty, sweet, elegant. Very good backbone! No rush. Complex, lovely wine. Outstanding. (18)

1955:

Top shoulder fill. Deep colour. Slightly pruny, leathery nose (overripe). Much sweeter than 1952 or 1953, but short finish. Too pruny and a bit musty. Tiring, fading, toffee quality to it. (16.5)

1949 to 1945

This was a "golden era" for Calon-Ségur.

1945:

Good neck level. Wonderful, deep, dark colour to rim. Intense, ripe nose of classic Claret; cedar, oak, earth, ripe fruit. Dense. Vanilla. Classic 1945. Powerful, tannic, ripe, rich. Excellent balance; ripe, rich fruit. Lots of life ahead. No rush. (19)

1947:

Bottom neck fill. Very good, dark colour; evolved, orangy rim. Not as dark as the 1945 or 1949. Sweet, rich, and lovely fruit. Intense. Long, less ripe than the 1945, but tannic backbone. Rich, fruity, powerful. Masculine. Very St. Estèphe. Still good fruit. Held extremely well. (18) A magnum tasted later that year was sensational!

1948:

Bottom neck fill. Very good deep colour; mature orangy rim. Full, fruity, rich, long. Tea leaves, sweet. Evolved; perfect drinking now. Some sharpness at finish after 30 minutes. Very good fruit. A lot of flavour. Leaner finish. (17)

1949:

Good neck level. Dark colour; quite evolved rim. Silky, rich, mellow, perfect balance. Lovely, intense, rich, complex. Perfect. Most enjoyable for drinking now. (19)

1926 TO 1929

Another great decade for Calon-Ségur. Why can't they reproduce this standard of quality nowadays? All three wines were purchased by Brad three years ago at Vinexpo. All three had very good neck levels and have been recorked at the château in 1989.

1926:

Dark, maturing colour. Not unlike the 1961. Sweet, round, elegant. Slightly acidic finish. Good fruit; drying out a bit. Still very good. Lovely bottle. Not unlike the 1953, yet not as great as the 1949. (18)

1928:

Deep colour to rim. Darkest of flight. Incredible depth, power, length. Like a great 1945 or 1961. Incredibly great. Tannic, powerful, rich, loads of ripe fruit. As in 1985 (at the German-American Tasting in San Francisco), a great bottle. This surely must be one of the finest 1928s, regardless of "official" classification. (19.5)

1929:

Lovely nose. Fruity, mature. Still lively. Powerful, tannic, rich. Livelier fruit than most 1929s today. Sweet, ripe fruit. Drying out at finish. (17.5)

1934 to 1918

1934:

Purchased at Christie's a few years ago. Excellent, low neck fill. Minty nose. Odd. Medium-dark, very evolved colour. Most forward colour. Sharp, but had some fruit. Ending dry, acidic. Needs drinking. Not as rich as the others. (16)

1918:

Recorked at the château in 1990. Purchased from Draper and Esquin's in San Francisco. Excellent top neck level. Not as dark as the flight of the 1920s, yet certainly as dark as the 1961 or 1962! Very good depth. Slightly orangy rim. Stemmy, herbaceous, still lively. Flavourful, spicy. Leaner style, but nice, sweet fruit. The acidity and the sweet fruit made it last surprisingly well. (17.5)

Outstanding tasting. Great and consistent wines. Far more consistent than some greater and more famous châteaux!

1945 MARCOBRUNER BEERENAUSLESE:

Silver-lead capsule, shipper unknown, label illegible. Odd, green, dark-colour label. Like a mature 1976 or 1967 Sauternes. Very slight nose. Hint of Riesling-Muscat. Earthy, too. Not unlike a Muscat de Beaumes-de-Venise. Very dry, dull, no aftertaste. Unpleasant, watery. Totally dried out. (No score)

1975 CHÂTEAU CALON-SÉGUR:

The 1975 and 1982 were served to the ladies next door. Nice fruit, quite tannic, typical of 1975s. Good fruit. Spicy Cabernet. No rush. Not as powerful or rich as the 1945 or 1928, but very good. (17)

1982 CHÂTEAU CALON-SÉGUR:

Very good, dark colour; typical of 1982s. Very grapey, fruity. Way too young. Ripe tannins. Closed. No complexity. Needs ten to 12 years. Should make a fine bottle in ten years. (17 or 18)

1963 CROFT'S VINTAGE PORT:

Decanted only 30 minutes before tasting; unfair to the wine. It should have been decanted four to five hours earlier. Good, dark colour. Spirity, sweet nose. Full, round, classic, spicy, elegant, sweet Port. Not as ripe as Graham's, or as powerful as Dow's. Needs four to five hours of breathing time. Very fine. (17.5)

A very exciting event. Calon-Ségur is a great property, producing outstanding wines . . . until the mid 1950s.

January 1992

Vertical tasting of Vega Sicilia "Unico" 1936 to 1962, at "Patina," in Los Angeles.

The event was organized by Ed Lazarus and John Brincko. The participants were Ed Lazarus, John Brincko (who provided several wines), John Tilson, myself, Stephen Klein, Wolfgang Grunewald, Bipin Desai, Frank Robinson, and Russ Buchan. Very good food served, compatible with the wines.

Vega Sicilia "Unico" 1936, 1941, and 1942

All three had new corks: one waxed, others very new-looking. Recorked at the winery.

1936:

Most mature-looking. Orange-brick rim. Evolved. Leathery, sweet, pruny nose. Acidic, lemony, yet sweet. Powerful. Light fruit, but power. Hint of vanilla, American oak. Pruny. Old, yet acidity kept it alive; like old Brunellos! Produced the year the Spanish Civil War started! (16)

1941:

Very good, deep colour. Slight maturity at rim. Intense fruit on nose. Concentrated. Full, rich, powerful. Excellent tannins, ripe fruit. Very good structure. No rush! Best colour, best fruit, best structure of flight. Incredible youth and structure. Clearly better than the 1936 or 1942. After one hour, it got even better! Later, still outstanding. Best of all. Great. Chocolaty, silky, round, rich, long! Super wine by any standard. Surely this must be a "once in a lifetime" experience. (19)

1942:

Deep, dark colour. Palish rim. Earthy, oaky nose. Leaner, harder than the 1941, but more youthful than 1936. Fresh, crisp, long, quite acidic. Stemmy. Not as ripe or complete as the 1941, but good structure. Wet-concrete nose. Later, nose opened up; sweet, forthcoming. (16.5)

Vega Sicilia "Unico" 1948, 1949, and 1953

1948:

Very good, dark colour. Not as much ruby as the 1941, more amber edge. Some wood. Creamy, lactic nose. Full, sweet, fruity, hard, yet very intense and concentrated. These wines taste a lot like big St. Estèphes. Nice, sweet, fruit. Not dried out. Sharper, more acidic than the 1941, but much livelier than the 1936 or 1942. Severe, hard wine, but good fruit. (17.5)

1949:

Purchased in Texas many years ago by Ed Lazarus, at an auction? Good depth, very evolved colour, orange rim. Not very clean-looking. Vegetal nose; tart fruit. Pungent, acidic, unpleasant. Original, shrunken cork, which fell into the bottle when it was opened. The only wine among the older bottles to have an original cork. All others must have been recorked at the winery. (12)

1953:

Pretty, youthful colour. Very good depth, but not as dark as the 1941. Ruby colour. American oak, sweet, truffles on nose. Concentrated, sweet fruit. Very good extract. Surprisingly youthful. Other tasters thought this was better than the 1948. Hard to choose between this and the 1948; the 1948 is harder, but both are excellent. (17.5)

Vega Sicilia "Unico" 1957, 1960, 1962 and "Reserva Especial" N/V

1957:

Excellent, deep colour. Not unlike 1970 Bordeaux. Still very youthful, concentrated nose. Fresh, lots of fruit on palate. Very good depth, length; powerful, intense. Very good. Lovely extract. Hard wine. (17)

1960:

Deep colour. More evolved than the 1957, but very dark. Clean, concentrated, ripe. Sweeter, softer than the 1957. Rounder, yet very ripe, sweet, rich. Elegant. (17.5)

1962:

Very good, dark colour to rim. Better appearance than the 1957 or 1960. Clean, fruity nose. Lovely balance. Rich, concentrated. Excellent, youthful fruit. Very good length. Great extract. This is a really fine bottle. (18)

"RESERVA ESPECIAL":

Bottled in 1984; about 7,800 bottles produced from 28 barrels. Dark, but more-evolved colour than the 1962. Nice fruit. Very much like the 1962. Not as hard or acidic as most. Made to appeal earlier. Probably a blend of various wines from the 1960s and early 1970s. (17.5)

Overall impressions

Great and rare event. Only one poor wine. Excellent quality. A truly fine property. Structure resembles a fine St. Estèphe; hard, tannic, serious wines, but with the higher acidity level of fine, old Brunellos. Group's overall favourite: the 1941, followed by the 1962, 1953, and 1948. This very rare event enabled us to learn about the style, structure, and staying power of the finest and rarest of Spanish red wines.

DESSERT WINE

RARE AMOROSO SWEET SHERRY "LANDED AGE" N/V, E. LUSTAU:

Dark amber. Rich, sweet, nutty, not cloying. Very good balance, intensity, and length.

Vega Sicilia Statistics

They have 300 acres under vine, with 60% Tempranillo; 25% Cabernet Sauvignon (increasing), 8% Merlot, the rest being Malbec and Albillo (white); only 20 hectolitres per hectare average production. Wines are aged in 70% American oak and 30% French oak. "Unico" is aged for seven to ten years in wood, and three to five years in bottle. "Valbuena" is aged only three to five years in wood. "Unico" average production is 5,000 cases per year.

The end of this Vega Sicilia historic tasting was marred by two discussions that—at a certain point—almost got out of hand. Somehow, Bipin Desai stood up and commented that, in his opinion, Mouton Rothschild makes one of the best—if not the best—First Growth. Others disagreed. A discussion ensued. Most tasters argued that while Mouton has been under one administration and one team for over 60 (!) years, it has been a "Dr. Jekyll and Mr. Hyde" wine. Mouton either makes great wines (1929, 1945, 1949, 1959, 1961, 1975, 1982, 1986) or disappoints when it should have done better (1928, 1955, 1966, 1970, 1978, 1979, 1981, etc.). I tend to agree with this argument. It seems to be "hit or miss." Then, out of the blue, one of our hosts, known for his very right-wing attitude, stood up and proposed a toast to "El Caudillo" (Francisco Franco). One could have almost cut the tension in the air with a knife. In the end, I got up and suggested that we "stick to wine."

January 23, 1992

Penfold's Grange Hermitage tasting for Le Tastevin Wine Club, at the Park Royal hotel, in West Vancouver.

APERITIF

PENFOLD'S CHARDONNAY 1988, BAROSSA VALLEY:

Delicate, flowery, elegant, well-balanced Chardonnay; spoiled by way too much new oak. Like chewing furniture!

FLIGHT #1

Cabernet-Shiraz

1. PENFOLD'S CABERNET-SHIRAZ 1987 BIN 389:

Very good, deep, cherry-red colour. Purplish rim. Spicy, stemmy, ripe, American oak nose. Good acidity. Long. Slightly tannic, vanilla-oak. Ripe, long aftertaste. (16)

2. PENFOLD'S CABERNET-SHIRAZ 1986 BIN 389:

Similar appearance to the 1987, but slightly paler rim. Much more subdued nose than the 1987. Some ripe fruit, but tight. Creamy, rich; more tannic, less acidic, riper fruit than the 1987. Fresher fruit than the 1983. (16.5)

3. PENFOLD'S CABERNET-SHIRAZ 1983 BIN 389:

Sent to us by the winery for this tasting. Far darker than the 1987 or 1986. Deep colour to rim. Similar nose to the 1987, but riper, rounder. Oak, sweet vanilla. Tannic; harder than 1986. Very good extract. Leather, ripe, rich, fat. Very good length. Chocolaty, forward nose. (17)

The above three blends were 65% to 75% Cabernet Sauvignon and 25% to 35% Shiraz. The overall quality was good. Good value. Nicely made wines. Not too heavy. Good food wines.

FLIGHT #2

Penfold's Grange Hermitage Bin 95, 1981 to 1985

1981:

Subdued, earthy, leathery nose. Full, new oak, rich, long, sweet. Loads of ripe fruit. Quite tannic. Rich, oak and vanilla. Very good. Needs four years. (18)

1982:

Slightly lighter rim than the 1981. More open, stemmy, peppery, leathery. Full, rich, ripe. Not as intense as the 1981, or as tannic, but riper, rounder. Lovely length. More stewed fruit, riper than the 1981. Some chocolate. Some overripeness. Needs two to four years. (18.5)

1983:

Very dark, almost black. Rubbery, spicy nose; some vanilla and ripe berries. Not unlike young Vintage Port! Full, powerful, intense. Loads of ripe fruit and tannins. Very long; needs six years. Some mint. Powerful. (17.5)

1984:

Very good, deep colour. Slightly palish rim. More forthcoming, more Bordeaux-like on nose. Lighter, leaner, without the sweet fruit of the previous three. Less ripe, less weight. Good acidity. Some French oak. Slightly hot finish. Elegant, soft (compared to the others). (16.5)

1985:

Sweet, ripe nose. Medium depth, very good balance. Elegant, oak, vanilla. Lovely length; cleaner, more elegant than the older vintages. Different, more "complete" style. Needs three to five years or more. (18)

Overall impressions

Show wines, impeccably made. Intense, rich, powerful, long. Full of ripe fruit, rich, oak, vanilla, spices. Difficult to drink more than a glass at a time. Popular event.

February 8, 1992

Dinner of "Group of Ten." Each couple brought a bottle. The two Domaine de la Romanée-Contis were our group wines.

CHAMPAGNE ROEDERER BRUT 1971, IN MAGNUM:

Yeasty, creamy Champagne. Held very well in magnum. Rich, generous, tiny bubbles, good acidity, yet soft. Very good. (18)

1978 CORTON-CHARLEMAGNE, LOUIS JADOT:

Deep, mature gold. Intense, open, nutty, oaky, rich, toasty nose. Typical Corton and 1978. Soft, rich, full, creamy. A bit acidic at finish, but long. Will not improve, but lovely now. (18)

1978 Chevalier-Montrachet, Remoissenet:

Slightly paler colour, but good depth. Subdued, buttery, elegant nose. Some oak. Lovely balance. Full of life. Very good balance. Complex, honeyed, flowery, long. No rush. Top quality. Great wine from a great vintage. (18.5)

1978 Romanée-St.-Vivant, Marey-Monges, Domaine de la Romanée-Conti

and

1978 La Tâche, Domaine de la Romanée-Conti:

(Group wines) Both had very good depth, the La Tâche slightly darker.

The St. Vivant: Superb, spicy, classic, Pinot Noir nose. Complex, sweet cherries. Full, rich, ripe, long. Great depth. Great length and intensity. No rush, has ten to 15 years to go. (18.5)

The La Tâche: Tighter nose, great backbone, long, complex. Harder, leaner, but great future. Too tight. Needs time. A great red Burgundy! The depth and extract is pure essence. Will be a perfect (20).

Romanée-St.-Vivant "Les Quatres Journaux" 1959, Louis Latour:

Very good, deep colour. Excellent level. Maturing rim. Lovely, jammy, rich. Barnyardy. A bit dull, but good depth. Subdued, candied. Drying out. Good, but not in the class of the Domaine de la Romanée-Contis. (17)

Château Leoville, Nathaniel Johnson and Sons, Bordeaux, vintage unknown:

Very good, deep colour. Mature, evolved rim. Not unlike a 1955 or 1959. Possibly a pre-World War I or earlier; possibly even prephylloxera. Cigar-box, cedar, sweet. Very good backbone and length. Outstanding cigar, cedar, tobacco on nose and palate. Not unlike an 1870. Not unlike Lascases. Old, yet authentic. Pity we do not know which vintage this could be. Amazing depth of colour. Hard to fault it, except for a trace of acidity at finish. Acquired in the 1920s by the father of one of Ian Mottershead's partners. Shipped from Bordeaux to Victoria for the Hudson's Bay Company around 1907 to 1910. (18.5)

Château Gilette "Crème de Tête" 1953, Christian Medeville:

Very good neck level. Brilliant, deep gold. Caramel candy rather than botrytis on nose. Without the cement smell typical of many vintages of this property. (They keep their wines in cement vats for up to 20 or 25 years before bottling.) Sweet, rich, long; not much character or individuality, but nice, clean, sweet fruit. (17)

Outstanding wines tonight; good food, too.

My research on the Château Leoville

The shape of the bottle is definitely 19th century, without the line on the side of the bottle, and with a very deep punt. Very similar shape to that of a bottle of 1870 Cos d'Estournel tasted recently. I also compared the glass to an 1899 Latour, 1920 Ausone, and 1928 Pichon-Lalande, and the Leoville bottle was almost identical to the 1870 Cos. Penning-Rousell's The Wines of Bordeaux indicates that until the latter part of the 19th century, the three properties [wines] were customarily sold just as "Leoville." Broadbent's Great Vintage Wine Book *mentions "Leoville" up to 1888; then from 1889 onward, he mentions "Leoville" under its proper ownership names (Lascases, Barton, Poyferré). Clearly, we drank a prephylloxera wine of great quality. A letter from Nat Johnson confirmed it as being from around 1880 to 1905.*

Further research by Ian Mottershead

The hunting lodge in the Fraser Valley where this wine was stored was owned by Clarie Wallace, who was a Lieutenant Governor of BC. The Wallaces sold the lodge to the McClelland family. Beth Hager married a McClelland; she died in the early 1930s. Ian is a partner of a grandson of Mrs. Hager. During Prohibition in the US, there was a fear there would be Prohibition in Canada, too, so wine was hoarded at the lodge. Norm Hager's grandfather had such guests at the lodge as Herbert Hoover. These wines were purchased from the Hudson's Bay Co. in the 1920s. There are eight to ten cases of mixed wines, aperitifs, liqueurs, and Brandies.

February 21, 1992

Vertical tasting and dinner, featuring Château Cheval-Blanc 1934 to 1982, at the "William Tell" restaurant, in Vancouver.

There were 30 participants, including the Vancouver crowd and Dr. Stan Schwartz of Danville, California. I organized this event. All wines were from my cellar, collected over the past six years. All were bottle-size (750 mL). All were château-bottled, except the 1947 (bottled by Cruse et Fils, Bordeaux). All had good-to-very-good levels. The worst, upper to very high shoulder.

Château Cheval-Blanc 1982 to 1970

1979:

Medium red, browning rim. Herbaceous, open nose. Round, sweet, forward. Complex, elegant, soft. Drink up. (16) Can be very good.

1978:

Slightly darker, deeper than the 1979. Younger nose, spicy, herbaceous. Some oak. Better backbone. No rush, but ready. Very long, complex. Very fine. Hint of tea leaves. Clearly better than the 1979 tonight. (17)

1982:

Very deep colour to rim. Sweet, lovely, rich, ripe berries on nose. Fat, luscious, hint of herbs. Classic, long, full. New oak, vanilla. Lovely balance. Chocolaty. Rich. (19)

1975:

Very dark, evolved colour. Some brown at rim. Tight nose. Full, powerful. Typical 1975, yet very good, ripe fruit. Not stemmy. More austere. Full, rich, long. (18)

1971:

Medium colour, good depth. Very evolved. Spicy, herbaceous nose. Forward, soft, past its prime, but still Cheval character. Smooth, stemmy, round. Elegant. Needs drinking. Very enjoyable. (17)

1970:

Better appearance, darker than the 1971, but not as dark as the 1975. Sweet, delicate nose. More backbone than the 1971. Rich, full, long. Ready, but if well stored, will last. Nice fruit. Hint of oak. (17.5)

1983 whites

1983 CHABLIS GRAND CRU "GRENOUILLES," CHÂTEAU DE GRENOUILLES:

Pale. Spicy, herbaceous nose. Good Chablis. Flinty, yet rich, ripe, alcoholic; typical 1983. A bit too sweet and alcoholic. (15.5)

1983 PULIGNY-MONTRACHET "CHAMPS CANET," E. SAUZET:

Bright green-gold. Classic Chardonnay; oaky nose, hint of sulphur. Round, complex, rich, mineral, long. Best of the three whites. Most complex, elegant, substantial. Very good balance. (17.5)

1983 CORTON-CHARLEMAGNE "DIAMOND JUBILEE," REMOISSENET:

Deepest; bright, deep gold. Full, rich, intense. Loaded with ripe fruit. Almost too alcoholic. Sweet. Very heavy. A bit too much of a good thing. (17)

Cheval-Blanc 1967, 1964, 1934

1967:

Medium-dark, evolved colour, good depth. Subdued, slightly leathery nose. Herbaceous, too. Stemmy, drying out. Quite lean. Certainly sound, but needs drinking. Surprisingly good. Better than Lafite, Mouton, or Margaux in 1967! (15)

1964:

Very good, deep colour to rim. Slight maturity. Subdued nose. Some sweet chocolate. Almost Pomerol-like. Full, fat, rich, long. Very good balance, depth. Complex, like Figeac 1964. (18)

1934:

Very good, top shoulder level. Original cork disintegrated. Brick colour. Old, sweet nose. Round, very delicate, Lafite-like. Elegant, smoky, complex, herbaceous. Spicy, some mushrooms. Has seen better days, but certainly sound and a pleasant drink. (16.5)

Château Cheval-Blanc 1966 to 1952

1966:

Good, dark colour; orangy rim. Subdued, sweet nose. Full, rich, sweeter than most 1966s. Long, complex, loads of fruit. Acid and tannins in harmony. Round, rich. Fresh fruit. Hint of mustiness, meaty. (17) I have tasted better examples of this wine in the past.

1959:

Excellent, deep colour to rim. Darker than the 1966. Very ripe, rich, leathery nose. Sweet, rich, ripe. Starting to oxidize. Sharp finish, unbalanced. Not as good as it can be. Port-like. Has seen better days. (15)

1953:

Toasty, burnt, oaky nose. Full, deep colour. Full, powerful, tannic, rich, long. Not unlike a big 1970. Coffee, crème-brûlée. Lovely nose. Intense, long, fabulous. (18)

1952:

Subdued, clean nose. Full, powerful, rich. Very 1952, yet sweet fruit. Even sweeter than the 1953. Not unlike a 1975. Hard, yet backed by good, sweet fruit. Solid, austere. One of the best 1952s. (17)

Cheval-Blanc 1955, 1948, and 1949

1955:

Very good, deep colour; slightly orange rim; impressive depth. Full, rich, loads of ripe fruit. Slightly crème-brûlée. Lovely wine. Top quality. No rush. Sweet, spicy. Great extract. (18.5)

1948:

Impressive, deep-red colour to rim. Like a 1982 but with more age! Meaty, iron; sweet, ripe fruit on nose. Ageless! Great extract, intense, full, rich, long. No rush. Darkest of flight. Not as well balanced as the 1955 or 1949, though. Massive wine. (17.5)

1949:

Very good, deep colour to rim. Impressive depth. Lovely, elegant, toasty, Cabernet Franc nose. Full, rich, complex, even tannic. Lots of depth, extract. Cannot detract anything from this wine. Great balance, length, complexity. Superb! No rush. (19.5)

Cheval-Blanc 1961 and 1947

1961:

Very deep, dark colour. Great depth to rim. Fabulous, ripe fruit. Classic. Intensity and ripe fruit typical of 1961. Hint of herbaceousness. Ripe, full, rich wine. Great extract, lovely depth, balance, yet drying out a bit at finish. Very good, though. Outclassed tonight by the 1949 and 1955. (18)

1947:

Bordeaux-bottled by Cruse et Fils, the only non-château-bottled. Good level, bottom neck. Excellent appearance. Incredibly youthful. Great extract, depth, length, balance. Solid, powerful. Not Port-like. A bit dry but very good! This is a historic wine. Outclassed on this occasion by the sublime 1955 and 1949. Maybe the fact that it wasn't château-bottled? Very fine, nevertheless. (18.5)

1967 CHÂTEAU CLIMENS, BARSAC:

Medium gold, still youthful. Subdued, botrytis nose. Round, complex, long. Rich, but not cloying. Does not have the fat or intensity of d'Yquem or Suduiraut, but then it is a Barsac. Very good. (17)

Overall impressions

A very successful evening. The clear favourites, and greatest wines were (in order) 1949, 1955, 1953, 1982. The least-favourites: 1979 and 1967, but even they were very good. No bad bottles. All excellent. The 1947 was not Port-like; rather austere Bordeaux; very good, but outshone by the 1949. Only the 1959 was a bit of a letdown.

March 21, 1992

Commanderie de Bordeaux Dinner and vertical tasting, featuring Château Palmer 1949 to 1985, at the Ramada Renaissance hotel, in Vancouver.

Peter Sichel generously shipped us the 1959 to 1967 vintages. The younger wines were from our extensive cellar.

THE TASTING

Château Palmer 1985 to 1978

1985:

Purplish, youthful colour. Cedary, complex nose. Full, yet not powerful. Oak. Elegant, complex, refined. Needs five to seven years. Very good balance. Not as rich as the 1983. (18)

1983:

Darker, more evolved than the 1985. Lovely, perfumy, chocolaty nose. Lots of elegance. Full, rich, more tannic and riper than the 1985. Very rich, chocolaty. Not quite ready. Tight, closed up. Try from 1995. Great potential. (18.5)

1982:

Similar in appearance to the 1983. Slightly paler rim. Very elegant, subdued nose. Hint of oak, vanilla. Rich, long, rounder, more evolved than the 1983. (17)

1981:

Lighter colour than all of the above. Evolved, brown-orange rim. Herbal, elegant nose. Hint of straw. Softer than all above. Hint of acidity. Elegant, forward, ready. (16)

1979:

Very good, dark colour; evolved rim. Chocolaty, coffee nose. Rich and ripe. Full, long, a bit tannic. Hint of acidity at finish, but a lot of extract. Fine, long. Ready, but no rush. (17.5)

1978:

Dark, but much more evolved colour than the 1979. Typical, spicy, herbaceous nose of the 1978s. Fairly evolved, ready. Elegant, spicy, complex. Very good, but lack of Merlot makes this wine atypical. (18)

APERITIF

CHAMPAGNE AYALA BRUT N/V:

Yeasty, round, smooth, much better than expected. Rich, creamy, lively. Obviously has some age, but very good.

CHÂTEAU PALMER 1975 TO 1949 (WHICH WE HAD IN FLIGHTS, THROUGH THE MEAL)

1976, 1967, 1964 (the "lesser" vintages)

1976:

Medium colour, evolved rim. Open, forward, ripe, but short finish. Slightly pruny. Ready. Needs drinking. Not bad, but some excessive acidity. Drink up. (15.5)

1967:

Evolved colour; lighter than the 1976; orange rim. Acidic finish, typical of the 1967s. Nice fruit, complex, better than expected. Needs drinking. (15)

1964:

Medium red, evolved, orangy-brown rim. Cedar, coffee, toffee, evolved nose. Soft, elegant, better than expected on palate. Round, sweet, complex. Fragile. Soft, sweet, surprisingly good. After 15 minutes, drying out. (16)

1975 and 1970

1975:

Deep colour. Herbaceous, tight nose. Very good fruit but hard tannins, typical of the vintage. Needs five to ten years. Very good quality. Powerful. Lovely. (18)

1970:

Very good, deep colour. Chocolaty, rich, ripe. Loads of ripe fruit. Very long, very full, rich, magnificent. Great bottle. Needs more time. I have had the good fortune of tasting this wine on at least 15 occasions. At 12 years old, it is not ready yet, but it is a beauty. Drink from 1993 to 2002. (19)

1962, 1959, 1949, in magnum

1962:

Similar appearance to the 1964, but less evolved. Open, cedar, straw, delicate, fruit nose. Richer, better backbone than 1964. Nice, sweet, forward. Two other bottles drying out. (16)

1959:

Very good, deep colour. Darkest of flight. Fullest, too. Good depth, structure, balance. Not as round and elegant as in past experiences, but very good. I've tasted better. Drying out at finish. Good, but not great. Pity, because this can be great. (17)

1949, FROM MAGNUM:

Evolved colour, orangy rim. Like the 1964. Elegant, old Margaux nose. Quite sweet, even tannic; acidic, but nice, ripe fruit. Forward, yet good balance. Lovely, but fading, even from magnum. Very good, though. Not La Mission or Cheval-Blanc or Lafite, but very enjoyable. (17)

1966, 1961

1966:

Impressive, deep colour. Mature rim. Lovely, chocolaty, cedary nose. Full, rich, long. Lovely length and balance. Full, powerful. Excellent. Classy. Ready, of course, but enough stuffing to last (if well stored) until 1998 or beyond. (18.5)

1961:

Even darker than the 1966. Full, luscious. Bigger, riper, sweeter, even more intense than the 1966. Great extract. Very ripe, sweet. Not as smooth as during past experiences, but lovely. As great as the 1970. Together with the 1970, best wine of the evening. (19.5)

Impressions

My personal favourites (in that order) were: 1961, 1970, 1966, 1975, 1983, 1985, 1978, 1979. When good, the 1959 definitely belongs to this group. Food was excellent. Presentation and service were great.

DESSERT WINE

1975 FONSECA'S VINTAGE PORT:

Soft, forward, very smooth, round, nice fruit. One of the top 1975s. Ready.

Early May, 1992

Special Robert Mondavi tasting, at the "Prow" restaurant, with Michael Mondavi.

A vertical of Robert Mondavi Cabernet Sauvignons "Reserve," Napa Valley.

FLIGHT #1

1984 to 1988

1984:

Good red colour, maturing rim, medium depth. Spicy, oak; a bit dank. Quite full, rich, even a bit tannic. Trace of acidity at finish. Medium-bodied. Good length, but too lean, acidic. Sharp finish. Not in the same class as the following wines. (16)

1985:

More youthful, deeper red than the 1984. Closed nose. Slight hint of tar. More body, more depth, more extract. Riper fruit than the 1984. Very good balance. Closed up. 11% Cabernet Franc in the blend. (17.5)

1986:

Darker, deeper than the 1985. Lovely, spicy, cedary, intense, Cabernet nose. Full, rich, long, loads of ripe fruit. Even riper and richer than the 1985. Only 17 months in oak. Shortest time in oak of flight. Very ripe tannins. (18)

1987:

Very good, dark inky colour to rim. Tight nose. Very ripe, great extract. Lovely on palate. Not as powerful as the 1986. Softer, riper tannins. Will be excellent. (18.5)

1988:

Deep, youthful colour; hint of purple. Noticeable eucalyptus, some fruit on nose. Ripe, rich, youthful. Intense. Slightly too acidic. Soft tannins, sweet. (17.5)

FLIGHT #2

1974 to 1979

1974:

Dark, but mature colour. Earthy Claret nose. Sweet, leathery, a bit seaweedy, inky. Good depth, balance. Surprisingly forward. My bottles are great. This was merely good. Long, complex, earthy finish. The score does not reflect the true quality of the 1974. Can be great. (17) Second bottle much better. Mint, eucalyptus, long, complex, livelier. Hint of tobacco. (18.5)

1975:

Similar appearance to the 1974, but slightly paler. Coffee, tobacco nose. Sweet. Full, rich, candied, tannic, but aftertaste very slightly oxidizing. Good acidity makes this a keeper. Better on nose than on palate. Longest time in oak (80% new): 33 months. (17.5)

1976:

Dark, but very mature, orange-brown rim. Tight, closed nose. Like an older 1966 Claret. Earthy, sweet, old fruit, but good backbone. Sweet, leathery, yet elegant. Harsh, dry, tannic finish. Not as hot as most "drought" 1976s. (16)

1977:

Dark, maturing colour. Nice, minty nose. Some oak, too. Harmonious. Round, sweet, rich, ripe. Ready and soft. Needs drinking. Slightly lemony finish. Another drought year. (16)

1978, IN MAGNUM:

Cooler vintage wine. Stemmy, green nose. Rounder on palate. Not as big or clumsy as the 1976 or 1977. Light, elegant, leathery, earthy Cabernet. Nice, long, but soft. (16.5)

1979:

Very good, dark, mature colour. Minty, open nose. Ripe fruit. Not leathery. Tannic finish. Intense, rich, still youthful. Very good. Classy, old style. Mint-eucalyptus. (17.5)

Overall impressions

The 1987, 1979, and 1974 showed best; 1985 and 1986 promising. We also discussed the devastation of many Napa Valley vineyards by the phylloxera louse. It is really serious. Many vineyards are being uprooted.

May 9, 1992

Dinner at "La Belle Auberge," in Ladner.

With Carol, John and Marcena Levine, Dr. Allan and Sally Tobe. Chef-owner Bruno Marti prepared a superb meal, as usual. The occasion was Carol's 46th birthday and Marcena's 47th birthday. Each couple brought along two bottles.

CHAMPAGNE BOLLINGER "VIEILLES VIGNES FRANÇAISES" 1979 "BLANC DE NOIRS" BRUT:

(My bottle) Two tiny plots of one acre each with 100% Pinot Noir grapes, ungrafted, with original prephylloxera root stocks. Very rare. Everyone agreed that this was a superb Champagne. Together with the Krug "Collection" 1955 (magnums), this is the greatest Champagne we've ever had. Deep, gold, maturing colour. Very fine yet lively mousse. Superb, rich, ripe, long, slightly yeasty, "liqueur of Champagne." Full-flavoured, off-dry, rich, creamy, perfect balance, length. Flavours went on and on in glass, on palate, and on nose. A magnificent bottle! A perfect (20).

MONTRACHET 1986, LOUIS LATOUR:

(Allan's bottle) Still too young, needs three to five years, but less lean or steely than the tight 1985. Unyielding at first, but opened up after 30 minutes in glass. Exotic, rich, long, with a serious, lean, acidic backbone. Will still improve. (18)

1946 "CLOS DES LAMBRAYS," HÉRITIERS COSSON:

(My bottle) Given to us by our Los Angeles friend, Ed Lazarus. An extremely rare 1946, on the occasion of Carol's birthday (born in 1946). Excellent level and appearance, good cork, and clean label. Fair bit of sediment (was not decanted, though). Very impressive, dark, deep colour. Some maturity at rim. Very smoky nose, not unlike 1945 Clos de Vougeot from René Engel. Toasty, lean, good structure, serious tannins and acidity, but some fruit there, too. Surprisingly rich, youthful, and serious for such a mediocre vintage. A rare experience. (17)

CHÂTEAU CHEVAL-BLANC 1947, LONDON-BOTTLED BY CHRISTOPHER AND CO.:

(John's bottle) Very good neck level. I had this bottling before, about five years ago. Although this bottle was very good, it was better, fresher, five years ago. Incredibly dark, deep colour to rim. Very ripe, almost leathery; but one-dimensional. Very full, very rich, very powerful, and long on palate. Not much class or complexity there, but lots of stuffing, power, depth. Will last for many years, but will not improve. Starting to lose its fruit, yet great extract. Stunning depth and weight. A rare wine and a great experience. (18.5)

CHÂTEAU D'YQUEM 1967:

(Allan's bottle) This great bottle had a deep, rich, golden colour. Magnificent, intense botrytis, caramelly, grapey nose. Full, long, extremely rich, fair bit of acidity. Lovely length, weight, complexity. The ultimate Sauternes, yet clearly at its peak, and losing some of its freshness and liveliness. Was superb five years ago. Still great, but will definitely not improve. Easily rated (19) to a perfect (20).

A most enjoyable evening. Great wines and excellent food.

May 29 to June 7, 1992

Trip to Los Angeles, Napa Valley, and Chicago.

May 29 to 30, 1992

Two-day tasting of Krug Champagnes, in Los Angeles.

Organized by Bipin Desai, with the participation of Rémy Krug. Two whole Krug wine collections were purchased at auction in London and New York. Also, Rémy Krug completed the collection. The proceeds of this event went to "Meals on Wheels," which Rémy Krug sponsors.

THE FIRST EVENT WAS HELD AT "MICHAEL'S" RESTAURANT.

Krug 1928 to 1982 "Collection"

"Collection" from 1973 back to 1928 only; 1976 to 1982 not called "Collection."

APERITIF

CHAMPAGNE KRUG "GRAND CUVÉE" N/V:

Quite youthful, fresh, long, well balanced. As good as most other houses' "Grandes Marques." Needs two to four extra years of bottle-age.

FLIGHT #1

1982, 1962, 1952, and 1942

(No 1972 made; a terrible year.)

1982:

Lovely, toasty, intense, creamy nose. Full, rich, tiny bubbles. Very long and full. Sparkling Bâtard-Montrachet-like. Will become a 1962 some day? Large volume. Complex. Disgorged July 1990. (18.5)

1962:

Noticeably darker than the 1982. Toasty, nutty, mature. Wonderful length. Complex, sweeter, rich. Very long. Fabulous depth. Lots of class. A complete Champagne that has held extremely well. Very good fruit. A classic. Elegance, finesse, etc. Disgorged in 1987; 24 years on its lees! Only 38% Pinot Noir and 26% Meunier; the balance is Chardonnay. (18.5) to (19).

1952:

Even darker than the 1962; like a mature, white Burgundy. Smells older; mushrooms, caramel, hint of oxidation. Very little fizz, but hint of it on palate. Like a fine old white Burgundy. Long. Too old for most, but certainly sound. Slightly honeyed. Long, sweet. Disgorged in 1960 at eight years of age. Made from 38% Chardonnay; unusually high. (17)

1942:

Still darker than the 1952, but not really old-looking. Very little fizz, yet livelier by far than the 1952. Incredible depth and length. Much fresher than the 1942; livelier, too. Slightly earthy nose. Quite earthy on palate. Round, complex, long. Hint of mushrooms. Not as fat as the 1962, but excellent. Lovely, complex, nutty, woody aftertaste. Very fine. Has held amazingly well. Disgorged in 1954. (18)

Overall impressions

In flight #1, best was 1962 and potentially the 1982. The 1942 has held amazingly well. The 1952 is old, but still very good. At Krug, they have no particular rule of disgorging. They disgorge when they have to ship.

FLIGHT #2

1976, 1971, and 1947

1976:

Quite deep gold; surprisingly evolved. The ripeness of the year. Quite sweet. Noticeably higher alcohol. Similar structure to 1976 white Burgundies. Made in a drought year. Picked September 1, 1976; very early. High yield, low acidity. Disgorged October 1987. (17) The 1976 can be superb: rich, oaky, luscious, long. Excellent! On other occasions (18) to (18.5).

1971:

Similar appearance to the 1976, but fresher. Toasty nose. Crisp. Full, long, complex. Lively, tiny bubbles. Lots of class. This is superb. Great depth. Clearly the wine of the flight. Good acidity. High Pinot Noir. Excellent. Disgorged in 1989. (18.5)

1947:

Brilliant, deep-gold colour. Nutty, herbaceous. No caramel or oxidation. Amazingly youthful. Full, rich, long, chewy, nutty. A meal by itself. Lovely length. Great extract. Has held extremely well. Toasty, rich, yet mature. Disgorged January 1956. This is really very fine. (18)

Comments

All three wines were big, rich vintages. Rémy decided on the vintages (flights). Rémy mentioned that their Pinot Meunier is from choice lots. A lot more variety in terms of quality between different vineyards of Meunier than in Chardonnay or Pinot Noir.

FLIGHT #3

1966, 1945, 1938, and 1928

1966:

Similar colour to 1976. Very good for age. Buttery, herbaceous nose. Hint of sulphur. Smells like a Chevalier-Montrachet. Full of life. Amazing. Spicy, fresh, well balanced. Much livelier than the 1976. Great length. Disgorged in 1986. (18)

1945:

Excellent, deep, gold colour. Nice mousse and tiny bubbles. Very ripe, like an older white Graves. Superb depth. Very good acidity, great extract. Wonderful, long. Liqueur of Champagne. Perfect balance. Outstanding. A meal by itself. No need for food! Very long. Almost Barsac-like. Magnificent! Has 42% Chardonnay in blend. Disgorged in 1965. (20)

1938:

Very impressive, youthful colour! Lovely, flowery, complex, long. Not as much extract as the 1945. Off-dry, touch of sweetness. Lively, long, complex, very fine. Almost a dessert wine. Fair bit of residual sugar. Disgorged in 1957. Excellent, but not quite the extract of the 1945 tasted above. (18)

1928:

Tighter, more serious backbone. Hint of residual sugar. Spicier, more herbaceous than the 1945, but great extract. Lovely length. Full, rich, tiny bubbles. Really a wine rather than a Champagne. Outstanding. Disgorged in 1989!!! After 60 years on its lees. Very high Pinot Noir (70%). (19.5)

Comments

Clearly, the 1928, 1938, and 1945 are made in a sweeter style. Pity to have put the 1966 in the same flight, yet it demonstrates difference in style of Champagne-making.

The 1928 Krug is now a legend. A large stock of this was sold to their English agents before World War II, and it was stored as a paid "Reserve" at Krug. When the War started, some British 1928 "Reserve" was still cellared at the winery. Rémy's grandfather destroyed the pre-war invoices and purchased the stock himself so it would not be confiscated by the Germans as enemy property. When the War ended, he reoffered the 1928s to the British agent, who did not want it; thus, they had 1928 left over at Krug. We drank 1928 Krug from Rémy's grandfather's private reserve. Only ten bottles are left at the property!

Second event, at "Spago's" restaurant, on the following day

The food was much better than at "Michael's" the previous night. The chefs of "Patina's" and "Chinois" were there, too, for a joint effort. As on the previous night, the aperitif was Champagne Krug "Grande Cuvée" N/V. Bipin asked me to speak about the first flight (1981, 1961, 1953).

FLIGHT #1

1981, 1961, and 1953

1981:

Bright gold. Good depth. Lovely, yeasty, fruity nose. Mellow, off-dry. Very good fruit/acidity balance. Lots of Chardonnay (50%). Tiny production. Very good acidity, excellent balance. No rush, yet soft, elegant. Difficult year. Disgorged June 1988. (17.5)

1961:

Amazing appearance. Like the 1981; very slightly darker. Toasty, oaky nose. Surprisingly fresh. Lots of Pinot Noir (over 50%). The intensity and depth of the vintage. Backbone, too. Lots of extract. Still very alive, long. Disgorged June 1990; 18 years on lees. Best of flight. Large production. (18.5)

1953:

Incredibly similar appearance to the 1961. Tiny bubbles. Toasty, ripe nose. Sweet on entry, very good acidity, hint of caramel. Very slightly starting to oxidize, but excellent and long. Good acidity, full, long, a bit citric. Small production. Disgorged in June 1986. (17)

Comments

1961 clearly best; 1953 getting tired; 1981 light "Blanc de Blancs" style (lots of Chardonnay). Oddly, 1961 large production, yet most concentrated. Other two vintages: small production.

FLIGHT #2

1973, 1964, 1955, and 1937

1973:

Bright gold. Herbal; surprisingly fresh-smelling. Lovely fruit, full of life, long, complex, sweet, but not over-the-hill. At its peak. Great length and balance. No rush. Needs food. Rich, big, but young! Disgorged 1983. (18)

1955:

Not part of the "Collection." Very deep gold; old Sauternes-like. Very rich, sweet nose. Fully mature, but not over-the-hill. Sweet, a "sipping" liqueur Champagne. Not nearly as great as the magnums tasted in 1988. Must have been disgorged a long time ago. They have none at the property, so Rémy acquired it in London from a private source. (16.5)

1964:

Fresh, buttery, lovely nose. Sweet on palate. Great length, but clearly sweeter than most. Very long. Full of life. Delicate, yet long and complex. Not very fat or rich, but very good. Not as rich as the 1973. Disgorged August 1987. (17.5)

1937:

Very deep gold, similar to the 1955. Softer than the 1955; sweeter, too. Very rich and soft. Went well with a spicy Chinese course. Flowery, delicate, yet rich. In the class of the 1945 and 1928. Great extract. Lovely depth and length. Luscious. Superb depth. Disgorged September 1957. 1937 is Henri Krug's birth year. Henri is Rémy's brother. He is the winemaker—a master. (19)

FLIGHT #3

1979, 1969, 1959, 1949, and 1929

1979:

Deepish gold. Elegant, softened quite a bit. Round, very elegant, classy. It is all there; ready, but very good depth and class. Very good fruit. Lots of Meunier (28%); much higher than usual. (18)

1969:

Much bigger, richer, fuller wine than the 1979. Lots of depth, extract, oak, lees, fabulous length. Great wine. Very long aftertaste. Still loads of fruit, very lively; tiny bubbles. A classic. At its peak, but no rush! Ageless! (19)

1959:

Darker than the 1969. Bottle-age showing. Crème-brûlée, caramel nose. Softer, biscuity, creamy, sweet aftertaste. Great balance. Great length and sweetness. Amazing depth. At its peak. (18.5)

1949:

Slightly darker than the 1959. Very good backbone, acidity, freshness, yet underlying fruit is soft. But under the acidity, the fruit fell apart. Still good, but not great. Too sweet on entry. Low acidity (6.5 grams). (16.5)

1929:

Surprisingly, lighter colour than the 1949 or 1959. Still lively. Not as complex as the 1928 of the previous evening, but sweet, soft. Has fizz. The 1928 hardly had any. Mushrooms, long, youthful. Very good fruit/acidity finish. Excellent. Has held very well. Great for its age. (18)

"Patina's," "Spago's," and "Chinois's" chefs were all in one place, cooking together—and with Krug Champagne. What more does one need?

The food at this second event was fabulous.

My overall greats

1945, 1928, 1971, 1962, 1982, 1947, 1937, 1961, 1969, 1959, 1966, 1973, 1979.

Rémy commented that this high standard of quality could not have been achieved without small oak-cask fermentation.

My comments were well received. I also mentioned my visit to Krug and meeting their father in 1980, as well as the outstanding performance of Krug Collection 1955 magnums during a 1955 First Growth Event (International Wine and Food Society) held three years ago—at which Krug was served at the very end, after 1955 d'Yquem, and was still the greatest wine of the evening.

Most of the wines, especially the older "Collections," are extremely rare. This will probably be the last time these wines will be tasted together, and especially from such a reliable source. No poor or mediocre wines. Only very good, or great!

June 5 to 6, 1992

Chicago.

I flew from San Francisco to visit Stephen Kaplan, in whose house I stayed. Stephen took me to an NBA basketball game—a playoff game #2— between the Chicago Bulls and the Portland Blazers. Michael Jordan was great, as usual. This was my very first live NBA game.

Visit to the Chicago Wine Company Auction, and later that day, to Christie's Wine Auction.

Both held on the same day. Talk about competition! Obviously, they are trying to undercut each other! Both boring affairs, and both seemed irregular. At the Chicago Wine Company, it seemed like a farce—bidding against the house. The minimum catalogue price is the house reserve price—obviously they own the wines rather than acting as a middleman, and they will not sell the wine under the suggested opening bid. They are really selling their own wines, and are trying to "get a higher price for it."

At Christie's, they let floor bidders know that "one more increase will get you the wine, because my written bidder will not go any higher!" At the Christie's auction, I made a successful bid on some large format bottles: 1978 Trotanoy and 1978 Gruaud-Larose (jeroboams), for my daughter Orly who was born that year. Also, an imperial of 1975 Mouton-Rothschild, for my son Michael who was born in 1975.

Pre-Auction tasting at Christie's

CHÂTEAU MOUTON-ROTHSCHILD 1961:

Low neck level. Dark, deep colour; mature rim. Lovely, ripe, expansive, cedar nose. Very long. Hint of mint. Full, rich, softer than expected, round. Lovely extract and finish. Very good. Can be even greater. (18.5)

CHÂTEAU LA MISSION HAUT-BRION 1962, NICOLAS:

Deep, almost-youthful colour of the 1962s. Open, fruity, earthy nose. Surprisingly fresh. Round, long, some tobacco. Rich, complex. Without the extract of a 1961, but excellent balance and fruit. One of the top 1962s. (18)

CHÂTEAU HAUT-BRION 1961:

Deep colour. Full, ripe, tobacco, earthy nose. Very long, rich, yet silky on palate. Classy wine. Lovely fruit. Excellent. Soft, ready, but no rush! (19)

CHÂTEAU MOUTON-ROTHSCHILD 1966:

Darker than expected. Not much complexity or ripeness on nose. Some cedar; stemmy, too. Medium-bodied, some acidity, and short finish. Lacks middle and depth, but some complexity on palate. Quite good, but not First Growth quality. (Latour, Palmer, La Mission, Ducru, Lascases, Margaux, Gruaud-Larose, all much better than this. Even La Lagune.) (16)

CHÂTEAU CHEVAL-BLANC 1970:

Evolved, forward, mature red colour. Good depth. Spicy, chocolaty, herbaceous nose. Round, soft, very complex wine. Long, well balanced. Easy to drink. Very long aftertaste. Will not improve. Perfect now. (18)

CHÂTEAU FERRIÈRE 1970, MARGAUX:

Good, deep colour of the 1970 Médocs. Peppery, spicy Cabernet nose. A bit stemmy. Quite acidic and sharp, but good body and tannins. Some fruit still there. Nice entry. Ready. Better than expected. Sharp edge, but enjoyable. (16.5)

CHÂTEAU LA TOUR-HAUT-BRION 1975:

Reported to be in reality La Mission 1975, bottled in small quantities as "La Tour-Haut-Brion" for some customers. Very dark, youthful colour. Tight nose. Herbal, concentrated Cabernet. Earthy. Typical structure of the good 1975s. Very tannic, very concentrated. Lots of fruit underneath. Needs at least ten years. Ripe, yet aggressive tannins. Will be very good someday, yet not quite as great as the "true" La Mission 1975. (17.5)

CHÂTEAU MARGAUX 1978:

Medium-red, good depth. Toasty, oaky, elegant nose. Herbaceous, rich, chocolaty; good acidity underneath. Almost ready, but needs four to six more years. Very good fruit and length. Complex. A historic wine, marking the return of this great property. (18)

CHÂTEAU CERTAN-DE-MAY 1979:

This must be the best Pomerol of the vintage. Dark, concentrated, lead-pencil, fruit on nose and palate. Approachable, but not really ready yet. Very full, round, rich, long. Lovely wine. (18)

CHÂTEAU LA CONSEILLANTE 1981:

Again, the Pomerol of the vintage! Very youthful colour. Lovely, fresh fruit on nose. Steelier style. Long, well balanced. Good structure. Not ready, but will be excellent in five to ten years. (18)

MUSIGNY "CUVÉE VIEILLES VIGNES" 1959, COMTE DE VOGÜÉ:

Very pale, mature colour. Slightly leathery, baked, oxidizing nose. Similar impressions on palate. A shadow of itself. Still drinkable, some sweetness, but really long over-the-hill! (14)

CHAMBERTIN 1978, DOMAINE A. ROUSSEAU:

Medium red, maturing colour with good depth. Surprisingly youthful on palate. Concentrated, tannic backbone. Very good herbal fruit. Classy, big, serious Chambertin. Hint of burnt toast on palate. Very good. Almost ready, but no rush. (18)

HEITZ CELLARS CABERNET SAUVIGNON 1970, NAPA VALLEY:

The "regular" bottling. Medium red, good depth. Very spicy, stemmy nose. Vegetable garden. Quite lean and acidic on palate. Not bad. Will probably be better with food, but nowhere near the extract, concentration, or complexity of the "Martha's Vineyard." (15)

Dinner at "Charlie Trotter's," in Chicago.

That night, Stephen Kaplan took me, as well as another guest and a lady friend of his, to Chicago's top restaurant, "Charlie Trotter's." Chef-owner Charlie Trotter prepared a fabulous almost-all-seafood meal. Great presentation and food quality! All wines, except the dessert wine, came from Stephen Kaplan's cellar.

CHAMPAGNE KRUG VINTAGE 1975:

Not the "Collection," but exciting nevertheless, especially since on the previous weekend, I had tasted all the Krug "Collection" from 1928 to 1982, yet no 1975! Pale gold, tiny bubbles. Very tight, lean, acidic, yet concentrated. Typical of the vintage and of "younger" Krugs. Needs five to ten years if well stored. Lovely fruit, concentration. After an hour in glass, it became a bit creamier and mellower, but not by much. Lovely balance and extract. (18.5)

CHÂTEAU COS D'ESTOURNEL 1985:

This wine seemed forward two to three years ago, but it has now closed up. Very deep, purplish-red colour to rim. Spicy, oaky, very fresh Cabernet, vanilla nose. Concentrated, tannic, but not a monster; lovely fruit, but really a baby. Excellent balance. Needs seven to ten extra years, at least, but will be lovely. All the components are there. (18)

CHÂTEAU BELAIR 1959 ST. GEORGES, ST. EMILION, CALVET SÉLECTION (DANISH-BOTTLING BY KJAER UND SOHNE):

Good, low neck level; young-looking (if shorter) cork. Nice, mature red colour. Clean, elegant, sweet, Cabernet, mature nose. Soft, well balanced, delicate, but certainly not tired. Not much complexity or depth, but for a "satellite" wine, certainly good, and has held very well! (17)

GIRARD CABERNET SAUVIGNON 1987, NAPA VALLEY:

(Sent to us by a guest at another table, Stephen's friend) Good, dark colour. Nice, cedary, Cabernet nose. Round, full-bodied, good acidity. Still too young, but quite enjoyable. (16.5)

1970 BEAULIEU VINEYARDS GEORGES DE LATOUR "PRIVATE RESERVE" CABERNET SAUVIGNON, NAPA VALLEY

AND

1970 CHÂTEAU LATOUR:

The Beaulieu Vineyards wine was more forward-looking, evolved. Open, forthcoming, sweet, American oak, stemmy, earthy nose. Round, open, forward. I remember it being more concentrated, with more depth than this. Quite good but not great. (16.5)

The Latour, on the other hand, was outstanding, but years away from being ready. Very deep, dark colour. Concentrated, cedary, spicy Cabernet nose. Full, very tannic, loads of tight fruit on palate. If well stored, will need ten more years to reach maturity, and will last 20 to 30 more years! Great quality here. (19)

NEDERBURG ESTATE "EDELKEUR" SUPERIOR 1978, WINE OF ORIGIN, SOUTH AFRICA, IN HALF-BOTTLE:

(I brought this as a gift for Stephen.) Made from about three-quarters Steen (Chenin Blanc) and one-quarter Johannisberg Riesling, approximately. Botrytized. Extremely rare. Deep gold. Like a 35- to 40-year-old Sauternes. Lovely, orange-apricot jam on nose and palate. Full, round, well balanced. Very good acidity, and mellow. Lovely, long aftertaste of ripe fruit. Really fine quality here. Went very well with a selection of apricot desserts. (18)

September 22, 1992

Commanderie de Bordeaux Tasting and Dinner, featuring ten-year-old 1982 Pomerols and St. Emilions, at the Hotel Vancouver.

We knew which châteaux were being tasted, but not the order within the respective communes.

1982 St. Emilions

1. CHÂTEAU MAGDELAINE 1982:

Very good colour; orange rim. Subdued oak, herbaceous nose. Full, ripe, rich. A bit metallic. Severe, rich, tight. Good depth, though. Needs three to five years. Good extract. Some tasters found it too lean. This wine is made almost exclusively from Merlot grapes. (17.5)

2. CHÂTEAU CANON 1982:

Similar colour to #1, but less evolved; no orange. Finer, herbaceous, stemmy nose. Full, rich, long, luscious. Lovely finish. Very good finish. Top quality. (18)

3. CHÂTEAU CHEVAL-BLANC 1982:

Impressive, deep colour to rim. Open, buttered popcorn, toasty, spicy, herbal nose. Slight hint of dill. Full, rich, still tannic, complex, long. Lovely, but needs time. Vanilla-oak. Less fat than most, at this stage, but classy. New oak. (18)

4. CHÂTEAU L'ARROSÉE 1982:

Excellent, dark colour. Sweet, ripe fruit on nose. Very ripe, very rich. Fabulous ripe fruit. Tannic. Needs time. Lots of extract. Classy, powerful. Fine St. Emilion, yet much harder style. (17.5)

5. CHÂTEAU FIGEAC 1982:

Dark, evolving colour. Pruny, perfumy nose. Hint of dill. Full, rich, tannic, very Cabernet Franc. Vegetal. Good extract. Lots of body, rich. Roundest. Lots of spicy, herbaceous nose and palate. Typical Figeac. Oddly, at this stage, showing better than the Cheval-Blanc. (18.5)

6. CHÂTEAU SOUTARD 1982:

Excellent, deep colour to rim. Subdued, clean nose. Loaded with ripe fruit, tannic, lots of extract, but needs many years. Most backward of flight. Good depth. Lots of extract. A bit simple, but big and chunky. Needs time to soften up, but lacks elegance or class. (16.5)

1982 Pomerols

7. CHÂTEAU CERTAN-GUIRAUD 1982:

Good, deep colour. Ripe nose. Sweet, round, complex, forward. Nice. Some tannin. Good acidity. Well balanced, sweet fruit. Needs two to four years. (16.5)

8. CHÂTEAU L'EVANGILE 1982:

Very impressive, deep colour to rim. Full, rich, ripe, luscious. Loaded with extract and ripe fruit. Lovely. Obvious l'Evangile. Very ripe, fat. Gobs of ripe fruit, yet not overdone. No rush. Needs three to ten years. (19)

9. CHÂTEAU LA CONSEILLANTE 1982:

Very good, dark colour; maturing rim. Ripe, sweet Merlot nose. Full, rich, sweet, long, loaded with ripe fruit. Superb. Hint of mint-eucalyptus. Tannic. Classy; elegant rather than fat. (18.5)

10. VIEUX CHÂTEAU CERTAN 1982:

Excellent, deep colour. Spicy, herbal nose. Lovely, more elegant style. More "St. Emilion." Lovely length, clean oak, rich, yet without the intensity or depth of #9. Will improve. (17.5)

11. CHÂTEAU LE GAY 1982:

Very ripe fruit. Lactic, tobacco, straw nose. Full, rich, fat, sweet, long. Straightforward. Less concentrated or complex than #7 to #10. Older barrels. Rich, chunky, but simple. (16)

12. CHÂTEAU LA FLEUR-PETRUS 1982:

Good, deep colour. Some maturity at rim. Tight, closed nose. Full, rich, tannic; needs time. Very good. This has great class and complexity. Needs five to ten years. Will be great! (17.5) to (18).

These 1982s, especially the Pomerols, need more time.

September 25 to October 10, 1992

Trip with Carol to Paris, Champagne, Brittany, and Normandy.

We stayed in a small hotel near La Madeleine, in Paris.

Dinner at Raoul Salama's home.

He is a writer for the Revue du Vin de France, *and travels often to Los Angeles for tastings. All wines were served blind. When possible, I insist on that.*

CHABLIS GRAND CRU "LES PREUSES" 1981, RENÉ DAUVISSAT:

I thought it was a Puligny. Round, oak, Chardonnay nose. Fairly lean (I thought 1987), but good length and complexity.

1975 Gruaud-Larose

and

1975 Leoville-Barton:

I guessed Haut-Médocs and 1975 right, but I thought they were Pauillacs.

The Leoville-Barton had a lovely, cedary, open nose (I thought Lynch-Bages), and was quite evolved, with some aggressive tannins, but a bit short, and lacking fruit on palate.

The Gruaud-Larose was unyielding on nose, much darker, deeper, more intense, but very tannic. If well stored, this wine will need five to ten extra years of bottle-age to come around.

Château Nairac 1983:

Subdued, clean, botrytis nose. Creamy, sweet, round. A bit too candied. Good, straightforward, round. Not much complexity.

September 28, 1992

Dinner at "Lucas Carton."

Three stars in Michelin and close to our hotel at Place de la Madeleine. We had a good night. Outstanding food; lovely seafood and pigeon. Very extensive wine list. Very expensive, too. We chose a great "unknown" wine. Not many tourists have heard of this wine made by the "Master of Meursault."

Meursault "Les Casse Têtes" 1986, J. F. Coche-Dury:

Typical Coche-Dury, and typical 1986. Rich, fat, long, full. New oak in harmony. Fabulous, nutty Chardonnay. Great balance. Needs three to five years. Excellent fruit, character, and class. Lovely wine.

September 30 to October 2, 1992

Three-day visit to Champagne.

We stayed at "Les Crayères" in Reims (Boyer), in one of the three rooms away from the main building (Room #1). Nice grounds. As we arrived, a caravan of ten cars with the Russian Chief of Staff (General Kalishnikov) showed up! We set appointments with Rémy Krug, Antoine Gosset, Christian Pol Roger, and Christian and Guy Bizot (Bollinger).

September 30, 1992

Visit and dinner with Rémy Krug.

At 5:00, we visited the Krug offices in Reims. Rémy's cousin gave us a nice tour. Back in the office, Henri and Rémy joined us. We tasted these wines.

Champagne Krug "Clos du Mesnil" 1982:

Made from 100% Chardonnay from the clos, replanted gradually over six years, after the purchase of this clos in 1971. First commercial vintage was 1979.

Champagne Krug Vintage 1982:

Both had the excellent structure, and concentration (beneath the fruit) typical of Krug. This gives them the fantastic staying power. The Clos du Mesnil had a ripe-raisins nose, an elegant, leaner style, but classic mousse, tiny bubbles, etc. Ripeness on nose because of abundant, yet excellent 1982 vintage. Rémy compared 1982 to 1966 or 1976, but not quite as big. Nice length, but for me, a Blanc de Blancs should be less hard. Personally, I clearly preferred the fabulous 1982 vintage blend! Lovely, complex, yeasty nose. Beautiful, golden colour. Ripe, yet structured to last for many years. Great length, concentration and class. Fabulous Champagne, will last for another ten to 15 years, but great now. I told both Rémy and Henri (who makes the wine) that I preferred the Vintage over the Mesnil.

They buy about 10% new oak each year. Wine stays in oak for six months (first fermentation). They buy their corks now from Spain (Catalunia) because it is difficult to get cork from the traditional source, Portugal. Also, in Portugal, peasants plant vegetables between the rows of cork trees and use pesticides, chemicals, and fertilizers; at Krug, they worry about what that might do to the corks. Their father Paul, whom I met in 1980, is 80 years old and still active.

I gave Rémy a half-bottle of Freemark Abbey Edelwein Gold TBA 1982, and a nice book on Haida Indians. He gave me a set of Krug glasses. They now keep a stock of seven years. They release the "Grande Cuvée" (80% of production) after six years, and the vintage after seven years. The "Clos du Mesnil" produces only 1,000 to 1,150 cases per year, when a vintage is declared.

Later that evening

Carol and I were guests of Rémy's at Boyer "Les Crayères" restaurant. We had a nice meal.

Champagne Krug "Grande Cuvée" N/V:

Still youthful, fresh, long, complex, but for me, too young. I prefer it to have two to three years of extra bottle-age after release.

Rémy then served a red wine blind from a decanter. Good, dark, but evolved colour. I smelled it and said right away that the minty, cedary, open nose reminded me either of Mouton or Lynch-Bages. Rémy was shocked. He said that the only other person he knew that could do this so fast was his father! He was impressed. I said "Possibly 1961 Lynch-Bages," but it turned out to be 1959 Lynch-Bages. I wouldn't have

March 24, 1984: Barrel Sample dinner, at Vancouver's Four Seasons hotel. Part of the Vancouver Wine Festival. L to R: Allan Hemphill (President, Château St. Jean); Jim Fetzer (VP, Fetzer Vineyards); Dr. Terry Leighton (President, Kalin Cellars); Tary Salinger (Marketing Director, Rutherford Hill Winery); Harry McWatters, (Sumac Ridge, BC); David Lake (Winemaker, M. W. Associates Vintners, Washington); Dawnine Dyer (Winemaker, Domaine Chandon); the author; John Lawson (Export Manager, Robert Mondavi); Walter Raymond (Raymond Vineyard); John Levine; Eric Wente; (President, Wente Bros.). Missing: Ken Toth (President, J. W. Morris). With the exception of Albert Givton and John Levine, wines from each of these individuals were represented at this event.

March 1984: Lunch and tasting at "Le Gavroche" restaurant, in honour of wine author Hugh Johnson, a guest speaker at the Vancouver Wine Festival. L to R: Sid Cross, Hugh Johnson, John Levine, the author, and Bernard Hoeter (R).

1985: First German-American "Rarities and Prephylloxera" weekend tasting, in San Francisco.

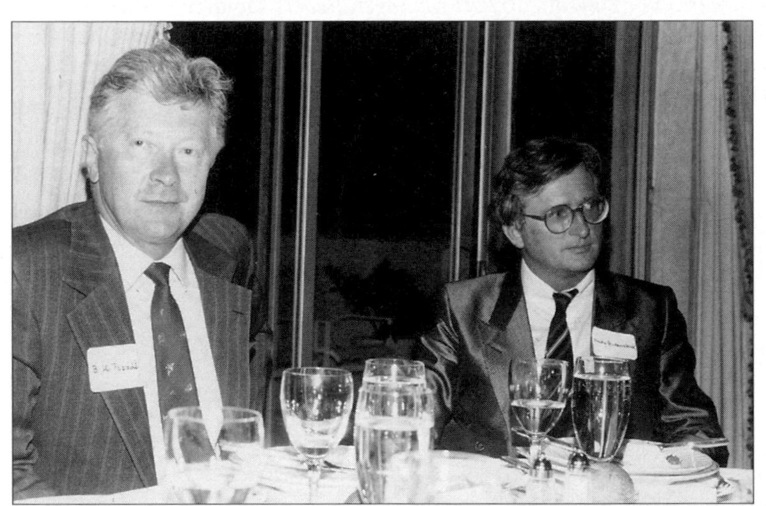

1985: Same "Rarities and Prephylloxera" weekend. Bill Poschel (L), one of the organizers, with Hardy Rodenstock, a German collector of rare old wines.

1985: With Paul Pinski, at German-American "Rarities and Prephylloxera" weekend.

June 1986: The 1986 vintage resting in the cellars of Château Ausone, St. Emilion.

November 1987: Vancouver's Commanderie de Bordeaux 1970 Claret tasting, with Harry and Prue Waugh.

1987: The author at
Château Leoville-Lascases.

April 1987: Pouring in preparation for a Château Palmer vertical tasting (1961 to 1985), at the Vancouver Club.

April 1987: Commanderie de Bordeaux tasting of Château Palmer/Château d'Angludet, at the Vancouver Club. With Peter A. Sichel (standing), our guest speaker, owner of Château d'Angludet and part-owner of Château Palmer, and Maître David Freeman (seated).

September 1987: Conducting Vancouver Museum charity wine auction.

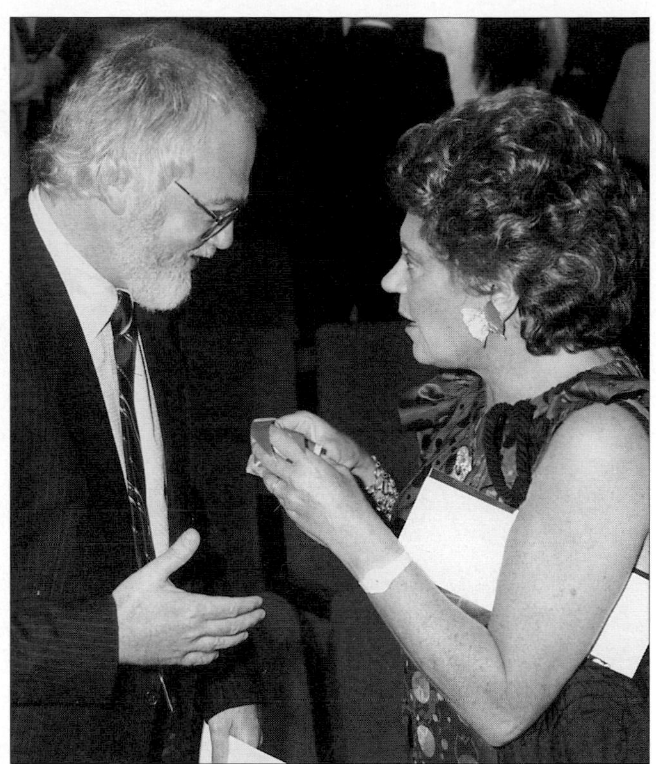

September 1987: With Philippine de Rothschild of Château Mouton-Rothschild, at Vancouver Museum charity wine auction.

April 1988: Another German-American "Rarities" weekend in Los Angeles. Tasting a mature Stony Hill Chardonnay.

1988: Salmanazar of Champagne Bollinger, in my wine cellar.

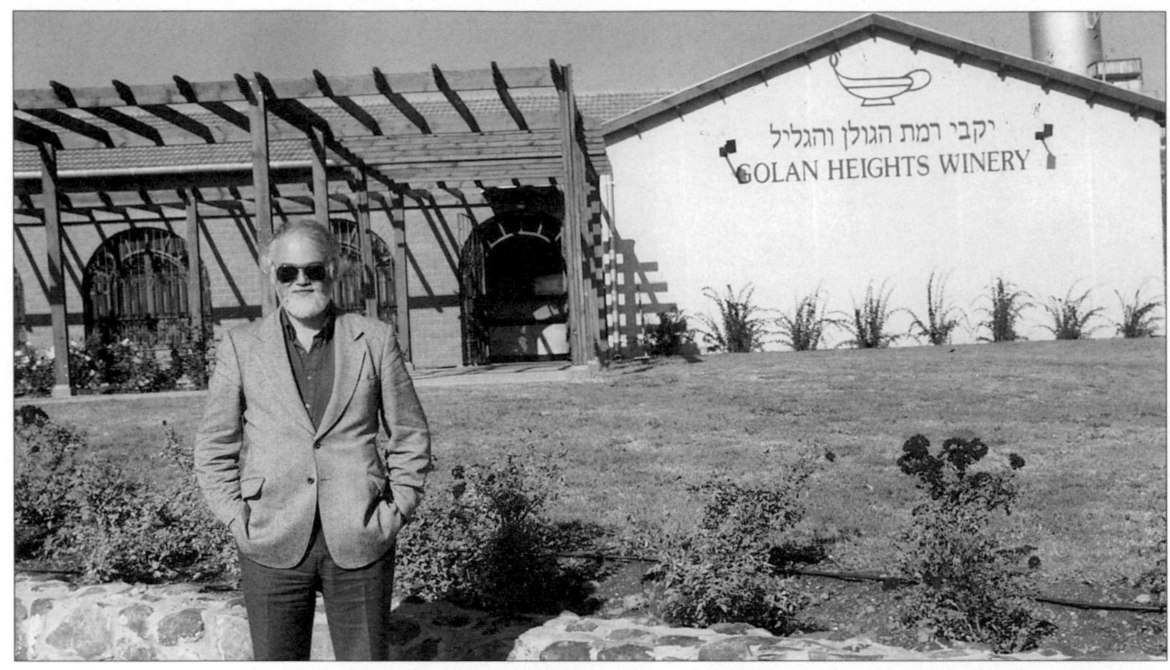

November 1988: Visiting Yarden Winery, Golan Heights.

1988: Panel of The Wine Consumer *newsletter relaxing after an exhaustive tasting. L to R: Dr. Allan Tobe, John Levine, Joan Cross, Dave Spurrell, Tony Gismondi, Marcena Croy, and Sid Cross.*

November 1989: In the cellar.

December 2, 1989: With Harry Waugh, in front of Brad Klein's 1956 Rolls, prior to big Château Latour tasting, in Los Angeles.

1989: Commanderie de Bordeaux event, with participation of a delegation from Bordeaux, including Jean-Michel Cazes (L).

1990: Harry Waugh's 86th birthday party in The Napa Valley. L to R: The author, Dr. Barney Rhodes, Dr. Haskell Norman, and Dr. Brad Klein.

Spring 1991: With Joe Heitz (centre) and John Levine, at American Wine Society vertical tasting of Heitz Cellars "Bella Oaks" 1976 to 1985, in Vancouver.

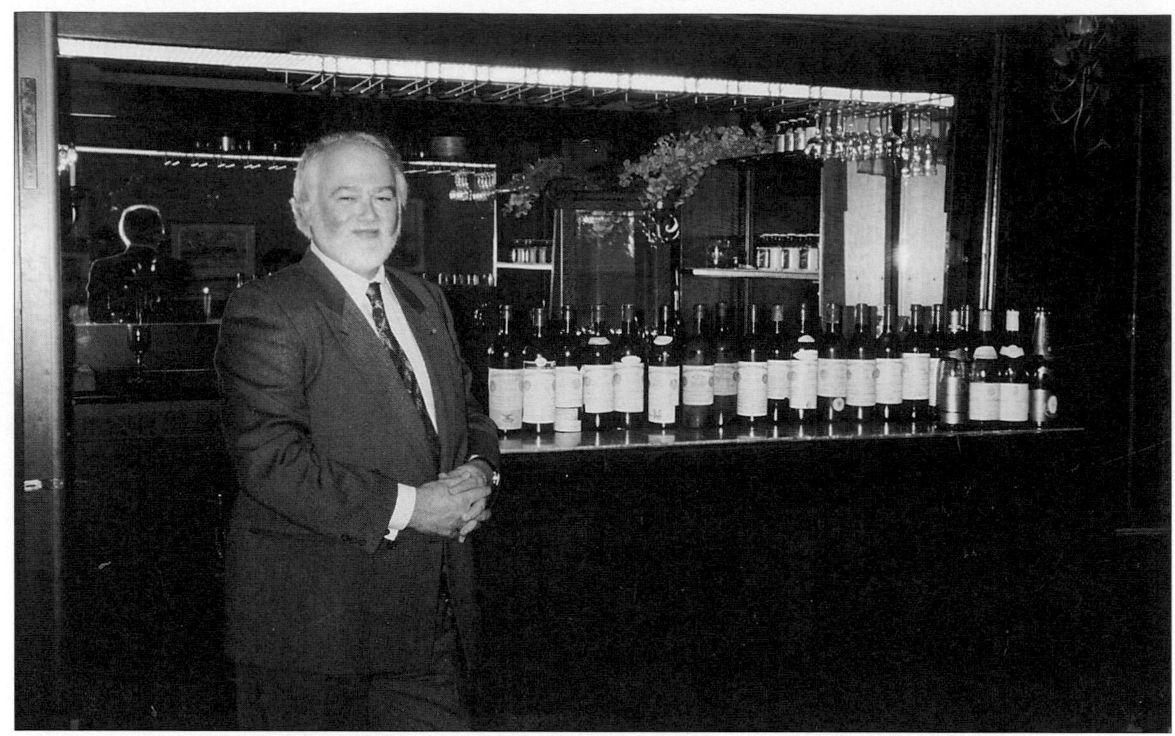

February 1992: Vertical tasting of Château Cheval-Blanc 1934 to 1982, at "William Tell" restaurant, Vancouver. All wines were from my cellar.

October 1992: Grandma Jenny's 80th birthday. Three generations: Mother, Orly, and me. Jenny's last wine: 1912 Niepoort Colheita Port . . . her birth year.

1992: Savouring d'Yquem 1967.

guessed 1959, because it was leaner than expected. Yet lovely length; great, spicy bouquet; and lovely, long finish. Boyer came over, and he was impressed, too. He said that it was their last bottle. We had a very nice, long evening. We also talked a fair bit about Hardy Rodenstock and his mysterious old bottles, and about Michael Broadbent and his personality.

October 1, 1992

Visit with Christian Pol Roger.

A very nice visit. According to Christian, the picking ended last week, and this will not be a "Vintage Year." It took more grapes to make less juice of sound, good (but not great) quality. We visited the operation. No oak. Seven kilometres of underground cellars, 30 metres deep. Christian is a very pleasant man. He has no children. He showed me my comments in the guest book from a previous visit 12 years ago, on September 10, 1980.

We tasted these wines.

CHAMPAGNE POL ROGER 1986 VINTAGE BRUT:

Made from 60% Pinot Noir, 40% Chardonnay. Smooth, elegant, yet rich, long. Very long and complex. This is a very fine wine.

We had lunch with Christian, in Epernay, at a small restaurant called "Chez Pierrot," where we had his Champagne.

1986 CHARDONNAY, POL ROGER:

Very elegant, long, complex. Well balanced. Lovely fruit. Made from 100% Chardonnay. Another wine to buy.

He does not believe in Pinot Meunier (early maturing), yet at Krug, the philosophy is opposite. Krug uses 15% to 20% Meunier. Christian gave us two bottles of Champagne, plus the one he sent earlier to "Les Crayères" for us. We gave him a nice Native Indian print.

Christian likes Dominus better than Opus One. I'll see him in Vancouver at the end of October (Club Pol Roger tasting), and let him taste a bottle of the 1985 Dominus.

We spent five hours at Pol Roger and lunch. A very nice visit. The subject of Hardy Rodenstock came up again (about the fake old wines). Christian is a friend of Gerard Jaboulet.

Dinner that evening at "Les Crayères."

GEVREY-CHAMBERTIN PREMIER CRU "LES CAZETIERS" 1985, A. ROUSSEAU:

Classic 1985 and classic Rousseau. Deep, youthful colour. Intense, fresh cherries on nose. Full-bodied, rich, long. Great balance, concentration, and long finish. Needs five to ten more years of bottle-age.

October 2, 1992

Visit to Gosset.

Antoine Gosset is a very nice man. He used to be in the sailboat business in Brittany, but when his brother died, he took over the wine operation. His father passed away in 1991. He admitted that the economy and exchange rates are hurting Champagne. They buy almost all their grapes from traditional suppliers. No oak. Clean operation. They age their liqueur for dosage in small oak barrels. Most wriggling is done by hand, shaking the bottles so that lees spread all over wine for uniform flavours. I suggested some ways to increase his sales in BC (half-bottles, a more active agent, etc.). He gave me a bottle of his Chinon, and one of a Brut Champagne especially produced for a unified Europe.

Then he took us out to lunch at "Au Vieux Pressoir," a small restaurant in Aÿ, converted from a private residence.

We enjoyed this bottle of wine.

CHAMPAGNE GOSSET "GRANDE RÉSERVE" BRUT N/V:

Round, creamy, fresh, elegant, well balanced. A favourite of mine.

Gosset make Rosé by blending white and red, rather than fermenting Pinot Noir juice on the skins, because they do not want a Rosé that is too tannic. Their winery was destroyed in 1944 by the US Air Force, who mistook the government distillery next door for a German fuel-storage facility.

October 2, 1992

Visit to Bollinger.

Then we met Guy Bizot, the son of Christian Bizot, owner of Bollinger. We visited the "clos" and vineyard. Oak fermentation (only old oak barrels from Burgundy). In about 10% to 15% of production. Bottles, magnums, and jeroboams age in their own sizes. Larger bottles and half-bottles are transferred from regular bottles. They produced ten barrels of "Vieilles Vignes Françaises" in 1992. The 1992 may not be a great vintage. Lots of rot due to rain in early September. The 1985 is being released now. The 1988 will be the next release. The ungrafted prephylloxera wine is from two tiny "clos" around the property. They plant 24,000 vines per hectare, as opposed to the usual 8,000! This is a great Champagne. Made from 100% Pinot Noir. Their cellars are very damp.

We went to the tasting room. (They are looking for new agents in BC.)

Champagne Bollinger "Special Cuvée" Brut N/V:

Light gold. Spicy, yeasty nose. Elegant and fruity. Tiny bubbles. Slightly off-dry. Fresh. Good length and intensity. Very good acidity. Can age two to four years. Made from 60% to 65% Pinot Noir, 10% to 15% Pinot Meunier, and 20% to 25% Chardonnay. Base wine is the 1988 vintage. Released after three to four years. About 80% of grapes come from Premier and Grand Crus; 20% from other vineyards. No oak in this N/V.

Champagne Bollinger "Grande Année" 1985 Brut:

Made from 45% Chardonnay (higher than normal), 55% Pinot Noir. Slightly deeper gold than the Special Cuvée. Nose subdued, yet ripe raisins. Rounder, less acidic. Complex, creamy, long, and sweeter. Frothier, too. Lovely intensity. He compared this to the 1975 R.D., and potentially a great, long-lasting year (1985). I agree. No rush!

Champagne Bollinger "RD" 1982 Extra Brut:

Disgorged in May 1992. Slightly darker yet than the above. Round, straw, yeasty character. Ripe, long, creamy. Intense nose. Ready. In the long run, I think that the 1985 "Grande Année" will be better. (The 1985 is a great vintage to buy!)

Nice visit to Champagne. Lovely weather, nice meals, friendly hosts.

October 3 to 7, 1992

Normandy and Brittany.

We travelled by car from Champagne to Normandy and Brittany. We visited the Beaches of Normandy, St. Mère Eglise, Bayeux, Granville, St. Malo, Fort La Latte, and Cap Ferret. We had various Beaujolais and Pouilly-Fumées. On the night of October 5 (Eve of Kippur and my father's memorial day), we stayed in a little place in Locmaria Berrien, near Heuglegoat, south of Morlaix, called "Auberge de la Truite." It is a converted railway station—small and quaint, with decent food.

It was a dreary, rainy night. We were the only guests. Fantastic wine list, going back to 1918, with many wines from the 1940s and 1950s. Nothing younger than 1969 for Burgundies, and 1966 for red Bordeaux. A Danish couple was there for dinner, although they didn't stay the night. They ordered a 1959, and we ordered a 1949, and I suggested that we exchange a glass, which we did. (A bat flew over our heads while we were having dinner!)

Beaune Premier Cru "Vigne de l'Enfant Jesus" 1959, Domaine du Château de Beaune, Bouchard Père et Fils

and

Beaune Premier Cru "Clos de la Mousse" 1949, Bouchard Père et Fils, both Monopole:

The 1959 "Vigne de l'Enfant Jesus" was darker, livelier, still very intense. Rich, ripe fruit. Classic Pinot Noir. Perfectly stored.

The 1949 "Clos de la Mousse" was browning, mature, superb. Barnyardy, Pinot Noir nose. Toasty, rich. Soft on palate, but long, still full of life, but at its peak. Needs drinking. Great nose! Fair bit of sediment. These wines haven't travelled much, obviously. The owner must have been a collector, and his wife inherited this fantastic cellar.

October 8 to 10, 1992

Chartres and Paris.

We stayed one night in Chartres, then back to Paris for three nights before taking our flight back to Vancouver. In Chartres, I happened to walk past a new wine shop that was only going to be officially opened the following week. I managed to convince the owner to let me in. He wasn't set up for credit cards yet, so Carol and I found enough francs to buy three bottles of rare old wines: 1926 Brane-Cantenac, 1953 Laville-Haut-Brion, and 1928 Montrose.

October 9, 1992

Dinner at "Chez Josephine" (Chez Dumonet).

A nice bistro in the 6ème. We had a very nice confit de canard and boeuf bourguignon.

Clos de la Roche 1985, A. Rousseau:

Medium red, palish rim. Very elegant, subdued, spicy Pinot Noir. Less intense than Rousseau's various Gevreys. Clean, long finish. Ready in two to five years.

October 24, 1992

Club Pol Roger Dinner at Hotel Le Meridien, with Christian Pol Roger, and the new French Ambassador to Ottawa, Alfred Siefer-Gaillardin.

I gave Christian a bottle of Dominus 1985. That night, the Toronto Blue Jays won the World Series, against the Atlanta Braves.

Champagne Pol Roger Brut 1986, in magnums:

Crisp, clean, fairly hard. No rush. Complex, but still tight and closed. Give it two to three years. Will be very good.

Champagne Pol Roger Chardonnay 1985:

Probably his best-made wine. Elegant, yeasty, rich, flowery nose. Delicate, lively, complex. Very long, elegant finish. Hard to beat this house's "Blanc de Blancs" style. Also, it is reasonably priced for the quality.

Champagne Pol Roger Rosé 1985:

Salmon-pink. Fine mousse. Dry, hard, yet good fruit underneath. Harder, masculine wine. I'm not a fan of Rosés.

Champagne Pol Roger "Réserve Spéciale" 1985:

Solid, yet not heavy. Needs time. Excellent fruit; fine, lively bubbles; long, lovely balance. This will be great in two to four years.

Champagne Pol Roger "Cuvée Winston Churchill" 1985:

This is the "Réserve Spéciale" for the Anglo-Saxon market. Comments as above.

Overall

The 1985s are excellent. A fine Champagne vintage.

October 25, 1992

Lunch at Jean Doise's, with Christian Pol Roger as guest.

Champagne Pol Roger PR "Réserve Spéciale" 1982:

Better at this stage than any of the younger Champagnes tasted the previous night. Obviously, three years of extra age make all the difference.

Château Giscours 1970:

Very deep, impressive colour to rim. Cedary, ripe, Cabernet nose. Sweet. Full, rich, excellent balance. Lots of depth. Still tannic. Will last for 10 more years, if well stored. Best Giscours of any vintage I've had to date.

October 28 to November 3, 1992

Trip to San Francisco and Yountville.

October 28, 1992

Marin County International Wine and Food Society Dinner, at "La Folie" restaurant, in San Francisco.

With Count de Lur Saluces, owner of the great Château d'Yquem and the excellent Château de Fargues

d'Yquem and de Fargues 1987 to 1983

"Y," dry wine of d'Yquem 1988:

Light gold. Lovely, hint of Sauternes, oaky, spicy, youthful nose. Too young. Needs three to five years of bottle-age. Not very big. Moderate acidity, but rich fruit. Long on palate. Clean, oak, vanilla, and ripe fruit.

Château de Fargues 1987

and

Château d'Yquem 1987:

de Fargues: Surprisingly dark gold for such a young wine. Subdued, elegant nose. Sweet, round. Very good acidity. Classy, clean wine. Not fat, but still very good depth. Better than many 1983s or 1986s! Impeccably made. No rush. Enough fruit and acidity to last. (16.5)

d'Yquem: Tighter, more closed than the de Fargues. Slightly spicier, more vegetal, but very good length. Lots of depth. Not cloying or fat, and somehow lacking a bit in botrytis, but very good nevertheless. Later, d'Yquem improved. More depth, less sweet, but better balanced. Tighter. Developed an odd, vegetal, egg-yolk smell in glass. (17)

Both 1987s are surprisingly good.

Château de Fargues 1986

and

Château d'Yquem 1986:

de Fargues: Bright gold, less forthcoming than the 1987, but more depth. Fabulous length. Excellent balance and acidity. Full, long. Great fruit extract, acidity, oak, and botrytis, all in harmony. Needs at least five to ten extra years. (17.5)

d'Yquem: Subdued, yet fabulous, intense, rich, botrytis nose. Great depth. Lovely balance. Still a baby. New oak. Great balance of vanilla, oak, botrytis, and ripe fruit. Needs ten to 15 years. Goes on and on, on palate. Has the extra dimension, and is more restrained at this stage than the de Fargues. (18)

1985 de Fargues

and

1985 d'Yquem:

Both most elegant pair of flight. Round, elegant, spicy, delicate, clean, refined. The d'Yquem is fatter, richer, more intense, but elegant, without the depth of the 1986 or the "nerveux" of the 1987. Little or no botrytis in 1985. The de Fargues (17), d'Yquem (17.5)

Château de Fargues 1983

and

Château d'Yquem 1983:

de Fargues: Great extract, depth. Clearly best de Fargues of the evening. Slightly earthy, wet cement nose, but lovely botrytis. Fabulous fruit/acidity balance. Classy, not cloying. Needs ten more years, like the 1975. Will be great. The 1986 is fatter, heavier, thicker, but more alcoholic and more heavy-handed. I prefer the 1983. (18)

d'Yquem: Superb overall. Great nose. Still subdued, but magnificent fruit. Great balance and depth. Superb finish. Impossible to fault this. By far, the greatest wine of the evening. Hard to find words to describe this! This wine needs until 1997 (to 2020) to reach its peak and plateau. Must buy! (19.5)

Fargues came into the Lur Saluce family through marriage in 1472 (13 hectares). Fargues has homogeneous soil. D'Yquem has very varied soils; it has been owned by the family since 1785. In 1787, the Jeffersons came to visit d'Yquem.

The food was extraordinary, and the presentation was fantastic. Chef/owner Roland Passot has done an excellent job. Then, at midnight, we drove to Yountville.

November 28, 1992

Paul Pinski's official 80th birthday party, at the Concordia-Argonaut Club, in San Francisco.

Paul very generously paid for this outstanding event for 120 people. The Crosses and Tobes were there, too.

CHAMPAGNE KRUG VINTAGE 1982:

They opened 30 bottles! As always, fabulous. Great depth, complex, long, tiny bubbles, rich, very good backbone, yeast, ripe fruit. Smoother than the 1979. Excellent and no rush.

MEURSAULT-BLAGNY 1985, FRANÇOIS JOBARD:

Pale gold. Tight on nose and palate. Leaner style. Lacks the extract of Coche-Dury's Meursaults. May improve with time. Just lacks fat, and too tight.

BÂTARD-MONTRACHET 1985, ANDRÉ RAMONET:

Much better than the above. Yellow-gold. Fruity, delicate, oak on nose. Almost sweet, smooth, elegant, and round on palate. Classy, long. Very fine quality, but not a big or very intense wine.

LA TÂCHE 1971, DOMAINE DE LA ROMANÉE-CONTI, IN JEROBOAMS:

No fewer than six jeroboams were opened! A jeroboam is equivalent to a Bordeaux double-magnum. Four were from North American retailers, two (the best) from England. Jeroboams of this wine now cost $1,800 to $2,000 each! All levels excellent. Some forward, a bit more leathery and more mature colour. Ours was the best. (We sampled five jeroboams, out of six.) Great colour and extract. Fabulous, spicy raspberries on nose. Great depth, length, balance, and fruit. Very long. One of the greatest red Burgundies of our time. No rush. Fabulous fruit.

CHÂTEAU D'YQUEM 1983:

15 bottles were served! This is the best d'Yquem between 1967 and 1988, or even 1990. Still too young. Very bright gold. Lovely, yet subdued botrytis; buttery nose. Very long, smooth, yet not cloying. Great fruit extract. Superb acidity and balance. Lots of depth here. By 1995 and beyond, this will be a great d'Yquem. A real treat!

Chef Hubert Keller of "Fleur de Lys" restaurant, in San Francisco, prepared an excellent meal.

The Concordia-Argonaut Club was established in 1864, mostly Jewish members. Miriam, one of Paul's daughters, pulled a fast one on Sid Cross, and stole his empty jeroboam of La Tâche. Sid was very upset. Eventually, she gave it back to him. Everybody was amused . . . except for Sid.

December 1, 1992

Dinner at Ramada Renaissance hotel, with Sid and Joan Cross, Ian and Rosemary Mottershead, Carol and myself. Trial dinner for the December 16, 1992, "Tenth Anniversary" Chevaliers du Tastevin La Tâche vertical tasting.

CHAMPAGNE KRUG "GRANDE CUVÉE" BRUT N/V:

(Purchased in 1983) Finally reaching its peak, but no rush. Fabulous body; ripe, yeasty, complex nose. Full, long, very masculine, but ripe underneath. Great.

PULIGNY-MONTRACHET PREMIER CRU "LES PUCELLES" 1978, LEFLAIVE:

(Sid's bottle) Delicate, subdued, yet tight. Leaner, drier than expected, but good. Somehow lacks the depth this wine had five years ago, yet no sign of madeirization. Odd. Good, but not great. Disappointing.

CORTON 1961, DOUDET-NAUDIN:

Deep colour. Slightly musty nose of old barrels. Rustic. Hard, acidic, charmless, dry, yet certainly has character and power. Will last for many years, but will not improve. Least complex of all the wines of the evening. Doudet-Naudin makes very rustic, old-style Burgundies. This was Sid Cross's bottle.

Somehow, Sid's two bottles were the least enjoyable of the evening.

CORTON 1962, JOSEPH DROUHIN:

(Ian's bottle, given to him by David Freeman) Light, evolved colour. Impeccable, clean, mature, cherry, classic Pinot Noir nose. Round, soft, elegant, long. Lovely fruit and balance. Clean, complex finish. Most enjoyable. Amazing at 30 years of age!

CHAMBERTIN 1971, BOUCHARD PÈRE ET FILS:

(My bottle) Unfiltered. Darkest wine of the evening. Deep red, maturing rim. Typical, rustic Chambertin. Typical 1971. Stemmy, spicy nose. Full, powerful, hard. Very good extract, but hard. No rush. Solid wine.

LA TÂCHE 1957, DOMAINE DE LA ROMANÉE-CONTI:

(My bottle, purchased at auction a few months ago) Level one-and-a-half inches below cork. Not decanted, fair bit of sediment. Cork brittle, but good. Mature, lighter, bright red colour. Superb, spicy, herbal, ripe-raspberry nose. Soft, round, long, great balance. Classic wine. Hard to believe that it is a 1957 and it is 35 years of age! Best wine of the evening. Great length and class. Not very powerful or rich, but classy, elegant, clean, and long.

December 16, 1992

Chevaliers du Tastevin Tenth Anniversary Black Tie Dinner and tasting, at the Ramada Renaissance hotel, in Vancouver, on the occasion of our Club's tenth anniversary (to the day!).

I acquired the wines (from auction and purchases in California and Chicago), and put the tasting together.

Subject: A Vertical tasting of La Tâche 1963 to 1978

APERITIF

CHAMPAGNE POL ROGER PR "PRIVATE RESERVE" 1975:

Our last three bottles. Deep, golden colour. One bottle almost flat, second OK, third best; but all three need drinking. Hint of caramel and oxidation. Some fruit and some fizz left.

CHASSAGNE-MONTRACHET PREMIER CRU "CHAUMÉES" 1986, JEAN-MARC MOREY:

Nutty, lovely, ripe, oak, Chardonnay on nose and palate. Rich, luscious, full-bodied. Very good acidity and finish. Good depth. Lots of fruit. Ready, but no rush.

LA TÂCHE 1963, IN MAGNUM:

Very good level, one inch below cork. A wine I've had three times since I purchased a case at auction last June, at Butterfield and Butterfield, in San Francisco. Mature, old-Port colour. Lovely, mature, raspberry liqueur, oak nose. Spicy, long. Very surprising for a "terrible" 1963. Still has fruit. Elegant, spicy, "goût de terroir." I did not decant this, but poured it carefully into 17 glasses (the number of participants) to not shock the wine too much. After 20 minutes, it started to dry out. (16)

LA TÂCHE 1976 AND 1972:

Three bottles of each.

Typical 1976, not my favourite year. Orangy, evolved, yet dark colour. Very ripe, baked nose, with hint of raspberries. Full, rich, hard, tannic. Very masculine, hard wine. Lots of depth and weight, but too robust and overmature. Low acidity, very tannic. Will last, but will not improve. (17)

I preferred the 1972, which was brighter, deeper red, more youthful, fresher. Crisp, acidic, but very good fruit. Lots of life. Lovely bouquet and flavour. (17.5)

LA TÂCHE 1966:

Two bottles from Atherton Wine Imports. One bottle drier and harder, other softer and rounder, but overall, quite similar. Superb, evolved nose. Complex, spicy, round, soft. The most elegant wine of the whole flight. Silky, spicy, ripe raspberries. Hint of new oak. Round, at its peak. Lovely wine. (18)

LA TÂCHE 1971, IN MAGNUM:

One magnum from Atherton Wine Imports. Excellent, very top level; wine almost touching cork. Original cork. Always great. Mature, yet dark colour. Brilliant. Great, herbaceous, yet spicy, raspberries and oak nose. Toast, too. Lots of sediment. Full, intense, long. At its peak. Great depth and class here. Loads of ripe, mature fruit. Grand Vin. (19.5)

LA TÂCHE 1978:

Three bottles. Consistent. Incredibly youthful, deep colour to rim. Superb, spicy, ripe raspberries, fresh nose. Oak, toast, all in harmony. Still very young and tight. Full, long, complex. Great balance and length. Intense, ripe fruit, acidity, and tannin. Perfect harmony. Will peak in five to ten years, and last forever! Great, great wine. Perfection! (20)

CHÂTEAU DE FARGUES 1976, SAUTERNES:

Two bottles. Deep, bright gold. Oak, botrytis, ripe, yet the acidity was good. Fatter 1976 style, but not cloying. Clean, long, complex. At is peak. Excellent. (17.5)

Chef Peter Bucher prepared a superb meal. "Three stars" by any yardstick. Great event! Well worth the four years it took me to collect all the wines. We had room for—and had planned for—24 participants. Only 17 members bothered to participate. We did not charge for the wines, as they were acquired through our yearly dues. Other than the advent of a terrible disease or accident, I cannot understand why anyone would not come to this tasting. The human brain sometimes puzzles me.

December 18, 1992

Chanukah dinner, at the Levines'.

EDNA VALLEY VINEYARD CHARDONNAY 1990:

Too young but promising. Complex, subdued Chardonnay. Very good balance and length. Hint of new oak. Not too ripe. Needs two to three years. (16.5)

SAVIGNY-LÈS-BEAUNE "GUETTES" PREMIER CRU 1971, JAFFELIN:

Rather coarse and getting tired. Browning colour. Herbaceous nose. Too dry. Some spicy Pinot Noir on palate, but harsh and lean. (13.5)

CHÂTEAU GRAND-PUY-LACOSTE 1979:

Bright, medium-red colour. Clean, fresh, round, soft. Very good, spicy, Cabernet flavour. Medium-bodied. Ready, but no rush. Clean, spicy, cherries finish. Good. (16.5)

CHÂTEAU LAFITE "GRAND VIN" N/V, BIRKEDAL-HARTMANN, BORDEAUX:

(I brought this along.) Low shoulder level. Very dark, wet, soft cork (unbranded). Lots of sediment. Old prune juice. Musty, earthy, pruny nose. Sharp, very rich, but not very pleasant on palate. Poor storage? Disappointing. This is a pre-1905 wine, discovered in a hunting lodge in the Fraser Valley, BC.

Ian Mottershead gave me this, as well as other old bottles to try and assess. One bottle of Lafite has a good, low neck level. Hopefully it will be better than this.

FONSECA'S VINTAGE PORT 1975:

One of the top 1975s; the other is Taylor's. Most others are too light. This Port had a good, dark, bright colour. Sweet, spicy nose. Full, rich, sweet, yet soft on palate. Ready, but no rush. Will last for another ten years before declining. Was decanted ten hours before serving. (17)

That day, December 19, 1992, my mother passed away, apparently after a massive heart attack. I found her body in her dining room on the following day, when she didn't answer the phone. May she rest in peace. She was a loving, dedicated, and caring mother, wife, and grandmother. Unfortunately, the children were with me when we discovered her. They loved her very much.

January 16, 1993

Dinner of "Group of Ten," at our home.

The two magnums were our group wines.

CHAMPAGNE KRUG "GRANDE CUVÉE" BRUT N/V:

(John Levine's wine. Purchased in 1987. Possibly ten to 12 years old.) Classic Krug. Full, creamy, rich, long. Great extract. Yeast, toast. Complex, long. Lovely balance and length. Serious Champagne.

CHAMPAGNE POL ROGER PR "PRIVATE RESERVE" 1982:

(Sid Cross's bottle) Much lighter than the Krug, more elegant. Toasty, spicy, herbaceous. A bit flat (few bubbles). Needs drinking, but elegant and complex.

1985 AND 1986 CHEVALIER-MONTRACHET "LES DEMOISELLES," LOUIS LATOUR:

(Allan Tobe's and Ken Cross's bottles)

The 1985: Leaner, spicier, harder. At first, a big musty, wet cement. Hint of brown sugar. (Oxidation?) I've had better examples.

The 1986: Deeper gold, more extract, higher alcohol, ripe fruit, oak, rich, long, full. Typical 1986. Tonight, the 1986 is clearly better. Top quality Grand Cru. Ripe fruit, long. Very good balance.

CHÂTEAU LAFITE 1962, IN MAGNUM:

(Group wine) Upper shoulder level. Lots of sediment, cloudy. Not the brilliant red colour of the top 1962s. Classic Lafite on nose and palate, though. Great elegance; long, biscuity nose. Round, soft, long. Very nice drinking now. Soft fruit. Medium-light colour. Maybe was shaken recently. Elegant finish.

CHÂTEAU LES CARMES HAUT-BRION 1961, GRAVES:

(My bottle) Good, top shoulder level. Served blind because we had the 1947 in magnum (see below). Much deeper than the 1962 Lafite. Great extract, dark brilliant colour. Earthy, chocolaty, ripe nose. Hard tannins, but lots of depth, extract, and ripe fruit. Typical 1961. Very good, well made, long, complex.

CHÂTEAU LES CARMES HAUT-BRION 1947, IN MAGNUM:

(Group wine) Very good top shoulder level. Great surprise. Very good, deep colour; mature rim. Earthy, rich, chocolaty nose. Long, full, tannic. Fantastic depth and extract for a 45-year-old wine. Loads of ripe fruit. Very long finish. Solid backbone. Clean, long, chocolaty, earthy finish. Hard, but ripe tannins. This was a pleasant surprise.

CHÂTEAU SUDUIRAUT 1959, SAUTERNES:

(My bottle) Excellent neck level. Fabulous amber, deep red, gold colour. Brilliant. For me, the wine of the night. Crème-brûlée. Oak, botrytis, ripe fruit. Full, creamy, long. Great fruit/acidity balance. At its peak. Full, rich, long. Lovely. True, classic Sauternes. They don't come much better!

January 21, 1993

Le Tastevin tasting of 1985 California Cabernet Sauvignons, at the Park Royal hotel.

Wines known to participants, but not the order. Also, the Israeli wine was served as a ringer (double-blind).

FLIGHTS OF FOUR WINES

1. IRONHORSE VINEYARDS CABERNET SAUVIGNON 1985, SONOMA VALLEY:

Good, dark colour; purplish hue; spicy, fresh, cherries, oak, vanilla nose. Full, rich, yet elegant. Good balance. Nice clean finish. (15.5)

2. ARROWOOD CABERNET SAUVIGNON 1985, SONOMA VALLEY:

More evolved colour than #1, palish rim, hint of orange. Warmer nose, hint of rubber, some vanilla-oak. Fuller, richer, more tannic than above. Riper, too. (16)

3. YARDEN "GALIL" CABERNET SAUVIGNON 1985, GOLAN, ISRAEL:

Very good, deep, dense colour. Rich, ripe cherries on nose. Hint of vanilla. Leaner, elegant, well balanced. Good concentration. A bit closed up at this stage. Hot finish. Needs time. Complex. More French-like. More elegant, leaner than #1, 2, or 4. (16.5)

4. BERINGER "KNIGHTS' VALLEY" CABERNET SAUVIGNON 1985, SONOMA VALLEY:

Good depth; orangy, evolved rim. Tight nose, some ripeness. Very good concentration and body. Needs time. Serious, solid, long. Very good balance. Vanilla. Favourite of the group for the flight #1 to #4. (17)

5. NEWTON VINEYARDS CABERNET SAUVIGNON 1985, NAPA VALLEY:

Very good, deep, dense colour to rim. Rich nose, yet subdued. Full, rich, plummy, ripe cherries. Ripe, full, long. Very good potential. Good length. (17)

6. ROUND HILL "RESERVE" CABERNET SAUVIGNON 1985, NAPA VALLEY:

Deep, youthful colour; brighter than #5. Odd nose, hint of rubber, sulphur. A bit vegetal. Leaner, higher acidity, but wanting in more fruit. More elegant than #5. Aggressive, leaner tannins. (15)

7. WILLIAM HILL "SILVER LABEL" CABERNET SAUVIGNON 1985, NAPA VALLEY:

Very good, dark colour; palish rim. Herbaceous, yet sweet nose. Hint of straw, too. Full, rich, round, structured like #5, but less complex. Good balance. (16)

8. INGLENOOK-NIEBAUM "RESERVE CLARET" 1985, NAPA VALLEY:

Lightest of flight #5 to #8. Orangy rim. Tight nose, some toast and oak. Good entry, tannic, nice fruit/acidity finish. Somehow dull middle. Quite tannic. Claret-like. A bit too lean. Only 40% or so Cabernet Sauvignon; the rest is Merlot and Cabernet Franc. (16.5)

9. ROBERT MONDAVI "RESERVE" CABERNET SAUVIGNON 1985, NAPA VALLEY:

Excellent, deep colour. Rich, very good extract. Lots of depth and concentration. Lovely, ripe, long, full. New oak. Hint of vanilla. Lots of toast and oak. Will be earlier maturing. (17.5) Possibly (18).

10. BEAULIEU VINEYARDS GEORGES DE LATOUR "PRIVATE RESERVE" CABERNET SAUVIGNON 1985, NAPA VALLEY:

Very deep, dark colour to rim. Musty nose. Full, rich—but odd, acidic. Piqué. Musty on palate, too. All three bottles were poor! (0) I have tasted far better examples of this. Poor batch?

11. J. PHELPS "INSIGNIA" CABERNET SAUVIGNON 1985, NAPA VALLEY:

Excellent, deep colour. Eucalyptus, minty nose. Full, rich, long, complex. Great balance. Lots of depth here. Very good extract, ripe fruit, and depth. Trying to be "Martha's" style. This is top quality. (18.5)

12. STAG'S LEAP CELLARS "SLV" CABERNET SAUVIGNON 1985, NAPA VALLEY:

Very deep, dark colour. Warm, toasty, ripe nose. Great extract. Rich, ripe, loads of excellent fruit. Powerful, fat, rich, supple, long. Great potential. Great depth of character. Needs time. (18)

Overall

Last flight (#9 to #12) clearly best. Most need more time. Pity that all three bottles of Beaulieu Vineyards were bad!

I added the Yarden (#3) as a ringer. No one guessed it or was even close! It showed well.

February 5 to 7, 1993

Marin County International Food and Wine Society weekend, including two dinners and two Port tastings, featuring Cockburn's Port.

My good friends Harry and Prue Waugh were guests at all four events.

Friday, February 5, 1993

Dinner at the Ritz-Carleton hotel in San Francisco, featuring an imperial of 1945 Château Leoville-Poyferré and a jeroboam of 1945 Château Gruaud-Larose, both St. Juliens.

Both had excellent levels and appearances.

CHÂTEAU LEOVILLE-POYFERRÉ 1945, IN IMPERIAL:

We expected a jeroboam, but actually discovered that it was an imperial, contributed by Dr. Haskell Norman. A remarkable 1945. Medium, evolved colour. Lovely, mature, complex nose of mature Claret, with earthy overtones. Soft, round, silky, long on palate. Still had impressive fruit and the tannic backbone of the 1945 vintage. Perfect drinking now. For me, a sign of a great wine is that the empty glass smell fabulous. It did. (18.5)

CHÂTEAU GRUAUD-LAROSE 1945, IN JEROBOAM:

Supplied by Stephen Kaplan of Chicago. Typical 1945 and typical Gruaud. Very impressive, deep, youthful colour, not unlike a 1970! Tight nose that took a good 30 minutes to open up. Concentrated, ripe berries on nose. Full, big wine, with loads of tannin. A typical 1945 that was well made and well cellared. Intense, much bigger, harder, more concentrated, and more focused than the Poyferré. No rush. If well stored, and in large format, it will last for many years. (18.5)

While most participants preferred the Gruaud-Larose because of its youth, concentration, and appearance, I—together with a substantial minority—preferred the Poyferré because of its elegance and complexity. My identical scores for both wines reflects the difficulty in choosing a "winner" between these two fine wines.

CHÂTEAU DE FARGUES 1975 SAUTERNES:

Deep, bright-gold in colour. Lovely botrytis, yet fresh fruit on nose. Full, rich, long, well balanced. Very good acidity/fruit ratio. Ready, but if well stored, no rush drinking this. Top quality Sauternes. Just below d'Yquem. (18)

Saturday, February 6, 1993

Lunch and tasting, featuring Cockburn's Vintage Ports from 1985 back to 1896, at the Park Hyatt hotel in San Francisco.

Guest Speaker was Peter Cobb of Cockburn's.

APERITIF

FINEST WHITE PORT N/V "XSR 120" MARTÍNEZ-GASSIOT:

Bright, deep-gold, Sauternes-like colour. Nutty, rich nose. Impeccably made. Round, sweet, long, and complex. Lovely balance, depth, and finish. Highly recommended. (17.5)

FIRST SESSION

Cockburn's Vintage Port 1985 to 1950

1985:

Purplish, youthful colour to rim. Closed nose with hint of ripe berries coming through. Sweet on entry, medium-bodied, very good backbone and depth. Not overly spirity. Round, complex, typical 1985. Probably ready by 1999 to 2005. Lovely, clean finish. (17.5)

1983:

Deep colour, palish rim. Delicate, hint of straw and sweet fruit on nose. More stylish, less fresh than the 1985. Clean, long, more Cockburn's style; leaner, yet not as hard as Dow's. Clean finish. Complex. Needs five to eight extra years. A bit too tight and unyielding. Will improve. (17)

1970:

Good, youthful colour; palish rim. More subdued on nose than either the 1983 or the 1985. Sweet on entry, quite big and spicy. Medium-bodied, but lacks the power of a Taylor's 1970, or the depth and richness of the 1970 Warre's. Just about ready. (17)

1967:

Quite evolved, medium-browning colour. Subdued nose. Soft, round, pleasant, and elegant. Lacks depth and grip, but still enjoyable at this stage. Will not get any better. Well balanced, not too spirity. (16)

1963:

Even more evolved colour than the 1967. Lovely, delicate, mature nose. Clean, complex. Has the extra depth and intensity that the 1967 does not have. Lighter style, not unlike Croft's, but very good depth. At its peak now. Hint of leather. (18)

1960:

Bottled by Harvey's of Bristol in 1962. Deeper, yet more mature-looking than the 1963. Earthy nose. Nice ripe fruit coming through. Odd medicinal flavour on entry, but nice sweet finish. A bit harsh, with fruit thinning out. Drink up before the spirit takes over. (16)

1955:

Deep, maturing colour. Lovely, delicate, flowery bouquet. Similar to the 1963, but a bit softer. Complex, round, classic, elegant Port. Good balance, length, and finish. This and the 1963 are clearly the best wines this afternoon. At its peak. The 1963 has this little extra dimension. (18)

1950:

Palish, mature colour; orange rim. Unpleasant mothball nose follows on palate. It later cleared a bit. Elegant, some fruit and clean aftertaste, but really hard to get past the nose and initial entry. Flawed wine. Pity, because on the palate, it actually tasted quite decent. (No score)

The 1985 was one of the three favourites, although it was atypical of Cockburn's style.

Saturday, February 6, 1993

Dinner at the Park Hyatt hotel, featuring 1959 Château Leoville-Lascases in bottles, magnums, and jeroboam.

Good service, mediocre food.

Champagne Perrier-Jouët Grand Brut N/V:

Fresh, clean, crisp. Nice fruit/acidity balance. Not big or yeasty, but clean, fruity. (16)

Meursault-Perrières Premier Cru 1982, Pierre Morey:

Classic Meursault and classic 1982. Very good intensity. Lovely fruit/acidity balance. Full, rich, yet soft. At its peak, but all there. Very good depth. (17.5)

Bâtard-Montrachet Grand Cru 1983, Pierre Morey:

Fortunately, not a typical alcoholic 1983! Fabulous exotic fruit on nose. Lots of dimension, extract, and depth. No rush, but drinking very well now. Excellent balance; lovely long finish. This is very good. (18)

Champagne Perrier-Jouët "Fleur de Champagne" 1976, in magnums:

Much better, richer, fuller than the nonvintage, with that extra yeasty character. Holding extremely well. Rich, creamy. Tiny bubbles. Full, long, and still lively. (17.5)

Château Leoville-Lascases 1959 (six bottles, three magnums, and a jeroboam):

There was quite a bit of bottle variation among the six bottles. The best was what it should be: classic Lascases and classic 1959. Deep colour, chocolaty, rich, full, with lots of life. Ripe, long, complex, cedary Cabernet. Fabulous. (18)

Another bottle seemed a bit tired, leaner, with a bit shorter finish. The other bottles were very good, but not quite up to the best. There was a slight difference between the three magnums. The best was as great as the best bottle, but more tannic, livelier, with deeper colour, and intensity. No rush. Great wine. (19)

The other two magnums would rate an (18). Strangely, compared with the best magnum and best bottle, the jeroboam was softer, rounder, very elegant, and complex, but lacked the "fat" of the best magnum. Yet it was excellent, too. (18)

This was an exciting comparative tasting and, as wine ages, it is definitely a matter of great individual bottles, rather than general properties or vintages.

DESSERT WINE

Château Rieussec 1975:

Bright, medium-gold colour. Lighter, more elegant by far, than the very ripe and rich 1976. Lovely botrytis, fruity nose. The good acidity of the 1975s is there. Well balanced. Clean, long aftertaste. (17.5)

Sunday, February 7, 1993

At the Park Hyatt hotel, in San Francisco.

Second session

Cockburn's Vintage Port, 1947 back to 1896

1947:

Mature, browning colour. Lovely, ripe fruit on nose. Classic Vintage Port. Ripe raisins. Round, sweet, and well balanced. Fine, delicate fruit. Very long on palate, well balanced. Not too spirity. Less extract than the 1945. Less sweetness, too, but certainly elegant. (18)

1945:

Rare. This bottle was contributed by Dr. Barney Rhodes. "The Port that never was." Peter Cobb, of Cockburn's, told us that this Port, bottled in 1947 (1945 was never declared by Cockburn's), came from a 63-litre demijohn jar bottled in 1947. Good, dark, maturing colour; slightly darker than the 1904 or 1912. Fruity, ripe, raisiny nose. Rich; full of life and extract. Great balance; sweet and ripe. Sweeter than Cockburn's usually is. Very good! (18.5)

What a pity that Cockburn did not declare the 1945 vintage.

1935, bottled by Grant's and Co., London:

Good, dark colour. Some maturity at rim, but nice red, too. Subdued nose, some spices coming through. Sweet, round, softer, less intense than the 1945. Looser-knit, good fruit, but hotter, spirity finish. Good extract and character. Holding very well. (17.5)

1927, London-bottled by Grant's and Co.:

Cigarette-smoke nose, not in the negative sense, although this is a paradox these days. Sweet, soft, round on palate. Elegant. Does not have the depth, complexity, or length of the 1912 or 1904, but nice fruit. Clean finish. Leaner, true Cockburn's style. (17)

1912:

Whitwham's label. Very good level and dark colour. Quite a bit of red left. Dull, spirity nose. Sweet, rich, yet drier, harder finish. Typical Cockburn's style. Topped up by younger wine! Surprisingly youthful. Tastes like a 1955. (18)

1908:

Whitwham's label. Pale, Tawny colour. Subdued, nutty nose. Hint of vanilla on both nose and palate. Quite soft on entry, but spirity, too. Good fruit. A bit harsh. Not as good extract as the 1904. The only wine in this whole flight that was tired and not up to par. (15.5)

1904:

Impressive, dark colour; green-Tawny rim. True Vintage Port character. Earthy overtones, but very good extract. Full, rich, sweet, and long. Fabulous aftertaste. Full, rich, fruity, and lovely extract. (19)

1900:

Very pale, yet darker than the 1908. Dark, Tawny colour. More Tawny than vintage on nose. Nutty, rich, better (more Vintage Port-like) on palate. Round, long. Spirity, but surprisingly good fruit. Very good. (17.5)

1896:

Very deep, Tawny colour; yellow rim. Smells of Vintage Port, though. Good, spicy, fruity nose. Good extract. Lots of depth and sweet fruit, but spirity, too. Surprisingly good. Has held extremely well. Earthy, old nose, but certainly livelier than the 1908. Very slightly Madeira-like. (17.5)

Notes

Peter Cobb said that his uncle, who was responsible for the vinification in the 1940s, bought a lot of 1944 and had no money left to buy the 1945, so they did not buy much 1945, nor bottle any.

It is interesting to note that Cockburn's did not declare any Port between 1912 and 1927. (No 1917, 1920, 1922, or 1924!) Apparently, the 1904 and the 1945 were made with grain spirit, rather than with grape spirit. This was not to their detriment, though.

Overall impressions

This tasting clearly showed that the old Cockburn's were outstanding, and, with the 1983 and 1985 showing well, it is to be hoped that in the future, they will produce wines of the same standard as in the past. The 1950s through the 1970s were a bit less than the potential of this fine property.

This article is courtesy of The Quarterly Review of Wines, *Autumn 1993*

"Cockburn's Through The Ages," by Peter Cobb

"*Question:* What do you do when a complete stranger invites you to a vertical tasting, featuring every Cockburn's Vintage Port declared this century, when the Company in question is the one you have worked for, man and boy, for over 30 years?

"*Answer:* You accept as gracefully as you can, and pray to God the wines do themselves justice.

"So it was that in early February this year, I packed my bags, crossed my fingers, and headed West. The tasting itself was organized by Haskell Norman, who presides over the International Food and Wine Society's Marin County Chapter like a very benevolent dictator.

"Rumour has it that Norman founded that chapter once he discovered that the San Francisco branch was predominantly stag. He obviously agrees with the adage that wine and women provide two of the three greatest pleasures in life. Where he stands on song is unclear.

"Not all the members come from the Bay Area. Stephen Kaplan was there from Chicago, and another notable collector had flown in from Memphis. As an added bonus, the amazing nonagenarian Harry Waugh and his wife Prue were—like me—invited guests. Harry had been one of my bosses in England in the mid-60s, and I had not seen him since then. Unlike his erstwhile employee, he had not changed an iota.

"Norman himself is an extremely distinguished psychiatrist, now retired, who once numbered an aged cousin of mine among his patients. This was at a time, in her own words, 'When I thought I was going crazy.' Haskell cannot remember her, but he must have done her some good because she lives contentedly with her husband in Sonoma County, owns a small vineyard of mostly Chardonnay and Gewürztraminer, and enjoys supplementing the family budget with some lovely watercoloring—a highly cultured lady and anything but crazy.

"Dr. Norman got the wine bug comparatively late in life, and only became an avid collector of fine wine once he had given up his practice. Port has become one of his great and abiding passions, but it is one he is happy to share with Bordeaux, Burgundy, and indeed all the really fine wines of the world. This particular weekend featured not only the unique two-day tasting of Cockburn's Port, but two black tie dinners involving the small matter of the 1945

Leoville-Poyferré and Gruaud-Larose in jeroboams, and the 1959 Leoville-Lascases in bottles, magnums and jeroboams, served as a tribute to another distinguished physician, Marvin Overton.

"A hard act to follow, you might think. So did I; by now, in addition to crossed fingers, the palms of my hands were getting decidedly clammy.

"The tasting was in two parts, split over Saturday and Sunday afternoon. Both were preceded—a nice touch, this—by a delicious glass of chilled, 20-year-old white Port, shipped by Martínez specially for Corti Bros, in Sacramento.

"Palates thus suitably cleansed, we got down to work. Saturday showed us the 1985 and all declared years back to 1950. The 1950 itself was a disaster: dried out, the fruit gone. The other wines were good, with perhaps only one being heralded as 'great' by the tasters. This was the 1963, very Cockburny in that it was lighter than some houses' offerings, but with a wonderfully fine, deep vintage nose and satisfying grip.

"My own favourite was the 1970, a year I consider to be rather neglected so far. It was a huge and magnificent year by any standards and this example was not yet—even after 20 years in bottle—at its peak.

"Of the younger wines, the Cockburn's 1983, is surely destined to become a classic. It has great complexity of fruit flavours, and at the moment is a blockbuster. It virtually has to be, to make up for the company's curious decision not to declare the 1977.

"The declaration of Vintage Port is a personal decision. You have to put your head on the block and predict that the wine you are offering—purple, tannic, and undrinkable now—will soften into something outstanding 30 or more years hence.

"It was said at the time that the 1977 was not declared because Cockburn's required all their fine wine to build up stocks of Special Reserve, the company's premium Ruby brand.

"Whatever the reason, the decision was not as controversial as that taken two generations earlier, when they went from 1912 to 1927 without declaring a vintage at all.

"Many good years like 1917, 1922, and 1924 came in between, but were not quite good enough (in my grandfather's subjective opinion) for Cockburn's to offer a vintage. It was doubly strange in that in those days, vintage was the only Port to be sold under a company's name.

"Actually, Cockburn's 1977 does exist as an undeclared vintage. I had endeavoured to get a couple of bottles over as a small contribution to the tasting, but fell afoul of the US Customs. It is a pity that they were not cleared in time because I think I could have proved a point. That the 1977s are fine wines is not in dispute. I maintain, however, that they have tended to be overpraised. Having seen others, I can say that the Cockburn's would-be 1977 is fairly typical of the year. Very good indeed, but not quite great. [Here, I disagree with Peter. Maybe 1977 is not as consistently great as the 1963s, or the still-underrated 1966s, but who can argue about the great quality of the 1977 Fonseca's, Taylor's, Dow's, or Graham's? AG]

"Otherwise, the 1985 has a long way to go; the 1967 was lovely but light; the 1960 was disappointing (particularly to me, as it was the first vintage I saw in the Douro and that has been a favourite of mine ever since); and the 1955 was classically elegant, a great wine, showing at its peak.

"So, Saturday proved a nice aperitif, predictable and unsurprising. Sunday, on the other hand, was neither.

"The wines went from the 1947 to the 1896 and included the (undeclared) 1945. They were all, in their different ways, quite remarkable.

"The three really old wines, the 1904, 1900, and 1896, as one would expect, were past their prime, although the tasters' average marks put the 1904 in third position, a singular compliment as 1904 had never been considered a top-flight year. It was thought to have been fortified with German grain spirit. The remarkable thing about these wines was that every one of them was, unlike the 1950, totally drinkable and in condition. Like Haskell Norman, they are enjoying a healthy and vigorous retirement.

"Everyone's undisputed star of the whole tasting was the 1912. It had a remarkable deep, ruby colour, a full luscious nose, and was wonderfully fruity and mature on the palate. My tasting note reads simply 'fabulous.'

"Six years previously, I had taken the last two bottles of 1908 from our cellars in Gaia to New York (thereby invoking the considerable anger of my colleagues, but that is another story). On that occasion, I had thought the 1908 was remarkable, and the 1912 past its prime. On this occasion, the situation was exactly the reverse.

"Nowadays, the most sought-after Cockburn's vintage at auction is the 1927. It's light in colour now, but the wine's sheer quality and breed is still very much in evidence; it's chocolaty, with excellent length. The 1947 is similar in style. There is subtlety on the nose, a little spirit, but holding up very well. I personally marked it third behind the 1912 and 1927.

"The wine that excited the most comment was the undeclared 1945. My uncle Reg, who effectively owned Cockburn's at the time, told me once that he thought WW II would end earlier than it did, and consequently he bought as much wine in 1944 as he could to have enough stock to restart business when hostilities stopped. The year 1944 was useful but not outstanding. By the time the 1945s came up, he was short of money and had to drastically reduce his vintage purchase. The only 1945 we have had in recent years was in a huge 65-litre demijohn. This was decanted and put into bottles in 1985, yielding around seven cases. It shows the considerable ingenuity of Barney Rhodes—who had collected many of the wines for the tasting—that he had managed to get hold of a couple of bottles. He must have a mole in Gaia! It was voted into second place by the tasters. Not by me, though, because as good as it was, it did not seem to have the classic Cockburn's style. The colour was excellent, it had a raisiny nose and good fruit on taste, but it lacked grip; it was almost too smooth—which highlights the main point to be made about a tasting of this kind. So much depends on when and how these old Ports were bottled, even by whom. Only in 1975 did the Port Wine Institute insist that all Vintage Port be bottled in Portugal.

"Until then, more often than not, the wines would have been shipped in bulk, two years after the vintage in question. After that, you were totally in the hands of the customer. There was a debate in the trade about which was better, Oporto or London-bottled. To my eternal shame, working in Britain in the Swinging Sixties, I supported the latter. Now I put such an aberration down to youthful British chauvinism.

"This was an extraordinary tasting. I doubt it can ever be repeated. Surely, it could only have taken place in America. Norman and Rhodes conducted it with skill, charm, professionalism, and considerable wit. By the end of the day, even my palms had dried out, because—thank God—only one of our wines had."

March 31, 1993

Council of Commanderie de Bordeaux lunch, at Pan Pacific hotel.

With Grand Maître Francis Fouquet and Jacques Hebrard, owner/manager of Cheval-Blanc (and their spouses), both representing the Grand Counseil de Bordeaux. All wines from our Club's cellar.

CHAMPAGNE ROEDERER "CRISTAL" 1983:

Perfect now. Creamy, round, soft; still lively with tiny bubbles and a fine, long mousse. Full, creamy, long. Lovely balance.

CHÂTEAU LA TOUR-MARTILLAC BLANC 1990, GRAVES:

Quite oaky on nose. Semillon predominant on both nose and palate. Full, rich, not quite "together" yet, but relatively low acidity. Try around 1995. Very good.

CHÂTEAU GRUAUD-LAROSE 1979 AND 1981:

The 1981 was corked, with a musty nose, but very good fruit and surprisingly deep, bright, red colour.

The 1979 was more evolved; old style, earthy, chocolaty, vegetal nose. Full, long, still a bit tannic. Long, cedary, earthy, fruity, spicy Cabernet finish. Drink now to 1998. The 1981 is clearly the better wine, but not on this occasion.

CHÂTEAU MARGAUX 1981:

Too young. Impressive, youthful colour. Lovely, elegant, cedar and new oak and Cabernet nose. Fruity, medium-bodied. Pity to drink this before 1995 or 1997. Will last until 2005 at least. Very long. Excellent balance. The best 1981.

CHÂTEAU SUDUIRAUT 1983:

Medium-bright gold. Hint of egg-sulphur on nose. Medium-bodied. Too much egg on palate. The 1982 is better. This lacks the class and botrytis of the classic 1983s. Drink now through 1998. Good, but not great.

Before lunch, I was awarded a diploma of Conseiller du Vin de Bordeaux by the Grand Maître, Francis Fouquet.

Saturday, April 3, 1993

Commanderie de Bordeaux Black Tie Tasting and Dinner, featuring Château Latour 1959 to 1989, at the Four Seasons hotel.

It was also a ceremony in which I awarded Certificates of Appreciation to our former Maîtres and long-serving council members.

THE TASTING
Château Latour
The vintages were known to us, but not the order in which they were tasted.

1. 1989:

Medium-bright red. Cedary, elegant, clean nose. Low fruit, hard tannins, fairly acidic. Surprisingly ripe (later). Of course, a baby! But without the depth this great property achieved in the 1970s. (17.5)

2. 1988:

Purple, deep, youthful colour to rim. Fresh fruit, new oak; powerful, tight, closed. Good acidity, good fruit. Not fat, but complex. Very closed. Possibly higher mark. Needs time, but will be very good. (17.5)

3. 1985:

Very good, deep colour, evolved rim. Lovely cedary nose. A bit stemmy, herbaceous, round. Odd for a 1985. I thought it was the 1983. Too vegetal. I expected fresher, more youthful fruit, and better balance. (17)

4. 1983:

More evolved than #3. Dark colour; lovely cedar nose. Chocolaty. Round and fruity. The backbone of Latour. Better than the 1985 but a bit diluted. (17.5)

5. 1986:

Deep colour. Tight nose; some oak, cedar. Full, tannic, powerful, and loaded with ripe tannins. Needs time. Typical, deep, broodingly tannic. Needs at least ten more years. Should be excellent, yet one wishes it had more fruit extract. (18)

6. 1982:

Dense, deep colour. Maturing wine. Lovely, cedary, spicy, ripe nose. Ripe, sweet fruit loaded with tannins. Very full, very long; starting to evolve. Great ripe fruit extract. Hint of leather. Fat, rich, ripe. Typical 1982. Needs ten more years. Opulence of this ripe vintage. (19.5)

#3 and #4 are the only ones I got wrong.

CEREMONY

CHAMPAGNE DOM RUINART 1982, BLANC DE BLANCS:

Classy, elegant, spicy, yeasty nose. Round, tiny bubbles, clean, and long. Fine on both nose and palate.

The ceremony included my handing over Certificates of Appreciation to former Maîtres Dr. Allan Tobe and David Freeman, and long-serving council members Tom Fleming and Ken Cross, and to Dr. Bernard Hoeter and Dr. Harold Kester.

The ceremony was followed by a sit-down dinner in which several older vintages of Château Latour were served in three flights.

FLIGHT #1

LATOUR 1979:

Deep colour. Tight cedary nose. Full, rich, and still tannic! Powerful. Good balance, length, and surprisingly youthful. A bit thin and acidic at finish. (16.5)

LATOUR 1978:

Impressive deep colour, darker than the 1979, with some age showing at rim. Sweet, spicy Cabernet nose. Full, rich, and loaded with ripe fruit; fabulous, concentrated fruit. Best wine of the flight. A classic 1978, slightly herbaceous and spicy, with good acidity. Needs five more years. (17.5)

LATOUR 1971, IN BOTTLE AND MAGNUM:

From the magnum, it was chocolaty, more evolved, with some cedar and tobacco. Lovely, sweet fruit, with a hint of chaptalization. Good flavour and fruit. At its peak, will not improve. (17)

The bottle was a bit drier, tighter, less charming. Can be excellent. Rated (16.5).

FLIGHT #2

All four wines below were sent directly from the château.

LATOUR 1975:

Very good, deep colour; evolved rim. Tight, hard tannins, but excellent fruit. Has power behind it. This must be one of the best 1975s. It will be excellent in five to ten years. Long, classic, cedary Latour that will last forever! (18)

LATOUR 1970:

Incredibly deep, youthful colour to rim. Full, powerful, and rich. Great extract and concentration. Great depth, ripe fruit. Not ready. A classic wine. Needs ten, 20, or 30 years. Superb extract that will last forever. (19)

LATOUR 1966:

Deep colour, mature rim; beautiful, chocolaty, cedary nose. Great intensity; sweet, ripe, and rich. Hard tannins of the 1966s, but more forthcoming fruit than the 1970. Not as great or ripe extract as the 1970. Too acidic, but very good. I prefer the 1975 on this occasion. I have tasted better examples of this wine. (17.5)

LATOUR 1964:

Deep colour; mature rim. Chocolaty, full, ripe, with great extract. Not as concentrated as the 1966, but with less aggressive tannins. Great length, chocolate, ripe fruit. The best, of all the Latours tasted tonight, for drinking now. (18.5)

FLIGHT #3

These two wines were also sent to us directly from the château.

LATOUR 1959:

Very impressive, deep colour. Superb ripe fruit on nose, full, rich, long, with fabulous depth and great extract. Still tannic, but with the ripe extract of the 1959s. Great cedary, chocolaty fruit. No rush; if it is well stored, it will have another ten to 20 years of life! (19)

LATOUR 1961:

Dense colour to rim. Full, powerful, rich, ripe, with great tannic extract. Lots of life ahead. Gobs of ripe fruit. Great intensity. Needs time! An all-time classic. Ageless. Perfect balance. $800 per bottle! (20)

DESSERT WINE

1980 CHÂTEAU DE FARGUES:

Bright gold. Evolved, but no rush. Lovely balance, nice botrytis. Not fat or "truly great," but certainly very good. Nice balance, fruit, new oak, and botrytis. (17.5)

Excellent dinner, really outstanding. I also awarded a certificate of appreciation to the Four Seasons hotel and its general manager, Ruy Paes-Braga.

Overall impressions

It is obvious, as expected, that Latour is a wine for the long run. It took the 1964 a good two decades to reach its peak. The 1975 was a revelation, although I knew that it was one of the best 1975s; more evolved than the 1970, but needing five to ten more years. The 1970 will be an all-time great, as is the 1961, with the 1959 very close behind. With the exception of the 1986, the style has changed in the 1980s. The only letdown for me was the 1985. The 1983 was surprisingly good. A great château, and a great event.

April 20 to 25, 1993

Trip to Yountville.

Visit to Duckhorn Vineyards.

With Margaret Duckhorn, a very nice lady. We tasted the 1991 Cabernet now being bottled, and some different lots of 1992 Merlots and Cabernets. These 1992s will be in cask for another year. We also visited the vineyard next to the winery where some Semillon is planted. (Last year, they had botrytis and bottled some sweet Semillon for their own use.) Their various vineyards have been attacked by phylloxera.

They still get grapes from "Three Palm Vineyard," as does Sterling Vineyards. Margaret gave me a half-bottle of their first year (1989) blend of Cabernet Sauvignon, Merlot, and Cabernet Franc wine called "Howell Mountain." In 1990, 1991, and 1992, they have increased the proportion of Merlot at the expense of the Cabernets.

May 10, 1993

Le Tastevin Wine Club special "Rarities" tasting, at the Park Royal hotel, in West Vancouver.

All wines were from my cellar. We had set up three tables, and people walked around and tasted the various wines. Wines appear in the order in which they were tasted.

APERITIF

CHÂTEAU CHALON 1982, VIN JAUNE, ARBOIS, HENRI MAÎRE, JURA, IN CLAVELIN BOTTLES (63 CL.):

Bright gold, sherry-like, solid, alcoholic, woody, ripe, with very good fruit. Full, long, and concentrated.. Will last for a long time in bottle. Reminiscent of a good dry Fino. This wine is produced from the Savagnin grape.

LA TÂCHE 1963, DOMAINE DE LA ROMANÉE-CONTI, MAGNUM:

Drier than on past occasions. Very light, pale colour. Some raspberry on nose. Classic Pinot Noir, but quite dry. Very soft, a bit watery, and chaptalized. Fell apart after ten minutes in the glass. Not a bad effort for such a miserable vintage. Previous two magnums, tasted in 1990 and 1991, were livelier.

MAS DE DAUMAS GASSAC 1981, DE LA VASSIÈRE:

Made from 100% Cabernet Sauvignon. Deep purple-red colour. Not much complexity, but great extract. Solid, massive, tannic. Very good backbone. Needs ten years. Very lively and youthful. Very good Cabernet-style wine from the South of France.

GEMELLO "35TH ANNIVERSARY" CABERNET SAUVIGNON N/V, CALIFORNIA:

Made from a blend of the 1959 and 1960 vintages. Soft, delicate, yet fleshy and round. Good fruit extract. Old Cabernet nose. Off-dry, full, rich, but ready. A bit short finish. Has held very well.

SPRING MOUNTAIN CABERNET SAUVIGNON N/V, LOT H, 68-69 LN:

Joe Heitz sold 50% each of the 1968 and 1969 "Martha's Vineyard" and regular Napa Cabernet Sauvignons in cask to the above winery, as he needed cash. "LN" stands for Limousin (1968) and Nevers Oak (1969). The letter "H" stands for Heitz. Some mint-eucalyptus, full, loads of ripe fruit. Fleshy, round, rich, concentrated. One bottle was drier. Surprisingly good.

CHÂTEAU CALON-SÉGUR 1918:

Topped off with the 1959 vintage and recorked at the château in 1990. Excellent top-neck level. Pale, mature Claret. Fair bit of sediment. Classic old Cabernet nose. Sweet, earthy, tobacco, biscuits. Round on palate, very long, lovely complex aftertaste. After 15 minutes, it started to dry out. Excellent.

LA TÂCHE 1976, DOMAINE DE LA ROMANÉE-CONTI:

Relatively evolved for a 1976. Trademark: expansive raspberry jam and Pinot Noir nose. Round, long, complex, elegant. Quite soft. Needs drinking. Very long aftertaste. However, the 1971 and 1978 are far greater wines. I even find the 1972 clearly superior to the 1976. Oddly, this wine did not have the baked, overripe character of this hot, dry vintage.

HERMITAGE "LA CHAPELLE" 1978, PAUL JABOULET AÎNÉ:

14 hectolitres per hectare! A great wine from a great vintage. Unbelievable deep-purple, youthful colour. Incredible extract. Tannic, powerful, loaded with ripe, but tight, fruit. At 15 years of age, it needs another 15

years, at least! Lovely, spicy, ripe, rich. Perfect balance. Great.

Heitz Cellars "Martha's Vineyard" 1974 Cabernet Sauvignon, Napa Valley:

Retails (1993) for US$250 per bottle! Very good, dark colour showing some maturity at rim. Classic "Martha's" eucalyptus, mint, Cabernet. Full, sweet, ripe fruit. Long, complex, lively, very special. Ready, but no rush if well cellared.

DESSERT WINE

Edelkeur Superior 1978, Wine of Origin, Nederburg Estate, South Africa, in half-bottles:

Made from mostly Steen (Chenin Blanc) and some Johannisberg Riesling, by the legendary Günter Brazil. Deep, bright gold, almost amber colour. Lovely botrytis, and spicy, ripe peaches and apricots on nose. Full, long, creamy, yet not cloying. Excellent balance and acidity. Great length. Ready, but no rush. Ranks with the finest TBAs. Great wine!

May 21 to 23, 1993

Trip to San Francisco, for an International Wine and Food Society weekend.

Dinner at "Elka's" restaurant, in Japantown.

With Brad Klein, Ed Lazarus, John Tilson, and John's wife Laurie. We each brought a bottle of 1978 Domaine de la Romanée-Conti wine. The La Tâche was mine, Richebourg was Brad's, and Grands Echézeaux was Ed's. All other wines brought by John. Very good Oriental food, but a bit too spicy for the wines. Wines were served a bit too warm, too. The term "chambré" means "room temperature." But at the turn of the century, room temperature meant 67° to 68° F. Nowadays, we tend to serve red wines at modern room temperatures of 72° to 74° F. This is too warm.

Champagne Ayala Brut N/V:

Quite nice, yeasty, fresh, fine mousse and bubbles, good fruit, round, and with some age. This was the only wine ordered from the restaurant's wine list. (16.5)

Bâtard-Montrachet 1982, Blain-Gagnard

and

Criots-Bâtard-Montrachet 1982, Fontaine Gagnard:

Both Gagnard daughters married and the estate split. Both wines are very well made, but with different philosophies of winemaking.

The Bâtard was a classic. Some sulphur on nose. Lovely oak, leaner, elegant, intense, long. Very well structured, with the elegance of the 1982s.

The Criots was almost a Condrieu-like wine, yet not as alcoholic. Exotic fruit; full, sweet, rich, very long. Loads of ripe fruit. Softer than the Bâtard. All seemed to prefer the nose on the Bâtard, and the flavour of the Criots. Both excellent. Both rated (18).

La Tâche 1978,

Richebourg 1978,

and

Grands Echézeaux 1978, all Domaine de la Romanée-Conti:

All three had very good, deep colours, with some maturity at rim.

The Richebourg (made from old vines before they replanted in 1979, and only 500 cases or so were made) was the biggest, tightest, and most solid. Lovely, but closed nose of ripe Pinot Noir. Full, intense, and powerful. A great mouthful. (19)

The La Tâche was classic raspberry jam on nose. Full, very long, great extract. No rush. Great balance and intensity; superb long finish. Great, but no rush. (19)

The Grands Echézeaux was as good as the two above, having the power and serious structure of the Richebourg, yet a hint of the raspberry fruit of the La Tâche. Also great. An underrated Domaine de la Romanée-Conti. Just very slightly less complex than the other two. All three are great wines. No rush and superb extract. As good as red Burgundies can be. (18.5)

From there, we dropped Laurie off at the hotel, and the four of us went to the "Cornelian Room" for more (!) wine and cheese (at 11:30 p.m.).

1980 La Tâche:

Very good reputation, but suffered by being served one hour after the great 1978s. Also a bit "piqué." Hint of fizz, edgy, but fresh, youthful raspberry fruit. Full, very good balance, and long. Can be excellent. This bottle merely good. (17)

This was followed by an extraordinarily intense white Burgundy.

Chevalier-Montrachet 1982, Georges Deleger:

The structure and intensity of a Montrachet! Almost hint of botrytis. Great depth, extract; sweet, very ripe fruit; long. At its peak. (18.5) John Tilson and I purchased their remaining two bottles at $100 per bottle. A very good price.

Saturday, May 22, 1993

Lunch with Brad and Randy Sultan, at "Geordy's" restaurant.

Very good food.

Brad brought along this bottle.

1952 Château Calon-Ségur:

Top shoulder level. Christian Moueix happened to be at the same restaurant with his girlfriend, Cherise Chen. We sent him a glass. He thought it was a 1949. Surprisingly dark, full, rich, and still tannic, without the excessive acidity of many 1952s. Very good depth. Chocolaty, almost plummy, but not oxidized. Very good, solid wine. (17.5)

Saturday, May 22, 1993

International Wine and Food Society Black Tie Dinner, at "Ernie's" restaurant, in San Francisco, featuring double-magnums of 1959 Lafite, Mouton, and Haut-Brion.

The dinner was mediocre and went on forever (over five hours).

Condrieu "Côteau de Vernon" 1988, Georges Vernay:

Lychees, exotic fruit nose. Brilliant, deep-golden colour. Fairly alcoholic (typical). Fat, lots of extract. Full, long, luscious. Excellent wine. Some people believe in ageing this wine, others in drinking it young. This was perfect. (18)

1959 Lafite,

1959 Mouton,

and

1959 Haut-Brion, in double-magnums:

The Mouton has an upper shoulder level. The other two, good neck level.

The Haut-Brion was the soundest, roundest, most elegant, and best for drinking now. Earthy, tobacco typical Haut-Brion overtones. Sweet, round, elegant, clean fruit. Very good balance; long, complex. Lovely wine. (18.5)

The Mouton was the most impressive. Very youthful colour. Intense eucalyptus-mint nose like "Martha's Vineyard." Very concentrated on palate. Powerful, intense, yet some medicinal, tarry aftertaste. Very good nevertheless. (18) I have definitely tasted better examples of this wine in the past. Can be great.

The Lafite was very good, but, in the context of what the great 1959 should be, it was a letdown. Tight nose. Some ripe Cabernet and cedar coming through. Quite dry, hard, tannic. Hard, short finish. A bit astringent. Can be magnificent. (17)

Pity that neither the food nor the wines has turned out great tonight. None of the double-magnums was spectacular.

Sunday, May 23, 1993

International Wine and Food Society vertical tasting of Grange Hermitage, at the Park Hyatt hotel, in San Francisco.

Mick Schroeder came up from Penfold's to conduct this event. (Geyser Peak Vineyards and Penfold's have merged.) I told Mr. Schroeder that Ian Huntley, the North American agent for Penfold's, and Darryl Groom, former winemaker for Penfold's and now at Geyser Peak, would conduct a similar tasting in Vancouver next week. Max Schubert started producing Grange Hermitage in 1955. He actually started earlier, in 1951, but the 1951 Grange Hermitage is very rare. All the wines were served through lunch. Two bottles of each vintage were opened.

FLIGHT #1

Grange Hermitage 1966 to 1972

1966:

Good, mature colour; orange hue. American oak, some leather, rich nose. Sweet, almost like very old, dry Port. Rich, long. Good acidity and balance; that is what is holding this wine together. (17)

1967:

Deeper and darker than the above. Darker rim, too. Cleaner, fresher nose than the 1966. Some Leather. Hint of eucalyptus. Big, rich, tannic, sweet, intense. Great depth. Long, full, very ripe. (17.5)

1968:

Deeper than the 1967, but browner rim. Toasty nose. Full, rich, softer than the 1967, leaner, more elegant. Atypical, more mature Bordeaux-like (like a ripe 1959), but more alcoholic. (17.5)

1969:

Medium-dark, mature colour. Similar to the 1966. Delicate, fruity nose. Hint of leather. Fresh butter and oak on nose. Hint of vanilla. Well balanced, clean finish. Slightly acidic. (17)

1970:

Evolved colour, orangy rim. Subdued nose. Some toast. Lightest on palate. Fairly acidic, leanest of flight. Some oak and toast coming through. Hint of prunes on nose. (16.5)

1971:

Darkest, most youthful colour of flight. Some age at rim, but excellent depth. Intense nose; hint of tar, cedar, some leather, very ripe. Full, rich, intense. Massive wine. Even very tannic. No rush. Very good balance. Starting to show some of the leathery "sweaty saddle," cigar-box character. (18)

1972:

Good, dark colour. Mature, orangy rim. Clean, toasty nose. Sweet on entry. Tannic, acidic, but good extract. Solid St. Estèphe style. Hint of vanilla, sweet American oak. Mature, at its peak. (16.5)

I spoke about the above flight. These wines are filtered twice before bottling: one coarse filtration and one finer filtration during the 20 months that Grange spends in barrel.

FLIGHT #2

Grange Hermitage 1973 to 1979

1973:

Lightest of flight. Medium, good depth. Orangy rim. Some leather on nose. Tannic, good extract, lovely flavour. Full, round, sweet. Good acidity, clean finish. Nice American oak. Some tar. Hint of coffee and leather. (17)

1974:

Darker than the 1973, orange rim. Subdued, earthy nose. Minty on entry. Very sweet, rich, long. Well balanced. Intense. Much more extract than the 1973. At first, a bit musty. (17.5)

1975:

Deeper yet than the 1974, to rim. Hint of mint. Full, rich, raisiny, tannic, solid, long. No rush. Great depth. Loads of fine, ripe, sweet fruit. (18)

1976:

Good, deep colour to rim. Darkest of flight. Fresh, youthful nose. Very ripe, leathery, intense. Loaded with ripe fruit. Great extract. Long. No rush. A "monster." Huge. Minty character. (17.5)

1977:

Very deep, dark colour. Minty, ripe nose. Sweetest, most tannic yet! Incredible extract. Needs ten years. Great extract, balance. Loaded with very ripe fruit. No rush. Like a Late Harvest Zinfandel. (18)

The second bottle of this wine was lighter and weaker, overall.

1978:

Deep, youthful colour. Chocolate/coffee nose. Full, sweet, rounder than the 1977, softer, but still sweet, chocolaty, rich, long. Well balanced. A bit simpler than the others, yet good concentration. Sweet, raisiny finish. (16.5)

1979:

Good, deep colour. Tight nose. Very young, sweet, rich, long, full, round; softer than the 1978 or the 1977. About ready, forward. Nice clean finish. Not in the same class as the others. (16)

An impressive flight.

FLIGHT #3

Grange Hermitage 1980 to 1987

1980:

Deep red colour to rim. Youthful, fresh, rubbery, woody, minty nose. Full, sweet, yet good acidity and balance. Softer than the others in this flight. Elegant. Ready by 1995 to 1997. (16.5)

1981:

Denser appearance than the 1980. Ripe nose. Full, sweet, long, leaner, drier than the 1980, but more tannic. Almost a hint of bitterness at finish. (17)

1982:

Deep colour to rim. Sweet, full, rich, powerful, long. Fuller, richer, riper, more tannic than the 1980 or 1981. Lots of depth, extract, power. Needs ten more years. (18)

1983:

Deep purplish-red colour. Tight, rich, full, sweet, long. Even bigger than the 1982, but more acidic, leaner, more aggressive tannins. Smoky, oaky. Needs seven to ten years. Drought; difficult year. Tiny production. (17)

1984:

Sweet, toasty, ripe. Looser-knit than the 1982 or 1983. Similar to the 1981. Hard, tannic finish, but medium-bodied with nice, round fruit. Needs five to six years. (16.5)

1985:

Deep, youthful, purplish colour. Unyielding nose. Ripe cherries and raspberries. Sweet, round, looser finish than the 1982 or 1983, but very good depth. Well balanced. Good complexity. Only needs three to five more years. More elegant style. Sweet, round, clean. Good extract. (17.5)

1986:

Candied fruit nose. Very soft, very forward. Different style. Elegant, soft, almost ready. Complete departure from the older style. Lacks depth. Not much liked. Like a simple Margaux! (16)

1987:

Deep, purplish colour. Toasty nose. Ripe fruit. Back to the classic structure. Full, powerful, solid, rich. Needs ten years. Not as big as the 1982 or 1983. Very good balance. Nice fruit. (17.5)

Nota Bene

It seems that with the wines of the 1980s, there is a clear change in style: lighter, more stylish wines, but, of course, still rich. They are not the massive wines of the 1960s or the 1970s, the 1987 being the exception.

This is clearly and consistently the best Australian red wine made to date.

Wednesday, May 26, 1993

Dinner at the Tobes', with Sid and Joan Cross, and Paul and Sara Pinski, our old, dear friends from San Francisco.

Wines served double-blind.

CHAMPAGNE KRUG VINTAGE 1979:

Typical 1979 Krug. Leaner style, but developing great, complex bouquet. Steely, tight, very good balance. No rush. Excellent. (18.5)

1985 AND 1986 MONTRACHET, LOUIS LATOUR:

The 1985 was slightly oxidized, earthy. Odd. Some fruit. The 1986 was fresher, more intense, and round. Very good fruit/acidity balance. Lovely, complex, flowery, intense, long.

The 1986 had a hint of apricots. Rich, complex. The 1986 needs more time. Will be very good. Very good intensity. Rated 1985 (16.5); 1986 (18).

CHÂTEAU GRUAUD-LAROSE 1961, IN MAGNUM:

Excellent depth to rim. Chocolate, cedar, intense nose. A little harsher, leaner than expected, but excellent depth. Very good extract, depth, chocolate, cedar. Great! Fabulous ripe fruit. Round and rich. Very long. (18.5)

CHÂTEAU DE FARGUES 1975:

I thought it was a 1976 or a 1983 Rieussec. Deep, dark, brilliant-gold colour. Much darker than expected. Buttery, oaky, rich botrytis, caramel nose. Full, luscious, rich. Good acidity, yet fatter, rounder than expected. Rich, ripe, botrytized fruit. Lovely. (17.5)

The 1961 Gruaud was the star of the evening, followed by the Krug.

Sunday, May 30, 1993

Lunch, featuring a tasting of Corton-Charlemagnes, in Victoria, at Ocean Point Resort.

FLIGHT #1

CORTON-CHARLEMAGNE 1989, CHARTRON ET TREBUCHET:

Tight, lemony, buttery nose. Very slight hint of oak. Full, tight, unyielding. Good fruit. A bit simple. Lacking the depth of this vineyard and vintage. (16.5)

CORTON-CHARLEMAGNE 1989, BONNEAU DU MARTRAY:

Fruitier wine than above, but tight and closed. Fuller, rounder, more intense on palate. Fairly lemony finish, but good extract and oak. Good, but does not have Latour's class or depth. (17.5)

CORTON-CHARLEMAGNE 1989, LOUIS LATOUR:

Tight nose. Fabulous balance. Best extract, depth, intensity of all three 1989s. Honeyed, nutty. Needs at least three to four more years. Fabulous length. (18.5)

CHEVALIER-MONTRACHET "DEMOISELLES" 1989, LOUIS LATOUR:

(I brought this bottle along by accident, instead of a second bottle of Latour's Corton-Charlemagne 1989). Still very tight nose. Superb depth, length. Great extract. Great white wine by any standard. Try again around 1995 or 1996. (19)

FLIGHT #2

CORTON-CHARLEMAGNE 1988, CHARTRON ET TREBUCHET:

Deep-gold colour for age. Also a bit madeirized. Similar impression on palate. Sweet, oaky, soft. Prematurely oxidized. Drink up! (14)

CORTON-CHARLEMAGNE 1985, LOUIS LATOUR:

Bright gold, very good depth, subdued nose, elegance of the 1985s, yet the depth of Corton-Charlemagne. Very good length, balance, lovely finish. Classic 1985. Round, nutty, complex, very long. (18)

CORTON-CHARLEMAGNE "DIAMOND JUBILEE" 1983, REMOISSENET:

Bright deep-gold colour. Buttery, almost light Sauternes nose. High alcohol, dramatic, full, hot, rich, yet not very complex. Like a ripe Alsace Pinot Blanc. Too alcoholic for me. Almost late harvest. (16)

CORTON "CLOS DE LA VIGNE AU SAINT" 1971, LOUIS LATOUR:

(Four bottles purchased at a Christie's auction for our club) Decanted, fair bit of sediment. Very good mature colour and depth. Lively, herbaceous, ripe nose. Round, long, clean finish. (17)

June 16, 1993

Le Tastevin tasting at the Four Seasons hotel, featuring a vertical tasting of Dominus Estate 1983 (First Vintage) through 1989.

Our guest speaker was Daniel Baron, manager of Dominus Estate (John Daniel Society), a joint venture of Christian Moueix and the two daughters of the late John Daniel. The property, called Napanook, is located in Yountville.

Dominus 1983 to 1989

1. 1983:

(Only 2,000 cases produced) Medium colour, evolved rim. Delicate, flowery nose. Hint of lilacs. Medium-bodied, nice elegant fruit. Well balanced, long. Quite soft yet tannic (but not excessive). Long, clean finish. Elegant wine, a bit angular. (16.5)

2. 1984:

Darker colour than the #1, not as evolved rim. Subdued nose, hint of oak-rubber-toast. Fruitier, richer, more intense than the 1983. More extract. Bigger, well balanced, good length. Needs time. 20% new oak. (17)

3. 1985:

Youthful, dark colour, slightly evolved rim. Subdued nose, little coming through. Rounder, riper than the 1984. More "fondu," yet powerful but riper tannins. Very good extract, depth. Ripe fruit and rich. (18)

4. 1986:

Similar appearance to the 1985, but a bit more purple. Fresher cherry nose than the subdued 1985. Higher acidity, greener tannins, less ripe. More aggressive tannins than the 1985. Like a younger 1984. Does not have the ripe extract and balance of the 1985, at this stage, but very good. Needs time. (17)

Starting with the 1987, Cabernet Franc was added to the blend. This was a cool year.

5. 1987:

(6,500 cases produced) Nice, dark colour, but not as deep as the 1985. Lighter, round, silky, more forward, most evolved, softest of flight yet very good backbone. Clean, long, fresh. Hint of bitterness, new oak, vanilla. Needs time. Raw tannins. (16.5)

6. 1988:

Dark, but with a youthful, purple colour. Baked bread, toast, delicate vanilla nose. Lighter on entry, then an explosion of tannins. Needs five years, at least. Hint of bitter tannins. Solid. Does not have the ripe extract of the 1985. Prefer this at this stage to the 1989. (Bloom interrupted, two sets of blooms—three weeks apart.) (16.5)

7. 1989:

(6,000 cases, 89% Cabernet Sauvignon, 10% Merlot, 1% Petit Verdot) Medium-dark colour. New Cabernet-oak nose. Medium-bodied, very good balance, very young. Needs five to eight years. Does not have the extract of the 1985, but very good. More aggressive than the 1988. A bit too hard, aggressive. First vintage that Petit Verdot was included in the blend. (17)

Other comments

Their Merlot is from cuttings from Petrus (First Vintage). About 79% Cabernet Sauvignon, 21% Cabernet Franc and Merlot (approximate). Old vineyard that was thought to be Cabernet Franc turned out to be old Merlot. Approximate yield is 50 hectolitres per hectare. 25% new oak in 1987, 15% in 1988, and 33% in 1989. The latter seems to be the new percentage of oak barrels that fits best the style of Dominus, according to Daniel Baron.

Daniel's lecture was very interesting and informative. The wines were all good, all had some similarity, yet all were different from each other. Overall group favourites were the 1985, 1989, and 1987 (in that order).

Friday, July 16, 1993

Dinner at "Geordy's" restaurant, in San Francisco.

Also there were Brad Klein and Ed Lazarus from Los Angeles, and Jeffrey and Jane Troy from New York. Jeffrey is in the wine business there. It was the eve of my 48th birthday. Each individual contributed a bottle.

CHAMPAGNE VEUVE CLICQUOT "CARTE OR" 1985:

Still lean. Needs time to round up. Fine, long, tight; good fruit and balance. Try around 1995.

DOMAINE DE CHEVALIER BLANC 1970

AND

LAVILLE-HAUT-BRION 1970:

(Domaine de Chevalier was my bottle.)

Domaine de Chevalier was paler, still youthful colour. At first, tight, leaner, crisper. Fresh for a 23-year-old white wine. Later, developed a lovely, flowery bouquet, hint of oak; long, very good fruit on entry, but a bit dry at finish. Crisp, fresh, very nice.

The Laville had a deeper gold colour; thicker, richer, hint of age. Long, intense. Not as complex as the Domaine, but full, buttery, ripe fruit. Starting to decline, but still very good.

VIEUX CHÂTEAU CERTAN 1966

AND

LATOUR-À-POMEROL 1970:

The Vieux Château Certan has a good, dark colour. Spicy, a bit stemmy on nose. Tight, hard, drying out. Little fruit left. Hard, not unlike a 1966 Cos d'Estournel. Too dry.

The Latour-à-Pomerol was a typical 1970. Very deep, intense, still youthful colour. Sweet, spicy nose. Full, hint of iron; intense, ripe fruit. Still very much alive. No rush. Loads of ripe fruit, long, not very complex, but good extract.

CHÂTEAU LYNCH-BAGES 1959:

Upper shoulder level. While sound, this wine, which can be great, was a bit over-the-hill. Hint of oxidation due to storage or low level. Sweet, rich, intense, true 1959, but this bottle was tired. Last time I tasted this (October 1992) with Rémy Krug at "Les Crayères," it was superb and full of life and extract.

Château L'Enclos 1945, Pomerol, bottled and shipped by Cruse:

Brad Klein brought this bottle along on the occasion of my birthday. Good bottom neck level. Classic 1945 and classic Pomerol. Deep, mature colour. Chocolaty with woody-biscuity-earthy nose. Full, round, still very good extract and backbone. These 1945s are great! Still nice ripe fruit, full, long, very good. Classic ripe Pomerol-Merlot fruit.

July 17, 1993

My 48th birthday.

I went with Carol and kids to "Auberge du Soleil." We took our own bottle.

Nuits-St.-Georges Premier Cru 1978 "Château Gris," Monopole, Lupé-Cholet:

(Purchased a few months ago from Draper and Esquin's in San Francisco) Classic 1978. Good colour, some sediment (decanted). Spicy, barnyardy, ripe nose. Full, round, well balanced, rich, long. Ready, but no rush. Top quality for a Nuits-St.-Georges.

1982 Opus One, magnum:

Most evolved colour, orangy rim. Sweet, cedary, toasty, vanilla nose. Round, soft, complex. At its peak, but well balanced. Delicate finish, quite Bordeaux-like, but Napa-style cedar-eucalyptus. Quite a bit of "Mondavi" grapes here. (17.5)

1983 Opus One:

Not tasted tonight. Could not get any in time for this event. See September 28, 1993, for comments on Opus 1983.

1984 Opus One, in magnum:

Darker, brighter, younger-looking than the 1982. Good colour to rim. Prunier, more meaty (more Merlot than Cabernet character, in the Pomerol style). Soft, evolved, sweet, good balance, delicate. Oddly, no Merlot in the blend. (16.5)

1985 Opus One, in magnum:

Bright, deep-red colour. Tight nose, ripe berries. Intense, fresh fruit, still youthful. Spicy, cedary, ripe cherries and grapes. Full, rich, very good balance. No rush. (The 1984 and the 1982 are ready, even from magnums.) Slightly oaky nose. Fine wine. (17.5)

1986 Opus One, in magnum:

Very good, deep colour to rim. Lovely, yet closed, sweet, ripe Cabernet nose. Serious, solid. Great fruit extract, ripe yet tannins evident. Needs five to ten years. Great future. Long, rich, full, yet serious. St. Julien-like. (18)

1987 Opus One:

As with the 1986, great depth. Even darker than the 1986. Very good colour to rim. More open, slightly oakier, and more herbaceous nose than the 1986. Softer tannins, too; not quite as much extract or depth. Overall very good, but the 1986 is more serious, with better extract. Later, developed very good depth and length. (17.5)

1988 Opus One:

Good, dark colour; purplish rim. Lovely, fresh, oak-vanilla, ripe, yet delicate fruit. Intense, tannic, hard, aggressive, but lovely fruit underneath. A bit green finish, but good extract. (17)

1989 Opus One:

Dark, purplish colour. Spicy, cedary nose. Softer than the 1988; lighter, looser knit, earlier maturing. Delicate, stylish, elegant, softer. A bit overripe grapes? More evolved colour. Almost ready. (16.5)

1990 Opus One:

Very dark colour to rim. Very fresh, youthful, oak-vanilla nose; great depth, very good extract. Full, rich; structured like the 1986, yet more complex and sweeter fruit; softer tannins. (18)

Overall impressions

Clearly improved overall quality as the vineyard matures (now very badly damaged by phylloxera, and being replanted). If one could compare this wine to Bordeaux, closer to a Ducru-Beaucaillou or Pichon-Lalande style (or a blend of both) rather than First Growth quality.

September 28, 1993

Commanderie de Bordeaux Dinner and tasting, featuring 1983 Clarets, at the Hotel Vancouver.

APERITIF

Champagne Bollinger "RD" 1982:

Disgorged April 1992. Big, hard, fairly dry, but lovely complex nose and palate. Fine mousse, long, yeasty, rich. Serious Champagne. (18)

FLIGHT #1

Château Giscours 1983:

Medium-dark colour. Evolved, orangy rim. Spicy, chocolaty, yet herbaceous nose. Medium-bodied, round; good balance, fruit. (16)

Château Clerc-Milon 1983:

Slightly brighter appearance than the Giscours. Tighter, fresher Cabernet nose. Solid, straightforward, chunky, well balanced, but a bit dry and not too complex. (15.5)

CHÂTEAU COS D'ESTOURNEL 1983:

Good colour. Pale rim. Smoky, oaky nose. Leaner on palate. Aggressive tannins, but nice fruit. Very St. Estèphe style. The fruit is soft, but the tannins are tough. Will the tannins outlast the fruit? (16.5)

CHÂTEAU CANTEMERLE 1983:

Very good, deep colour. Evolved rim. Closed, unyielding nose. Full, rich, round, long, tannic, spicy. Good depth and structure. Needs five years. Together with the Gruaud-Larose, best wine of flight. (17.5)

CHÂTEAU TALBOT 1983:

Deep youthful colour. Ripe, rich, full; good depth, lots of fruit. Good St. Julien style. Nice sweet fruit. Straightforward. Very enjoyable. (16.5)

CHÂTEAU LEOVILLE-BARTON 1983:

Not as dark as the Talbot, more evolved rim. Subdued nose. Harder, more forward, yet more aggressive tannins, too. Lacks fat. Too lean, lacks fruit. (15.5)

CHÂTEAU LEOVILLE-POYFERRÉ 1983:

Bright, youthful colour to rim. Subdued oak, berries, clean nose. Not stemmy. Full, rich, sweet fruit. Ripe tannins. Needs time. This property is finally starting to produce fine wines, after an absence of two generations from the "true" Second Growth scene. (17)

CHÂTEAU GRUAUD-LAROSE 1983:

Bright, deep purple to rim. Animal, leathery bouquet. Hard tannins, intense wine. Full, rich, long, ripe, chunky. Very good potential. Try around 1996 to 1998. (17.5)

FLIGHT #2

CHÂTEAU DUCRU-BEAUCAILLOU 1983:

Lightest of flight; bright-red colour, palish rim. Spicy, toasty, cedary, elegant nose. Subdued, elegant on palate. Very perfumy flavour. Long, complex, delicate. Almost ready. (17)

CHÂTEAU LEOVILLE-LASCASES 1983:

Very good, deep colour to rim. Essence of Cabernet. Full, rich, long. Fuller, deeper, riper than the Ducru. Lots of flesh here. Very well balanced. Not as complex or enjoyable at this stage as the Ducru or Pichon-Lalande. (17.5)

CHÂTEAU PICHON-LALANDE 1983:

Similar appearance to the Ducru. Spicier, toastier, more evolved, and more elegant nose. Great class. Round, yet harder tannic backbone. Very good depth. Lovely. (18)

CHÂTEAU LAFITE-ROTHSCHILD 1983:

Medium-dark, evolved colour. Tight, unyielding nose. Full, hint of tea leaves. Elegant, yet good backbone. On the lean side. Most disappointing of flight. Too lean, hard, acidic. Good, complex wine, but too hard. Needs time? (16.5)

CHÂTEAU MOUTON-ROTHSCHILD 1983:

Deep, red colour. Tar, intense Cabernet nose. Not much cedar or mint. Fuller, richer, denser than the Lafite. Rich, intense, long. Needs three to five years. Good Cabernet complexity. (18)

CHÂTEAU MARGAUX 1983:

Very good, deep colour. Darkest of both flights. Tight, unyielding nose. Full, intense, long, rich, powerful. Superb depth, great length, lovely structure. Needs ten more years. Lots of extract. Best wine. This wine was served double-blind at the end of the tasting. Most participants thought it was a 1986 or even a big California Cabernet. Absolutely no doubt that this is the Claret of the vintage. (19)

MONDAVI-ROTHSCHILD OPUS ONE 1983:

I served this wine blind by itself at the end of the tasting because many of our members participated the previous night in the Opus One vertical tasting, where the 1983 was missing. Leaner style, new oak, complex, spicy, elegant. No rush, but hard. Better and more complex than the 1982 or 1984 (both riper). Good wine, but lacks a bit in fat. (17)

DESSERT WINE

CHÂTEAU CLIMENS 1964, BARSAC:

Surprisingly light, green-gold, bright colour. Buttery, delicate nose. Nice oak. very slight hint of botrytis. Vanilla ice cream. Soft, round, elegant. (Difficult vintage, rare wine; no d'Yquem produced in 1964.)

October 5 to 17, 1993

Trip to London, Israel, and Athens.

October 8, 1993

Dinner at the home of Harry and Prue Waugh, in London.

Harry has very little wine left, as he sold most of it to finance the studies of his twin children, Harriet and Jamie. They are 23 now. Harry will be 90 next year! Harry is still a director of Château Latour, although Latour was sold earlier this year to M. Pinault, a Frenchman. Harry said that he may never come to North America again, as he has little money left.

He said that the International Wine and Food Society treated him poorly over a trip to South Africa, which he was supposed to organize, and which did not work out quite right. He is upset with them as they blamed him for the problems.

He repeated the story about his experiences during World War II, when he was an officer with the Welsh Guards, protecting Winston Churchill at "Chequers."

Sir Bernard Baruch was a guest. Also at that dinner were Churchill, Harry, and another young officer. They had Champagne, steak and kidney pie, cigars, etc.—rare during the war!

At the end of the dinner, the subject arose of how the British Army Officer Corps would vote in the upcoming elections. Harry commented that the Corps was left wing and most of the army would vote Labour. Churchill apparently did not want Baruch to know this, so he dismissed Harry and the other officer!

With dinner, we had the following wines.

HARVEY'S BRISTOL CREAM:

(Bottled in 1973; 20 years old) Much better than today's version. Creamy, nutty, long, full, rich, and complex.

CHAMBERTIN "CLOS DE BÈZE" 1980, A. ROUSSEAU:

Round, long, spicy, clean Pinot Noir. Holding very well. Elegant, but good fruit. Rich, good finish.

FONSECA'S VINTAGE PORT 1963:

The wine of the evening. Great nose, body, length, balance. Approaching its peak. Superb fruit, length. Not as ripe as Graham's or as hard as Taylor's. Better balance, length. Excellent.

With Sam and Joan Fromowitz, at the US Embassy, in Athens.

An unknown, but good, Greek Cabernet Sauvignon 1986, a pleasant Mumm's Champagne N/V, and a nice 1988 Gewürztraminer "Roncières," Dopff et Irion.

Sam serves now as Political Attaché, a delicate posting, requiring a balancing act between two NATO members, Greece and Turkey, plus the Cyprus problem to boot!

November 3, 1993

Tasting of the Union des Grands Crus de Bordeaux, at Hotel Le Meridien, in Vancouver, with most of the owners participating.

DOMAINE DE CHEVALIER BLANC 1990:

A lovely white Graves. Medium-gold colour. Subdued oak-vanilla, spicy Sauvignon nose. Round, complex, long; lovely length and balance. Very fine. Ready from 1995 to 2000. (18)

DOMAINE DE CHEVALIER ROUGE 1990:

Medium-deep, youthful colour. Elegant, spicy, ripe berries, oaky nose. Fairly tannic; clean, fruity finish, but lacks middle. Very nice, but not great. A bit thin. I expected more from this property in 1990. Time will tell. (16.5)

DOMAINE DE CHEVALIER ROUGE 1988:

For me, the best wine of the whole evening. Medium-red colour. Elegant, subdued, toasty, oak-vanilla, nice fruit nose. Medium-bodied, medium depth, but classic balance and length. Classic Domaine de Chevalier elegance. Lovely, long, clean finish. Ready from 1998 to 2005. (18)

CHÂTEAU L'ANGÉLUS 1988:

Medium depth, youthful, herbaceous, good St. Emilion. Medium-bodied, a bit austere, tannic. Needs time. (16.5)

CHÂTEAU L'ANGÉLUS 1990:

Very deep, dark colour. Great extract of ripe fruit. A mouthful. Soft, early maturing; loads of ripe yet soft (low acidity) fruit. Easy to like and drink, but will it hold? (17.5)

CHÂTEAU PICHON-LALANDE 1990:

A disappointing wine. Not that it is not good, but not up to the standard of this property's 1986, 1983, or 1982. Medium to light red colour (for a great Pauillac from a fine vintage). Subdued, clean, elegant nose. Soft, lacks middle, a bit thin. Good. (17)

Had a nice chat with Claire Villars (daughter of the late Bernadette Villars).

Also tasted her two wines.

CHÂTEAU CHASSE-SPLEEN 1990:

Dark colour. The "simplicity" of a Cru Bourgeois, yet very well made. Solid, full, well balanced. Nice fruit. Good tannic backbone. Clean, long. (17)

CHÂTEAU LA GURGUE 1990, MARGAUX:

Lighter colour, rounder, more elegant, more forward than the Chasse-Spleen. Pleasant. (15.5)

These were followed by these wines.

CHÂTEAU DURFORT-VIVENS 1990, MARGAUX:

Too light, thin, herbaceous. Pleasant, but not much more. Certainly not a top Classed Growth. (15)

CHÂTEAU FIGEAC 1988 AND 1990:

The 1988 a bit too thin. Herbaceous, spicy, Figeac style, but too light, and leaner tannins. Good, but not great (16.5)

The 1990 was elegant, soft, darker, generous, better, riper fruit. Drink from 1997 to 2003. Nice, spicy fruit and new oak in harmony. (17.5)

CHÂTEAU PAVIE 1988 AND 1990:

Had a nice chat with the owner, Mr. Valette.

The 1988 was leaner, drier, but nice fruit. Needs time. (16.5)

The 1990 was darker, richer, yet not fat. Elegant, clean, long, fruity. Herbaceous yet ripe. Well made. (17.5)

November 19, 1993

Vertical tasting and dinner, featuring Château Trotanoy (Pomerol) 1924 to 1990, at "Spago's" restaurant, in West Hollywood.

Organized by Bipin Desai. Wolfgang Puck prepared the meal. Lovely pizza and white truffles hors d'oeuvres.

FLIGHT #1

1987:

Medium-dark, youthful colour; pale rim. Light, elegant, spicy, crisp, round. Some oak. For early drinking. Fine effort in an off-year. (15)

1983:

More St. Emilion than Pomerol-like. Herbaceous, spicy, medium-bodied. Round, but a bit sharp finish. Lacks flesh. Will lose its fruit soon. Unbalanced. (16)

1981:

Medium-dark colour. Sweeter, more forthcoming on nose than the 1979. Not as much weight, though. Lacks middle, but ready and pleasant. (16)

1979:

Medium-dark, mature rim, good depth. Sweet, clean, subdued nose. Full, rich, sweet, fleshy; backed by enough fruit. Not ready. Still has some aggressive tannins. (17.5)

1967, IN MAGNUM:

Deep, maturing colour. Subdued nose. Hint of lead pencil. Round, elegant; most complete and best-balanced wine of flight. (17.5)

1962:

Deep, mature colour. Tobacco and cedar on nose; smoky, cedary. Fruit drying up a bit, but nice, smoky, mocha wine. Drink up. (16.5)

1952:

(Not château-bottled, but Trotanoy label) Evolved, medium-dark colour. Subdued nose. The tannic, acidic backbone typical of the 1952s, but some fruit there. Dryish, austere, but still drinkable. Clean, long finish. Tannic finish. (16) Petrus 1952, tasted last year, is outstanding.

1934:

Bright, mature orange-red colour. Delicate, earthy, sweet fruit on nose. Dry, well balanced, but fruit going fast. Short finish; better on entry. Has seen better days. (15) The second bottle was better, more concentrated, more intense. Lovely, ripe. Very good balance. Lively. (17)

1924:

(Whitwham-bottling) Sherry-orangy colour. Sweet, old Claret nose. Hint of old wood. Dry, sour finish. Better on nose than on palate. Pruny. Gone. (No score)

1926:

Good, deep colour. Very good appearance. Sweet barley sugar on nose. Rich, concentrated; slight sourness at finish, but very good ripe fruit. Still enjoyable. Good appearance. (17.5)

FLIGHT #2

1988:

Deep purple, youthful colour. Tight, closed nose. Very "1988." Hard, austere, tannic; new oak. Good length, but tannins a bit too aggressive. Needs at least seven years. Time will tell. (16.5)

1986:

Similar appearance to the 1985, but more evolved rim. Riper tannins than the 1985, but overall, not as well balanced. Hard to choose a favourite. I prefer the 1985: better balance, better acidity. (16.5)

1985:

Bright-purple colour. Spicy, new oak, ripe raisins on nose. Round, elegant, well balanced, medium-bodied, good extract. Mid-term (1997 to 2003). Not as rich as the 1979, but good. (17)

1966:

Impressive, deep colour; orange-brick rim. Subdued, duller nose than the 1964. Full, rich, long, complex, surprisingly youthful. Quite spicy, herbaceous nose. St. Emilion/Cheval-Blanc-like. Unsure about its future, but impressive. (17)

1964:

A wine I know well. Dark, maturing colour. Ripe, chocolaty nose. Sweet, smoky, rich mouthful. Lots of depth, very good balance. Full, rich, long, surprisingly youthful. Very good. Great depth. (18).

1959, IN MAGNUM:

Very good, deep colour and appearance. Ripe raisins, Merlot nose. Full, sweet, low acidity, ripe tannins; typical 1959. What the 1982s will turn into in due course? Rich, full, lots of ripe extract. (17.5)

1955, IN MAGNUM:

Medium, mature colour. Good depth. Hint of barley sugar. Delicate, more extract, but slightly less complexity than the 1949. Finer than the 1949, sweeter, richer. Classic sweet Merlot, but not as complex as the 1949. Excellent balance. (18)

1949:

Good colour, appearance; orangy rim. Warm, clean nose. Lovely cedar. Round, full. Trace of acidity at finish, but still nice fruit. Delicate, clean, well balanced. (17.5). The second bottle had better depth; richer, fuller middle; long cedar-tobacco finish. (18)

My overall favourite of this flight was the magnum of 1955, with the 1964 very close behind. The 1959 and 1949 were lovely, too, and the 1985 had the best balance of the young wines.

FLIGHT #3

1990:

Purplish, youthful colour. Even riper, richer, and sweeter than the 1989. Loads of ripe fruit, extract. Good balance. Slightly fatter, richer than the 1989, but both excellent. (18)

1989:

Bright, deep purplish-red colour. Very youthful, spicy nose. Lovely balance, fruit, length, and depth. Very good extract. Best of the 1980s in all three flights in terms of balance and length. Very promising. (18.5)

1982:

One bottle nicer, more elegant nose, but leaner, too acidic and thin on palate. Second bottle richer, riper, typical 1982, yet lacks complexity and is too tight. Maybe needs time, but unsure. Good, ripe fruit. I have definitely tasted better samples of this wine. Can be great. (16.5)

1975:

Young-looking for a 1975. Lovely, fruity nose. Full, rich, excellent balance, especially for a 1975. Very good. Lovely, long finish. Spicy. Excellent depth. (18) This, together with l'Evangile and Lafleur, are the best Pomerols of the 1975 Vintage. Petrus may belong to this group, too, but it needs more time.

1971:

Deeper, but more evolved than the 1970. More open, cedary, ripe Merlot nose. Round, complex, richer, more forward than the 1970. Chocolaty, lovely extract. Ripe fruit. The 1970 is livelier, richer; has a better future. Of course, the 1970 was tasted from a magnum. (17.5)

1971 was the most successful in the commune of Pomerol, followed by the St. Juliens.

1970, IN MAGNUM:

Impressive, classic "1970s" colour and depth. Lovely extract on nose. Concentrated, still youthful. Full, rich. Loads of ripe, fresh fruit. Excellent balance, long finish. Not ready from magnums! Impressive wine. (19)

FLIGHT #4

1945:

Both 1945s were good, but the second bottle was fruitier and had better extract, better colour and depth. Good, ripe fruit. Ripe, rich. Our bottle was a bit tired, sharper, with a trace of acidity. Hint of sweetness at finish. Can be great. Rated our bottle (16), and the second bottle (17).

1947:

Good, dark colour. Herbaceous, leathery, wet wood nose. A bit lean, acidic, tight; a bit too sharp and spirity. Odd, not very good, but not bad. One bottle was fresher, richer, riper. Cracked up after 15 minutes. This was a letdown. I know this wine well; it can be great. (15)

1961, IN MAGNUM:

Deepest, darkest of flight, by far. Essence of Merlot. Full, rich; great extract, lovely depth, excellent balance. Loaded with ripe, rich fruit and tannic backbone. No rush, if well stored. (19)

My overall favourites (in order)

The 1961 (magnum), 1970 (magnum), 1964, 1971, 1975, and 1955 (magnum). Most disappointing and worrisome (in terms of expectations) were the 1982 and the 1983. Best young wines were the 1989 and the 1990; both excellent.

Saturday, November 20, 1993

Lunch at "Opus" restaurant, featuring Château Latour-à-Pomerol, 1990 back to 1945.

Part of Bipin Desai's "Pomerol Weekend"

FLIGHT #1

1949:

Impressive colour, good depth. Sweet, ripe, mature nose. Quite a bit of age, but good depth, extract, and backbone. Hint of ripe leather. Powerful, tannic, but fruit starting to weaken. Long aftertaste. Drying out. Drink up. (17)

1953:

More evolved colour than the 1949, paler rim. Very mature nose. Soft, tired, yet has some fruit and elegance. At the end of its useful life, but still a pleasant drink. No faults. (16.5)

1962:

Better colour than the 1953, but not quite as dark as the 1949. Toasty-oak and ripe fruit on nose. Lovely fruit, good extract; clean, still lively. Nice drinking now. As good as the 1949 or the 1953, if not better. (17)

1976:

Good, dark colour (surprising for a 1976). Sweet, clean Merlot nose. Ripe on entry, but drying out. Better on nose than on palate, but still enjoyable. Hint of sharpness at finish. (15)

1983:

Good, dark colour. Cigar, cedary, herbal nose. Leaner style, too steely, light, sharp. Good backbone, but lacks extract and ripe fruit. Good, but not great. (16)

1986:

Youthful colour, but not very dark. Subdued, sweet nose of young berries. Better extract than the 1983. "Late picked" ripe wine. Hint of new oak. Very good. (17)

FLIGHT #2

1945:

Dark, evolved colour. Toasty, ripe nose (good extract). Sweet on entry, with the aggressive tannins of the 1945s, but thin, acidic fruit. Later, improved in glass. Solid, but too dry finish. Nice flavour, though. (16)

1955:

Deep, maturing colour. Not quite clean. Subdued nose. Better balanced than the 1945; sweeter, riper fruit that is drying out at finish. Getting tired, but still enjoyable. (16.5)

1959:

Dark, mature colour. Ripe Merlot, lead pencil nose. Full, sweet; good balance, sweet fruit, very good extract. Lovely, sweet, rich. No rush. Impressive. Chocolaty, classic Pomerol. (18.5)

1979:

Medium, evolved colour. Buttery, toasty nose. Hint of oak. Too sharp, acidic; lacks depth (the Trotanoy 1979 is much better). (14.5)

1981:

Medium colour. More subdued on nose than the 1979. Spicy, better structured than the 1979; richer, well balanced. Needs five years. (16.5)

1988:

Purplish colour. Tight on nose; hint of new oak. Full, rich, long; very good extract, lovely fruit. Classic, leaner 1988 style, yet good Merlot fruit extract. Needs time. (17.5)

FLIGHT #3

1952:

Good, dark colour; mature rim. Lovely, ripe nose. Full, rich tannins and acidity coming through, but has enough extract. Very good. Aggressive tannins after one swallows (typical 1952). Holding very well. (17.5)

1964, IN MAGNUM:

Deep, impressive colour. Closed nose; hint of ripe, concentrated berries. Full, lively, solid, concentrated. Excellent extract. A mouthful of rich, serious (very well-balanced) wine. Lots of power and depth here. Overblown and simple, but big and rich. For lovers of powerful wines. (18)

1966:

Lighter colour than the 1964, but good depth. Browning rim. Youthful, sweet Merlot nose. Quite a bit leaner, sharper, than the 1964, but nice, delicate fruit and good acidity and tannic backbone. Elegant, smoky, cedary nose. A bit acidic, green. Drink up. (17)

1985:

Medium depth, purplish rim. Evolved, spicy Merlot nose. Medium-bodied, light, elegant, mid-term. Nowhere near the depth of the 1964. Lacks concentration. (16)

1989:

Deep red colour. Much more serious than the 1985, yet not quite the Trotanoy level. Solid, rich, very good fruit extract, new oak. Long. (17.5)

1990:

Very deep, purplish colour. Tight nose. Very young, of course. Softer, riper than the 1989, great fruit extract. Great depth. Lovely wine. Impressive future. Very good balance. Possibly better than the 1990 Trotanoy. (18)

Very good flight, overall. 1985 too light and uninteresting.

FLIGHT #4

1947:

Darker than the 1961. Oxidized, madeirized nose. Gone (both bottles). Sweet prune juice! The second bottle was slightly livelier, but also starting to oxidize, yet it had some fruit. Impossible to rate. (No score) Latour-à-Pomerol has produced an outstanding 1947; unfortunately, these two bottles were very poor.

1961:

Good, dark colour; mature rim. Lovely, sweet extract. Like a 1961 Petrus. Great depth, luscious, sweet, long; almost Syrah extract. Gobs of ripe fruit. No rush. Perfect balance. Will last for a long time. Great reputation and great price ($1,000 per bottle!). Held well in glass. (19)

1970:

Good, dark colour. Maturing rim. Woody, vanilla, new oak nose. Amazing for a 23-year-old wine! Lots of extract; rich, solid, serious. No rush. Loaded with good ripe fruit. Excellent. Good backbone, youthful. (18.5)

1971, IN MAGNUM:

Not quite as deep as the 1970. Subdued, almost overripe nose. Solid, dry, not as "fresh" as the 1970, but riper tannins. Very slight hint of oxidation. Prefer the youth of the 1970. (17.5)

1975:

Similar appearance to the 1971, but even deeper. Subdued, meaty, ripe fruit nose. Still tannic, but lovely, ripe, sweet fruit. Very promising. Good extract and fruit. Hint of coffee beans. I liked it more than most. (17)

1982:

Excellent colour. Toasty, herbaceous nose. Full-bodied, well balanced, good depth. Not as fat or rich as the 1982 l'Evangile, but better than the 1982 Trotanoy at this tasting. Lots of potential here. No rush. Will become excellent in five to seven years. (17.5)

The 1961 costs as much as two-and-one-half bottles of 1961 Latour! Although I liked it very much, I do not think it is worth that kind of money. But then, it is a matter of supply and demand.

Overall impression

Better wines than the Trotanoys on this occasion, more consistent. True Pomerols: straightforward, delicious fruit, sweet, rich, and well balanced. Yet I cannot help but feel that Trotanoy would have shown better, had the 1945 and 1982 been better bottles.

November 23, 1993

Lunch at "Mustard's," in Yountville, with Daniel Baron, vineyard manager at Napanook (Dominus Estate).

DOMINUS 1987:

Quite dark. Cedary Cabernet nose. Quite dry at first, and tannic, but better with food. Concentrated, good backbone. Needs another five years.

We also tried some wines that Daniel is producing himself.

CHARDONNAY 1991, SALMON CREEK, LOS CARNEROS "BAD DOG RANCH":

(Named after a sign by the vineyard) 100% barrel-fermented. 20% new Burgundian oak casks. Produced at Monticello. According to Daniel, he wants the oak-toast to be the frame of the picture, and the "fruit bowl" to be the actual painting. Indeed, this wine has nice, pure fruit. Complex, well balanced, and the oak-vanilla is subdued and in the background. Well made.

1992 CABERNET SAUVIGNON, BARREL SAMPLE:

Aged in older barrels, planted on 3309 rootstocks (same as Petrus). 75% Cabernet Sauvignon, 15% Merlot, and the balance is Cabernet Franc and Petit Verdot. This rootstock needs irrigation in dry years—this goes against Christian Moueix's philosophy of not irrigating, even in California. Planted in the Napanook Vineyard, the Merlot is original French Merlot, and the Cabernet Franc cuttings come from Vieux Château Certan, the best Cabernet Franc, according to Jean-Claude Berrouet, Moueix's winemaker. Hint of licorice, lovely, mellow fruit, well balanced. Very nice wine.

Daniel thinks that Christian should concentrate on making Merlot in California, "which is what he knows best." He thinks that the focus on Cabernet Sauvignon is a mistake, and that the wines are too tannic (Dominus), too slow-maturing, and "misunderstood," by both wine writers and consumers.

I also learned, confidentially, that Daniel is leaving Dominus in about six months. He got in trouble with Christian's partners, especially Jim Smith, Robin Lail's brother-in-law. Christian is 50% owner in the setup at Napanook and the two Daniel daughters have 25% each. He told me about the problems with the delay in finding a winery, problems with marketing, hesitant indecision by management, and more. Looks like Christian wants to renegotiate or even cancel the joint venture when renewal comes due in 1997, and take over the whole operation.

Daniel reminded me how I served as Harry Waugh's "nose" when we visited Napanook together and tasted the 1983, 1984, and 1985, back in 1989. Harry cannot smell any more as a result of a car accident in France a few years ago.

Daniel has to start to look for another job, or maybe start a winery, if he can find backers. His prospects at Dominus are dim.

It is a pity that things are not going well at Dominus.

I guess Christian thought that he would manage and have a free hand at Dominus, as his father did at Petrus or Lafleur—where the other partners or owners are silent and let him have a free hand. Robert Parker's rave reviews of the earlier vintages were a mistake. These are tight wines, hard to appreciate when young. Many people purchased these wines upon Parker's rave reviews and were disappointed. Consumers are trying these wines too soon. I find this to be a problem with Château Ausone, too. It needs several years to show its true class.

November 26, 1993

Thanksgiving Dinner and Paul Pinski's 81st Birthday, at the Pinski's home, in San Francisco.

MEURSAULT-PORUZOTS PREMIER CRU 1985, F. JOBARD:

An elegant Meursault, typical 1985. Delicate, long, smooth, yet nutty. Nice Meursault character. Ready.

MEURSAULT 1985, J. F. COCHE-DURY:

The master of Meursault. This was much more backward than the Jobard, yet so much more depth, weight, extract. Excellent. Not quite ready, but lots of stuffing.

VOLNAY 1985, J. F. COCHE-DURY:

The light colour of Volnay and the fruity extract of the 1985s. Lively fruit, spicy Pinot Noir. Very enjoyable. Long, clean, impeccable.

GRAHAM'S VINTAGE PORT 1945:

Both bottles had excellent neck levels. Oddly, both had broken corks with the bottom-half of the cork floating in the wine. More forward than expected. Usually 1945 Graham's is deep, jammy, and intense. These had a lovely balance, smooth, long, lively fruit but soft. One bottle was slightly more spirity than the other, but both were very good. Lovely Port.

Paul was very generous with his wines, as usual.

January 18 to 23, 1994

Trip to Yountville and Los Angeles.

The day before my departure, there was a major earthquake in Los Angeles, which left 53 dead and five highways out of commission.

January 21 and 22, 1994 (Los Angeles)

Two events, featuring Château d'Yquem 1988 back to 1847.

January 21, 1994

FIRST EVENT: LUNCH AT "SPAGO'S"

FLIGHT #1

Château d'Yquem 1988, 1986, and 1983

1988:

Bright gold. Fresh, elegant nose. Slightly herbaceous, quite sweet, medium-bodied, round, soft. Lovely, clean, oak, caramel, custard. Lovely balance and depth, but I wish it had a little more weight and intensity. (18) Great potential, nevertheless.

1986:

Similar appearance to the 1988; more subdued, buttery nose. Bigger, richer, thicker than the 1988. Very good acidity and backbone. For the long run. Luscious. A bit too spirity for me. Otherwise excellent. (18.5)

1983:

Darker, more-evolved colour than the above two. Lovely, creamy, custard, caramel, botrytis nose. Still youthful. A blend of 1986 and 1988, with even greater extract; starting to show some maturity, but no rush. Luscious peaches, ripe pears, apricots. Lots of length and depth here. For me, clearly the best of the 1980s. A "must" in any cellar. (19.5)

FLIGHT #2

Château d'Yquem 1959, 1955, 1947, 1945, and 1937

All wines in this flight had good neck levels.

1959:

Lightest of flight, but good amber colour. Excellent appearance for its age. Superb botrytis, caramel nose. Great length, balance, fruit, weight, depth. It was hard to produce a poor 1959 Sauternes. Surprisingly youthful. This is a great wine! (19.5)

1955:

Deeper than the 1959. More subdued on nose. Lovely, clean, peaches-apricot jam. Full, rich, long. Very good extract. Lots of body, depth. Slightly sharper than the 1959, but excellent. This is a lovely wine that had a hard time competing because of the great extract of the other wines in the flight. (18)

1947:

Darker yet than the 1955. Superb depth, length. Candied, caramel, ripe fruit. Very youthful. No rush. Great depth, extract, length. Full, rich, fat, yet very good acidity. Surprisingly, quite youthful on palate. Great wine. (19.5)

1945:

Deep-amber colour. Brilliant. Subdued nose; lovely, youthful(!) botrytis. Rich, long, full, creamy, fat. Lots of fruit extract. Exploded in the mouth. Great depth, acidity, all in harmony. No rush drinking this. A perfect wine. Sensational! (20)

1937:

As expected, darkest amber colour of flight. Pale Sherry-colour. Older, caramelized nose. Surprisingly round and youthful. Acidity kept this wine alive. Lovely fruit, botrytis; rich finish. Stylish. Even in this great company, it has held its own! The best 1937 Sauternes I have ever tasted. (18.5)

A great flight. Only the 1955 was slightly "less than great," but even that wine was excellent.

FLIGHT #3

Château d'Yquem 1874 and 1870

Both very good bottom neck levels.

1870:

Recorked at the château in 1989. Amber-green Madeira colour. Smell of old Sauternes, but Sauternes nevertheless! Slightly stemmy, old nose. Ripe raisins, Madeira nose. Slightly Sherry-like, but still long and complex. A very rare and fine wine. (18.5)

1874:

Brighter, cleaner colour than the 1870. Subdued nose. Full, rich on entry, but thinner and a bit more acidic finish. Some decay on nose, but better on palate. (16) as a wine and (18) for its age.

These two old d'Yquems were certainly better than many red wines of that venerable age.

FLIGHT #4

1869 and 1847

1869:

Recorked at the château in 1989. Green-gold, mature Madeira colour. Old, caramel, botrytis, slightly off, musty nose. Sweet, elegant, round, nice fruit. Good backbone. Rich, long, and ripe. (18)

1847:

The oldest d'Yquem I have ever tasted. Coffee beans, chocolaty nose. Not unlike chocolate liqueur. Sweet, lovely fruit, rich, long, concentrated. Still has fruit, acidity. Surprisingly lively. This is the most famous of all old Sauternes vintages. Exciting wine. Not as clear as the 1869 in glass. Decanting problem. A legend. (19) Original cork with the name of the château and the vintage clearly legible.

Really hard to give specific marks to these old treasures. No bad, poor, or even mediocre wines. 1847 was the first year that they made wine at d'Yquem that was affected by botrytis. This 1847 was acquired from a source in England.

1977 Graham's Vintage Port:

Good, dark colour. Still closed nose. Full, rich, tight. Too young, of course. Quite sweet and rich, typical Graham's. I could think of a hundred other wines that would have been better suited to end this great event. Actually, why serve any wine to follow these great Sauternes?

Saturday, January 22, 1994

Second Event: lunch at "Patina's" in Los Angeles.

Chef-owner Joachim Spichal prepared an excellent lunch.

FLIGHT #1

Château d'Yquem 1864 and 1865

1864:

Recorked at the château in 1992. Bright, amber, Madeira colour. Olive-green rim. Unmistakable, old, caramelized Sauternes nose. Earthy overtones, wet cement. Raisins, too. Sweet, full, rich. Lovely fruit; thick, caramel-candy. Hint of Madeira on palate. Trace of "hot," acidic finish. I wonder if any Madeira was added to this? Long, complex, ripe, raisiny, rich aftertaste. Lovely. Well structured. Nice balance. (18)

1865:

Deeper, darker amber than the 1864. Odd, earthy, unclean nose, yet ripe raisins and even a hint of botrytis coming through. Less lively, less fresh than the 1864; sharper, acidic, yet good, ripe, caramel-Madeira fruit. This was recorked at the château in 1993 (purchased from a French collector). Was this topped up with Madeira, too? In any event, both are very good. (18)

FLIGHT #2

Château d'Yquem 1893 and 1900

Both not quite as dark as the above two, but similar amber with olive-green rim. The 1893 slightly paler.

1893:

Recorked in 1993. Spicy, raisiny, old-Sauternes nose. Earthy overtones. Elegant, long, complex; lovely balance. Livelier than either 1864 or 1865. Long, lovely aftertaste. Still fresh fruit. Excellent structure. Buttery, caramel, sweet raisins nose. Still hint of botrytis. (19)

1900:

Duller, stemmier nose than the 1893. Drier on palate, too. A bit foursquare, hot, but still nice raisins and even hint of botrytis. Higher acidity, lower fruit; a tired wine. While good, it lacks in structure and balance. (16.5)

FLIGHT #3

Château d'Yquem 1962, 1967, 1975 and 1976

1962:

Great, intense botrytis nose. Ripe peaches and apricot jam. Full, rich, round, long, almost creamy. Great extract, depth, balance. Lots of stuffing here. Long, complex, lively. Elegant, flavourful, easy drinking. (18.5)

Sauternes were more successful in 1962 than in 1961. This is also true of the 1967s, which are better than the 1966s. With red Bordeaux, it is the reverse.

1967:

Similar appearance to, very slightly darker than, the 1962. Subdued, complex nose. Essence of Sauternes. Sweeter, richer than the 1962. Great depth, extract, length. Superb, with very good acidity underneath. Lovely, very long finish. Full, rich, creamy, mellow. Perfect harmony. Great. Very special. (19.5)

1975:

Bright, deep-gold colour to rim. Great depth. Excellent acidity. Lovely length. Will last well for a long time. Lots of depth. This is serious stuff. Ready, but no rush; great wine. (19)

1976:

Medium-dark gold; palish rim. Fresh, ripe pineapples and peaches on nose. Excellent balance. Rich, without the extract of the 1967, but very good. Trace of vegetal finish. Still fresh. Both this and the 1975 will last well. (18) However, the 1975 has better underlying acidity.

FLIGHT #4
Château d'Yquem 1929 and 1921

1929:

Very deep-amber colour. Like a mid-19th century Madeira. Luscious, candied Madeira nose. Full, rich, luscious. Great extract, depth. Great balance, acidity, fruit. Superb. A legendary bottle. Full, rich, creamy. Hint of brown sugar. Original cork. (19.5)

1921:

Two bottles tasted of this wine.

First bottle: Recorked at the château in 1991; green sticker. Slightly paler than the second bottle. Amber, deep gold. Tight, cardboardy nose. A bit thin, hot finish. Lacks extract and depth. Later, sour, acidic, sharp. Faulty, but still drinkable. (14)

Second bottle: Original cork; red sticker. Very much a Trockenbeerenauslese nose. More Riesling than Sauternes. Superb depth, great length. Complex. Great balance; smooth, rich, luscious, but not cloying. Lovely fruit. Has held extremely well. Sensational! A perfect (20)!

Two excellent events

With the exception of the "poor" bottle of 1921, all were exceptional wines. My favourites among the 20th century wines: 1945, 1967, 1921, 1929, 1975, 1959, 1983, and 1947.

Quinta do Noval 1985:

Purplish, red colour. Spicy, youthful, round. Needs ten to 15 years. Nice fruit, rich, not very big, but good length. Again, why serve a Port (or any wine, for that matter) after these great d'Yquems?

That afternoon

I drove around Santa Monica and other areas hit by the earthquake last Monday. Quite a bit of damage. Brad also lost several bottles of wine due to wine-bottle breakage in his cellar, as did wine merchants and others in the area. Los Angeles was unusually quiet and there was very little traffic!

That evening

Dinner at "Chinois" restaurant.

Brad brought along two bottles of wine.

Champagne Jacquesson "Signature" 1982:

Like so many 1982s, excellent balance, lovely fruit and depth, tiny bubbles. Very enjoyable.

Domaine de Chevalier Blanc 1960:

A minor year, yet a lovely white Graves. Evolved in glass; after an hour, it was nutty, elegant, oak-vanilla, complex, yet delicate and subdued.

It occurred to me that within 36 hours, I will have had four (!) lovely meals: at "Spago's," "Patina," "Chinois," and "Opus"—four of the leading restaurants in Los Angeles. Plus a vertical of d'Yquem 1847 to 1988, and a vertical of La Tâche and Romanée-Conti!

During the night, I experienced two aftershocks, one mild and one quite violent, lasting three to four seconds.

Sunday, January 23, 1994

Lunch at "Opus" restaurant, in Los Angeles, featuring a vertical tasting of La Tâche and Romanée-Conti.

After a sensational two-day tasting, featuring Château d'Yquem 1847 to 1988, held at both "Spago's" and "Patina" restaurants in Los Angeles, I had the pleasure (and good fortune!) of participating in the third and final event of this great January 21 to 23, 1994 weekend—on the heels of the earthquake of the previous Monday.

I approached this tasting with trepidation because it featured mostly large-format bottles, mostly double-magnums (called jeroboams in Burgundy). The reason for my worry was that at a previous tasting of large Domaine de la Romanée-Conti bottles—organized several years ago in San Diego by Toufiq Khouri—several of the large bottles seemed prematurely tired. A debate ensued as to how well corks can seal large bottles of Burgundy because of the tapered shape of the neck. My worries turned out to be unfounded. These wines came from the excellent cellar of San Francisco Bay-area collector, Doctor Ben Ichinose, and they were in excellent shape.

As with the d'Yquems, this tasting was organized by the indefatigable Dr. Bipin Desai. The tasting featured magnums and double-magnums (jeroboams) of older La Tâche, and Romanée-Conti wines from the late 1950s and 1960s.

FLIGHT #1
1964 La Tâche and Romanée-Conti, in double-magnums

Very similar appearance. Brick-red, mature colours with good depth.

Romanée-Conti:

Smoky, rich nose. Full, rich in a masculine sense. Velvety, yet tannic and powerful. Serious, solid, rich, hard; backed by good fruit. A bit drier finish. More concentrated than the La Tâche, but less elegant. Within 30 minutes, this wine dried out and displayed a tannic, unyielding finish. (17.5)

LA TÂCHE:

More subdued, classic raspberries on nose. Lively, fresher than the Romanée-Conti. Lovely fruit, complex; spicy, long finish. No rush. Years of life ahead. Both wines tasted fresher than colour would indicate, but the La Tâche was clearly the more enjoyable and better-balanced wine. (18)

FLIGHT #2

1971 La Tâche and Romanée-Conti, in double-magnums.

Both slightly deeper colour than the first flight, with mature, orangy rims.

La Tâche slightly darker.

LA TÂCHE:

One of my all-time favourite red Burgundies. Classic raspberries, rich, herbaceous (typical 1971). Loads of fruit and years of life ahead. Big, rich, impeccable. Spicy with great extract. Very long. No rush. (19)

ROMANÉE-CONTI:

Fuller, harder, richer. Like the 1964 but riper fruit, better intensity, sweeter, and Oriental spices. The 1971s are livelier than the 1964s. Pure essence of Pinot Noir, great fruit extract. Will last for a long time. Impressive, solid, serious, rich wine. (19.5)

The 1971 Romanée-Conti definitely better than the 1964 Romanée-Conti. The La Tâches were closer to each other, with the 1964 being more forward.

FLIGHT #3

La Tâche and Romanée-Conti 1959, in magnums. Colour quite similar to the 1971s, but a bit lighter, more evolved.

LA TÂCHE:

A typical La Tâche. Not quite as raspberry-like, yet lovely fruit. Surprisingly youthful. Rich, long, full, smooth, elegant, clean. No sharp edges. (18)

ROMANÉE-CONTI:

Spicy, full, rich, solid. Great chocolaty, spicy extract. Perfect balance. Lovely fruit. (18.5)

Both of the 1959s did not have the extract of the 1971s and were more subdued. Better balanced than the 1964s, though.

1959 was a great year for red Burgundies. These two wines, while certainly very fine, did not have the depth or breadth that I expected from them.

Also tasted

1962 LA TÂCHE, IN DOUBLE-MAGNUM:

Darkest of all the wines tasted. Sensational. Great depth, class, length. Leaving both 1959s behind. Smooth, mellow, perfect balance, and lovely fruit. A mouthful of silky, perfect fruit. Possibly the best 1962 red Burgundy I have tasted to date. Impossible not to like this wine. Lovely, harmonious. At its peak. (19.5)

Dollar for dollar, the La Tâche is definitely the better buy. And while we are on the subject of value, my experience has shown that the best buy of all Domaine de la Romanée-Conti wines, and consistently good, is the Grands Echézeaux.

Chef Thomas Keller did a superb job. Great food. The restaurant survived the earthquake. Some cracks were visible in the ceiling, and on the walls, and several windows were shattered, sealed by sheets of plywood.

February 3, 1994

The following is an article I sent to *The Vine*, published by Clive Coates.

"Dear Clive:

I have read the latest edition of *The Vine*, #107, with great interest. While I may not always agree with your tasting notes, the background on properties and the overall vintage reviews and progress reports give me a good 'feel' for various properties.

"What hit a raw nerve with me in this particular issue is your report and review of red Burgundies of the (in)famous 1983 vintage.

"Since I started seriously tasting and collecting wines over 20 years ago, I have always made an absolute rule never to purchase red Burgundies without first tasting them, whether at the vineyards (from barrel) or after bottling (in France or in various parts of Canada or the USA, where these wines are offered for sale).

"The exception was 1983. Circumstances just did not allow me to travel to Burgundy in mid/late 1984, so, based on generally glowing reports of such experts as yourself, Robert Parker, and others, I gambled (as did so many others). The first sign that I had made a terrible mistake was when I had a private lunch in Vancouver with Johnny Hugel, of Alsace fame, in early 1985. He told me how he had driven to Burgundy one day in the fall of 1983, intending to visit some growers and see how the vintage was progressing. When he saw the miserable conditions in the vineyards and the spread of rot in northern Burgundy, he turned around and drove back to Riquewihr. I had been had! I deserved it, because I had broken my own rule.

"Since then, I have conducted and participated in many tastings featuring 1983 red Burgundies, some blind and some double-blind tastings. Overall, the wines (including many Grand Crus from reputable producers and négociants) were rotten, prematurely tired, and browning. They tasted like Chiantis that were very old, from mediocre vintages that had been poorly stored—plus rot and mustiness. There were exceptions, of course. Some ordinary Village Vosne-

Romanées from Grivot, the range of wines from Faiveley, and a few others, but overall—OH, MY!

"At first, my anger was directed at the immoral, greedy producers who, disregarding any damage to their reputation in selling these foul wines to the public—or the damage this would cause Burgundy in the long run—went ahead and produced and sold these wines because they 'needed the vintage.' (They hadn't had one since 1978, and watched with envy what Bordeaux did with their 1982s.)

"Like so many other collectors, I started to look for 'suckers' who would take these wines off my hands. However, auction houses and wine shops were inundated with people trying to get rid of their 1983s. Prices dropped rapidly, and the auction market is still flooded with these wines at give-away prices. There are very few takers.

"At no point did I get angry at wine experts like yourself, because I should have known better.

"I do not know what you or Parker or other journalists and experts are given to taste when you visit vineyards in Burgundy. Is it really possible that what you tasted and what you reviewed had nothing to do with what was eventually bottled and shipped to London, Vancouver, New York, Los Angeles, Chicago, or San Francisco?

"Clive, we all make mistakes. It is only human. Robert Finnigan was 'lukewarm' in his review of the great 1982 Clarets. It cost him his wine career—permanently! You and Parker recommended the 1983 red Burgundies, yet somehow you both survived. I guess you were luckier than Finnigan.

"When stockbrokers recommend certain stocks that eventually turn out to be no good, they distance themselves from those stocks, ask for forgiveness from their clients, or pray and hope that the 'evil' will go away and be forgotten. That is exactly what has happened to you and to Robert Parker. But here is where you and Parker part ways.

"Parker, sheepishly and ever so gradually, downgraded the 1983 red Burgundies. Every subsequent report/review was cooler, more critical, putting as wide a distance as possible between himself and these wine reviews, hoping that his subscribers would forgive and forget. He never came out openly with a 'mea culpa,' but he was lucky and got away with it—this time.

"Not you! This glowing review and high marks you have given so many 1983 red Burgundies in your issue #107 of *The Vine* puts you on the spot again.

"Give it up, Clive! You got away with it this time. Your readers have forgiven and forgotten; why look for trouble?

"Ending on a more positive note, I will continue to read and enjoy your publication but, as always, take it with a grain of salt."

Best regards,
Albert Givton

The following are several comments and responses, published in *Rarities* wine magazine, by various writers/contributors to this magazine.

Another opinion

"The above letter is, in my opinion, much too strong and ignores the many good, very good, and great wines in the 1983 vintage. It also conveniently ignores that *The Wine Journal* also said at the very beginning that there were many fine wines in that vintage. Is Albert saying that there are no very good or great wines in 1983 in Burgundy? He would be very much in the minority if that is his opinion.

"On the subject of Mr. Hugel's observation of rot in the vineyards, the point is that all producers of Burgundy in 1983 knew that a rigorous selection was going to be necessary, not only because of rot, but also hail damage. The selection was first in the bunches of grapes, or even in trimming off parts of bunches. Then, after the wines were made, there was a second selection in the cellar where much wine was either discarded or mixed into Bourgogne Rouge blends. The occurrence of rot in Burgundy is fairly common and the Burgundian winemakers know how to make good wines in spite of it."

[A comparative tasting of 1978 and 1983 red Burgundies deleted.]

Dennis Foley

Yet another opinion

"I still stand 100% behind the letter I wrote to Clive Coates in 1994. The 1983 Burgundy vintage is almost entirely composed of wines that are rotten, prematurely tired, and browning. In reading Dennis's notes, I cannot believe the wines were as good as he says. It is my opinion that Dennis is insensitive to the taste of rot and is so enamoured of ancient wines that he cannot tell a tired wine when he tastes one!

"Now I will admit that I have tasted the odd 1983 Burgundy that is acceptable, but only very few and far between. Furthermore, they can only be said to be acceptable in the context of the dismal 1983 vintage, and would not be seen as acceptable when compared to wines from better vintages such as 1985, 1988, or 1990.

"Take my advice: Avoid the 1983 Burgundies completely!"

Albert Givton

Still another opinion

"Dennis Foley is certainly to be congratulated on the completeness of opinions he assembled in his *'Historical Review of the 1983 (red) Burgundy Vintage.'* We see everything from champions of the vintage, such as Clive Coates and Dennis, to the outspokenly negative Albert Givton.

"One would think that too many opinions have already been presented, but, perhaps because the powers that be in our grand publication are not quite comfortable with any of them, I have been asked for my opinion, which I will attempt to state as briefly as possible.

"Certainly the basic growing conditions and degree of maturity and ripeness of the grapes in 1983 were such that a great vintage could have been produced, were it not for two tragedies of nature. In July, there was hail, and in September, heavy rainfall a good part of the month. The rain can cause rot in the grapes and hail produces 'off' aromas and flavours in the wine, not dissimilar from rot. These 'little' problems with the vintage were not dwelled upon while John Tilson and I were in Burgundy, tasting the vintage from barrel. In many cases, we were presented with quite impressive tasting samples and came away with the idea that the vintage, though variable, was going to produce a good many very fine wines.

"Later, we found that some of the same wines we tasted out of barrel bore little resemblance to what was ultimately bottled. What had obviously happened was that, in many instances, we tasted out of specially selected barrels containing wine devoid of 'off' characteristics. These barrels were later blended with the rest, which either had 'off' characteristics or had been heavily fined, thus leaving the wine light and stripped of much of its character.

"With all respect to Dennis Foley—for whom I have much admiration—in my opinion, it is obscene to attempt to compare 1983 with 1978. I think 1978 is one of the truly fine red Burgundy vintages of the century. It was virtually trouble free and the wines were of a uniform high quality, limited only by the particular vineyard or the skill of the vintner.

"I do not quite understand Dennis's statistics. All I know is that I have attended comprehensive tastings of both vintages. The tasters at the 1983 event were not particularly happy campers. I reviewed my own scores and found there were many, many more wines rated 'outstanding' among the 1978s. Also the general scores of the 1978s were a good deal higher. The 1983s contained a good many notes such as 'rot,' off,' and 'musty.' The great majority of the top names produced wines not quite up to the quality one would expect from a first-rate vintage.

"Dennis is certainly correct that the 1983s are dirt cheap. Since there are some very fine wines from the vintage, they can represent excellent value. Obviously, extreme selectivity is required."

Edward Lazarus

More

"This pretty well covers the subject of the 1983 red Burgundy vintage. What I wrote in *The Underground Wine Journal* proved to be very accurate. Robert Parker early on (August 1984) was quite enthusiastic: "... 20% of the wines I have tasted have the potential ... to be considered great.

"A year later, in August 1985, he was a bit more pessimistic, but still quite enthusiastic, as the quote from Dennis's article indicates: 'approximately 20% of the red wines are among the finest produced since 1964.' The point is that there was a lot of early hype about the vintage. Then we burst the bubble. Later opinion on the vintage really soured, as Albert Givton states in no uncertain terms. But, like Ed says, the wines were better out of barrel and even then, we found under 10% that we rated potentially outstanding, 50% very good, and 40% good or below average!

"And, again, Ed is right on when he criticizes Dennis for comparing 1983 with 1978. 1978 is a great vintage. 1983 is not. End of conversation. But, part of the confusion is that Dennis has misinterpreted the percentage ratings that *The Underground Wine Journal* published on 1983 and 1978. The 1983s were tasted from barrel, and ratings represent only potential. Indeed, many of the wines turned out to be even worse than our apprehensive early assessment. In fact, 40% of all the wines that were cherry-picked to taste from the best producers did not even rate a 'very good potential' rating of 15 to 17. The 40% rated 14 and below. On the other hand, while we rated only 10% of the 1978s outstanding, we tasted from a wider sampling of producers, and nearly everything else was very good. And, virtually nothing was below average. Clearly, this reflects much greater consistency with the 1978s as compared with the 1983s.

"The problem with the 1983s, in my opinion, is not so much the lack of colour (some of the very best Burgundies I have ever drunk were very light in colour, even pale: Faiveley's 1923 Musigny and Frederick Mugnier's 1949 Clos Vougeot, for example). Great Burgundy is not about colour. Great Burgundy is about balance, haunting perfume, and exquisite flavours! Unfortunately, few 1983s have these characteristics. Some are too dry. Some are too thin. But the real problem with most of the wines is the smell of rot. It ranges from a slight mustiness to a decided earthiness and, in the very worst wines, a decidedly dirty smell and taste. If you're not sensitive to these characteristics (and perhaps Dennis is in this group), then you may not find the wines too offensive. However, what I've noticed with people tasting the 1983s is that they first react to the colours, as most are lighter red—some with a decidedly amber tone—and in the worst wines, a tell-tale brown hue that is a sure sign of decay. These latter wines are generally to be avoided, but most people pay no attention to the hue, only to whether the wine is light or dark, and if it's light, it's already 'no good.' Too bad. For with older Burgundy (virtually anything over ten years old), this is a grievous mistake. Let those people slurp up the young, purple, cold-fermented Burgundies so impressive because of a purple colour, but devoid of complexity and character, and totally without the potential to age! But that's a story for another day.

"Finally, there is no question in my mind that Dennis has greatly overstated the number of great 1983s. No way has this vintage produced 23 outstanding wines. And some of his 'picks' are way off the mark. For example, all of the 1983 Henri Jayers have proven to be very poor. Ditto for Dujac. And, to call the Villages Nuits-St.-Georges from Labouré-Roi outstanding, again is way off the mark, in my opinion. For the record, here is my list of outstanding 1983s, ranked in order of preference: Mazis-Chambertin (Leroy), Musigny (G. Roumier), Ruchottes-Chambertin (G. Roumier), Mazis-Chambertin (Maume), Musigny (G. Roumier), Bonnes Mares (G. Roumier), Bonnes Mares (Bertheau), Charmes-Chambertin (Leroy), Charmes-Chambertin (Bachelet), Clos Vougeot (J. Gros), and Clos Vougeot (G. Roumier).

"You will note there are no wines from Vosne-Romanée on my list, although wines from this commune are generally among the greatest of all Burgundies for me. The reason is, although many have good concentration, nearly all have, to my smell and taste, the telltale musty, earthy character that renders them less attractive. Contrast these wines to the wines of Clos Vougeot, where few of the wines have this character. Certainly it would appear that Vosne-Romanée was much more affected by hail and rot than Clos Vougeot and this, in a nutshell, says it all about the 1983 vintage—variable!"

John Tilson

February 9, 1994

Chevaliers du Tastevin Dinner and vertical tasting of Corton "Clos des Cortons," Faiveley, at the "William Tell" restaurant, in Vancouver.

Corton "Clos des Cortons," Monopole, Faiveley

1986:

Dark, round, rich. Good, but soft, ripe fruit. Lighter-bodied wine, with a spicy, clean finish. Ready. Typical for the vintage. (16)

1987:

Lighter colour. Herbal, spicy, vegetal Pinot Noir nose. Leaner, sharper, more acidic, yet good fruit. Raspberries. Sharpness annoying, yet more style and character than the softer 1986. (16)

1983:

Darker than both the above, and than the 1989. Good depth. Tight, unyielding nose; hint of rubber. Full, rich, tannic, austere, solid. A big wine, yet not rotten or musty. Needs time. Resembles the 1976s. (17)

1989:

Buttery, fresh, oaky, complex nose. Lovely fruit. Most likeable so far. Good body, long, complex. A lovely bottle for mid-term drinking. (17)

1985:

Deep colour, slight maturity at rim. Intense, rich, ripe fruit, yet has the charm of the 1985 vintage. Luscious, rich, long. Great depth. Miles ahead of the above four. Enjoyable now, but will last. (18.5)

1988:

Like the 1985, yet more austere, harder. Great depth, balance, extract. Lovely. This is serious stuff. Has lots of body, flesh; rich, clean, impeccable. Needs five to eight more years to mature. Darkest of flight, and ultimately the best. (18.5)

February 25, 1994

Trip to South Africa with members of the International Wine and Food Society.

A dream come true—and just in time. I wonder what will happen next month when free elections will be held for the first time in the republic of South Africa? If Nelson Mandela wins, and there is no "wholesale" revenge and settling of accounts, this country may survive. If not...?

The following is a selection of wines tasted on this trip... and a few comments

THELEMA CHARDONNAY 1988:

Best wine of the evening. Very California, oaky, cedary. Good maturity. Bright, dark-golden colour. Long, complex, full, well balanced. Ready.

Monday, February 28, 1994

Visit to Shaft #5, "President Brand" gold mine in the Free State, near Welkom.

We went down 2,000 metres (!) to the drilling area and also saw how the ore is melted. It takes 8,000 metric tons of ore to produce one ingot of 25 kilograms of 80% pure gold!

Wednesday, March 2, 1994

24-hour trip by "Blue Train" to Capetown.

With our lunch on the Blue Train, our member from Marin County, Caryl Saunders, and I shared this wine.

ALTO CABERNET SAUVIGNON 1984:

Mature colour. (Too much shaking on the train?) Leathery, full, solid wine. At its peak, even slight hint of oxidation, some tannin. Has character. This can be very good.

1982 "LE BONHEUR" CABERNET SAUVIGNON, SIMONSIG, STELLENBOSCH:

At its peak. Nice, dark colour. Cabernet character; rich yet complex. More delicate than the Shiraz, yet quite tannic. Far better than the food, which was very disappointing!

The "Blue Train" was a disappointment. Elegant dining room and bar, tiny cabins, and really terrible food at lunch and dinner, 'though breakfast was OK.

Friday, March 4, 1994

Visit to Stellenbosch and some fine wineries. The Cape and the vineyards area is a piece of paradise!

A combination of Vancouver, the Napa Valley, and the Grand Canyon—all in one location!

Visit to Meerlust Winery.

James Mitchener stayed at this 300-year-old winery while he wrote The Covenant.

CHARDONNAY 1992:

A solid, well-made Chardonnay from ten-year-old vines. Barrel-fermented, some toast. In Allier oak casks for nine months. Elegant, oaky, fruity nose. Nice fruit, complex, long; California style, but elegant. (16)

PINOT NOIR 1989:

Evolved colour; nice varietal nose. American oak with some sweetness. Volnay-like, but sweeter; yet tannic backbone. Good length, complex. Long finish. (16.5)

CABERNET SAUVIGNON 1986:

Bright red. Nice varietal nose. Hint of rubber. Medium-bodied. Claret-like. A bit tannic. Good fruit, good balance. A bit stemmy. 100% Cabernet Sauvignon. (16)

MERLOT 1987:

Darker than the Cabernet Sauvignon. Sweet, varietal nose. Long, well balanced, easy to drink. Longer, cleaner, and overall better made than the Cabernet Sauvignon. 10% Cabernet Sauvignon in the blend. (16.5)

RUBICON 1987:

Darker than the Merlot. Subdued Claret nose. Quite tannic, dry; nice length and complexity. 65% Cabernet Sauvignon, 25% Merlot, and 10% Cabernet Franc. (16)

All Meerlust wines were of high standard.

Visit and lunch at Delaire Winery.

Superb setting, formerly owned by the South African wine writer, John Platter.

Visit to Thelema Vineyard.

The winemaker, Gyles Webb, did some of his apprenticeship with Joe Heitz, where I met him a few years ago. He remembered me. They use French oak, mostly Seguin-Moreau, François Frères, and Dargaud and Jaegle.

CABERNET SAUVIGNON 1990:

Very good, deep colour. Complex nose. Long, spicy, complex. Fine wine. Needs two to three years, but will be good. Clearly the best red wine of Thelema's range tasted. (16.5)

Saturday evening

Dinner at the home of Mr. Uwe Koetter, a member of the Capetown branch of the International Wine and Food Society.

The German Mr. Koetter, a local jeweller—and a racist and an anti-Semite—was outwardly a pleasant man. His beautiful home had a great setting overlooking the bay off Capetown. According to him, blacks are not very intelligent, and the Jews are running away from South Africa with their money. Later that night, I learned from him that most of his money is Overseas, and that he has a German passport and he can leave any time—as soon as trouble starts. Then he asked me where I was from. I told him that I was born in Cairo, Egypt, and that I had fought in the Six Day War—on the Israeli side. He managed to keep a straight face.

Sunday, March 6, 1994

Lunch at Boschendal Winery, with Caryl Saunders, Stan and Helene Schwartz, Stan and Anna Bernhard, and the group.

Boschendal Gewürztraminer "Jean Gardé Vineyard" 1990:

A fine wine by any standard. Dry, Alsace style. Flowery, subdued nose. Nice, spicy varietal character. Well balanced. Clean, lovely fruit. The most enjoyable white wine I have had on this trip so far. (17)

Wine laws in South Africa are similar to those in California. Acidifying and irrigation are allowed. Addition of sugar (chaptalization) is not allowed (the opposite of France).

Dinner at the Lord Charles hotel, in Heldenberg.

I decided not to go on a dinner tour. Stan Bernhard of San Francisco and I had a quiet dinner at the hotel. I purchased a half-bottle of Edelkeur 1986 (Nederburg) that the restaurant kindly allowed me to take away. We also ordered what turned out to be the best wine of the trip so far. (They had a very extensive South African wine list.)

Nederburg Cabernet Sauvignon 1973:

Mid shoulder level (I was worried). Like a 1959 Claret! Full, older Cabernet character. Chocolate overtones. Round, mellow, very long. Cedary, complex. Long, clean aftertaste. Best red wine so far, by a mile! (18)

March 10 and 11, 1994

Itala Wilderness Game Reserve, in Natal (Zululand).

We (Stan and Helene Schwartz, Stan and Anna Bernhard, Caryl Saunders, and I) purchased our own wines in Plattenburg.

Klein Constantia Chardonnay 1991:

A well-made wine; oak and fruit in harmony. Long, complex, well balanced. Long, clean finish. Nice complexity. Rich, not too acidic. Good. (16.5)

Alto Cabernet Sauvignon 1986:

Classy wine. Very good Cabernet character. Some oak. Well balanced. Not too big or overripe. Elegant, yet good depth. Ready, but no rush. (16.5)

Nederburg Cabernet Sauvignon 1981:

Too vegetal, stemmy, sharp. Some Cabernet Sauvignon character, but too green and sharp. (14.5)

Champagne Veuve Clicquot "Carte Or" 1985:

The only "foreign" wine tasted on this trip. We purchased two bottles in a wine shop. Lovely! No comment, just great—and a welcome change. This is not to say that some of the South African sparkling wines were not very good. It is just a case of my palate getting overtired tasting so many different wines in such a short period of time.

Klein Constantia Shiraz 1987:

Medium-bodied; spicy, ripe fruit. A bit acidic, but complex. Nice wine. Not very big. (16)

L'Ormarins Cabernet Sauvignon 1985, "La Maison du Roi," Franschoek Valley:

Elegant, complex Cabernet nose. Too acidic, obviously acidified and sharp. Good ripe fruit, though. Acidity spoiled it. (15)

De Wetshof Estate "Edeloes" Noble Late Harvest 1991, in 500 mL bottle:

Bright, deep amber-gold. Lovely ripe apricots and botrytis nose. Sweet, yet not cloying. Lovely, long, complex, full, rich, luscious. (17.5)

Edelkeur "Superior" Noble Late Harvest 1986, Nederburg:

Bright, deep-gold. Botrytis, ripe apricots. Not as luscious or as deep as the great 1978 I have at home, but full, rich, long; good botrytis. Almost TBA style. (17)

We also visited a Zulu village, and had a traditional lunch there, with a native dance and "witch doctor" performance. Stan Schwartz was accused, by the witch doctor, of stealing a goat! He was tried and found guilty. He was, however, pardoned, as he promised to replace the goat.

March 13, 1994

Black Tie Dinner at the "Royal Grill," in the Royal hotel, in Durban, with local members of the International Wine and Food Society.

Le Bonheur Cabernet Sauvignon 1984:

Clos du Val style. A California Cabernet trying to be a Bordeaux. Not bad. Good fruit, oak, cedar, all in harmony. (16.5)

Klein Constantia "Vin de Constance" 1987:

In old-looking 50 cl bottles. This is an attempt at reproducing the famous Constantia wine of the 18th and 19th centuries, and a favourite of Napoleon Bonaparte. (This wine has now disappeared.) Muscat-based, lychees, but not enough depth. Too light, a bit overalcoholic. Simple. Nowhere near the quality, depth, and complexity of the various Noble Late Harvest wines tasted on this trip. (15)

Monday, March 14, 1994

Lunch at the "Razzmatazz" restaurant, in Umhlanga Rocks, Durban.

The last event of this International Wine and Food Society tour of South Africa featured game, including porcupine, gazelle, wild boar, and ostrich.

NEETHLINGSHOF GEWÜRZTRAMINER 1993:

Really good, spicy Gewürztraminer. Very good balance, fruit, length. Off-dry. Lovely, complex finish. Very good. (17)

KANONKOP PINOTAGE 1989:

Classic Pinotage. deep colour. Full, rich, spicy, sweet American oak. Long, straightforward, good depth. Not my style of wine, but very good nevertheless. Good fruit extract. (16)

LA RÊVE DE SAXENBOURG "PRIVATE COLLECTION" 1991 NOBLE LATE HARVEST:

Bright, deep-gold. Ripe peaches and apricots on nose. Full, rich, luscious, long. Very good acidity and length. Will age well. (17)

Clearly, South Africa's best "world class" wines are their botrytis-affected, Steen (Chenin Blanc)-based Noble Late Harvest wines. Also excellent are their Noble Late Harvest Rhine Rieslings and Sauvignon Blancs. The older (and now exceedingly rare) Cabernets can be excellent, too. Most local people we met on this trip were very nice. The potential of this country is great, but civil war must be avoided at all cost.

Monday night

After the flight back to Johannesburg, Caryl Saunders, Roger and Stella Sinclair, and I were guests at dinner at the home of some of the local members.

At that point, and being very tired, I do not recall the Chardonnay or Pinotage we had. However, the dessert wine was, again, excellent.

DELHEIM EDELSPATZ NOBLE LATE HARVEST 1991:

Luscious apricots-botrytis nose and palate. Excellent acidity/fruit balance. Rich, long, complex, spicy. A perfect ending to a very special trip. (17)

The next day, the long, long, long trip back home, via the Azores, New York, and Montreal to Vancouver.

April 9, 1994

Dinner of "Group of Ten."

CHAMPAGNE ROEDERER "CRISTAL" 1979:

Bright gold. Tiny bubbles. Smooth, mellow. Hint of sweetness. Complex, delicate, elegant. At its peak. Round. Lovely fruit. Soft, very fine.

CHAMPAGNE KRUG VINTAGE 1979:

Solid, lean, high acidity. Serious. Drier, more austere, harder than the "Cristal." Needs food. Needs time.

1978 BÂTARD-MONTRACHET, LEFLAIVE

AND

1978 CORTON-CHARLEMAGNE, REMOISSENET:

The Bâtard had a hint of mustiness, but was not corked. Mushrooms, earthy overtones. Very good backbone. Full, rich, long. Very good acidity, fruit, oak, all in harmony. Lots of depth. Pity the nose spoils this.

The Corton-Charlemagne had a tighter, honeyed nose. Full, rich, long, sweet. Very good balance. Honeyed, oaky, fruity finish. Very long. Great depth. Acidic with a fruity backbone. Lovely wine.

1966 CHÂTEAU LA MISSION HAUT-BRION:

(Served double-blind) Surprisingly forward. Cedary, earthy, chocolaty, mature, long Claret nose. Round, full, rich, complex. Mellowing. Lovely now, but enough depth to last well. I thought it was a 1966 Gruaud-Larose.

1928 CHÂTEAU GRUAUD-LAROSE, IN MAGNUM:

(Group bottle) Very good neck level; cork disintegrated. Good, dark colour; a bit unclear (murky). Old Claret nose. Some volatility, but round, soft. Has the tannic backbone typical of the 1928s. Long, earthy. Nice fruit. Dried out in glass after 20 minutes, but still long and complex.

CROFT'S VINTAGE PORT 1963, LONDON-BOTTLED BY CHARLES KINLOCH:

At its peak now. Elegant, long, spicy, round. Very good depth. Evolved colour and fruit. Complex, stylish, elegant.

April 14 to 20, 1994

Trip to Yountville.

1976 VEGA SICILIA "VALBUENA" 5 AÑOS, COSECHA:

This is the second wine of Vega Sicilia, a notch under their great "Unico." Aged five years in oak (vintage 1976), it is a combination of the style of Beaulieu Vineyards Private Reserve Cabernet (American oak-vanilla) and Australia's Grange Hermitage (full, rich, solid, leathery). Dark, some sediment, surprisingly bright-red in spite of spending five years in wood. Full, rich, long; loads of fruit. No rush.

Chambertin 1955, Leroy:

(Valued in 1994 at US$750 per bottle) Dark, mature, evolved colour. Decanted 45 minutes. Fair bit of sediment. Sweet, intense Pinot Noir on both nose and palate. Very forward and mature, yet sturdy, rich, full, and big. Lots of extract and ripe, intense, spicy fruit. A treat. Great wine.

Lunch at "Mustard's."

With Daniel Baron of Dominus Estate, who is leaving Dominus shortly, after a disagreement with Christian Moueix's partners—the husbands of Marcia Cain and Robin Lail.

Château La Conseillante 1981:

Decanted. At first metallic, acidic, lean; nice, elegant fruit. It improved dramatically after 30 minutes in glass. The stylish elegance of this property; spicy, complex, long, and excellent ripe fruit. Ready, but no rush.

Duckhorn Sauvignon Blanc 1992, Napa Valley, in half-bottle:

Lovely, fruity, fresh wine. Clean, crisp, well balanced, spicy, and long. Will improve in one to two years.

Daniel will start work as vineyard manager at Silver Oaks Vineyards near Oakville, owned by Justin Meyer. Justin was a Franciscan monk selected by Brother Timothy to replace him as winemaker at Christian Brothers. He left the Order, married, and started the now-famous Franciscan Winery near St. Helena. At Silver Oaks, they produce Cabernet Sauvignons, an Alexander Valley, a Napa, and a small plot (four acres) called Bonny's. Wines from the different regions are bottled separately. Total production is 30,000 cases.

Going back to La Conseillante, and based on soil and style of this wine, I think that the top Pomerols and St. Emilions should be reclassified into three appellations: the Pomerols, the Côte St. Emilions, and a third appellation to include Cheval-Blanc, Figeac, Vieux Château Certan, and La Conseillante, as these wines are very similar in style.

Diary 15

Friday, May 13, 1994

A two-day visit to Vancouver by Christian Moueix and his girlfriend, Cherise Chen.

Dinner at "Bishop's" restaurant.

After a glass of Paul Bara Champagne at our home, we went to "Bishop's" restaurant where we had two bottles I brought along: a Spring Mountain Napa Cabernet Sauvignon, Lot H 68/69 LN, and a superb 1945 Château Magdelaine, bottled by Hannapier. Christian told me that the firm of Hannapier was taken over in the 1950s by Calvet.

The Spring Mountain story, as related to me by from Joe Heitz

The late 1960s were years of struggle for winemakers and grape growers. Money was short, and bankers' fists were tight. Joe had to sell some of his wines to come up with much-needed cash. The designation Lot H means "Heitz," and 68/69 means a blend of the 1968 and 1969 vintages (two fine vintages). Actually, each vintage was further blended: 50% "Martha's Vineyard" and 50% Napa Valley grapes. "LN" stands for the type of oak in which each vintage/blend was aged. In the case of the 1968, "L" stands for Limousin. In 1969, the wines were aged in "N"—Nevers oak—casks.

SPRING MOUNTAIN CABERNET SAUVIGNON, LOT H 68/69 LN, NAPA VALLEY:

Even now, at 25 and 26 years of age, the wine is still cedary, rich on nose, with a hint of eucalyptus. Full, soft, yet quite intense on palate, with a very slight hint of oxidation. Needs drinking, but still very good nevertheless.

CHÂTEAU MAGDELAINE 1945:

Impressive, deep colour, not unlike a 1961 or 1966. Fine, clean, herbaceous, fruity nose. The tannic backbone of the 1945s combined with fabulously fresh fruit. A great bottle. Superb. Still full of life!

At the end of the meal, John Bishop, the restaurant owner, kindly offered us all a glass of wine without identifying it.

1967 CHÂTEAU GILETTE "CRÈME DE TÊTE," SAUTERNES:

Light colour. Lilacs on nose. Alcoholic, thick, no botrytis. Christian and I thought it was a Beaumes-de-Venise or a mysterious, unknown new-world dessert wine. Nothing like Sauternes, let alone a great or expensive one! I think that Christian Medeville, the owner, is making a mistake by keeping his Sauternes in concrete vats for 20 or more years before bottling.

John Bishop reserved us a parking spot at the back of his restaurant by putting an empty wooden asparagus crate with the words "Reserved for A. Givton" in the space where my car was to be parked.

Saturday, May 14, 1994

Commanderie de Bordeaux event, featuring Christian Moueix's Wines, at the Four Seasons hotel.

I organized this event for Christian Moueix with the wines that he sent us for this occasion. Christian conducted the tasting. During the day, I took Christian and Cherise for a drive around town in my 1961 Jaguar Mark II, and we had lunch at a nice Chinese restaurant.

THE TASTING

ALL 1989S AND 1990S, IN PAIRS, EXCEPT FOR THE DOMINUS, WHICH WAS 1990 AND 1991.

1989 and 1990 Château Magdelaine, St. Emilion

THE 1989:

40% new oak. About 80% Merlot and 20% Cabernet Franc. Not very dark, but excellent depth. Superb, complex nose. Spicy, oaky Cabernet Franc and Merlot nose. Long on palate, very good balance. Complex, elegant. I preferred this to the 1990. (18)

THE 1990:

Deeper colour. Tight nose. Ripeness coming through. Full, rich, very good extract. More concentrated, bigger than the 1989. Solid, tannic. A bit overmature. Christian agreed that, overall, the 1989 was better, and that the 1990 was a bit overripe for its own good. But he said that the 1947s were like this, and they turned out to be great St. Emilions and Pomerols. (17.5)

1989 and 1990 Château La Grave-à-Pomerol (formerly La Grave Trigant- de-Boisset), Pomerol

THE 1989:

Medium-red. Forthcoming, herbal nose. Elegant, some dry tannins. A bit unripe and lacks depth (Christian's own comments). (16.5)

THE 1990:

Much more impressive. Deep red to rim. Intense, ripe fruit on nose. Gamey, a bit leathery. Solid. More rustic. Loads of ripe fruit. A favourite of most tasters. (17.5)

1989 and 1990 Château La Fleur-Petrus, Pomerol

Average 70% Merlot and 30% Cabernet Franc.

THE 1989:

Bright, red colour. Very good depth. Elegant, complex, leaner style (like Vieux Château Certan or La

Conseillante). Long. Vanilla-oak. Complex. Very good balance and finesse. (17)

THE 1990:

Richer, darker, full, and more solid. Ripe, good extract, slightly better depth than the 1989, yet not as impressive or intense as the 1990 La Grave. Very good. (17.5)

1989 and 1990 Petrus, Pomerol

Both are great wines by any yardstick.

THE 1989:

Great colour and extract to rim. Subdued, closed nose at this stage. Full, rich, solid, superb balance. Massive. Needs 15 or more years. Drier oak finish. Will be great in ten years time. (19.5)

THE 1990:

Similar colour/appearance to the 1989. More toasty, oaky nose. Christian agreed with my comments that the oak used for this was different from the 1989. Heavier, more obvious than the 1989. Excellent, ripe fruit. Try around 2005. (19)

Both 1989 and 1990 will make great bottles some day.

1990 and 1991 Dominus Estate, Napa Valley

About 30% to 40% new oak.

THE 1990:

Obvious California. Good, dark colour. Minty, riper, more leathery. Subdued nose. Full, rich, yet elegant. (17.5)

THE 1991:

An uncanny resemblance and taste to the 1990 La Grave-à-Pomerol. Very intense, rich, ripe. Very big, Pomerol-like. Will be very good. (18)

WITH DINNER

The food and service were, as usual at this fine hotel, very good.

1982 CHÂTEAU BELAIR, ST. EMILION:

A wine for connoisseurs. Elegant, hint of mushrooms. Almost at its peak. Full, lovely fruit. Long and smooth. Like Ausone, but in a less obvious way. A wine of finesse. Understated. Not a "show" wine.

1982 CHÂTEAU LATOUR-À-POMEROL:

Almost 100% gravel soil. Finesse, elegance, yet richer fruit, and deeper than the Belair. Almost ready. Superb balance, length, depth. Great extract. Lots of class here. Ready, but no rush. At the top of a long plateau; should last well into the next decade.

1982 CHÂTEAU TROTANOY:

The best 1982 Trotanoy I have tasted to date. One-half gravel and one-half peat soil. Petrus is 100% peat. Over 80% Merlot. Great future. Much more masculine than the La Fleur-Petrus. Deep, ripe, tannic, rich. Needs five more years. Lovely extract, very impressive. The Latour-à-Pomerol more enjoyable tonight, but Trotanoy will have the edge in five to ten years. Great wine.

1962 CHÂTEAU SUDUIRAUT:

We opened six bottles. All good bottles, but quite a bit of variation. Deep amber, light tea colour. Subdued, earthy, mushroomy, botrytis, brown sugar on nose and palate. Good intensity. Very mature, good acidity, medium-bodied. Needs drinking, though.

This was a most enjoyable and memorable event and Christian, as usual, was a gracious guest speaker.

Incidentally, Christian told me that several years ago, he accepted, for the only time, an invitation to a vertical tasting of "old Petrus" held in Germany by H. Frericks. Some imperials of 1921 Petrus were opened. Christian asked his father, J. P. Moueix, about it; his father said he could not believe that in 1921, Petrus would bottle imperials. The source? Hardy Rodenstock, that mysterious German wine connoisseur/provider. When Christian asked Hardy's sommelier to show him the cork, the sommelier replied "nein," and put the cork into his pocket. The same thing happened to me with Rodenstock a few years ago. Coincidence?

May 21 to June 6, 1994

Two-week trip to London, Israel, and Paris, with my 19-year-old son, Michael. Little wine tasted on this trip.

1989 CHÂTEAU MUSAR WHITE:

(In London, at Harvey Nicholl's "Fifth Floor" restaurant) Bright, deep-golden colour. Very ripe, Rhône-like wine. Full, rich, heavy, fairly alcoholic. Almost Spanish but cleaner, good fruit. Too heavy for my taste.

1986 CHÂTEAU LEOVILLE-POYFERRÉ:

(In Paris, at "Bistro-à-Vins," near Place de la Madeleine) Typical 1986. Deep, dark, solid. Good, ripe tannins. Needs three to five more years. Very good fruit and backbone.

In Paris, we also had lunch at a Bistro with Christian Moueix, his two children, and his friend, Cherise Chen. We had a Bordeaux Ordinaire with lunch.

June 14, 1994

A meal at "Bishop's" restaurant, with Mark and Tracy Schonfeld.

Mark has just become President of the British Columbia Medical Association. I brought along the wines.

1978 PULIGNY-MONTRACHET "PUCELLES," LEFLAIVE AND
POMMARD "RUGIENS" 1959, MICHEL GAUNOUX:

Still lively at 18 years of age. These 1978 white Burgundies have amazing staying power. It helps, of course, if they were made by masters such as Vincent Leflaive. Round, soft, spicy oak and Chardonnay nose. Full, round, well balanced. Perfect now and will not improve. I purchased this wine in Portland in 1981. It cost then US$12 per bottle. How times have changed!

POMMARD "RUGIENS" 1959, MICHEL GAUNOUX:

Rather soft for such a ripe year as 1959. Evolved colour; spicy, open Pinot Noir nose. Mature and soft on palate. Needs drinking. Fair bit of sediment.

Saturday, June 25, 1994

International Wine and Food Society Black Tie Dinner, celebrating Harry Waugh's 90th Birthday, at the Stanford Court hotel, San Francisco.

FINE OLD RED BURGUNDIES OF THE DR. BAROLET COLLECTION WERE FEATURED.

Comment on the Dr. Barolet wines

Harry Waugh was instrumental in the discovery of those 30,000 bottles that Dr. Barolet inherited from his father, a wine merchant. Harry contacted Christie's after tasting them, and the wines were auctioned off in the early 1970s. These wines have had the reputation of being "doctored" with Brandy and/or Rhône wines.

In 1968, a broker in Beaujolais contacted Harry Waugh and offered him these wines. Dr. Barolet's father collected them from different producers. Some of the wines from the 1950s were still in barrel when Harry Waugh went down into the cellar in 1968!

1982 and 1986 Puligny-Montrachet Premier Cru "Les Folatières," Domaine Henri Clerc

THE 1986:

Bright, deep colour. Rich, intense Chardonnay on nose and palate. Full, rich, luscious, oak/vanilla. Good acidity. Very ripe. Hint of honey, acacia. Forward, typical Henri Clerc structure—his wines age too fast.

THE 1982:

Deeper still. Very California-like. Full, sweet, rich, very ripe. Very intense. Honeyed. Almost a dessert wine!

All wines below are from the collection of Dr. Barolet. Two bottles of each wine were tasted.

1951 CHAMBOLLE-MUSIGNY, MARTENOT:

Light-red colour (like a 1964). Clean, a bit chaptalized, acidic fruit. Obviously sugar added, but good Pinot Noir character. Hint of rotting wood. Not bad for an off-year. (14)

1952 CHAMBOLLE-MUSIGNY, MARTENOT:

More smoky, toasty nose than the 1951. Harder, richer, more tannic, too. Similar appearance to the 1951. Good backbone. Sweet aftertaste. After 20 minutes, dull and simple. (15)

1934 CHAMBOLLE-MUSIGNY, MARTENOT:

Deeper, yet more elegant than the 1952. Clearly more depth, yet sweeter, too. Good fruit. Quite hot. Cognac added? Surprisingly youthful. (17)

1925 CHAMBOLLE-MUSIGNY, MARTENOT:

Very mature colour; orange rim. Caramelized, herbaceous nose. Stemmy, candied. Acidic, sharp, over-the-hill. Still drinkable, with some Pinot Noir character, but barely. (14)

1939 POMMARD "RUGIENS," MARTENOT:

Good medium-red colour. Palish rim. Clean, fruity nose. Hint of toast. Very sweet on entry. Nice fruit; too sweet, candied, yet some fruit there. Pleasant. (15)

1950 NUITS-ST.-GEORGES, MARTENOT:

Palish colour and orangy rim. Old, very soft, acidic, sharp. Still alive, but too sour. Has seen better days. (12.5) Second bottle: better structure, long, richer. (14.5)

1934 GEVREY-CHAMBERTIN, H. DE VILLAMONT:

The two bottles were good, yet one was bigger, harder, richer than the other. Good backbone, full, masculine. Lovely toast, smoky. Best of flight. Very nice. (16.5)

1935 VOSNE-ROMANÉE, H. DE VILLAMONT:

Ullage two-and-one-half inches. Pale rose colour. Candied, Kool-Aid. Sharp, sour. Not worth bothering. (0)

1928 POMMARD "EPENOTS," H. DE VILLAMONT:

Very good, mature colour.

First bottle: pruny, sharp, acidic. Some fruit, but too sharp. (14)

Second bottle: Better character. Fuller, richer. Harder tannins. Powerful. Typical of the vintage. Hearty. Noticeably sweet after 30 minutes in glass. (16)

1923 SAVIGNY-FONQUERAUD "HOSPICES DE BEAUNE":

Ullage two-and-one-half inches. Old appearance. Earthy, rotting wood nose. Candied, sharp, obviously brandy added, but to no avail. Sharp, sour, but drinkable. (12)

1970 GRAHAM'S VINTAGE PORT:

As expected, excellent, youthful colour. Classic Graham's. Sweet, rich, full, still too young. Very good balance and extract. The 1970s are underrated, and almost always "very good to excellent." This Port needs another five to ten years to reach its peak. (18)

It was nice to see Harry again. That night after the tasting, while I was sleeping at the home of a friend, there was a mild earthquake at around 1:30 am that woke me up. It rated 4.8 on the Richter scale.

July 13 to 18, 1994

Trip to Los Angeles and the Napa Valley.

July 17, 1994

My birthday. Dinner at the "Four Oaks" restaurant, in Bel Air, with Brad Klein.

World Cup soccer final, between Italy and Brazil.

Last time these two met in the finals was in Mexico, in 1970 (Brazil won 4 to 1). The game ended 0 to 0 after overtime, and had to be settled in penalty shots. Brazil won, after three misses by Franco Baresi, Massaro, and Roberto Baggio!

Brad contributed these wines for my birthday.

1982 CHAMPAGNE SALON "LE MESNIL," BLANC DE BLANCS:

The elegance of Chardonnay, yet the depth, weight, length, and very good acidity of the ripe 1982 vintage, and of a Pinot Noir Champagne! Lots of depth, balance. At 12 years, ready but no rush. Fine mousse. Very long. (18)

1978 CHEVALIER-MONTRACHET "LES DEMOISELLES," LOUIS JADOT:

A great wine from a great and very familiar vintage. Spicy, herbaceous nose. Very intense, typical 1978. Great depth, length, and extract. Luscious, ripe. Great balance, extract, depth, and complexity. A super wine. (19)

1945 DOMAINE DE CHEVALIER ROUGE, GRAVES:

Top shoulder level. Another lovely bottle. Very good, dark, deep colour to rim for a 49-year-old. Earthy, ripe, typical Graves. Full, tannic backbone, very good fruit. Lots of life and very long finish. Lasted well in glass for an hour or more. A classic wine from a classic year. (18)

How fortunate I am to have been born in 1945, such a great all-round vintage!

Saturday, July 30, 1994

Dinner at John and Marcena Levine's home, on the occasion of John's 56th birthday.

The following four red wines were served together (blind) in the following order. Major fault: it was a warm day and the wines were served at a temperature of at least 24°C. Way too warm! This tends to bring out the faults in a wine.

1976 CHÂTEAU PETRUS:

Medium-dark colour, evolved rim. Tannic, very dry, hard. Little charm, little fruit associated with Merlot. Powerful. Not at all your typical 1976 or Petrus! I thought it was a 1975 Haut-Médoc of average quality.

1978 SHAFER CABERNET SAUVIGNON, NAPA VALLEY, STAG'S LEAP DISTRICT:

This was their first vintage, and a rare wine. Obviously California, and very different from the other three wines. Darkest, deepest colour. Fresh, ripe berries, and leather on nose. Full, rich, intense. Years of life ahead. Lots of ripe sweet fruit. Little complexity. Better on nose than on palate.

At the end of the meal, John served this wine, also double-blind.

CAYMUS 1976 CHARDONNAY "SPECIAL SELECT," NAPA VALLEY:

A very rare, botrytized Chardonnay. Not made before, or since, by Charlie Wagner of Caymus. Deep-gold colour. Spicy, delicate nose, but full, rich, sweet. Well made, well balanced. Lacked complexity, but clean, long finish. 9° residual sugar. John was willing to bet $10,000 that no one would identify this wine, but he barely gave me time to guess what it was. He was shocked when he found out that I had some of this in my cellar. He thought he owned the "only bottle in the world!"

August 25 to September 3, 1994

Trip with family to Yountville.

Dinner at "French Laundry" restaurant, in Yountville.

With Barney and Belle Rhodes. Chef Thomas Keller's "new" restaurant opened two-and-one-half weeks ago. Very good meal.

With dinner

1991 ZD Chardonnay, Napa Valley, and 1992 Crighton Hall Chardonnay, Napa Valley, both in half-bottles

THE 1991 ZD:

Good fruit, acidity, balance. Complex, spicy fruit. Clean, medium-bodied. Nice finish. Well made.

THE 1992 CRIGHTON HALL:

Clumsy. Marzipan nose. Flat, fat, low acidity, too alcoholic, lacking acidity, noticeable residual sugar.

1987 BONNES MARES, DE VOGÜÉ:

(I brought this bottle along.) Medium-depth. Fine Pinot Noir "cherries" nose. Hint of singed oak.

Round, well balanced. The elegance of Chambolle. Long, complex. Easy to drink. Lots of charm here.

We also discussed a book I'm planning to write about my wine experiences over the past 20 to 25 years, and the tactfulness (or the lack thereof) of writing unpleasant things about such people as Michael Broadbent, Robert Parker, and others. Belle said that seeing that I'm "only" 49 years old, I should wait a few more years before I "tell all." Barney, on the other hand, didn't see anything wrong in telling it as it is. As yet, I have not decided what to do.

Since 1991, Barney has been replanting his "Bella Oaks" vineyard in thirds, one-third each year (14 acres total), after the ravages of phylloxera.

The Rhodes purchased "Bella Oaks" in 1969. At that time, the land was planted in prune trees. But the trees developed a disease and were uprooted. The Rhodes planted grapes in 1971. First crop was 1975, but it was, too young, so they sold most of the crop to Louis Martini. As of 1976 (the first official vintage), it has been produced, bottled, and sold by Joe Heitz. There is no short or long-term contract—only a handshake! Barney Rhodes is on the board, as are several of his doctor friends from Kaiser Permanente. Also Joe Heitz, and Rolly, David, and Kathleen (the Heitz kids). Nine people in total on the board of directors.

September 21, 1994

Commanderie de Bordeaux tasting of 1985 Clarets, at "The Prow" restaurant.

As Maître of our Commanderie, I conducted the tasting.

CHAMPAGNE KRUG "GRANDE CUVÉE" BRUT N/V:

(Purchased in 1991) Lovely, as usual. Complex, long. At Krug, they pick as at d'Yquem—four to five passages, all individually handpicked. Great length and complexity. Will age very well. (18)

1988 DOMAINE DE CHEVALIER, GRAVES BLANC:

Totally fermented in oak. Complex, smells of oak, lees, Sauvignon Blanc, etc. Fabulous. Racey, long, complex. Drink from 1997 onward. (18)

FLIGHT #1

1. 1985 CHÂTEAU SOUTARD, ST. EMILION:

Very good, deep colour to rim. Rich, ripe Cabernet Franc and Merlot nose. Hint of oak. Full, very good depth, rich, ripe, long. Solid, yet not aggressive tannins. (16)

2. 1985 CHÂTEAU LA LAGUNE, HAUT-MÉDOC:

Similar appearance to #1. New oak-vanilla nose. Expansive. Leaner, less depth than the Soutard. A bit acidic at first. Very good, though. In retrospect, maybe 100% new oak was a mistake for such a soft, elegant vintage. Oak dominates this wine.(16)

3. 1985 CHÂTEAU LEOVILLE-POYFERRÉ, ST. JULIEN:

Similar appearance to #1 and #2. Lovely, earthy, ripe Cabernet nose. Elegant, good depth. Medium-bodied. Complex. A bit thin (diluted), but very elegant and complex. (17)

4. 1985 CHÂTEAU GRAND-PUY-LACOSTE, PAUILLAC:

Deep, bright colour. Very Cabernet nose. Very Pauillac. Ripe, rich. Full, chocolaty, intense, long. Sweet ripe fruit, backed by good tannins. (18)

5. 1985 CHÂTEAU SOCIANDO-MALLET, HAUT-MÉDOC:

Lighter colour than #4. Good depth, though. Classy, oaky Cabernet nose. Medium-full, yet not as powerful as I expected. Nice balance and fruit. Long. Fairly aggressive tannins. (16)

6. 1985 DOMINUS ESTATE CABERNET SAUVIGNON, NAPANOOK, NAPA VALLEY:

This wine was added as a ringer. Dense, red colour. Baked, leathery nose. Solid, fairly aggressive tannins. Made from 80% Cabernet Sauvignon and 20% Merlot. Very good potential, from 1995 onward. (17)

FLIGHT #2

7. 1985 CHÂTEAU AUSONE:

Medium, evolved colour. Elegant, evolved nose. Round, soft, classy. Nice fruit. Herbaceous, forward. Has class but is light. Complex, elegant, stylish. Very good. (17.5) The 1986, and especially the 1989 and 1990, are superior.

8. 1985 CHÂTEAU CHEVAL-BLANC:

Good, dark colour and depth. Much darker, deeper colour than the Ausone. Intense, herbaceous, stemmy, ripe, spicy nose. Full, rich, new oak, very herbaceous. Great depth and intensity; a spicy, rich, luscious wine. (18.5)

9. 1985 CHÂTEAU PALMER:

Very good, deep colour. Evolved rim. Slight hint of stemminess. Fuller, harder, but less opulent than Cheval-Blanc. Very good structure. Long, complex, spicy. Needs five to eight years, yet even nice now. Lots of depth and class. (18)

10. 1985 CHÂTEAU LYNCH-BAGES:

Impressive deep colour. Spicy, ripe Cabernet nose. Very ripe, intense, sweet fruit. Lots of depth, ripe fruit. Almost ready. Not as austere as the Grand-Puy-Lacoste. Very good, with excellent depth and weight. (18)

11. 1985 CHÂTEAU MOUTON-ROTHSCHILD:

Very good, dark colour to rim. Tight, closed nose. Full, solid. Needs ten years. Great depth, intensity. By far the biggest wine of the night. Backward, cedary, cigar-box. Lovely. (18.5)

1967 CHÂTEAU D'YQUEM:

Amber-gold. Some sediment. Sensational caramel, botrytis, and exotic ripe fruit on nose. Intense botrytis. Rich, long, complex. Very forward, round, long. Great depth. At its peak. Will not improve. How can it?! (19)

COGNAC FERRAND "SÉLECTION DES ANGES" (30 YEARS OLD):

Lovely Cognac. Great nose, long complex. Very good. Smooth, perfect.

October 12 to 16, 1994

Trip to Yountville.

Friday, October 14, 1994

Dinner at Joe and Alice Heitz's.

I gave Joe a bottle of Gewürztraminer "Bergheim" Domaine Marcel Deiss of the excellent 1990 vintage, (Joe likes Gewürztraminer), and a bottle of Domaine de Chevalier Rouge 1981. Perfect for drinking now.

We had dinner at their home, just the three of us (Alice, Joe, and myself). Before dinner, Joe took me to the winery across from their home. A batch of Cabernet Sauvignon from "Martha's Vineyard" had just come in, and his son Rolly was supervising the sorting-out. Here and there were leaves of eucalyptus trees. There are eucalyptus trees around the vineyard, and during picking, the odd leaf ends up in the basket (containers of grapes shipped to the winery). All the grapes were picked before the one-night downpour of early October. Then they stopped picking for two weeks. This is relatively late for picking in California (mid-October).

With dinner, we had some white mushrooms that grow under nearby trees. They can grow to the size of a small cantaloupe, but these were the size of small apples. Sautéed in butter, they had the texture and flavour of sweetbreads. Joe calls these mushrooms "furry bears." With dinner, we had the two wines I had brought along.

1990 GEWÜRZTRAMINER "BERGHEIM," DOMAINE MARCEL DEISS:

Definitely "Late Harvest." Thick, rich, long, lychees, perfumy. Pity they didn't indicate on the label that it was a "vendange tardive." More of a sipping wine than a dinner wine. Nevertheless, it was excellent.

1981 DOMAINE DE CHEVALIER, GRAVES ROUGE:

Typical of the vintage, and of this property. Delicate, ready, complex, long. Perfumy, earthy, chocolaty nose. Very nice.

DESSERT WINE

1976 HEITZ CELLARS ANGELICA:

Sweeter, more alcoholic than the 1974. Very good, sweet, Sherry-like, but I prefer the 1974, which is great.

October 18, 1994

Private tasting at "Le Gavroche" restaurant, in Vancouver.

I organized this tasting; all wines were from my cellar. 16 participants, including Carol and myself. Featuring verticals of older vintages of Château Malescot-St.-Exupéry (Margaux), Château Pontet-Canet, and Château Pichon-Longueville-Baron (Pauillacs), from 1945 to 1966. All single bottles. Three properties that used to produce excellent wines, and have the potential to do so once again . . . if the owners wish to do so.

All Pontet-Canets were château- or Bordeaux-bottled by Cruse (the then-owners), except 1945, which was London-bottled by Block, Gray and Block.

FLIGHT #1

1964 CHÂTEAU MALESCOT-ST.-EXUPÉRY:

Mature colour. Good depth. Smoky, toasty nose. Nice fruit at entry, fairly dry, acidic finish. Long aftertaste. Past its prime, but still drinking well. (15.5)

1966 CHÂTEAU MALESCOT-ST.-EXUPÉRY:

A bit darker, deeper than the 1964. A little more herbaceous on nose. Rounder, better fruit, sweeter than the 1964. Complex, long, elegant. (16.5)

1966 CHÂTEAU PONTET-CANET:

Tobacco-like, complex, smoky, rich nose. A bit acidic at finish, but still has class. Later improved. Rich, long, sweet. Excellent, at its peak. (17.5)

FLIGHT #2

1952 CHÂTEAU PICHON-BARON:

Good, deep colour. Classic, tobacco, cedar, old ripe Claret. Full, impressive, rich, long. Ripe fruit, especially for a 1952! Lovely for about 20 minutes, then started to fade. (17.5)

1952 CHÂTEAU PONTET-CANET:

Very good depth. Toasty. Leaner, harder than the 1952 Pichon-Baron. Quite lively. Very good. More elegant, less extract than the 1952 Pichon-Baron. (17)

1947 Château Pontet-Canet:

Corked nose. Pity, because it had a nice, ripe, fruity flavour. 1947 ripeness. Full, long, can be excellent. This bottle was off.

1945 Château Pontet-Canet, London-bottled by Block, Gray and Block:

Classic 1945. Fairly alcoholic, ripe nose. Very rich, full, ripe, tannic. Typical 1945 Claret. No rush, in excellent condition. Great extract. (18)

FLIGHT #3

1959 Malescot-St.-Exupéry:

Excellent dark colour. Subdued nose. Rich, ripe, sweet fruit. Lovely, long, complex. Excellent wine. Ready. Perfect now. Chunky, rich, ripe wine. (18)

1959 Pontet-Canet:

Dark colour, tobacco nose. Open, cedary, sweet, ripe, long, soft, elegant. Most complex, yet lightest of the three. Lots of class and complexity here. (18.5)

1959 Pichon-Baron:

Like a ripe California Cabernet. Rich, great extract. Solid, full, long. Loads of ripe fruit. Tannic, too. A bit hard, and dry finish. (17.5)

The three 1959s expressed almost to perfection the ripe character of the 1959 vintage. I hope that some day, the 1982s will turn out to be as good as these 1959s.

FLIGHT #4

1961 Malescot-St.-Exupéry:

Very deep colour. Masculine, solid, intense, loads of ripe fruit. More solid, yet less sweet than the 1959. More tannic, good backbone. (18.5)

1961 Pontet-Canet:

Subdued, toasty, tobacco nose. As elegant as the 1959, yet riper, with more extract with good intensity. Classic 1961! Sweet fruit. Great drinking now. (18.5)

1961 Pichon-Baron:

Very good, deep colour. Sweet, great depth, extract. This is almost St. Estèphe-like, but this solid wine is very good, too. Classic, serious Pauillac. (18)

DESSERT WINE

1964 Tokay Aszú Essencia (500 mL bottle):

Tiny cork. Amber, deep colour. Nose of old California Johannisberg Riesling BA or TBA. Citrus flavour, and lemony, candied aftertaste. Lovely extract. TBA-like, yet not cloying. Long, complex, quite soft. Very good. (17.5)

Yellow Chartreuse:

Maybe it was actually the green, as the colour was that of virgin olive oil. 55° proof. Litre bottle. Produced in Tarragona, Spain, around 1903, when the monks were expelled from France. Fine sediment. Chartreuse is the only known liqueur that can actually mature in bottle. Intense, spicy nose. Full, thick, rich, sweet, very spirity, and hot. A historic liqueur. We compared it to modern Yellow Chartreuse, which was much thinner, drier, and less intense. Made from 120 to 150 different herbs and spices.

Great evening.

October 29, 1994

Commanderie de Bordeaux Black Tie blind tasting and Dinner, featuring a vertical tasting of Château Haut-Brion 1959 to 1986, at the Pan Pacific hotel, in Vancouver.

This was a blind tasting. It took me 18 months to collect all the wines for this event, from sources in New York, Chicago, San Francisco, Vancouver, and Victoria. As Maître, I conducted the tasting.

FLIGHT #1

1. 1981:

Good depth, mature rim. Subdued, earthy nose. Full, round, sweet, hint of oak. Forward, elegant, ready. Lots of class. No rush, but will not improve. (17)

2. 1985:

Tighter nose. Deeper colour. A bit stemmy on nose. Better balanced than the 1981. Needs time. Good backbone, length. Five to ten years. (17.5)

3. 1983:

Good, dark colour. Toasty, perfumy nose. Full, more tannic than either #1 or #2. Good balance. Dill, stemmy. Fairly dry, leaner style. Not very ripe. Elegant finish. Stood out in its stemminess. I've had better bottles of this. (16.5)

4. 1986:

Bright, red colour. Fresh nose of sweet, ripe fruit. Clean, long, still very tannic. Concentrated. Very rich, ripe. Excellent potential. Needs time. Seven to 12 years. (18)

5. 1982:

Bright, young colour. Fresh, lovely fruit, ripe, long, quite solid, but less aggressive than the 1986. Very young, powerful. 1986? Lots of depth. Needs a long time. (18.5)

Overall

I was really surprised to discover that the 1982 was bigger than the 1986, and that I had switched them around. Very good wines—typical Haut-Brion and true (overall) to the vintages. Only the 1981 is ready. The others need more time.

With dinner

1988 CHÂTEAU HAUT-BRION BLANC:

Bright, light, golden colour. Buttery, oaky, vanilla, fresh nose. Still very youthful. Lots of class here, but really too young. Excellent potential. (18)

FLIGHT #2 (WITH MAIN COURSE)

1979:

Good depth. Mature rim. Lovely oak, chocolate, spicy nose. Full, silky, round, rich, and long. Fabulous flavour. This is really excellent. Lots of depth, rich, ripe fruit. Perfect now, but no rush. One of the best 1979s! For me, best of flight. (18)

1978:

Lighter colour than the 1979. Leaner, more herbaceous, yet toasty nose. More Cabernet, more acidic than the 1979. Toasty, smoky. Typical "Cabernet" year. Very good fruit, leaner than 1979, but very good structure. Sweet, leathery, oaky finish. At its peak. (17)

1975:

Very 1975. Dusty, earthy. Tannins blending better than most 1975s, though. Nice fruit, well balanced. A bit "green," but overall excellent. Earthy. Solid tannins. (17)

1970:

Full, rich, surprisingly powerful and tannic. A solid wine. Fairly dry, more tannic, bigger, and more powerful than the 1975! Earthy, oaky, toasty nose. Very ripe fruit. Second bottle more elegant, maybe even better balanced, but lacks the depth of the first bottle. (16) to (17), depending on bottle.

FLIGHT #3 (WITH THE CHEESES)

1966, IN MAGNUM:

Impressive, deep colour. Subdued, ripe, toasty nose. Full, sweet fruit, ripe, rich. Smooth, lovely fruit, long. Superb. (18)

1964, IN MAGNUM:

Riper, tea leaves. Sweet, forward nose. Oddly, over-the-hill, yet from a magnum. Drying out. I've had far better bottles of this. Leathery, tight, losing its fruit. Much weaker, and more tired than the 1966. Poor storage? Can be very good. (14)

1961:

Again, tea leaves on nose. Great depth of colour. Full, sweet, rich, tannic (but in a very ripe way). Ready, no rush. Bigger, tougher than the riper, rounder 1959. (18.5)

1959:

Good, dark colour. Rich, round, long. Very soft, but very good backbone. Not as lively or tannic as the 1961, but great for drinking now. Excellent fruit, though. Better than the 1961 tonight, but the 1961 will keep longer. (19)

Overall impressions

Very good property producing consistently good wines, true to the vintages.

Saturday, January 21, 1995

Commanderie de Bordeaux Dinner, at the Vancouver Club.

I thought this one up while reading Charles Walter Berry's book Viniana, *published in 1929. One of three dinners described in the book is the Claret Dinner with First Growths. Menu was exactly as described in the book, so are all the wines and the Armagnac. The vintages are, of course, younger!*

CHAMPAGNE BOLLINGER "GRANDE ANNÉE" 1985:

Full, rich, complex. Fine mousse. Yeasty, rich Champagne. Very good backbone, acidity, and fruit. Serious stuff. Lots of class and length, too. Ready, but lively. No rush. (18)

1978 CHÂTEAU MOUTON-ROTHSCHILD:

The least impressive of the reds. Mature colour. Oak and spices, but vegetal on both nose and palate (very little Merlot in 1978). Loosely knit. Some sharpness at finish. Stylish, but lacks depth. (16.5)

1983 CHÂTEAU LATOUR:

Much deeper, darker, richer Cabernet than the 1978 Mouton, yet in Latour terms, surprisingly forward. Overproduction? Nevertheless, chunky, rich, yet soft. Good Cabernet concentration. Not a heavyweight. (17.5)

DIEZ HERMANOS "FINO IMPERIAL":

A very old—19th century—Sherry. Fine sediment. Very mature. A Solera, going back to the 1870s. Probably 30 years in bottle. Dry, smooth. Old, but nutty and complex. (17)

1981 Château Haut-Brion and 1981 Château Margaux

THE HAUT-BRION:

Perfect now. Elegant, medium depth. Complex earthy, perfumy nose. Lots of class. Round, soft, lovely balance, lingering aftertaste. (17.5)

THE MARGAUX:

(The wine of the vintage) Very youthful, purplish, deep colour. Complex oak-vanilla and ripe berries on nose. Full, rich, a bit tannic. Needs five to ten more years. Will be lovely. Very fine. (18)

1976 CHÂTEAU LAFITE-ROTHSCHILD:

Perfect now. Cannot improve. Velvety, complex, soft, round. Very good balance. Elegant cedary nose. A complete wine. Lafite turned around in 1976, after over a decade of mediocre wines. Drink up. Lovely. (18)

1969 Madeira Bastardo, Cossart-Gordon:

Too young, of course. Amber, brilliant colour. Nutty, earthy, spicy nose. Very spirity. Acidic, youthful on palate. Good extract and length. Drink from 2010 and beyond. (17)

Good, classic "Club" dinner. Nice event.

February 4 to 12, 1995

Trip to San Francisco, Yountville, and Las Vegas.

International Wine and Food Society Event (Lunch), featuring a vertical tasting of Fonseca's Ports, at the Park Hyatt hotel, in San Francisco

First session

Fonseca's Vintage Port 1992 to 1963

Bruce Guimaraens conducted this tasting. I have known Bruce for over 15 years now. A very charming man and as gifted a winemaker as can be. He has been making the wines at Fonseca's, where he is one of the owners, for over 40 years.

1992:

Very deep purple to rim. Clean, oak, fruity nose. Subdued. Lovely balance and depth, great fruit. Clean, long finish. Very good extract. Tannins not as hard as in older vintages when young. Do I detect a change in style? Are Port producers starting to make "apartment" wines for early consumption and quick turnover? I hope not. 8,000 cases produced. (18)

1985:

More evolved colour than the 1992. Less depth, yet very good, purplish colour. Unyielding nose, a bit more spirity than the ripe 1992. Sweet, medium-bodied, fairly tannic. Lacks the flesh of the 1992, leaner. Hint of bitter tannins. Needs seven to ten years to harmonize. Bruce loves the 1985. He thinks it will be a great classic. He said that Port goes through a "dumb" period, between seven and 12 years in bottle. (17)

1983:

Surprisingly evolved colour, good depth, mature rim. Hint of maturity on nose. Starting to smell like Port rather than black-fruit juice. Light, evolved fruit, yet quite spirity. Probably would be more harmonious if allowed to air for three to four hours. A bit dumb now. Maybe needs a little more ripe fruit. (16.5)

1980:

Lighter colour than the 1983. Quite evolved. Hint of leather and raisins. Ready, well balanced, forward, complex. All in harmony. Does not have the depth of the 1985, 1977, or 1992, but very elegant. No rush, but will not improve. (17)

1977:

Better depth than the 1983. Good colour to rim. Tight, unyielding nose. Yet the extract is definitely there. Good balance, fruit. Very good depth, extract. Serious wine. Better balanced than any of the previous vintages, save 1992. Huge wine. Needs time. (18)

1975:

Evolved colour, yet deeper than the 1980. Elegant, open bouquet; complex, lovely nose. Velvety, round, great balance and class. To most, this was surprisingly good. I knew it would be as I have had this Port several times before. (17.5) Taylor's and Fonseca's produced the best 1975s.

1970:

The largest vintage declared since 1927. Very good, deep colour. Tight, yet elegant, spicy nose. As lovely as the 1975, yet so much more depth and extract. Great depth. Perfect now, but no rush. Excellent quality. The 1977 is a bit fresher and has more backbone, yet this 1970 is great. With the 1970, a decision was made to reduce the sweetness 3.3° to 3.4° boeme, as opposed to older vintage at 3.7° boeme average. (18)

1966:

Even deeper than the 1970. Great colour extract. Ripe berries on nose. Silky, yet great depth. Very full, loads of ripe fruit. Perfect now, but so much fruit that there is no rush. Great Port. Fatter, sweeter, deeper than the 1963, yet the 1963 is more complex, with better backbone, leaner. (18.5)

1963:

Excellent dark, colour. Similar to the 1966, yet totally different. Leaner, racier, great extract. The best wine of the flight for me, yet hard to decide as there were so many fine wines. Needs time. Best-pronounced nose. (19)

Overall impressions

In the 1990s, more Tourriga Nacional was added to the blend than in the 1960s and 1970s, therefore the tannins are marked by very ripe, rich fruit.

This was a lovely flight. Maybe the 1983 is going through a phase. All others were excellent. One historical note: Bruce said that they should have declared the 1931, but because of a recession, they didn't, and that was a mistake. Importers did not want Port houses to declare the 1966. I am happy they did.

Normally, Taylor's declare more than Fonseca's (by 30% to 40%), yet in 1992, Fonseca's produced 8,000 cases, and Taylor's only 6,000 cases. In 1927, Fonseca's produced 25,000 cases!

Same evening

International Wine and Food Society Black Tie Dinner, featuring a vertical tasting of Château Pichon-Longueville, Comtesse de Lalande, at the Park Hyatt hotel, with May de Lencquesaing, and Bruce Guimaraens.

Both sat with me at the head table.

1986 CORTON-CHARLEMAGNE, BONNEAU DU MARTRAY:

At its peak. Good, earthy, Chardonnay nose, hint of sulphur. Fairly rich, open, evolved on palate. Long, clean finish. Lacks the fat and depth of some other 1986 Corton-Charlemagnes, such a Jadot or Coche-Dury, but good.

Château Pichon-Lalande:
FLIGHT #1:

1947, IN MAGNUMS:

Evolved colour. Earthy, old Claret nose. Wet earth, some Cabernet. Soft on palate, round. Good acidity and backbone, but fragile. Chocolaty. The acidity is holding this together. Clearly the best wine of the flight. Soft, but very good. Similar weather conditions to 1982. (18)

1949, IN BOTTLES:

Oddly, less-mature colour than the 1947. More concentrated berries on nose. Mushrooms. More tannic than the 1947, yet drier finish. Was better ten years ago. Picked from September 29 onward. (17)

1952, IN MAGNUMS:

Fresher than the wines of the 1940s. Mature Claret nose, but freshness, too. Quite hard and tannic. Acidic backbone, but good fruit. After 20 minutes, drying out. Yet chocolaty background. Picking started on September 18. (17.5)

1955, IN MAGNUMS:

Good, mature colour. Typical 1955. Very soft, round, without the solid backbone of the 1952. After a few minutes in glass, it was losing its fruit. (16.5)

1978, IN MAGNUMS:

Typical 1978. Herbaceous, stemmy, very good extract. Maybe needed an extra hour of airing (and five to ten more years in magnums). Very good fruit, solid backbone. Only 36 hectolitres per hectare, a small crop. The first vintage produced under May de Lencquesaing's management. (17.5)

FLIGHT #2

1959, IN MAGNUMS:

Good, dark colour. Evolved, orangy rim. Lovely sweet fruit. Lacks fat, which is odd for such a ripe vintage. Noticeable acidity at finish, but complex, clean, a bit lean. Later, velvety, complex, long, lovely. Drink up (even from magnums). (18)

1970, IN MAGNUMS:

Very good, dark colour. Cedary, earthy "sous-bois" nose and flavour. Old style, solid, full. Great fruit concentration. Excellent from magnums. Classic 1970. Ripe, sweet fruit. Super wine. (18.5)

1975, IN MAGNUMS:

Good, deep colour. Classic Claret nose with hint of ripe berries. Full on palate, not too green or tannic. Tannins backed by great fruit. No rush. Will improve. Excellent wine. This wine was made under the supervision of Michel Delon of Leoville-Lascases. (18)

1990, IN MAGNUMS:

Purple colour. Great extract, deep, full, yet, oddly, too soft. Why so soft? Overproduction? Very seductive wine. Almost too seductive. Almost too good, too soon. (17.5)

1994, IN MAGNUMS:

(Not tasted; these were May's comments) Made from 50% Cabernet Sauvignon, 35% Merlot, 15% Cabernet Franc, all picked before the rain. According to May de Lencquesaing, they are excellent, soft wines. Rain caused no botrytis until the end. Lots of tannins. May turn out to be like the 1975.

FLIGHT #3

1945, IN MAGNUMS:

Upper shoulder level. Darkest of flight. Smell of wet cement and wet earth. Solid, good fruit, tannic. Concentrated. The structure of the 1945s, yet lacks the complex fruit and coffee/mocha that I associate with 1945 Pichon-Lalande. Solid. A bit "dirty."(17.5)

1953, IN MAGNUMS:

Everything a 1953 should be. Harmonious, velvety, concentrated, elegant. Lovely fruit. Complex, very soft, yet all there. (18)

1961, IN MAGNUMS:

Classic 1961. Concentrated, rich, solid. Almost unready. Compact, no rush. Very good extract. Maybe doesn't have the chocolate ripeness of other 1961s, but nevertheless very good, ripe fruit. (18)

After the tasting and dinner we had the following.

CHAMPAGNE ROEDERER "CRISTAL" BRUT ROSÉ 1988:

Salmon colour. Clean, crisp, fairly dry. I wonder why people insist on serving dry Champagne at the end of a meal. It is inappropriate and a waste. Bruce Guimaraens agreed with me.

1970 FONSECA'S VINTAGE PORT, IN MAGNUMS:

Great, dark colour, depth. Ripe intense fruit. As expected, deeper, tighter than the 1970 tasted from bottles earlier that day. Lots of depth. No rush. Should last well for another 20 years.

Sunday, February 5, 1995

Second session of vertical Fonseca's Vintage Port tasting, 1960 to 1912.

1960, Oporto-bottled:

Medium-evolved colour. Bright-red middle. Sweet, open, fruity nose. Round, straightforward. Very nice drinking now. A bit spirity at edge. (16.5)

1955, bottled by Avery's of Bristol:

Oddly, the cork was branded: Taylor's! Evolved, mature colour. More extract and burnt caramel on nose than the 1960. Sweet, rich, full, lots of depth. Nutty nose. Very nice. Small year, quantity-wise. Depressed market. Originally released at $2.20/case or 18¢ per bottle! (18)

1948, Oporto-bottled:

Similar appearance to the 1955, but slightly lighter. Subdued nose. Round, not as much spice or extract as the 1955. Elegant, velvety, round. Mouth-filling, lots of class. Bruce's favourite . . . "Vintage Port at its best." (18.5)

1947:

A little more depth than the 1948. Delicate, clean nose. Bigger, richer than the 1948. Very good extract, backbone. Lovely. More depth and complexity than either 1948 or 1955. This is great. Not shipped, but they bottled two single quintas. We tasted one of them. Flowery, delicate, lovely. (19)

The 1947 was bottled as "Guimaraens" rather than "Fonseca's." I was in the minority here, as most tasters preferred the 1948. Anyway, this is academic, as no Fonseca's 1947 was produced or shipped as such.

1945, Oporto-bottled:

Mature, evolved colour. Rich, caramel, evolved nose. Sweeter, softer than the 1947. A bit sweeter, more syrupy than the 1948. Great wine. Hot year. (19)

1934:

Similar appearance as the 1945. Dull, earthy, vegetal nose. Only a hint of Port wine. Very good backbone, drier than the others, yet elegant. Remarkable colour. A bit earthy, dry finish. (17)

1927:

Impressive, deep, mature colour. Deeper than the 1948 or 1945! Earthy nose. Excellent balance, full of life. Drier, but excellent extract. Long, lovely. Top quality. Holding extremely well. Hard finish, yet lovely fruit. (18)

1922:

Deeper colour than 1927; even deeper than the 1945! Full of life. Lovely fruit, length, balance. Lots of extract. A bit simpler, sweet, good flavour. (17.5)

1912:

Deeper than all the 1920s and most 1940s and the 1934! Sweet, elegant, lemon-tea nose, yet lively and fruity. Extraordinary wine! Very good backbone, depth, complexity. The greatest 1912 I've ever tasted, and a great Port. (19.5)

Overall impressions

Extraordinary tasting. Consistently great for over a century. The best, most consistent Port vertical tasting that I have participated in. Dr. Barney Rhodes agreed.

Only "Fred" Guimaraens and Bruce himself have produced the wines from 1896 to 1995! Bruce will retire next year (1996); he has been the winemaker since 1956, for 40 years! According to Bruce, the common denominator of a true Vintage Port is no precipitation during the harvest, and picking the fruit at the right stage of maturity. The weather is relatively secondary in importance. For example, 1945: hot and dry; 1963: cool and wet.

February 13, 1995

Le Tastevin Dinner, featuring 1982 red Bordeaux, in Vancouver.

1985 Champagne Deutz "Cuvée William Deutz":

Spicy, elegant, fruity on nose and palate. Not a big Champagne, but is stylish, complex, and easy to sip.

FLIGHT #1

1. 1982 Château Batailley:

Medium-dark colour, orange rim. Herbaceous nose. Nice toast. Round, forward, good fruit. Ready. (15.5)

2. 1982 Château Branaire-Ducru:

Very good, deep colour. Ripe, leathery nose. Tight, hard, a bit sharp. Odd bottle. Can be very good. Hard, tannic, low fruit. Must retaste. (14)

3. 1982 Château Malartic-Lagravière:

Medium-red, evolved rim. Flowery, slightly raisiny nose. Harder, round, forward. Hint of Cassis. Most complex of flight. (16.5)

4. 1982 Château Certan-Guiraud :

Deep colour, darkest of flight. Full, rich, tannic. Solid wine. Most popular wine of flight. Food was spicy and Merlot went well with it. (16)

FLIGHT #2

5. 1982 Château Calon-Ségur:

Great depth of colour to rim. Luscious fruit. Classic, rich, full, long. Excellent extract. Fairly tannic. Needs three to five more years. After many years of underperforming, it is nice to see a good Calon-Ségur again. (17)

6. 1982 CHÂTEAU MONTROSE:

As dark as the Calon. Tighter nose. Some oak, ripe berries. Less fat than #5. Classy, nice fruit. Not as fat or rich, yet very good fruit. Many "wine authorities" have underrated this wine. (17)

7. 1982 CHÂTEAU GRAND-PUY-LACOSTE:

Incredible deep, purplish colour to rim. Tight nose. Hint of oak, vanilla. Full, solid, rich, better balance than #5 or #6. Great fruit extract. Lots of depth here. Classic Pauillac. "The poor man's Latour!" (18)

8. 1982 CHÂTEAU DUCRU-BEAUCAILLOU:

Very good, deep colour, yet not as impressive as #7. Flowery, elegant nose. Long, flavourful. Lovely, complex finish. Classy. Almost ready. (18.5)

9. 1982 CHÂTEAU LEOVILLE-BARTON:

One bottle corked. (We served three bottles of each wine.) Good depth. Slightly evolved rim. Cedary nose. Leaner, harder, but very good fruit. Lovely finish. Cedar, spices. A bit high in acidity. (17.5)

10. 1982 CHÂTEAU LA LAGUNE:

Excellent deep colour. Warm walnuts and toast on nose. Sweet on entry. Full, rich, solid, long. Sweet fruit. Less complexity than any other wines in this flight, but lots of sweet fruit. (17.5)

FLIGHT #3

11. 1982 CHÂTEAU L'EVANGILE:

Good, deep colour. Iron, lead pencil, ripe, earthy, fruity nose. Full, sweet, rich, very Merlot. Lots of depth and extract. Great wine. (18.5)

12. 1982 CHÂTEAU LEOVILLE-LASCASES:

Very good, deep colour. Purplish rim. Tight, closed nose. Some Cabernet coming through. Full, rich, solid. Very good depth. Lots of extract and length. Needs time. Try again in 1998 or beyond. This is a very serious wine. (19)

13. 1982 CHÂTEAU MOUTON-ROTHSCHILD:

Almost opaque, black colour. Tight, closed nose. Very big, massive wine. Great extract. Solid. Not nearly ready. Needs ten extra years. Superb ripe fruit and tannins, all in harmony. (20)

DESSERT WINE

1982 CHÂTEAU SUDUIRAUT:

A very good Sauternes, and better than the 1983 Suduiraut. Luscious, deep gold. Rich, long, botrytis nose. Full, rich, long on palate. Excellent fruit/acidity balance. No rush. Very good. (18)

Overall impressions

The 1982s, especially the second and third flights, proved that this is a great vintage.

Saturday, February 18, 1995

Dinner of "Group of Ten," at our home.

CHAMPAGNE POL ROGER PR "PRIVATE RESERVE" 1982:

(The equivalent of Cuvée Winston Churchill) Evolved, soft, feminine, elegant, long. Tiny bubbles. Clean yeasty, flowery nose. Lots of elegance.

1989 CORTON-CHARLEMAGNE, LOUIS LATOUR:

Nutty, rich, oaky, lovely, vanilla-fruit balance. Full, quite evolved. Rich, honeyed. Long finish. Richer, more open than the Chevalier. Very different style.

1989 CHEVALIER-MONTRACHET "DEMOISELLES," LOUIS LATOUR:

Tighter than the Corton. Flowery. Very long, very complex. Lots of depth, but a bit closed. Needs three to five years. Serious stuff. Higher alcohol, more intense. Both excellent.

1952 LA TÂCHE, DOMAINE DE LA ROMANÉE-CONTI:

(My bottle. I did not decant. Fair bit of sediment.) I was unnecessarily worried because of the two-and-one-half inch ullage. Medium to light colour. Good depth. Raspberries and essence of Pinot Noir on nose. Very intense. Even fresh! Sweet fruit on palate. Fairly acidic, which is probably why it has held so well for 43 years and with two-and-one-half inch ullage. Very, very long on palate; spicy, round. Great depth. Top quality, especially for what was only an average vintage.

1947 CHÂTEAU CALON-SÉGUR, IN MAGNUM:

(Our group bottle) Shipped directly from the château. Superb level. Like a new wine. Cork seemed ten to 15 years old, so probably recorked at the château (and topped up?). Excellent, deep colour, mature rim. Spicy, yet ripe on both nose and palate. Tannic, as a St. Estèphe should be, yet rich, sweet fruit, typical of the 1947s. Lots of depth. No rush. Incredible quality. Calon made very good wines in the 1920s, 1930s, and 1940s.

1963 QUINTA DO NOVAL VINTAGE PORT:

One of the most feminine, soft, and elegant 1963s. Very good balance, stylish. Medium colour. Easy to drink, good fruit/acidity and bouquet. All in harmony. Ready. Not very deep or heavy, but certainly very stylish.

Overall

All wines were excellent tonight.

March 22, 1995

Commanderie de Bordeaux Dinner and tasting, celebrating the 20th anniversary of the 1975 vintage, at the Sutton Place hotel.

All wines were from my cellar. All wines were known to us in advance, as was the order (except for flight #2, which was tasted blind).

FLIGHT #1

1975 CHÂTEAU PAPE CLÉMENT:

Dark, maturing colour. Spicy, elegant nose. Very nice fruit. Round, tannic backbone blending nicely with the fruit; long finish. Not drying out but ready. Surprisingly good. Later dried out (after one hour in glass). The most drinkable wine of flight. (16.5)

1975 CHÂTEAU LYNCH BAGES:

Similar appearance to the Pape Clément. Lovely, cedary Cabernet nose. Full, lively fruit. Tannic backbone. Very good depth and length. Good fruit extract. (17)

1975 CHÂTEAU MONTROSE:

Deeper colour to rim than above two. Tight, yet clean Cabernet nose. Solid, powerful, tannic, backed by good fruit. Serious wine. Excellent potential. Needs lots of time. (17.5)

1975 CHÂTEAU BRANAIRE-DUCRU:

Medium-red, evolved colour; orange rim. Tight, slightly leathery nose. Leaner, yet more forward. Tannins becoming aggressive. Starting to lose its fruit. What a pity. This wine was fruity and lovely five years ago. Drink up. (14)

1975 CHÂTEAU LEOVILLE-BARTON:

Typical 1975. Herbaceous, stemmy Cabernet nose. Medium colour, orangy rim. Quite complex, evolved (later). Hint of oak. Best complexity of the three St. Juliens. (16)

1975 CHÂTEAU GRUAUD-LAROSE:

Less-pronounced herbs than the Leoville-Barton. Dry, tannic, low fruit. Solid. More depth than the two other St. Juliens. Too hard. Needs fruit (that it doesn't have). Too dry for its own good. (15.5)

FLIGHT #2

(This flight was tasted blind.)

1. 1975 CHÂTEAU PALMER

Very good colour, slightly evolved rim. Ripe berries on nose, but unyielding. Very good fruit, rich, solid. Sweet. Not too aggressive tannins. Very good extract. No rush. I thought this was the Lascases. (18)

2. 1975 CHÂTEAU LEOVILLE-LASCASES:

Very good, deep colour. More delicate, less ripe fruit than the Palmer. Full, solid, very good depth, long, complex. Excellent, tobacco. Soft, ready. Second bottle oxidizing, pruny. I thought this was the Mouton. (17.5)

3. 1975 CHÂTEAU MOUTON-ROTHSCHILD:

Most evolved-looking of flight. Orange rim. Good depth. Cedar, tobacco nose. Hint of herbs. Very complex. Most ready of flight. "Margaux" elegance. A complete, lovely wine. I thought this was the Palmer. (18)

4. 1975 CHÂTEAU LATOUR:

Very good, deep colour to rim. Solid, cedary Cabernet. Very clean nose. Loads of ripe fruit. Rich, long, complex. Perfect balance. Excellent extract. Tobacco, fruit. I guessed this as Latour right away. (18.5)

5. 1975 CHÂTEAU LA MISSION HAUT-BRION:

Excellent deep red. Slightly evolved rim. Stemmy, 1975-style Cabernet nose. Solid, leathery, tannic, full. Lots of serious Cabernet fruit here. Excellent, but has the aggressive tannins of the 1975s. Needs lots of time. Great potential. Obviously La Mission. (18.5) to (19)

Overall impressions

Second flight not only clearly better than first flight, but great wines by any yardstick. This tasting was important as it proved that not all 1975s are dried out and "lean and mean," as is the trend to the 1975s now. Indeed, many 1975s were never good. Others were good, but have lost their fruit after 20 years (Branaire-Ducru), yet others are truly classic, great wines.

DESSERT WINE

1976 TOKAY ASZÚ ESSENCIA, MONIMPEX:

The last Tokay Essencia made by the Communists in Hungary. (The 1981 and 1983 will be finished by private owners.) (The 1981 is being downgraded to 6 Puttonyos.) Nutty, raisiny on nose. Amber-gold. Some sediment. Full, luscious. Little acidity, low alcohol.

The food and service were excellent.

April 1995

At home.

1942 LA TÂCHE, DOMAINE DE LA ROMANÉE-CONTI:

Very low level (three inches). Evolved colour. Lots of sediment. Part of a lot of four bottles I purchased at Butterfield and Butterfield auction earlier this year. The other three bottles have much better levels (two inches) and deeper red colour. Wax capsule. Made in the depths of World War II.

I must admit that this bottle surprised me more than any other wine I have ever drunk. I have a fairly wide experience tasting La Tâche, and know that even in poor or mediocre vintages, it can produce surprisingly fine wines, but this bottle beat them all. Very, very low level. Cork black and crumbly. Unmistakable smell of old raspberry jam. Classic La Tâche! Full, surprisingly rich. Excellent backbone. Very forward, but great intensity and depth. Very slight hint of decay. Sweet, long fruit. For the vintage and especially the ullage, this is a sensational wine!!! Even after a full hour, it still held its own.

June 8 to 11, 1995

Trip to Yountville as guest of Christian Moueix, on the occasion of the Napa Valley Hospital Wine Auction.

Dinner at "Don Giovanni" restaurant.

On Highway 29, south of Yountville. On Thursday night, Christian and his wife of six months, Cherise, invited me to dinner, with their John Daniel/Dominus estate manager Jean-Marie Maurèze, and former manager Daniel Baron, now managing Silver Oak in Rutherford.

1966 CHÂTEAU LAGRANGE, POMEROL:

(I brought it along.) Decanted. Very good colour. Good depth to rim. At first it had an off nose (metallic and dusty), and was hard, tight, and dry. After 45 minutes, a dramatic transformation. Nice, evolved, tobacco, fruity, sweet-berries nose. Round, rich, very good depth, and fruit extract. No rush. A good 1966.

This wine was produced by Christian's father who purchased the winery in 1955. I purchased this bottle on my previous trip to Napa in April, from the Oakville Grocery, where I was told that it came from the private cellar of Joseph Phelp (who also owns the Oakville Grocery). Christian said that the varietal is mostly Merlot, and that the quality of Lagrange varies because half the soil is good Pomerol soil and the other side is lesser-quality soil. He also said that his new agent in Washington State, Andy Lench, has been supplied with several cases of the 1990 Château Lagrange.

1990 SILVER OAK WINERY CABERNET SAUVIGNON, NAPA VALLEY:

(In honour of Daniel Baron) Very young, a baby, and totally unready. Bright, deep, youthful colour. Pronounced oak on both nose and palate. Somehow off-balance, a bit short, and acidic at finish. Leave it alone for five to seven years.

Christian was wearing a neck brace. It seems that he has the same neck problem as I do—aggravated by air travel and sleeping in hotels and on poor pillows.

Friday, June 9, 1995

Vintners' Ball at Meadowood, the opening session of the 1995 Napa Valley Wine Auction.

Before the Ball, we met at Napanook for a glass of Champagne with Christian, Cherise, and their staff. I had had tickets for the following day's auction and dinner, but as I hate crowds, I gave my two tickets away.

CHAMPAGNE PERRIER-JOUËT "FLOWER BOTTLE" 1988, IN MAGNUMS:

I prefer it to the 1985. Smooth, round, very stylish, elegant, nice fruit.

From there, Christian and I drove to a meeting point at Sutter Home Winery for the shuttle to Meadowood. About 1,500 people participated! Various California Champagnes, Beluga caviar, and smoked-salmon reception. Among the guests at our table were Michael Aaron, owner of Sherry-Lehmann in New York, and his wife Christine Aaron.

During a table conversation with Michael, it turned out that he lives in a penthouse flat in Manhattan at the Coronado, where I bought an apartment late last year. What a coincidence! On my next trip to New York, I'll visit them. His wife was born in 1945, same year as I was, and Michael complained about the difficulty of finding 1945s, especially in 1995, the 50th anniversary of VE Day.

WITH DINNER

DOMINUS ESTATE 1991, IN DOUBLE-MAGNUM:

A great wine. A baby, of course, but superb depth, length, balance. More French than California. Lovely ripe berries, fruit. Iron, minerals, and oak on palate. Superb, very long finish. I hope to get some of this.

The evening ended with a dance, and then we drove back home to Yountville.

Saturday, July 8, 1995

Dinner at the Tobes'.

Also Sid and Joan Cross. Allan organized a small dinner, on the occasion of my 50th birthday. All wines served double-blind.

CHAMPAGNE KRUG VINTAGE 1979:

Much improved. Not as lean as it used to be. Creamy, long, lovely nose. Round, not big, but lots of depth and excellent balance. Complex, yeasty. (18.5)

1985 CHEVALIER-MONTRACHET "DEMOISELLES," LOUIS LATOUR:

Surprisingly forward, butterscotch, earthy overtones on nose. I thought it was a 1979 or 1982 or even a

1978. Very soft, starting to oxidize. I'm worried, as I own a few bottles. (15)

1986 Chevalier-Montrachet "Demoiselles," Louis Latour:

Allan opened this because he didn't like the 1985. Livelier, fresher than the 1985, yet also hint of butterscotch on nose. Very good depth, complex, surprisingly forward. Made from good, ripe grapes. (17)

1970 and 1975 Château Latour:

I guessed Pauillac and the Latour 1970(!), but I thought the 1975 was the 1971. In retrospect, I should have guessed this, too, as it had the backbone of the 1975s.

The 1975 is excellent. Has the tannic backbone of the vintage, yet is open and accessible. Cedary, classic nose. Long, spicy Cabernet, good depth, full. Ready but no rush. A bit herbaceous, not a generous wine (1975 Médocs are anything but generous), yet surely one of the top wines of that vintage. Solid, excellent fruit. (18)

The 1970 was sensational. Much deeper, darker than the 1975. Essence of Cabernet on nose. Still tight. On palate, it was full, generous, solid. At first, I thought it was the 1970 Montrose. Great fruit extract. Not ready at 25 years of age! This is great stuff. Classic 1970 and classic Latour. Needs another five to seven years to reach its peak, and will last until 2020 or longer! A great bottle. (19.5)

Sunday, July 9, 1995

I took Bruno and France Prats of Château Cos d'Estournel on a day trip to Turnagain Island, on the Sunshine Coast of British Columbia.

After a short jeep ride and a walk in the rain, we went back to the cottage where we had some cheese and fruit with the following two wines.

1988 Corton-Charlemagne, Tollot-Beaut:

(Bruno's favourite white Burgundy) Superb. Tollot-Beaut is a major producer of Corton and Beaune reds, but its "secret weapon" is a tiny production (only four barrels or 100 cases) of superb, leaner, stylish, long-lived Corton-Charlemagne. It was also the first Charlemagne I ever tasted back in 1974 (the 1969 vintage), so I have a weak spot for it. Classic. Leaner style, of course, due both to the vintage and the style of this domaine, but impeccable balance, fruit, depth, and complexity. I should not really rave too much about it, as I do not want this little secret to get out!

1974 Beaulieu Vineyards Georges de Latour "Private Reserve" Cabernet Sauvignon, Napa Valley:

Excellent. Some people seem to have bad luck with this wine. The eight bottles I have tried so far from the case I bought in 1980 were all of superior quality. Classic American oak-vanilla combined with lovely ripe fruit, approaching its peak. Bruno loved it.

Monday, July 10, 1995

Joint dinner of the International Wine and Food Society and the Commanderie de Bordeaux, featuring the French Domaines Prats Wines.

Bruno Prats was the guest speaker. After some pleasant Maître d'Estournel 1993 (both red and white), we tasted the following wines through dinner.

1992 and 1993 Château de Marbuzet:

Produced from seven hectares of vines and juice from grapes of Cos d'Estournel that are three to 20 years old. In effect, this is the second wine of Cos.

The 1992 was thinner, more evolved on both nose and palate, pleasant fruit, crisp, forward.

The 1993 had more depth; noticeably darker, fuller, riper grapes. Clean, cedar-oak on nose. Nice berry fruit on palate.

1992 and 1993 Château Cos d'Estournel:

Two mediocre, rainy vintages.

As with the Marbuzet, the 1992 is more evolved. Nice vanilla, toasty nose. A bit vegetal, clean, long, forward.

The 1993 is much richer, darker, deeper. Bruno compared the quality of the 1993 to "between 1987 and 1981."

1989 and 1990 Château Cos d'Estournel:

Two great vintages. Both very deep in colour. Lots of fruit extract; ripe, rich, full, very long.

The 1989 is velvety.

The 1990 has more depth and more flesh. Needs five to seven years to approach its peak. Bruno compared the 1990 to the 1945! Impossible. The 1945 was a massive, tannic, hard (yet great) St. Estèphe. The modern wines have 60% Cabernet Sauvignon and 40% Merlot. Much rounder, richer, smoother, mellower. Hard to detect the tough St. Estèphe character in these wines, yet they are very flavourful, ripe, and long. Definitely "new style" Clarets.

1983 Château Cos d'Estournel:

Now fully mature. Mature colour. Cedary, evolved Cabernet nose. Not fat on palate. Rather lean, but nice fruit; spicy, cedary. Ready, but no rush.

Comments by Bruno Prats

He gets along well with Professor Ribereau-Gayon who "advises," but not with Emile Peynaud who "instructs." Bruno likes California wines that have "come of age" and have developed their own style. He is a proponent of the importance of soil (terroir). He doesn't like most Australian wines, "too boring and one-dimensional." He likes Rieslings (Alsace) and Corton-Charlemagne. He is not crazy about sweet wines, not even Sauternes.

July 14 to July 16, 1995

Corton-Charlemagne Weekend.

I have been planning this event for over two years, to coincide with my 50th birthday on July 17 (Monday). All the wines were from my cellar. Most participants (26 per event) were from Vancouver, but also some friends from San Francisco, Los Angeles, and Hawaii. The majority of participants took part in both events. Other than Champagnes and some fine Clarets and Sauternes, this weekend featured 32 Corton-Charlemagnes from 12 vintages (1976 to 1992) and 19 producers.

Friday, July 14, 1995

A Corton-Charlemagne Grand Cru Dinner, at the Pan Pacific hotel.

APERITIF

CHAMPAGNE BOLLINGER "SPECIAL CUVÉE" BRUT N/V, IN JEROBOAM:

Has developed depth and yeastiness. Full, round, solid, rich, soft. Mature, but still had fine mousse.

FLIGHT #1

THE CORTON-CHARLEMAGNES

1992s

1. 1992 BERNARD AMBOISE:

Best bright-yellow colour of the flight. Full, expansive, nutty nose with oak overtones. Great extract. Intense. Oak blends well. A generous wine. Fairly low acidity and forward. Almost too forward for such a young wine. (17.5)

2. 1992 CLOS FRANTIN, A. BICHOT:

Tight, closed on both nose and palate. Earthy, mineral overtones. Higher acidity, leaner than #1, but also much less depth or intensity. Hard to guess this as a Corton-Charlemagne. Good fruit, but lacks character. Also sharp and alcoholic finish. Tart. Hint of anise. (15)

3. 1992 "DIAMOND JUBILEE," REMOISSENET:

Tight nose. Hint of sulphur. Good extract, fruit, and balance. Elegant. Needs time to develop. Lighter style, but good. Remoissenet whites tend to age well. (16.5)

4. 1992 TOLLOT-BEAUT:

Nutty, almonds, oak nose. Classic. Tight, leaner style of this house. Great intensity and balance. Backward, but great potential. Lovely fruit extract, all in harmony. Needs five years. These wines age well. (18)

FLIGHT #2

In this flight, we tasted ripe, mature 1976s, a perfectly balanced and stylish 1985, and a great effort in a mediocre vintage, the 1987.

1. 1976 BONNEAU DU MARTRAY:

Bright gold. Quite alcoholic on both nose and palate, typical of this hot vintage. Rich, nutty, a little oak. Soft, earthy overtones, wet cement. Has held well, but needs drinking. (16.5)

2. 1976 "DIAMOND JUBILEE," REMOISSENET:

Nuttier, more typical Corton-Charlemagne than the Martray. Oak, toast on nose. More class and complexity. Good fruit/acidity balance. Very slight hint of butterscotch. Needs drinking. (17)

3. 1985 LOUIS LATOUR:

A perfectly balanced year; a perfectly balanced wine. At ten years of age, at its optimum peak. Classic Latour. Elegance rather than power, yet unmistakable Corton-Charlemagne nuttiness. Spicy, clean, long. Lovely bottle. (18)

4. 1987 J. F. COCHE-DURY:

Intense new oak, toast on nose. Hint of sulphur. Needs time to "get it together." The leanness of the vintage, yet a great effort. Excellent length and complexity. Intense oak blended nicely. Try in 1997 to 1999. (17.5) What a gifted winemaker Jean-François is!

FLIGHT #3

1989s

This was the biggest comparative flight of the whole weekend, with eight different 1989s, a very successful vintage.

1. 1989 BONNEAU DU MARTRAY:

Lovely, buttery, fresh nose. Hint of toast. Medium-bodied, round, elegant style of the house. Good depth and length. Good acidity/fruit balance. Almost ready. A very enjoyable wine. (17.5)

2. 1989 CHARTRON ET TREBUCHET:

Tighter, greener than #1 on both nose and palate. Lighter style of this house. Hint of toast. Elegant and fresh, but lacks depth and intensity. Good balance. Hint of vanilla and bubble gum on nose. Too much oak was used for this elegant wine. Doesn't have the power of a Corton-Charlemagne from a very good year. (16)

3. 1989 Faiveley:

For me, as well as for most participants, this was the greatest Corton-Charlemagne of the evening. Bright golden colour. Hint of sulphur on nose. Tight. Needs many years! Great balance. Serious, great depth and fruit. A sleeper. Solid, excellent extract. Only 1,800 bottles produced, and only 18 to 20 hectolitres per hectare! This will be very great some day. (19)

4. 1989 Joseph Drouhin:

Darkest golden colour of flight. Round, soft, rich, low acidity. Most forward of the whole flight of 1989s. Earthy, mineral overtones. A bit, too obvious. (17)

5. 1989 Domaine Leroy:

Very tight, very hard, very backward wine. Hard to judge both quality and maturity date. Closed on both nose and palate. Impeccable balance. Earthy overtones. Little hint of oak. (17)

6. 1989 Louis Latour:

As classic as Faiveley's, but in a more forward style. Perfect balance, lovely fruit. Nutty, clean, long. Lovely to drink now, but no rush. Harmonious. Very good extract, long finish. (18.5)

7. 1989 Domaine Maldant:

Some tasters thought the wine was corked. Most disagreed, as did I. A bit sweaty, cabbage nose. Good balance, nice ripe fruit, but lacks depth or complexity. Bad bottle? or so-so wine? Forward, a bit vegetal. Some hint of oak. (15)

8. 1989 Domaine Georges Roumier:

A great producer in the Commune of Chambolle-Musigny. His 1989 Corton-Charlemagne was a bit disappointing. Tight nose. Sweeter, straightforward style. Lacks complexity or Corton-Charlemagne nuttiness. Well made technically, but lacks interest. (16.5)

With the cheese course, we had the following.

1970 Château Pavie, in magnum:

Good neck level. Classic 1970s colour. Deep, bright-red to rim. Unmistakable St. Emilion. Lovely fruit, fresh at 25 years, and for a St. Emilion, surprisingly lively. Lovely, round fruit. Clean, long finish. Spicy, yet ripe. (17.5)

1959 Château Pape Clément, in magnum:

Perfect top neck level. Very perfumy, velvety wine. Classic, cedary, earthy, sweet, cigar-box nose. Very soft, elegant, long. Lots of class here, but definitely needs drinking, even from magnums. Most enjoyable. (18)

1967 Château Climens:

Typical Barsac. Bright, yet not deep gold (again, typical of this property). Buttery, oak, botrytis nose. Still fresh, very good acidity. Lovely fruit. Crisp, definitely not heavy-handed. Long, complex. No rush. (17.5)

Grande Champagne Cognac, "Abel" of Maison Ferrand, 45 years old:

Abel is the given name of Pierre Ferrand's grandfather. Amber colour. Great depth. Smooth, long. Complex, oak. No artificial caramel here! Lovely.

Sunday, July 16, 1995

Second Corton-Charlemagne session. Lunch at "Seasons in the Park" restaurant, in Queen Elizabeth Park.

This session featured the remaining 16 Corton-Charlemagnes of the 1978, 1982, 1983, 1986, 1988, and 1990 vintages.

The food was excellent, and Chef Pierre Delacote did an excellent job.

APERITIF

Champagne Veuve Clicquot "Carte Or" 1985:

Lively, fresh, crisp, good mousse. Has enough weight and backbone to last a few more years, yet drinking very well now.

FLIGHT #1

1990s

1. 1990 Faiveley:

Deepest golden colour of flight. Luscious, ripe Chardonnay on nose, with subdued oak. Hint of roasted almonds. Round, rich on palate. Excellent balance. Not as fat or rich as the 1989 tasted two days earlier, but excellent extract. Full-blown nose. Rich, more mature than the superb 1989. (18)

2. 1990 Marius Delarche:

Bright green-gold. Citrus, candied, open nose. Round, forward, elegant, and buttery. Easy to drink. Slight hint of madeirization. (16)

3. 1990 Pierre Bitouzet:

Green-gold. Herbaceous, hint of sulphur on nose (cleared after 30 minutes). Round, elegant, medium-bodied, a bit tight. Good weight. Full, clean finish. A good wine that was overshadowed by #1 and #4. (17)

4. 1990 Tollot-Beaut:

Bright-golden colour. Tight, yet ripe nutty nose. Hint of oak. Full, intense, solid backbone, as usual. Exotic, ripe pineapples. Needs time. Lovely wine. I preferred this slightly over Faiveley's 1990. (18.5)

5. 1990 Bouchard Père et Fils:

Fairly dark-golden colour, like #1. Tight nose. Clean, Quite alcoholic, but good fruit. Heavy-handed. Low acidity and not complex enough. (16)

FLIGHT #2
1988s and 1986s

1. 1988 Louis Latour:

Bright green-gold. Honeyed. Full, rich, long, impressive. Superb depth and length. Great extract. Ready, but no rush. (18)

2. 1988 Tollot-Beaut:

I tasted the 1988 last weekend on Turnagain Island, with Bruno and France Prats of Château Cos d'Estournel. Bright green-gold. Hint of sulphur, oak, nuts. Full yet youthful. Tight backbone, typical of this property's style. Solid, needs time. Excellent, but not, at this stage, as charming as #1. (17.5)

3. 1988 Corton Blanc, Chandon de Briaille:

Not a Grand Cru; made from 50% Chardonnay and 50% Pinot Blanc. Tight, straightforward. The solid structure of the Pinot Blanc is obvious. Flowery, oaky nose. Harder, less luscious and complex than the others, but very well made. Good depth. No rush, but may never develop great complexity. (16.5)

4. 1986 Louis Jadot:

Classic Corton-Charlemagne; classic 1986. Rich, luscious. Bravo Jadot! Ripe green apples on nose and toasty oak. Great extract. Explosive ripe fruit. Very long, excellent balance. Ready, but no rush. (18.5)

5. 1986 Michel Juillot:

Honeyed nose. Sweet, rich, very good acidity/fruit balance. Pineapples, exotic fruit. Rich, oaky Chardonnay flavours. Lively, long. I seemed to like it more than other participants. (17.5)

6. 1986 Louis Latour:

I liked this less than other participants, yet a very good wine in its own way. Tight nose, hint of caramel. Deep, golden colour. Luscious, intense, very sweet, soft, needs drinking. Too ripe, yet went well with the lovely lobster course. (17)

FLIGHT #3
1983, 1982, and 1978

1. 1983 Louis Latour:

Bright gold. Good acidity and fruit. Not, too alcoholic (a problem with many 1983s). Well balanced. Intense, nutty, oaky fruit. Very good extract. Ready. (17.5)

2. 1982 Louis Latour:

Deep gold. Exotic, ripe fruit on nose. Pineapples, peaches. Very soft (most 1982s are by now). Round, slight hint of oxidation. Good depth and ripe fruit. Drink up. (17)

3. 1982 Tollot-Beaut:

Bright gold. Straw and ripe fruit on nose. Fully mature, but holding well, thanks to excellent acidity. Great balance, length, weight. All there. Exotic fruit. Ripe, yet solid. Lovely. (18)

4. 1978 Louis Latour:

The 1978s are great white Burgundies. I love them. They are holding extremely well. Brilliant golden colour. Herbal, stemmy overtones on nose, typical 1978. Great balance, backbone, fruit intensity. Full of life, but ready. Great depth. Lovely fruit, yet not quite as lively as the Remoissenet. (18.5)

5. 1978 "Diamond Jubilee," Remoissenet:

This house's white wines are usually excellent, and they age extremely well. Similar colour and nose to the 1978 Latour. Full of life! Lovely extract, fruit, exotic spices. Hazelnut, cinnamon. Very long. Superb. (19)

Amazingly, no poor wine in this 32-wine, two-day marathon.

1962 Château Gruaud-Larose, in magnum:

Has held extremely well. Bright, deep colour typical of the 1962s. Tobacco, spicy Cabernet nose. Sweet, round, lovely fruit balance. Long, ripe, fruity finish. This is a fine Claret. (17.5)

1945 Château Senejac, Cru Bourgeois, Haut-Médoc:

I brought this along as a surprise, my birth year, 50 years ago! Two bottles. Recorked at the château in 1984. Excellent level. Very 1945! Deep, mature colour. Earthy, sweet, ripe, tobacco, cigar-box nose. Solid backbone. Excellent fruit. Long, complex. Clean finish. (18)

1962 Château Suduiraut:

Two bottles, both excellent. Very deep, amber-gold colour. Very ripe, botrytis, citrus, flowery nose. Full, rich, soft, yet very good acidity. Great explosion of exotic, ripe fruit on palate. Very mature, but lovely. (18)

Thus ended this marathon weekend. Great food, great wines, great weather, and good company. It took me over ten years to collect all these wines. It was well worth it.

I scored a dozen of the 32 Corton-Charlemagnes (18) and over, with 1989 Faiveley and 1978 Remoissenet my overall favourites. Latour and Tollot-Beaut were consistent overall and excellent. I remarked to the participants that we were very fortunate that one of the largest producers of Corton-Charlemagne, Louis Latour, makes such great Charlemagnes that are both reasonably priced, in terms of Grand Cru quality, and widely available.

Sunday, August 27, 1995

Marin County International Wine and Food Society Dinner, featuring 1970 Premier Grand Crus Classés, at the "Heights" restaurant, in San Francisco, on the occasion of members Barry and Joan Boothe's 30th wedding anniversary.

We arrived one hour late. What a mess traffic was on the Golden Gate bridge! It took us two hours from Yountville! Consequently, we missed the hors d'oeuvres and the 1970 Bollinger R.D. in jeroboam.

1970 CHASSAGNE-MONTRACHET "MORGEOT," GEORGES DELEGER:

Tight, deep gold. Herbaceous, vegetal Chardonnay nose (like the 1978s). Dry, lean, sharp, acidic finish, but excellent backbone helped this wine last this long. Low fruit. Drink up.

FLIGHT #1

1970 CHÂTEAU AUSONE

AND

1970 CHÂTEAU HAUT-BRION:

The Ausone was more evolved, browning, mature. Unmistakable, spicy, herbaceous, stemmy St. Emilion. A bit dry, hard, yet soft and drinkable. Somehow seemed to be made from unripe grapes. Sharp, acidic finish. Hint of oak and tobacco. Better on entry than at finish. (15) This was not a good period for Ausone. Things turned around there with the arrival of the gifted winemaker, and friend, Pascal Delbeck.

The Haut-Brion had a much deeper colour; mature, evolved rim. Leathery, chocolaty nose. Harder than the Ausone. More backbone, tighter, but lacks charm or ripe fruit. Bitter, tannic finish. Surprisingly closed, yet will not improve. The 1966 is definitely better. (16) I have tasted better examples of this.

FLIGHT #2

1970 CHÂTEAU CHEVAL-BLANC:

The best wine of the first two flights. Herbaceous, ripe nose. Classic St. Emilion. Good, dark colour of the 1970s. Great extract, lovely fruit. Ready, soft, yet very good fruit. Fine wine. (18)

1970 CHÂTEAU LAFITE:

Lafite was palest. Almost Burgundian in appearance and nose. Subdued toasted oak. Elegant fruit. A bit soupy, acidic, lean finish, lacking middle. (16) Produced in the midst of a low ebb at Lafite (1963 to 1975). The best "Clos Vougeot" of the night!

1970 CHÂTEAU MARGAUX:

Had the appearance of a great 1970. Excellent, deep, bright colour. A bit green, yet spicy and complex Cabernet Sauvignon on nose. But on palate it was a lean, mean, citrusy, acidic, sharp wine. No future. (14) Another wine produced during a difficult time for this great property.

FLIGHT #3

1970 CHÂTEAU PETRUS:

Very dark. Superb, earthy, mineral, ripe Merlot nose. Full, tannic, solid, backed by loads of ripe fruit. Will last for a long time. Very ripe, approachable, but no rush. Luscious. (18.5)

1970 CHÂTEAU MOUTON-ROTHSCHILD:

Mouton was leaner, very fine, complex, tobacco, cedar. Ready, evolved. Maybe slightly acidic, sharp finish, but tobacco, long fruit, complex. Lots of class here. (18)

1970 CHÂTEAU LATOUR:

As expected, this was the wine of the evening. Incredibly dark, deep colour to rim. Tight nose, yet classic cedary Cabernet. Superb balance and depth, solid, with ripe fruit. At 25 years of age, not ready. Approachable and drinkable (decant for at least two hours), but will last for another 20 years or more if well cellared. A great wine. (19.5)

As expected, the 1970 Latour was by far the best wine of the whole flight of the 1970s.

1970 CHÂTEAU D'YQUEM:

Bright, medium-gold. Clean vanilla-oak, buttery, botrytis nose. Round, soft, complex on palate. Does not have the weight or intensity of the 1967 or the liveliness of the 1975 or the depth of the 1971, but very good. Very long. Lovely and soft. Ready. (18)

1970 TAYLOR'S VINTAGE PORT, IN HALF-BOTTLES:

Served from four half-bottles. Even in half-bottles, this was very good. Approaching its peak. Good, deep colour. Spicy, complex fruit. Not jammy like Graham's or soft like Croft's. The "Latour" of Port. In full bottles, this wine will last for another 15 to 20 years. (18)

I had a chance to taste the

CHAMPAGNE BOLLINGER "RD" 1970, IN JEROBOAM:

Still full of life, fine bubbles, yeasty, heavier style, yet fresh. Very fine.

The food was excellent, all through the meal.

Dinner at "Bistro Don Giovanni."

With Barney and Belle Rhodes, John Bender (Professor of English at Stanford University), and his guests Eddie Penning-Rowsell and his wife Meg, from London. I brought along two bottles, the 1992 Stony Hill Chardonnay and the 1986 Château Leoville-Poyferré.

1992 STONY HILL CHARDONNAY
AND
1993 TREFETHEN CHARDONNAY, NAPA VALLEY:

The Stony Hill, according to Barney, was made from young vines. Quite golden, a bit lean, hard. Hopefully will improve, but lacks the depth this wine possessed in older vintages.

The Trefethen was forthcoming, fruity, crisp, round. Good acidity, long.

1986 CHÂTEAU LEOVILLE-POYFERRÉ:

The Leoville-Poyferré was the best wine of the evening. Classic St. Julien. Very good depth of colour. Solid Cabernet. Spicy extract; full, rich, yet approachable, for a 1986. No rush, though. Very good balance, long. Clean oak-vanilla Cabernet on both nose and palate. Concentrated, fruity, rich. Penning-Rowsell liked it, too. Poyferré is making a come-back, since 1982, after several decades of producing mediocre wines.

1980 HEITZ CELLARS "BELLA OAKS" CABERNET SAUVIGNON, NAPA VALLEY:

Paler, more-evolved colour than the Poyferré. Open, spicy, leather, and eucalyptus on nose. Round, forward, rich, quite intense on palate. Sweet fruit, and ripe raisins predominate. An odd wine. Usually "Bella Oaks" is more subdued, less "Martha's Vineyard" style than this. A very "obvious" wine. This stressed the elegance and class of the Leoville-Poyferré.

Penning-Rowsell is now 83. He did not remember me from our previous meeting at Christie's in London, back in 1977, at an auction dedicated exclusively to Château Latour. That was 18 years ago! He seems to have mellowed quite a bit. He agreed that the 1986 Clarets were overall "forgotten" by the public. He also admitted that Bordeaux overcrops these days. Legally 56 hectolitres per hectare, actually more like 60 or 65 hectolitres per hectare.

Thursday, August 31, 1995

Dinner at "La Folie" restaurant, in San Francisco.

With George Derbalian, who arranged this event, accompanied by his wife; Dr. Lee Smith and his wife, May; Dr. Dick Fleming (a plastic surgeon who has operated on many stars in Hollywood) and his companion, Margaret (an actress); Jim Gaby from Washington, DC, (an engineer and avid wine collector); Carol and myself. We shared the cost of this event. The wines, all from George's cellar in Atherton, were top class. George is an Armenian by birth, an engineer by profession, and runs a wine import business called "Atherton Wine Imports." We had an incredible eight-course meal, prepared by chef /owner Rolland Passot. Superb food. George is a very nice man and he knows his wines.

CHAMPAGNE SALON "LE MESNIL" 1982:

A Champagne I have had on several occasions. It is quite mature now. 100% Chardonnay. Round, elegant, delicate. Good depth, complex, tiny bubbles and long. Hint of sweetness, mature, and round. (18)

Then we tasted two giants among white Burgundies.

1983 MONTRACHET, DOMAINE DE LA ROMANÉE-CONTI:

The Romanée-Conti expressed itself from the beginning. Deep golden colour. Superb Chardonnay, intense nose. Even hint of botrytis, not unlike a fine Barsac! I described it as Beethoven's Fifth Symphony. Full, rich, very long, yet not the high alcoholic character of so many 1983s. A gigantic marble column from the beginning. No change, after two hours in glass. Great extract, luscious fruit, great intensity. Maybe not quite as great as the 1970 or 1978, but close. (19)

1983 MONTRACHET, DOMAINE RAMONET:

The Ramonet started more shyly. Paler colour. Subdued, flowery, spicy nose. Perfect balance, elegance, spicy Chardonnay complexity. But after one hour, it evolved, and developed in the glass into a glorious, lovely, long, flowery, classic Chardonnay. Superb balance, extract, length. Both wines were so different from each other, yet both were great. (19)

1949 CHÂTEAU D'YQUEM:

Served with superb warm Sonoma foie gras. Excellent level, well into neck. Amber-gold, deep colour. Lovely, mature, botrytis, apricots, ripe peaches on nose. Full, round, soft, eminently drinkable. Softer, rounder than the 1945 or 1947. Perhaps not as great, but a lovely, complex wine nevertheless. (19)

1971 LA TÂCHE, DOMAINE DE LA ROMANÉE-CONTI, IN JEROBOAM:

Classic 1971 La Tâche. Kept developing in glass. Spicy, classic ripe raspberries. Deep colour, concentrated, full, rich, long. Full of life. A great La Tâche, as usual. (19.5)

Too much wine for only eight people! Two of the ladies drank very little; I paced myself carefully so I was able to drive back to Yountville, where I arrived safely at almost 2:00 a.m. A great evening. Superb food and great wines.

September 14, 1995

Commanderie de Bordeaux Dinner at "Pastel" restaurant, in Vancouver, featuring the "Super Second" face-off of the 1981, 1982, and 1983 vintages: Châteaux Palmer, Leoville-Lascases, Pichon-Lalande, and Cos d'Estournel.

FLIGHT #1
1981s

1981 COS D'ESTOURNEL:

Good depth, evolved rim. Hint of oak, straw on nose. Full, sweet fruit. Rich, solid, yet soft tannins. (17)

1981 PICHON-LALANDE:

Slightly deeper than the Cos. A bit more herbal nose. Deep, riper, richer, bigger than the Cos. Lots of ripe fruit. Good extract. Best extract of the flight. Tobacco, rich, long. (18)

1981 LEOVILLE-LASCASES:

Similar appearance to the Pichon. Lovely oak, Cabernet nose. Rich, tannic on entry. Solid. Lacks the elegance of Pichon, but big and rich. Most tannic, most backward of flight. No rush. (17.5)

1981 PALMER:

Lightest colour of flight. Open, delicate, fruity nose. Delicate, complex. Most elegant, most forward, yet lovely, silky, ready. Drink soon. (16.5)

FLIGHT #2
1983s

1983 COS D'ESTOURNEL:

Deep red. Palish rim. Herbal, straw, oak nose. Tighter than the 1981, more vegetal. Nice fruit. Better than expected. (17)

1983 CHÂTEAU PICHON-LALANDE:

Good, dark colour. Deeper than the 1981. Tight, concentrated nose. Solid, spicy, yet elegant. Lovely extract, complexity. Great depth. Still tannic. (18.5)

1983 CHÂTEAU LEOVILLE-LASCASES:

Still youthful, tannic, rich, solid. Full, great extract. Very Cabernet. Trying (and in 1983, succeeding) to be Latour. (18) Actually, in 1983, better than Latour.

1983 CHÂTEAU PALMER:

Excellent deep colour. Lovely, complex, tobacco, Cabernet nose. Very long, sweet, elegant. Lovely extract. Classic Margaux. (18.5) This must be the best Palmer since the great 1970.

I had a hard time deciding on my favourite of the two first flights, between the 1983 Palmer and 1983 Pichon-Lalande. Both are great wines.

FLIGHT #3
1982s

1982 COS D'ESTOURNEL:

Very good, deep colour to rim. Ripe, cedary, intense fruit on nose. Full, rich, long. Loads of ripe fruit. Great extract, yet, for a St. Estèphe, ready. (18)

1982 CHÂTEAU PICHON-LALANDE:

Superb deep colour. Great nose of ripe fruit. Superb extract on palate. Loads of ripe fruit. Great depth, long. Toast, oak. Complex. Still not "put together." Lovely, ripe fruit. (19)

1982 CHÂTEAU LEOVILLE-LASCASES:

Very deep colour. Intense, ripe Cabernet nose. Red currant jam. Loads of ripe fruit. Intense, great extract. Tobacco, chocolate, sensational. Essence of Cabernet. Great bottle. Latour-like. (19)

1982 CHÂTEAU PALMER:

Lightest colour of flight. Elegant nose. Soft, complex, sweet fruit, but definitely doesn't have the extract and depth of the other three. Yet surprisingly good. (17.5)

1982 CHÂTEAU RIEUSSEC:

Bright gold. Elegant botrytis nose. Round. Medium-bodied. Lacks the depth and extract of the 1983 Rieussec, but good acidity, fruit, and depth.

Chef-owner Marcus Wheelan did an excellent job. Great food. Marcus formerly worked at "Chartwell's," at the Four Seasons hotel, in Vancouver.

November 17 to 23, 1995

Trip to Los Angeles and Yountville.

Friday, November 17, 1995

Noon tasting in Los Angeles, at Dr. Brad Klein's, featuring 1961 First Growths, plus Palmer and La Mission Haut-Brion.

Serena Sutcliffe of Sotheby's was among the participants. Brad belongs to a group of tasters who meet once a month. The host determines the subject and each participant brings a bottle. I brought along a bottle of 1961 Lafite (my only remaining bottle), which I purchased in Seattle, in 1981. The wines are served blind. It is possible to have more than one wine of the same property and vintage, as participants don't know what others are bringing along. This is going to be a long day, as after the lunch, I have a tasting in the evening, featuring 1945 Sauternes, Rhônes, Barolos, and Russian Ports, organized by Bipin Desai.

Diary 15

APERITIF

CHAMPAGNE JACQUESSON "SIGNATURE" 1982:

Unusual. Fine mousse and bubbles. Flowery, lilacs, grapey nose, rather than yeasty. I've never experienced this taste in a Champagne before. Fine, delicate, elegant. Good fruit. Unusual.

The wines were served blind. Order and exact châteaux unknown. All wines are in the exact order in which they were tasted. We did not know the order, nor did we know which was our own bottle.

1. 1961 CHÂTEAU LAFITE-ROTHSCHILD:

Palest of flight. Very slightly cloudy. Delicate, flowery nose. A bit dry and leathery, yet good depth. Complex, spicy flavours of a fine, yet delicate wine. Very much Lafite style. A bit acidic. Later this wine fell apart and dried out. Disappointing. (17)

2. 1961 CHÂTEAU HAUT-BRION:

Impressive, dark colour. Slightly evolved rim. Closed nose. Ripe fruit. Full, powerful, tannic, massive. Very Cabernet. Not ready! Latour? Sweet, more earthy. Maybe Haut-Brion? Later, ripened quite a bit. Leathery, raisiny. Concentrated. Lovely. (18.5)

3. 1961 CHÂTEAU LATOUR:

Even deeper than #2. Very slight hint of mustiness. A bit sharper, more evolved than #2. More acidic, too. Later, obviously corked. Too bad, because it has the solid structure to be a serious contender. (No score)

4. 1961 CHÂTEAU MOUTON ROTHSCHILD:

Slightly lighter than #2 or #3. Evolved, browning rim. Lovely, classic, cedary nose. Best nose so far. Lovely, complex, leathery character. Classy, superb, sweet, evolved, cedary fruit. Excellent backbone. Superb. Very youthful. A great bottle. (19.5)

5. 1961 CHÂTEAU HAUT-BRION:

Excellent, dark colour. Orangy, mature rim. Cedar, ripe fruit on nose. Solid, sweet, tight. Very ripe fruit, tannic. Somehow, short finish. Has the structure but not the complexity of a great 1961. Sweet fruit. Later improved. Complex, ripe, sweet, long, slightly more life than #2, yet both great. (18.5)

6. 1961 CHÂTEAU LATOUR:

Medium-dark. Good depth. Orangy rim. Tight, classic, cedary nose. Full, solid, tannic, very ripe, very rich, very long. Loads of ripe fruit. Serious. More tannic than ripe fruit, yet fruit is undoubtedly there. All there, yet not that extra notch of complexity as the other greats in this flight. A bit vegetal; nice, complex wine. Maybe Cheval-Blanc? (17.5)

7. 1961 CHÂTEAU LATOUR:

Excellent depth and appearance. Closed, lovely, cedar, ripe fruit on nose. Full, rich, tannic, earthy. Great character, masculine. Latour? Loads of ripe tannins. Classic. Superb. (19)

8. 1961 CHÂTEAU CHEVAL-BLANC:

One of the darkest of flight. Coffee, cedar, classic nose. Great depth. Loads of sweet fruit, yet very youthful. Solid, tannic, loads of very ripe, massive fruit. Great wine. Needs years. Bags of life and fruit. Superb. Cinnamon. A great bottle. Best 1961 Cheval-Blanc I've ever tasted. (19.5)

9. 1961 CHÂTEAU LA MISSION HAUT-BRION:

Good, dark colour, but lighter than #6, #7, or #8. Evolved, orangy rim. Odd nose. Hint of mint. A bit "off" nose. "Piqué" on palate. Sharp, acidic, yet complex, very sweet. Unusual sweetness. Right Bank? Cheval-Blanc? (17.5) Very elegant, yet not as great as 1961 La Mission can be. (I added that last comment when we found out what the wines were.)

10. 1961 CHÂTEAU LAFITE:

Medium-mature colour. Tea leaves, delicate nose. Sweet on palate, forward, soft. A bit acidic. Maybe was better five to seven years ago. Hint of sharpness on palate. Soft, leathery, forward, tobacco. Very enjoyable. Needs drinking. Later, weakened a bit. Lafite? Classic, elegant. (18) Afterward, I found out that this was my bottle. I am glad that it held its own.

11. 1961 CHÂTEAU PALMER:

Medium-dark, good depth. Orange rim. Very mature nose, flowery, hint of leather. Ripe on palate, soft, sweet, classy, elegant. Lovely, ripe, soft fruit. Cedar, tobacco. Most enjoyable. Later a bit soupy, sweet finish, yet very good. (18) Not as great as when experienced with Carol and Peter and Diana Sichel at d'Angludet in April, 1984, and on several occasions since.

DESSERT WINE

1861 CHÂTEAU LA TOUR BLANCHE:

A full-century older than the above. Mid shoulder level. Purchased from Sotheby's. Very dark, almost red colour. Original cork. Smell of molasses, prunes. Medium green-reddish colour. Very Sherry-like on nose. Drying out. Good acidity, soft fruit, even a little sweetness. Drinking history. Certainly sound. After three hours, opened up, clean, almost Madeira, raisiny nose, yet hint of botrytis.

Overall impressions

A great tasting. Only one poor wines (#1). Oddly, two of the three Latours were excellent, yet they were overshadowed by two other wines. I expected Latour to be the greatest wine of the tasting. In this case, Mouton and Cheval-Blanc won. No participant brought along either Margaux or Petrus.

It is painfully clear that there will always be bottle variation when people bring their own bottles, stored and handled under different circumstances and purchased from different sources, over many years.

That evening

FIRST SESSION

Tasting of 1945 wines, at "Fenix" restaurant, on Sunset Boulevard.

Serena and I went to Bipin Desai's first-of-three tasting marathons of 1945s (except Clarets), to taste 1945 Sauternes, red Rhônes, Barolos, Brunellos, and Russian Ports.

FLIGHT #1
1945 Sauternes

1. 1945 CHÂTEAU DOISY-DAËNE:

Palest of flight. Bright, mature gold. Delicate, earthy nose. Hint of raisins, some botrytis. Soft, delicate, sweet, yet not cloying. Good acidity. Long aftertaste. (17.5)

2. 1945 CHÂTEAU LAFAURIE-PEYRAGUEY:

Deeper, amber gold than #1. Subdued, delicate nose. Lovely, full, rich, very soft; nice sweet finish. Not too fat. Clean, elegant, classic, mature Sauternes. (18)

3. 1945 CHÂTEAU RAYNE-VIGNEAU:

Colour similar to #2, but very slightly deeper. Hint of vegetables on nose. Slight hint of mustiness. Much older-tasting than #1 or #2. Some sweetness. Wet cement. A bit bitter, hard finish. Unclean. Pity, because this can be great. (15.5)

4. 1945 CHÂTEAU SUDUIRAUT:

Deep amber-gold, similar to Rayne-Vigneau. Subdued, clean nose. Beautiful balance, length, delicate. Sweet, yet not cloying. Impeccably made. More depth and botrytis than #2. Caramel, extract, length. Fine peach jam, perfect balance. (18.5)

5. 1945 CHÂTEAU D'YQUEM:

Two bottles were tasted. First bottle was darkest of flight. Deep amber-gold. Second bottle similar in appearance to Suduiraut. First bottle fatter, richer, sweeter, intense. Great extract. Superb. The second bottle slightly lighter, fresher, less fat, slightly higher acidity. Both great. First bottle a little more caramel. Second bottle livelier. First bottle very sweet, concentrated. A dessert by itself. Rated both (19.5).

FLIGHT #2
Sangiovese and Côte-Rôtie

1. 1945 CHIANTI CASTELLANA RISERVA:

Palish colour, orangy rim. Nose a bit cheesy. Off-smell. Hard, tannic, acidic. Dried out. (12)

2. 1945 BRUNELLO DI MONTALCINO BIONDI SANTI" RISERVA":

Better colour than #1. Still palish red. Off, hint of sulphur on nose. Hard, tannic, solid. Cleaner on palate, better balanced than #1, but lacks fruit. Nowhere near as good as when tasted a few years ago at a vertical of Biondi Santi (1891 to 1970). Fairly high acidity, lean. Powerful, solid. Later, good fruit. The most expensive bottle of the whole evening, including d'Yquem 1945! (16)

3. 1945 CÔTE-RÔTIE, VIDAL-FLEURY:

Deepest, darkest of flight. A bit cloudy. Soupy, oxidized, over-the-hill. Leathery, dead. (0)

A wasted flight. Poor wines. The Brunello was drinkable. Unfortunately, I had to talk about this flight. Not much to say. As usual, Bipin picks on me to talk about the "poor" flights. This time, even I couldn't say much about these wines. Had we tasted 1947s, rather than 1945 Italian wines, I'm sure that it would have been a different story altogether.

FLIGHT #3
1945 Barolos

1. 1945 BAROLO BORGOGNO "RISERVA":

Palish, evolved colour. Classic, leathery, plum-pudding nose of old Barolos. Sweet on entry, good backbone, hint of oxidation, but sound. Complex, spicy. Needs drinking. (15.5)

2. 1945 BAROLO ALDO CONTERNO "RISERVA":

Best, darkest colour by far. Clean, fresh, spicy nose. Full, solid, rich, tannic. Excellent ripe tannins backed by fine fruit. The best 1945 Barolo I've ever tasted. Impressive. (17.5)

3. 1945 BAROLO MARCHESI "RISERVA":

Good depth, more evolved colour than #2. Baked bread on nose. Cherry pit. Very good extract; lovely ripe fruit. Full, solid, powerful. Good extract. (16.5)

4. 1945 BAROLO MARCHESI CASTELLANA:

Pale, orangy colour. Neutral, strawberry jam nose. Light, acidic, some fruit, but tired. Needs drinking. Still sound. Hint of coffee beans. (14)

5. 1945 BAROLO RINALDI "RISERVA":

Medium, mature red. Oxidizing nose, sharp, acidic, some fruit, but needs drinking. Slightly sweeter than #4. (15)

FLIGHT #4
Russian (Georgian/Crimean) Ports from the Massandra Collection

1. 1945 LIVADIA:

Very pale red, almost Rosé. Light Muscat. Quite nice. Like a very pale 1958 or 1950 Port. A pleasant surprise. Well balanced. Plummy. (16)

2. 1945 SUROZH:

Very pale colour. Light, Sherry-like. Sweet, cloying, spicy. Hint of mustiness. Very sweet. Quite alcoholic. (15) as a wine, (17) as a curiosity. Not unlike a Pineau des Charentes, but too spirity.

Serena said that the Massandra Cellars are Imperial cellars in Crimea, near the Black Sea, near Yalta. This cellar was built for the Czar and his court. After the Revolution, the top Soviet leaders used it for themselves. Livadia is the name of a location near Yalta. The greatest are the Russian Pink and white Muscats. Wines from the Imperial Reserve are embossed with the Czar's Eagle. A large lot of these wines was sold at an exclusive Sotheby's auction recently.

Saturday, November 18, 1995

Dinner at "La Cachette" restaurant, in Los Angeles, with Brad Klein and Serena Sutcliffe.

A very pleasant, quiet evening. Brad's 1956 Rolls Royce was the talk of the evening with the waiters. A beautiful one-of-a-kind car.

1987 CORTON-CHARLEMAGNE, TOLLOT-BEAUT:

Typical 1987 and typical of this producer. Bright, light gold. Flowery, clean, fresh nose of pears, hint of oak. Crisp, lean, high acidity, yet good length. Will last well for another four to five years. Fine effort.

1982 CHEVALIER-MONTRACHET "DEMOISELLES"

AND

1986 CHEVALIER-MONTRACHET "DEMOISELLES," BOTH OF DOMAINE LOUIS LATOUR:

(1982 was my bottle; 1986 was Brad's bottle)

The 1982 was deep, golden, oxidized, undrinkable. Can be excellent.

The 1986 was the best wine of the evening: Classic, soft 1986, rich, pears, peaches, oak/vanilla. Elegant. Not a big or stunning wine, but classy. At its peak.

1961 CHÂTEAU PONTET-CANET, CRUSE, BORDEAUX-BOTTLED:

Oxidized, prune juice. Two bad bottles out of four that night. This can be, and usually is, an excellent Claret.

Sunday, November 19, 1995

Lunch at "Spago's." Second session of Bipin Desai's event, featuring 1945 Ports.

The Croft's was my bottle, which I brought down from Vancouver. Serena participated in this event, as well.

1945 CHÂTEAU LAVILLE-HAUT-BRION

AND

1945 CHÂTEAU LAVILLE-HAUT-BRION "CRÈME DE TÊTE":

The "regular" was brilliant gold, more like a white Graves, 20 or 25 years younger. Subdued, buttery, citrusy nose. Fairly dry, high acidity. Later, oak-lemony aftertaste. Very good intensity.

The "Crème de Tête" was amber gold, like a 1947 Sauternes. Peaches, hint of botrytis on nose. More intense, richer than the "regular." Not as great as when last tasted three years ago, but very good. The "regular" had some herbaceous Sauvignon character on nose. The "Crème de Tête" had a hint of honey, botrytis. Both good, even very good, but not great. Both rated (17).

FLIGHT #1

1945 Dow's, Fonseca's, Ferreira's, Offley's

1. 1945 OFFLEY'S:

Mature, red colour. Light, palish rim. Spicy, clean, fruity nose. Classic Port. Quite sweet, long, a bit spirity, hot finish. On the sweet side. Typical Offley's. Not very complex, but certainly very good. (17)

2. 1945 FERREIRA'S:

Palest, most mature wine of the flight. Very light, browning. More subdued nose than #1. Softer, too, less spirity. A bit sharp finish. Brown, evolved. (16.5)

3. 1945 FONSECA'S:

Lighter red than #1, but more youthful than #2. Best nose; most classic, ripe fruit. Creamy, smooth, no sharp edges. Long, delicate, less intense than the great 1948, but very elegant and plummy. Plummy. (17.5)

4. 1945 DOW'S:

Medium-red. Mature rim. Fresher nose than most. Full, rich. Classic Port. Fairly spirity, but backed by lots of fruit. A masculine wine, in spite of its sweetness. Best depth of flight. Very good. Roses and minerals on nose. (18)

All four are at their peak. Dow's, no rush. Others at their peak or in decline (especially Ferreira's).

FLIGHT #2

Warre's, Taylor's, Graham's, Croft's, Quinta do Noval

1. 1945 QUINTA DO NOVAL:

Palest of flight. Lighter than the Dow's in flight #1. Sweet, mature nose. Elegant, raisiny. Structured like the Fonseca's, but sweeter. Unusual. Quite sweet. Orangy nose. (17) In retrospect, this should have been included in the first flight, and the Dow's should have been inserted here.

2. 1945 CROFT'S:

(My bottle) Good, bright-red colour. Light, evolved rim. Spicy, spirity nose. Good depth, solid, still youthful. A bit hard, even drier than Dow's. Still fresh, yet hard, even slightly bitter finish. Very good. Best 1945 Croft's I've ever tasted. (18)

3. 1945 GRAHAM'S:

Good, youthful colour to rim. Sweet, youthful on nose. Full, intense, rich. Excellent balance. Lots of depth here. No rush. A great Port. (19)

4. 1945 TAYLOR'S:

Good, dark colour. Most closed, tightest nose. Great sweet fruit extract. Big, solid, youthful. Drier than the Graham's, as it should be, but lovely fruit. Freshest. Great Port. Years of life ahead. (19.5)

5. 1945 WARRE'S:

Slightly leathery, ripe nose. Subdued, closed. Nice sweet, elegant, well balanced, spicy. Very good sweet fruit. Long, rich. Surprisingly good. Actually excellent. Sweetness of Graham's with structure of Taylor's. (18.5)

Most were at their zenith or just past it, but the Taylor's has a great future. The Warre's was a very pleasant surprise.

No doubt that 1945 Ports are great wines, as are the 1945 Sauternes.

In retrospect, I'm glad I missed the 1945 red Burgundies event. I have tasted most of them before, and although there were a few very good wines, several were disappointing. Apparently, even the Romanée-Conti was slightly oxidized.

Serena Sutcliffe made a good impression on me. I tasted with her three times in three days (1961 Clarets, Sauternes 1945, Barolos 1945, and 1945 Ports). She knows her wines, and she is a good taster. Oddly, although we marked our wines individually, we seemed to agree on almost every wine, and we gave most of them identical points.

Discussion with Serena on Michael Broadbent

She said that as he ages, Michael is getting more egocentric, and doesn't tolerate people who disagree with him. Broadbent does have an interest in Lafite. That must be why he defends Lafite when it underperforms, such as is the case with the 1945. My suspicions that he was biased were correct. (Apparently, Eric de Rothschild has an interest in Christie's.) I told her that Broadbent also committed himself and backed Hardy Rodenstock and, fake wines or not, he has to play the game, because he was the "expert" who said that Hardy's wines were authentic. (I think that many of them are fakes.)

Serena's comments on Hardy Rodenstock's discovery of a "mysterious" Venezuelan cellar

In the late 19th century, there was a lot of wealth in Venezuela. Many people imported fine French wines. At the turn of the century, their economy went downhill. Some families still imported French wines in bulk, and used the old empty bottles of fine French wines as containers for the bulk wines they were importing.

Serena said that these days, there is a flood of fake wines, Sotheby's have to turn away many "impeccable-looking" wines, and that sellers are looking at other venues to find victims to sell these wines to.

Eddy Penning-Rowsell is a very good writer, but not as good a taster. He just wrote down what Baron Philippe, the Woltners, Hermann Cruse, and other great wine personalities told him. I have heard this from other sources, too.

I told Serena that, on the other hand, Harry Waugh was an excellent taster. A "buyer's" taster, who could correctly assess the potential quality and expected maturity of young wines. This gift can, of course, be improved upon with tastings, but if one doesn't have that gift to begin with, then it just isn't there. Broadbent is a fine wine writer. But he is not a very good taster. This is obvious at blind tastings.

Serena was on her way to South Korea, and spent the weekend tasting with us as the guest of Bipin Desai. She speaks French fluently. Nice lady, and a very knowledgeable taster.

In Yountville, dinner with Joe and Alice Heitz.

I drove to the Heitz's for a "shot of Macallan, 17 years old." Then we went for dinner to the old "Christian Brothers Culinary Institute of America Kitchen." Food was OK, but nothing special.

I brought along a bottle that Joe produced but that he hadn't tasted for many years.

1959 HEITZ CELLARS/HANZELL CABERNET SAUVIGNON:

This was Hanzell's first vintage. At the time, Joe was the winemaker there. Joe bought the juice, and aged and bottled it in 1962. Excellent top neck level.

Original cork was in very good shape. We decanted the wine at Joe's home. It had very little sediment. Very much like a good 1966 Claret. Drying, yet good fruit. Complex, cedary Cabernet. Lovely nose. Good length. Very good, but needs drinking. It made Joe's day. He kept the bottle as a souvenir.

I gave Joe a half-bottle of 1988 Château Sociando-Mallet. He told me that Nestlé's have put Beringer up for sale. He told me that the 1974 vintage was his son David's first vintage. Joe was in bed then with a bad back, and he instructed David and Alice how to make the 1974 "Martha's" over the phone. Not a bad effort! Later we drove back to his house for a glass of this wine.

1974 HEITZ CELLARS ANGELICA:

Nutty, complex, long, lovely balance, depth. Smooth, full-bodied. Very good.

Sunday, December 10, 1995

International Wine and Food Society (Marin County) Dinner, at the Ritz-Carlton hotel, in San Francisco, celebrating Dr. Barney Rhodes' 75th birthday, featuring some great prephylloxera Lafites, in magnums, (the great 1870 and the 1864).

This was a repeat of Barney's 70th birthday held five years ago at "Stars" restaurant, in San Francisco, but this time the food was absolutely exquisite. Chef Gary Danko is a very gifted young man.

1985 BÂTARD-MONTRACHET, DOMAINE LEFLAIVE:

Classic 1985 and classic Leflaive, leaner, herbaceous style. Lots of depth, length. Very good fruit/acidity balance. Lovely, honeyed, oak on nose. No rush. Quite youthful at ten years of age, yet round and long. Lovely wine. Very stylish. (18.5)

1959 CHÂTEAU LAFITE:

Six bottles of this wine were opened. Over the years, this wine has become a legend. It is one of the few great Lafites of this century. Superb, classic Lafite bouquet. Chocolaty, cedary; typical ripe 1959. Lovely balance, fruit. Rich, very good backbone, yet aggressive, dry finish. Deep colour. Loads of ripe fruit. Bigger, darker, more tannic than the 1953 that follows here. After 45 minutes, it overtook the 1953, which started to dry up. No rush. (19)

1953 CHÂTEAU LAFITE, IN MAGNUMS:

Lighter in colour than the 1959. More evolved, softer, more velvety, as befits a 1953 at 42 years of age—even in magnums. Lovely, flowery, elegant bouquet. Really classic nose. Cedar, roses, expansive. Silky on palate. Superb. Great balance, sweet, delicate fruit. Lasted well in glass for 45 minutes, then the depth of the 1959 took over. (19.5)

Intermission

CHAMPAGNE DOM PÉRIGNON 1962, IN MAGNUMS:

This was a most pleasant surprise. Bright, deep, mature-golden colour. Sweet, ripe on palate. Tiny bubbles, fine mousse. Creamy, rich, round, elegant. Nice sweet fruit and balance. Has held extremely well. (18)

1870 CHÂTEAU LAFITE, IN MAGNUM:

This was the 125-year-old miracle of the evening. Of course, 1870 was a magnificent, very slow-maturing vintage for red Bordeaux. I have had the incredibly good fortune to have tasted this wine on four occasions previously! The first three were magnums from the famed Scottish Glamis Castle collection. This magnum was also bottled in Scotland, by Cockburn. No label, good silver/gold capsule, and level well into neck. Surely there must be only five or six magnums of this left on the planet, if that. Capsule read: 1870 Claret-Lafite, Cockburn. The rest was illegible.

Similar appearance to the 1953(!), and lighter that the three Glamis Castle 1870 Lafites I tasted previously. Sweet, roses, classic Lafite, plus sealing-wax nose. Great depth, silky, elegant, still very much alive. Lovely, soft fruit. This is an incredible wine. Very slight, almost unnoticeable, bottle decay on nose. Perfection. (20) The amazing thing is that the 1870 left the great 1959 behind! It saddens me to think that this may be the last time in my life that I will taste this superb wine.

1864 CHÂTEAU LAFITE, IN MAGNUM:

Wax capsule, no label. Very good neck level. Purchased from Christie's, London, in the late 1970s. Darker colour than the 1870, but noticeably browner. Green salad, herbal nose, yet rich, with nice clean fruit. Good acidity. Not great, yet a very enjoyable wine. Not merely "sound" or "alive," but actually good. Overshadowed by the historic 1870. (17.5)

1975 CHÂTEAU D'YQUEM, IN MAGNUMS:

Bright, deep, brilliant-golden colour. Superb balance, botrytis. Has the good acidity of this fine vintage combined with the lovely, honeyed botrytis of this superb wine. Lively, caramelly fruit. Ready, but no rush. Fresher than the fine 1976. (19)

1920 OFFLEY'S VINTAGE PORT:

In honour of Barney Rhodes, who was born that year. Maybe the only disappointing wine of the evening, but let's put it into perspective. The others were great; this was merely good. Medium colour, good appearance. Cocoa aftertaste. More of a liqueur than a Port. Quite spirity. (16.5)

A memorable event. Congratulations to Dr. Haskell Norman for a great afternoon, and a word of gratitude to Dr. Barney Rhodes for making this event possible.

A fine ending to Diary #15.

February 19, 1996

Vertical tasting and dinner, featuring "50 Years of Château Calon-Ségur" 1916 to 1966, at "Star Anise" restaurant, in Vancouver.

That period was the golden age of this St. Estèphe property. Since the mid-1960s, Calon has produced rather underachieving wines—with the exception of the good 1975, 1982, and 1990. All the wines were from my cellar, and I organized this event. There were 16 participants. This tasting also featured a 200-year-old true Madeira (not a Solera).

APERITIF

Champagne Dom Pérignon 1982, in magnum:

Clean, fresh. Good backbone, tiny bubbles. Long on palate. Maybe without the weight of a great Krug or Bollinger, but very good. No rush from magnums. (17.5)

Hermitage "Chevalier de Sterimberg" 1959, Paul Jaboulet Aîné, in magnum:

Bright, palish-gold colour for such a mature white wine. At first, the nose was a bit dull. Quite dry, even lean. After 15 minutes in glass, it opened up a bit, with some fruit and hint of honey. Somehow, this wine lacked the ripeness and intensity, especially when coming from such a generous and ripe vintage. A bit dull. Has held well, though. (15)

FLIGHT #1

Château Calon-Ségur

1916:

(Recorked at the château in 1995. Purchased in London from Sotheby's last month.) Excellent level. Excellent appearance. Lovely, cedary nose. Round, complex, long. Lovely fruit. Roses, flowers, silky, elegant. Very long on palate. Beautiful colour. The best wine of the flight. Has held extremely well. (18.5)

1918:

(Recorked at the château in 1990. Excellent level. Purchased from the Chicago Wine Co.) Harder than the 1916. Leaner, yet very good fruit. After 20 minutes, the 1916 was better, the 1918 drying out. Classic St. Estèphe. Good. (17.5)

1934:

Oxidized. Cork fell into bottle. Earthy, sour, Madeira. Poor bottle. (0)

1952:

Deep, dark colour. Mature. A bit overripe, oxidizing nose. Tired, yet hard, tannic, solid. I wish this were a good bottle. Tasted better than it smelled. I have definitely tasted better examples of this wine. Nose (13) Palate (16)

FLIGHT #2

1948:

Bright red; good depth. Lovely, cedary, minty nose. Long, velvety, classic. Lovely, delicate fruit. Held well in glass. Clean, long finish. (18)

1943, in magnum:

Much deeper, darker than the 1948. Tight, earthy, cigar-box nose. Ripe, full, tannic, hard, solid, chunky. Not nearly as elegant or complex as the 1948. Earthier, yet backed by ripe fruit and solid tannins. Very good. Hint of mushrooms, wet earth. Long, full, solid. Very St. Estèphe. (17)

1966:

Lilacs, violets on nose. Medium colour, some depth. A bit herbaceous, vegetal. Leaner finish. Odd but nice. Drink up. (16)

1961:

Deeper, darker than the 1966. Cedary, ripe, sweet nose. Not concentrated enough. Some ripe fruit. Tannic, yet a bit acidic. Fine, but not great for a 1961. Short finish. (17)

1959, in magnum:

Slight oxidation on nose. A bit danky-dirty on palate, yet solid, ripe, tannic. Heavy, rich, sweet fruit. Seemed a bit heavyhanded. Good, but these last three wines are clearly not among the leaders in their respective vintages. The beginning of the decline of Calon-Ségur. (17)

I preferred the 1948 in this flight. Other tasters preferred the magnum of 1943.

FLIGHT #3

1949:

Very good neck level. Superb tobacco nose. Classic old-style St. Estèphe. Lovely fruit. Long, silky, superb fruit, rich. Ready. Needs drinking. In retrospect, it was a bit light for this flight. More depth, better fruit than the very good 1948, though. (18.5)

1947, London-bottled by Corney and Barrow:

Excellent level. Deep, youthful, bright colour. Silky, delicate, lovely fruit. Superb, lovely fruit, elegant. Perfect balance. A great "Palmer" from St. Estèphe. Layers of complexity. The only nonchâteau-bottled wine of the tasting. This wine definitely deserves its fine reputation. (19)

1945, in magnum:

Superb level and appearance. Excellent, deep colour to rim. Darkest of the 1940s. Will go on for years. Massive, ripe, sweet. Great extract. Super 1945. Great, tannic backbone. A masterpiece. All a great 1945 should be. Layers of fruit. (20)

1928:

Very deep, bright, red colour. Classic. Great tannic extract, typical 1928. A "more mature 1945." Very slight oxidation. This is one of the truly great 1928s. (18.5)

Flight #3 was by far the best. These are great wines—by any standard. This tasting showed how great Calon-Ségur can be. What a pity that the present owners are not as dedicated to quality as they should be.

The finale was a classic 200-year-old Madeira.

TERRANTEZ 1795, BARBEITO:

Shipped from Funchal last fall. Originally purchased by them in cask in 1972, and bottled in 1991—after spending 196 years in cask! The structure and sweetness level of a Bual (mid-range between a very sweet Malvasia and a drier Verdelho). Bright, deep golden-amber colour. Lovely, nutty, maple-syrup nose. Great extract, length, acidity, and fruit. Full of life. Will last forever. Tangy, austere. Fabulous, spicy bouquet. A historic wine. (19)

It took me about a decade to collect all these wines; a lot of work went into organizing this event—and it was well worth it.

March 27, 1996

Le Tastevin tasting, featuring a vertical of Robert Mondavi Napa Valley Cabernet Sauvignon "Reserve" 1974 to 1990.

APERITIF

GEWÜRZTRAMINER "CUVÉE DES FOLASTRIES" 1992, JOSMEYER, ALSACE:

Classy, lychees, spicy nose. Long, full, rich, well balanced. Packed with fresh, clean fruit. Very good.

Robert Mondavi Vertical tasting of Cabernet Sauvignon "Reserve"

1990:

Deep, purplish colour to rim. Still fresh, ripe fruit. Toasty-oak. Not a very big wine, but still youthful. Needs three to five more years. Not as big as one would expect, though. (17.5)

1989:

Similar depth to the 1990, but a little more evolved at rim. Cleaner fruit on nose (rather than toast/mint). Softer than the 1990. Sweeter fruit, more evolved. Softer tannins. Drink from 1998 to 2003. (16.5)

1988:

Bright-red colour; good depth, yet more evolved than the 1989. Hint of leather, rubber, lilacs. Drier than the 1989 or 1990. Sharper, more aggressive tannins; less fruit and a bit short at finish. A bit spirity, too. (15.5)

1987:

Lovely, deep, brilliant colour to rim. Most impressive. Fruity, ripe nose of leather, mint, cherries. Full, rich, solid; excellent, ripe tannins. Most "complete" wine so far. Creamy, long; lovely balance. Drink from 1998 to 2005. Excellent. (18)

1986:

Bright, deep colour. Sweet, open Cabernet nose. Some mint. Soft, forward, elegant. As forward as the 1988 but riper, rounder fruit, and no aggressive acidity. (16)

1985:

Bright, red colour. Slightly evolved rim. Full, rich, round; ripe cherry fruit. Lovely balance. Ready, but no rush. Clean, cherry/Cabernet fruit. Elegant, long finish. My favourite of the flight. (18.5)

1980:

Good depth, evolved orange rim. Tight nose, hint of rubber. Jam, molasses. Hint of eucalyptus on palate. Soft fruit, but aggressive tannins. Drink now, before the fruit disappears and one is left with dry tannins. A bit hollow and sharp at end. Better on entry than at finish. (15.5)

1979:

Evolved colour. Orange rim. Mint, rubbery nose; some eucalyptus, too. Full, rich, round, well put together. Ripe fruit, some tannins. Very good. Well balanced, long, clean. Ready, but no rush. (17)

1974:

Evolved colour, less depth than the 1979. Superb, minty-eucalyptus, evolved nose. Classic California Cabernet. Very long, very intense. Ready of course, yet enough depth to last. Smooth, minty, long, complex. Lovely. (18.5)

Overall impressions

The 1987, 1985, and 1974 excellent. The 1988, 1986, and 1980 a bit disappointing. The 1979 very much like 1979 Clarets. A pleasure to drink now.

DESSERT WINE

CHÂTEAU LAFAURIE-PEYRAGUEY 1983, IN HALF-BOTTLE:

A great vintage and a comeback for Lafaurie after two decades of unimpressive performance. Bright gold. Complex botrytis, ripe fruit on nose and palate. Long, full; excellent balance. No rush. Drink from 1998 to 2010.

April 28, 1996

Stopover in London for a couple of days, on the way back to Vancouver.

Lunch with Harry Waugh (who is now 92!), at his club—"Boodles," on St. James Street. I had excellent steak and kidney pie and a glass of this wine.

VOSNE-ROMANÉE 1990:

(One of their house wines. Shipper unknown.) The fruit and depth of this fine vintage, but slight acidity at finish.

Harry repeated to me the story of his dinner (at Chequers) with Churchill and Sir Bernard Baruch. Harry was stationed then at the Wellington Barracks with the Welsh guards.

That same night, I met Serena Sutcliffe and her husband David Peppercorn, at their home for a glass of Fino Sherry.

Then we went to a restaurant on Regent Street, called "L'Odéon." Serena and David were in Israel to judge wines for the "Jerusalem 3000" celebrations. They liked the Castel wines very much; small production, non-Kosher.

At "L'Odéon," we tasted these two wines.

VOUVRAY "CLOS DE BOURG" 1992, A. HUET:

Excellent balance, dry, orange blossoms, long. Not as tight as other young Vouvrays. Lovely fruit, good length. (Huet's older Vouvrays, notably the 1921, 1945, and 1947, are extraordinary.)

LES COLLINES DE LAURE 1994, JEAN-LUC COLOMBA, RHODANIENNES:

Located near Cornas. It is a Vin de Pays made from a blend of Syrah, Carignan, and Grenache. Full, youthful, deep purple-red colour. Lovely fruit extract. Not very tannic or big, but good balance.

Serena and David are a very nice couple. We discussed the possibility of my selling some wine in Los Angeles at Sotheby's. David is very interested in international politics, especially of World War II, a subject I am quite interested in myself and with which I am familiar. This was also my major at university.

May 7, 1996

Le Tastevin tasting, featuring the 1988 red Burgundy vintage. This was the last tasting held by Le Tastevin.

On June 10, we will have a farewell Tastevin dinner, after being in existence for 20 years. I have decided to step down and disband the club. Our council was unanimous in its advice to fold the club; they argued that it was my creation and no one could be found to replace me, and do an efficient job. We will divide the remaining wines in our cellar among our 80 members.

During Le Tastevin's 20 years, I have planned, organized, acquired the wines for, and conducted most of the 120 tastings (six tastings yearly). We covered every subject, country, region, and important vintage—from verticals of Vega Sicilia, Tokai, Sassicaia, single vineyards, Côte Rôtie (Guigal), Grange Hermitage, Château Musar—to Ports, Champagne Burgundy, Bordeaux, (every good vintage since 1961), California Cabernets, Germany, Alsace, etc.

APERITIF

CHÂTEAU LA LOUVIÈRE 1988, GRAVES BLANC:

Elegant structure of the 1982s. Nice oak, vanilla, and fruit. Well balanced, honeyed, subdued, spicy Sauvignon Blanc. Well made.

1988 Côte de Beaune

1. SAVIGNY-VERGELESSES "BATAILLÈRE," A. MOROT:

Nice red colour; palish rim. Fruity, subdued nose. Solid, rich, good fruit. Ready but no rush. Straightforward. Nose a bit tight. A bit austere. Rustic. One-dimensional. (15.5)

2. VOLNAY PREMIER CRU "CAILLERETS," DOMAINE DE LA POUSSE D'OR:

Similar appearance to #1. More cherry-red colour. Lovely, fruity nose. Sweet fruit. Elegant, ripe, rich, long. Lovely flavour. Well balanced. Very good. (17)

3. BEAUNE PREMIER CRU "CLOS DES MOUCHES," JOSEPH DROUHIN:

Brighter, deeper colour than #1 or #2. Younger-looking. Full, rich, a bit tannic. Lovely fruit. Very youthful, fresh; trace of acidity. Livelier than #1 or #2, yet #2 has better depth. Typical, fresh, spicy-cherries Drouhin style. Ready. (17)

4. BEAUNE PREMIER CRU "TEURONS," A. MOROT:

Very good, deep colour. Denser than #1 to #3. Full, solid, powerful. Rich, tannic. No rush. Backed by very good fruit, but tannins still a bit aggressive. Needs time. May rate higher, in due course. (16.5)

5. POMMARD PREMIER CRU "JAROLLIÈRES," DOMAINE DE LA POUSSE D'OR:

Good, dark colour. More evolved than #4. Lovely, spicy Pinot Noir nose. Loads of ripe fruit, yet tannic backbone. As austere as #4, but more complex and multidimensional. Drink from 1998. (18)

6. CORTON GRAND CRU, MOILLARD:

Clearly deepest, darkest of flight. Gamey, ripe-fruit nose. Very solid, very big; massive fruit, powerful tannins. Great extract, but doesn't have the complexity of #5. Needs time. (17.5)

1988 Côte de Nuits

7. CHAMBOLLE-MUSIGNY, YVES CHALEY:

Bright red. Fresh fruit on nose. Full of fruit, flavour, length. Ready. Less tannic than the wines of the first flight. (16.5)

8. CHAMBOLLE-MUSIGNY "ORVEAUX," FAIVELEY:

More evolved colour than #7. More smoky, oaky. Elegant fruit. Long, classic, complex, velvety. Ready. A bit dry at finish. (17)

9. GEVREY-CHAMBERTIN, A. ROUSSEAU:

Deeper than #7 or #8. Palish rim. Smoky, toasty Pinot Noir nose. Full, sweet, tight, solid. Needs time. Very good fruit extract. (17)

10. CLOS DE LA ROCHE GRAND CRU, JOSEPH DROUHIN:

Deeper than #7 to #9. Palish rim. Lighter than #6. Smoky, toasty; new oak. Very complex, long. No aggressive tannins. Lovely fruit. Grand Cru quality. (18.5)

11. ECHÉZEAUX GRAND CRU, MOILLARD:

Deep colour. Very sweet, very rich. Not very complex. Lots of extract. Needs time. Chunky style of Moillard. (17.5)

12. CHARMES-CHAMBERTIN GRAND CRU, MOILLARD:

Deepest colour of both flights. Very dark to rim. Full, very ripe, tannic fruit. Loads of extract. A very big wine. Needs five to seven years. (18)

Overall impressions of the vintage

More tannic, bigger, harder wines than the elegant 1985s, and the intense, fruity 1990s. The backbone similar to 1976 or 1983, yet more fruit than 1976, and no rot—a problem with so many 1983s. A vintage for keeping. Solid wines. Most are well made.

May 11, 1996

FA Cup Final.

Liverpool 0, Manchester United 1. Eric Cantona scored in the 85th minute. Manchester United is my favourite soccer team.

May 14, 1996

Commanderie de Bordeaux Dinner, featuring 1989 red Bordeaux, at the "Five Sails" restaurant, Pan Pacific hotel.

I was the speaker at this event.

CHAMPAGNE DEUTZ "CUVÉE WILLIAM DEUTZ" 1985:

Soft, delicate, spicy; nice fruit, good mousse. Ready, well made. Has the elegance and balance of this fine vintage.

FLIGHT #1

Pomerols and St. Emilions

1. CHÂTEAU LA DOMINIQUE 1989:

Good depth, palish rim. Delicate, fruity, subdued nose. Ripe, sweet, intense fruit. A bit stemmy. Powerful. Fairly alcoholic. Drink around 1998 to 2002. (17)

2. CHÂTEAU L'ARROSÉE 1989:

Good depth, palish rim; still some purple. Stemmy, spicy, ripe Cabernet nose. Tannic, sweet. Very good depth. Very Cabernet wine. Austere; almost Haut-Médoc-like. Try around 1998 to 2002. (16.5)

3. CHÂTEAU MAGDELAINE 1989:

Dense, deep colour. Spicy, sweet Merlot nose. Open, spicy, sweet, buttery, oaky. Soft yet intense. Very Merlot; over 90% Merlot. Drink in 1999 to 2005. (17.5)

4. CHÂTEAU TROTANOY 1989:

Deep red colour. Subdued, toasty, oaky nose. Full, tannic, big, round. Very ripe fruit. Perfect balance. Almost 100% Merlot. Excellent, deep, full, generous wine. Needs five to seven years. (18.5)

FLIGHT #2

1. CHÂTEAU CANTEMERLE 1989:

Deep colour to rim. Spicy, clean, fruity Cabernet nose. Vanilla. Very good fruit, depth. Ripe. A bit rustic. Very good potential. (17)

2. CHÂTEAU MONBRISSON 1989:

Buttery, oaky nose. Good depth. Harder, more tannic than #1. Good fruit extract. A bit hard, edgy finish. Surprisingly hard, yet backed by good fruit. (16)

3. CHÂTEAU TALBOT 1989:

Deep purplish colour to rim. Austere, tight nose. Full, solid, tannic. Good extract. Very powerful; loads of ripe fruit. Needs time. Very ripe. (17)

4. CHÂTEAU LA LAGUNE 1989:

New oak, vanilla nose. Round, elegant, yet good sweet fruit and depth. Obvious new oak. Lovely now, but will hold. Not as deep as the Talbot, more evolved. (17)

5. CHÂTEAU CALON-SÉGUR 1989:

Good, deep, red colour. Subdued, tight nose. Hard, tannic, sweet, yet lacks depth. Fairly alcoholic. Off balance. Best part is bouquet. Tobacco, toast. St. Estèphe style. (15.5)

FLIGHT #3

1. CHÂTEAU PALMER 1989:

Good depth. Subdued cedar nose. Vanilla. Elegant, round. Very good acidity/fruit balance. Not a big wine, yet fairly high alcohol and ripe, chocolaty fruit.

Superb complexity, yet surprisingly forward. Very long. Classic Margaux. (18.5)

2. CHÂTEAU LEOVILLE-BARTON 1989:

Deeper colour than the Palmer. Subdued, delicate, yet closed nose. Full, luscious. Very ripe, rich tannins. Great balance. Lots of extract. Depth. (18)

3. CHÂTEAU PICHON-LONGUEVILLE-BARON 1989:

Deepest, densest wine of the whole tasting. Tight, closed nose. Some rubber. Massive, tannic, full, rich. Loads of very ripe fruit. Great potential. Needs many years. Try around 2003 or beyond. (19) Finally, this property is back on track.

4. CHÂTEAU MONTROSE 1989:

Deep, yet not as dark as #3. Subdued nose. Tannic, austere; not as fat as #2 or #3, but more austere. Classic St. Estèphe. Needs many years. Doesn't have the fruit intensity of #2 or #3 at this stage, or the elegance of #4. (17.5)

Overall impression of the vintage

Very good, ripe, well-balanced wines. Some are much bigger than others. Others, surprisingly forward. This vintage seems to have produced looser-knit, more forward wines than the concentrated, ripe 1990s. Overproduction?

May 22, 1996

Dinner at "Umberto's" restaurant, with guest winemaker Angelo Gaja, featuring Gaja's Wines.

1. SAUVIGNON BLANC 1994 "ALTENI DE BRASSICA":

Pale gold. Fresh, vegetal, oak-vanilla nose. Vineyard planted in 1982; first released vintage was 1986. Buttery nose. Good acidity, fairly alcoholic; aggressive tannins and oak. Will be very good, but needs three to four extra years of bottle-age. (16.5)

2. CHARDONNAY 1994 "GAIA & REY":

This vineyard was planted in 1979; "Gaia" is the name of his daughter and "Rey" is Angelo's grandmother's family name. Bright gold. Subdued, elegant, vanilla-oak, Chardonnay, buttery nose. Full, rich, luscious. Very Bâtard-Montrachet-like. Lots of extract, depth, and sweet fruit. Very ripe; almost slight residual sugar. Impeccably clean. Very long. Impressive. (18.5)

3. BRUNELLO DI MONTALCINO 1990 "SUGARILLE":

Medium red, good depth. Almost Claret-like appearance, nose, and palate. Like a 1988 Claret. Classy Sangiovese straw nose. Fairly acidic, a "keeping" factor for Tuscan wines. Long, spicy, well balanced. 100% Sangiovese. Gaja likes to work with a single varietal. He purchased this property recently. (17)

4. BAROLO 1989 "SPRESS":

"Spress" means nostalgia. Much deeper than #3. Purplish rim. Tar and concentrated fresh ripe berries on nose. Full, intense. Loads of ripe fruit, tannins, oak. Good acidity. Very long. Not massive, but lots of depth. Needs five to seven years. Very good. His first Barolo. Since 1962, Gaja and his father looked for a fine Barolo vineyard; they finally found this one in 1988. (17.5)

5. BAROLO 1970 "GROMIS":

Browning, very evolved colour. Leathery. Quite oxidized, losing its grip. Acidic, sharp. Past its best. Disappointing. Gaja did not make the wine. They bought the property and stock in January 1995. (13)

We tasted none of his Barbarescos tonight, yet this is their "Fame and Glory" wine! Most wines are very good to excellent. The Chardonnay is outstanding.

May 23 to 27, 1996

Short weekend trip to Yountville.

VOSNE-ROMANÉE PREMIER CRU "LES SUCHOTS" 1990, MANIÈRE-NOIROT, IN HALF-BOTTLE:

Still youthful colour. Clean, impeccable Pinot Noir and ripe cherries on nose. Round, full, long. Drinking well now in half-bottles, but no rush.

1990 HEITZ CELLARS "MARTHA'S VINEYARD" NAPA CABERNET SAUVIGNON:

(At "Piatti" restaurant, in Sonoma) Deep, youthful colour to rim. Hint of eucalyptus; vanilla, oak, ripe Cabernet nose. Fabulous on palate. Still too young of course, but excellent depth, balance. Creamy, rich, fruit. Great balance. Very long. Full, intense, yet approachable even now. A lovely wine that has a great future.

May 31, 1996

1991 PINOT NOIR, OREGON, DOMAINE DROUHIN:

Classic, fruity Pinot Noir nose. Good depth, colour. Spicy Pinot Noir nose. Full, round. Like a fine Volnay from a good vintage. Fine effort. Good fruit and balance.

June 1, 1996

"Group of Eight" dinner, at the Tobes'.

One couple of the "Group of Ten" has separated, and both individuals withdrew from our group. Thus we are only "eight little Indians" now.

CHAMPAGNE BOLLINGER "RD" 1982:

Very elegant. Lovely bouquet. Complex, yeasty, rich, long. Tiny bubbles. Great length. Exquisite. Very fine.

1985 AND 1986 PULIGNY-MONTRACHET "LES COMBETTES" PREMIER CRU, ETIENNE SAUZET:

The 1985 leaner, lighter, higher alcohol, fresher. The 1986 a bit fatter; hint of botrytis. Both surprisingly youthful. Lovely fruit; very elegant, yet certainly lots of depth underneath. Both great. I preferred the freshness of the 1985.

The 1986 has a more developed nose. Classic, stylish Puligny Gerard Boudot of Domaine Sauzet produces fine Pulignys.

1953 CHÂTEAU GRUAUD-LAROSE, IN MAGNUM:

(Our group wine, which I purchased from the Chicago Wine Co. two years ago) Excellent neck level and appearance. Decanted. Fair bit of sediment. Excellent cork/appearance. Maybe recorked at the château. Very delicate, soft, silky. Beautiful, delicate, long nose. Nice, sweet fruit. Very good colour. Bright red, palish rim. Classic, silky, typical 1953. Quite a bit of breeding for a Gruaud-Larose. Lovely, complex, cedar, cigar-box. Sweet, delicate finish. Very clean. Needs drinking.

1966 CHÂTEAU LATOUR:

Served double-blind by our host. Very Latour and very 1966. At first, both Sid Cross and I thought that it was a 1961 Montrose. Very deep colour. Very Cabernet nose. Spicy, rich, tannic, hard. Dry 1966 style, yet so much intensity behind that it will last for a long time. Slightly dusty nose. Very serious, solid wine. No rush.

TAYLOR'S VINTAGE PORT 1963:

I guessed this one right on—both property and vintage. Unfortunately, this Port was decanted only one hour before tasting, so it was quite spirity. Lovely, expansive, ripe nose. Very obvious style of Taylor's or Dow's (leaner, more masculine), rather than the richer, thicker Graham's style. Lots of class on both nose and palate. Very long, very serious, very complex. Amazing that at 33 years of age, this Port is not quite ready yet.

All the wines tasted tonight were of the very best quality.

Monday, June 10, 1996

Farewell event of Le Tastevin Wine Club, after 20 years in existence. Tasting and dinner, at the Pan Pacific hotel.

We accommodated everyone who wished to attend: 80 participants in all, out of a membership of 88. My children, Michael and Orly, attended this event, too. The host table had several different wines because of the limited quantities and the large number of participants. The tasting and dinner featured 1982 red Bordeaux—a great vintage to end a 20-year experience.

APERITIF

CHAMPAGNE VEUVE CLICQUOT BRUT N/V, IN BOTH JEROBOAM AND MAGNUMS:

The jeroboam was more evolved, more mature, toasty, rich. The magnums were fresher, livelier. Both very good.

CHÂTEAU LA TOUR-MARTILLAC, GRAVES BLANC 1990:

Pale green-gold colour. Toasty-oak. Vanilla, herbaceous Sauvignon Blanc. Medium-bodied, clean, round. Very good.

MEURSAULT-GENEVRIÈRES PREMIER CRU 1989, LOUIS LATOUR:

Very good for both a Meursault and a 1989. Nutty, clean oak, buttery Chardonnay on both nose and palate. Medium-bodied, quite long, complex, round, soft, yet with good fruit and acidity to last.

1982 RED BORDEAUX

FLIGHT #1

1. CHÂTEAU BATAILLEY 1982:

Medium, red colour, good depth. Evolved, clean, spicy Cabernet nose. Slight sharpness at finish. Clean, elegant, ready, but no rush. Cedar, oak. Nice fruit. (15.5)

2. CHÂTEAU MALARTIC-LAGRAVIÈRE 1982, GRAVES:

A good, enjoyable wine, but little 1982 character. The most evolved colour of all the red wines. Mature, medium-light red. Open, spicy, earthy, clean, ripe nose. Slightly sharp (acidic), open, flowery, soft. At its peak. (14.5)

3. CHÂTEAU CHASSE-SPLEEN 1982, MOULIS:

Deep, youthful colour to rim. Tight nose of fruity, ripe black fruit. Spicy, fruity, ripe; good depth. Still a bit tannic. Doesn't have the complexity of #1 or #2, but much more backward. Very good Cru Bourgeois. (16.5)

4. CHÂTEAU SOUTARD 1982, ST. EMILION:

Even deeper than #3. Full, tannic; unusually big and hefty for a St. Emilion, yet the spicy, herbaceous character of Cabernet Franc. Tannic, solid, chunky. Needs time, but somewhat one-dimensional. (15.5)

FLIGHT #2

5. CHÂTEAU BRANAIRE-DUCRU 1982:

The most straightforward, least complex of this flight. Deep colour to rim. Full, ripe, fairly evolved, spicy Cabernet. Well structured. Ready but no rush. (16.5)

6. CHÂTEAU LA LAGUNE 1982:

Very good, deep colour; even purplish. Clean, spicy, ripe Cabernet, earthy nose. Hint of oak. Fresh, youthful, rich, full-bodied. Very good depth. No rush; actually needs three to five more years. (17.5)

7. CHÂTEAU CALON-SÉGUR 1982:

Medium, deep colour. Very good, ripe fruit. Tannic, yet softer than expected. More evolved, too. Classy, complex, spicy Cabernet. Ripe fruit. Very good 1982. Long. OK to drink now, but no rush. Class here. (17.5)

8. CHÂTEAU LEOVILLE-POYFERRÉ 1982:

Deep colour. Ripe Cabernet; very good ripe fruit extract. More backward than the Calon. Full, still a bit tannic. Very good extract. Serious. Lots of ripe St. Julien fruit. No rush. (17.5)

Host Table, 1982s

CHÂTEAU LYNCH-BAGES 1982:

Deep (as above), yet dry, hard, tannic. Very good, impressive colour. Needs time. Closed, tight, solid. Reserve judgement. (17) This score reflects the way this wine tasted tonight. Can be much finer.

CHÂTEAU MONTROSE 1982:

Better than the "experts" say. Very St. Estèphe, very 1982. Solid, deep, full. Lots of extract, yet lovely ripe fruit. Long, spicy, oaky Cabernet. No rush; actually needs time. (17.5)

CHÂTEAU LEOVILLE-POYFERRÉ 1982:

We had our own bottle and it was not only better than the two above, but even more impressive than the other Leoville-Poyferré. (See comment above.) Bags of fruit. Full, rich, long. Great extract, fruit, depth. Needs time. Impressive. (18)

FLIGHT #3

CHÂTEAU FIGEAC 1982:

Typical Figeac, typical 1982. Herbaceous, spicy, oaky on nose and palate. Expansive, open, almost ready. Very classy, unmistakable St. Emilion. Spicy, very long. Round, clean. Very good, deep colour. Ready, but no rush. Clean vanilla-oak. Lovely. (18.5)

CHÂTEAU PALMER 1982:

This wine is not liked by the experts; they prefer the 1983. Maybe so, but this 1982 was excellent. Very soft, evolved, classic Margaux, perfumy, chocolaty, cedary nose. Most classy wine of the whole flight. Deep, yet round, soft, silky. Ready but will hold. A lovely bottle. (18)

Then we had the last red wine of the evening, served all by itself.

CHÂTEAU MOUTON-ROTHSCHILD 1982:

As expected, a shining star! By far the deepest, darkest, most intense wine. Fabulous, clean, ripe berries on nose; also cedar, oak. Very long, very full. Perfect balance. Great extract, intensity. Impeccably clean and well balanced. Needs ten more years to reach its peak. Tannic backbone, but all in perfect harmony. A great finale for a 20-year experience. (19.5)

DESSERT WINE

MOSCATEL DE SETÚBAL, 25 YEARS OLD, J. M. DE FONSECA:

(Group tables) I purchased this wine ten years ago, so it is at least 35 to 40 years old now. Amber Madeira, aged colour. Subdued, caramel, spicy Muscat nose. Medium-bodied, round. A bit "old" on palate, but good, acidic, fruity backbone.

After many accolades and expressions of gratitude, the club—through its council—gave me a lovely silver Champagne platter, in which were etched the words: "To Albert Givton, Le Tastevin Wine Club, 1976 to 1996, with gratitude."

A nice finale to a great and satisfying experience. I have enjoyed creating this club, educating so many people about wine, and I'm also content that it is over. Time to try new adventures in life. Farewell "Le Tastevin"!

Sunday, June 16, 1996

Father's Day Dinner, at the Spurrells'.

All wines served double-blind.

1979 Diamond Hill Cabernet Sauvignons "Graveley Meadow," "Red Rock Terrace," and "Volcanic Hill," Napa Valley

These were three of the greatest California Cabernet Sauvignons I have tasted in recent years. True classics. All three had incredibly deep, youthful colours. "Graveley Meadow" was lightest, most evolved, yet still very deep. "Volcanic Hill" was black. I thought that all three were either 1986 Montrose, Cos d'Estournel, Calon-Ségur, or even Latour (or at one point, Mouton 1986!). Classic, cedary Pauillac style: big Cabernets, very tannic; powerful; excellent acidity/fruit balance. No other California Cabernet that I've tasted is so Pauillac-like in its balance, nose, flavour, or structure.

"GRAVELEY MEADOW":

Most evolved, sweet fruit, good depth, some tannins to close. Complex, spicy Cabernet. Great length. Essence of Cabernet.

"RED ROCK TERRACE":

Deeper, sweeter fruit; roundest of all three, yet great tannic and ripe-berries extract. Lovely, deep, cedary, powerful. Not unlike Mouton 1986.

"VOLCANIC HILL":

Deepest, darkest, most backward. Exotic fruit, essence of Cabernet. Full, tannic, very ripe. I even thought at one point that they were 1986 Lafite, Mouton, and

Latour (in that order!). I was really fooled this time, but these are not California Cabernets in the classic sense. They are an accident of nature. And 1979s to boot! 18 years old. Lots of sediment. Massive, great Cabernets. Rated all three (18.5).

1975 CHÂTEAU D'YQUEM, IN HALF-BOTTLE:

Bright, deep, gold colour. Exotic, yet tight, buttery, oaky, botrytis nose. Excellent, youthful acidity. Very long, very lovely. No rush.

June 17 to 23, 1996

Trip to Yountville.

Talking to Belle Rhodes over the phone, I found out that Joe Heitz had had a stroke in late May. I spoke to Alice Heitz over the phone, and she told me that Joe had just arrived back home from the hospital. He is doing a lot better. The problem now is how to tell him to ease up on the wines and single malts he likes so much!

June 20, 1996

Visit to Duckhorn, with Margaret Duckhorn.

Fascinating barrel-sampling of various 1995s. She said that the 1994s are the best wines they made in the early 1990s.

We tried the following 1995s from the cask.

1995 MERLOT "HOWELL MOUNTAIN":

(100% Merlot) In Seguin-Moreau "Chêne Russe" (Russian oak). The softest, easiest to taste of the bunch. Sweet fruit. Fruity, evolved nose. Round, soft on palate. Very little oak character. Very soft. Even a beginner could like and identify this as being very soft, sweet Merlot.

SAME MERLOT, IN FRENCH SYLVAIN OAK:

Tannic, hard, dry, leaner, tight. Good fruit. Tobacco, some dill.

SAME MERLOT, IN FRENCH SANSAUD OAK:

Noticeably oakier, more aggressive tannins, tighter than above.

SAME MERLOT, IN FRENCH SEGUIN-MOREAU OAK:

Very French. Toasty, oaky, vanilla nose. Tight, closed. A bit more acidic than the above three.

SAME MERLOT, IN AMERICAN OAK:

Classic, sweet "red wood," vanilla, expansive nose. Round, sweet aftertaste.

All above are the same Merlot from the northern Napa Valley. Amazing how much oak casks change the character of the wine. All above will be blended, of course, and Cabernet Sauvignon and Cabernet Franc will be added to the blend.

1995 MERLOT "THREE PALMS VINEYARD":

100% Merlot in second-year Haut-Brion casks. Deeper, darker, more exotic and expansive than all above. No wonder this is their top-of-the-line Merlot. Full, very deep, great extract. Lots of depth.

1995 CABERNET SAUVIGNON:

From their own vineyard. Young, eight-year-old vines; planted in 1987. Will be used for blending. Herbaceous, medium-deep, spicy, tannic, fresh. Good acidity/fruit balance.

1995 MERLOT:

Margaret called it "Down Valley"—from the cooler Carneros district. Will be used for blending. More dill. Obviously cooler region. Deep colour. Crisp, fresh, spicy; good acidity, leaner style.

The winemaker told me that the Russian oak is difficult to get. It's grown near Chechnya, where there is presently a civil war. Cost is high to get the oak to France and source is uncertain. Seguin-Moreau had their special saws (shipped from France) stolen when they arrived in Russia. Cost is no cheaper than French oak, and Duckhorn may discontinue its use.

Then we went into another chais to taste several casks of "Howell Mountain" Cabernets and Merlots.

1995 "HOWELL MOUNTAIN" MERLOT:

Very hard, acidic, tannic, good fruit. The 1995 Cabernet Sauvignon "Howell Mountain" is similar, as is the Cabernet Franc.

Margaret said that they are holding these wines for an extra year before release, as people tend to drink them too young. This wine is very tight. Their problem is how to manage the aggressive tannins in the "Howell Mountain" wines. The "Three Palms," on the other hand, is safe to release as soon as it is bottled because connoisseurs will keep it longer. Not so with "Howell Mountain." That's why they release it later.

Last, we tasted this wine.

1994 "HOWELL MOUNTAIN" BLEND:

Harmonious, spicy berries, oak, tobacco nose. Tannic, tight on palate. Will be bottled shortly and released in 1997.

Nice educational visit.

Same day: Visit to Viader Vineyards, on Howell Mountain.

Met with Delia Viader. Delia is the mother of four. Born in Argentina, she has lived in Chile and all over Europe and Lebanon. Her father was a diplomat for the United Nations. She has a PhD in Philosophy from the Sorbonne and speaks fluent French.

She was married to Mr. Fouquet, who runs the Seguin-Moreau Tonellerie in Napa. Her father bought the land and she built a lovely home there and an 18-acre vineyard. (Steep, all the way to a lake at the bottom.) Planted in 60% Cabernet Sauvignon and 40% Cabernet Franc. No Merlot. All 2,500 cases produced in the first vintage—1989—are from her own vineyards. No second wine. "Meritage" style. Usual blend in wine is 50% Cabernet Sauvignon and 50% Cabernet Franc, as the Cabernet Franc produces more fruit.

Tasted the following wines.

1992 VIADER:

Very deep colour; slightly evolved rim. Tobacco. Full, very round, rich, long. Loads of ripe, sweet fruit. Well balanced. More forward.

1993 VIADER:

Even better, tighter, higher acidity, more "serious" than the 1992. Needs five to seven years. Excellent. Very concentrated.

They produced 2,000 cases of the 1992, and 2,500 cases of the 1993. Delia hopes to increase production to 4,000 to 5,000 cases by the late 1990s. Delia likes Cheval-Blanc, but says she doesn't want to produce that style. "Only Cheval can produce Cheval." I agree. Nice lady; well educated and gifted. She makes the wines herself.

June 29, 1996

Back in Vancouver, dinner at Ken and Barb Cross's home.

CHAMPAGNE BOLLINGER BRUT 1985, IN MAGNUM:

Fresh, yeasty. Lovely fruit, lively, long, complex. No rush. Excellent.

HERMITAGE BLANC 1983, J. L. CHAVE,

MUSIGNY BLANC 1983, DE VOGÜÉ,

AND

MEURSAULT-GENEVRIÈRES 1983 "CUVÉE BAUDOT," HOSPICES DE BEAUNE, REMOISSENET:

Three white wines served double-blind. After tasting the first wine, I thought that they were all Chave Hermitages! All three noticeably alcoholic. The Meursault was the darkest, but all three were bright gold. The Hermitage was exotic, spicy, rich. A bit candied nose. Ripe, fat.

The Musigny later became obvious Pinot Blanc style. Hard, solid, almost one-dimensional. Oaky, rich, and round. A bit spirity.

The Meursault was my favourite. Best balance, hint of sulphur. Good acidity/fruit balance. Sweet, complex, yet lacked the nutty Meursault/Chardonnay character. Odd wine and difficult tasting. Apparently, according to Hugh Johnson, the Musigny Blanc is 100% Chardonnay. Hard to believe, as it has little (if any) Chardonnay character.

1970 CHÂTEAU LAFON-ROCHET,

1970 CHÂTEAU COS D'ESTOURNEL,

AND

1970 CHÂTEAU MONTROSE, ALL ST. ESTÈPHES:

Three red wines served double-blind, too. All three were typical St. Estèphes, with that typical dry, tannic, masculine backbone. I thought that they were 1966s.

The Lafon-Rochet was the most evolved and had the lightest colour. Clean, tobacco, lean. Mature, evolved fruit. Better than expected, but ready. A bit herbaceous. Toasty.

I never liked the Cos 1970 d'Estournel. Similar to Margaux 1970 (both then under Ginestet). Lemony, citric, sharp. Nice tobacco, toasty nose. Lean, tannic, low fruit. Disappointing.

Montrose clearly—by far—the best, as expected. Deepest colour. Concentrated ripe fruit. Tannic, solid backbone. Excellent fruit extract. Very good. No rush.

STERLING CABERNET SAUVIGNON "RESERVE" 1974, NAPA VALLEY:

One of my favourite 1974 Napa Cabernets. Deep colour. Very California, sweet, cedary nose. Evolved, sweet fruit. Not as complex as the St. Estèphes, but sweeter, fruitier, more evolved. Very good.

CHÂTEAU GUIRAUD 1967, SAUTERNES:

Then under the ownership of P. Rival. Deep amber-gold colour. Subdued nose. Concentrated on palate. Extract, botrytis, good fruit/acidity balance. Has held extremely well.

July 3, 1996

Farewell Dinner for the council of Le Tastevin Wine Club, at Bruno Marti's "La Belle Auberge" restaurant, in Ladner.

Participants: Tony Gismondi, Dave Spurrell, Merv Isert, Jim Davidson, Marcena Croy, my secretary Dorothy McFee, and myself

CHAMPAGNE LOUIS ROEDERER "BRUT PREMIER" N/V:

Some age. Yeasty, toasty, clean nose. Round, fine mousse, long. Benefitted from three years of cellaring. Good fruit; spicy, clean. Well balanced.

CHASSAGNE-MONTRACHET PREMIER CRU "LES VERGERS" 1985, MME. FRANÇOIS COLIN:

Very 1985. Elegant. At ten years, fully mature. Good fruit. Hint of sulphur on nose; oak, toast, too. Nice fruit; elegant, subdued, well balanced. Ready. Good quality.

Gevrey-Chambertin Premier Cru 1990 "Clos du Fonteny" Monopole, Bruno Clair:

Very youthful, purplish-cherry, deep colour. Tight nose, yet ripe, clean berries, too. Full, great balance, depth, soft tannins. Needs three to four years of extra bottle-age. Spicy, rich fruit. Impeccably made. Great vintage.

1985 Dominus, Napa Valley (Napanook), John Daniel Society:

A favourite of mine, this 1985 has a perfect balance, is succulent, rich, round, full. Subdued, spicy Cabernet nose; slightly herbal. Perfect, round, long. Ready, yet lots of body and fruit extract. No rush. The best Dominus between 1983 and 1987, in my opinion.

Château Lynch-Bages 1983:

Ready, yet still a bit tannic. Minty, spicy character typical of Mouton or Lynch-Bages. Good, dark colour; not as deep as the Dominus 1985. Spicy nose. Full, round, long. Well balanced. Certainly one of the better 1983s. An underrated vintage. Drink now to 2005.

Château St. Jean "Select Late Harvest" Johannisberg Riesling 1978 "Belle Terre Vineyard," Alexander Valley, Sonoma Valley:

(10.8° residual sugar) In full 750 mL bottles. Classic BA style. Deep gold-amber colour. Apricots and spices on nose and palate. Very good acidity. Long, sweet, yet not cloying. Has held very well, thanks to full-bottle size. Petroleum-Riesling character. A fine wine.

Thus comes to an official and final end the era of Le Tastevin Wine Club. The food was excellent, too, as we've grown to expect from this gifted chef/owner, Swiss-born Bruno Marti.

July 16 to 21, 1996

Trip to Yountville, with my son Michael Dinner at Paul and Sara Pinski's.

Also attending: the Crosses, Steve and Babette, who are Paul's son and daughter-in-law, Dr. and Mrs. Eugene (Debbie) Wong from Honolulu.

Champagne Krug Vintage 1982:

We tried three bottles of this—all great— with fine Oceitra caviar and blinis. First bottle was best. Classic round, ripe 1982; long, full, great. The second bottle was a bit fresher, but earthier, too. Third bottle a combination of #1 and #2. All three were excellent, with that great balance and extract typical of Krug.

Bâtard-Montrachet 1985, Leflaive:

Three bottles; all three superb, with the racey elegance of the 1985s, yet the fruity extract and backbone of great Bâtard. At ten years of age, no rush drinking this. As the wine warmed up in the glass, hints of apricots, peaches, lovely exotic fruit came through. Good acidity/fruit balance. Lovely.

1971 Clos de la Roche, Leroy:

Two bottles. These two reds were a letdown. Both had good fills. One bottle was a bit musty, volatile, sharp, with some toasty oak. The second bottle was cleaner with good, deep colour, quite a bit of burnt toast; dry, lacking classic fruit extract. Even the better of the two bottles was a bit sharp—too dry. These wines cost a fortune, and they should taste better than this. Paul himself was disappointed.

I'm developing quite a head cold, but even so, I could identify the disappointing quality of this wine. That night, I slept very poorly. The following day (Saturday, July 20), I decided to go home and to forfeit my participation in the IW&FS dinner and the 81st birthday celebrations for Haskell Norman tomorrow. I just can't smell or taste a thing!

August 12, 1996

At "Cascabel" restaurant, in Vancouver, with Val Wilson, my editor for this book.

Château Trotanoy 1983:

At first, a bit metallic, astringent. Later, opened up nicely. Evolved colour. Spicy, expansive nose. Soft, round; good depth and fruit. Doesn't have the extract and class of the 1982 or 1989, but quite good. Ready.

September 19, 1996

Confrérie des Chevaliers du Tastevin Dinner, featuring the recently arrived 1993 Vintage red Burgundies, at "Cascabel" restaurant, in Vancouver.

Côte de Nuits 1993s

1. Vosne-Romanée 1993, Daniel Rion:

Young, cherry-red colour. Slightly pale rim. Clean, vanilla, subdued fruit on nose. Fairly acidic on entry. Light-bodied. Some sharpness at finish. Elegant, complex, Vosne style. (15.5)

2. Nuits-St.-Georges "Roncières" Premier Cru 1993, R. Chevillon:

Medium cherry-red. Good depth. Watery rim. Straw-oak nose. Light-bodied, fairly high acidity, low fruit. Less dry than #1, but less backbone. Later, developed some spicy complexity. (15.5)

3. Gevrey-Chambertin "En Pallud" 1993, Maume:

Deepest of flight. Deep purple colour to rim. Closed nose. Ripe fruit, but not much complexity at this stage. Solid, sturdy, full, powerful. Tight, aggressive tannins, unyielding. Rustic, masculine wine. (15)

4. CHAMBOLLE-MUSIGNY 1993, J. F. MUGNIER:

Good depth, slightly palish rim. Unyielding nose. Dull. Fairly dry, yet some fruit underneath. Some acidity at finish. Solid, but finishes short. Nice fruit, though. (15)

5. NUITS-ST.-GEORGES "PORRETS ST. GEORGES" PREMIER CRU 1993, FAIVELEY:

Bright cherry-red colour; palish rim. Elegant, forthcoming on nose; cherries and ripe fruit. Light on entry, yet tannic. Good extract. Best balanced of flight. Long, spicy Pinot Noir finish. (16.5)

6. VOSNE-ROMANÉE 1993, RENÉ ANGEL:

Clearly palest of flight; medium to light red. Watery rim. Dull nose. Light, watery, short finish, yet tannic. Not enough depth or ripe fruit. Too lean. (14.5)

Later, with dinner, we had the following two wines.

1985 NUITS-ST.-GEORGES "AUX MURGERS," MÉO-CAMUZET:

This put the 1993s in perspective. Lovely, deep, cherry colour. As dark as #3, yet so much finer, as 1985s should be. Lovely, clean, cherry-fruit nose. Hint of oak. A bit of toast, too. Lovely aftertaste. Long, complex, round. So much better, more complete than the 1993s tasted above. (17.5)

Overall impressions on the 1993 red Burgundies

Obviously a cool, difficult vintage. With the exception of #5, the wines were relatively light, a bit too acidic/lean, yet clean and well made (under the circumstances). Not a vintage to cellar too long, or to pay too much for. Unfortunately, this is not the case, as these wines cost more than the much finer 1990 vintage.

October 14, 1996

Meeting at the Grand Conseil de Bordeaux in downtown Bordeaux, with the Grand Maître, Francis Fouquet, and the cellerier, Mr. Grillet.

I announced to Mr. Fouquet that during the summer of 1997, I would step down as Maître of the Commanderie de Bordeaux in Vancouver, and that Ian Mottershead would take over. We discussed wine, politics, liquor monopolies in Canada (and their hopeful demise), and special awards to restaurateurs who have assisted us in organizing our various tastings and dinners.

The Grand Maître also awarded me—at a small ceremony—a Grand Conseil de Bordeaux medallion, with gold background, confirming my title of Conseiller du Vin de Bordeaux and Chevalier. We later went for lunch to the restaurant "Chez Lasserre, La Chamade," where we had a very good lunch, with the following wines.

CLOS FLORIDÈRE 1993, BLANC GRAVES:

Produced by Debourdieux in a new technical method; 100% new oak, 50% Sauvignon Blanc, and 50% Semillon. Clean, impeccable wine. Smells of herbaceous Sauvignon Blanc and new oak, with taste of round, soft, rich Semillon. We all agreed that while impeccably made, this wine lacked the "terroir" character. A "Parker" wine.

CHÂTEAU BÂLESTARD-LA-TONNELLE 1989:

As usual for this property: rich, solid, full, not quite ready. Very good fruit. A relatively big St. Emilion.

Mr. Grillet admitted that young French people, even the children of winemakers, lack the experience of tasting older wines. They therefore don't understand them and find them too hard and harsh. He also agreed that wines are standardized too much these days, and that many lose their individual "terroir" character.

Dinner at the home of Bruno and France Prats, in Bordeaux.

Also present were his son Jean-Guillaume and his wife, and other friends, including Mrs. Hughes Lawton (who came without her husband), Mr. and Mrs. de Beaumel, a serious wine collector from Zurich. We had an interesting and lively evening, during which a couple of guests (a surgeon and his wife) were informed by phone that their daughter-in-law had just given birth to a (third) girl.

CHAMPAGNE TAITTINGER "COMTES DE CHAMPAGNE" 1988:

As this wine was a Blanc de Blancs, I found it unusually hard and tight. Maybe it needs more time. Good fruit and structure underneath, though. The 1988s are tight, slow maturing Champagnes. Potentially, they are very promising.

CORTON-CHARLEMAGNE 1990, LOUIS JADOT:

Jadot's Corton-Charlemagne is one of my favourites, and this fine 1990 did not disappoint. Nutty, toasty Charlemagne character, yet so much body and intensity. Could use an extra two to four years of bottle-age. Fabulous length, great extract and balance. Lovely wine.

CHÂTEAU COS D'ESTOURNEL 1975:

In the past, I found Cos 1975 too lean and too dry. This was much better. Not quite ready (at 21 years!), yet very good extract and fruit. Shedding its aggressive tannins. Impressive dark colour. Good Cabernet extract. No rush. Very good.

COS D'ESTOURNEL 1955, NICOLAS:

Bruno told me that the Nicolas-bottling is better than the château-bottling in 1955. At 41 years of age, this wine is impressive. Good, dark, evolved colour at rim. Open, cedary, ripe, fruity nose. The elegance on palate of the 1955s, yet the backbone of a St. Estèphe. Round, cedary, complex; backed by good fruit. Perfect now. Slightly musty nose. Cleared after 20 minutes in glass.

1977 GRAHAM'S VINTAGE PORT:

Still a bit young, but classic, sweet; great extract, Graham's style. Needs another five to ten years.

Bruno compares the 1996 Clarets to the 1986s, and the 1995s to the 1985s in Bordeaux. He said that 1996 was a Médoc year. Merlots are a bit weak, but very ripe, concentrated Cabernets. In short, a vintage for Haut-Médocs rather than St. Emilions and Pomerols (Right Bank).

Tuesday, October 15, 1996

Morning visit to Château Margaux, with Corinne Mentzelopoulos.

We discussed in detail the possibility of her visiting Vancouver in 1997, to celebrate the 20th anniversary of her family's ownership of Château Margaux and our 20th anniversary as a Commanderie de Bordeaux à Vancouver.

After a short visit to the chais, we discussed the 1996 vintage. In her opinion, the 1996s will be harder than the 1995s; riper tannins. She said that the 1996s have better structure, are more solid, with more pigmentation than the 1995s. In general terms, she seems to think that the 1995s will resemble the 1985s, and the 1996s the 1986s, with maybe less depth. It seems that 1996 was saved in the Médoc, after a fair bit of rain from late August to mid-September, but a lovely Indian Summer.

We then tasted two 1995s.

1995 PAVILLON BLANC DE CHÂTEAU MARGAUX:

100% Sauvignon Blanc and already in bottle. Hint of oak; ripe, slightly vegetal nose. Fuller, rounder, and richer on palate, with relatively low acidity. Round, complex. Oak dominates a bit. Needs two to four years. Will be very good.

Paul Pontallier is experimenting with Russian oak barrels. They also produce about 30% of their own oak barrels, and buy the rest from five or six suppliers of Allier oak. (I learned about Russian oak barrels during a visit earlier this year with Margaret Duckhorn, in the Napa Valley.)

1995 CHÂTEAU MARGAUX, BARREL SAMPLE:

This wine will be bottled in October/November 1997, a year from now. First impression is of an elegant wine. Purple colour, good depth, yet not black. Lovely ripe berries on nose, but oak-vanilla dominates at this stage. Medium-bodied. Lovely fruit, elegant, long. Hint of bitterness at finish because of new oak. All this will, of course, become harmonious once the wine is bottled.

We will see Corinne at Château Palmer at dinner with Peter and Diana Sichel tonight.

Visit to Château Pichon-Longueville Comtesse de Lalande.

With May Eliane de Lencquesaing. A tasting followed by lunch.

TASTING

1995 PICHON-LALANDE, BARREL SAMPLE:

45% Cabernet Sauvignon, 40% Merlot, 15% Cabernet Franc; no Petit Verdot in 1995. (The Petit Verdot, a late ripener, can produce excellent wines, but its window of peak maturity is very short—sometimes as short as 24 hours—and it has to be picked right there and then.) Lovely, deep colour. Sweet fruit and new oak on nose. Even softer than usual, with 40% Merlot. Forward, round. Lovely fruit. I hope that in another year's time in barrel, it will develop more extract and weight. Lots of class and elegance here.

1994 PICHON-LALANDE:

Just bottled last June. 45% Cabernet Sauvignon, 35% Merlot, 12% Cabernet Franc, and 8% Petit Verdot, reflecting the exact planted (proportional) area of this property. Quite similar to the 1988 in structure. A bit looser-knit. Good acidity and tannic backbone, yet slightly thinner middle. One almost wishes for the structure of the 1994, and the ripeness and fruit of the 1995, blended together! Well made, though. Serious, classic, leaner Pauillac.

May's favourite ("mon bébé," as she calls it) is the 1986—mine, too. Yet, she agreed with me that it is an unusual Pichon-Lalande because of its solid backbone and Cabernet extract. Almost Latour-like.

May talked about her late husband (Le Général), who had a tendency to forget his passport (or lose it), and who liked to argue with customs officials, which got her into trouble more than once. She said that now she doesn't have to worry about an "extra child."

I told her that my daughter Orly is planning to spend an academic year in Paris at the American University of Paris. She very generously offered her flat in Paris for a while, while we looked for a flat there. As it happens, May's flat is on Rue Bosquet, the same street as the American University. She also said that Orly could spend some time with the oldest of her nine grandchildren, Sophie, who is also 18, and born in April 1978. (Orly was born in March 1978.)

May's son-in-law, Comte Gildas d'Ollone, joined us for lunch; he said he'll also try to find a flat for us in Paris. We were joined for lunch by Fiona Morrison, M.W., a public relations lady with the CIVB in Bordeaux.

With lunch

CHAMPAGNE DE VENOGE CORDON BLEU N/V:

Slightly sweet for my taste. Not very complex, but clean, good fruit. Not much toast or character there. Not bad, though.

RÉSERVE DE LA COMTESSE 1993:

Spicy, sweet, forward, round. Pleasant fruit, hint of new oak. Easy to drink. This is the second wine of Pichon-Lalande.

CHÂTEAU PICHON-LALANDE 1985:

A classic 1985 and typical of this property. Lovely fruit; deep, slightly evolved colour; elegant, drinking well now. Good fruit, looser-knit, softer than the great 1986.

As on past visits, the Canadian flag was flying when we arrived at Pichon-Lalande—an elegant gesture.

That evening

Dinner at Château Palmer.

Dr. Larry Burr, a fellow member of the Commanderie de Bordeaux, and I drove to Château Palmer for dinner with Peter and Diana Sichel. Also present were Anthony Barton and his wife (of Leoville and Langoa-Barton), Corinne Mentzelopoulos of Château Margaux, and three other guests from England—friends of the Sichels. It was nice to see Peter and Diana again. Although we did talk over the phone and correspond frequently by mail and fax, we hadn't seen each other since 1990!

After a glass of Champagne, we sat down for dinner to a glass of this wine.

SIRIUS WHITE 1993:

Clean, crisp, round. Nice fruit, good ripeness. This is produced by Maison Sichel. There is also a red version.

This was followed by these wines, all served double-blind.

CHÂTEAU PALMER 1983:

Quite evolved colour. Lovely, chocolaty, elegant nose. Good structure, yet some noticeable acidity. I thought it was the 1975. When I found out that it was the 1983, I was a bit surprised. Not that the wine wasn't superb, but somehow it seemed too evolved. The 1983 Palmers in my cellar are still tight, much more youthful.

CHÂTEAU PALMER 1961:

Superb! Evolved colour. Explosive, elegant, chocolaty, flowery nose. Round, silky on palate, yet great depth. Still has lovely fruit. The sheer concentration and complexity made this the ultimate Margaux. I thought it was the 1966—another great Palmer. The reason I did not guess 1961 was that it was very evolved. This 1961 cannot get any better; it is definitely ready. Pity to wait any longer. It can only decline from now on.

CHÂTEAU MARGAUX 1945:

I was right on this one. As soon as I tasted it, I whispered to Corinne that this was a 1945. The fabulous concentration, yet solid, masculine backbone and tannins so typical of the 1945s. Layers of fruit; still full of life. Even fresher than the 1961 Palmer. While the 1961s are very ripe and round, the 1945s—having great tannic structure—are still amazingly fresh. This was a truly great 1945. These 1945s have a herbaceous taste, yet are incredibly concentrated. This is the best 1945 Château Margaux I have ever tasted, and I have tasted it four times previously. I know that this wine does not have a great reputation, but this bottle was superb.

CHÂTEAU D'YQUEM 1980:

I guessed this right on, too. I've had the good fortune of tasting this wine twice earlier this year (in Vancouver). Bright, yet still youthful golden colour. Impeccable nose. Clean botrytis, oak-vanilla, fruity nose. Elegant; lovely balance on palate. Clean, long finish. Exotic, yet not fat like a 1967 or still powerful, youthful like a 1975. It had the excellent acidity of the 1975s, but lighter, looser-knit middle. This structure is what made me think of 1980.

Peter Sichel, Anthony Barton, and Corinne Mentzelopoulos all commented on how difficult it was to do business in Japan. They found the Japanese aloof, tough, not willing to speak English (yet understanding it well), chauvinistic, and quite anti-American and anti-any-kind of foreigners.

A most enjoyable evening. Good friends, great wines, and fine food. What more could one ask for?

Little did I know at the time that this would be the last time that I would see our dear friend Peter Sichel. He passed away in early 1998.

Wednesday, October 16, 1996

Spent the day with Jean-Michel Cazes.

And in Pauillac, with visits to Pichon-Baron, Lynch-Bages, lunch at Cordeillan Bages (where we were staying), and an afternoon visit to Château Latour

Morning visit to Château Pichon-Baron.

A visit with Malou Le Sommer, secretary to J.-M. Cazes. Last time I visited this property, it was in full construction. This time I saw it completed. Quite a fascinating place. After a tour of the modern winery and an exhibit by J.-M. Cazes of their computer-controlled fermentation room, we went into the tasting room.

1995 CHÂTEAU PIBRAN, BARREL SAMPLE:

A Cru Bourgeois owned by the AXA group. Château Pibran was purchased in 1987, same year as Pichon-Baron. Bright, deep colour. Ripe, good fruit, extract concentration. A fine Cru Bourgeois. Rich, sweet fruit. Very good.

We tasted the Grand Vin, produced from approximately 82% Cabernet Sauvignon and 18% Merlot. No Cabernet Franc or Petit Verdot.

1995 CHÂTEAU PICHON-BARON, FROM CASK:

One year in oak so far. Will not be bottled until July 1997. Excellent colour. Soft fruit. Elegant, classic 1995, yet not the solid Pauillac-style Pichon-Baron is. Sweeter, more feminine. Soft, elegant, classy. For medium-term.

1994 CHÂTEAU PICHON-BARON:

Just bottled last month. Lovely oak-toast on nose. Not as deep as the 1995, or even the 1994 Pibran, but good. Hard, higher acidity. Needs time. Good fruit, but a leaner-style wine.

We also met the winemaker of Pichon-Baron, Jean-René Matignon. He knows Harry MacWaters well, the winemaker of Sumac Ridge in BC.

I learned that the Japanese owners of the Cru Bourgeois Château Citran had just sold this property to the Villars group (Chasse-Spleen, etc.) for 50% less than what it cost them!

At Pichon-Baron, as elsewhere, they are experimenting with Russian oak. It is a bit premature to decide on the quality and on the proportion to be used in the wine. At Pichon-Baron, they used 60% new oak for the 1996 and 50% new oak for the 1995s—mostly Tronçais oak.

Back at our hotel, Cordeillan Bages.

We had a lovely lunch with Jean-Michel Cazes and Malou Le Sommer.

We tasted the following wines.

NUITS-ST.-GEORGES PREMIER CRU BLANC "CLOS DE L'ARLOT" 1992, DOMAINE DE L'ARLOT:

Owned by the AXA group. Made from 100% Chardonnay; the only white Côte de Nuits, Nuits-St.-Georges, made from 100% Chardonnay. Surprisingly good—much better than expected. Lovely fruit, excellent balance, classy nose and palate, long. Very good acidity and fruit backbone. A bit young. Drink from 1998 to 2002. Highly recommended.

CHÂTEAU PETIT VILLAGES 1987:

This Pomerol property was purchased by the AXA group from Bruno Prats of Cos d'Estournel around 1989. Very good effort for a 1987. Good fruit, good acidity. Soft, forward, a bit lean. Evolved, forward. Nice effort.

The AXA group

The group sold Château Franc-Mayne in St. Emilion as they decided that this small property (seven hectares) is more suitable to a local gentleman-farmer than a large corporation that doesn't have the time and doesn't want to spend valuable resources on it. The AXA group also own Château Suduiraut in Sauternes (where they are making the first vintage since they purchased it in 1991—there has been no fine Sauternes vintage between 1991 and 1994.), and they purchased Quinta do Noval from the Van Zellers in 1992.

About their property in Tokay, Hungary

When they purchased this property, they found the wines too oxidized and not acceptable to the Western palate. They discovered that the old Tokay producers (the Communist government monopoly Bor Kombinat) didn't allow a second fermentation, they simply added Brandy, which was a cheap way to produce wine, but illegal in the West (because then it becomes a fortified wine, with its own tax ramifications).

When the AXA group, under J.-M. Cazes, allowed the local Hungarian old-timers to taste the new wine produced after the fall of Communism, they said that this was the way they remembered old Tokay.

André Cazes—Jean-Michel's father, who is 83—had a stroke last week. He is still in the hospital, but everyone hopes he will recover soon.

Afternoon visit to Lynch-Bages.

After lunch, Larry and I went to Lynch-Bages to taste more wines.

1995 BLANC DE LYNCH-BAGES:

40% Semillon, 40% Sauvignon Blanc, and 20% Muscadelle. Clean, spicy, herbaceous. Very good balance. Not big, yet crisp, with good depth and fruit.

Hint of oak. Needs two to three years of bottle-age. Fine effort.

1994 ORMES DE PEZ:

This is an unusually soft St. Estèphe, with 30% Merlot in the blend. Good depth. Subdued, toasty, oaky nose. On palate, like most 1994s, fairly lean. Crisp, good tannins/acidity balance. A bit hollow in middle. "Needs a bit of 1995 in the blend!"

1994 HAUT-BAGES-AVÉROUX:

The second wine of Lynch-Bages. Subdued, delicate nose. Medium colour. Tight, a bit green. Young vines. Reasonably good.

1994 LYNCH-BAGES:

Medium colour. Very good depth. Lovely, exotic fruit on both nose and palate. Better fruit concentration than many other 1994s. Very good extract. Good tannic backbone. By 2003, this will be a fine bottle.

1995 ORMES DE PEZ:

Deeper than the 1994. Cherry, ripe fruit on nose. Typical 1995. Lovely, soft, evolved fruit; long. Will be bottled next spring. Good potential.

1995 HAUT-BAGES-AVÉROUX:

Deep-purple colour. More tannic, more solid than the 1995 Ormes de Pez. Concentrated fruit, good structure. Will make a very pleasant bottle. Well made, a very pleasant bottle.

1995 LYNCH-BAGES:

Will spend another year in wood. Deep, dense colour. Exotic fruit on nose. Great concentration, solid backbone. Lots of depth here. Very good, ripe tannins. Tighter, riper fruit. Less obvious oak than the 1995 Pichon-Baron.

Visit to Château Latour.

With Malou's husband, Christian Le Sommer, manager of Latour, and Frederic Engerer, the commercial director of Latour. We tasted the following wines.

1995 LES-FORTS-DE-LATOUR:

Deep colour. Fresh, ripe berries. Very 1995 style. Good flesh; rich long. Very good potential. Will be bottled next summer.

1994 LATOUR:

Very elegant, toasty, oaky, accessible nose. Quite similar to the 1988, but the 1988 is better overall. Less acidity and backbone than the 1988. Cedar, coffee overtones. Prunes, too. Good depth. Needs seven years.

1995 LATOUR:

Great fruit extract; concentrated, supple (surprising for Latour). Almost too supple? Will be bottled in June 1997, not later, because they don't want the new oak to be too dominant. Sweet fruit. Elegant, lovely wine, but not the big Latour structure.

1991 LES-FORTS-DE-LATOUR:

Evolved, sweet, smooth on nose and palate. Almost creamy. Ready soon. Noticeable acidity.

1991 LATOUR:

One of the best wines of that weak vintage (fortunately, little frost at Latour because of proximity to the river). Sweet, cedary, elegant fruit on nose and palate. Almost ready. Drink over the next five to seven years. Fine effort.

That evening

Jean-Michel Cazes invited me to Château Kirwan.

Mr. Schÿler, owner of Kirwan, inducted the German Consul General to Bordeaux into the Commanderie du Bontemps. I also met Jean-Eugene Borie of Ducru-Beaucaillou and other growers. Jean-Michel introduced me to the guests. Back at Cordeillan Bages, I had a chat with Jean-Michel's sister Sylvie; I hadn't seen her since 1980!

Thursday, October 17, 1996

LIBOURNE AND ST. EMILION

Visit to Château Petrus.

1995 PETRUS:

Lovely, deep colour. Great concentration, but—as elsewhere—a soft, elegant wine. This will spend another year in barrel, and the first assemblage won't be done for a while yet. Oak blends nicely. Impeccable balance, lots of extract. A fine bottle. The peat topsoil at Petrus (underneath, there is gravel) is excellent for Petrus. It retains the moisture during the dry months, yet because the vineyard is on a hill, there is good drainage. The roots are lazy; they get their nutrition mostly from the peat, therefore they are only a half-metre deep and grow sideways, rather than down.

From there, we went for lunch to La Fleur-Petrus.

With about 40 other people: the permanent staff and stagières (students). Christian Moueix, his wife Cherise, and Jean-Claude Berrouet (their principal winemaker and a good friend of mine who has visited us at Turnagain Island) joined us for lunch. They have purchased the Château of Le Gay (but not the vineyard) from Mrs. Robin (owner of Lafleur), so the new château will become the official château of La Fleur-Petrus, rather than the old barn where we had lunch.

Before leaving Pauillac.

That morning, we had a flat tire; we wasted time having it fixed, and had to cancel our morning appointment at Château Canon. Later, Christian Moueix told me that Eric Fournier had sold Canon recently to the Chanel (perfume) group. What a pity; hopefully this will not reduce the quality of Canon. (Chanel also owns Rausan-Ségla—a good omen.)

Christian's Comments, regarding the 1996 Vintage

Yes, better in the Médoc than in Pomerol and St. Emilion, but he doubts the Médoc owners' claim that 1996 "will be like the 1986." He said that it was just too wet in the summer (and even in September) to make a great vintage. Good, maybe; great, no!

He also told me that Pascal Delbeck only makes Belair and the other properties of Mme. Dubois-Chalon, but that he is not involved with Ausone any more because of the row with the other 50% owner. What a pity! He is a fine winemaker who turned Ausone around from 1976 onward.

Christian also confirmed the sale of Franc-Mayne by the AXA group for $4,000,000. He said that this property would have been ideal for me. Nice small château; compact seven-hectare vineyard. He said he has some great 1928s and 1929s of that property. I have tasted the 1945, 1949, 1959, and 1970 in the past, and they were all excellent. He also said that at Ausone, they had, in their archives, invoices of Russian oak barrels purchased at the beginning of this century, before World War I. About Modern oak barrels, Christian said that in his opinion—and for his wines—Taransson made the best barrels, then Demptos, and then Seguin-Moreau, in that order.

I told him about the Russian barrel (Seguin-Moreau) experiments at Duckhorn, Margaux, and Pichon-Baron. Jean-Claude Berrouet told me that they were experimenting with Russian oak, too, at Trotanoy. He made one barrel of Trotanoy 1994 in Russian oak, and next time I'm in Libourne, he'll let me taste it.

Visit to Figeac.

We met Thierry Manoncourt's daughter, Laure d'Aramon. Her three sisters live in Paris, and she is involved at Figeac daily. At Figeac, they are not on good terms with Parker these days They are in the category of Domaine de Chevalier, Ausone, Palmer, and other elegant wines. They have tried for many years to obtain Premier Grand Cru "A" category (like Cheval-Blanc and Ausone); the committee looking into this accepted it in most categories, except in terms of price.

Ironically, they decided that Figeac doesn't fetch enough money to justify Premier Grand Cru "A" classification. In the past, they sold all their wines to the négociants, in one lot. In future, Laure wants to release it in tranches—at higher prices—to play the "ego" game of many Super Seconds. It seems that nowadays, creating an artificially low supply increases demand—and prices.

After a visit of the chais, we tasted the following.

FIGEAC 1983, IN HALF-BOTTLE:

Like many 1983s, evolved. Complex, spicy, herbaceous Figeac style. Elegant, ready, but no rush.

Friday, October 18, 1996

Visit to Château Cheval-Blanc.

This was the only disappointing part of the whole week in Bordeaux. For me, it was a rather important visit, because I was hoping to organize two tastings of Cheval-Blanc in British Columbia, one on behalf of the French Trade Commission (of younger vintages, to be held in Victoria), and the other for the Commanderie de Bordeaux in Vancouver.

Pierre Lurton, the régisseur who has replaced Jacques Hebrard, wasn't there—although I had written him in advance, and the Grand Conseil had set an appointment for me. There wasn't even an office or anyone to talk to—just three lady tourguides who were extremely busy with Japanese tourists.

First, our visit was delayed by 30 minutes, which put a stress on the rest of the morning. Then we were told by an impatient tourguide that we would have to wait a bit longer for our "tour" because they were very busy. When I explained to her who I was and the purpose of my visit, she told me that only Pierre Lurton could make these decisions, that he wasn't there, and she was extremely busy. After waiting for 15 more minutes in the hallway, we just left and went to our next château. On every trip, there usually is a disappointing episode. Cheval-Blanc was ours.

Visit to Vieux Château Certan.

At this property, I almost joined my ancestors in the autumn of 1982. I almost fell into an open vat (of the great 1982!), overcome by gas from the fermentation. Leon Thienpont, the father of the present owner, Alexandre, grabbed me by the tail of my jacket and pulled me back up! Leon has since passed away. Alexandre was very busy racking, so his assistant took us on a tour of the winery and a tasting.

1996:

Difficult year in Pomerol, a lot of rain. Thankfully, they thinned the leaves in the summer to allow more sunshine (the little that was there) to get through to the grapes, and they thinned the crop. Vieux Château Certan's vineyard average age is 35 years, comprised of

30% Cabernet Franc, 10% Cabernet Sauvignon, and 60% Merlot. The 1996 growing season compared to 1993 here. Vieux Château Certan's blend makes it the most Médoc-like of the Pomerols.

VIEUX CHÂTEAU CERTAN 1994:

Bottled last summer. 75% Merlot. Very good fruit. Not vegetal or herbaceous. Fairly full-bodied, closed up, tannic. A serious wine that should be aged for seven to ten years.

VIEUX CHÂTEAU CERTAN 1993:

65% Merlot. Purple colour, not as dark as the 1994. Ripe, good extract. Herbaceous, a bit stemmy. More typical of this property than the riper 1994. Good finish. Needs seven to eight more years or longer.

At Vieux Château Certan, they share the same cellar manager as La Conseillante, but Alexandre Thienpont makes the wine.

Visit to Ausone and Belair.

Visit and lunch with Pascal Delbeck, and his charming wife Madeleine. As of this year, Pascal is not involved with Ausone at all. He lives at Belair and makes the Château Belair wines, as well as wines in other properties in St. Emilion's satellites belonging to Mme. Dubois-Chalon. (She lives in her half of Château Ausone. The other half belongs to a group headed by her nephew.)

Pascal said that the best thing for Ausone is for it to be sold because the situation there has become impossible. He said that Mme. Dubois-Chalon's nephew (the other 50% partner) is trying to push her out. Now that Pascal has been removed from his position of winemaker at Ausone, the other partner has hired Michel Roland to supervise the vinification. This will produce wines in a style that Robert Parker likes—bigger, fatter wines. Parker doesn't like (or understand) elegance. He likes to use terms such as "hedonistic, oozing, gobs of succulent fruit, massive, lush, etc." And this goes against the style of Ausone and the philosophy of Delbeck.

The other owner, of course, hopes that if Parker will like the wines in future, then the price will go up. Pascal describes the former style of Ausone as "Royalist" and the new style as "Imperialist." Delbeck also worries that even when the "Parker phenomenon" disappears, the damage will have been done in the vineyard, with new rootstocks, different wines, etc., forever affecting the style of Ausone.

He likes Pavie and Canon very much—and the potential there. He is not worried about the sale of Canon to Chanel because he knows the people at Chanel, and perfume and wines have similar philosophies.

Pascal said that 1990 was the last true traditional Ausone. He said that Parker tastes in a Russian "Kalachnikov" (assault rifle) fashion—one wine per minute—and how can anyone do justice to wines or concentrate while dedicating only one minute per wine. He's not angry at Parker, but rather at Parker's followers, and says that many winemakers are starting to make "Parker" wines.

He said that Ausone has seven hectares under vine and that Belair has 13 hectares. At Belair, they use Demptos oak barrels, usually 50% new, depending on the vintage. Cost of oak in a top-classed growth amounts to about $5 per bottle!

He stopped working for Cazes/AXA because he's busy with ventures in Spain, Chile, and in the Napa Valley. He said that Franc-Mayne sold for too much because, while the house was already renovated, a lot of new money would have to be invested in the chais and in the vineyard.

Pascal is now involved with a winery (Abadia Retuerta) in Ribera del Duero, as the advisor to Swiss investors. This is near Vega Sicilia. Grape composition is 70% Tempranillo, 20% Cabernet Sauvignon, and 10% Merlot. He is also involved as advisor in a Napa Valley venture with Gordon Getty and at Stagling (a vineyard just above Robert Mondavi's in Oakville).

About the discord at Ausone

Delbeck said that we all have an appointment with God, but that there are many ways to get there! In other words, there is more than one way to make wine, and that having so many owners trying to make Parker-style wines is a mistake.

We also visited the fabulous caves and cellars at Belair.

To show how fussy the consumer is, Pascal said that he had made a really decent red Bordeaux Ordinaire, but because it was a blend of two vintages, he decided not to put a vintage on it. It was "too cheap," and didn't sell well. He then put a vintage on the magnums of a second batch of the same wine (he only bottled magnums of this wine), and it sold like hotcakes—and at a much higher price!

We then started our tasting.

DOMAINE CHALLON 1995 "CUVÉE DU MANOIR":

He sells this white wine wholesale for US$46 per case! This vineyard was planted in the past with the dull Ugni Blanc. He ferments it in oak, and now the grape varietal composition is 60% Semillon, 35% Sauvignon Blanc, and 5% Muscadelle. A lovely sipping wine that should be a "favourite poolside aperitif with ladies in California." Smells of Asti Spumanti, with the 5% Muscadelle really coming through. Off-dry, round, flowery, easy-sipping wine.

1993 AND 1995 CHÂTEAU BELAIR:

The 1993 a bit harder; good backbone, fruit; hint of the calcareous/sandy soil; very good length, balance.

The 1995 is deeper, riper, softer, fruitier. Both excellent in their own way.

CHÂTEAU AUSONE 1993:

Elegant, subdued nose. Lovely fruit, excellent backbone and structure. Very long. Needs eight to ten years. Top quality.

CHÂTEAU AUSONE 1990:

Luscious. The last great Ausone, according to Pascal. Deep, round, lots of depth, extract, fairly low acidity. Great concentration. Will be a great bottle some day. Here, too, there is soil character in the wine—calcareous and sandy.

We then proceeded to their home (at Belair) for lunch, prepared by Madeleine. We had crêpes, omelette, and young pheasant, shot by Pascal's friend. (We had to watch for lead pellets in the pheasant!)

CHÂTEAU BELAIR 1982:

Excellent wine, exhibiting all the characteristics of this fine vintage. Full, luscious fruit. Soft, ripe tannins. Ready now, but so much concentration that it will last well for many more years. Long, spicy, slightly herbaceous. Very good quality.

CHÂTEAU AUSONE 1942:

Incredibly structured like a 1945! Good, mature colour. Cedar, cinnamon, spices on nose. Round, yet a streak of tannic backbone, not unlike 1945 or even 1928. Very good fruit. Round, long, full of life. Who would have believed this from a 1942!? Pascal wanted us to compare two wines that are 40 years apart, a 1942 and a 1982. Surprisingly, still very good fruit. Of the very few 1942s I've tasted, this is by far the best. If well cellared, this can last for a few more years. A great experience.

CHÂTEAU AUSONE 1983:

I wanted to taste the 1983, because I hadn't tasted it since an impressive barrel sample in the spring of 1985. Great now, but no rush. Very good structure and backbone. Good fruit. Earthy, truffles on nose. Full, yet not fat. (Ausone never is.) Very long. Very good. No rush.

There was a problem with the smell of some of the glasses. According to Pascal, some smells in glasses won't go away, even after thorough rinsing, and these glasses have to be destroyed.

What a fabulous reception, visit, and lunch to end a great week in Bordeaux. Larry Burr was (or seemed to be) in heaven. This was a great ending to a most enjoyable trip. Even the weather was reasonable. Pity that the visit at Cheval-Blanc was a disappointment.

The day we left Pauillac for St. Emilion, we had breakfast with J.-M. Cazes, who mentioned that earlier in the year, Pierre Trudeau visited Lynch-Bages; he seemed sick and very tired. He had to sit down every few minutes and left early. Trudeau is now 76. Maybe his conscience is starting to bother him as to the permanent damage he has caused our country in his 16 years as dictator of Canada.

November 2 to 7, 1996

Trip to Yountville.

Visit to Joe and Alice Heitz.

Joe is recovering from his stroke (earlier this year), but has lost his sense of smell and taste! He says that this is the pits, not only because he enjoys wines and single malts so much, but because it is his livelihood, too. This must really hurt. The doctors promise him that his sense of smell and taste will come back. He's pessimistic. I hope that the doctors are right. Alice kindly opened this bottle for us.

1991 HEITZ CELLARS CABERNET SAUVIGNON "TRAILSIDE VINEYARD," NAPA VALLEY:

Planted about eight years ago, near Howell Mountain. About 2,800 cases produced—small production so far. The wine promises to be very good. Without the explosive eucalyptus bouquet and intensity of "Martha's Vineyard," it is styled more like his "Bella Oaks," but with riper, sweeter fruit. Good Cabernet cedar/oak, spicy character. Long, good fruit. Rounder than expected at this stage, yet very good tannic backbone. Needs three to five extra years of bottle-age.

Dinner at "Meadowood."

From the Heitz's, I drove back to Yountville to meet Christian Moueix, his wife Cherise, and his son Edouard. We drove up to Meadowood for dinner. Christian's vineyard/winery manager, Jean-Marie Maurèze, and his wife Françoise joined us for dinner, as did another couple of friends.

Christian ordered two bottles of this wine.

CHAMPAGNE DOM PÉRIGNON 1988:

Both good, but unimpressive; certainly not up to their fine 1982 or 1985 standards. What was odd was the bottle variation. One bottle was clearly drier, more herbaceous, hint of yeast, quite lean and acidic. The second bottle was markedly softer, rounder, even sweeter, but without the toasty complexity and extract that this fine Champagne can produce.

I brought along two bottles of wine.

CHEVALIER-MONTRACHET "LES DEMOISELLES" 1988, LOUIS LATOUR

AND

CHÂTEAU DUCRU-BEAUCAILLOU 1978:

The Chevalier was certainly the wine of the evening. Quite forward and in full blossom, to be expected from a relatively forward vintage for white Burgundies. Almonds, exotic fruit on nose. Very long, yet not big on palate. Superb complexity, great class, elegance, fresh-roasted almonds, hint of oak. Very long, ripe (yet not big) aftertaste. A lovely bottle.

The Ducru-Beaucaillou was very good, too, but typical 1978. Obviously stemmy, herbaceous on nose and palate.

1978 was the miracle year in Bordeaux, saved by a late outburst of sunshine that ripened the Cabernets somewhat, but it came too late for the Merlots—thus, the wines are quite stemmy and lack that extra dimension of ripeness that Merlot generally imparts. Several properties have produced fine wines nevertheless, such as Latour, Leoville-Lascases, Ducru, Palmer, Margaux, La Mission Haut-Brion. It was really a "Left Bank" year, as both Pomerols and St. Emilions suffered from the absence of ripe Merlot.

Christian's Comments on the 1996 red Bordeaux

He looked back at his records on the 1978s, and was surprised as to how much the 1996 vintage resembled the 1978s. With rain spoiling the Merlot and late sunshine saving the Cabernets, it was another Haut-Médoc year, rather than St. Emilion/Pomerol.

Christian also said that, in his opinion, Roederer Estate makes the finest Californian sparkling wine, the closest in style to a good quality French Champagne.

Then we tasted a wine Christian brought along.

1989 DOMINUS:

A vintage written-off by wine writers, yet several properties produced good Cabernets—softer, more forward in style. This wine was typical. Quite approachable. Round, stylish. Good, soft, ripe fruit. Clean, spicy Cabernet.

Long, good depth.

November 16, 1996

Commanderie de Bordeaux Dinner, featuring a vertical tasting of Château Lynch-Bages 1981 to 1992, at the Hotel Vancouver.

FLIGHT #1

Château Lynch-Bages, 1992 to 1988

1992:

Medium cherry-red. Spicy, herbaceous. A bit stemmy, grassy. Typical 1992 (rained a lot). Soft, forward. Not bad, drinkable, pleasant. Low fruit. Good for the vintage. (14)

1990:

Deeper, darker than the 1989. Loads of ripe fruit. Better, more tannic backbone than the 1989. Ripe tannins. Very good intensity. Powerful, yet all in harmony. Overall, a bigger, more serious version of the 1989. (17.5)

1989:

Good, deep colour to rim. Subdued, clean nose. Ripe, soft, sweet fruit. Not as tight as the 1988. Looser-knit. Long, lovely ripe fruit. Spicy, smoky nose. Perfumy, aromatic, almost a bit too soft for a Pauillac. But then this seems to be a problem with many 1989 Haut-Médocs. (17)

1988:

Good depth, palish rim. Closed nose. A bit spicy, vegetal. Tighter on palate. Good fruit, but not very ripe. Clean, long. Needs time. Lacks ripeness in middle. A bit hollow. (16)

Guest speaker of the first flight was Dan Kleck, winemaker at Taylor Cellars, New York State, who came along as the guest of one of our Commandeurs.

FLIGHT #2

1981, 1983, and 1986

1981, IN MAGNUMS:

Evolved colour. Spicy, a bit vegetal on nose. Sweet on entry, straightforward, some acidity/sharpness at finish, yet nice fruit. A bit lean, but nice complexity. Ready, even in magnums. (16.5)

1983, IN MAGNUMS:

As evolved in the glass as the 1981, but a bit more depth. Odd, beet-root, jammy nose. Quite ripe, sweet, with a good tannic backbone; riper than the 1981, but less elegant. Spicy, classic Claret. Cedar overtones. Ready. (17)

1986, IN MAGNUM AND BOTTLES:

Clearly deepest colour. Great extract. Still too young. Fabulous fruit, rich, ripe. Excellent balance. Needs five to seven years. Spicy, cedary on nose and palate. Exotic. (17.5)

FLIGHT #3
1985 and 1982

1985:

Very good, deep, dense colour. Cedary, rich, with the elegance of the vintage. Perfect balance. Lovely, long, approachable. Very long aftertaste. Without the stuffing of the 1982, but excellent. (18)

1982, IN MAGNUM AND BOTTLES:

While the 1986 (previous flight) was luscious and sweet, it seemed dry when compared to this fabulous, ripe 1982. Deep colour, purplish. Subdued, elegant, cedary, ripe on nose and palate. Very ripe, long, complex. Ready, but no rush. Great fruit extract. As lovely as the 1985 is, this has an edge. Sweeter, riper fruit, with excellent intensity. (18.5)

Comments

The 1990 bigger than the 1989, but both surprisingly soft. The new trend of winemaking? The Lynch-Bages were excellent. Overall high standards, reflecting the serious winemaking abilities of the people who head this property, notably J.-M. Cazes.

November 22, 1996

Confrérie des Chevaliers du Tastevin Black Tie Dinner.

MEURSAULT 1992, LOUIS JADOT:

This négociant's wines, whether simple Villages wines or Grands Crus, are always well made and reliable. Nice almonds, oak, Chardonnay on nose. Round, clean, soft, forward. Good, ripe fruit. Clean, nutty flavours.

PULIGNY-MONTRACHET PREMIER CRU "CLOS DU CAILLERET" 1990, DOMAINE JEAN CHARTRON:

This monopole vineyard is outstanding. When Joseph Drouhin had the exclusivity on this property, the wine was fuller, richer. Now that it is back in the owner's hands, it is made in the lighter, more elegant style. I preferred the older style. Lovely, spicy, elegant nose. Round, crisp, clean, well balanced; hint of exotic fruit. Ready.

CHAMBERTIN "CLOS DE BÈZE" 1987, A. ROUSSEAU:

An excellent producer. Toasty, intense, clean, spicy Pinot Noir on nose. Deceptively forward on entry, but lots of body, and fairly high acidity (a trademark of the 1987 red Burgundies, not unlike 1972). Very long, complex, spicy. Excellent effort. Not ready. This was the most complex of all the red wines of the evening.

CHAMBERTIN "CLOS DE BÈZE" 1989, LOUIS JADOT:

Very different from the 1987; typical, soft, ripe fruit of the vintage. Closed nose. Rich, ripe, intense. Very good extract. Needs an extra two to three years of bottle-age. Has more flesh and extract than most 1989s, which are too soft in general. Lovely. Very good potential, but Rousseau's 1987 had more complexity.

CLOS DE LA ROCHE 1983, JOSEPH DROUHIN:

This is one of the few good 1983s. Thankfully, no sign of gray rot—"goût de grêle." Medium, evolved colour. Tight, herbaceous, stemmy nose; some oak. Hard, tannic on palate. Good fruit, but dry, lean style. No rush, but if kept much longer, it may lose its fruit.

The Jadot was the deepest, ripest of the red, and the Rousseau by far the most complex.

The dinner was held at the Metropolitan hotel in Vancouver.

Chef Michael Noble prepared an excellent meal to accompany the fine wines. The loin of fallow deer was the best deer I've tasted to date. Orly joined me at this event as my guest.

November 1996

Excerpt from an article written by me, and sent to various leading newspapers in North America and to *Decanter* magazine in London, which chose not to publish it; it is entitled "It Is Not Too Late!"

" 'This is a corpulent, broad-flavoured, muscular, opulently fleshy and hedonistic wine… it is crammed with oozing, unctuous fruit; decadently intense, utterly profound, big framed, hugely complex… with hints of licorice, jammy plums, and black currants… an enormous, awesome bruiser, splendidly concentrated and absolutely full of velvety tannins, superripe with fat, chunky flavours ... a ponderous, luscious, shimmering, and authoritative wine with multidimensional personality.

'In short, it is simply the greatest wine of this estate since the monumental 1949 (AD). It has gobs of sweet tannins and a huge, soaring bouquet. A power-monger that is astonishing in its depth, unbelievably exciting, with a mind-boggling finish… an olfactory smorgasbord. Drink from next year… 95 out of 100.'

"Robert Parker Jr. had entered our wine lives.

"This open letter is not aimed at criticizing Robert Parker, the individual, nor to question his honesty or even his winetasting ability (although negative—even nasty—comments abound, but often off the record). No, it is an attempt to save, before it is too late, what makes the whole subject of fine wines so fascinating: the individuality and character of each wine.

"Parker's popularity has dramatically impacted the price and availability of wines. As one leading New York wine retailer put it, 'If it scores over 90 points, I can't get it. If it scores under 90 points, I can't sell it.' Consider the caricature of a customer tasting a sample of a wine and commenting that the wine tasted foul. When told by the clerk at the wine shop that Parker had given this wine 92 points, the customer replied: 'I'll take two cases.'

"Parker's *Wine Advocate* was just one of a flood for wine magazines and newsletters that appeared on the North American wine scene in the late 1970s and early 1980s. Then came the 1982 vintage in Bordeaux. Parker took the plunge of his life and went all out, raving about and exalting the 1982 vintage. Other wine writers advocated caution. Parker won. From then on, there was no stopping his dazzling success.

"No matter that he had made a mess of his overoptimistic early accolade of the 1983 red Burgundy vintage. No matter that he wrote and commented on varietals and wine regions about which he knew less than other wine writers. The rocket had been launched. Parker had become not only the Ralph Nader of the wine world, but the final word on the most prestigious wine areas of the world.

"His thumbs-up (over 90 points) or his thumbs-down (under 90 points) decided the fate of the wine gladiators. Over the past decade-and-a-half, his verdict has become the 'live or die.' And, let us not kid ourselves, at stake are millions of dollars in profits or losses in the short term, and indeed, the fate of whole vineyards and wineries in the long run.

"During the 1980s, I began to worry about California wines, both whites and reds (notably Cabernet Sauvignons and Chardonnays). UC Davis [University of California, Davis] was producing cloned winemakers, all learning from the same masters and producing wines that tasted alike. The individualistic wines were there all right, but few and far between. Soon Italy started to produce 'Super Barolos' and 'Super Tuscans,' with foreign varietals (notably Cabernet Sauvignon in Tuscany).

"Again, they were starting to taste alike. Even Porto began to produce different wines. Softer, early maturing Ports for the near future. In my 25-odd years of extensive tastings, I have never associated Vintage Port with 'early consumption.' This is a paradox. Burgundy, with its small, prestigious vineyards, had little to worry about—especially the whites, as they had little or no competition from outside. Indeed, Burgundian producers have cleaned up their act dramatically over the past decade, with a few hiccups here or there. Parker's impact on them has been relatively minor, as they could always find individuals and restaurants who would buy their whole production.

"As a passionate of red Bordeaux wines, I have followed the developments there with interest over the past two-and-a-half decades. It has been fascinating to watch the improvements in the overall quality of the fine red wines of Bordeaux.

"After 'Wine-Gate' of the early 1970s, things improved fast. Technology, methods of vinification, and vineyard management all helped improve the quality. The blessed decade of the 1980s, with no fewer than eight good or great vintages, certainly helped. But the main trump card of Bordeaux was their 'terroir.' I was beginning to worry about Parker's influence, and the danger of following one prophet with a very special taste for big, soft, and early maturing wines.

"Actually, I viewed his influence as positive. After all, to give credit where credit is due, Parker had forced many indifferent or unscrupulous estates to produce better wines, and to clean up their act. He has also been instrumental in putting on the map and/or increasing the popularity and quality of several minor or out-of-the-way wine-growing regions that otherwise would have probably remained anonymous to this day.

"Relatively obscure but dedicated properties such as Château l'Arrosée or Tertre Rôteboeuf in St. Emilion, several small estates in Pomerol, several Crus Bourgeois in the Médoc, notably Sociando-Mallet, started to receive their well-deserved recognition, and in no small way, thanks to Robert Parker's *Wine Advocate.*

"Other properties started to produce better wines. The combination of fine weather conditions in the 1980s, a younger, dedicated generation of winemakers, advances in technology, and seeing their neighbours profit from producing better wines added to the general quality improvements in Bordeaux.

"Dedicated winemakers, such as Bruno Prats of Cos d'Estournel and others, stressed the importance of 'terroir,' a fact that gave the great châteaux of Bordeaux their individual character. One gray cloud on the horizon has been, and still is, overproduction; [production of] 60 or more hectolitres per hectare was becoming the norm—not a good sign.

"Wine is my passion, especially the red wines of Bordeaux. I have spent many years learning and studying them—inside out. I have tasted Clarets going back to the early 19th century, and have read every book on the subject—recent and ancient—that I could lay my hands on. I discovered that the best way to taste wine—any wine—was double-blind. When I guessed right, it was a source of great satisfaction. And, when I was wrong—sometimes very wrong—I learned a lot and fine-tuned my tasting abilities and memory.

"A Pomerol always tasted like a Pomerol, whether it was the rich, fatter wines—predominantly Merlot-based—such as l'Evangile or Lafleur, or the crisper, more elegant style of Vieux Château Certan or La Conseillante, with their higher proportion of Cabernets. The same was true of Pauillac, St. Estèphe, and all the other communes.

"Then, over the years, I started to notice that wines from different communes started to taste alike. Was it my palate, or were wines being produced in such a way that they would all appeal when young, fruitier, richer, softer, at the expense of their individual character? On many visits to Bordeaux, I started to notice a worrisome trend: the Parker 'bulldozer' was crushing everything that stood in its way.

"His influence had grown to the point where, if the top châteaux of Bordeaux wanted to sell their wines and make a profit, they had to produce 'Parker wines' or suffer the consequences. I also noticed that owners and winemakers were trembling because Parker was 'coming to Bordeaux next month, and I hope that he will like my wines,' or were pleading with him to retaste their wines and give them a second chance.

"My latest trip to Bordeaux, in October 1996, confirmed this trend. Great and gifted winemakers were let go by the owners because Parker didn't like the style, and therefore the price of the wine was not soaring. And—the worst tragedy of them all—new varietals and new clones were planted, causing very long-term damage. And the great variety, characterized by different soils, different winemaking approaches, and different ageing procedures, is disappearing.

"What has happened to 'vive la différence'? In short, the best argument of Bordeaux has collapsed: the individual 'terroir' character. A St. Estèphe tastes like a Pomerol, and a Pauillac like a St. Emilion, and a St. Emilion like a St. Julien, and sometimes they taste like California Cabernets. If it all tastes the same, why bother to buy a case of each leading château? Why not just buy ten cases of one leading property, keep two to three cases for drinking (always in the near future, these days), and sell the rest at auction?

"Several producers are trying to resist, especially the non-Parker style of elegant wines such as Domaine de Chevalier, Figeac, Ausone (until the recent, tragic replacement of Pascal Delbeck as winemaker), Palmer, and a few other properties. But most could not resist the pressure. The new wine consumers were clamouring for Parker wines. Soft, fruity, early maturing, lacking individual character, but loaded with 'hedonistic, massive fruit, with gobs of blah, blah, blah.' In short, wines that are on steroids.

"The new wine press—not just Parker, but *The Wine Spectator* and other leading wine publications from America and Britain—has created a new generation of wine snobs who are buying wines because of the score and scarcity (exemplified by the Château Le Pin farce).

"More and more winemakers and famous châteaux are jumping on the bandwagon of technically correct, clean wines—all tasting alike. Winemakers—and not only in Bordeaux—fail to train the new generation in tasting older wines and seeing the difference in vintages, styles of wines, and differences in communes. The Guy Accads and Michel Rolands have taken over.

"Wines that for generations have been renowned for their elegance, their velvety structure, and lighter style are made to fit Parker's palate. Fermentation procedures are changing, robbing many wines of their character—and what made them famous for generations.

"As a consumer, and a 'passionate' of wine, I see a tragedy-in-the-making here. Wine newsletters come and go. One day, Robert Parker will retire to write his memoirs, but the producers will be stuck with indifferent, neutral, technically correct wines and vineyards planted with the wrong varietals and root stocks. The consumers will own cases upon cases of the same wine in their cellars, but with different labels.

"There is nothing wrong with Rubens, but what about Matisse, Van Gogh, or Picasso? Just imagine for a moment that an art critic walks into the Louvre. He walks out three hours later, having reviewed and rated the 160 leading paintings there, giving Leonardo da Vinci's Mona Lisa 94 points, a Matisse 89, a Picasso 87, and a Rubens 97 (big, hedonistic, unctuous).

"Now imagine what would happen if this art critic had such influence that every artist started to paint 'Rubens style,' because that is what sells.

"The critic's opinion is one thing. But the artists, art dealers, and collectors all clamouring for only that one art critic's favourite style of painting becomes a threat to the art world as a whole.

"You, the consumers, have created this 'Parker Mania.' Continue to read Robert Parker's valuable wine reviews. Subscribe to other newsletters to get a wide range of views. But also taste, taste, taste—and form your own opinion. And let the producers know that you don't want all the wines to be made the same way and to taste the same.

"Let your wine retailers know that you are sick and tired of their selling wines almost always through Parker's or *The Wine Spectator's* comments and scores. And once in a while, try some wines that the experts didn't like. You may be pleasantly surprised. If you keep silent and allow wine writers, producers, retailers, and auction houses to continue with this farce, then you—the consumer—will pay the ultimate price.

"For the fact that you buy wines and read these lines means that you care about the subject of fine wines. Those among you who are business people will surely identify the danger of following blindly the advice of one expert on all investments, all business sectors, all commodities, all stocks. And, for the artistically oriented among you, what would the world be without the variety of taste, opinion, colour, dress, landscape, tune?"

December 14 to 21, 1996

Trip to Las Vegas and Los Angeles, with Carol and Orly.

Dinner with Brad Klein, at "Chinois" restaurant, in Los Angeles

We brought along our own bottles.

CHAMPAGNE JACQUESSON "SIGNATURE" ROSÉ 1989:

A fine Champagne. Pale salmon-pink colour. Spicy, fresh nose. Fairly dry, leaner style, good fruit, tiny bubbles, long. Well made. Will last well until 1998 to 2000. (17)

MONTRACHET 1985, LOUIS LATOUR:

The elegant structure of the 1985s. At its peak. Flowery, elegant, ripe nose. Medium-bodied. Lacks a bit in weight or length for a Montrachet. Hint of wet cement on nose, but good overall. (17.5)

PRADO ENEA 1976 "GRAN RESERVA" RIOJA, MUGA:

This is considered to be Muga's best wine from the 1970s. It spent one year in large oak tintas and four years in small oak barricas. Made mostly from Garnacha grapes (Grenache) and Tempranillo (Rioja's cousin of the Pinot Noir). Fairly evolved, mature colour. Very little sediment. The nose would fool anyone—very Pinot Noir (Côte de Nuits). Some ripeness on palate, yet still a bit tannic and woody. Good fruit. Long, spicy, complex, very Burgundy-like, herbaceous rich. A fine wine. (17)

The food at "Chinois" was excellent, as usual; especially the tuna (ahi) sashimi and the catfish.

IN SANTA MONICA

Dinner with Brad Klein, at "Jiraffe" restaurant.

This time, we had dinner by ourselves, without the ladies.

BÂTARD-MONTRACHET 1985, LOUIS LATOUR:

More forward than the 1985 Montrachet (Latour's) that we had two nights ago. Quite sweet, round, and very soft; starting to oxidize a bit. Most 1985s need drinking. They're not as good as the 1986s; yet, when younger, they were very promising. (17)

HEITZ CELLARS "MARTHA'S VINEYARD" CABERNET SAUVIGNON 1969, NAPA VALLEY:

A classic. Joe Heitz prefers this to his 1968 "Martha's." Deep colour. Very youthful-looking. Unmistakable "Martha's" nose of eucalyptus-mint. Very big, rich; loaded with ripe fruit. Long aftertaste. No rush. Bags of life. Top quality. (18)

Haskell Norman passes away

Last week, Dr. Haskell Norman, Chairman of the Marin County International Wine and Food Society, passed away at age 82, after a bout with brain and lung cancer. A dear friend of many and a wine enthusiast who has created many a memorable winetasting and dinner. He will be missed. I wonder if the Marin County branch of the IW&FS will survive. It certainly won't be the same.

January 16, 1997

Dinner and vertical tasting of Sassicaia, at "Lola's" restaurant, in Vancouver.

Organized by Bill Spohn, a former member of Le Tastevin Wine Club and with the participation of several other former members. Each participant brought along a bottle.

1975 SERRIGER WURZBERG RIESLING AUSLESE, HERRENBERG, MOSEL

AND

1976 STAADTER MAXIMINER PRÄLAT RIESLING AUSLESE, MOSEL:

Both excellent, both reflecting the respective styles of the vintages.

The 1975 lighter gold, yet good depth. Excellent, spicy Riesling, petroleum nose. Lovely acidity, ripe fruit; some residual sugar. Very long.

The 1976 deeper colour, slightly tighter nose, fatter, richer, a slight hint of vegetables. Quite soft at finish. Overall, 1975 was fresher, and 1976 richer, even slightly sweeter.

FLIGHT #1

SASSICAIA

1989, 1987, and 1983

1989:

Good depth, quite evolved at rim. Delicate, clean, straw, oak, vanilla, and ripe berries on nose. Quite soft, evolved on palate. Somehow lacks middle and a bit short at finish. Silky, elegant, very stylish and velvety. Just about ready. (17)

1987:

Noticeably darker than the 1989. Intense, deep berry colour to rim. Tight, unyielding on nose. Deeper, bigger than the 1989, yet backed by good, ripe fruit. Noticeable high acidity at finish. Lacks the elegance and balance of the 1989. Hint of rubber. Later, rounded up a bit and developed nice depth. A fine effort in a difficult year. (16.5)

1983:

Colour deeper than the 1989. Not as deep as the 1987 and more mature rim. Slight hint of wet earth, mushrooms on nose. A serious wine. Fruit quite mature, but starting to dry out. Hint of rubber. Masculine, tough. (16.5)

FLIGHT #2

1979, 1980, and 1981

1979:

Impressive depth, mature rim. Subdued, Bordeaux-like on nose. Slightly vegetal. Round, lovely, classy. Very good fruit. Soft, yet excellent structure. Ripe, round. Lovely bottle now. Experts have rated it low—amazing; clearly best wine of the first two flights. (18)

1980:

Impressive colour for the vintage. Good depth. Delicate hint of fruit and oak. Quite dry. Closed. Still fairly tannic; hollow middle. (15.5)

1981:

Deep colour to rim. Surprisingly youthful for a 15-year-old wine. Closed nose, with some ripe fruit coming through. Aggressive tannins, backed by good fruit. Not quite ready. Maybe too much new oak and not enough ripe fruit. Very good, nevertheless. (17)

FLIGHT #3

1982 and 1978

1982:

Very good appearance/colour to rim. Ripe, clean fruit on nose. Almost a blast of fruit—then it dies. Nice fruit, good backbone. Still lots of life ahead. Even some aggressive tannins. Suffered, in terms of ranking, from the extract of the 1978. (See below.) (17)

1978:

Amazing, deep, bright colour to rim. Best of all! massive, tannic; great ripe-fruit extract. At the risk of sounding prejudiced—this being my bottle—this was the biggest, greatest, and most intense wine of the evening. Tight, closed nose; a bit herbaceous. Excellent extract. Creamy, luscious, rich, very long. Almost Latour 1970 in style. After one hour, hint of cinnamon. (19)

Comment

At the end of the evening, after the wines had two hours to breathe, the 1978 turned out to be superior to the lovely 1985 (flight #4). Bigger, deeper, more extract, older-style wine. Very impressive. Sassicaia does not produce wines of the calibre nowadays.

FLIGHT #4

1985, 1986, and 1988

1985:

Almost as deep as the 1978. Ripe, luscious, intense nose; not unlike a 1982 Pichon-Lalande. Superb extract. Luscious. Very ripe tannins. A huge wine. Lovely fruit yet good acidity and balance. Great bottle. (18.5)

1986:

Good depth to rim, but surprisingly light compared to the 1985. Herbaceous St. Emilion style. Round, soft, elegant. Good depth, rich. Needs two to three years, and will last until 2000. Nice fruit. Warm and charming. (17) Robert Parker rated this wine a perfect 100 points! Go figure!

1988:

Good, dark colour. Lovely toast on nose. Full, not as fat and ripe as the 1985, but excellent. Lovely fruit. Needs five to seven years. At this stage, still too young and not quite together, but will be very good. Like the Bordeaux 1988s at this stage. The acidity bothers me a bit. Very good nevertheless. (17.5)

In hindsight, the 1982 and 1986 should have been paired. These two suffered from being paired with two giants (1978 and 1985, respectively).

Overall impressions

Excellent range of wines. Value-wise, it is a different story. One-for-one, these wines are almost as good as Pichon-Lalande or Cos d'Estournel. But price-wise, they cost almost double.

January 23 to 28, 1997

Trip to Yountville, Napa Valley.

January 23, 1997

Evening visit and dinner at Viader Vineyards, as Delia Viader's guest.

Also present was a group of about ten Canadian journalists and representatives of the Quebec and BC liquor monopolies, and several representatives of wineries, including Bernard Portet of Clos du Val, and representatives from Cakebread, Beringer, and Frog's Leap Vineyard.

1992 CAKEBREAD CABERNET SAUVIGNON "RESERVE," NAPA VALLEY:

Sweet, fruity nose. Hint of rubber. Round, surprisingly forward for such a young wine. Loosely knit. Nice, minty Cabernet flavours. Sweet finish. Pleasant, but somehow lacks character and depth. (15)

1992 CLOS DU VAL CABERNET SAUVIGNON "RESERVE," NAPA VALLEY:

Made from 89% Cabernet Sauvignon, 3% Merlot, and 8% Cabernet Franc. One of the best wines of the evening. Very good, deep colour. Cedary, ripe berries on nose, with hint of vanilla and oak. Fruit and acidity in harmony. Full, rich, needing three to five extra years of bottle-age. (17)

1986 DUCKHORN CABERNET SAUVIGNON, NAPA VALLEY:

Very French style. Medium, red colour, evolved rim. Spicy Cabernet/oak nose. Fairly dry. Tannic, still a big aggressive wine—even at ten years. Yet, odd sweetness at finish. Good now, but should improve over the next two to three years. (16.5)

1989 FROG'S LEAP CABERNET SAUVIGNON "RESERVE," NAPA VALLEY:

Richer, riper, sweeter, yet more forward than the 1986 Duckhorn. Good, ripe tannins; hint of vanilla-oak. Enjoyable now, or over the next five years. (17)

Bernard Portet said that the wine media had done an injustice to the 1989 vintage in Napa, writing it off, yet some excellent wines were produced.

1991 ST. SUPÉRY CABERNET SAUVIGNON "LIMITED EDITION RESERVE, DOLLARIDGE RANCH," NAPA VALLEY:

An impressive wine. Deep colour to rim. Lovely, ripe fruit on nose; vanilla and oak and ripe cherries. Full, ripe tannins; well balanced. Still very youthful, of course. Drink from 1999 onward. (17.5)

1989 VIADER VINEYARDS, IN DOUBLE-MAGNUM:

60% Cabernet Sauvignon and 40% Cabernet Franc. This was Delia's first vintage, and a fine effort indeed. Even in double-magnums, this wine is ready; typical of the softer, early maturing 1989 vintage. Understated, spicy Cabernet nose. Round, nice fruit, spicy, yet no sharp edges. Soft tannins, round, and long. Very good. (17)

1990 BERINGER CABERNET SAUVIGNON "PRIVATE RESERVE," NAPA VALLEY:

The most solid, most masculine of all the red wines tasted tonight. Made from 96% Cabernet Sauvignon, 1% Merlot, and 3% Cabernet Franc from Howell Mountain. Biggest, deepest, darkest. Sturdy, ripe yet solid tannins. Not nearly ready. Drink from 2000 to 2005. Very rich, ripe fruit. (18)

An impressive effort. The representative of Beringer told me that there is mostly Chardonnay planted in their vineyard in Yountville across from my townhouse.

Bernard Portet will be the chairman this year of the Napa Valley charity wine auction to be held this summer. At the end of the tasting and dinner, Bernard Portet got up to thank our hostess Delia Viader, and to welcome "our Canadian friends"—to which the representative of the SAQ (Société des Alcools du Québec) mumbled: "and Québec friends." I had a very hard time controlling myself and not reacting.

Later that night

The group drove in a bus to "Ana's Bar and Pool Hall" in St. Helena

Delia and I joined them. Bernard Portet and I shot a game of pool and others joined us, too. It was fun. I didn't realize that Bernard is a fun-loving guy, but then it is the French blood in his veins.

Friday, January 24, 1997

Visit to Groezinger's Wine Shop, in Yountville, with owner Martin Blomberg.

I tasted two wines.

NEWTON 1994 ZINFANDEL, NAPA VALLEY:

Parker raved about this wine. Neither Martin nor I were that impressed. It is an in-your-face wine, all right. Big, chunky, tannic. Very ripe, youthful, but no Zinfandel character. None of that spicy berries. In fairness to Parker, he tasted a barrel sample. Maybe he should be more careful with his assessments.

MULDERBOSCH SAUVIGNON BLANC 1995, STELLENBOSCH, SOUTH AFRICA:

Still very youthful. Intense, spicy, herbal Sauvignon Blanc nose. Fresh, crisp, fairly acidic, but lots of tight extract and depth there. Should make a fine bottle by 2000 and beyond.

We also discussed the influence of Parker on winemaking in France, Portugal, and even in the USA. So many newcomers and novices with money know so little about wine, and don't have the time or can't be bothered to learn that they must rely on Parker and The Wine Spectator. *They drink their Ports at 10 years (!) and they like fruity, early maturing wines.*

We also discussed the new threat in the Napa Valley—Pierce disease (PD), a virus that attacks the veins under the vine leaves and eventually destroys the vine. The leaves lose their greenness (chlorophyll) and show burning at the edges. There is no known cure. Several vineyards have been damaged very seriously. As an example, Martin told me that Phillip Togni has lost about 40% of his vines to this disease. It is even worse than phylloxera, about which people at least have a fair bit of knowledge and can manage, fight, and control it.

Same day

Lunch at the Culinary Institute of America.

With Dan and Margaret Duckhorn. Dan had just got back from Mendocino and he told me that he had just purchased an 80-acre vineyard and winery in Anderson Valley, where he will plant up to 50 acres of only one varietal, Pinot Noir. He has retained the winemaker there, but they are gutting the winery and adding new equipment.

We discussed Russian oak, and he agreed that no more than 5% of the crop should be aged in Russian oak barrels. It produces perfumed, soft wines. He is also going to use more American oak in the future. When asked about Pierce disease, Dan smiled—a worried smile. He told me that it is a virus that is carried by grasshoppers; it attacks the leaves and eventually the roots, killing the vine. There is no known cure.

Especially vulnerable are vineyards near tall grass and humid, wet soils. On Howell Mountain and on other hills, it seems that vineyards are safe because of drier soils. The flats are another story. He will send me some information on this disease. Locals know it also as Anaheim disease, because that seems to be the geographic source.

About trends in winemaking and wine drinking, Dan said that it is a fact of life that people do not want to age wines, but drink them right away. No one these days, it seems, can be bothered with intellectual wines. Pity.

Dan is fond of French Sauvignon Blancs, so I brought one along.

CHÂTEAU LAVILLE-HAUT-BRION 1978:

Amazingly youthful in appearance and taste, even at 18 years old! Pale gold. Buttery, oaky, spicy Sauvignon nose. Full. Excellent fruit/acidity balance. Lots of class here. Will last well for another ten years or more. A lovely bottle. (18)

On the way out, Margaret showed me her new present from Santa, her husband: a brand new Jaguar Sedan, in British racing-green.

Dinner at the "French Laundry"

In Yountville, with Delia Viader and another couple, good friends of Delia, from San Francisco. Chef Hubert Keller produced an excellent menu for us.

PULIGNY-MONTRACHET 1994, ETIENNE SAUZET:

Gerard Boudot, the owner and winemaker of Sauzet, has made excellent 1994s, even at the Villages level. The wine was light and elegant—as most 1994 white Burgundies are. Lovely, subdued Chardonnay/oak nose. Crisp, quite soft, clean, and elegant on palate. Drink now to 1999. His Premiers Crus and Grands Crus are more intense, of course, but still elegant in 1994. (16.5)

I brought along this bottle.

CHÂTEAU COS D'ESTOURNEL 1986:

Superb. Possibly the best Cos in the 1980s; even better than the 1982, and certainly better structured that either their 1989 or 1990. Impressive, deep colour to rim. Essence of Cabernet and ripe fruit on nose. Full, intense, solid; loaded with ripe tannins and fruit. Not yet ready and will last well, if well stored, for at least another 15 years. (18)

It rained all night, renewing fears of flooding in the Napa Valley.

Dinner at the Condo.

With Delia Viader of Viader Vineyard. I cooked dinner.

Delia brought me a bottle of her 1994 Viader as a gift. She hopes to increase her production from 3,600 to 5,000 cases (maximum). Her vineyard is planted with 50% each of Cabernet Sauvignon and Cabernet Franc. She has also planted a few rows of Petit Verdot, and may add it in future as 1% to 2% of the blend.

She uses about 60% new oak yearly. Presently, the winemaking facility is at Rombauer's—same as Christian Moueix's Dominus. She also plans to plant some Syrah in a flat, sheltered area near the entrance to the vineyard, where the soil is very poor.

Delia is a dedicated, hard-working person. She makes the wine herself—all aspects—not just winemaking and vineyard management, but public relations and sales, too, worldwide. Switzerland and Germany are major importers of her wines.

January 29, 1997

Back in Vancouver.

CHÂTEAU FIGEAC 1982:

With lovely veal-kidney dinner. Classic Figeac and classic 1982. Deep, rich colour to rim. Cedar, spicy, expansive, ripe fruit and oak on nose. Full, round, ripe, soft tannins on palate. Very long, luscious. This reminds me a lot of Figeac's 1964—another great wine. (18)

February 4, 1997

Dinner and tasting of Château Latour, at "Rover's" restaurant, in Seattle.

Drove to Seattle with Sid Cross. This event was organized by Andy Lench of Bordeaux Wine Locators, Latour's agents in Seattle. Frederic Engerer, the export manager of Château Latour, represented the château.

Before the tasting, Frederic said that the 1996 is starting to develop good backbone and better structure than the 1995. He confirmed my impression when I visited Latour last October that Latour's 1995 was a bit too soft, yet he said that it is just a reflection of the 1995 vintage.

We started the tasting with the following two wines.

LES-FORTS-DE-LATOUR 1991 AND 1989:

Les-Forts-de-Latour is usually aged in 40% to 60% new oak barrels. It is made up not only of wines not judged quite great enough to be included in the Grand Vin, but also from three plots called "Comtesse de Lalande," "Petit Batailley," and "Santa Anna," as well as Latour's young vines.

LES-FORTS-DE-LATOUR 1991:

Bright cherry-red; evolved rim. Forthcoming, warm, fruity, straw/oak nose. Acidic on entry, little tannin. Quite forward, soft. Fine effort in an indifferent year, but too sharp. (14)

LES FORT DE LATOUR 1989:

Similar appearance to the 1991, but more depth. Riper, sweet, subdued nose. Round, medium-bodied; still a bit tannic, of course, but not a big wine. Ready now to 2002. The fruit is a bit soft. (16)

Château Latour 1991, 1990, 1989, 1988, 1985, 1982, and 1978

CHÂTEAU LATOUR 1991:

Deeper colour than the 1991 Les Forts. Less vegetal on nose. Hint of chocolate, dried fruit, exotic. Fairly high acidity, but backed by good fruit. Fine effort for 1991. (17)

Small production because a lot of Latour had to go into Les Forts in 1991 (because of frost that damaged and reduced drastically the production of Les Forts). What saved Latour in 1991, and even more so in 1964, is their closeness to the river and warmer temperature, allowing them to pick a few days before Mouton or Lafite—a major advantage. This 1991 was bottled sooner than in riper vintages, thus avoiding too much oak impact in a difficult, diluted year.

Since 1990, Latour has been bottling a third wine, an A/C Pauillac, about 30,000 to 40,000 bottles. Average production of Les Forts is 130,000 to 140,000 bottles, and Latour approximately 240,000 bottles, or 20,000 cases.

CHÂTEAU LATOUR 1990:

Deep, dense colour to rim; youthful-looking. Black currants, oak, toast, all in harmony. Full, rich, ripe, tannic. Powerful tannins, and the fruit is as backward as expected. Almost salty on lips. Needs at least ten more years to open up. Too closed; hard to judge with precision, but certainly great potential. Layers of fruit, cinnamon, Cassis, cedar, all in harmony. Also tobacco and mocha. (19)

CHÂTEAU LATOUR 1989:

As deep as the 1990, but slightly paler rim. More subdued on nose. Quite tannic, solid, backed by ripe fruit, but a bit looser-knit than the 1990. No doubt needing an extra eight to ten years of bottle-age. The overall structure of a 1985 in terms of fruit, and 1988 in terms of tannins. A bit more leathery and ripe than the 1990, but the 1990 is classier, with better depth. Almost California-like. (17.5)

CHÂTEAU LATOUR 1988:

Excellent, deep colour to rim. Straw, oak, subdued nose. Still tight. Solid, serious, classic Bordeaux/ Cabernet on palate. Excellent fruit, tannins, acidity, all in harmony. Very young, of course. Hint of ripe raisins on nose. Starting—ever so modestly—to open up, but still a baby. More focused and better defined than the 1989. Drink from 2002 onward. (18)

Robert Parker isn't too excited over the 1988s, and they are, therefore, still underrated and reasonably priced. The 1988 Latour is excellent.

The 1989 is Bordeaux's "California wine"—almost too ripe—at the very edge of ripeness. At the estate, they believe that the 1990 has even greater potential than the 1982. They believe that the 1990 has even greater potential than the 1982. Time will tell.

CHÂTEAU LATOUR 1985:

Bright, deep colour to rim. Delicate, herbaceous nose with hint of toast/oak. Typical 1985 on palate; loosely knit, soft fruit, yet still fair bit of acidity and even noticeable tannins. One of the better 1985s, yet one wishes it had more depth and riper fruit. Ready, but no rush. A bit too weedy and too accessible. (17)

CHÂTEAU LATOUR 1982:

Deep, dense colour, showing just a little maturity at rim. Ripe, rich, raisiny, sweet, cedary on nose. Full, round; already approachable as the fruit is softening up, yet still has a tannic backbone. Not as tight as the 1990; a broader, more open wine. It seems that the 1990 is more focused. This 1982 has a sensational bouquet. Surprisingly evolved. Superb now. Great, great nose. (19)

Château Latour 1978:

Mature colour, good depth. Palish rim. Delicate, straw, oak, chocolate, cedar, ripe nose. Not as vegetal as some 1978s. Full, rich, solid; lovely ripe tannins. Full-bodied, excellent depth. Truffles on nose (atypical for Latour) and black olives. Luscious, long, full. A great 1978; possibly, together with La Mission, Pichon-Lalande, and Margaux, the best 1978. No rush. Lovely bottle. (18)

Before dinner, at the reception

Champagne Jacquesson 1985 "Signature":

Too green, too sharp, too acidic. Very fresh at ten years of age, but lacks ripeness and depth. Far inferior to the fine Jacquesson 1989 "Signature" and 1989 "Rosé" tasted last December in Los Angeles.

Then we sat down for dinner.

Les-Forts-de-Latour 1975:

Good colour, still deep red. Pale rim. Very 1975 nose; stemmy, almost a bit rustic. Sweeter on entry than expected, and riper fruit. Quite rich, full, solid. At this stage the tannins are soft, well blended in the wine. Serious Cabernet. Went very well with oxtail terrine. Ready, but no rush. (17)

Château Latour 1971:

Deep, brick-red colour. Slightly watery rim. Some volatile acidity on nose. Quite forward on palate, yet still tannic. Definitely the liveliest 1971 around, yet fairly acidic finish. Definitely better with food than by itself. Somehow unbalanced. Lacks a bit in fruit. (17)

Château Latour 1970:

Massive, deep colour to rim. At 26 years of age, still very impressive appearance. Very concentrated, unyielding. Black fruit, sensational ripeness, perfect balance. Ripe, rich tannins, acidity, fruit, all in harmony. Superb weight. Approachable, but no rush. Will last forever. Blows the 1971 away. More backward than the 1982! (19.5)

Château Latour 1966 and 1967:

It is a pity that they were served in this order. A better pairing would have been the 1971 with the 1967, and the 1970 with the 1966. The 1971 had to compete against the great 1970. An impossible task.

The 1967: Good, deep colour; impressive for a 30-year-old and from a good, rather than great, vintage. The problem with the 1967s was their relatively high acidity. The Latour had it, too, but at least it was backed by enough fruit. Better than the 1971; riper fruit. Certainly the best 1967 around. Lovely now. Cigar-box, cedar, earthy overtones. Good, ripe fruit. Slightly acidic finish. Intense, long. Fine bottle. Hint of chaptalization. (17)

The 1966: Not much deeper than the 1967. Cedar, ripe, tobacco, oak nose. Oddly, a bit stemmy, too. Beefy, rich, solid; quite dry and fairly acidic, but backed by tight fruit. Cinnamon, Cassis nose. Somehow I remember the 1966 as being richer. This bottle, while lovely in appearance and on nose, was just a bit too acidic on palate, even sour, against the 1967! The 1970 is so much richer. A bit "piqué." Definitely off. Something wrong here. How can the 1967 be better balanced than the 1966? Not a good bottle. (16) Yet all the bottles were shipped from the château, and had impeccable appearances. This can be excellent.

Château Latour 1964:

As with the above, impressive deep colour. Amazingly youthful for its age. Very ripe on nose. Prunes, sweet raisins, intense. Full, chocolaty, ripe tannins, rich. Definitely the best Haut-Médoc in 1964. Very long. Still full of life. Very rich, luscious. Perfect now, but no rush. (18)

Château Latour 1959:

Opaque; impressive, deep, dark colour to rim. Great, earthy, chocolaty, cedary nose. Even more intense (by far) than the 1964. Classic, ripe 1959. Dark chocolate truffles on nose. Solid. There was some bottle variation on nose. Other bottles had a more delicate, cedar, cigar-box nose. Very dense, very big, still full of life. Lovely. (19)

Taylor's 1963 Vintage Port:

Classic Port and now fully mature at over 33 years old. Evolved colour with good depth. Elegant, complex, clean nose. Long, round, perfectly balanced. Lots of class and layers of spicy fruit. (18.5)

As far as the Latours are concerned, my choice for stardom (in order) are: 1970, 1982, 1990, and 1959. The big surprise was the fine quality of the 1988, a wine and vintage overlooked by the influential wine experts on both sides of the Atlantic. The 1989 was surprisingly forward, but then, most 1989s are.

February 11, 1997

Commanderie de Bordeaux "Members Only" Dinner and tasting, featuring the 1986 Claret vintage, at "The Beach House" restaurant, in West Vancouver.

This was a tenth-anniversary assessment tasting of the 1986 Haut-Médocs. The food was excellent. Chef Sonny Mendoza is a gifted young chef.

APERITIF

CHAMPAGNE BILLECART-SALMON BRUT "RESERVE" N/V:

Clean, fruity nose. Round, crisp, well balanced. Good fruit, lingering aftertaste. Fine.

FLIGHT #1

CHÂTEAU HAUT-BAGES-LIBÉRAL 1986:

Dark colour, orangy rim. Clean fruit and oak on nose. A bit tannic, but diluted middle. The late Bernadette Villars of Château Chasse-Spleen had just taken over this property, and did her best with what she had. Pleasant, cedary, clean finish. Just the middle is lacking. Good Cabernet spiciness. One-dimensional. Not a bad effort, but outclassed. (15)

CHÂTEAU LA LAGUNE 1986:

Bright red. Subdued nose. Round, yet quite tannic. Good stuffing backed by ripe fruit. Ready, but no rush. Clean, long finish. A rich, solid wine. (16.5)

CHÂTEAU LEOVILLE-POYFERRÉ 1986:

Excellent, dense colour—best of flight. Tight, closed nose. Hint of Cassis and ripe fruit. Spicy, rich, solid. Tannins backed up by lots of fruit. Fine extract. Needs five to seven years or more. One bottle was slightly musty; the other two were fine. (17.5)

CHÂTEAU RAUSAN-SÉGLA 1986:

Lovely, deep colour. Very Margaux. elegant, cedary, subdued nose. Round, "fondu," elegant, yet good fruit. Best complexity of flight. Finally Rausan-Ségla is back. More approachable than the Leoville-Poyferré, but needs two more years. (17.5)

CHÂTEAU LA LAGUNE 1985:

Added for comparison against the 1986s. Much more evolved colour. Toasty, clean oak. Soft, forward, well balanced. A mistake to use 100% new oak in such a soft year. Too much oak for structure. (16)

FLIGHT #2

CHÂTEAU LEOVILLE-BARTON 1986:

Impressive, deep colour. Full, rich; great concentration of fruit. Lovely, concentrated, serious, tight. Roughest of flight. Hard, solid wine. Higher acidity than the Gruaud. Needs five years or more. (17.5)

CHÂTEAU GRUAUD-LAROSE 1986:

Denser colour than the above, but not as bright. Closed, unyielding nose, yet hint of ripe fruit. Powerful, tannic, rich, solid wine. Needs lots of time (ten or more years). Deep, powerful wine. (17)

CHÂTEAU LYNCH-BAGES 1986:

Bright, deep-red colour. Exotic, cedary, lovely sweet fruit. Not as tight as above two. Lingering aftertaste. Very good balance; fruit and tannins in harmony. Oddly, more forward than Gruaud or Leoville-Barton. (17)

CHÂTEAU PAPE CLÉMENT 1986:

Bright, yet evolved colour. Sweet fruit on nose. Sweet on palate. Round, long, approachable, yet excellent backbone. Fairly evolved, rich, long, Leather, ripe fruit. Beautiful now. This was the only non-Haut-Médoc wine of the whole tasting, and a fine effort. (17.5) Nice to see this property back in form.

FLIGHT #3

CHÂTEAU COS D'ESTOURNEL 1986:

Dense, deep colour. Excellent extract. Tight nose, hint of oak, very closed. Like a four-year-old Claret. Ripe, powerful tannins. Concentrated wine. Very dense, very serious. Multidimensional. Lovely, ripe fruit. Grand Vin! (18.5)

CHÂTEAU PICHON-LALANDE 1986:

Not as dark as the Cos, but good, deep colour. More evolved at rim. Slightly rubbery nose. Surprisingly forward, soft, yet quite powerful tannins underneath. Lovely, sweet fruit. Great class and stuffing. The elegance and breed are there, too. (18)

CHÂTEAU LATOUR 1986:

Good, dark colour. Evolved rim. Tight, yet slightly rubbery nose. Solid, powerful on entry. Lacks middle, though. Ponderous, serious Pauillac that somehow lacks the middle concentration. Needs five to seven years. Disappointing in the context of a First Growth. Very good nevertheless. (17.5)

CHÂTEAU MOUTON-ROTHSCHILD 1986:

Impressive, deep colour to rim. Ripe, superb extract, cedar on nose. Great. The wine of the evening. Sensational. Great extract, fruit. Needs ten to 15 years. Loads of clean, fruity, oaky lusciousness. Must be the wine of the vintage. (19.5)

CHÂTEAU MOUTON-ROTHSCHILD 1985:

Included in this flight to put the two vintages into perspective. Quite evolved colour; orangy rim. Cedary, open, herbaceous nose. Classic, typical Mouton. Complex cedar, oak, fruit, and toast. Lovely now and should hold well. All in harmony. (18)

We ended this fine and educational evening with Port.

CROFT'S 1963 VINTAGE PORT:

As expected at 33 years of age, evolved colour. Clean, delicate, yet expansive nose. Spicy fruit. Silky, round, very long on palate. Lovely now. (17.5) I purchased these Ports back in 1974 and they have rested in my cool cellar (11°C/52°F) since then.

Overall impressions on the 1986 Vintage in the Médoc

This is a great year. Maybe less ripe than 1982, but more stuffing, more serious, and will be as long-lived (if not longer) than the 1982s. With the exception of the Haut-Bages-Libéral, they were all super wines.

Some, like Rausan-Ségla and Pape Clément, were more evolved. Others will need several more years, around the turn of the millennium, if not later, to reach their peak.

My guess is that Mouton 1982 and 1986 will eventually resemble the Mouton 1959 and 1961, respectively. The only relatively weak effort—but a fine, serious wine nevertheless—was the Latour. In terms of value, the three best buys—and by any yardstick, all three are great wines—are the Cos d'Estournel, Pichon-Lalande, and potentially, Leoville-Barton.

Thursday, February 13, 1997

Dinner and tasting, at "Etoile" restaurant, in Vancouver, with a small group of friends, featuring some fine mature wines.

1976 HATTENHEIMER WISSELBRUNNEN RIESLING AUSLESE, LANG, MOSEL:

Bright, deep, evolved golden colour. Lovely, spicy, oily, petroleum, rich, ripe nose. Quite evolved. Lovely fruit, acidity. Fairly rich; some bitterness at finish, but good fruit. Quite rich and sweet for an Auslese. Classic Riesling. (17)

1975 URZIGER WURZGARTEN RIESLING AUSLESE, NICOLAY, RHEINGAU:

Totally different from the above. Palish-golden colour. More delicate, more subdued nose. Flowery, elegant. Lighter, crisper acidity, livelier, fresher. Nice, spicy, long finish. (17)

GRANDS ECHÉZEAUX 1971, DOMAINE DE LA ROMANÉE-CONTI, IN MAGNUM:

Excellent, deep colour. Lovely, expansive, raspberries, Pinot Noir nose. Full, rich; great concentration of fruit. Spicy, slightly stemmy. Loads of fruit. Very long finish. Perfect now, but if well stored, should hold well for another decade or longer. After an hour in glass, still full of life, with great, exotic, spicy extract. (18.5)

CARRUADES DE CHÂTEAU LAFITE 1966:

Excellent appearance; good depth, orange rim. Toasty, baked oak on nose. Later, cleared and delicate, spicy fruit came through. On palate: drying up a bit. Smoky, a bit short, simple. A hard act to follow (after the 1971 Grands Echézeaux). After ten minutes in glass, fragile, drying out. Some elegance. Drink up. (15.5) This is the second wine of Château Lafite.

CHÂTEAU DUCRU-BEAUCAILLOU 1961:

Mid shoulder level, which worried us. Slightly dank-cellar on nose. Deep colour; palish rim. Lovely, toasty, ripe fruit on nose. Sweet on entry. Rich, long, full, ripe. Great, sweet fruit extract. Better on palate than on nose. Impressive level of ripe fruit, in spite of the low ullage. Mocha, coffee aftertaste. (17.5)

While very good, this wine did not quite achieve the level of quality it can produce. Low ullage and poor cellaring must have had something to do with the result. Can be superb.

CHÂTEAU DUCRU-BEAUCAILLOU 1970, IN MAGNUM:

A superb magnum! Excellent level. Youthful appearance of the best 1970s. Deep, purplish colour to rim. Very fresh, youthful, fruity nose. Great extract, great balance. Lots of fruit. Very young; needs more time from magnums. The best 1970 St. Julien. (18.5)

CHÂTEAU RIEUSSEC 1983:

Typical, early maturing, deep-golden colour. Peaches, apricots, exotic fruit. Lots of depth here. Lovely botrytis on nose. Full, sweet, luscious. Perfect now. (18)

March 12, 1997

Farewell and dinner, at home, for the council of the Commanderie de Bordeaux.

On April 26, 1997, at our Gala Induction Dinner and Ceremony, I will transfer the duties of Maître from myself to Ian Mottershead. That event will feature a vertical tasting of Château Margaux, with the participation of Corinne Mentzelopoulos, the owner of Château Margaux.

To this farewell dinner, I have invited our regular council, our founding Maître, Dr. Allan Tobe, and long-time council member, Sid Cross. All the wines were from my cellar. All wines were served double-blind.

CHAMPAGNE DOM PÉRIGNON 1982, IN MAGNUM:

Superb, especially from magnum, and from a great vintage. Creamy, smooth, long, complex. Perfect balance. Lovely, long finish and extract. The master blender at Moët et Chandon may not appreciate the comparison, but this 1982 really resembles a good Roederer Cristal. Nothing wrong with that comparison.

CHASSAGNE-MONTRACHET PREMIER CRU "MORGEOT," DOMAINE DU DUC DE MAGENTA, 1978:

Alas, I waited too long. Bright, youthful colour, but lean, acidic, vegetal, hard; low fruit, and lacking Chardonnay character. Most tasters thought that it was a Rhône.

CHÂTEAU DE LUCQUES 1924, BARSAC:

Shipped by Eschenauer. Served with a foie gras salad. I acquired this bottle from a wine shop last October, during a visit to St. Emilion. The owner of the shop wanted 1,700 francs.

After lengthy negotiation, we settled on 1,250 francs. He told me that before World War I, this property was an Appellation Sauternes; Lur Saluces (owner of d'Yquem) threatened to sue the owner if he didn't change his Appellation, because most of the vineyard was in Barsac. Therefore, after World War I, the name Barsac appeared on the label. The property fell on hard times during the recession and "disappeared."

In recent editions of Feret, *the property reappears as producing only red wine. Consequently, we tasted an irreplaceable bit of history.*

Very good top shoulder level. No sediment. Decanted 15 minutes. Cork was sound but fragile. Very deep amber-gold colour. Not unlike a fine 1959 Sauternes, which is what most tasters thought this was. Clean, delicate, slightly earthy nose, but ripe raisins and botrytis, too. Round, very much alive, still some sweetness, good acidity. Long and nutty with some botrytis. Lovely wine. Went very well with the foie gras.

1979 Pommard "Clos de Verger," Pothier-Rieusset

and

1979 Hermitage Rouge, J. L. Chave:

Most participants had a good tasting, guessing the former as being Rhône and the latter as Burgundy.

The Pommard is one of the finest 1979s made. A reliable producer. Good, dark, evolved colour. Spicy, expansive, ripe, yet slightly vegetal Pinot Noir on nose. Full yet round; good fruit and acidity underneath. Ready, but still holding well.

The Hermitage was classic Chave. Spicy, leathery, peppery Syrah. Dark colour. Full, yet getting a bit softer. Drinking well now, but no rush. Lots of extract. Not as intense as the great 1978, but very good.

Château Latour 1962, in magnum:

I acquired this magnum in 1975, 22 years ago, and it has remained undisturbed in my cellar since, at a constant temperature of 11°C. What a superb wine! Most tasters thought that it was a 1982, Mouton or Latour! The incredibly youthful, deep, bright colour of the 1962s. Level was excellent, well into neck. Finally a Latour one can drink rather than taste (they take forever to come around). Great, chocolaty, cedary, clean, spicy, ripe fruit on nose. Superb length, balance, and ripe fruit on palate. Very long, smooth, round, yet full of life. Really impossible to fault this magnificent magnum. (19)

I will refrain from trying to acquire more of this because I want to keep in my memory the fantastic quality of this 35-year-old great Claret. Acquiring it now may entail the risk of poor storage and/or bottle variation—and of course, crazy prices! Back in 1975, I paid $40 for this magnum.

Warre's 1934 Vintage Port "Directors' Reserve":

Bottled by Arthur Bell and Sons, Perth, Scotland. Very pale colour. Unmistakable, spicy Vintage Port on nose. Quite spirity, yet soft, delicate fruit. Long, spicy, complex. Clean, long finish. Very fine.

At the end of the evening, I thanked my council for helping me run our Commanderie de Bordeaux, where I have served as Maître since February 1988. How time flies!

March 26, 1997

Morey-St.-Denis Blanc "En la Rue de Vergy" 1990, Domaine Bruno Clair:

Bright green-gold colour. Crisp, spicy, slightly herbaceous nose. Crisp on palate, too, yet has good depth, fruit, and acidity, all in harmony. The structure of a Chablis Grand Cru, yet without the flinty taste. Drinking well now, but no rush. Bruno Clair is a gifted winemaker. White Burgundy from the Côte de Nuits is a rather uncommon wine. Fine effort. (17)

Meursault "Désirée" 1990, Comtes Lafon:

Lafon and Coche-Dury are the undisputed masters of Meursault, and it shows, even in this lieu dit, rather than a Premier Cru. Brilliant golden colour. Clean, nutty, oaky, and impeccably clean and long fruit on nose. Similar impressions on palate. Lots of class here. Great balance. Ready but no rush. Clean, complex, long finish. Even hint of exotic fruit. (17.5)

Bonnes Mares 1989, Louis Jadot:

Bright cherry-red, youthful colour. Nose still a bit closed, but clean, fresh, spicy, and fruity. Quite evolved on palate, as expected of a 1989. Lovely fruit, round, no hint of tannins. Ready, at this youthful stage. (17.5)

What a pity that producers of red Burgundy overproduced in 1989. A little more conscientious pruning would have given these 1989s the extra depth that would have turned them from very good to excellent, even great. Greed was the damaging factor in 1989, as far as red Burgundies are concerned. In terms of weather conditions, there was no reason not to produce wines with the concentration of the 1990s in 1989.

Saturday, April 26, 1997

Commanderie de Bordeaux Gala Black Tie Dinner and vertical tasting of Château Margaux, at the Four Seasons hotel, Vancouver.

On this occasion, we are celebrating the 20th anniversary of our Commanderie's charter in 1977. We also celebrate the 20th anniversary of the ownership of Château Margaux by the Mentzelopoulos family. I will also induct four new Commandeurs. Last, but not least, I shall be stepping down as Maître of our Commanderie, after nine years (since February 1988), and I will induct Ian Mottershead as our new Maître.

Corinne Mentzelopoulos, the owner, arrived last night; she will join us, as will Delia Viader, owner/winemaker of Viader Vineyards in Napa, at this event. Corinne very generously shipped us all the Margaux wines for this event. We will start with a sit-down tasting, followed by a Champagne reception and ceremonies, followed by dinner.

THE TASTING

Château Margaux

1994:

Dark, youthful colour. Tight on nose, hint of oak, but little fruit coming through at this early stage. Quite tight on palate. Some fruit, but still very backward, of course. Does not seem to be a rich wine in the 1990 style. Very good fruit concentration, though. Obvious high Cabernet, hard, leaner-style wine. Very good potential in ten to 12 years. (17.5)

1990:

All the components are there. This wine is a true representative of this excellent, ripe vintage. Very deep colour to rim. Fabulous, ripe Cassis fruit on nose. Great balance, fruit extract, soft tannins, oak—all in harmony. Very long on palate. Some bitterness at finish from the oak. An exotic, great wine. Will mature relatively early, by 2002, but it is so well balanced and so rich, it will last well at least until 2015. Grand Vin! (19.5)

1989:

Good, dark colour, showing slight evolution at rim. Looser-knit than the ripe 1990 and not as tight as the 1994. Higher acidity than the 1990; softer, more forward overall. Good backbone. Long, complex. This will mature before the 1990 and have a relatively shorter plateau. Drink from 1999 to 2010. (18)

1988:

The forgotten vintage of this excellent decade of the 1980s. Dark colour; excellent depth. Tight, unyielding nose. Hard, tannic, almost aggressive, but underneath this masculine façade, there is enough fruit. Tannic, oaky, powerful. Not a charmer at this stage. Classic old-style, traditional Claret of great quality. This is one of the best wines of that vintage. More personality, more "serious" than the 1989. Needs at least another 12 years to approach maturity. Excellent potential. (18.5)

1986:

A massive, opaque, mighty wine that is totally unready and will last for decades! Closed nose; hint of oak and very ripe Cassis fruit. Great tannic concentration backed by loads of tight fruit. This reminds me of the 1970 Latour in its youth. Inky. By far the greatest extract of all the wines tasted tonight. If well stored and a sound bottle, don't even think of trying this wine, or expect it to be ready before the year 2005. Will last well for many decades after that. (19.5)

1978:

The first vintage produced by the new regime. Ready now. Classic, old-style, herbaceous Margaux. This stemminess is also typical of the 1978 vintage. Round, well balanced, good depth. Has lost its youth, but at 19 years of age, it is at its peak. Not a generous, fat wine; rather elegant. Very long on palate. (18.5)

These were followed by two white wines.

Pavillon Blanc du Château Margaux

1995:

Youthful, crisp "nerveux," spicy, and long, as such a youthful wine should be. This wine is made from 100% Sauvignon Blanc grapes, and is barrel-fermented in 100% new oak. Some sharpness, but in a positive, youthful sense. Should be drinking well by 2002 to 2005. (17)

1986:

Fully mature at ten years old. Rich, long, quite powerful, with excellent ripe-fruit extract. Even hint of some residual sugar on palate. Made from very ripe grapes. Almost has the weight of a fine Chardonnay. Very good quality. (17.5)

Corinne wanted the whites to be served after the reds at this tasting because, according to her, the Sauvignon Blanc grape is very spicy, and interferes in the tasting of red wines once the palate has been exposed to this varietal.

At the reception, before the induction and transfer of the title of Maître, we tasted two fine Champagnes.

Champagne Veuve Clicquot Brut Rosé 1985:

Bright-pink rather than salmon colour. Quite evolved in appearance. Fine mousse. Long, full on palate; showing the excellent fruit extract of that fine vintage in Champagne. Very good.

CHAMPAGNE VEUVE CLICQUOT BRUT "RESERVE" 1989:

Still youthful and tight, typical of this property's wines when they are young. Needs two to three extra years of bottle-age. Very good fruit. Well balanced, fairly solid Champagne. Excellent potential. "Reserve" is the new name of "Carte Or," the designation of this Champagne in earlier vintages. It is the same wine.

After the ceremonies, we sat down for an exquisite meal, prepared by Executive Chef Marc Miron, with the following wines.

PAVILLON ROUGE DU CHÂTEAU MARGAUX 1990 AND 1982:

The 1990 was youthful, softer than the Grand Vin; more Merlot was obvious. Round, charming, nice oak-vanilla (100% new oak barrels) and ripe fruit in harmony. Approachable but not quite ready. Drink around 1998 to 2003.

The 1982 had the typical very ripe fruit, charm, and exotic character of that very ripe vintage. Lovely ripe fruit extract. Very long. Oak and fruit in harmony. At its peak. A fine bottle. Rated the 1990 (17) and the 1982 (17.5). Both are as good as—or better than—several Haut-Médoc Classed Growths.

CHÂTEAU MARGAUX 1983:

I will repeat what I have said several times before. This is the wine of the vintage, as far as Bordeaux is concerned. Fabulous, deep, bright, youthful colour. Cedary, spicy, ripe Cassis, Cabernet nose. Still very closed; not nearly ready. Lots of depth, but still tannic and very tight. Great concentration. Did not have the charm and ripe, sweet fruit at this stage of the 1982, but a very long-distance runner. Great potential. (19)

CHÂTEAU MARGAUX 1982:

The corks indicated that the wine was recorked at the château in 1994. Corinne said that Paul Pontallier, the general manager of Margaux, decided to recork several batches of the 1982 because he was a bit worried about the quality of some of the original corks. Very deep colour. Marvellous, ripe nose of ripe Cassis. Full, round, soft tannins, sweet fruit on palate. Totally atypical. A mouthful of charming, rich, sweet fruit that is eminently drinkable now, but has so much fruit (and soft, ripe tannins underneath) that it will hold well at this plateau for another decade, or more. Much more approachable and enjoyable tonight than the 1983. (19)

CHÂTEAU MARGAUX 1966, IN MAGNUMS:

Recorked at the château in 1994. Impeccable condition and appearance. This was the last great vintage produced at this château under the ownership of the Ginestets. After the mid-1960s, a difficult period followed for Margaux, with disappointing wines produced in 1970, 1971, 1975, and 1976, culminating in the sale of this property to Corinne's father in 1977.

Everything one could possibly expect from a fine, great, mature Claret. The colour is still impressive and dark, showing some maturity at rim, but surprisingly deep for a 30-year-old wine. Fabulous nose of classic Claret. Cedary, elegant, perfumy nose. Hint of wood. Full, rich, long; great fruit/acidity balance. Spicy, chocolaty Cabernet. A magnificent wine. (19)

The final wine of the evening.

WARRE'S VINTAGE PORT 1977:

In its 20th year, and approaching full maturity. Bright, red colour. Rich, spicy, fruity nose. Full, yet not too spirity. Excellent backbone and balance. Ready, but will last well for another decade, or more. Very good fruit extract. A solid, medium-sweet, spicy Port.

The 1977 vintage is, in my opinion, the last of the classic vintages of Oporto. While the 1980s and 1983s are certainly fine, they do not have the sheer size of the 1977s. From 1985 onward, the Vintage Ports seem to have been made in an earlier-maturing, charming style. This is obviously a business decision, and a practical one, made by the Oporto Trade. Consumers these days do not have the storage space and the patience to wait 20 or more years until a Vintage Port reaches maturity.

We ended this excellent and historic event with Cognac.

COGNAC "RESERVE," 20 YEARS OLD, PIERRE FERRAND:

Generously contributed by one of our members. Unadulterated, solid, excellent Cognac. While I personally prefer the silkier "Sélection des Anges" (30 years old) of this house, the "Reserve" is a top-quality Cognac.

I have served as Maître of our Commanderie de Bordeaux for nine years. I feel good about stepping down now, and I know that Ian Mottershead will do an excellent job.

May 7 to 17, 1997

Trip to New York and Paris, with Orly.

In New York: Dinner at "Café des Artistes," with Orly and Delia Viader of Viader Vineyards, who was in New York that week.

We tried two wines.

CORTON-CHARLEMAGNE 1994, LOUIS JADOT:

Too young, of course, but a classic wine from a fine producer. The tell-tale character of this fine vineyard. Oak, elegant, yet fruity; all in harmony. Still tight. Fresh, very long. Not really a big wine; rather classy and elegant. Nutty, fruity character. Very good. Should be ready by 2000 to 2002. (17.5)

CHÂTEAU GRUAUD-LAROSE 1989:

As with the above, still youthful but surprisingly soft. Usually, Gruaud-Larose produces tighter, harder Cabernets, but it seems that most châteaux produced fairly soft wines in 1989. Another 1985? Dark, cedary-oaky, rich, yet soft, spicy Cabernet. A bit herbaceous, but backed by good ripe fruit. Drink by 1998 to 2000. (17.5)

IN PARIS

Dinner at restaurant "Violon d'Ingre," with Orly.

SANCERRE 1995, PAUL PRIEUR:

Fine, typical herbaceous Sauvignon Blanc. Fresh, round, crisp, long. A well-made Sancerre.

Lunch at the classy Hotel du Crillon "Restaurant des Ambassadeurs," near the La Place de la Concorde, with Orly.

CHAMPAGNE BOLLINGER "GRANDE ANNÉE" 1989:

Rounder, softer, more forward than the tighter 1988. Most 1989 Champagnes are quite soft. This wine is rich, yeasty, long, soft, creamy. Very good. For drinking over the next two to five years.

That night, we went to see the ballet *La Sylphide*, at the Palais Garnier (French Opera House). Most enjoyable performance and a great, classic hall.

Next day

Dinner at "Le Grand Véfour," near the Palais du Louvre.

A good but scandalously expensive meal with a pleasant bottle of Champagne. This was our last evening in Paris before our return to Vancouver.

CHAMPAGNE ROEDERER "BRUT PREMIER" N/V:

Fresh, herbaceous, long, crisp. Well balanced and enjoyable.

June 5, 1997

Today is the 30th anniversary of the Six Day War in the Middle East.

Exactly 30 years ago today, I went to war.

CHÂTEAU GRAND-PUY-LACOSTE 1978:

At almost 19 years, fully mature. Medium colour, orangy rim. Open, cedary-fruity nose. Round, slightly stemmy (typical 1978) with good, spicy Cabernet extract. Quite full. Has lost its tannins, but still has good fruit. Drink now to 2002. (17)

June 23, 1997

Commanderie de Bordeaux "Rarities" Dinner, at "Lumière" restaurant.

Chef Rob Feenie prepared an outstanding meal to accompany the wines.

CHEVALIER-MONTRACHET "LES DEMOISELLES" 1985, LOUIS LATOUR:

Deep, golden colour. Starting to oxidize. Still drinkable, but not nearly as good as it should be. Allan Tobe, who was the Vancouver agent for Louis Latour in the 1970s and 1980s, said that in the mid-1980s, Latour did not add enough sulphur to their Chardonnays, and therefore, they did not last as well as the 1989 and onward, or as well as the older wines from the 1970s and early 1980s. (14)

CHÂTEAU LAVILLE-HAUT-BRION 1978:

At 18, a superb white Graves that has finally come around. Exotic fruit, vanilla, oak; all in harmony. Mellow, very long. An excellent wine. (18)

Most of the wines were from my cellar. We opened sets of two bottles of each wine. I have purchased all the following wines from various sources in the USA and the UK, over the past ten years. With the exception of the Brane-Cantenac 1926, all were good to excellent. The 1928 Palmer deserves its reputation as being one of the greatest Clarets of the century.

FLIGHT #1

CHÂTEAU LAFLEUR-DE-GAZIN 1945, POMEROL:

Orange, evolved colour. Pale-orange rim. Atypical. Ripe raisins on nose. Sweet, soft, forward. Was probably better ten years ago. Lacks the backbone so typical of the 1945s. Pleasant, nice fruit, but getting tired. Drink up. Good top shoulder levels and healthy corks. (16)

CHÂTEAU GRUAUD-LAROSE 1916:

Recorked at the château in 1991. Top neck level. Very good, deep colour. Mature orange rim. Burnt oak, toasty, quite dry. Woody overtones, but good fruit, too. Rustic, solid, a bit too dry. After 15 minutes in glass, the fruit disappeared. (17)

CHÂTEAU CALON-SÉGUR 1918:

Best of flight. Top neck level. Recorked at the château in 1990. Deep, bright colour. Clean, fruity nose. A bit austere on palate, but long, clean, and fresh. Fruit held well in glass for 30 minutes. Most enjoyable—and almost 70 years old. (18)

CHÂTEAU BRANE-CANTENAC 1926:

Top shoulder levels. Both corks disintegrated. Not recorked. Madeira colour. Heavily oxidized. Pity, because this wine can be very good. (No score)

FLIGHT #2

CHÂTEAU PONTET-CANET 1961, BORDEAUX-BOTTLED BY CRUSE, THE THEN-OWNERS:

Round, soft, nice fruit. Both bottles lacked the extract and the chocolaty-cedary character typical of this property in 1961, but they did have that extra dimension and sweet, ripe fruit of the vintage. Good, but not great. (16)

CHÂTEAU LA LAGUNE 1961:

Lightest of flight. Stemmy, spicy, herbaceous Pinot Noir on both nose and palate! This wine would fool any experienced taster into thinking that it is a red Burgundy. After the frost of 1956, La Lagune had to replant the whole vineyard, so in 1961, the vines were very young. Nice fruit, round, good backbone. Tastes not unlike a Nuits or Gevrey Premier Cru! (17)

CHÂTEAU L'ARROSÉE 1961:

As usual, a sturdy and solid wine. Very dark, ripe, still tannic, even a bit rustic, but has the unmistakable extract and ripeness of the vintage. Obviously high Cabernet (of both kinds) in the blend. Not a wine for the faint-hearted or for lovers of true St. Emilion. (17.5)

CHÂTEAU MOUTON-BARON-PHILIPPE 1961, IN MAGNUM:

Clearly best appearance of flight. Excellent depth. Full, sweet, elegant. Lovely fruit. Perfection now—out of magnum. Best wine of flight. Over the past two decades, I have tasted this wine on at least eight occasions. Consistently excellent. (18.5)

CHÂTEAU L'ARROSÉE 1966:

Almost as good as the 1961, but a bit harder and less ripe, yet surely one of the better 1966s. Has held extremely well. Still lively, good fruit, solid, even tannic. No rush, and the fruit should last for another four to five years. (17)

FLIGHT #3

CHÂTEAU PALMER 1970:

Deep colour to rim. Good extract, but where is the great bouquet and the lovely fruit so typical of this wine?! Both bottles were a letdown. Maybe poor storage? Not oxidized or pruny, just unyielding, hard, tight. Most unusual. Good, but not what it should be. This wine was outstanding when tasted last month at the same restaurant. (16.5) The Palmer 1970 was contributed by one of our members.

CHÂTEAU PALMER 1928:

Original label: Nicolas Stamp. Both bottles recorked by Nicolas. One bottle recorked in 1968, the other in 1980. Slight difference, but both great bottles. The 1968 recorked bottle had a more open, expansive bouquet: an explosion of exotic smells. The second bottle, recorked in 1980, was a little more subdued on nose, but slightly fresher on palate. Impressive dark colour for an almost 70-year-old wine. Lovely fruit, very long, complete, perfectly balanced. Great complexity; just a hint of the solid backbone so typical of the 1928s. Very long aftertaste. A smorgasbord of flavours. Magnificent wine, well deserving of its reputation as being one of the great Clarets, not only of that great but slow-maturing vintage, but of this century. Superb. A great experience. (19.5)

CHÂTEAU D'YQUEM 1975:

Bright, deep-gold, almost amber colour. Darker than I expected. An explosion of botrytis, exotic fruit, ripe apricots on both nose and palate. Very long, round. Perfect now. My bottles are slightly fresher. Very fine, even great. Superb length, balance, and fruit. The best d'Yquem between 1967 and 1983. (19)

A memorable evening, at the end of which our new Maître, Ian Mottershead, surprised me with a lovely gift, presented on behalf of the Commanderie, in recognition of my many years as Maître and member of council. It was a magnificent silver "Claret" wine label and chain, recently acquired in London by Ian, from George II era. Of escutcheon form and superb quality, it has engraved inside borders, chased with grapes and wine leaves, produced by Sandilands Drinkwater, London, circa 1745.

Friday, July 18, 1997

An International Wine and Food Society Dinner, in San Francisco, in memory of the late Dr. Haskell Norman, our founding chairman, who passed away last fall.

This event was held at the Ritz-Carlton hotel. Chef Jean-Pierre Dubray prepared an outstanding dinner for us: the best dinner I have experienced at that hotel.

Champagne Pommery Brut N/V, in magnums:

Round, elegant, good fruit, creamy, well balanced. Hint of yeast. We must have aged this Champagne in our Society's cellars for a couple of years, at least.

Corton-Charlemagne 1992, Michel Voarick:

Surprisingly soft and evolved for such a young wine. Ripe, clean, appley fruit. Round, very soft, fairly rich, lacking a bit in complexity, but quite good. (17)

Château Lanessan 1975:

Typical 1975 structure and a good Cru Bourgeois. A bit dusty on nose. Rustic, hard, fairly tannic, but thankfully backed by good fruit. Lacks complexity. Solid, hard, trace of acidity at finish. (15)

Château Cheval-Blanc 1975, in magnum:

Superb wine. Clearly the best 1975 St. Emilion. (Figeac is also a good 1975, if not quite up to the standard of the Cheval. Other 1975 St. Emilions are well below this class.) Lovely, deep colour to rim. Spicy, sweet Cassis nose with hint of stemminess. Full, round, great extract. Very well balanced. Still a bit tannic (in magnum), but excellent ripe-fruit concentration. At its peak. Magnums should last well for another decade. (18)

Château La Mission Haut-Brion 1975:

Very dark, dense colour to rim. Ripe berries, earthy, yet still unyielding nose. This wine is not ready yet. Solid tannins backed by excellent ripe fruit. Very full, very long on palate. A very serious wine. Very 1975 , though. Not for lovers of modern-day, charming, fruity, soft Clarets. This wine should last well into the 21st century and, well-cellared bottles (and especially magnums) may last for another 30 years. (18.5)

Robert Parker rated this wine a perfect 100. This is a matter of opinion and personal taste. No doubt, this is a fabulous wine, but, if it is rated 100, then the same château's 1961 vintage would rate 110; the 1959, 115; the 1945, 115; and the unbelievably great 1949, 125 points.

Château Lafite 1961, in jeroboam:

Our new chairman Jack Rubyn described this wine as being an imperial, but we discovered, when we inspected the bottle, that it was a jeroboam. Our new chairman is not very knowledgeable in wine, as he has been interested in the subject and involved actively for only a couple of years. He will hopefully learn about it, because he is surrounded by knowledgeable wine advisors, and our extensive cellar is packed with great, irreplaceable treasures, collected over the years by the late Dr. Norman.

One of the best 1961 Lafites I have tasted. It can be variable, as in those days, Lafite bottled the wines in batches, over several months, and without doing an assemblage of a few casks to achieve uniformity and consistency. Classic, velvety wine on both nose and palate. Vanilla, oak, lovely perfumy nose. Round on palate, very long, elegant, without having the massive fruit extract of a 1961 Mouton, or especially Latour. (18.5)

Château Rieussec 1979:

Bright gold. Creamy, buttery wine, typical of this property. Not much botrytis, but the little that is there is good. Needs drinking. (17)

In Yountville.

Marsannay Blanc, Chardonnay "Vieilles Vignes" 1992, Phillipe Nadeff:

Nadeff produces a small quantity of white wines from a vineyard located in this extreme northern area of the Côte-de-Nuits, on the road to Dijon. Very similar in style to a good Pouilly-Fuissé from a rich year. Round, straightforward, ripe, appley character. At five years old, it is at its peak. Round, rich, most enjoyable, and reasonably priced.

Sunday, July 10, 1997

At a party in Ross, in memory of our late chairman, Dr. Haskell Norman.

The food was excellent, as is usual at such events. The wines were very disappointing, however. Mostly "unwanted" wines from our cellar that our new and very inexperienced chairman, Jack Rubyn, is trying to get rid of.

This was the only red wine served.

Clos de Vougeot 1983, Domaine Rebourseau:

Typical 1983. Pale, mature, evolved colour. Musty on both nose and palate, low fruit, tannic. Not very impressive. Cloudy (should have been decanted, but was not). The other wines were downhill from there. Haskell would never have dared serve such wines, not at his birthday party, anyway. All other wines served were white. and even poorer than this.

July 29, 1997

Kistler Chardonnay "Dutton Ranch" 1989, Alexander Valley:

At its peak. Buttery, fairly full on palate, but well balanced. Nice, long finish with ripe fruit overtones. Low acidity indicates that this wine will not last much longer. Kistler's Chardonnays are now very hard to find and very expensive. They now cost more than fine Premier Cru Pulignys and Chassagnes from such excellent producers as Sauzet and Niellon.

Also tasted that night

July 29, 1997

Spring Mountain Cabernet Sauvignon 1973, Napa Valley:

Made in the days when Mike Grgich was the winemaker there. An impressive 24-year-old wine. Decanted 45 minutes. Fair bit of sediment. Deep, mature colour. Classy nose of cedar, eucalyptus, and ripe fruit. Full, rich, with a hint of sweetness on palate. Very long, soft, no tannins left, but still retains a fair bit of rich, luscious fruit. A very good Cabernet.

August 6, 1997

This morning, I learned that Gerard Jaboulet passed away last week, following a heart attack.

He was a very nice man, a friend, and a gifted winemaker. This is a sad loss to the wine community. He was the man behind (among other wines) all the recent outstanding Hermitages "La Chapelle," notably the great 1978, 1983, 1986, 1989, and 1990. He was only 55 years old.

August 17, 1997

Château Ducru-Beaucaillou 1961:

Purchased in London during an eight-month stay there 20 years ago, back in 1977, for £110 per case. Nowadays this wine fetches an unbelievable £4600 per case at auction. The wine scene is going mad! Aged in my cellar these past 20 years under ideal conditions, at 52°F (under 12°C). A magnificent bottle. A combination of 1961 Palmer and 1959 Lafite! Evolved, mature colour. Superb, expansive nose of ripe, but soft fruit, sealing wax, slightly toasty oak. Velvety, round, soft. Superb balance and length. Classic elegance so typical of Ducru. At the end of its plateau. Magnums should still be great, if well cellared. A very great wine. (19.5)

September 4, 1997

At "Lumière" restaurant.

Château Ausone 1979:

Dark, spicy, herbaceous nose, yet ripe, too, typical of the vintage. Full, complex, mellow, but with enough backbone to last well for another decade. Long aftertaste. Top quality. This, as well as Lafite and Haut-Brion, have produced the best First Growths in 1979.

Pascal Delbeck, the gifted winemaker, did an excellent job at Ausone between 1976 and 1995. He single-handedly turned this property around. It is sad that he was caught in the row between the two owners, Madame Dubois-Chalon and her late husband's nephew, Mr. Vauthier. Now that the Vauthiers have acquired 100% control of Ausone, Pascal is dedicating his time to Château Belair next door, owned outright by Madame Dubois-Chalon.

How sad that the Vauthiers have chosen to produce "Robert Parker and Michel Rolland" wines: hefty, rich, early maturing, robbing Ausone of its character as a true connoisseur's long-ageing wine. Pascal, however, has put Belair on the map now, producing one of the top St. Emilions.

Niersteiner Rehbach Riesling Eiswein 1989, Weingut Hermannshof, Rheinhessen, in half-bottle:

A superb wine from a great vintage. Lovely, ripe raisins, botrytis and hint of petroleum jelly on nose. Full, luscious, rich, sweet, yet not cloying. Excellent fruit/acidity balance. Exotic fruit. A dessert all by itself.

September 16, 1997

At a Commanderie de Bordeaux council meeting, at the residence of our new Maître, Ian Mottershead.

All wines were served double-blind.

Bollinger "RD" 1982, disgorged February 1996:

At first, I thought that it was a 1979 Krug. Steely, lean, hard, with surprisingly fresh fruit. I also ventured to guess Veuve Clicquot Grande Dame 1988. When tasted last May, this Champagne was rich, nutty, almost butterscotch, yeasty, and mellow. This was surprisingly masculine. A "food" Champagne.

Bâtard-Montrachet 1992, Joseph Drouhin:

As is so often the case with Drouhin's whites, this wine is surprisingly forward for a five-year-old Grand Cru. Bright gold. Buttery, intense, ripe Chardonnay nose. Round, buttery, low acidity, full, and creamy on palate. Very fine quality, but needs drinking over the next two years.

LEONETTI CELLARS MERLOT 1993, WASHINGTON STATE:

Deep, bright purple colour. Typical herbaceous yet sweet Merlot on nose. Where it lost it was on the palate. Sour, citric, low tannins. The acidity (was it acidified?) totally dominated the fruit through and through. I thought that it was an Italian wine that was not well balanced. Leonetti Cellars have a reputation of producing fine Merlots. If so, then in 1993, the winemaker blew it.

NUITS-ST.-GEORGES, HOSPICES DE NUITS, "LES DIDIERS" 1988, CUVÉE JACQUES DURET:

How different the 1988 red Burgundies are from the charming 1985s and the exotic, fruity 1990s. The 1988s are much more masculine, tannic, serious wines that will require at least five extra years of bottle-age, and the best will last well into the 21st century. Evolved colour. Spicy, rich, herbaceous Pinot Noir on nose. Elegant on entry, but an explosion of tannins and sweet fruit on palate. Good, clean finish. Drink from 2000 to 2005 or beyond. Very good.

CHÂTEAU CHEVAL-BLANC 1966:

Mid shoulder level. Evolved, orange-red colour. Crumbly cork. Very slight hint of oxidation, but fine, slightly charred oak on nose. Round, classy, but much softer and more evolved, due, of course, to the poor level. Other bottles can be excellent. This, if from a good bottle or magnum, is the best Cheval-Blanc between 1966 and 1982, although I have tasted excellent examples of this property's 1975 vintage.

CHÂTEAU LEOVILLE-LASCASES 1953:

Very good low neck level for a 44-year-old wine. Palish red colour, but with good depth. Classic, elegant 1953 that has held very well, but that is now past its prime. Sweet, soft, cedary, on both nose and palate. A velvety wine that has a trace of acidity at finish. Drink up!

CHÂTEAU LA CONSEILLANTE 1982:

What a surprise this was! We all thought at first that it was a red Burgundy! Surprisingly evolved for a 15-year-old and from such a reputable vintage. An elegant, spicy, herbaceous wine. Lots of class here, but it does not have the sheer weight and ripe fruit intensity of other 1982 Pomerols, notably l'Evangile, Trotanoy, or Lafleur, but then La Conseillante is made in the more elegant, leaner style (as is Vieux Château Certan), with a higher proportion of Cabernets and relatively less Merlot.

September 24, 1997

Dinner with Carol and our children, Michael and Orly.

Michael is now 22 years old and has just started Law School. Orly is 19.

VEUVE CLICQUOT "LA GRANDE DAME" 1985:

A superb Champagne from an excellent vintage. Halfway in weight between a Taittinger Comtes de Champagne and a Bollinger "RD." Excellent mousse. Tiny, persistent bubbles. Very long on palate. Medium weight, complex, excellent fruit. At its peak, but no rush. Lots of class here.

CHÂTEAU PALMER 1970:

From an original case purchased in Vancouver back in December 1975, 22 years ago. What a superb wine! Decanted 30 minutes. Still has excellent colour and depth. Classic Margaux and classic Palmer on both nose and palate. Ripe, elegant, velvety. Long legs, superbly complex. Layers of elegant, well-balanced fruit. At 27, a magnificent Claret. I believe that the key is in the cellaring, because other people's Palmer 1970s have not been as good as mine, showing signs of cracking up. Anyway, tonight this was absolutely superb!

September 1997

Dinner at "Uforia" restaurant.

BAROLO "RISERVA" 1952, BORGOGNO:

Recorked at the property around 1994 or 1995, according to the owner of the restaurant. Surprisingly little sediment. I did the decanting myself. At first the wine was a bit astringent, but after 30 minutes, it turned into a superb, old-style Barolo, with hint of tar, leather, and ripe figs on both nose and palate. Full, rich, fair bit of acidity, but excellent fruit, too. At 45 years old, an impressive wine.

October 6 to November 1, 1997

Trip to Paris, St. Petersburg, Israel, and Tuscany.

October 9, 1997

Dinner at "Alain Ducasse," in Paris, the latest Michelin three-star restaurant that is the talk of the town.

The only certainty is that it is very, very expensive. Some say it is overrated. Other than most of the staff being a bit too reserved, I found the decor, service, and food excellent. Great presentation, too. Very extensive and impressive wine list. As usual in starred French restaurants, the prices are ridiculously high. Not uncommon to see wine prices marked up by 400% from the already expensive retail prices in Paris. Had they marked their wines up by only 200% (already a rip-off), they probably would have sold more wine. So, I stuck to this good, relatively reasonably priced bottle.

CHOREY-LES-BEAUNE 1989, TOLLOT-BEAUT:

A reliable producer whose wines (both their reds and their superb Corton-Charlemagne) I know well. Bright colour, good depth. Clean, expansive Pinot Noir nose. Round, well balanced. Spicy. Good depth and backbone, especially for a 1989. Fine effort.

October 10 to 14

St. Petersburg (formerly Leningrad).

No wines tasted there, with the exception of a rather ordinary local sparkling wine. Imported wines, notably French, are ridiculously overpriced.

IN ST. PETERSBURG

I was met by the Russian secretary of an acquaintance of mine from Vancouver who has a sawmill business in Siberia. A very nice lady who was helpful in arranging tickets to shows and trips to palaces outside the city. Visited the great Hermitage Museum and palace, the cruiser "Aurora" (whose shells started the October 1917 Revolution), the Peter and Paul Fortress, St. Isaac's Church, and a day trip to Pushkin and Pavlovsk and the castles there. In the city, saw a good Russian folklore show and an excellent performance of Tchaikovsky's ballet Romeo and Juliet *at the Meryinsky (formerly Kirov) Ballet. The new Russia has its work cut out for it. After 75 years of Communist hibernation and brain washing, the road will be long. I feel sorry for the older generation who, even after six years of democracy, still seem at a loss to comprehend what has happened. The potential of this vast country is great, though.*

October 15 to 22

In Israel. Tasted mostly local white wines, all made by the famous Yarden Winery in Katzrin (on the Golan heights).

"GAMLA" CHARDONNAY 1995, YARDEN:

Not unlike a French Chardonnay from Vin de Pays d'Oc or a Macon. Clean, crisp Chardonnay character on both nose and palate. Good fruit, well balanced. This is the second wine of Yarden's Chardonnay.

"GALIL" CHARDONNAY 1995 ,YARDEN:

Tasted twice. Their top Chardonnay. Hint of oak and vanilla. More depth, character, and balance than their regular (Gamla) Chardonnay. Nose similar to a good California Chardonnay, but structure more typical of a white Burgundy. More refined and higher acidity. Nice wine.

"GALIL" CABERNET SAUVIGNON 1993, YARDEN:

Impressive dark colour to rim. Spicy Cabernet nose, hint of oak and vanilla. Structured and tasted very much like a "new wave" Italian Cabernet with trace of acidity, but tannins, too. A good wine. Try it in two to three years. The vintage of this wine I know best is the 1985, which I have tasted in Vancouver on several occasions. A very good wine that is now (at 12 years old) approaching its peak.

IN FLORENCE

CHIANTI CLASSICO RISERVA 1990, LUCIANO BRUNI:

Purchased in a little Enoteca in San Gemignano and drunk in a rented flat where I was staying with my friend, Marie-José Aubin, for a week in the old part of Florence, near the Palazzo Vecchio. Considering the reputation of the vintage, a bit disappointing. Quite evolved colour. Orange rim. Fruity, straw on nose, but quite acidic, fairly lean. Lacking in fat. Not a bad wine, but not up to the standard of this fine vintage.

Visit to Castello Nipozzano, Marchesi Frescobaldi's vineyard and winery.

Visited the old cellars and the family reserve wines, going back to the 1860s. The Frescobaldis have been making wine there for over seven centuries: 30 generations of winemakers. The Castello itself dates from the 11th century. They use various French oak barrels for their top wines, usually some new (up to 50%, in the case of Mormoretto), and large Slovenian oak barrels (up to 50 years old) for their Nipozzano Chianti. The winery is located north-east of Florence, in the Ruffina area.

Their Pomino Bianco is made up of a blend of approximately 40% Chardonnay and 60% Pinot Blanc (the Chardonnay will increase to 50% with the 1997 vintage).

Mormoretto is usually made from 80% Cabernet Sauvignon and 20% Cabernet Franc, and aged in up to 50% new French oak barrels.

Their Pomino Rosso is a blend of about 60% Sangiovese, 20% Pinot Noir and 10% each of Merlot and Cabernet Sauvignon.

The Montesodi, their top Chianti Ruffino, is made from 100% Sangiovese, only declared in good vintages. Average production is very limited, about 2,500 to 3,000 cases.

The Nipozzano "Riserva" is aged in large, used (sometimes very old) Slovenian oak vats. It is a Chianti Ruffina, of course. Aged between 18 to 24 months in those large vats, plus six to 12 months of bottle-age before release.

The 1997 vintage seems very promising. Ideal growing conditions. Possibly as good as the 1990, and the best vintage since then, according to our guide.

I tasted the following wines (all presently released).

POMINO BIANCO 1996:

No oak ageing. 60% Pinot Blanc and 40% Chardonnay. Fresh, fruity, crisp. Nice clean fruit. A reasonably priced everyday white wine. Recommended, if it can be purchased for under $15 per bottle.

POMINO CHARDONNAY 1994:

Made from 85% Chardonnay and 15% Pinot Blanc. Fermented and aged in oak for ten months before bottling. From the fine "Vignetto" vineyard. Oak/vanilla and nice, sweet, ripe fruit on both nose and palate. Crisp, good depth, well balanced, long aftertaste. A very well-made wine. Drink now to 2002.

POMINO ROSSO 1994:

Medium depth, palish rim, medium-bodied, fairly tannic. Sweet fruit on entry, yet lean with trace of acidity at finish, but backed by decent fruit. Drink now to 2004.

NIPOZZANO "RISERVA," CHIANTI RUFFINA 1994:

100% Sangiovese. Paler, looser knit than the Pomino Rosso. Classic straw, fruity nose. A bit lean, dry, fairly acidic, tannic. Lacking fruit, but not a bad wine overall.

MONTESODI 1993:

No 1994 was made, as the quality was judged not up to the standard of this fine vineyard. Matured two years in French oak casks. I did not find out what the percentage of new oak was. Deep garnet colour to rim. Solid, full, concentrated. Very good fruit extract. Ripe, too. Needs at least five to seven more years of bottle-age. Hint of tar and truffles on both nose and palate.

MORMORETTO 1994:

A very different style altogether. Obvious Cabernet Sauvignon. Deepest of all the red wines tasted. Very young looking, smelling, and tasting. Aggressive tannins, powerful. Spicy, rich. Good structure and balance. No sense trying this wine before 2004.

Frescobaldi also produce a very fine olive oil and Grappa, as well as a Vin Santo, made from Chardonnay and Pinot Blanc, and usually picked very late, in December. The grapes are sun-dried and they are not affected by botrytis. They expose the wine to temperature extremes, in both summer and winter, by storing the barrels under the roof. Thus, the wine heats up and ferments in summer and rests in winter. This exposure lasts for four years and the variation in temperature gives this wine an aged look and an old taste, even when it is only five or six years old.

VIN SANTO 1991, POMINO:

Four years in used Pomino Rosso barrels. Deep amber-gold colour. Fresh, raisiny nose. Good acidity. Fairly sweet and noticeable spirit. Hint of ripe figs and exotic fruit. I am not a fan of Vin Santo, but this is not bad at all.

Frescobaldi have entered into a joint venture with Robert Mondavi of the Napa Valley. They produce a wine called Luca, made from 100% Sangiovese grown in the Chianti Ruffina region.

That evening

I had a most interesting visit and tasting in old Florence, at a small wine bar called "Cantinetta Dei Verrazzano"

Featuring a wide range of wines: red, white, sparkling, Vin Santo and Grappa, of Castello di Verrazzano, which is located in the heart of Chianti Classico, between Florence and Sienna. The wine steward, a young man by the name of Paolo, was friendly, helpful, and very enthusiastic. With various fine Crostinis, I tasted the following wines (all made at the Castello di Verrazzano, which is owned by the Cappellini family).

CHIANTI CLASSICO "RISERVA" 1985:

Aged for 28 months in large Slovenian oak vats. At 12 years old, fully mature, yet good cherry-red colour. Hint of tar, good fruit, well balanced. Clean, crisp fruit. Drink now through 2000.

SASSELLO 1994:

Also made from 100% Sangiovese. Only 6,000 bottles produced on average. Deep, youthful colour. Powerful, tight, restrained at this early stage, but the fruit is there, as is a fair bit of tannin and acidity. This wine will not reach its peak until 2002, and will last at least until 2010. Very good potential. Aged for 14 months in 25% Vosges and 75% Allier oak barrels, and a further 15 months in bottle before its release. Sassello is produced from a single vineyard called "La Querciolina."

BOTIGLIA PARTICOLARE 1994:

Made from 85% Sangiovese and 15% Cabernet Sauvignon, therefore, it is a Vino da Tavola. Aged in Tronçais and Vosges oak casks for 12 months, and a further 15 months of bottle-age before release. As with the Sassello, only 6,000 bottles produced, and only in good vintages. In 1990, the Sangiovese grape was so successful, that they decided not to include any Cabernet Sauvignon that year. Similar bright appearance of the Sassello, but sweeter, rounder, more forthcoming fruit, with hint of cedary fruit on nose.

Long, round, excellent balance. Enjoyable now, but will improve with three extra years of bottle-age. More approachable than the Sassello at this stage.

BOTIGLIA PARTICOLARE 1986:

Similar blend to the 1994. A superb, fully mature Tuscan wine. Hint of licorice; evolved colour with orange rim at 11 years. Velvety, smooth, perfect balance. Full bodied, generous, soft tannins. Hint of leather. A beautifully made wine in a year that is not known for its great Chiantis or other Tuscan wines. A real treat.

BOTIGLIA PARTICOLARE 1981:

Quite similar in appearance and body to the beautiful 1986, but slightly drier, with a hint of tar.

On the following day, I went back to the Enoteca di Verrazzano, and tasted the following two wines.

CHIANTI CLASSICO "RISERVA" 1988:

Good depth, orange rim. Subdued, still a bit closed on nose, hint of straw. Good fruit, well balanced, and not too lean. Ready, but well structured and should hold well for another three to four years.

CHIANTI CLASSICO "RISERVA" 1981:

Older vintages such as this had 20% white grape varietals in the blend (15% Malvoisie, and 5% Trebbiano). Hint of tar and licorice on nose. Very evolved, brown/orange colour. Smooth, round, soft, yet still has good backbone. Ready now and will not improve. Hint of toast (from the Slovenian large oak casks in which it was aged). Label read "Denominazione di Origine Controllata," without the words "E Garantita –DOCG," introduced several years later. Actually, this wine was structured like a good 1966 Haut-Médoc. Not bad at all, considering that there is 20% white juice in the blend.

Dinner at "Enoteca Ristorante Pinchiorri," one of the very best (and most expensive) restaurants in Florence.

One dish I had there that I will never forget was a superb rissotto, with a whole quail and porcinni mushrooms. The best rissotto I have tasted to date, anywhere. The wine that I ordered is exclusively bottled for, and can be found only at, "Ristorante Pinchiorri."

CASTELLO DI VERRAZZANO "QUERCIOLINO" 1990:

Made from 100% Sangiovese Piccolo. A heavenly wine from a great vintage. This wine was recommended to me by Paolo, the friendly young waiter at the Verrazzano wine bar the previous day. Very deep, intense red colour to rim. Decanted and after 30 minutes in glass, an explosion of intense, yet smooth, round and very ripe, sweet fruit. Not unlike drinking a 1982 Château Cheval-Blanc! Great length, complexity, and extract. Together with 1978 Sassicaia (a wine I had the good fortune of tasting on seven occasions to date), the greatest Italian wine I have tasted in my 25 years of tasting wines. Not only was it a superbly crafted wine, but the sheer pleasure of drinking it was ecstatic. A memorable evening.

Visit to Antinori at Badia a Pessignano, in Chianti Classico.

By coincidence, Umberto Menghi was there, with a group of two-dozen doctors and their spouses from Vancouver. Along with managing several restaurants in Vancouver, Umberto runs a cooking school located near Piza. A cold, rainy day, unfortunately. Actually, other than the first two days in Sienna and one day in Florence that were all nice, the rest of the week has been very cold, windy, and rainy.

After a very basic and uninteresting "PR show" by their public relations lady, we drove to Badia a Passignano for lunch.

CERVARO DELLA SALA, CASTELLO DELLA SALLA 1995, IN HALF-BOTTLE:

A white wine produced from 80% Chardonnay and 20% Grecetto. Woody, hint of residual sugar. Fairly acidic, even hint of cheese on nose, yet very little Chardonnay character, in spite of the fact that about 80% of the juice in this wine is from the Chardonnay grape. A solid, unusual wine. Hint of honeyed aftertaste. This wine was both barrel-fermented and barrel-aged.

That afternoon
Back in Florence, tasted some sensational ice creams, at the Gelateria Vivoli, near Santa Croce, in the heart of old Florence.

November 3, 1997

Commanderie de Bordeaux event, hosting several producers.

Notably the owners of Châteaux Gazin, Canon La Gaffelière, Pontet-Canet, Branaire, and Smith-Haut-Lafitte, who are travelling as an organization established four years ago, calling itself "Les Cinq," each representing a property in one of the five major communes of Bordeaux.

CHÂTEAU SMITH-HAUT-LAFITTE BLANC 1995:

Out of 55 hectares planted, only ten hectares are dedicated to the white wine, planted only in Sauvignon Blanc (Gris). According to the owner, Florence Cathiard, the 1995 is softer, early maturing, and rounder, while the 1996 has better acidity and will take longer to mature. Hint of grapefruit on nose, as well as ripe white peaches. Round, complex, delicate. Little hint of oak. Almost ready, even at this early stage. A pleasant wine, but not, I'm afraid, in the same league as Laville-Haut-Brion or Domaine de Chevalier Blanc. (16) In fairness to this wine, one does not have to pay the high price demanded for those two great wines.

Château Smith-Haut-Lafitte Rouge 1993:

Hint of tobacco, licorice, and earth on nose. Good extract, round, well balanced, but I noticed some astringency and bitterness at finish. Drink from 1999 to 2003. The Cathiards have owned this property since the late 1980s. (16)

Château Gazin 1990

and

Château Pontet-Canet 1990:

Gazin: Garnet colour to rim. Stemmy, slightly pruny on nose. Good fruit on entry, but short finish. Fairly spirity. Somehow off-balance; lacking in depth and middle. Maybe this is due to the sale to Petrus, over two decades ago, of their five best hectares. At a blind tasting, I would have mistaken it for a St. Emilion, even though this wine is made up of 95% Merlot and only 5% Cabernet Franc. An easy-to-like and easy-to-drink wine, but certainly not a big, serious Pomerol from a ripe year. (16.5)

Pontet-Canet: Obviously, a serious Pauillac from a ripe year. Deep, dense red colour to rim. Tight, unyielding nose. Closed up. Needs at least seven more years to approach maturity. Later, nose opened up into a rich, leathery bouquet with hint of prunes. How nice to see that the Tesserons have finally decided to produce a fine Pauillac at Pontet-Canet, after 20 years of underachievement there. The last fine vintage produced there (under the Cruse regime) was 1966. (17.5)

To quote the late Maurice Healy, from his excellent book *Stay Me With Flagons*, (first published in 1940), "Finally, what on earth is Pontet Canet doing down amongst the Fifth Growths? Here is a wine which is never commonplace and almost always seems… to have much of the breed of its neighbour, Lafite; and it is the least temperamental of Clarets, always conscious of its duty to please."

Château Canon La Gaffelière 1988

and

Château Branaire Ducru 1988:

The Canon had a medium-red colour, orange, evolved rim. Spicy, herbaceous, classic St. Emilion nose. Leaner, but good 1988 structure. Fairly forward. Spicy, bell peppers, too. Still a bit tannic, good fruit, but lacking a bit in fat and ripeness. Made up of 45% Cabernet Franc, 40% Merlot, and 15% Cabernet Sauvignon, mostly older 40 to 60-year-old vines. (16.5)

The Branaire is made from 75% Cabernet Sauvignon, 20% Merlot, and 5% Cabernet Franc. 1988 was the first vintage produced by the new owners. Deep, bright colour, but quite evolved, orangy rim. Sweet fruit, ripe, rich, solid on palate with good backbone. The fruit is forward, yet the tannins and acidity are still quite tight. Needs two to four more years. 40% of the production that year went into the second wine. (17)

Château Pontet-Canet 1952:

Very evolved, pale colour. Superb, expansive nose of earth, mushrooms, wet wood, and sealing wax, but charming fruit. Very soft on palate, little fruit, but noticeable acidity, typical of this once-tight, hard vintage. Was much better ten years ago, but still enjoyable. (17)

This wine was a gift from our Maître, Ian Mottershead, to our guest Michel Tesseron, owner of Pontet-Canet (and Lafon-Rochet in St. Estèphe). Michel very generously opened it and allowed us all to taste it. Michel's wife is a former Cruse, the owners of Pontet-Canet until the Tesserons purchased it in the mid-1970s, after the "Wine-Gate" scandals that saw, among others, the fall of the Cruse family from grace.

November 1997

Hermitage "La Chapelle" 1970, Jaboulet:

Opened it in memory of Gerard Jaboulet, a dear friend and excellent winemaker, who passed away earlier this year at age 55. A superb bottle! Good depth at 27 years old, fair bit of sediment. On nose and palate, a combination of great Burgundy and classic Claret. Exotic, spicy, leathery, but very clean, mature fruit. Serious, solid, yet round and complex on palate. Surely the best La Chapelle between 1961 and 1978. How great these old Hermitages are compared to the softer, early maturing, younger vintages! A memorable bottle.

November 27, 1997

Thanksgiving family dinner, at Paul and Sara Pinski's, in San Francisco.

Paul will be celebrating his 85th birthday on Saturday, November 30, 1997.

Krug "Clos du Mesnil," Blanc de Blancs 1985 Champagne:

Four bottles opened. Two were sweeter, rounder, approachable. The other two were a bit drier and leaner. This excellent, rare Champagne has the elegance and ripe fruit typical of a 100% Chardonnay wine and of the superb 1985 vintage, combined with the classic, masculine backbone of Krug. Very tiny bubbles, fine mousse. Lovely, elegant fruit on nose, with hint of green apples and ripe pears. Great class here. Drink now to 2005.

MEURSAULT-PERRIÈRES PREMIER CRU 1987, J. F. COCHE-DURY:

This master can produce superb Meursaults in a difficult vintage, which 1987 was. Bright, deep-golden colour. More obvious oak/vanilla than in riper years, yet Jean-François managed to capture enough extract out of the grapes so that the oak was not allowed to overwhelm the wine. Long, very complex. At its peak. A bit lean; hint of bitterness at finish. Four bottles opened. Two were a bit riper. The other two were slightly leaner with more bitterness at finish. Overall, an excellent Meursault. Perrières is Coche-Dury's only Premier Cru in Meursault. All his other Meursaults are "lieux dits," such as "Narvaux," "Rougeots," etc.

BEAUNE PREMIER CRU 1978, LEROY:

Three bottles opened. Quite a bit of bottle variation here. The best example had a good, dark colour, evolved rim. Fair bit of sediment. Classic 1978 on both nose and palate. Herbaceous, stemmy, yet backed by lovely fruit extract. Hint of toast, charred oak. Long and ripe. Ready at 19 years, but no rush. The second bottle was a bit drier, otherwise quite similar to the first. The third bottle was a bit earthier, with a slight hint of mustiness. Why so much bottle variation in such a fine year, and from such a reputable firm?

QUINTA DO NOVAL "NACIONAL" 1947, A.J. DA SILVA, SHIPPED TO LONDON BY RUTHERFORD, OSBORNE, AND PERKINS:

The star of the evening. Label read: "Produced from prephylloxera grapes." This, technically, is not quite correct. It is produced from the sole Tourriga Nacional grape and ungrafted vines (therefore susceptible to attack by the phylloxera louse), but not from actual prephylloxera vines. I decanted the wine about one hour before serving it. The cork crumbled. As expected, fair bit of sediment. Bright, youthful garnet colour for a 50-year-old Port. Superb nose of oriental spices and ripe grapes. Perfectly balanced on palate. No harsh edges here. Lovely, velvety fruit. Lingering aftertaste. The best Vintage Port I have tasted in a long time. Surprisingly lively.

In Yountville.

CHÂTEAU LA GRANDE ROCHE 1991, NAPA VALLEY PINOT NOIR:

The grapes for this wine are from Atlas Peak, from young, seven-year-old vines. Made by Rick Forman and Bruce Scotland. Two rackings were done, thus producing this lovely, velvety, Volnay-like Pinot Noir. Evolved colour, spicy, herbaceous. Long, round, well balanced, backed by excellent ripe fruit. An impressive effort.

Saturday, November 29, 1997

85th birthday celebrations for our dear friend, Paul Pinski.

Over 120 relatives and guests were invited to the Concordia Argonaut Club, in San Francisco.

CHAMPAGNE KRUG 1985, IN MAGNUMS:

So good; complex, yeasty, ripe fruit, and elegant, yet so different from previous vintages of Krug Champagnes. Elegance, round, easy to sip, while older vintages are much more masculine, muscular, steely, and tight, needing food and years of maturity before offering everything to the taster.

BIENVENUES BÂTARD-MONTRACHET 1986, DOMAINE RAMONET:

Bright, deep-golden colour. Expansive nose of exotic fruit, combined with vanilla and oak. Full-bodied, rich, luscious wine, backed by excellent acidity and fruit. A mouthful of exquisite Chardonnay. Solid backbone and extract should enable this wine to last well, at least for another two to three years.

BÂTARD-MONTRACHET 1988, DOMAINE RAMONET:

More serious, more solid, and more restrained than the 1986 Bienvenues. The tightness and noticeable acidity is typical of this vintage, yet, contrary to most 1988 white Burgundies, this one is backed by concentrated, ripe fruit. Needs two to three extra years to come around. As a rule, 1988 white Burgundies suffer from overproduction. The fruit is diluted and only the leanness of the vintage comes to the fore. This wine, on the other hand, has excellent fruit extract and layers of complexity. But then, Ramonet is a great winemaker.

RICHEBOURG 1985, DOMAINE DE LA ROMANÉE-CONTI:

In bottles, magnums, and jeroboams (equivalent to four bottles in Burgundy). A total of three jeroboams, six magnums, and 12 bottles were opened by our generous host, Paul Pinski. While all three sizes came through as superb examples of what a great vineyard, dedicated winemaking, and excellent vintage can produce, there were definite differences, not only in terms of evolution, but also in structure and taste. The bottles were obviously the most approachable, yet even they were not quite ready, and should last for quite some time. Excellent, deep colour. Lovely nose of ripe cherries, raspberries, and black currants, combined with a hint of charred oak. On palate, quite solid, good fruit, excellent structure, and long finish. Lovely.

The magnums showed best, with that extra ripe, sweet fruit that was much in evidence. The jeroboams were the dullest, tightest. Some say that these large-format bottles need more time. That may well be true, but, judging from personal experience, I am skeptical about the final result. As always, magnums are still the ideal size in which to age great wine. In any event, these were merely nuances. 1985 Richebourg DRC, in any size bottle, is a great Burgundy.

CHÂTEAU D'YQUEM 1976:

Deep, golden colour, almost amber. Luscious nose of crème brûlée combined with oak, vanilla, and ripe botrytized fruit. Full, soft, round. Very sweet and noticeably flatter than the 1975 Château d'Yquem which is livelier and fresher, due to its better acidity. A great wine, nevertheless. The food was superb, too. A memorable evening.

December 1, 1997

Dinner with Delia Viader of Viader Vineyards.

Delia brought along a sample of her recent release.

VIADER VINEYARDS 1995, NAPA VALLEY:

Made from a blend of approximately 50% Cabernet Sauvignon and 50% Cabernet Franc, this, in my opinion, is her finest effort to date. Just released last August and sold out already. (Production is approximately 4,000 cases annually. There is no second wine. 28 acres under vines, of which four have been recently planted with Syrah and will produce a separate wine in a few years.) The wine is aged in Seguin-Moreau French oak casks, including about 1% of Russian oak, also supplied by Seguin-Moreau. The wine is lush, concentrated, tannic, serious, yet not bitter, and extremely well balanced and long. Full, rich, excellent potential in ten to 12 years. More St. Julien than California in style.

With dinner I served the following two wines.

CHAMPAGNE CHARBAUT BRUT N/V:

Fresh, flowery lilacs on nose. Medium bubbles and the foam went flat instantly. Pleasant, but lacks depth, yeast, and character. A rather simple Champagne.

VIEUX CHÂTEAU CERTAN 1989:

Bright red colour, evolved at rim. Some sediment. Subdued, elegant nose of ripe fruit. Slight hint of herbaceousness. Mellow, round, complex, and long on palate. Surprisingly forward, but then this seems to be the style of the 1989s. Loosely knit. Most enjoyable. Drink now to 2003. This property, together with Château La Conseillante, has a higher than usual proportion of Cabernets for a Pomerol; therefore, it produces more elegant and more herbaceous wines than the mostly Merlot-based other top properties of that commune, such as l'Evangile and Lafleur.

December 2, 1997

A visit with the Heitz family.

Joe Heitz was away on an errand; he had forgotten about my visit. His wife Alice said that he is feeling better after last year's stroke, and that he is slowly recovering his sense of taste and smell, but that he still cannot taste red wines. Apparently, Jack Davies, the owner of Schramsberg, is seriously ill with a severely debilitating, muscular disease.

At the Winery

I spoke to Joe's daughter Kathleen. She said that the 1997 harvest will be excellent and abundant. They have not produced any "Martha's Vineyard" in 1993, 1994, or 1995. The next vintage, 1996, will be released around 2001 or 2002. The vineyard was uprooted due to phylloxera. Her younger brother Rolly has sold his share in the family business and is seeking other ventures. The older brother David is the winemaker, as he has been for many years now.

They only produced their superb Angelica dessert wine in two vintages, 1974 and 1976 (released on their respective 20th anniversaries). No other vintage Angelica has been produced since, as they could not find a good-enough source for the juice. This excellent Tawny-style wine is well worth the effort of finding, notably the 1974.

David has just released his first vintage, 1994, of Heitz Cellars Napa Valley Port. Only 150 cases produced and now sold out. It is made from the eight traditional grape varietals used to produce Vintage Port (Tinta Cao, Tourriga Francesa, Souzao, Tinta Amerla, Alvaralhao, Tinta Barroca, Tinta Madeira, and Bastardo), aged for two years in oak barrels.

HEITZ CELLARS NAPA VALLEY 1994 PORT:

Bright, ruby-red colour to rim. Fresh black fruit and ripe, red fruit on nose. Sweeter on entry than true, young-Vintage Port and more accessible, too, yet it needs a good five to seven extra years of bottle-age, or longer, to reach maturity. A fine first effort.

December 1997

CHÂTEAU LAFITE 1975:

Fairly dense colour; orange rim. Cedary, expansive on nose, with slight vegetal overtones. Quite mature on palate. Still some tannins, yet the fruit is very soft. The backbone is typical of the vintage. A very good Claret that has held well, but not quite up to First Growth quality. Just lacks a bit of extra dimension. This vintage represents the comeback of Lafite, after underperforming since 1962.

For a very long time, Lafite owed its fame and reputation to the superb vintages of the 19th century, notably the incredibly great 1870, which I have had the good fortune of tasting on five occasions, all from magnums, including four times from the famous Glamis Castle collection. With one exception, they were all perfect wines, at over a century old. After 1900, and until the great 1953 and 1959 came along, Lafite really did not produce any memorable wines. Even the 1945 has been variable and often pale and disappointing. After the good 1962, and until the beginning of the comeback in 1975/1976, Lafite produced disappointing wines, in terms of First Growth class. This is puzzling, because this property has been under one ownership since the 1860s.

Thankfully, Lafite is back on track, with possibly the best 1976, a good 1978 (if a bit too herbaceous for my taste), a very good 1979, a pleasant 1981, a superb 1982. 1983 is good, but not great; 1985 and 1986 excellent, each reflecting the style of the respective vintages. The 1985 is elegant, round, and classy. The 1986 is solid, with excellent balance and potential (after the year 2000). This property produced a very fine 1988, a superb but soft 1989, and a great 1990. Welcome back, Lafite!

December 1997

LA TÂCHE 1955, DOMAINE DE LA ROMANÉE-CONTI:

This magnum was acquired at a Sotheby's auction in New York last September, as part of a DRC mixed lot. Two and one-half inch ullage, but when I unpacked the box, the cork was floating in the wine! Only the capsule prevented this from leaking. Orangy, very mature colour. Still had a hint of raspberries but, alas, badly oxidized. Undrinkable. One of the risks of buying at auction. However, over the past 25 years of buying wines at auction, I would say that I was lucky over 80% of the time. I proceeded to open another wine.

December 1997

CORTON-CHARLEMAGNE 1989, LOUIS LATOUR

AND

CHEVALIER-MONTRACHET "LES DEMOISELLES" 1989, LOUIS LATOUR:

Both represent the finest white Burgundies from this producer's stable. The source of the grapes is from their own vineyard holdings, while Latour's other Grands Crus, such as Montrachet, Bâtard-Montrachet, and Bienvenues, are made from purchased grapes, under contract. Also, the 1989 vintage was outstanding for white Burgundies. Both have a brilliant, golden colour.

The Corton-Charlemagne is rich, luscious, with nutty and oak overtones. Even a hint of minerals. Full on palate, long, exquisite, rich flavours. While approachable now, it will last well until at least 2003, if well cellared. Grand Vin.

The Chevalier-Montrachet is a winner. At this stage, it is a bit tighter, concentrated, yet rich. Excellent fruit/acidity balance and great complexity. Drink from 1999 to 2005 or beyond. Another great wine.

December 1997

HEITZ CELLARS "MARTHA'S VINEYARD" CABERNET SAUVIGNON 1980, NAPA VALLEY:

Impressive, deep colour for a 17-year-old, evolved rim. Oddly, classic cedary, Cabernet nose, without this vineyard's typical mint/eucalyptus overtones. Fairly dry, still tannic, but little fruit. A good wine, but somehow I fear that the tannins will outlast the fruit. Clean, fruity finish. Drink up.

(The above notes were written just after decanting, as I was sipping the wine while waiting for the lamb to cook. When I finally sat down to dinner an hour later, the wine had developed a lot more concentration, depth, and ripe fruit. I have made a "beginner's mistake" in jumping to conclusions before giving the wine enough time to breathe. A lovely wine.)

December 1997

Dinner with friends.

CHAMPAGNE BOLLINGER "GRANDE ANNÉE" 1985:

Everything one could expect from an excellent Champagne. Great vintage, excellent producer, lovely wine. Full, rich, very well balanced, yeasty. Tiny bubbles and fine mousse. A generous Champagne.

DOMAINE DE CHEVALIER BLANC 1988:

Palish gold. Flowery nose of fresh apples, oak, and vanilla. While not as intense and rich as this fine property's 1983, it is long, complex, and has a lot of class. Approachable now, but should hold at least until 2005.

VEGA SICILIA "UNICO" 1962, RIBERA DEL DUERO:

This wine is my personal all-time favourite Spanish red wine. The body, depth, weight, fruit extract are all there, but somehow the winemaker has managed to maintain a fantastic elegance here. Not unlike a 1966 Château Palmer, but with a little more woody overtones. At its peak. Superb wine.

BARBARESCO 1978, ANGELO GAJA:

I was fortunate enough to acquire a case of this wine in its youth (in 1984), before the world went crazy over Gaja's wines. The price then was US$265 per case. As expected, still youthful at almost 20 years old. Unusually long cork. Deep, garnet colour to rim. Fair bit of sediment. Decanted one and one-half hours. Tar and ripe, spicy fruit on nose. Full, luscious, still a bit tannic. A serious, solid wine. If well cellared, it should last at least until 2010.

CHÂTEAU D'YQUEM 1980, IN HALF-BOTTLE:

Like the 1987, the 1980 d'Yquem has been overlooked, yet it is a lovely Sauternes. Brilliant, golden colour. Ripe botrytis mingled with oak and vanilla on nose. Crème brûlée on palate, but in an elegant sense. Not big or luscious, but the ripe fruit is backed by very good acidity. A lovely wine. This will last well until 2005 or beyond.

January 1998

Dinner at home, with friends.

MONTRACHET, MARQUIS DE LAGUICHE, 1989, JOSEPH DROUHIN:

A sublime wine. Perfect now. Exotic fruit, ripe pears on nose. Hint of vanilla and oak. Full, round, perfectly balanced. Loads of fruit.

CHÂTEAU MUSAR 1977, SERGE HOCHAR, LEBANON:

Evolved colour, orangy rim. On nose, this wine has a smell of ripe prunes, leather, and spices. Round on palate. Some fruit there, but seems a bit tired. Drink up. Not unlike a mature Rioja.

SASSICAIA 1981, BOLGHERI:

Impressive, bright-red colour to rim. Cedar, ripe fruit on nose. Clean and fruity. Full on palate, losing its tannins. Harmonious, long. Very well balanced, backed by lovely, ripe fruit. Top quality. Drink now to 2002.

CHÂTEAU PALMER 1978:

Evolved, red colour. Orange rim. The spicy, herbaceous nose typical of this Cabernet year. Round, quite forward, lacking the fat that Merlot imparts to this fine wine. Merlot is such an important component at Palmer (around 40%). Drinking well now. Spicy and elegant.

CHÂTEAU LA MISSION HAUT-BRION 1975:

Still a blockbuster! Dense, deep colour to rim. Nose of very ripe fruit, cedar, and earth. Full, powerful, tannic. Great fruit extract, perfect balance. Grand Vin! This wine has been in my cellar since its youth, stored at a constant 52°F. Great potential. Drink from 2000 to 2015 or beyond. How fortunate I am to have acquired two cases of this in London in 1977 (as futures), at a cost of £63—per case!

WARRE'S 1970 VINTAGE PORT:

Decanted three hours before serving. Deep colour. Ripe, fruity, forthcoming nose. Full, velvety, sweet, well balanced. Very long and mouthfilling. Ready, but no rush if well cellared. A beautiful, undervalued Port.

January 1998

Dinner with Carol, Orly, and Michael.

CHÂTEAU AUSONE 1979:

A wine I know well, and one that has given me a lot of pleasure over the years. Fully mature now. Classic 1979. Chocolaty, rich, round, spicy, herbaceous Cabernet Franc backed by good, ripe fruit. Round, velvety, very well balanced, and long. An excellent wine and one of the top handful of 1979s. Probably the best 1979 St. Emilion, as Certan-de-May is the best Pomerol in that vintage.

Other good 1979s are Haut-Brion, La Mission, Domaine de Chevalier (surprisingly full-bodied for this property), Palmer, Lafite, and Pichon-Lalande. Lascases can be very good, too, but it is spicy, cedary, and tight, reflecting the high proportion of Cabernet Sauvignon (around 85%) in this wine.

January 1998

A tasting, featuring St. Emilions of the great 1982 vintage, celebrating the 15th anniversary of this vintage.

CHÂTEAU PAVIE 1982:

Most forward of flight, and the least luscious, yet it still has the character of this ripe vintage. Medium colour, good depth, orange rim. A bit on the dry side, but good fruit. Ready now. (17)

CHÂTEAU L'ARROSÉE 1982:

Typical l'Arrosée, with its high proportion of Cabernets. Tight, serious, dark, backed by solid, ripe fruit. Not too complex at this stage, but rich and a bit tannic. Try around 2000 to 2005. (17.5)

CHÂTEAU CANON 1982:

More evolved colour than the l'Arrosée, but still excellent depth. A charmer. The most pleasurable to drink now, along with Figeac. Lovely, ripe fruit. Not really a big wine, but lots of nice fruit, soft tannins, and good acidity. (18)

CHÂTEAU FIGEAC 1982:

A beauty! Cedar, ripe black fruit, oak, and vanilla on nose. Still a bit tannic. Not quite at its peak, but almost there. Lingering aftertaste. (18.5)

Château Magdelaine 1982:

With over 80% Merlot in the blend, this wine is structured more like a Pomerol than a St. Emilion. Good depth, but not as dark as the Figeac. Iron, mineral, and black currant on nose. Full, intense. Great fruit extract. Drink now to 2007 or beyond. (18)

Château Ausone 1982:

An unusual Ausone. This château produces "intellectual" wines, more elegant than "in your face" fruit and ripeness. Usually, Ausone is tighter in its youth, but this 1982 is quite forward. Very similar in structure to the Canon. Lingering oak, cedar, and ripe fruit aftertaste. It also seems to have more sediment than the others. (All wines were decanted one hour before the tasting.) Very good, but I prefer the serious structure of this château's 1983 and the smooth, creamy 1979. Excellent, nevertheless. (18)

Château Cheval-Blanc 1982:

As expected, the superstar in this star-studded tasting. First, the colour gave it away. Very deep, dense colour to rim. Incredible nose of very ripe black and red fruit. Lots of extract, full, creamy. Perfect balance and great intensity. At the risk of boring the reader, and having tasted the great Cheval-Blanc 1947 on seven occasions (including twice from magnums and twice London-bottlings), I have to compare the 1982 to the glorious 1947. The only other Cheval-Blanc that approaches this great 1982 is a sensational bottle of the 1961 Cheval-Blanc I tasted four years ago in Los Angeles. (19.5)

This tasting did not disclose anything new. The wines tasted the way we expected them to taste. How fortunate I am to have acquired quantities of these and other 1982s very early, shortly after their release (and several "En Primeur"). A case of Cheval-Blanc 1982 cost me, in 1984, US$385 and Figeac a mere $180 per case. Had I known then what I know now…

January 1998

Château L'Evangile 1983

and

Château Le Pin 1983:

Tasted double-blind. Obviously Pomerols or very ripe St. Emilions.

The l'Evangile was excellent. Deep colour, evolved rim. At first, nose was stemmy, but later developed hint of licorice and chocolate. Masculine, still tannic at 14. Lots of extract and ripe fruit. No rush. An excellent wine and possibly the best Pomerol of the vintage.

The Le Pin had a brighter, more youthful red colour. Forthcoming, sweet, ripe fruit on nose. Rounder, softer, less serious than the l'Evangile. Sweet fruit on palate. Flowery. At this tasting, the l'Evangile was clearly the more serious of the two and, considering the price Le Pin goes for these days, it is nothing short of a farce. A good buy at a tenth of the price!

Mid-January 1998:

Champagne Billecart-Salmon "Cuvée N. F. Billecart" Brut 1989:

This is a lovely, elegant Champagne made in the Taittinger "Comtes de Champagne" style. Long, smooth, well balanced, creamy; rich and round. Excellent fruit and structure. Also has the typical elegance of the vintage. Very good.

Château Palmer 1970:

A masterpiece that is at its absolute peak now and will not improve. Evolved colour, good depth, fair bit of sediment. Decanted 45 minutes. Classy, chocolaty, elegant nose. Round, smooth on palate. Classic Margaux. All there, but in a soft way. No sense keeping this much longer, even if well cellared, as this bottle was, since its youth. Magnums should last well until 2003 to 2005.

Duckhorn Vineyards "Three Palms Vineyard" 1978 Merlot, Napa Valley:

Dan Duckhorn's first vintage and the "Three Palms Vineyard" is his top-of-the-line Merlot. Thus, this is now very rare and expensive. Several years ago, Margaret Duckhorn, Dan's wife, told me that as they needed cash badly in the early 1980s, they did not keep any in reserve, so none is available at the winery. Retails now for well over US$150 per bottle, if it can be found.

One interesting comment

I have tasted this wine on six occasions. The levels of all the bottles were mediocre at best (upper to top shoulder). Maybe they had a problem with the corks. Not fitting right? Enjoyed this bottle with Carol and Michael. Soft, forward, and will not improve, but it is all there. Classic, sweet red fruit on both nose and palate. Well balanced, very good, sweet fruit extract. Not very complex, but a pleasure to drink now. Better than the bottle tasted last month.

Montrachet 1985, Louis Latour:

Louis Latour must have undergone some sort of crisis in the mid-80s. This is obvious in both their 1985 and 1986 whites, and from their own Domaine (Chevalier-Montrachet "Demoiselles" and Corton-Charlemagne) and their purchased grapes-négociant wines (Montrachet, Bâtard, and Bienvenues). All the above were quite good when young, but they have definitely not aged well. This is true of this Montrachet, too. Impressive, deep-golden colour. Flowery, delicate nose with hint of oxidation and wet cement. Tired, soft, lacking depth and fruit on palate. Very disappointing. Barely Villages quality, let alone Grand Cru!

EDELKEUR "NOBLE LATE HARVEST" WINE OF ORIGIN 1978, NEDERBURG ESTATE, SOUTH AFRICA, IN HALF-BOTTLE:

Sold at the Nederburg auction. This wine was produced by Gunther Bröezel, the then-winemaker at Nederburg Estate. Made from botrytized Chenin Blanc grapes (called Steen in South Africa) and sometimes with a little Johannisberg Riesling. Impressive amber-gold colour. Intense nose of ripe apricots and botrytis. Luscious, full, great fruit extract and excellent acidity on palate. At 20 years old, fully mature. A superb dessert wine made in the Trockenbeerenauslese old style.

Several years ago, a case of 24 half-bottles of this came up for sale at an auction in Chicago. The estimate was $15 per half-bottle. Having tasted this wine previously, I could not believe my eyes, because I knew that in South Africa, connoisseurs were ready to kill for this, and, if one could find it, it would retail for five times that price. I bid only $13 per half. I was very upset with myself for bidding so low but, unbelievably, I got the lot! I was very fortunate that no one else picked this one up. This is one of the pleasures of buying at auction.

January 20, 1998

Commanderie de Bordeaux Tasting and Dinner, featuring various wines from the commune of St. Emilion.

With dinner
(Wine served in pairs)

CHÂTEAU AUSONE 1985:

Evolved, orangy rim. Odd, cheesy nose. No sign of oak or cedar. Much better on palate. Charming, sweet fruit. good depth. At its peak. Lovely now. Typical, sweet, elegant 1985. Well balanced and very good extract. Spicy, peppery aftertaste. (18)

CHÂTEAU CANON 1983:

Good colour. Elegant, cedary, and fruity nose. Lovely balance and depth. At its peak. Round, good backbone. Clean, long finish. (17.5)

Both the above châteaux were from the Côtes region of St. Emilion.

SECOND PAIR
From the Graves region of St. Emilion

CHÂTEAU LA DOMINIQUE 1982:

Similar appearance to the 1982 Figeac. Less obvious, less ripe on nose. Full, sweet, luscious, round. Great extract, rich, hint of new oak, spicy Merlot. The sweetness of a Pomerol! Lovely bottle. Sweeter than the Figeac, but more straightforward. (17.5)

CHÂTEAU FIGEAC 1982:

Deep, dense colour. Classic, ripe 1982 nose. Full, flavourful. Ripe tannins and ripe fruit. Great length. Hint of prunes, but in a very positive way. Hint of bell peppers, too. (18.5)

Note
La Dominique is located near Figeac and Cheval-Blanc, in the Graves region of St. Emilion, nearer to Pomerol, but while the latter two great Domaines have a fair bit of gravel in their soil, there is only a tiny section of gravel at La Dominique, in a corner of the vineyard.

THIRD PAIR

CHÂTEAU SOUTARD 1985:

Medium cherry-red colour. Palish rim. Ripe, leathery nose. Full, solid, quite big for a 1985, yet typical of this property. Still tannic, powerful, ripe, rich, straightforward. Drink now to 2002. (17)

CHÂTEAU TERTRE RÔTEBOEUF 1988:

Made from almost 80% Merlot. Aged in 100% new oak. Obviously very selective breeding and handling. Impressive, deep colour. Palish rim. Clean, impeccable nose of ripe Merlot. Big, impressive, powerful, ripe. A "Parker" wine. Unfortunately, lacks class. Fullness, yes, but lacking terroir character. Solid, tannic, very serious. Drink around 2002 to 2005 or beyond. Tastes like a young 1978 Taltarni Cabernet Sauvignon from Australia (tasted in 1983 and predicted by some experts to be the next Château Latour; rubbish, of course!). (17.5)

DESSERT WINE
Served double-blind

CHÂTEAU MAJON 1982, MENDOCINO COUNTY "SAUTERNE" (NO. "5"), PRODUCED BY JOHN PARDUCCI:

A rare, tiny production, that is now extremely hard to find. Made mostly from grapes produced in Talmadge Vineyard, with natural botrytis (not induced), and from 100% Chardonnay! The sugar content at fermentation was so high, permission was needed from the authorities to add water to the juice! This wine would fool anyone. Smells and tastes like a 1975 Barsac or a young Suduiraut. Lovely botrytis, full, rich, good fruit, and backed by excellent acidity, which is why I thought that it was a 1975. An impressive effort.

January 1998

CÔTE RÔTIE "LA MOULINE" 1983, E. GUIGAL:

14 years old and approaching its peak. Impressive, deep colour. Very slight orange at rim. Intense, expansive black currants, oriental spices, and hint of leather on nose. A mouthful of lovely, ripe fruit, yet it definitely is a refined wine. Complex, fruity, well balanced. Guigal adds some white varietals to this single-vineyard wine (mostly Roussanne), which he does not do at "La Landonne." Quite approachable now, but, if well cellared, should last well into the 21st century.

January 1998

HEITZ CELLARS "MARTHA'S VINEYARD" CABERNET SAUVIGNON 1985, NAPA VALLEY:

A great vineyard and an excellent vintage combine here to produce a classic "Martha's," yet without the "in your face" mint and eucalyptus so typical of this vineyard's great 1974. The above characteristics of this vineyard are there, of course, but in a more subdued way. Deep colour to rim. Lovely nose of ripe berries, oak, and eucalyptus. Full, rich, well balanced. Excellent fruit extract. Still a bit tannic. Drink from 2000 to 2008 or beyond. Top quality.

January 1998

Dinner with friends.

PULIGNY MONTRACHET "CLOS DU CAILLERET" 1989, DOMAINE JEAN CHARTRON:

Until 1984, this "monopole" vineyard, possibly the greatest single vineyard in Puligny, other than the Grands Crus, was leased to the négociant Joseph Drouhin. Part of the agreement of returning it to its owners was that they would refrain from bottling it as a vineyard designate for five years. Thus, there was no "Le Cailleret" between 1984 and 1988, with the 1989 being the first vintage produced.

The wine was a bright, green-golden colour with good depth. Some sulphur, pronounced oak on both nose and palate. Good, but delicate Chardonnay is dominated by the oak. What could and should be great is merely good. Chartron is apparently trying to upgrade "Le Caillerets" from Premier to Grand Cru, because of the excellent location of this vineyard. In my opinion, to do so will require him to start producing a great wine there, as Drouhin did, notably with their superb 1978 and 1982.

CHÂTEAU LEOVILLE-LASCASES 1966, IN MAGNUM:

Classic 1966 and classic (high Cabernet) Lascases. Even from a magnum, this wine was better ten years ago. Excellent level. Good depth, mature rim. Cedary, spicy, slightly vegetal Cabernet on nose. Tannic, on the dry side, masculine. Not unlike a St. Estèphe, yet some fruit is still there. Fairly tight. Lingering aftertaste with trace of acidity.

MUSIGNY 1964, COMTE DE VOGÜÉ, BOTTLED BY CORON PÈRE ET FILS:

Impressive, youthful colour for a 33-year-old. Maybe some Syrah was added? Not only does the colour seem to indicate that, but on the nose, too, it seemed unusually peppery for a Pinot Noir, although it had the obvious character of a fine red Burgundy. Fleshy, rich, trace of acidity. Its main fault was, maybe, lack of finesse and complexity. Also, the fruit seemed to be drying up a bit. Most enjoyable, nevertheless.

February 1998

TOKAI ASZÚ 5 PUTTONYOS "BOJTA" 1991, ROYAL TOKAI WINE COMPANY:

Made in the new style. More Sauternes-like, botrytis-affected than the Communist regime's madeirized style. Palish-gold colour. Elegant, delicate, ripe, botrytized fruit on nose. Not cloying, good fruit, and sweet aftertaste. Very good fruit/acidity balance. Drink now to 2010.

This new wave of post-Communism Tokai wines, financed chiefly by foreign interests, will have to remain a mystery to our generation. The last true, great Escenssia was the pre-Communism 1947. These new Tokais should, theoretically, show their true character when 30, 40, or even 50 years old, around 2030. Young people of today may live long enough to enjoy them. For us it is, alas, too late, unless a "Viagra"-style pill that extends life to age 120 or 150 is invented soon.

February 4 to 9, 1998

Trip to Yountville, Napa Valley.

Incredible storms, rain, and floods that week.

Lunch with Martin Blomberg, owner of "Groezinger's Wine Shop" in Yountville, at the "Napa Valley Grille" restaurant

BONNY DOON VINEYARDS VIOGNIER 1996, CENTRAL COAST, IN HALF-BOTTLE:

Martin brought this one along. As soon as it was poured, we knew we had trouble on our hands. Peachy-gold colour, way too dark for such a young wine. Early signs of oxidation. Quite spirity Viognier, and big, but little spicy character so typical of this varietal. Heavy handed. Obviously a bad bottle. The cork was made of plastic. I hope that these corks will never be used in premium wines. Besides the ceremony and aesthetics of traditional corks, what effect will plastic have on fine wines over time?

I brought along two bottles.

CORTON-CHARLEMAGNE 1992, BONNEAU DU MARTRAY:

At first, tight, fairly closed up, but as the wine warmed up in the glass, it developed lovely complexity. Hint of almonds, acacia, and oak backed by a fair bit of power and alcohol underneath. Understated, elegant, classy. Very different from the more intense, more forthcoming, and more luscious examples of Louis Latour's or Coche-Dury's Charlemagnes.

I have tasted over the years just about every good vintage of Bonneau du Martray's Corton-Charlemagnes since the mid-1960s vintages, and my impression has always been that the wine is reliable, well made, but always restrained, almost as if the producer did not want to risk leaving the grapes on the vines for another week of sunshine to reach optimum maturity and extra dimension. Very good, nevertheless.

CHÂTEAU GRAND-PUY-LACOSTE 1989, IN HALF-BOTTLE:

Impressive, youthful colour. Subdued, restrained nose of fine, classic Pauillac/Cabernet. Still youthful on palate. Excellent balance, tight fruit, even in half-bottle. Drink from 2000 to 2008. This is an excellent wine. If Lynch-Bages is the "poor man's Mouton," then this wine is the "poor man's Latour," although with the crazy price of fine Claret, nobody who loves Claret can afford to be poor these days.

Martin Blomberg told me that back in 1959, Joe Heitz was one of his teachers in Fresno, where he studied oenology, and that Joe had the reputation of being a "tough cookie" even then. We also discussed old South African wines (Martin is originally from there, where his family was involved in the wine business in Capetown). Martin said that in the old days, Nederburg and other producers could not afford American oak barrels, so they put blocks of American wood in holding tanks to impart the character of American oak and vanilla to their Cabernets. In the early 1970s, while living and working in the UK, Martin acquired ten cases of 1970 Château Palmer at £2 per bottle, which he still owns. This is even cheaper than what I paid in 1975 for that wine in Vancouver, Can$10.50 per bottle!

Saturday, February 7, 1998

Torrential rains and floods all week. Today is the second session of the three-day marathon tasting of Diamond Creek Cabernet Sauvignons.

Going back to 1972 (up to 1995), all the vintages and individual vineyards produced, with the participation of the owner, Al Brounstein, and organized by Bipin Desai. The first event was held last night at "Postrio" restaurant in San Francisco. I missed the first event, but I shall incorporate other tasters' comments on the wines tasted last night. This second event (and tomorrow's third) are being held at the "French Laundry" restaurant in Yountville, right next door to my place. I'm glad I don't have to drive far in this torrential rain. Chef/owner Thomas Keller is preparing two outstanding lunches for us.

DIAMOND CREEK TASTING

FIRST SESSION

Friday, February 6, 1998

"Postrio" restaurant, San Francisco.

In this session only, the wines are listed in chronological order and not in the flights in which they were tasted.

VOLCANIC HILL 1974:

Good ruby-red colour for age. Mature nose of minerals, tea, and black cherries. Fully mature, spicy, some fruit there, and soft tannins. A fine effort, but not one of the great 1974s. (17)

VOLCANIC HILL 1975:

Rounder, more lush, with fresher fruit, but less solid than the 1974. Very good, nevertheless. (16.5)

GRAVELLY MEADOW 1976:

Riper than the two above; the first of twin-drought vintages in the Napa Valley. Red currant, Cassis, and cedar on nose. Full, ripe, hint of leather. Fully mature. (16)

GRAVELLY MEADOW 1978:

Most Médoc/Pauillac-like so far. Cedary, hint of tar, and very good fruit extract. Ready, but no rush, yet it is already 20 years old. (17.5)

VOLCANIC HILL 1979:

This is a rich, solid wine. Dense colour, cedary, cigar box on nose. Full, solid tannic, not unlike a big Château Montrose. (17.5)

VOLCANIC HILL 1980:

Fruity, jammy, black fruit on entry, but trace of acidity of finish. Quite good, though. (16.5)

VOLCANIC HILL 1981:

The least impressive so far. Fairly sturdy, but fruit seems to be fading a bit. Drink up. (16)

RED ROCK TERRACE 1982:

A nice, fruity wine that has a trace of acidity. Good flavours and spicy finish. (16)

RED ROCK TERRACE "SPECIAL SELECT" 1982:

Bigger, more tannic than the regular 1982 Red Rock Terrace, with fragrant, lush fruit and lingering aftertaste. The grapes were picked a month later than the rest of Red Rock, because the grapes came from the cooler part of the vineyard. This is excellent. (18)

GRAVELLY MEADOW 1983:

Spicy fruit, hint of licorice and Cassis, but a bit loosely knit. Drying up a bit. Needs drinking. (16.5)

GRAVELLY MEADOW 1984:

A ripe, earthy wine with good depth, but not very complex and a tart finish. Ready now. (16)

LAKE 1984:

Minty black fruit on nose. Slightly stemmy on palate, but backed by excellent fruit and tobacco flavours. Lingering, luscious aftertaste. (17.5)

RED ROCK TERRACE 1985:

Hint of charred oak and licorice on nose and on entry, and earthy, tobacco, mineral finish. But—and this is a major "but"—hollow middle. Diluted, loosely knit. Will not improve. (15.5)

VOLCANIC HILL 1986:

Earthy, meaty on both nose and palate. Backed by good, ripe fruit. Quite concentrated. Drink now to 2003. (17)

VOLCANIC HILL 1987:

Not really a big wine, but not quite ready yet. Cherries and tobacco on nose. A leaner wine. Tight, fairly acidic and tannic—lacks charm. (15.5)

GRAVELLY MEADOW 1988:

Herbal, flowery nose. Quite evolved. Hint of oak, soft fruit. Good, but not great. (16)

VOLCANIC HILL 1988:

Better than that vintage's Gravelly Meadow. More concentration, more character, better depth. Toast, oak, cherry fruit and cedar in harmony. (17)

GRAVELLY MEADOW 1989:

Approachable, ripe, soft, round. "New style"? Attractive, long finish. (17)

THREE VINEYARD BLEND 1989:

Hint of mint, black fruit, ripe tannins, some licorice. Most enjoyable. A pleasure to drink now. (18)

RED ROCK TERRACE 1990:

Very forward, soft, round, luscious. Definitely "new wave" wine. Easy to drink and understand. (17)

GRAVELLY MEADOW 1991:

Fruity, round, ripe. Very approachable. Flowery on nose. Hint of new oak and spicy, fruity finish. (17)

GRAVELLY MEADOW "MICROCLIMATE" 1991:

More concentration than the above, better structured, backed by ripe tannins. Dark berry fruit is backed by good acidity. Very good potential. Drink from 2002 to 2006. (17.5)

GRAVELLY MEADOW 1992:

Flowery, elegant, almost silky texture. Lingering finish, fragrant. Nice "modern" wine. (16.5)

LAKE 1992:

Quite similar in structure to the 1992 Gravelly, but has that extra dimension and extract. (17)

RED ROCK TERRACE 1994:

Still youthful. Nice bouquet of black fruit, violets, and mint. Clean, well-balanced, ripe, but not overly so. Will mature by 2002. (16.5)

RED ROCK TERRACE "MICROCLIMATE" 1994:

Riper than the above, more concentration of black fruit and dark chocolate. Hint of oak/vanilla. Not quite blended together yet but very good potential. If you are used to—and prefer—Diamond Hill's older style, this one's not for you. A very good "Pomerol." (18) Hard to fault it. A matter of taste.

LAKE 1994:

Forward, soft, fleshy, round, luscious. Amazingly forward. Very ripe, soft fruit. Almost ready. (17.5)

VOLCANIC HILL 1995:

Lush black currant, oak, vanilla on nose. Full, rich, ripe tannins. Good—but not too obvious—acidity. Long aftertaste. Drink from 2003 onward. (18)

VOLCANIC HILL 1997 (BARREL SAMPLE):

Peppery; Cassis and oak on both nose and palate. Rich and luscious. (No score: barrel sample)

Saturday, February 7, 1998

SECOND SESSION

"French Laundry," Yountville.

Belle Rhodes called to let me know that they have lost their power and could not open their garage door. I drove to Bella Oaks to pick up Belle and Barney and take them to the "French Laundry." In addition to Belle and Barney Rhodes, I also had at my table Robert Finnigan and Michel Bettane of the Revue du Vin de France, *as well as Serena Sutcliffe, MW, Director of Sotheby's wine department. Nice to be at a table with knowledgeable tasters.*

FLIGHT #1

RED ROCK TERRACE 1979:

Good depth, mature orange rim. Sweet, herbaceous, ripe, evolved fruit on nose. Still a bit tannic; good intensity, but the fruit is definitely softening up. Slightly cloudy, probably due to faulty decanting. (16)

RED ROCK TERRACE "FIRST PICK" 1977:

Mature red colour; orange rim. Hint of rubber. Picked from the top of Red Rock Terrace. The "second pick" ripened three to four weeks later, and was not quite as good because ripening was uneven. Slightly pruny, noticeable acidity, tired fruit. (15)

RED ROCK TERRACE "SECOND PICK" 1977:

Similar appearance to the "First Pick," but cleaner, fruitier nose. Tighter, more acidic, leaner, yet livelier than the first pick. Drink up. Both are not very impressive. (15.5)

RED ROCK TERRACE 1976:

Excellent depth to rim. Hint of rubber on nose is backed by good fruit. Quite acidic, tannic, too, but thankfully, backed by enough fruit. (16.5)

GRAVELLY MEADOW 1974:

Deep, intense colour. Evolved rim. Lovely, mature, expansive, minty nose. Also, excellent, ripe fruit. Beautiful balance, depth, length. How good these 1974s are, especially if well cellared. Almost structured like 1945 red Bordeaux. A serious wine. (18)

VOLCANIC HILL 1988:

Brilliant colour, good depth. Full, fruity, intense. Very good depth. Lots of ripe fruit, combined with solid, tannic backbone. Very good. Drink now to 2005. (17)

VOLCANIC HILL 1978:

Bright red, good depth. Full, fruity, intense. Very good extract. Lots of ripe fruit. Combined with solid, tannic backbone. Drink now to 2005. (17.5)

In this flight, the 1974 Gravelly Meadow was clearly the best wine, followed closely by the 1978 Volcanic Hill.

FLIGHT #2

THREE VINEYARD BLEND "NOVEMBER PICKED" 1981:

Good depth. Hint of rubber. Good fruit, but a bit too lemony. Pleasant, soft, needs food. Too citric for me. This was produced from a second crop of all three vineyards. (15)

GRAVELLY MEADOW 1982:

Tight on nose. Unyielding. Lovely fruit concentration. Warm, classic old Claret nose. Full, tannic, serious. Fairly high acidity, but backed by good fruit. Later, supple, elegant. (17)

GRAVELLY MEADOW "SPECIAL SELECT" 1982:

Tighter on nose than the "regular." Made by fining the wine with two egg whites only, and not beating them too much, so that they go down faster by gravity. The regular was cleared with the standard number (six) of egg whites. Sold to the restaurant trade; brighter than the regular. The only time at Diamond Creek that they used this nomenclature. Rounder. Not as aggressive or tannic as the regular 1982, but less impressive overall. (16)

RED ROCK TERRACE 1983:

Good depth, orange, evolved rim. Tight, unyielding nose. Surprisingly closed for a 14-year-old. Fruity, well balanced. Solid, tight tannins. Too acidic/citric. (15)

GRAVELLY MEADOW 1975:

Excellent depth, mature rim. Rubbery, tannic, intense. Loads of depth and ripe fruit. Again, quite noticeable acidity, yet no tartaric acid was added, but rather natural acidity. Lovely depth. Serious wine. Complex, long. Very good fruit. Well balanced, all there. (18)

RED ROCK TERRACE 1984:

Fresh, buttery/oak on nose. Still youthful, tannic, fairly lean. More obvious soil character, but less noble than the Gravelly Meadow. Fine wine, nevertheless. (16.5)

GRAVELLY MEADOW 1981:

Unyielding on nose, at 15 years old! A bit herbaceous. Sweet, ripe tannins and fruit. The first wine of this flight so far that does not seem to have excessive acidity. Very good fruit extract. Soft, ready, yet enough tannic backbone to last until 2000 or beyond. Very good. (17)

RED ROCK TERRACE 1980:

Deep, dense colour. Youthful to rim. An odd wine. Very tannic, aggressive on entry, but then a short finish. Soft fruit. Tannins say "wait," but fruit says "drink me." Lacks the noble structure of the other wines in this flight. Too sharp. Other bottles were better. Mellow, complex, well balanced. Good fruit. (Four to five bottles of each wine were opened.) (16)

THREE VINEYARD BLEND 1985:

Hint of rubber on nose. Good fruit. Still very young. Noticeable acidity, backed by good, ripe fruit. Solid. Drink from 1999 to 2004. Sweet, complex. (17)

RED ROCK TERRACE 1986:

Good depth, evolved rim. I know that this sounds repetitious, but all the wines had an impressive colour.

Very consistent, whether young or old! Good fruit. Still lively. Ripe tannins are backed by nice fruit. Drink now to 2005. (16.5)

RED ROCK TERRACE 1987:

Youthful colour. Buttery, oaky, ripe fruit on nose. Noticeable vegetal/Cabernet Franc greenness on entry. Well balanced. Complex, less tannic, less acidic, less serious than the 1970s and early 1980s; more approachable. Drink now to 2004. (17)

THREE VINEYARD BLEND 1990:

Classic 1990. Fruity, elegant, complex. Less tannic than older vintages, less serious, more approachable. Lovely fruit. This particular blend has not been produced since. (17)

GRAVELLY MEADOW 1990:

Well balanced, leaner "old" style. Complex, forward, spicy, crisp. Nice, rich fruit. But acidity too obvious; lacks flesh. Too green, too lean. Pity. One wishes it had more ripe fruit. (16)

Al Brounstein said that Jerry Luper was their advisor for several years. He has been replaced now by Dick Peterson and Dick's daughter Heidi.

VOLCANIC HILL 1991:

Certainly less masculine than wines made in the early 1980s and the late 1970s, but lovely fruit, ripe tannins, and acidity all in harmony. Charming, feminine wine that is very well balanced. Drink now to 2003. (18)

VOLCANIC HILL "MICRO CLIMATE" 1991:

Very similar in colour and structure to the regular 1991 Volcanic Hill, but just more concentrated. Yet oddly, sweet Pomerol-like, rather than serious Haut-Médoc. (17.5)

GRAVELLY MEADOW 1990:

Acidity too obvious; lacks flesh. Too green, too lean. Pity. One wishes it had more ripe fruit. (15.5)

FLIGHT #4

GRAVELLY MEADOW/LAKE 1992 BLEND:

Purplish red colour. New oak/cedar on nose. Fruity, rich, less aggressive tannins than the older vintages. Riper tannins, more harmonious, but less masculine. More refined, less rustic. These two vineyards are close together and both are exposed to cool air from the sea. (17.5)

VOLCANIC HILL 1992:

Sweeter, less earthy than the Gravelly Meadow. Complex, sweet, elegant. Very forward. (17)

GRAVELLY MEADOW 1994:

Very good, deep, intense colour. Sweet vanilla, delicate, round, harmonious, rich, oaky fruit. Lovely, forward Pomerol style. (17.5)

RED ROCK TERRACE 1995:

Bright, deep colour to rim. Fresh, fruity, ripe cherries on nose. Sweet, round, elegant. Totally different style. More harmonious, more elegant, hint of vanilla, sweet fruit. Early maturing and approachable. A charmer. Drink 2002 to 2008. A "modern" wine, not unlike Château L'Angélus 1989 or 1990. (17.5)

LAKE VINEYARD 1987:

Dense colour. Slightly cloudy rather than brilliant. Ripe, almost pruny nose. A bit diluted, yet good intensity. Slightly herbaceous. Nice, sweet fruit. Drink now to 2003. (17)

LAKE VINEYARD 1990:

Less intensity than the Lake 1987, less concentrated. More friendly. Good quality. Drink now to 2004. (17.5)

RED ROCK TERRACE 1997, BARREL SAMPLE:

Deep, youthful colour to rim. Fresh fruit. Intense, perfectly balanced, ripe tannins, all in harmony. Very good potential. No score, as this is a barrel sample.

Overall impressions

There is clearly a change in style of winemaking at Diamond Creek, from big, old-style, Montrose-like wines in the 1970s and early 1980s, to leaner wines, more acidic in the mid-to-late 1980s and fruitier, softer, riper, earlier-maturing "modern" wines in the 1990s. The wines are now impeccably made, with lovely fruit, riper tannins, and are much earlier maturing. Whether they will have the staying power of the older wines, only time will tell.

DESSERT WINE

ROBERT PECOTA "MOSCATO D'ANDREA" 1996:

Fairly oily, rich, spirity, with good Muscat and lychee nuts character. Well made, but definitely not my style of wine.

During the tasting, I discussed the following matters with Michel Bettane and Serena Sutcliffe.

On Mouton Rothschild

Bettane called it "Delila" (I call it "an expensive mistress"), a property that produces a great wine once per decade or so and underachieves and is frustrating otherwise. Yet, oddly, all this has happened under the same ownership for over seven decades and now under the Baron's daughter and heir.

On Dominus

Christian Moueix's property in the Napa Valley. They both seem to feel that the wines are too unyielding, and hard, but that there is noticeable improvement from the mid-1990s onward, maybe due to old incompatible vines during the first decade of Dominus production. I do not agree with them, because the 1985 is quite fruity and both the 1990 and 1991 were in excellent shape when I tasted them both from cask and again upon release. I have found the wines from the late 1980s and early 1990s to be very well made.

Bettane seemed to indicate that now that Pascal Delbeck has been removed from Ausone, the wine should improve. He seems to be closer to Vauthier, the then-half (and now full) owner of Ausone. It seems that Vauthier and Delbeck had very different philosophies on how to make the wine at Ausone. Pascal, however, is doing an excellent job at Belair. Delbeck has become another victim of the new-style "in your face" fruit, and soft, oaky, early maturing wines. At Ausone, Michel Rolland and Robert Parker have won, tragically. Now Ausone will become another technically correct, hedonistic, unctuous, massively fruity, early maturing, easy-to-understand wine. Too bad.

I also learned that the lovely restaurant "Chez Robin" in Chenas, in the heart of the Beaujolais, has closed down. Michel Bettane suggested (more of wishful thinking than fact) that Freddy Girardet, who was apparently forced out of the famous restaurant that bore his name, might start his own place, maybe reviving the old "Chez Robin." Who knows?

Bettane and I also discussed Corton-Charlemagnes. He is very fond of Bonneau du Martray, which I think is good, even very good in some vintages, but an underachiever. He said that Louis Latour's and Coche-Dury's Corton-Charlemagnes are more impressive in their youth, but that the Bonneau du Martray is the long runner. I tend to disagree there. No doubt du Martray has great potential, but they must allow the grapes to ripen a little more before picking. A matter of taste, I guess. Michel also said that he did not like Tollot-Beaut's Corton-Charlemagnes too much. There I disagreed with him emphatically. I think that this producer's Charlemagnes are superb and made to age. Again, a matter of taste. As Tollot-Beaut only produces four barrels of their exquisite Corton-Charlemagne yearly, I am happy that other wine aficionados don't find it appealing. We both agreed, however, that François Faiveley makes excellent Corton-Charlemagnes.

Serena and I briefly discussed generalizations made by journalists that "1963 Ports and 1970 red Bordeaux are over-the-hill. In my cellar, at a constant 52ºF, these (and other) vintages are still very much alive. For instance, 1963 Croft's Vintage Port, always elegant (the "Lafite" of Port) made a superb 1963 that is still alive. Serena said that Robin Reid had told her that it was the best Croft's he had produced in 35 years of winemaking there.

About the 1970 Bordeaux

Bettane surprised me when he said that 1970 Château Palmer was not as great as some say. I do agree that it is now fully mature, and that maybe it does not have the concentration of that property's great 1961 or 1966, but the 1970 is still a superb—even a great—Claret. I have tasted it on over 30 occasions and it has never disappointed me.

About Château Le Pin

Bettane agreed with me that this is the wine-marketing farce of the century. Serena, who is head of Sotheby's wine department, just smiled and did not say a thing!

Al Brounstein closed the session by saying that in recent vintages, he does not declare "second picking" at Diamond Creek, but rather bottles it as "microclimates." An excellent marketing ploy. I think that Brounstein is an excellent businessman. He knows how to attract avid collectors by creating small quantities of "designer's" Cabernets. Nothing like very limited production to arouse interest. Just imagine five single-vineyard Château Latours each year! Al also said that now they leave less foliage on the vines than they did in the 1980s, thus less protection from the sun, producing riper, softer, fruitier, and earlier-maturing wines.

February 8, 1998

Third session, also at "The French Laundry" restaurant, in Yountville.

Thankfully, there is a reprieve in the rain. I do not think that the soil here can take another drop of rain! (Unfortunately, just as I left for a short walk to "The French Laundry," the rain started again.)

FLIGHT #1

RED ROCK TERRACE 1978:

Cedary, subdued fruit on nose. Hard, tannic on entry. Fruit is disappearing fast in this wine. Very old style, masculine. Later, some fruit came through, but still the wine seems to be past its prime. (16.5)

RED ROCK TERRACE 1974:

Surprisingly, colour is as dark as the 1978. Classic Claret on nose. Mature, cedary, earthy overtones, almost La Mission Haut-Brion-like (the "old style," that is). Less aggressive tannins than the 1978, rounder, better balanced, overall. (17.5)

VOLCANIC HILL 1976:

A drought year. Tighter on nose than above two. Even leaner than the 1978. Very dry, very little fruit left, and very noticeable acidity. Hardly any fruit left. (15)

Volcanic Hill "First Pick" 1979:

Deep, dense colour to rim. Buttery, oaky, ripe nose. The nose alone seems to indicate that this is a very heavy, rich wine. Indeed, on palate, the tannins are ripe, the fruit is still excellent, and the balance is there. What this wine lacks in character or complexity is compensated by the sheer ripeness of fruit. Made from fruit of the first three rows at the top of this vineyard. Impressive concentration. (18)

Volcanic Hill 1979:

Not as ripe as the "first pick," but more elegant, spicier. Round, smooth, no aggressive tannins. Lots of class. Fully mature now. (17.5)

Volcanic Hill 1973:

Similar colour to the 1979; soft, round, sweet fruit; perfect balance. All in harmony. Nice, ripe tannins. Only the second vintage at this winery, and excellent. The balance is most impressive. (17.5)

Volcanic Hill 1972:

Still tannic, but good, ripe fruit, and balance, especially considering that this was their first vintage, the vines were young, and it was a difficult year in the Napa Valley. (17.5)

Red Rock Terrace 1972:

Very different from the 1972 Volcanic Hill. More eucalyptus and cedar is obvious here. Not unlike a 1970 Château Lynch-Bages. Lovely concentration of fruit. Fairly aggressive tannins, but backed by ripe fruit. Most impressive. (18)

Al Brounstein started his winery in 1965, and 1972 was his first commercial release. He said that the above (first) flight, represented some of the blockbuster wines that made his early reputation.

FLIGHT #2

Volcanic Hill 1982:

Rich, rubbery nose. Volatile, fairly hard, acidic, but certainly backed by good fruit. Unfortunately, the acidity is too obvious. (16.5)

Volcanic Hill "Special Select" 1982:

Fresh, fruity, but unyielding nose. Lovely, sweet, rich, much better balanced than the "regular." Better structure, riper. Very good. (17.5)

Volcanic Hill 1983:

Loosely knit, compared to the above two. Sweet, elegant fruit, backed by good, ripe tannins. At its peak. Good quality, but without the weight of the older wines. (17)

Red Rock Terrace 1988:

Very ripe, very dense. Good concentration of fruit. Ripe, solid tannins. Very good length. (17)

Red Rock Terrace 1975:

Impressive, dense colour. Tight, unyielding nose. Similar on palate. Excellent concentration, still full of ripe, sweet fruit. Lively. No rush! This is a great wine, by any standard. (19) Grand Vin!

Volcanic Hill 1984:

Deep, youthful colour to rim. Much younger-looking than its age would indicate. Quite spirity, intense cedary fruit. Noticeable acidity. Too sour. The acidity overwhelms even the ripe fruit! Unbalanced. The least favourite. Too aggressive. Second sample tasted had more fruit, which masked the high acidity. Rated first sample (14) and second sample (16)

Red Rock Terrace 1981:

Good depth, evolved rim. Delicate, cedary nose. Surprisingly soft and forward. Elegant, fruity, still solid tannins. Slightly vegetal aftertaste. (16)

Three Vineyard Blend 1981:

Impressive, very dense, dark colour. Herbaceous, barnyardy on nose. Almost Chambertin-like from a very ripe year. Similar impressions on palate. Very green, stemmy, yet oddly, very ripe. Lovely fruit. Very different, easy to like and drink. (17.5)

FLIGHT #3

Three Vineyard Blend 1985:

Excellent balance, lovely fruit concentration, rich, easy to drink and like. No aggressive tannins. Ready, but no rush. (17.5)

Gravelly Meadow 1986:

Straw, cedary, evolved nose. Well balanced, good, ripe fruit. Soft tannins, but somehow a bit too acidic at finish. Nice, sweet fruit. (16)

Gravelly Meadow 1987:

Hint of rubber on nose. Better than the 1986. Riper tannins, better structured, less obvious acidity. Very good balance. More complete wine than the 1986. (17)

Volcanic Hill 1985:

Classic 1985. Nice, fruity wine. Fruit (cherry, ripe black fruit), oak, tannins, and acidity in harmony. Solid, powerful, but excellent balance. Lovely, rich wine. Drink now to 2007. (18)

Volcanic Hill 1990:

Fresh, cedar, French vanilla and oak on nose. Sweeter, lovely fruit concentration. Yet very different style from the mid-to-late 1970s. So much softer, more charming, riper fruit. Very good. This is top quality. (18)

Red Rock Terrace 1991:

One of the most feminine wines of the whole tasting. Very Margaux-like. Out of character with the others.

A bit too minty, but so different, so classy, and much softer, while retaining good fruit concentration. (18)

RED ROCK TERRACE 1992:

Oak, vanilla. Sweet, odd, not nearly as well balanced as the 1991. Sweeter, easier to drink, richer. May last longer, but will not have the class of the 1991. (17)

THREE VINEYARD BLEND 1983:

Sweet fruit. Approachable, easy to like, but lacking the sheer concentration of the 1985 Three Vineyard Blend. (17)

VOLCANIC HILL 1989:

Looser knit than the 1990 Volcanic Hill. Very "new style," more forward, softer, easy to drink. Now to 2003. (17)

FLIGHT #4

GRAVELLY MEADOW 1989:

More character on nose than the 1989 Volcanic Hill. More depth, more character, riper fruit. Yet not as tannic or ripe as the older vintages. (18)

VOLCANIC HILL 1993:

Lovely vanilla, oak, and young fruit on nose. Excellent balance. Very St. Julien, fruity style. Obvious new oak/vanilla. Well balanced. (17.5)

VOLCANIC HILL 1994:

Good acidity, fruit, oak. Very long, complex, rich, sweet wine. Excellent quality. Hint of rubber, but not in a negative sense. Lovely concentration. (18)

GRAVELLY MEADOW 1995:

Sweet fruit. Very "new style." Lovely extract, ripe fruit, soft tannins. Drink from 2003 to 2012. Good fruit intensity, soft, round. (17.5)

LAKE 1992:

Excellent fruit, acidity, tannins. Long, complex, round. This is top quality. Superb balance. Great extract, but what makes this special is the sheer class of the wine. Marvellous wine. (18.5)

LAKE 1978:

The rarest, most collectible wine made at Diamond Creek. Only one barrel (25 cases) made, and Al has only two bottles left! Absolutely magnificent wine. Great, sweet fruit extract, structure, oak, intensity. At almost 20, a masterpiece. Slightly stemmy, but great. All there. (19)

GRAVELLY MEADOW 1997:

(barrel sample)

Good concentration of ripe, sweet fruit. Hard to rate a barrel sample, but this will be beautiful. Great concentration, lovely fruit, excellent balance. Great potential. (No score)

A few facts and personal observations on the Diamond Creek Cabernets

The earlier vintages resemble, both in structure and taste, the big St. Estèphes of the early 1970s, such as Montrose 1970 and 1975. In the late 1970s—notably the 1979s—the style seemed to switch to either Pauillac (Grand-Puy-Lacoste style) or Graves, but more La Mission in structure than the elegance of Haut-Brion. These wines will fool any experienced wine taster at a blind tasting into believing that they are big Haut-Médocs.

The exception might be the 1974, with its typical eucalyptus "California" character. With the younger vintages, however, there is a clear shift to more charming, earlier-maturing, softer wines. For the perfectionist, this is good news. It means that younger Diamond Creeks taste like fine California Cabernets rather than great, classic Médocs. The wines from the mid-to-late 1980s were relatively less interesting.

Among the participants who made closing remarks were Terry Robarts and Mat Kramer, both noted wine writers.

At the end of the Diamond Creek tastings, Serena Sutcliffe seemed to prefer the Gravelly Meadow among the three regular single-vineyard bottlings, because of its excellent balance. Serena was born in 1945, my birth year; lucky lady! Vintages do not come any greater than this.

Gossip

Serena said that among the Royals, the Queen Mother was the most avid wine drinker. Prince Charles started to get interested in wines, but Diana, with her diet mania, did not approve, so he was temporarily "off" the subject of wine. Prince Phillip is the first to admit that he is a "navy man," not really interested in fine wines, rather more into rum or whiskey.

Some basic statistics on the various microclimates of Diamond Creek Vineyards: the largest vineyard is Volcanic Hill (eight acres), then Red Rock Terrace (seven acres), and Gravelly Meadow (five acres). The tiny "Lake" Vineyard (three-quarter acre) is located to the south-west of the other vineyards, and is bottled separately only in outstanding years.

Also tasted on this trip to the Napa Valley were three great 1978s, all so different from each other but each superb in its own way.

HERMITAGE ROUGE 1978, J. L. CHAVE:

Together with the late Gerard Jaboulet's 1978 Hermitage "La Chapelle," this is the greatest Rhône produced in that stunning vintage. A dramatic wine approaching its peak. Classic spicy, peppery, and concentrated Syrah. Less fruity than "La Chapelle"

1978. An intellectual wine. Drink now to 2010. A great Hermitage. (19)

RIDGE "MONTE BELLO" CABERNET SAUVIGNON 1978, CALIFORNIA:

When I first tasted this wine back in 1983, I knew that this was going to be something very special some day, and it is! Inky, deep colour. Intense, ripe, spicy Cabernet nose with hint of leather. Loaded with ripe fruit, ripe tannins, and great extract. Ready, but no rush. Drink through 2005. Top class. (18.5)

CHÂTEAU LATOUR 1978:

The best 1978 First Growth. Herbaceous nose, typical 1978 (a low Merlot year, and producing greener wines). Excellent fruit extract and tannic backbone. Just about fully mature, but enough structure to last for another decade or so. Top quality, classic, cedary Claret. (18.5)

February 11, 1998

CHAMPAGNE POL ROGER "BLANC DE CHARDONNAY" 1988:

Unusual for this house, yet typical for the vintage. A masculine wine. The 1988s are structured for the long run. Excellent fruit/acidity balance. Lovely, yeasty, complex bouquet. Full, rich, solid. No rush. Would fool anyone at a blind tasting. Tasted more like a young Bollinger or Krug, rather than an elegant Pol Roger.

CLOS DE TART 1989:

This monopole, owned by Mommessin, is located in Morey-St.-Denis. Much lighter, more evolved colour than the above two. Expansive, open, fully mature on both nose and palate. Definitely higher class, length, and complexity, but loosely knit. Lacks concentration. Drink up. The problem with many 1989 red Burgundies was not the weather, but overproduction, and Pinot Noir never forgives that mistake. One can get away with "stretching" Cabernet, but not Pinot Noir. Clos de Tart's 1985, 1988, and 1990 are finer wines than this.

February 1998

Dinner at "Le Crocodile" restaurant, in Vancouver.

With Andy Lench, owner of "Bordeaux Wine Locators," a wine-importing company in Ranier, Washington State. Among others, they are the agents of Château Latour for the north-western USA.

I brought along this bottle.

CORTON-CHARLEMAGNE 1992, JOSEPH DROUHIN:

Typical Drouhin white and typical 1992. Bright-golden colour. Expansive, forthcoming bouquet of ripe Chardonnay, almonds, and vanilla/oak. Soft, round, luscious on palate. Drouhin's whites mature relatively early. This excellent wine is at its peak now. Fairly low acidity, yet quite full-bodied. Lovely fruit extract. Very good.

Andy brought along this fine bottle.

CHÂTEAU ROUGET 1959, POMEROL:

Excellent neck level. Deep, maturing colour. Fair bit of sediment. Classic chocolaty, iron, ripe fruit on nose. Full-bodied, still even a bit tannic, but backed by excellent fruit. An impressive wine that has held extremely well, especially considering the fact that much of Pomerol (and other parts of Bordeaux) were severely damaged during the terrible frost of 1956. Top-quality wine. As good as a 1959 Leoville-Lascases or l'Evangile (tasted recently).

A note on some Burgundy négociants

And how to differentiate between their domaine wines, produced from their own grapes, and négociant wines, acquired from other sources. In Joseph Drouhin's case, if the words "Recolte du Domaine" are printed (in green lettering) on the label, such as is the case, for instance, with their Corton-Charlemagne, Chambolle Musigny "Les Amoureuses," or Griottes Chambertin, then it is produced from their own grapes. Otherwise, the wine is made from purchased grapes.

In the case of Louis Latour, the wines from the Domaine (such as their superb Corton-Charlemagne or Chevalier-Montrachet "Demoiselles" or their very good Chambertin "Heritiers Latour"), the vintage will be printed on the actual label, and for their Grands Crus whites, the lettering will be in gold. If the wine is made from purchased grapes, such as their Montrachet or Bâtard Montrachet, the vintage will be printed on the neck round label only. Those are their "Maison" (négociant) wines, rather than "Domaine." The case of Faiveley is different. Their regular labels are ivory or yellow colour.

Depending on whether the wine is white or red, the lettering and frame will be in green for the whites and in red for the reds. However, if the wine is a product of a monopole estate (Faiveley owning the whole vineyard), the labels will have a gray background (example: Nuits-St.-Georges "Clos de la Maréchale," or Mercurey "Clos des Myglands," or their excellent Corton "Clos des Cortons").

February 1998

Commanderie de Bordeaux council meeting.

All wines served double-blind.

MEURSAULT "DÉSIRÉE" 1993, COMTES LAFON:

This was a shocker! Obvious Chardonnay, but tasted like a "new wave" Chablis! Not my style of wine, and not at all what a Meursault should be, especially considering the reputation of the producer. Pale gold. Herbaceous, mineral, (but understated) nose. Diluted, soft, pleasant. 1993 was not a particularly good vintage for white Burgundies, but Lafon should have definitely done better, or downgraded this to Bourgogne Ordinaire.

CHÂTEAU TROTANOY 1993:

Bright, ruby-red colour. Charming, fruity nose of nice, spicy Merlot and hint of new oak. Soft, round, clean finish. A bit diluted, to be expected in that difficult, wet vintage. Drink now. Worth buying, if reasonably priced.

BEAULIEU VINEYARDS "TAPESTRY" 1991, NAPA VALLEY:

This is Beaulieu Vineyard's entry into the "Meritage" game. Made from 80% Cabernet Sauvignon, 17% Merlot, and 3% Cabernet Franc. Dark, but surprisingly evolved colour. Sweet, pruny fruit on nose. Hint of volatile acidity. Seems a bit chemical, pruny on palate. Sweet on entry and short finish. This wine needs a lot of improvement. Not very impressive.

VIEUX CHÂTEAU CERTAN 1988:

I thought that it was a 1978 St. Emilion or Margaux. Evolved colour. Spicy, stemmy nose, typical of Cabernet Franc and not-quite-ripe-enough Cabernet Sauvignon. This property uses an unusually large proportion of Cabernets in the blend for a Pomerol. A bit too lean for my taste, lacking fat, but certainly an elegant, stylish, well-crafted wine. 1988 has its shares of successes, but most are in the Médoc, notably Lafite, Mouton, Latour, Leoville-Barton, and from the Graves, I like both Pape Clement and Domaine de Chevalier.

GROTH VINEYARD CABERNET SAUVIGNON "RESERVE" 1985, NAPA VALLEY:

An excellent wine from a very good vintage. Luscious. Deep colour to rim. Tannic, but backed by excellent, ripe fruit. Well balanced; minty on nose, typical Napa Valley Cabernet. An impressive wine that is drinking well now, but it should hold well until 2005 or beyond. Excellent.

CHÂTEAU L'EVANGILE 1982:

Just the appearance of this wine in the glass was impressive. Deep, dense colour to rim. Superb nose of ripe Merlot. Great extract. Ripe tannins, backed by lovely, ripe fruit. Most enjoyable now, but full of life. Drink now to 2010. The best wine of the evening, by far. Very long aftertaste and thick legs on side of glass.

February 1998

Various wines tasted this month.

HERMITAGE "LA CHAPELLE" 1985, JABOULET:

Now 12 years old. Like everywhere else in France, 1985 is an elegant vintage rather than a big, tannic one. Surprisingly youthful, deep colour to rim. Spicy, leathery nose of Syrah. Round on palate. Little sediment. Trace of acidity, but, overall, very good. Somehow lacks the ripeness of the 1982 or the solid, tannic structure of the 1983. Ready, but should hold well for another five years.

SMITH-WOODHOUSE 1977 VINTAGE PORT:

A lovely Port and a sleeper, until recently. I have been acquiring this Port for several years now, but, unfortunately, it has now been "discovered," and the price is climbing fast. Impressive, deep, dense colour to rim. 20 years old, and still solid. Ripe fruit, very sweet, made in Graham's fruity style. Lots of life ahead, and very well balanced. A lovely Port. Drink now to 2015.

February 26 to March 3, 1998

Trip to Yountville, with my friend Marie-José Aubin.

Fortunately, the torrential rains of the past three weeks have now stopped and the weather has cleared.

NUITS-ST.-GEORGES PREMIER CRU "LES CAILLES" 1990, ALAIN MICHELOT:

A lovely wine. Bright, deep, cherry-red colour to rim. Superb nose of ripe, clean fruit. Concentrated mouthful of lovely, fresh, intense, red fruit. Lots of depth and class here. Ready, but structured to last well for another decade. How fine these 1990s are turning out to be!

At "The French Laundry," in Yountville.

As usual, an excellent meal.

CHÂTEAU LEOVILLE-POYFERRÉ 1986:

I brought this bottle along. This wine confirms the comeback, after many decades of underachievement, of this potentially great property. From 1982 and particularly from 1983, Leoville-Poyferré has been producing very good wines. While this 1986 does not have the massive tannic backbone typical of the greatest 1986s, such a Mouton Rothschild, Margaux, Leoville-Barton, or Pichon-Lalande, it is a well-crafted wine. Very good, dark colour to rim. Cedary, spicy Cabernet on nose with hint of ripe Cassis fruit. Solid on palate. Well balanced, long, complex. Drinking well now, but should hold for another decade, if well cellared. A fine effort.

March 4, 1998

Today I received the very sad news that our dear friend Peter Sichel, owner of Château d'Angludet and part-owner of Château Palmer, passed away last week in Bordeaux.

Peter was a true gentleman, and a very knowledgeable and generous man. I last saw him 15 months ago at Château Palmer, where we had a most enjoyable visit with Peter and Diana, and an excellent dinner, accompanied by such great wines as Château Palmer 1983 and 1966, Château Margaux 1945, and Château d'Yquem 1980. Peter will be sorely missed. Fortunately, he has trained and prepared a gifted generation of sons to take over the family business.

Early March 1998

CHÂTEAU DUCRU-BEAUCAILLOU 1975:

Decanted one hour. Deep colour, evolved rim. Stemmy, herbaceous nose typical of the vintage. Full, rich, still a bit tannic at 22 years old, but backed by very good fruit. Does not have the elegance associated with this property, but then 1975 was anything but an elegant vintage. A well-crafted wine that is at its peak. Hint of truffles and earth, with good black fruit in the background. Drink now to 2005.

March 1998

Reception and "free for all" tasting, at the residence of Ray Signorello, in West Vancouver.

His son (whose first name is Ray Jr.) produces a variety of fine wines in the Napa Valley. Each of the numerous guests brought along a bottle, plus several bottles were opened by our generous hosts. My contribution was this bottle.

BAROLO "RISERVA" 1978, GINESTRA, PRUNOTTO:

Almost 20 years old and now fully mature. Brick-red colour. Orange rim. Tar, spices, and straw on nose. Good acidity, still a bit tannic, but soft fruit. An elegant, well-made wine.

I had the opportunity to taste the following wines, in the order tasted.

CAYMUS CABERNET SAUVIGNON 1982, NAPA VALLEY:

Ripe, leathery, and cedary nose with good, rich fruit extract. A solid, ripe wine with good fruit and acidity. Fully mature, but enough stuffing to last till 2005.

SPOTTSWOODE CABERNET SAUVIGNON 1990, NAPA VALLEY:

Deep, dark colour to rim. Ripe black fruit on nose. Clean, cedary, spicy black fruit on palate, too. Well balanced. Oak blends nicely. Not nearly ready. Try around 2002.

CHÂTEAU CHASSE-SPLEEN 1989, MOULIS:

Evolved, elegant, soft. Typical 1989, but worrisome nose. Skunky, even hint of sulphur. Too loosely knit and soft. Lacks depth. Nowhere near as fine as this property's 1986.

LEONETTI CELLARS "RESERVE," "SEVEN HILLS VINEYARD" CABERNET SAUVIGNON 1990, WASHINGTON STATE:

Very deep, dense colour to rim. Like smelling and chewing new oak. Sweet, American oak and vanilla. Massive, tannic, yet charming, easy to like. Quite herbaceous, but a wine I have some difficulty taking seriously. Too much oak for its own good. Future uncertain.

GRGICH CELLARS CABERNET SAUVIGNON 1990, NAPA VALLEY:

A tight, lean, acidic wine that lacks depth. This is disappointing, especially from such a renowned winemaker as Mike Grgich. Loosely knit, too sharp, acidic, lacking ripe fruit. Colour is relatively light, as well. Too vegetal and sharp. Lacks charm and extract.

CHÂTEAUNEUF-DU-PAPE 1994, CHÂTEAU DE BEAUCASTEL:

Deep, dense colour. Animal, leathery, spicy, ripe nose. A hefty, rich, solid wine that is very far from being ready. Well crafted, solid, tannic. Very good fruit extract. Drink from 2004 to 2010. Very good potential.

CHÂTEAU PALMER 1982:

Quite evolved colour, nose, and palate. While it lacks the classic, ripe intensity of the best 1982s, it is an elegant, complex wine. Now fully mature and will not improve. One wishes it had a little more extract, though.

CHALONE VINEYARDS PINOT NOIR 1985, CALIFORNIA:

Good, bright-red colour. Evolved, elegant, yet sweet fruit on both nose and palate. Spicy, hint of oak. Clean, impeccably made, and now fully mature.

Spottswoode Cabernet Sauvignon 1986, Napa Valley:

An excellent Cabernet. It is 11 years old, and not nearly ready. Excellent, deep colour to rim. Ripe, expansive nose of black fruit and oak. Even a hint of cedar. Full, tannic (but ripe tannins), very well balanced. A lovely bottle. Drink from 2000 onward.

Marqués de Riscal "Reserva" 1993, Rioja, Spain:

Bright, cherry-red colour. Sweet oak, clean, modern wine. Elegant, complex, spicy cherry fruit. Soft, drinking well now. This property went through a low after the excellent 1970 vintage, with a string of very mediocre vintages. Nice to see it back in form.

Then our host's son, Ray Signorello Jr., opened the following wines.

Château d'Yquem 1959:

An older version of the great 1967. Crème-brûlée, coconut, exotic, rich, lovely botrytis, and ripe apricots on both nose and palate. Very evolved. Will not improve. A great Sauternes.

This great nectar was followed, after a light pasta meal, by some exciting red wines.

Signorello Vineyards Petite Syrah "110 Year Old Vineyard" 1995, Napa Valley:

Only 40 cases produced with a yield of a diminutive 14 hectolitres per hectare. Needs at least ten years of bottle-age. Totally unready. Great fruit extract, leather, rich, black fruit, with hint of oak and vanilla blending very nicely. Ripe black currants. Try around 2005.

Alas, the 1996 (not yet released) will be the last vintage, as the vines have been uprooted after that vintage.

Geyser Peak Petite Syrah "Unfiltered" 1976, Centennial Bottling, California:

A combination of 1990 Château Montrose and 1975 Château Latour! Impossible to guess this wine as a Petite Syrah. The reason I compare this wine to two solid Médocs, 15 years apart in age, is that this wine is behaving on both nose and palate like a youthful wine, yet it shows signs of maturity when swallowed. At a blind tasting, this wine would fool any taster into thinking that it is a great Médoc! This is very odd. An excellent wine, and a stunning effort, especially in a drought year. A revelation. Every day, I learn something new about wines.

Signorello Vineyards "Los Amigos" Pinot Noir 1995, Napa Valley:

Aged in 55% new oak barrels for 18 months, this wine is made from purchased grapes picked from 35 year-old vines in the Carneros district, planted originally by Louis Martini. Very dark colour to rim. Very young and youthful, of course. Very different in style from red Burgundy. California, spicy, ripe style. Lots of extract, but very well balanced, elegant, yet ripe. Herbaceous fruit, acidity, and tannins all in harmony. Drink from 2002 to 2005 or beyond.

Caymus "Special Selection" Cabernet Sauvignon 1984, Napa Valley:

A disappointing wine. Matchstick, burnt nose which is quite unpleasant. Better on palate. Solid, sturdy, relatively lean with obvious acidity and lacking enough fruit extract and ripeness to counter the aggressive tannins. Something very wrong here.

Penfold's Grange Hermitage 1984, Australia:

An excellent wine. Superbly crafted. Definitely "new style," elegant wine, without the leathery, tarry, spicy Syrah character of older vintages of Grange, but what a lovely wine! "Beautiful" is the best way to describe it. Elegant fruit, oak, vanilla on both nose and palate. Great breed here. Drink now to 2003. Superb effort. A charmer.

On the following few days

I had the opportunity to taste several superb bottles at various restaurants, at home, and with friends.

La Tâche 1985, Domaine de la Romanée-Conti:

A superb, classic Pinot Noir. Typical raspberry fruit. Quite evolved, as most 1985s are, but great balance and fruit extract. Drink over the next ten to 15 years. The best La Tâche since the great 1978, but without the solid backbone and powerful structure of the latter. Great quality.

Champagne Veuve Clicquot "La Grande Dame" 1985:

Now fully mature. Smooth, creamy, rich Champagne from an excellent vintage. Good yeast, fine, persistent mousse, tiny bubbles. Full, ripe fruit backed by excellent acidity. A real pleasure to sip.

Grange Hermitage 1981

and

1982, Penfold's, Australia:

These two wines have a lot in common, yet they are very different from each other in terms of structure.

The 1981 is more masculine, tannic, drier, with good fruit underneath, which is quite evolved, in spite of the tannic backbone.

The 1982 is fatter, richer, with riper, softer tannins. Both have the telltale character of Syrah: leather, tar, oriental spices. Drink the 1981 now to 2003. the 1982 now to 2008. Grange Hermitage is still the greatest Australian red wine, at least in my opinion.

Vega Sicilia "Unico" 1968, Ribera del Duero, Spain:

Lighter, leaner, less chocolaty than the superb 1962, which I know well, but a lovely wine, nevertheless.

Fully mature, but with excellent backbone, good fruit, hint of charred oak and vanilla. Lots of class here.

MONTRACHET, MARQUIS DE LAGUICHE 1989, JOSEPH DROUHIN:

Classic Chardonnay, and a great Montrachet from an excellent vintage. Honeyed, rich, appley Chardonnay. Flowery, full, smooth. Very long, fully mature. Lots of ripe fruit extract here and at its peak. Great bottle.

SASSICAIA 1985, BOLGHERI (TUSCANY):

The best Sassicaia, in my opinion, since the massive 1978, yet so different from it. More forward, more elegant. Clean oak-toast-vanilla, and ripe fruit on both nose and palate. Impeccably made. Excellent balance, long; nice, ripe, clean fruit. Drink now to 2007. An excellent Sassicaia. The "dark horse" and surprisingly good wine of this property is the 1979. Do not overlook it!

March 11, 13, and 15, 1998

Three-day extravaganza, featuring the 1970 red Bordeaux vintage.

I have been planning this event for over five years. A total of 54 various châteaux will be tasted, as well as unusual aperitif and dessert wines. All the wines are from my cellar, and they have been perfectly cellared for up to two decades at 52°F constant. The exceptions are the 1970 Haut-Brion, La Mission Haut-Brion, and Trotanoy, which were purchased recently from a wine merchant in Washington State. All levels and appearances are very good. The 16 participants will take part in all three sessions.

Each session will feature several communes. These wines are now 27 years old and they have spent a full quarter-of-a-century in bottle. These tastings will give all participants an excellent opportunity to appraise this highly touted vintage. No doubt there will be disappointments and a few pleasant surprises. However, due to excellent storage, I think that this should be a most enjoyable weekend.

Wednesday, March 11, 1998

FIRST SESSION

At "The William Tell" restaurant.

APERITIF

"Y" 1979, DRY WINE OF CHÂTEAU D'YQUEM:

Bright, green-gold colour with good depth. Expansive, oak, vanilla, and ripe fruit, with hint of botrytis on nose (no doubt due to storage in used d'Yquem casks). Surprisingly dry on palate, but with excellent balance and length. Later developed even a hint of sweetness. This wine is made from the Sauvignon Blanc grape. It is only bottled when there is excessive Sauvignon Blanc left over after the production of the Grand Vin, as d'Yquem does not produce a second wine.

FLIGHT #1

Graves

1. CHÂTEAU CARBONNIEUX 1970:

Dark colour, orange rim. Earthy, truffles on nose. Bell pepper, too. Still tannic, surprisingly solid. Good fruit. A bit coarse, with noticeable acidity at finish. (15)

2. CHÂTEAU HAUT-BAILLY 1970:

Good depth, evolved orange rim. More forward-looking than #1. Delicate, cedary nose. Hint of coffee beans. Softer, round, elegant. Noticeable acidity at finish, but good, toasty oak and fruit, too. Fully mature. The elegance is a trademark of this property. (17)

3. DOMAINE DE CHEVALIER 1970:

Similar appearance to #1. Subdued, perfumy nose. Has breed. Fairly soft, yet tannic backbone. A bit too dry, without the charm it had in the past. Later improved. Elegant, long. Needs drinking. I have tasted better examples of this. (17)

4. CHÂTEAU LATOUR-HAUT-BRION 1970:

Excellent, deep colour. Darkest so far. Fruity, cedary, toasty on nose. Hefty, lively fruit and flesh. Still surprisingly youthful, yet simple. I have tasted better examples of this, too. (16)

5. CHÂTEAU LA MISSION HAUT-BRION 1970:

Good colour; pale orange rim. Volatile on nose. Powerful, but coarse. Lemony, sour. Good structure, but too acidic. For some mysterious reason, La Mission blew the 1970 vintage. This and Leoville-Lascases are two great properties, but both have produced disappointing 1970s. (15)

6. CHÂTEAU HAUT-BRION 1970:

Deepest, darkest, and best wine of flight. Ripe, earthy, hint of truffles on nose. Surprisingly deep, ripe, rich, and long. A lovely mouthful of ripe, fully mature wine. Hint of leather. The biggest, richest, best 1970 Haut-Brion I have tasted to date. Can be variable. (18.5)

FLIGHT #2

Margaux and Haut-Médocs

1. CHÂTEAU LA LAGUNE 1970:

Impressive, deep colour to rim. Cedary, spicy on nose. Full, sweet, solid. Very slight hint of mustiness. Nice fruit, still a bit tannic, masculine. Spicy, cedary complex, and sweet. (16.5)

2. CHÂTEAU DAUZAC 1970:

Similar appearance to the 1970 La Lagune, but more evolved rim. Earthy, wet cement on nose. Lean, acidic, sour. Poor wine. Hint of cork, too. (12) Only in the late 1980s has Dauzac started to produce good wines.

3. CHÂTEAU PRIEURÉ-LICHINE 1970:

Evolved colour with red tinge. Dull, vegetal nose. Sweet, solid, yet sour on palate. Too sharp, but still has retained some fruit. (14.5)

4. CHÂTEAU MALESCOT-ST.-EXUPÉRY 1970, IN MAGNUM:

Deep colour to rim. Impressive, full, rich, solid. Backed by ripe fruit. Steely finish with noticeable acidity, but good, ripe fruit, too. Zesty, slightly citrusy. Has held very well in magnums. A bit rustic. (16)

5. CHÂTEAU LASCOMBES 1970, IN MAGNUM:

Deep-red colour. Subdued nose. Full, cedary/toasty, with good fruit, but some noticeable acidity. Surprisingly lively. Elegant, well balanced. (16.5)

6. CHÂTEAU PALMER 1970:

We toasted the memory of our dear friend, Peter A. Sichel, who passed away two weeks ago. Perfection now, but approaching the end of its plateau. Very soft, evolved, perfumy, complex, velvety, and chocolaty. Such a pleasure to drink now. The epitome of Margaux. (18)

7. CHÂTEAU MARGAUX 1970:

Impressive, deep colour. Spicy, cedary, but rustic on nose. Extremely acidic and sharp on palate. Clearly overshadowed by the 1970 Palmer. Michael Broadbent rates this a five-star, which puzzles me. A poor effort, and the beginning of Margaux's decline—until the new regime took over in 1977/1978. (14.5)

FLIGHT #3

St. Estèphes

1. CHÂTEAU MEYNEY 1970:

Dark colour to rim. Stemmy, subdued nose. Sweet, but noticeable acidity on nose. Too sour. Lean finish. Drink up. (14)

2. CHÂTEAU DE PEZ 1970:

Bright red. Not quite as dark as the Meyney. Orangy rim. Green, stemmy, charred oak on nose. Quite sweet, long, rich, still solid, at 27 years old. Sweet, cedary, but was better five years ago. (16)

3. CHÂTEAU LAFON-ROCHET 1970:

Sweet, leathery, baked, and pruny on nose. Sweet on palate. Soft tannins, but too ripe, and very sharp, acidic finish. Past its prime, but then, this was never a very good wine. (14)

4. CHÂTEAU COS D'ESTOURNEL 1970:

Bright, deep colour. Excessive acidity, lacking ripe fruit. Some greenness, unripe tannins. Otherwise, quite a pleasant wine, with enough complexity to show the class this property is capable of producing. (16.5)

5. CHÂTEAU MONTROSE 1970:

As expected, a brooding giant. Very deep, very youthful colour to rim. Cedary, slightly herbaceous nose, backed by ripe black fruit. Very big, very hard, very tight, with great concentration. Drink from 2000 to 2020. If there is one criticism, it is that this wine lacks the complexity and class of that other 1970 monster, Château Latour. This is clearly the best St. Estèphe of the vintage. (18)

Overall impressions

The first flight (Graves) was clearly the best and most complex. The Margaux flight, as expected in 1970, was disappointing, with the exception, of course, of the lovely (but now fully mature) Palmer. The St. Estèphe flight was good overall, with the classic, old style, tight, hard wines typical to that commune. How sad it is that the modern St. Estèphes have lost their true commune character, producing softer wines, more Merlot, maybe more immediately pleasing to the palate, but totally uncharacteristic to this fine commune.

Tonight's stars were the 1970 Haut-Brion, Palmer, and Montrose. No surprises here.

DESSERT WINE

VOUVRAY MOELLEUX "LE HAUT-LIEU" 1947, HUET:

What a superb dessert wine! The best sweet Vouvray I have ever tasted. Brilliant, deep amber-gold colour. Ripe apricots and peaches, superb nose. Full, creamy, yet backed by excellent acidity. Very long. A mouthful of lovely, ripe Chenin Blanc. A great effort from a gifted producer. Huet himself feels that this is the best wine he has ever produced. (19) I purchased this wine, together with Huet's 1945, last year from the "Sonoma Rare Wine Company," at a cost of US$200 per bottle.

Friday, March 13, 1998

SECOND SESSION

At "Le Crocodile" restaurant, in Vancouver, featuring Haut-Médocs, St. Juliens, and Pomerols.

We sat down to a glass of this wine.

CHÂTEAU CHALON, VIN JAUNE 1966, BOUVRET:

This famous wine comes from the Jura; it is made in the Jerez method, from the Savagnin grape. It is allowed to oxidize and develop a nutty character and bottled in a short, squat, 630 mL bottle called a Clavelin. Bright, palish gold. Subdued ripe nutty nose. Full, yet crisp on palate with good acidity. Very long, bone-dry. Lots of class here.

Today's tasting features Haut-Médoc Crus Bourgeois (all from the southern Médoc and Moulis), and Château Gloria (as the lead wine for the St. Juliens, which will be the second flight). The third flight will feature Pomerols.

FLIGHT #1
Haut-Médocs/Crus Bourgeois

1. Château Lanessan 1970:

London-bottled by Corney and Barrow.

Medium-red, evolved colour. Very slight hint of dill on nose. Soft, evolved on palate. Nice fruit, but tired, with hint of acidity and sharpness at finish. Was much finer ten years ago. (14.5)

2. Château Beaumont 1970:

Darker, deeper, more youthful than the Lanessan. Slightly earthy, herbaceous nose. Still a bit tannic with pleasant fruit. Surprisingly lively. After 20 minutes in glass, became astringent. (14.5)

3. Château Chasse-Spleen 1970, Moulis:

Very good, youthful colour. Palish rim. Cedary, spicy nose of fine Cabernet. Full, but lactic on palate. Very evolved, yet sweet fruit coming through with good backbone. I have tasted finer examples of this wine in the past. (15)

4. Château Gloria 1970, St. Julien:

This wine introduced us to the St. Julien flight. Subdued nose. Some fruit coming through. Very soft, very evolved. Was much better ten years ago. Drink up. Quite pleasant, nevertheless. (16)

The first three wines of the above flight were certainly sound, but a bit pedestrian. They have obviously seen better days.

FLIGHT #2
St. Juliens

1. Château Branaire-Ducru 1970:

Evolved colour, orangy rim. Slightly oxidized, vegetal nose. Quite sweet on entry, but seems artificial. Candied, soft, tired, yet some cedary character there. Needed drinking ten years ago. (14)

2. Château Beychevelle 1970:

Similar appearance to the Branaire, but slightly brighter. Stemmy, spicy nose. Pleasant, soft fruit. Hint of toasted oak. Good length and complexity. Has the typical elegance of this property. Drink up. (16.5)

3. Château Gruaud-Larose 1970:

Deeper colour than the above two with orange-green rim. Tight, subdued nose of cedar, earth, and mushrooms. Quite aggressive on palate. Lively fruit, fresh, but slightly too sharp and acidic. Not well balanced. Gruaud-Larose produced superb wines until, and including, 1966. Their wine clearly declined in quality for over a decade. From 1981 onward, this property has been back in form. (15)

4. Château Leoville-Poyferré 1970:

Medium-red colour, orange rim. Stemmy nose. Quite sour, acidic, but backed by pleasant fruit. Too musty, but not corked. Nothing exciting has been produced by this potentially great property after the 1940s. From 1982 onward, it is finally back in shape. (14)

5. Château Leoville-Barton 1970:

Hint of chocolate, coconut on nose. Cedary, dill, too. Solid structure, but a bit lean, yet has pleasant fruit. I wish it had more flesh. Hint of iodine, which was characteristic of this property from the 1950s through the 1970s. (17)

6. Château Leoville-Lascases 1970:

Similar appearance to #4, but more depth. Neutral, lactic nose with hint of cedar. Solid, ripe, tannic. Good terroir character. Best 1970 Lascases I have tasted to date. Usually it is a disappointing wine. Good, but not great. (16.5)

7. Château Ducru-Beaucaillou 1970:

As expected, the best St. Julien of the 1970 vintage. Now fully evolved, it approaches the quality and elegance of the 1970 Palmer, but has slightly livelier fruit. Spicy, cedary nose. Round, perfectly balanced on palate. Very long, velvety, with enough fruit to last for five more years. Top quality and a pleasure to drink now. (18)

FLIGHT #3
Pomerols

1. Château du Domaine de l'Eglise 1970:

Good, dark colour. Licorice, minty, almost California nose. Fairly acidic, yet good, ripe fruit underneath. Was riper, richer ten years ago, but has held very well. The last fine Domaine de l'Eglise to date. After 1970, this property was acquired by the Bordeaux négociant firm of Borie-Manoux, a firm that strives to produce correct, reliable, commercial products, rather than top-flight wines. (17)

2. Château Le Gay 1970:

Similar appearance to the above, but darker rim. Unyielding nose, with hint of iron and mushrooms. Sweet, solid, rich, trace of acidity at finish, but good, ripe intensity. After 15 minutes, it ended a bit short and astringent. Was better ten years ago. (16)

3. Vieux Château Certan 1970:

Lovely, bright colour. Complex, long, cedary nose of great breed. Obviously high Cabernet content. Spicy, complex, long. A classy, elegant wine. Has breed. The best 1970 Vieux Château Certan I have tasted to date. (18)

4. CHÂTEAU LAFLEUR-PETRUS 1970:

Deep colour. Ripe, plummy, solid, even tannic. A surprisingly big wine. Lots of depth here. Very good extract and still surprisingly lively. (17.5)

5. CHÂTEAU TROTANOY 1970:

Very impressive, deep colour. Deepest colour so far. Sensational, rich, cedary, and earthy nose with truffles overtones. Superb, lively, great fruit extract. Best 1970 Trotanoy tasted to date. Made from old vines. Great bottle. (19)

6. CHÂTEAU LAFLEUR 1970:

Very impressive, deep colour. Unfortunately, oxidized. Tannic, rich, solid, but losing its fruit. Too tough and leathery. Not a very good bottle. Seemed baked. Maybe slightly oxidized. This was very disappointing, because when last tasted five years ago, it was superb. I purchased several bottles of this in Portland, Oregon, back in 1979, at a cost of US$18 per bottle. This wine retails now for over US$350 per bottle! (15)

7. CHÂTEAU PETRUS 1970:

A near-perfect wine. Now approaching its peak. Stunning quality. Great depth of colour to rim. Superb nose of ripe fruit, iron, and hint of truffles, but still fresh and lively. A mouthful of great, rich, round, well-balanced wine. Cannot get any better. The star of the evening. (19.5)

The Pomerol flight was stunning—not only in the overall quality of the wines, but in how lively and fresh the best wines still are. Of course, proper storage is the key, and all these wines were very well cellared for almost two decades (or more). Who said that Pomerols do not age or develop complexity?

DESSERT WINE

1945 RUSSIAN PORT, CRIMEA, FROM THE MASSANDRA COLLECTION:

This wine was auctioned off at a special Sotheby's sale in the early 1990s. Cellophane wrapper with a Sotheby's label reading "South Coast Red Port from the Massandra Collection." Tiny, but healthy, cork. Some sediment. Pale, Rosé colour, not unlike a Tavel Rosé. Clean, spicy Muscat on both nose and palate. Good sweetness and acidity, with perfumy Muscat flavours. Quite long. An experience.

The cellars, located at the Livadia Palace of the Czars, near Yalta, were established in the 1890s by Czar Nicholas II. With the break-up of the Soviet Union, the winery began to sell off a few hundred cases of Port, Sherry, and Muscat, dating from 1923 to the early 1960s.

Sunday Noon, March 15, 1998

THIRD AND FINAL SESSION

At "Lumière" restaurant, headed by the gifted Executive Chef Rob Feenie, featuring St. Emilions and Pauillacs.

APERITIF

CHAMPAGNE POL ROGER "RESERVE" 1985, IN MAGNUM:

A lovely Champagne from an excellent vintage. Creamy, smooth, round, long, with fine mousse and tiny bubbles. Still lively. Very long on palate. Bravo, Pol Roger!

SAVENNIÈRES GRAND CRU "CLOS DE LA COULÉE DE SERRANT" 1980, MME. JOLY:

Made from Chenin Blanc grapes and surely one of the very finest Savennières, and from such a difficult vintage. Palish, youthful, golden colour. Neutral nose. Hint of petroleum jelly, but not in the flowery Riesling sense. Full, fairly acidic, but round, long, and well balanced. No rush drinking this 17-year-old. Very good aftertaste.

FLIGHT #1

St. Emilions

1. CHÂTEAU FRANC-MAYNE 1970:

Evolved colour, orangy rim. Toasted oak, cedary nose with hint of dill. Typical St. Emilion. Expansive, round, elegant, still has good, sweet fruit. Very long. Finishes a bit astringent. Needs drinking, but certainly a very fine effort. This tiny seven-hectare property has produced lovely wines over the decades. (16.5)

2. CHÂTEAU FONPLÉGADE 1970:

Darker than the Franc-Mayne. Subdued, toasted almonds and black fruit on nose. Slightly metallic. Surprisingly, quite tannic, with hint of truffles. Tight, low fruit. Drink up. (15.5)

3. CHÂTEAU LA GAFFELIÈRE 1970:

Very evolved colour. Leafy, elegant, subdued nose. Soft, velvety, sweet fruit. Lovely balance, intensity, and class here. Still surprisingly lively. Sweet, soft on entry, but flavours lingered on palate. Very fine wine. (17.5)

4. CHÂTEAU PAVIE 1970, IN MAGNUM:

Good, dark colour. Stemmy, yet ripe and evolved wine. Full, luscious, round on palate. Seared oak. More impressive on entry than at finish. Drink up. (16.5)

5. CHÂTEAU L'ARROSÉE 1970:

Good, dark colour to rim. Smoky, meaty, big wine (as expected). Lots of Cabernets here. Not a very complex wine, but certainly sturdy. Still lively, but getting slightly astringent. A bit metallic. Was better five years ago. (16.5)

6. CHÂTEAU CHEVAL-BLANC 1970:

Superb nose. Toasty, lovely oak and cedar. Great extract. Lots of class here. Clearly, best wine of flight. Only the La Gaffelière approaches it in terms of complexity, but this Cheval-Blanc is so much classier. Better than expected. Certainly soft and evolved, but very fine. (18.5)

Overall impressions

Clearly, the Cheval-Blanc was the best wine of the flight. However, the real surprise was the elegance and complexity (and longevity) of the La Gaffelière.

FLIGHT #2

Pauillacs

1. CHÂTEAU CROIZETS-BAGES 1970:

Quite evolved colour. Metallic, dull nose. Sharp, acidic, low fruit. Hard, steely. Having said that, the wine was better than expected. When will this property turn around? (14)

2. CHÂTEAU MOUTON-BARON-PHILIPPE 1970:

More evolved colour than #1. Sweet, cedary, toasty, cherry. Fair bit of acidity is backed by good, cedary, stemmy Cabernet. Better than expected. Clearly best complexity of the first three Pauillacs. (16)

3. CHÂTEAU PONTET-CANET 1970:

Deeper colour than above two. Subdued, slightly candied nose. Closed and unyielding. Nice sweetness. Better than its reputation would indicate. Soft, evolved, elegant fruit. Clean, fruity aftertaste. (15)

4. CHÂTEAU BATAILLEY 1970:

Deep bright-red colour. Sweet, cedary, and wet earth on nose. Round, still surprisingly fruity. Not much complexity here, but certainly still lively and fruity. Better structure than the Pontet-Canet. This is the only Borie-Manoux property that attempts to achieve some complexity. Sadly, this is not the case with Trottevieille, Domaine de l'Eglise, etc. (16)

5. CHÂTEAU HAUT-BATAILLEY 1970:

Lovely, dark-red colour. Youthful rim. Metallic, dusty nose. Hint of toast and dill, too. Nice, sweetness on entry. Very good fruit. Elegant, cedary, well balanced. Lasted surprisingly well. Classy, yet elegant Pauillac. (17)

6. LES-FORTS-DE-LATOUR 1970:

This is the second wine of Château Latour. Clearly, deepest, darkest, most youthful wine of flight. Sweet, ripe nose of cedary Cabernet, with ripe, cedary extract. Full of life. Some greenness, due, no doubt, to younger vines, but an excellent wine, nevertheless. (17.5)

With the exception of Les-Forts-de-Latour, I did not expect much from this flight. I was pleasantly surprised.

FLIGHT #3

Pauillacs

1. CHÂTEAU PICHON-LALANDE 1970:

Dark colour, palish, orangy rim. Subdued nose with hint of cedar. Sweet, elegant fruit on entry. Coffee beans, cigar box. Leaner, tighter, more masculine than expected for a wine as elegant as this. Has class. (17.5)

2. CHÂTEAU GRAND-PUY-LACOSTE 1970:

Medium red. Surprisingly evolved. Cedary, open, plummy nose. Quite evolved on palate. Black currants, hint of tar. Not as youthful as on past occasions, but certainly a very fine, classic Pauillac. I have tasted several better examples of this, over the past two decades. (17.5)

3. CHÂTEAU LYNCH-BAGES 1970:

Very impressive, deep colour. Cedary, minty nose. Very ripe, California-style Cabernet. Ripe, fruity, tannic, minty wine. So obvious Lynch-Bages and so easy to like! Great fruit extract. Loads of ripe, rich fruit. Drink now to 2005. (18.5)

4. CHÂTEAU LAFITE-ROTHSCHILD 1970:

Clearly palest, most evolved wine of all three flights today. Smoky, elegant, but very tired on both nose and palate. Bacon bits, perfumy, but thin, loosely knit, tired. Having said that, it was better than expected. (16.5)

5. CHÂTEAU MOUTON-ROTHSCHILD 1970:

Much darker than the Lafite. Lovely, cedary, cigar box, classic Mouton nose. Full, rich, round, evolved, yet lovely extract. Noticeable acidity at end, but toasty cedar, oak, and ripe fruit, too. Surprisingly fine. (18)

6. CHÂTEAU LATOUR 1970:

Together with Petrus and Trotanoy, the greatest wine of this three-day event. Still not ready! Deep, dark colour. Lovely, cedary black fruit and truffles on nose. A mouthful of very rich fruit and tannins. If well cellared, should reach its peak around 2005 and last well at least until 2025. A great Claret with a great future. A mouthful of great Cabernet extract towering over all other wines in this (or any other) flight. Deserves its reputation of being the greatest, longest-lived wine of this fine vintage. A fitting finale. (19.5)

DESSERT WINE

SETÚBAL "COLHEITA" 1934, J. M. DA FONSECA:

Celebrating the 100th Anniversary of that house, established in 1834.

This Setúbal is made from Moscatel and other varietals, all from the 1934 vintage, and bottled in the early 1990s, so that it has spent over 50 years in cask before bottling. A luscious, intensely rich, nutty, sweet wine. Lingering aftertaste of roasted almonds and maple syrup. Superb quality.

Chef Rob Feenie produced, as is usual at "Lumière," a superb and innovative meal.

Conclusions

Are the 1970s, now 27 years old, over-the-hill? No, provided (and this is absolutely crucial) that they were very well cellared through their lives, and that the levels are good. How many times have we read, over the past decade, that the 1970 Bordeaux are over-the-hill? Even as recently as a month ago, at an extensive tasting of Diamond Creek Winery's wines in San Francisco and Yountville, I was told by Michel Betanne and other knowledgeable tasters to expect many disappointments. Well, these experts were wrong.

Of course, 1970s that were stored in warm cellars and/or that have poor levels will taste washed-out and tired, but the best are still superb. Wines such as 1970 Latour, Montrose, Petrus, Trotanoy, Lynch-Bages, and others are still full of life. And if The Wine Spectator *or other leading magazines or experts tell you that the 1970s are over-the-hill, tell yourselves that these expert tasters have tasted wines that were not well stored and that came from many varied sources. The same is true of 1963 Vintage Ports, for instance. (Mine are full of life. Some are not ready yet at 35 years. Yet when you read comments on these wines, you would think that they have already kicked the bucket.) Other successful 1970 Bordeaux, such as Palmer, Ducru-Beaucaillou, Grand-Puy-Lacoste, Haut-Brion, Cheval-Blanc, etc., are drinking very well now, but they will not improve.*

Another point of view
Comments on the 1970 red Bordeaux tastings, written by one of the participants, Bill Spohn, an avid wine taster and collector

"I would like to state a caveat for Robert Parker fans. Although I understand that he is now finishing up a new edition of his *Bordeaux* book, the tasting notes in his previous book are mostly from tastings he did in 1989 and 1990, with a scattering of wines not tasted for some time before that. In comparing his notes to mine, I find many differences, most of which can be accounted for by the development of the wines in the intervening eight years. So use his older edition as a guide if you will (and I think he is quite useful for this) but, as always, don't treat it as gospel on these wines, or for that matter, any other.

Here are a few selected notes from Bill Spohn.

"HAUT-BRION:

Here is a wine that points out the changes from Parker's notes. He gave it an 84 rating and said it was light, lean, and innocuous. This wine was very dark, with a bricky rim, and mature nose. It was medium-bodied and well integrated, a bit dusty and dry with a touch of astringency at the end, but little if any tannins left. One knowledgeable taster commented that this wasn't the first time he had seen a wine put on weight compared to earlier tastings (he had tried the wine when it was about nine years old, and basically agreed with Parker), but that he didn't really know wine could do that. This wine was an ageing, elegant gentleman, and the favourite of many in the flight.

"MARGAUX:

An aged, custardy nose, very acidic almost immediately, which overcomes what fruit is lurking behind, and drying and astringent at the end. The only First Growth that I haven't bothered to finish! One iconoclastic member chose this as his favourite, but I expect that he would say that Hitler was a good inspirational speaker, or that Saddam is kind to dogs. You can find something good to say about anything, I suppose, but for this wine, it seems a waste of time.

"MONTROSE

Dark, oak, and alcohol, big on the palate with fruit and a lot of acid; not unbalanced but very concentrated and very long finish. A monumental wine that needs time.

"TROTANOY:

Either my favourite or second-favourite wine of the evening, depending on whether you choose drinking it now or in the future. Big, dark wine and a big dark-berry nose, followed by wonderful fruit and exceptional length; it is no longer too tannic, but smooth, velvety, and sensuous. One that I wish lived in my cellar!

"PETRUS:

An expansive nose like a cherry-custard tart, a huge wine; very concentrated, filled with soft tannins, with wonderful flavours coming in waves across the palate, and a finish that seems to persist indefinitely. I definitely took my time over this wine. It is a relative baby and has many years ahead of it, although it seems fully mature. I truly wish that some resided in my cellar, but at Can$1,200 to $1,400 a bottle, I'm afraid that I shall have to monitor its future development from afar, like a child without a nickel, looking in the window of a candy store. The prices for this wine (in any year) are paid more for its status as a cultural icon than as a wine, but believe me, there is substance behind the reputation.

"The person responsible for this, one of the most profoundly interesting events in my tasting career, is Albert Givton—gentleman, raconteur, and palate par excellence. What has always astounded me is not only his memory for taste and aroma, but his ability to relate, at a moment's notice, his personal experience with any given wine going back over many years of tasting. If you ask me about a wine, I will sometimes know immediately if I have tasted it, occasionally be able to recount the distinguishing characteristics of the wine, but more frequently, unless the wine was exceptionally memorable, require recourse to my notes, which are not, shall we say, in the most ordered state possible.

"Remarkably, people like Albert and Sid Cross, (who also attended the event), can rattle off their entire experience of a wine over the years, giving a unique perspective on the development of just about any given wine.

"This series of tastings has given us an almost unique view of the 1970 vintage, not tasting them one at a time from various sources, but all within a few days. And all (or all but three) from the same cellar, as storage can greatly affect older wines like these. To those who criticize this vintage, I say: don't knock it until you have tried them this way!

"LYNCH-BAGES:

Great colour, very cedary nose, with a nice touch of mint/eucalyptus, marvellous intensity, very long. It wasn't elegant, but so what—you can't have everything. A really pleasurable mouthful!!

"LATOUR:

Very dark and clear, without any appreciable browning, this wine was my favourite of the day. It has everything you would want: fruit, chocolate, spice, weight, all in Spades, ending in the great length. A magnificent wine!!"

End of Bill Spohn's notes.

March 1998

JOSEPH PHELPS "INSIGNIA" CABERNET SAUVIGNON 1985, NAPA VALLEY:

Dark colour showing a fair bit of maturity. At first the bouquet was quite leathery, not unlike an Australian Cabernet or Shiraz, but after decanting for one hour, the wine developed a lovely, cedary, minty, eucalyptus nose. Full-bodied, rich wine of very good intensity. Fully mature now, but has enough stuffing to last well for another five to seven years, if well cellared.

PULIGNY-MONTRACHET PREMIER CRU "CLOS DU CAILLERET" 1993, DOMAINE JEAN CHARTRON:

But red! Made from 100% Pinot Noir. While red Chassagne-Montrachet is quite common, it is rare to find a red Puligny-Montrachet, especially from such a fine Premier Cru. I cannot help but wonder why Chartron would plant Pinot Noir in such a reputable Clos, in view of the fact that the white would fetch a much higher price. In any event, the wine was very good. Lovely, bright cherry-red colour. Already drinking very well. Clean, round, ripe fruit with very good depth and balance. Clean, spicy, long, fruity finish. Most enjoyable. Drink now to 2001.

Late March 1998

CHÂTEAU GRUAUD-LAROSE 1966:

Excellent neck level. Impressive, deep colour with some maturity at rim. Intense, rich, cedary, chocolaty nose of fine Claret. Full, very well balanced, ripe, yet soft fruit. At its absolute peak. Lovely fruit extract. Drink now to 2003. It is clear today that this is the best 1966 St. Julien. Beychevelle and Ducru-Beaucaillou were lovely, but elegant, and they peaked in the early to mid-1980s. The Lascases, even when tasted from a magnum a couple of months ago, was not nearly as rich, ripe, or fresh as this lovely bottle. The best Gruaud-Larose between 1966 and 1982s.

March 1998

We are in the midst of the Asian financial crisis.

There is the feeling out there that the price of wine will halt its upward spiral and that prices, both at auction and retail, may start to drop and come back to a more realistic level. Time will tell. However, there is a very real danger out there to the unaware wine aficionado. If and when the flood of fine wines changes direction, from going to the Far East back to the more traditional European and North American markets, the future bargain hunter will have to be very cautious. There is no wine tradition in the Far East. Therefore, two dangers loom. The first is the problem of shipment and storage. How have these wines been shipped and stored in the heat and humidity so predominant in Asia? The second is, and this is true of the top wines only, how many fakes (imitations) are out there? If there has ever been a reason to say "caveat emptor," now is definitely the time to say so.

Late March 1998

GRANDS ECHÉZEAUX 1972, DOMAINE DE LA ROMANÉE-CONTI

AND

BONNES MARES 1978, ROBERT GROFFIER:

The Grands Echézeaux was excellent, at over 25 years old and from a very underrated vintage. It took these wines over 15 years to show their real quality, yet even today, they are undervalued, and a bargain at auction. Excellent, bright colour with good depth. Spicy, stemmy, charred oak, and mature, ripe fruit on nose. Superb balance of fruit extract, acidity, and excellent backbone. Very long. Will last for another decade, if well cellared. All 1972 Domaine de la Romanée-Conti wines are excellent, notably La Tâche.

The 1978 Groffier Bonnes Mares is a classic. A wine I know well, from an excellent vintage and a gifted winemaker. The elegance, complexity, and class of a Musigny combines with excellent fruit extract to produce this marvellous bottle. At its absolute peak. Cannot get any better.

Late March and Early April 1998

CHÂTEAU HAUT-MARBUZET 1982

AND

CHÂTEAU SOCIANDO-MALLET 1982:

The Château Haut-Marbuzet is officially a St. Estèphe, while the latter is a Haut-Médoc, yet the actual style of these two wines couldn't have been more reversed, with the Haut-Marbuzet the softer, rounder, more forthcoming, backed by rich, sweet fruit (high proportion of Merlot in the blend).

The Sociando-Mallet behaving like an old-style Montrose! A brooding giant. Very dark, deep, tannic, but ripe. A serious, solid, big wine requiring at least an extra five years of bottle-age to reach its optimum drinkability. Both impressive, yet so different. Haut-Marbuzet for the beginner—Sociando-Mallet for the connoisseur.

CORTON-CHARLEMAGNE 1989, LOUIS LATOUR

AND

CORTON-CHARLEMAGNE 1989, TOLLOT-BEAUT:

I know both producers well, and their Corton-Charlemagnes are excellent, but very different in style.

Latour's is excellent, their best effort between 1978 and 1995. Luscious, exotic, rich fruit with hint of almonds and new oak. Very long, at its peak now, but with enough fruit extract to last well until at least 2003. Excellent.

Tollot-Beaut's is so different! Leaner, racier, hint of lilacs, almonds, and vanilla/oak. Masculine, solid backbone, backed by excellent fruit. The "Krug" of Corton-Charlemagne. Alas, only about 100 cases are produced. Great future, not quite ready. Drink from 2001 to 2006. Rated both a solid (18.5).

LA TÂCHE 1976, DOMAINE DE LA ROMANÉE-CONTI:

Dark colour, but showing quite a bit of evolution at rim. Lots of sediment. Decanted one hour. Ripe, almost leathery, on nose. Made in a drought year, obviously. Still tannic, yet "old" fruit. Trace of leanness and acidity at finish. May last for a long time, but will not improve, as the soft fruit may disappear. Of course, this is a very good wine, but in the context of this property's other successes in the 1970s (the excellent 1972 and the sublime 1971 and 1978), it lacks that extra dimension and distinction.

CHÂTEAU LAFITE-ROTHSCHILD 1988

AND

CHÂTEAU CHEVAL-BLANC 1988:

These must surely be two of the finest 1988s around. It seems that this vintage has been forgotten in the excitement over the solid 1986s, the elegant 1985s, and the ripe and abundant 1989s and 1990s.

Lafite has a good, dark colour, palish rim. Lovely nose of cedar, new oak, and slightly herbaceous (but ripe) fruit. Excellent backbone and balance. Very good black fruit, backed by good acidity. Still a bit tannic. Try around 2001 to 2008. Will make an excellent bottle. (18.5)

The Cheval-Blanc is slightly darker, hint of toast and charred oak, backed by good, ripe black fruit and just a hint of dill. Full, riper than the Lafite, more forward, but with excellent fruit extract. Another great bottle. Drink now to 2005. Both rated (18.5).

CHÂTEAU D'YQUEM 1980 AND 1987, FROM HALF-BOTTLES:

Two excellent Château d'Yquems from "forgotten" vintages, yet how good they both are!

The 1980 is more evolved, of course. Hint of crème brûlée, lovely botrytis, vanilla, oak, and ripe fruit on both nose and palate. Went superbly well with fresh foie gras.

The 1987 is fresher, slightly paler gold. Long, expansive, slightly noticeable acidity, but excellent fruit, too. Drink now to 2005 or beyond. Great value. I'd rather buy and cellar these than any other Sauternes or Barsac from a great vintage, save, perhaps, Climens, a favourite of mine.

Early April 1998

A tasting, featuring the 1985 vintage, "A Global Perspective."

CHAMPAGNE BATISTE PERTOIS, 1985, 100% GRAND CRU, BLANC DE BLANCS:

Over 12 years of age and still surprisingly fresh. Clean fruit on nose. Tiny bubbles. Long, fairly ripe. Will not improve, but backed by nice fruit and good acidity. The elegance of Chardonnay combined with the ripeness of the vintage. (17.5)

MAS DE DAUMAS GASSAC 1985, DE LA VASSIÈRE:

Impressive, deep colour to rim, with purple hue. Spicy, ripe black currants and oak on nose. Full, rich, loaded with ripe fruit. Very well balanced and succulent. Approachable now, but should hold well for another decade. Needs decanting. (17.5)

Robert Mondavi Cabernet Sauvignon "Reserve" 1985, Napa Valley:

Good depth of colour, evolved at rim. Cedary, hint of eucalyptus and mint on nose, combined with very good, ripe fruit. Fairly loosely knit, fully mature. Will not improve, but drinking very well now. Velvety, round fruit. Totally different in structure from the very concentrated Mas de Daumas Gassac. (17.5)

Sassicaia 1985, Marchesi Incisa Della Rocchetta, Tuscany:

In structure, halfway between the Mas Gassac and the Mondavi Cabernet. Bright, deep-red colour to rim. Lovely, cedary, spicy, oak, and vanilla on nose. Still fairly rich, even a bit tight, but backed by lovely fruit and very good balance. A very stylish wine of great class. Impeccable structure. Drink now to 2007. (18)

Hermitage "La Chapelle" 1985, Jaboulet:

Similar appearance to the Sassicaia, but paler at rim. Spicy, rich, sweet berry fruit on nose. Quite forward, but with good, ripe, tannic backbone. Not as masculine as the solid 1983, or as concentrated as the superb 1978. More approachable. Hint of leather and ripe fruit at finish. Drink now to 2004. (17.5)

Richebourg 1985, Domaine de la Romanée-Conti:

A masterpiece! Clearly the greatest (and most expensive) wine of the flight. Bright, cherry-red colour, typical of the vintage. Toasty, charred oak combine with superb, ripe, spicy Pinot Noir to create a great, exotic bouquet. Full, round on palate, with excellent backbone and even some tannins to loose. Lots of depth and length here. Enjoyable now, but will be better by 2003, and last well beyond 2010. (19)

Château Latour 1985:

The only disappointing wine of the tasting. Not that the wine is not good, but, for Latour, it is too loosely knit. Both Lafite and Mouton produced better, more complex, and even more concentrated wines than this in 1985. Lacks the concentration, power, cedary extract, and black fruit backbone so typical of this great property. Ready now, but should hold until 2003. The other problem with this wine is its lack of the multidimension that is expected from a First Growth. Good, but not great. (17)

Barbaresco 1985, Angelo Gaja:

Together with the Mas Gassac, the darkest wine of the flight. As usual with Gaja's wines, an unusually long cork. Rich, ripe, leathery, and tarry on nose. Still big, chewy, solid. Not ready. Try around 2002 to 2005. Very concentrated and well balanced. Hint of new oak and vanilla is complemented by rich, ripe fruit. A very fine effort. (18)

Graham's 1985 Vintage Port:

Still very youthful. Lovely, fruity nose. Not really a big Port, but certainly very concentrated. Excellent sweet, ripe fruit; typical style of this fine property. Possibly the best Port made in 1985. Excellent concentration and length. Drink from 2002 to 2010 or beyond. (18)

Conclusions

1985 was one of those rare vintages where almost everywhere, the wines were either excellent, or at least, very good. "The year of the comet." How lucky we have been with this vintage, and with the decade of the 1980s, in general!

April 2, 1998

1988 CONDRIEU "CÔTEAU DE VERNON," GEORGES VERNAY:

Vernay's regular Condrieu is a yardstick for Condrieu producers, but the Côteau de Vernon is as excellent as any great Condrieu can be. Made from a small plot of land at the top of the Condrieu hill. Bright, deep-golden colour. Clean, exotic nose of ripe pineapple, pear, and lychee nut. Full, rich, round on palate, but not cloying. So rich in glycerine that the first impression is that the wine is actually sweet, which it is not. Fairly high alcohol (over 14°), typical of the Viognier grape in that part of the world, but the fruit intensity and rich structure mask the high alcohol. Absolutely superb. Some tasters argue that Condrieu (and Château Grillet, which is also made from Viognier grapes) should be drunk while young and fresh. That may be true in most cases, but this ten-year-old is just magnificent now. Wish I had more!

April 3, 1998

A bring-your-own-bottle buffet dinner at Ray Signorello's residence.

I tasted the following wines.

CHÂTEAU BRANAIRE-DUCRU 1982:

(My bottle) Deep, maturing colour to rim. Classic nose of very ripe "California style" Cabernet Sauvignon. Full, rich, round. Perfect drinking now, but chewy, rich, very ripe. Excellent black fruit. No rush. What a lovely, but unusually ripe, the 1982 vintage is turning out to be. (17.5)

1995 ROSSO DI MONTALCINO, CIACCI PICCOLOMINI, D'ARAGONA:

Bright, red colour. Elegant, clean cherry fruit. Sweet, round, soft. Most enjoyable, even at this early stage. Not a keeper. (15)

1985 WILLIAM HILL CABERNET SAUVIGNON "GOLD LABEL RESERVE," NAPA VALLEY:

Deep colour, maturing at rim. Spicy, herbaceous Cabernet nose. Fairly full, yet soft on palate, backed by ripe fruit. At its peak. The only drawback is a trace of nagging acidity. Will not improve, but should last well in bottle until 2002, if well cellared. (16)

1985 BERINGER CABERNET SAUVIGNON "RESERVE," NAPA VALLEY:

Bright, deep colour. Luscious, cedary, minty fruit on nose. Very intense, rich on palate, but surprisingly approachable. Lots of depth here. Well balanced, long, ripe, spicy fruit. Better extract and better balanced than the William Hill (see above). Drink now to 2005. A multilayered, interesting wine. (17)

CHÂTEAU MOUTON-ROTHSCHILD 1986:

The star of the evening! Very deep, dense colour to rim. 12 years old and not nearly ready. Drink from 2003 to 2020 or even beyond, if well cellared. Great classic, cedar, ripe black fruit with hint of new oak on nose. Superb depth, ripe tannins, and great fruit extract. Lingering aftertaste and perfect balance. Grand Vin! (19)

ST. HALLETT "OLD STOCK" 1994 SHIRAZ, BAROSSA VALLEY, AUSTRALIA:

Surprisingly light and evolved colour for such a young wine, and a Shiraz at that! Light ruby-red colour. Soft, round, very approachable. The elegance of a Volnay, with some leathery and spicy character of Syrah. Ready. (15)

1994 ANDERSON'S "CONN VALLEY VINEYARDS" ESTATE RESERVE CABERNET SAUVIGNON, NAPA VALLEY:

Bright red colour. Hint of leather and rubber on both nose and palate is backed by good, ripe fruit. Still tight. Drink from 2000 to 2005. Good potential. (16.5)

1990 SOLAIA, ANTINORI:

A super star from a super-star vintage, but consumed way too soon. Will not be ready until 2002 or beyond. Like chewing chalk! Very deep colour (but lighter than the superb 1986 Mouton-Rothschild) to rim. Powerful, tannic. Ripe fruit is there, but it is hidden by the tannins at this stage. Great potential in five to ten years. Pity to open this too soon. Acting like a young Château Latour. May have had some charm in its youth when first bottled, but totally closed up now. (17.5), potentially (18).

CHÂTEAU LEOVILLE-POYFERRÉ 1990:

Does not have the sheer ripeness of the 1982 or the masculine, tannic backbone of the fine 1986 of this property, but a charming wine nevertheless. Medium bright red colour to rim. Fruity, cedary, and round on both nose and palate. Surprisingly soft, but lovely to drink now. Most enjoyable. (17.5)

CHÂTEAU GRUAUD-LAROSE 1986:

Very deep colour. Typical Gruaud and typical 1986. Solid, chewy, tannic; cedary, ripe black fruit. Very tight, but the fruit is there. Requiring patience. Drink from 2001 to 2010 or beyond. A very fine wine. (18)

1994 VIGNA FLAMINIO (BRINDISI) ROSSO, AGRICOLE VALLONE:

Evolved, pale, ruby-red colour. Structured like an elegant wine from the north of Italy, rather than a rustic, rich, chewy wine from the hot south, which is where this wine comes from. Sweet, elegant, yet has excellent backbone. Rich, fruity, hint of ripe cherries.

Drink now to 2002. A new experience for me and a most pleasant surprise. (16.5)

Early April 1998

1985 MEURSAULT-PORUZOTS, FRANÇOIS JOBARD:

This is not a wine for the faint of heart. Bright, green-golden colour. Amazingly fresh and tight for a 13-year-old. Pronounced oak, minerals, and lemony Chardonnay on nose. Tight, leaner style, but steely fruit on palate. Full of life, excellent backbone, fruit, and acidity. Will live for at least another seven years, if well stored. A serious wine with mineral, nutty overtones.

April 10, 1998

Passover dinner with the family.

CHAMPAGNE BOLLINGER "GRANDE ANNÉE" 1985:

Classic masculine Bollinger. Brilliant colour, yeasty, herbaceous nose. Full, solid, excellent depth. The elegance and class of the vintage combined with the serious structure of this house's style. Will last well until 2003 or beyond, if well cellared.

BÂTARD-MONTRACHET 1986, LOUIS JADOT:

At its absolute peak. Bright, deep golden colour. Mineral, expansive, oak, and ripe Chardonnay on nose. Full, round, clean, and very long on palate. Ripe, yet has excellent acidity. Definitely Grand Cru class here. Drink now to 2000.

CHÂTEAU CANON 1981:

Herbal, velvety, elegant, and very well balanced. A lovely bottle that is at its peak. Long, velvety, good backbone. Will not improve. Most enjoyable.

CHÂTEAU D'YQUEM 1980 IN HALF-BOTTLE:

The class of this great property is all there, but in an understated manner, 1980 being an elegant vintage for Sauternes (by far more successful than for both red and dry white Bordeaux). Clean, elegant botrytis, oak, buttery fruit, and good acidity. A perfect accompaniment to foie gras. An excellent Sauternes.

April 1998

At a private dinner.

CHAMPAGNE BOLLINGER "RD" 1979:

Fully mature, rich, yeasty, yet very elegant and smooth Champagne. Tiny bubbles, creamy mousse. Beautifully round and long; still lots of fruit there at almost 20 years old. A beauty.

BÂTARD-MONTRACHET 1978, LEFLAIVE:

Well, 20 years old, and no rush! Green-gold colour. Superb mineral ripe nose. Still has a hint of oak and rich, ripe pineapple. Full of life, ripe fruit, and excellent balance underneath. A great vintage and a very gifted producer. A classic!

1971 ROMANÉE-ST.-VIVANT, DOMAINE DE LA ROMANÉE-CONTI:

Deep colour. Spicy, vegetal, ripe Pinot Noir on nose. Classic, long, full with solid backbone. Still full of life and complex, spicy finish. Hint of toasted oak. Drink now to 2005. Top quality.

TAYLOR'S 1970 VINTAGE PORT:

Top shoulder level. Decanted three hours before serving. A magnificent Port. Solid, masculine, typical Taylor's. Spicy red fruit on nose and palate. Fruit, tannins, and acidity blend beautifully. A pleasure to drink now to 2005, if well cellared.

April 18, 1998

Commanderie de Bordeaux Gala Dinner and Induction Ceremony.

We are inducting three new members tonight and this will be our new Maître Ian Mottershead's first induction ceremony. We are featuring tonight the 1982 vintage. How fortunate that I have purchased a fair amount of 1982s for our cellar just in time, in the mid-1980s. Today, prices for these wines are prohibitive.

April 1998

Tasted at a seafood restaurant in Vancouver.

1996 HAWTHORNE MOUNTAIN RIESLING VQA, OKANAGAN FALLS, BRITISH COLUMBIA, CANADA:

Pale gold. Flowery, good varietal character on nose. Elegant, slightly off-dry Kabinett-like wine. Clean, fruity finish.

1996 HESTER CREEK PINOT BLANC VQA, GOLDEN MILE, OLIVER, BRITISH COLUMBIA, CANADA:

Palish gold. Subdued, clean nose of green apples. Solid backbone, as a Pinot Blanc should be. Good, but subdued fruit. Needs two to three extra years of bottle-age, but already drinking well.

1996 HAWTHORNE MOUNTAIN PINOT GRIS VQA, OKANAGAN FALLS, BRITISH COLUMBIA, CANADA:

A dreadful, commercial, nail polish drink, reminiscent of what all Canadian wines tasted like before Free Trade (back in 1987) was introduced, when local chemical factories, calling themselves "wineries" were protected by the liquor monopolies from outside competition. Soapy, nail polish nose of cheap plastic. Acidified water and alcohol on palate. Forget it.

1995 SAUVIGNON BLANC "BARRELLI CREEK," GALLO, SONOMA:

Bright, deep golden colour. Totally dominated by smoky oak on both nose and palate, without any Sauvignon Blanc character whatsoever. Tastes and smells like an old style, artificially oaked, cheap Australian Chardonnay from the early 1980s. The restaurant wine list indicated that this wine had won a gold medal at a recent San Francisco competition. Maybe there should be stiffer sentences for judges who award any medals, let alone gold, for such wines.

In desperation, after trying one glass each of the above four wines, we ordered this bottle.

1995 FERRARI-CARANO CHARDONNAY, ALEXANDER VALLEY:

Almost Chablis-like, green-gold colour. Subdued, elegant nose with hint of green apples. Slight hint of buttery oak. Quite fresh on palate, elegant, easy drinking, not unlike a good Pouilly Fuissé.

April 23 to 30, 1998

Trip to Yountville, Napa Valley, with my daughter, Orly. Dinner at "Bistro Don Giovanni."

We brought along this bottle.

1992 STONY HILL CHARDONNAY, NAPA VALLEY:

In the context of this good but not great vintage, a very good Chardonnay that is now fully mature. Bright golden colour. Nose of ripe apples and pears. Round, elegant with good fruit/acidity balance. Long, complex, yet delicate. Most enjoyable.

Afternoon visit with Joe and Alice Heitz.

I brought along this bottle.

1993 WACHENHEIMER ALTENBERG RIESLING SPÄTLESE, WEINGUT JOSEPH BIFFAR (RHEINPFALTZ):

A perfect sipping wine on a glorious sunny spring afternoon. Bright, green-golden colour. Flowery, spicy, petroleum jelly nose. Classic Riesling. Excellent fruit/acidity balance. Hint of residual sugar, long, flowery fruit extract.

After his stroke almost two years ago, Joe is finally starting to get his tasting abilities back. He is now frail, but still has in him the feisty character for which he has been renowned. Joe is very fond of Gewürztraminer, but he said that there is very little good Gewürztraminer fruit in California. He would have loved to try and produce some himself, but never had the opportunity or the access to good fruit. They produced a little 1996 and 1997 "Martha's Vineyard" Cabernet (after having to uproot the vines, following the 1992 vintage, due to phylloxera). These will be released after the turn of the century. His daughter Kathleen is the manager of the business and of the estate, and his eldest son David is the winemaker. His youngest son, Rolly, left the family business recently, and is not even on talking terms with the family. These conflicts are unfortunately common in families, especially when a family business is at stake, but there is always hope that things will sort themselves out eventually.

In Yountville.

At "Mustard's."

Brought along our own bottle.

1987 RITCHIE CREEK NAPA VALLEY CABERNET SAUVIGNON:

Ten years old and fully mature. Deep colour to rim. Spicy, cedary nose of ripe Cabernet with some greenness. Round, well balanced, good mature fruit, but trace of nagging acidity which was still obvious even an hour after decanting. Not a bad Cabernet, but somehow lacks that extra dimension and extract.

Also tasted in Yountville on this trip.

1995 NEVERS CABERNET SAUVIGNON, NAPA VALLEY:

Only 775 cases produced and the vines were uprooted after the 1995 vintage, due to the ravages of phylloxera. Made from 90% Cabernet Sauvignon (I'm told that the source of the Cabernet is the Eisele Vineyard near Calistoga) and 10% Merlot. Produced by Ehren Jordan, winemaker at Turley Vineyards. Bright, very youthful, purplish colour to rim. Fresh, ripe, young black fruit on nose with hint of vanilla and oak. Similar impressions on palate. The only surprise is how forward and soft this wine is. Almost enjoyable now. Not really a distance runner. Drink from 2000 to 2005.

1990 MCCREA CELLARS "MARIAH," DON GRAVES VINEYARD, COLUMBIA VALLEY, WASHINGTON STATE:

Made from 25-year-old Grenache vines, producing only 1.5 tons per acre. According to the label, Mariah is named for the wind that sweeps through the Columbia River Gorge. The farthest thing to Grenache and as close to a mature Volnay as can be. Uncanny resemblance to a soft, round, fruity, Pinot Noir. Spicy, sweet, soft fruit. Pleasant, but not much complexity there. Seven years old, and already starting to decline. Drink up!

1996 AU BON CLIMAT CHARDONNAY, SANTA BARBARA COUNTY:

Pale golden colour. Green apples and butter on nose. Little oak, crisp, round, good fruit/acidity balance. Not unlike a pleasant Mâconnais.

1994 DOMINUS, NAPANOOK, NAPA VALLEY:

Intense, deep, inky colour to rim. Expansive nose of lovely, ripe black fruit combined with oak and cedar. Great extract on palate. Fairly tannic, but fabulous ripe fruit. Pity to try this before 2003 to 2006 or beyond. Great potential.

1991 ROBERT MONDAVI CABERNET SAUVIGNON "RESERVE," NAPA VALLEY:

Very good, deep colour, palish rim. Expansive, cedary, eucalyptus nose. Full, rich, yet elegant. Lovely cedar and ripe black fruit. Still a bit tannic, but approachable. Excellent balance and length. Drink from 2000 to 2006. A fine effort.

CHÂTEAU CLIMENS 1976, BARSAC:

Typical Barsac and classic Climens. Surprisingly pale for a 21-year-old Sauternes. Sweet, rich, yet superb balance, acidity, fruit, and youth. Honeyed, botrytis nose. Taste went on and on, on the palate. Perfect now, but, if well cellared, will last for another two decades. Superb.

May 1998

Dinner with the family and friends.

CHAMPAGNE CHARLES HEIDSIECK BRUT 1990:

As usual, reliable and well made. Yeasty, ripe, rich, yet lively. Good length, lovely fruit, and good backbone. Clean finish, tiny bubbles, and fine mousse.

1978 PULIGNY-MONTRACHET PREMIER CRU "PUCELLES," HENRI BOILLOT:

How great these 1978 white Burgundies have turned out to be! 20 years old and certainly not over-the-hill. Mature, rich, nutty-oaky flavours, backed by excellent exotic Chardonnay fruit. Mellow, well balanced, and complex on both nose and palate. One of the finest vintages for white Burgundies over the past quarter-century, and definitely the longest-lived.

1982 MAZIS-CHAMBERTIN, DOMAINE MAUME:

Surprisingly lively and rich. Fair bit of sediment. Rustic, but in a positive sense. Excellent ripe fruit on both nose and palate. Clean, long, spicy, and rich. Layers of fruit and very long aftertaste. Over 15 years old and an impressive effort in a "soft, early maturing" vintage. A great effort.

CHÂTEAU LA LAGUNE 1966, NICOLAS BOTTLE:

Level like a recently bottled wine. I have owned this wine (as part of a lot of three cases of 1966 La Lagune) since 1974, and have tasted it well over two dozen times since. Bright, deep colour to rim. Cedary, chocolaty, rich black fruit on nose. Similar impressions on palate. Excellent balance, depth, and ripe, lively fruit. One of the best 1966s and a great La Lagune. Perfectly mature at over 31 years old, but no rush! These bottles have been exceptionally well cellared, of course.

May 1998

A tasting, featuring 1983 Margaux and other southern Haut-Médocs, 15 years on

APERITIF

CHAMPAGNE ROEDERER "CRISTAL" 1983:

A smooth, excellent Champagne of great class. Fully mature, fine mousse, tiny bubbles. Clean, yeasty, creamy nose. Mellow, velvety, rich, and smooth on palate. Cannot get any better and needs drinking. A real treat.

THE TASTING

CHÂTEAU CANTEMERLE 1983:

This vintage signalled a comeback for a château that used to produce excellent wines in the 1940s, 1950s, and early 1960s, but that has been an underachiever since. Impressive, deep colour to rim. Ripe, chocolaty, cedary nose. Full, round, well balanced, with layers of ripe fruit, and ripe tannins. Very good length. Ready, but no rush. (17)

CHÂTEAU LA LAGUNE 1983:

While this wine does not have the sheer ripeness and intensity of the superb 1982 vintage, it is an understated, elegant wine. Slightly herbaceous, cedary, earthy nose with good fruit in the background. Fairly dry, noticeable acidity, but backed by good fruit. Hint of oak and vanilla. Quite good. (16)

CHÂTEAU PRIEURÉ-LICHINE 1983:

Medium colour, evolved at rim. Elegant, herbaceous, forthcoming nose of classic Margaux. Round, fully mature on palate. Not much depth or weight, but certainly an elegant, well-made wine. Ready and will not improve. (16)

CHÂTEAU BRANE-CANTENAC 1983:

This underachieving, overproduced property is finally starting to make wines that are stylish, elegant, and well structured. Overall, very similar to the Prieuré-Lichine, but with a little more depth and slightly more noticeable acidity. Ready. (16)

CHÂTEAU MALESCOT-ST.-EXUPÉRY 1983:

Another property that used to produce excellent, deep-coloured, rich wines, notably in 1959 and 1961, but, alas, a property that has produced rather rustic, ordinary wines for over two decades. This property also has a fairly large proportion of Petit Verdot in the blend, around 8% to 10%. Deep colour, cedary, black fruit on nose. Fairly tight and hard on palate. Noticeable acidity, lacking oak, vanilla, or complexity. Good, but not great. (15)

CHÂTEAU RAUSAN-SÉGLA 1983:

1983 represents the beginning of the comeback of another potentially great château. Fairly evolved colour, palish rim. Classy, elegant nose of black fruit, cedar, fresh herbs. Round, long, well balanced, with nice complexity. Ready now. (17)

Château Palmer 1983:

While the 1975, 1978, and 1979 Palmers are very good, true to both the character of the respective vintages, and to Palmer's chocolaty elegance, the 1983 is clearly the best effort of this fine property since the superb 1970. Medium to dark colour, showing some maturity at rim. Lovely chocolaty, cedary, perfumy nose. Classic Margaux! Round, smooth, elegant, very well balanced, and as long and persistent on palate as one could possibly wish. Definitely one of a handful of stars in 1983 in the Médoc. Drink now to 2003 or beyond. (18.5)

Château Margaux 1983:

The "Grand Maître" of the 1983 vintage in the whole of the Médoc, no doubt. Deepest, most youthful wine of flight, by a mile. Intense black, herbaceous, cedary fruit on nose. Still surprisingly tight, tannic, and youthful on palate, but backed by excellent fruit. Not nearly ready, yet it is already 15 years old! A very big, very serious wine that should approach its peak around 2003 to 2008. Grand Vin! (19.5)

Château de Fargues 1983:

The grand finale to a fascinating tasting. Not quite 1983 d'Yquem, but certainly one of the very best wines of that superb vintage in Sauternes. Brilliant golden colour. Buttery, oaky, vanilla, botrytis, and ripe fruit on nose. Similar impressions on palate. Taste went on and on. Very rich, creamy, but backed by excellent fruit. Drink now to 2010. (18.5)

May 25, 1998

Chevaliers du Tastevin dinner, featuring various Pommards.

1993 Chablis Grand Cru "Les Clos," William Febvre:

Oh, how I long for real, old-style Grand Cru Chablis! Back in the 1970s, one could get an excellent Grand Cru for $6 to $10, and what one got was the real thing. Nowadays one pays five to seven times the price and all one gets is an ordinary Chablis, masquerading as "Grand Cru." Some greenness, a little bit of flint, and hint of green apples, but where is the extract, ripe fruit, and terroir complexity? One or two producers, notably Raveneau, still produce the real thing, but at a cost! Overplanting, and especially in the wrong soils, has all but destroyed this once great wine-producing area. A sad state of affairs, indeed. This Chablis fit the mold. A decent petit vin, no more. Even Moreau, Laroche, and other once famous Chablis producers are now only a shadow of their past glories.

1990 Pommard, J. M. Boillot

and

1990 Pommard "Les Noizons," J. L. Joillot:

Both had the charming, velvety, elegant, and ripe fruit, so typical of this fine vintage.

The Noizons (not a Premier Cru, but rather a lieu-dit) is slightly deeper in colour, and spicier, riper fruit. Both fine efforts and fully mature.

1988 Pommard "Clos des Epeneaux" Premier Cru, Comte Armand

and

1988 Pommard "Les Jarollières," Domaine de la Pousse d'Or:

The latter is a monopole of this Domaine. Both Premier Crus, and both from another excellent, but much tighter and more masculine vintage.

The Clos de Epeneaux has an excellent, deep, youthful colour, spicy, slightly green nose that is backed by very good, ripe, dark fruit. Concentrated, tannic, not quite ready. A lovely bottle that should be drinking well from next year (1999) to 2005 or even beyond, if well cellared.

The Jarollières is every bit as good, but even more tannic, more concentrated, and more complex. Drink from 2000 to 2008. Excellent potential.

1983 Pommard "Rugiens" Premier Cru, de Courcel

and

1985 Pommard "Clos des Epeneaux" Premier Cru, Comte Armand:

Fortunately this 1983 was not affected by the rot that was so pervasive that year, but this pair showed the difference between the excellent 1985 and the mediocre 1983. While unfair, this pairing was most educational.

The 1983 is prematurely brown, soft fruit, yet, oddly, fairly tannic, and masculine. No sense waiting for the tannins to soften, because the little fruit that is there will disappear shortly. Fortunately, no taste or smell of rot.

The 1985 is clearly the star of the evening. Superb depth of colour, ripe cherry fruit on nose. Beautiful balance, fruit extract combined with velvety complexity. Ready now, but should hold well for another five to seven years. Most enjoyable.

Late May 1998

A comparative tasting, featuring the 1985 and 1986 vintages in the Médoc and Graves.

One leading château was chosen from each commune or region, tasted in pairs.

1. Château Sociando-Mallet 1985 and 1986, Haut-Médoc:

This is a very well-run property in the northern Médoc, producing masculine wines that can take on any St. Estèphe any day in terms of sheer structure and weight.

The 1985 is dark, youthful, cedary, with a clean Cabernet nose. Quite forward in terms of the style of this property, yet even so, one of the bigger 1985s. Lovely fruit extract and spicy, cedary finish. Not quite ready. Drink now to 2007. (17)

The 1986 is massive, tight, masculine, tannic. Totally unready. Deep, dark colour to rim. Black currants, oak, and green spices on nose. Very dry on palate, but the fruit is definitely there. Pity to drink this before 2003 or well beyond, if well cellared. (18)

The following pairs were served "geographically," from south to north.

2. Château La Mission Haut-Brion 1985 and 1986:

If one discounts the 1984 vintage, these were the first vintages produced wholly under the stewardship of Jean Delmas, the gifted manager of the Dillon stable, Haut-Brion, et al. When the sale of La Mission, Laville, and Latour-Haut-Brion was announced, I viewed it as a tragedy and the end of an era. The same would be true if Palmer were to be acquired by Margaux, Lafite by Mouton, Montrose by Cos d'Estournel, etc. At this level, wine is art, and one artist cannot "sell" his style to another artist with no consequences. I took it, therefore, with a grain of salt when Delmas announced that "nothing would change" at La Mission. In the case of Graves, this sale was a double tragedy. It removed the only true competitor to Haut-Brion, as if we do not have enough commonality in so many châteaux, planting similar root stocks and varietals. Now, here was a great style disappearing forever. Not that Delmas and Haut-Brion do not produce great wines; they do, of course, but competition and style difference is vital for everybody's sake. Now that I have vented my frustration, I shall describe the wines.

The 1985: Even in "soft and elegant" vintages, La Mission used to produce big, sturdy, earthy, long-ageing wines. Not this 1985. Certainly very good, elegant, fruity, ready, charming, and soft, but no statement here and certainly no "Super Second" quality. Sociando Mallet, a Cru Bourgeois level "newcomer" is sturdier, and has more stuffing. (17)

The 1986 is, as expected, bigger, tighter, more tannic. Very good potential and not ready yet. I slightly prefer the Haut-Brion 1986 to the La Mission 1986. (17.5)

Footnote

When I first heard the news that Haut-Brion had acquired La Mission, I bought every La Mission between 1959 and 1982 that came my way, just to be on the safe side!

3. Château Palmer 1985 and 1986:

If 1985 is an elegant vintage and Palmer is an elegant wine then, in theory, this would produce a very early maturing wine that is too soft. Well, that is not the case. The wine is elegant, all right, but it has good depth, acidity, and fruit. It is fully mature now and should be consumed over the next three to five years. More extract than both the 1981 and 1982 of this château, but less depth or complexity than the superb 1983. A very complex wine nevertheless, that is a pleasure to drink now. (18)

The 1986 is not really a big wine in terms of the vintage, but it is more solid, less refined, and slightly greener than the 1985. Hint of chocolate and cedar, soft tannins (but they are there), and clean, spicy finish. Not up to the 1983 or 1989 standard, but certainly very good. (17.5)

4. Château Leoville-Barton 1985 and 1986:

Until the early 1980s, 1959 was the last great vintage for this property. Ronald Barton produced fairly tight, green, slightly undermatured wines, which is a pity, because the location of the vineyard, its exposure, and soil can potentially produce great wines. Ronald's last fine effort was the 1982, but then who could miss that vintage? After his death, his nephew, Anthony Barton took over. With the twin 1985, 1986 vintages, Anthony blazed his property back into glory. Both are superb efforts and, since then, Leoville-Barton has never looked back. Unfortunately for the consumer, the price has not looked back either, especially since the early 1990s.

The 1985 has excellent, deep, youthful colour to rim. Black currants, hint of cedar and chocolate on nose. Round, fruity, excellent backbone, and great fruit extract. One of the most concentrated 1985s around. Drink now to 2005. (18)

The 1986 is a classic. Even deeper, darker, denser colour. Cedar, oak, slightly vegetal on nose. Excellent tannic backbone. Surely the best Leoville-Barton since the superb 1959. Drink from 2000 to 2010 or beyond. (18.5)

Château Pichon-Lalande 1985 and 1986:

Two very good wines (the 1986 outstanding), yet so different! Not only do they reflect the differences of the vintages, but two extremes in terms of structure. Pichon-Lalande is the "St. Julien of Pauillac," making relatively feminine, early maturing, high Merlot proportion wines.

The 1985 is all of the above, but in an even more exaggerated way. It tries desperately to be a Margaux! Soft, velvety, forward, and elegant. Ready, charming, and will not improve. (17)

The 1986 is the first true Pauillac made at Pichon-Lalande in a generation. Classic 1986! Spicy, complex, and solid wine. Lots of extract and solid tannins. Needs more time. A great effort. Drink from 2000 to 2015. (18.5)

CHÂTEAU COS D'ESTOURNEL 1985 AND 1986:

Together with the superb 1982, this pair of vintages heralded a comeback of a reputable château that had been an underachiever after 1961. What has been worrying me is the alarming increase in Merlot, producing softer, rounder wines that are of excellent quality overall, but that are losing their tannic, masculine character so typical of St. Estèphes. These two vintages are the best wines produced at Cos d'Estournel between 1982 and the mid-1990s nevertheless.

1985: Deep colour to rim. Black currant, oak, and vanilla nose. Lots of colour and fruit extract. Round, yet full, rich, and very long. A pleasure to drink now through 2005. (18)

1986: Appearance very close to the 1985, but, as expected, more tannic, more masculine, great concentration, but not ready. Drink from 2001 to 2010 or beyond. Great potential. (18.5)

Late May 1998

1989 MONTRACHET, MARQUIS DE LAGUICHE, JOSEPH DROUHIN:

Bright, golden colour. Exotic bouquet of ripe fruit, oak, vanilla, all in harmony. Full, yet not big. Complex, velvety, very long aftertaste. An excellent wine. At nine years old it is fully mature and may start to decline shortly.

CHÂTEAU PALMER 1970:

A superb Margaux that I have had the good fortune of tasting over two dozen times since 1975. Absolutely ready and exquisite. Good, dark colour, typical of this fine vintage. Chocolaty, perfumy nose. Velvety, round, cedary, and long on palate. All one could wish in a Margaux. The closest vintage to this Palmer in the past quarter-century is the excellent 1983.

Early June 1998

A short two-day trip to Yountville. I ate at the new "Bistro Jeanty" in Yountville, owned and operated by the former chef of Domaine Chandon. I had an excellent coq au vin following a very good smoked-trout salad. I brought my own bottle along.

CHÂTEAU PATACHE D'AUX 1982, MÉDOC:

I purchased this upon its release in 1984. Paid $5.50 per bottle. Very impressive. Not much complexity there, but the tell-tale deep colour and lovely ripe fruit so typical of this excellent vintage. Full, round, fully mature, but so much ripe fruit there, that there is no rush drinking this. Very good.

Everybody in the Napa Valley is talking about the latest disease of the vine, "Pierce Disease," carried by grasshoppers, and destroying the vines. Unfortunately, there is no known cure. Even in a recent issue of Decanter *magazine, there is an article on this. I guess that the wine world is finally becoming aware of this new danger. Also recently, a scandal in Bordeaux with the authorities charging Château Giscours' management with adulterating this classed growth's wine with other wines and oak chips instead of real oak barrels. The problem , from the consumer's point of view, is that, if they have been doing this at Giscours, what about other properties?*

In May and June, the weather in the Napa Valley has been quite wet and cool. A lot of coulure? No one knows how the vintage (1998) will turn out quality-wise, but it is already clear that the quantity will be below average.

June 1998

CHÂTEAU LEOVILLE-LASCASES 1978:

Shared it with Carol as a prelude to tomorrow night's Commanderie dinner which will feature the 1978 vintage, 20 years on. I have owned this wine since it first came on the market in 1981. The level was not unlike a wine just bottled. Medium-red colour with very good depth. Slightly herbaceous on nose, very pronounced Cabernet. 1978, the "miracle year" according to Harry Waugh, was a year of poor weather that was saved at the last moment by a few sunny days, just before the vintage. Alas, this came too late for the Merlot grape, the "softening agent" of the Médoc, so the wines are herbaceous and stemmy, but those that are well made have a very fine structure, and excellent extract nevertheless. Thus, this is a "Left Bank" year. The Pomerols and St. Emilions fared less well as a group, including Petrus. The Lascases is excellent. Essence of Cabernet. Fully mature, spicy with layers of complexity. Ready, but should hold well for another five to seven years.

My favourite 1978s are the Latour, Pichon-Lalande, Leoville-Lascases, Ducru-Beaucaillou, Palmer, and La Mission Haut-Brion. Notable failures are Montrose (way too soft for a St. Estèphe), Mouton-Rothschild, Lynch-Bages (washed out), and Beychevelle. On the

Right Bank, the best 1978 I have tasted is Cheval-Blanc, which will not come as a surprise.

June 9, 1998

Commanderie de Bordeaux dinner, at the Wedgewood hotel, featuring the 1978 vintage at 20 years old.

We started with a red wine tasted double-blind.

CHÂTEAU TROTANOY 1993:

I thought right away that it was a 1988. It had a good, youthful colour and depth; spicy, fresh black cherries, and some cedar on nose; fairly lean, tannic, but with good fruit. A fine effort in an indifferent vintage. Drink now to 2004.

Two whites followed.

1988 CORTON-CHARLEMAGNE, LOUIS LATOUR

AND

1989 CORTON-CHARLEMAGNE, LEROY:

Both good, but not great. The 1988 was complex, nutty, very soft, and evolved, but had good style, and some exotic fruit, with hint of oak. The 1989 should have been much better, but it wasn't. Paler, softer, slightly earthy. Lacked depth or weight. Overall, I preferred the style of the 1988 Louis Latour.

We then sat down to the tasting, served in flights, through a very well-prepared meal.

FLIGHT #1

CHÂTEAU LANESSAN 1978, HAUT-MÉDOC:

Evolved colour, orange rim. Rustic on nose with hint of residual sugar. (Chaptalized?) Thin, very soft, almost no fruit left. Was better eight years ago. Drink up. Dull. (13)

CHÂTEAU L'ARROSÉE 1978, ST. EMILION:

Better colour than the above. Palish rim. Elegant, subdued nose. Serious, masculine, even a bit tannic. Has withstood the test of time very well, no doubt due to the high proportion of Cabernets. (15.5)

CHÂTEAU FIGEAC 1978, ST. EMILION:

Similar appearance to the l'Arrosée, but spicy, stemmy, green on nose. Hint of dill. Some sweetness on palate. Good fruit. Fairly lean, acidic finish, but some pleasant fruit there too. More complexity and class than the above two. (16)

DOMAINE DE CHEVALIER 1978:

Evolved colour with palish rim. Hint of toasted oak. Elegant, subdued, lean. The fruit is disappearing fast. I much prefer the Domaine's 1979. This is too lean and watery. (15)

Overall, not too impressive a flight. The wines were clearly better eight to ten years ago.

FLIGHT #2

CHÂTEAU D'ANGLUDET 1978:

Medium red, evolved colour. Dull nose. Too lean, sour, acidic. Not very good. Rustic. (13.5)

CHÂTEAU PALMER 1978:

Very evolved colour. Orangy rim. Lovely, perfumy, elegant, and toasty nose. Quite soft, most enjoyable, but no future. The most elegant wine of the flight. Needs drinking, however. (17.5)

CHÂTEAU MARGAUX 1978:

Our bottle was corked, unfortunately. The second bottle was much better. Deepest, darkest wine of flight. Solid, tannic, unyielding, even at 20. Very good depth, extract, and ripe fruit. No rush. Drink now to 2008. Surprisingly tight. (18.5)

CHÂTEAU MONTROSE 1978:

Fairly evolved colour. Lean, acidic, weak, light finish. Not one of Montrose's better efforts. Drink up. (14.5)

CHÂTEAU COS D'ESTOURNEL 1978:

Far superior to the Montrose, and a "comeback" year for Cos which has been underachieving after 1961. Masculine, good fruit. Ready, but still tannic. Drink now to 2005. (17)

FLIGHT #3

CHÂTEAU BEYCHEVELLE 1978:

Very pale colour. Almost a Rosé. Stemmy, cheesy, sweet water on nose. Sharp, acidic, sour. This was a poor wine when it was young, so what could one expect two decades on? Very disappointing. (13)

CHÂTEAU GRUAUD-LAROSE 1978:

Medium to dark colour. Evolved rim Leathery, sweaty, and stemmy nose. Sharp, acidic, chunky, with good fruit, but spoiled by too much acidity. (15)

CHÂTEAU BATAILLEY 1978:

Spicy, herbaceous nose. Some toast. Citric on palate. Nose much better than palate, but some elegance and class there. Clearly better than the preceding two wines. Drink up. (16)

CHÂTEAU PICHON-LALANDE 1978:

Possibly the best wine tonight together with Palmer and Margaux. Cedary spice, toasted oak, good fruit. Long complex finish. At its peak, but with enough fruit to last five more years. (17.5)

WITH DESSERT

CHÂTEAU COUTET 1975, BARSAC:

A wine I know well, and the finest effort at Coutet, after their very good 1962, until the more recent 1989 and 1990 twins. Still fairly youthful colour (typical for a Barsac), but this was not as good as in the past. A bit earthy, good acidity (a trademark of the 1975s), but lacked fat, and rich, fruity botrytis. Not bad, though.

June 20, 1998

Dinner at "Lumière" restaurant, with a group of friends.

Our group bottles were the 1978 Montrachet, DRC (now worth an astronomical US$800 per bottle!), and 1978 La Tâche, Monopole, DRC. We each brought along an extra bottle and turned it into a feast. Chef Rob Feenie produced an excellent, innovative meal. My contribution was the bottle of 1985 Bollinger "Grande Année."

1985 PERRIER JOUET'S "FLOWER BOTTLE:"

80% Chardonnay in the blend, and it showed. Crisp, fresh, clean, and elegant. Slight touch of sharpness, but elegant fruit, too. This was followed by

BOLLINGER "GRANDE ANNÉE" 1985:

Much creamier, smoother, richer; hint of yeast and ripe fruit. Excellent, and at its peak.

The next wine was a most unusual one.

1978 ROYALE CLUB (FOUR STAR CUVÉE), A/C BOURGOGNE, REMOISSENET:

(This is overproduction and thus, declassified Montrachet from Remoissenet's own vineyard.) Deep, golden colour. Acacia and hint of botrytis and oak on both nose and palate. Very ripe, quite mature, but not oxidized. Layers of rich, ripe fruit. Impressive at 20 years old. This was followed by probably the greatest white wine in the world, and consequently, very rare and very expensive.

1978 MONTRACHET, DOMAINE DE LA ROMANÉE-CONTI, BOTTLE #2412:

Impressive, youthful golden colour for a 20-year-old white wine. Still full of life and should last for another decade, or longer! Great complex nose of ripe, flowery Chardonnay, combined with oak, vanilla, and layers of ripe fruit. Still has excellent acidity and fruit. Absolutely magnificent. The late André Noblet, winemaker at the Domaine at that time, really outdid himself here. A memorable experience. Worth its weight in gold!

1990 ROMANÉE-SAINT-VIVANT, DOMAINE DE LA ROMANÉE-CONTI:

A classic Pinot Noir from a great vintage. Bright, deep cherry-red colour. Superb nose of spicy, ripe fruit, and oak. Not quite ready yet. Drink from 2002 to 2015. An excellent wine.

Then we tasted our second group wine, and one I have had the good fortune of tasting on at least a dozen occasions to date.

LA TÂCHE 1978, MONOPOLE DU DOMAINE DE LA ROMANÉE-CONTI:

As expected, wild raspberries on nose and palate, a trademark of this great property. Still full of life, rich, luscious, with excellent backbone, length, fruit, and spicy acidity, all in harmony. Will last for many more years. Drink now to 2015. Grand Vin!

WE ENDED THIS SUMPTUOUS EVENING WITH AN EXCELLENT BOTTLE OF 1975 CHÂTEAU DE FARGUES, SAUTERNES, LUR SALUCES:

Bright, deep golden colour. Full mature, and has held extremely well, due to the excellent acidity level typical of the finer 1975 Sauternes. Luscious, rich botrytis, and clean, buttery, vanilla fruit. Very long. A memorable dinner.

Monday, June 22, 1998

The World Cup soccer games are in full swing.

Shocking defeat for England today by Romania! Romania's second (and winning) goal came in the 90th minute!

June 22, 1998

1990 CORTON-CHARLEMAGNE, FAIVELEY:

Until the Mid-1980s, this was sold as Corton Blanc. Since 1986, François Faiveley has been producing a superb, masculine, slow-maturing, and full-bodied Corton-Charlemagne, notably the excellent 1989. This 1990 is a bit leaner, harder, but it already exhibits the class, intensity, mineral, and exotic fruit flavours, combined with new oak. Solid backbone and very good fruit/acidity balance. Drink now to 2002 or beyond.

June 27, 1998

Small-group tasting.

There were ten participants, some of whom are former members of my Le Tastevin Wine Club. This group is one of the offshoots of that club. Each participant brought along a bottle. Mine was the 1978 Château Palmer. The food was prepared by Chef Scott Kidd, former chef of "Lola's" restaurant, in Vancouver.

CHÂTEAU D'YQUEM 1970:

With terrine of foie gras. Fully mature, rich, great botrytis, oak, and ripe fruit on both nose and palate. Soft, round, and elegant. Perfect now. The 1971 is better structured and, overall, a longer-lasting, and more complex wine. This is really fine, however.

A trio of 1978 Clarets
Margaux,

Pichon-Lalande,

and
Palmer:

Now 20 years old.

The Pichon-Lalande was badly corked, sadly. It can be an excellent wine.

The Margaux is still youthful, purplish, deep colour to rim Restrained nose of cedary Cabernet, slightly herbaceous. (Very little Merlot in 1978. The sunny weather in September that year came too late to save the Merlot.) Tight, fairly solid, even youthful on palate. Not a generous wine, still tannic. The fruit is there, but somehow one must be concerned that in a decade or so, the fruit will disappear and the green tannins will remain. Time will tell.

The Palmer was the most elegant, velvety, with a hint of chocolate. Fully mature, soft, but with that classic elegance typical of this fine property. Needs drinking, though.

Then came the turn of three 1982s
Château Grand-Puy-Lacoste,

Château Mouton-Rothschild,

and
Château Cos d'Estournel:

The Grand-Puy-Lacoste is a lovely, classic Claret. Deep colour to rim. Reserved on nose, but certainly ripe black fruit there. Full, perfectly balanced, spicy Cabernet. Long finish. Enjoyable now, but it has a good decade at this plateau ahead of it. A well run, reliable, and, until the recent price madness, always good value. A safe bet.

The Mouton-Rothschild is a masterpiece. What a pity that this great property has been inconsistent, especially after 1962 and before 1982. Ironically, the same Maître de Chais, Raoul Blondin, and owner, Baron Philippe (both now deceased), have produced this wine for over five decades. Textbook Claret, and definitely First Growth quality here. Very deep colour; great extract. Vanilla, oak, ripe black fruit, and tobacco on nose. Full, solid, superb balance and fruit extract on palate. Ripe tannins, very long finish. Grand Vin! Drink from 2002 to 2020 or beyond, if well cellared.

The Cos d'Estournel was odd. Again, deep, dark colour to rim. Leather, truffles, and prunes on nose, reminiscent of an older-style Barolo or fine Spanish Rioja. Full, fat, but, again, pruny on palate. Must be a poorly stored bottle, because, when tasted previously, this was excellent.

These were followed by two Châteauneuf-du-Papes. The order puzzles me because, good as they may be (and in spite of Robert Parker's rave reviews of several southern Rhône properties), they are pedestrian wines when compared to fine Clarets or great red Burgundies or the top northern Rhône properties.

Château Rayas 1983 and 1989:

The 1983 is now fully evolved, velvety, yet has excellent balance and fruit extract. Spicy, slightly off-dry. (Rayas is made almost exclusively from Grenache grapes). Fine wine.

The 1989 is youthful, dark, peppery, but noticeably sweet, not unlike a Late Harvest Zinfandel. Heavy-handed and pedestrian. According to one of the participants, Parker has "awarded" this wine 96 points. A chacun son goût!

We ended the evening with a classic Port from a great vintage.
Fonseca's 1963 Vintage Port:

At 35 years old, it is fully mature now. Velvety, smooth, round. Very complex, spicy, and long aftertaste. The "Château Margaux" of Port. Bravo Bruce Guimaraens!

Late June 1998

Dow's 1966 Vintage Port:

(London-bottled by Charles Kinloch) Fortunately, tasted on a cool June day! 32 years old and fully mature. An underrated vintage that has produced some excellent Ports, notably Croft's, Graham's, Fonseca's, and Dow's. Evolved colour. Fair bit of sediment. Decanted one-and-a-half hours. Spicy fruit, fairly dry, as Ports go, finesse, and great texture. Long, complex finish. Not quite as concentrated as Dow's 1963, which I know well, but pretty close to it in quality. The 1963 is less evolved.

Early July 1998

Dinner at "La Belle Auberge," in Ladner.

Chef/owner Bruno Marti prepared us an excellent meal, as usual. All the wines were supplied by our host, David Freeman, QC.

1955 Hermitage "La Sizeranne," Chapoutier:

Two bottles tasted. Both had excellent levels and appearance. How nice it is to see the firm of Chapoutier now back to its past glorious form, since the early 1990s, after almost a quarter-century in the wilderness, a wasted generation. These 1955s were made before the "wilderness" period. One bottle was a bit thin and hard, losing its fruit, and slightly musty. The second was far fresher and livelier. Toasted oak, ripe (but lean and tight) fruit, hint of charred wood. A solid, serious wine, as a Hermitage should be. May last another decade (in spite of its 43 years), but may lose its fruit. Long, spicy finish.

Early July 1998

Dinner with friends, featuring a superb magnum of Château Gruaud-Larose 1961.

CHÂTEAU GRUAUD-LAROSE 1961, IN MAGNUM:

Superb! The wine of the evening. One could not wish for a greater 1961 (with the exception, maybe, of Latour, Palmer, La Mission, or Mouton). Full of life, great chocolaty extract, mouth-filling. Very long with layers of ripe, cedary fruit. No rush drinking this magnum. Bottles are fully mature now. Grand Vin! While the 1961 Ducru-Beaucaillou is still velvety, elegant, and most enjoyable, it is past its prime now. No other St. Julien even approaches the quality of this Gruaud-Larose in 1961.

CHÂTEAU DUCRU-BEAUCAILLOU 1975:

Decanted two hours. Together with Leoville-Lascases, the best 1975 St. Julien, by far. Very 1975. Tight, stemmy, but backed by vital ripe fruit. No rush drinking this. Cedary, spicy fruit. Long on palate. A gentleman's Claret of the "old school." Today's Clarets are charming, vanilla puff-cakes compared to this!

July 1998

1985 AND 1990 RICHEBOURG, DOMAINE DE LA ROMANÉE-CONTI:

The 1985 was mine, the 1990 a friend's. Two great wines from two excellent vintages.

1985: Deep coloured, showing no sign of maturity. Exquisite, charming black cherries and lightly toasted oak on nose. Oriental spices, too. Luscious on palate. Perfectly balanced and will obviously last for another ten or even 20 years, if well cellared, but so lovely drinking now! Rich, full-bodied, luscious. Grand Vin.

1990: As expected, tighter, more tannic than the 1985, but not more concentrated. Very similar to the 1985, actually. The oak is more pronounced, of course. These are two superb examples of what great Burgundies are all about. Drink from 2005 to 2020, or beyond.

CHÂTEAU RAYAS 1990, CHÂTEAUNEUF-DU-PAPE:

Having tasted this property's 1983 and 1989 recently, I was very curious to taste this 1990. According to my host, Robert Parker has rated this wine a perfect 100 points. Even jammier, riper, sweeter, and more spicy and leathery than the overripe 1989. This wine will suit lovers of very late-harvest Zinfandels. Impossible to drink this with food. Desperately trying to be a Graham's Vintage Port. A curiosity rather than a wine. "A chacun son goût." Sweeter, richer, and riper than any Grange Hermitage from Australia I have tasted to date. This wine has recently been offered at auction for over US$600 per bottle! Is there no end to this madness?

The following day, I had the opportunity to taste three very good Italian wines.

1988 BRUNELLO DI MONTALCINO, PERTIMALI:

Deep, ruby-red colour to rim. Toast, almonds, and ripe black fruit on nose. Tighter on palate (not as charming as the excellent 1985, or as sweet and ripe as the superb 1990). Actually, Italian reds from the 1988 vintage resemble the 1988 red Bordeaux and, oddly, red Burgundies of the same vintage. Tighter, restrained, slow-maturing wines. Very good potential. Drink from 2002 to 2010.

1990 ORNELLAIA, ANTINORI:

A beautifully crafted, rich, luscious wine, with hint of new oak, still fairly tannic, black fruit. Full-bodied and very rich. Drink from 2003.

1990 BAROLO, BUSSIA "VIGNA CIGALA," ALDO CONTERNO:

An outstanding Barolo. How great the 1990 vintage has been in both Tuscany and Piedmont! Luscious, ripe, peppery, slightly leathery. Layers of exotic, ripe fruit. Great potential. Pity to try this before 2005 to 2010, or beyond. Conterno must surely be one of the greatest producers in all of Italy. You could buy five bottles of this superb Barolo for the price of a single bottle of the famous French "Late Harvest Zinfandel," Château Rayas 1990, Châteauneuf-du-Pape. Go figure! I guess there is no accounting for taste.

July 1998

Dinner with friends, featuring a string of superb, mature Heitz Cellars "Martha's Vineyard" Napa Cabernet Sauvignons, from 1968 to 1974:

After that period, "Martha's" seemed to be more patchy, producing good wines, of course, but peaking only in 1985 and 1990. I haven't tasted the 1991 or 1992 recently.

1968:

Evolved colour. Classic, minty/eucalyptus, and cedary Cabernet on nose. Soft, round, forward, but, at 30, still fruity. Velvety, long finish. Excellent. (18)

1969:

Overall, very similar to the 1968, but a little more concentration, and intensity. A mouthful of rich, cedary Cabernet. Oriental spices. Great bottle. Joe Heitz told me on several occasions that he tends to prefer the 1969 to the 1968. (18.5)

1969 Lot C-91:

This is a blend of "Martha's Vineyard" and regular Napa Valley Cabernet. Sweet fruit, rich, complex, and long. The Eucalyptus is slightly less pronounced, but it is still a lovely wine. Amazing how well these wines have lasted. (17.5)

1970:

Another great bottle. Not as ripe as the 1969. Actually resembles the 1968 in structure, but a little tighter, more restrained. Classic, cedary Cabernet of great class. Ready, of course, but no rush. Excellent fruit/acidity balance. I have purchased these Cabernets from the now-defunct San Francisco wine merchant, Draper and Esquin's, back in the mid-1980s. (18)

1974:

24 years old and still youthful and intense. Most pronounced eucalyptus and cedary mint of flight. Luscious, ripe fruit on both nose and palate. An exotic wine. So intense that some people like it and others don't. It can overwhelm. For me, a great experience. (19)

A personal view on the 1975 red Bordeaux vintage

After the hype from 1975 to 1977, when the Negoce of Bordeaux desperately needed a "great" vintage to kick-start a dormant wine market, it has gradually become fashionable to denigrate this "tough" vintage. By the early 1990s, I was finding myself in an ever decreasing minority, supporting this vintage.

Obviously, there were many failures in 1975. Many wines lack the fruit concentration to compete with the green, aggressive tannins. Others are diluted and thin. Yet others are too acidic and "never had it" in the first place. And yet, having tasted the 1975s on so many occasions, I have reached the conclusion that the consumer still has a fine array of good, even great 1975s to choose from. Some are rounder, more evolved. Others are still very tannic, made in the "old style," not unlike the 1945s and 1928s.

I do realize that 1945 and 1928 were very great vintages, but so are (or will be) some of the 1975s listed below. Obviously, they are 22 years old now, and one crucial factor to take into account, that goes with any wine, is how the wines were cellared and handled. No 1975s can truly be called charmers (à la 1985 or 1953). Nor can they be called fat or ripe (such as 1947 or 1982).

Best 1975 Pomerols:
Petrus, l'Evangile, Lafleur, Nenin, La Conseillante, and Trotanoy.

Best 1975 St. Emilions:
Cheval-Blanc and Figeac.

Best 1975 Graves:
La Mission Haut-Brion.

(Rumours have it that Latour-Haut-Brion is actually the La Mission, a special-bottling for certain clients. My personal experience differs. While good, it is not quite La Mission.)

Best 1975 Margaux:
Palmer.

Best 1975 St. Juliens:
Leoville-Lascases, and Ducru-Beaucaillou.

Best 1975 Pauillacs:
Latour, Mouton-Rothschild, Lynch-Bages, and Pichon-Lalande.

Best 1975 St. Estèphe:
Montrose.

Other good 1975s:
Domaine de Chevalier, Calon-Ségur, Beychevelle, Grand-Puy-Lacoste, Vieux Château Certan, etc.

Some people may have tasted poor examples of some of the above or better examples of wines not listed. Most of the wines listed above are ready and enjoyable. Others, such as Latour, Montrose, and La Mission, need more time.

Among the disappointing wines:
Margaux, Ausone, Cos d'Estournel, Lafite, and Gruaud-Larose.

I personally consider this vintage, based on the above list, as being the last "old style" vintage to date. After the "miracle" vintage of 1978 and the rich, round 1979, there appeared a new decade, a new era in wine making in Bordeaux, a totally new style of wine. More reliable? Yes. Earlier maturing? Yes. More Merlot and more new oak? Yes. More production in terms of hectolitres per hectare? Yes. Better and more classic wines overall? Not necessarily.

Short trip to Yountville, Napa Valley.

Bastille Day, July 14, 1998

Reception at Dominus on the occasion of the Inauguration of their newly-completed winery.

An interesting, practical, and very modern winery. At the reception, two wines were poured.

Champagne Perrier Jouët Brut N/V, in magnums:

Flowery, crisp, elegant, and clean fruit. A perfect summer sipping Champagne.

1994 DOMINUS:

A baby, of course, but this has excellent potential. Deep, purplish colour to rim. Cedary, vanilla, and ripe Cabernet on nose. In structure this resembles a 1996 Haut-Médoc, such as Grand-Puy-Lacoste or Leoville-Barton. Impeccably made and excellent potential by 2005.

Later this year, Yountville will get its own appellation. If so, Dominus will be the star of the appellation. Other wineries located within the proposed Yountville viticultural area are: Domaine Chandon, Goosecross Cellars, Bell Winery, Havens Wine Cellars, Bernard Pradel Cellars, and Château Chevre.

Lunch with Ray Signorello Jr., owner of Signorello Vineyards, at "Bistro Jeanty" in Yountville.

Philippe Jeanty is the former chef of Domaine Chandon and he is doing an excellent job with his new Bistro.

I brought along this bottle.

1992 CORTON-CHARLEMAGNE, LOUIS JADOT:

A chilled, welcome relief, as the temperature outside the restaurant soared to almost 100ºF. A classy, nutty, honeyed, and oaky Chardonnay. Not particularly big, but beautifully crafted. Complex, long, lovely ripe fruit. Approaching its peak.

Ray brought along this bottle.

1988 VOSNE-ROMANÉE PREMIER CRU "AUX RÉAS," DOMAINE LEROY:

Solid backbone, typical of the 1988s combined with the elegance of this commune. Bright cherry-red colour. Spicy, ripe Pinot Noir on nose. Impeccable balance and length. Drink now to 2008.

We also tried this wine.

SIGNORELLO'S OWN 1995 PINOT NOIR "LOS AMIGOS VINEYARD," CARNEROS:

35-year-old vines. Ray had to pay $3,000 per ton for the fruit, and produced only 400 cases. A fine example of a classic, fruity, charming Pinot Noir.

July 16, 1998

Dinner, again at "Bistro Jeanty" (excellent coq au vin), with Delia Viader, owner/winemaker of Viader Vineyards.

I brought along this bottle.

CHÂTEAU LEOVILLE-POYFERRÉ 1986:

How nice to see this property back in form, after many decades of producing mediocre, undistinguished wines. Classic 1986, approaching its peak. Good depth, cedary, oak, vanilla, and spicy Cabernet on both nose and palate. Still a bit tannic, but a well-made—and undervalued—wine. Drink now to 2008.

Delia told me that on the previous day, she had tasted a 1986 Château Beychevelle that was weak and forward. I used to like Beychevelle. In the 1950s and 1960s, and even early 1970s (up to 1975), Beychevelle produced elegant, distinguished wines. I liked to call this property "the Palmer of St. Julien." Alas, with overproduction, this fine property has become the "Brane Cantenac" of St. Julien, producing weak, early maturing wine.

Talking to a few members of the wine trade in California

They are confirming my fears that poorly stored wine is making its way back from the Far East. I feel sorry for European and North American buyers who think that they are getting bargains at auction, when they may actually be getting expensive prune juice.

Evening, July 17, 1998

Just got back from Yountville.

Dinner with the family, celebrating my 53rd birthday.

1945 BEAUNE PREMIER CRU, "MONTÉE ROUGE," LEON VIOLLAND:

Excellent level and appearance. Wax capsule wrapped around a string, the purpose of which is to pull the string and crack the wax. Evolved colour, but with very good depth. At first, nose expressed the smell of truffles, earth, and ripe prunes. After 15 minutes in glass, the bouquet evolved into mature, spicy Pinot Noir. Lovely fruit on palate, with good tannic backbone. After an hour, the wine reached its peak. Velvety, complex, spicy, slightly barnyardy, but long. Great effort and a fine 53-year-old wine. Montée Rouge is a tiny Premier Cru Appellation, at the top of a hill, and close to the boundary of Beaune to the east. The soil has an unusual reddish colour. An excellent wine.

Saturday, July 25, 1998

Lunch at "Seasons" restaurant, in Queen Elizabeth Park, Vancouver, featuring La Tâche, Domaine de la Romanée-Conti, "Monopole" 1942 to 1978.

I was the organizer and all the wines came from my cellar. Most of the vintages tasted were acquired several years ago, with the exception of the 1953, 1947, 1969, and 1961, which were purchased as a single lot at auction over a year ago. We were 17 participants, with several guests from out of town, including Ray Signorello Jr., owner/winemaker of Signorello Vineyards, Napa; Dr. Brad Klein from Los Angeles; and Mr. Paul Pinski from San Francisco, who has been tasting fine Burgundies for many decades and is an authority on the Domaine de la Romanée-Conti wines.

"Seasons" is the venue where Presidents Yeltsin and Clinton had their formal dinner, during their Vancouver Summit four years ago. Executive Chef is Pierre Delacote.

A superb lunch accompanied the wines.

Only one bottle, the 1953, had a low ullage (three inches). The older bottles had lower levels than the younger ones, which is to be expected. The appearance of the wines was fairly evolved. This is very misleading with Pinot Noir, because almost all the wines had great intensity, body, and flavour. Approaching a tasting of this kind, one must forget Claret or Rhône. Pinot Noir just behaves differently.

CHAMPAGNE CHARLES HEIDSIECK BRUT 1990:

A very well-crafted Champagne from an excellent vintage. Creamy, smooth, yet crisp and fresh. Good, yeasty character, backed by excellent fruit. A fine effort.

NB: All wines are La Tâche, unless otherwise indicated.

FLIGHT #1

1951:

Evolved, browning colour. Slightly oxidized nose. Solid, acidic, hint of fruit, but over-the-hill. Some charred oak. Still drinkable, but barely. (14.5)

1958:

Spicy, vegetal, stemmy, good Pinot Noir, mature nose. Lovely fruit. Sweet. Most enjoyable. Still alive. Peppery, good impact on palate, and classic, elegant character. (17)

1958 RICHEBOURG, DOMAINE DE LA ROMANÉE-CONTI:

More toasty, roasted, oaky, and spicy than the 1958 La Tâche. More backbone, but less fresh fruit. Overall, better structured than the La Tâche. However, the La Tâche had livelier fruit and was more complex. Both excellent. A matter of taste. (17)

1952:

Very evolved colour. Nice, mature Pinot Noir nose. Hint of raspberries on palate (the only wine in this flight that had this). Clearly, best wine of flight, and a superb 46-year-old! (18)

1953:

Mid shoulder fill. Very evolved, pale colour. Waxy, mushroomy, over-the-hill. Cork disintegrated. Still drinkable, but barely. Pity, because the 1953 can be great. After all, in the case of wines of this age, one drinks individual bottles and not vintages. (13)

FLIGHT #2

1942:

Evolved orange-brown colour. Charred, toasty oak and herbaceous, mature Pinot Noir on nose. Spicy, rich, still full of life. Excellent fruit balance. Cork disintegrated. The smell and taste lasted for a long time. A great war year effort. Wax capsule (shortage of lead during the war), and thinner green-blue glass (one grabbed what one could during the war). (18)

1947:

Superb, mature raspberry-jam nose. Hint of dill. Mature, evolved colour. Sweet fruit, long, ripe, rich. Excellent raspberry character. A complete 50-year-old. One could not ask for much better red Burgundy than this. (19)

1961:

Darkest of flight. Orange tinge and browning rim. Smoky, toasty. Not as complex as the 1947 on nose, but lovely, ripe, spicy fruit on palate. (Overall, Burgundy produced greater wines in 1959 than in 1961.) This is fully mature, but it has enough ripeness to last further. (16.5)

1966:

Musty on nose. Very sweet (much better) on palate. Very rich, but foursquare. Seems to have been poorly stored (cooked). Acidic finish. After 30 minutes in glass, hint of mocha, and a dramatic change for the better. Round, elegant, complex. Hint of toast and lovely fruit. (17)

FLIGHT #3

1969:

Orangy rim. Evolved colour. Hint of raspberry jam. Full, rich, powerful. Surprisingly spirity, and acidity helped this wine last. Hint of cinnamon on nose. A bit tired. 1964, 1966, and 1962 are better. Somehow, it seems that Domaine de la Romanée-Conti didn't pull it off in 1969. (16.5)

1972:

Lovely, spicy fruity, and toasty nose. Full, lively, good fruit/acidity balance. Bright red colour. These 1972s are turning out to be superb wines, contrary to most experts' predictions (Bordeaux influence?). Lots of life left in it. An excellent bottle. (18)

1976:

More evolved colour than the 1972, orange rim. Ripe, tannic, very 1976. Solid, powerful. A drought year. Has weight, body, and structure, but lacks the fresh fruit, and complexity (and vital acidity) of the 1972. (16.5)

1972 GRANDS ECHÉZEAUX, DOMAINE DE LA ROMANÉE-CONTI:

I served this as a "mystery wine" (all other wines and the order of pouring were known to the participants).

I included this to show how good these 1972s have turned out to be. As with the 1972 La Tâche, bright, youthful red colour. Charred oak, ripe black fruit on nose. Full, solid, well balanced. Great extract and fine fruit. Does not have the layers of complexity of La Tâche, however. Very good nevertheless. (17)

Domaine de la Romanée-Conti's Grands Echézeaux represents the best value in the context of the various Grands Crus produced by this great house.

FLIGHT #4

1971:

Essence of fruit. Deeper colour (and younger) than the previous flights. Spicy raspberry fruit, toasted oak on nose. Full, rich, intense, and long; very concentrated. Still full of life. As a matter of fact, this has so much intensity that it would be difficult for a couple to drink a full bottle of this over dinner, especially if preceded by a glass of Champagne or white wine. This is solid, serious stuff. If well cellared, this wine will last well into the 21st century. (19)

1978:

The other "big gun" of the 1970s decade, and almost too young! Bright red, youthful colour. Great raspberry fruit extract. Full, solid, superbly balanced. Has it all, but not quite ready at 20 years old! Luscious, tight, concentrated. Opened up after one hour in glass. Grand Vin. Drink now to 2010, or beyond. (19)

The great wines at this event (this seemed unanimous), in no particular order were: 1978, 1971, 1972, 1947, 1952, and 1942. We did not taste the 1964 or 1962, also two excellent La Tâches.

The final wine of this memorable tasting was one of my all-time favourite Sauternes.

Château Suduiraut 1959:

Amber-gold colour. Luscious nose of ripe apricots, honey, and botrytis. Full, creamy, long. Fruit, acidity, and extract all in harmony. A noble Sauternes; as good as it gets. (19)

This has been a most successful and educational vertical tasting, confirming both the quality and the staying power of this truly great red Burgundy.

Late July 1998

Also tasted two wines that share a similar commune, a common history, but yet are so different!

Château Pichon-Longueville Baron 1989

and

Château Pichon-Lalande 1989:

The former signalling a great comeback of this superb property, after a quarter-century of mediocrity. Powerful, cedary, rich, masculine, spicy Pauillac/Cabernet wine. Hint of oak. Great fruit extract, and depth. In my opinion, bigger than the 1989 Mouton-Rothschild. Drink from 2004 to 2010, or beyond. An excellent Pauillac.

The latter, so different, so feminine (even more so than usual!). Elegant, ripe, soft, and charming. A pleasure to drink now, but really not a Pauillac! Pichon-Lalande has produced great classics in that blessed decade of the 1980s, notably 1982, 1983, 1986, and 1990. The 1985 and 1989, while charming and a pleasure to drink now, are just below that fine quartet.

August 1998

We are having one of the nicest, sunniest summers in a long while.

1986 Nuits-St.-Georges Premier Cru "Les Roncières," Joseph Drouhin:

Bright red colour. Ripe cherry fruit on nose. Round, generous, well balanced, long. It has excellent depth for a relatively light year. A pleasure to drink now.

Champagne Bollinger "Grande Année" 1985:

Grande Année indeed! All there. The weight, yeasty character, and depth, plus ripe fruit, typical of this house's style, combined with the elegance of the vintage. At its absolute peak. Excellent!

Champagne Veuve Clicquot "Rosé" Reserve 1988:

Salmon pink colour. Lively, fresh, clean fruit combined with the masculine backbone of this fine, long-lasting vintage.

Champagne Louis Roederer "Cristal" 1983:

My last bottle of this fine wine. Still surprisingly lively mousse and tiny, persistent bubbles. Creamy, long, lovely fruit, velvety. One could not ask for a more pleasant sipping Champagne.

1980 Duckhorn Vineyards Cabernet Sauvignon, Napa Valley:

At 18 years, perfection now. Impressive, deep colour to rim. Luscious nose of ripe berries and cedar. Full, round, long mouthful of ripe, well-balanced fruit. Lingering aftertaste. Will not improve, but it has enough depth and ripe fruit to last at this plateau for another decade. A fine wine.

Château Sociando-Mallet 1983:

While technically this is a Haut-Médoc, it is as St. Estèphe-like as one could wish. Serious, masculine Cabernet. Full, solid, still a bit tannic at 15. Lovely fruit extract, black currant and cedar on both nose and palate. Ready, but no rush.

MEURSAULT-PORUZOTS 1986, FRANÇOIS JOBART:

Fully mature, exotic, ripe wine. Brilliant, deep-golden colour. Nose reminiscent of ripe pears, and melon. Full, rich, low acidity, luscious. Almost residual sugar there. Great depth and extract. Has held very well, but will not improve. Needs drinking. An excellent Meursault.

CHÂTEAU MOUTON-ROTHSCHILD 1975:

23 years old and only now reaching its peak. Excellent, deep, maturing colour to rim. Cedary, minty, tobacco nose with hint of dill. Full, solid, excellent tannic backbone, backed by very good, ripe fruit. No rush drinking this "old style" wine. The best Mouton between 1961 and 1982. Those who criticize the 1975 vintage as a whole are missing the opportunity of tasting and experiencing some truly classic Clarets. A serious Pauillac.

1995 KISTLER VINEYARDS CHARDONNAY "DUTTON RANCH," SONOMA VALLEY:

A lovely Chardonnay from a very fine vintage. Bright gold, subdued, understated nose of golden apples, flowers, oak, and vanilla, all in harmony. Well balanced, long. Not ready, of course, but very good potential. Kistler's Chardonnays are becoming very expensive, but the quality is certainly there.

1994 VIADER VINEYARDS, HOWELL MOUNTAIN, NAPA VALLEY:

Deep, inky red colour. Cedary, ripe Cabernet Sauvignon predominates (this wine is made from a blend of approximately 50% Cabernet Sauvignon and 50% Cabernet Franc). Rich, sweet fruit, tannic, luscious, but masculine. Impeccably made. Not ready yet, of course. Drink from 2003 to 2010. Hint of toast and black currant.

1991 DUNN VINEYARDS CABERNET SAUVIGNON, HOWELL MOUNTAIN, NAPA VALLEY:

Deep colour, very little evolution. Rich, clean black fruit. Hint of oak. Very good intensity. Full-bodied and generous. Drink from 2002 to 2010.

CHÂTEAU FIGEAC 1989:

Impeccably made but, like so many 1989s, loosely knit and early maturing. Clean, stemmy, herbaceous fruit. New oak, vanilla, and ripe black fruit in harmony. Approaching its peak. Drink now to 2004. The 1990 has better definition and extract.

1994 PESQUERA "JANUS," RESERVA, RIBERA DEL DUERO, SPAIN:

Produced previously only in 1982, 1986, and 1991. Profound, rich, concentrated fruit. Hint of vanilla and toasted oak. Excellent balance. A serious wine. Not nearly ready. Drink from 2004 to 2015, or beyond.

1982 CORNAS, AUGUST CLAPE, FROM MAGNUM:

16 years old and not quite ready yet! Deep colour to rim. Oriental spices, leather, tar, and ripe black fruit on both nose and palate. Full, rich, great extract. A mouthful of ripe, tannic fruit. Bottles should be drinking well now. Magnums from 2000 and beyond. Clape is a master. Only Noël Verset approaches him in this high standard, 100% Syrah, northern Rhône wine.

CHÂTEAU PETRUS 1971:

Clearly, the best, most successful commune in 1971 was Pomerol, and Petrus is the best 1971 Pomerol, followed closely by Châteaux Trotanoy, and Lafleur-Petrus. Good depth, evolved rim. Ripe, expansive black fruit on nose. Sweet, hint of oak. Generous, rich, but still retains a little tannin. Mouth-filling, luscious. Very long aftertaste, with hint of oriental spices. Ready, but no rush, if well cellared.

CHÂTEAU CLIMENS 1983, BARSAC:

Elegance, class, intensity, structure, botrytis; all there. (Totally different from the other excellent 1983 Rieussec, which is deeper, heavier, more luscious.) Drink from 2000 to 2020. Great Barsac.

September 9, 1998

A Commanderie de Bordeaux Dinner, featuring the 1983 vintage, held at the Pan Pacific hotel. Executive Chef, Ernst Dorfler.

This is a good assessment tasting, last held in 1993, when the wines were 10 years old. Now they are 15 years old, and they should be at or near their peak.

After a fine bottle of Champagne Charles Heidsieck Brut 1990, we proceeded with the tasting (through dinner), in flights.

FLIGHT #1
Graves and Haut-Médocs

1. CHÂTEAU MALARTIC LAGRAVIÈRE 1983:

Mature red colour. Evolved rim. Toasted oak, mature fruit, and earth on nose. Past its prime, but still enjoyable. Early signs of cracking up. Needs drinking. Drier than most, but has character. Somehow lacks fruit. Was better five years ago. (15)

2. CHÂTEAU CANTEMERLE 1983:

Deeper colour, more youthful looking than #1. Elegant, understated, ripe fruit on nose. Lovely mouthful of fruit, still slightly tannic. Very good extract. Not a very complex wine, but certainly at its peak, and showing no signs of declining. Drink now to 2002. However, after 30 minutes, it started to dry up, which is very odd. Storage? (16)

3. 1983 ZINFANDEL (GRAPES FROM PARDUCCI VINEYARDS), CALIFORNIA:

This wine was served double-blind. Similar appearance to #1. Slightly herbaceous, stemmy nose. Generous, slightly tannic. Less complex, less sweet than #2, but has good fruit extract. Drink now to 2004. Later improved and tasted better than #2. This was produced by one of our members in his basement. Fooled us all! (15)

4. CHÂTEAU LA MISSION HAUT-BRION 1983:

Very good, deep colour, orangy rim. Subdued, unyielding nose. Some charred oak. Full, generous, round, rich, yet velvety. Best extract so far. No rush drinking this. Rich, sweet fruit, well balanced and long. Excellent. (18)

5. DOMAINE DE CHEVALIER 1983:

More evolved than #4 in appearance. Vanilla, flowery nose. Different from the others. Less earthy, more open, and forthcoming. Toasted oak, delicate fruit on nose. Elegant, classy, fully mature. Complex, long finish. Most complex of flight. (18)

This flight was served blind with a wine introduced as the ringer (#3). Most participants preferred the La Mission to the Domaine de Chevalier. A matter of taste.

FLIGHT #2
St. Juliens

1. CHÂTEAU LEOVILLE-BARTON 1983:

Most evolved colour of flight. Elegant, herbaceous nose. Leanest of flight on palate. Some fruit, but aggressive acidity. Needs drinking. Will not improve. (16)

This was Ronald Barton's last vintage. From 1985 onward, his nephew, Anthony Barton, took over.

2. CHÂTEAU LEOVILLE-POYFERRÉ 1983:

Delicate, toasty/oaky nose. Good fruit extract. Better balanced than the Leoville-Barton, better depth. Ready, but no rush. Drink now to 2004. Good, ripe tannins. (17)

3. CHÂTEAU SAINT-PIERRE 1983:

Deepest colour of flight. Charred oak and very ripe fruit on nose. Generous, rich, round, velvety, yet with ripe extract and tannins. Best wine of flight. Leathery, spicy black fruit. A relatively inexpensive and fine wine. (17.5)

4. CHÂTEAU TALBOT 1983:

Classic St. Julien. Fruity, slightly herbaceous, generous. Maybe without the complexity of the St. Pierre, but certainly a good St. Julien. Drink now to 2003. Cedar and ripe fruit. (16.5)

FLIGHT #3
Pauillacs and St. Estèphe

1. CHÂTEAU GRAND-PUY-LACOSTE 1983:

Most evolved of flight in appearance, on nose, and on palate. Cedary, classy Cabernet. At its peak. Will not improve. Good all-round Pauillac. (16.5)

2. CHÂTEAU LYNCH-BAGES 1983:

Quite similar in appearance to the Grand-Puy-Lacoste, but slightly richer, livelier fruit, and hint of mint. Also at its peak. Very good, but not up to this property's excellent 1982, 1985, or 1986. (17)

3. CHÂTEAU COS D'ESTOURNEL 1983:

Better than expected. Also at its peak, but slightly more tannic backbone. Well balanced, hint of oak, round. Again, as with Lynch-Bages, the 1982, 1985, and 1986 are superior, but this is most enjoyable for drinking now. (17)

4. CHÂTEAU MOUTON-ROTHSCHILD 1983:

Deepest colour of flight, as expected. Noticeable oak, vanilla, cedar, and black fruit on nose. Tannins are still a bit aggressive. Not quite ready. Drink from 2000 to 2010. Very good potential. (18)

DESSERT WINE

CHÂTEAU RIEUSSEC 1986:

Round, generous, well balanced, clean vanilla, and botrytized fruit on both nose and palate. Without the depth and intensity of the superb 1983, but very good nevertheless. (17.5)

Conclusions

1983 is an underrated vintage, and most châteaux (other than Margaux and Palmer) still represent good value. Château Margaux (not tasted on this occasion, but well known to me) is clearly the wine of the vintage, and the only wine that needs more time to mature. All others are ready. Lesser châteaux are past their prime.

Mid-September 1998

1983 HERMITAGE BLANC, J. L. CHAVE:

15 years old and finally approachable. Rich, exotic fruit. Full-bodied, with excellent ripe fruit extract. Ready, but no rush. I do not know of any producer of white Hermitage who can approach the sheer depth of this producer's wine. During my last visit with Gerard Chave four years ago, I tasted the white Hermitage 1952 and 1959. Both were still excellent.

1967 BAROLO "RISERVA," BORGOGNO:

At over 30 years, this wine is still at its peak. Evolved colour. Fair bit of sediment. Tar, oriental spices on nose, not unlike a big Chambertin, which is what most participants thought it was, but it had this unmistakable, tannic backbone so typical of old-style

Barolos. What a pity that most Piedmontese producers have departed from producing this serious style of wine. Lingering aftertaste. Excellent quality. Will not improve.

CHÂTEAU D'YQUEM 1980:

While this excellent Sauternes does not have the sheer weight and intensity of this property's great 1967, 1975, or 1983, it is an exquisite Sauternes. Vanilla, oak, and botrytis all in harmony on both nose and palate. True breed here. Great class and length. Another underestimated vintage. Drink now to 2008, or beyond. Actually, this is elegant enough to be served at the beginning of a meal, with foie gras or lobster.

September 1998

1989 GEVREY-CHAMBERTIN PREMIER CRU "CAZETIERS," BRUNO CLAIR:

It is interesting to see how similar the 1989 red Burgundies are to red Bordeaux of the same vintage in terms of structure. Fleshy, soft, round, elegant, and relatively early maturing (overproduction?). There are some big wines, such as Rousseau's Chambertin or Château Haut-Brion, but overall, it is a charming, rather than solid vintage. This well-made wine fits the mold. Classy, spicy, black cherries, and hint of oak on nose. Fleshy, round, complex, and spicy on palate. Fairly evolved, not unlike the 1985s at that stage. A pleasure to drink now. Bruno Clair is a reliable winemaker.

1985 JOSEPH PHELPS CABERNET SAUVIGNON "EISELE," NAPA VALLEY:

A reputable producer, a very good vineyard, and an outstanding vintage combine here to produce this excellent Cabernet. Rich, full, hint of cedar, spicy, still a bit tannic (decanted one hour). Mouthfilling, long, and rich. Drink now to 2005.

1983 DUNN VINEYARDS CABERNET SAUVIGNON, HOWELL MOUNTAIN, NAPA:

15 years old and no rush drinking this. Deep colour to rim. Cedar, oak, ripe black fruit in harmony. Still a bit tannic, but backed by very good fruit. Long aftertaste. Randy Dunn in a master of his craft, no doubt. Drink now to 2003.

Visit with Margaret Duckhorn at Duckhorn Vineyards.

They are in the process of building a new winery. They are also starting to offer for sale their Decoy range of wines, notably the Pinot Noir from a recently acquired vineyard in Anderson Valley. I tasted several individual casks (before final blending) of 1996 Merlots and Cabernet Sauvignons:

1996 MERLOT FROM SELBY VINEYARD:

Low yielding, soil compatible to Cabernet Sauvignon. Deep purplish colour. Intense fruit, fairly aggressive and tannic. Will add body and structure to the final blend.

1996 MERLOT, COHN VINEYARD (OFF NIEBAUM LANE):

Blackberry, jammy red fruit. A charming Merlot.

1996 CABERNET SAUVIGNON FROM THE YOUNTVILLE AREA:

Toasty, generous, rich. Fairly tannic. Their experiment with Russian oak has ended. The wine aged in the above casks produced a fairly light, elegant product, but lacking in structure.

1996 MERLOT, NAPA VALLEY (FINAL BLEND):

Made from 75% Merlot, 15% Cabernet Franc, and 10% Cabernet Sauvignon. Presently being released. Full, sweet fruit, generous. Firm tannic backbone at this early stage. Will be very fine by 2004.

1996 PARADUXX:

A Zinfandel-based wine (61% Zinfandel, 1% Petit Verdot, and 38% Cabernets). Fairly dry, tannic, yet relatively evolved colour. Has retained the black fruit character of the Zinfandel grape. For mid-term drinking, say from 2002 to 2005.

I also saw Alice and Joe Heitz briefly when I went to the winery to pick up several bottles of Joe Heitz's recently released 1997 Chardonnay, "Cellar Selection." Joe looks well and is recovering nicely from his stroke.

October 3, 1998

Vertical tasting and dinner, featuring Château d'Yquem 1967 to 1990.

I am the organizer of this event and all the wines are from my cellar. The older vintages (1967, 1971, 1975, and 1976) have been in my cellar since their infancy. This event is being held at the Four Seasons hotel. 18 participants.

APERITIF

CHAMPAGNE LOUIS ROEDERER "BRUT PREMIER" N/V:

As usual, good yeast, fruit, depth, and balance. Very good.

Château d'Yquem 1987 and 1980

1987:

Delicate, flowery, subdued. Vanilla, ripe peaches. Most elegant. Very good length. Subtle. Drink now to 2005. (17)

1980:

More obvious botrytis, richer, excellent acidity. Vanilla, oak. Great effort. Drink now to 2007. (18)

Château d'Yquem 1990, 1989, and 1988

1990:

Bright gold (but slightly paler than the other two). Still fresh, hint of new oak-vanilla. Sweet, round, complex, less "liquoreux," more elegant, but good flavours. Long, complex finish. Needs at least seven more years. Will be a top-notch bottle. (18.5)

1989:

Sweeter, better acidity, better balanced than the 1990. Luscious, complex, fabulous botrytis. Very good. Powerful and more extract rich, long. Drink from 2002 onward. (18.5)

1988:

Leaner, excellent balance, good acidity. All there, but in a more restrained and masculine form. Superb potential. Drink from 2005 onward. (19)

At this stage, the 1989 is the most approachable, the richest, most obvious. Great, luscious botrytis. The 1988 is the raciest, tightest, but with, possibly, the best acidity and balance. The 1990 is not quite together yet, but it is very promising. Difficult flight. All three are very fine wines, indeed.

Château d'Yquem 1986 and 1982

1986:

Made in the same mold as the 1989 and 1990. Rich, luscious, botrytis. Full, generous, but not cloying. Excellent potential, and better than when tasted on previous occasions. (18.5)

1982:

Spicier, greener, less botrytis, but a wine in which the herbaceousness of the Sauvignon Blanc is allowed to express itself. Drink now to 2008. (18)

Château d'Yquem 1970, 1971, and 1976

1970:

Dark-golden colour; top shoulder level. Earthy, mushrooms, slightly oxidized. Has seen better days. (16.5)

1971:

A bit earthy (but not corked). Intense, rich, solid, concentrated, old style. Excellent length, acidity, and balance. However, I have tasted better examples. (17.5)

1976:

Best wine of flight at this event. Rich, luscious. Very good acidity, great concentration, and length. Tonight, clearly the best wine of this flight. Fully mature. (18.5)

1989 CHAMBOLLE-MUSIGNY PREMIER CRU "LES AMOUREUSES," JOSEPH DROUHIN:

The elegance of both the commune and the vintage. Bright, cherry-red colour. Clean, expansive, fruity nose. Round, silky, elegant on palate. Most stylish. Good fruit and clean, long finish. Drink now to 2003. (17.5) This was served with the meat course.

CHÂTEAU D'YQUEM 1983, 1975, AND 1967:

These are the three "big guns" of Château d'Yquem in the decades of the 1960s, 1970s, and 1980s, and it showed. I doubt that even the string of excellent vintages of the late 1980s will match the sheer extract, intensity, and size of these three masterpieces.

1983:

Bright golden colour. Fabulous nose of nectar of peaches, vanilla, oak, and botrytis, all in harmony. Full, but not cloying on palate. Great, ripe fruit extract, backed by excellent acidity. A brooding giant. Will live for at least another two decades or more. Drink from 2003 onward. Fabulous. (19.5)

1975:

Surprisingly, colour is only very slightly darker than the magnificent 1983. More subdued on nose, more restrained on palate, but it is all there! Great extract. Lovely, thanks to superb acidity balance, a trademark of the 1975 Sauternes vintage (while the 1976s are fatter, softer, and more forward). Superb fruit and length. Over 20 years old and decades ahead of it. Drink until 2025, or beyond, if well cellared. (19.5)

1967:

I have cellared this wine since 1975, and have had the good fortune of tasting it on at least two dozen occasions to date. Perfect neck level. Bright, deep gold, not quite amber yet. Far livelier and fresher than when tasted in the past from other cellars. Essence of Sauternes! Luscious, rich botrytis, ripe apricot jam. Superb balance, and enough acidity to last for at least another decade at its peak. A masterpiece. (20) (Perfect Score). Fully mature, or course, but, at least as far as "my" 1967 d'Yquems are concerned, no rush drinking it.

Overall impressions

No doubt d'Yquem is a great work of art. The wines are all excellent, and the best are sheer nectar. There is a clear change in style of winemaking here. While the younger vintages (1990, 1989, 1988, and 1986) are all excellent in their own way, they are more approachable, less masculine than the great 1983, 1975, or 1967. Only time will tell if the younger vintages will last as well, for as long.

Chef Doug Anderson (formerly of the Four Seasons hotel in Chicago) produced an imaginative, exquisite meal to accompany these great wines. Not an easy task, I assure you! A memorable evening.

Mid-October 1998

1997 BURROWING OWL VINEYARDS, OKANAGAN VALLEY, OLIVER, BRITISH COLUMBIA, CANADA:

Both Pinot Gris and Chardonnay tasted. The Pinot Gris is flowery, clean, crisp, and fruity. Pale golden colour. Correct wine, but not much complexity at this early stage. The Chardonnay is slightly deeper gold. Hint of oak and golden apples on both nose and palate. Better definition, complexity, and style than the Pinot Gris, but, again, a bit too young. Not a bad effort at all.

CHÂTEAU MARGAUX 1981:

Decanted one-and-one-half hours. Impressive, deep garnet colour to rim. Cedar, black fruit, slightly stemmy on nose. Very long. Full, complex on palate. Tannins clearly are softening up, but still has excellent fruit extract. At 17, no rush drinking it. Clearly, the best 1981 Claret. Top quality. (18.5)

October 1998

Club Pol Roger, Chevaliers du Tastevin, and Commanderie de Bordeaux combined Gala Dinner, with the participation of Christian Pol Roger.

I learned tonight from Christian that Château Cos d'Estournel has been sold by the Prats family. This was one of the last of the top Haut-Médoc properties that was still family run. Usually, succession duties and family feuds spell the end of many dynasties.

CHAMPAGNE POL ROGER 1988, "CUVÉE SIR WINSTON CHURCHILL:"

Produced predominantly from the Pinot Noir grape, this is an excellent, long-lived Champagne. Solid backbone; very good, yet restrained fruit. Clean, layers of complexity, toast, and yeast. No rush drinking it. As time goes by, it seems that the lovely, elegant, and generous 1989s, and the very ripe, rich 1990s will ultimately be outlived, and maybe outperformed, by the masculine, serious 1988s.

October 1998

Dinner with friends.

CHAMPAGNE KRUG 1985:

A beautifully crafted, exquisite Champagne that is unusually charming and forward for Krug. The 1982 is richer and the 1979 steelier and tighter. All three are top class.

1990 CORTON-CHARLEMAGNE, FAIVELEY:

While still dominated by new oak, this is a luscious, rich, slow-maturing, serious Grand Cru white Burgundy. Layers of fruit, roasted almonds, and hint of minerals. Very good. Drink now to 2005.

1982, 1985, AND 1990 TIGNANELLO, ANTINORI:

If this "super Tuscan" property's wines from the 1970s were more rustic, the vintages of the 1980s are more generous, rounder, and more approachable.

The 1982 is fully mature now. Fairly evolved colour. Spicy nose of ripe cherries, straw, and hint of oak. Generous, round, with good, fruity aftertaste. (17.5)

The 1985 has a brighter red colour, fresher, maybe slightly less solid, but more generous. Excellent. Drink now to 2004. (18)

The 1990 has a deep, dark colour to rim. Ripe black fruit and oak on nose. Full-bodied, spicy fruit. Try around 2002 to 2008. A lovely wine. (18)

CHÂTEAU RIEUSSEC 1988:

Brilliant golden colour. Butter, oak, botrytis, and ripe peaches on nose. Full, generous fruit backed by good acidity. Drink now to 2008.

October 1998

Dinner at the gifted Chef Robert Feenie's "Lumière" restaurant, with Sam and Joan Fromowitz, and Marie-José Aubin.

I brought the following wines along, and I let Robert taste them all. He is becoming very interested in wine.

1989 CORTON-CHARLEMAGNE, MALDANT:

A good Chardonnay, but in the context of the vintage, and being a Grand Cru, a bit disappointing. First, excessive sulphur (it dissipated a bit, but not by much). Straightforward, clean fruit, but without the extract, ripeness, and nutty overtones. A good "Villages" Chassagne, at best.

1975 CUVAISON CABERNET SAUVIGNON "SIGNATURE," NAPA VALLEY:

A rare, limited production made by the then winemaker at Cuvaison, Phillip Togni (who now operates his own winery). Many years ago, Togni told me that this wine would last 20 years. He was right. At 23 years old, still impressively deep, and dark to rim. Cedary, minty nose with ripe, rich black fruit. Still full, even a bit tannic. Excellent extract and depth. Decanted one hour. Drink now to 2005, if you can find it.

CHÂTEAU LA MISSION HAUT-BRION 1981:

Total contrast to the Cuvaison. If the Cuvaison has the classic, old style, briary California fruit, the La Mission has the elegance and class of fine Claret. Fairly evolved colour and fully mature at 16. Complex, elegant, spicy Cabernet nose. Velvety, smooth, and round on palate.

Great complexity and long aftertaste. A pleasure to drink now, while it is still at its peak.

Late October 1998

1980 CHALONE PINOT BLANC, CALIFORNIA:

Approximately 500 cases produced. Years ago, Joe Heitz told me that good Pinot Blanc needs at least a decade or more to show its true character and class. This advice proved itself with this excellent 18-year-old wine. Deep, brilliant golden colour. Displaying the character of fine old white Hermitage with exotic fruit, melon, Bartlett pear, and honey on both nose and palate, backed by good acidity, and depth. Lingering aftertaste. This wine would fool any expert at a blind tasting. Most impressive.

Early November 1998

GRAHAM'S 1985 VINTAGE PORT:

When this Port was barely declared, back in 1987, Harry Waugh told me that this was probably the Port of the Vintage. How glad I am to have listened to him, and purchased several cases of this. Very deep colour to rim. Still too young, of course, but already displaying the typical Graham's richness and sweetness. Full, tarry, great extract. Drink from 2003 until 2025, or beyond.

1965 AND 1968 VEGA SICILIA "UNICO," RIBERA DEL DUERO, SPAIN:

Two very poor vintages all over Europe, with very few exceptions, yet these two wines are excellent, especially the 1968.

1965: Impressive, youthful colour, evolved at rim. Tobacco and leather on nose. Still fairly full, but a lot of class and elegance, too. Perfect drinking now.

1968: Approaches my favourite (the 1962) in its class and elegance. Rich, smoky, less evolved than either the 1965 or the 1962. Amazingly youthful at 30 years! Very long, great balance, extract, and depth. A combination of 1966 Palmer and 1982 Lafite. No rush!

Mid-November 1998

Short trip to Yountville, Napa Valley.

Meeting at Stag's Leap Wine Cellars with the owner, Warren Winiarski, Barney and Belle Rhodes, and Caryl Saunders for a photo session and discussions about the "Napa 2000" events to be held in the Napa Valley in May 2000, for the International Wine and Food Society's Convention, which is held every three years. I have contacted Christian Moueix and he has agreed to organize a vertical of Dominus as part of the convention events. We will probably cohost this event.

Warren gave us each a slice of a gigantic mushroom (the size of a basketball), called Hericium Crinaceus. It means "lion's mane," and it grows on a tree at the winery (one mushroom per year). From there we drove to the restaurant "Pinot Blanc" in St. Helena, owned by Joachim Spichal, the chef/owner of "Patina" in Los Angeles. We tried a bottle of this wine.

1995 HARRISON ESTATE CHARDONNAY "UNFILTERED," NAPA VALLEY:

A big, luscious, rich Chardonnay. Fruity, generous, subdued oak, and fairly high alcohol. Its only fault is noticeably low acidity. Most pleasant drinking now, but in two to three years, as the fruit softens, there is a danger that the low acidity will result in the wine oxidizing, and declining fast.

I chose the red wine, which was served double-blind.

1995 FORMAN CABERNET SAUVIGNON, NAPA VALLEY:

A food wine, rather than a show wine. Bright red. Cedar, oak, and clean fruit on nose. Still tannic, but not aggressive. Well balanced, long, elegant rather than chewy, or beefy. Lots of class and length. Ric Forman has produced an excellent wine here. Oddly, when Barney tasted it, he said: "this is not a Cabernet." To me it was very obvious, but then I knew what the wine was.

November 1998

CHÂTEAU TROTANOY 1964:

At 35, a superb Pomerol! As good as (if not better than) the 1964 Petrus. Excellent, deep colour, mature rim. Truffles, chocolate, and iron on nose. A mouthful of luscious, rich, generous, velvety fruit. Very well balanced, soft, lingering aftertaste. After 45 minutes, it started to become a bit astringent. A great experience.

December 1998

1990 CHIANTI CLASSICO "RISERVA," TENUTA DI VERRAZZANO:

An excellent Chianti from a great vintage and a reliable producer. Deep garnet colour to rim. Ripe cherries on nose. Full, rich, yet elegant, and smooth on palate. Perfect drinking now. How good 1990 has turned out to be in Italy!

1987 ROMANÉE-ST.-VIVANT, DOMAINE DE LA ROMANÉE-CONTI:

It seems that 1987 red Burgundies suffer from the same stigma that the 1972 red Burgundies suffered from when the media (and consumers) neglected to acquire them because of the poor reputation of both vintages in Bordeaux. As with many 1972s, the 1987 red Burgundies are turning out to be very good wines, indeed. This 1987 is excellent drinking now and, at least until 2004. Bright, cherry-red colour to rim Toasted oak and spicy Pinot Noir on nose with very slight hint of dill. Medium-bodied, good fruit/acidity balance, and layers of complexity and length. Very good indeed.

1998 has seen the passing of two great wine makers and leading figures in the Bordeaux wine scene. Earlier this year, our dear friend, Peter A. Sichel (d'Angludet and Palmer) passed away. As we approach the end of this year, Jean-Eugene Borie (Château Ducru-Beaucaillou, et al) has also passed away. Jean-Eugene presided over Ducru for almost five decades, and produced superb wines. In his case, it is the man, not the soil, that has made the difference. He shall be sorely missed.

Mid-December 1998

1978 MAS DE DAUMAS GASSAC:

Their first vintage, made exclusively from Cabernet Sauvignon grapes. At 20 years old, this wine is still amazingly youthful. Very deep colour to rim. Fair bit of sediment. Decanted one hour. Full, generous, youthful, slightly leathery, but backed by excellent fruit on palate. Long and spicy. The tannins have softened quite a bit since I last tasted this almost a decade ago. A great inaugural effort.

1969 HEITZ CELLARS "MARTHA'S VINEYARD" CABERNET SAUVIGNON, NAPA VALLEY:

Impressive colour, mature rim. Unmistakable eucalyptus, spicy, evolved nose. Still has excellent fruit and good backbone. Some dryness at finish. Among the older vintages, this is Joe Heitz's favourite. Those were difficult financial times for Joe. He had to sell a portion of the 1969 "Martha's Vineyard" as a blend with regular Napa Cabernet (Lot C-91), and some to Spring Mountain as a blend, to satisfy his bankers.

Chanukah Dinner, with family and friends.

A glass of the always-reliable Champagne Louis Roederer "Brut Premier" N/V, was followed by this.

1989 HERMITAGE BLANC, "CHEVALIER DE STERIMBERG," JABOULET:

Still surprisingly youthful colour for a nine-year-old. Ripe pears and spices on nose. Full, generous, rich, well balanced. Very long, fruity aftertaste. While enjoyable now, this will last for many more years, if well cellared.

1957 VOLNAY PREMIER CRU "CLOS DES DUCS," MARQUIS D'ANGERVILLE:

Ullage two inches. Very pale, almost Rosé colour. Very mature, but unmistakable spicy Pinot Noir on nose. Soft, old-tasting but the acidity (typical of both red Bordeaux and red Burgundies in 1957), is what kept this wine alive for this long. After 20 minutes in glass, it fell apart. Well past its prime, but still enjoyable.

1966 HERMITAGE "LA SIZERANNE," CHAPOUTIER:

One of the last good vintages from this venerable house until the advent of a new generation of owners/winemakers in the early 1990s. Impressive, deep colour, mature rim. Leathery, spicy, rich, sweet nose. Similar impressions on palate. Full, long, and generous. Very slight hint of oxidation (barely noticeable). Fair bit of sediment. Very good, but needs drinking.

CHÂTEAU MOUTON-ROTHSCHILD 1959:

Ullage upper shoulder. The ullage worried me, needlessly. The great, deep, dense colour so typical of the best 1959s. Luscious, chocolaty, cedary nose. Full, fat, round, generous on palate. Still full of life. A great wine.

CHÂTEAU CLIMENS 1976, BARSAC:

The best Barsac year in and year out, and behaving like one! Surprisingly pale, youthful, golden colour for a 22-year-old. Lovely, peachy, botrytized fruit on nose. Full, rich, but not cloying on palate. Excellent acidity and backbone. This will easily last well until 2010, or beyond. (The 1949 is still superb!)

A most enjoyable evening.

December 1998

Oh my! Another oxidized bottle of this Champagne.

1988 CORTON-CHARLEMAGNE, TOLLOT-BEAUT:

I have always had great bottles of Corton-Charlemagne from this producer. The 1988 seems the exception. I wonder why?

Dr. Barney Rhodes, owner of "Bella Oaks" Vineyard in the Napa Valley, had a stroke earlier this month. It seems that it was quite a serious stroke. I hope that he will recover soon. I last saw Barney in the Napa Valley for lunch last month. Harry Waugh, on the other hand, who is now 95 years old, is doing just fine. As a matter of fact, he hopes to give his daughter, Harriet, away next spring, when she gets married. Harriet and her twin brother Jamie are 25 years old!

Mid-to-Late December 1998

1979 DUNN VINEYARDS CABERNET SAUVIGNON, HOWELL MOUNTAIN:

Randy Dunn's first release, and a wine that I purchased several bottles of in Carmel, California, for $18 per bottle, back in 1983. Now a collector's item. 19 years old and fully mature. Cedary, ripe Cabernet nose with hint of stemminess. Generous on palate;

soft, round tannins, backed by very good fruit. Ready, but no rush, if well cellared. A fine first effort.

CHÂTEAU RAUSAN-SÉGLA 1995:

How nice to see a once-great property back in form. After almost four decades of producing uninspiring wines, this property has turned around with a fine effort in 1986. This 1995 is true to the vintage and to the elegance of the commune of Margaux. Bright, cherry-red colour to rim. Oak, vanilla, ripe red fruit, all in harmony on both nose and palate. Quite rich and full, but the tannins are soft. A charmer. Drink from 2003.

1985 RICHEBOURG, DOMAINE DE LA ROMANÉE-CONTI:

An absolutely great Richebourg! The charm of the lovely 1985 vintage is there, all right, but oh! The depth and extract! Black fruit, intense nose, with hint of charred oak, and oriental spices. Truffles, too. Great length and extract on palate. While already approachable, this will be sensational over the next 25 years. Très Grand Vin!

CHÂTEAU LATOUR 1970:

Jean-Paul Gardère, the old régisseur of Château Latour described this wine a decade ago, during one of my many visits to Latour, as a "Charles de Gaulle" of a wine. It still is! Almost three decades old, and not ready yet! It should be noted that all my bottles of this wine were acquired in the mid-to-late 1970s, have excellent levels well into neck, and have spent their life at a perfect, constant 52°F. Inky red colour to rim. Essence of spicy, cedary Cabernet. Still tannic, very ripe, very big. Luscious. Magnificent. Every serious student of wines should taste a good sample of this wine at least once in his or her lifetime. Drink from 2005 to 2025. Superb Claret.

I doubt that anyone in Bordeaux, including Château Latour, is capable of reproducing this magnificent nectar nowadays. According to modern palates, used to charming, sweet, Merlot-loaded, and super-extraction wines, this wine would probably have rated only 88 to 90 points in its youth, when it was tight, aggressive, and totally charmless—the texture of a green banana.

December 1998

A vertical tasting of the greatest Graham's Vintage Ports of the Post-WW II Era.

1985:

Classic Graham's. Deep, ruby colour, youthful at rim. Sweet, ripe, spicy fruit on both nose and palate. Not as tight as expected, but great fruit extract. Lingering aftertaste. Not quite ready. Drink from 2005. (18)

1977:

Eight years older than the above and not just more mature, but more masculine. Less elegance than the 1985, more solid, tannic, but it has the trademark sweet fruit and extract so typical of this property. Can be enjoyed now (decant at least five hours before serving), but should peak around 2004. Drink until 2020, or beyond. (18.5)

Unfortunately, we did not taste the excellent 1966 on this occasion.

1963:

Deep colour, mature-looking. Dense, sweet, generous. Velvety, but this is misleading, because there is a lot of depth and ripe fruit extract here. Fully mature, but no rush. Oriental spices, lingering aftertaste. Drink now to 2010. A superb Port. (19)

1945:

The three Ports tasted above are great wines by any yardstick. The 1945 towered over them all. Sensational black colour to rim. Ripe black fruit jam on both nose and palate. Very rich, sweet, very intense. Aftertaste went on forever. As luscious as one could possibly hope. Superb. Drink now to 2020, or beyond! A truly great Port. (19.5)

December 1998

1976 TOKAI ASZÚ ESSENCIA, MONIMPEX, HUNGARY:

In traditional 500 mL bottle. Amber, deep golden colour. Lovely nose of ripe apricots, raisings, and hint of oxidation (quite natural). Sweet, rich, but not cloying, backed by very good acidity. This is an historic wine. The last Aszú Essencia before the fall of communism in Hungary. Both the 1983 and 1988 vintages were already handled and bottled by free entrepreneurs, both Hungarian and foreign.

A small vertical tasting of Château Cos d'Estournel 1985, 1986, and 1989

This famous property has recently been sold. How sad to see so many great Bordeaux châteaux being sold by traditional families with lengthy Bordeaux roots to outsiders and to megacorporations. The French government must do something very soon to change the laws of inheritance or else most of the great properties will end up as "portfolio holdings" of corporations! Cos, Leoville-Lascases, Leoville-Barton, and Gruaud-Larose all produced superb "twin" vintages in 1985 and 1986. (One should include Pichon-Lalande but, while the 1986 is superb, I have found the 1985 a bit too feminine, and more diluted than it should be. It is a lovely wine for drinking now nevertheless.)

Back to Cos d'Estournel

1985:

Approaching its peak, but still deep, dark, with great, cedary bouquet. Hint of new oak. Full, round, generous. Ripe tannins and fruit in harmony. Has the elegance of this fine, but velvety, vintage, yet the ripe fruit extract is there. Superb wine. Drink now to 2005, or beyond. (18)

1986:

A brooding giant, but it is all there! A serious St. Estèphe. Very deep colour to rim. Cedar, oak, and Cassis fruit on nose. Still a bit tight. Solid tannins, true St. Estèphe. Very big, chewy, ripe. Great intensity. Grand Vin! Drink from 2004, or beyond. (18.5)

1989:

As is so often the case with the 1989s, elegant, supple, but a bit too loosely knit. A very nice wine for the mid-term, but doesn't even have the extract of the "elegant" 1985. Most enjoyable, but too much Merlot (especially for a St. Estèphe), and maybe too much wine produced for its own good. The great 1989 Left Bank wines still seem to be the "Graves twins" (Haut-Brion and La Mission), as well as Palmer, Pichon-Baron, Montrose, and Leoville-Lascases. The other leading châteaux could have been great, if only they had produced less wine! (17)

Diary 18

The Performance of Selected Châteaux of Bordeaux

In the second half of the 20th century, based on the personal experience of the author

Several of the leading châteaux of Bordeaux have had ups and downs over the decades. Some more so than others. One of the properties that has had a noticeable gap in the quality of its wines is Château Margaux, between 1962 and 1977, a time when the Ginestet family went through hardships, and few financial resources were available until the advent, in late 1977, of the Mentzelopoulos family, at which time Margaux was turned around in a dramatic fashion.

More puzzling has been the performance at Château Lafite. Before 1962, they bottled by cask at Lafite, rather than producing an assemblage. This created inconsistencies. Overall, however, Lafite produced good wines in the early part of the century without ever achieving the heights of the 1870s (the prephylloxera era). In modern times, Lafite had a very noticeable "down" period, between 1963 and 1975. From 1976 onward, there has been a clear improvement in the quality, with the 1976 itself being possibly the best Claret of the vintage. Before that time, their "Twin Peaks" were the 1953 and 1959. The 1945 has been variable, mostly disappointing, and weak, with only one exception; this is also true of the 1961.

Another property that used to make reliable wines in the earlier part of this century, until and up to 1966, is Château Cantemerle, which produced very little in terms of quality, between 1967 and 1982. I am pleased to see, however, that from 1983 onward, Château Cantemerle has been producing fine wines once again.

Yet another very reliable and reasonably priced property in the Médoc has been Château Pontet-Canet, a property that produced superb wines under the stewardship of the Cruse family; however, just before and during the period of "Wine-Gate," the oil crisis, and the wine bust of 1973, Pontet-Canet went downhill dramatically. From 1986 onward, and notably from 1989 and 1990, this property is back to its former high-quality standards.

The same is true of Château Pichon-Baron, the great Pauillac Second Growth that produced superb wines in the 1940s and 1950s and 1961, but which underperformed from the early 1960s until 1988. After the purchase of the property by the AXA insurance group—and under the winemaking stewardship of Jean-Michel Cazes, owner of Château Lynch-Bages—fundamental changes have occurred there for the better.

Château Ausone, the great Premier Grand Cru "A" of St. Emilion, was, and still remains, an intellectual's wine. Even that property, however, which produced superb long-lived wines in the 19th century and early 20th century, went through a weak period from the late 1920s until 1975. In 1976, the gifted young winemaker Pascal Delbeck took over, and the change was dramatic—if not to the liking of wine guru Robert Parker Jr.

Château Calon-Ségur is another property that produced great wines in the earlier part of the century, including a superb 1928, and great wines at the end of World War II—notably the 1945, 1949, and the magnificent 1947. The potential there is great; the dedication of the present owners, however, has not always matched the quality of the early post-War era. Two good vintages of this property are the 1975 (better than Cos d'Estournel) and the 1982 (better than Montrose).

Château Rausan-Ségla, which produced memorable wines in the early part of the century, has gone through a very long period, of almost five decades, in which its wines have been noticeably lower in quality than its high ranking as a Second Growth might indicate. I am pleased to say, however, that from 1986 onward, this property has started to produce excellent wines once again.

Château Cos d'Estournel, which of course was connected to the Ginestet family, owners of the famed Château Margaux, has gone through the same hardships as Château Margaux, and the property's destiny has been parallel—with one difference: in 1977, Château Margaux was purchased by an "outsider" (Mentzelopoulos), while Bruno Prats took over at Cos. Bruno's mother is a Ginestet.

Château Leoville-Barton, under the stewardship of the late Ronald Barton, produced rather lean and uninspiring wines, although the 1945 and the superb 1959 are exceptions. Very little was made there in terms of quality until Ronald's nephew, Anthony Barton, took over in the mid-1980s, and turned this property around. Once again, Leoville-Barton is at the very top-rank of the St. Juliens.

Château Leoville-Poyferré has probably had one of the longest periods of underachieving. After the great 1929, very little quality was produced here, even in great years such as 1945, 1959, or 1961; however, from 1982, and notably from 1983 onward, this property is producing excellent wines once again.

Great wine properties that have had minor hiccups include Château Latour, between 1979 and 1985; and Château Lynch-Bages, between 1971 and 1981 (with the exception of the fine 1975). Château Figeac, which produced great wines in the 1940s, 1950s, and 1960s, experienced a short drought from 1976 through 1981, and then, after producing an extraordinary wine in 1982, was rather lukewarm until the advent of the superb 1989 and 1990 vintages.

Château Gruaud-Larose has been a consistent château over the decades—actually going back to 1865, the oldest vintage of this wine that I have had the pleasure and the good fortune of tasting. Even there, after a magnificent 1966, little was produced to match the quality of that property's earlier vintages, until the advent of the early 1980s; the 1981, 1982, 1983, 1985, and 1986 are all superb wines. This property stands firmly rooted in the ranks of the "Super Seconds."

Château Montrose, which again has been consistent for many years, was less so between 1978 and 1985—but this is a very short period of underachievement for a property of such reputation, one that has delivered so many great wines over the decades.

The great Château Petrus has had its own share of problems, but again, only for a short spell, from 1972 through 1981—the exception being a very good 1975, but even that vintage was certainly not in the class of that property's great 1970 or 1982.

The property that has been puzzling me through all my years of tastings is Château Mouton-Rothschild. This property has been behaving like a great actor, but one who is very temperamental—Dr. Jekyll and Mr. Hyde, if you like. What makes it really odd is that it has been under the same management—both in terms of ownership (under the stewardship of the late Baron Philippe) and the winemaker (Raoul Blondin, the late winemaker of that property for almost 50 years)—yet it has produced many mediocre vintages, with the odd great peaks, over the years. Very little was produced at Mouton in terms of quality after 1962—with a good but not great 1970, a good but not great 1975, and nothing else until 1982. So really, from 1961 through 1982, little was produced there in terms of memorable wines.

Wines just starting to turn the corner after many decades of underachieving are Château Rausan-Gassies in Margaux, Clos Fourtet in St. Emilion, and Lynch Moussas in Pauillac.

Château Ducru-Beaucaillou has been consistent in terms of quality, with a fine 1959, and notably, wines produced from 1961 onward. This property made superb wines—with a very short spell of lower quality—rather than "Super Second" class, from 1984 through 1989.

Properties that have given me great pleasure over the years, with very few disappointing vintages, have been Domaine de Chevalier, and notably Château La Mission Haut-Brion, in the Graves district. The great Château Palmer, which was doing well during the period when Château Margaux was underperforming, has been making excellent wines from 1959 to date—regardless of what some experts who enjoy hefty wines may think and say of more recent vintages. Château Grand-Puy-Lacoste has given me a lot of pleasure over the years. This is also true of Château Climens, a great Barsac property that has been producing magnificent wines since the early 1920s.

Late-December 1998

A tasting of four producers' 1995 Corton Charlemagnes.

BONNEAU DU MARTRAY:

The roundest, most forward, most elegant of the flight. Bright, yellow-gold. Toast, oak, vanilla, and elegant fruit on nose. Similar impressions on palate. Round, soft, medium acidity, but good, ripe fruit. A charmer. Drink from 2000 to 2003. (18)

TOLLOT-BEAUT:

Green-gold. Tight, herbaceous, oak, and green apples on nose. Some toast, too. Most backward, fairly high acidity, but good, tight fruit behind. The least evolved. Very good potential. Only four or five barrels (100 to 125 cases) produced. Needs at least five more years to reach maturity. (18)

REMOISSENET "DIAMOND JUBILEE":

Bright yellow-gold. Brilliant colour with touch of green. Toasted almonds, slightly vegetal nose. Good oak, too. Fruity, intense, excellent backbone. No rush; try around 2002 to 2004. Very long, flavourful aftertaste. (18.5)

LOUIS LATOUR "COMTES DE GRANCEY":

The fattest, richest of the lot. Very different, rich, luscious. Great ripe fruit extract. Generous, well balanced, long, ripe fruit, and almonds aftertaste. Drink from 2001. A lovely bottle. (18.5)

All four are excellent Chardonnays. Very different in style, but all express the individual characters of the respective producers, combined with the generosity and elegance of the 1995 vintage.

December 1998

Trip to Los Angeles. Dinner at the residence of Dr. Brad Klein.

CHAMPAGNE HEIDSIECK MONOPOLE 1989 "DIAMANT BLEU," IN MAGNUM:

An elegant, fruity, rich, and creamy Champagne. However, it was surprisingly sweet, almost "extra dry," rather than "Brut." A pleasant sipping Champagne.

PULIGNY MONTRACHET 1994 PREMIER CRU "FOLATIÈRES," PAUL PERNOT:

Palish gold. Toast, oak, and green apples, as well as minerals. Fairly tight, leaner style, 1994 not being particularly generous in Burgundy. Clean, fresh finish. Drink from now to 2002. This was followed by two Second Growth St. Juliens, both of the 1966 vintage, and both from magnums.

CHÂTEAU GRUAUD-LAROSE 1966:

Clearly the freshest, most youthful, and brightest of the two. Not unlike a ten-year-old fine Claret, rather than a 32-year-old. It was a bit one-dimensional with a fairly straightforward finish, however. Regular bottles tasted at home over the past decade were much finer.

CHÂTEAU LEOVILLE-BARTON 1966:

Much more evolved colour, orangy rim, showing its age. Hint of charred oak. Very complex, cedary, even chocolaty nose. Soft, round, silky, and elegant on palate. On this occasion, definitely the more complex and elegant of the two.

EITELSBACHER KARTHAÜLER HOFBERGER (WACHSTUM) 1959 RIESLING BEERENAUSLESE, HANS WILHELM RAUENSTRAUCH (MOSEL-SAAR-RUHR):

Amber-gold colour. Spicy, rich botrytis, and apricot jam on nose. Excellent fruit/acidity balance. Still full of life at almost 40 years old! Very long, classic Riesling/petroleum nose. Luscious, concentrated, lingering aftertaste. Top quality, and from a marvellous vintage in the Mosel.

SANDEMAN'S 1945 VINTAGE PORT:

The last wine of the evening, and my birth year. Far better than expected. Evolved colour. Lovely scented nose of spicy, mature fruit. Velvety, forward on palate, but still all there. Sweet, delicate fruit, and complex, long finish. Most enjoyable.

Late-December 1998

Dinner at "Chinois" restaurant, in Los Angeles, with my daughter Orly, Brad Klein, and Marie-José.

CHÂTEAU LAVILLE-HAUT-BRION 1978:

Incredibly youthful, bright-golden colour. Toast, oak, vanilla, and ripe pears on nose. Mouth-filling, still full of life at 20. Lingering aftertaste. An excellent wine.

CHÂTEAUNEUF-DU-PAPE 1978, DOMAINE DU VIEUX TÉLÉGRAPHE:

How great these 1978 Rhône wines are! Deep, dense colour to rim. Oriental spices and very ripe, black fruit on nose. Mouth-filling, rich, long. Great concentration of fruit. Enjoyable now, but should last at its peak for another decade, or even longer.

Dinner at "Spago's," in Los Angeles, the following night.

The Montrachet and the d'Yquem were my contribution. The reds were Dr. Brad Klein's bottles.

1992: *La Tâche . . . toujours La Tâche! With Ian Mottershead, who would succeed me in 1997 as Maître of the Commanderie de Bordeaux.*

February 1992: Concentrating at a Cheval-Blanc 1934 to 1982 tasting, in Vancouver.

1992: New inductees into the Commanderie de Bordeaux. L to R: Pierre Doise, the author, Kostie Killas, Bernard Ledun, French Consul General to Vancouver, and Dr. David McLean.

1992: After receiving Ordre du Mérite Agricole. With Menashe Arbel (L) and Bernard Ledun, French Consul General to Vancouver.

Golden Treasures from 1945.

February 1993: Being awarded title of Conseiller du Vin de Bordeaux. L to R: Albert Givton, Maître, Commanderie de Bordeaux à Vancouver; Jacques Hebrard, Château Cheval-Blanc; Francis Fouquet, Grand Maître, GCB.

1993: Migniardises at a Gala dinner for the Commanderie de Bordeaux, Four Seasons hotel, Vancouver.

March 1994: IW&FS trip to South Africa. Enjoying the only non-South African wine of whole trip, Veuve Clicquot. L to R: The Bernhards, Dr. Stan Schwartz, the author, Caryl Saunders, and Helene Schwartz.

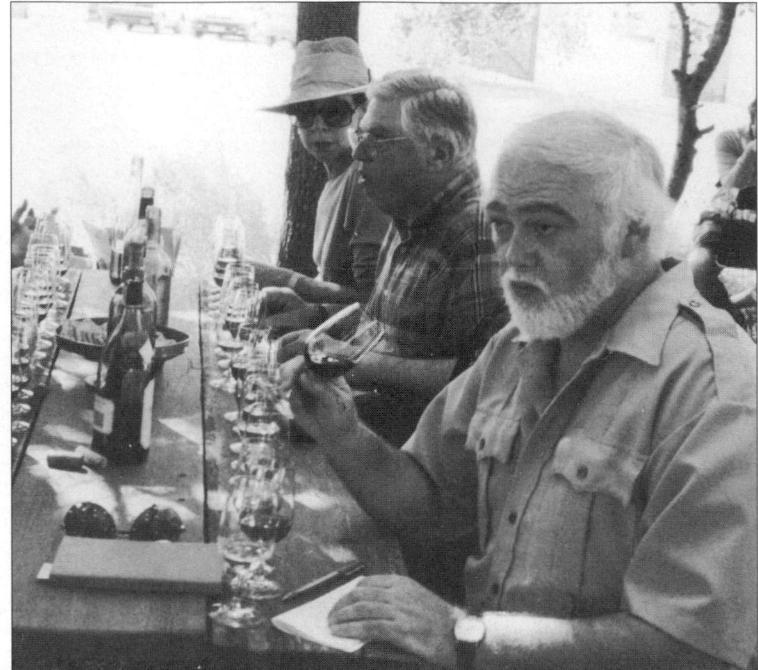

1994: Tasting in the garden of a winery, Stellenbosch, South Africa.

1996: Last induction by Maître Albert Givton before stepping down. L to R: John Withers, Marcena Croy, the author, Dr. Alvin Nirnberg, and Dr. Nathan Maltz.

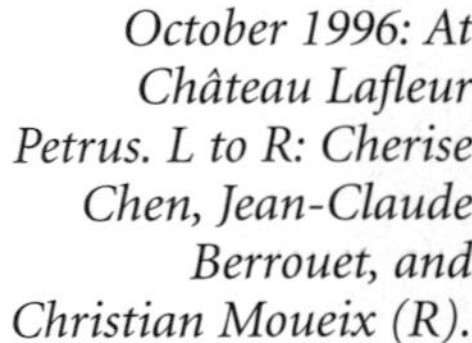

October 1996: At Château Lafleur Petrus. L to R: Cherise Chen, Jean-Claude Berrouet, and Christian Moueix (R).

October 1996: Fermentation vats at Château Petrus.

October 1996: Fermentation vats at Vieux Château Certan. "1982–a threatening vintage!" In October 1982, overcome by fermentation fumes, I almost met my end there!

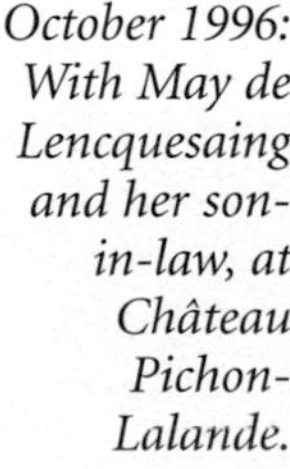

October 1996: With May de Lencquesaing and her son-in-law, at Château Pichon-Lalande.

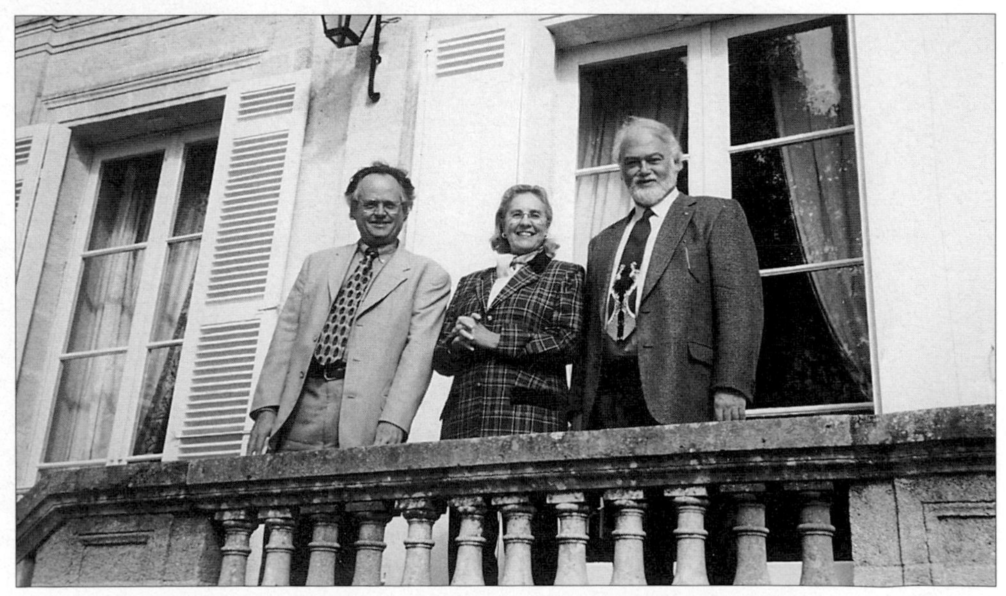

October 1996: Château Latour, Pauillac.

October 1996: With Laure d'Aramon, in the vineyard of Château Figeac, St. Emilion.

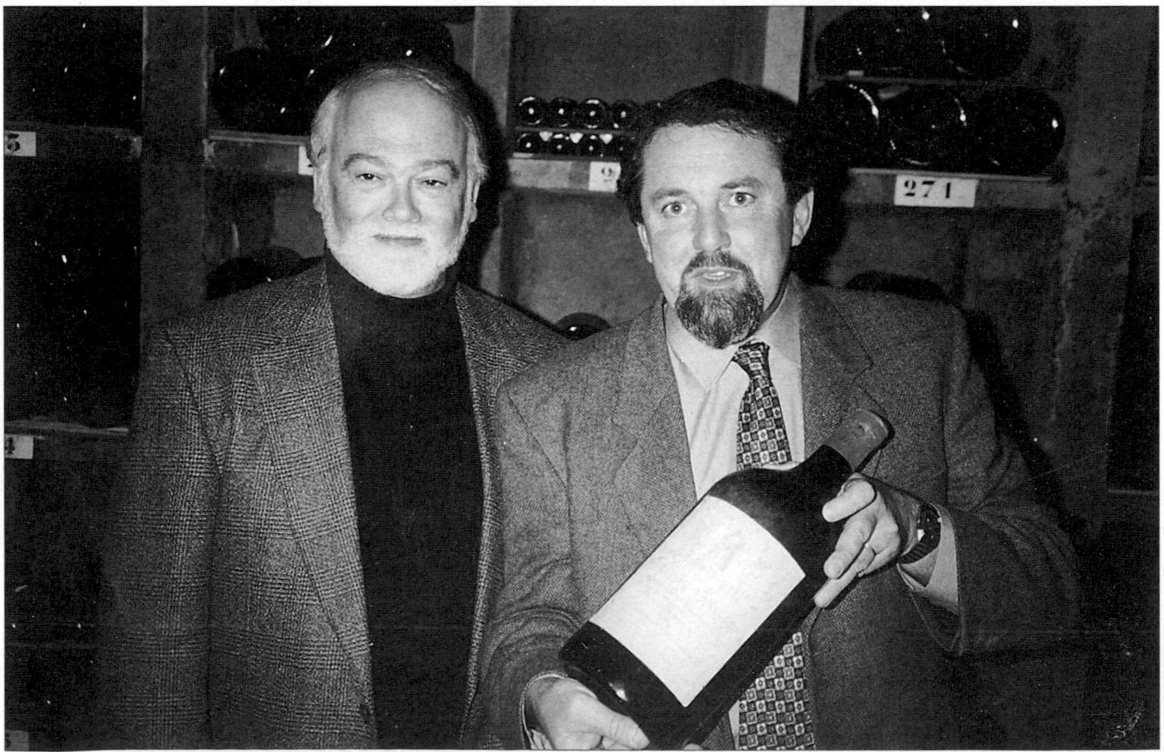

October 1996: With Christian Le Sommer, régisseur of Château Latour. The "baby" is a double-magnum of the great 1961.

October 1996: With Corrine Mentzelopoulos, in the courtyard of Château Margaux.

October 1996: Château Margaux.

October 1996: With Pascal Delbeck, Château Belair, St. Emilion.

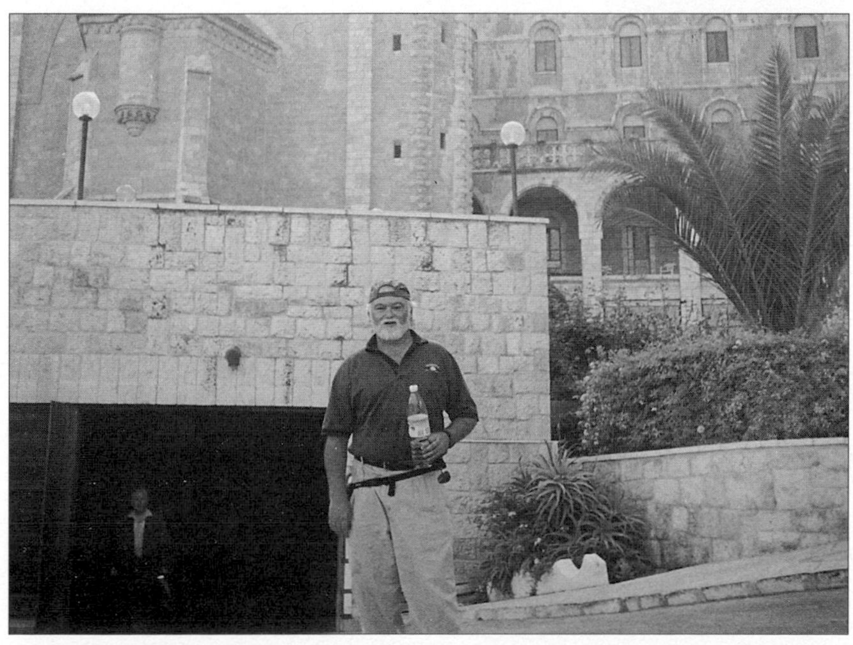

1997: Notre Dame de France, Jerusalem. The author as tourist . . . not soldier.

1997: Handing over the reins of The Commanderie de Bordeaux à Vancouver to Ian Mottershead.

December 1997: "The Givtons" at a Staff Christmas party. With Michael, Carol, and Orly.

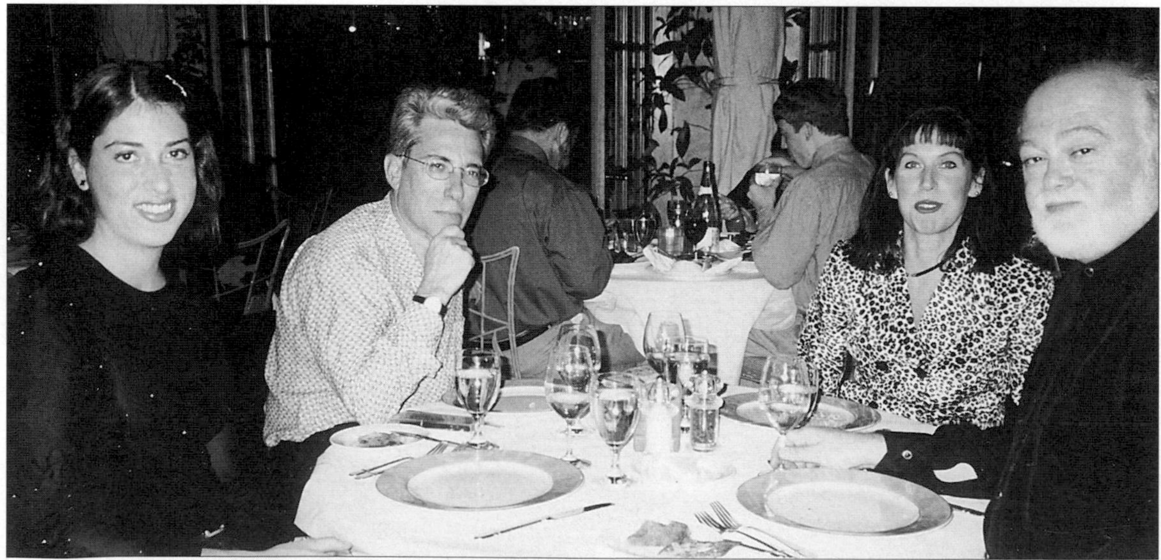

December 1998: At "Spago's," Los Angeles, with Orly, Brad Klein, Marie-José, and a glass of Montrachet 1989, Marquis de Laguiche.

MONTRACHET 1989, MARQUIS DE LAGUICHE, DROUHIN:

Nine years old and approaching maturity. Bright-golden colour. Delicate, subdued nose of golden apples, ripe raisins, and oak, all in harmony. Delicate, understated, rather than explosive on palate. Long, rich, round, well balanced, with the generosity typical of this fine vintage. However, one should not keep this wine much longer, as it will decline soon.

CHALONE 1978 PINOT NOIR, CALIFORNIA:

Only 600 cases produced, and there cannot be much of this wine still available out there. Surprisingly youthful colour to rim. Spicy, herbaceous, lovely, sweet fruit on nose. Fairly rich on palate, with good intensity. Still very much alive, with the acidity balancing the fruit to perfection. Surely one of the best California Pinot Noirs of the past 20 years. A lovely bottle.

MUSIGNY 1961, JACQUES PRIEUR:

While in Bordeaux, both the 1959 and 1961 vintages produced superb wines, in Burgundy the 1959s are clearly finer wines than the 1961s. This wine fits the mold. Evolved colour, browning at rim. Spicy, ripe Pinot Noir on nose. Rustic, fairly solid. Hint of residual sugar. A rich, mouth-filling wine, but where is the elegance for which this vineyard is so famous?

CHÂTEAU D'YQUEM 1975, IN HALF-BOTTLE:

The star of the evening! Even in half-bottle, this wine is full of life! There is something very special about the structure of 1975 Sauternes. While they are generous wines, with lovely botrytis and intensity, they also have a very obvious acidic streak (in a positive sense) that will make the best, long-lived wines. The great 1967s are more generous and riper. The 1971s have a very good balance and class. The 1976s are rich, luscious, and soft, but the 1975s are still full of life. While the 1975 d'Yquem is not as honeyed and luscious as the 1967, it will outlast its senior stablemate by at least two decades. This 1975 d'Yquem is superb. Fruit, oak, botrytis, steely acidity, and slight hint of greenness, all in harmony. Un Grand Vin!

The food at "Spago's" was very good, too, but the service needs improving. Also, I found that their smaller (Hollywood) operation was overall finer, both in terms of food quality and service (as well as ambience). Maybe this fine eating establishment has become too big (277seats) for its own good?

New Year's 1999

A short four-day cruise around the coast of Baja, California, and San Diego.

CHAMPAGNE ROEDERER "CRISTAL" 1990:

A lovely way to welcome the last year of the millennium. Generous, creamy. Velvety, smooth. An elegant Champagne of great distinction. Lovely ripe fruit, backed by good, but not too obvious, acidity. Drinking extremely well now.

FAR NIENTE VINEYARDS 1994 CABERNET SAUVIGNON, NAPA VALLEY:

Deep red, garnet colour. Spicy, slightly stemmy nose. Hint of oak, cedar, and black fruit. Not a blockbuster, but not quite ready. Try around 2002. Good extract, well structured, and generous.

ZD 1996 CHARDONNAY, CALIFORNIA:

Made from a blend of grapes from both Napa and Sonoma Valleys. Typical herbaceous, spicy ZD style. Fresh fruit. Crisp, clean, with just a hint of honeydew and ripe pears.

Early 1999

CHAMPAGNE VEUVE CLICQUOT "RESERVE" 1989:

As on past occasions, rich, yeasty, full-bodied, generous. Excellent ripe fruit is backed up by good acidity, but, as is the case of most 1989 Champagnes (a ripe year), the wine is ready and will not improve.

CHÂTEAU LEOVILLE-LASCASES 1959:

Classic 1959, classic cedary Lascases! Deep colour, evolved rim. Cedar, black fruit on nose. Full, rich, mouth-filling. A generous, extremely well-balanced wine. Better, in my opinion, than Lascases 1961. Lingering aftertaste. This wine has been at its plateau of perfection now for over 15 years! One could not hope for a better St. Julien. Definitely in the same class as 1961 Ducru-Beaucaillou and 1961 Gruaud-Larose. Grand Vin!

CHASSAGNE MONTRACHET "LES CAILLERETS," 1989 PREMIER CRU, BLAIN-GAGNARD:

Complexity and elegance combine here to produce a lovely, smooth, mineral Chardonnay. Very good length. Soft fruit is backed by good acidity. At its peak. A pleasure to drink now. Very well made.

Early January 1999

A small vertical tasting of recent vintages of Château Haut-Brion.

Three pairs were tasted, all from the great decade of the 1980s.

FIRST PAIR

1982 AND 1983:

The 1982 has an excellent, deep colour to rim, typical of the vintage. Very ripe black fruit on nose with hint of oak. Mouth-filling, warm, generous. The tannins are soft, but the wine has excellent extract and depth. A typical, lovely 1982, but very different from what one would expect from Haut-Brion. It is not an elegant, earthy, flowery wine. Anything but! Enjoyable now, but has a long life ahead of it. Drink now to 2010. (18.5)

The 1983 is very different all round. Medium-red colour, palish rim, but has good depth. Tight on nose, but some earth, truffles, and cedar coming through. Leaner, tighter on palate. Needs at least two hours of airing. Tightly knit wine, still a bit tannic, trace of acidity, but lovely, long, elegant aftertaste. Enough fruit to last at least until 2005, and, if well cellared, until 2015. (17.5)

SECOND PAIR

1985 AND 1986:

The difference between these two wines is even more obvious than between the 1982 and 1983.

The 1985 has a typical cherry-red colour to rim. Cedar, vanilla, lovely red fruit on nose. Round, very well balanced. Elegant. Velvety, long finish. Typical 1985 that will not improve, as it is perfect for current drinking, but it has enough extract to last for another few years. (18)

The 1986 is a totally different story. Structured like the 1983, but more so all round. Deeper colour, tighter on nose (hint of earth, mushrooms, and oak). Solid tannins. The fruit is there, but it is still closed up. Will be a very fine bottle, and may live longer than the 1982. Drink from 2004 to 2020. Pity to open this too soon. Great potential. (18.5)

THIRD PAIR

1989 AND 1990:

The 1989 has lived up to its reputation. Very deep, almost black colour to rim. Fabulous fruit extract on nose, oriental spices, and oak. Not as fat and forthcoming as it was just after bottling. A bit tight and closed up. If you must try a bottle now, let it breathe and decant for at least two hours. A mouthful of ripe, intense fruit. The tannins are there, but they are very ripe. Even riper than the 1982 was in its youth. This is a total departure from Haut-Brion's elegant style. Great extract and future. Drink from 2002. If well cellared, should live to be 50 years old! (19.5)

The 1990 would have been the best, ripest, most luscious Haut-Brion since 1982, had it not been for the massive 1989. Bright, deep colour to rim. Still very youthful colour. Even touch of purple. Spicy, ripe, fresh. Oak and vanilla not quite blended together yet, but I noticed that it is (relatively speaking) only medium-bodied with good, but not massive, extract. Obviously made in a ripe year. Haut-Brion usually picks early, but in both 1989 and 1990, they picked even earlier than usual. Excellent potential from 2005. (18.5)

I noticed that the 1990 sells at auction for only 40% to 45% of the price of the 1989. If so, then it is a bargain!

Overall, a most impressive and educational tasting.

January 1999

Dinner at "Diva's" restaurant, at the Metropolitan hotel, in Vancouver, celebrating my girlfriend Marie-José's birthday.

I brought along two red wines.

CHAMPAGNE DE VENOGE "BLANC DE BLANCS" 1990:

Elegant, smooth, round, easy sipping. Then we opened and decanted very carefully a bottle of this wine.

CHÂTEAU MOUTON-ROTHSCHILD 1957:

Marie-José's birth year. Excellent neck level. Surprisingly bright-red colour, with good depth and evolved orangy rim. Tobacco, cedar, some greenness on nose. Lean on palate, a bit tannic. Noticeable acidity, but still has fruit and excellent length and classic tobacco complexity so typical of Mouton. This must surely be the best 1957 and the longest-lived. The 1957 vintage produced lean, hard, acidic wines (due in part to the terrible frost of the previous year). This fine bottle has lived up to its reputation. Another fine 1957 was Lynch-Bages, when last tasted almost a decade ago.

This was followed by a very different Claret.

CHÂTEAU CERTAN-DE-MAY 1979, POMEROL:

If the Mouton 1957 is masculine, almost all Cabernet, then this 1979 is almost 100% Merlot, deep-red colour, ripe, sweet Merlot fruit. Luscious! Possibly the best, ripest Pomerol in 1979, including Petrus.

Mid-January 1999

Corton "Clos des Cortons" 1986, Monopole, Faiveley:

Fortunately, François Faiveley has bottled this wine without filtering, as the 1986s are turning out to be soft, elegant red Burgundies, a total contrast from both 1986 Clarets and 1986 Rhône Valley wines. Spicy Pinot Noir, soft, round, elegant, forward. No sediment. Needs drinking soon.

January 19, 1999

Dinner and tasting of the Commanderie de Bordeaux, at "La Toque Blanche" restaurant, in West Vancouver.

The food and service were outstanding. The subject of this event was the commune of St. Julien.

The wines were tasted in three flights through the meal, as follows.

FLIGHT #1
1989s

Château Beychevelle:

Garnet-red colour. Palish rim. Elegant, forthcoming, flowery nose. Hint of new oak. Soft on entry, round, soft tannins. Elegant, clean finish. There were two faults in this wine: a bit hollow in middle and slight hint of bitterness at finish. Most herbaceous of flight and most elegant. (16.5)

Château Branaire Ducru:

Similar appearance to the Beychevelle, but a little more depth. Still closed on nose, some ripe black fruit. Bigger, richer on palate. More tannic, too, but a bit short finish. A bit dull, and later, some noticeable volatile acidity.

Château Lagrange:

55% Cabernet Sauvignon, 45% Merlot. No Petit Verdot. The last year where no Petit Verdot was used at this property. As of 1990 Petit Verdot has been added; around 10% on average. Bright-red colour. Evolved rim. Subdued, unyielding nose. Hint of vanilla and oak. Yet harder, more tannic, more masculine than the above two. Aggressive tannins are backed by enough fruit. Will probably be ready by 2002. (The first two wines are ready now.) A stylish wine with good potential. Quite herbaceous (young vines). (16.5)

Château Talbot:

Deepest, darkest of flight. Totally closed nose with very little fruit coming through. Very masculine, ripe, chunky. At this stage, it is also one-dimensional, however. Not nearly ready. Try around 2004 or beyond. Almost rustic, typical of this property. (16.5)

Overall impressions

None are truly great, but overall, a consistent flight. The impression is that in 1989, many properties have overproduced.

FLIGHT #2
A vertical tasting of Château Gruaud-Larose

1985:

Cherry red, youthful colour. Spicy, sweet red fruit, stemmy nose. Lovely, sweet fruit on entry. Rich, intense, impressive structure, especially for a 1985. Clean, spicy black-cherry finish. Approachable and enjoyable now, but has enough extract to last well into the first decade of the 21st century. (17.5)

1983:

Very impressive, deep colour, almost as deep as the 1982. Very similar nose to the 1985, but in a more restrained way. Full, rich, masculine. Hard tannins, yet has lovely fruit, too. The opposite in structure to the 1985, which is fruity, elegant, and feminine. Serious wine. Around 60% Cabernet Sauvignon is used in the blend to make this wine. The average age of the vines is around 30 years. Smoky oak, concentrated. A lovely wine. Drink now to 2010. Excellent potential. (18)

1982:

Densest, most youthful colour of the flight. Subdued nose. Hint of very sweet, ripe fruit. Very rich, sweet mouthful. Classic 1982. Enjoyable now, but with enough extract to last for another decade or even longer. Very 1959 in style. Great, sweet fruit extract. (18.5)

1981:

Similar appearance to the 1983. One of the best 1981 Haut-Médocs made. Oddly, more restrained on nose than the 1983! Full, rich, sweet fruit. More evolved than the 1983; drinking very well now, but should remain at this plateau until at least 2005. (17.5)

1979:

Subdued, sweet, peppery nose. Round, sweet ripe fruit. Typical 1979. Not much class here, but sweet and generous. Perfect now. Spicy, stemmy; hint of charred oak. (17)

Overall impressions

An outstanding flight that justifies this great property's position as a Second Growth. Consistent and extraordinary wines.

FLIGHT #3
1985s

Château Leoville-Poyferré:

A complete wine. Classic, elegant 1985. Perfection now. Flowery, elegant nose. Clean and charming. Round on palate. Sweet fruit, a lovely mouthful of clean, long, velvety fruit. Bravo! Great balance. (18) How nice to see this great property back in form.

CHÂTEAU LEOVILLE-BARTON:

Deeper colour than the above. Overall, more masculine, slower to mature, but lovely fruit extract. Classic St. Julien. Rich, sweet. Very long, cedary. Drink from 2000 to 2015. Another lovely bottle. (18.5)

CHÂTEAU DUCRU-BEAUCAILLOU:

Good, dark colour, evolved rim. Slightly dusty nose. Volatile, coarser, sharp, acidic. The sweet fruit is slightly artificial (candied). Maybe made at a time when this property had problems with the paint used to coat the outside of the cement holding tanks and walls of the winery. (16)

DESSERT WINE

CHÂTEAU LAFAURIE PEYRAGUEY 1986:

An outstanding Sauternes. Bright-golden colour. Clean, understated, buttered, honeyed botrytis nose. A lovely mouthful of ripe fruit, botrytis, and spices. Impeccable balance will help this wine age for many years to come. Lovely now, but great potential. Drink at least until 2015. (18.5)

Late January 1999

CORTON CHARLEMAGNE 1992, JOSEPH DROUHIN:

A classic Grand Cru, but also typical Drouhin. Bright, deep gold. Rich, nutty, honeyed Chardonnay. Good acidity, but as with most of this négociant's whites, very forward and soft. Drink up soon, before it oxidizes. Lovely now.

LA QUADRATURA DEL CERCHIO 1995, "SECONDO VIAGGIO," TUSCANY:

Made from a blend of approximately 80% Sangiovese and 20% Cabernet Sauvignon. A "new wave" Italian wine. Very deep colour to rim. Ripe black fruit on nose. Still closed and tannic, but the ripe fruit is definitely there. Hard to guess this as being Italian (in terms of style or terroir). The only hint is that, in spite of its great, ripe fruit extract, it has noticeable acidity, a trait of Italian red wines.

CHÂTEAU LA MISSION HAUT-BRION 1975:

I have had the good fortune of tasting this wine, both from cask in the spring of 1977, and on six occasions since, mostly at tastings. I have finally decided to break open one of my two cases of this great wine, and try one of my own bottles. Decanted one hour. Fair bit of sediment. Amazing depth of colour at over 23 years old, but starting to show slight maturity at rim. Black truffles, wet earth, ripe black fruit, and cedar on nose. Full, solid, masculine, still tannic (but ripe tannins). Great fruit extract. My cellar is very cold, with constant temperature of 52°F, and I have owned this wine since it was bottled in 1977. Other bottles, cellared in warmer storage facilities, or bottles that have travelled a lot, may be at their peak. The bottle tasted needs at least another five to seven years to reach its peak, however. The last great "independent" La Mission.

While the 1978 and 1979 are among the best wines of their respective vintages, and the 1982 is excellent, too, modern vintages of this property, under the control of its arch rival, Château Haut-Brion, from 1983 onward, are "merely" very good, and rarely, if ever, challenge Haut-Brion in quality. Up to 1975, while Haut-Brion produced some lovely wines, it rarely matched, and never surpassed, the sheer depth and stature of La Mission. I am glad that the Woltner brothers, Henri and Fernand, are not around to see the finely tuned, but nevertheless downgrading, of this great property.

January 1999

1981 AND 1982 CORNAS, AUGUST CLAPE:

Clape is one of the best producers in Cornas (the other being Noël Verset).

The 1981 displayed an impressive, deep colour, a rich, peppery/leathery/ripe black fruit bouquet, and a round, sweet, generous body. Excellent length. At its peak at 16 years, and will stay at this plateau for a while, if well cellared.

The 1982 displayed the same appearance and bouquet, but it was still a bit tannic, with great fruit extract. Fabulous, fleshy wine. Very well balanced. Drink now to 2005. Both wines require decanting.

CORTON CHARLEMAGNE 1992, TOLLOT-BEAUT:

Thankfully, far better than the prematurely aged 1988. Bright gold. Oak, vanilla, and green apples on nose. Fairly crisp on palate, but very good extract, and fruit underneath. Not a massive wine. Approachable now, but no rush. Very good.

BOTIGLIA PARTICOLARA 1986, VINO DA TAVOLA DI GREVE, CASTELLO DI VERRAZZANO:

Produced in the Chianti Classico region, from 100% Sangiovese Piccolo grapes. Evolved red colour. Hint of tar and straw on nose. Medium weight and depth, good acidity, but the fruit is very soft. Good quality.

Early February 1999

CHÂTEAU MOUTON-ROTHSCHILD 1970:

One of the better examples of this wine that I have tasted recently. Bright-red colour, evolved rim. Cedar and spicy Cabernet jump out of glass. Medium-bodied, good acidity, and fruit is very soft. Fully mature. Excellent length, with the typical cedary character of Mouton.

Corton Charlemagne 1989, Joseph Drouhin:

Bright, deep gold. Generous, rich fruit (yellow golden apples) with excellent acidity and weight. Impressive depth and aftertaste. Top quality, but requires drinking soon.

In an Italian restaurant, in New York.

1990 Ghemme "Collis Breclemae," Antichi Vignetti di Cantaluppo, Tuscany:

As is the case with so many Tuscan and Piedmontese wines in this outstanding vintage, lush, full, generous, rich, very well balanced. Deep-garnet colour. A joy to drink now, but enough depth and intensity to last well into the 21st century.

February 1999

A tasting, featuring Ets. J. P. Moueix's 1996 vintage wines, as well as selected other wines, mostly Pomerols, and several St. Emilions.

There is a paradox in Bordeaux. The decade of the 1990s has been one of the busiest and one of the best for the négoce of Bordeaux, yet the overall quality has been only average. On the other hand, the decade of the 1980s was one of the greatest ever. Yet, overall, the markets were tame, especially when compared to the hectic (and upward) markets of the 1990s.

According to J. P. Moueix's export director, Laurent Navarre (who conducted the tasting), the 1998 vintage in the Libournais will be the best since 1990, surpassing even the very good 1995s. This is also true of the Graves St. Emilion region, notably Cheval-Blanc and Figeac.

In 1998, some vats attained a natural alcohol level of 13.5º or 14º! Navarre also confirmed that overall, the quality of the Right Bank wines was better in 1995 than in 1996. At Moueix, they toast the barrels only lightly, to avoid imparting too much burnt-oak flavour to the wine. In 1996, they started picking around September 20, and the harvest was picked in two weeks, by three teams: one team for their Fronsac properties, the second for their Pomerol properties and Château Magdelaine, and the third for their other St. Emilion properties, as well as Château Lafleur in Pomerol, which they manage.

Château Canon de Brem 1996, Canon Fronsac:

This 12-acre property, producing 2,000 cases annually, was acquired in 1984, together with Château La Dauphine. This wine was bottled in April 1998, aged in 30% new oak barrels. Made from 70% Merlot and 30% Cabernet Franc. Bright cherry-red colour. Slight hint of oak. Generous, sweet fruit on palate. Ripe and long.

Château La Croix Canon 1996, Canon Fronsac:

The estate comprises 35 acres under vine, the soil is clay and limestone, and the vines are old. Some as old as 60 or even 70 years! 70% Merlot and 25% Cabernet Franc, plus 5% Cabernet Sauvignon, producing an average of 5,000 cases yearly. Similar in appearance to the Canon de Brem, but that is where the similarity ends. Stemmier on nose, less-pronounced new oak, hint of candy. Less acidic than the above, richer, denser, and more generous. It is also less elegant, however. A heftier wine, in short.

J. P. Moueix are also the sole agents for the following châteaux: Certan-de-May, Lafleur, Gazin, and Belair in St. Emilion. Between 1951 and 1960, they acquired Magdelaine, Trotanoy, and in 1964, 50% of Petrus, which they own jointly with the late Mme. Loubat's heirs. In 1969, they acquired five hectares of the best part of Château Gazin, and this is included in Petrus. J. P. Moueix divided his holdings in two: the elder son, Jean-François, took over the very important Duclos négociant house, and Christian manages the Ets. J. P. Moueix, including the Pomerol, St. Emilion, and Fronsac properties.

Their very gifted supervising winemaker, Jean-Claude Berrouet, has been producing the wines of the various estates since 1964!

Château Moulin du Cadet 1996, St. Emilion Grand Cru:

Subdued, elegant nose. Oak, charming with good fruit extract. A generous wine. A little stemmier, typical St. Emilion, yet it has an unusually high proportion of Merlot (85%), with 15% Cabernet Franc. The soil is similar to Fronsac (clay on chalk). 12 acres produce an average of 2,400 cases.

Château Magdelaine 1996:

This is the earliest property acquired by J. P. Moueix, and their most important St. Emilion estate. Again, the proportion of Merlot is unusually high (90%!) with 10% Cabernet Franc. Production is 3,250 cases, aged in 50% new oak barrels on average. Average age of the vineyard is 30 years. Best extraction of colour so far. Bright cherry-red. Lovely oak/vanilla, and ripe fruit on nose. Elegant, sweet fruit. Lovely.

Château Belair 1996:

24 acres planted in 70% Merlot and 30% Cabernet Franc. Produced by the gifted Pascal Delbeck who, until 1996, produced Château Ausone, as well. Similar appearance to the Magdelaine, but richer, fuller. Top quality and great concentration of fruit. Rich and generous. Drink from 2002 to 2010 or beyond.

The Pomerols

CHÂTEAU LA GRAVE 1996:

Acquired by Christian Moueix back in 1971, this 20-acre estate produces about 3,500 cases. 90% Merlot and 10% Cabernet Franc vines are planted on gravelly soil, not unlike the soil composition at Château Figeac. Deep colour. Rich, ripe, almost a baked nose. Full, good weight, but less elegance or charm at this stage than the St. Emilions or Fronsacs tasted above. Good acidity, tannic, and solid. A good wine. Drink from 2002 to 2008.

CHÂTEAU LATOUR 1996, POMEROL:

This property is owned by the Lacoste family, co-owners of Château Petrus, but vinified and distributed by Moueix. 20 acres planted in 85% Merlot and 15% Cabernet Franc, producing on average 3,000 cases yearly. Less obvious, more refined and elegant than the La Grave. Hint of new oak/vanilla, with elegant fruit and good acidity. Drink from 2002. A subtle wine.

CHÂTEAU GAZIN 1996:

Moueix are sole agents for this property's wines. 50 acres under vine, producing around 8,000 to 10,000 cases annually. 80% Merlot, 15% Cabernet Franc, and 5% Cabernet Sauvignon. Very different from all the other wines on both nose and palate. Obviously matured in heavily toasted-oak barrels. Smoky, sweet, generous fruit on both nose and palate. Ripe fruit and tannin. Solid, concentrated. Needs ten years to reach its peak.

At Gazin, the wine goes through the secondary (malolactic) fermentation in barrels. This is never the case at the Moueix properties, where the malolactic fermentation is made in vats, and only then is the wine put in ageing barrels. They also use the batonnage method at Gazin, the stirring of the wine in vat, and the breaking of the cap during fermentation. Again, this method is not used at the Moueix's properties.

CHÂTEAU CERTAN-DE-MAY 1996:

Here, too, Moueix is the sole agent. This is a property that I usually admire, notably for the excellent 1979 (the best Pomerol of the vintage), the 1982, and even the 1986; but, alas, not this time. The nine acres under vine, producing an average of only 1,500 cases annually, are planted in 60% Merlot, 25% Cabernet Franc, and 15% Cabernet Sauvignon. Subdued, unyielding nose. Has good backbone; solid, tannic, masculine, but lacks ripe fruit and it is charmless. Very little Merlot/generosity here. I expected much more from this property.

CHÂTEAU PETRUS 1996:

Deepest, densest colour of both flights. Rich, sweet, excellent extract, but not really a massive wine. Sweet fruit, oak, and vanilla, all in harmony. Lingering aftertaste. 27 acres under vines. 95% Merlot and 5% Cabernet Franc (although it is safe to describe this wine as being 100% Merlot). Planted on mainly clay soil. It is usually rare to produce great wine on clay soil. The roots go down one metre to reach moisture (while in the great properties of the Médoc, the roots go down as deep at 15 or even 18 metres!). Average age of vines is 45 years, but some of the older vines go back to the beginning of the century. In 1996, Petrus produced 2,600 cases (3,000 cases in 1995). Navarre mentioned that in 1998, the volume was a relatively low 35 hectolitres per hectare.

This was a useful tasting. The wines were not great, but certainly most had a lot of class. From a consumer's point of view, the Fronsacs should be the best buys here. Certan-de-May was disappointing. Of the St. Emilions tasted, Château Belair is definitely one to seek.

February 1999

CHÂTEAU LAFAURIE-PEYRAGUEY 1995, IN HALF-BOTTLE:

A lovely, charming Sauternes. Bright-golden colour. Botrytis, delicately oaked fruit and flowers. Jumps out of the glass. Very long, flowery. A classy wine. The only surprise is that it is already so approachable. Is it made in a modern "early maturing" style?

RIDGE 1996 ZINFANDEL "GEYSERVILLE," CALIFORNIA:

Made from 75% Zinfandel, 17% Carignan, 6% Petite Syrah, and 2% Mataro grapes. Garnet colour. Sweet, spicy fruit, but well balanced, and not overwhelming. Full, round, generous, but still too young. Try around 2003 to 2005. Good potential.

Mid-February 1999

A tasting of 1986 St. Juliens.

APERITIF

CHAMPAGNE BILLECART-SALMON 1990 "CUVÉE N.F. BILLECART":

A lovely Champagne, from an excellent vintage and a top-notch producer. Tiny bubbles, slightly yeasty, flowery, but ripe nose, as well. Full, creamy, generous. Elegance rather than weight here. Very fine indeed.

THE TASTING

CHÂTEAU GLORIA 1986:

Most evolved colour of flight, and the only nonclassified wine. Fruity nose, hardly any hint of oak. Fairly tannic, pleasant fruit, but lacks extract and ripeness. Mid-term. Drink from now to 2002. Waiting any longer may cause fruit to dry out. (15)

Château Beychevelle 1986:

After the 1982, this is probably Beychevelle's best effort of the 1980s decade. Bright, deep-red colour. Palish rim. Forthcoming, cedary nose. Rich, in the context of this property's style, but fairly forward, in the context of the vintage. Ripe fruit, spicy, and complex. Enjoyable now to 2004. (17.5)

Château Talbot 1986:

Total contrast to the Beychevelle. Deeper, beefy, rich, almost rustic. Impressive structure, ripe fruit, and tannins. Try around 2002 to 2006. Little elegance or complexity, but rich fruit. (17)

Château Ducru-Beaucaillou 1986:

A combination of the complexity and elegance of the Beychevelle, and the serious tannic backbone of the Talbot. Quite restrained, some noticeable acidity, but lots of class here. At this stage, I hesitate to give this wine a higher mark. Drink from 2003 to 2008. (17)

Château Branaire Ducru 1986:

More Talbot than Beychevelle in structure, but not quite as big as the Talbot. Nice cedary fruit, ripe tannins, clean finish. Enjoyable now to 2005, if well cellared. The 1982 of this property is riper and better overall. (16.5)

Château St. Pierre 1986:

Very similar structure to the Branaire, but more oak, toast, and cedar on both nose and palate. Nice fruit. Slightly high acidity, but good overall. Drink now to 2004. (16.5)

Château Leoville-Poyferré 1986:

As good as this property's 1982 and 1983, if not better. Classic Cabernet. Cedary, spicy, still tannic, but backed by excellent fruit. Well balanced, long, spicy black fruit. Drink from 2002 to 2010. Finally, Poyferré is back, after decades of underachievements. (17.5)

Château Gruaud-Larose 1986:

Impressive, deep-garnet colour. An explosion of cedar and ripe black fruit on nose. Full, rich, well balanced. Lots of ripe, rich fruit, and ripe tannins. While enjoyable now, this wine will be even better by 2002 to 2010. Until and including 1966, and from 1981 onward, this property has been producing top-class Clarets. (17.5) Deserves to be a "Super Second."

Château Leoville-Barton 1986:

A superb wine! 1985 has signalled a new era at this property, when Anthony Barton took over from his late uncle, Ronald Barton. The 1986 is even better, more serious. Great, ripe fruit extract, oak, rich, solid tannins, yet a lot of class and complexity, too. This is a lovely wine. Drink now to 2010. Top quality. Now should be counted among the "Super Seconds." (18)

Château Leoville-Lascases 1986:

Essence of Cabernet on both nose and palate. The most backward, hardest, most masculine wine of the lot, but great concentration, balance, and complexity. Noticeable hard tannins, which will soften up by 2004 onward. Great potential. Deserving its "Super Second" status. (18)

Château Langoa-Barton 1986:

Very good, deep colour. Palish rim. Herbaceous, spicy Cabernet nose. Very good fruit, soft tannins (but they're there); clean, complex, long finish. Very good now to 2004. (16.5)

Concluding remarks

An excellent, serious Cabernet vintage. St. Julien must surely be the most successful and most consistent commune of the Haut-Médoc and Graves.

Early March 1999

A trip to Yountville.

Champagne Paul Bara Brut 1986, Bouzy 100% Grand Cru:

Generous, round, toasty, backed by good fruit. A ripe wine from a ripe vintage. Tiny bubbles and fine mousse. This has held surprisingly well. Velvety, yet rich, not unlike Veuve Clicquot Grande Dame in style, at a fraction of the cost.

Dinner at "Bouchon" restaurant, in Yountville, the new bistro owned by Thomas Keller, chef/owner of "The French Laundry," with Christian Moueix and his wife Cherise, and Marie-José Aubin.

I brought along this bottle.

Corton Charlemagne 1992, Bonneau du Martray:

Fully mature, evolved on both nose and palate. A wine of class and elegance, rather than power or depth, reflecting both the character of the vintage and the style of this grower. Lingering, flowery aftertaste, with hint of fresh butter, and oak. A lovely bottle

We also ordered a half-bottle of this wine.

Araujo "Eisele Vineyard" 1995 Cabernet Sauvignon, Napa Valley:

Very dense, very deep colour. Black fruit jam, oak, and vanilla, on both nose and palate. Way too young, of course. Although we were four people, we could not finish the half-bottle! It was too overwhelming. This wine is made to score high marks and win awards in its youth, but I have no idea how it will age. Nor does Christian.

Christian agreed with me about the danger of commonality in wines, in general, and in those of Bordeaux, in particular. Too many wines smell and taste the same, losing their terroir character. He also told me that, although most proprietors will not admit to their exact amount of Merlot in the blend, a staggering 70% of all red varietals planted in "greater Bordeaux" are Merlots! No wonder so many wines taste alike nowadays. Christian said that he had just completed the assemblage of the Dominus 1998 vintage, a difficult year, but he is very optimistic. He said that too often, he encounters wines that are spoiled (poor shipping and/or storage conditions) on his trip to the Far East. It seems that many wine collectors over there are preoccupied with the cost, increase in value, and scarcity of the wines, rather than in the actual quality of the product.

There is another worrisome trend. Ten years ago, over 40% of fine wines were shipped in refrigerated reefers. Nowadays, it is down to only 10%! Apparently it costs US$1,500 to ship by reefer rather than by nonrefrigerated containers. Buyer beware!

Christian kindly brought along two bottles of Château Petrus 1982, which will be tasted in my upcoming marathon, three-day tastings of over 60 of the best châteaux of the great 1982 vintage. This tasting will be held in late September, early October 1999.

Other wines tasted in Yountville

CHÂTEAU MAGDELAINE 1988:

The leanness and style of the 1988 combines nicely with the elegant Merlot fruit. At its peak, but has good backbone. A stylish, most enjoyable wine. Good length and spicy, complex fruit. Drink now to 2004.

CÔTE DU RHÔNE 1979 RED, E. GUIGAL:

This "simple" wine has held very well, amazingly. Chocolaty, complex, hint of leather and spices. I acquired this back in 1984, for $45 per case. This was my last bottle. Drink up.

Tasted at the Winery

CLOS PEGASE "MITSUKO'S VINEYARD" 1996 CHARDONNAY, NAPA VALLEY:

Typical, oaky/buttery, generous, and ripe Chardonnay on nose. Good fruit and rich, but unfortunately, excessive oak and high alcohol (overmature grapes) robs this wine of its freshness. It reminds me of the old blockbuster Chardonnays of the late 1970s and early 1980s. (14.5)

CLOS PEGASE 1996 MERLOT, CARNEROS/NAPA VALLEY:

10% Cabernet Sauvignon in the blend. Much better structured than the Chardonnay. The addition of some Cabernet Sauvignon gives this elegant, spicy, well balanced, and fruity wine a little backbone and good structure. Drink from 2001 to 2005. (16)

CLOS PEGASE 1996 CABERNET SAUVIGNON, NAPA VALLEY:

From the Palisades area, made with a blend of 4% Merlot and 3% Petit Verdot. Medium weight, cedary, hint of oak and vanilla. Very nice fruit, ripe tannins, and good length. A good Cabernet. Drink from 2002 to 2007. (17)

March 9, 1999

An extensive tasting, at "Le Gavroche" restaurant, in Vancouver, celebrating the 20th anniversary of the great 1978 Rhône vintage.

APERITIF

CHAMPAGNE BOLLINGER "GRANDE ANNÉE" 1985:

A classic "gôut anglais" Champagne. Rich, creamy, hint of caramel, luscious. Needs drinking, though. A serious, ripe Champagne.

HERMITAGE BLANC 1978, J. L. CHAVE:

Deep, mature-golden colour. Cantaloupe, honeydew melon on nose. Full, rich, but not oily. Good acidity, solid. The fruit is still there, but the wine is starting to show some butterscotch/caramel. Needs drinking.

FLIGHT #1

1978 GIGONDAS, JABOULET:

Past its peak, but nice candied fruit and the depth of colour so typical of this great, very low-yield vintage. Soft fruit and ripe tannins. Very slight hint of acidity at finish. Hint of leather and oriental spices. Needs drinking soon. (14.5)

1978 CROZES-HERMITAGE "THALABERT," JABOULET:

Best, most impressive colour of flight, like a five-year-old wine! Ripe fruit, toasted oak on both nose and palate. Still masculine, tight, lively, and tannic, backed by excellent fruit. Clearly the best wine of this flight. Drink now to 2007. (16.5)

1978 HERMITAGE "LA SIZERANNE," CHAPOUTIER:

Most evolved, palest of flight. Smells and tastes like a mature Pinot Noir. Cedary, elegant nose, but dry, little fruit left, past its prime. This was never a great wine. How nice to see the house of Chapoutier back in form, beginning in 1989, after a "lost generation." (15)

Flight #2

1978 HERMITAGE, E. GUIGAL:

Good depth, evolved colour. Classic Syrah on nose. Spicy, mineral, fruity, and gamey. Similar impressions on palate, but the fruit is very evolved, and there is some nagging acidity at finish. Better than

Chapoutier's La Sizeranne, but needs drinking soon. (16.5)

1978 CÔTE RÔTIE "BRUNE ET BLONDE," E. GUIGAL:

Similar appearance to Guigal's Hermitage, but more complex, toasty on nose, and clearly more complex and elegant on palate. Beautiful balance, length, and depth. An elegant wine that is perfection now, at 20 years old. (17.5)

1978 CHÂTEAUNEUF-DU-PAPE, DOMAINE DU VIEUX TÉLÉGRAPHE:

Much deeper, more youthful colour than the above two wines. The colour of a five-year-old! Spicy, intense, youthful, licorice nose. Still tight, hard, unyielding on palate, amazingly. Masculine, solid, but not very complex. May last for another 20 years, but will the fruit last, and will it ever develop complexity? (17)

FLIGHT #3

This was the flight of the two masterpieces of the great 1978 Rhône vintage.

1978 HERMITAGE ROUGE, J. L. CHAVE:

Impressive, deep colour; slightly evolved at rim. Understated, complex, long, and beautiful bouquet of licorice, tar, ripe red fruit, even cedar. It is all there. Impressive on palate, as well. Magnificent balance, mouth-filling, but understated and not explosive. Ripe tannins are blending beautifully. Very long. Drink now to 2015, if well cellared. Grand Vin! (19)

On one of my visits to Gerard Chave, back in 1982, I mentioned to him that my daughter Orly was born in 1978; I asked him if I could acquire a case of the great 1978. Gerard told me that he had none left for sale, and that he was now shipping the 1979 to Kermit Lynch (retailing in California for US$120 per case). Three months after my return from France, I received a phone call from Kermit Lynch, telling me that with the shipment of the 1979, Gerard had sent a case of the 1978 "for Mr. Givton's daughter." There was no charge. It was a gift.

1978 HERMITAGE "LA CHAPELLE," JABOULET:

Incredibly dense, deep, purplish, youthful colour to rim! Very ripe, black fruit, youthful nose. Amazing for a 20-year-old. Powerful, mouth-filling, still tannic, very ripe (almost overripe). A powerhouse that will last for at least another two decades. On this occasion, I must admit that Chave's Hermitage was more complex, more refined, however. Both are great wines, though. (18.5)

I have had the good fortune of tasting this wine on eight occasions previously, including a barrel sample back in 1980 and from bottle in 1982, with the late Gerard Jaboulet. Gerard told me back in 1982 that in 1978, they produced between nine and 14 hectolitres per hectare! This is essence, not wine! On a later visit, he also told me that he had offered a barrel (25 dozen bottles) of this great 1978 to the British Columbia liquor monopoly, but that they were not interested because it was a new vintage, and that Gerard would have to submit samples. The bureaucrats would rather get more 1974, which they already had listed. After all taxes, the 1978 would have cost the consumer Can$25 per bottle. So Gerard had to contact his Hamburg agent and offer him 25 cases of the great 1978 in exchange for 25 cases of the mediocre 1974, which he shipped to Vancouver. Why has the Lord created bureaucrats?

We ended this event with two rare South African dessert wines

1978 EDELKEUR "NOBLE LATE HARVEST," WINE OF ORIGIN, NEDERBURG ESTATE, IN HALF-BOTTLES:

An extremely rare wine, sold only at the Nederburg Auction in South Africa. Made from Steen (Chenin Blanc), with a little Riesling. Amber colour. Ripe apricots and orange marmalade on both nose and palate. Excellent acidity (typical Chenin Blanc structure), full, rich, sweet, but not cloying. Made by the great Gunther Bröezel, who was, at the time, the winemaker at Nederburg Estate. (17.5)

1963 CRUSTED VINTAGE PORT, BOBERG:

Deep, dark colour, amber rim, not unlike a 30- or 40-year-old Tawny Port. On palate, it had a combination of flavours of Tawny and Vintage Port. Excellent fruit, good structure, full, generous. A fine effort and a rare 35-year-old dessert wine from South Africa. (17)

Coincidentally, Delia Viader, owner of Viader Vineyards in the Napa Valley, was in Vancouver for a one-day wine trade show and she joined us, as another participant did not show up. Her comments on the two great 1978 Hermitages were similar to mine. On my previous extensive tasting of 1978 Rhône wines, back in 1991, Jaboulet's "La Chapelle" had the upper hand. This time, Chave seemed the better wine, but not by much. It comes down to a matter of taste.

March 10, 1999

My daughter Orly's 21st birthday, celebrated at "Chartwell's" restaurant, Four Season's hotel.

I brought along two bottles of wine from the 1978 vintage, Orly's birth year.

1978 CHEVALIER MONTRACHET, REMOISSENET:

An excellent Grand Cru white Burgundy from a superb vintage, and from a house that produces tight, solid Chardonnays of excellent quality that age gracefully. Toasted bread, hint of dill, honey, and lovely fruit on palate. The aftertaste is superb. Will not improve, of course (after all, it is 21 years old), but still at its peak. Great fruit extract. Tasted on 11 previous occasions. Always great. (18.5)

HEITZ CELLARS "MARTHA'S VINEYARD" 1978 CABERNET SAUVIGNON, NAPA VALLEY:

After the twin drought years (1976 and 1977), 1978 produced elegant, well-balanced wines in the Napa Valley. This wine fit the mold. Subdued, fruity bouquet of eucalyptus and mint. Cedar, oak, and elegant fruit, all in harmony on both nose and palate. Soft tannins, spicy fruit. Bottles are ready. Magnums should last well for another decade, if well cellared. (17.5)

Mid-March 1999

CHALONE 1979 PINOT NOIR, CALIFORNIA:

Almost 20 years old now. Evolved colour. Spicy, generous, and forthcoming Pinot Noir character on both nose and palate. Well balanced, still has nice, but mature, fruit. Not as youthful or rich as the 1978 tasted three months ago in Los Angeles, but certainly a fine wine. Very Burgundian in style.

CHÂTEAU MONTROSE 1975:

A classic, cedary, masculine, "old-style" Claret. Impressive, deep colour. Cedary, ripe, slightly earthy/vegetal nose. Full, powerful, tannic wine that is backed by excellent fruit. The top St. Estèphe in 1975. Far better than Cos d'Estournel that year. This is still great value at auction. An excellent wine. No rush, if well cellared. Drink now to 2010. Decanting and airing for an hour is a must.

1987 MEURSAULT-PERRIÈRES, J. F. COCHE-DURY:

Not too many producers of white burgundies can claim that they made a fine 1987, and that 12 years later, their wines are still at their prime. Coche-Dury is one of those few master-producers. Bright gold, oak, roasted nuts, and green apples on nose. Fairly tight on palate, lean (typical 1987), but still has enough stuffing and fruit to last. Amazing! Definitely tight and ready, but no rush. An impressive effort.

Late March 1999

A trip to Hawaii.

CORNAS 1978, NOEL VERSET:

Fully mature now, but with very good, ripe fruit extract. Mouth-filling, black fruit, ripe tannins, and generous, fruity finish. Verset and Clape are two excellent producers of Cornas.

At "La Mer" restaurant, Halekalani hotel, Waikiki.

DOMAINE DE CHEVALIER 1995 RED:

Still a baby, of course, but lovely class and elegance here. The fine 1995s resemble the 1985s in their youth; elegance and charm, combined with excellent balance. New oak/vanilla still predominate. Bright-red colour to rim. Lovely fruit, and clean, lingering aftertaste. Definitely not a "Parker" wine. Drink from 2003 onward.

1990 CHEVALIER MONTRACHET, DOMAINE JEAN CHARTRON:

True to the elegant, leaner style of both the vintage and the producer. Fresh; golden apples and minerals on nose. Honeyed, elegant, well balanced, with charming, soft fruit. Clean finish. At its peak.

Dinner at Alan Wong's restaurant, in Honolulu, with Dr. Eugene Wong, Dr. Steven Berman, and spouses.

The Corton Charlemagne was my bottle. The de Fargues was Dr. Berman's. All the other wines were very generously contributed by Eugene Wong, our host. The food was artistic and outstanding.

1988 BOLLINGER "GRANDE ANNÉE" CHAMPAGNE BRUT, FROM MAGNUM:

As "goût anglais" as one could wish a Champagne to be. Even the colour was deeper gold. Yeasty, hint of caramel on nose. Full, generous, rich. A solid good Champagne, true to this house's style, and to the solid, masculine 1988 vintage. Definitely not a "sipping" Champagne. Serious stuff.

MEURSAULT 1979

AND

1983 "NARVAUX," LEROY:

Both impressively deep, golden colours. Both had a very rich, nutty, appley/pear nose. Both even had a touch of butterscotch and hint of botrytis. The difference was in the structure.

The 1979 was elegant, surprisingly crisp. Good acidity backed the generous, ripe fruit. Excellent, especially for a Villages wine.

The 1983 was much richer, fatter, more intense, but it had an obvious spirity, hot aftertaste that I do not like, and that is prevalent in so many 1983 white Burgundies. Impressive on entry, too alcoholic finish.

1985 CORTON CHARLEMAGNE "COMTES DE GRANCEY," LOUIS LATOUR:

Much paler colour than the two Leroy Meursaults. Charming, spicy, mineral nose. Round, elegant, well balanced. The trouble was that, after two such hefty Meursaults, this wine almost seemed feminine and soft. Perfect for drinking now.

Château Rouget 1959 and 1945, Pomerol:

Both with excellent levels and appearances.

The 1959 was a charmer. Less rich or intense than I would have expected from that generous vintage. Sweet Merlot, stemmy, ripe nose. Medium-bodied, soft, elegant, and fully evolved fruit, but showing signs of astringency at finish. Needs drinking.

The 1945 was superb! All there. Deep colour. Ripe, even very ripe nose of black fruit and mushrooms. Full, solid, mouth-filling. Loads of ripe tannins, too. Very long, ripe aftertaste. My age, and still all there. A superb, classic 1945.

Château de Fargues 1967:

Deep, golden colour. Intense, ripe botrytis on nose. Soft, luscious on palate, but past its prime. Not as lively and fat as ten years ago. Trace of dryness and acidity at finish. Drink up. This would be beautiful with foie gras.

Late March 1999

Back in Vancouver.

Château Lafite 1970:

Good neck level. Very pale colour, almost a dark Rosé. Flowery, elegant nose. Quite soft, very low fruit, and astringent. Acidity taking over. After 1962 and before 1975, Lafite went through a "low" period, to put it mildly.

Early April 1999

Dinner, at home, with my son Michael.

Château Haut-Brion 1979:

Evolved colour, excellent depth. Charming wine. Chocolaty, earthy, mature fruit on nose. Velvety, round on palate. Very well balanced, good length, and rich. A pleasure drinking now, in its 20th year. One of the top wines of the vintage, surely. (18.5)

Also tasted in early April 1999

Château Margaux 1981:

Still not quite ready, amazingly. At first, hard, tannic, obvious oak/vanilla, and steely. Impressive, youthful colour. After an hour, it mellowed a bit. Lovely fruit extract, solid backbone, even a bit tannic, backed by excellent fruit. This must be not only the best Claret of the 1981 vintage, but possibly the only one that is not quite ready, yet it is already over 17 years old. (18.5)

Château Petrus 1950:

A legendary Petrus. I have owned this bottle for over ten years, and have tasted it only once before, with Christian Moueix in Libourne, back in 1984. Bright red, evolved colour. Decanted and tasted right away. Lovely nose of truffles, surprisingly ripe fruit. Very slight hint of oxidation. Full, generous, rich, with layers of ripe fruit. Will certainly not improve. Drink up. (Another excellent 1950 tasted recently is Figeac.)

A tasting of E. Guigal's three single-vineyard-designated Côte Rôties of the excellent 1988 vintage

1988 Côte Rôtie "La Mouline":

Made with some white juice in the blend. Impressive, deep, youthful colour to rim. Hint of licorice, tar, spicy black fruit on nose. Full, still a bit tannic, but approachable. At this stage, the most complex and forthcoming of the three. Drink now to 2008.

1988 Côte Rôtie "La Landonne":

Made from 100% Syrah. The deepest, darkest of the three, to rim. Intense yet restrained nose of cedar, black truffles, and licorice. Full, powerful, masculine; quite tannic. Needs at least another five to seven years of bottle-age. Pity to open this too soon. Will be a great bottle by 2005.

1988 Côte Rôtie "La Turque":

Produced only since 1985. Most intense, sweetest, ripest fruit of the three. Exotic fruit, oriental spices. Still a bit tannic. A glorious mouthful of great Syrah. Drink from 2003 onward.

In terms of structure or impact on palate, the easiest comparison of these fine wines would be to Bordeaux or Vintage Port.

La Mouline has the elegance of Lafite or Croft's.

La Landonne has the power of Latour or Taylor's.

La Turque has the exuberant, ripe fruit of Mouton or Graham's.

April 1999

Dinner at a friend's home.

I brought along the Champagne. All wines were outstanding.

Champagne Bollinger 1988 "Vieilles Vignes Françaises":

Made from 100% Pinot Noir from two plots adjoining the estate. Ungrafted vines (French rootstocks). A tiny proportion of this Champagne is produced, only in very good vintages. One of the very greatest Champagnes one could possibly taste, and from a tight, slow-maturing vintage. Bright, deep-golden colour. Tiny, persistent bubbles, and excellent mousse. Ripe, rich nose of yeast, toast, and ripe fruit. This is a "Blanc de Noirs." Great extract. An explosion of ripe, tight fruit, and serious backbone. Drink from 2001 to 2012, if well cellared. Grand Vin! (19)

CHÂTEAU MOUTON-ROTHSCHILD 1985

AND

OPUS ONE 1985, MONDAVI-ROTHSCHILD:

The Mouton displayed a combination of the cedary-Cabernet concentration of this property, with the elegance of the vintage. Soft tannins, complex, lingering fruit. Well balanced and very long. Lovely drinking now to 2008. (18.5)

The Opus One had a slightly more evolved colour, hint of eucalyptus, slightly herbaceous. More aggressive tannins than the Mouton, but less charming fruit at this stage. Excellent concentration, though. Drink now to 2008. This wine was produced before phylloxera ravaged Opus One's budding vineyard. (18)

1976 RIESLING, SELECTION DE GRAINS NOBLES, HUGEL:

A historic, superb dessert wine, in the light Beerenauslese style. Bright, deep-golden colour. Amazingly fresh, ripe fruit for a 23-year-old wine. Hint of petroleum and ripe raisins on nose. Full, rich, but not cloying. Very long, mouth-filling. The aftertaste went on forever. (18.5). While perfect now, it will last for another two decades, or longer, if well cellared. Johnny Hugel is very proud of this, and of his magnificent 1976 Gewürztraminer SGN.

April 1999

A tasting of the 1985 Pomerol "Top Guns."

We started with a young, not nearly ready, but excellent white Burgundy.

1995 CORTON CHARLEMAGNE "DIAMOND JUBILEE," REMOISSENET:

This house purchases a portion of their Chardonnay from Louis Latour, apparently. As is usual with this property's style, this wine exhibits excellent backbone, green apples, honeysuckle, hint of toast, and very good length. Not quite ready. Drink from 2002 onward. Lots of stuffing here and very good ageing potential. This producer's 1978 Corton Charlemagne is still drinking well! (18)

THE TASTING

CHÂTEAU CONSEILLANTE 1985:

Couldn't get any better than now! At a perfect plateau. This is a lovely Pomerol. Oriental spices, herbaceous Cabernets, and ripe Merlot in harmony. Beautifully balanced, long, round, and absolutely charming. This is a very reliable property. (18.5)

VIEUX CHÂTEAU CERTAN 1985:

Together with the La Conseillante, the best for drinking now. Charming, fruity nose. Hint of oak and black fruit. Trace of acidity does not detract a thing from this charming wine. Very long, easy to drink and enjoy. Thienpont is a gifted winemaker. (18)

CHÂTEAU TROTANOY 1985:

Somehow, I expected more concentration, more ripe Merlot from this great property. Loosely knit, elegant, spicy fruit. Does not have the size, extract, and concentration of this property's superb 1982, 1975, 1971, or 1970. From 1989 onward, Trotanoy is back in form. Another vintage of this Château that somewhat disappoints is the 1983. (17)

CHÂTEAU CERTAN-DE-MAY 1985:

Fairly evolved colour with good depth. Stemmy nose. Fairly dry on palate, lacking the ripe concentration of other Merlot-based Pomerols. Ready now. Does not have the sheer power, concentration, and ripe fruit extract of this property's superb 1982 and 1979. Even the 1986 is better, more concentrated, by far. (16.5)

CHÂTEAU LAFLEUR 1985:

Even in an elegant year, Lafleur produced a rich, concentrated, ripe wine. Darkest so far. Ripe Merlot on both nose and palate, hint of iron, rich fruit. Exotic. Ready, but no rush. (18)

CHÂTEAU LE PIN 1985:

Halfway between the elegance and complexity of La Conseillante and the ripeness of Lafleur. Impeccably made. Lovely fruit, elegant, yet ripe. Ripe tannins blend nicely. Long, complex, some oak and vanilla coming through. However, at ten (or more) times the price of La Conseillante, this is a joke, and not a funny one, at that! (18)

CHÂTEAU PETRUS 1985:

May not be as great as the 1982 or 1989, but it still has that extra dimension that clearly puts this wine above all the other 1985 Pomerols. Bright, ruby-red colour to rim. New oak, cedar, and vanilla blend with hint of iron and ripe, sweet Merlot fruit. Very long, rich, but not massive. Approachable now, but will be even better by 2002 to 2007. (19)

CHÂTEAU L'EVANGILE 1985:

A lovely wine from a great property. Who can forget the magnificent 1961, 1975, 1982, or even 1983 l'Evangile? And, of course, the superb 1990. This 1985 is a charming wine, but l'Evangile is renowned for its ripe, fruity concentration, rather than for its subtlety. Well balanced, clean, soft fruit. The 1983 (best Pomerol of that vintage) is superior. Having said that, it is still a lovely wine that is fully evolved now. (17.5)

With the exception of the good, but not great, Trotanoy, and the rather disappointing Certan-de-May, these are excellent wines, giving a lot of pleasure. Most will not improve as they are offering everything they have to offer now.

April 1999

With my son Michael.

1979 DOMAINE DE CHEVALIER ROUGE:

This property produced better wines in 1979 and 1983 than it did in 1978 or 1982. Impressive, deep but evolved colour. Earthy, truffles, and hint of chocolate on nose. Very similar to the 1979 Palmer on nose and in structure. Perfect now at 20. Will not improve, but has held very well. Bravo Domaine de Chevalier! A charming wine.

April 24, 1999

Commanderie de Bordeaux Gala Dinner and Induction of new members.

CHAMPAGNE CHARLES HEIDSIECK BRUT 1990:

The cat is out of the bag! For three years now, we could get this Champagne locally for Can$44 per bottle. Now that *The Wine Spectator* has discovered it, it has disappeared. The Americans are now paying US$50 to $60 a bottle for this. Rich, masculine, fine mousse, solid. Excellent backbone and fruit extract. Very long. No rush drinking it. This is a very reliable Champagne, as good as many other houses' Grandes Marques. One to buy, if it can still be found.

CHÂTEAU CARBONNIEUX 1990, GRAVES BLANC:

Green-golden colour. Oak and ripe fruit on nose. Well balanced, clean, and now fairly rich and round. It has shed its green-apple freshness of five years ago. Mouth-filling, but not really fat. A well-made wine. I always prefer this property's white to its red version.

The theme tonight is a small vertical of Château Grand-Puy-Lacoste, Pauillac.

1989:

Typical 1989 and a classic Pauillac. Generous, rich, relatively soft tannins. Quite evolved. Very well balanced, charming, cedary fruit. Lingering aftertaste. Ready now but has just achieved its plateau, so it should be drinking well for another five to seven years.

1985:

Surprisingly more extract than the 1989 and even fresher. Bright, deep-red colour. Oak, cedar, and spicy black fruit in harmony. Round tannins, mouth-filling. Drink now to 2007. May not be as lovely as the 1985 Lynch-Bages, but I prefer this to the 1985 Pichon-Lalande. An excellent wine.

1983 AND 1982:

The 1983 is leaner, more forward, slightly stemmy. Good fruit and drinking well now, but, unfortunately, it suffered from competing against riper, fruitier vintages such as 1989 and 1985, and the pairing with the superb 1982 did not exactly help it, either.

The 1982 is as great as expected. Visually, clearly the deepest, darkest of all four. Very ripe fruit on nose. Full, very ripe, rich, mouth-filling. An explosion of ripe, black fruit, soft tannins, and oak, all in harmony on palate. This wine will last well for at least another decade. Superb wine and a classic 1982. All there!

DESSERT WINE

CHÂTEAU CLIMENS 1986:

What a safe bet Climens is! Always reliable and always impeccably made. I have never had a disappointing wine from this excellent Barsac, having tasted most good or great vintages of this property, going back to 1945. Bright gold. Superb botrytis, vanilla/oak, ripe, exotic fruit on both nose and palate. Not as tight as the great 1983. Fatter, richer, especially for a Barsac. Drink now to 2015. A great wine.

April 24, 1999

Lunch at "Le Gavroche," with François Faiveley, who is visiting us in Vancouver, and his local agent, Pierre Doise.

I brought along two bottles.

1985 "BARON DE L," POUILLY FUMÉ, DE LADOUCETTE:

14 years old and still an excellent Sauvignon Blanc. Everything about this wine was classy. The slightly herbaceous but generous and expansive nose; the roundness on palate; the lively fruit and lingering aftertaste.

CHÂTEAU CALON-SÉGUR 1918:

Excellent appearance and level. Recorked at the château in 1990. Heavy, thick glass, and deep punt. On nose, an explosion of truffles, cedary bouquet, and even fruit. The fruit was still there, amazingly, as was the excellent, tannic backbone of classic old St. Estèphes. Very long on palate, no sign of decay. After 20 minutes in glass, the wine started to dry up. A great experience and a superb Claret.

Every young oenologist must try one of the great old wines, if only to learn and understand how wines used to be made. I doubt that any wine made today would last seven decades, let alone taste this great. François was extremely excited to taste this old, majestic Calon-Ségur. It turned out that today is François's birthday. He was born in what I like to call an "Armagnac year," one of the vintages when it is almost impossible to find good wines, 1951. Other than a decent La Tâche and a superb Beaulieu Vineyards Napa Valley Cabernet Sauvignon "Private Reserve, Georges de Latour," there is not much out there worth seeking in 1951.

Faiveley hopes for a large crop in 1999, because he hardly has any wine left to sell. He said that, like Bordeaux, Burgundy producers have made a short-sighted, greedy decision to jack up the price of the 1997s, but he lays the blame with Bordeaux, who started this trend. Now wholesalers and retailers are stuck with warehouses full of 1997 Clarets that they cannot sell, as the demand is almost nonexistent. We also discussed my next trip to Burgundy, and his unpleasant experience with Robert Parker. He also expressed puzzlement over Hardy Rodenstock's "treasures." We briefly discussed Michael Broadbent's ability, or lack thereof, to taste wines blind.

François and I share a love for Vega Sicilia, the magnificent Spanish red wine. He said that when still in cask (the "Unico" spends up to ten years in cask), Vega Sicilia is undrinkable, yet, with age, it turns out to be superb. I can well imagine "expert" wine writers tasting Vega Sicilia in its youth and rating it below 80 points!

A most interesting and enjoyable lunch.

That night, the Confrérie des Chevaliers du Tastevin hosted a dinner in honour of our guest, François Faiveley.

We started with a tasting of Faiveley's 1995 reds. During our lunch, I told François that I was worried about how these wines would taste now, as they have been in bottle for almost three years, a period when many red wines close up and become unyielding, only to "reopen" two to three years later. As it turned out, I was right, and François agreed with me that the wines were not showing their best. There was a clear gap in quality, structure, intensity, and flavour between the Premier Crus and the Grands Crus.

THE TASTING
All wines were bottled in the Spring 1997.

1995 NUITS-ST.-GEORGES PREMIER CRU "CLOS DE LA MARÉCHALE," MONOPOLE:

Average age of vines is 32 years. Approximately 24 acres planted. This Clos is wholly owned by Faiveley. Surprisingly light colour. Slightly volatile on nose. Austere, tight, astringent, yet the depth is there. Obviously going through its "closed" phase. Not tasting very well tonight. Must retaste in two to three years.

1995 GEVREY CHAMBERTIN PREMIER CRU, "LA COMBE AUX MOINES":

Only three acres of this is owned by Faiveley. Average vineyard age is 32 years. Even more evolved colour than the Nuits. Perfumy, flowery, delicate nose, not at all what one would expect from Gevrey. Yet tight, unyielding on palate. Totally closed up. Must retaste.

All of Faiveley's Grands Crus are hand-bottled and unfiltered.

1995 CLOS DE VOUGEOT:

Average age of vines is 30 years, planted on just over three acres. Clearly darker, deeper than the two Premier Crus. Bright red. Animal, ripe, leathery on nose, with hint of vanilla and oak. Ripe, rich, forceful. Good fruit extract. Masculine. Needs ten years. Very good potential.

1995 LATRICIÈRES CHAMBERTIN:

Average age of vines is 27 years, planted on just under three acres. Production in 1995 was 28.5 hectolitres per hectare, 400 cases. Very good depth, evolved rim. Oak and vanilla predominant at this stage. Some fruit coming through. Lovely, elegant, less powerful than the Clos de Vougeot, more finesse. Drink from 2005 onward. Very good potential.

1995 CHAMBERTIN "CLOS DE BÈZE":

3.2 acres under vine. Age of vines on average is 37 years. 23 hectolitres per hectare produced in 1995, approximately 4,000 bottles (320 cases). Bottled on June 16, 1997. Deepest, darkest of flight. Very ripe red and black fruit on nose, with hint of charred oak. Superb depth, great ripe fruit extract. Hint of violets. Great breed. One to buy! Drink from 2006.

1995 CORTON "CLOS DE CORTONS FAIVELEY," MONOPOLE:

Old vines (37 years). Total production of 7.35 acres is 775 cases. Excellent deep colour. Restrained, tight, masculine. Superb fruit extract. Hefty. Biggest, richest, deepest wine of flight. Another "must buy." This vineyard was acquired by François' great-great grandfather in 1864. He gave his daughter in marriage to the last Duke of Burgundy, a Habsburg, and gave her this vineyard as dowry. He told the cartographer to add the name "Rognet" to this vineyard (Rognet means "split from"). Thus, a portion of this Corton vineyard is known officially as "Corton Rognet."

Faiveley does not like artificial yeast inducement, because it eliminates "terroir" character. The yeasts vary from commune to commune, and sometimes even from one vineyard to the next. He practices clonal selection.

About the Côte Chalonnaise, François said that, as the vineyards of the Côte d'Or are planted to their maximum capacity, the Côte Chalonnaise will become the "bread and butter" of new Burgundy expansion. The potential is there.

THE DINNER

1992 MEURSAULT "CLOS DE LA BARRE," COMTES LAFON:

A beautifully crafted, complex, long, nutty Meursault. Not as fat as Lafon's Meursaults usually are, due no doubt to the elegant, rather than rich, 1992 vintage. Stylish, elegant, very well balanced. A pleasure to drink now.

1996 CORTON CHARLEMAGNE, FAIVELEY:

Produced from only 22 hectolitres per hectare, from a small plot at the top of the Corton hill. Too young, of course, but great potential by 2003 to 2007. At this stage, the oak dominates on both nose and palate. While the fruit is tight, it is definitely there, however. Great extract and depth. Pity to drink this "before its time." Grand Vin!

1991 GEVREY CHAMBERTIN PREMIER CRU "LES CAZETIERS," FAIVELEY:

An impressive effort for the vintage. Fully mature. Excellent, bright, cherry-red colour. Spicy, open bouquet of ripe cherries, with just a hint of oak. Nice fruit. A charming wine.

1989 NUITS-ST.-GEORGES PREMIER CRU "LES PORRETS ST. GEORGES," FAIVELEY:

A rich, ripe wine, yet soft and approachable, typical of both the vintage and this commune's style. Deep colour. Ripe, rich fruit on nose. Mouth-filling, very well balanced, hint of oak. Very soft, ripe tannins. Drink now to 2003. This is very good.

1988 CHÂTEAU SUDUIRAUT, SAUTERNES:

Still too young, tight, on both nose and palate. Not a fat or luscious wine, but very good botrytis, and ripe fruit underneath. Very good potential. Drink from 2003 onward.

Chef Doug Anderson and the Four Season's hotel staff prepared an outstanding dinner for us, as usual.

April 28 to May 4, 1999

Short trip to Yountville, Napa Valley.

Met Ray Signorello Jr. at the winery, on the Silverado Trail, and tasted several wines.

1997 SEMILLON, NAPA VALLEY:

Made from purchased grapes, with 20% Sauvignon Blanc in the blend. Some oak on nose. Rich fruit, luscious, very young. The addition of Sauvignon Blanc imparts just a hint of greenness and good acidity. Ready soon.

1997 CHARDONNAY "ESTATE":

Made with their own grapes, grown in the Napa Valley. Aged in 50% new French oak barrels. Ripe, golden apples on nose. Some vanilla and oak. Quite rich, full-bodied. Very "California" style, but thankfully, backed by good acidity. Still a bit young. Needs an extra two years in barrel to reach its peak. A fine effort.

1997 ZINFANDEL, NAPA VALLEY:

5% Syrah in the blend. Only 100 cases (four barrels) produced and available locally "to friends." An amazing 16.9° alcohol after fermentation is masked nicely, thanks no doubt to the excellent ripe fruit. Purplish colour. Fresh, spicy, hint of oak. Will be released next month. This is very good, but I have never been a fan of Zinfandel (with the exception of Ridge's great old Geyservilles, such as the superb 1973).

1997 PINOT NOIR, CARNEROS, "LOS AMIGOS VINEYARD":

This is one of Ray Signorello's favourites among the wines that he produces. He is definitely a Burgundy fan, in spite of his substantial Cabernet Sauvignon vineyard holdings. Made from 38-year-old vines, and matured for 17 months in 65% new French oak casks. Only 1.5 tons per acre and no filtration. Bright, cherry-red colour, not unlike the charming 1985 red Burgundies in their youth. Lovely fruit extract, purity, and balance. Clean, long, very well made. Drink from 2003 onward.

Then I served Ray, double-blind, a wine I had brought along.

1997 DOMAINE COMTE PERALDI, AJACCIO A/C, COMTE DE POIX:

A Corsican wine, made from 100% Sangiovese grapes. Bright, light-red colour, not unlike a young Santenay or Volnay. Very Pinot Noir on nose! Would fool anyone. Fruity, light, elegant, and clean, with a trace of acidity, typical of Sangiovese. A revelation to both of us, and a good buy at $15 per bottle.

Ray Signorello and I went to "The French Laundry" restaurant, in Yountville, for dinner.

Chef Thomas Keller's staff prepared an amazing array of no fewer than 24 miniature courses for us! Ray and I each got to taste different courses, but we tried each other's dish (12 courses each). We brought along the following wines to accompany this superb meal.

CHAMPAGNE DOM PÉRIGNON 1982:

A superb Champagne that is amazingly youthful at 17, yet it displays the yeast and toast of mature Champagne. Excellent balance, layers of complex fruit. Superb! I wonder why there is such a gap in quality between this and Moët et Chandon's other Champagnes. It must be that they put all their finest fruit in the Dom, a very large production for a Grande Marque (yet the winery will not disclose quantities produced), and there is little else of quality left for their other Champagnes.

1992 CHASSAGNE MONTRACHET PREMIER CUR "LES CAILLERETS," DELAGRANGE-BACHELET:

Noticeable sulphur on nose dissipated after a few minutes. Crisp, fresh, complex, honeyed overtones. An elegant, very well-made Chardonnay. Slightly mineral. Most enjoyable and at its peak.

1988 ECHÉZEAUX, EMMANUEL ROUGET:

Ray thought that it was slightly corked. I did not think so, although it was hard, tannic, masculine, a bit rustic, maybe—but this is the character of the slow-maturing 1988s. Anyway, as it was Ray's bottle, he decided to make up for the Echézeaux, and ordered a half-bottle of this wine.

1995 SYRAH, ARAUJO, "EISELE VINEYARD":

A superb baby! Classic spicy, rich Syrah. A mouthful of superbly balanced, rich, ripe fruit. This will be an excellent wine in seven to eight years.

Our waiter and the sommelier tasted all the wines we brought along. I always insist on that—to allow the staff to taste wines they would not otherwise have a chance to taste. One criticism of the restaurant is that their mark-up policy is ridiculous, and discouraging. 200% to 250% mark-up is a bit too much. Keller is following in the footsteps of top European restaurants. At least in California restaurants, though, one can bring along one's own bottle!

Spoke to Joe Heitz over the phone. He is doing much better and is recovering from his stroke. He can taste wine now, "especially Gewürztraminer." No wonder. First, Gewürztraminer is intense and spicy, and has an immediate impact on the palate. Second, it is one of Joe's favourite varietals, especially the Alsatian kind. He can also taste reds now, but complains that so many California Cabernets taste too fruity and round, while young, and that they offer everything they will ever have, right away. Gone are the days when one had to wait five to ten years for a great red to reach it speak, and develop complexity. I think that he has a very valid point here.

I told him about a tasting of California Cabernet rarities that I am organizing in Vancouver for late June, featuring rare wines from 1969 back to 1947, including Heitz's own 1968 and 1969 "Martha's Vineyard," 1968 Georges de Latour "Private Reserve" (BV), Hallcrest 1959, Hanzell 1959 (their first vintage, and made by Joe Heitz), old Inglenook from the 1950s, and the eccentric Martin Ray's 1947 Cabernet Sauvignon (Saratoga), bottled in a Champagne bottle (Champagne cork and wire included!). Alas, the notes on this tasting will not appear in this book as it is going to print very shortly, before the tasting in June.

Sunday, May 2, 1999

Visited Barney and Belle Rhodes.

Barney is recovering nicely from his stroke. I arrived at their home one hour after John Avery left—John is retiring in a few months. Belle told me that Harry Waugh fulfilled his dream of escorting his daughter Harriet down the aisle; she was married last month. Harry will be 95 next June.

Belle and I discussed briefly the fate of the once-famous Marin County branch of the International Wine and Food Society. Since the death of its founding head, Dr. Haskell Norman, the membership is declining fast. I wonder why London does not react, as it must be losing a bundle in membership dues. The new "self-appointed" head of the branch, Jack Rubyn, has stepped on many toes. I wonder what the fate of our extensive cellar will be? Haskell Norman built a superb cellar over the years, worth well over half-a-million dollars today. With a little knowledge and imagination, we could have had at least another decade of great and rare wine tastings. We shall see.

I am writing these words while sipping a cappuccino at "Barbara Gordon's Café," in Yountville. It is a strange feeling to be writing one of my last entries before the book goes to press—after taking wine notes for a quarter-century, and editing and consolidating the material for three years. I trust it was worth the effort, and that the readers will enjoy it.

May 1999

1978 CHÂTEAU LEOVILLE-LASCASES:

20 years old, and at its absolute peak. Together with Ducru-Beaucaillou, surely the best St. Julien of the vintage, and one of the top Haut-Médocs. Cedary, stemmy nose. Full, round, spicy, very Cabernet, with trace of green, a characteristic of the vintage. Lingering aftertaste.

1985 TIGNANELLO, ANTINORI:

A beautifully crafted wine from a successful vintage in Tuscany. Ripe cherry fruit. Hint of oak; very well balanced, smooth, but with enough depth and ripe tannic backbone to last another five to seven years. Tasted with my editor for this book, Val Wilson.

1972 GRANDS ECHÉZEAUX, DOMAINE DE LA ROMANÉE-CONTI:

How wonderful the much-maligned top producers' 1972 red Burgundies are at 27 years! Palish, evolved colour. Scent of oriental spices, stemmy, raspberry jam on both nose and palate. The acidity barely noticeable. Lingering aftertaste, with hint of charred oak. A lovely bottle.

Reception at a friend's house, in West Vancouver, in honour of the 80-year-old French painter, Bernard Cathelin.

I was surprised to see Gerard Chave there, accompanied by his spouse. We had a very pleasant chat. Gerard is an avid fisherman, and spends many of his vacations fishing in Québec. As was the case with Christian Moueix and François Faiveley, Gerard is also worried about so many French wines, notably Bordeaux, tasting so similar to each other and losing their terroir character. He thinks that the damage will be long term. Coming from so many reliable sources, this must be a real problem. How sad it is to see this great art downgraded to a mere competition for high scores upon release, and maximum extraction for early appeal and consumption. I shall, hopefully, visit Chave next spring.

1986 CHEVALIER MONTRACHET, JEAN CHARTRON:

Green-gold colour, not unlike a Chablis Grand Cru. Ripe green apples on nose, with very slight hint of oak. Elegant, subdued, yet it has very good fruit extract. Long, ripe, but not very intense. Has held very well, but will not improve. Most enjoyable.

1961 CHÂTEAU GRUAUD-LAROSE:

This is an exceptionally fine wine. Deep brick-red; mature Cabernet, truffles, and spices. Beautifully balanced on palate. Soft, round, still displaying magnificent ripe fruit and great length. At its absolute peak. Grand Vin!

June 24, 1999

A very special wine event featuring California Cabernet Sauvignon Rarities.

The word "Rarities" is an understatement—the youngest wine was a 1969, the oldest a 1947. Several of these wineries are extinct now, and most of the great pioneering figures who created these wines have now departed from this world, or have been in retirement for some years. This was a once-in-a-lifetime opportunity for a group of 15 tasters to taste historic and extremely rare California Cabernets. All wines came from my cellar; one bottle of each wine was tasted.

After a glass of Champagne, Veuve Clicquot, Brut Gold Label nonvintage, and a slightly overoaked Sonoma Cutrer Chardonnay 1995, "The Cutrer," we sat down to an excellent dinner at "La Belle Auberge" restaurant, in Ladner. The dinner was prepared by Chef/Owner Bruno Marti, who has in the past prepared many very fine meals for us to accompany some great wines.

FLIGHT #1

RIDGE VINEYARDS, CABERNET SAUVIGNON N/V:

This is a blend of the 1966 and 1971 vintages, bottled in April 1972. The Cabernet Sauvignon grapes are from the Monte Bello Vineyard. Dark colour, impressive for its age; sweet, rich, slightly herbaceous, probably some young vines in there. Because the wine was bottled in April 1972, the portion of the wine that is from the 1971 vintage probably must have been from very young vines. Good, ripe fruit, just a hint of rubber, but rich, excellent balance, and has held very well in the glass. An impressive effort for a wine that is almost 32 years old.

GEMELLO VINEYARDS CABERNET SAUVIGNON N/V "35TH ANNIVERSARY," CALIFORNIA:

From the Santa Cruz mountains. This is a blend of the 1959 and 1960 vintages. The wine had an evolved orange colour at rim, but otherwise, very good depth. Full, fruity, cedary, rich. Slightly acidic, and a bit short after 15 minutes in the glass. Hint of chocolate, cocoa; a rustic wine typical of this winery's style. An impressive effort, nevertheless, and a wine that has certainly survived the test of time.

HEITZ CELLARS CABERNET SAUVIGNON 1968, NAPA VALLEY:

The best wine overall in the first flight. Mature colour with good depth, orangy rim; slightly stemmy, but a lot of elegance, hint of cedar, even of eucalyptus, although it's not the "Martha's Vineyard" but the regular Cabernet. Complex, stylish, very long, and it has held in the glass at least an hour before drying up. Most impressive effort.

SPRING MOUNTAIN VINEYARDS, NAPA VALLEY CABERNET SAUVIGNON N/V "LOT H, L/N 1968/69":

This is actually a Heitz Vineyards wine (Lot H) aged in Limousin and Nevers Oak (L/N), respectively, in the 1968 and 1969 Vintages (1968/69). It is a blend of about 50% Napa Valley Cabernet and 50% "Martha's Vineyard." Joe Heitz was short of cash at the time, and had to sell off some of this great juice to satisfy his bankers. The owners of Spring Mountain thought it only fair to bottle it . . . but to give the credit to Joe Heitz. Minty, slightly rubbery, very good deep colour; good fruit, rich; hint of roasted almonds, but noticeable acidity and dry finish. Having tasted this wine on five previous occasions, I would say this wasn't the best bottle. It was a good wine, nevertheless; however, it lacked the complexity and class of the Heitz's 1968 Cabernet that preceded it.

HEITZ CELLARS NAPA VALLEY CABERNET SAUVIGNON:

No vintage or vineyard indication. This is actually the 1959 HANZELL, their first vintage produced by Joe Heitz. Joe told me he produced this wine, and bottled it in 1962. Dr. Barney Rhodes confirmed that this is the Hanzell. Heitz said that Ivan Shaw, who helped finance Heitz Cellars, bottled this lot for himself and stored it in his grandmother's cellar. This was my third experience with this wine, having bought a lot of three bottles at auction a few years ago. This was the most evolved wine—and most evolved colour, orangy rim. The wine was cracking up; noticeable acidity, low fruit, but some fruit was there; certainly drinkable, but without the depth, weight, and fruit concentration of the first two and the fourth wines of this flight, and without the complexity of Heitz's 1968 Cabernet. Pleasant, nevertheless, and of course, a historic wine.

FLIGHT #2

MARTIN RAY CABERNET SAUVIGNON 1947, SARATOGA:

This was produced by the legendary eccentric man himself. One of the very rarest California Cabernets! Pre-1953, this wine was bottled in heavy Champagne bottles, with Champagne corks and wire. Very impressive, dark colour to rim, like a wine 25 years its junior. Hint of ether, burnt smell at first, but a rich, solid wine that was brilliant in its colour; most impressive appearance. The nose, however, bothered most tasters. The fruit was there, but it was a rustic wine with a hint of rubber. Surprisingly, after about 45 minutes in the glass, the unpleasant smells dissipated, and the wine improved dramatically. It displayed rich fruit, solid backbone, and impressive balance. A historic, irreplaceable treasure.

INGLENOOK VINEYARDS NAPA VALLEY CABERNET SAUVIGNON 1959 "CLASSIC CLARET":

Deep, bright colour; Port-like, a lot of fruit extraction, jammy, ripe, and rich. A rather simple wine, however, with no sign of new oak or complexity, yet it held its own in the glass for half-an-hour without drying up.

INGLENOOK VINEYARDS NAPA VALLEY CABERNET SAUVIGNON 1968, LOT H-12 "LIMITED CASK":

This was the best wine of the second flight. Very impressive, deep colour, even more brilliant than the 1959 Inglenook. Lovely concentrated black and red fruit on nose; not much complexity, but well balanced and full of life. This wine, if well cellared, could easily last another decade or so. Most enjoyable.

HALLCREST VINEYARD CABERNET SAUVIGNON 1959:

Produced from grapes grown on a mountain vineyard in Santa Cruz. Founded by Chafiee Hall, a San Francisco attorney in the 1940s, this boutique winery was closed in the mid-1960s. Another once-in-a-lifetime experience. Again, the appearance of the wine was very impressive: bright, deep colour, slightly evolved rim. Stemmy, herbaceous, hint of dill on nose. On palate, very concentrated, well-balanced, ripe fruit; not much complexity, but a lot of body and depth, and it held its own in the glass for a good hour before the acidity took over.

The last wine of this flight was a mystery wine. It was served to the participants double-blind. Paul Draper, winemaker at Ridge Vineyards, spent some time with Dourthe Frères, the negoçiant house from Bordeaux. When he joined Ridge Vineyards in 1969, he acquired, from Dourthe Frères, two barrels each of Château Montrose and Château Leoville-Lascases, all from the 1966 vintage. We tasted the Lascases. He bottled them at Ridge Vineyards. Needless to say, this is an extremely rare wine. The reason I introduced it to the tasting was because of the connection between this particular bottling and Ridge Vineyards.

The wine was slightly musty but not corked. Very much Haut-Médoc style, rather than California, without the youthful ripe fruit concentration that is typical of most 1966 Haut-Médocs nowadays. In other words, it is a masculine, fairly hard wine that is starting to lose its fruit. Good complexity and class, but outperformed in this flight by much more concentrated and fruity wines. Of course, one does not know how much time this wine spent in barrel before being bottled, and whether it saw any new oak at all, and how it was treated in transit between Bordeaux and California.

FLIGHT #3

The third flight was made up of three of the greatest California Cabernet Sauvignons produced by the previous generation, and wines that, indeed, were very, very different from the way California wines, notably Cabernet Sauvignons, are made today. These wines have personality and individuality, which modern Cabernet Sauvignons lack; modern Cabernets boast great extract and use of new oak, but have no personality.

BEAULIEU VINEYARDS "GEORGES DE LATOUR - PRIVATE RESERVE" CABERNET SAUVIGNON 1968, NAPA VALLEY:

Produced by the great André Tschelitcheff. An absolutely magnificent wine. Very impressive, deep colour; one would guess at a blind tasting that this was a wine from the 1980s, not the 1960s. Solid bright-red colour to rim; fabulous ripe, rich fruit; sweet vanilla, American oak on nose; similar impressions on palate. Great fruit extract, great balance, and lingering aftertaste. A lovely, magnificent wine that is almost ageless. This wine could easily last half-a-century. Superb effort.

HEITZ CELLARS "MARTHA'S VINEYARD" CABERNET SAUVIGNON 1968, NAPA VALLEY:

A wine of great reputation and class. Fabulous cedary fruit, hint of eucalyptus and mint, gorgeous bright deep-red colour to rim. Leaner, tighter, racier than the B.V., very, very different in style of course, expressing the terroir of "Martha's Vineyard," with its eucalyptus trees. Another great bottle, although I slightly preferred the sheer fruit concentration of the Beaulieu Vineyards tonight.

HEITZ CELLARS "MARTHA'S VINEYARD" CABERNET SAUVIGNON 1969, NAPA VALLEY:

While the 1968 is more famous and sought-after, the 1969 is one of Joe Heitz's all-time favourites. Very similar colour to the 1968. More forthcoming, open nose—again of cedar, eucalyptus, and hint of mint. On palate, however, a little more evolved, a little more loosely knit—not quite as tight and concentrated as the 1968. Another great bottle and a memorable wine.

Thus ended one of the rarest possible California Cabernet Sauvignon tastings. We all had the opportunity to taste wines that will never again be available; they were made by the true pioneers in California. Nowadays, the philosophy of wine production and ageing has changed so dramatically that this experience may always belong to the past. The wines may not have been as impeccably made—or as clean or as oaky—and did not have the clean, fruity taste of today's Cabernet Sauvignons, but they did have one very important attribute that today's Cabernets—even the most expensive, rarest, and most sought-after—lack, and that is personality.

What a great and historic way to end this book.

Some day, I may write another book, if I have the energy to do so. I do not doubt that the passion will remain, so… au revoir!

Albert Givton

Selected Cellar Notes

Selected Cellar Notes

Bordeaux 532
Margaux and Southern Haut-Médocs 532
St. Juliens 543
Pauillac First Growths 551
Other Pauillacs 556
St. Estèphes 561
Other Haut-Médocs 565
Pessac-Léognan and Graves 567
Saint Emilions 571
Pomerols 576
Red Burgundy 581
Côte de Nuits 581
Côte de Beaune, Côte Chalonnaise, and Some Beaujolais Grands Crus 590
White Burgundy 592
Côte de Beaune, Côte de Nuits, Chablis, Mâconnais, and Côte Chalonnaise 592
Sauternes, Barsac 602
Loupiac, Ste. Croix-du-Mont 602
Sweet Wines from the Loire Valley, Rhône Valley, and Other French Dessert Wines 606
Champagne 607
White Graves and Other Dry White Bordeaux 615
Rhône Valley Reds and Whites 616
Alsace 621
Loire Valley Reds and Whites 623
Corsica 624
Provence 624
California Cabernet Sauvignons 626
Zinfandels and Other California Reds 632
Merlots 633
Grignolino 634
Pinot Noirs 634
Petite Syrah 636
California Chardonnays 636
Miscellaneous California White Wines 641
American Dessert Wines 641
Vintage and Other Ports 644
Tokai, Madeira, and Other European Dessert Wines 648
Red, White, and Dessert Wines from South Africa and Australia 650
South Africa 650
Selected Dry White Wines from Australia 651
Selected Red Wines from Australia 652
Some Australian Dessert Wines 653
Wines from Italy, Spain, Lebanon, and Israel 654

BORDEAUX

MARGAUX AND SOUTHERN HAUT-MÉDOCS

CHÂTEAU MARGAUX 1924:

Purchased in June 1977 from Christie's (written bid).

July 17, 1977

My 32nd birthday. Low shoulder level. Cork rotten and disintegrated. Decanted. Colour was quite dark and fairly brown, but clear. Lots of sediment. Bouquet of rotten wood and musty. Taste: departed this world. Vinegar. Yet some experts who have tasted it only eight years ago said that it was still very pleasant. Needless to say, it was a disappointment, but I didn't expect much. After all, it is 53 years old, and who knows how it has been cared for?

CHÂTEAU MARGAUX 1943:

February 1983

From the Oster-Taylor mansion collection. Low shoulder level. Good cork. Crusted sediment. Pale-red colour and in a white glass bottle used for white Graves (War years' shortage). Very elegant nose, typical Margaux. Elegant, still had some fruit, acidity, tannins, but very forward. Velvety. A very pleasant surprise. Good aftertaste. After 30 minutes, it started to dry out.

CHÂTEAU MARGAUX 1952:

June 1977

At the "Toastmaster's Inn," in Rochester, Kent. A touch of brown, mature wine. Fine, delicate bouquet. Good wine. Still lively, with trace of acidity, typical of this vintage. A pleasant experience.

CHÂTEAU MARGAUX 1953:

July 17, 1986

On the occasion of my 45th birthday. Tasted it at home, with lovely osso bucco. Decanted 30 minutes. Fair bit of sediment. Brick, mature colour with good depth. Elegant, open, mature nose. Sweet, complex, delicate. An absolute masterpiece and a famous Margaux. Round, soft, forward on palate. Needs drinking, especially in bottles. Lovely, long, spicy flavours with delicate, complex finish. The nose was superb. A memorable bottle. Magnums should last well until 1990, but risky.

CHÂTEAU MARGAUX 1959:

October 1976

With Carol, at the Raphael hotel, in San Francisco. In half-bottle. Beautiful bouquet. Fully matured, dark, and soft. I wish I could purchase a case of this wine. Becoming rare and expensive.

November 1977

Last half-bottle, tasted at home. Comments as above. We'll miss this one. Delicate, supple, and complete wine. Held very well considering that it was in half-bottles.

July 17, 1980

From a regular-size bottle. My 35th birthday. Opened and decanted 30 minutes before dinner. Darkish brick-orange colour. Quite a bit of sediment. Lovely, sweet, elegant nose. At first, a bit "lead pencil" flavour, but after 45 minutes, it softened. Very elegant. After one-and-a-half hours, it started to dry out. The best part was the superb, chocolaty bouquet. Supreme elegance. Some tannin left, but definitely at its peak. Great wine. Nowadays it sells for $150 per bottle!

CHÂTEAU MARGAUX 1961:

Purchased a bottle in a wine shop in Soho on Greek Street in London, and made a successful bid for a lot of six bottles at Christie's in June 1977 (£15 per bottle).

July 1977

In London. Decanted one hour. Beautiful wine. Dark colour, medium sediment. Typical great Margaux bouquet. Long aftertaste, full bodied, soft. A complete wine. One bottle of the lot, which was shipped via the liquor monopoly, arrived in Vancouver broken. What a shame and loss!

May 1980

Dark colour, a touch of brick. Long, healthy cork. Lots of sediment. Lovely Margaux bouquet, typical "goût de terroir." Some tannin left; good balance, lovely flavour. Complex and elegant. Beautiful, great wine. The little that was left in the glass after one-and-a-half hours started to dry out and the tannins took over.

March 1984

Served blind at our residence, with Peter Sichel of Château Palmer, and Joan and Sid Cross. Some sediment, decanted one hour. Good dark colour, like a 1966. Some age, yet good colour to rim. Lovely, fragrant, complex, elegant, chocolaty bouquet. Full and long on palate. Very well balanced. At its peak, but will hold. Peter thought it was a 1959 or even a 1949 St. Julien. Sid wasn't quite sure. Nobody guessed 1961. A magnificent wine, and a great experience. This wine retails these days for US$250! I wonder how far this price increase madness will go?

CHÂTEAU MARGAUX 1966:

January 2, 1984

At home, with Carol. This wine sells today for $150 per bottle. (Equivalent to £80 or eight times as much as when I purchased it seven years ago!) Dark, still youthful colour. Good depth. Fair bit of sediment. Decanted 45 minutes, but it needed one-and-a-half hours. Lovely, elegant, and complex nose so typical of Margaux. Spicy, earthy, vegetal, sweet nose. Beautiful. On palate: a bit lean and hard at first (the 1966s are structured this way), but later became round and mellowed. Should be rounder and more complex in three to four years. The best thing about this wine is its wonderful bouquet, so typical of Château Margaux.

❧ December 13, 1986
Impressive deep, dark colour, showing some maturity. Quite solid and full on palate. After an hour, it developed a complex bouquet typical of Margaux. Good depth, complexity, and class. A bit acidic, but not in an unpleasant way. May not be as fine as the 1961, but it is much better than some "experts" say it is. Very good.

❧ May 1995
At "Bishop's" restaurant, with friends. I brought along all the wines: 1989 Montrachet, Marquis de Laguiche; 1955 Clos de la Roche, Charles Vienot; and 1980 Château d'Yquem in half-bottle. All wines that evening were great. So was this fine bottle. At 29 years of age, great depth of colour. Lovely, mature, elegant, chocolaty Margaux nose. Full, rich, round, long. Very lively! Good neck level. Lovely fruit, balance. Full, long on palate. A classic. No rush. I have owned this since 1977.

CHÂTEAU MARGAUX 1967:

❧ November 1975
Beautiful dark colour, perfumed, violet-scented. Very good wine. Long-lasting flavour. At its peak and will stay there for another few years. Good fruit, backed by some noticeable acidity.

❧ March 17, 1978
First fine bottle of wine after Orly's birth March 10. Comments as above. Fine, long-lasting bouquet. Some tannin. Ready, but will still improve in one to two years. Slight touch of brown, but deep colour. Finishes well. Try as I may, I cannot see in this wine the failure and disappointment that so many critics find in it. It isn't a great wine, but a very pleasant and good wine. Certainly better than Lafite or Mouton 1967!

❧ August 16, 1979
At home, on the occasion of our fifth wedding anniversary. Lovely oak, delicate nose. Good, elegant Margaux flavour, but too much acidity, and a bit short at the end. Lovely bouquet, nevertheless. At 12 years old, the acidity is showing signs of taking over, a problem most 1967 Clarets faced five years ago.

❧ September 1982
At home, with friends. Our last bottle of what was a fine wine that Carol and I enjoyed over the last seven years. The 1967 Margaux has always been criticized as a poor example of what that wine could produce. Yet it has never disappointed us. We tasted it against 1967 La Mission Haut-Brion and 1967 Ducru-Beaucaillou. All three were very similar in colour. Fairly dark, good depth to rim. They are now 15 years old. The Margaux was the most complex and elegant. Lovely vanilla bouquet of new oak barrels. Long, elegant, good flavour, not too much acidity. At its peak. A bit lean.

With the benefit of hindsight, the most successful, and longest lasting 1967s were the traditionally bigger wines, such as Latour and La Mission.

CHÂTEAU MARGAUX 1969:

❧ October 1976
Opened a bottle and a half-bottle of this wine on the same day. Pleasant. Fairly light and nice bouquet. But for a Margaux and for the price, it is disappointing. A fair price for this wine would be more like $17 to $20. (Paid $30)

❧ February 1980
Tasted against 1969 Château Petrus and 1969 Charles Krug Vintage Selection Cabernet Sauvignon. Lightest colour, most elegant, and complex of all three. However, after one hour, it was first to fade and dry out. Even in a mediocre year, the elegance of Margaux was there. Drink up.

CHÂTEAU MARGAUX 1978:

❧ December 1990
Decanted one hour. Some sediment. Deep, youthful colour. Vinous, spicy nose with lots of oak and vanilla. Very youthful nose. Perfumy, complex. Velvety, yet rich on palate. Good Cabernet structure. Great depth, slightly stemmy (typical 1978), but lots of fruit. Will make an excellent bottle in five to ten years. Not quite ready. The first vintage produced under the new Mentzelopoulos management (if one disregards the 1977), and what a turnaround!

❧ June 1992
Against Palmer 1978 with council of Le Tastevin. Both fine wines, but Margaux deeper, more solid, more backward. Needs five to seven years. Lovely fruit, great extract. Very good and promising. Other comments as above.

❧ April 30, 1995
Basic comments as three years ago. Still purplish colour. Superb, classy Margaux nose. Cassis and oak/vanilla. Very youthful. Great concentration on palate. Very long. If this is not the greatest 1978 Claret,

it surely is one of the two or three greatest! The elegance of Margaux and the classic structure of a true Premier Cru thoroughbred. Just about ready, but should last well until 2005, if well stored.

CHÂTEAU MARGAUX 1981:

April 1992
Decanted one-and-a-half hours. Some sediment. Impressive, deep-purplish colour to rim. Lots of extract. Still a baby on nose. Oak, vanilla, very fresh fruit. Medium-bodied, lovely fruit, ripe, mellow tannins. Very long, yet closed and fresh. Needs at least five more years of bottle-age. Doesn't have the explosive ripe fruit of the 1982 or the serious backbone of the 1983 or 1986, but an excellent wine, nevertheless. One of the best, if not the best, 1981 Claret.

CHÂTEAU PALMER 1928, NICOLAS LABEL:

Excellent top neck levels.

August 17, 1994
With Carol, celebrating our 20th wedding anniversary at "Petit Genève" restaurant in Vancouver. Not decanted. Cork indicated that it was recorked by Nicolas in 1988. Fair bit of sediment. Medium-dark, mature colour. Orange-brown rim. Classic Margaux nose. Cedar, earth, perfume; lovely and long. Nice fruit, tannic backbone, typical of the 1928s, which is why they lasted this long. Great complexity and length. Dryish finish, but superb. Classic old Claret! (19)

CHÂTEAU CANTENAC-BROWN 1955:

Purchased a lot of eight bottles at auction at Sotheby's in May 1977, at a cost of £4 per bottle. Decanted 20 minutes. Cork read "Vintage 1955." Bottled by Lalande et Co. Bordeaux. A.C. but not château-bottled.

May 1977
At first, smell of rotting wood, but improved after an hour. Dark colour, a touch of brown, quite a bit of sediment. Pleasant, still powerful wine but over-the-hill. An experience. Resold three bottles at auction at Christie's in November 1977 as part of a mixed lot. Brought back two bottles to Vancouver.

June 1978
Good cedary nose, deep colour, lots of sediment. Soft, still some tannin left. A bit dry. Starting to decline, yet still intense. A good 1955 that lasted well. Better than when last tasted in London a year ago.

December 1981
Last bottle, 26 years old, at home, with friends. Good colour, brown-orange rim. Fair amount of sediment. Lovely, elegant, old Claret nose. Margaux elegance and sweetness. Good flavour; however after 30 minutes, it started to deteriorate, and the acidity came through. Quite an experience. A good wine, overall. Everybody liked it.

CHÂTEAU D'ISSAN 1955:

November 1986
With friends, against 1957 Château Lynch-Bages. Soft, forward, still elegant, but getting tired. Nose of straw, without too much complexity. A soft vintage and a soft (but sound) wine. At the same dinner, I also served the 1961 Château Haut-Bages-Avéroux and 1961 Château Pavie-Decesse.

CHÂTEAU PALMER 1959:

August 1984
At 25 years of age, lovely, dark, yet browning colour. Good depth, almost like the 1961. Magnificent, complex, perfumy, elegant, classic Cabernet nose. Typical Margaux elegance. Lovely, round, mature, long on palate, slightly high acidity, and showing its age. Definitely at its peak. Had this wine twice before last year: once with the Commanderie de Bordeaux, and once during the International Wine and Food Society's 50th Anniversary Convention last October in Vancouver.

December 30, 1985
Last great bottle for 1985. Comments as above. Maybe not as great as Palmer 1961 or 1966 (or potentially 1970), but very lovely. Elegant, complex with good depth. A lovely bottle!

July 16, 1987
One day before my 42nd birthday, and two days before leaving for a week's holiday in San Francisco and Yountville with Carol, Michael, and Orly. Deep, mature colour. Fair bit of sediment, excellent level. Lovely, elegant, long, complex nose of delicate Margaux. Ripe, chocolaty fruit. Round, flavourful. Lovely balance. A typical, stylish Margaux. Classic nose. Lovely wine. One of the very best Palmers. At 28 years of age, it has held extremely well.

December 1991
Upper shoulder level. Classic, sweet, delicate, complex nose. Silky, long, elegant on palate. A beauty. After 40 minutes in glass, started to dry out. Decant and drink right away!

July 30, 1993
At home, at the end of the rainiest July on record. Comments as in December 1991, but even softer. Good, dark colour. Lovely, velvety, complex. Needs drinking. Has held extremely well for 34 years.

CHÂTEAU PALMER 1961:

April 1984
At the beginning of a trip to Bordeaux and Oporto. We had dinner with Peter and Diana Sichel at

Château d'Angludet and Peter opened a bottle of 1961 Château Palmer. Perfection. Fabulous, rich, long, well balanced. Palmer and Claret at its ultimate best. I have been hoping to taste this wine for a long time, having previously tasted a London-bottling by Berry Bros. that was good, but not great. This bottle was perfection. (20)

CHÂTEAU LA LAGUNE 1961:

Purchased from John Walker in San Francisco earlier this year. Cost $18.

October 1977

Decanted one hour. Very dark, bright colour. Quite a bit of sediment. Nice bouquet, but not great. Reminiscent of caramel or chocolate (that's probably because of the addition of sugar). Good, powerful wine. Faded away after two hours. Had an uncanny resemblance to a full, rich Pinot Noir.

CHÂTEAU GISCOURS 1961, IN HALF-BOTTLE:

April 1977

In London. Delicate, soft Margaux. Bright colour, medium body. Not too great a bouquet. Quite a bit of sediment. Maybe the fact that it was a half-bottle harmed the wine; it wasn't as great as one would expect from a 1961. Purchased on Greek Street in Soho (£3.50).

CHÂTEAU LASCOMBES 1961:

April 1977

In London. We found it better than the Giscours 1961. Fine bouquet, finishes well. Quite powerful, needs more time. Also purchased on Greek Street, Soho (£3.75).

June 1983

At home, at a blind tasting of 1961 Clarets. Very good wine. The elegance of the Margaux Commune combined with the ripeness and concentration of this great vintage.

CHÂTEAU BRANE-CANTENAC 1961:

Purchased in Seattle last October (1977) for $25 per bottle. Expensive.

February 1978

First great bottle of Claret in our new home on Adera Street. Carol still pregnant so I ended up drinking most of it by myself. After 45 minutes, decanted and tasted. Medium colour with a touch of brown. Earthy bouquet. Tasted tired, very dry, and powerful. One hour later, it developed a beautiful, complex flavour, and the fruit came through. Not a very big bouquet, but splendid taste. A very good wine.

CHÂTEAU MALESCOT-ST.-EXUPÉRY 1961:

February 1992

Very impressive, deep, dark colour to rim. Like a 1982, with a little more maturity! Very ripe, slightly leathery, rich nose. Lots of sediment. Full; loads of rich, ripe, leathery fruit. Lots of ripe Petit Verdot here. Long, not elegant at all, but very full, and rich. Will not improve, but will last well. Very good. Why can't this property produce such fine wines nowadays?

CHÂTEAU CANTEMERLE 1961:

Purchased six bottles at auction (Butterfield and Butterfield). Low neck, high shoulder levels.

June 1991

With council of Le Tastevin. Mature, evolved colour. Sweet, ripe, forward, open, evolved nose. Round, soft, mellow, yet good, ripe backbone. Very forward. At its peak. Elegant and classy.

February 1993

Comments as in June 1991. At its peak. Needs drinking. Will not improve, but lovely, velvety, elegant. Most enjoyable.

CHÂTEAU RAUSAN-SÉGLA 1964:

October 1976

Typical Margaux. Smooth and pleasant. A bit light in texture, but dark in colour. Short aftertaste and bouquet. Will not live long.

CHÂTEAU CANTEMERLE 1964:

Summer 1976

Fairly light, fruity, and very pleasant. Good wine. Displayed good chocolaty ripeness, but needs drinking.

Los Angeles

CHÂTEAU GISCOURS 1964:

Spring 1976

Dark colour. Quite fruity, but little bouquet or lasting taste. A little disappointing; dry, acidic finish.

CHÂTEAU BRANE-CANTENAC 1964:

May 1976

In Amsterdam. Dark, excellent bouquet. Soft, very good wine. Classic, elegant Margaux. Will not improve.

Purchased a case at auction at Sotheby's in June 1977. Paid £42 per case.

August 1977

In London. A very fine wine. Full, dark, mellow, chocolaty bouquet. Some sediment.

April 1978

This bottle wasn't too dark, and the chocolate bouquet was only slightly there. Mellow, delicate Margaux nose and bouquet. Medium sediment.

Decanted one-and-a-half hours. No trace of acidity. At its peak.

❧ March 1979

At dinner, against the Malescot 1964. Lighter in colour and body than the Malescot, but more delicate and complex bouquet. At its peak. Not a great wine, but very pleasant.

❧ December 1981

Medium colour, browning, some sediment. Decanted 45 minutes. Soft, elegant bouquet; sweet, soft on palate. Clean, starting to decline. Slightly high acidity. Drink up.

CHÂTEAU MALESCOT-ST.-EXUPÉRY 1964:

Tasted four times at home, during 1976. Very dark colour. Quite a bit of sediment. Decanted and left to breathe for two hours. Powerful, rich wine, yet soft and pleasant aftertaste. Good quality. Lots of Cabernet Sauvignon. A bit short on bouquet.

❧ March 1979

Served double-blind. Big, sturdy wine. Everyone thought it was a Pauillac or big St. Julien. Deep colour. Good nose, cassis-like, good body, some tannin left. Ready, but will stay there for some time. A bit on the dry side.

❧ October 1981

High shoulder level, good cork. Medium-dark colour, good, mature, and cedary Haut-Médoc nose. Thinning, woody, some fruit, but high acidity on palate. Starting to decline. Drink up. Hard like a 1957 or 1952 Pauillac; not Margaux style.

❧ April 1982

This bottle was far superior to the previous one in October 1981. Lovely dark colour. Minty, spicy nose. Very big wine, some tannin. Dry, a bit high in acidity. Good long aftertaste and impressive colour. Nobody guessed this wine. Not a usual Margaux. Too big for that commune. Lynch-Bages "cassis" nose.

❧ May 1984

Last bottle. Tasted against my last bottle of 1964 Brane-Cantenac. Served blind to friends. Decanted 30 minutes. Both wines had a fair bit of sediment. Level was very good on the Brane and high shoulder on the Malescot.

The Malescot was the better wine. Comments very similar to April 1982 in all respects.

The Brane was a bit lighter in colour (yet fairly dark), softer, more elegant, but getting tired. High acidity, soft, forward; reaching the end of its useful life.

The Malescot still had a fair bit of life in it. Similar nose as when last tasted in April 1982, but acidity starting to show. Very good wine. Both wines are 20 years old and they have both followed me through the past seven or eight years and given me a lot of pleasure.

Purchased a few more bottles of this wine from Christie's, Chicago in 1986. Low neck levels.

❧ July 1989

With panel of *The Wine Consumer*. Fair bit of sediment; decanted 30 minutes. Complex, flowery/herbaceous Margaux nose. Quite mature-smelling. Fuller, yet also quite old on palate, like a 1955. Maybe because of relatively low level in bottle. Still a very good wine.

CHÂTEAU CANTEMERLE 1964:

Acquired four bottles from the Chicago Wine Company auction earlier this year. Very good neck levels.

❧ May 1989

Mature colour, but with very good depth and clarity. Open, mature, long nose of older Claret; tobacco, earth, coffee. Lovely complexity. Soft and round on palate, yet not tired. Good fruit, delicate, long finish. Holding very well at 25 years of age.

❧ June 1989

With council of Le Tastevin. Even better than first bottle! Deep mature colour. Impressive nose of tobacco, chocolate, and coffee, typical of the successful 1964s. Outstanding bottle. Long, mature, soft, complex. Still fruity. Top quality and one of the last, really fine Cantemerles in two decades (until 1983). Everyone was impressed.

❧ November 1991

With friends. Much softer than in June 1989, yet best of the three wines tasted. Others were 1964 Haut-Bailly and 1964 Gruaud-Larose. Drier, tighter than in June 1989, but elegant and complex. Ready. Needs drinking.

CHÂTEAU MALESCOT-ST.-EXUPÉRY 1966:

Good neck level. Poor but legible label.

❧ March 1992

Medium sediment. Decanted 45 minutes. Good, dark, maturing colour. Earthy, lead pencil and herbs on nose. Full, dryish, but good fruit. Leaner style, but very good depth and good fruit. Hint of smoky oak. Long, complex. Ready, but no rush.

❧ March 1993

Decanted 30 minutes. Fair bit of sediment. Evolved colour, good depth. Spicy, delicate, herbaceous Margaux nose. Leaner 1966 style, but well balanced, with nice delicate fruit. Not much depth or complexity, but has held well. Clean, spicy, delicate Cabernet finish. Will not improve, but nice wine.

Malescot hasn't produced too many impressive wines since the mid-1960s.

CHÂTEAU PALMER 1966:

❧ December 1976
With Carol, at a restaurant, in Seattle. Dark, powerful wine. Needs more time. Paid $23 which was a fair price in a restaurant. After one-and-a-half hours, it mellowed a bit. Fine bouquet, but not very forthcoming at this stage. Will make an even greater wine in five years. Seems more intense and deeper than the 1970, but not as elegant and complex. Loads of ripe, chocolaty fruit. Great potential. This wine needs time. It is only ten years old.

❧ March 1986
Decanted one hour. Good dark, mature colour. Lovely, "old," complex, rich nose. Quite long. A bit lean finish. One of the better 1966s. Good complexity. This wine is now 20 years old.

❧ May 1988
My last bottle. Excellent level, wine almost touching cork. Decanted 30 minutes. Good dark colour to rim. Elegant, chocolaty nose of mature Claret. Subdued, soft, round, forward. Noticeable acidity and finishes a bit short. Better on nose and on entry than at finish. Drink up!

CHÂTEAU DURFORT-VIVENS 1966:

❧ September 1977
In London (£4). Delicate bouquet, medium colour, otherwise, disappointing. Thin, some acidity, and short finish.

❧ September 1978
A 1966 Claret tasting. A pleasant surprise. Came second after La Lagune 1966. Good fruit and bouquet. Dark colour, some tannin left. Fine delicate bouquet. A good wine. Much better than last year's experience (see above).

CHÂTEAU GISCOURS 1966:

Indications are that this is going to be a fine wine by 1978 and at $10, I would buy a few bottles, had it not been for the artificially high price of our mismanaged BC liquor monopoly, selling it for $20 per bottle in 1976. Purchased some of this in Seattle for $8.50.

❧ April 1978
Dark colour, full bouquet. Medium sediment. Decanted one-and-a-half hours. Even after two hours, it was deep, full, and beefy ("fleshy"). Will be at its peak in two years and should last for many more. Fine, delicate Margaux bouquet, yet powerful. Tannins almost gone. A fine wine.

❧ April 1979
Deep colour with slight touch of brown. Elegant, flowery nose. Good texture and long-lasting aftertaste. Some tannin to lose. A "together" wine that will last for quite some time. A bit stemmy and fairly dry. Good overall.

❧ January 1983
Lovely dark, mature colour. Touch of orange at rim. Elegant, "sweet," mature, oak/vanilla bouquet. Fair amount of sediment. Slightly high acidity. Good fruit. Elegant, yet has enough extract to last. Ready, but no rush; should be enjoyed while it is still at its peak.

CHÂTEAU D'ISSAN 1966, IN HALF-BOTTLE:

❧ March 1977
In London. Medium brown colour. Typical Margaux bouquet, soft and very pleasant. A good wine. Ready. Bottled by Berry Bros.

CHÂTEAU KIRWAN 1966:

❧ May 1975
A very soft, light, pleasant wine. 1966 was the last year that Kirwan was not château-bottled, but rather Bordeaux-bottled by Schröder and Schÿler, the owners, who are also important wine négociants.

❧ November 1977
At home, as part of a 1966 Claret tasting. This bottle tasted a little harsher than the others, and had a trace of acidity. The colour was dark/bright, and the bouquet delicate.

❧ September 1978
At a blind tasting of 1966 Clarets. Came in fourth out of six. A first it was well balanced, quite deep. Good fruit and delicate nose. Later it dried up. All in all, a good wine that is at its peak.

CHÂTEAU BRANE-CANTENAC 1966:

Served blind to friends at a dinner, against the 1971 and 1967 Brane-Cantenac.

Most elegant and complex of the three. Round, soft, subdued, elegant nose. Well balanced, forward. Ready. Good Margaux style. Herbaceous nose. Pleasant.

CHÂTEAU BRANE-CANTENAC 1967

Darker than the other two, but all three very close in appearance. Medium depth, touch of orange, mature. Best body. Bigger than the others, a bit acidic (typical 1967) but good flavours and structure.

CHÂTEAU BRANE-CANTENAC 1971:

The least good. Not as elegant on nose. Lean, hard, dull, woody, sharp. None of the guests thought it was Bordeaux (they guessed Spain, Italy, etc.). Only one guest said "Bordeaux" (she thought that I was serving a vertical of Pontet-Canet).

Cellar Notes

Château La Lagune 1966:

❧ December 1975 and April 1976

Needs more time. A big, powerful wine. Quite dark, nice, rich bouquet. Will be a very good wine in three to four years, and for many years beyond that. Very ripe, intense. I acquired two cases of this wine in Montreal in 1974, for Can$200 per case.

❧ September 1978

At home, as part of a blind tasting of 1966s. The winner! (Others were 1966 Corton Coron, a Burgundy ringer; Talbot, Kirwan, Giscours, Durfort-Vivens.) Beautiful, deep colour. Good, rich, ripe nose (cedar). Good fruit, quite a bit of sediment; lingering aftertaste, some tannin left. Needs another four years or more.

❧ November 1980

Medium-dark colour, fair bit of sediment. Lovely earthy/fruit nose, intense, yet elegant. Big, fruity, full, rich wine. Very little tannin left, but it is so nicely balanced that it will keep for some time. Long, lovely aftertaste. Great bottle! Full of flavour, yet elegant. (18)

❧ January 2, 1983

Medium-dark, brilliant colour. Slightly orangy rim. Complex, beautiful cedar/Cabernet nose. Lovely, long on palate, without the leanness of most 1966s. Good flavour, well balanced. Ready, yet with enough fruit to last for quite some time. This is first or top Second Growth quality! It should be noted that this property was devastated during the terrible 1956 frost, and most vines had to be uprooted. The 1966 vintage represents a turning point here, with the vines approaching maturity. The result is outstanding.

❧ November 1984

What a lovely bottle! At its absolute peak and perfection. Comments as above. Deep, mature, healthy colour. Round, full, rich, complex. Beautiful Claret at its peak. (18)

❧ May 1986

First day of Expo 86, celebrating Vancouver's Centennial. Comments as above, yet quite soft. Drink now to 1990. A lovely, well-balanced wine. Not as dry or lean as most 1966s.

❧ April 5, 1987

At home, with Serge Hochar of Château Musar in Lebanon. Serge is in Vancouver for the International Wine Festival. Comments as above. A lovely wine. La Lagune is one of Serge's favourite Médocs. He was, at one time, hoping to purchase that property. Touch of greenness (young vines), but otherwise a lovely wine.

❧ August 1988

With Harry and Prue Waugh. As usual, consistently good. Rich, round, good fruit, especially for a 1966. Holding very well. Cedar, oak, spices. Complex, long. A lovely wine. Top quality. One of the better 1966s. We finished the evening with a glass of very good 20-year-old Croft's Tawny Port.

❧ May 1990

At home, upon our return from a trip to Prague, Budapest, and Tokai. Comments as above. Impressive, deep colour, slightly mature rim. Chocolate, earth, and cedar on nose. Full, long, superb balance. A really lovely wine. Has so much depth and balance that, if well stored, will last for many more years.

❧ April 1991

Tasted a bottle purchased in San Francisco earlier this year. Deep, maturing colour. Fabulous nose of wet earth, cedar, chocolate. Lovely balance, length, and depth. Fully mature; great intensity, fruit. Perfectly balanced finish. This, as usual, is really very good.

❧ November 1992

Purchased two more bottles from Draper and Esquin's.

❧ December 1992

A Draper and Esquin's bottle. Very good level. Beefy, deep, dark colour. Almost Burgundy on nose. Full on palate, soft, but loads of ripe chocolaty, sweet fruit. Still lively, but getting soft. Very rich, long, succulent wine.

❧ January 1997

At home, with Michael and Orly. Forward, mature colour. Excellent level. Decanted 30 minutes. Chocolaty/cedar nose. Good depth. Sweet on entry. At 30 years old, holding extremely well. Ripe fruit, oak in harmony. Round, forward, yet excellent fruit. One of the best 1966s. Lovely wine. I have tasted this wine on 16 previous occasions. It has never disappointed me. Little did I know, back in 1975, that this wine would last so long. Maybe due to good, cool storage.

Château Palmer 1967:

❧ January 14, 1990

This 23-year-old has held extremely well. Medium, mature colour; fair bit of sediment. Decanted 15 minutes. Elegant, complex, delicate nose. Round, delicate, soft, yet still very good; good level and well stored. After one hour acidity coming through. At the end of its useful life, but still most pleasant and elegant.

CHÂTEAU BRANE-CANTENAC 1967:

❧ January 1977

Beautiful, soft, full, dark, and perfumed. Typical Margaux. This wine is fully mature, but it will last for quite some time. Fine bouquet.

❧ February 1977

Before our extensive eight-month trip to England. Started with Dom Pérignon 1969, then enjoyed a comparative tasting with dinner of Brane Cantenac 1967 and Heitz Cellars "Martha's Vineyard" 1967 Cabernet Sauvignon, Napa Valley. I decanted both one hour before dinner. The Brane had a typical Margaux bouquet. See other comments above. The Heitz "Martha's Vineyard" had a very definite and different taste. Minty and earthy (not in the negative sense of the word). It had a more definite character and is just about ready. Shouldn't be kept much longer. We ended with a 1971 Ockfener Bockstein Riesling Auslese, Weingut Gebert, Mosel-Saar-Ruhr. Light, fruity, and refreshing.

❧ June 1981

Tasted blind against Palmer 1967 and Margaux 1967.

CHÂTEAU BRANE:

Most disappointing of the three. Grassy nose, high acidity, a bit short; not too much bouquet. Medium colour. A bit thin. By itself a fairly good wine, but against the other two, not as good. This will not improve.

CHÂTEAU PALMER:

The darkest and biggest of the three. Some tannin, good, deep, bright colour, elegant nose; not too open. Not very complex.

CHÂTEAU MARGAUX:

Lightest colour, touch of orange. Sweet, elegant nose and flavour. More delicate and complex than the other two. The best of all three because it is true to the style of the commune. A good wine that has never disappointed me. All three wines need drinking, and will not last much longer.

CHÂTEAU PALMER 1970:

Three cases purchased at the new liquor monopoly specialty shop, on Pender Street, Vancouver, in December 1975. The fourth case purchased in the same store a year later. I discovered it lying in a back room. Same price ($10.50 per bottle)!!

❧ June 1976

Dark colour. Rich, fruity bouquet. Still tight. Will make an excellent wine in five years and for a long time after that. This is one of the best red Bordeaux I have tasted to date. Very promising.

❧ October 1977

Upon our return from a seven-month trip to London. Decanted two hours. Beautiful, bright ruby colour. Some sediment. Typical delicate Margaux bouquet. Full taste, but still very powerful. This wine should be ready in seven years, and will live for quite some time. Lots of tannin and powerful.

❧ August 1978

Decanted. Deep-purple colour. Intense, fruity nose at first, then developed a delicate Margaux character. Superbly balanced. Quite a bit of tannins left. Loads of fruit. Should reach its peak in five years' time. Great! I hope that this wine will last for quite some time so that we may enjoy it for many years to come.

❧ December 1980

Some sediment. Decanted one hour. Dark, deep colour, little tannin left. Lovely, concentrated wine. Good fruit/acidity balance. Elegant bouquet. Will last for many years, but very enjoyable now. No trace of orange or brown in colour.

❧ October 1983

At home, to celebrate the arrival from England, after five years, of my eight cases of 1975 Clarets (La Mission Haut-Brion and Palmer) and 1963 Ports (Dow's and Croft's). Decanted one hour. Fair bit of sediment. Beautiful 1970 colour, deep, dark, slight touch of age at rim. Lovely, elegant, long, complex nose. Full, rich, round on palate. Great balance and complexity. Lovely mouthful. Long aftertaste. A lovely bottle.

❧ December 1984

Deep colour to rim, still very youthful. Fair bit of sediment. Decanted two hours. Still has tannins to lose. Fabulous, complex, rich, chocolaty nose. Long, full, perfectly balanced on palate. Fabulous bottle. Enjoyable now, but will hold for many years. Great! (19)

❧ June 1985

With friends, who helped me move my cellar to our new home. Comments as above. Reaching maturity, but no rush. Fabulous bottle. A classic wine. At its peak in four to ten years. When I first tasted this wine in 1976, I underestimated its ageing potential. This wine will last for a long time, if well cellared.

❧ January 2, 1988

First great bottle of 1988. Superb, lively, deep, bright-red colour to rim. Still closed nose. Lots of class, perfume, and ripe fruit. Full, rich, long, perfect balance. Lots of extract. A great wine. Not quite ready. Drink from 1990 to 2005. Superb. This is now 18 years old.

❧ June 1990

Decanted one hour. Excellent level, deep colour to rim. Superb nose of violets, perfumy, elegant Margaux and chocolate. Full, long, great balance. Still very good backbone and depth. Lots of class. Starting to get ready, but no rush. Long on palate, excellent fruit. A great wine. It is vital to store fine wines in a cool cellar.

❧ February 1993

This wine now costs US$150 per bottle! That is 40% more than what I paid for whole cases 17 years ago (Can$10.50 per bottle).

❧ April 1994

Decanted one hour. Deep-red colour. Excellent extract to rim. Superb, elegant, ripe, perfumy Margaux nose. Round, velvety, elegant, perfect balance and length on palate. A great wine at its peak, but no rush.

❧ September 1995

25 years old and still superb; deep, dark, rich, long, chocolate/tobacco nose. Full, rich, yet silky Margaux elegance. At its peak, but will last for several more years until it starts to decline (if well stored). Great breed. How fortunate I am to have purchased a fair bit of this wine back in December 1975, at what now seems a ridiculous $10.50 per bottle. But, then, Petrus 1970 was retailing in New York for $18 per bottle, and Latour 1970 for $16. I feel that I am becoming the world expert on 1970 Château Palmer!

CHÂTEAU CANTEMERLE 1970:

❧ May 1976

In Amsterdam. Still youthful, but nice wine. Fruity, and not too dark, with slight trace of acidity. Not quite as good as the 1961 or the 1964 of this property, though.

❧ July 1978

At a blind tasting, featuring 1970 Clarets. Very closed. Must be going through a phase. Hard and difficult to taste. However, it is promising. Lots of alcohol, deep colour. Try it again in two years.

❧ February 1982

Lovely, deep, young-looking colour typical of the 1970 vintage. Good, fruity Cabernet Sauvignon nose. However, fairly high acidity spoils what could have been a good wine. Not too much tannin. Good fruit. Lacks a bit middle but by far its main fault is too much acidity. I was mistaken with my early positive assessment of this wine.

CHÂTEAU MALESCOT-ST.-EXUPÉRY 1970

❧ July 1985

With the panel of *The Wine Consumer*. Deep, dark colour, typical of the 1970s. Complex, long, lovely mature nose. Full and round. Rather lean and hard on palate. Tannic and a bit low in fruit. A "hard" Margaux. The nose is the best part. Will last for many years, especially from magnums, but will not improve, and may lose its fruit. Drink now to 1990.

CHÂTEAU LA LAGUNE 1970:

Purchased at Christie's in 1977 for £46 per case. Arrived in Vancouver in April 1978.

❧ January 1982

Deep, lovely colour, typical of the 1970 vintage. Not very complex on nose. At first, quite acidy, but later improved and softened remarkably. Lovely drinking now, but a bit disappointing in that it lacks complexity, a fine wine, nevertheless.

❧ August 1989

As a ringer, in tasting of 1970 Graves. Very good, youthful, rich, fruity. Has improved dramatically since 1982. At its peak, but no rush. Sweet, fruity, well-structured wine.

CHÂTEAU LASCOMBES 1970, IN MAGNUMS:

❧ December 1985

At home, with Joan and Marcel Olivier, the French Consul General to Vancouver, and other guests. Good depth, long, complex, delicate, herbaceous nose typical of Margaux. At first a bit lean, but later opened up, and developed depth. The typical, deep colour of the 1970 vintage. Very enjoyable. Ready, even in magnums.

CHÂTEAU PALMER 1975:

Purchased through A. Nugent. Lying at the château. Paid £60 per case. September 1979 lying in London at A. Nugent's. Cleared from Bond. Finally arrived in Vancouver October 1983.

❧ March 1986

This wine retails today for US$80 to US$90 per bottle!

❧ April 1986

At a blind tasting, with *The Wine Consumer* panel. Decanted four hours in advance. Very dark, deep colour to rim. Closed, unyielding nose. Big, slightly minty. Hard, tannic, closed, yet well balanced, and a lot of fruit underneath. Dumb at this stage. Great potential, but needs at least five to seven more years to open up. Maybe longer.

❧ April 1, 1993

At our residence, with Jacques Hebrard of Cheval-Blanc and Francis Fouquet, Grand Maître of the Commanderie de Bordeaux. Typical 1975, typical Palmer. Deep, mature rim. Spicy, herbaceous, yet elegant, chocolaty nose. Tight. Full, aggressive tannins. Needs time. Will be excellent. Impressive structure for an 18-year-old Claret.

❧ November 1993
Some sediment. Very good, deep colour, little maturity at rim (many 1975s are browning already). Good depth. At first, subdued tar, cedar, Cabernet nose. Full, rich, quite tannic, yet starting to round up a bit. Still a bit tannic aftertaste. Trace of sharpness, but lots of flesh. Hint of tobacco and dark chocolate (after 30 minutes). After one-and-a-half hours, a bit softer, developed more extract, still some aggressive tannins, but good fruit underneath. Promising. Try again in 1995 or beyond.

❧ April 1995
20 years old and holding its own. Decanted one hour. Fair bit of sediment. Classic 1975 and classic Palmer. Impressive, deep, maturing colour. Chocolaty, cedar, evolved nose. A bit vegetal. Tannic (typical 1975), yet good fruit extract. Lots of depth; solid, rich wine, yet the elegant complexity of this Margaux property. Very good. No rush.

❧ June 1995
First wine at our new home on 12th Avenue. We moved four days ago, on May 29. Comments as in April 1995. Cedary/tobacco, mature, yet deep colour.

❧ August 1996
On Turnagain Island, with Orly and Carol at the end of summer, Labour Day weekend. Next week Orly starts university at UBC. At 21 years of age, this wine has mellowed quite a bit. Perfect drinking now.

❧ July 1997
Upper shoulder level. Dark, evolved colour. Cedary, chocolaty, yet stemmy nose. Full, round, softened up quite a bit. At its peak. Tannins and fruit in harmony. Lovely wine. Ready, but should hold for another decade, if well stored.

CHÂTEAU MALESCOT-ST.-EXUPÉRY 1975:

❧ February 1993
Decanted 45 minutes. Very little sediment. Mature, medium-red/browning colour. Herbaceous, stemmy, almost Pinot Noir nose. Soft, most tannins gone. Old fruit, but certainly alive. Surprisingly evolved for a 1975. Hint of leather. Needs drinking.

❧ May 1996
Now 21 years old, starting to show signs of age. Decanted 45 minutes. Vegetal, spicy Cabernet, evolved nose, typical of this hard vintage. The wine is becoming a little beet-rooty/sweet. Straightforward, soft, round, good extract. Not much complexity. Tannins all soft and mellow by now. Other comments as in February 1993.

CHÂTEAU PALMER 1976:

❧ May 1983
Medium colour, bright, and young. Open, vanilla/oak Cabernet nose. Not the mintiness I found in this wine last March. Medium body. Very good flavours. Needs two extra years to lose its tannin, but not a sleeper. Lacks middle. Elegant, very nice, well made, but a typical 1976 (a bit diluted because of heavy rains).

❧ July 1984
Comments as above, but more forward on nose and colour, as well as body. Browning at rim, soft, forward, elegant, easy to drink. Not too many 1976s have impressed me so far, and I have tasted quite a few. Needs drinking. I wonder how good the 1976 vintage would have been in the Médoc, a drought and hot year, had it not rained so much during the harvest.

❧ May 1985
Medium colour, starting to show signs of age. Lovely, elegant, open Margaux nose. Soft, forward, clean, very pleasant on palate, but lacks complexity or the depth or tannin to last. Should be consumed over the next two years. Not one of the great vintages, but stylish. Bouquet is best part.

❧ June 1996
On Turnagain Island. Last bottle. The wine is now 20 years old. Comments in general as in 1985, but starting to go down hill. Very evolved. Very soft, cracking up. Evolved, palish-red colour. Delicate bouquet. Has held well, but now past its prime. I do not doubt that it has lasted this long only due to my cool cellar.

CHÂTEAU PALMER 1978:

❧ July 1986
Tasted a bottle at the office with Tony Gismondi and Dave Scholefield of the BC liquor monopoly. Very deep colour, showing some maturity at rim. Spicy, concentrated Cabernet nose. (1978 was a year of little Merlot. Therefore, Palmer is made from mostly Cabernet, which is unusual because they usually have a high proportion of Merlot in the blend.) Big, still tannic. Lovely bouquet. Not as massive as the 1975 but big, nevertheless. Excellent balance, requiring another three to five years of bottle-age. Will last well.

❧ June 1992
With council of Le Tastevin against 1978 Château Margaux. Lovely deep colour to rim. Elegant, cedary, cassis, chocolate nose. Round, soft. Very good extract on palate. Lovely length, elegance. Vegetal nose blended nicely now. Almost ready, but no rush. Really nice wine.

❧ February 1997

On Turnagain Island. This wine is now showing quite a bit of evolution. Medium-red. Good depth. Spicy, elegant nose of Margaux, yet a bit herbaceous, typical of the 1978s (low Merlot year). Forward, soft, round, long on palate. Complex and elegant. At its peak now.

CHÂTEAU PALMER 1979:

❧ September 1990

Decanted one hour. Good, dark colour to rim. Some sediment. Ripe, yet elegant, chocolaty, spicy Cabernet nose. Still youthful, yet round, complex, well balanced, long, mellow. Low tannins, but good balance, and fruit will ensure five to ten extra years, if well stored. Very good.

❧ May 1995

A bad bottle. Not corked, but rather "piqué." Metallic on nose. Sharp, sour, acidic. Some kind of bacteria must have been in the cork. Flawed. I had to open another bottle of wine (from an almost empty cellar, as most of our wines were moved this week to the new cellar at 12th Avenue). I opened a 1980 Gevrey-Chambertin "Champeaux," Domaine Maume. Comments under "Burgundy."

CHÂTEAU DU TERTRE 1979:

❧ October 16, 1992

My mother's 80th birthday. Some sediment. Good depth, round, elegant, nice fruit. Good intensity. Clean, complex finish. Actually surprisingly good. Ready. Also served that night: 1979 Château Haut-Brion and 1912 Niepoort Colheita Port. Mother was born in 1912.

This was my mother's last birthday, and these were the last bottles of wine she ever tasted. She passed away December 19, 1992.

CHÂTEAU PALMER 1981:

❧ January 1992

Little sediment. Elegant, oak, vanilla, spicy, open, Cabernet nose. Round, elegant, long. Drinking well now to 1995. Flavourful, elegant, stylish wine. Much better than its reputation would seem to indicate. Having said that, it is soft and loosely knit.

CHÂTEAU LA LAGUNE 1982:

❧ December 1987

At home, with the panel of *The Wine Consumer*, against a range of Napa Valley Cabernets, such as 1983 Opus One, 1982 Robert Mondavi "Reserve" Cabernet Sauvignon, 1982 Beaulieu Vineyards Georges de Latour, 1983 William Hill Gold Label, etc. The La Lagune was as good as, if not better than, all of the above, which are far more expensive these days. Deep, purplish colour. Ripe Cabernet and oak on nose. Full, rich, chunky, yet complex. Lovely ripe fruit intensity. Should make a lovely bottle in eight to ten years. Great charm and class. I am very pleased to have acquired three cases of this in 1984, at $92 per case. Drink from 1994 to 2005 or beyond.

CHÂTEAU PALMER 1983:

❧ January 1997

Took a bottle along to "Le Gavroche" restaurant, in Vancouver. Just my daughter Orly and I. Superb bottle! Classic Margaux, classic Palmer. Cedar, spicy, herbaceous, chocolaty bouquet. Mellow, silky on palate, yet fruity with excellent ripe berries, and rich, long finish. Perfect now, but will last for several more years. A great wine. Potentially as good as the 1970!

CHÂTEAU CANTEMERLE 1985:

❧ April 1989

With the panel of *The Wine Consumer*, served blind against various 1985 California Cabernets. Very good and typical 1985. Charming, delicate, young, fruity. Very good depth, complexity, length, good oak/fruit balance. Try around 1993 to 1995. After 1966, Cantemerle was underperforming, but from 1983, this property has started to produce fine wines once again.

ST. JULIENS

CHÂTEAU LEOVILLE N/V:

Shipped by Nathaniel Johnson. Nonvintage. Pre-WW I, possibly late 19th century.

❧ July 1995

Upper shoulder level. Crumbly cork. Still surprisingly alive. Delicate, flowery nose. A bit tired on palate, but certainly alive. Nice fruit. Super sealing-wax nose. A bit dry finish. Good, very old Claret.

CHÂTEAU GRUAUD-LAROSE 1916:

Purchased at auction. One of three lots of six bottles each, at Butterfield and Butterfield, in September 1996. Recorked at the château in 1993. Original heavy, hand-blown bottle. Superb level (topped up). The 1916 vintage has produced some superb wines. I hope that this is one of them.

❧ March 1997

Decanted 15 minutes. Lots of sediment. Excellent appearance. Good depth, mature rim. Old Claret-smelling, earthy, woody, some fruit. At first, dry and acidic on palate. Quite firm, lively, even a bit tannic, not unlike a 1945. Actually, surprisingly alive for an 80-year-old wine! Later it became smoother, cedary-woody. Good fruit. Trace of acidity, but still very much alive and enjoyable.

CHÂTEAU GRUAUD-LAROSE 1928, CHÂTEAU-BOTTLED:

Purchased at auction in 1991. When this wine arrived, one of the two magnums cracked as I lifted it from the box. Bottom fell off. What a mess! What a disaster!! Excellent neck level and appearance. The surviving magnum will be tasted with the "Group of 10." Comments in my wine diary.

CHÂTEAU LANGOA-BARTON 1928:

Shipped by Louis Eschenauer Bordeaux. Bottled by Green and Co. and S. H. Day Ltd., Cornwall, England. Good neck level.

❧ November 1989

Deep, dark, youthful colour. Lean, hard, tannic. Too dry, but has style and class. Has held very well. A bit too acidic; like a 1952 Haut-Médoc, but with even less fruit.

CHÂTEAU LEOVILLE-BARTON 1945:

London-bottled by Justerini and Brooks

❧ July 17, 1995

My 50th birthday, at home, with family and friends. Excellent neck level. Tight, but solid cork. Decanted 45 minutes. A classic 1945. Superb, sealing-wax, old Claret nose. Lovely, deep colour. Solid backbone typical of the classic 1945s, backed by ripe fruit and great extract. Incredible at 50 years! Great complexity. Ripe, solid, long. Empty glass still offered superb Claret bouquet. A top-class 1945. No rush! (19)

CHÂTEAU LEOVILLE-BARTON 1945:

Purchased two bottles of this at a wine shop in Chelsea, on Kings Road, London, in 1977. London-bottled by Block, Gray and Block. Wax sealed top. Excellent levels. Short but firm corks. Cost £18 per bottle.

❧ September 1977

In London, before returning to Vancouver. Opened 20 minutes and decanted. Fair bit of sediment. Bright, dark colour with a touch of brown. Musty smell at first, but cleared later on. This wine is over-the-hill, but still drinkable. At first, it had a very powerful, earthy taste, loaded with tannin. On the thin side. A bit green. This wine must have been at its peak ten years ago. With so much tannin, it will live for a long time, but it is losing its fruit. It was an experience, anyway.

❧ March 9, 1982

At home, with Harry Waugh, Joe Heitz, and his daughter Kathleen, and the Tobes, during the Vancouver Wine Festival. Harry was staying with us that week. I have waited for just such an occasion to open this bottle. 1945 is my birth year, and the wine was bottled by the firm Harry worked for before the War.

Finally the day arrived to open it in honour of Harry Waugh. Short but hard cork came out easily. Neck level. Original cork, according to Harry. Fair amount of sediment. Decanted 15 minutes before serving. Dark, youthful colour; incredible! Big, lovely, spicy, fruity nose. Slightly high acidity, but very good mouthful. Joe Heitz called it "the star of the evening." Long, good flavour, will hold for some time. What a great experience. Harry said that this wine was actually made by Ronald Barton. So much better than the first bottle tasted in 1977.

CHÂTEAU LEOVILLE-BARTON 1945:

London-bottled by Block, Gray and Block. Purchased a case at auction. Arrived September 1987. I paid £400 for this case.

❧ September 1987

Opened first bottle. Lowest level, mid shoulder, with some concern about the quality. I was pleasantly surprised. Deep, dark, mature colour. Ripe raisins, complex nose of mature Claret of a hot vintage. Slight hint of oxidation, but not enough to take away a thing from this wine. Round, full, fruity, long, and complex. Has held extremely well, and typical structure of the 1945s. Still full and, yes, even a bit tannic. A lovely, complex, very mature 42-year-old Claret.

❧ November 9, 1987
At home, with Prue and Harry Waugh, and other friends. Comments as above.

❧ December 1987
Superb! Best example so far from this case. Comments as above, yet this time no sign of oxidation. Lovely depth, complexity. A great bottle!

❧ April 1988
Mid shoulder level. Decanted 15 minutes. Not quite as lively as last December. Dark, mature mushrooms and wet earth on nose (old Claret). Full, soft, round, complex. Sweet. Very good. Bottle variation is to be expected with such old wines.

❧ June 1988
With panel of *The Wine Consumer*, following a vertical tasting of Stag's Leap Cabernet Sauvignons Lot 2 and Cask 23, 1976 to 1979. Medium to dark colour, a bit cloudy, mature-looking. Mid/high shoulder. Very small, shrunken cork. Lots of sediment. Chocolate on nose, sweet, round, soft; early signs of oxidation. I've had better bottles. This one was tired, but drinkable. Sweet, soft, perfumy. Not quite the structure or depth of the better 1945s. Can be excellent, though.

❧ July 1991
At "The Prow" restaurant, in Vancouver, with John Tilson, Ed Lazarus, Stephen Kaplan, and Brad Klein. Getting tired. Sweet, old fruit. Good, dark colour. High shoulder fill. Drink up. Variable bottles.

❧ February 1994
At home, with friends, against 1945 Château Pontet-Canet bottled by same shipper (Block, Gray and Block). Upper shoulder level. Spicy, cedary, open nose. Round, a bit astringent, but lingering aftertaste. The tannic backbone of the 1945s, but nice fruit. A bit dry; typical of the property. Lots of class, and a very good bottle. The Pontet-Canet was better, though.

CHÂTEAU GRUAUD-LAROSE 1949:

❧ October 1982
At home, with friends. This wine retails today, in 1982, for US$85. Opened, decanted, and served right away. Low neck level. Good cork. A lovely, 33-year-old wine. Elegant, sweet, complex nose. Good colour; a bit mature, but fairly dark. Good flavours, very well balanced. Ready, but with enough fruit to last. Better than expected. Bigger and better balanced than the 1949 Talbot I tasted in 1979. A lovely wine that has held very well. I should have bought two or three more bottles!

CHÂTEAU TALBOT 1949:

❧ December 1, 1979
Opened, decanted, and tasted within ten minutes. At first, nose "woody," but after five minutes, clean, pleasant nose. Cork clean, firm, came out easily. Medium-bright, clean colour. Fair amount of sediment. Touch of brown at rim, but very good appearance. Sweet, clean bouquet. A bit chaptalized. A bit watery on palate. Quite sweet, very little fruit left, but still had some tannin. Over-the-hill, but delicate and still drinkable. Pleasant aftertaste. Tasted a bit like a 1959 Beychevelle, but darker in colour. A pleasant surprise, since I didn't know what to expect.

CHÂTEAU DUCRU-BEAUCAILLOU 1955:

❧ April 1990
On the eve of a trip to Prague and Budapest with Carol. Lots of sediment, decanted 30 minutes. Good cork. Very good, deep, yet mature, browning colour. Expansive, perfumy, rich, ripe nose of truffles, ripe raisins, and cedar. Perfect balance, long, complex, elegant. Lots of fruit, class, and character. Soft, smooth, no sharp edges. A very, very good wine. One of the best 1955s I've tasted to date. This is the "Lafite" of St. Julien.

CHÂTEAU TALBOT 1955:

❧ May 1988
With several friends and Debbie Guimaraens, Bruce Guimaraens' daughter, who was staying with us. Served together with Hermitage "Sizeranne" Chapoutier 1955. Excellent level. Fair bit of sediment. Sturdy, rich, full, well balanced, long. Very good quality. Full, impressive. Has held very well. Didn't have quite the complexity and spice on nose of the Hermitage, but it was very good.

CHÂTEAU GRUAUD-LAROSE 1958:

Very good low neck level. René Rondeau, of Draper and Esquin's in San Francisco, praised this wine, so I took a chance and purchased two bottles.

❧ June 1989
With the council of Le Tastevin Wine Club. Decanted, some sediment, but not a lot. Impressive, dark colour for a 1958. Mature rim. It's 30 years old, from a poor vintage, and yet very impressive! Delicate, tobacco, expansive nose. Medium-bodied, soft, mature, a bit dry and acidic, yet chunky, especially for a 1958. Quite long and clean on palate. No sign of oxidation. Very good and a rare treat. A week ago, we tasted, with the Commanderie de Bordeaux, a vertical of Gruaud 1945 to 1985. This wine fit Gruaud's pattern. Even in mediocre vintages, it manages to pull it off!

CHÂTEAU LEOVILLE-LASCASES 1959:

❧ July 15, 1977

In London, when we hosted Harry and Prue Waugh for dinner. It was an "emergency" bottle, opened after a disappointing Meyney 1961. Beautiful dark colour. Harry Waugh isn't too fond of the 1959s, but he was impressed. Fine, ripe bouquet, yet powerful. Lots of body and sediment. Carol loved it, too. The next day, I purchased the last two bottles of this at a wine shop in Greek Street, Soho. I paid £8 per bottle. A reasonable price for the quality.

❧ January 2, 1980

Finally had enough courage to open the second bottle. Our first bottle of wine for 1980, and what an experience! Deep, bright, dark colour to rim. Lots of sediment. Firm cork. Decanted 30 minutes. Lovely nose, sweet, chocolaty, fruity. Medium body, elegant, typical fruity and mature St. Julien. What a lovely wine. Very little tannin left after 60 minutes. At its peak. Harry Waugh rated it first out of five good 1959s (in his Diary of a Wine Taster, Volume 8). A great wine and a great experience. Long-lasting aftertaste. Fabulous. I'm sorry I only have one bottle left.

Purchased another bottle in San Francisco in 1981. Paid $60. This is becoming expensive.

❧ June 4, 1987

A day before leaving for a two week trip to Bordeaux with Tony Gismondi, and a visit to Paris with Menashe. This was the Draper and Esquin's bottle. It was also in celebration of 20 years, on June 5, 1987, since the Six Day War, in which I was a soldier and fought on the Jerusalem front. Lots of sediment, excellent level. Deep, mature, browning colour. Complex, spicy, and cedary nose of great, mature Claret. Round, soft, forward, elegant, long, and classy. Well balanced, good fruit. A classic Claret, holding well, but definitely at its peak. A lovely wine! Long, ripe, complex aftertaste. YUM!

CHÂTEAU BEYCHEVELLE 1959:

Part of a lot of six bottles purchased at a Sotheby's auction. Paid £10 per bottle last year (1978).

❧ February 1979

Top shoulder level. Medium mature colour, brick and brown, thinning a bit at the edge. Sweet nose, a bit woody. Opened and decanted 30 minutes. Smell improved after another 30 minutes. Very sweet on palate. Most tannins gone; lacks fruit. Some alcohol left, and very (unusually so) sweet. A touch of acidity at finish. Medium-light body. Not bad, but has not lasted well, maybe due to poor storage before I purchased it.

❧ July 1979

Served blind, against Château Pichon-Baron 1959. Very elegant nose; very soft, sweet wine. Medium to light colour, pleasant, clean bouquet. One guest mistook it for a Pinot Noir. Lots of sediment. Definitely ready, and starting to decline. The Pichon-Baron was the exact opposite. Darker, much drier, closed up nose, less complex, and less elegant. Very sturdy and big. Has a long life ahead. An ideal wine would be a blend of both.

❧ September 1981

Last bottle, and the best so far. Fits almost all descriptions above, but has a bit more depth of colour. Sweet, spicy, almost Pinot Noir nose. Past its peak, yet very pleasant and elegant. The end of a chapter. Cannot improve and needs drinking.

CHÂTEAU LEOVILLE-BARTON 1961:

❧ October 1985

Decanted one hour. Medium sediment. Fairly dark, mature colour; orangy rim. Lovely, complex, open, and fruity, mature nose of classic Claret. Very well balanced, fruity (typical St. Julien structure), round, very little tannin. At 24 years of age, this wine is at its peak. Lingering aftertaste. It has enough fruit to last for a few years, but is drinking very well now. However, it is outclassed by the excellent 1959 of this property.

❧ June 1988

With the panel of *The Wine Consumer*. Lighter, weedier, leaner than the 1961 Pontet-Canet, against which it was tasted. Rich, solid backbone, typical of the 1961s; complex, spicy. Quite classy and elegant, if without the depth of some great 1961s. Very good, nevertheless. At its peak. Better on nose than on palate.

CHÂTEAU TALBOT 1961:

❧ January 4, 1977

Opened 90 minutes before dinner and decanted. Powerful wine. May live many more years. Lots of sediment. Beautiful, rich bouquet that lasted a long time. After two hours, the empty glasses still had a nice, rich bouquet. I wish I had a case of this wine! A typical fruity, yet powerful St. Julien.

❧ August 1977

In London, at our Ealing Commons flat. I paid £9 last month for this bottle. A trace of acidity, medium sediment; dark, bright colour; typical, good St. Julien taste. A good solid wine, but in the summer it is hard to drink powerful wines, and Carol is losing her taste for wine. I guess she's really pregnant.

CHÂTEAU LANGOA-BARTON 1961:

❧ May 1978
At an International Wine and Food Society dinner. Solid, dark, powerful wine. Some tannin left. Very dry and too little fruit. Otherwise a good example of the concentration of the great 1961s.

CHÂTEAU GRUAUD-LAROSE 1961:

Purchased a six-bottle lot at Christie's in May 1977, and a lot of 12 bottles in November 1977 (written bid). Had two bottles in London, with four more shipped, plus 12 lying at A. Nugent's. The shipment arrived in December 1978. Only 11 bottles. One had "disappeared." Quite expensive (£12 per bottle), but well worth it.

❧ August 1977
Harry Waugh spoke highly of this wine. This wine is perfect now. Haven't tasted anything like this before. Very dark colour; beautiful, smooth, chocolaty bouquet. Decanted one-and-a-half hours. Lots of sediment, still very powerful. Full, rich, yet supple wine. Lasted long on palate. A beauty!

❧ September 30, 1977
Our last bottle of wine in London, ending a seven-month trip to England. Superb wine. How happy I am to have another 16 bottles to enjoy in the years to come. At £12 per bottle, this is a bargain for the quality. Of the four bottles sent via the LDB, one arrived smashed by the idiots at the liquor monopoly. What a waste!

❧ January 1980
The ultimate Claret. Needs at least another two years and should last until the end of the century. Still lots of tannins, very dark, intense nose/bouquet. I cannot find words to describe this wine. Superb! Other comments as above. (20)

❧ March 1982
At home, with lovely lamb roast on the night of the 1982 Oscars. *Chariots of Fire* was the winning movie. Superb! Beautiful, dark colour; mature-looking, great, complex, deep, sweet berry/fruity nose. Lovely mouthful of perfection. Some tannin. Great balance. Lovely, long aftertaste. What more can I say? Should hold at its peak for at least another five years.

❧ October 1984
At home, with the Allan Tobes and Sid Crosses, after tasting 1970 and 1971 Château La Fleur-Petrus. Served double-blind. Magnificent, deep, dark colour to rim. Incredible, complex, fruity, mature Cabernet Sauvignon nose. As long as eternity. One of the finest wines we all ever tasted! Great complexity on palate. Soft, like a fabulous 1959, but with the depth of the 1961s. Sid thought at first that it was Latour 1961, but it wasn't hard enough. Very long aftertaste. Full, rich, round, mature, complex. A mouthful of perfection. At its peak, but no rush. (19.5) or (20)!

❧ February 1986
Good deep colour to rim, showing some age. Fair bit of sediment. Decanted one hour. Lovely, long, complex nose. Ripe, full, mature. Rich, long, very well balanced on palate. Still has some tannin. No rush drinking it. Great length and quality. A classic! This wine retails today for $175 or more.

❧ March 17, 1988
A different bottle, purchased in San Francisco in 1986. Hoping for it to be a going-away present for Carol before her trip to Nepal. Disappointing bottle. Very deep, browning colour. Good neck level. Big, rich, chunky, but oxidizing too. Still drinkable, but nowhere near the true greatness this wine can achieve. Pity. Probably poor storage.

Acquired a case of six magnums from the Chicago Wine Co. from the Nicolas (Paris) stock. Excellent level. Recorked? Paid $275 per magnum.

❧ March 1993
This wine now costs $250 per bottle, $500 per magnum.

CHÂTEAU DUCRU-BEAUCAILLOU 1961:

Purchased a case at Christie's, London, in 1977 for £140 per case. Lying at A. Nugent's. Arrived in Vancouver in July 1978.

❧ August 1978
Opened first bottle. Deep colour. Quite a bit of sediment. At first, a strong oak smell and powerful, rich wine. After an hour, the fruit and elegance came through. Excellent wine of great quality. Lovely nose and long finish. Long legs in glass. Very ripe, rich, and at 17, still powerful and youthful. A great wine!

❧ April 1979
Comments as above. Elegant, softening, yet intense, very well balanced, long finish. Had it against the 1961 Leoville-Barton. The Ducru is clearly a better wine in 1961.

❧ May 1980
My "worst" bottle. High shoulder level, and cork came out too easily. Dark colour, touch of brick; lots of sediment. Opened and decanted one hour. Clean, "old" nose. Fruity St. Julien. No mistake there. Very little tannin left. Complex, flavourful, and fruity wine. Very well balanced. Soft and elegant. At its peak. But not the "massive" wine one would expect from a 1961. Clearly, ullage was a factor.

❧ March 1982

At home, with Harry Waugh and Joe Heitz. Lovely, great wine. As good as the best 1961 Ducru-Beaucaillou tasted to date. The Lafite of St. Julien.

❧ February 1986

This bottle was much better than when tasted three months ago at a Commanderie 1961 tasting. High shoulder level. Mature brown-orange rim colour with good depth. Open, chocolaty, woody, mature Cabernet nose. Round, well structured, and balanced. At its peak. Great length. A very fine bottle. Fair bit of sediment. Decanted 45 minutes. At first it had an odd, slightly corked nose, which cleared after 20 minutes. This wine retails today for US$125 (almost Can$200).

❧ February 1987

Most comments as in February 1986, but this bottle was clean and lovely from the beginning. At its peak. Soft, complex, with great elegance. A lovely wine that is now definitely ready. Excellent length in glass. This wine has held at its peak now for almost a decade.

❧ March 1989

At home, with lovely osso bucco I prepared. Comments as in February 1987. Superb wine. Chocolate and cigar-box nose, ripe, long, elegant. Velvet! Lovely length, delicate, good depth of colour, and ripe fruit, as a fine 1961 should be. Truly top quality.

❧ March 1993

This wine now fetches US$250 per bottle! The price of fine wine is getting out of hand.

CHÂTEAU GRUAUD-LAROSE 1962:

❧ March 1993

Served from magnum as part of my 50th birthday and Corton-Charlemagne weekend. Gruaud made an excellent 1962. Bright, deep-red colour. Expansive, cedary, ripe fruit on nose. Velvety, perfectly balanced, very long. An excellent 1962.

CHÂTEAU GRUAUD-LAROSE 1964:

❧ May 1977

Tasted it at a Christie's presale tasting. Very pleasant and fruity. A bit harsh (tannic). A good wine. Roasted, smoky character, even gamey.

❧ September 24, 1989

On the eve of Carol's trip to Bhutan. Decanted 45 minutes. Very good, bright-red colour, like a 1962. Slight maturity at rim. Cedary, spicy, fruity, mature Cabernet nose. Slight hint of charred oak. Solid, quite dry, but still has good fruit. This wine is 25 years old. Good depth, backbone, concentration, and balance. Solid, as Gruaud usually is. At its peak. Excellent wine.

❧ December 1989

Very good level. Decanted 30 minutes. Good, dark colour. Lovely, ripe, chocolaty, cedary, Cabernet nose. Full, long, fruity, and ripe. Great concentration. At its peak, but no rush. Ripe, chocolaty on palate, too. Full, rich, sturdy St. Julien, yet mellow and mature. Lovely.

❧ March 1991

Odd, smoky-oaky. They had a fire at Gruaud in 1965 and 60% of the 1964 vintage was destroyed. Maybe the smoke affected some casks? Quite dark, fruity, rich, chunky.

❧ November 1991

At home, with friends. Tasted against 1964 Haut-Bailly, and 1964 Cantemerle. Darkest. Weedy. Very Cabernet. Tight, hard, losing its fruit, yet still tannic. Like an "older 1975." Not as smoky as in March 1991. Quite solid. Hard St. Estèphe-like.

CHÂTEAU DUCRU-BEAUCAILLOU 1964:

❧ August 1976

Beautiful, dark colour. A big wine. Nice bouquet, dark and fleshy wine. The St. Juliens, as a whole, produced superior wines in 1964 to all other Haut-Médoc communes. Only Latour is better.

CHÂTEAU LEOVILLE-LASCASES 1966, LONDON-BOTTLED BY BERRY BROS.:

❧ March 1977

In London. Powerful, fine wine. Needs more time. Typical fruity St. Julien, a bit brownish colour. Should be ready in three years. 80% Cabernet Sauvignon! At £3.75 per bottle, a very good buy.

❧ September 1977

Had a half-bottle, in London. Lots of flesh. Dark. Excellent fruit extract. Very "Cabernet"-cedary. This was Château-bottled. Drink from 1980.

CHÂTEAU LEOVILLE-LASCASES 1966:

Purchased from Draper and Esquin's. Shipped by Dourthe Frères in Moulis (Médoc) in cask to California. A single barrel (25 cases) was shipped and bottled by Paul Draper at Ridge Vineyards, Cupertino, California. Good low neck/high shoulder level. Very rare! Bottled in standard Ridge bottles, no punt, unusual label portraying the chais of Lascases, rather than the Gate and Lion. René Rondeau of Draper and Esquin's told me that they tasted recently a bottle with lower fill and it was very good.

❧ February 1, 1991

At farewell dinner for *The Wine Consumer*. Chunkier, bigger, and drier than the château-bottling. Impressively lively. Not unlike a 1966 St. Estèphe. Good fruit, straightforward, spicy.

CHÂTEAU TALBOT 1966:

❧ March 1978

Had a bottle at a blind tasting of six Margaux and St. Juliens of the 1966 vintage. Came in last. Fairly forward, finished short, Medium-light colour; not too complex. Too dry. A good wine, but not a great one.

CHÂTEAU GRUAUD-LAROSE 1966:

❧ June 1976

Superior, in my opinion, to Talbot 1966. More character, more body (definitely) and a longer-lasting aftertaste. Very good wine and a good value at $11.40 per bottle. Tasted it twice in 1976. Dark and fruity, a typical, good St. Julien. Great fruit extract, and structured to last for another decade or more.

❧ November 30, 1978

Decanted two hours. A big, deep-coloured wine. Lots of tannins, some acidity, too. Good fruit, excellent bouquet. Needs at least another two years. A great wine. One of my favourites. It is selling now at the BC government liquor monopoly stores for $23.50! That is more than double the price paid two years ago.

❧ January 1982

Fairly deep colour with touch of orange-brown at rim. Good, spicy Médoc nose; good fruit, well balanced. Softening up. Ready, but should hold for a few years before declining. Not very complex, but a typical, fruity St. Julien.

❧ September 1993

Decanted 45 minutes. Good, dark, maturing colour. Lovely, complex, oak, Cabernet, warm-biscuit nose. Round, full, rich. Very good balance and extract. Has lost its aggressive edge. At its peak, but no rush. Full, long, spicy Cabernet finish. Very good. Not dry, not hard. Round and lovely. This wine retails now for US$75 (Can$100).

❧ Late September 1995

29 years old and still full of life. Typical Gruaud-Larose, typical St. Julien. Dark, full of fruit extract. Chunky, well balanced. Long. Not very complex, but developing classic, mature, Cabernet/cedar character. Chocolate, too. Lots of fruit. No rush. Will last another ten years. One of the best 1966s (many are drying up).

CHÂTEAU GLORIA 1970:

❧ September 1979

Lovely deep colour, nose still closed (decanted one hour), but elegant, "oaky." Lovely, intense flavour. Excellent fruit/acidity balance, some tannin left. Powerful wine. Needs one to three years. Long-lived. Best Gloria I have tasted to date. Purchased a case in Seattle last May. Paid $76 for the case.

❧ February 1985

Dark, maturing colour to rim. Typical 1970 appearance. Open, round, elegant, charming Cabernet nose. Round on palate. No tannins left. At its absolute peak. Has held very well for 14 years. Long, round, rich. Very enjoyable, but not too complex. Very good. Better than any other Gloria made to date.

❧ October 25, 1993

Federal election night in Canada, and the day we sold our house on Montgomery Street in Vancouver. Looks like a majority Liberal government under Jean Chretien. Back to a weak dollar, more spending, more taxes, and more alienation of Quebec. Decanted 15 minutes. Good dark, maturing colour. Mature Cabernet nose. Very good fruit, but soft, getting a bit tired. However, good extract has kept this wine going. Now past its prime, but still enjoyable.

CHÂTEAU LEOVILLE-BARTON 1970:

Purchased three cases of this wine in Montreal for $90 per case in November 1975.

❧ June 1991

Good neck level. Decanted 45 minutes. Medium sediment. Mature, brick-red. Earthy, spicy, open, evolved nose. Soft on palate. Round, delicate, fruity. Well balanced. Soft tannins. Clean, long, earthy, Cabernet (slightly vegetal) flavours. Needs drinking.

CHÂTEAU GRUAUD-LAROSE 1970:

❧ April 1991

Excellent, deep-red colour to rim, typical of 1970 Clarets. Full, spicy Cabernet nose. Round, rich, very good fruit concentration. Not very tannic, but well balanced and nice, concentrated fruit. Long. No rush. A bit one-dimensional.

CHÂTEAU DUCRU-BEAUCAILLOU 1970:

Purchased two cases in Vancouver in 1977. Cost $12.20 per bottle.

❧ November 1977

Quite a bit of sediment. Bright, dark colour. Decanted one-and-a-half hours. Powerful wine. At first, it seemed a bit "green," but improved in glass and after two hours, was very good. Needs at least another five years of bottle-age.

❧ March 1987

Deep, bright colour to rim, showing no sign of age. Fair bit of sediment. Decanted one hour. Spicy, open, fresh, herbaceous nose. Complex, long, full. Well balanced, good fruit. Little tannin, but still youthful. Very good. No rush. Holding extremely well at 17 years old.

❧ June 1993

At the Four Seasons hotel, with Daniel Baron of Dominus Estate (Moueix), and council of Le Tastevin. Superb colour. Deep, still youthful. Lovely tobacco/cedar, ripe nose. Very young (excellent storage, level). Fair bit of sediment. Decanted one hour. Full, rich, reaching its peak, but lots of extract, ripe fruit, and balance. No rush. If well cellared, will last until 2002 or beyond.

❧ December 1995

Decanted 45 minutes. Excellent dark colour. Slightly mature rim. Classic, fruity St. Julien. Mature, evolved nose of ripe fruit, chocolate, and cedar. Full, rich, round, velvety. Great length, body, and balance. At its peak. Lovely wine. Top quality. Best St. Julien in 1970.

CHÂTEAU GRUAUD-LAROSE 1971:

❧ March 1982

Deep, dark colour, still youthful. Decanted one-and-a-half hours; vegetal, intense nose. Has fair amount of intensity, fairly high acidity, even tannic. A hard wine. Lacks middle and that worries me. A lean wine that will last for a long time, but will it lose its fruit? Resembles a 1952!

❧ October 1987

Queen Elizabeth II and Prince Philip were in Vancouver last month on an official visit, and stayed at the Four Seasons hotel. The hotel's general manager phoned me and said that the Queen's representatives requested Château Gruaud-Larose 1971 for a private dinner with Canada's Prime Minister Brian Mulroney, and his wife Mila. They asked me if I could supply two bottles of this wine and I agreed.

They also requested a bottle of Fonseca's 1963 Vintage Port. I agreed reluctantly, because I only have three bottles left of this fine Port. Somehow I doubt that Her Majesty, the Queen, and the Prime Minister were made aware of the fact that they were drinking wines from my cellar. I wonder why 1971 Gruaud-Larose was specified, when I could have supplied much finer wines.

CHÂTEAU BEYCHEVELLE 1971:

❧ April 1982

On Turnagain Island. Good colour, starting to show its age. Lovely, long, sweet, cedary bouquet. Very little tannin left, but should hold for another four to five years. Well balanced, long aftertaste. One of the most enjoyable 1971 Haut-Médocs I've tasted to date.

❧ May 1985

With Bruce Guimaraens, the owner/winemaker of the great Fonseca's Ports, and a good friend. Very nice wine. Comments similar to three years ago.

❧ January 1989

I had the whole bottle by myself, as Carol is "off wine" for a month. Comments as in 1985, yet good concentration of fruit; rich, round, very soft, good depth. Needs drinking, but by no means "dead." Good fruit, trace of acidity at finish. Quite pleasant, but can only decline at this stage.

This is the best effort at Beychevelle between 1970 and 1985. The wine is delicate enough as is, but they generally overproduce at Beychevelle. A little more concentration can turn this property into a much finer product.

❧ January 1994

Last bottle. Decanted 30 minutes. Some sediment. Impressive depth, yet evolved colour. Lovely, cedary, open, forthcoming, spicy Cabernet nose. Round, very soft; was better three years ago, yet most enjoyable. Most 1971 St. Juliens were very good, but they are getting tired. Based on my experience with them, I can safely say that the best 1971 St. Juliens were Beychevelle and Leoville-Lascases. Talbot was good, too. I've had this Beychevelle well over a dozen times since 1975 and it has never disappointed. Definitely needs drinking, even if very well cellared. I shall keep a fond memory of this wine. Back in 1977, I paid $12.50 per bottle. It was well worth it.

CHÂTEAU LANGOA-BARTON 1971:

❧ February 18, 1980

Still big, some tannin, dark, good fruit, grassy nose. Needs at least another two years. Otherwise, a sad day. Pierre Trudeau's Liberals got into office again, but I won't spoil this Cellar Book with lousy politics!

❧ June 1989

Served blind, to the panel of *The Wine Consumer*. Decanted 30 minutes. Excellent top neck level. Most thought it was an Italian 1971. Leathery, palish colour. Odd nose. Soft, tired, still pleasant, but stemmy; trace of acidity. Past its prime. Odd. A disappointing wine. Passé! This wine was much better when it was ten years old.

CHÂTEAU LEOVILLE-LASCASES 1971:

Tasted it twice in 1979. Deep colour, good fruit, needs one to two more years. Not as elegant and complex as Beychevelle 1971, but a serious, masculine Cabernet wine.

❧ September 1991

Very good neck level. Some sediment. Dark, mature appearance. Complex, elegant, evolved, spicy Cabernet nose. Round, well balanced. Soft, but still has fruit. Silky, classy. Better balanced, and a finer wine than the Lascases 1970. Very good. At its peak, if well stored. Magnums should be very good.

CHÂTEAU DUCRU-BEAUCAILLOU 1972:

❧ February 1981

At a blind tasting against 1972 Lafite and 1972 Haut-Brion. Ducru was dark, a bit jammy. Very little on nose. All three wines had an unpleasant grassy-green nose. (Lafite had the nicest nose of all three. A minty bouquet reminiscent of Heitz "Martha's Vineyard"). Haut-Brion had the lightest colour. All three were short, very acidy. The poorest year of the 1970s and an experience for all of us. Lafite came first, Haut-Brion second, and Ducru third. A vintage best forgotten.

CHÂTEAU LEOVILLE-LASCASES 1975:

❧ January 1983

Decanted one-and-a-half hours (it needed it!). Very good, deep, dark colour to rim. Some sediment. Great Cabernet extract. Pauillac structure, but St. Julien fruit. Typical tannic, powerful 1975, but lots of excellent fruit. Very good length. Rich, intense, lots of depth. Will improve at least until 2000, and last well beyond. Acquired in London in 1977 from Justerini and Brooks. Paid £56 per case. Drink from 1988 to 2000.

CHÂTEAU BRANAIRE-DUCRU 1975:

❧ June 1985

Decanted one-and-a-half hours. Fair bit of sediment. Deep, dense colour to rim. Still young-looking. Complex, spicy, but still closed, cedary Cabernet nose. Clean and very fine. Full, rich on palate. A chunky wine. Good fruit, some tannins to lose. Needs at least two to three more years. Will last for another decade. Clive Coates described this wine as simple, soft, and forward. Nonsense!

❧ August 1990

On Turnagain Island, with friends. A bit more evolved than five years ago, but otherwise as good. Approaching its peak, but no rush. Will last to the end of the century. Spicy tobacco, old-style Cabernet. good backbone, depth, Cabernet fruit. Very well balanced. A very good, underrated wine. I am glad that back in 1979, I purchased a case of this wine. Paid $165 per case.

❧ June 1997

An excellent bottle for a 22-year-old. Dark, evolved colour. Cedary, spicy, sweet Cabernet nose. Round, good backbone, rich, long. A very fine bottle. Ready, but no rush. Has enough fruit to last. Has developed the classy, chocolaty character of mature Clarets from good vintages.

CHÂTEAU LEOVILLE-LASCASES 1976:

❧ November 1993

With council of Le Tastevin. Very good level. Fair bit of sediment. Decanted 40 minutes. Excellent, deep colour to rim. Not unlike a 1975. Subdued, clean, cedary Cabernet nose. Fairly solid, good fruit, full-bodied. Not at all what one would expect from a 1976. Most 1976s are well past their prime today. Good length, solid, backed by nice fruit. This bottle had an excellent level, and was well cellared at a constant 52°F. A pleasant surprise.

CHÂTEAU LEOVILLE-LASCASES 1978:

❧ August 1996

Good, deep colour, mature rim. Fair bit of sediment. Rich, concentrated, yet mature, cedary Cabernet on both nose and palate. Has the unmistakable herbaceous character of the vintage (lack of Merlot). Long, round, complex; lovely bottle. Ready, but no rush, yet this wine is already 18 years old. Purchased in New York in 1981 at a cost of $212 per case.

CHÂTEAU DUCRU-BEAUCAILLOU 1978:

❧ February 1995

At almost 17 years old, lovely, deep colour. Complex, flowery-cedary Cabernet nose. Typical elegant style of this property. Good depth, fruit, and balance. Ready, but no rush. A velvety wine. Not too stemmy; a problem with several 1978s.

❧ March 1997

Excellent neck fill. Originally purchased in 1981. Comments as in February 1995, but a bit more evolved. Good, dark colour. Typical stemmy, bell pepper nose of the 1978s (lack of Merlot). Complex, spicy, fruit/acidity in harmony. Leaner style, but good depth. Lovely now.

CHÂTEAU LEOVILLE-BARTON 1978:

❧ May 1995

Upper shoulder level. Decanted 30 minutes. Elegance combined with the stemminess of the vintage. Level (low), some weepage, may have caused this bottle to mature fast. Cedary, elegant Cabernet nose. Nice evolved colour, good depth. Forward, round, elegant. At its peak. Pleasant, but not very complex. Nice wine, though. Some tasters may find it too stemmy, bell-peppery.

CHÂTEAU LEOVILLE-POYFERRÉ 1978:

❧ September 1996

With Orly. Very good, deep colour. Spicy. Herbaceous Cabernet nose. A bit vegetal, a problem with many 1978s (little or no Merlot in blend), but good fruit. A bit too acidic. Complex, long, spicy. Better than expected. At 18 years, it has held very well.

CHÂTEAU GRUAUD-LAROSE 1978:

❧ March 1997

With Val Wilson, the editor helping me write this extensive wine book. Decanted one hour. Some sediment. After a few minutes in glass, opened up very nicely. Good depth, mature, orangy rim, but excellent appearance at over 18 years of age. Slightly herbal-cedary nose. Rounder, smoother, better balanced than expected. Ripe, yet not a heavy-handed wine. At its peak. Not too stemmy, as many 1978s can be. Actually very good. Best 1978 Gruaud tasted recently.

CHÂTEAU GRUAUD-LAROSE 1981:

❧ April 1997

Impressive, deep colour to rim. Lovely, cedary, ripe black currants on nose. Softening a lot on palate, but still great fruit extract. Very rich, long, cedary, ripe fruit. Certainly one of the top 1981s. No rush.

CHÂTEAU SAINT-PIERRE 1982:

This property was purchased in 1982 by Henri Martin, owner of Château Gloria. He dropped the name "Savaistre" and changed the label.

❧ March 1994

At the Renaissance hotel, in Vancouver, for a trial dinner for the Commanderie de Bordeaux. Tasted against 1982 Leoville-Barton and 1982 Gruaud-Larose. Most forward of the three. Nice fruit, rich, round, long, elegant. Ready, soft, but good, concentrated fruit.

The Leoville-Barton was a bit drier, more vegetal, better backbone. Long, no rush. Very good.

The Gruaud-Larose showed best. Great extract, rich, deep, dark, loads of ripe fruit. Intense, full. Excellent balance. Years ahead of it.

CHÂTEAU GRUAUD-LAROSE 1983:

❧ June 1988

With the panel of *The Wine Consumer*. Very deep, dark, purplish colour to rim. Impressive, spicy, ripe Cabernet fruit on nose. Long, full, rich, tannic, layers of fruit. Big, intense wine. Loaded with ripe fruit and tannins. Very well balanced. Needs ten more years. Will be lovely. Surely one of the top 1983 Haut-Médocs, and a bargain at $24 per bottle.

PAUILLAC FIRST GROWTHS

CHÂTEAU LAFITE N/V (PRE-1905):

Shipped by Birkedal-Hartmann. Label read: "Barons Alphonse, Gustave, Edmond de Rothschild." These are the three sons of James de Rothschild, who acquired Lafite in 1868, and died that same year. One very good neck level. The others, upper shoulder or lower levels. Possibly late 19th Century. These wines were among several cases of old wines and liqueurs discovered at a hunting lodge in the Fraser Valley, just east of Vancouver. According to Nathaniel Johnson, this wine is a blend of several vintages, all prior to 1905.

❧ January 1993

Mid shoulder level. Brighter than previous bottles. Cork disintegrated. Decanted. After 15 minutes: sour, thick, prune juice. After two-and-a-half hours: Old Claret nose. Ripe fruit, woody, wet earth, but ripe raisins, too. Full, rich, powerful. Concentrated. Very deep, dark colour. Over-the-hill, but certainly drinkable. Hint of oxidation. Not bad at all.

❧ January 26, 1993

Mid shoulder level. Served to council of the Commanderie de Bordeaux. Great bottle! Pulled cork two hours in advance. Decanted 15 minutes. Bright, deep, mature colour. Orangy rim. Like a 1955 or 1953! Lovely, complex, oak, cedar, ripe raisins, sealing wax, complex Claret nose. Full, rich, still tannic, great extract. A bit astringent, but long, and complex. Rich, lovely flavours. Fabulous bottle! Top quality by any standard. Cork crumbled into dust. Great experience.

CHÂTEAU LAFITE 1959:

❧ 1977

Purchased six bottles in Amsterdam. Paid $30 per bottle. This wine is being offered in San Francisco now for $70 to $75, so if it is really excellent, as its reputation indicates, I have made a good buy.

❧ 1978

For sale in San Francisco for $120!!

❧ March 5, 1978

We finally decided to open a bottle. Top shoulder level (that's what worried me). Opened and decanted 45 minutes before dinner. Very long, clean-smelling cork. Colour was deep red, very bright, no trace of brown at 19 years! Did not fade at rim. Smell/bouquet was musty at first, but later developed a clean, long-lasting, cedary Pauillac bouquet, quite delicate, yet powerful. Taste of a fine, big, chocolaty wine. Improved an hour later. Good, long-lasting aftertaste, some tannin left, and quite fruity. Amazing for such an old wine. A tiny bit of acidity identified by both Carol and myself at the end, but otherwise excellent. I'm happy we have another five bottles left. We will try it when it is around 25 years old (around 1984). One of the five or six best Clarets we have tasted to date. These days, if it can still be found, this wine retails for over $150 in the US.

❧ August 1984

On the occasion of our tenth wedding anniversary. This superb wine is 25 years old now. Decanted 45 minutes. Impressive, deep colour, showing some maturity at rim. Superb nose of ripe, chocolaty fruit, cedar, oriental spices, combined with the elegant style so typical of this property. Great balance on palate. Magnificent ripe, round, very long fruit. A perfect wine. Lafite has not made a wine of this level since. Maybe the 1982 will be as good, some day. I have purchased two cases of the 1982 as "futures" recently. It was quite expensive, at $480 per case ($100 more per case than Mouton-Rothschild of the same vintage).

CHÂTEAU LAFITE 1962:

❧ December 1976

A wine of very good quality. Fair bit of sediment; decanted one hour before dinner. Bright colour, not too dark. Not a bargain at $32. Has the appeal and elegance of this early maturing, yet long-lasting vintage, which was overshadowed by the great 1961s.

❧ July 17, 1978

My 33rd birthday. Decanted at home, and had it at "La Quiche" restaurant. Far better than first bottle. Bright, dark colour. Quite a bit of sediment. Generous nose. Well balanced. Some tannin left. At its peak after one hour. A touch of brown. Very good. Sells nowadays in San Francisco for $45 per bottle.

❧ March 1983

It is always hard to part with the last bottle of any fine wine, but wine is a living thing, and when its time comes, it has to be drunk. Definitely at its peak. Decanted 30 minutes. Fair amount of sediment. The typical, bright-red colour of the 1962s, slightly orangy-watery at rim. Typical sweet, delicate bouquet of Lafite. Not very intense. A soft and elegant wine. No tannins, good clean, fruity flavour. Slightly high acidity, but not unpleasant. Well balanced. Nothing to be gained by keeping this wine any longer. Today this wine sells in San Francisco wine shops for around US$125 to US$150. A very pleasant experience.

CHÂTEAU LAFITE 1966:

❧ June 1985

While moving my cellar to our new house on Montgomery Street, a friend who was helping me dropped a case containing this bottle. It broke. This is the only bottle that broke out of over 4,000 bottles moved. But did it have to be this one? Replacement cost today is over $220, and it was my only bottle!

CHÂTEAU LAFITE 1967:

❧ 1976

Way overpriced at $42 per bottle. I paid too much for this. Shouldn't have bought it for this high price. Lighter than the Margaux 1967 in colour. Pleasant aftertaste. Noticeable acidity, however. Not nearly as good as the 1967 Latour, La Mission, or Margaux.

❧ October 1979

At a blind tasting of Margaux and Pauillacs. Light colour. Elegant nose, soft, and delicate. Chaptalized. Noticeable acidity. Drink up.

CHÂTEAU LAFITE 1968:

❧ September 1976

New York. For $5 per bottle, an excellent buy. Very light and fading, but typical Lafite bouquet. Pleasant wine. Pale colour. Elegant, silky, soft. Will not last much longer, though.

CHÂTEAU LAFITE 1971:

❧ July 17, 1981

My birthday. Pale, evolved colour. Orangy, a bit thin at rim. Sweet, elegant, scented bouquet. Open. Lacks middle and a bit short finish. Tired, fairly high acidity. Nose/bouquet the only good thing. Otherwise disappointing.

❧ May 1982

With the two Cross families, against 1971 Beaulieu Vineyards Georges de Latour "Private Reserve" Cabernet Sauvignon, and 1971 Château La Fleur-Petrus. Lightest colour. Comments as above. Had more complexity than the two others, but not a great wine. Dill-vegetal. Later, sweet caramel. Disappointing for Lafite, and expensive at $40 per bottle. (By now, this wine retails for $80 to $90 per bottle.)

CHÂTEAU LAFITE 1975:

❧ December 1990

At home, with French Consul Bernard Ledun. Decanted 45 minutes. Typical 1975. Good, deep colour. Some sediment. Tight, serious, spicy Cabernet nose. Solid, hard 1975 on palate. Good fruit, but a bit too dry. Lacking generosity, and has some bitterness at finish. Quite good, though. Will last for several years, but may not improve.

CHÂTEAU LAFITE 1976:

❧ August 1994

Perfect top neck level. At 18 years of age, perfection. Satin and lace. Lovely balance. Medium red, good depth. Elegant, long bouquet of oak/vanilla/ripe fruit.

Similar impressions on palate. Long, complex, round. Must be the best 1976! Lovely.

CHÂTEAU LAFITE 1979:

❧ July 1995

16 years old. Decanted one hour. Good, deep colour to rim. Lovely, sweet cedary, perfumy nose. Ripe, round on palate. Typical soft, rich, sweet 1979, and typical elegance of Lafite. Classy, long, fruity. Ready. Will not improve, but should hold well. Very good. Better than either 1979 Mouton or 1979 Latour.

CHÂTEAU LAFITE 1983:

❧ September 1993

A bit lean and tight. Needs time. Medium to dark colour. Tight on nose, but some elegance and fruit coming through. Still fairly hard on palate. Needs five more years, or longer.

CHÂTEAU LAFITE 1985:

❧ June 1997

Bright, deep, cherry-red colour. Expansive nose of oak, vanilla, ripe cherry fruit. Round, typical 1985 style, exotic fruit, mellow tannins. Very long. Approachable now, but well balanced and enough fruit to last for another decade or more. Lingering aftertaste. Classic Lafite and classic 1985, "the year of the comet."

CHÂTEAU LATOUR 1952:

❧ March 1977

Tasted with Carol. Last dinner before our departure March 11, 1977, to spend several months in London. Beautiful, dark colour. Lots of sediment. Opened and decanted one-and-a-half hours before drinking. This was the best red Bordeaux we've had in a while. Superb. Velvety-smooth. No trace of acidity or tannin. The bouquet was fantastic and rich, and lasted for a long time in glass. Truly a great wine. Not nearly as hard or acidic as I expected it to be. Purchased at a special Château Latour auction at Christie's in June 1977. I made a successful bid for a lot of six bottles. These bottles were recorked in 1967 at the château, and have been lying there until final shipment to Christie's. Harry Waugh and Penning-Rowsell were at the auction, too, and we had a brief chat.

❧ April 1980

At home, with the Sid Crosses. Decanted one hour. A lot of sediment. Dark colour. Lovely, big Cabernet Sauvignon bouquet; hint of mint and cedar on nose. Easily identified as a big Pauillac or St. Estèphe (served blind, as usual). Lots of tannin, very dry. A bit short on fruit. Will last for years without declining, but will not improve. Its fault: very dry and relatively low fruit. Otherwise an excellent 28-year-old wine. 1952 produced good, but hard, slow-maturing wines. The key is having enough fruit to outlast the tannins and acidity.

CHÂTEAU LATOUR 1962, MAGNUM:

❧ March 1997

At a farewell council meeting/dinner of the Commanderie de Bordeaux, before my stepping down as Maître. Magnificent magnum! Absolutely stunning! Bright-red colour, typical of the vintage. Superb chocolaty, cedary nose. Full, round, velvety, yet with great, ripe fruit extract. Superb balance. A great 35-year-old Claret.

CHÂTEAU LATOUR 1964:

❧ June 1985

One of the last great bottles of wine we had on Adera Street before moving to our new house on Montgomery Street. I selected a bottle that had a low fill (low neck/high shoulder). Decanted one hour. Deep colour, still fairly youthful-looking. Very slightly watery rim. Lovely, mature, open, yet ripe fruit impressions of classic Pauillac. Spicy and rich. Full, round, long, masculine on palate. Perfect balance. Very long. At its peak, but has enough depth and is so well balanced, it will stay at its peak for many years, and will decline very slowly. Very long aftertaste. A superb bottle and possibly the greatest 1964. (Other fine 1964s I have enjoyed and that are, in my opinion, the best of the vintage are La Mission, Trotanoy, Petrus, Haut-Brion, and Figeac.) Great wine.

❧ July 1988

Excellent level. Beautiful appearance. Deep, mature colour to rim. Lovely nose of truffles, black fruit, and other ripe red fruit. Superb, sweet, complex, soft, elegant, yet has lots of stuffing. A fabulous bottle. Still at its perfect peak. A lovely 1964. Wish I had more!! Textbook, mature Pauillac. Great!

❧ November 1993

Great wine. Amazingly, comments as in July 1983, ten years ago. Identical. A great classic wine. No rush, if well stored.

CHÂTEAU LATOUR 1966:

❧ September 1977

Tasted a half-bottle in London, purchased from Berry Bros. (£5). Excellent. Deep colour, fruity, rich. Fine bouquet. Needs another three to five years. Should be ready by 1986.

❧ November 1983

This wine is 17 years old and, even in a half-bottle, it is showing fantastic characteristics. Deep colour, slightly maturing at rim. Complex, cedary, round, beautiful nose. Full, rich, very long on palate. Intense, complex, some tannin to lose. Well balanced. Even in a half-bottle, this wine will hold for quite some time. A great and marvellous Claret experience. Pity I only have one bottle left. This wine retails now for US$100 or more per bottle! Even at this high price, I must try to get some more.

CHÂTEAU LATOUR 1967:

❧ November 1980
After our return from an extensive, two-month trip to France. Dark colour, touch of brown. Lovely nose. Some tannin. Good flavour and long aftertaste, but seems to lack "middle." A bit watery. If it weren't for this fault, it would have been an excellent bottle.

❧ March 1996
At 29 years of age, excellent level/appearance. Decanted 45 minutes. Fair bit of sediment. Good colour, mature rim. Unmistakable Latour/Cabernet Sauvignon/cedar nose. Round, soft, and mellow on palate. Quite long, spicy, complex. Good, cedary fruit, yet acidic finish typical of 1967. Latour must be the longest-lived 1967. Almost all others are over-the-hill. Will not improve. Very good. Probably the best 1967 made. Drink up over the next two to three years.

CHÂTEAU LATOUR 1970:

❧ June 1996
On Turnagain Island. The one bottle that is top shoulder. (All other bottles well into neck.) At 25-and-a-half years old, still not ready! Essence of Cabernet/cedar/oak nose. Very deep colour to rim. Decanted one-and-a-half hours. Very full, intense, ripe fruit. Great extract. A wine for the next generation. Fabulous, intense, full, long. A classic. It retails now (1996) for US$350 per bottle. How fortunate I am to have acquired two cases of this wine in Seattle back in 1976. The cost was $225 per case.

Purchased three cases from Christie's Chicago in 1987. (Some high shoulder and a few low neck levels.)

❧ April 1987
Opened first two bottles at home when Serge Hochar of Château Musar came over for dinner. Both corks fell into the wine. A disaster. Wine oxidized, sour, dead. Am contacting Christie's Chicago to return the wine to them! What a disappointing and disgusting experience! Yet, Christie's catalogue did not indicate that the wines (in all three cases) were leaking, and most were upper shoulder levels. "Buyer beware" or not, they must give me a refund for this. Paid US$1100 per case, plus border taxes (into Canada).

❧ May to July 1987
Opened another five bottles, two with best fill of bunch. Oxidized, sour. Woody. Dead. A disaster! At least I got my refund from Christie's. They should not have allowed this wine to be sold at auction. The levels were too low, and most bottles showed obvious signs of leakage. Stains on wooden cases, too. Several corks fell into wine when tapped gently. Fortunately, I own two cases, purchased in Seattle back in 1976, and these are magnificent.

CHÂTEAU LATOUR 1971:

❧ September 1991
Decanted 45 minutes. Very good top neck level, and dark, still youthful appearance. Spicy, cedary, complex Cabernet nose. Very good fruit-acid-tannin balance. Long, complex. No rush if well cellared.

❧ January 1995
Decanted one hour. Dark, impressive colour. Ripe, rich, spicy Cabernet nose. Full, round, much more forward than the 1970. Lots of fruit, good extract, slight dryness at finish. At its peak, but no rush. Lots of class, even some chocolate. Rich, long. First Growth extract and quality.

CHÂTEAU LATOUR 1975:

❧ February 1992
Decanted two hours. Some sediment, but not much. Very impressive, deep, dark, opaque colour to rim. Tight Cabernet-cedar nose. Full, tannic, ripe fruit. Very big, intense, loads of Cabernet. Hard, but backed up by enough fruit. Needs many years. Try around 1997 to 2000 or beyond. Excellent potential.

CHÂTEAU LATOUR 1976:

❧ April 1992
Good neck level; dark colour to rim. Some maturity. Cedary, spicy, slightly green nose. Quite full, ripe on palate. Soft, trace of acidity, dry, yet good fruit. Long, serious Pauillac. Certainly very good, and one of the top 1976s. Has held very well. Will not improve.

CHÂTEAU MOUTON-ROTHSCHILD 1934:

❧ March 1991
From a half-bottle. Very good neck level. Solid, healthy cork. Heavy glass, deep punt. Excellent appearance. Good, dark, mature colour. Superb, spicy, complex, tobacco-cinnamon-cedar, mature nose. Round, excellent backbone. Good, lively fruit. Complex, long. A bit short-acidic finish, but overall outstanding. Has held extremely well, especially in half-bottle. Great depth and classic Mouton nose. A memorable wine.

CHÂTEAU MOUTON-ROTHSCHILD 1957:

❧ 1977
Better than Latour 1957; fairly dark, a touch of brown, still fruity and delicate, even after one-and-a-half hours. Spicy Cabernet on nose. Trace of acidity, typical of this hard vintage, but backed by good fruit.

CHÂTEAU MOUTON-ROTHSCHILD 1959:

❧ November 1994
Decanted 40 minutes. Impressive, deep colour to rim. Superb, classic Mouton nose: cedar, tobacco, some mint, and ripe berries. Great depth and extract. Full, rich, yet round. Very long aftertaste. Complex, rich, cedary. A classic. This wine is becoming very expensive. Retails now for US$500 per bottle.

CHÂTEAU MOUTON-ROTHSCHILD 1962:

❧ June 1977
Lunch with Carol, at the Tate Gallery, in London. They have a very fine wine list. Superb wine. Dark, soft, round. Fine bouquet. Mellow, but with enough extract to last. Cedary, minty, rich, and long. At £7 per bottle, at the restaurant, this is a bargain.

❧ March 1980
This bottle was purchased from Cockburn and Campbell in London, in September 1977. Quite a bit of sediment. Very good, firm cork. Clean-smelling. Dark, clear, deep colour all the way to rim. Lovely bouquet, fruity, sweet, cedary nose so typical of Mouton. Impressive appearance for a wine of this age. Decanted and tasted after 45 minutes. When first tasted, it had quite a bit of acidity, lots of alcohol, very little tannin. Held very well for two hours, but quite high acidity; good flavours. The acidity bothered Carol more than it did me.

CHÂTEAU MOUTON-ROTHSCHILD 1967:

❧ June 1980
Lovely cedar-woody nose. Good, dark colour. Sweet on nose and palate. Soft, ready, elegant, but after one hour, the excessive acidity came through; a problem with so many 1967s. Other than Latour, Petrus, or La Mission, I doubt that any 1967 will improve. Many have reached their peak and others are declining fast.

CHÂTEAU MOUTON-ROTHSCHILD 1969:

❧ July 1977
In London. Medium colour, with a touch of brown, a thin wine. Dull bouquet. A very disappointing, acidic wine. Not worth the £6 I paid for it. A poor vintage.

CHÂTEAU MOUTON-ROTHSCHILD 1970:

❧ March 1983
With Bob Sinclair. Bob gave me this bottle when he lost a bet about Pierre Trudeau retiring after the Constitution was brought back from Great Britain. Of course, Trudeau didn't retire, but I felt guilty and I shared this bottle with Bob (five years too soon). Lovely, dark colour. Big, cedary, lead-pencil nose. Rich Cabernet nose and flavour. Very well balanced. Some tannin to lose. Concentrated. A fine wine from a great year. Try around 1988.

❧ September 1990
I have tasted this wine on at least six occasions since 1983, but this is the first of my own bottles tasted since then. Fair bit of sediment. Decanted one hour. Good, dark colour with some maturity at rim. The depth of the 1970s. Complex, cedary, mature Cabernet nose. No tannins left, but good fruit, and backbone. Complex, long, serious Pauillac, yet trace of acidity/astringency at finish. Will hold well, but as fruit softens further, this astringency might become more obvious. Better than Lafite, but without the structure and intensity of Latour or Montrose 1970. Very good, and classy nevertheless.

CHÂTEAU MOUTON-ROTHSCHILD 1975:

❧ December 21, 1994
First bottle of case, and last wine at home for 1994, as on the following morning, the family is leaving for a two-week holiday to New Orleans, Houston, San Antonio, where we will celebrate New Year's Eve, and Austin, Texas. This wine retails now, December 1994, for about US$110 per bottle or Can$150. Decanted one hour. Some sediment. Good, dark colour, maturing rim. Spicy, cedary/earthy nose. Full on palate, good fruit/acidity. Surprisingly, not as tannic as expected. Long, spicy, clean finish. Ready in bottles at 20 years of age, but no rush. Try magnums around 1997 to 2005.

❧ June 1995
Tasted against a 1986 Heitz Cellars "Martha's Vineyard." Comments as in December 1994. Lovely, complex, not as ripe or luscious as Mouton 1959, 1961, or 1982, but fruity, and with good stuffing. A fine classic Claret.

CHÂTEAU MOUTON-ROTHSCHILD 1976:

❧ July 1985
I opened a bottle on my 40th birthday in our new home on Montgomery Street. Medium colour. Good depth. Round, soft, complex, forward. Lovely, cedary, evolved nose. Medium body and depth. At its peak. Not a great wine, but quite enjoyable.

❧ August 1989
Good, dark colour. Slightly maturing rim, but with good depth. Warm, open, spicy nose, with cedar, tobacco, ripe raisins, and oak in harmony. Full, yet soft, elegant, and no sharp edges. At its very best. Drink up.

CHÂTEAU MOUTON-ROTHSCHILD 1978:

❧ September 15, 1986
At a charity auction at the Vancouver Museum. I commented on the auction wines in a printout. Fairly deep colour, starting to show some age. Spicy, cedar nose, slightly green, and stemmy, but later improved.

Medium body and complexity; spicy Cabernet. Quite a good wine. Drink now to 1995, but not as good as the 1970, 1975, or the great 1982. Somehow lacking in extract and ripe fruit.

❧ May 1991

General comments as six years ago, but quite a bit more evolved. Too vegetal, lacking fruit, and too acidic. Disappointing.

CHÂTEAU MOUTON-ROTHSCHILD 1983:

❧ October 8, 1989

While Carol was in Bhutan, I opened a half-bottle with lovely osso bucco I made that was popular with the kids. Good, dark, still youthful colour. Spicy, clean, long nose, some cedar. Medium-bodied, well balanced, slightly tannic, but quite enjoyable in half-bottle. Clean, complex finish. Full bottles will reach their peak in four to six years. Not as great or intense as the 1982, but certainly top-class. Promising. Leaner style, typical 1983.

❧ November 1992

Half-bottle, at home. Comments similar to three years ago, but a bit more forward. Just about ready. Well-stored bottles should peak around 1996 and last well into the 21st century.

CHÂTEAU MOUTON-ROTHSCHILD 1984:

Bottle signed by artist (Yakov Agam), and by Baronesse Philippine de Rothschild, in appreciation of my assistance at a Mouton/Vancouver Museum charity auction.

❧ September 16, 1986

Medium-red colour. Not too much depth. Clean, spicy, herbaceous on nose with hint of oak. Similar impressions on palate. A medium-bodied, mid-term wine. Pleasant. Drink from 1990 to 1992.

OTHER PAUILLACS

CHÂTEAU PONTET-CANET 1945:

London-bottled by Block, Gray and Block. Purchased a case at auction in 1986 in London for £360. Most bottles have excellent levels. Some labels do not indicate vintage.

❧ August 1987

First bottle, after allowing the wine to rest for three weeks, with Joe and Alice Heitz, who were our guests for three days. Good level (top shoulder). Lots of sediment, impressive dark colour. Nose a bit oxidized, pruny, and leathery. Wet wood. Still tannic on palate. Full and solid, but not very pleasant taste. Hopefully, the other bottles are better.

❧ November 9, 1987

At home, against 1945 Leoville-Barton (same London-bottling). Served blind. Guests were Harry and Prue Waugh (Harry worked for Block, Gray and Block before World War II.) The Leoville-Barton was more concentrated, fruitier, livelier, and excellent. Both excellent low neck levels. This Pontet-Canet had lovely depth of colour; round, complex, drying out a bit, but still fruity. Good flavour and had the tannic backbone typical of the 1945s. A great experience for us all.

❧ June 1988

With the panel of *The Wine Consumer*, against 1945 Leoville-Barton (same London-bottling), 1961 Leoville-Barton, and 1961 Pontet-Canet. Superb bottle, much livelier and better than the 1945 Leoville-Barton. Blue-green glass bottle. Low neck level. Good, long, solid cork. Lots of sediment. Deep, impressive colour, like a 1961, but some orange at rim. Lots of ripe, mature Cabernet on nose. Wet earth, wood, mushrooms, oriental spices. Full, tannic (backbone of the 1945s), lots of fruit, classy. One of the best of this case so far, and best wine of the evening.

❧ July 1990

At "La Belle Auberge," in Ladner, with friends, celebrating my 45th birthday. (Also tasted 1985 Montrachet, Louis Latour, and 1979 Roederer Cristal. Bruno Marti, owner/chef, tasted all three, too.) High shoulder fill. Decanted 15 minutes. Cork disintegrated. Deep, mature colour. Very good depth. Lots of open, warm cedar, solid Cabernet nose. Chocolate, leather. Very good intensity. Depth and structure typical of the 1945s. Tannic, masculine. After a half-hour, acidity obvious, but still very good, full, rich. Has held extremely well. Very good. How fortunate I am to have been born in 1945. Vintages do not come much better than this, and not just in Bordeaux!

❧ July 17, 1992

On my 47th birthday, with family and Mother. Good, top shoulder level. Cork disintegrated. Fair bit of sediment. Impressive dark colour of a much younger wine. Heavily oxidized on nose. Solid, but sour and too pruny. Almost undrinkable. Disappointing. C'est la vie! Served a back-up wine (a 1972 Grands Echézeaux, DRC), which was excellent.

❧ February 1994

At home, with friends. Served blind against the Leoville-Barton 1945 (same shipper). Comments about cork and appearance as above, but quality excellent. Good neck level. Superb, ripe, clean, mature, and intense, cedary Cabernet nose. Full, solid, rich, and long on palate. Still tannic (typical 1945), but loads of fruit. Guests thought it was a First Growth (Latour!). Very long. Richer, fuller, and longer than the Leoville-Barton.

CHÂTEAU PONTET-CANET 1949:

❧ December 1985

Impressive, dark colour, quite young-looking for its age, like a good 1966 or 1970 (at 36 years of age!). Good cork. Complex, meaty, slightly dusty nose. Full, round, rich, long on palate. A lovely, sturdy 1949 that has held very well. After 20 minutes in glass, it started to show some excessive acidity. A typical, old-style Pontet-Canet, and a great experience.

CHÂTEAU LYNCH-BAGES 1957:

❧ August 1981

Quite dark and very dry. After 45 minutes, developed a lovely, minty-eucalyptus nose, and softened a bit. Hard, dry Pauillac. Good style. Definitely a success for a 1957. Lynch-Bages resembles Mouton-Rothschild on nose, and is described as "the poor man's Mouton."

❧ November 1986

At home, with friends, served against 1955 Château d'Issan. Dark colour; dill, eucalyptus, and mint, both on nose and palate. Solid, masculine, dry, but has some fruit. Typical of both the property and the vintage. Very good quality.

❧ January 1991

Very good neck level. Fair bit of sediment. Still impressive, dark, spicy, lean, yet has good fruit. A success in that difficult vintage. Surprisingly good, and holding well.

CHÂTEAU PONTET-CANET 1959:

❧ March 1988

Excellent depth, length, and complexity. Smooth, perfect balance, long. At its peak. A lovely wine. Super quality. Classic Pauillac.

CHÂTEAU PICHON-LONGUEVILLE-BARON 1959:

❧ July 1977

Tasted a half-bottle, at the "Toastmaster's Inn," in Kent. Dark colour to rim. Rich, chocolaty, cedary, long-lasting bouquet. Ripe, full-bodied. Very good wine. (paid £4.25). Had it on the same day as the Château Margaux 1952, also in half-bottle.

Comments under Margaux 1952.

❧ August 1977

Purchased six bottles at Hedges and Butler on Regent Street, London, for £7 per bottle. Shipped to Vancouver.

❧ September 1977

In London. Very dark, full, powerful wine. Fine bouquet, quite a bit of sediment. Cedary, ripe fruit, yet masculine Pauillac. One of the last great Pichon-Barons to date. It has a long life ahead.

❧ February 1986

Mature, yet deep colour. Not unlike a fine 1961 or 1970. Very good depth. Fair bit of sediment. Decanted 45 minutes. Good neck level. Complex, mature, spicy-ripe, cigar nose. Long and complex. Full, austere, yet round, and well balanced. Finished a bit dry, but had good length. A solid, typical, sturdy Pauillac of excellent quality. Ready, but no rush.

❧ December 1991

With Sid and Joan Cross, the Mottersheads, and Bernard Ledun, French Consul General to Vancouver. Upper shoulder level. Very impressive, deep, dark colour. Essence of Pauillac/Cabernet nose, concentrated. Latour-like. Intense, hard, concentrated. A bit dry and austere at finish, yet still has fruit. Powerful wine. No rush.

CHÂTEAU HAUT-BAGES-AVÉROUX 1961:

Purchased five bottles in Seattle in 1976 for $9.50 per bottle.

❧ January 1977

At home, with friends. Everybody agreed that it is an excellent wine. Not a big nose, yet superb taste; nice dark colour, lots of tannin. Decanted 45 minutes. Long-lasting bouquet in empty glass. I hope I can get some more. It is a real bargain at $9.50. Will live for many years, and maybe even improve. (Haut-Bages-Avéroux is owned by the Cazes family. This wine is the second wine of Lynch-Bages.)

❧ November 1986

Last bottle, with friends against Pavie-Decesse 1961 (St. Emilion). Good, dark colour. Complex, elegant, mature nose of ripe Cabernet and tar. Full, round, good backbone. At its peak, but holding well. A very good bottle.

CHÂTEAU LYNCH-BAGES 1961:

❧ April 1977
In London, with Carol. Powerful wine, dark colour, some sediment. Will be ready in three to four years, and last for a long time. If there's anything for which I have to reproach this wine, it is a slight lack of bouquet. However, it is a typical Pauillac, powerful, and very good. We will spend the next seven months in London.

CHÂTEAU MOUTON-BARON-PHILIPPE 1961:

❧ July 1978
At a tasting of five vintages of Mouton-Baron (1961, 1966, 1970, 1973, and 1975). Sturdy, big wine. An ideal wine would have been the depth and body of the 1961, combined with the bouquet and finesse of the 1966.

❧ August 1991
A bottle purchased in San Francisco in 1990. Very good, dark, maturing colour. Complex, earthy, long nose. Quite rich on palate, but drying up a bit at finish. Good, but not great. Previous two samples were much better. Maybe storage wasn't ideal before I purchased it. Can be excellent.

❧ May 1994
Sign of weepage. Mid shoulder level, cracked/oxidized capsule. Decanted 30 minutes. Clean, cedary, ripe, old Cabernet nose. Deep colour to rim. Good fruit, rich, sweet/ripe, yet acidic finish. I've had better bottles. Faulty cork, but wine held up. Nice, cedary, long finish. Hint of tobacco. Magnums should be very good now.

CHÂTEAU PICHON-LONGUEVILLE-BARON 1961:

One bottle is original, château-bottled, purchased from Draper and Esquin's. The other, very high fill, is from the château, recorked and topped by Jean-Michel Cazes, who now manages the property on behalf of the new owners, the AXA Group. Original bottling: traditional red capsule and silver top. Recorked bottle: copper-colour capsule, level almost touching cork.

❧ March 1992
Tasted both the original bottling and the recorked bottle. Both were in very good shape. The recorked bottle was a bit fresher, cedary, spicy, with very good depth, weight, and length. The other bottle (original cork), was a bit more evolved, ripe, chocolaty, intense. Both displaying the depth and extract of this fine vintage and of this great property. What a pity that the former owners of this property, the Bouteillers, produced mediocre wines between 1967 and 1985. Jean-Michel Cazes and the AXA Group have now turned this property around, especially with the superb 1989 vintage.

CHÂTEAU GRAND-PUY-LACOSTE 1961:

❧ February 1986
Purchased a case at Christie's Chicago auction for $750.

❧ April 1986
High shoulder level. Decanted 45 minutes. Medium mature colour. Fair bit of sediment. Complex, yet very mature nose. Round, soft, forward, long. Mature, but still perfectly sound. Quite forward, but very good complexity. This bottle needed drinking. Others may be bigger and harder. Must re-taste.

❧ April 1991
Good, low neck level. Decanted 45 minutes. Garnet, maturing colour. Good depth and clean. Lovely mature, ripe, cedary, spicy, chocolaty, wet earth nose. Classic Cabernet and Pauillac. Quite soft, but rich. At its peak, yet good depth, long, and complex. Very good. Ready; it will last well for three to four more years, but it will not improve.

❧ September 1995
Comments almost identical to four years ago!

CHÂTEAU PONTET-CANET 1961:

❧ May 1985
Deep colour, typical of the big 1961s. Chocolate, spices, tobacco on nose. Full, rich, long, complex. Very 1961. Classic Pauillac. Serious, ripe, fruity. An excellent bottle. At its peak, but no rush. What a pity that this fine property ceased to produce fine wines after 1966.

CHÂTEAU PONTET-CANET 1961:

It should be noted that older vintages of Pontet-Canet were bottled in Bordeaux by the then-owner, the négociant firm of Cruse.

❧ November 1987
Lowest level of case, but level still well into neck. Some sediment. Excellent deep, dark colour to rim, showing some maturity. Complex, rich nose. Fruity, intense, mature, old Claret, rich, round, and chunky on palate. Finishes long and clean. An excellent Claret from a great vintage. Ready, but no rush.

❧ June 1988
With the panel of *The Wine Consumer*, against 1961 Leoville-Barton, 1945 Leoville-Barton, and 1945 Pontet-Canet. Deep colour, typical of the big 1961s. Chocolate, spices, tobacco on nose. Full, rich, long, complex. Very 1961. Classic Pauillac. Serious, ripe fruit. An excellent bottle. At its peak, but no rush.

❧ November 4, 1991
Low neck level. Decanted 45 minutes. Fair bit of sediment. Impressive, deep colour, mature rim. Superb oak, tea leaves, complex, warm nose of classic

Cabernet. Ripe, excellent backbone, balance, length. Full, rich, intense, long. Lovely bottle. Without the perfume of Lafite or the power of Latour, but very fine bottle nevertheless. The last excellent Pontet-Canet for many years. What a great vintage 1961 was! The following day, I had surgery on my right hand for carpal tunnel syndrome. I should stop writing so much!

❧ January 1995
One bottle of a lot of four bottles purchased with Brad Klein at a London Christie's auction in 1994. Decanted 30 minutes. Browning (but clean), very mature colour. Hint of oxidation on both nose and palate. Sound, drinkable, but not a patch on good bottles of this excellent wine. Poorly stored?

CHÂTEAU PONTET-CANET 1964:

❧ February 1996
Now 32 years old. Dark, brick-red colour. Expansive, cedary nose. Classic Claret. Soft, round, fully mature, yet certainly long with good fruit. After 30 minutes, some acidity coming through (drying out). Overall, most enjoyable. Drink up. Up to 1966, Pontet-Canet produced excellent wines. With the 1986 vintage, this property seems to be making a comeback.

CHÂTEAU GRAND-PUY-LACOSTE 1964:

❧ June 1990
Tasted against 1964 Gruaud-Larose. Very good, maturing colour. Nose of earth, mushrooms, mature Cabernet. Quite dry, but still has fruit. Severe, austere, but very good length. Will not improve, but no rush.

CHÂTEAU BATAILLEY 1966:

❧ February 1984
Very nice wine. Good depth of colour, maturing at rim. Lovely, open, and complex Cabernet nose. Long, round, well balanced on palate. Not as lean as some 1966s. Very enjoyable. A good 1966 and a good Pauillac.

❧ January 1994
Very good neck level. Decanted 45 minutes, some sediment. Good, dark colour. Some maturity. Surprisingly dark. 28 years old and still at its peak! Lovely, mellow, silky smooth wine. Good Cabernet extract. Long, delicate, yet not tired or over-the-hill. Lovely drinking now. Holding very well. An underrated wine. Still lots of fruit there. As good as ten years ago! I underestimated the staying power of this wine.

CHÂTEAU LYNCH-BAGES 1966:

❧ February 1994
Before trip to South Africa with the International Wine and Food Society. Top shoulder level, fair bit of sediment. Very impressive, deep colour. Classic cedary/mint, cigar-box nose of Lynch-Bages. Full, rich, youthful. Lots of life ahead. A bit obvious acidity, but very good fruit, and even some tannin at 28 years of age.

LES-FORTS-DE-LATOUR 1966:

The second wine of Château Latour. Very good appearance/neck level. This is the first vintage in which Les-Forts-de-Latour was produced.

❧ January 1993
With the panel of Le Tastevin. Very good, dark colour. Slight maturity at rim. Cedary, spicy, classic Cabernet nose. Some greenness on nose and palate (young vines). Very good depth, fruit, oak, soft tannins. Cedary, spicy. Classy 1966 Cabernet that is almost 27 years old.

❧ July 17, 1985
On my 40th birthday with friends. (That night, we also had an extraordinary bottle of 1945 Château Mazeyres, Pomerol.) Tasted Les Forts against the Grand Vin, Latour 1967. Both were fairly dark, mature at rim. Les Forts was slightly paler. Spicy, forward, complex, a bit edgy, but good length, and complexity. At its peak, and will not improve. Fairly dark. Latour was more complex, rounder, fuller, richer, and longer, but similar in style. Lovely, spicy nose. One of the best, if not the best, 1967s. Without the nagging acidity of other 1967s. Round, forward, soft. At its peak. A lovely bottle! Les Forts was slightly leaner. Both very good, but overshadowed by the marvellous bottle of 1945 Château Mazeyres.

CHÂTEAU PONTET-CANET 1968:

❧ 1980
Still available in some BC government liquor monopoly stores. They must have bought a lot of this garbage. Sells at an exorbitant $12.50!! The government monopoly must have bought the whole production of this wine, made in a dreadful year. If one needs proof that bureaucrats have no brains and/or do not care, this is it!

CHÂTEAU LYNCH-BAGES 1970:

Purchased 14 bottles in Seattle in 1982. Paid $465 for the lot. A good buy and a great 1970.

❧ November 1, 1989
Decanted one hour. Very dark, deep, still youthful colour. Ripe raisins, cedar, rich, spicy, warm Cabernet nose. Full, powerful, rich, long intense on palate. Surprisingly youthful. No rush. Drink 1992 to 2005 or even beyond, if well stored.

❧ October 1992
Very good mid neck level. Decanted one hour. Fair bit of sediment. Deep, impressive, dark colour. Little sign of age at 22 years of age! Fabulous ripe fruit, cedar,

and minty nose of a "poor man's Mouton," or fine Napa Cabernet Sauvignon. Full, intense, ripe, rich on palate. Loads of ripe fruit. Rich, full-bodied, long. No rush. Excellent.

❧ May 1997

Against 1970 Palmer and 1970 Ducru-Beaucaillou. Superb bottle, full of life at 27 years of age. Far more intense and youthful than both the 1970 Palmer and Ducru, (which were excellent, too).

CHÂTEAU GRAND-PUY-LACOSTE 1970:

❧ November 1980

Tasted double-blind with friends. Everybody thought this was a California Cabernet. Big, cedary-spicy nose. Closed, powerful. Decanted two-and-a-half hours. Needs a good five extra years. A big, slow-maturing Pauillac of excellent quality. Compared to Lynch-Bages, which is sweeter, more charming, and lovely to drink now (but it has a fine future ahead of it). Drink from 1985 to 2000, if well cellared.

❧ September 1983

Tasted blind against Château Leoville-Barton 1970. Both decanted one-and-a-half hours. The Leoville-Barton was the older-looking. Medium dark, orangy rim. Lovely, complex Haut-Médoc nose; no mistake there. Round, long, lovely bouquet, and flavour. Fairly high acidity. There is a danger that if left too long, the fruit will disappear, and the acidity will remain.

The Grand-Puy-Lacoste had a massive, deep-purplish colour to rim, not at all showing its age. Concentrated berry, Cabernet nose. Not as complex as the Leoville-Barton, but a lot of depth and weight. Such great concentration of fruit, good acidity, and some tannin will make this wine a keeper. Lovely!

❧ December 1988

Deep, bright-red colour to rim with little sign of maturity for an 18-year-old wine. True to the vintage and to the property's style and classic Pauillac. Truffles, spicy Cabernet on nose. Round, complex, long, sturdy, yet nothing sharp. Full, rich. A lovely bottle at its peak, but the fruit and the balance are so good that it will live another decade or more, especially if well stored. Robert Parker Jr. does not like this wine. He gave it a low rating, which is great news, because I have just acquired a second case at a Chicago wine auction for only $350 per case!

❧ August 1996

On Turnagain Island. Decanted 45 minutes. Mature, yet deep colour. Lovely, cedary Cabernet, spicy Pauillac nose. Full, rich, long, soft; has lost its tannin. Very long, full. The "poor man's Latour." Very good and ready at 26 years old.

CHÂTEAU LYNCH-BAGES 1975:

❧ August 25, 1988

On the occasion of Michael's Bar Mitzvah and his birth year, 1975. Some 12 guests had a chance to taste it. Best red wine of the evening, and an excellent 1975. Without the hard tannins of many 1975s. Round, deep, rich, complex, approaching maturity, but no rush. Consistently good. Tasted at least ten times previously. Ready, yet with enough depth to last another decade. Loads of fruit, mint, cedar, good length. Top quality.

❧ November 1995

At a full 20 years old, this wine is one of the better 1975s. Impressive, dark colour. A little maturity at rim. Decanted one hour. Cedary, spicy, fruity nose. Full, solid, good tannic backbone, typical of the 1975s, but backed by excellent ripe fruit. No rush. Ready, but enough depth and balance to last another ten years, if well stored. Lovely, rich, classic Pauillac. Very good.

CHÂTEAU PICHON-LALANDE 1975:

Purchased a case in Portland, Oregon, in 1979 for a reasonable $140 per case.

❧ March 1988

At home, with the panel of *The Wine Consumer.* I have tasted this wine on four previous occasions, but this was the first bottle from my own stock. Excellent level. Quite a bit of sediment. Decanted one-and-a-half hours. Very dark, maturing colour. Cedar, oak, spices, complex Cabernet nose. Opening up. Slightly vegetal. Backbone and tannins typical of the 1975s. Good fruit, fairly solid, on the dry side. Lots of class. No rush. Drink from 1990 onward. Some tasters thought it was too dry. I disagree. A very good wine.

CHÂTEAU PICHON-LALANDE 1978:

Two cases purchased in New York and Alberta in 1982, at an average cost of $16 per bottle.

❧ May 1992

Decanted one hour. Some sediment. Herbaceous, oak-Cabernet nose. Typical of vintage. Very good colour, little maturity. Spicy, leaner, but not sharp on palate. Elegant, but good fruit, and structure. Long and complex. Almost ready; will last well until 2000. One of the top 1978 Haut-Médocs and, together with Château Latour, the best Pauillac of the vintage. On the other hand, both Mouton and Lynch-Bages made disappointing wines in 1978.

❧ August 1996

On Turnagain Island. Comments very similar to May 1992, but definitely more evolved, both in colour and on palate. No rush, but ready. Elegant, well made. A beautiful, fully mature Claret.

CHÂTEAU PICHON-LALANDE 1979:

❧ December 1992

Still-dark, youthful colour. Little maturity at rim. Lovely, complex, cedary, oaky, spicy Cabernet nose. At 13 years, this wine is soft, ready to drink, but backed by lots of fruit. Will hold at the plateau for some years. Complex, long, spicy. Clean, cedary-fruity finish. Elegant St. Julien style rather than masculine Pauillac. This wine retails for $65 per bottle. I purchased two cases of it in 1982 for $14 per bottle!

❧ July 1993

On Turnagain Island, with Nelly and Jean-Claude Berrouet, winemaker for 30 years of the Moueix estates, including Petrus and Trotanoy. At its peak. Ripe, soft tannins, spicy, fruity, St. Julien style rather than powerful Pauillac. Classy, elegant, spicy. All in harmony. Very good.

CHÂTEAU PICHON-LALANDE 1981:

Two cases purchased in Napa and Los Angeles in 1984 for $160 per case.

❧ January 1994

At home, after trip with family to Hong Kong, Bangkok, and Hawaii. Decanted 45 minutes. Some sediment. A velvety wine. Excellent balance, elegant, spicy, new oak-fruit in harmony. Complex, spicy, soft, Very good balance. Nice fruit. A lovely wine. Ready. Drink now to 1998.

CHÂTEAU GRAND-PUY-LACOSTE 1982:

Two cases purchased in San Francisco in 1983 (as futures) for $100 per case.

❧ March 1997

Fair bit of sediment. Deep, youthful colour to rim. At 15 years of age, dense colour. Typical ripe nose of the 1982s, not unlike a big California Cabernet. Cedar, sweet, ripe fruit on nose. Intense, full, rich, very ripe tannins. Approachable now, but with so much extract that it could last well for another ten years or more. Very concentrated, yet ripe, and charming. A lovely wine. This wine retails now (in 1997) for an incredible US$1,200 per case!

ST. ESTÈPHES

CHÂTEAU CALON-SÉGUR 1916:

Purchased three bottles at Sotheby's in London for £140 per bottle, October 1995. One bottle broke during shipping. Serena Sutcliffe highly recommended that I buy this wine for my Calon-Ségur vertical. Recorked at the château in 1995.

❧ February 19, 1996

As part of a Calon-Ségur vertical tasting, 1916 to 1966. One of the four greatest wines of the tasting, together with the magnum of 1945 and the bottles of 1928 and 1947. Superb fruit, balance, depth. Grand Vin. Silky, full of life. How great this property was in the first half of this century! Its eclipse these days is due, no doubt, to less than dedicated owners. Hopefully, the 1982 may herald a much-needed change there.

CHÂTEAU CALON-SÉGUR 1918:

Purchased two bottles in San Francisco in 1990 for $200 per bottle, from Draper and Esquin's. Very high neck levels. Obviously topped up at the château. Direct sale from the château. René Rondeau of Draper and Esquin's told me that the source is impeccable. One plain capsule and shorter bottle. The other is a regular bottle and capsule. Hand-blown glass.

❧ July 1, 1992

Old bottle, deep punt, heavy glass. Lots of air bubbles in glass. Decanted 15 minutes. Wine almost touching cork. Cork reads "Rebouchonné au château en 1990." Good, medium, mature colour. Orange rim. Sweet, forthcoming nose of old Claret. Clean. A bit lean on entry, but after ten minutes mellow, sweet, long. Soft, good acidity which is what has kept this wine alive. Sweet, long aftertaste. Some earthiness. Very good, especially at 74 years of age!

❧ February 1994

Recorked at the château in 1990. Very good level. Lots of sediment. Earthy nose, yet fruity. Hard, tannic, yet nice fruit. Long, complex, held well in glass for 30 minutes before drying out. Very good length. Earthy overtones.

CHÂTEAU CALON-SÉGUR 1918:

From the Chicago Wine Co. Direct from the château. Excellent top neck levels. Original bottles. Topped up and recorked at the château with the 1955 and 1962 vintages. Very good wine.

❧ December 1992

Following Calon-Ségur 1961, 1966, and 1975. Good, dark colour. Lovely cedary, minty nose. Good fruit, dry, tannic. Best during first 20 minutes. After that, drying out fast. Held extremely well. Amazing resemblance in style to the three younger vintages tasted the same night.

❧ January 1996
As all above, recorked at the château in 1990. This is indicated on cork. Comments as three years ago, but a bit softer, more evolved. Classy, old cedar/Claret nose. Round, good fruit, delicate. Long on palate. Medium mature colour with good depth. Certainly soft, but very fine.

CHÂTEAU CALON-SÉGUR 1928:

Recorked at the château.

❧ February 19, 1996
At a Calon-Ségur vertical tasting, 1916 to 1966. Superb bottle. Deep, dark, intense, solid. Like an old, great 1945! Detailed comments in my wine diary. This is consistent with past experiences I have had with this 1928.

CHÂTEAU CALON-SÉGUR 1943, IN MAGNUM:

❧ February 19, 1996
At a Calon-Ségur vertical tasting, 1916 to 1966. Impressive dark colour. Earthy, cigar/cedar nose. Ripe, full, tannic. A fine effort for a War year, and a very good wine; especially from a magnum.

CHÂTEAU CALON-SÉGUR 1945, IN MAGNUM:

❧ February 19, 1996
As part of a Calon-Ségur vertical tasting, 1916 to 1966. The star of the evening. A superb magnum. Deep, rich, fruity, tannic. Perfect balance. Great extract. No rush at 50! A classic St. Estèphe. Grand Vin! Perfect score. (20)

CHÂTEAU COS D'ESTOURNEL 1947:

Bordeaux-bottled by Fernand Ginestet (the then-owner).

❧ February 1997
Very good cork. Bottom neck level. Excellent, deep red, bright colour. After 15 minutes in decanter, nose of cedar, ripe fruit, mushrooms. Very St. Estèphe, very ripe 1947 style. Full, solid, still tannic, masculine, yet backed by very good fruit. After one hour in glass, even better. Lots of extract, solid, cedary Cabernet. Has held very well. An excellent bottle.

CHÂTEAU CALON-SÉGUR 1947:

London-bottled by Corney and Barrow.

❧ February 19, 1996
At a vertical tasting of Calon-Ségur, 1916 to 1966. Silky, sweet, ripe, velvety, elegant. Excellent fruit extract. Great balance. Perfect now. Lovely wine. The only wine at the tasting that was not château-bottled.

CHÂTEAU CALON-SÉGUR 1948:

❧ February 19, 1996
At a Calon-Ségur vertical tasting, 1916 to 1966. Silky, Lovely, long, complex. Perfect now. Surprisingly good. Lovely fruit, elegant.

CHÂTEAU CALON-SÉGUR 1949:

❧ February 19, 1996
As part of a Calon-Ségur vertical tasting, 1916 to 1966. Silky, long. Very complex, clean, sweet fruit. Lovely. How good these old Calon-Ségurs are. The lacklustre performance of this property in the past three decades must be due to less than dedicated efforts by the owners.

CHÂTEAU CALON-SÉGUR 1952:

Recorked at the château recently. Pristine condition.

❧ February 19, 1996
At a Calon-Ségur vertical tasting, 1916 to 1966. Served in a flight that also included the 1916, 1918, and 1934. Very rich, solid, big, a bit oxidizing on nose, but full and long on palate.

Detailed tasting notes on Calon-Ségur 1916 to 1966 in wine diary.

CHÂTEAU MONTROSE 1953:

English-bottled by ICEW.

❧ October 1986
As part of a Château Montrose vertical tasting, 1953 to 1983. The star of the evening. Lovely. A very fine bottle. Detailed comments in wine diary.

CHÂTEAU COS D'ESTOURNEL 1959:

Purchased a case at a Sotheby's auction in 1977. Paid £120 per case.

❧ March 1979
Opened lowest level bottle (top shoulder), and decanted 30 minutes before dinner. Medium-dark colour, a touch of brown, and some brick at edge. Cork disintegrated, and fell into wine. Good clean nose; some fruit, cedar. Well balanced, quite evolved for a St. Estèphe, but after all, it is 20 years old. Typical dry, austere wine. Some tannin/fruit/acidity left. A touch of excessive acidity in background, but all in all, an excellent wine. I was a bit worried after tasting the tired 1959 Beychevelle purchased at the same auction.

❧ May 2, 1979
Against 1959 Beychevelle and 1959 Meyney. Best wine of the lot. Darkest colour, cigar-box nose, intense. Some tannins left. Will live for quite some time. Big, solid, typical St. Estèphe. Ready. Much better than the bottle tasted two months ago.

❧ May 1984
At home, with Carol and our Tastevin Club council. Served double-blind. Mid shoulder level. Decanted 40

minutes. Fair bit of sediment. Very dark, deep, mature Claret. Some tasters thought it was a 1961. Lovely, complex, mature, round, cedary Haut-Médoc nose. Great depth and complexity. On palate, it was chocolaty, round, full, intense, very long. Well structured, and will hold. At 25 years old, a fabulous bottle! Everybody loved it.

❧ February 1989

This wine is in its 30th year. High shoulder level, lots of sediment. Decanted 30 minutes. Impressive, deep colour, showing some age at rim, but not much. Serious, lovely bouquet of mature Claret made from very ripe grapes. Full, still solid, and chunky, even a bit tannic. Great depth, length, and balance. Lovely depth, rich, serious, old-style St. Estèphe. Fabulous flavours. A great wine that, if well stored, will hold well for another decade. Indeed, not unlike an excellent 1961!

CHÂTEAU COS D'ESTOURNEL 1959:

Bottled by Ginestet, whose sister owns Cos d'Estournel. She is the mother of Bruno Prats. Thus, a Ginestet-bottling of this fine wine is just as good and as safe a bet as the château-bottling.

❧ September 1991

Decanted 45 minutes. Excellent deep colour to rim. Much younger-looking than a 32-year-old wine is expected to be. Not unlike a good 1970. Lovely ripe, rich nose of spicy, mature Cabernet; chocolate and coffee. Ripe (which the better 1959s are). Full, rich, intense, long on palate. Still has loads of life. Has held extremely well. Slight astringency at finish, but rich, full, long. Really lovely bottle. Top class!

❧ December 1994

At "La Belle Auberge," in Ladner, with Menashe, Dafna, and Carol. Also tasted that night, a bottle of 1950 Clos des Lambrays, 1950 being Dafna's birth year. Superb, classic St. Estèphe and classic, ripe 1959! Very deep colour to rim. Classic cedary, chocolaty, mature Cabernet nose. Typical, hard, tannic St. Estèphe, yet loaded with ripe, rich fruit. Long on palate. Lasted well for one-and-a-half hours in glass. Full. A mouthful of rich, ripe, tannic St. Estèphe. A great bottle! No rush.

CHÂTEAU MONTROSE 1959:

❧ April 1985

Opened first bottle at home, with Sid and Joan Cross. Also served Chevalier-Montrachet 1978, Remoissenet, and 1969 Chambertin, Rousseau. Mid shoulder fill. Very dark, deep colour, like a mature 1970 or big 1961! Long, complex, cedary nose of a big, mature Haut-Médoc. A "broad-shouldered" wine. Masculine, hard, some tannin, steely, yet well balanced. After one hour, softened up, but also started to dry out. This wine will last for many years, but needs drinking 30 to 45 minutes after decanting. A true, hard, big St. Estèphe. Great wine.

CHÂTEAU MEYNEY 1961:

❧ July 1977

In London, with Harry Waugh. Light colour, dull taste, thin. Acidy aftertaste. Had a "dusty" smell according to Harry. What a disappointment for a 1961!

CHÂTEAU CALON-SÉGUR 1961:

❧ December 1992

With friends. Served against 1966, 1975, and followed by 1918 of the same property. The rich, ripe depth of the 1961s and the tannic backbone of St. Estèphe. Full, rich, long. Good. No rush.

❧ July 1994

With council of the Commanderie de Bordeaux. Lots of class. Tobacco, ripe nose. Full, yet more 1962 or even 1959 in style, rather than the depth of 1961. Softer than above. Complex. Very good, but not truly great.

CHÂTEAU CALON-SÉGUR 1966:

❧ June 1976

Not quite ready. Light colour, quite powerful, yet little bouquet. For the price and the reputation, this was a disappointment. Paid $14 per bottle last month.

❧ October 1984

At 18 years, this wine is at its peak. Medium colour, showing its age. Some sediment. Spicy Cabernet, slightly stemmy nose; medium body, a bit high in acidity, lean, rather than full, round, elegant, or long. Quite a pleasant Claret.

❧ December 1992

At home, with friends, against Calon 1961, 1975, and 1918. Softest, most accessible, roundest. At its peak. Will not improve. Soft, round, but tannic backbone typical of St. Estèphe. Needs drinking. Has nice fruit, but soft.

CHÂTEAU DE PEZ 1966:

❧ September 1993

Decanted 40 minutes. Some sediment. Dark, maturing colour. Lovely earthy, ripe Cabernet; cedar, spicy, ripe berries on nose. Expansive. Excellent balance. Not dry at all. Round, long, with soft, mature fruit, but good depth. Obviously at its peak at 27 years of age. Better, in my opinion, than Montrose or Cos of that year.

Cellar Notes

CHÂTEAU COS D'ESTOURNEL 1966:

Purchased a case in London, at a Sotheby's auction in 1977. Paid £70 per case.

❧ July 1986

Reaching perfect maturity. Dark, maturing colour. Fair bit of sediment. Complex, yet not as oaky-perfumy nose as more recent vintages of Cos. Round, well balanced, good backbone, and structure, without the dryness and hardness of most 1966s. It needed 20 years to finally mature. Long, round, good fruit. A good wine. Ready, but no rush drinking it.

❧ June 1988

This wine has finally come around. Medium colour, good depth, orangy, mature rim. Delicate, complex, cedar nose of fine, mature Claret. Quite subdued on both nose and palate. Fair bit of sediment. Decanted one hour. Soft, fruity, round, complex. At its peak. Without the hard tannins or edginess it had previously.

CHÂTEAU COS D'ESTOURNEL 1970:

❧ May 1977

At a pre-auction tasting at Christie's. Powerful, not ready, tight, unyielding. Hard to judge. Successfully bid on one case. Paid £42 per case.

❧ February 1983

Tasted blind against the 1966 Cos. Both opened and decanted one hour before serving. Both very dark, full, very similar colours. Both had a fair bit of sediment. The 1966 label still has the "Ginestet" label, while the 1970 names Prats as the owner (Bruno Prats' mother is a Ginestet). Still youthful colour. The 1966 is more open, more complex, woody/earthy on nose. Hard and fairly tannic. Typical structure of the 1966s. One guest thought that these were two different wines, and the other thought they were both Merlots. Way too big and hard for Merlots! The 1970 was more closed on nose, but a bit softer on palate. Not as complex (needs more time?) as the 1966. However, both are massive wines that need years to reach maturity. Actually the 1966 may start to decline before it is ready, due to excessive tannins. Try again in two to three years.

❧ October 1989

More evolved colour than six years ago. Cedary, earthy nose. Hard, lean on palate, losing its fruit. Trace of acidity at finish. The fact that I tasted it against the massive 1970 Montrose didn't exactly help the cause of this wine. Drink up before what is left of the fruit disappears. Clearly, Montrose made a much finer 1970 than Cos d'Estournel did.

CHÂTEAU DE PEZ 1970:

Cru Bourgeois. Purchased a case in Vancouver for Can$8.60 per bottle in 1976.

❧ February 1985

Full, deepish colour to rim, typical of the 1970 vintage. Quite youthful-looking, very little orange here. Spicy, slightly stemmy, round Cabernet nose. Decanted one hour. Fair bit of sediment. Full wine, loaded with fruit, well balanced. Very little tannins left, but its structure will enable it to last for quite some time. A lovely bottle. Much better than some more reputable châteaux in this great vintage. No rush.

❧ June 1996

Full, ready; even soft, but the good dark colour typical of the 1970s is there. Very good depth. Soft, elegant. Fully mature. Very pleasant. Not a complex wine, but well balanced.

CHÂTEAU MONTROSE 1970:

Purchased a case in Vancouver in 1984. Paid $42 per bottle. The reason I paid such a high price is that it is cheaper than in the US, and I can't get anyone to exchange a few bottles against 1970 Cos d'Estournel, of which I have a fair bit. Also, this is a classic and massive 1970! One bottle broken in luggage on the way back from a trip to San Francisco. What a waste!

❧ October 1986

One of the stars of a vertical tasting of Montrose 1953 to 1983. Outstanding. Try again in 1992. Massive wine. Great extract. Structured not unlike a 1970 Latour. Great future ahead.

CHÂTEAU CALON-SÉGUR 1975:

❧ December 1992

At home, with French Consul Bernard Ledun and other friends. Also tasted that night: Calon-Ségur 1918, 1966, and 1961. Deep, darkest colour. Typical St. Estèphe and 1975. Lean, herbaceous, tannic, but good fruit behind. No rush. Very good, cedary flavour. Hard. Not quite as powerful as the 1975 Montrose, but better structured that the 1975 Cos d'Estournel.

CHÂTEAU MONTROSE 1975:

❧ October 1986

At a Montrose vertical tasting, 1953 to 1983. One of the best wines of the evening. No rush. Needs ten years. A big, powerful, sturdy wine.

CHÂTEAU MONTROSE 1976:

❧ May 1982

A bit expensive ($32 per bottle in 1982), but this wine impressed me at a dinner at the "Pavillon" restaurant in Vancouver with Brother Timothy (Christian Bros.) and Harry Waugh. Big, deep dark, meaty, sweet, fat, rich wine. Needs five more years. One of the few serious 1976s.

CHÂTEAU MONTROSE 1982:

❧ October 1986
As part of Montrose vertical tasting, 1953 to 1983. Very good wine. But surprisingly soft for a Montrose. Much more open and evolved than the 1970 or 1975.

❧ June 1997
Bright, red colour. Fairly evolved rim. Cedary, spicy nose. Neither on the nose nor on palate does this wine express the ripeness of the vintage, as do both Calon-Ségur and Cos d'Estournel in 1982. Certainly a very good 1982, quite evolved, less fat, more elegant than most, in the Palmer 1982 or Domaine de Chevalier 1982 style. Ready, but no rush. Fair bit of sediment. Decanted 45 minutes.

CHÂTEAU HAUT-MARBUZET 1982:

❧ November 1995
With the council of the Commanderie de Bordeaux. Purple, dense, youthful colour, like a five-year-old. Black. Spicy, ripe Cabernet nose, not unlike a ripe California Cabernet. Hard, coarse, tannic on palate. Very big, very impressive, yet simple. Lacks class or complexity. No rush drinking it, but will it ever develop complexity or class?

CHÂTEAU CALON-SÉGUR 1982:

❧ February 1993
Decanted two-and-a-half hours. Some sediment. Deep, dense colour, little maturity at rim. Closed nose, but after two hours, some very ripe fruit and oak coming through. Very full, sweet, rich, ripe fruit on palate. Intense, sweet, ripe tannins. Well balanced. Long, but still very youthful and closed. Lots of extract. If well stored, should peak around 1996 to 1998, and last at least until 2010. Very fine wine!

OTHER HAUT-MÉDOCS

CHÂTEAU SENEJAC 1945, HAUT-MÉDOC:

This Cru Bourgeois Supérieur was topped with the same wine and recorked at the château in 1986.

Excellent fill. René Rondeau, of Draper and Esquin's in San Francisco, was at Senejac when they topped it, and tried it himself.

❧ July 1989
At home, on my 44th birthday, with friends. Good, dark, maturing colour. Very good depth. New, branded cork. Very good fill. Fair bit of sediment. Lovely, ripe, yet old, chocolate, tobacco nose of classic Claret. Still tannic, good backbone, very good length and fruit. Old, yet well structured, and most enjoyable. Much better than when tasted in Los Angeles at a 1945 tasting at Brad Klein's last year. Very good. After 30 minutes in glass, started to dry out a bit. A rare experience.

❧ July 16, 1995
On the day before my 50th birthday, opened last two bottles for 26 participants at my extensive Corton-Charlemagne event, at which we tasted 32 different Corton-Charlemagnes. The Senejac was added at the end, as a surprise. Comments similar to six years ago. Has held extremely well.

CHÂTEAU MAUCAILLOU 1970, MOULIS:

❧ January 1979
Very pleasant surprise. Deep colour; good, clean Cabernet nose. Complex, earthy bouquet. Good fruit/acidity balance, lots of tannin. A much bigger wine than expected. Needs two to three years. After two hours, it lost some of its harshness, but still had lots of tannin. Wish I had a few more, at the price. Purchased three bottles in Hawaii in 1975 for $7 per bottle.

❧ December 1986
Second bottle. How well it has held. Deep, mature colour, so typical of this vintage. Complex, open, ripe, and mature nose. Full, soft, at its peak. Well balanced, lovely flavours, and clean, long aftertaste. A very enjoyable wine, and a bit of nostalgia. I have seen this wine "grow" in my cellar since the early days that I had a cellar. I started collecting wines in the fall of 1973.

CHÂTEAU BEAUMONT 1970, HAUT-MÉDOC:

Purchased two cases in London from Corney and Barrow, for £3.25 per bottle. Due to lack of space and also due to our planned long trip to Britain, I had to resell one case at auction.

❧ July 1982
On Turnagain Island. Dark, good, spicy Cabernet nose, but has the high acidity that it doesn't seem to

be able to get rid of. Simple, pleasant. Should hold well. That day, I caught my largest salmon to date: a 15 pound Coho!

CHÂTEAU LANESSAN 1970, HAUT-MÉDOC:

London-bottled by Corney and Barrow. Purchased two cases for £30 per case.

❧ December 1978

At a tasting against 1973 Gemello and 1974 Mondavi Cabernet Sauvignons. Big, dry Bordeaux; earthy, some oak, some sediment, a slight touch of brown. Almost ready, some tannin left to lose. "Sturdy."

❧ September 1985

Fairly deep, maturing colour. Spicy, complex, and jammy on both nose and palate. Full and rich, but a bit one-dimensional. It is developing a chocolaty/stemmy flavour, not uncommon with older Clarets that start out being full and heavy. Needs drinking, yet a couple of bottles should be allowed to age longer, just to see how they last.

CHÂTEAU CHASSE-SPLEEN 1970, MOULIS:

❧ July 1977

During lunch with A. Nugent in Surrey, England. Fine dark wine. Good bouquet. Should be ready in five years. Loads of ripe fruit, but quite tight at this stage.

❧ August 1981

At home, with friends. However, had it after a 1957 Lynch-Bages. The Lynch-Bages, while older and from a hard vintage, was much more complex.

❧ January 1984

This time I noticed a change in the wine. Good concentration of colour, typical of the 1970 vintage and of Chasse-Spleen. Spicy Cabernet nose. Well structured, but leaner, a bit drier. Is it losing its fruit, or is it going through a phase? Nevertheless, a very fine, big, dry wine of good quality.

❧ February 1988

Excellent bottle. Deep red to rim. Impressive colour of the better 1970s. Lots of fruit, depth, still a bit tannic. Long, clean, full, beefy. Very good balance. An excellent Cru Bourgeois. No rush. Drink now to 1993 or beyond. Best bottle so far, out of a case purchased in London in 1977 for £30 per case.

❧ January 1993

At home, upon reading the news that the manager/régisseur and part-owner, Bernadette Villars and her husband Philippe, died recently in a hiking accident in the Pyrenées. I met Bernadette Villars several times on my trips to Bordeaux at Chasse-Spleen, Haut-Bages-Libéral and La Gurgue (in Margaux). She was only 48. A loss to the world of wine and a tragic accident.

Comments as in February 1988, but a bit more evolved. Very good. Softer tannins, and rounder. Will keep. Bernadette will be sorely missed.

CHÂTEAU CISSAC 1970, HAUT-MÉDOC:

Purchased two cases in London in 1977. Paid £32 per case.

❧ May 1977

At a Christie's pre-auction tasting in London. Very dark, powerful, lots of tannin. Fine bouquet. A very good wine in four to five years?

❧ August 1983

On Turnagain Island. Fairly dark, 1970-style colour. Fairly closed nose (even after one hour decanting). A very lean and hard wine. This wine seems to have lost its fruit, and retained some tannin and acidity. Rather simple. Similar to the style of 1952 Clarets?

CHÂTEAU CHASSE-SPLEEN 1975, MOULIS:

❧ April 1985

At almost ten years old, some sediment. Deep, dark, still young colour to rim. Lovely cedar/spice Cabernet nose. Very big, tannic, full, rich, and hard. Decanted one hour. This wine needs another four to five years to reach its peak, and will stay there for some time. Excellent potential. Classic Haut-Médoc.

❧ November 1995

At 20 years of age, excellent, deep, maturing colour. Very good extract. Mature, spicy, herbaceous Cabernet nose. One of the better 1975s because of excellent balance and concentrated, ripe fruit, backed by a solid tannic backbone. Very good. Approaching its peak, but no rush. Drink now to 2005. Not a complex wine, but a good Cru Bourgeois.

CHÂTEAU SOCIANDO-MALLET 1979, HAUT-MÉDOC:

❧ February 1991

Deep, very slightly maturing colour. Good depth. Rich, concentrated fruit, straightforward, full-bodied. Ready, but will last five to ten more years. Good extract and Cabernet character. Not very complex, but a solid, serious wine.

CHÂTEAU POTENSAC 1982, MÉDOC:

❧ July 17, 1990

At my 45th birthday party. Rich, deep-red colour. Herbaceous, yet ripe. Clean, young, spicy, long, elegant. No rush. Most pleasant. This wine is made by the gifted winemaker/owner of Château Leoville-Lascases, Michel Delon.

PESSAC-LÉOGNAN AND GRAVES

CHÂTEAU HAUT-BRION 1959:

❧ November 1976

Dark, still powerful, yet smooth. Very fine aftertaste, but a bit overpriced at $15 for a half-bottle. The bouquet wasn't too long-lasting. Maybe the fact that it was a half-bottle did not allow this wine, which can be superb, to mature properly. (Note: Tasted on five occasions since then from 1988 to 1996. All superb bottles.)

CHÂTEAU HAUT-BRION 1961:

❧ February 1986

Had this wine at home twice before (in 1983 and 1985), other than at several tastings, of course. Both extraordinary bottles (in September 1985 from a magnum). Great depth, concentration, and class. Rich, luscious, chocolaty. Intense ripe fruit, typical for the vintage. Purchased six bottles in London in 1977 for £23 per bottle.

❧ January 1989

Retails now for $425 to $450 per bottle!

CHÂTEAU HAUT-BRION 1962:

❧ October 31, 1976

Excellent Graves. Still powerful, although it had one-and-a-half hours to breathe, and was decanted. Lasting bouquet, medium-dark colour; could last in bottle for many more years. Lovely, cedary fruit, which is still surprisingly fresh.

❧ September 1986

Before a trip to Burgundy and the Rhône Valley. This wine retails today for US$90 to US$120. Decanted 30 minutes. Some sediment. The typical deep-red colour of the better 1962s. Outstanding young colour for its age! Complex, mature, open, and elegant nose, reminiscent of mature oak, earth (rich), very much Graves and Haut-Brion style. Lovely complexity. Full, yet round, elegant, and long on palate. Cigar box. At its absolute peak. A lovely wine. I'm sorry that I do not have any more of this! This wine was purchased in London in 1977 for £10 per bottle.

CHÂTEAU HAUT-BRION 1964:

❧ June 1977

In London. Big, powerful wine. Medium-dark colour, fine, chocolaty bouquet. Typical ripe, earthy Graves. Has a few years ahead of it. Complex and very fine. One of the best 1964s.

❧ September 1, 1986

Having purchased a case recently at Christie's Chicago for $650 per case, I decided to try this one bottle purchased a long time ago. Little sediment. Decanted 30 minutes. Cork came out too easily (loose?). Amber browning-colour to rim. Good depth. Chocolaty-woody-earthy-prunes nose. Dry, hard, acidic, and oxidized on palate. A decaying wine. I could only drink one glass. Pity, because this wine can be outstanding. Also, its value today is a small fortune (over US$100 per bottle!). Very disappointing. I was looking forward to a great experience.

❧ October 1986

Having tasted the single bottle I had last month, before purchasing this lot, l was worried. However, pleasant surprise. Deep mature colour. Spicy, earthy-chocolate nose. Decanted 45 minutes. Complex, long, full. Still has good fruit, and excellent complexity, but it is forward and needs drinking. Very enjoyable.

❧ February 1988

Delicate, ready, needs drinking. At the end, hint of leather, and slight oxidation. Lovely, delicate, earthy complexity. Perfect drinking now. A wine of distinction and class. Very good! Retails now for US$130 to $180 a bottle.

❧ December 29, 1989

Intended to be the last great wine of the year. Unfortunately, it was a corked bottle. Deep, dark, earthy, but corked on nose and palate. What a pity!

❧ Friday, May 26, 1995

The last bottle of wine we drank at our old home on Montgomery Street. Next Monday, May 29, we will move to our new home on 12th Avenue. A very mature but lovely wine. Deep mature colour. Fair bit of sediment. Decanted 30 minutes. Silky, soft, elegant, round, chocolaty, smooth. Good mature fruit, earthy overtones. Lovely. Needs drinking, at 31 years of age. Very stylish and elegant.

❧ November 1995

At home, with friends. Also tasted that night 1937 Richebourg DRC and 1976 d'Yquem. This was one of the best 1964 Haut-Brions I've ever tasted. Very dark, velvety, earthy-chocolaty-cedary. Full, long. Great balance. Mouth-filling. A lovely bottle. There is a lot of bottle variation in this case.

CHÂTEAU HAUT-BRION 1966:

❧ April 1989

Fairly dark, maturing colour. Earthy, particularly cedary-cigar nose. Fairly lean, hard, yet round, with delicate complexity. Trace of acidity at finish. Not great, but certainly very good, long, and complex. Ready. Will not improve. Has the extra dimension of a Premier Grand Cru on both nose and palate. Retails now for US$175 per bottle.

CHÂTEAU HAUT-BRION 1967:

❧ December 1981
Before a trip to Hawaii with the family. Surprisingly dark, young-looking colour. Like a 1962. Good nose, earthy flavour, good complexity. At first, it had the "curse" of the 1967s: high acidity. But after an hour, it improved. Certainly one of the better 1967s.

CHÂTEAU HAUT-BRION 1969:

❧ June 1976
In New York, with friends. Ready to drink. Quite dark colour. A good effort in a mediocre year. A bit chaptalized, but at $5 per bottle, not bad.

CHÂTEAU HAUT-BRION 1970:

❧ October 1982
Surprising how similar this wine is to the 1970 Lafite (but with a bit more body and depth). Caramel-sweet, plummy nose. Lovely long bouquet. Medium colour, good depth, but ageing, mature, brick-red. Good colour to rim (slightly orange). Very little sediment. Lovely mouthful. Some tannin (not much). Well balanced, and long aftertaste. Elegant, but does not have much power or depth.

❧ October 1985
Medium deep, maturing colour at rim. Spicy, truffles nose with hint of caramel. Fairly full on palate, yet delicate. Somehow lacking in complexity (in the context of a 1970 First Growth), and its major fault is high acidity on the finish. A very enjoyable wine, nevertheless. No rush, but I'm afraid it will never lose its high acidity.

❧ August 1989
Last bottle, at a blind tasting of 1970s, with the panel of *The Wine Consumer*. This wine is getting tired and now has noticeable acidity. Not very successful.

CHÂTEAU HAUT-BRION 1972:

Purchased two cases in London in September 1977, at a Sotheby's auction. Paid £30 per case.

❧ December 1977
Two weeks after the wine's arrival in Vancouver. Wine still upset. Medium-bright colour. Earthy bouquet, some noticeable chaptalization, quite thin in texture, and some acidity all along. Finished short. This wine needs rest and time. In two to three years, it will improve (I hope). It will mellow and ripen, but one cannot expect much from such a poor vintage. Purchased at a bargain price, of course.

❧ January 1987
Last bottle, served blind after a tasting of 1976 Clarets. Has held surprisingly well, and developed complexity. Much better than expected, but of course, not really a good wine. Drink up.

CHÂTEAU HAUT-BRION 1976:

❧ March 1995
Last bottle. Excellent top neck level. Very good appearance. Decanted 45 minutes. Some sediment. Evolved, mature Claret colour, but good depth. Earthy, gamey nose. Hint of chocolate. Round, soft on palate. Mellow, yet good fruit. Trace of acidity at finish. Well stored in my cellar all these years. Even so, needs drinking. Silky, most enjoyable.

CHÂTEAU HAUT-BRION 1979:

❧ September 1991
Decanted 45 minutes. Some sediment. Medium to dark colour. Some maturity. Very good level. Lovely sweet, ripe, earthy nose. Sweet, luscious, long; round, complex on palate. Full of ripe, soft fruit. Long aftertaste. Very good balance. At its peak, but if well stored, no rush. Very fine and enjoyable.

❧ May 1992
Before Carol's one-week cruise to the Queen Charlotte Islands. Impressive, deep, dark colour to rim; like a 1970, browning at rim. Some sediment. Decanted 45 minutes. Lovely exotic, spicy-earthy, herbal, open nose of classic Graves and truffles. Full, long, soft, but extremely well balanced. Lovely fruit, length, and extract. Little tannin left. Excellent now, but no rush.

❧ October 16, 1992
My mother's 80th birthday, with friends. (Also served 1979 Château du Tertre and 1912 Niepoort "Colheita" Port.) Very deep, ripe, full, rich, smooth. Great depth. Creamy. Lovely extract. Round, new oak, rich, fat, fleshy. This is lovely. One of the best 1979s, surely. Ready, but no rush.

CHÂTEAU LA GARDE 1953, A/C GRAVES, LOUIS ESCHENAUER:

Very good appearance and neck level. Bottled at the château.

❧ June 1990
With the council of Le Tastevin. Dark, maturing colour, like a 1961 or 1964. Sweet, delicate, slightly earthy nose. Round, delicate, straightforward on palate. Some acidity, nice fruit, but severe, hard finish. Certainly still alive. An experience. Entry like a delicate 1953 Graves, and finish like a 1952 or 1964 St. Estèphe. A new experience for us all.

CHÂTEAU HAUT-BAILLY 1955:

Two half-bottles purchased in New York in 1976, for $5 per half-bottle.

❧ October 1978
At home, for a small tasting with friends. Good "old" nose, lots of sediment. Sweet, woody, "molasses"

bouquet. Drying out and over-the-hill. We drank it as soon as it was decanted.

CHÂTEAU LA MISSION HAUT-BRION 1959:

I decided to buy a few bottles in 1976, after finding out that the catalogue price of this wine in San Francisco (Connoisseurs Wine Imports) is $50, so at $31 locally, it is a bargain!

❧ January 1977

A superb, dark, full-bodied wine. Has typical "goût de terroir" and superb bouquet. Powerful Graves of great quality. Opened 90 minutes before dinner, and decanted. Quite a bit of sediment. This wine will live on for quite some years. (In 1985 this wine retails for over $180!)

DOMAINE DE CHEVALIER 1961:

❧ February 1, 1991

At a farewell dinner for *The Wine Consumer.* Earthy, spicy, herbaceous nose typical of this property. Full colour typical of the 1961s. Nice fruit, earthy, fairly chunky. Concentrated. Best on nose (complex). Three days earlier, we had a vertical of this Château 1959 to 1983 at the Commanderie de Bordeaux, in which the 1961 was missing, so this filled a gap.

CHÂTEAU LES CARMES-HAUT-BRION 1961:

❧ January 1993

At home, with "Group of Ten." Served blind. (Our group bottle was a magnum of 1947 Les Carmes!) Excellent wine. The depth of colour typical of the 1961s. Earthy-chocolaty. Full-bodied. Long. Great extract. No rush drinking it.

CHÂTEAU MALARTIC-LAGRAVIÈRE 1961: AND CHÂTEAU MALARTIC-LAGRAVIÈRE 1962:

Both were given to me by Mr. Marly, owner of Malartic-Lagravière.

❧ June 1986

At home, with members of *The Wine Consumer* tasting panel. The 1961 had a lovely, deep dark colour. Complex, long, earthy, plus ripeness and spices on nose. Round, perfectly balanced, long, and complex, full of life. A lovely bottle. No rush at 25 years of age! The 1962 was much lighter in colour. Elegant, open nose. Complex, delicate, light to medium body. Noticeable acidity at finish. Nice, but needs drinking. I wrote to Mr. Marly, and reported to him on the tasting and thanked him.

CHÂTEAU HAUT-BAILLY 1964:

❧ June 1990

With council of Le Tastevin. Very good depth, mature rim. Cedar, earthy, mature nose. Quite dry on palate and soft, but good depth. Needs drinking, but not dead. Good soft fruit. Hint of chocolate, earth. Dry finish. Nose is best part.

CHÂTEAU LA MISSION HAUT-BRION 1966:

❧ July 1977

A half-bottle purchased from Berry Bros. and Rudd for £3.50. In London. Excellent, still very powerful. Will be great in four or five years. Typical Graves, earthy, and truffles bouquet. Finer than the 1967. "Smoky" and very earthy. Intense wine. Deep and big and still closed. Will be great some day.

❧ October 1978

For dinner, with friends, served against the 1967 La Mission. The 1967 was more elegant, forward, and pleasant. The 1966, at first, had a "burnt" nose and a deeper colour. After one hour, it lost most of its burnt nose. Big on palate, lots of fruit, and tannin. Needs at least another five to eight years. A giant with a lot of potential.

CHÂTEAU LA TOUR-HAUT-BRION 1966:

❧ August 1988

High shoulder level. Browning, oxidized, baked. That worries me. If the other bottles are the same, it means trouble!

❧ October 5, 1988

Tasted second bottle. Superb wine! Medium mature colour. Open, complex, long nose of earth, gravel, and mature Cabernet/oak. Round, soft, long, well balanced. At its peak but no rush. Lovely bottle.

❧ December 1988

Another disappointment. Too much bottle variation. Low neck level. Getting tired. Oxidizing. Too bad. Not a consistent lot; one of the risks of buying wine at auction.

❧ April 1995

Decanted 45 minutes. Some sediment. A great and lovely wine. Very much like 1966 La Lagune, but with that extra dimension and complexity. Very mature, soft, earthy, round, complex. Soft, long, round, chocolaty-earthy. Very complex, silky. At 29 years of age, fully mature, but a lovely Claret.

CHÂTEAU LA MISSION HAUT-BRION 1967:

Two cases purchased in Vancouver in 1975 for Can$19.50 per bottle.

❧ October 1976

Both Carol and I were very impressed. Beautiful, soft wine, yet very dark and very intense bouquet. Will live a long time. Should improve in two to three years. Our feeling, after tasting this wine, made us agree that La Mission should be at the very top (officially) with other First Growths. As soon as we tasted it, we knew we had something great there.

❧ July 1978
Never disappointing. Good body, flavour, and fine bouquet. Deep colour. Needs at least one-and-a-half hours of breathing and decanting. No sign of acidity, which is a problem with many 1967s.

❧ November 1983
Medium dark colour, orangy rim. Earthy-woody, complex, open nose of classic Claret. Mellow on palate, soft, at its peak, with a bit too much acidity (the curse of most 1967s). A bit lean, but long aftertaste. Based on this bottle, starting to decline. Drink up. Has held very well.

❧ March 1987
Impressive, dark colour for a 1967. Complex, open, rich Cabernet nose with some earthiness. Full, getting a bit dry, but excellent depth. Other than Petrus and Trotanoy, this is one of the great successes of 1967. Has held very well, but should be drunk up before it looses its fruit. A serious, masculine wine. Very good. Almost luscious for a 1967. Excellent fill, and fair bit of sediment.

❧ March 1992
Excellent top neck level. Mature colour, very good depth. Earthy, sweet, oak, spicy Cabernet nose. Mellow, round, great complexity. Has held extremely well for 25 years. Lovely fruit, round. Needs drinking. Most enjoyable. Really very good.

❧ August 1993
Last bottle, at home. At 26 years of age, very good level, good mature red colour. Medium depth. Elegant/meaty/earthy Cabernet nose. Round, soft, mellow, still has some fruit. Trace of acidity, typical of vintage. Soft, delicate. Good level bottles like this one (or magnums) have held extremely well. One of the best 1967s. Most enjoyable. I have been drinking this wine since 1976, and I will keep fond memories of it.

DOMAINE DE CHEVALIER 1970:

❧ June 1989
Excellent level. Decanted 45 minutes. Fair bit of sediment. Nice dark, slightly mature colour, typical for the vintage. Lovely, expansive, warm nose of fine, mature Claret. Chocolate, earth, tobacco. Full, round, well balanced, long, and complex. Good backbone and depth. Complex and superb, rich, round finish. One of the very top wines of this fine vintage. Great. In my experience, this is better than both 1970 La Mission (which has volatile acidity) and 1970 Haut-Brion, which is a bit too loosely knit and not as well balanced.

CHÂTEAU HAUT-BAILLY 1970

Two cases purchased at Sotheby's London in 1978, for £54 per case.

❧ November 1979
Lovely nose, medium-bright colour. Typical of this château. Elegant, soft, very pleasant, and well made. Old vines and high percentage of Merlot. Its only drawback: lacks Graves characteristic. More like a soft Margaux, but it has lot of class.

❧ November 1983
At home, against the 1970 Château Pape Clément. Both had the good dark colour of the 1970s. The Haut-Bailly had more elegance on nose and palate, softer, more complex. A lovely bottle at its peak. The Pape Clément was a bit earthier on nose, bigger, and a bit leaner on palate. A good, sturdy wine. Better than expected. Both very enjoyable.

❧ February 1987
Decanted 45 minutes. Lovely, fairly dark, mature colour, typical of the 1970s. Open, elegant, complex nose. Some earthiness. Round, forward, well balanced, elegant, clean finish. At its peak, yet holding very well. One of the best Haut-Baillys of the past 25 years!

❧ April 1992
Very good level. Decanted 30 minutes. As above, but very soft, slight acidic finish. Still enjoyable, but definitely needs drinking.

CHÂTEAU LA MISSION HAUT-BRION 1978:

Purchased half-a-case from a warehouse in Berkeley, California, run by a veterinarian who has a place full of odd and rare wines. The price was the same as for the 1976 vintage. Paid $22 per bottle. This wine sells now (1982) at double the price at John Walker's and at Draper and Esquin's.

❧ June 1992
Decanted one hour. Very good, deep colour, slight maturity at rim. Earthy, chocolaty, complex nose. Round, long, little tannin left, but excellent balance. Long, rich, chocolate-earthy-herbal. A complete wine. Delicious, but no rush. Should hold well for ten more years.

DOMAINE DE CHEVALIER 1979:

❧ July 1996
On Turnagain Island, with friends. Dark, evolved colour. Quite ripe for a 1979, yet it has the elegance typical of Domaine de Chevalier. (Tasted it against 1979 Beaulieu Vineyards Georges de Latour "Private Reserve" Napa Cabernet Sauvignon.) Spicy, earthy, herbaceous nose. Medium-bodied, soft, round. At its peak. Elegance, rather than power. Long, complex. Fine wine.

CHÂTEAU LA MISSION HAUT-BRION 1981:

❧ February 1994

At home, with the council of the Commanderie de Bordeaux. Deep dark, impressive colour. A bit tarry; almost Rhône-like. Quite hard, a bit lean, with hint of rubber. Not ready. Some tasters said it was too hard, lean, and hollow. I don't think so. It needs time. Try again around 1997 to 1999. A bit hard, especially for a 1981. Will be very good by 1999.

❧ May 1996

On Turnagain Island. Much mellower than in 1994. Deep colour. Cedar, earthy nose. Lovely fruit. Perfect balance. Good backbone. Soft tannins. Intense fruit extract. Long, fruity aftertaste. Ready, but no rush. Spicy, rich, full.

CHÂTEAU LATOUR-HAUT-BRION 1981:

❧ July 1997

At 16 years of age, this wine is at its perfect plateau. Good, dark colour. A velvety, round, perfectly balanced wine. Long, earthy-cedary nose. Lovely fruit and balance. Great quality. Some of the 1981s are turning into lovely wines. Most are being overlooked, because of the reputation of the 1982s, 1986s, and 1990s.

SAINT EMILIONS

CHÂTEAU AUSONE 1945:

❧ May 28, 1993

For lunch, on Carol's birthday, with Paul and Sara Pinski from San Francisco. Cork crumbled. Top shoulder level. Good, dark colour. Orangy rim. Earthy-tobacco, slightly herbaceous nose of mature Claret. Medium-bodied. Leaner finish. Tannic, typical for the vintage. Nose was best part. Better on entry (soft, elegant, some fruit) than on finish. Quite good, and a rare treat. We also drank a fine 1964 Beaune "Clos de la Mousse," Bouchard Père et Fils.

CHÂTEAU AUSONE 1964:

❧ June 1977

In London. Bright colour, little sediment. Very fine bouquet, dry, and powerful, long-lasting aftertaste. A good wine, and at a reasonable price (£14 per bottle), from Hedges and Butler.

CHÂTEAU AUSONE 1970:

❧ December 1978

Fairly forward, medium colour, orangy-brown. Nice, delicate berry nose, some sweetness on nose, but fairly dry on palate. Lacks extract. After about two hours, it dried up and seemed tough and charmless. Almost at its peak. Not enough fruit there to be a keeper. Together with Château Margaux, Ausone produced the most disappointing First Growth in 1970, with Lafite not too far behind.

CHÂTEAU AUSONE 1976:

❧ March 6, 1990

Given to me by Pascal Delbeck of Château Ausone, during a visit there. His first vintage at Ausone, and a turning point for that property.

❧ September 1992

Excellent level and appearance. Fair bit of sediment. Decanted 45 minutes. Impressive dark, youthful colour. Lovely oak-cedar-Cabernet/herbaceous nose. Lots of class. Velvety, lively, rich, long. Lovely fruit, classy bouquet, and flavours. One of the best, liveliest 1976s. No rush. Very good indeed.

CHÂTEAU AUSONE 1979:

❧ May 1997

Fully mature. Very good, deep colour to rim. Spicy, herbaceous, rich, chocolaty nose. Velvety, round, very good extract on palate. Ausone, Haut-Brion, and Lafite produced the best First Growths in 1979. Cheval-Blanc can be good, too, but variable. I have found Mouton, Latour, and Petrus disappointing that year. Margaux is not bad, but not nearly as good as that property's 1978 or 1981.

CHÂTEAU CHEVAL-BLANC 1955:

❧ April 27, 1994

At "Diva at the Met" restaurant, with Delia Viader of Viader Vineyards, Napa. Superb wine. Lovely deep, evolved colour. Great, clean, fruity nose. Hint of cedar. Round, perfect balance. Good body, layers of complexity on palate. Very long finish. Still full of life, yet soft and elegant. A great bottle. Delia loved it, too. Cheval-Blanc is her favourite St. Emilion (actually, it is her favourite red Bordeaux).

CHÂTEAU CHEVAL-BLANC 1966:

❧ June 1977

In London. £7.50 per bottle from Justerini and Brooks. A beautiful St. Emilion. Very powerful, not ready. Beautiful bouquet. Very dark colour. Bouquet lasted forever! A great wine. Loads of ripe black fruit. Should be approachable by 1982, and last well beyond that.

❧ August 17, 1980

Had a half-bottle with cheeses, to celebrate our sixth wedding anniversary, and one day after tasting the great 1947 Cheval-Blanc at home. Truly a fine St. Emilion. Dark colour, slightly browning. Lovely, big, herbaceous nose. Intense flavours. Still some tannins left. This wine in full bottles will live for a long time. In half-bottles, it should reach its peak in two to three years. Perfect fruit/acidity balance. Lingering aftertaste. After two hours, it was still excellent.

CHÂTEAU CHEVAL-BLANC 1970:

Purchased several bottles in London from Berry Bros., at a cost of £8.50 per bottle.

❧ April 1985

At home. (I had this wine on five previous occasions at dinners and tastings.) Medium dark, mature Claret colour. Orangy rim, slightly pale. Complex, warm, mature "obvious" Cabernet Franc/St. Emilion nose (vegetal-herbaceous). Soft, forward, elegant, unmistakable St. Emilion. Long, complex finish. This wine may have some time to go in magnums, but in bottle size, it is at its peak. Soft, elegant, very good, but not great. If Cheval-Blanc had more Merlot and less Cabernet Franc (two-thirds!), it would be a greater, more concentrated wine. Very enjoyable, though. I paid Can$15 for this wine. It retails now, in 1985, for Can$125!!

CHÂTEAU CHEVAL-BLANC 1971:

❧ June 1980

Lovely, deep, dark colour. Elegant (but not very open yet), toasty, herbaceous nose. Complex wine of very fine quality. Really stylish and aristocratic. Intense and excellent aftertaste. Good balance. Needs two to three years, and will last for some time.

❧ October 1986

Upon my return from a trip to Peru with my 11-year-old son Michael. Ageing colour. Lovely, mature, complex, stemmy nose of fine St. Emilion. Soft, round, and very forward on palate. A bit sharp at the end. Needs drinking.

CHÂTEAU CHEVAL-BLANC 1975:

❧ December 1993

Very good, deep colour. Spicy, expansive, herbaceous Cabernet Franc nose. Full, rich, long. Very good tannic backbone (typical 1975), but with good fruit extract. Ready, but will last for ten more years, if well stored. Very good fruit, complexity, and length.

CHÂTEAU CHEVAL-BLANC 1978:

❧ August 1996

At "Le Gavroche," in Vancouver, with Ingo Grady, a wine merchant and local agent of Moueix, and Delia Viader, owner of Viader Vineyard on Howell Mountain, Napa. Mellow, spicy, hint of scorched oak barrels, a bit herbaceous, elegant, long, soft, complex. This property is Delia's favourite in Bordeaux.

CHÂTEAU CHEVAL-BLANC 1979:

❧ November 1995

Decanted one hour. Good, dark, maturing colour. Lovely, ripe, spicy, mineral/chocolaty nose. Full, round, good depth, quite sweet, rich fruit. Ready, but no rush, if well stored. A mouthful of rich, herbaceous/sweet, ripe Boucher/Merlot. Actually, bigger and sweeter than expected. Impeccable level in bottle. Very good. Not unlike 1979 Palmer, but bigger and sweeter.

CHÂTEAU MAGDELAINE 1945:

Good level. Purchased from Draper and Esquin's in 1983. Variation in shape of bottles. This wine was bottled by Hannapier, Peyrelongue and Co. in Bordeaux, not château-bottled.

❧ May 13, 1994

At "Bishop's" restaurant, in Vancouver, with Christian Moueix and his friend Cherise Chen. It was Christian's first visit to Vancouver and first tasting of Hannapier's bottling of this 1945.

Decanted 30 minutes. Sensational wine. Great, dark colour and appearance. Superb nose of fine old Claret; lots of fruit and life in it. Velvety, yet the iron-fist tannic background of the 1945s. (My birth year. Christian was born in 1946.) Great length, balance, depth. Full, surprisingly youthful, long, rich. Great aftertaste. A great bottle, and the best 1945 Magdelaine that Christian or I have ever tasted. A great experience. John Bishop had a taste and raved about it, too. I have waited ten years to serve this to Christian, whose family owns this fine property.

CHÂTEAU PAVIE 1947:

Bordeaux-bottled by Eschenauer; shipped to England by Whitwham's Wines Ltd. I'm usually worried about Whitwham bottlings, but looks like an authentic bottle.

❧ February 3, 1990

Very good neck level. Cork disintegrated. Fair bit of sediment. Very good, deep, dark, maturing colour. Decanted 30 minutes. Complex, earthy-mushrooms, rich, older Claret nose. Quite full, solid wine. On the lean side, but still has fruit. Not adulterated. Held well. Good structure and long on palate.

CHÂTEAU MAGDELAINE 1961:

❧ June 1988

Deep maturing, impressive colour to rim. Lovely perfumy, ripe, complex, chocolate nose of mature Claret. Full, rich, yet soft, with excellent backbone. Great depth, complexity, and lots of fruit. This lovely, ripe wine has held extremely well. The wine was almost touching the cork; and clean labels, too.

CHÂTEAU LA GAFFELIÈRE-NAUDES 1961:

❧ May 1977

In London. Opened and decanted one-and-a-half hours. Almost at its peak. Fine bouquet, dark colour, medium sediment, mellow. Fine wine. Rich, chocolaty fruit with stemmy, cedary overtones.

❧ July 1977

Purchased a case at a Christie's auction. Paid £80 per case, including commission. Tasted in London that same month. Comments as above.

CHÂTEAU L'ARROSÉE 1961:

❧ March 1982

At home, with Harry Waugh (who tasted the 1966 of this property in the afternoon at a Tastevin 1966 tasting, and who has never tasted the 1961 vintage of this château before), as well as with Joe Heitz and his daughter Kathleen, and the Tobes. Joe Heitz said that he thought this wine was made more in the style of the older California Cabernet Sauvignons (sturdy, big, dark, hard), while the 1961 Ducru-Beaucaillou we had against it was more Bordeaux style. Elegant, complex, lovely, long, cedary nose; good fruit flavours and well balanced. Quite forward. Very good.

❧ November 1990

Impressive, deep, dark colour. Slight maturity at rim. Fair bit of sediment. Very ripe, lovely, complex, cedary nose. Full, almost sweet Cabernet on palate. Soft, yet rich, loaded with ripe fruit. Great extract. More complex on nose than on palate, but a very special, very rich wine. No rush. Riper and heftier than expected. Very good.

❧ November 1992

Decanted 45 minutes. Some sediment. Good, youthful, dark colour. Lovely, sweet, concentrated chocolaty fruit on both nose and palate. Not very complex, but excellent balance and depth. No rush. Lovely wine. Classic 1961, if not of Ducru or Palmer level.

CHÂTEAU FIGEAC 1964:

Harry Waugh spoke very highly of this wine. This wine should be soft and very rich. 1964 was a very good year in both St. Emilion and Pomerol.

❧ December 20, 1976

Dark colour. Very nice ripe bouquet. Luscious wine. The Merlot grape is prevailing. Very little sediment. This wine is at its peak and can stay there for some time. An elegant and perfumed wine of excellent quality. Ripe, rich, very long, mouth filling. Lovely bottle. Must buy some.

I was very happy to find two remaining bottles in a wine shop in San Francisco in May 1978, during a trip to the Napa Valley by car. Paid $15 per bottle.

❧ November 1981

Superb bottle! Dark mature colour, brown-orange rim. Lovely, subdued, sweet, elegant nose. Not very complex, but rich yet velvety wine. Elegant, soft, well rounded, good length, easy to drink and enjoy. Better than the previous bottle. At first, a bit harsh, but after 45 minutes, it softened up. Lovely wine. I'd love to own some more!

CHÂTEAU FIGEAC 1966:

❧ April 1984

This wine retails today for Can$65. It has gone up over 400% in six-and-a-half years. Tasted it with Carol, a few days before our trip to Bordeaux and Oporto. Lovely, dark, deep colour, maturing at rim. Elegant, fragrant, sweet nose. Some sediment. Decanted one hour. Perfectly balanced, delicate, yet full, rich, and round. At its peak.

My memories of the 1966 Cheval-Blanc (another lovely St. Emilion) indicate that this wine is as good! A great experience. In two weeks time, I will have lunch with Thierry Manoncourt at Figeac.

❧ October 1985

Excellent appearance and level. Good, mature colour. Good depth. Decanted 30 minutes. Cork soft, black. Very volatile acidity on nose. Cleared after 45 minutes. Drier, leaner than expected, but good. Not as great as it can be, but round. Too dry, acidic finish. I've had better bottles of this. Poor storage?

❧ October 1989

Excellent level. Medium sediment. Decanted 30 minutes. Deep, maturing colour. Expansive, spicy, herbal/oak nose. Full, soft, mellow. At its absolute peak. Round, elegant, fruity. Long, delicate finish. Very nice wine. Unmistakable Figeac or Cheval-Blanc style, although the Cheval-Blanc 1966 is a bit richer.

❧ November 1996
At home, with Carol, Michael, and Orly. Perfect level/appearance. Decanted 30 minutes. Superb wine. Together with Cheval-Blanc, the best 1966 St. Emilion, and among the very best 1966s overall. Classic vegetal/spicy Figeac nose. Ripe fruit, too. Luscious, long, round, soft. Perfect balance. Very long aftertaste. At 30 years, perfection.

CHÂTEAU L'ARROSÉE 1966:

Purchased a case in Seattle in 1980. Paid $190 per case.

❧ December 1988
Deep colour to rim with some orange, sign of age. Spicy, long, complex nose, more Cabernet Sauvignon than Right Bank (Merlot, Cabernet Franc). Rich, good fruit, without the leanness of many 1966s. Long, spicy, mature, some oak, tobacco, trace of acidity at end. Overall, very good, and holding very well. Excellent bottle. Better than many 1966s Classed Growths.

❧ July 1995
Now it is rounder and more forward. Excellent classic Claret (high Cabernet Sauvignon content obvious). Cigar-box, round, complex. Lovely, forward, mature wine. Needs drinking over the next two to three years.

CHÂTEAU LA GAFFELIÈRE 1970:

❧ March 1978
At a blind tasting of various Clarets. Came in third behind Palmer 1970 and La Mission 1967. Good wine. Fruity, velvety, rich Merlot nose. However, more forward than expected. Almost ready.

❧ March 4, 1982
Harry Waugh arrived today, and will be staying with us for eight days, through the Vancouver Wine Festival. (He brought me a nice decanter and two bottles of Les-Forts-de-Latour 1966 for a special Tastevin tasting next week.) We enjoyed the wine. Had slightly high acidity, but very good. Typical, deep 1970 colour. Good fruity/spicy nose. Long aftertaste, elegant, and ready.

CHÂTEAU SIMARD 1970:

❧ November 1994
(24 years old!) With the council of Le Tastevin. Evolved, mature colour, yet good depth. Clean, elegant Merlot/Cabernet Franc nose. Obviously from a ripe year. The fact that it has been in my cellar for 18 years at 52°F has helped. Still nice fruit. Velvety, even complex. Long, clean finish. At its peak, and will not improve. A pleasant surprise. Most enjoyable.

CHÂTEAU FRANC-MAYNE 1970:

❧ March 1990
Very good neck level. Medium colour. Browning. Elegant, earthy/sweet, mature nose. Round, soft. Not bad. Was better five years ago. I have tasted this wine on five previous occasions, since 1982. On past experiences, it was much livelier. Past its prime. A small property to watch.

CHÂTEAU L'ARROSÉE 1970:

❧ December 1978
Deep colour, not nearly ready. For a St. Emilion, it has quite a Cabernet, cedary nose. Would mislead me at a blind tasting. Needs at least two to three more years. Big wine. Very good. The proportion of Cabernets (both Sauvignon and Franc) in this wine is quite substantial.

❧ January 1987
Bright, dark, maturing colour, typical of this vintage. Complex, herbaceous nose. Good fruit, well balanced, with enough fruit to last. Yet it is getting ready and drinking very well now (but no rush). Clean, long aftertaste. A very well-made wine. The most "Haut-Médoc" St. Emilion.

❧ September 1990
At home, before Carol's trip to New Mexico and Arizona. Lovely dark colour, typical of the 1970s. Spicy Cabernet nose (l'Arrosée has a high proportion of Cabernet Sauvignon for a St. Emilion). More Pauillac-like in structure (or St. Julien), yet it has the herbaceousness of St. Emilion. Full, rich, long. Very good balance and length. Ready, but enough backbone to last another ten years. Very good. Loads of ripe fruit.

❧ July 1994
Top shoulder level. Fair bit of sediment. Dark, but evolved colour. Full, round, stemmy St. Emilion, yet sturdy. Quite forward, soft, at its peak. Ready and will not improve. Good.

CHÂTEAU PAVIE 1970:

❧ November 1991
Last bottle, at home. At 21 years of age, good neck level, fair sediment, decanted 45 minutes. Good dark colour, typical of the 1970s. Very little maturity at rim. Chocolate, herbaceous, ripe nose. Round, soft, very good balance. Long, clean, spicy. At its peak. Needs drinking before it starts to decline. Very nice, round, smooth. Nice sweet fruit. Most enjoyable. Magnums will hold.

CHÂTEAU PAVIE 1970, MAGNUM:

❧ July 1995
As part of my Corton-Charlemagne and 50th birthday marathon weekend. Very good. Holding well.

Ripe fruit on nose, round, velvety, well balanced. Still very much alive and nice, deep-red colour, typical for the vintage.

CHÂTEAU FIGEAC 1975:

❧ July 1985

Medium, mature brick colour. Lovely, complex, fruity, leathery, ripe nose. Medium body, round, long, and at its peak at ten years old. Drink now to 1995. One of the very best St. Emilions that year.

❧ August 1988

On Turnagain Island. A lovely wine at its peak. Dark, but maturing colour. Spicy, herbaceous nose with hint of oak. Lots of complexity on nose. Round, fruity, excellent balance, ripe fruit. Long, clean, and complex finish. One of the very best 1975 St. Emilions. Ready, but no rush (good balance and fruit). Softer tannins than most 1975s.

❧ December 1993

At 18 years of age, it is still at its peak. Good depth, mature colour. Herbaceous nose (typical St. Emilion). Spicy, good backbone, and balance. Long, flavourful, spicy Cabernets (Sauvignon and Franc). Lost its tannic backbone. Round, complex, and spicy.

CHÂTEAU FIGEAC 1978:

❧ July 1989

On Turnagain Island. Medium dark colour, showing some maturity at rim. Little sediment. Decanted 45 minutes. Very good level. Very St. Emilion, spicy Cabernet Franc, and new oak on nose. Complex, sound, a bit leaner (typical 1978), but good length and balance. Little tannin. Ready, but good backbone and structure. If well stored, will stay at this plateau until 1992 to 1994. As with the 1975 vintage, the two best St. Emilions in 1978 are Cheval-Blanc and Figeac. The latter, by the way, is the only non-First Growth of that commune to age its wines in 100% new oak barrels.

❧ June 1994

With the council of Le Tastevin. (also tasted the 1975 and 1981 Figeac). Better than the 1981. Medium dark colour. Fresh, spicy, herbaceous, nice fruit, good extract. Other comments as above. Very nice, long.

CHÂTEAU FIGEAC 1978, DOUBLE-MAGNUM:

❧ September 1982

This bottle was given to me by Thierry Manoncourt, the owner of Château Figeac when I told him that Orly, my daughter, was born in 1978. What a lovely present, and what a nice, and interesting, man. This has been my third visit to Château Figeac. This bottle should hold for many years and will be opened some day to celebrate one of Orly's birthdays.

CHÂTEAU CANON 1981:

❧ October 30, 1995

With council of Le Tastevin. (This was the night of the Referendum in Quebec over "Separation." The "No" camp won; 50.6% to 49.4% for the "Yes." Close call, until the next round.) Decanted one hour. Little sediment. Surprisingly dark for a 1981. A classy, elegant wine. Surely one of the better 1981s, especially from St. Emilion. Spicy, herbal, elegant nose. Round on palate. Not much weight, but excellent balance. Velvety, smooth, good depth. Long, complex. Structured like a Domaine de Chevalier, but herbal Cabernet Franc character. Ready, but no rush.

CHÂTEAU FIGEAC 1982:

❧ January 1997

Retails now for an unbelievable US$150 per bottle. I purchased a case as "futures" in 1984, and paid that price per case! At 15 years, this wine is perfect now. Deep colour to rim. Ripe, luscious, expansive nose. Full, intense, ripe with soft, ripe tannins. Long aftertaste. Has the herbaceous character of Figeac (high proportion of Cabernets) but in a ripe way. Lovely. No rush. This must surely be the best Figeac since 1966, or even since the great 1964 or 1961!

CHÂTEAU MAGDELAINE 1989:

❧ February 1997

In the Barbados. I brought along several bottles of wine on this trip. Still very young. Purplish colour. Lovely ripe Merlot/oak/vanilla on nose. This wine is made almost entirely of Merlot. Very unusual for a St. Emilion, but then it belongs to Moueix, who has Merlot running in his veins! Rich, round in a soft way. Very stylish. Fleshy, opulent. Clean, rich fruit. Drink around 1999 to 2004.

POMEROLS

CHÂTEAU PETRUS 1961:

❧ Spring 1983

Purchased through a Seattle wine merchant, from a private collector in Oregon. This wine sells today for almost double what I paid ($180). Finally, a dream come true! I own my very own bottle of this great and rare wine!

❧ Fall 1987

Traded this bottle (having had the good fortune of tasting this wine on five previous occasions) for 20 bottles, including two bottles of d'Yquem 1975, six bottles of Pichon-Lalande 1983, and a case of Gruaud-Larose 1982. In effect, I have traded one great experience for 20 great experiences. Not a bad deal!

CHÂTEAU PETRUS 1967:

Purchased this wine In San Francisco in 1976 at John Walker's, for $24 per bottle.

❧ September 1986

At home, the day before I left for a trip to Burgundy and the northern Rhône Valley. This wine has become rare now, and retails for US$250 to $300 per bottle. Decanted 45 minutes. Fair bit of sediment. Impressive colour for a 1967, and at 19 years of age. Deep, still bright, young colour. Licorice, spices, and fine complexity. At first, it was hard, dry, and tannic on palate. After 45 minutes, it softened quite a bit. Round, full, rich, with good backbone. Essence of Merlot, yet a serious, solid wine. Does not have the complexity of a fine Médoc (it is made from almost 100% Merlot), but excellent depth and length. Ready, yet no rush. A sturdy wine, on the dry side. Very good and a great experience. I should have bought some more, especially at $24 per bottle.

CHÂTEAU PETRUS 1970:

❧ September 1982

At home, with friends. Opened and decanted one hour before tasting. Very dark colour. Little sediment. Unusual California bouquet (like a Beaulieu Vineyards Reserve or a Mondavi Reserve Cabernet Sauvignon). Spicy, minty, licorice. Ready, yet with enough backbone, tannin, and acidity to last for quite some time. More California than French. Not as soft and elegant as the 1971, and not as fat and rich as the 1961, but very good. Unusually tight for Petrus. Has great potential. Lovely bouquet in empty glass! This bottle was from a lot of three bottles purchased in New York in 1976 for $23 per bottle, from "67 Wines and Spirits," in Manhattan. Three other bottles purchased at Macy's in New York that same year cost me $18 per bottle.

CHÂTEAU LA FLEUR DE GAZIN 1945:

Six bottles, acquired at a Christie's London auction in 1992. Capsule reads: "1er Cru Haut-Pomerol 1945, Borderie Propriétaire." According to Feret's 13th Edition, *this Pomerol property belongs to Jean-Jacques Borderie, and produces 25 tonneaux (100 barrels, equivalent to 2,500 dozen).*

❧ June 1993

Opened first bottle three days after it arrived. Cork actually branded "Ch. Lafleur-Gazin." Fair bit of sediment. Beefy, sweet, round, no aggressive tannins, but too oxidized. Really undrinkable with any enjoyment, but not "awful." We didn't bother to drink it.

❧ July 1993

With the council of Le Tastevin. Lovely! Much better than first bottle. Cork came out whole. Mature, barnyardy/straw, old Cabernet nose. Biscuity, rich, long. Round on palate, yet backbone typical of the 1945s. Complex, round, elegant. Old-looking, but clean colour. Nice fruit, long on palate. Very good. First bottle really worried me. This bottle was very good.

CHÂTEAU MAZEYRES 1945:

This Pomerol vineyard was completely decimated during the terrible frost of 1956. This wine is château-bottled. Very good level. Owner Mr. Theophile Querre purchased this château early this century. Fairly large proportion of Cabernets.

❧ July 17, 1985

On my 40th birthday, with friends. Also tasted 1967 Les-Forts-de-Latour, 1967 Latour, etc. The star of the evening. Healthy, solid cork with no information. except vintage. Incredible, complex, long bouquet. Round, opulent, perfumy, mature, and marvellous! Decanted 30 minutes. Fair amount of sediment. Good depth of colour, showing maturity at rim, but more like a 1961, rather than a 1945. Round, complex, very long, and flavourful on palate. At its peak. No noticeable tannins left, but well balanced and will hold. At its absolute peak. A great bottle. Memorable! (19.5)

About one-third of the vineyard (15 to 18 hectares) is planted with Cabernet Sauvignon, which is unusual for a Pomerol.

CHÂTEAU LA POINTE 1947:

❧ February 5,1992

At "Bishop's" restaurant, for Menashe's 45th birthday. Lovely, elegant, light, but a still lively and fruity wine. Very good.

CHÂTEAU PETIT-VILLAGE 1959:

❧ April 1992

With Tony Gismondi and Jean-Guillaume Prats, the 23-year-old son of Bruno Prats, whose great uncle Ginestet produced this wine. Deep, dark colour and extract. Very good chocolaty, rich, ripe, iron Pomerol nose. Full, yet soft, long. Complex and rich. Trace of acidity at finish, but ripe fruit, too. Very good. Jean-Guillaume has never tasted an old Petit Village before. Nice young man. Plans to work at Cos d'Estournel some day. Very good wine, too. Surprisingly lively, but ready.

VIEUX CHÂTEAU CERTAN 1959:

❧ March 18, 1981

Quite a bit of sediment. Decanted 30 minutes before dinner. Lovely, chocolaty/oak on nose. Medium dark colour, a bit watery at rim. Good long legs. Delicate, but not too intense. At first, tasted quite dry, some tannin, and quite a bit of acidity. Then it turned into a round and elegant wine. This wine was made three years after the frost disaster of 1956, and it has held very well. Quite an experience. After one-and-a-half hours, the acidity took over, and the wine was quite harsh—but it didn't lose its elegance on nose.

CHÂTEAU L'EVANGILE 1961:

❧ January 20, 1991

High shoulder fill. Very ripe, rich, intense wine. Deep colour. Fat, complex, smooth, round, and long. Expansive. Very fine wine and a rare experience. (Remaining bottle has better neck level.) (Other wines tasted that night were 1979 Pol Roger "Winston Churchill," Puligny-Montrachet "Clos du Cailleret" 1982, Drouhin, 1957 Château Lynch-Bages, and a half-bottle St. Jean Johannisberg Riesling BA "Belle Terre," Sonoma.)

CHÂTEAU TROTANOY 1964:

❧ July 1976

Very powerful wine. Dark colour, fleshy. Nice, but not great bouquet. Needs more time in bottle (three to four years?). Will live for a long time. Selling locally (in Vancouver) for $20 per bottle. Purchased eight bottles.

❧ March 1978

Very dark deep colour. Fine Pomerol (Merlot) bouquet. Rich wine. Will live for a long time. Decanted one-and-a-half hours. Medium sediment. Luscious, chocolaty fruit. A big wine.

❧ April 1979

Very dry, a bit bitter/unpleasant bouquet. Corked bottle.

❧ November 1979

This time it seemed fruitier than in the past. Much more pleasant and round. Can it be that the fruit is finally coming through?

❧ August 16, 1980

At a special group dinner, with five couples. Also tasted that night: 1947 Cheval-Blanc, 1955 Petrus, etc. Comments as above, but tannin is taking over. Decanted two-and-a-half hours. Actually showed better than the 1955 Petrus.

❧ January 1984

Decanted one hour. Some sediment. Good, dark colour, some sign of age. This wine is in its 20th year! Lovely, spicy, complex nose of a classic Pomerol. A lean and hard wine. Good structure and backbone. In the years to come, it may lose its fruit, but it still has tannin and depth, and will hold for a long time. Not a jammy or rich wine, but rather lean, yet very complex, and definitely an excellent wine.

❧ August 1987

At home, with Joe and Alice Heitz, who spent a couple of days with us. I decided to open it after a disappointing 1945 Pontet-Canet. Full, rich, long, spicy, some tar. Well balanced, and full of life. Other comments as above. A lovely bottle. Joe thought it was a California Cabernet! This example was the fruitiest so far, and at 23 years old.

❧ January 1996

Decanted 45 minutes. Superb, deep colour to rim. Iron, ripe Merlot nose. Full, rich, long. Exquisitely full, rich, minerals, iron. Lots of ripe fruit. Perfect balance. At 31, a great Pomerol. Years of life ahead. Great wine. It is amazing how long it took this wine to come around.

CHÂTEAU LE GAY 1970:

Purchased from Christie's London, shipped via Chicago. Arrived March 1987. Owned by the Robin sisters, owners of the famous Château Lafleur. This 1970 Le Gay is a very good wine.

❧ May 1987

This bottle had the lowest level (high shoulder). Disappointing. Dark, mature-looking. Still drinkable, but acidic, oxidized. All other bottles have better levels. Let us hope that they are better than this.

❧ August 1988

On Turnagain Island, with Prue and Harry Waugh. A good bottle. Ripe, deep colour typical of the 1970s. Some maturity. Rich, round, full. Soft, at its peak. Quite good. Impressive at 18 years old, and from a relatively minor property.

CHÂTEAU LAFLEUR 1970:

❧ December 1975
Had it in our hotel room in Portland, Oregon, on our way back from San Francisco. Michael is six months old, and we took him along on this trip. Dark, fruity, and rich. A very good wine. Great, intense fruit extract. A baby, with great potential. Excellent value at $11 per bottle.

❧ October 1982
First bottle, at home. Massive wine! Very dark, young, purplish colour to rim. Quite a bit of sediment. Decanted one hour. Closed, lead-pencil, sweet nose. Not very complex. Well balanced. Still tannins to lose; quite a hard wine. Thick, serious. Needs at least five more years. If this wine doesn't lose its fruit, it will last for a long time. Pity to open it too soon, yet it is already 12 years old!.

CHÂTEAU DU DOMAINE DE L'EGLISE 1970:

Acquired a case of this wine in Vancouver, in 1976. Paid $11 per bottle.

❧ September 1976
Dark colour, nice bouquet, soft, and pleasant. A surprisingly good wine. Ready to drink, and will stay at its peak for a few years. After reading Harry Waugh's enthusiastic comments on this wine, I decided to buy three more bottles in January 1977.

❧ June 1978
At a Tastevin Club dinner, at "La Quiche." Very popular wine. Still not ready (again at blind tasting October 1978). Lots of tannin, deep, big wine. Very good quality. Came first against La Fleur-Petrus 1971 and Clinet 1970.

❧ April 1989
After one hour, long, mellow, rich, complex, well balanced. Lots of fruit. At its peak, but no rush. For the equivalent of a Crus Bourgeois, this is excellent. Last good year produced at this property before the Castejas (of Batailley, Trottevieille, etc.) took over, and lowered the quality.

❧ October 1995
While general comments are similar to six years ago (in 1989), the wine is definitely mature. Perfect now, at 25 years! Round, hint (but only just) of drying out. Needs drinking. This is the last really good Domaine de l'Eglise in 25 years. The Castejas who have owned this property since 1971 or 1972 haven't done much good to it.

CHÂTEAU LA FLEUR-PETRUS 1970:

Purchased several bottles in London, in 1977, from Corney and Barrow. Paid £3.80 per bottle.

❧ October 1984
At home, with friends, against 1971 La Fleur-Petrus. Served double-blind. This wine sells today for ten times (!) the price of seven years ago. The two wines were similar, yet different. They both had the same good, dark colour, slightly maturing at rim. The 1970 was the more austere of the two. Closed, harder, leaner, more tannic, lead pencil nose. No rush drinking it, but will it improve? Overall, a fine bottle. The 1971 had a lovely open, complex, lead-pencil, fruity Merlot nose. Rounder, more delicate, more open, and forthcoming on palate. Everybody preferred the 1971 (Harry Waugh indicated to me that the 1971s in Pomerol were better overall than the 1970s). A lovely mouthful that is at its peak, but will hold. Both excellent. Sid Cross thought that they were two vintages of Sassicaia, or maybe Australian reds. Odd.

CHÂTEAU TROTANOY 1970:

❧ September 1978
A half-bottle at " Rossellini's - The Other Place" restaurant (paid $14). Good, rich wine. Lots of fruit and tannins. Developed well in glass after one-and-a-half hours. Medium colour, and body. Very good. Full bottles should be left alone for at least another five years. Great potential.

CHÂTEAU NENIN 1971:

❧ 1976
In New York, with friends. Nice wine, but a bit hard. Quite dark. Good, rich structure. Should age another two to three years. A fruity wine. A wine I know well. Purchased a case locally, at the government liquor monopoly. Paid $12 per bottle. Quite expensive, but a good wine.

❧ January 1977
Typical Pomerol. Bright and dark colour, quite powerful, but rather tight, and not very intense bouquet. I hope it will improve in three years.

❧ July 1981
On Turnagain Island. Deep, browning colour. Little tannin, but good fruit/acidity balance. Ready, but with enough fruit concentration to last for some time. Nenin made very good wines in both 1971 and 1975. Alas, this property has not been producing fine wines since then.

❧ July 1982
At home, upon my return from the World Cup soccer games, in Spain. Dark, deep colour, touch of brick-orange. Good, spicy-sweet nose. Lovely, full, fat,

concentrated fruit, yet maturing. Good acidity, very little tannin. The fruit should make it last, but it is ready and enjoyable.

❧ August 1987

On Turnagain Island, with Joe and Alice Heitz, who spent a few days with us in Vancouver and Secret Cove. Better than above. Complex, rich, round, long, elegant. Well balanced and at its peak. A lovely bottle.

❧ August 1988

At home, with dinner, against five other 1971 Pomerols. Guests for dinner were Harry and Prue Waugh, the Levines, Freemans, and Spurrells.

Here are my notes.

FLIGHT #1
Taillefer, Gazin, Nenin, all 1971

TAILLEFER:

Deep in colour, spicy, minty nose, not unlike a California Cabernet Sauvignon. Full, solid, good fruit. Rather simple, but sound. No rush.

GAZIN:

Paler, more mature, thinner, simpler, watery, finishing acidic. the most disappointing wine of the flight.

NENIN:

Best of flight. See comments in August 1987.

FLIGHT #2
La Fleur-Petrus, Trotanoy, Petrus, all 1971

LA FLEUR-PETRUS

Elegant, deep colour; fruity, spicy-herbaceous Merlot. Leaner, but very good. No tannins left. At its peak. Very enjoyable.

TROTANOY:

Most complex of the flight. Medium dark colour. Lovely, expansive, spicy-herbal, complex nose. Good backbone. Not quite ready due to good storage. Great length, depth, and complexity. A very good wine!

PETRUS:

Darkest, deepest, most extract, and most solid structure of flight. Fairly hard and tannic on entry, but silky, complex finish. Needs at least five more years, especially from a cool cellar, yet somehow at this stage, it doesn't have the class or complexity of the Trotanoy. Good tasting. 1971 Pomerols have been very successful and are holding well.

❧ August 1994

Six years have gone by since I last tasted this wine (1971 Nenin). Deep, maturing colour. Roasted, rich iron/Merlot nose. Sweet, full, fairly intense. Good, ripe, round, mature fruit. Clean, long finish. Hint of cedar and good backbone. Still at its peak, but will not improve. Very good. Possibly the last fine vintage for Nenin to date.

CHÂTEAU LA FLEUR-PETRUS 1971:

Purchased a case in London in 1977 for £33 per case, from Corney and Barrow.

❧ June 1983

Decanted one hour. Fair amount of sediment. Good, dark colour, some browning. Sweet, "lead-pencil" Merlot nose, typical Pomerol. Well balanced, good fruit, good depth, quite forward, yet with enough body and structure to last. A fine bottle, and a good example of Pomerol. Long on palate.

❧ August 1988

Decanted 45 minutes. Some sediment, but not much. Excellent level. Medium red, good depth, a bit pale, mature rim. Lovely, forthcoming, open, spicy-herbaceous Merlot/Cabernet Franc nose. Flowery. Forward, round, fruity, and clean on palate. At its peak. Trace of acidity at finish. Stylish, leaner Pomerol. Quite typical of both the property and the vintage. Very good. This wine is now rare and expensive.

Traded six bottles of this wine for four bottles of Château Trotanoy 1971.

CHÂTEAU L'EVANGILE 1971:

❧ March 1983

Decanted 45 minutes. Dark but evolved colour. Complex, elegant, spicy Merlot nose. At its peak. Structured like a leaner La Conseillante rather than l'Evangile's traditional rich, luscious style. Lead-pencil bouquet, typical of Pomerols. Round, well balanced. Will not improve. This is the first time I have tasted this property's wines from bottle (other than barrel samples on three previous occasions, tasted at the château). Long aftertaste. A lovely bottle, at its peak. I wish I had some more of this in my cellar. The 1975 vintage of this property, tasted twice from barrel and once in bottle with old Mr. Ducasse (the owner), will be a superb wine some day.

CHÂTEAU LA CONSEILLANTE 1975:

❧ May 1984

Decanted two hours. Some sediment. Deep, maturing colour, yet purplish rim. Very good, thick legs (glycerine). At first, harsh and lean, but after 90 minutes, it opened up. Lovely, sweet, slightly vegetal, complex nose. Round, full, long on palate, yet solid structure (a typical 1975 vintage Pomerol). Very enjoyable now, but with enough structure, tannins, and fruit to last for quite some time. Not quite as big as Trotanoy 1975; rather like a fine St. Emilion. Try again in 1986.

❧ January 1993

Decanted one hour. Little sediment. Good, medium-dark, slightly mature rim colour. Spicy, stemmy, herbal nose. Hint of oak. Round, some tannins, sweet fruit. Quite intense, yet spicy. Very good length and balance. Leaner style Pomerol, typical of this property. Approaching its peak, but really no rush. Will last well beyond 2000, if well stored. Other comments as in May 1984 (eight years ago!).

❧ April 1997

At "La Belle Auberge" restaurant. An excellent wine. Deep colour for a 22-year-old Claret. Expansive, herbaceous yet ripe nose, typical of this property. Holding extremely well. Long on palate, good backbone, lovely spicy, complex fruit. A fine wine. Overall, 1975 Pomerols have been more successful than St. Emilions of that vintage, Cheval-Blanc and Figeac being the exceptions.

CHÂTEAU NENIN 1975:

❧ February 1992

Decanted one hour. Fair bit of sediment. Deep, dark colour typical of the 1975s. Palish rim. Iron, earth, and subdued fruit on nose. Full, rich, still some tannins. Straightforward, well balanced. Ready, but has good backbone. Will last until 2000. Rich, fleshy, not drying out yet. Purchased in Honolulu in 1980. This is the last good vintage for this large Pomerol property, to date.

CHÂTEAU LATOUR-À-POMEROL 1975:

❧ September 1984

First bottle out of a case purchased in Seattle, in 1980 ($190 per case). Deep, maturing colour. Sweet fruit, complex, long, spicy-herbaceous nose. Long, full on palate with the backbone (tannins) typical of the 1975s. A very fine bottle needing two to three extra years to reach its peak, but will hold for quite some time after that, if well stored.

CHÂTEAU LAFLEUR 1975:

❧ September 1986

Deep, dark colour to rim. Impressive! Lead-pencil, ripe, rich, earthy (wet earth) nose. Still closed. Big, masculine, tannic, and hard. Decanted one-and-a-half hours. Fair bit of sediment. Later, rounded up a bit, but not by much. A solid, chunky wine. Well balanced, though. Try again in 1990 to 1995. Acquired this wine in 1983 for $28 per bottle. Now, in 1986, it is worth a small fortune!

CHÂTEAU L'EVANGILE 1975:

Mr. Ducasse gave me a bottle during a visit to his château in October 1980. (In October 1982, during a visit to Bordeaux, I found out that he had passed away three weeks earlier. He was 83 years old.) A rare wine. Almost never seen at auction.

❧ November 5, 1993

Finally decided to open a bottle. Hadn't tasted this wine since May 1977, when I tasted it with Carol and Mr. Ducasse at l'Evangile (from barrel). Almost a 1947 Cheval-Blanc structure! Deep, maturing colour. Ripe fruit, lead-pencil/Merlot ripe nose. Full, fat, rich. Very good balance. Tannins softening. Very rich, very full. Ripe fruit (loads of it). An intense, ripe, very rich wine. Most un-1975! Great extract. Ready but no rush. Classic Pomerol. Sells now for US$150 per bottle!

CHÂTEAU LATOUR-À-POMEROL 1978:

❧ May 1995

Top shoulder level. Decanted 45 minutes. Fair bit of sediment. Good, bright colour, palish rim. Comments as in May 1992. Good depth, balanced, fruity. Still full of life. At a plateau. Long, spicy, rich/minerals. Very good.

My poor back is showing signs of giving up. Over the past three months, I have been packing and lifting almost 500 cases of wine. Thankfully, my son and a few of his friends will help me move the wine to our new cellar next week.

CHÂTEAU L'EVANGILE 1978:

❧ April 1985

Opened a bottle for *The Wine Consumer* panel. Decanted one-and-a half hours. Deep colour, but quite brown. Like a 1966 or older-looking, but good depth. Spicy, herbaceous, warm nose. Round, forward, elegant on palate, but soft (yet well structured). I suspect a faulty cork may have done something to this wine. Must try again.

❧ July 1985

At our new home on Montgomery Street. Much better than first bottle. Dark colour, slightly mature rim. Complex, rich, full, needs two to four more years. Lead pencil/iron character. At this point, not very complex. Rich, full wine. Well structured. "Beefy." Good potential, but not nearly as good as the impressive 1975 or the "soon to be great " 1982.

CHÂTEAU CERTAN-DE-MAY 1979:

❧ February 1987

At home, with the panel of *The Wine Consumer*. Low neck level. Impressive, young, very deep, dark colour. Lead pencil, loads of fruit, a bit vegetal, rich, spicy on nose. Typical Pomerol. Full of life, loads of fruit. One of the best, if not the best, 1979 Pomerol. Has a long life ahead of it. Try again in 1990 to 1995 or later.

❧ February 1992

Impressive dark colour to rim. Plummy, rich, ripe fruit on nose. Still tannic, excellent depth, ripe fruit, balance. Long, complex. Lovely aftertaste. Sweet, ripe fruit. No rush. Drink through 1997 or beyond. The best 1979 Pomerol?

CHÂTEAU LA CONSEILLANTE 1981:

❧ October 1987

At home, with the panel of *The Wine Consumer.* Surprisingly deep, dark, youthful colour for a 1981. Lovely spicy, rich, young Merlot nose, with delicate overtones of oak and vanilla. Lovely depth on palate. Rich, yet good backbone, some tannin, long, very good fruit. A wine of top quality. Drink starting 1990. This must surely be one of the very top Pomerols in 1981.

CHÂTEAU DE SALES 1982:

❧ January 1995

Deep, youthful colour, typical of the 1982s. Luscious, rich; lots of sweet, ripe fruit. Soft, round, ready, but backed by enough fruit to last well for another five to seven years. Surprisingly good for this large property (by Pomerol standards). Succulent. Easy to drink.

CHÂTEAU L'EVANGILE 1983:

❧ March 1996

First bottle of case, at 13 years old. I have tasted this wine in barrel in 1984 and twice at tastings, but this is the first bottle from my own cellar. Classic Pomerol, and surely one of the very best Pomerols in 1983, if not the best. Deep colour. Loads of ripe, sweet fruit, minerals, iron, classic Pomerol, and classic Merlot. Full, rich, long. Ready, but has enough depth and extract to last several more years. Surprisingly, very little sediment.

RED BURGUNDY

CÔTE DE NUITS

CLOS DE LA ROCHE 1934, COMMUNE DE MOREY-ST.-DENIS, DOMAINE DES GRANDS CRUS DE VOUGEOT, PREMIER GRAND CRU

❧ August 1988

Purchased a lot of four bottles at auction. Tasted in Yountville, before bringing the wine back to Vancouver. Tried the bottle with the lowest (two-and-one-half inches) ullage. Has held extremely well. Pale, evolved colour. Spicy Pinot Noir and truffles on nose. Soft, a bit citric, but some sweet fruit still in evidence.

❧ January 1989

At home, with the panel of *The Wine Consumer.* Deeper, very mature colour. Cork disintegrated. Mature on nose. Hard to guess Pinot Noir. Still alive, rich, long, wet earth, and wood, but some ripe, leathery fruit, too. Quite good. The first bottle tasted better.

❧ November 1989

At home, with friends, including the US Consul General to Vancouver, Sam Fromowitz, and his wife Joan. Very good level, one inch below cork. Cork came out OK, but disintegrated. Decanted at the last minute. Lots of sediment. Deep mature colour, not unlike a 1959. Spicy, unmistakable Pinot Noir, "old style" nose. Full, quite solid. Old-tasting, yet still alive and kicking with good depth. Improved in glass after 15 minutes. This 55-year-old Grand Cru has held extremely well. A great buy in retrospect, and a "once-in-a-lifetime" experience for all participants.

❧ February 1994

At home, with guests, one of whom was born in 1934, so it was a special 60th birthday present. General comments as in November 1989, yet this was the best bottle so far! Loads of fruit, rich, full, long, solid. Excellent. I also served that night, the following: 1963 Grands Echézeaux DRC in magnum (superb! Yes, a 1963), 1970 Krug, 1971 Pol Roger "Chardonnay," two 1945 Clarets, both London-bottled by Block, Gray and Block (Pontet Canet and Leoville-Barton), and 1966 Croft's Vintage Port. All great wines!

RICHEBOURG 1937, DOMAINE DE LA ROMANÉE-CONTI:

From a Davis and Co. auction in Chicago. Low levels, all three bottles at two to three inches ullage. Hopefully, the wine will be sound.

❧ September 1995

Opened the bottle with the lowest level (three inches). An oxidized, browning wine. Cork came out whole, but disintegrated. Old, Madeira-earthy on nose. Some structure and depth on palate. Even hint of Pinot Noir, but gone. This is the risk of buying at auction. "Win a few, lose a few." Hopefully, the other two bottles will be better. Anyway, they have better levels at only two inches ullage.

❧ November 1995
Did not decant. Old crumbly cork. I expected very little and, boy, was I surprised! Deep colour. Mature rim. Leathery, ripe berries (raspberry jam) on nose. Full, intense, mouthfilling. Great extract and complexity. Loads of ripe fruit. Got even better after 30 minutes in glass. Not adulterated, just very low yields. Superb, deep, mouthfilling wine. It amazed us all! A true classic.

LA TÂCHE 1942, DOMAINE DE LA ROMANÉE-CONTI:

Purchased four bottles at a Butterfield auction in February 1995. Approximately two-inch ullage. Wax capsules. Opened the bottle with the lowest fill, three inches below cork, yet the wine was very good. Delicate raspberries on nose and palate. Long, lovely. A stunning surprise!

❧ July 16, 1995
With Dr. Stan Schwartz and Mannie and Willette Klausner, who came up from California for my Corton-Charlemagne/50th birthday weekend. Even better than the above. Two-and-one-half inch ullage. Not decanted. Opened one hour (!) before serving. Great, complex, mature raspberry/classic Pinot Noir/La Tâche nose. Tiny cork (there was a shortage of everything in France during the War years). Lasted in the glass for over one-and-a-half hours. A bit lean, but excellent fruit, and very long. For its age and the vintage, a stunning wine! I stole this (paying only $75 per bottle at auction). I recently saw it listed in San Francisco for $350 per bottle.

CLOS DE VOUGEOT 1945, RENÉ ENGEL:

❧ February 1, 1991
At a farewell dinner for the panel of *The Wine Consumer*. Smoky, toasty, bacon-bits nose. Full, chunky, rich, powerful. Like a 1961 Hermitage with some Pinot Noir. Impressive, still lots of life, fruit, and power. A fine bottle… and my birth year.

NUITS-ST.-GEORGE 1945, JOHN HARVEY:

Simple, typed label. Good level. Purchased from Draper and Esquin's. This is an English-bottling.

❧ November 1985
At home, before a trip to Bordeaux. Cork came out OK, but fell apart. Medium-pale, mature colour. At first, a caramel, slightly earthy, oily nose. Later, it cleared. Smell of very mature Pinot Noir. Round, high alcohol (added to wine?); hot, a bit harsh. After 30 minutes, it opened up. A chunky, old, yet sound and enjoyable wine. Has seen better days. Earthy, caramel, high acidity, and alcohol. Quite an experience, though.

CLOS DES LAMBRAYS 1946, HERITIERS COSSON:

This bottle was given to us by Ed Lazarus of Los Angeles. Carol's birth year. This is one of the few good 1946s. Excellent level and appearance.

❧ May 1992
On the Occasion of Carol's 45th birthday. Very good, especially for the vintage. Pristine condition. Charred oak, backed by good fruit on both nose and palate. Surprisingly well balanced and lively. Most enjoyable.

CHAMBOLLE-MUSIGNY 1949, CAVES DE LA BUSSEROLLE:

From a Butterfield auction. Excellent level and appearance.

❧ January 1996
At home, with friends. Decanted. Fair bit of sediment. Light, evolved colour, not unlike a good 1969. Spicy Pinot Noir, mature nose. Surprisingly full, long, intense, powerful on palate. Lots of depth, character, excellent structure. Far above the quality expected from a simple Villages wine. Full of life! Held well in glass for over an hour. This is the kind of wine that makes Burgundy's reputation.

CLOS DES LAMBRAYS 1950, DOMAINE DES LAMBRAYS, HERITIERS COSSON:

❧ December 1994
Not decanted. Lots of sediment. Mature, medium light-red colour. Mushrooms, old, yet definitely Pinot Noir nose. Round, soft, clean fruit. Fragile, yet alive. Well balanced. Nice fruit. Dried out after 20 minutes in glass. We also tasted a superb 1959 Cos d'Estournel that night.

LA TÂCHE 1951, DOMAINE DE LA ROMANÉE-CONTI:

Good appearance. Levels two inches below cork. One bottle two-and-one-half inches.

❧ November 1994
Opened first bottle for the council of the Commanderie de Bordeaux. Black cork. Totally oxidized and mushroomy. Dead.

LA TÂCHE 1952, DOMAINE DE LA ROMANÉE-CONTI:

Acceptable levels (two inches below cork). Good appearance. One bottle has a two-and-one-half-inch ullage.

❧ February 1995
At home, with "Group of Ten." Fabulous. Pale colour, very good depth, intense spicy-raspberries, Pinot Noir nose. High acidity, but very long, and certainly very lively at 43 years of age. Excellent.

RUCHOTTES-CHAMBERTIN 1953, CHARLES VIENOT:

Excellent, top neck level. New label.

❧ December 1991

With the Crosses, Mottersheads, and Bernard Ledun, French Consul General to Vancouver. Impressive dark colour. Serious, spicy, clean Pinot Noir nose. Not unlike a 1971! Lovely structure. Solid, yet elegant, spicy fruit, long, clean, impeccably made. Lots of stuffing, yet not heavy. Classy, long, spicy on palate. Has held extremely well. No rush at 38 years of age! Excellent quality.

CLOS DE LA ROCHE 1955, CHARLES VIENOT:

❧ May 1995

At "Bishop's" restaurant, with friends. (Also tasted the 1966 Château Margaux, 1989 Montrachet Laguiche and a half-bottle of 1980 d'Yquem) Excellent neck level. Recorked at the winery (new unbranded cork). Fair bit of sediment. Not decanted. Mature colour, good depth. At first, green olives, vegetal nose. Later, complex, spicy Pinot Noir. Quite lively, full, rich, long. Not unlike a 1978, but older colour. Very good complexity, depth, length. This was very good. I wish I had more.

CLOS DE VOUGEOT GRAND CRU "GRAND MAUPERTUIS" 1955, JEAN GROS:

Direct from the property. Superb levels and appearance.

❧ March 1992

Lots of sediment. Dark, mature colour. Sweet Pinot Noir nose. Quite ripe, on the sweet side. Obviously chaptalized. Sweet fruit, round, straightforward. Somehow does not have the complexity of the 1972 La Tâche that preceded it. Good, but not great.

LA TÂCHE 1957, DOMAINE DE LA ROMANÉE-CONTI:

Chicago Wine Co. auction. One-and-a-half-inch ullage. Very good appearance.

❧ December 1992

With friends. Best wine of the evening. Great class, complex, raspberries. Long, round, lovely. Amazingly alive at 35 years and still fresh, thanks to good acidity and careful selection.

RICHEBOURG 1958, DOMAINE DE LA ROMANÉE-CONTI:

Good appearance and level only one inch below cork.

❧ November 1994

With the council of the Commanderie de Bordeaux. Mature, palish, evolved colour. Lovely, charred (toasted oak), cherries, Pinot Noir nose. Intense, superb complexity, length. Rich, yet elegant. Excellent, especially for such a difficult vintage!

LA TÂCHE 1958, DOMAINE DE LA ROMANÉE-CONTI:

Good appearance.

❧ September 1994

Opened the three-inch-level bottle. Cork crumbled. Did not decant. Fair bit of sediment. Browning rim. Very mature colour, good depth. Unmistakable nose of raspberries and Pinot Noir, a trademark of this property. Quite acidic on palate, but nice fruit, depth, and clean Pinot Noir. Mature and lean. Held well in glass for an hour. Surprisingly good.

CHAMBERTIN "CUVÉE HERITIERS LATOUR" 1959, LOUIS LATOUR:

Purchased a bottle from Draper and Esquin's in 1987. Expensive! ($135 per bottle)

❧ July 1988

My 43rd birthday. Heavy glass bottle. Decanted 30 minutes. Fair bit of sediment. Brick colour, with excellent depth. Nuances of mocha, chocolate on nose, combined with ripe berries. Lovely, intense, complex nose. Full, yet soft on palate. Long, typical manly Chambertin with great class. Still fruity. Will last for a few more years. Great length and complexity on palate. A superb, classic Burgundy. Wish I had more! (19)

CLOS DE VOUGEOT GRAND CRU "GRAND MAUPERTUIS" 1959, JEAN GROS:

Direct from the producer. Superb levels and appearance.

❧ April 1993

Impressive dark colour, good depth to rim, showing some maturity. Not unlike a good 1971 or 1978. Fresh, spicy-fruity Pinot Noir on nose. Some charred oak. Full, rich, even sweet. What this wine lacks is complexity. It has the depth, fruit, and body, yet it is simple, straightforward. Pleasant. No rush. Has it been topped up with younger wine at the winery?

LE RICHEBOURG 1959, A. BICHOT, VOSNE ROMANÉE:

Purchased a case from the Quebec liquor monopoly in 1975. Paid $28 per bottle. Tasted three bottles during 1976. Exquisite, rich wine of great quality. Soft, yet powerful. Complex, very good, spicy bouquet. Lots of sediment. Has to be decanted. We let it breathe for approximately two hours.

❧ January 27, 1978

Last great wine before moving to our new home on Adera Street. Great wine. Earthy bouquet of a mature, great 19-year-old! Dark colour, still powerful after two-and-a-half hours. Lots of sediment. Bouquet lasted in empty glass for two hours. This wine will live for many years. One of the few Burgundies that still gives me hope that maybe not all Burgundies are light, and fade after a few years.

❧ December 29, 1979
Was hoping to taste the last really fine wine of the decade, and after two weeks of abstention due to my tonsillectomy on December 17, I was disappointed. Lovely nose, beautiful, deep, dark colour with a touch of brown, but on the palate, a bad bottle! Sour, acidic, dry wine! It is hard to believe that the wine is deteriorating so fast after being so good, so consistently. Disappointing experience.

❧ December 29, 1983
The last great bottle of wine for 1983. Decanted 45 minutes. Fair bit of sediment, good level. Incredible bouquet! Truffles, spices, complex, mature; long, beautiful nose of great Pinot Noir. Medium-bright colour, slightly brown rim. Younger-looking than its age (24 years) would indicate. At first, a bit harsh and lean on palate, but later, fuller, round, a beautiful mouthful. I am sorry to see this wine go, but what better comment than that. One of Carol's favourites, as well. Drank it slowly, and enjoyed every drop. It should hold another few years, but, surely, cannot get any better. Magnificent bouquet! Only two disappointing bottles out of the case. A real experience. I will miss it.

ROMANÉE-ST.-VIVANT 1961, LONDON-BOTTLED, BOUCHARD PÈRE ET FILS:

❧ April 1977
In London. Beautiful wine. Decanted and after 30 minutes, it was smooth, soft, and rich. Very dark colour, some sediment. At its peak. Excellent ripe fruit extract. Well balanced, mouthfilling. A bargain at £4.50 per bottle.

LA TÂCHE 1963, DOMAINE DE LA ROMANÉE-CONTI:

Purchased at a Butterfield and Butterfield auction. Very good levels and appearance. Price extremely good. Hopefully, wine is decent. Five magnums purchased for $70 per magnum.

❧ July 1992
With the council of the Commanderie de Bordeaux. Decanted just before serving. Fair bit of sediment. A disastrous year, yet a very good wine by any yardstick! Medium depth, very mature brown-orangy colour. Lovely truffles, spicy Pinot Noir, clean nose. Long, rich, round; nice fruit on palate. Dry finish, but very good. Hint of acidity at finish. Served blind. Most tasters thought it was a wine from the 1950s or 1940s. Very fine effort.

❧ November 1992
Not decanted. Comments as above; even better, fresher, spicy fruit! Incredible quality for such a poor vintage. Obviously, being in magnum and well cellared has helped. I'm glad I purchased this at auction, at a ridiculously low price. Thanks to the late André Noblet, régisseur of Domaine de la Romanée-Conti, who let me taste these 1963s in 1977, during a visit to the winery, I appreciate what can be done in a poor year if the selection is very strict.

GRANDS ECHÉZEAUX 1963, DOMAINE DE LA ROMANÉE-CONTI:

❧ February 1994
Spicy, raspberries, Pinot Noir nose. A bit acidic, but lovely fruit, and intensity. Full, rich, long. Has held extremely well. Really surprisingly good.

MUSIGNY 1964, JOSEPH DROUHIN:

❧ August 1987
With Joe and Alice Heitz, who spent a couple of days with us. Bright, cherry-red colour. Fair bit of sediment. Forthcoming, intense nose. Long, spicy, elegant, hint of barnyard. Superb on palate, too. Long, well balanced, with excellent fruit. The star of the evening. Joe was impressed. Great wine at 23 years of age. (19)

MUSIGNY 1964, COMTE DE VOGÜÉ:

❧ November 1982
At home, before my departure for Jerusalem and Bordeaux. I had this wine exactly a year ago at one of our "Group of Ten" special dinners. After reading the notes on the previous bottle, I decided that it is time to drink this bottle. A masterpiece. My only bottle of 1964 red Burgundy left. A true Musigny. Elegant, complex, soft, long, fabulous tea leaves/spice, sweet nose. Very long and very complex. Decanted 30 minutes. Velvety, clean aftertaste. Bright, red colour, and not tired-looking. Although the flavour and aftertaste are excellent, the greatest thing about this wine is its incredibly complex, elegant bouquet. Great bottle. One of the best red Burgundies I have tasted to date.

CLOS VOUGEOT 1964, RENÉ ENGEL:

Excellent level and appearance.

❧ November 1995
One of the best Clos Vougeots I've tasted to date. Very good colour. Lovely, spicy/fruity nose and palate. Full, rich, long. Much livelier than many other 31-year-old Pinot Noirs! Great fruity extract, yet mellow, velvety. At its peak, but no rush. Excellent effort.

RICHEBOURG 1966, CHARLES NOËLLAT:

❧ November 1992
Very good neck level. Some sediment. Mature orange-red colour. Good depth. Delicate, subdued, spicy Pinot Noir nose. Round, silky, elegant, long. Good

flavour. At its peak. Good, clean fruit. Classy. Will not improve.

BONNES MARES 1969, DOMAINE CLAIR-DAÜ:

❧ August 1977

In London. Delicate bouquet, medium colour. No sediment. We had it on a hot afternoon, which is unfair to the wine. Nevertheless, it was velvety, chocolaty, rich, spicy, and very well balanced. Good value at £6.50 per bottle. This producer's Bonnes Mares is located in the commune of Morey-St.-Denis.

BONNES MARES 1969, AVERY'S (BRISTOL):

From Butterfield and Butterfield auction February 1995. Mixed case, excellent top neck levels.

❧ June 1995

With the council of Le Tastevin. Did not decant. Fair bit of sediment. Good, deep, maturing colour. Expansive nose of ripe, mature, barnyardy Pinot Noir. Full, rich, round, lively fruit, and good length. Even a fair bit of alcohol (but not excessive. Avery's is reputed for adding Brandy into their older Burgundies. If so, they did an excellent job). Long, complex Pinot Noir/sweet-fruit aftertaste. Very good. No rush. Impressive wine that is a quarter-of-a-century old.

RICHEBOURG 1969, JEAN GROS:

❧ May 27, 1986

On the eve of Carol's 40th birthday. Very good level, medium sediment. Decanted 45 minutes. Medium colour with good depth, and orange-brown rim. Quite mature-looking. Complex, spicy, fruity, opulent Pinot Noir nose. Round, mature, at its peak. Great length, and complexity on palate. Long, clean finish. Very good fruit, well balanced. Ready, but will hold. A superb bottle! Outstanding. (18.5) at least.

CHAMBERTIN CLOS DE BÈZE, DOMAINE GENERAL REBOURSEAU 1969, PIAT PÈRE ET FILS:

❧ February 1980

Decanted one hour. Hardly any sediment. Bright-red colour, some brick-brown. Lovely fruit. Spicy, complex, and intense nose. Really great on palate. Full-bodied, enough extract to last a few more years. Very well balanced, good fruit, very little tannin. A velvety wine, yet manly and intense. To date, probably one of the finest great red Burgundies we've tasted. Wish they made such red Burgundies more often.

CHAMBOLLE-MUSIGNY "CHARMES" 1969, NICOLAS:

❧ May 1983

Dark colour, little sediment, decanted 45 minutes. Big wine, barnyard-spicy Pinot Noir nose. Not very complex, rustic, and still youthful. Similar in style to Doudet-Naudin. While this wine will not improve, it will last for a long time. Lacks the elegance of a good Chambolle. Rather like a Gevrey Chambertin, or Morey-St.-Denis. Served it blind. One knowledgeable guest thought it was a St. Emilion or St. Julien! As usual, he does poorly at blind tastings.

CHAMBERTIN 1969, DOMAINE A. ROUSSEAU:

❧ April 1985

At home, with Sid and Joan Cross. Medium colour, mature rim, good depth. Lovely, open, long, complex Pinot Noir nose. After one hour decanting, opened up. Fabulous length, and perfectly balanced. A long, fabulous bottle of wine. Lovely complexity, length, and depth. Delicate, yet excellent backbone. A classic. At its peak, but should hold there for at least two to three more years. (19)

ROMANÉE-ST.-VIVANT 1969, MAREY-MONGES:

❧ October 1978

I read a report in *Decanter* magazine a few months ago that this wine is over-the-hill, so I decided not to wait any longer to open it. Medium sediment, dark bright colour. Nose developed from spicy to sugary (burnt sugar). Very good flavour, well balanced; long-lasting aftertaste. A good, solid, complex Burgundy. I wish I had waited, and not trusted 's report. Will keep for quite a few years. Vinified, bottled, and shipped by the Domaine de la Romanée-Conti.

LA TÂCHE 1971, DOMAINE DE LA ROMANÉE-CONTI:

Purchased a case at a Butterfield and Butterfield auction, November 1992. From an "impeccable" cellar. Very good levels and appearance. Cost a fortune (US$3000 a case), but this is a great wine.

❧ January 1993

First bottle from this case. Bright, deep colour; orangy, mature rim. Classic, spicy raspberries, toasted oak, and Pinot Noir on nose. Full, rich, long, and very intense on palate. Evolved, open, forthcoming, but so much extract, and excellent structure that there is no rush drinking this. Will stay at this plateau until the year 2000 or beyond, and will decline very slowly, if well cellared. Great wine!

❧ August 17, 1993

Our 19th wedding anniversary. We went to John Bishop's restaurant in Vancouver for dinner, and brought our own bottle of 1971 La Tâche. Comments as in January 1993. So big, so intense, so rich, full, and long that we felt it was actually filling, not unlike food! Great raspberry depth, length, balance. No rush. A classic. We also sent a glass over to Dave Freeman, who happened to be at the restaurant at the same time. (John Bishop generously let us taste some 1986 d'Yquem in half-bottle. Very young, but superb! Not as rich as the 1983 but great depth, elegance, balance. In ten years, this will be a great wine.)

❧ April 1997
The 1971 La Tâche retails now for US$600 per bottle!

LE MUSIGNY 1971 AND 1972, LOUIS JADOT:

❧ April 1984
Purchased the 1972 in Bath, England. Paid £9.

❧ March 1985
At home, with friends. Tasted against the 1971 Musigny from Jadot, purchased ten years ago in Seattle. Both had some sediment and both were decanted one hour before serving. The 1972 had a medium colour, good depth, elegant, complex, long, lovely, spicy-complex bouquet. It did not have the excessive acidity typical of the 1972s. A fine bottle.

Now to the 1971. I purchased this bottle a long time ago, and have waited ten years to try it. The wine was darker than the 1972, fuller to the rim. An extraordinary, complex, deep, spicy nose, still a bit closed. Great depth, full, very well balanced, some tannin to lose. Incredible length. Almost a "Chambertin" in style. While drinking well now, this wine will reach its peak in three to five years, and hold well beyond. An absolutely fabulous bottle, possibly one of the three or four greatest red Burgundies I have tasted in my 12 years of wine tasting to date. Fabulous. (19.5)

GRANDS ECHÉZEAUX 1972, DOMAINE DE LA ROMANÉE-CONTI:

❧ September 1980
Last great bottle of wine before leaving for our extensive, ten-week tour of France (from September 6, 1980).

A bit thin and acidy, but after 90 minutes, it developed a lovely, rich, complex, spicy bouquet. Still powerful, some tannins, rich. Needs another two to three years. Good, long cork. Very good. It has the size and depth of a fine Côte de Nuits. Try again around 1985 or beyond.

Purchased a case at auction from Butterfield and Butterfield in June 1991. Paid $900 per case. An excellent buy. Replacement value $175 per bottle. Most have very good levels. Three have levels one inch from cork.

❧ August 1991
In Yountville, with Belle and Barney Rhodes. The wine was soft, forward, superb, complex, very elegant. Classic spicy-raspberry character with hint of charred oak. Holding extremely well. We drank it at "The French Laundry" restaurant.

❧ October 1991
I took a bottle to a friend's for dinner. Corked! Very poor wine, totally undrinkable. This is the second time I've taken a "fine" bottle to that friend's home for dinner, and it turned out to be corked. The first was a 1964 Haut-Brion, six months ago.

❧ May 1992
Level one-and-one-quarter inch from bottom of cork. Did not decant. Fair bit of sediment. Good dark, but quite mature colour; orange rim. Intense Pinot Noir, truffles, herbal nose. Spicy, very good intensity. The acidity of the better 1972s is all important! Good fruit, long, spicy, oak/Pinot Noir. Fairly lean, but very good fruit and balance. At its perfect plateau, but because of good fruit and acidity, no rush drinking this. Very good! Serious stuff.

❧ July 1997
My 52nd birthday, at "Lumière" restaurant with Carol, Orly, and Michael. Excellent level. Good appearance, fairly evolved colour. Lots of sediment. Classic spicy, raspberries nose. Round, well balanced; trace of high acidity, typical of this vintage. Long, lots of extract. At 25, this wine has held extremely well, thanks, no doubt, to fairly high acidity backed by enough fruit. Excellent wine.

RICHEBOURG 1972, DOMAINE DE LA ROMANÉE-CONTI:

❧ March 1991
At the office. With friends, after moving the Commanderie de Bordeaux cellar. Good neck level. Medium colour, fair bit of sediment, mature-looking, a bit cloudy. Smoky, expansive, ripe, intense raspberry jam on nose. Full, sweet, rich, and spicy on palate. Round, yet full and long. Classy, complex, sweet, mature fruit finish. Very good, but had it been better stored, it would have been livelier. Typical, spicy complexity of Richebourg.

BONNES MARES 1972, JOSEPH DROUHIN:

❧ January 1993
With the council of Le Tastevin. Brick, mature colour. Classic, spicy, perfumy, toasty Pinot Noir. Ripe berries, classic Drouhin. Round, soft, with spicy, delicate fruit. At 20, has held extremely well. Top quality. Great spicy Pinot Noir aftertaste. Ready. (18)

LA TÂCHE 1972, DOMAINE DE LA ROMANÉE-CONTI:

❧ December 1982
This wine is a full ten years old now. Brick-red colour, orange rim. Some sediment. Decanted 45 minutes. Lovely, plummy, spicy, raspberries, and complex Pinot Noir nose. A lot of class. A bit high acidity (a characteristic of the 1972s), but long on palate. A bit lean, and maybe lacks middle for a Côte de Nuits of this class, but certainly a very good wine. Ready, but seems to have a long period of levelling off, and should still be very good for another four years. This wine, if it can be found, retails today for over $120 a

bottle. How fortunate I am to have purchased a case of this at a local government liquor monopoly store in 1976, for $24 per bottle.

❧ March 1992
With Dr. Brad Klein. (Also tasted that night a 1955 Clos Vougeot, Jean Gros) Brilliant, dark, mature colour. Lovely nose of raspberries, ripe Pinot Noir. Lots of class here. Fair bit of sediment. Good acidity and fruit extract. Complex, long, spicy, intense. The acidity has helped this wine retain its lively fruit. Classy, intense, long finish. A beauty. No rush. Most enjoyable.

❧ May 1997
With Carol, before my departure with Orly to New York and Paris. Excellent level and appearance. This wine is now a quarter-of-a-century old. Fabulous, spicy Pinot Noir/raspberries on nose, a trademark of La Tâche. Great fruit extract and intensity. Has lost the acidic character of the vintage. Long, round, smooth. At its peak, but no rush. Great character, class, and length.

CHARMES-CHAMBERTIN 1972, JOSEPH DROUHIN:

❧ September 1982
Against 1972 Grands Echézeaux DRC, with Harry Waugh, the Freemans, and the Helmers. The Grands Echézeaux was darker, more intense, higher acidity, typical of the 1972s. Good fruit, solid, ready, but should hold. Mind you, it was not much darker than the Charmes Chambertin of Joseph Drouhin's, which was a bit lighter, more orange at rim, softer, sweeter, more open, spicy Pinot Noir nose, more elegant. Forward, ready, will not improve. Very good.

ECHÉZEAUX 1973, DOMAINE DE LA ROMANÉE-CONTI:

❧ May 1979
Very pale colour, quite brown. Pleasant, open bouquet, which faded away after 45 minutes. One can tell that this wine comes from a fine vineyard, but the body, intensity, and colour are disappointing. Mind you, 1973 was a very light year for red Burgundies. The whites, on the other hand, are superb.

LA TÂCHE 1976, DOMAINE DE LA ROMANÉE-CONTI:

❧ December 1991
All 12 bottles have excellent neck levels. Decanted one hour. Fair bit of sediment. Good depth of colour, but very evolved; brick/browning. Lovely, open, expansive nose of spicy Pinot Noir, dill, oak/toast/smoky, all in harmony. Round, full, at its peak, but lots of intensity; spicy, sweet fruit; evolved, rich, and long.

❧ March 1992
With council of Le Tastevin. Deep, mature colour, orange-brown rim. Not as brilliant colour as the La Tâche 1972 served later that night. Fair bit of sediment. Intense, spicy Pinot Noir nose. Full, rich, mature, yet with the ripe backbone typical of the 1976s, a drought year. A bit rustic. At its peak, but no rush. Long aftertaste. Certainly Grand Cru quality. Very fine wine. However, it is not quite up to this fine property's great 1971 or 1978.

NUITS-ST.-GEORGES PREMIER CRU "CHÂTEAU GRIS," MONOPOLE 1978, LUPÉ-CHOLET:

A rarely seen wine.

❧ November 1993
With the council of Le Tastevin. Decanted 45 minutes. Very good level. Deep, dark, mature colour. Good, spicy Pinot Noir/barnyardy nose (in a clean way). Full, rich, solid wine. Lots of extract; rich, serious, long. Old-style rustic Nuits, yet clean, full, ripe fruit. Not very complex, but certainly good.

BONNES MARES 1978, ROBERT GROFFIER:

This wine has an excellent reputation. Very high neck levels.

❧ April 1993
At "Le Gavroche," in Vancouver. Fair bit of sediment. Mature, evolved colour, yet good depth. The nose of La Tâche! Ripe cherries, intense, evolved Pinot Noir; classic nose. Similar impressions on palate. Lovely mature fruit. Full, velvety, ripe-cherry fruit. Long, clean finish. This is great stuff. Will not improve, but no rush. Great length, class, and complexity. (19)

RICHEBOURG 1978, CHANSON PÈRE ET FILS:

❧ February 1985
The name of the wine and vintage are excellent. The shipper, unfortunately, is not. Had it on the day I purchased it. Like a 1978 Côte de Nuits Villages with a lot of acidity. Very disappointing and dull. An insult to Richebourg!

GEVREY-CHAMBERTIN PREMIER CRU "CAZETIERS" 1980, PHILIPPE LECLERC:

Purchased from Draper and Esquin's in San Francisco and was rated "outstanding." The Underground Wineletter, Vol. V #6).

❧ May 1989
Impressive, youthful, medium-dark colour. Some sediment. Decanted 45 minutes. Classic, rich, youthful, spicy Pinot Noir "barnyard" nose. Good fruit. Good backbone and depth. Still young. Very good balance. Surprisingly good for a 1980. Enjoyable now, but will get even better by 1991 to 1993. Very good! Leclerc is a gifted winemaker.

❧ September 1996
Amazingly, as good as seven years ago. A great effort by a fine winemaker. Lovely, spicy fruit. Evolved

colour, yet good depth. Long, lovely fruit, balance. Excellent.

CHARMES-CHAMBERTIN 1982, DOMAINE MAUME:

March 1992

Decanted one hour. Little sediment. Palish, light colour. Lovely, spicy, herbaceous, forthcoming, classic Pinot Noir. Round, yet has good backbone. Long, complex, at its peak. Maume's Charmes actually comes from the Mazoyères vineyard. Very good. Ready, but no rush.

June 1997

At home, with Carol, Michael, and Orly. Surprisingly, hardly any sediment. Pale, evolved colour. Subdued, delicate Pinot nose. Clean, hint of raspberries. Silky on palate, yet still has good fruit at 15 years of age, and from a "soft" vintage. Sweet, spicy, elegant, round fruit. Perfect now. A credit to this serious producer.

MAZIS-CHAMBERTIN 1982, DOMAINE MAUME:

December 1989

With the panel of *The Wine Consumer*. Quite dark colour for a 1982. Some sediment. Obviously unfiltered (not a brilliant colour). Big, rich, rustic nose of Pinot Noir. Still powerful. Full, rich, quite hot. Needs at least five more years (not before 1993) or longer. Very good intensity. Later, nose opened up. Complex, rich, and long.

GEVREY-CHAMBERTIN "EN PALLUD" 1982, DOMAINE MAUME:

This is a "lieu-dit," not a Premier Cru.

August 1987

With Charles Brossier, export manager of Borie-Manoux. Quite pale-red colour, typical of the vintage. Open, forthcoming, lovely Pinot Noir/oak nose. Expansive. Fuller and harder on palate than colour would indicate. Fruity, well balanced. Some sediment (not filtered). Very good. Will peak two to three years.

June 1995

Tasted against Kalin's Pinot Noir 1980, Santa Barbara. The Maume was a bit more aged in colour, and had thrown a fair bit of sediment. Quite solid for a 1982; more like a 1983. Rustic, earthy smells. Quite dry and hard. Totally uncharacteristic for a "soft" vintage like 1982. A bit "dirty" smelling, and sharp, acidic finish. Yet, unmistakable Pinot Noir character. Seemed better when tasted in 1987. It was fresher, and had better fruit.

GEVREY-CHAMBERTIN PREMIER CRU "LAVAUX SAINT-JACQUES" 1982, DOMAINE MAUME:

February 1996

Some sediment. Surprisingly full for a 1982. Maturing at rim. Rustic, old-style Pinot Noir. Spicy, full, rich, even solid on palate. Still has some fruit. May lack elegance, but very Gevrey. Fine effort.

CLOS DE LA ROCHE GRAND CRU 1983, JOSEPH DROUHIN:

April 1992

With Jean-Guillaume Prats (Bruno Prats' son), and Tony Gismondi. (Also served the 1959 Petit Village.) No sign of rot (a problem with many 1983 red Burgundies). No sediment. Lovely fruit, brilliant colour. Lots of life ahead. No sediment. Full, long, spicy Pinot Noir. Very good potential. Try around 1994 to 1997.

GEVREY-CHAMBERTIN 1983, PHILIPPE ROSSIGNOL:

Gold medal winner, Macon Wine Fair.

March 1993

Some sediment, evolved colour. Good depth, though. Thankfully, no sign of rot! Clean, spicy Pinot Noir on both nose and palate. Full, rich, round; very good fruit and structure. Lovely, clean, spicy Pinot Noir aftertaste. Very good. Drink from 1995 to 2000.

NUITS-ST.-GEORGES PREMIER CRU "LES CAILLES" 1983, ROBERT CHEVILLON:

July 1991

No sediment. Medium-red colour and depth, without the premature browning or the smell and taste of rot of so many 1983s. Very good depth, balance, length. Complex, spicy, classic Nuits and Pinot Noir. No rush but enjoyable now. Very good fruit. Encouraging, after so many poor 1983s. Drink 1993 to 1998.

ECHÉZEAUX 1983, MUGNERET-GOUACHON:

February 1991

No sediment, no decanting, opened one hour. Light-red colour, starting to turn prematurely brown. Spicy, open Pinot Noir nose that is a bit musty. Some fruit, evolved, but not very complex. Some sign of rot. After one hour, finished sharp, acidic, bitter, and musty. Not bad, but not Grand Cru quality. Like so many 1983s, disappointing.

NUITS-ST.-GEORGES PREMIER CRU "LES VAUCRAINS" 1983, ROBERT CHEVILLON:

June 1990

For once (a rare occurrence), an excellent 1983! No sign of rot. Good, dark colour. Little sediment. Lovely scented, spicy Pinot Noir nose; quite evolved. Round, full, rich, long, spicy, and clean on palate. Good depth. Ready, but no rush. Drink now to 1997.

MAZIS-CHAMBERTIN 1983, PHILIPPE NADEFF:

April 1990

Little sediment. Bright cherry-red colour. Slight browning at rim. Slightly musty-sugary (chaptalized) nose. Cherry fruit. Full, serious on palate. Not charming. Obviously chaptalized, but solid backbone, nice fruit. Little sign of rot (a problem with many 1983s). Good structure. Retry in three to four years.

VOSNE-ROMANÉE 1983, JEAN GRIVOT:

❧ January 30, 1991
Not decanted. Little sediment. Medium bright-red colour. No browning. Spicy, complex, still subdued nose. No sign of rot or mustiness, either on nose or on palate. Good fruit, delicate on entry, but good backbone, and some tannins left. Very good. Will reach its peak in two to four years. Much better and cleaner than many prestigious Grands and Premiers Crus 1983 that are foul, falling apart, and smell of rot!

BONNES MARES GRAND CRU 1983, LOUIS LATOUR:

❧ September 1992
Dark colour. Some maturity at rim. No sediment. Open, spicy, intense, barnyardy nose. Classic Pinot Noir. Full, rich, tannic. Long. Needs three to five more years of bottle-age. Trace of mustiness in aftertaste (a curse of many 1983s!), but enough fruit to mask it at this stage.

VOUGEOT "CLOS DE LA PERRIÈRE" 1985, DOMAINE BERTAGNA:

❧ September 1995
Quite evolved, mature rim. Medium-bodied, little sediment. Clean, yet barnyardy Pinot Noir nose. Round, soft, good depth. Nice fruit. Ready, but no rush. This is a "Premier Cru," unusual for Vougeot.

VOSNE-ROMANÉE PREMIER CRU "BEAUX-MONTS" 1985, DANIEL RION:

❧ February 1989
Bright, cherry-red colour, typical of the vintage. Lovely cherry fruit with hint of oak and vanilla. Full, round, spicy, and long on palate, with excellent, ripe fruit. One bottle broke when other bottles fell on it in my cellar. A rare accident, but these things happen.

CLOS DE VOUGEOT 1985, CHARLES MORTET:

❧ May 1991
With French Consul General to Vancouver, Bernard Ledun. Super wine! Great depth of colour. Intense nose, essence of Pinot Noir. Luscious, excellent balance; long, complex. Lovely wine. Great fruit extract. Enjoyable now, but will add complexity in three to four years. Bernard enjoyed it very much as well. How charming these 1985s are turning out to be.

ECHÉZEAUX GRAND CRU 1985, MOILLARD:

❧ March 1992
Good dark, still purplish, youthful colour. Palish rim. Lovely, ripe, cherry nose; hint of oak, vanilla. Warm. Rich, round, charming fruit. Long. Very good. Good depth, balance, long. Excellent. No rush. Still very young. Try from 1995 onward.

❧ May 1996
On Turnagain Island, with French Consul General to Vancouver, Maryse Berniau. Comments as in 1992. Holding extremely well. No rush. The following morning, the phone rang. When I asked the caller for his name, he said, "Monsieur Giscard d'Estaing." The call from Paris was for Maryse, who is trying to organize a three-day whale-watching trip for the former President of France.

❧ July 1997
At home, with Michael and Orly. Fully mature now, at 12 years old, but no rush. No sediment. Nice bright cherry-red colour. Ripe, cherry-fruit nose, typical of the vintage. Round, fruity, sweet, charming wine. Moillard's wines are not very complex. They are certainly not delicate. But they are fleshy and have good fruit extract.

GEVREY-CHAMBERTIN 1985, PHILIPPE ROSSIGNOL:

❧ October 1995
First bottle at ten years of age. Bright-red colour. Good depth, still youthful-looking. Spicy Pinot Noir nose. Clean, ripe berries. Quite full, solid. Very good depth, extract, and balance. Not very complex (after all, it is only a Villages wine), but lots of stuffing. No rush. Typical, well-made 1985. Rossignol is a gifted winemaker.

CHAMBERTIN "HERITIERS LATOUR" 1985, LOUIS LATOUR:

❧ January 2, 1996
Little sediment. Decanted. Classic 1985 and classic Chambertin. Bright cherry-red. Good depth. Spicy, black cherries on nose. Full, solid, lovely fruit. Good acidity/backbone. Not a massive wine, but not quite ready, yet. Will peak around 1998 to 2004. Long, spicy, complex. Very good to excellent.

NUITS-ST.-GEORGES PREMIER CRU "LES RONCIÈRES" 1986, JOSEPH DROUHIN:

❧ August 1991
Very good, dark colour, like a 1985. No sediment. Fresh, lively. Very good balance. Rich, ripe fruit. Complex, elegant, yet very good depth, especially for a 1986. Not light at all. Very fresh. Needs two to three extra years.

CLOS DE VOUGEOT 1987, MEO-CAMUZET:

❧ September 1995
Bright cherry-red colour. Spicy Pinot Noir/oak nose. Ripe fruit. Clean, long. Very good depth, well balanced. Lighter 1987 style with underlying acidity, typical of the vintage. Improved in glass after one-and-a-half hours. Quite rich, long. Ready, but thanks to acidity, will hold until 1998 to 2000. A very well-made and most pleasant wine. Complex, spicy, long.

An underrated vintage, because of the poor reputation of Bordeaux that year, no doubt.

RUCHOTTES-CHAMBERTIN "CLOS DES RUCHOTTES-MONOPOLE" 1987, ARMAND ROUSSEAU:

October 1995
At "Star Anise" restaurant, in Vancouver. Bright cherry-red. Delicate, spicy, clean Pinot Noir nose. Good acidity/backbone/fruit balance. Most enjoyable, yet will improve over the next two to four years. A very good wine. This was once the property of the house of Thomas Bassot, acquired by Charles Rousseau.

NUITS-ST.-GEORGES PREMIER CRU "CLOS DES ARGILLIÈRES" 1987, DANIEL RION:

August 1995
Comments as in 1992! Surprisingly fresh. Are these 1987s going to turn out to be like the 1972 red Burgundies? Very good fruit/acidity balance. Oak/spicy cherries/Pinot Noir on both nose and palate. Surprising depth and intensity. Definitely more backbone, and fresher than the soft 1986s. Very good. Classic, solid Nuits.

CHAMBERTIN "CLOS DE BÈZE" 1989, BRUNO CLAIR:

April 1997
Took a bottle to Puerto Vallarta. The softness of the vintage, combined with the depth of Chambertin. Medium colour. Clean, spicy, fairly intense Pinot Noir on nose. Full, round, silky, but some tannins underneath. Good fruit extract, well balanced. Lovely mouthful. Ready now to 2002. Bruno is a very gifted winemaker.

CÔTE DE BEAUNE, CÔTE CHALONNAISE, AND SOME BEAUJOLAIS GRANDS CRUS

Pommard Premier Cru "Epenots" 1934, Collection du Dr. Barolet (François Martenot):

September 10, 1996
At home, with council of the Commanderie de Bordeaux. At that meeting, I announced that I would be retiring as Maître in May 1997, and Ian Mottershead would be taking over. I have served as Maître for nine years, and on council for four years before that.

Very pale, evolved colour. Almost Rosé. Sweet, spicy, soft, open nose, unmistakable Pinot Noir, very forward; yet good fruit on palate. Maybe "doctored" a bit, but good length; nice sweetness, fruit, not drying out. Very soft and forward. A rare treat. Two council members who enjoyed this wine were born in 1934.

POMMARD PREMIER CRU "RUGIENS" 1959, MICHEL GAUNOUX:

June 15, 1994
At "Bishop's" restaurant, in Vancouver.

With Mark and Tracy Schonfeld. Mark has just been elected president of the British Columbia Medical Association. (Also tasted the 1978 Puligny Montrachet "Pucelles," Leflaive.) Not decanted. Fair bit of sediment. Mature, medium red-brick colour. Subdued, delicate, clean Pinot Noir nose. Round, silky on palate. Nice fruit, long, smooth wine. Trace of acidity at finish. Needs drinking. Impressive for a 35-year-old.

POMMARD "CLOS DES EPENOTS" 1959, DOMAINE DE COURCEL:

Morell and Co., New York. From the original cellar of "Monsieur Henri."

December 1981
Fair amount of sediment. Decanted and tasted right away. Bright colour. Sweet, spicy nose, not very intense. On the palate: Oh, what a disappointment! No acidity, no tannin or fruit, or complexity. Simply old, sweet tea. Didn't even seem to have any alcohol! Not fit to drink. Very disappointing. Ended up drinking beer with our steaks. It is always a gamble buying older bottles. Can't win them all.

BEAUNE PREMIER CRU "CLOS DE LA MOUSSE" 1964, BOUCHARD PÈRE ET FILS:

May 1993
Lunch, at home. Excellent mature colour, good depth and appearance. Lovely tea leaves, ripe, spicy cherries,

mature nose. Full, rich, long. No doctoring here! Just excellent fruit extract. Long, complex, no rush. Very full, very rich, very long. A lovely bottle.

BEAUNE-GRÈVES PREMIER CRU 1969, ROPITEAU:

❧ September 1985
Opened first bottle. Its content had nothing to do with the label. The cork was branded: "1971-Monthélie-Hospices de Beaune, Cuvée J. Lebelin." Fair bit of sediment. Palish, mature colour. Lovely scented nose of mature Pinot Noir. Round, soft, forward, perfumy, and long on palate. At its peak. Elegant wine of very good quality. Like a mature 1964. Needs drinking.

❧ December 1985
Second bottle. Cork indicated same information as the first bottle. Comments as above, yet this bottle seemed a bit tired, and with higher acidity. Definitely should be drunk up. Obviously, Ropiteau put the wrong labels on these bottles.

BEAUNE "CLOS DES MOUCHES" 1969, JOSEPH DROUHIN:

❧ January 2, 1989
Mature, medium-depth colour. Lovely, open, complex, chocolate/spicy Pinot Noir nose. Round, complex, well balanced, long, and clean. Fair bit of sediment. A most enjoyable bottle that is at its peak. Impressive for a 20-year-old. Still has good fruit.

BEAUNE "CLOS DE LA FEGUINE" 1969, DOMAINE PRIEUR, CALVET:

❧ September 1976
A wine of very fine quality. Surprising, ready to drink. Dark colour, mature, full taste. Considering Vancouver prices, it's a good buy at $11.50 per bottle.

❧ September 1979
Full, deep colour, still young-looking. Good Pinot Noir bouquet. Still big in mouth, "fleshy," yet rounded and very drinkable. A relatively unknown vineyard, yet such a fine wine.

❧ November 1981
Last bottle. This is one of the few red Burgundies I really enjoyed on several occasions over the years. Had it eight times. Eight great experiences. This last bottle, at 12 years old, is at its peak. Good depth of colour. Spicy-fruity, mature nose. Lovely flavours. Good aftertaste. Well rounded, mature. Couldn't get any better.

CORTON 1971, BONNEAU DU MARTRAY:

❧ June 1978
Excellent wine, well rounded, fruity, a touch of brown. Beautiful, rich bouquet, still "solid," with some tannin to lose. Should last for quite a few years. An excellent wine all around and typical manly Corton. Paid $8.50 for this in a wine shop in Carmel, California. I should have bought some more.

HOSPICES DE BEAUNE, "CUVÉE GUIGONE-DE-SALINS" 1972, BEYERMANN:

Purchased a case in Vancouver for $12.50 per bottle in 1977. Quite expensive.

❧ December 1986
Last bottle of this wine. Before a Caribbean cruise with the family. Very soft, complex, delicate, and enjoyable. Long, spicy finish. A lovely bottle, at its peak. I have enjoyed this wine a dozen times over the past nine years, and it has always been a very pleasant experience. It has held surprisingly well for 14 years.

CORTON "CLOS DE LA VIGNE AU SAINT" 1976, LOUIS LATOUR:

❧ June 1995
At our new home on 12th Avenue. In the midst of a terrible lower-back pain! Moving 500 cases of wine last month to our new home has taken its toll. One of the best 1976 red Burgundies I've tasted recently. Decanted. Fair bit of sediment. Dark, maturing colour. Vinous, classy, intense, evolved Pinot Noir on both nose and palate. Full, very good backbone, fruit, and intensity. Lots of depth. Ready, but no rush. Lingering aftertaste.

"CUVÉE REMOINA" 1976, REMOISSENET (AVERY'S):

❧ October 1983
This wine is overproduction Beaune-Marconnets, but sold to Avery's in bulk, therefore has Appellation Contrôlée Bourgogne only. Dark, deep colour; some sediment. Decanted one hour. Spicy Pinot Noir nose, but not very complex, or open. At first, harsh on palate, but improved after one hour. Rustic style. Big, deep, hard wine. Good fruit, but one-dimensional. 1976 being a drought year, the wines are (or should be) ripe, dark, and big. This wine reflects the vintage. Quite good.

❧ November 1990
Last bottle. Decanted 45 minutes. Some sediment. Impressive, deep, dark colour. Barnyardy, sweet, ripe, "old style" red Burgundy. Similar impressions on palate. Hefty, some fruit, but softer tannins at 14 years of age. Good length, beefy, rich wine. No rush. Should hold well for five to six more years. After that, it may turn pruny.

POMMARD "CLOS DE VERGER" 1979, POTHIER-RIEUSSET:

❧ August 1989
Impressive dark, still youthful colour. Comments as above, but a bit more evolved. Approachable, but not yet at its peak. Needs two to three extra years, and

should hold well for some time. Very good fruit extract, balance, and depth. Impressive effort, especially for a soft, early maturing vintage.

CORTON "CLOS DES CORTONS" 1985 MONOPOLE, FAIVELEY:

❧ July 1992
No sediment. Good deep colour, maturing at rim. Lovely, spicy, ripe berries, clean nose. Full, rich, long, excellent balance. Essence of Pinot Noir. Very long finish. Soft tannins, but great depth, and rich fruit will help this wine keep for ten more years, if well cellared. Top class.

CORTON "CLOS DES CORTONS" 1986 MONOPOLE, FAIVELEY, UNFILTERED:

❧ January 1995
No sediment. Bright cherry-red colour. Clean, spicy cherries/Pinot Noir nose. Very drinkable. Good fruit, round, fresh. Not much depth (typical 1986). Fortunately, François Faiveley bottled it unfiltered. Otherwise the wine would have had no body left. Elegant, ready. Well made, but lacks the depth of the excellent 1985.

BEAUNE PREMIER CRU "TOUSSAINTS" 1987, ALBERT MOROT:

❧ January 1992
The fools at the BCLDB monopoly halved the price as a "discounted" item! Good cherry-red colour. Maturing rim. Spicy, rich Pinot Noir nose. Full, rich, well balanced. Good depth. Needs two to three extra years of bottle-age. Nice sweet fruit. Clean, long finish. At the discounted price of Can$16 per bottle, I purchased every bottle I could find.

BEAUNE PREMIER CRU "LES TEURONS" 1988, ALBERT MOROT:

❧ November 1990
Austere. Deep, dark colour. Solid, powerful, old style. Needs four to seven years. Very good fruit. Serious wine. Most masculine of this house's Beaune stable.

VOLNAY PREMIER CRU "CLOS DE LA BOUSSE D'OR" 1988, DOMAINE DE LA POUSSE D'OR:

❧ August 1996
Some sediment. Decanted one hour. Good depth of colour, maturing rim. Still fairly big, rich, lovely fruit, and elegance, yet the unmistakable backbone of the vintage. No rush. Long, full, rich, well balanced. This is a "Monopole" of the Domaine de la Pousse d'Or. Drink from 1999 to 2004.

WHITE BURGUNDY

CÔTE DE BEAUNE, CÔTE DE NUITS, CHABLIS, MÂCONNAIS, AND CÔTE CHALONNAISE

MEURSAULT N/V, BIRKEDALL HARTMANN:

This wine is listed in the government monopoly liquor stores.

❧ June 1974 to May 1975
Poor value at $11 for a nonvintage blend. One of the bottles was spoiled. I hope my future experiences with Meursault will be better. Each time I tried it, it tasted foul. Took the remaining four bottles back for a refund. How sad it is to be a wine enthusiast in Canada, with its bureaucratic wine monopolies and high taxes.

BEAUNE DU CHÂTEAU N/V, BOUCHARD PÈRE ET FILS:

❧ November 1976
Clean bouquet. Resembles a good Pouilly Fuissé, but at $11, overpriced. It sells in Alberta for approximately $7.

POUILLY-FUISSÉ N/V, BOUCHARD AINÉ ET FILS:

❧ 1974
Tasted several times. This was Carol's and my first experience with white Burgundies. Clean, fruity wine, but a bit thin. It is a nonvintage, therefore a blend of various vintages. There is so little to choose from at the BC government liquor stores!

❧ Tried it twice in 1978
Unpleasant, sulphuric, mediocre wine selling for $22! When will it ever end?! Our government monopoly stores are full of this, and other wines like this.

LE MONTRACHET, MARQUIS DE LAGUICHE 1969, JOSEPH DROUHIN:

❧ July 15, 1977
In London. With a fine seafood flan Carol made. Our guests were Harry and Prue Waugh. A big, powerful wine. Harry said that it needed four to five more years. After an hour, it improved and softened. A great wine. Fine bouquet; clean, and very typical, ripe Montrachet. Excellent potential.

PULIGNY-MONTRACHET "LES PUCELLES" 1969, HENRY BOILLOT:

❧ May 1977
At the Toastmaster's Inn in Kent, England. Beautiful wine; full, mineral, fruity bouquet. One of the best white Burgundies we've had to date on this trip.

Toasty, long on palate. Not really rich, but a distinguished, elegant wine.

LE MONTRACHET 1970, FLEUROT:

❧ August 1976

Purchased at Macy's wine department in New York. Paid $14 per bottle. Beautiful bouquet. Fine wine, on the mellow side. We had great expectations and were a bit disappointed. A bit too sweet and not crisp enough. Not as good as the Bâtard 1973, Joseph Drouhin we drank earlier in 1976.

CORTON-CHARLEMAGNE 1971, COMTES DE GRANCEY, LOUIS LATOUR:

❧ June 1977

In London. Excellent nose, pale-gold colour. Very powerful, not ready. This wine is great, and it will live for many years. Superb depth, nutty, ripe Chardonnay. Expensive; paid £6 per bottle.

CORTON-CHARLEMAGNE 1971, TOLLOT-BEAULT:

❧ December 1976

Has quite a bit of sediment for a five-year-old white Burgundy. Dark gold, very bright colour. Beautiful, mellow bouquet. Superb taste. A bit flinty (very little), and rich in texture. This is the greatest white Burgundy we've tasted to date. Must find some more of this. Purchased in New York earlier this year at the very high price of $9 per bottle.

CHASSAGNE-MONTRACHET PREMIER CRU "RUCHOTTES" 1973, RAMONET:

From a wine shop in Seattle. Paid $11 per bottle in 1977. Not cheap!

❧ November 1978

Bright, golden colour. Fine nose, well balanced. Nice fruit, ready, yet has enough fruit and acidity to last for some time. Complex, good wine. Excellent. Exotic fruit with hint of vanilla. Ready, but no rush. Ramonet is a great producer, but good white Burgundies are so expensive these days.

BÂTARD-MONTRACHET 1973, L. GROS:

❧ March 1976

The greatest white Burgundy we've tasted to date. Maybe a bit young. Beautiful distinguished bouquet. We were sorry to finish it. Had it with lovely trout. Intense, rich, luscious wine. Great wine.

BÂTARD-MONTRACHET 1973, GAGNARD-DELAGRANGE:

❧ June 1981

A masterpiece. Almost as good and as intense as the great 1970 Le Montrachet, Domaine de la Romanée-Conti I tasted at the Domaine recently. Bright, golden colour. What a great bouquet! Toasty, forthcoming, intense, incredibly good. Perfect fruit/acidity balance, good body, and very long aftertaste. I wish I had more of this wine. Near perfection. Great! Purchased at Hedges and Butler in London in 1977 at £5.50 per bottle. (19.5)

CORTON-CHARLEMAGNE 1973, COMTES DE GRANCEY, LOUIS LATOUR:

❧ March 1983

At home, just before our Passover/Easter trip to London and Israel with the family. Fabulous wine! Almost ten years old and holding very well; very little sign of age. Bright, medium-gold, clear colour. Lovely, subdued, nutty nose. Very well balanced, long, clean aftertaste. Seems ageless for a white wine! Big, powerful wine of excellent quality. An aristocrat! Louis Latour kept these wines in oak for 15 months, according to Broadbent.

❧ January 1986

My last bottle. Surprisingly young-looking for its age. Bright gold. Complex, long, delicate nose of roasted almonds, oak, and toast. Very well balanced. Long, round, mature. At its absolute peak. Ripe, forward, layers of incredible complexity, and depth. This, my last bottle, was memorable. A lovely experience! I'm sorry to see it gone, but it will not improve with any more ageing. Great. (18.5)

CORTON-CHARLEMAGNE 1973, BONNEAU DU MARTRAY:

Purchased a couple of bottles of this wine at Justerini's in London last year. Paid £5 per bottle.

❧ April 1980

Tasted against 1973 Corton-Charlemagne of Louis Latour's. Both wines had approximately the same colour. Bouquet more open in this wine, more oak on nose, a bit drier. Very good. Ready. Well made. Louis Latour's was fresher, a bit more complex, well balanced, and will last for some time. Both are great wines; different in style, with Louis Latour's indicating a better future. Nice nutty noses, fine complexity. Great wines.

POUILLY-FUISSÉ "TÊTE DE CRU" 1975, J. LORON:

❧ July 1983

This wine has held very well, and is lovely drinking now. One of the few good Pouilly Fuissés I have tasted to date. Medium-gold, clear colour. Crisp, yet complex nose. Well balanced. Unmistakable Mâconnais, yet complex, elegant, and very well made. Ready. Oddly, both Chablis in the extreme north and the Mâconnais in the extreme south have produced far better white wines in 1975 than did the finer vineyards of the Côte d'Or.

CORTON-CHARLEMAGNE 1976, LOUIS LATOUR:

❧ November 1984
At home. With friends, against 1976 Puligny-Montrachet "Pucelles" of Leflaive's. The guests, all experienced tasters, had a poor tasting, thinking that the wines were Rhône or Sauvignon Blanc or California Chardonnay! Toasty, forward, low acidity, typically 1976, yet very classy wines. The Corton-Charlemagne was fuller, nuttier, more intense. The Pucelles was toastier, a bit leaner (as a fine Puligny should be), with mineral overtones. Both very fine, but mature wines.

PULIGNY-MONTRACHET "LES PUCELLES" 1976, V. LEFLAIVE:

❧ January 1982
What a great wine! A masterpiece. Beautiful medium-gold colour; round, toasty bouquet. Creamy, long on palate. Well rounded, clean, yet rich. At its peak. The lack of acidity suggests that this wine may not live much longer, but at the moment, it is just perfect. White Burgundy at its optimum.

❧ April 1984
A few days before our departure for London, Bordeaux, and Oporto. Comments as above. Very impressive; at its peak, round, long; beautiful complexity on nose, and palate. Toasty, complex Chardonnay nose. Beautiful, very enjoyable wine. I haven't enjoyed such a fine white Burgundy for some time.

❧ February 1985
Last bottle, with a "Group of Ten" dinner. This wine was fabulous over the years, but has started to decline lately. Very successful for a 1976. Rich, but soft and early maturing for white Burgundies. Great experience. This wine has been my introduction to the fine Leflaive estate.

CHASSAGNE-MONTRACHET PREMIER CRU "CAILLERETS" 1976, REMOISSENET:

❧ March 5, 1982
With Harry Waugh. Tasted it against 1976 Puligny-Montrachet "Combettes," also from Remoissenet. The Caillerets was more luscious, open, opulent; lovely, toasty nose, very good. Ready. The Combettes was a bit more subdued. Good acidity, not as forward, opened up later. Lovely. Both very good, but Combettes slightly fresher-tasting.

❧ November 1986
Against Remoissenet's Puligny Montrachet "Combettes" 1976. The Caillerets was lighter, crisper, younger tasting, with good complexity. The Combettes was richer, fuller, more voluptuous, less acidic, with excellent depth, and more class. Both wines are excellent and both have held extremely well (at ten years of age) for 1976s. Most other 1976 white Burgundies are over-the-hill now, tired, and clumsy. These two bottles are very good. While I'm not a fan of Remoissenet's reds, I find that their whites age well, and have good structure and class.

PULIGNY-MONTRACHET PREMIER CRU "PUCELLES" 1978, V. LEFLAIVE:

Purchased in Portland, Oregon for $18 per bottle in 1981.

❧ June 1985
Green-gold colour. Very complex, open, long Chardonnay-toast nose. Full, complex, leanness of Puligny. Great length and intensity. A classic approaching its peak. No rush. A fine wine from a great vintage.

❧ June 1987
Before a trip to Bordeaux. Brilliant-gold colour with hint of green. Intense, lovely, long, round nose. Full, round, long, complex. Loaded with fruit. Excellent balance. Ready, but will hold. A lovely bottle!

❧ May 1989
Brilliant, deep yellow-gold colour. Superb nose of ripe, intense Chardonnay with oak and vanilla. Full, rich, long. Serious. Great concentration and body. Superb length. Holding very well, with good acidity and backbone. Great extract. At its peak. Retails now (if it can be found) for US$85 per bottle; this is over four times what I paid for this wine eight years ago.

BÂTARD-MONTRACHET 1978, V. LEFLAIVE:

Purchased in Oregon in 1981. Paid $30 per bottle.

❧ July 17, 1985
My 40th birthday. Also tasted: 1967 Les-Forts-de-Latour, 1967 Château Latour, and 1945 Château Mazeyres-Pomerol. Great length and complexity. Full, round, rich, good fruit/acidity balance. New oak, lovely aftertaste. A classic, approaching its peak. Great quality. (19)

❧ May 1988
After hearing other people, such as Sid Cross, saying that the wine is declining and "odd," I was worried, and I opened a bottle. Deep, bright green-gold. At first it was closed and unyielding, but after 45 minutes, it exploded! Superb depth, elegance, charm, and complexity. Quite soft, at its peak. A lovely bottle. Definitely ready. Drink now to 1992. Great quality, thank heaven!

❧ January 22, 1990
Before a Trip to San Francisco. This wine is worth its weight in gold these days! Bright, deep, green-gold. Oak, hint of sulphur, and ripe, mature Chardonnay

nose. Rich, full, long, soft. Holding well. Fabulous length and great extract. Super wine! A rare treasure.

NUITS-ST.-GEORGE "CLOS DE L'ARLOT" 1978, TÊTE DE CUVÉE, JULES BELIN:

❧ June 1983
Medium-bright, clean gold colour. Ripe pineapple on nose, fruity on palate. Elegant, soft, very well balanced. Not as toasty or complex as big Cortons, or Montrachets, but very elegant and delicate. An unusual white wine from the Côte de Nuits.

❧ June 1991
At an International Wine and Food Society Dinner in Vancouver. Surprisingly, comments as five years ago! Holding extremely well. Deep gold, straightforward, and solid; typical for Pinot Blanc. Fruity, rich, long. Lovely fruit. Ageless. These 1978s are just great.

CORTON-CHARLEMAGNE 1978, COMTES DE GRANCEY, LOUIS LATOUR:

❧ August 1985
At a vertical tasting of Latour's Corton-Charlemagnes 1971 to 1983. Great intensity and power. This wine will be a keeper. Purchased a case in 1983 for $300.

❧ August 1987
I'm worried. This magnificent wine is starting to age fast. Deep gold. Intense, woody nose. Rich and ripe fruit, too. Hint of oxidation. A bit sour and acidic on palate, yet very big, intense, and rich. What a shame. Two years ago, this was a magnificent wine. Drink up?!

❧ December 29, 1987
Last great bottle for 1987. Good news! I must have had a bad bottle last August because this bottle was superb! A great wine. Great depth, intensity, lush fruit. Great balance. Full, rich, good fruit, and acidity. A classic. Drink now to 1993. What a relief! Essence of Chardonnay at its best.

CHEVALIER-MONTRACHET 1978, REMOISSENET:

❧ April 1985
Bright gold. Fabulous, complex, delicately toasty, long on nose. Good length, perfectly balanced. Lovely complexity, good fruit and acidity on palate. Still a bit hard on the finish. Fabulous now, but will hold for some time. Great wine. (18.5)

❧ April 1987
Oh, what a wine! Every time I taste fine 1978 white Burgundies, I realize how great they are. Comments as above. A superb bottle. At its peak, but perfect balance suggests no rush.

❧ March 1990
Upon my Return from a 19-day trip to Burgundy and Bordeaux. Brilliant green-gold colour. Toasty, fruity, expansive, appley Chardonnay nose. Leaner, steely Remoissenet style, yet rich, long, and full on palate. At its peak. Great concentration of fruit. Superb Chardonnay from a great vintage! This classic retails today for over $175 a bottle. I acquired this in Seattle in 1982 for $35 per bottle.

CORTON-CHARLEMAGNE "SILVER JUBILEE" 1978, REMOISSENET:

❧ February 1985
Curious gold-green colour. Bright, almost Chablis-like. Lovely, nutty, complex, rich nose. Full, big on palate. Very well balanced. A "noble" yet austere wine. Not as intense and ripe as Latour's Corton-Charlemagne 1978, but very rich. Top quality.

❧ May 1985
At home, with Bruce Guimaraens of Fonseca's Port, who is staying with us. Fine bottle. Comments as above. Remoissenet's Corton-Charlemagne is apparently made from purchased grapes from Domaine Louis Latour.

❧ November 1986
Medium bright-gold. Great, complex, elegant, mature nose. Clean and long. Round, elegant, great balance on palate. Everything about this wine is perfect, yet it is not as powerful or luscious as Latour's or Leflaive's wines. A lovely bottle at its peak, but no rush. Excellent.

❧ January 1994
At "Le Petit Genève" restaurant, in Vancouver. Very soft, elegant, brilliant-golden colour. Honeyed nose, complex, round, reaching the end of its peak, but still lovely and long. Elegant, lovely wine. Needs drinking, through 1994. This wine is now 15 years old.

PULIGNY-MONTRACHET PREMIER CRU "PUCELLES" 1978, HENRI BOILLOT:

❧ August 1983
With lovely Chinook salmon that I caught that same morning off Campbell River on a fishing trip with friends. Medium-gold colour. Complex, elegant, toasty Chardonnay nose. Beautifully balanced (fruit, acidity, intensity). Fine wine, long on palate. Will hold for quite some time. One of the loveliest white Burgundies I have tasted in the past two years. (18)

❧ February 1, 1991
At home, during farewell dinner for the panel of *The Wine Consumer*. Quite green, toasty, sulphuric, lean, yet good fruit and lively. Other comments as above. Drink up. After all, this wine is now in its 13th year.

CORTON-VERGENNES 1978, "CHÂTEAU DE BLIGNY," PIERRE-YVES MASSON:

A rare white Corton.

❧ April 1989
At first, a bit sulphury, but opened up nicely. Complex, long, elegant, soft, drier than most older white Burgundies. Good depth, clean, long finish, well balanced. Got better as it opened up in glass. Has held well.

MOREY-SAINT-DENNIS PREMIER CRU "MONTS-LUISANTS" 1979, DOMAINE PONSOT (MONOPOLE):

A rare wine. Very little made; produced from Pinot Blanc grapes.

❧ August 1988
At home, with Harry and Prue Waugh. Bright, deep green-gold colour. Some sulphur, but good nose of mature Pinot Blanc. When well made, Pinot Blanc can be an ager. Good fruit, fairly rich, soft; low acidity, round, clean, long finish. Has held extremely well.

❧ July 1989
Last bottle, with friends. Served blind against 1980 Chalone Pinot Blanc "Reserve." Medium-golden colour. Some sulphur. Crisp, quite lean, yet has fruit underneath. Improved after 20 minutes in glass. An unusual wine, not unlike a white Corton. Quite good. A rare experience.

CORTON-CHARLEMAGNE 1979, TOLLOT-BEAUT:

❧ February 1984
Lovely wine! Bright-golden colour. Spicy, complex nose of nutty Chardonnay and oak blending nicely. Leaner style, yet long and complex. Great fruit extract. A collector's item; only four barrels produced.

❧ January 3, 1987
First great wine of 1987. A superb, well-balanced, nutty, complex, long, lovely wine. Great quality. At its peak, but no rush. Expansive, intense. A lovely, memorable bottle! Taste lasted forever.

❧ January 2, 1990
First great wine of 1990. Oddly, comments as three years ago. Leaner style, typical of this house's Corton-Charlemagne. Restrained, understated, very good aftertaste. This house produces a tiny amount of Corton-Charlemagne, only four barrels annually (100 cases!).

❧ July 8, 1990
Last bottle. World Cup soccer final match. Germany wins, beating Argentina 1 to 0. Bright green-gold. Toasty, spicy Chardonnay nose. Leaner style, surprisingly lively for an 11-year-old. Steely, excellent fruit. Great balance. An excellent wine that has held very well. Herbaceous, long, complex. Great!

PULIGNY-MONTRACHET "LES REFERTS" 1979, LOUIS LATOUR:

❧ April 1985
Bright gold with green tinge. Complex, delicate, classy, toasty Chardonnay nose. Forward, beautifully balanced, long, complex, delicate on palate. At its peak. A lovely bottle. Very fine. Bravo Latour! (18)

MEURSAULT 1979, JEAN MICHELOT:

❧ February 1989
Opened my last bottle. Green gold. Complex, full, well balanced, still exquisite. Rich, long, full. A lovely bottle. In its tenth year, and still holding very well. Michelot makes superb Meursaults. Really impressive. Balance, fruit, depth, complexity. It is all there.

CORTON BLANC 1980, FAIVELEY:

Now upgraded to Corton-Charlemagne (since 1986).

❧ March 1992
With the council of Le Tastevin. Darkish gold. Rubbery-Chardonnay, hint of sulphur on nose and palate. A bit short, but still has fruit. Not great but certainly sound at 12 years old, and from a mediocre vintage.

CHABLIS GRAND CRU "VALMUR" 1982, J. M. RAVENEAU:

❧ September 1984
Fabulous, rich, yet still a bit closed nose. An explosion of intensity and complexity on palate. Long, full, rich, well balanced. Needs two years to develop and round up. A lovely, classy Chablis. Purchased a case of this in San Francisco last year. Paid $135 per case.

❧ October 1987
Pineapple on nose. Oak, too. A bit simple. Certainly Chardonnay, but lacking the crispness, and smoky-flinty flavours of Chablis. Also, not enough complexity. Overall, this 1982 Valmur of Raveneau seems inconsistent.

❧ July 1988
On Turnagain Island. Comments as above, yet round, soft, and pleasant. Easy drinking. Top Chablis from the best producers has tripled in price over the past five years, yet they keep planting more and more vines there, and not always on the best soils. This is worrisome.

❧ January 1992
Better than five years ago! Spicy, flinty, yet sweet and creamy. Rich, full, long. Very good intensity. Has held well, and actually improved. Best bottle since 1985. Odd bottle variation. Elegant and complex. Now fully mature.

PULIGNY-MONTRACHET PREMIER CRU "CLOS DU CAILLERET" 1982, JOSEPH DROUHIN:

❧ March 1992
Deep gold (too dark). Sweet, woody, heavily oxidized. Pity. Until 1985, Drouhin vinified this whole "monopole" vineyard. From 1986 onward, it reverted back to Jean Chartron who now vinifies and bottles this wine under his own label. Apparently, Chartron is trying to reclassify this vineyard as a Grand Cru.

CHEVALIER-MONTRACHET 1982, GEORGES DELEGER:

❧ May 1993
In San Francisco, at the "Carnelian Room." John Tilson and I purchased their last remaining two bottles after tasting the wine off their wine list. Great extract and depth. Fabulous, rich, honeyed.

❧ October 1994
With Carol, at "Le Petit Genève" restaurant, in Vancouver. Deep, mature, golden colour. Superb, ripe, honeyed nose of classic Chardonnay. Full, long, very soft, yet rich, intense, with great fruit/acidity balance. Few "Montrachets" could compete with this. Will not improve, but a superb classic Grand Cru. Great wine. Very long, full. Lovely!

BÂTARD-MONTRACHET 1982, JOSEPH DROUHIN:

❧ March 1989
Deep gold. Intense, rich, oaky, full, but starting to oxidize. Drink up. A poor sample, or is this the usual Drouhin problem of early maturing whites?

❧ August 1989
Comments as above. Has fallen apart. Very disappointing. A letdown. Drouhin should do better than this! Oxidizing, acidic, some depth, but tired. Over-the-hill. I have finally figured out that Drouhin's white wines are very good, even excellent, in their youth. Most do not seem to age well, however.

POUILLY-FUISSÉ "LA ROCHE" 1982, GUFFENS-HEYNEN:

❧ May 28, 1986
A magnum, at "Le Petit Genève" restaurant, in Vancouver. At a surprise party with 14 friends for Carol's 40th birthday. Rich, big, oaky, forward. Losing its fruit, and too oaky. Better on nose than on palate. Needs drinking. The excessive oak has overwhelmed this wine.

MERCUREY BLANC 1982, MICHEL JUILLOT:

❧ May 1984
A stunning surprise! This is a fabulous wine. Medium gold, lovely, complex, oak/vanilla nose. At a blind tasting, it would probably be mistaken for a fine Puligny or Chassagne Premier Cru. Well balanced, long, rich, complex. True to the 1982 vintage. A lovely and promising bottle. Excellent.

❧ December 31, 1990
Last bottle, on New Year's Eve. Disappointing. Hasn't held very well. Should have consumed it three years ago, when it was still at its peak.

CORTON-CHARLEMAGNE 1982, TOLLOT-BEAUT:

❧ October 1988
With the panel of *The Wine Consumer*. Complex, toasty, long nose. Leaner style. High acidity, good fruit, long, complex. Serious. Lovely length. Top quality. No rush drinking this. Excellent potential.

❧ March 31, 1989
Comments as above. Clean oak and ripe fruit. Very good depth and balance. Good acidity. Long, intense, fruity. At its peak, but should hold for two to three more years. Great quality. Only 100 cases (four barrels) produced.

❧ October 1993
At "Le Petit Genève" restaurant, in Vancouver. At its absolute peak. Comments as in March 1989, but rounder, softer. Still-lovely fruit. Excellent Corton-Charlemagne.

CHEVALIER-MONTRACHET 1982, V. LEFLAIVE:

❧ February 1, 1991
At a farewell dinner for *The Wine Consumer*. Creamy, elegant, at its peak; complex, smooth, toasty, oaky, vanilla, elegant fruit. Lovely bottle.

PULIGNY-MONTRACHET PREMIER CRU "CLOS DU CAILLERET" 1982, JOSEPH DROUHIN:

❧ January 20, 1991
Superb length, balance, complexity, and depth. Great fruit, toasty, velvety, rich. Really a "Grand Cru." Great fruit extract, yet not heavy. This is excellent. As of 1986, "Caillerets" is produced by Jean Chartron (who leased the vineyard to Drouhin for 20 years).

BÂTARD-MONTRACHET 1983, LOUIS LATOUR:

Would retail locally for $90 to $100 in January 1987. Purchased in 1984 for $36 per bottle across the border. It should be noted that among Louis Latour's Grands Crus whites, the Corton-Charlemagne and Chevalier-Montrachet "Demoiselles" are produced from fruit picked in their own vineyards, while the Montrachet, Bâtard, and Bienvenues-Bâtard are produced from purchased grapes.

❧ June 1993
At the Four Seasons hotel, with Daniel Baron, vineyard manager of Dominus, and the council of Le Tastevin. Off-dry. Round, rich, full-bodied, soft, yet intense, and honeyed. Very good balance, but low

acidity. Typical 1983, but, thankfully, not too alcoholic. At its peak.

❧ August 1997
At 14 years old, still very good. Bright, deep-golden colour. Lilacs, honey, oak, ripe Chardonnay nose. Full, rich, fairly alcoholic, but backed by good fruit. Soft, round, long, and complex. Will not improve.

CORTON-CHARLEMAGNE 1983, REMOISSENET:

❧ August 1989
At dinner of "Group of Ten." Very good. Rich, oaky, intense. Luscious, nutty fruit, backed by good acidity, thankfully. Too many 1983s are too spirity and clumsy.

CHABLIS PREMIER CRU "VAILLON" 1983, MOREAU:

❧ December 5, 1993
Last bottle, at a memorial dinner to Grandma Jenny, (my mother). Spicy, crisp, flinty, lively, very good balance/fruit. Long. Nice wine holding very well. No rush, even at ten years! Moreau doesn't make Chablis like this anymore. Pity.

PULIGNY-MONTRACHET PREMIER CRU "CHAMPS-CANET" 1983, ETIENNE SAUZET:

❧ December 1985
With panel of *The Wine Consumer*. Rich, full, oaky, high alcohol. Still closed at this stage. A big, rich wine needing two to three extra years to develop more complexity. Almost too spirity for me. Excellent potential, though. Try again in 1987.

❧ May 1995
At its peak. Bright gold. Oak-Chardonnay-ripe nose. Very intense, long. Lots of depth here. Fairly high alcohol, and low acidity, a problem with many 1983 white Burgundies, but made by a master. Lots of depth, weight, and intensity. Needs drinking, but has lasted well.

CORTON-CHARLEMAGNE 1983, LOUIS LATOUR:

❧ April 1992
At "Le Gavroche," With Andy Lench, the Seattle agent for Château Latour. Deep bright-gold. Nutty, oaky, complex nose. Full, rich. Very good balance (not too alcoholic). Great depth, good fruit, even fine acidity. Excellent wine. No rush. Solid, serious Chardonnay.

MEURSAULT "LES CASSE-TÊTES" 1983, J. F. COCHE-DURY

Rare and superb wine. Most of the production is sold to "Taillevent," a three-star restaurant in Paris. Purchased in California in 1985. Paid an exorbitant $32 per bottle!

❧ August 1989
Bright green-gold colour with good depth. Superb, forthcoming, yet fresh nose of lovely ripe Chardonnay, with hint of new oak and almonds. Full, rich, long. Great balance and depth, without the excessive alcohol typical of this vintage. Great length. No rush, but already showing how good it is. A superb Meursault! Coche-Dury is a master.

PULIGNY-MONTRACHET PREMIER CRU "FOLATIÈRES" 1983, MONNIER-VAIVRAND:

❧ August 1988
On Turnagain Island, with Harry and Prue Waugh, as well as their twin children, Harriet and Jamie. Green gold. Crisp, fresh, not as heavy or alcoholic as many 1983s. Still young. Hint of sulphur on nose. Crisp, fruity. No rush. Does not, however, have the depth or complexity of a fine Premier Cru. But considering the fact that I purchased this wine in San Francisco in 1985 for $130 per case, not bad at all.

MEURSAULT "LES NARVAUX" 1983, J. F. COCHE-DURY

Coche-Dury is a master winemaker. His wines are of great class, and are becoming expensive, unfortunately.

❧ August 24, 1988
Lovely and lively. Textbook Meursault. Oak, Chardonnay, intensity, fruit, excellent balance. Great depth. Ready, but will hold three to five more years. Fairly alcoholic, yet not as exaggerated as many 1983s.

❧ December 1989
Comments as above, but slightly rounder. At its peak, but no rush. Excellent, as Coche-Dury's wines usually are.

MEURSAULT PREMIER CRU "LES LURAULES" 1985, MONCEAU-BOCH, MME GUIDOT:

❧ September 1987
At a Le Tastevin tasting, and later in September, at home. The four bottles at Le Tastevin had an odd smell of acetone, and may have been stored in poor barrels. The bottle at home was better, more nutty Meursault character, a bit too sharp (acidic), and odd signs of premature oxidation. Earlier this month, I tasted the wine at Kermit Lynch's, and it was much better. Maybe a poor batch. Kermit Lynch agreed to ship me another case free of charge.

❧ October 1987
Comments as above. Too alcoholic, low fruit. Not very good. Lacks Chardonnay extract and complexity.

❧ December 1987
Kermit Lynch gave me a second case free because I told him that I was disappointed with the quality of the first case. They said that the first case must have been stored poorly. This is an odd comment, as all my wines are cellared at an ideal 52°F temperature.

CORTON-CHARLEMAGNE "COMTES DE GRANCEY" 1985, LOUIS LATOUR:

❧ March 1993
Reaching its peak. Classic 1985 and classic Corton-Charlemagne. Brilliant green-gold colour. Nutty, complex, oaky nose. Elegant, lovely balance, very long, lovely finish. Beautiful wine. Ready, but should hold for three to five more years.

❧ September 1994
Before a business trip to Toronto, New York, and Montreal. Youthful, golden colour. Honeyed, nutty Chardonnay nose. Hint of oak/vanilla, long, complex on palate. The elegance, acidity, and balance of the 1985 vintage. Still youthful, even fresh. No rush. Classic Corton-Charlemagne from a good, elegant vintage.

❧ April 1996
Perfect now at ten years. Round, complex, spicy, elegant wine. Very "1985" style (elegance rather than weight). Soft, round, nice fruit. No rush, but definitely ready.

❧ June 1996
Comments as in April. Soft, delicate. Doesn't have the backbone of the 1978, 1983, or 1989, but perfect now. Needs drinking.

❧ July 1997
Over-the-hill, oxidizing. I have waited too long to drink this.

BÂTARD-MONTRACHET 1985, LOUIS LATOUR:

❧ January 1995
Leaner, elegant structure of the 1985s, yet unmistakable Grand Cru quality. Subdued, elegant, toasty, ripe raisins on nose. Medium-bodied, excellent balance, spicy, good depth. Lovely, long finish. Very complex, yet understated. No rush. Very good.

❧ December 1996
This bottle worried me. Fairly dark, starting to oxidize. Honeyed, full, rich, good depth, but soft, with some madeirized sweetness. I hope that other bottles are better. This is over-the-hill.

❧ April 1997
Appearance and early impressions on both nose and palate similar to December 1996, but after 15 minutes, opened up nicely. Exotic fruit, ripe pears, long. Very fine, but definitely forward, and needs drinking soon.

CHEVALIER-MONTRACHET "LES DEMOISELLES" 1985, LOUIS LATOUR:

❧ March 1988
With the panel of *The Wine Consumer*. Too young, of course, but I was curious to see how it tasted. Brilliant depth. New oak and ripe, complex Chardonnay of great class on nose. Still closed. Full, rich, big wine. Great balance, lots of depth, and class here. Full, fruity. Lovely wine. Needs four to six years. Will be excellent. Everyone loved it.

❧ October 1990
Superb! Ultimate Chardonnay. Subdued, complex elegance of the 1985s on both nose and palate. Oak, vanilla, fruit, all in harmony. Lovely now, but no rush. Will even improve in one to two years. Long, complex, delicate. A noble wine. Perfect balance. Needs time!

❧ August 1995
What a mistake I made in October 1990, assuming this wine needed time! It has collapsed. Very disappointing. Had it last month at Dr. Tobe's. Same thing. The wine is starting to oxidize. Nice, but flat, soft, hint of caramel, wood, tired. Sweetness coming through. What a let-down. Should have drunk this wine in 1992!

❧ March 1997
Mature, evolved, golden colour. Sweet, very ripe on nose, with hint of oak. Full, rich, sweet. Very ripe. Slightly spirity. Fortunately, better than when tasted in August 1995, but definitely needs drinking.

BEAUNE "CLOS DES MOUCHES" BLANC 1985, JOSEPH DROUHIN:

❧ May 1997
At 12 years of age, has held extremely well. A surprise, because Drouhin's whites are usually early maturing. Bright gold. Flowery, ripe Chardonnay nose. Full, round, long, surprisingly rich for a 1985. Ripe, exotic fruit. Very soft, yet rich, almost sweet fruit. Unusual, but excellent.

CHEVALIER-MONTRACHET GRAND CRU 1986, CHARTRON ET TREBUCHET:

❧ August 1986
With Carol, Michael, and Orly. Bright gold. The delicacy on nose and palate typical of this producer. Complex, mature, but good fruit, medium-bodied, honeyed, ripe aftertaste. Very good, but somehow should have more depth for a Grand Cru and from a very good vintage.

BIENVENUES-BÂTARD-MONTRACHET 1986, JAFFELIN:

❧ June 1992
At home, with council of Le Tastevin. Deep, very mature colour. Looks ten years older. Honeyed, oaky, oxidizing nose. Full, heavy, oxidizing; lemony on palate. Poor and over-the-hill. Tasted this twice before in 1989 and 1990 at tastings. Always disappointing. I've rarely had a "good" bottle of wine produced by this house. The price ($89 per bottle) is a rip-off too.

Puligny-Montrachet Premier Cru "Les Folatières" 1986, Joseph Drouhin:

❧ January 1993

Better than Drouhin's Meursault Perrières 1986, but very mature, showing signs of cracking up. Rich, full, long, nutty, but a bit old-tasting. Drink up before it collapses. Many of Drouhin's whites collapse suddenly when five or six years old. They can be great one day, and totally oxidized six months later, even when stored under ideal conditions. Their reds seem to age much better.

Chevalier-Montrachet "Les Demoiselles" 1986, Louis Latour:

❧ October 1994

Bright, youthful gold. Hint of oak, honey. Lovely complex nose. Flowery, fresh, crisp, excellent length, and balance. Not very fat, but good weight. Not quite ready. Needs two to three years to reach its peak. Noble.

❧ Twice in January 1996

A very ripe, almost overripe, wine. Luscious, rich, low acidity, fat. Hint of residual sugar. Slight hint of oxidation, too. Full, fat, long. Needs drinking. I wish it had a little more acidity and fresh fruit.

❧ Later that month

Far superior to the bottle tasted earlier this month! Why this bottle variation from the same case? Honeyed/oak nose. Lovely fruit, lively, crisp, well balanced. Great depth, body, spicy, vanilla/oak/honey Chardonnay. True Grand Cru quality. Superb wine.

Corton-Charlemagne "Comtes de Grancey" 1986, Louis Latour:

❧ April 1992

Classy oak, spicy Chardonnay, nutty nose. Full, round, rich, long. Surprisingly, ready, and low in acidity. Usually Latour's Corton-Charlemagnes from fine vintages need eight to ten years to approach maturity, but this six-year-old is ready. No rush, though. Very good, long finish.

❧ April 1, 1993

Against Corton-Charlemagne 1986, Moillard, with Jacques Hebrard of Château Cheval-Blanc, and Francis Fouquet, Grand Maître of the Grand Conseil du Vin de Bordeaux. Tighter than above. Needs time. Complex, long, "nerveux." Very good length.

Corton-Charlemagne 1986, Moillard:

❧ April 1, 1993

Against Louis Latour's 1986 Corton-Charlemagne with Jacques Hebrard of Cheval-Blanc and Francis Fouquet, Grand Maître of the Grand Conseil du Vin de Bordeaux. Forward, soft, perfect now. Nutty, rich, creamy; low acidity. Other comments as in November 1990, but softer. Has held well.

Corton-Charlemagne 1986, Louis Jadot:

❧ October 1991

Lovely, bright-golden colour, touch of green. Superb, intense, toasty, oaky, spicy herbaceous, ripe Chardonnay nose. Full, rich, long. Excellent balance and length. No rush. Should peak around 1993 to 1995. Great depth and class. Top quality!

❧ December 1995

Acacias, honey, oak, toasty nose. Perfect balance. Lovely length, fruit, balance. Soft, yet has very good extract. Drink now to 1998. Classic Burgundy. Fine effort.

❧ July 1997

With Carol and Orly, upon my return from a trip to the Napa Valley. At over ten years old, this wine is as magnificent as ever! Comments as in December 1995. Superb length, balance, class. A great Corton-Charlemagne. Ready, but no rush. Bravo Jadot!

Bâtard-Montrachet 1986, Louis Jadot:

❧ April 1992

Bright green-gold. Steely, oaky, spicy, intense Chardonnay nose. Tight, yet rich. Excellent backbone, length, balance. Lots of depth, yet really too young. Will be great, but pity to open another bottle before 1995 or beyond. Lots of stuffing here.

❧ January 2, 1994

At home. First great wine of 1994. Superb wine. Comments as above, but more evolved. Great quality, balance, oak-fruit-acidity-length. Fabulous. Classic Bâtard!

Meursault Premier Cru "Les Perrières" 1987, Coche-Dury:

❧ May 1993

This wine, from a very mediocre vintage, and at six years old, is still too young! As if it needs confirmation, Coche-Dury is a master. Great wine, great structure, intensity. Nutty, oaky, fruity Chardonnay on both nose and palate. Very big, still tight. Excellent fruit/acidity balance. Long, complex. Les Perrières is Coche-Dury's only Premier Cru Meursault.

Meursault "Les Rougeots" 1987, Coche-Dury:

❧ November 1992

Palish gold. Spicy oak, fresh fruit on nose. Very long, yet steely, hard, excellent fruit/acidity balance. Obviously leaner year, but impeccably made. Long, lots of class. No rush.

❧ November 1995

Last bottle, at home, with friends. Served fresh Sonoma duck foie gras I prepared. Softer than above. Leaner 1987 style. Oaky, nutty nose. Round, soft, yet acidic finish. A fine effort in a mediocre vintage. That night I also served a Champagne Bollinger 1982 RD, 1937 Richebourg DRC (great), 1964 Clos Vougeot, René Engel, 1964 Château Haut-Brion, and a half-bottle of 1976 Château d'Yquem. In this great company, this Meursault held its own.

MEURSAULT "LES CHEVALIÈRES" 1987, COCHE-DURY:

❧ August 3, 1992

Superb effort for 1987. Classic Coche-Dury. Had it with barbecued, 16-lb. spring salmon I caught that morning. Brilliant gold. Clean, buttery-oaky-fruity-nutty Meursault on both nose and palate. Lovely balance, length. No rush. Excellent wine!

❧ February 22, 1994

The night before my trip to South Africa. Comments as in August 1992. Still full of life, nutty-oaky, lovely fruit, the leanness of 1987, yet great depth, and length. Superb effort in an "off" year.

❧ November 1997

Amazingly, most comments as in 1992. All positive notes except for the high acidity of this lean vintage. This is a great effort in a mediocre vintage (at best) for white Burgundies. Obviously, Jean-François Coche is a master.

MOREY-ST.-DENIS PREMIER CRU "MONTS LUISANTS" 1988, DOMAINE PONSOT:

❧ September 1995

Clean, crisp, fruity. Well made, long, good balance, and depth, yet does not taste like a white Burgundy. Technically, it is, of course; but it lacks the Chardonnay character. More "Chave Hermitage Blanc" style. Unusual wine.

BÂTARD-MONTRACHET 1988, LOUIS LATOUR:

❧ October 1997

With Michael and Orly. Bright gold. Buttery oak, good Chardonnay fruit on nose. Leaner 1988 style on palate, typical of the vintage, yet it has good depth and length. At nine years old, it is at its peak. Michael is now 22 years old, studying Law at the University of British Columbia. Orly is 19, and she, too, is a student at the same university.

CHEVALIER-MONTRACHET "LES DEMOISELLES" 1988, LOUIS LATOUR:

❧ November 1995

Still youthful, yet round and elegant. Not a big wine, but lots of class, length, and spicy Chardonnay complexity. The leaner structure of the 1988s. Somehow less weight than I expected, but lovely nevertheless. Drink now to 2000.

❧ July 1997

At "Lumière" restaurant, on my 52nd birthday, with Carol, Michael, and Orly. Already evolved. Leaner 1988 style. Honey-oak nose. Delicate, subdued, fair bit of acidity. On nose quite developed, but on palate, still fairly fresh. Needs drinking before it loses its delicate, subdued fruit. Complex, long finish. Lacks the fat of the fine 1989s.

CORTON-CHARLEMAGNE 1988, TOLLOT-BEAUT:

With the exception of one bottle, I got the whole lot (one case) allocated to a leading wine shop in San Francisco. Tollot-Beaut produces only four barrels per year of this wine (100 cases!).

❧ March 1993

Lean, typical 1988 style. Needs time. Try in 1995 and beyond. Steely, tight, yet underneath all this there is fruit and excellent balance. I know this producer's Corton-Charlemagne well; it needs at least eight to ten years to reach its peak.

❧ July 1995

On Turnagain Island, with Bruno Prats and his wife France, owners of Château Cos d'Estournel. Bruno said that Corton-Charlemagne is his favourite white Burgundy, but he had never heard of Tollot-Beaut. Lovely lime-nutty nose. The leanness of the vintage and true to this property's style, yet round, long, and complex. Lovely weight and depth. Classic nutty aftertaste. Excellent now. Long and clean. This is top quality Charlemagne.

MONTRACHET, MARQUIS DE LAGUICHE 1989, JOSEPH DROUHIN:

❧ May 1995

At "Bishop's" restaurant. Forward, ready at six years of age, yet a perfect, classic wine. Lovely nose, spicy oak/vanilla/Chardonnay. Complex, elegant, long. As it opened up in glass, it developed more depth. Ready, but no rush. One word of caution, though. Being a Drouhin product, it may collapse and oxidize suddenly, with no warning. Keep an eye on this.

PULIGNY-MONTRACHET PREMIER CRU "CLOS DU CAILLERET" 1989, JEAN CHARTRON:

❧ October 30, 1995

Night of the Quebec Referendum, with council of Le Tastevin. Comments as in March this year. Classy and elegant. Somehow, in spite of the incompetence of our Federal Liberal government, under Jean Chretien, the country has survived, this time around.

Corton-Charlemagne "Comtes de Grancey" 1989, Louis Latour:

❧ July 1995

At the Corton-Charlemagne weekend marathon. A lovely wine! Still too young, but exotic fruit, oak, and acidity all in harmony. Drink from 1997 to 2000 or beyond.

Pouilly-Fuissé "Clos la Roche" 1994, Saumaize:

❧ August 1996

Barely two years old, yet already impressive. Bright green-gold. Clean, green apples/Chardonnay nose. Quite full, ripe, hint of oak. Very good extract, lots of ripe fruit, yet soft. Drink 1997 to 2000.

Pouilly-Fuissé "Ronchevats" 1994, Saumaize:

❧ September 1996

I prefer this slightly to this producer's "Clos la Roche." Surprisingly intense, ripe, lovely, deep fruit, some new oak. Great extract, soft, but clean, long. A mouthful of fine Chardonnay. Maybe too much oak? Time will tell.

SAUTERNES, BARSAC

LOUPIAC, STE. CROIX-DU-MONT

Château d'Yquem 1967:

Said to be the greatest d'Yquem since 1949.

❧ May 1977

In London, from a half-bottle. Purchased from Berry Bros. at £6.50 per half. Complex wine of great quality. Rich, yet delicate, luscious botrytis on nose. I do not go for dessert wines, but this is something special. Even Carol, who does not like Sauternes, said "mmm." Crême brûlée, lovely, long, complex flavours. I am glad that I purchased a case of this wine in full-size bottles in Vancouver last year. It was, however, expensive. I paid $27.40 per bottle.

❧ June 1978

Excellent, rich, long-lasting, botrytized nose, and taste. Dark gold colour with lingering aftertaste. A masterpiece. Had it with Carol's cheesecake and fresh strawberries. Everyone was very excited.

❧ 1978 and 1979

Tasted three times. Deep golden colour; very intense botrytis nose. Beautiful, big, intense flavours. A giant of a wine. I also tasted the 1966 d'Yquem in 1978 at a Commanderie de Bordeaux dinner. Also a big, dark wine, but not nearly as complex, and fine as the 1967.

❧ December 1981

At a special dinner of Le Tastevin wine group. Lovely, deep bright colour, great, luscious nose. Honey-botrytis, great complexity. Intense. "Too big to drink." Must sip.

❧ May 1989

This wine retails now for an incredible $400 per bottle, almost 20 times what I paid for it 12 years ago! Bright, deep, mature golden colour. At its absolute peak now. Luscious botrytis and crême brûlée on nose and palate. Perfect balance, thick, rich, yet backed by very good fruit and acidity. A great Sauternes. Oak and vanilla blend beautifully.

Château d'Yquem 1971:

❧ January 1984

Not as fat or cloying a wine as the 1967. Elegant, complex botrytis, and oak on nose. Excellent balance, good acidity, medium bright-gold. Good fruit, long, delicate. Very intense, yet in a delicate way. Should hold for quite some time. An exquisite experience. In a class by itself.

CHÂTEAU D'YQUEM 1975:

❧ March 1981

This wine sells today for almost $100 a bottle. I am glad that I purchased a half-dozen bottles of this wine in 1979 for $60 per bottle, 1975 being my son Michael's birth year. I hope that when he grows up, he will appreciate it, if there's any left!

❧ November 1984

From half-bottle at home, with friends, following a half-bottle of 1976 Château Guiraud. Medium-deep (but not dark) gold. Complex, very long, beautiful nose. Absolutely perfect balance. Great botrytis, but not overwhelming. Good acidity, fruit. Will last for a long time. A magnificent work of art. (20)

❧ October 1987

Purchased two more bottles from the Chicago Wine Company, as part of an exchange for a bottle of 1961 Petrus. Total exchange for that single bottle of Petrus: two bottles of 1975 d'Yquem, 12 bottles of 1982 Gruaud-Larose, and six bottles of 1983 Pichon Lalande! I think that I made a good deal here.

❧ November 9, 1987

At home, with Harry and Prue Waugh, and other guests. Very young, golden colour, with the good acidity typical of the 1975s. Crisp, youthful; lovely complexity, and length. Yet some guests did not like it as much as I did, commenting that it was a bit lightweight for d'Yquem. I think that it just needs more time. It is going to be a great wine by 1992.

❧ September 18, 1990

A half-bottle, at the last tasting with the panel of *The Wine Consumer*, ending six years of publication. Bright-golden colour. Complex, rich botrytis, ripe fruit, oak, and vanilla on nose. Great length and harmony. Good acidity, not as fat as the 1967 or the 1976. Racier, yet creamy, long, complex; superb balance. Lovely wine. Its excellent structure will make this wine last for many years.

❧ November 1996

This wine retails now for US$400 per bottle.

CHÂTEAU D'YQUEM 1976:

❧ November 1995

From a half-bottle. Bright deep-gold. Intense, full, excellent fruit/acidity balance, creamy, botrytis all in harmony. Superb nose. Great flavours. A lovely bottle. Ready, but no rush.

❧ February 1997

At "Le Gavroche." Also tasted that night a 1947 Cos d'Estournel. In half-bottle, more evolved than when tasted last year. Crème-brûlée, soft, lots of botrytis, yet not cloying. Good extract, multidimensional, oak, fruit all in harmony. Quite soft. Lovely.

CHÂTEAU D'YQUEM 1980:

❧ March 1986

At home, with panel of *The Wine Consumer*. Palish gold. Delicate, clean, fresh, long nose with nice botrytis. Complex, delicate, long on palate. Needs four to five years. Beautiful, clean Sauternes. Impeccably made.

❧ April 1989

Comments as above. Impeccable, brilliant, lovely botrytis, new oak, fruit, and acidity, all in harmony. Everyone loved it. No rush. Great quality. This is superb with foie gras!

❧ May 1995

At "Bishop's" restaurant, with friends. Also tasted that night a superb bottle of 1966 Château Margaux, 1955 Clos de la Roche, Charles Vienot, and 1989 Montrachet-Laguiche (Drouhin). Elegant, soft, complex. Ready, Not much depth or weight, but lots of class. Perfect balance, and elegance. As d'Yquem goes, this represents very good value, retailing at half the price of finer vintages of this property, such as the great 1983 and the very good 1986. Same is true of the excellent 1987, an underrated wine.

❧ January 1996

With Sid Cross, Dr. Larry Burr, and Dave Freeman. Tasted it with home-made Muskovy-duck whole foie gras. Superb Sauternes. The acidity went well with the foie gras. Lots of depth. Impeccable on nose and palate. Botrytis, oak, vanilla, intensity, medium body. Great length, lots of class here.

CHÂTEAU D'YQUEM 1984:

Given to me by Bernard Ledun, French Consul General to Vancouver, who is leaving us for his new posting in Mexico City. (Note: A month later, before his new posting, Bernard died at age 52 after open-heart surgery in France. He never made it to Mexico.)

❧ June 1995

With the council of the Commanderie de Bordeaux, in memory of Bernard. Structured like a great Climens! A great "Barsac." Superb balance, new oak, vanilla, even lovely botrytis, all in harmony. What a great effort for such a poor vintage! Classic, long, fabulous aftertaste. Spicy, complex, smooth. Superb on both nose and palate. I wrote "Barsac-great" because in 1984, d'Yquem made a relatively lighter-style wine. Buttery, lovely. Grand Vin! May not last for half-a-century, but at 11 years old, it is a great bottle.

CHÂTEAU DE RAYNE VIGNEAU 1917, VICOMTE DE PONTAC:

❧ April 1988

Excellent low neck level. Very deep-gold, light-amber colour. Vintage printed on cork. Clean label.

Purchased second bottle in February 1989. Comes from the cellar of an old San Francisco gentleman who stopped drinking because of ill health.

❧ August 1989
At home, at the end of a blind tasting of 1970 red Graves with panel of *The Wine Consumer*. Very old, yet brilliant, deep-gold colour. Still drinkable. Little botrytis on nose, hint of wet earth, but some raisiny fruit, and even some sweetness. Not bad at all at 72 years old, and from a difficult vintage.

CHÂTEAU DE RICAUD 1920, LOUPIAC:

Owner: Maurice Wells. Purchased from St. Helena Wine Merchants from a private source. This fine property is situated in "Haut Loupiac," and according to Feret's 12th Edition, *it had quite a reputation. Excellent, deep, dark gold colour. Level low neck. Lovely artistic label.*

❧ March 1989
Served it to the panel of *The Wine Consumer*. A rare treat. Cork disintegrated. Fair bit of sediment. Nose of old wine, ripe raisins, and wood. Clean, sound, and ripe. Fairly dry, yet rich, and full on palate; even a trace of sweetness left. Still alive at almost 70 years of age! Recent vintages, under new ownership, have very similar labels. After one hour, still rich nose and structure. A once-in-a-lifetime experience.

CHÂTEAU DE LUCQUES 1924, BARSAC-ESCHENAUER:

Purchased in a wine shop in St. Emilion during a visit to Bordeaux in October 1996. This property now produces red wines, but in the early part of the century, it produced Sauternes. At the end of World War I, the Lur Saluces (owners of Château d'Yquem) sued the owners of this property for using the term "Sauternes," because the majority of the estate was actually in Barsac. So the owners had to change the appellation to "Barsac." Amber-gold colour. Top shoulder level. Asking price Ffr1,700, but I negotiated the store owner down to Ffr1,350.

❧ March 1997
With foie gras, at a farewell council meeting of the Commanderie de Bordeaux. Lovely. Elegant Barsac style. Incredibly lively at almost 73 years old! Still had good botrytized fruit and elegant, long finish. A rare treat.

CHÂTEAU FILHOT 1928:

❧ January 1993
With the council of Le Tastevin. Half-bottle. Deep amber-gold. Cork came out in one piece. Some crusted sediment. Classic caramel-botrytis Sauternes nose. Hint of crème brûlée. Still sweet, but finished a bit dry. Very good, rich fruit. Very good length and depth. Hard to fault this wine. The power of the 1928s. Excellent.

CHÂTEAU DE REINE VIGNEAU 1933:

Amber colour. Upper shoulder level. Owned by the Vicomte de Pontac.

❧ June 1993
With the council of the Commanderie de Bordeaux. Cork came out easily; slightly crumbly. Little sediment. Bright colour. Crème-brûlée nose with hint of botrytis. Quite dry, yet some sweetness there. Long, complex, good. Hint of wet earth. Exactly 60 years old and from a difficult vintage. Would be perfect with foie gras. Very good acidity, balance. Lovely! Dryish finish, but very good structure.

LOUPIAC 1955:

Odd bottle; like a large, one-litre soda bottle. Label reads: "Caves du Château de la Fot Creuse - Vicomte Charles de Curel." Apparently, Draper and Esquin's got two cases and all 24 bottles were of different shapes!

❧ January 1983
At a special dinner. Held surprisingly well, and very youthful. Served blind. People thought it was a 1971 or 1975 Sauternes! Indeed, it has very good botrytis, ripe fruit flavours. Well balanced, long, and complex. Still full of life.

CHÂTEAU SUDUIRAUT 1959:

❧ January 1993
At home, with "Group of Ten." Superb! Great depth, crème-brûlée. Perfect balance, ripe fruit. Must be one of the greatest Sauternes since 1945! I have had the good fortune of tasting this wine on at least half-a-dozen occasions previously. Always brilliant. One of my all-time favourite Sauternes.

CHÂTEAU CLIMENS 1964:

❧ December 1988
Served blind to panel of *The Wine Consumer*. Much younger-looking than its age would indicate. Most guessed 1983, 1982, or maybe 1976! A rare wine. Very little 1964 was made. Poor year for Sauternes. (No d'Yquem produced that year.) Lovely, delicate, mature nose with hint of botrytis and oak. Excellent balance. Long, rich, yet not overly so. Great class! A real treat. Surprising how well it has held.

CHÂTEAU SUDUIRAUT 1967:

❧ February 1, 1991
At a farewell dinner for *The Wine Consumer*. Deep gold, soft, creamy, complex. Not big or cloying, but very elegant, low acidity. At its peak. Tasted several times between 1980 and 1990, and in the past, this wine showed much better.

CHÂTEAU RIEUSSEC 1970:

❧ October 1983

At home, with guests of the International Wine and Food Society Convention. Medium gold. Good botrytis nose. Clean on palate, but seemed younger in appearance and weight than a 13-year-old should be. Yet it was delicate and soft. Not big or very complex; rather elegant, easy to enjoy. Good botrytis nose. Overall, 1970 Sauternes were not as successful as the 1971s, which is the opposite of red Bordeaux. The same is true with the 1961s and 1962s, and 1966s and 1967s (the 1962s and 1967s being the better vintages in Sauternes).

CHÂTEAU SUDUIRAUT 1971:

❧ February 1981

At the end of a blind tasting of 1978 Clarets that have just arrived in Vancouver. Medium-gold colour. Some sediment. Good, ripe botrytis on nose. Not a typical Suduiraut on palate. A bit on the dry side for a Sauternes. Some people like this style, but I rather like the sweeter, richer Sauternes, with the exception of the superb Climens, of course. A good, delicate wine. The 1967 of this property is better.

CHÂTEAU COUTET 1975, MAGNUM:

❧ June 1980

At a Commanderie de Bordeaux dinner. Too young. Good balance, excellent botrytis on nose. This will be a very fine wine in four to five years. Beautiful style, and richness. Will last for many years. Best Coutet since 1962.

CHÂTEAU FILHOT 1975:

❧ March 1981

Pale greenish colour. Subdued nose; elegant. A bit buttery, not very sweet. Elegant, rather simple. Lacks intensity. In the 1950s, and especially in the 1920s and 1940s, this property used to produce superb Sauternes. Maybe someday, they will pull it off again.

CHÂTEAU DE FARGUES 1975:

❧ February 1990

With the panel of *The Wine Consumer*. Retails now for over US$100 per bottle. Fair bit of sediment. Excellent level, and bright, deep golden colour. Ripe, rich, and intense botrytis on nose. Great extract. Unctuous, full, creamy, and long. Very good balance, with good acidity (backbone typical of the 1975s). At its peak. Will hold, but will not get any better. Superb Sauternes.

CHÂTEAU RIEUSSEC 1976:

❧ May 1980

In half-bottle, at "Chez Panisse," in Berkeley, California, and at home, in December 1980. Lovely, dark-gold colour. Very thick, long legs. Good botrytis nose; ripe peaches and apricots. Sweet and long aftertaste. Very dark for such a young wine, and not too much acidity to last for many years. But at present, it is lovely. Usually, Rieussec matures earlier than other top-flight Sauternes. Had some two days later. Still very good. One of my favourites.

❧ April 1, 1993

Dinner, at home, with Jacques Hebrard of Château Cheval-Blanc, Francis Fouquet, Grand Maître of the Commanderie de Bordeaux, and other guests. Very deep amber-gold. Brilliant. Soft, sweet, rich, round, long. Very mature, but still has good fruit and acidity. Will not improve. Top quality. Typical ripe, full Rieussec.

❧ July 1997

Last bottle. At over 20 years of age, comments as in April 1993. Honeyed, amber gold. Full, rich, yet signs of drying up a bit. Lovely botrytis, long, complex. Has lasted very well.

CHÂTEAU CLIMENS 1976:

❧ September 1982

A top-quality Barsac. Light in colour; lemony, botrytis nose. Great elegance, length, good fruit/acidity balance. What a lovely wine! Needs a few more years to age and develop complexity. Great potential. Drink from 1986 to 2006 or beyond.

CHÂTEAU CLIMENS 1983, BARSAC:

❧ April 1997

A half-bottle. Bright pale-gold, typical of this property. Delicate, yet complex, exotic fruit, ripe pears, and botrytis on nose. Fabulous balance, length, and class on palate. Approaching its peak, but should last for many years. Lovely Barsac. Full bottles should last for another two decades. Climens ages very well and retains its pale colour for many years.

CHÂTEAU RIEUSSEC 1983:

❧ March 1992

With the council of Le Tastevin and my friend from Los Angeles, Dr. Brad Klein. Great extract, balance, depth. Brilliant deep-gold. Very good acidity; thick, rich, long. Certainly one of the best 1983 Sauternes. Not as tight as d'Yquem, but almost as good, and certainly, more enjoyable now. Drink now to 2005.

CHÂTEAU LAFAURIE-PEYRAGUEY 1983:

❧ June 1992

Half-bottle, with the council of Le Tastevin. Classic Sauternes. Still full of life. Clean, superb balance, botrytis, and exotic fruit. Great length. Truly a lovely Sauternes. Enjoyable now in half-bottle, but no rush. How nice it is to see this property back at the top flight of Sauternes, after two decades of underperforming. This property made great wines in the 1900s to 1950s era.

CHÂTEAU LAFAURIE-PEYRAGUEY 1986:

❧ July 1992
Subdued, peaches-botrytis, clean, long nose. Fabulous depth, balance, length. Still very young. Lovely, creamy, long, rich fruit, botrytis, all in harmony. Will be a very fine wine by the year 2000, and well beyond.

CHÂTEAU DE RICAUD 1986, LOUPIAC. OWNER ALAIN THIENOT:

❧ March 1989
With the panel of *The Wine Consumer*. Comparing it to the 1920 of the same property. Bright gold. Clean, impeccable on nose and on palate. Long, a bit nutty, sweet, yet not cloying. Little botrytis, but most enjoyable. Well balanced. Interesting to compare this property (two vintages), 66 years apart! Good fruit and very clean. Well balanced.

SWEET WINES FROM THE LOIRE VALLEY, RHÔNE VALLEY, AND OTHER FRENCH DESSERT WINES

MOULIN TOUCHAIS, ANJOU 1933:

Made from Chenin Blanc, this wine is 50 years old now. Upper shoulder level, but being a sweet wine, I hope that it has held well. Purchased earlier this year (1983) from a wine shop in Amsterdam.

❧ June 1983
At home, as a finale for a fabulous tasting of 1961 Clarets. The Chenin Blanc grape is usually high in acidity and lasts well for many years. Bright-golden colour. No sign of botrytis, but nice fruit and fairly long on palate. Hint of earth and minerals. Good, sweet fruit, but not too complex.

MOULIN TOUCHAIS, ANJOU 1947:

❧ August 1988
Bright gold. Some cloudy sediment. Heavy glass bottle. Good cork. Perfumed, slightly earthy-cement nose. Medium sweet, quite acidic (typical of Chenin Blanc), fairly spirity. Clean, long finish. Has held extremely well.

MOULIN TOUCHAIS, ANJOU 1959:

❧ June 1991
With Jack and Ellen Orlando. Jack is the US Consul, leaving Vancouver shortly for a posting in Brasilia. Bright lemon-gold colour. Incredibly lively and fresh for a 1959. Clean, perfumy, sweet nose. Round, medium sweet, not too cloying, good fruit/acidity balance. Even refreshing. Went very well with a light cheesecake and raspberry coulis. Nice, long, clean finish.

QUART DE CHAUME 1978, CHÂTEAU DE SURONDE:

❧ June 1995
With the council of the Commanderie de Bordeaux. Bright yellow-gold. Very Chenin Blanc. Dull, full, fat, quite sweet, yet not sweet enough to be a dessert wine. A bit cloying. Not as stylish as Moulin Touchais, yet holding very well at 17 years. Round, creamy, good acidity, but not complex. A matter of taste.

SAVENNIÈRES, "CLOS DE LA COULÉE DE SERRANT" 1980, MME JOLY, LOIRE:

❧ April 1990
Neutral nose, some ripeness. Medium gold. Full, dry, complex, rich. No residual sugar. Quite dry, yet rich, and long. Very nice. Made from Chenin Blanc. (Coulée de Serrant is a Grand Cru.)

CHAMPAGNE

BOLLINGER "SPECIAL CUVÉE" BRUT N/V:

❧ December 1990

Comments below are of several bottles acquired in 1988. Yeasty, rich, long, well balanced. Serious, long, complex. Very good fruit and fizz. Fine bottle.

❧ March 1997

Not a very good bottle. Too green, sharp, citric, steely. Purchased recently; maybe an extra year of bottle-age would have made a difference. Bollinger's Vintage, RD (recently disgorged), and Vieilles Vignes Françaises are matured in oak. The nonvintage does not see any oak, however.

❧ August 1997

From a magnum, at a party at home. Fairly steely and still youthful. Purchased and cellared since 1991. Solid, good mousse. Yeasty, yet herbaceous nose. Good depth, rich, long finish. Very good for a nonvintage. The structure is typical of the more serious, solid style of Bollinger's.

LANSON BLACK LABEL BRUT N/V:

❧ 1980 to 1987

Tasted on at least a dozen occasions. All from the same lot.

❧ Last tasted in February 1987

Good, yeasty, fresh nose. Acidic, lean, hard, and short. A lot of bottle variation. Can be good. Complex, round, and pleasant. Several examples were disappointing, though. This inconsistency seems to be typical of this Champagne house. I never know what to expect when I open a bottle.

VEUVE CLICQUOT PONSARDIN BRUT N/V, MAGNUMS:

When bottled in magnums, it is even harder and more acidy than the regular bottles. It needs three to five years of extra bottle-age to reach maturity, and develop the weight, roundness, and complexity this Champagne is known to possess.

❧ May 1986

Last magnum from this case, with the panel of *The Wine Consumer*. Has held extremely well since it was purchased in 1980. Rich, long, complex; good mousse and tiny bubbles. Slightly sweeter, heavier wine. Extremely enjoyable. Very good, still. Ready, but no rush in magnums. This wine is probably a blend of the 1975, 1976, and 1977 vintages.

GOSSET "GRANDE RESERVE" BRUT N/V:

❧ January 15, 1991

Back from Los Angeles, on the eve of a possible war between the USA and Iraq over Kuwait. Smooth, creamy, just off-dry; complex and long. Very fine. Ready, easy to drink, and easy to like. Excellent Champagne.

❧ October 10, 1991

Celebrating the purchase today of Poise Island, in Sechelt. (A beautiful, uninhabited, 9.5-acre island located on British Columbia's Sunshine Coast.) Comments as above. Elegant, delicate, creamy, complex, forward.

❧ August 1993

At home, by the pool, during one of the few nice days of the miserable spring and summer of 1993, weatherise. Smooth, round, ripe, off-dry. Very good length and balance.

❧ December 24, 1995

Last bottle from this particular case, acquired in 1990. As above. Very good. This Champagne has given us a lot of pleasure, and having tasted it two-dozen times to date, it has never disappointed.

KRUG "ROSÉ" N/V:

❧ October 8, 1995

Thanksgiving with Carol, Michael, and Orly. Light, salmon colour. Ripe, fruity nose. Fuller, richer, rounder on palate than most Rosés, which are fairly dry. Full, long, fine mousse, rich, complex, soft. Very good.

JACQUES SELOSSE "BLANC DE BLANCS" N/V, GRAND CRU-BRUT:

Oak-fermented and aged

❧ January 1996

An excellent Champagne. 100% Chardonnay Grand Cru, from Verzay. Serious. More Brut than Blanc de Blancs. Yeasty, yet delicate on nose. Fine bubbles and mousse. Long. Excellent balance. At its peak, yet no rush. Lovely fruit. Clean, long aftertaste. Fresh! Very fine.

PLOYEZ-JACQUEMART BRUT N/V:

❧ June 1992

With the council of Le Tastevin. Delicate, tiny bubbles; forward, round, clean. Not unlike a Taittinger N/V, but more extract and body. Quite pleasant.

E. BARNAUT "GRANDE RESERVE" BRUT N/V:

❧ February 1988

With the council of Le Tastevin. Excellent mousse and tiny bubbles. Yeasty, complex, herbal, slightly green nose, yet open and ripe. Quite lean and green on palate, backed by good fruit. High acidity. This wine needs an extra year of bottle-age to round up a bit. Quite good.

GOSSET "NAISSANCE DE L'EUROPE" BRUT N/V:

❧ September 1992
Given to me by Antoine Gosset during a trip to Champagne, Normandy, Brittany, and Paris last year. A special bottling for Europe's Union (The Maastricht Accord) in January 1993.

❧ December 1992
With friends, including French Consul General Bernard Ledun. Creamy, yet full, rich, and long. Very good, clean, yeasty nose. Very good fruit. Still youthful. Will age well for an extra two to four years. Fine effort.

MICHEL NOIROT BRUT N/V, "LES RICEYS:"

❧ February 1, 1991
At a farewell dinner, for *The Wine Consumer*. Good, toasty, a bit green, tight. Their "Clos St. Roch" is rounder, more complex. None of us had tasted Champagnes of this house previously.

MICHEL NOIROT BRUT N/V, "CUVÉE DU CLOS ST. ROCH-LES RICEYS":

❧ February 1, 1991
At a farewell dinner, for *The Wine Consumer*. Round, toasty, complex, elegant, well balanced. Nice fruit, small bubbles. Rounder and better than their regular Brut. This was my first experience with this Champagne house.

KRUG "GRANDE CUVÉE" N/V:

❧ May 1987
Lovely complexity, length; lively, tiny bubbles. Lots of class. A top-quality Champagne. Leaner, yet has excellent depth. Great fruity-yeasty aftertaste. This nonvintage Champagne, usually made from a blend of seven to ten vintages and 20 to 30 different growths, can age gracefully for at least a decade.

❧ June 1987
Purchased several cases of this Champagne earlier this year in the province of Saskatchewan, where it retailed this year for $36 per bottle, just about half the price it is in British Columbia.

A note to the reader

Saskatchewan is considered the "Cradle of Socialism" in Canada. In the 1930s, the Socialists in that province decided to really "punish the rich" by marking up Champagne by a flat $5 per bottle. A very high tax at the time. In the 1980s, they are still persisting with this policy, making that province's Champagne prices the cheapest in Canada! Who said that bureaucrats (and especially those of the Socialist persuasion) have no brains? Or, could it be that they have acquired a taste for Champagne?

❧ January 9, 1992
Mellow, yeasty, complex, oaky nose. Full, long, rich. Lovely depth, balance, length. Great class. Hint of ripe, citrusy fruit. Very fine bottle. Lovely stuff!

❧ January 1995
Smooth, complex, tiny bubbles; rich, round, creamy. Very elegant, long, mature. Great stuff. I purchased these bottles eight years ago, so this Champagne is now at least 15 years old.

❧ April 1996
I have owned this Champagne since 1987. This is the Saskatchewan batch. Every bottle has been superb and holding well. Lovely, as usual. Creamy, long, full, rich. Smooth.

❧ September 23, 1996
With Carol and Orly, from a lot I purchased in Vancouver in 1989. Superb. Full of life, long, complex, yeasty, perfect balance, tiny bubbles. Great extract and length. Krug is Krug.

❧ November 1996
Comments as in last September, but softer, rounder, elegant. Very good depth. Has held very well. Lovely bottle, relatively soft. When young, Krug can be steely and rather lean. It develops significantly with age, as do most great wines.

❧ July 1997
Comments as last May. This bottle was purchased in 1988 in Alberta, so it must be at least 15 years old. Still full of life, crisp, steely backbone. Very long.

LECHÈRE BRUT N/V, "VENICE-SYMPLON-ORIENT-EXPRESS," AVIZE, PREMIER CRU:

❧ June 1989
Earlier this year, I acquired a case of this from D & M Liquors in San Francisco at the excellent price of $215 per case. An elegant, stylish Champagne. Quite forward. Clean, yeasty nose. Complex, soft, long. Not unlike a fine Blanc de Blancs. Well balanced. Clean, long finish. Drink now to 1993. Very good.

CANARD-DUCHÊNE "CHARLES VII" BRUT N/V:

❧ August 1984
Tasted for the first time. The prestige cuvée of Canard-Duchêne, a blend of their finest cuvées from more than one vintage. A lovely, elegant, soft, velvety, rich Champagne. Clean and fragrant on nose. Excellent balance. Very well made and classy. At its peak. It is unusual to see a prestige cuvée that is nonvintage.

POL ROGER "CHARDONNAY" 1969:

❧ 1978 and 1979
Tasted several times. Crisp, pleasant golden colour. Elegant, clean nose, tiny bubbles. Good Chardonnay

nose and flavour. Not very intense. Easy to drink. An elegant, delicate wine.

❧ March 1982
At home, with Harry Waugh, Joe Heitz, and his daughter Kathleen, and the Tobes. Well balanced, elegant, mellow. Holding very well. Bright colour for age. Very good. One of Harry Waugh's favourite Champagne houses, and the late Sir Winston Churchill's, as well.

❧ June 1991
With the council of Le Tastevin. At 22 years of age, this is excellent. Tiny bubbles, fine, still lively, and persistent mousse. Yeasty, yet elegant, flowery, mature, clean, long nose. Soft, round, excellent balance. Very "Blanc de Blancs," elegant style. Smooth and creamy. Will not get better, but a lovely, stylish, complex Champagne. Impressive quality. Hint of mature "caramel" finish.

DOM PÉRIGNON 1970:

❧ September 1980
Last great bottle before our departure for our two-month trip through the vineyards of France. Elegant, clean nose, medium-full flavour. Quite complex. Today it retails for $43, which is quite unjustifiable, because some very fine champagnes sell at half the price. Overall, very good quality, tiny bubbles. Elegant fruit; at its peak.

DOM PÉRIGNON 1971:

❧ November 1984
A fabulous bottle, full of life, yet soft, round, mature. Tiny bubbles, elegant, complex nose. Long, clean on palate. Has held very well, and showing better than the bottle I tasted in June this year in San Francisco, at the 80th birthday celebration honouring Harry Waugh. This wine has become rare, and sells now in New York for over US$100. An enjoyable experience, especially since I feel that overall, Dom Pérignon is overrated and overpriced these days.

HENRIOT 1971:

❧ January 1986
Marvellous Champagne. Tiny bubbles. Great length, complex, mature, delicate, well balanced. At its absolute peak. What else can I say? They do not come any better. As great as the finest Krugs or Bollingers! (19)

POL ROGER "CHARDONNAY" 1971:

❧ February 1994
Last bottle. At 23 years of age, superb! "Goût anglais," yeasty, soft, elegant, excellent balance. Very long, full aftertaste. Truly great, and a Chardonnay, at that! This was really a surprise!

POL ROGER "CHARDONNAY" 1973:

❧ April 1982
Their flagship "Blanc de Blancs." Good balance, clean, delicate, very pleasant, soft. Maybe not as complex as the 1969 or 1971, but quite good nevertheless.

❧ March 1986
Last bottle. At almost 13 years of age, this wine has held very well. At its peak. Comments as above. Very enjoyable.

MUMM'S RENÉ LALOU 1973:

❧ November 1983
Elegant Champagne. Subdued, fruity nose. Good bubbles. This wine is now ten years old, and at its peak. Not the very long aftertaste or complexity that one would expect from a Grande Marque Champagne. Today the 1978 vintage sells for $42; very overpriced.

❧ July 1986
Medium-gold, young colour. Slightly toasty, and yeasty, delicate, mature nose. Fine bubbles, but not much fizz at twelve-and-a-half years of age. On palate it is round, delicate, soft, and slightly sweet (high dosage?), showing signs of getting tired. Pleasant, but needs drinking.

BOLLINGER BRUT "RD" 1973:

❧ August 1986
At "Chartwell's" restaurant, at the Four Seasons hotel. On our 12th wedding anniversary. Round, elegant, soft, forward, yet still very much alive. At its peak. Complex, yeasty, delicate nose. Long, round, and flavourful on palate. Persistent, tiny bubbles and well balanced. Very good.

POL ROGER BRUT "PRIVATE RESERVE" 1973:

❧ January 1993
Very "goût anglais." Deep gold. Full, rich, creamy, ripe, almost sweet. Hint of caramel candy. (Hint of oxidation, too.) Very tasty, but really a food wine. A bit too "old" for me. After all, it is over 19 years old.

DOM PÉRIGNON BRUT 1973:

❧ June 17, 1985
At our new home on Montgomery Street. We just moved two days ago, and it is our first bottle of wine here. Medium gold. Very good, lively, yet delicate bubbles. Complex, yeasty, but overall, a delicate wine. Starting to lose its fruit, but still sound and very elegant. Needs drinking.

ROEDERER CRISTAL 1974:

❧ December 1979
A rarely seen vintage, made under difficult weather conditions. Very well-made, delicate wine. Good fruity, yeasty nose. A bit high in acidity. It seems that

this wine will improve with age. Lovely flavours. Made in the creamy, elegant style typical of this Champagne.

BOLLINGER BRUT 1975, METHUSELAH:

❧ July 17, 1985

Opened the first methuselah on the occasion of my 40th birthday. And our housewarming on Montgomery Street. Lovely, long, complex. Well balanced, yeasty, and very fine indeed! Better than expected, because large formats (larger than magnums) are produced by the transfer of the wine from regular bottles into larger bottles.

ROEDERER CRISTAL 1975:

❧ February 1982

Lovely, elegant, tiny bubbles, soft, complex. Very good nose. A wine possessing a lot of class. Had it with three different (all fresh) Beluga caviars: Romanian, Russian, and Chinese. The Romanian was the best.

❧ July 16, 1985

Classy, long, complex; touch of yeast, and sugar. Fine bubbles. Well structured with the good acidity typical of the 1975s. Long, clean aftertaste. Lovely. At its peak.

POL ROGER "RESERVE" 1975:

❧ December 1988

Round, delicate, yet complex, with excellent depth and balance. Lovely, clean, long bouquet. Full, round, soft. An excellent Champagne that, at 13 years of age, has held extremely well. But then, 1975 was a great year in Champagne.

DOM PÉRIGNON BRUT 1975:

❧ June 1983

Elegant, complex nose. Long, clean, almost creamy on palate. Great class. An aristocratic Champagne of great quality. Lots of life; no rush drinking it. 1975 was a very good year in Champagne.

❧ May 1989

Fairly deep, golden colour (mature-looking). Ripe raisins; complex, long, lovely nose. Mellow, rich, ripe, mature on palate. Tiny bubbles. Surprisingly lively for its age. Definitely mature, but still very good. Lots of class here. This bottle came from a lot purchased in Saskatchewan in 1984, at a cost of $30 per bottle. At that time, it was selling locally, in Vancouver, for $46 per bottle.

❧ June 1990

Rare and expensive now. It sells for over $150 per bottle. Great Champagne! Superb mousse, very lively, tiny bubbles. Mellow, smooth, long, complex nose. Similar on palate. A complete Champagne that has held very well. Great class, elegance, and length. I have underestimated the staying power of this wine.

CHARLES HEIDSIECK BRUT 1975:

❧ August 1987

At home, with Joe and Alice Heitz, who spent a couple of days with us in Vancouver and on Turnagain Island. Complex, long, elegant, lively, mature on both nose and palate; yeasty, clean, rich, and long. Very good. Has held extremely well.

BOLLINGER BRUT "R.D." 1975:

R.D. means "recently disgorged" (September 3, 1984) after nine years on its lees. Comments below are from a lot of six bottles purchased in 1986.

❧ May 1986

I have had this Champagne three times before at various tastings. Complex, long, elegant, yeasty, mature nose. Very classy. Full, round, beautifully balanced. At its peak. Tiny mousse. A superb Champagne.

❧ August 1997

This Champagne is now 22 years old, and it was disgorged back in September 1984, a full 13 years ago. Fine mousse; tiny bubbles, but they are there. Butterscotch, maple nose; very "goût anglais." Creamy, long, complex. Delicate, yet full, and rich. Went perfectly with veal. A superb Champagne that has held extremely well.

BOLLINGER "GRANDE ANNÉE" BRUT 1976:

❧ January 1985

Full, rich, luscious, almost too much dosage. Not unlike a sparkling, massive California Chardonnay! I have never experienced such a full and rich Champagne before. 1976 produced rich, ripe wines not only in Champagne, but in Burgundy, too (both reds and whites), the Rhône Valley, the Loire, and Alsace, where great late-harvest wines were produced that year.

❧ March 1985

Very different from the above bottle. Leaner, good yeast/complexity. Lively bubbles, and lots of them. Finished a bit bitter, and short. Not bad. Why this bottle variation?

J. LASALLE "BLANC DE BLANCS" BRUT, PREMIER CRU CHIGNY, 1976:

❧ February 1985

Medium gold, tiny bubbles, fine foam. Toasty, delicate, complex nose. Rich, round, complete on palate. Well balanced, extremely well made. For the price ($17), this Champagne is as good as many Grandes Marques. Top quality, long, complex, delicate Chardonnay. A new experience for me.

GOSSET BRUT "GRAND MILLÉSIME" 1976:

July 1987
Elegant, forward on nose. Good bubbles and mousse. Fairly lean and acidic, unusual for 1976. Crisp, elegant. At its peak. A stylish Champagne.

KRUG "BRUT" 1976:

January 1993
Opened the first bottle from a lot of four bottles acquired recently. Magnificent bottle! Bright gold. Tiny bubbles. Rich, off-dry, oaky, ripe, fruity nose. Full, long, complex. Perfect balance. Superb length, body, taste. A "food" Champagne. Great quality! Taste went on and on and on.

JULIEN TARIN BRUT, "BLANC DE BLANCS," LE MESNIL SUR OGER 1977:

April 1987
Rich mousse, tiny bubbles. Elegant, well balanced, rich, slightly sweeter style; unripe grapes require more "dosage," (syrup added). Getting tired, hint of madeirization, but still long and complex. A good effort in a difficult year.

BILLECART-SALMON BRUT, "CUVÉE N.F. BILLECART" 1978:

December 1985
At home, with the French Consul to Vancouver Marcel Olivier, and his wife Joan. Elegant, complex, and delicate Champagne. Well balanced, lovely nose, long, and very fine fruit. Has a lot of class.

August 1988
With Harry and Prue Waugh and their twins, Jamie and Harriet. Lots of complexity and class on nose. Long, round, not heavy or rich, but classy, elegant, and very stylish. At its peak. Very good! The Waugh family is spending a weekend with us on Turnagain Island.

May 1995
A few days before moving from Montgomery Street to 12th Avenue. Amazingly, comments identical to August 1988! Has not aged at all; at almost 17 years of age, has held extremely well. Good, yeasty fruit, round, well balanced, and stylish.

ROEDERER CRISTAL 1978:

January 1984
Quite forward for such a young Champagne, yet delicate, creamy, long, and complex. A lovely Champagne. Ready.

March 10, 1995
On the Occasion of Orly's 17th birthday. We took Orly to "Le Petit Genève" for dinner, and opened this fine bottle, her birth year. Amazingly, 11 years later, general comments as in 1984. Softer, nuttier, a bit older, but long and creamy. Still fine mousse and tiny bubbles, but soft. Lovely, long, ripe, mature finish. An excellent Champagne. Needs drinking.

LECLERC-BRIANT BRUT "SPECIAL CLUB" 1978:

October 1984
Fine bubbles, good foam. Complex, delicate on both nose and palate. Taittinger style. Still a bit young. Very good yeast. Made from a blend of Pinot Noir, Meunier, and Chardonnay. Excellent value. 1978 was a very small vintage, quantity-wise. Long and well balanced.

POL ROGER "CUVÉE WINSTON CHURCHILL" BRUT 1979:

January 20, 1991
At home, during the first week of the "Gulf War" against Iraq, with friends. After several disappointing examples, this bottle was very good. Creamy, rich, delicate, long. Well balanced, and stylish. Very good depth. This is the first vintage of this prestige Cuvée, honouring the memory of Sir Winston Churchill. Pol Roger was one of his favourite Champagnes.

ROEDERER CRISTAL 1979:

December 1987
Ordered a case from the Saskatchewan liquor monopoly, at an excellent $53 per bottle. Tasted the first bottle the week I took delivery of this Champagne. Tiny bubbles, delicate, expansive, creamy, fruity nose. Great length, complexity, good fruit, and lots of class on palate. A lovely, velvety wine!

June 1988
With the panel of *The Wine Consumer*, during a break in tastings. Forward, sweet, lovely complexity, class, and length. Full, soft, elegant, and silky. A superb Champagne at its peak. Great stuff!

June 1992
At a "Group of Ten" dinner. Lovely, smooth, creamy, rich Champagne.

BATISTE PERTOIS PREMIER CRU CRAMANT "BLANC DE BLANCS 100%" BRUT 1979:

June 1987
Before a trip to Bordeaux. Still lively, round, elegant. Tiny bubbles, fine mousse, round, and well balanced. Elegance of Chardonnay. A well-made Champagne.

MUMM'S RENÉ LALOU BRUT 1979:

April 1989
A bit harsh, metallic, and dry. OK but not outstanding. Lacks depth and complexity. No Grand Cru quality here, other than the high price!

DOM RUINART "BLANC DE BLANCS" BRUT 1979:

April 1987
At home, with Serge Hochar, of Château Musar in Lebanon. Serge came over for dinner and this is one

of his favourite Champagnes. Elegant, complex, delicate. A classy Champagne. Although I prefer the richer, more masculine Krug or Bollinger style, this is a very good Champagne.

❧ January 5, 1989
First Champagne of 1989. Lovely Champagne. Comments as above. Elegant, delicate, long nose. Round on palate. At its peak. Needs drinking. Has held well for a Blanc de Blancs.

R ET L LEGRAS PREMIER CRU BRUT, "BLANC DE BLANCS" 1979, CHOUILLY:

❧ November 1987
Pleasant fruity nose. Not very complex at this stage. Still fresh and foamy. A bit simple on palate. Too much "dosage" for a "Brut." Too sweet. Rather ordinary.

❧ June 1989
Substantial improvement over the first bottle tasted in 1987. Complex, yeasty nose. Very good mousse and tiny bubbles. At ten, and made from 100% Chardonnay, this has held very well. Full, rich, long, but not too heavy, as a Blanc de Blancs should be. Elegant. Delicate, long finish. At its peak.

KRUG VINTAGE 1979:

Blend of 36% Pinot Noir, 28% Pinot Meunier, 36% Chardonnay

❧ June 6, 1991
Leaner-style Champagne. No rush. Fine bubbles; complex, long. Lovely, yeasty, fruity, classy nose. Well balanced. Very good depth. Not a rich or fat Champagne, rather racey. Needs time.

❧ May 1992
Bright gold. Good depth. Very fine mousse. Fabulous, fruity, yeasty, expansive bouquet. Mellower, richer, rounder than previously. Full, rich, long, intense. Very good fruit/acidity balance. I have purchased two cases of this. It will be interesting to see how it evolves with age.

❧ September 1995
At 16 years of age, this wine has finally rounded up. It has lost its youthful, steely leanness. Round, long, great balance, depth. Tiny bubbles, fine mousse. Complex, yeasty bouquet. Solid backbone. At its peak, but no rush. Excellent.

BOLLINGER BLANC DE NOIRS "VIEILLES VIGNES FRANÇAISES" 1979:

❧ May 1992
Made from 100% Pinot Noir from ungrafted "prephylloxera" two one-acre plots adjacent to the winery. Extremely rare. Superb. One of the two greatest Champagnes I have ever tasted, (the other being 1928 Krug). Great wine!!! (20) Incredible depth, weight, and length. The smoothness of a great Cristal, combined with the body of a great Krug and the ripeness of Bollinger. All there!

BOLLINGER "R.D." 1979:

Disgorged in 1990.

❧ November 1995
Earthy, steely, serious Champagne. Tiny bubbles, fine mousse. Complex, spicy, medium-bodied. Long, complex, spicy aftertaste. Very good. Has held very well.

PAUL BARA BRUT "BOUZY" 1979:

❧ April 1984
At home, for a "Group of Ten" dinner. Fine Champagne. Made from 100% Grand Cru grapes. Quite elegant, good fruit. A well-made wine.

❧ November 1984
Although a blend of Chardonnay and Pinot Noir, it is delicate, similar to a Pol Roger "Chardonnay." Forward, elegant, long, very fine bottle. Very good quality.

❧ May 13, 1994
At home, with Christian Moueix. Christian is a guest of our Commanderie de Bordeaux, for a short visit which will include a tasting of several 1982s, including Petrus. Quite mature. Rich, round, older tasting. Needs drinking. Becoming very "goût anglais," but still fine mousse and bubbles. Good fruit, rich, long, well balanced. Off-dry. Was definitely better four years ago.

DOM PÉRIGNON 1980:

❧ August 1989
At home, with the panel of *The Wine Consumer*. Quite good, forward, buttery. Surprisingly rich for an "off" vintage. It is soft and needs drinking soon, however.

TAITTINGER "COMTES DE CHAMPAGNE," BLANC DE BLANCS 1981:

❧ April 26, 1990
With Carol, on the eve of our trip to Prague and Budapest. Lovely Champagne. Complex, yeasty, rich, delicate nose. Tiny, lively bubbles. Fine mousse. Great length, balance, and fruit. Lovely Champagne. Ready, but no rush. Made in the more elegant style, typical of this house.

BOLLINGER BLANC DE NOIRS "VIEILLES VIGNES FRANÇAISES" 1981:

Ungrafted, prephylloxera 100% Pinot Noir, from two small plots located near the estate.

❧ September 9, 1996
A superb Champagne! Layers of creamy, ripe fruit. Expansive, magnificent, ripe/yeasty nose. Fine mousse and bubbles. Each gulp was a special experience.

Certainly one of the two or three greatest Champagnes I have ever tasted. Very rich. Very smooth. Very long. Magnificent. Perfect. (20)

DOM RUINART "BLANC DE BLANCS" BRUT 1981:

❧ March 31, 1990
Crisp, leaner style. Delicate, elegant, lively. Tiny bubbles. Good length, fine complexity. Classy Champagne. This reminds me of the Billecart-Salmon Blanc de Blancs style.

DOM PÉRIGNON 1982:

❧ February 19, 1996
A magnum tasted at the beginning of a tasting featuring Château Calon-Ségur 1916 to 1966, and a 200-year-old Madeira "Terrantez" 1795, Barbeito. Lovely Champagne. Clean, crisp, ripe, long. Still full of life. Very good. An impressive wine from a very fine vintage.

❧ March 1997
At a farewell dinner, for the council of the Commanderie de Bordeaux. Before my stepping down as Maître. Superb, creamy, very long. Lovely now. (Also from a magnum.)

POL ROGER "CHARDONNAY" 1982:

❧ February 1992
With excellent fresh Siberian Beluga caviar. Tiny bubbles, fine mousse. Smooth, flowery, well balanced, good length. A lovely, complex, elegant wine. Really fine. Drinking very well, but no rush.

❧ April 1, 1993
With Jacques Hebrard of Cheval-Blanc and Francis Fouquet, the Grand Maître of the Grand Conseil de Bordeaux. Creamy, long, at its peak. Elegant; the ripeness of the 1982s. Very "Cristal" style. Lovely.

POL ROGER BRUT "EXTRA CUVÉE DE RESERVE" 1982:

❧ October 1993
Creamy, good extract. Mature, but not over-the-hill. Lovely fruit/mousse/bubbles. Creamy, yeasty, ripe nose. Lovely length, balance. Best example to date.

VEUVE CLICQUOT "CARTE OR" BRUT (GOLD LABEL) 1982:

❧ August 1987
Purchased two cases in Saskatchewan for $300 per case. The first bottle, (although I have tasted it twice previously), was rich, round, complex. Long and very elegant. A lovely Champagne. Will mature fairly early.

❧ May 1988
Two bottles, with Randy and Patsy Sultan of Los Angeles and other guests, including Debbie, daughter of Bruce Guimaraens of Fonseca's, who was staying with us. Comments as above.

❧ May 8, 1994
For Mother's Day. Full, rich, ripe. Perfect balance, lots of depth, complex, elegant, creamy. At its peak. Lovely Champagne from a very good year.

❧ May 1994
Construction crew on Turnagain Island helped themselves to a bottle as they were building our new home. This was part of a lot of over two cases of fine wines that have "disappeared." At least these guys have good taste!

❧ June 1994
While watching game seven of the Stanley Cup finals for 1994. Vancouver Canucks 2, New York Rangers 3. The Canucks had a great postseason! The wine was excellent, too. Now fully mature.

❧ July 1997
Has held incredibly well; it is 15 years old now. Creamy, smooth, round, yeasty, rich, and complex. Fine, lively mousse. Very long. No doubt that my cool cellar has helped this wine age gracefully.

BOLLINGER "R.D." 1982:

❧ September 1993
Disgorged April 2, 1992. Bright, deep-golden colour. Fine mousse, tiny bubbles. Ripe yeasty/oaky, rich nose. Full, rich, complex. Lots of depth and extract. A "dinner" Champagne. Very "goût anglais" in style.

❧ October 26, 1994
The day Jordan and Israel signed their Peace Treaty. Comments as in September 1993. Excellent Champagne.

Second batch. Disgorged January 1994

❧ December 1994
Great mousse, tiny bubbles. Rich, full, long, round, luscious. Other comments as in September 1993. This is a lovely, classy, "yeasty," ripe, fruity wine.

❧ August 1995
As in December 1994. Typical, ripe, rich 1982. Best with food. Creamy, long, almost "Extra Dry" rather that "Brut." Lovely.

❧ December 24, 1996
A "food" Champagne, yet smooth, round, not too acidic, rich. Lovely now. This bottle was disgorged April 2, 1992.

LANSON "RED LABEL" 1982:

❧ July 1990
During my 45th birthday party. Better than expected. Nice yeast, delicate to medium body, long, complex; not overly sugared (which happens often with Lanson, especially with the nonvintage Black Label). Most enjoyable.

❧ June 1993
On Turnagain Island. Creamy, yeasty, evolved, complex nose. Small bubbles, fine mousse. Surprisingly good. Of course, 1982 was an excellent year for Champagne. Round, creamy, smooth; still lively, but round, and at its peak. Long finish. Very nice.

POL ROGER "PR" 1982:

❧ November 1989
Made from a blend of Pinot Noir and Chardonnay from six vineyards rated 100% Grands Crus. Full, rich, ripe. Excellent fruit and intensity. A rich, serious Champagne. PR stands for "Private Reserve." I am told that the equivalent wine shipped to Anglo-Saxon countries is the "Cuvée Winston Churchill."

BOLLINGER "GRANDE ANNÉE" BRUT 1982:

❧ April 1992
Lovely, yeasty, rich nose. Full, long, tiny bubbles, Still very lively at ten years. Classic Bollinger from a fine vintage. Very good fruit, depth. Nose superb. Good fruit balance. No rush. Drink now to 2002.

ROEDERER CRISTAL 1983:

❧ September 1991
Delicate, creamy, subdued, off-dry. A perfect sipping Champagne. Not as yeasty or big as Bollinger or as steely as Krug. Lovely, round, mellow, and long. Very good balance.

❧ December 31, 1995 at Midnight
At home, on a quiet New Year's Eve, with fine Beluga caviar. The last wine of 1995 and the first of 1996! As back in 1991. Excellent.

❧ January 1, 1997
With Carol and Orly. At its peak. Superb balance, good fruit, still lively, fine mousse, long, delicate, yet lots of stuffing. Top quality. Has held extremely well. Welcome 1997!

VEUVE CLICQUOT BRUT "CARTE OR" 1983:

❧ June 1995
Last bottle, at home. Round, delicate, soft. Not as intense as the 1982, or as lively as the 1985, but smooth, full, creamy; made from ripe grapes. Very good. Classy. Needs drinking, though.

POL ROGER "CHARDONNAY" 1985:

❧ September/October 1992
Given to me by Christian Pol Roger during a recent trip to Champagne. I also purchased several bottles from the local government liquor monopoly.

❧ October 1996
Round, elegant, smooth. Tiny bubbles, nice fruit, complex, long. Ready. Lovely bottle. In my opinion, this 100% Chardonnay wine is consistently Pol Roger's best Champagne, reflecting the elegant style of this house.

VEUVE CLICQUOT ROSÉ 1985:

❧ December 1995
One of the finer Rosé Champagnes and from an excellent vintage. Salmon/pink colour. Fine mousse and bubbles. Went well with steak. Lovely fresh fruit. Well balanced. Long, clean. Not too dry or hard. Very good. No rush, but at its peak now. I prefer Rosé Champagnes with food rather than as an aperitif, because of their relative dryness and masculine structure.

VEUVE CLICQUOT "CARTE OR" 1985:

❧ August 17, 1995
On Turnagain Island, for our 21st wedding anniversary. Long, rich, complex. Creamy and smooth. Well balanced. Better than many Grandes Marques, and at less than half the price.

CHARLES HEIDSIECK BRUT 1985:

❧ October 1995
A well-made Champagne. One of the best efforts of this house in several years. Excellent balance, depth, and length. Yeasty, fine mousse, tiny bubbles. Ripe, rich, yet elegant fruit. Long, complex. Perfect now at ten years of age.

BATISTE PERTOIS PREMIER CRU "BLANC DE BLANCS 100%" 1985, CRAMANT:

❧ June 30, 1997
Michael's 22nd birthday. Fine mousse. A lovely, round, elegant Blanc de Blancs. At 12 years old, smooth, round, delicate. Nice fruit, soft.

VEUVE CLICQUOT "LA GRANDE DAME" 1985:

❧ May 1997
First bottle at 12 years old. Round, elegant, yeasty, lots of depth, ripe fruit. Not big, but quite rich and long. Very fine quality. Perfect now.

BILLECART-SALMON BRUT, "CUVÉE N.F. BILLECART" 1989:

❧ July 1997
Typical of the vintage and of the style of this fine house. Tiny bubbles, fine mousse. Soft, round, fruity. Very elegant, and long. Clean, fresh, yet round aftertaste. Most enjoyable. This is one of my favourite smaller Champagne producers.

CHARLES HEIDSIECK BRUT 1990:

❧ June 1997
With Orly. Surprisingly forward, and evolved for a six-year-old Champagne. Lovely, yeasty, rich, ripe, toasty nose. Full, round, soft, very forward on palate. Almost "Extra Dry" rather than "Brut." Fair bit of dosage or very ripe grapes. Most enjoyable, fine mousse. Ready

now. An excellent Champagne. I hope that this will remain a secret, because it is very reasonably priced at Can$44 per bottle.

WHITE GRAVES AND OTHER DRY WHITE BORDEAUX

CRU BEDAT 1943 AOC GRAVES BLANC:

Very good level, medium to dark gold. Some sediment. Clean label reads "Potensac Dry." Bottled and shipped by: "Société pour la Selection des Grands Crus de Graves, Sauternes et Barsac."

❧ August 23, 1989

At home, with the panel of *The Wine Consumer*. Surprisingly good. Almost dry Sauternes-like. Full, nutty botrytis, yet dry. Earthy, wet cement. Some fruit. Like a dry old Château Gilette.

CHÂTEAU CARBONNIEUX BLANC 1971:

❧ June 1977

In London. Rich, trace of sugar on nose. Light-golden colour. Quite dry on palate, but backed by good fruit. Good wine. A bargain at £2.50 per bottle.

CHÂTEAU LAVILLE-HAUT-BRION 1978:

❧ November 1995

With the council of the Commanderie de Bordeaux. Very youthful, bright-golden colour for a 17-year-old white wine. Scents of acacia, oak, vanilla, perfumy Semillon on nose. Round. Excellent balance, long, spicy, ripe, full finish. Ready, but no rush. These wines can last in bottle for a very long time. How happy I am to have acquired a case of this fine wine in San Francisco back in 1980, having paid $200 per case! While I have tasted this fine wine on half-a-dozen occasions since then, this was the first bottle from my case.

"R" (DRY WINE OF CHÂTEAU RIEUSSEC) 1979:

❧ 1980

At a restaurant in Bordeaux, with Peter A. Sichel of Châteaux Palmer and d'Angludet. Slight hint of Sauternes on nose, but lovely, dry, exotic flavours. Elegant, crisp, fruity. Needs one to two years, but showing very well. Clean and long aftertaste. A new experience for me.

"Y" 1979:

The dry wine of Château d'Yquem. Mostly Sauvignon Blanc grapes. An unusual and fairly rare wine.

❧ February 1991

With several friends, including Jean-Yves Conte, French Trade Commissioner to Vancouver. Lovely wine. Elegant, long. Touch of oak and botrytis (from old d'Yquem barrels?) on both nose and palate. Round, elegant. At its peak. Complex, creamy. Very good and very special.

CHÂTEAU PAPE CLEMENT BLANC 1980

❧ August 1989

This bottle was given to me back in 1985 by Mr. Marly, owner of Château Malartic Lagravière during a visit there. A rare and unusual white Graves. Only one tonneau (four barrels) or 100 cases produced. Made from one-third each Sauvignon Blanc, Semillon, and Muscadelle; unusual proportions indeed. Pale gold. Earthy, spicy green-apple on nose. Leaner on palate, but good fruit and hint of oak. Maybe some day, as (and if) the popularity of white Graves grows, Pape Clement will decide to produce more of it, and sell this commercially.

DOMAINE DE CHEVALIER BLANC 1983:

❧ March 1989

With the panel of *The Wine Consumer*, after an extensive tasting of 28 different California Sauvignon Blancs. Bright gold. Complex nose, just starting to open up. Lovely oak, vanilla, and ripe fruit on nose. Great depth and complexity on palate. Excellent balance, lovely intensity. A classy wine. Needs three to five more years, and should hold well beyond that. As good as one could hope a fine white Graves to be! Drink from 1994 to 2005 and beyond, if well stored.

RHÔNE VALLEY REDS AND WHITES

HERMITAGE "LA SIZERANNE" 1955, CHAPOUTIER:

❧ November 1987

Given to me by David Freeman when he came over for dinner with Harry and Prue Waugh.

❧ May 1988

At home, together with 1955 Château Talbot, bottled by Nicolas. Guests included Debbie, daughter of Bruce Guimaraens of Fonseca. Excellent level, fair bit of sediment. Medium red, very good depth. Spicy, complex, lovely elegance on nose, not unlike a sturdy, mature, and noble red Burgundy. Round, long, fruity. Lots of class. Nowadays, Chapoutier does not make wines nearly as good as these. If and when the new generation takes over at Chapoutier, they will, hopefully, restore the reputation of this potentially great estate.

CHÂTEAUNEUF-DU-PAPE 1961, DOMAINE DU MONT REDON:

❧ June 1993

With the council of the Commanderie de Bordeaux. Mature colour, good depth. Fair bit of sediment. Dry, tight cork crumbled. Spicy, ripe nose. Round, sweet, good depth. Old. Needs drinking, but very good quality.

CÔTE RÔTIE 1966, ANDRÉ PASSAT:

❧ August 1978

Lots of sediment; dark, bright colour. Good earthy, woody bouquet. Could be mistaken for a Cabernet Sauvignon type. Delicate, long-lasting bouquet, very flavourful, and feminine, yet with good structure. A very good wine. At its peak.

CHÂTEAUNEUF-DU-PAPE "LES CÈDRES" 1967, PAUL JABOULET AINÉ:

❧ January 1988

With the panel of *The Wine Consumer*. Served double-blind. Very good level. Some sediment. Full, dark colour. Spicy, hot, rich nose. Most tasters thought it was Italian or Spanish. Ripe, rich, lots of extract. Fruity, jammy. Long. Holding very well. Impressive at 20 years old.

HERMITAGE "LA CHAPELLE" 1970, PAUL JABOULET AINÉ:

❧ January 1977

Dinner at "Le Pavillon" restaurant, in the Four Seasons hotel, in Vancouver. Powerful, dark wine. Quite a bit of sediment. The texture and colour of a great Burgundy, but with the dryness of a very good Claret. Needs time.

❧ July 1977
In London. Purchased a bottle for £4.80 at Harrods. As good as the previous bottle in Vancouver. Big, powerful, masculine. An excellent wine. Needs at least two hours to breathe. Try again in three years.

❧ April 1978
One of Carol's favourites. Decanted two hours. Very dark, very powerful wine. Medium sediment. Delicate, yet not great, bouquet. A fat, peppery wine. Quite a bit of tannin and lots of alcohol. The dryness of Bordeaux and fullness of a great Burgundy. Needs at least two to three more years.

❧ June 1983
I have not tasted this wine since 1978. Dark, concentrated colour. Some sediment. Decanted one hour. Spicy, austere nose of a Burgundy, yet structured like a big Haut-Médoc. Lovely, intense nose. Still some tannins to lose. Well balanced. Good fruit, long aftertaste. A very well-made wine. Slight orange-brown rim, showing its age (almost 13 years old, and a long way to go!).

HERMITAGE LA "SIZERANNE" 1971, CHAPOUTIER:

❧ September 1981
Big, deep, dark colour; good fruity, complex, "hot" on nose, but not very open yet. Decanted one hour. Little tannin or sediment, big and very powerful. Slight touch of brown. Excellent fruit, good acidity, good aftertaste. This wine will live for a long time. Try again in a few years.

❧ April 1989
This is a superb bottle! The complexity on nose of a great Côte de Nuits, but a bit darker in colour. Lovely, long, complex, spicy nose, yet not unlike a fine Pinot Noir. Long and beautiful. Solid on palate. Perfect balance, great depth, class, length. Lots of mature fruit. Not tired, but at its perfect peak at 18 years of age! One of the stars of the evening. One of the last great Hermitages made by Chapoutier, which has been disappointing in the past 15 years. Great experience.

DOMAINE DU VIEUX TÉLÉGRAPHE 1978, CHÂTEAUNEUF-DU-PAPE:

❧ April 23, 1991
As part of a tasting of 1978 red and white Rhônes. Deep purple-red. Youthful, concentrated. Needs seven to ten extra years! Very good balance. Rich, ripe, intense, concentrated fruit. Ten years ago, this was a steal at $96 per case! Excellent potential. Drink from 1995 to 2003 or beyond.

HERMITAGE "LA SIZERANNE" 1978, CHAPOUTIER:

❧ September 1987
At home, with the panel of *The Wine Consumer*, against 1978 Hermitage, E. Guigal. Palish, old-looking, mature. A bit sharp, acidic, and citric. A pleasant wine with some complexity, but not what a 1978 Hermitage should be. The Guigal was much better.

❧ August 1993
On Turnagain Island. Some sediment; medium, mature colour. Round, soft, spicy, clean, pleasant, but of course, nowhere near the depth, extract, and intensity of such great 1978 Hermitages as Chave or La Chapelle of Jaboulet. Good, but certainly not great. Ready. The new generation that is taking over at Chapoutier must, and should, do better than this.

CROZES-HERMITAGE "THALABERT" 1978, PAUL JABOULET AINÉ:

Purchased a case of this in 1981 for $10.50 per bottle.

❧ April 23, 1991
As part of a tasting of 1978 red and white Rhônes. Very deep colour, purple-red. Youthful, tannic, intense. Needs time. Some tasters disagreed, noting that it was drying out. A matter of taste.

❧ February 1992
Excellent level and appearance. Deep, youthful colour to rim. Decanted. Fair bit of sediment. Luscious fruit, intense, rich, yet round, soft, full. At its peak, but no rush. Lots of extract, typical of this great, low-yield vintage. Good, spicy, fruity aftertaste.

HERMITAGE "LA CHAPELLE" 1978, PAUL JABOULET AINÉ:

Purchased a case locally through an agent, for $22.50 per bottle in 1981.

❧ April 23, 1991
As part of a tasting of 18 different 1978 red and white Rhônes. Intense, deep colour. Jammy, very ripe, intense, closed up. Needs ten more years! This is a great wine. Only 14 hectolitres per hectare were produced in 1978. Great future. Try around 1996 to 2010.

HERMITAGE 1978, J. L. CHAVE:

Probably the finest 1978 Hermitage and, according to some experts, the greatest Chave red since 1929! A rare and massive wine, which is worth a lot more than the actual amount paid ($125 per case). I had to talk Gerard Chave into releasing a case for me. I told him that 1978 is Orly's birth year, and he very kindly shipped a case for me via Kermit Lynch, in Berkeley, California, in 1982.

❧ April 23, 1991
As part of a tasting of 18 different 1978 red and white Rhônes. Greatest wine of the evening. Superb! Needs five to seven years. Deep, complex, concentrated, great balance. Jaboulet's "La Chapelle" is great, too, of course, but this had a slight edge at this tasting.

HERMITAGE 1978, E. GUIGAL:

❧ September 1987
At home, with the panel of *The Wine Consumer*, against Chapoutier's 1978 Hermitage "La Sizeranne." Very deep, dark colour. Spicy, rich, peppery Syrah nose. Full, rich, tannic, fruity, well balanced, and long. Will be an excellent bottle in seven to ten years. Not nearly ready. Much better than Chapoutier's, which is tired, a bit sour, and simple, lacking the intensity or extract typical of this great vintage.

❧ May 1995
At almost 17 years of age, approaching maturity. The depth of colour of this great vintage in the Rhône. Deep colour extract. Spicy, ripe berries on nose. Full, rich, very concentrated fruit. Does not have the massive depth and intensity of Chave's or Jaboulet's Hermitages 1978, but nevertheless, very good. Rich, spicy mouthful. Ready, but still a bit tannic. Very good length. Ready, but no rush. Drink now to 2003.

CÔTE RÔTIE "BRUNE ET BLONDE" 1978, E. GUIGAL:

❧ October 30, 1993
Tasted against 1978 Sassicaia, and 1978 Torres Black Label "Reserva," accompanying a Middle Eastern dinner. Great, deep red colour. Perfect balance. Approaching its peak, but no rush. Lovely, spicy nose. Full, rich, yet not too big. Elegant. Excellent extract. Long finish. Very good balance. Lovely wine.

HERMITAGE ROUGE 1979, J. L. CHAVE:

❧ February 1990
With the panel of *The Wine Consumer*. Fair bit of sediment. Decanted 45 minutes. Heavily stained bottle, excellent level. Very good, deep, dark, slightly maturing colour to rim. Intense, ripe, spicy/peppery Syrah nose. Full, long, not very hard any more, but intense, ripe, and rich. Approaching its peak, but no rush. Very good. A bargain back in 1981. Paid $135 per case.

HERMITAGE "LA CHAPELLE" 1979, PAUL JABOULET AINÉ:

Gerard Jaboulet gave me two bottles of this when I visited him in September 1980.

❧ March 1988
With the panel of *The Wine Consumer*. Deep, dark colour, showing some maturity at rim. Decanted one hour. Medium sediment. At first, an off, skunky nose that cleared completely after ten minutes in glass. Full, peppery, rich, yet getting ready. On the dry side, medium fruit. A fine effort for 1979. Drink from 1990 to 1995. Very enjoyable.

❧ October 8, 1994
On Turnagain Island, during the first weekend in our new house there. Very good, deep, mature colour. At its peak. Spicy, sweet fruit. Excellent balance. Rich, round, complex. Lots of ripe fruit. Very good depth. Lovely now, but no rush. This wine has improved quite a bit over the past six years.

HERMITAGE ROUGE 1980, J.L CHAVE:

❧ December 1993
With Bernard Ledun, French Consul General to Vancouver, before his departure to his new posting in Mexico City. Good, dark colour. Fair bit of sediment. Decanted one hour. Surprisingly good for a 1980. Spicy, rich, long, well balanced; very good depth, fruit extract. Long finish. Approaching its peak, but no rush.

HERMITAGE "LA CHAPELLE" 1982, PAUL JABOULET AINÉ:

❧ May 1986
Deep, dark colour. At first vegetal, spicy nose that cleared after a bit. Spicy, ripe, rich on palate, yet some tasters found it too hard and lean. Needs at least an extra three to four years in bottle.

❧ December 1988
Excellent, deep colour. Warm, spicy, leathery; long, rich nose. Full, fruity, ripe, very good balance. Lots of lively fruit. Drink from 1992 to 1998 or beyond. Excellent potential.

❧ March 1993
Comments as in December 1988, just slightly softer, but rich, spicy, ripe, long. Holding very well. Almost ready, but no rush.

CORNAS 1982, AUGUSTE CLAPE:

❧ October 1995
Fair bit of sediment. Decanted one hour. Bright, youthful, deep cherry colour. Very youthful for a 13-year-old Cornas. Lovely, classic, spicy, peppery Syrah nose. Very good fruit extract on palate. Well balanced, hint of tannins, good body. So well balanced that it is a pleasure to drink, even now. Long aftertaste. Ready, but no rush. An excellent Cornas.

HERMITAGE "LA CHAPELLE" 1985, PAUL JABOULET AINÉ:

❧ June 1993
With the council of the Commanderie de Bordeaux. Bright, deep-red, purplish colour. Rubbery, fresh strawberries, spicy nose. Hollow middle, finishing dry. Going through a phase? May improve, but does not

have the depth or weight of the 1983, or the ripeness of the 1982. Hopefully, it will improve.

HERMITAGE BLANC "CHEVALIER DE STERIMBERG" 1959, JABOULET:

❧ February 19, 1996

Served from a magnum at the beginning of a vertical tasting of Château Calon-Ségur 1916 to 1966. Lively fruit, but lacking extract, ripeness, and complexity. Tired; drink up.

CHÂTEAU GRILLET 1971:

❧ May 1977

In London. A famous, rare, and expensive white Rhônes wine made from 100% Viognier. Rich golden colour and texture. Fine, rich, flowery bouquet. Tangy at first, but then improved into a delicate, mellow wine. Hint of ripe pears. Paid £8 for this bottle at Jackson's of Piccadilly. Apparently, it is the smallest Appellation Controlée in France, producing approximately 500 cases yearly. This is my first experience with this wine.

CHÂTEAU GRILLET 1978:

❧ September 1980

At the château, tasted with Mr. Neiret-Gachet at his vineyard. Lovely, delicate, flowery. Very elegant. Has class. I will try to get some of the 1979 vintage, which he is releasing shortly.

❧ April 21, 1991

As an aperitif before extensive tasting of 1978 Rhônes. The debate about drinking young or old Château Grillet continues. I like both. This was the last vintage before they doubled production (from 450 cases to 850). Concentrated, rich, yet subtle. Some Viognier, lychees-Muscat. Fairly alcoholic. Well balanced. Long and clean. Classy.

HERMITAGE BLANC 1978, J. L. CHAVE:

❧ November 1983

A lovely bottle! Big, complex, clean, elegant nose. Very well structured. Drinking very well now, but will hold for many years. Quite big and powerful. A gentle giant. Probably the best Chave white Hermitage made in the past 20 years or more. Very promising. They only produced 12 hectolitres per hectare in 1978. Very concentrated. Magnificent.

❧ April 23, 1991

As part of a tasting of 1978 red and white Rhônes. Austere, tight. Much tighter, oddly, than seven years ago. Going through a phase? I know from personal experience that Chave's whites age well. A few years ago, I had the opportunity to taste some superb 1959 and 1929 white Hermitage at his property.

CHÂTEAU GRILLET 1979, NEIRET-GACHET:

❧ March 1982

At home, with Harry Waugh; also Joe Heitz, and his daughter Kathleen, and the Tobes. This wine was a discovery for Joe and his daughter, and for Harry Waugh, who has had it before, but never so young. Elegant, complex nose with hint of ripe pears, but maybe not as full-bodied as one would wish it to be (such as a great Condrieu), yet made from the same grape varietal (the Viognier). Understated, elegant. Still youthful.

❧ October 1983

Medium-gold colour. Fragrant, complex nose. "Dry" honey on palate, elegant, quite dry, and a bit lemony, which is a characteristic of white Rhônes. At first, it seemed elegant, but later it turned out to be quite full-bodied. Clean, long aftertaste. An unusual experience. A rare, and fine wine. Better than when last tasted over a year ago.

❧ March 1984

At home, with Peter Sichel of Château Palmer, and Sid and Joan Cross. Peter had mentioned to me in the past that he had never tasted this wine before. Comments as above, yet everybody thought that it would improve with age.

❧ June 1986

Lilacs and spices on nose. Brilliant green-gold colour. Elegant, delicate, complex, with breed, and length, yet not a big wine. At its peak.

HERMITAGE BLANC 1979, J. L. CHAVE:

Acquired in 1981 in San Francisco for $160 per case from Kermit Lynch.

❧ September 1982

I opened a bottle fully realizing that it is too young, but curious to find out for myself about the potential of this wine. A beauty. Medium-dark colour, lovely raisins/apricots on nose. Big on palate, long, clean, well balanced. Lots of fruit, and a ways to go. Should reach its peak in three to four years, and hold for quite some time. Solid, serious wine of great quality.

Gerard Chave told me during my visit to his winery in October 1980 that most of his white Hermitage of good or great years (such as 1978 and 1979) hold for 15 to 20 years before they start to decline.

❧ January 1984

Too young. Intense, big, round, yet lemony. Fabulous nose and flavour. Needs at least two to three more years.

❧ August 1988

Served against the same wine of the 1978 vintage, with Harry and Prue Waugh. Both similar appearance. Bright, young, gold colour. Both had a flowery, ripe nose. The 1979 was more complex, rounder, fruitier, more elegant. At its peak, but no rush. The 1978 is tight, drier, harder, more austere, lower fruit at this stage. Needs three to five extra years. Overall, the 1979 was the favourite.

❧ June 1995
Almost 16 years old. Deep golden colour. Pineapple/pear, spicy nose, yet subdued. Quite a heavy, rich wine. Very good fruit/acidity balance. Round, long, rich, exotic. Fairly alcoholic, but in harmony with good fruity and acidity. Needs food. Drink now to 2000 or beyond.

CHÂTEAU GRILLET 1980:

❧ February 1984
With lovely Dover sole. Medium-gold colour, delicate, fruity, complex nose. Very little of the "lemony" character of Rhône whites. On palate, thicker and creamier than the 1978 or 1979. Rich, yet delicate, lovely balance, long. A fine bottle. We visited Château Grillet on October 12, 1980, one day before they picked. The grapes were mature, sweet, and rich, and 1980 was a warm vintage in the Rhône. They did not suffer from the torrential rains of Bordeaux or Burgundy. We also happened to spend some time in the aforementioned areas, and the harvests weren't very promising at all. Way too much rain.

❧ June 1995
At home, after a lapse of 11 years since last tasted, and at 15 years of age. Bright golden colour. Exotic, yet subdued nose of honeydew, apricots, and melon. Round, smooth, fairly rich, and elegant on palate. Has held very well, but has certainly changed. Ready and mature, of course, but a classy, elegant wine.

HERMITAGE BLANC 1980, J. L. CHAVE:

❧ March 1987
With the panel of *The Wine Consumer*. Dark, deep, mature gold. Rich, sweet, ripe nose. Thick, yet soft on palate. Seems to be tiring, lacking acidity or exotic spices. Odd wine. Disappointing. Must retaste.

❧ August 1987
On Turnagain Island, with Joe and Alice Heitz, who spent a couple of days with us. Much better than above. Round, rich, lots of depth. Well balanced, clean. At its peak. Exotic fruit, ripe peaches. Joe had never tried a white Hermitage before, and he was impressed.

❧ February 1996
With the council of the Commanderie de Bordeaux. Deep, bright golden colour. Oak, flowery/honeyed nose. Solid, full, long. Like a Meursault of Coche-Dury's in structure, but not in taste, of course. Full, rich, solid.

HERMITAGE BLANC "CHEVALIER DE STERIMBERG" 1981, PAUL JABOULET AINÉ:

❧ August 1985
Elegance rather than power. Medium gold, touch of greenness. Delicate, lemony, fruity nose. Round, soft, yet power underneath on palate. Slightly woody. Enjoyable now but will develop more character in two to three years.

CONDRIEU "CÔTEAU DE VERNON" 1982, GEORGE VERNAY:

This is Vernay's very special, very small production of Côteau de Vernon. Only three cases arrived at Draper and Esquin's in San Francisco. About 300 to 400 cases produced yearly.

❧ April 1986
Deep, bright green-gold. Lovely, elegant, subdued nose of fresh peaches and apricots. Almost thick on palate. Round, clean, very long. Incredible complexity and breed. A marvellous bottle of wine. Beats any other Condrieu or Château Grillet I have tasted to date. Superb!

❧ February 1987
Deep, bright gold. Ripe raisins, peaches, and apricots on nose. Fabulous length. Full, rich, alcoholic, intense, with good acidity. Thick and well balanced. Loaded with ripe fruit. A lovely wine. In my opinion, this is the greatest Condrieu today.

CONDRIEU "CHÂTEAU DU ROZAY" 1983, P. MULTIER:

❧ August 1988
At home, as an aperitif with Harry and Prue Waugh. Complex, spicy lychees. Full, solid, fairly alcoholic. Good depth. Has lost some of its freshness, but still very good. Some oak.

HERMITAGE BLANC 1983, J. L. CHAVE:

❧ June 1996
The wine is now 13 years old. Bright, golden colour. Lovely, ripe, subdued peaches on nose. Full, excellent balance. Round, yet fresh. Very long, medium-bodied, clean, exotic fruit, peaches/melon. No rush. One of the best Chave whites I have tasted recently.

CONDRIEU "CÔTEAU DE VERNON" 1985, GEORGES VERNAY:

This is the rare single-vineyard Condrieu wine of Vernay's. Made from old vines at the top of the Condrieu vineyard.

❧ August 1987
At home, with Joe and Alice Heitz. Joe had never tried a Condrieu before. Peaches nectar on nose. Rich, flowery, full, fairly alcoholic, long. Excellent. Young, lively, and intense. Very good.

❧ November 9, 1987
With Harry and Prue Waugh, and several other tasters. Harry has never tasted the "Côteau de Vernon" before. Approximately 400 cases produced yearly. The best Condrieu, and from an excellent vintage. Comments as above.

❧ September 1989
At home, with Barney and Belle Rhodes, and Haskell and Rae Norman. Superb wine. Barney loved it. Haskell never had it before. Excellent. Very rare wine. This was my last bottle.

ALSACE

RIESLING "RESERVE EXCEPTIONNELLE" 1971, HUGEL:

❧ 1976 and 1977
Tasted on several occasions. Fine Riesling with quite a bit of depth. Mature, delicate, very pleasant. Not too sweet. Some bite, but improved after airing for a half-hour. Hint of petroleum jelly; classic Riesling from a very good vintage.

❧ May 1981
Tasted blind against other Alsatian wines of the 1971 and 1976 vintages. Sid Cross mistook them for Loire wines, which is odd. Good nose, smoky. The 1971 at first had more character, but later, the 1976 developed nice, ripe complexity, although for me the 1976 was a bit disappointing. A bit thin in the middle. Both elegant, crisp; the 1971 slightly spritzy at first.

❧ January 1984
Last bottle, and the best! Lovely, complex, elegant Riesling. Good fruit/acidity. Great balance. Lasted better than expected.

GEWÜRZTRAMINER "VENDANGE TARDIVE" 1976, DOPFF ET IRION:

❧ November 1989
Holding extremely well, and from a great vintage. Complex, mature, petroleum/Riesling nose. Dry, yet has weight. Complex, long, elegant. At its peak. No sweetness, but fairly thick, indicating a late-harvest wine. I am not a fan of Dopff et Irion, but this is good. Needs drinking.

GEWÜRZTRAMINER "VENDANGE TARDIVE" 1976, HUGEL :

❧ June 1985
At a tasting of late-harvest wines, including German Auslesen and California Johannisberg Rieslings. Great complexity and length. Spicy, yet not overwhelming. Round, well balanced. No rush. A classic, elegant wine of great character. Preferred it to Hugel's Riesling "Vendange Tardive," but not by much.

GEWÜRZTRAMINER "VENDANGE TARDIVE - SELECTION DE GRAINS NOBLES" 1976, HUGEL, CASKS 20, 28, AND 67:

Three of the bottles I have purchased are Fût #28, one bottle is Fût #67. "Fût" means cask. Jean "Johnny" Hugel told me that he produced three fûts of Gewürztraminer, Grains Nobles, in 1976: #67, #28, and #20. #67 is a bit less sweet. His Fût #20 is the best, the richest. Fût #28 achieved 13.4° alcohol and 132 oechsele. #28 was released first, then #67, and finally #20. He also suggested that one should taste them in that order. I also managed to get a couple of bottles of

Fût #20. This should make an interesting tasting some day.

❧ August 1987

Opened a half-bottle, at home (Fût #28), for Joe and Alice Heitz. The Heitzes spent a few days with us at home and on Turnagain Island. Ripe lychees on nose. Round, lively, well balanced, long, elegant. A great Gewürztraminer. Joe was impressed by it, and by the fact that it was so lively in half-bottle, and at 11 years of age. No rush. Not overly sweet. Essence of fruit. Great, lovely.

RIESLING "VENDANGE TARDIVE" 1976, HUGEL:

❧ June 1985

Round, complex, relatively dry, compared to 1976 German Auslesen, but fine, and with great length. Very fine indeed.

❧ April 1994

From a half-bottle. At 18 years of age, and in half-bottle, this is a superb Riesling. Has the characteristics of a rich Riesling, petroleum on nose, very ripe fruit. Slight hint of sweetness, or actually "off-dry." Full, long, superb balance, and length. Mouthfilling. A lovely wine. Will last for a long time!

RIESLING "VENDANGE TARDIVE - SELECTION DE GRAINS NOBLES" 1976, HUGEL:

❧ June 28, 1987

Opened a half-bottle for David and Kate Dougdale. David is a principal with O. W. Loeb wine merchants in London, and a friend of Belle and Barney Rhodes of California. A superb, late-harvest Riesling, even in half-bottle. Light-gold colour. Magnificent, delicate, subdued, noble Riesling nose. Not too sweet, round, delicate, long. At its peak, yet no rush. Such good balance, fruit, and class! A lovely wine. Rates 18 or higher.

GEWÜRZTRAMINER "VENDANGE TARDIVE" 1983, LEON BEYER:

❧ July 1993

Pale gold. Spicy lychees on nose. Muscat. Fairly rich, high alcohol, hint of residual sugar. Long, complex, soft. Ready. Very pleasant summer wine. Had it with Chinese food.

RIESLING "LES ECAILLERS" 1985, LEON BEYER:

❧ September 1991

With the council of the Commanderie de Bordeaux. Nice, green-gold colour. Lovely oak/petroleum, flowery Riesling nose. Intense, long, complex, elegant on palate. Excellent balance. Fresh, crisp, long, clean Riesling finish. Really fine bottle. No rush.

GEWÜRZTRAMINER "RESERVE CUVÉE EMILE WILLM" 1990, WILLM:

Rare in magnum. A tall, slim bottle. Also, 1990 was great for Alsace wines. A collector's item.

❧ December 28, 1995

On the day it was purchased, I accidentally dropped it on the kitchen floor, and it broke into little pieces. It wasn't meant to be. Fortunately, I managed to acquire another magnum. Had the opportunity to taste this in July 1996 at a friend's home. An impressive wine. Still very youthful. Complex, spicy, rich petroleum and fruit on nose. Long on palate. Very good fruit extract and depth. Drink now to 2005.

LOIRE VALLEY REDS AND WHITES

POUILLY-FUMÉ 1976, DE LADOUCETTE:

November 1979

Excellent, full-bodied. Nice, intense nose. Good fruit/acidity balance; will last for some time. Very good quality. Spicy Sauvignon Blanc from a ripe vintage. A bargain in Seattle at $6 per bottle.

April 1982

Good, herbaceous Sauvignon Blanc on nose. Fruity, well balanced; very good acidity makes this wine quite long-lived, but seems to have lost the flintiness so typical of this varietal.

March 1986

On Turnagain Island. Has held surprisingly well. A lovely, complex Pouilly-Fumé. Recent vintages of Ladoucette are not nearly as good. This was a lovely bottle. It had it all. Balance, fruit, nose, complexity.

CHINON "VIEILLES VIGNES," CUVÉE DU CLOS DE LA DIOTERIE 1978, CHARLES JOGUET:

Old vines, made from 100% Cabernet Franc. Already a fair bit of sediment in bottle (1982). Should be a lovely wine.

July 1983

Surprisingly evolved colour, some sediment. Intense, vegetal, stemmy nose typical of the Cabernet Franc. Now I know where the St. Emilions get their bouquet. (A fair bit of Cabernet Franc goes into St. Emilions, called "Boucher" there.) At first harsh and fairly hard, almost bitter. After being decanted for one hour, it improved and mellowed. Well balanced, pleasant, yet I find it lacking in depth, and a bit short. An experience, nevertheless.

POUILLY-FUMÉ "BARON DE L" 1979, DE LADOUCETTE:

February 1983

How much better this wine is than the regular Ladoucette 1979! Perfumed, elegant, complex, fruity, long on palate, and clean. A lovely Sauvignon Blanc. Real class. A bit expensive, but a good wine. Ready, but its balance will make it last for at least two more years (or longer). The regular 1979 is watery, thin, and ordinary. The regular Ladoucette 1975 and 1976 are fine examples of Pouilly-Fumé, however.

CHAVIGNOL "LA GRANDE CÔTE" 1982, SANCERRE, PAUL COTAT:

March 1984

Unmistakable Sauvignon Blanc; spicy nose, green-gold colour. Not as flinty as a Pouilly-Fumé; this wine is rounder, richer, fatter, almost California in style. Well balanced, complex, but not really my type of wine.

June 1984

Unusual, almost late-harvest wine, similar to an Alsace Gewürztraminer Vendange Tardive; pale golden colour. Well structured and balanced. An experience.

July 1994

With the council of the Commanderie de Bordeaux. 12 years old and still very good. Classy, herbaceous, spicy Sauvignon Blanc nose. Round, soft, long, clean. Very well made. Not too fat or flabby. Good acidity. At its peak.

POUILLY-FUMÉ "BARON DE L" 1985, DE LADOUCETTE:

August 1990

Price finally came down to a reasonable level ($30). Sold at one time for a ridiculous $50 a bottle!

October 1990

Pale gold. Nice, complex, spicy, elegant, flowery nose. Well balanced, flinty, green-grassy/ripe fruit on palate. Long, complex, spicy, elegant.

White and Red Wines from Bourg, Blaye, and other Bordeaux Regions, as well as Beaujolais, Languedoc-Rousillon, Corsica, and other parts of France

CORSICA

CLOS NICROSI BLANC DE BLANCS N/V, VIN DE CORSE, CÔTEAUX DU CAP CORSE, T. LUIGI:

Made from Malvoise and Ugni Blanc

❧ January 1987

Thick, rich, lemony, not unlike a white Hermitage. This nonvintage wine is probably a blend of 1981 and 1982.

PROVENCE

MAS DE GOURGONNIER 1981, CÔTEAUX DES BAUX, PROVENCE VDQS, NICOLAS CARTIER:

❧ May 1984

Deep, youthful, purplish, dark colour. Spicy Cabernet Sauvignon (Médoc) nose. Rich, deep, full, tannic wine; good fruit. Not a complex wine, but a good one. There are many single bottles retailing at the price of a whole case of this "simple" wine, and they are not worth it! Will improve in another two to three years. Not to expect great complexity, but very good. I purchased a case of this in San Francisco last year for everyday drinking. Reasonably priced at $45 per case.

MAS DE DAUMAS GASSAC 1978, VIN DE PAYS DE L'HERAULT, V. GUIBERT DE LA VAISSIÈRE:

Made from Cabernet Sauvignon grapes. Paid $6.50 per bottle in 1982. Now, this costs a small fortune.

❧ September 1985

Very deep, purplish colour; intense, and much younger-looking than its age would indicate. Fair bit of sediment; good, long cork. Unyielding on both nose and palate. Full, rich, intense, spicy essence of Cabernet. Lacks complexity at this stage. Incredible depth, loads of fruit. Needs six to eight extra years. Only 1,500 cases produced. Aged for 30 months in Merrain oak barrels. Reasonable production (40 hectolitres per hectare). This is the first vintage made by this winery (vines planted in 1970 and 1971).

MAS DE DAUMAS GASSAC 1980, VIN DE PAYS DE L'HERAULT, V. GUIBERT DE LA VAISSIÈRE:

100% Cabernet Sauvignon. Purchased in San Francisco in 1983 for $53 per case, a bargain!

❧ August 1984

Purplish, deep, dark, big, "hot" Cabernet and spicy Syrah style. Well made, fruity, well balanced. Some sediment. Should be ready in four to six years, and hold. Not very complex at this stage, but very good, and a great value.

❧ January 1993

With the council of the Commanderie de Bordeaux. Very dark, deep purple colour. Fair bit of sediment. Hot, spicy, very Rhône-like. Full, rich, tannic, young. Needs five to ten more years. Try again around 1996 to 1998. Great extract. Very good depth. Solid. Not complex, but big, and youthful. Pity to open this now.

MAS DE DAUMAS GASSAC 1981, VIN DE PAYS DE L'HERAULT, GUIBERT DE LA VAISSIÈRE:

Purchase price in 1984 is $64 per case.

❧ June 1984

Tried the first bottle of this vintage. Already throwing sediment. Long cork for good ageing. Very deep, dark, purplish colour. Young berry, fruity, concentrated Cabernet Sauvignon nose. Rich, full, well balanced, tannic (but not too much so). Excellent quality. Some day, this wine will become famous. I also have the 1980 and the 1978 (first commercial release).

❧ March 1988

With the panel of *The Wine Consumer.* 100% Cabernet Sauvignon. Deep, brilliant, purplish, young colour. Oak, spice, clean, intense, young fruit on nose. Some sediment. Decanted one hour. Tannic, firm, rich, spicy, fruity. Very Cabernet, yet spices of Rhône. Solid. Needs three to five years or more. Well balanced. Very good.

❧ December 26, 1996

Decanted one hour. Deep, dark, youthful colour to rim. Deep garnet. Spicy, "dusty," mineral on nose. Full, yet softening on palate. Excellent fruit extract. Approaching maturity, but no rush. Very good.

MAS DE DAUMAS GASSAC 1985, DE LA VAISSIÈRE:

❧ November 1990

With the council of the Commanderie de Bordeaux, Opened and decanted one-and-a-half hours. Some sediment. Very deep, youthful, purplish colour to rim. 80% Cabernet Sauvignon and 20% other Bordeaux varietals, plus Syrah, Tannat, and Pinot Noir! Very Cabernet nose, yet spicy, hot, even a bit leathery. Full, powerful, tannic, loads of ripe fruit. Not much complexity yet, but lots of power and fruit. Very good. At purchase, in 1988, this already cost $23 per bottle. Brochure included in box, with technical details, recommends waiting until the year 2000 to drink this. Too many people are discovering this wine and, consequently, the price is going up.

❧ August 1996

Comments as in 1990, but a bit more evolved, rounder on palate (not in glass: appearance is very deep purple of a one-year-old wine!). Luscious, fruity, round, long. Little tannin left. Straightforward, very fruity. Drink now to 2005.

MAS DE DAUMAS GASSAC "BLANC" 1991, DE LA VAISSIÈRE:

This is a blend of various white varietals. First vintage of this white wine was 1986. 40% Chardonnay, 40% Viognier, 10% Petit Manseng, 10% Muscat and Bourboulenc.

❧ November 1993

With the council of the Commanderie de Bordeaux. Bright gold. Low acidity, fat, fresh, elegant. Perfumy Viognier on nose and palate. Full, round, nice fruit. Forward. An unusual wine.

MAS DE DAUMAS GASSAC BLANC 1992, DE LA VASSIÈRE:

Made from a blend of Chardonnay, Petit Manseng, and Viognier.

❧ August 1996

At "Le Gavroche" restaurant, with Delia Viader, owner of Viader Vineyards on Howell Mountain, and Ingo Grady, the British Columbia agent for Dominus (Napanook Estate). Sturdy Pinot Blanc style. A bit hot and spicy (Viognier and geographic influence). Full, rich, a bit spicy, long. Good.

CALIFORNIA CABERNET SAUVIGNONS

SPRING MOUNTAIN "LES TROIS CUVÉES" CABERNET SAUVIGNON, NAPA VALLEY:

❧ May 1979

Deep colour, some tannin, minty, and cigar-box nose. Very rich wine. A blend of the 1975, 1976, and 1977 vintages. Very good quality. In spite of its depth, quite pleasant to drink now, but should last for quite a few years.

❧ August 2, 1981

Big, dark, peppery/fruity nose. Medium sediment. Good depth. Powerful. Very good now, but with enough fruit to last for quite some time. Very good value. (Paid $9 per bottle in 1978.)

❧ November 1985

Deep, dark, maturing colour. Big, chunky wine. Hot, high alcohol (has three vintages in it, including two drought years, 1976 and 1977, and the 1975). Starting to taste like an Australian beefy, mature Cabernet. Pruny. Needs drinking. Have I missed the boat?

SPRING MOUNTAIN "LOT H 68-69 LN" CABERNET SAUVIGNON N/V, NAPA VALLEY:

Purchased from Draper and Esquin's. Excellent neck level. Joe Heitz (with whom I had a bottle of this previously) told me that in the late 1960s, he was short of cash and had to sell "Martha's Vineyard" and Napa Cabernet as bulk wine! So "H" stands for Heitz, 68-69 is a blend of the 1968 and 1969 vintages, and LN means "Limousin/ Nevers." The 1968 was aged in Limousin oak, and the 1969 in Nevers oak.

❧ June 1991

With council of Le Tastevin Wine Club. Impressive, dark colour, with some maturity at rim. Intense, minty-eucalyptus nose. Full, solid, but losing some of its fruit. Dry and austere, yet still very much alive. Nose was the best part. A rare treat. This wine is now over 22 years old.

❧ December 1991

Mid shoulder level. Impressive, dark colour. Ripe, intense, cedary Cabernet nose. Full, rich, long on palate. Very good balance, depth, and ripe fruit. No rush. Surprisingly good! Better than when tasted previously, six months ago.

❧ New Year's Eve 1992

Upper shoulder level. Typical Heitz: minty-eucalyptus. Rich, long. Lovely nose. Very good on palate. Ready but no rush.

❧ May 13, 1994

At "Bishop's" restaurant, Vancouver, with Christian Moueix and Cherise Chen. Deep colour. Lovely cedary-minty, classic Heitz nose. Full, solid, rich, yet cracking up/high acidity at finish. An experience for Christian, who has never heard of this bottling.

GEMELLO "35TH ANNIVERSARY" CALIFORNIA CABERNET SAUVIGNON N/V:

According to a Butterfield and Butterfield auction catalogue, from whom I bid successfully on a lot of ten bottles, this is a blend of the 1959 and 1960 Vintages.

❧ New Year's Eve 1992:

Upper shoulder level. Toasty, bacon bits, rich, full, on nose. Powerful, sweet, yet drying out at finish. Good on palate. Excellent on nose. Impressive for a wine that is over 30 years old.

❧ January 26, 1993

Good neck level. Most tasters thought it was a 1961 or 1959 Bordeaux. Apparently in those days, most of the juice for Gemello's wines came from Ridge Vineyards. No "bacon bits" taste in this one. Round, rich, long. Claret-like. Surprisingly good. Better than above.

❧ February 1994

With council of the Commanderie de Bordeaux. Different from the January 1993 bottle. More rustic, harder, like a Shiraz. Full, woody/earthy, rich, spicy, and old-tasting. Seems to have some Shiraz in the blend.

HEITZ CELLARS NAPA CABERNET SAUVIGNON N/V:

This is the 1959 Hanzell Cabernet Sauvignon, their first vintage, bottled by Joe Heitz. Heitz told me that he remembers bottling it in 1962. Label doesn't indicate either vintage or Hanzell. Purchased at Butterfield and Butterfield auction. Barney Rhodes told me that this labelling is not unusual.

❧ February 1, 1991

Farewell dinner for the tasting panel of *The Wine Consumer*. Still full, dark, quite austere, and dry, but some fruit there. Nose subdued and spicy. Very little sediment. Joe Heitz told me in 1995 that Ivan Shaw—who helped finance Heitz Cellars so they could buy juice/grapes from Hanzell—produced and bottled some of this for himself, and stored it at his grandmother's cellar. That is where this wine came from originally.

❧ November 1995

Council of the Commanderie de Bordeaux. Served double-blind. Some sediment. Excellent level. Most participants thought it was a 1970 or 1966 Haut-Médoc. Cedar-eucalyptus nose. Some astringency/ acidity at finish; getting tired, yet still has good fruit.

Long on palate. Needs drinking, with food. Like drinking history.

INGLENOOK "CLASSIC CLARET" CABERNET SAUVIGNON 1958, NAPA VALLEY:

November 1994
Decanted 45 minutes. Some sediment. Classic cedar-vanilla-ripe fruit nose of older-style Napa Cabernets. Good, dark colour. At 36 years of age, it has held extremely well (good neck level). Full, rich, long, even a bit tannic! Loads of ripe fruit. Sweet, rich wine. Lovely extract, depth, and flavour. Excellent, and not even a "reserve" or "limited cask."

BEAULIEU VINEYARDS GEORGES DE LATOUR "PRIVATE RESERVE" CABERNET SAUVIGNON 1961, NAPA VALLEY:

September 12, 1996
Council meeting of the Commanderie de Bordeaux where I announced my intention to step down next year (April 1997). Ian Mottershead is to replace me as Maître. Good bottom neck level. Very pale, evolved colour, almost deep Rosé rather than red, yet lovely, spicy, sweet/vanilla nose. Light on palate, yet not flat. Hint of cedar and eucalyptus (the vineyard is located near "Martha's Vineyard"). Very forward, very soft. Was much better a decade ago but certainly not dead. Good "terroir" character. A rare experience.

INGLENOOK CABERNET SAUVIGNON 1962, ESTATE-BOTTLED, CASK F-3, NAPA VALLEY:

May 1985
From a private cellar. When I purchased this wine, it seemed (and was) expensive. Decanted 30 to 45 minutes. Fair bit of sediment. Deep, mature colour. Still some purple. Complex, eucalyptus, mint, spicy nose. Long and fabulous. Full, complex on palate. At its absolute perfection. Great intensity.

GEMELLO CALIFORNIA CABERNET SAUVIGNON 1968:

October 1978
Dark colour; oak and ripe fruit on nose; very little sediment. Opened one hour before tasting. Not as deep as the 1970 but a mature, clean Cabernet nose. Complex, "solid" wine. Wish I had a few more bottles of this. Spent five years in cask before being bottled!

BEAULIEU VINEYARDS GEORGES DE LATOUR "PRIVATE RESERVE" CABERNET SAUVIGNON 1969, NAPA VALLEY:

August 1978
Big, full wine. Decanted two hours. Good cedar nose; bright, deep colour. Will last for quite a few years. At the end of the evening, bouquet turned to vanilla and cedar. Very fine, complex wine. Overwhelmed the Château Fonplégade 1966 and the Grands Echézeaux 1970 (H. de Villamont), against which it was served.

CHARLES KRUG "RESERVE" CABERNET SAUVIGNON 1969, NAPA VALLEY:

February 1979
Served blind against 1969 Château Margaux 1969 and Château Petrus 1969. The nicest, fruitiest wine of the three but not as elegant as the Margaux. Nice California Cabernet Sauvignon bouquet, good fruit, some sediment. Very fine, round wine. Dark colour. Lasted best in glass, but then 1969 was a much finer year in California than in Bordeaux.

GEMELLO CALIFORNIA CABERNET SAUVIGNON 1970:

September 1986
With the panel of *The Wine Consumer*. Haven't tasted this wine since 1981. Deep, dark colour to rim with signs of maturity. Little sediment. Improved in the glass for an hour. Lovely, complex, open, ripe wine—not unlike a rich, ripe 1970 St. Estèphe, but darker and bigger. Fairly dry, still solid. At its absolute peak. Long, complex Cabernet Sauvignon finish. Very good.

BEAULIEU VINEYARD GEORGES DE LATOUR "PRIVATE RESERVE" CABERNET SAUVIGNON 1971, NAPA VALLEY:

December 1976
At the restaurant "Le Tastevin," in Seattle, after a fabulous bottle of 1966 Château Palmer. Good bouquet, bright colour. A wine of fine quality. Ready. American oak and vanilla obvious. Overshadowed by the superb 1966 Palmer.

May 1982
With friends, against 1971 Château Lafite and 1971 Château Lafleur Petrus. Dark colour, minty-eucalyptus bouquet, similar to a Mondavi Cabernet Sauvignon "Reserve." Not as pronounced as Heitz Cellar's "Martha's Vineyard." Not very complex, but most enjoyable. Fine bottle.

STERLING VINEYARDS "RESERVE" CABERNET SAUVIGNON 1973, NAPA VALLEY:

March 1981
At Sid Cross's, with Peter Sichel of Château Palmer. Dark colour, good Cabernet fruit on nose. Quite dry on palate. A bit short but pleasant. I liked it more than most. Other tasters thought it didn't have enough fruit.

January 1984
Tasted blind, against 1973 Petrus and 1973 Latour. A difficult and tricky tasting! Darkest (slightly darker than Latour). A relatively lean wine, much more Haut-Médoc than California in style, some mint on

nose. Good fruit. Long on palate. Overall, the favourite, but I preferred the nose on the Petrus.

❧ September 15, 1993
To celebrate Rosh Hashana, and my arrival in Vancouver exactly 20 years ago to the day. Surprisingly good. Fair bit of sediment. Mature but good, dark colour. Eucalyptus-spicy Cabernet nose. Round, complex, spicy. Has held very well. Both Sid Cross and I, 12 years ago, thought that this wine lacked fruit!

GEMELLO CABERNET SAUVIGNON 1974, CALIFORNIA:

❧ January 1988
Seldom-seen wine from a great vintage in California. Good, dark colour to rim, showing little sign of age. Some sediment. Rich, very-California nose and palate. Eucalyptus, spicy. Good depth, full, quite tannic, like a chewy 1975 Claret. Good length, complex. Needed two hours of airing. Intense, full, tannic. Very good. Drink now through 1994 or beyond.

ROBERT MONDAVI CABERNET SAUVIGNON 1974, NAPA VALLEY:

❧ January 1988
Surprisingly dark, deep colour to rim. Very good appearance. Spicy, herbal, oaky nose. Good extract. Deep, full, rich, very good balance, lots of fruit still. No rush drinking this. One-dimensional but good. Well-made wine; and this is only their regular, not the reserve wine!

❧ February 1991
Almost 17 years old and holding very well. Impressive deep colour for age. Perfumy, complex, cedary-Cabernet nose. Round, well balanced, long. Little tannin left but excellent fruit. Ready, but no rush. Very good. No doubt, my cool cellar (52°F) must have helped this wine last this long.

STERLING VINEYARDS "RESERVE" CABERNET SAUVIGNON 1974, NAPA VALLEY:

❧ May 1988
At home, against Robert Mondavi 1974 Cabernet Sauvignon" Reserve." Guests were Debbie Guimaraens, the young daughter of Bruce Guimaraens of Fonseca's, staying with us; the Gismondis; Mottersheads; and Randy and Patsy Sultan from Los Angeles. Sterling was deeper, livelier, crisper. More Bordeaux-like. Quite big, tannic, ripe, fruity. No rush. Well balanced. An excellent wine. Loads of fruit. The Mondavi was mintier, more eucalyptus, thicker, fatter, intense, big, and lovely. No rush there either. Two excellent bottles.

❧ May 1996
At 22 years of age, this is perfection now. More forward than eight years ago. Lovely, deep, maturing colour. Cedary, slightly minty nose. Long, spicy, rich, soft tannins, round. Very good depth and balance. At its peak now.

MAYACAMAS CABERNET SAUVIGNON 1974, NAPA VALLEY:

❧ April 1995
Impressive, deep colour for this 20-year-old. Eucalyptus, ripe berries, and American oak (sweet vanilla) nose. Full, intense, lots of fruit. Excellent backbone, even a bit tannic. Good fruit/acidity balance. If well cellared, this wine will last well into the 21st century.

BEAULIEU VINEYARDS GEORGES DE LATOUR "PRIVATE RESERVE" CABERNET SAUVIGNON 1974, NAPA VALLEY:

❧ February 1982
Had this wine twice previously, both times at tastings. Lovely dark colour, touch of orange. Some sediment. Flowery, spicy, sweet Cabernet Sauvignon bouquet. Little tannin left, but lovely concentration of fruit and flavour. Almost ready, elegant, but should hold well for some time. More "Lafite" than "Latour" in style.

❧ August 1985
Our 11th wedding anniversary. Deep colour to rim, good depth. Elegant, long, complex, and mature Cabernet nose. Full, long on palate, well balanced. Enjoyable now but will peak in two to three years. Its excellent structure will make this wine last for several more years.

❧ May 1989
Dark, maturing colour, orange rim. Pronounced, ripe American oak on nose. Full, rich, some sweetness noticeable. Smooth, velvety, long. Well balanced. Holding very well at 15 years of age. Many critics have been hard on this wine. I think that it is very good, made in the "old style," rich, American oak-aged fashion. Very good.

❧ July 1995
On Turnagain Island, with Bruno and France Prats, owners of Château Cos d'Estournel. (Also tasted 1988 Corton-Charlemagne of Tollot-Beaut's.) Bruno likes California Cabernets. At its peak. Red-browning colour at rim. Classic California-American oak/vanilla Cabernet. Long, round, soft, top quality. Great complexity, cigar box, sweet, mature Cabernet on both nose and palate. Will not improve. This wine is now 21 years old.

ROBERT MONDAVI "RESERVE" CABERNET SAUVIGNON 1974, NAPA VALLEY:

❧ December 29, 1984
While I have had this wine several times before, I have never opened a bottle of my own until tonight. Dark

colour, showing some age at rim. Warm, complex, open eucalyptus-spice nose. Full, rich, long, complex, soft (yet still tannic at ten years). Very fine quality. Almost ready, but will hold for many years.

❧ August 1985
Lots of sediment. Decanted one hour. Deep colour to rim. No sign of age (orange or brown). Spicy, complex Cabernet nose with hint of eucalyptus. Full, long, complex, little tannin left, but very well structured and should hold for many years. Lovely wine of great quality. This wine has 14% Merlot in it, and was aged in new French oak barrels for 30 months.

❧ April 1987
With Serge Hochar of Château Musar (Lebanon). A new experience for him. Dark, complex, long. Concentrated, fabulous mint-eucalyptus nose. Lovely fruit, some tannins, well balanced. A great wine! No rush. Serge agreed and was fascinated by its quality.

❧ July 1991
On Turnagain Island, with John Tilson, Ed Lazarus, and Stephen Kaplan. Very good wine. Getting ready. Other comments as above.

❧ June 11, 1994
That night, the Vancouver Canucks defeated the NY Rangers to force a seventh and final Stanley Cup game. Appearance as in February 1993. Other comments as above, with the eucalyptus typical of this wine. Long, rich, very good balance. Excellent wine. Now fully mature.

BURGESS "VINTAGE SELECTION" CABERNET SAUVIGNON 1975, NAPA VALLEY:

❧ July 1996
On Turnagain Island. After cellaring it for 18 years, at 21 years of age, it did not disappoint. Deep colour, ripe, American oak, Cabernet/minty, "California" nose. Ripe, sweet fruit on palate. Not very complex but certainly lots of fruit and length. Some sweetness, cedar. May not have "layers of complexity," but certainly alive and kicking.

CUVAISON "SIGNATURE" CABERNET SAUVIGNON 1975, NAPA VALLEY:

❧ September 1982
Signed by Philip Togni, the winemaker. Made with grapes from vineyards at the summit of Spring Mountain, St. Helena. Big, powerful, rich wine. Very tight. Needs many years of bottle-age. Inky, but backed by good, tight, concentrated fruit.

❧ March 1984
At home, with Peter Sichel of Château Palmer. Very dark, almost black. Decanted one-and-a-half hours. Some sediment. Structured like a big 1975 Bordeaux. Slight volatile acidity/alcohol on nose, which disappeared later. Big, massive wine. Needs years. Will the fruit outlast the tannin? Try again in 1987 or even 1990. One of the great successes of California Cabernets. Long, complex; magnificent, lingering Bordeaux bouquet in empty glass.

❧ November 9, 1987
Against 1975 Mondavi Cabernet Sauvignon "Reserve," with Harry and Prue Waugh. Mondavi better balanced and elegant. This Cuvaison "Signature" is massive. Very deep, dark, purplish colour. Briary, very intense, ripe fruit, powerful, tannic. Lacking charm. Lots of fruit, though. I think that it needs more time, however. At least five more years. Try again in 1992 or beyond.

SPRING MOUNTAIN CABERNET SAUVIGNON 1975, NAPA VALLEY:

❧ January 1992
Dense, deep colour to rim. Lots of sediment. Cedary, leathery, clean cigar-box nose. Full, powerful, long. Very rich. No rush. Loads of fruit. Very good. Powerful but excellent balance. Try again in 1994 to 1996.

❧ March 1994
Comments exactly as in January 1992. Who said California Cabernets do not age well?

ROBERT MONDAVI "RESERVE" CABERNET SAUVIGNON 1975, NAPA VALLEY:

❧ November 9, 1987
Against 1975 Chappellet Cabernet Sauvignon "Signature" with Harry and Prue Waugh, the Tobes, Freemans, and Ruy Paes-Braga, the General Manager of Vancouver's Four Seasons hotel. Elegant, very Claret-like. Spicy, well balanced, complex, delicate. Oak-vanilla, spicy. Very enjoyable. Ready, but no rush. Most preferred it to the massive Cuvaison.

❧ December 1990
At home, against 1975 Château Lafite with French Consul General Bernard Ledun, and several other guests. Very good, deep, lively colour. Some sediment. Spicy, yet tight, minty, oaky, eucalyptus nose. Medium-bodied, racey, elegant on palate. Good texture, smooth, but drying out a bit at the end.

❧ November 1993
Very good, deep colour. Decanted 30 minutes. Little sediment. Subdued cedar/Cabernet nose. Hint of smoky oak. Elegant, round, long. Very good balance, length, depth, fruit/acidity. All in harmony. Ready, but no rush if well cellared. Lovely wine that is now 18 years old.

STAG'S LEAP CABERNET SAUVIGNON 1977, LOT 2, NAPA VALLEY:

June 1986
Deep, young-looking. Intense. Spicy, "hot," alcoholic nose, due to the drought in 1977. Some sediment. After one hour it softened quite a bit. Well balanced, some cedar and spice. Round, long, clean finish. Solid, yet enjoyable. Ready, but no rush. Better than many 1977s I've tasted previously.

KEENAN CABERNET SAUVIGNON 1978, NAPA VALLEY:

June 1996
At 18 years, impressively purple, deep, youthful colour, like a six-year-old; big Cabernet! Spicy, rubber, oak/vanilla Cabernet nose. Ripe berries. Full, rich, certainly rounder than nine years ago, yet still very intense. Will last for a long time. One negative comment: in spite of its age, it has not developed complexity. One-dimensional. After the second glass, it became boring.

VILLA MOUNT EDEN CABERNET SAUVIGNON 1978, NAPA VALLEY:

November 1994
On Turnagain Island. My last bottle of this wine. Decanted 45 minutes. Some sediment. Maturing colour, good depth. Classy, spicy, minty nose of Napa Cabernets. Round, soft, forward, well balanced. Velvety fruit, long finish. At its peak. Most enjoyable. It has spent the past 12 years in my cellar, at a cool storage temperature of 52°F, which may explain why it lasted so long, so well.

HEITZ CELLARS "MARTHA'S VINEYARD" CABERNET SAUVIGNON 1978, NAPA VALLEY:

January 1996
At "Star Anise" restaurant in Vancouver. Deep colour to rim. Hint of eucalyptus. Full, rich, long. A bit sharp, acidic, but backed by good fruit. Ready, soft tannin, but enough concentration to last a few more years.

RIDGE "MONTE BELLO" CABERNET SAUVIGNON 1978:

"Santa Cruz Mountains." 94% Cabernet Sauvignon, 6% Merlot.

January 1984
This is a magnificent Cabernet needing at least five more years to reach its peak. A classic! Great extract, cedar, oak, ripe fruit all in harmony. I must get some more of this. Great potential.

STAG'S LEAP WINE CELLARS "CASK 23" CABERNET SAUVIGNON 1979, STAG'S LEAP VINEYARDS (THEIR RESERVE WINE):

July 1985
This bottle was given to me by Warren Winiarski, the owner, during a visit to the winery.

June 1988
Dinner at home, with panel of *The Wine Consumer*. I served a vertical of Stag's Leap Wine Cellars, as follows, double-blind. All four wines had impressive, deep, dark colours, much younger-looking than their age would indicate.

1978 LOT 2:

Deep colour to rim. Spicy, rich Cabernet nose. More elegant, leaner on palate. Soft tannins, long, spicy, complex. Ready, but no rush. Good fruit, stylish.

1976 LOT 2:

The favourite and most mature of the flight. Full, tobacco, rich, complex nose. Long, elegant, not too "hot" (yet 1976 and 1977 were drought years). Elegant, complex. Very good. Lots of class here. While ready, no rush drinking this wine. Very pleasant. Some mintiness.

1977 LOT 2:

Even darker than the 1976. Harder, more tannic. A solid wine. No rush. Full, serious, fruity, long, clean finish. Good Cabernet spiciness.

1979 CASK 23:

Different style than above three. More refined, more elegant, less weight. Not as intense. May need two to three more years. At this stage, I prefer the 1976 Lot 2. An elegant complex wine, though. Tobacco, spices on nose. Promising and very good.

BEAULIEU VINEYARDS GEORGES DE LATOUR "PRIVATE RESERVE" CABERNET SAUVIGNON 1979, NAPA VALLEY:

July 1996
Deep, youthful colour. Very California nose (mint, eucalyptus), yet not the vanilla and American-oak characteristics typical of Beaulieu Vineyards. Full, rich, mature. Very good fruit extract, ripe, sweet. Ready, but no rush. The best BV produced since 1974.

DUCKHORN CABERNET SAUVIGNON 1980, NAPA VALLEY:

July 1994
Incredibly inky, deep-purple colour, chunky, youthful. Very good balance. Lots of extract of very ripe fruit. Good acidity. This 14-year-old wine tastes like a four-year-old! Too young and intense. We couldn't finish the bottle. Needs five to ten more years. At this stage, it seems one-dimensional.

Château Chevalier Cabernet Sauvignon 1980, Napa Valley:

❧ November 1993

Decanted one hour. Very deep, dense, youthful colour to rim. Smells like a Rhône or an Australian Hermitage. Full, sturdy, tight, needs time. Dryish but good fruit. Solid, tannic, lots of depth. Too powerful for me. This winery does not exist any more.

Heitz Cellars "Martha's Vineyard" Cabernet Sauvignon 1980, Napa Valley:

❧ October 1991

Decanted 45 minutes. Little sediment. Youthful, dark colour to rim. Slightly leathery, eucalyptus, oak nose. Not overblown like the 1974. Elegant, subdued. Very good balance, fruit, tannins, acids. Should peak around 1993 or 1994 and last beyond 2000. Understated, in the context of this fine wine's style.

Heitz Cellars "Bella Oaks" Cabernet Sauvignon 1980, Napa Valley:

❧ December 5, 1993

Memorial to Grandma Jenny, my mother, who passed away a year ago. Unmistakable Heitz style. Hint of eucalyptus, spicy, still lively, well balanced, nice fruit. No rush. Little sediment.

Robert Mondavi "Reserve" Cabernet Sauvignon 1980, Napa Valley:

❧ April 1991

Dark colour; spicy oak, eucalyptus nose. Complex, soft, yet good fruit and balance. Long, nice drinking now, but no rush. Some sediment. Elegant rather than big. (Cool weather in 1980.)

Dominus Estate 1983, Napa Valley:

❧ May 1985

This is the first vintage produced by this winery. I tasted it from barrel with Harry Waugh and Daniel Baron, the manager of Christian Moueix's estate in Yountville. Then we had some at lunch at the Meadowood Club. The chef there prepared us some duck. Into the sauce, he put some of the 1983 Dominus we brought along. This must be the first time anywhere that this wine was used to produce a sauce!

Robin Lail is one of John Daniel's two daughters, partners of Moueix in this venture. She manages the Meadowood Club. She was there and we had a nice chat.

Mondavi-Rothschild "Opus One" 1983, Napa Valley:

❧ April 1, 1993

At home, with Jacques Hebrard of Château Cheval-Blanc and Francis Fouquet, Grand Maître of the Commanderie de Bordeaux. Medium dark colour. New oak, spicy Cabernet. Austere, leaner style. Good fruit. Still tight. Wait till 1996 to 2000. Promising.

Dominus Estate 1984, John Daniel Society, Napa Valley:

A box of six bottles was given to me by Daniel Baron, manager of Dominus (Napanook). He told me that Christian Moueix phoned and told him to set aside these bottles for me. Made from a blend of about 75% Cabernet Sauvignon and 25% Cabernet Franc and Merlot. 4,000 cases produced in 1984, their second vintage, which was released before the 1983.

❧ May 1990

Tried a bottle. Still very young, tight on both nose and palate. Not as luscious as the 1985; more austere. Try around 1995.

Dominus 1985, John Daniel Society, Napa Valley.

❧ April 1, 1993

At home, with Francis Fouquet, Grand Maître of the Commanderie de Bordeaux, and Mrs. Fouquet; Mr. and Mrs. Jacques Hebrard of Château Cheval-Blanc; and friends, including Bernard Ledun, French Consul General to Vancouver. (Also tasted 1983 Opus One, 1982 Pol Roger "Chardonnay," 1976 Rieussec, 1986 Corton-Charlemagne, both Moillard's and Latour's, 1975 Château Palmer, and 1961 Château l'Arrosée.) This wine was aged in second-year Cheval-Blanc barrels. The depth, ripeness, intensity typical of the 1985s. Excellent wine. Full, rich, long, very good balance, clean finish. Good now, but will improve. Better, in my opinion, than either the 1983 or 1984.

Heitz Cellars "Martha's Vineyard" Cabernet Sauvignon 1985, Napa Valley:

❧ June 1993

With council of the Commanderie de Bordeaux. Decanted one hour. Very deep, intense colour. Minty, eucalyptus, classic "Martha's" nose. Full, rich, very good balance. Slightly too alcoholic and finishes dry, but it needs time. Will be very good. Some tasters thought it was too dry, too alcoholic and that it had a sharp, dry finish. I disagree. Try again in 1998 or well into the 21st century.

Heitz Cellars "Martha's Vineyard" Cabernet Sauvignon 1986, Napa Valley:

❧ June 1995

At "Bishop's" restaurant. A classy wine that is not quite ready. Very good, deep red colour. Not as pronounced eucalyptus as the 1985, but very good, spicy, cedary Cabernet nose. Full, rich, long. Good, ripe tannins, acid, fruit balance. Drink from 1998 to 2003.

DUCKHORN "HOWELL MOUNTAIN" CABERNET SAUVIGNON 1989:

Given to me by Margaret Duckhorn during a visit to the winery in April 1993. This is their first vintage of this wine. Later vintages will include more Merlot and less Cabernet Sauvignon. Blend of the 1989: 41% Cabernet Sauvignon, 34% Merlot, 25% Cabernet Franc. A nice mid-term wine, say in three to four years.

ZINFANDELS AND OTHER CALIFORNIA REDS

ZINFANDELS

RIDGE GEYSERVILLE ZINFANDEL 1973, CALIFORNIA:

❧ May 28, 1983

On Carol's birthday. I had this wine previously in San Francisco in 1980, before a Hubelein wine auction. Dark, purplish colour, not showing its ten years! Sweet nose. Some sediment. Decanted one hour. Fruity, spirity wine (14.7° alcohol). Good acidity, no tannins. Long on palate. At first it could be mistaken for a Merlot, but later on the spicy flavour of Zinfandel came through. Also hint of St. Emilion, especially when left in the glass for some time. At its peak, but no rush. Excellent quality. One of the classic Zinfandels and a rare wine. Made from grapes from Lytton Springs Vineyards (old vines) and described as "late picked." An excellent Zinfandel.

MAYACAMAS LATE HARVEST ZINFANDEL 1974:

❧ September 1979

Tasted half-bottle, purchased at the winery. Very intense and bright. Very fruity and 16° alcohol. Needs at least four to five extra years. I do not like Late Harvest Zinfandels, but this is a real experience. I fear that it is not well balanced. Future uncertain, but impressive now. A curiosity.

JOSEPH SWAN ZINFANDEL 1974, SONOMA VALLEY:

❧ May 1985

Tasted against a bottle of 1975 by the same producer. The 1974 turned out to be the better wine, and quite outstanding. Almost Claret-like. Layers of cedary, earthy fruit, complex, spicy, long. Well balanced.

RIDGE "SHENANDOAH" ZINFANDEL 1978:

❧ March 1987

With panel of *The Wine Consumer*. Some sediment. Ridge wines usually hold their colour well. Made with 5% Syrah. "Late Harvest" 15.9° alcohol. 2.7% residual sugar. Ripe berries, intense, fruity nose. Full, rich, big. Good fruit. Not my type of wine. Too big, heavy. Others liked it.

❧ May 1992

On Turnagain Island. Good, dark, maturing colour. Some sediment. Decanted 45 minutes. Spicy, sweet nose. Full, yet soft, and round, not unlike a rich Merlot. Spicy, good fruit and length. Not too sweet. Has improved quite a bit.

MERLOTS

STERLING VINEYARDS MERLOT 1974, NAPA VALLEY:

❧ May 1985

Served blind against 1974 Sterling Vineyards Napa Cabernet Sauvignon. Both were surprisingly full, dark, and young for their age. The Merlot was sweeter, spicier, more herbaceous, simpler; easy to like. It has held extremely well. The Cabernet was more austere, drier, more solid, with some tannins. No rush drinking that one either. Both very good quality. 1974 was a great vintage in California.

❧ March 1987

Still youthful, well structured; dark, young colour. Fruity, complex, open nose; round, still a bit tannic. Long, clean finish. Not unlike a 1974 Cabernet. Sterling made excellent wines in the 1970s. Alas, this is not the case nowadays.

CHÂTEAU CHEVALIER MERLOT 1978, SONOMA VALLEY:

❧ January 1986

Fair bit of sediment. Very dark, deep colour. Spicy, sweet, rich nose, yet vegetal and sharp. Similar impressions on palate. Full, rich, but a bit sharp, and too herbaceous for me. Rich, "sweet" Merlot wine. Ready, but no rush. I don't like the style.

DUCKHORN "THREE PALMS VINEYARD" MERLOT 1978, NAPA VALLEY:

❧ May 1985

At home, with Bruce Guimaraens, the gifted winemaker of Fonseca's Ports. Rich, luscious fruit. Needs five more years. Very good potential. This first vintage retails now (1991) for US$100 a bottle! As of this year, practically the whole "Three Palms Vineyard" in the northern end of the Napa Valley is struck by phylloxera. The owner now sells grapes from this fine vineyard to Sterling Vineyards, too.

❧ August 1995

On Turnagain Island, with Brad Klein from Los Angeles. Upper neck level. Expansive, ripe, vegetal, open nose. Slightly leathery, and minty. Nose (bouquet) is the best part. Good fruit on palate. Good, deep colour. Complex, spicy, sweet, soft fruit. One flaw: a bit sharp and acidic finish. This wine is now a collector's item, selling for $150 per bottle. Not worth it, but that is what scarcity does. It is also this winery's first vintage.

ZD CALIFORNIA MERLOT 1979:

75% Napa, 25% Santa Barbara (100% Merlot)

❧ October 1990

Surprisingly youthful, deep colour for an 11-year-old. Mellow, round, sweet fruit. Spicy, rich Merlot. Well balanced, easy to drink. Will last for some time, but will not improve.

RUTHERFORD HILL MERLOT 1979, NAPA VALLEY:

❧ November 1983

At home, at a council meeting of Chaîne des Rôtisseurs. Dark, concentrated, fruity; a well-structured. Good fruit, easy to drink and enjoy. Will hold well. I am presently acting as cellerier of our branch of the Chaîne des Rôtisseurs.

GRIGNOLINO

Grignolino "Private Stock" N/V, Napa Valley:

Produced by Leon Brendel, Grignolino Vineyards and Cellars. This winery is now called Heitz Cellars. Joe Heitz gave me this rare bottle. He had seven bottles left. He bottled it in 1961 after he purchased the winery from Brendel in 1960 —and found this wine still in oak casks. Joe suspects it is made from the 1958 or 1959 vintages. The label read: "Only one— Grignolino, true varietal wine."

❧ June 1988

Dinner with the panel of *The Wine Consumer*. Appearance and nose of old Volnay; palish red. Sweet, spicy nose. Better on nose than on palate. Sweet, simple, little complexity. Not much stuffing. A little sediment. An historic, rare bottle. Quite unusual.

PINOT NOIRS

Beaulieu Vineyards "Los Carneros" Pinot Noir 1976, Napa Valley:

❧ May 1981

A massive wine. Very dark, fruity, sweet nose. Lots of fruit and tannin. Needs five to eight years. Not very complex or elegant, but big. Good aftertaste. Old-style, sturdy wine.

❧ June 1989

At home, with David and Kate Dougdale of O. W. Loeb & Co. of London. Big, rich, dark, ripe, herbaceous. Made in a drought year. Too alcoholic. Not my type of wine, but not bad. Old-style, blockbuster wine. First vintage ever for Beaulieu Vineyard's Pinot Noir from Carneros.

❧ November 1995

Probably some Syrah in the blend. Comments generally as eight years ago. Just slightly rounder and softer. Quite herbaceous, dark, very ripe. Unusual. Not my style and very little resemblance (if any) to true Pinot Noir.

Martin Ray "Winery Lake" Pinot Noir 1977, Carneros, Napa Valley:

❧ September 1996

With the council of the Commanderie de Bordeaux when I announced my intention of stepping down as Maître in April 1997. Had it against 1982 Kalin Sonoma Pinot Noir "Cuvée DD." Very Martin Ray style. Deep colour, big, herbaceous, stemmy. Lots of extract, body, little terroir-elegance character. Old-style California Pinot, yet had good fruit, complexity, exotic spices, and length. Interesting.

Martin Ray himself couldn't have made this wine as he passed away several years earlier. Probably produced by his son.

Caymus Pinot Noir 1977, Napa Valley:

❧ December 1987

Deep, dark, old-style California Pinot Noir. Chunky, spicy, but well balanced. Not at all French-style Pinot Noir, but lots of fruit extract, and rich. Not really my style of wine, though. Should hold for three to four more years.

❧ June 1991

With council of Le Tastevin. Very deep, intense colour. Ripe, intense, stemmy, vegetal nose. Not unlike a big Syrah. Too dry, very powerful, tannic, old-style California Pinot Noir. No charm or elegance, and little Pinot Noir character here.

SANFORD AND BENEDICT PINOT NOIR 1978:

October 1983
At a "Le Tastevin" tasting of Pinot Noirs. Big, dark wine. Very stemmy, old-style California Pinot Noir. Sturdy, hefty, not at all like the more stylish, modern California Pinots. Like drinking a green salad!

CAYMUS PINOT NOIR 1978, NAPA VALLEY:

January 1989
Against Villa Mount Eden 1978 Pinot Noir "Tres Niños," Napa Valley, and two 1978 Grand Cru Burgundies. Darkest, youngest-looking of flight. Medium dark, still youthful. Typical Caymus extract, yet not a blockbuster. Herbal, spicy nose. Fruity, clean, long, solid. Well balanced. If it lacks anything, it is complexity. Otherwise a sound, well-made Pinot Noir. No rush drinking it. Better than the 1977.

VILLA MOUNT EDEN "TRES NIÑOS VINEYARD" PINOT NOIR 1978, NAPA VALLEY:

January 1989
Tasted against Caymus Napa 1978 Pinot Noir and two 1978 red Burgundies. Ullage one-and-a-half inches (leakage?). Complex, spicy, herbaceous, Napa-style Pinot Noir. Fairly simple, at its peak. Well balanced, soft. Good fruit and clean, spicy finish.

TUALATIN OREGON PINOT NOIR 1979, WILLAMETTE VALLEY:

October 1983
At a tasting of Pinot Noirs. This wine was a "gold medallist." Undrinkable, pale, vegetal, "sweetened" soup.

BACIGALUPI PINOT NOIR 1979, SONOMA COUNTY:

June 1983
Medium colour, showing some age (yet it is a young wine). Good, French-character Pinot Noir, earthy, spicy. A bit high in acidity. Quite soft and forward. Not unlike a Volnay, but really maturing fast. Quite good.

July 1985
At my 40th birthday party. Comments as above. Soft, forward, and getting tired. Not bad, though.

KALIN CELLARS PINOT NOIR 1980, SANTA BARBARA:

June 1995
With council of the Commanderie de Bordeaux against 1982 Gevrey-Chambertin "En Pallud," Bernard Maume, both owners/winemakers being eccentric intellectuals. Nice fruit, good Pinot Noir character. Quite fresh and spicy for a 15-year-old. A bit herbaceous. Nice cherry character, clean. A bit acidic at finish. More Rhône-like spiciness. Made in a hot environment. A rustic wine.

KALIN CELLARS "CUVÉE DD" PINOT NOIR 1982, SONOMA VALLEY:

November 1989
US Consul General to Vancouver Sam Fromowitz brought this bottle along for dinner. Deep, bright colour. Fresh, spicy nose. Some oak. Fruity, youthful for its age. Spicy, straightforward. Good varietal character, but without the barnyardy smells and flavours of red Burgundies. Quite good. Tasted it against two 1982 red Burgundies.

September 1996
At 14 years of age, this wine has retained its Pinot Noir character but is tannic, hard, even unyielding, and a bit dry. Austere wine. Lacks charm. Not unlike 1983 red Burgundies, but without the rot. One wished it had retained more fruit and more elegance.

PETITE SYRAH

MIRASSOU "MONTEREY" PETITE SYRAH 1976, UNFILTERED:

❧ February 1980

Dark purple colour. Quite big, still very young, steely wine. Quite fruity. Should make a good bottle in two to three years.

❧ August 1991

Lots of sediment. Very good level. Dark, mature colour. Spicy, black fruit, warm nose. Full, warm, generous. Straightforward. Good fruit, well balanced. Ready, but no rush. Has held very well.

CALIFORNIA CHARDONNAYS

HEITZ CELLARS PINOT CHARDONNAY 1973, LOT Z-32, NAPA VALLEY:

Purchased it recently (1996) from a private source. Cost: $40. This is one of the last famous "Pinot Chardonnays" from Joe Heitz. At 23 years, it will hopefully still be good. In the past, this was an excellent wine. Tasted on four previous occasions since 1977. Each time it was outstanding.

❧ September 1996

With the council of the Commanderie de Bordeaux. Very deep gold. Hint of botrytis, oxidation on nose. Like a late harvest wine. Big, soft, little Chardonnay character (but it is there). Rich, nutty, full. Was much better 15 years or even ten years ago. Drinking history.

MAYACAMAS CHARDONNAY 1975, NAPA VALLEY:

❧ September 1978

This wine was available in various stores in Napa and San Francisco, but most merchants refused to sell more than a bottle per customer. Tasted a half-bottle, purchased from Bob Travers, the owner/winemaker of Mayacamas. Rich, golden colour. Intense bouquet, full taste. A wine of great quality. Will improve in one to two years.

❧ March 1982

At a dinner for Harry Waugh. Pale-gold colour. Delicate, complex nose, not too oaky, lemony, or pungent. Fabulous flavour and long aftertaste. Lovely fruit/acidity balance, and enough life in it to last for two more years at its peak. One of the three loveliest California Chardonnays I've tasted to date. Others were the 1973 Château Montelena, Napa Valley, and the 1979 Chalone. Really great. (18)

❧ February 1986

As great as they come! Superb wine. Perfect balance. At over ten years of age, it has held very well. Long, complex, yet delicate nose. Round, well balanced, and long on palate. A lot of class and breed. One of the very best California Chardonnays I have ever tasted. Magnificent wine. (18)

❧ June 1989

My last bottle, with the council of Le Tastevin Wine Club. Deep, brilliant gold colour. Oak and ripe, buttery, mature Chardonnay on nose. Full, rich, intense, ripe, yet with enough acidity. Great intensity but needs drinking. Lots of depth here. Impressive. Almost a meal by itself, yet not too alcoholic or "hot." Nose was best part. Was better three years ago, but still impressive.

Château Montelena Chardonnay 1975, Napa and Alexander Valleys:

❧ May 1982
"French-style" California Chardonnay. Good acidity, complex, clean, mature nose. Made by Mike Grgich, who now owns his own winery in the Napa Valley. Good wine and well balanced. Ready, yet with life in it. Unusual for California Chardonnays, which start their life as big "show" wines, yet seem to mature, go flat, and decline after only two to three years.

Sterling Vineyards Chardonnay 1975, Napa Valley:

❧ October 1986
Before a trip to Peru with my son Michael. Have kept this last bottle for quite some time. At 11 years of age, it has held surprisingly well. This is a rare wine today, retailing for US$35. Bright gold, young-looking. Complex, elegant, long, classic, and subdued nose. Full, yet round, perfectly balanced. Amazingly, no rush drinking it. Great length! One of the finest, classiest California Chardonnays I have tasted to date. Well worth the $9 paid back in 1979. Recent vintages of this winery's Chardonnays are not nearly as good.

Sterling Vineyards Chardonnay 1976, Napa Valley:

❧ October 1979
Against 1976 Meursault, Ropiteau. The Meursault was no match for this wine. Complex oak, honeyed nose; good flavours, but a bit too much oak and not very clean or crisp. Lacks a bit in acidity but overall a good wine. Obviously made in a drought year.

Mayacamas Chardonnay 1976, in magnums:

❧ August 1981
Quite fat, luscious, yet elegant, round, and very drinkable. Lovely wine, well made and well balanced. Good aftertaste. Ready, yet should hold well for at least two to three more years, especially in magnums.

❧ June 1988
Last magnum at special dinner with panel of *The Wine Consumer*. Served blind against magnum of 1976 Chante Alouette (Chapoutier, white Hermitage). Deep, mature gold (but not as deep as the Hermitage); buttery popcorn, fruity, oaky nose of mature Chardonnay. Full, complex, good acidity and backbone. Has held very well. Rich, long, not overly intense. Ready, even in magnums.

Château St. Jean "Beltane Ranch" Chardonnay 1976, Sonoma Valley:

❧ March 1981
Bright-gold colour. Elegant, complex, not too heavy oak on nose, yet typical California. Good flavour, well balanced. Not overwhelming, elegant. Good acidity and good aftertaste. At its peak and should hold there for at least two more years. Lately I've been disappointed with some Château St. Jean Chardonnays (even with the "Robert Young" Vineyard), going flat and flabby too early, so this is a pleasant surprise.

ZD Vineyards "Patusquet Vineyard" Chardonnay 1977, Santa Barbara:

❧ November 1980
Crisp, clean, intense nose. Full, fruity, quite high acidity. Sonoma style. Well made and a favourite Chardonnay of mine. Needs one to two years. Excellent.

❧ October 1981
Lovely bouquet, typical greenness, stemminess on palate. Good flavour and balance. Good acidity, well rounded. Similar in structure to white Burgundy rather than California Chardonnay. Very good.

❧ August 1983
On Turnagain Island. Had it with fabulous barbecued Coho salmon I caught that same afternoon. This wine has developed very well. Over the years, it has lost its intense vegetal, oak nose, has mellowed and become more elegant with good balance of acid, fruit, and long aftertaste. Very good wine.

Château St. Jean "Robert Young Vineyard" Chardonnay 1977, Sonoma Valley:

❧ November 1980
Bright gold in colour. Expansive, elegant, lovely nose. High alcohol, clean, a bit tight, fruity. Big wine of excellent quality. Needs one to two more years. One of the better California Chardonnays.

❧ June 1981
Green-gold. Elegant nose, not very intense. Not very long on palate. It is amazing how such a famous wine has deteriorated so fast. Still has class and elegance, but no intensity. Drink up.

Château St. Jean "Les Pierres Vineyard" Chardonnay 1977, Sonoma Valley:

❧ July 1981
On Turnagain with lovely barbecued salmon. (I caught it the same morning off Thormanby Island. The biggest Coho I've caught to date: 11 pounds.) Deep gold. Slightly fizzy. Fairly low acidity. Intense, oaky, honey nose. Good flavour, heavy, on the sweet side. A bigger, fatter Château St. Jean style. Ready.

Château St. Jean "Robert Young Vineyard" Chardonnay 1978, Sonoma Valley:

❧ April 1982
Lovely, elegant bouquet. Good oak, honey, but not very intense. Good acidity, well balanced, elegant,

long, well made. A hard-to-find wine (only 1,000 cases produced).

❧ February 1987
This wine has held surprisingly well for eight years. Bright, mature golden colour. Rich, oak-ripe Chardonnay nose; slightly vegetal, typical of Sonoma. Similar impressions on palate. Rich, full, still has good fruit. Round, long. A big, rich, mature Chardonnay.

GRGICH HILLS CHARDONNAY 1978, NAPA VALLEY:

❧ April 1982
Fabulous bottle! After so many Chardonnays which, when still young, start to age prematurely, finally a well-balanced wine with a good future. Lovely bouquet, not too intense; alcohol 13.5º; not too high. Good fruit/acidity balance, still youthful. No rush to drink this wine. Mike Grgich is the winemaker who brought Château Montelena to fame with their 1973 Chardonnay, which achieved a first-place medal in Paris in 1975 at a now-famous Burgundy versus California Chardonnays competition.

❧ October 1986
Disappointing. Dark, bright gold. Oxidized on both nose and palate. Some fruit, but clearly over-the-hill. Pity. I waited too long to drink this wine.

CHÂTEAU ST. JEAN "ROBERT YOUNG VINEYARD" CHARDONNAY 1979, SONOMA VALLEY :

❧ April 1983
Elegant, complex, oaky, green apples on nose. First impression when tasted: too sweet and heavy. Later on improved. Good acidity, well balanced. Ready. I wonder how long it will last. California Chardonnays have this tendency to win gold medals when young, but they fade fast, and their life span is so short. What a pity. Also, to my taste, they are too heavy and assertive to be enjoyed with food.

❧ December 1984
Bright-gold colour. Round, full, mature, long, luscious wine. Incredible intensity. Almost too rich for me but very good. A meal by itself.

❧ June 1987
With David and Kate Dougdale of O. W. Loeb and Co. of London. Very deep gold, yet not tired-looking. Intense, full, rich, well balanced. One of the last successes to date for St. Jean's "Robert Young" Chardonnay. Full, long, classy. At its peak, but no rush. Less heavy-handed, it seems, than when last tasted in 1984.

❧ April 1988
Surprisingly, the colour was not unlike Chablis (green-gold, very good depth). A well-made, well-balanced wine. Its rich structure has helped it age gracefully. Lots of fruit. Ready and very good. Maybe I was wrong in this instance about my comments in 1983. It has held better than expected.

STERLING VINEYARDS CHARDONNAY 1979, NAPA VALLEY:

❧ April 1987
At home, with Serge Hochar of Château Musar in Lebanon. Serge described this wine as "sweet-sour and salty," but still pretty good. Improved a lot after 45 minutes in the glass. Elegant, long, complex, well structured, but starting to show signs of age. Drink up.

MATANZAS CREEK WINERY CHARDONNAY 1979:

73% Sonoma and 27% Napa grapes. No alcoholic content indicated on label!

❧ June 1983
Upon my return from Napa and the purchase of a condominium in Yountville. Medium-gold, bright colour. Oak on nose, not overpowering. Good acidity, well balanced. Long and lovely, without being too big or too spirity. Clean, classy finish. Ready, but should hold.

❧ August 1987
On Turnagain Island, with Joe and Alice Heitz who spent a couple of days with us in Secret Cove. Joe had never tasted a Matanzas Chardonnay before and he was impressed by the quality. Deep, bright-gold colour. Great intensity. Vegetal, yet rich overtones typical of Sonoma. Round, well balanced. Good fruit and acidity. Very nice wine.

CHALONE VINEYARDS CHARDONNAY 1979, CALIFORNIA:

❧ December 1980
Very French in style. Medium-gold colour. Toasty nose. "Montrachet"-like. Lovely flavour, elegant, complex. Fabulous. Not the usual heavy Chalone style that does not appeal to me. Good fruit/acidity balance and needs one to two more years, but even now it is great. A very pleasant surprise!

❧ January 1983
Medium-gold, clear, bright colour. Good oak, some honey, clean nose, long. On palate: medium intensity, slightly high alcohol, and seemed a bit off balance, but long, elegant, full, rich, yet not too heavy. A most enjoyable Chardonnay. Had it been better balanced, it would have been a classic. Nevertheless, very good.

❧ February 1989
Holding extremely well. Soft at almost ten years of age, round, lots of depth, and rich, ripe, mature fruit. Full, long, complex. An excellent Chardonnay. Quite soft now. Drink up before it starts to decline.

❧ April 1990
Last bottle, on the eve of a trip to Prague and Budapest. Great bottle. Bright, deep-golden colour. Rich nose of fine Meursault or Corton-Charlemagne-1978 style. Full, rich, long, intense, well balanced. At 11 years of age, has held extremely well. Classic, long, full Chardonnay. Lots of depth. One of the best California Chardonnays I've tasted recently. Some California Chardonnays do age well after all.

KEENAN CHARDONNAY 1979, NAPA VALLEY:

❧ May 1981
With Charles Brossier of Borie-Manoux. Very young, just purchased. Deep-gold colour. Good, clean nose; slightly vegetal, but already showing well. Youthful fruit/acidity. Needs one to two years. Not massive by California standards. Very well made.

❧ May 2, 1986
Opening day of Expo 86 in Vancouver. This wine has held very well. Long, complex, a little fuller and more mature than it used to be, but still good. Very enjoyable, well balanced wine. Good length. I have underestimated the staying power of this wine. Maybe my cool cellar (52°F) had something to do with this.

KISTLER "CUTRER" CHARDONNAY 1979, SONOMA VALLEY:

❧ May 1982
Bright-gold colour; expansive bouquet. Actually on nose, it seemed more French than California (at first: toasty nose. Later, as it warmed up, it developed the characteristics of California Chardonnays: honey and oak). Long, clean flavour. Good acidity, which is promising in terms of longevity. Good fruit, good complexity, big yet not overwhelming, which is one of the main problems of many California Chardonnays. Lovely wine.

❧ October 1982
Darkish-gold colour. Toasty-oaky nose, almost resembling a Corton-Charlemagne. On palate: very little acidity, going flat and flabby. What a disappointment these "great" Californians are. With a few rare exceptions, these prize-winning wines (when they are young) tend to fall apart suddenly after one or two years!

KISTLER "DUTTON RANCH" CHARDONNAY 1979, SONOMA VALLEY:

❧ February 1983
At home, with Carol, and Eli Appelbaum, my "army days" friend, who is now an economics professor at York University in Toronto. Bright, clear-gold colour. Good oaky-fruity nose. Didn't seem as fat, flabby, or tired as the "Cutrer" Sonoma, but not very complex. However, because it wasn't "tired" and flabby, it was a pleasant surprise. (I had heard from people who had tasted it recently and didn't like it.) Crisp, good flavour.

❧ December 1985
Last bottle. The nose of a rich Corton-Charlemagne. On palate: unmistakable California, but long, complex, and well balanced. At its peak and, because of its balance, it has held very well.

KISTLER "WINERY LAKE" CHARDONNAY 1979, SONOMA VALLEY:

❧ October 1983
Production of only 3,900 bottles. A rare wine. Deep-gold colour; bright, almost mature Sauternes-like. Lovely, elegant, yet big oak-toast on nose. Big mouthful of wine. Buttery, fruity, rich, intense, and long; good acidity. For those who love big Chardonnays. In any event, a lovely bottle.

❧ March 1984
At home, with Peter Sichel of Château Palmer, and Joan and Sid Cross. Medium, deep-gold colour. Intense, toasty-oak nose. A blend of California and Burgundy. Not very massive, but full, rich, and forward. Ready, excellent quality. A new experience for Peter.

❧ June 1991
Now 12 years old. I was worried when I opened my last bottle. Very deep gold, like a 1976 Sauternes or 1962 or 1959 white Burgundy, or a Sherry. Very mature, sweet, intense Chardonnay nose, but not oxidized. Intense, rich raisins. Long. Good acidity has helped this wine last. Creamy, full, long. Unusual, not unlike a late harvest wine. I've had rich Meursaults 1945 that tasted like this! Amazing that comments are similar to first bottle I tasted back in 1983, when it was only four years old.

EDNA VALLEY VINEYARD CHARDONNAY 1980, SAN LUIS OBISPO:

❧ Early August 1985
As close to a Louis Latour Corton-Charlemagne as one could get! Nutty, complex, long, hard to guess this wine as California. Lovely.

❧ Late August 1985
At a vertical tasting of Louis Latour Corton-Charlemagnes: 1971, 1973, 1976, 1978, 1979, 1981, and 1982. Everyone thought the 1981 Corton-Charlemagne was the odd-man-out and assumed that the Edna Valley was a Corton-Charlemagne! That proves my point made above.

❧ December 1990
At home, with French Consul General Bernard Ledun. Deep, mature gold. Intense, oaky, complex nose. Full, rich, complex on palate. Still lots of fruit,

but needs drinking. Powerful, serious wine, yet good acidity and not off-balanced. Nutty, oaky, very long.

MAYACAMAS CHARDONNAY 1981, CALIFORNIA:

❧ May 1989

On Turnagain Island. Bright, deep green-gold colour. Rich nose with overtones of new oak predominating. Leaner style on palate, fair acidity, still crisp and clean, but for such a delicate, almost Chablis-like wine, there is too much new oak predominating, with its bitter tannins. Less new oak with this delicate wine would have produced a better-balanced wine. Good, nevertheless. Bob Travers has been trying to introduce an appellation "Napa Mountain" for his wines. As he hasn't been successful, his wines are now designated "California," rather than "Napa Valley."

ROBERT MONDAVI "RESERVE" CHARDONNAY 1981, NAPA VALLEY:

❧ May 1986

As when previously tasted, this is a superb Chardonnay. Round, complex, beautifully balanced with touch of oak. Good fruit and acidity. Top quality. Ready, but no rush. Possibly Mondavi's best Chardonnay to date.

❧ April 1987

Consistent notes. An excellent wine. Best Mondavi Chardonnay from 1975 to 1984, including all "Reserves." Green-gold, deep colour. Lovely, complex, rich nose of ripe Chardonnay, some oak. Great intensity of flavour. Rich, long, round, excellent balance. and long, rich aftertaste. Top quality.

MATANZAS CREEK CHARDONNAY 1987, SONOMA VALLEY:

❧ November 1992

Against 1987 Meursault "Rougeots," Coche-Dury. Sweeter than the Meursault. Typical Matanzas. Rich, herbaceous, full, long. Very good depth. Ripe fruit, some oak. Lots of rich, intense fruit, but overshadowed by the class and elegance of the Meursault. Softer, too. Less acidic than the Meursault. 1987 was a difficult year for white Burgundies, but Coche-Dury is a master winemaker.

ROBERT MONDAVI "RESERVE" CHARDONNAY 1987, NAPA VALLEY:

❧ May 1990

Bright green-gold. Spicy, clean Chardonnay, vanilla and oak on nose. Well balanced, long, good intensity; enough depth and balance to last three to four more years. Classy. Best Mondavi Chardonnay, in my opinion, since their fine 1981 "Reserve."

❧ April 1993

Bright green-gold. Flinty, oaky nose, like a Chablis Grand Cru. Well balanced, lively, good fruit. Long, complex, very good. Since the early 1980s, Mondavi's Reserve Chardonnays are variable and inconsistent. 1981 and 1987 are very good. Other vintages are good too, but too soft. Yet other vintages, notably the 1983 and 1984, are oxidizing and have fallen apart after a couple of years in bottle.

ZD "CALIFORNIA" CHARDONNAY 1988:

❧ July 1995

Typical ZD style: lemony, crisp, round, fresh, good Chardonnay character. Chablis-like structure, yet unmistakable California Chardonnay flavours. Most enjoyable.

KALIN CELLARS "CUVÉE W" CHARDONNAY 1988, LIVERMORE VALLEY:

❧ February 1995

At six years old, holding well. Ripe pineapple, oak on nose. Typical California Chardonnay. Straightforward, round, quite rich, full, well balanced. Fairly acidic, but backed by good fruit. Clean, long finish. Since the mid-1980s, California Chardonnays have improved dramatically, with better balance and acidity.

KISTLER "DUTTON RANCH" CHARDONNAY 1989, RUSSIAN RIVER:

❧ September 15, 1993

On the 20th anniversary to the day since my arrival in Vancouver. Honeyed, fat, rich, round. Oak, honey, vanilla on nose and palate, but a bit flat (low acidity). No use ageing this any further.

MISCELLANEOUS CALIFORNIA WHITE WINES

ROBERT MONDAVI FUMÉ BLANC 1978, NAPA VALLEY:

❧ June 1980
Bright, golden colour; very good Sauvignon Blanc, crisp nose. Flavourful and with good body. Ready. A well-made wine. Excellent value ($5.25). Lacks the complexity and acidity of Pouilly-Fumé, though. Best California Sauvignon Blanc tasted to date.

❧ May 1981
With Roland Kressman at home. Comments as above. Roland liked this wine very much; showing early signs of drying up, with a fair amount of acidity.

CHÂTEAU ST. JEAN PINOT BLANC 1979, SONOMA VALLEY:

❧ November 1983
Against 1979 Morey-St.-Denis Blanc "Mont Luisant," Domaine Ponsot, also made from Pinot Blanc. Flowery, subdued, California nose. A "gentle," elegant, and delicate wine, not overwhelming. Good fruit and acidity, forward.

CHALONE PINOT BLANC "RESERVE" 1980:

Very small production.

❧ July 1989
Bright, deep-golden colour. Rich oak, ripe fruit on nose. Full, intense, round, excellent length and balance. A rich, concentrated, yet not cloying or clumsy wine. Lots of class, character, and depth here. Concentrated fruit. Fine bottle. This varietal usually improves with age and, when well made, can last well for a decade or even longer.

AMERICAN DESSERT WINES

HEITZ CELLARS "ANGELICA" 1974:

Purchased from the winery. Joe Heitz told me that it was bottled in 1991 and I tasted this lovely dessert wine with him. It is his first effort to date with this wine, made from Mission grapes. 19° alcohol. Very "jammy," with hint of Muscat. Intense, long, rich. Lovely, nutty flavours. Not unlike a fine old East India Sherry.

❧ July 17, 1992
My 47th birthday party with family and friends. Comments as above. Very good. Bottled in a tall, slim, elegant glass container.

❧ December 5, 1993
At a memorial to Grandma Jenny, my mother. Nutty, Sherry-like. Full, rich, long, sweet, but not cloying. Excellent quality. Very long and complex. Heitz Cellars are now releasing the 1976 vintage of this fine dessert wine.

I have recently been told by the Heitz family that the 1976 will be their second and last bottling of this very special wine.

FREEMARK ABBEY "EDELWEIN" 1976, NAPA VALLEY:

Equivalent to a BA. Their TBA is called "Edelwein Gold" and sells (in 1980) for about US$20 per half-bottle. Made from botrytized Riesling grapes.

❧ 1980
Very different from Château St. Jean's BA. Lighter in colour, lemony (rather than apricot-peach) bouquet and flavour. Well made; clean, fruity nose. Touch of botrytis but, personally, I prefer the bigger Château St. Jean style. This resembles a German BA, but with more intensity.

CALERA ZINFANDEL ESSENCE 1976:

Made from botrytis-affected Zinfandel grapes.

❧ June 1981
Bright-red colour. No sediment. The nose had some hint of Zinfandel, but mostly of botrytis-Riesling! Very interesting (surprisingly, an elegant wine rather than a blockbuster). Medium sweet, yet fairly dry finish and easy to drink. An interesting experience.

CHÂTEAU ST. JEAN "BELLE TERRE VINEYARD" SELECT LATE HARVEST JOHANNISBERG RIESLING 1976, SONOMA VALLEY:

(15.4° residual sugar)

❧ November 1981
Dinner at Tony Gismondi's. (That night we also tasted a superb 1953 Château Margaux.) Very dark-golden colour. Typical, peach-apricot bouquet. Elegant, soft,

very enjoyable. Low alcohol, great mouthful. The only thing that worries me is its ageing potential, i.e., lack of acidity. Otherwise, a fine wine.

❧ July 1993

At home, with council of Le Tastevin. Deep amber. Spicy, herbal-dill nose. Intense. Full, rich, long, old TBA style. Some fruit left. Held well for 17 years. Spicy, sweet, yet not too cloying. Good. I have underestimated the staying power of this wine.

CAYMUS VINEYARDS "SPECIAL SELECTION" LATE HARVEST CHARDONNAY 1976, NAPA VALLEY:

(9% residual sugar)

❧ January 1987

At home, at the end of a tasting of 1976 red Bordeaux and other Cabernets. A lovely wine. Would fool anyone. Now very rare and expensive. Not unlike a Moulin Touchais (Anjou) Chenin Blanc dessert wine, but cleaner, less earthy, and with better, fresher fruit and botrytis.

ROBERT MONDAVI "OAK KNOLL VINEYARDS BOTRYTIS" JOHANNISBERG RIESLING 1977, NAPA VALLEY:

(21° residual sugar.)

❧ April 1992

With Tony Gismondi and Jean Guillaume Prats (Bruno Prats' son). Very dark amber. Fabulous, spicy-botrytis Riesling on nose. Sweet, rich, excellent spicy-acidity balance. Long and rich. Lovely wine. Very mature, but still lots of fruit and length.

CALLAWAY VINEYARD "SWEET NANCY" LATE HARVEST CHENIN BLANC 1977, TEMECULA, CALIFORNIA:

(10.7% alcohol, 9.0% residual sugar.)

❧ June 1989

Brilliant, deep (yet not too dark) gold colour. Flowery, spicy, intense, clean nose with spicy fruit, and botrytis coming through. Rich, yet not cloying, quite spicy, fairly high acidity (typical of Chenin Blanc). Well balanced, long, complex. Most enjoyable and has held very well, especially in half-bottle. No rush.

ROBERT MONDAVI "BOTRYTIS" SAUVIGNON BLANC 1978, NAPA VALLEY:

(13° residual sugar)

❧ October 1982

At the winery as a guest of John Lawson, Export Manager of Mondavi, and again in Vancouver. See comments below.

❧ March 1983

In Vancouver at a black tie dinner in honour of Robert Mondavi. Both times: fabulous wine, sweet, well balanced, lovely botrytis Sauternes-like. very good. Excellent fruit, acidity, and complexity. Very long on palate.

CHÂTEAU ST. JEAN "BELLE TERRE VINEYARD" "INDIVIDUAL BUNCH SELECT LATE HARVEST" JOHANNISBERG RIESLING 1978, SONOMA VALLEY:

(28.2° residual sugar)
This wine sells now (1980) in Vançouver for $42 per half-bottle.

❧ May 1980

At a special Château St. Jean tasting in Vancouver at which Dick Arrowood (the winemaker) lectured. Very sweet, dark, amber "Tokai" colour. Massive. Took some home and tried it two days later. Finally the bouquet had opened up. Fabulous apricot-peach bouquet. Still massive. Even in half-bottle, this wine needs at least ten more years to develop, and could keep for many more years. 1978 was Orly's birth year. I will keep a couple of bottles for her.

❧ June 1993

At the Four Seasons hotel, with Daniel Baron of Dominus Estate and council of Le Tastevin. Very deep, amber colour, not unlike a very old Muscat or Tawny Port. Rich, caramel, sweet nose. Soft, very sweet, rich, low acidity. Long, luscious. As a Riesling, over-the-hill. As a "dessert" wine, full, rich, impressive. No Riesling character left, unfortunately. Liquid maple syrup!

ROBERT MONDAVI "BOTRYTIZED" JOHANNISBERG RIESLING 1978, NAPA VALLEY:

❧ January 1996

Very deep, amber-gold-orange colour. Spicy, cinnamon, flowery Riesling nose. Better balanced than the old St. Jean TBAs. Good acidity, not cloying. Lovely length. Bigger than a German TBA but has held extremely well. Spicy, lovely fruit. Rich, full, hint of lemon/orange blossom. An excellent dessert wine. At 18 years old, fully mature, yet no rush drinking this.

FELTON-EMPIRE "TEPUSQUET VINEYARDS" LATE HARVEST GEWÜRZTRAMINER 1979, SANTA BARBARA:

(21° residual sugar)

❧ October 1987

With the panel of *The Wine Consumer*. Bright, deep-gold colour. Elegant, complex nose of botrytis and Gewürztraminer spice. Round, low alcohol (8.5°), good acidity. Fairly soft and light for a TBA. Great length and complexity. A very enjoyable bottle.

HINZERLING LATE HARVEST GEWÜRZTRAMINER 1979, YAKIMA VALLEY:

(11.1° residual sugar, BA style)

❧ June 1981

Spicy, flowery, intense nose. Fairly light in colour. Slightly spritzy at first. Clean, very pleasant. Still very young, but an experience. Similar nose to Muscat de Beaumes de Venise, but less alcohol and weight. Lychee nuts on nose. This wine is produced in Washington State.

CHÂTEAU ST. JEAN "JIMTOWN RANCH" SELECT LATE HARVEST GEWÜRZTRAMINER 1980, SONOMA VALLEY:

(15.1° residual sugar)

❧ July 1985

On the occasion of my 40th birthday. My favourite St. Jean Late Harvest wine so far. The reason: not as cloying, sweet, or thick as other St. Jean BAs or TBAs. Bigger and heavier than a German equivalent, but lovely fruit. Good acidity, medium body, very good length. Deep-gold colour. Spicy lychee nuts on nose. Ready, but no rush.

❧ March 1991

Deep gold. Exotic, fresh lychees on nose. Round, soft, full, sweet, and spicy. Nice botrytis. Evolved and ready. Very nice.

WINDSOR VINEYARDS SELECT LATE HARVEST JOHANNISBERG RIESLING 1982, RUSSIAN RIVER, SONOMA VALLEY:

(14.9° residual sugar)

❧ September 1996

With council of Commanderie de Bordeaux. Surprisingly good. Amber, deep-gold colour. More Sauternes than Riesling on nose. Very good balance, acidity, fruit, length. This winery is now defunct, its vineyards having been taken over by Piper-Sonoma and Rodney Strong. Always sad to drink a wine of a winery that does not exist any more.

FREEMARK ABBEY "EDELWEIN GOLD" JOHANNISBERG RIESLING 1982, NAPA VALLEY:

(21.9° residual sugar) TBA

❧ October 1984

Deep, bright amber-gold colour (quite deep!). Fruity, youthful on nose and palate. Good acidity at this stage. Lovely, mouth-filling, botrytized wine. A bit too sweet for me, but nevertheless a very good bottle. (Freemark's spicy style, rather than orange-apricot-peach style of Château St. Jean's.)

CHÂTEAU ST. JEAN "ROBERT YOUNG VINEYARD" SELECTED LATE HARVEST JOHANNISBERG RIESLING 1984, ALEXANDER VALLEY:

(18.4° residual sugar)

❧ February 1989

Two bottles broke when they fell from the shelf in my cellar and they, in turn, broke a bottle of 1985 Vosne-Romanée "Beaumonts," Daniel Rion. These accidents are rare, but they do happen.

Purchased two more half-bottles.

❧ August 1995

A lovely dessert wine. Peach nectar, botrytis, spicy fruit. Good fruit/acidity balance. Not as overwhelming as St. Jean's BAs and TBAs from the 1970s. Not "maple syrup," but fine German TBA style. Lovely, long, good fruit. No rush. Fine.

VINTAGE AND OTHER PORTS

NIEPOORT "COLHEITA" PORTO 1912:

Purchased during a trip to France in September 1992 for my mother. She was born October 16, 1912.

❧ Friday, October 16, 1992

On the occasion of my mother's 80th birthday. Other than the family, we invited several close friends. Colheita is a single-vintage Tawny. Matured in wood for at least 50 years. Possibly longer. Amber colour, olive-green rim. Intense, raisiny nose. Full, rich, nutty. Great length. Full of life. Ageless. Mother was very pleased. Lovely wine. Creamy, smooth, long. Lots of extract. Purchased in Paris in a wine shop off Place de la Madeleine. Post Script: This was the last bottle my mother tasted. She passed away two months later.

WARRE'S 1934 VINTAGE PORT, "DIRECTOR'S SPECIAL RESERVE":

Bottled 1936 in Perth, Scotland, by Arthur Bell and Sons Ltd.

❧ February 1, 1991

At a farewell dinner with panel of *The Wine Consumer*. Smooth, round, complex, elegant; perfect balance. Lovely Port. Decanted 30 minutes. Great class. Still at its peak! Not declining. Great stuff.

❧ March 1997

At home, for the final meeting with the council of the Commanderie de Bordeaux. In April, I step down as Maître, after serving for nine years, since February 1988. Decanted 45 minutes. Fair bit of sediment. Palish, evolved colour, not unlike a 1960. Flowery, spicy, evolved nose. Quite spirity, but soft fruit still there. Very much alive, and hasn't lost its Vintage Port character. Complex, long. A lovely, mature Port.

GRAHAM'S 1945 VINTAGE PORT, OPORTO-BOTTLED:

Purchased two bottles. One was drunk with our "Group of Ten" dinner a couple of years ago (1980). It was very spirity, very dark, still massive, good fruit, and will probably last forever. Great future ahead!

REBELLO VALENTE 1945 VINTAGE PORT:

❧ October 30, 1993

At the end of a Middle Eastern dinner. (Also tasted that night: 1978 Guigal Côte-Rôtie, 1978 Sassicaia, 1978 Torres Gran Coronas "Black Label," 1962 Vega Sicilia "Unico," etc., with several friends including the French Consul General to Vancouver, Bernard Ledun.) Bright red colour. Elegant style. Decanted 30 minutes. Fair bit of sediment. Lovely bouquet. Flowery, stylish. Well balanced. Nice fruit, no rush. Classy. Good length. Lovely bouquet and lingering on palate. Holding well.

TAYLOR'S 1955 VINTAGE PORT:

❧ June 1977

At a dinner, in London, with Harry and Prue Waugh. This is Prue's favourite Port. Excellent. Powerful, mature, yet lots of future. Fine bouquet. The next day it was still lively, with lingering aftertaste.

TAYLOR'S 1955 VINTAGE PORT:

Bottler unknown. Excellent bottom neck level. No label.

❧ December 1992

Decanted four hours. Lots of sediment. Cork disintegrated. At first, deceptively light. After three-and-a-half hours, quite spirity. Medium colour. Lovely spicy nose and palate. Lots of class, complex, long. Leaner style, very stylish. Good depth, length, and balance. Very good.

CROFT'S 1960 VINTAGE PORT:

Purchased at Cockburn and Campbell's, a London wine shop.

❧ September 1977

At its peak. Dark, lots of sediment; excellent bouquet. Decanted three hours. Soft, as most 1960s are, but spicy, elegant, complex, long. Very Good.

OFFLEY'S BOA VISTA 1960 VINTAGE PORT:

❧ January 1978

Medium colour, not as full and powerful as the 1963, but a good wine. Decanted four hours before tasting. Lots of sediment. Pleasant bouquet. A bit too much on the sweet side, but a fine Port, nevertheless.

QUINTA DO SIBIO 1960 VINTAGE PORT:

(Sociedad Vinicola)

❧ March 1981

Spicy nose. Medium body, medium colour, fairly high alcohol, quite sweet (alcohol taking over). Good flavour, lingering aftertaste.

❧ October 1981

Medium-light colour. Lots of sediment. Decanted three-and-a-half hours. Sweet, open, straightforward nose. Mature, pleasant, easy to drink. Ready, at its peak. True to the style and character of the 1960s.

❧ November 1983

Decanted two hours. Evolved colour; elegant, open nose. Soft on palate. Good fruit, not very complex, at its peak. Quite good.

GRAHAM'S 1962 VINTAGE PORT:

❧ February 1981

At "2601 Vaughan," a French-style restaurant in Portland. A vintage rarely seen. Orange-brick colour. Soft, spicy, fruity nose. Sweet, but not too much so. Mature, ready to drink, and very pleasant.

OFFLEY'S BOA VISTA 1963 VINTAGE PORT:

❧ November 1977

Opened and decanted five hours before tasting. Lots of sediment. Very powerful, yet seemed more evolved. A wine with an excellent future. Dark colour. Fine, powerful, spicy bouquet. Should be ready in five to six years. London-bottled by Hedges and Butler. How fine these 1963 Ports are turning out to be.

❧ March 5, 1982

At home, with Harry Waugh. Surprisingly forward. Medium-dark colour. Lots of sediment. Decanted four hours before dinner. Good flavour, not too complex, soft, elegant. Well made (Charles Kinloch-bottling).

❧ February 1983

This was a Charles Kinloch-bottling but different from all above. Much darker, bigger, heaps of fruit, and concentrated, sweet wine. Lovely nose. Needs at least three to five extra years and should hold for a very long time. A lovely port.

COCKBURN'S 1963 VINTAGE PORT:

❧ November 1976

Lots of fruit extract and taste. Decanted five hours. Needs another five years or more. Price was really cheap. As usual, the liquor monopoly (LCB) do not know what they are doing! I paid $6.45 per bottle for these fine 1963s, last year. Purchased a total of seven cases of various 1963s, notably Dow's, Croft's, and Fonseca's. These Ports retail now (in 1976) across the USA for around $14 to $20 a bottle.

DOW'S 1963 VINTAGE PORT:

❧ March 1978

Quite a bit of sediment. Decanted four hours. Medium-red colour; not too sweet, quite powerful. Very fine. Should be ready in five to ten years, yet it is quite forward for a 1963.

❧ September 1978

At dinner with friends. Decanted four hours. Deep colour, otherwise comments as above. What struck me was that it was quite dry (relatively speaking) and sturdy like the Cockburn's, but without the finesse of Cockburn's. Overall, an excellent 1963, with a great future.

❧ March 1982

At home, at a dinner for Harry Waugh, with Joe Heitz and his daughter Kathleen, and the Tobes. Lovely, fine, dark colour. Decanted five hours before serving. Big nose, massive, well made. Should be ready in five to seven years and last for a long time. Harry liked it very much, and had lots of it! This wine is holding better than expected.

❧ November 1993

With the council of the Commanderie de Bordeaux. (Charles Kinloch-bottling, London.) Decanted three hours. Medium-evolved colour. Exactly 30 years old, yet still lively and youthful. At first, quite spirity. Later, complex, delicate, long. The "Lafite of Port." Round, nice fruit, excellent balance. Spicy, complex, long. No rush. Excellent neck level. This Port had held extremely well, no doubt thanks, at least in part, to my cool cellar.

SANDEMAN'S 1963 VINTAGE PORT:

❧ February 1977

Full, powerful. Lots of sediment. Needs another five to ten years. Another great 1963. Quite sweet, Sandeman's style.

CROFT'S 1963 VINTAGE UK PORT, BOTTLED BY CHARLES KINLOCH:

❧ April 1981

Purchased a case in Vancouver. Dark colour, lovely, sweet, fruity nose. Good, intense fruit, very good flavour. Not too much tannin left, but enough fruit and acidity and alcohol to last for quite some time. Relatively soft, forward, yet lovely. An excellent buy, in 1976, for $6.45 per bottle.

CROFT'S 1963 VINTAGE PORT, THIS SECOND CASE BOTTLED IN OPORTO:

Purchased from Justerini and Brooks. Lying at A. Nugent's. Finally arrived in Vancouver in October 1983, after six years and shipping problems. Paid £36 per case.

❧ November 1984

Decanted three hours. Medium colour, lovely, long, elegant. At its peak, but no rush. Beautiful balance, length, and complexity. A noble, yet forward, elegant Port. Very good.

❧ February 1987

At home, with the panel of *The Wine Consumer*. Decanted four-and-a-half hours. Fair bit of sediment. Medium to dark colour. Mature rim. Lovely, elegant, spicy nose, typical of the fine 1963s. Full, rich, yet very elegant. Reaching its peak, but no rush. Great finesse, and the beautiful structure and length of this great vintage.

GRAHAM'S 1963 VINTAGE PORT:

❧ August 1986

Tasted at "Chartwell" restaurant at the Four Seasons hotel. This bottle was opened and decanted two days ago so the Port was quite forward. Yet it had the depth, complexity, and lovely bouquet of the fine 1963 vintage. An excellent Port. Must buy some more. Unfortunately, it retails now (1986) for $45 per bottle.

QUINTA DO NOVAL 1963 VINTAGE PORT:

❧ May 1978

A very good Port. Decanted four-and-a-half hours before tasting. Still quite powerful. Medium colour; good, long-lasting bouquet. One of the better 1963s and a bit darker and fuller than Croft's, but lighter than Dow's. Will be at its peak in three to five years. Purchased this case in London last year. Paid £40 per case.

❧ March 1982

Decanted five hours. Lots of sediment. Medium-dark colour. Lovely, intense, complex bouquet, so typical of the great 1963s. A great wine. Long, well balanced. Already elegant, but needs three to four years to reach its peak, and will hold for quite some time. Not as masculine as some (Dow's), and not as forward as others (Croft's).

❧ March 1985

Decanted five hours. Lots of sediment. Every comment I have read or heard or even my own experience with this wine (mostly London-bottlings) has been that the wine is soft, forward, and ready. This case of mine is very different. It is a Portuguese-bottling celebrating Da Silva's family's 250th anniversary. Could it have some "Nacional" grapes in it? Very dark, full, rich, intense, big, great complexity, and depth. Not unlike Fonseca's or Graham's in style. A fabulous bottle, needing another two to four years, and should hold well into the next century.

Looking at my previous notes since 1978, I agree with my March 1982 assessment.

❧ January 1989

A lovely Port. Decanted five hours. Bright-red colour. Elegant, spicy, complex nose. Velvety, silky on palate. Not unlike a fine 1955. Long, delicate, easy to drink. "Margaux" of Port. At its peak, but will stay there for a few more years. More forward than when last tasted in 1985, but lovely.

❧ February 1995

"Group of Ten" dinner. Basic comments as in 1989. Holding surprisingly well. Ready, but no rush. Yet it is already 32 years old.

QUINTA DO NOVAL 1966 VINTAGE PORT:

❧ December 1981

Good, dark colour; complex, quite intense. Decanted five hours. Approachable, but has enough depth/fruit to last for quite a few years. An excellent Port.

❧ December 1985

Decanted six hours. Shipper unknown, no label. Elegant, at its peak, yet quite full, rich, and round. Quite complex, not unlike a 1963 Croft's. Ready, but no rush. Fair bit of sediment. A very nice Port, indeed.

SANDEMAN'S 1966 VINTAGE PORT:

❧ November 1980

Decanted five hours. Big, sweet wine. Quite forward and fruity, yet it will last for a long time. Very good. Easy to drink. Not too complex. A straightforward, easy-to-understand "beginner's" Port.

❧ January 1984

Decanted five hours. Fair bit of sediment. Basically, comments as in 1980, yet seemed slightly leaner, not as sweet as previously, and a bit harder.

CROFT'S 1966 VINTAGE PORT:

❧ August 1978

Decanted three hours. Lots of sediment. Powerful wine; strong, oaky nose, and high alcohol. Similar to Cockburn's 1963, but sweeter. Needs five to eight more years. Very good. Paid $7.35 per bottle for this two years ago, in 1976.

❧ March 1980

Decanted five hours. Lots of sediment. Dark colour, big spicy nose, quite full. Quite spirity on nose. Youthful; needs another two to five years. A bit harsh and doesn't have the depth of the 1963 vintage, but very good, nevertheless. My guess is that in about three to four years time, the fruit may start to weaken, and the alcohol might take over.

❧ February 1994

Decanted four hours. Fair bit of sediment. Light, evolved colour. A gentle Port at its peak. Elegant, spicy, complex, round, long. Mellow. Will not improve, but has lasted much better than expected.

GRAHAM'S 1966 VINTAGE PORT:

❧ November 1992

Decanted three hours. Bright-red colour. Good depth, palish rim. Subdued, sweet, complex nose. Silky, superb balance. Long, Very good fruit. Lively, long, smooth. Perfection now. A classic Port. A good buy in Vancouver in 1977; paid $7.45 per bottle.

TAYLOR'S 1970 VINTAGE PORT:

❧ October 1984

Decanted five hours. Big, deep, fairly alcoholic wine. Already rounding a bit, but really needs another six to eight years. Should lose some of its harshness with age. Very good fruit and depth.

❧ September 1991

Bottom neck level. Decanted five hours. Good, medium-dark colour. Fair bit of sediment. Spicy, complex, long. Very fine. Softening up a bit. Not as fierce as seven years ago. Reaching its peak. Complex, spicy, not too jammy. Typical Taylor's. Lovely spice, length, balance, and fruit. Ready, but no rush. A serious, masculine Port.

FONSECA'S 1970 VINTAGE PORT, IN HALF-BOTTLE:

❧ January 1987

Deep, dark colour. Lovely, fruity, lively Port. Even in half-bottle, still full of life. Rich, fruity, concentrated, and complex. In full bottles, drink now to 2000 or beyond. Very good.

WARRE'S 1970 VINTAGE PORT:

Very highly rated in 1978 as second only to Taylor's in Decanter *magazine, and should be ready around 1990.*

❧ March 1992

At home, with council of the Commanderie de Bordeaux. Decanted five hours. Some sediment. Superb, dark, deep, youthful colour. Lovely, fruity nose. Complex, long. Superb balance, depth, length. Sweet, fruity, velvety, yet excellent backbone. Will last for 20 more years. Great quality. Very sweet, rich, "Graham's-like." This fine Port is still a bargain at auction.

1972 TAYLOR'S LATE-BOTTLED RESERVE:

❧ February 1985

Fair bit of sediment. Orangy, bright colour. Good, open, spicy, rich nose. Soft, forward, at its peak.

There are two basic philosophies on late-bottled Vintage Port. Some say that it should be consumed within two to four years after bottling (when the wine is eight to ten years old). Others maintain that as it ages further, it develops more "true" Vintage Port character. A matter of taste.

DOW'S 1975 VINTAGE PORT:

❧ November 1989

Decanted five hours. Fair bit of sediment. Medium colour, light (not much depth). Spicy, sweet nose. Medium-bodied. Not too spirity. Ready, but no rush, yet without the depth, complexity, and size of a great vintage. My experience leads me to conclude that the only really fine 1975 Vintage Ports are Fonseca's and Taylor's. All others are rather lightweight, including Graham's.

FONSECA'S 1975 VINTAGE PORT:

❧ February 1991

With French Trade Commissioner to Vancouver, Jean-Yves Conte, and other friends. Decanted six hours. One of the best 1975s. Good colour and body; clean, spicy, good backbone, long, complex, elegant. Very good. No rush. Drink now to 2000 or beyond.

GRAHAM'S 1975 VINTAGE PORT:

❧ November 1988

Fairly light for Graham's. Ready, some sharpness, but clean, spicy nose. A bit spirity. Typical of most 1975s, but atypical Graham's.

❧ November 1994

Decanted four hours. Lots of sediment. Light, elegant, not too spirity. At its peak. Mellow, soft; most enjoyable now. Nice, spicy fruit. Yet it lacks the depth of a truly great Vintage Port.

GRAHAM'S 1980 VINTAGE PORT:

❧ April 1997

A lovely, fully mature Port in half-bottle. Bright colour. Spicy, sweet nose. Soft, round, silky, yet has lots of fruit. A charmer. One of the best Ports of the vintage. In full bottles, drink now to 2005.

The following two bottles were among several bottles given to me by Joe Heitz in March 1987, after I helped him clean out and organize his private cellar at his home in St. Helena.

PORT WINE N/V:

Source or shipper unknown. Joe Heitz has various bottles, each in a different-shaped container, mostly beer or rum bottles. Purchased from the Crocker estate in 1975. All these bottles are pre-Prohibition (before 1920). Possibly produced around 1911 to 1919. Shipped and bottled by F. Cazanove, Bordeaux (indicated on lead capsule) in 1921. Excellent level. I tried a bottle with Joe in St. Helena and it was a fine old Tawny-style wine. Bottled in a "St. Thomas Bay" (Martens) rum bottle!

❧ May 20, 1987

With the panel of *The Wine Consumer*. Small, narrow cork, but in fairly good shape. Brown, bright, Tawny colour. Some sediment that looked greenish. Pale green at rim (olive green). Old woody nose. Spirity, a bit of varnish, and fairly alcoholic. Some hint of Port left. Still drinkable, but not too pleasant. Later improved on nose a bit. Cinnamon, spices (nutmeg). An interesting experience.

❧ May 24, 1987

Tried it again at a friend's home. I brought this bottle along. Cleaner, round, nutty, better than above; quite drinkable!

SUPERIOR LONDON DOCK PORT N/V:

Tried it with Joe Heitz in St. Helena at the winery (in 1987). Bottled in San Francisco by Goldberg, Bowen & Co. Pre-Prohibition stock. Story as above, but bottled in true Port-shaped bottle. Excellent level. Fine old Tawny style. Possibly made around 1910 to 1915 or even before.

TOKAI, MADEIRA, AND OTHER EUROPEAN DESSERT WINES

Since the end of World War II, Tokays have been produced and exported by the Hungarian Communist wine monopoly, Monimpex. Therefore, no producer/shipper is indicated in the case of post-1945 Tokai.

TOKAI ASZÚ 1969, 3 PUTTONYOS:

❧ May 1978

Deep, golden colour. Being only 3 Puttonyos, one should not expect much intensity. Nutty, almost like semisweet Sherry.

❧ January 1980

Dark colour, nutty nose. Not very sweet, but nice flavours. Good wine, pleasant, and easy to drink. At first it smelled a bit musty, but cleared up a few minutes later.

TOKAI ASZÚ 1966, 6 PUTTONYOS:

❧ March 1979

Deep colour, rich nose; sweet and intense. Far better than any 5 Puttonyos I've tasted previously. Lovely flavour. Will probably last for a long time. Clean and clear, no sediment. Almost like a fine Madeira, but more intense and "Muscaty."

TOKAI ASZÚ ESSENCIA 1964:

❧ November 1980

Very dark amber colour; nutty-raisiny nose. Lemony-sweet flavour, lingering aftertaste. Low alcohol, elegant, very pleasant. A rarity and an experience.

❧ May 1988

At home, with friends, including Debbie Guimaraens of Oporto (Bruce's daughter, owner of Fonseca's). Debbie is staying with us. Fair bit of sediment. Very deep, dark-amber colour. Quite mature, sweet, yet very good acidity. Comments as in 1980 overall, yet much more mature, both in appearance and on palate.

TOKAI ASZÚ 1971, 5 PUTTONYOS:

❧ February 1981

Dark-golden colour. Good, clean-crisp nose. Oxidized, typical nutty bouquet. Very good flavour. Not very sweet, but easy to drink. Clean flavours, good fruit/acidity balance. Goes well with sweet, fruity desserts because of its crispness. Lingering aftertaste.

TOKAI ASZÚ 1973, 5 PUTTONYOS:

❧ September 1982

Thick, milky/muddy sediment. Deep amber colour. Good "old Sherry" nose. Fruity, crisp, and long. Well balanced. Well made.

TOKAI ASZÚ 1974, 5 PUTTONYOS:

❧ November 1989

Deep amber colour. Lovely, rich, Muscat nose. Full, round, long. Will last until 2000 or beyond. Some crystal sediment. Very good length and complexity. Quite sweet, but not cloying, with good acidity.

❧ December 1990

Deep amber-gold. Crème brûlée nose. Spicy, sweet, rich, round. Very good acidity and fruit. No rush.

MADEIRA TERRANTEZ 1795, BARBEITO:

❧ February 19, 1996

At the end of a vertical tasting of Château Calon-Ségur 1916 to 1966. Fabulous Madeira. Bual-style weight. Amber-gold. Nutty. Brilliant, long, fruity. Great fruit/acidity balance. Tangy. Great stuff! An historic 200-year-old wine.

Following is a reproduction of a letter I have received from Vinos Barbeito (verbatim).

"Funchal 14, September 1995

Dear Sir:

We have received your letter dated September 7th.

Regarding your questions, I can inform you of the following:

All the wines have been bought by my grandfather in 1972. They have been purchased in casks of 420 litres each from the Hinton family.

This family has been established in Madeira since 1802 and it is quite difficult to know the exact origin of the wines. We believe that the wines have been in that family as a result of the many wines they used to receive from the small farmers in Madeira, in exchange for food supplies. This was very common procedure at that time.

The Hinton-Welsh family are the same Welshes who owned Welsh Brothers Madeiras; old wine producers. This company has not existed for many years.

The wines have been bottled in 1991 due to the fact that it is our company's procedure to maintain as much of the wine for as long as possible in casks because its improvement is much longer. As you may know, Madeira wine does not improve after eight to ten years in bottle.

This results that having the wine in casks will always improve its quality, allowing our company to have better and better wines.

We hope this information is suitable for you, even though we all know that the ancient age of the wines causes lack of information we may give you.

We hope you have a great success in the tasting.

Please be free to contact us in case you need any further information.

Sincerely yours,
Ricardo Diogo V. Freitas
Vinos Barbeito (Madeira) LDA"

WEISSBURGUNDER RUSTER BEERENAUSLESE 1976, MORANDELL, AUSTRIA:

❧ May 1980
Sauternes-like wine. Good botrytis on nose. Medium-gold colour. Flavourful, well balanced. Will keep for quite some time.

❧ New Year's Eve 1984
On Turnagain Island. Softening up. Delicate, round, not very intense or complex botrytis, but quite pleasant. At its peak.

1983 BINGER SCHARLACHBERG RIESLING EISWEIN, WEINGUT VILLA SACHSEN, RHEINHESSEN:

❧ October 1989
Bright-gold colour, touch of green. Lovely, complex, hint of petroleum on nose. Round, delicate, good depth, and acidity. Ripe raisins. No rush. Good backbone, and still fresh. Drink from 1995 to 2005.

❧ October 30, 1995
"Quebec Referendum" night with council of Le Tastevin. Comments as in 1989, but slightly more evolved. Perfect balance, sweetness; elegant, long. Stylish, classy wine. Clean, crisp, very long finish. No rush. Excellent Riesling "petroleum" character. Top quality. It tasted particularly good when we leaned that the "non" side won, and that Canada will not be torn apart… yet.

1989 OCKFENER BOCKSTEIN RIESLING EISWEIN, WEINGUT GEBERT, MOSEL/SAAR/RUHR, IN HALF-BOTTLE:

❧ October 1996
At home, before a trip to Paris and Bordeaux. Bright-golden colour. Petroleum jelly/classic nose. Round, delicate, perfectly balanced. Lovely fruit, nice sweet/spicy aftertaste. Beerenauslese style. Impressive balance and delicate, subdued fruit.

MOSCATEL DE SETÚBAL (25 YEARS OLD), J. M. DE FONSECA:

❧ September 3, 1980
At Le Tastevin's annual dinner. Nutty, Madeira-like nose. Not very sweet, but quite pleasant with a touch of bitter-almond. Not too heavy, and easy to drink. Woody-oaky-Muscaty flavour. Interesting.

CROFT'S 20-YEAR-OLD FINEST TAWNY PORT, BOTTLED 1984.

❧ 1985 and 1986
Tasted several times. Superb Tawny. Long, complex, full, rich, yet not overly cloying. Again in 1990, 1991. Nutty, creamy, long, and rich.

MÁLAGA "SOLERA" 1885, SCHOLTZ HERMANOS, MÁLAGA, SPAIN:

❧ 1991 to 1993
Tasted several times. Nutty, rich, complex, long. Very good balance, sweet, but not cloying. Very good length, depth, and aftertaste.

RED, WHITE, AND DESSERT WINES FROM SOUTH AFRICA AND AUSTRALIA

SOUTH AFRICA

ALTO CABERNET SAUVIGNON 1970:

❧ May and August 1977

Tasted it twice in London. An excellent South African wine, "discovered" by Alastair Nugent and Harry Waugh during a trip to South Africa in January 1977. A big, powerful wine that will need another four to five years of bottle-age. Lacks finesse. Very sturdy. A little Merlot would improve this wine a lot.

VERGENOEGD CABERNET SAUVIGNON 1975:

❧ August 1992

Similar to the Backsberg Cabernet 1976, but less chunky, less sweet, more elegant, and softer. Clean, lively. No rush. Holding surprisingly well.

PAARL "ROODEBERG" 1975:

❧ New Year's Eve 1990

On Turnagain Island, with friends. Some crystal sediment. Light-red colour. Spicy, hint of Pinot Noir on nose. Ripe, rich. Quite sweet, forward, light on palate. Getting tired. Not very pleasant. Purchased this bottle locally (in Vancouver) ten years ago.

BACKSBERG ESTATE CABERNET SAUVIGNON 1976:

❧ August 1992

Deep, mature colour. Surprisingly fresh Cabernet/vanilla nose. Good extract, youthful, sweet, American oak character on palate. Quite rich, straightforward. Lots of life ahead, but not much complexity. A solid, chunky wine.

❧ December 5, 1993

American oak, vanilla on nose. Round, herbaceous, slightly sweet. Soft, ready, will not improve, but nice balance. Enjoyable. Not much complexity, but pleasant. Has held well.

1930 MUSCADEL KWV, "LATE BOTTLED VINTAGE" "BIN B-14" WINE OF ORIGIN "BOBERG SUPERIOR":

❧ December 1990

Deep-brownish colour with orange, olive-green edge. Intense nose of Muscat raisins, luscious, sweet. Incredible length for a 60-year-old. Great complexity, fruit, and balance. Nutty, syrupy, yet acidity helps maintain some freshness. Very long, very special. The hit of the night.

❧ December 1991

Intense, spicy, rich, long. Apparently, this sells now at auction in South Africa for a small fortune! Purchased locally (in Vancouver) 12 years ago for a mere $29 per bottle.

CRUSTED VINTAGE PORT 1963, "WINE OF ORIGIN BOBERG SUPERIOR":

❧ September 1984

Surprisingly deep colour. Mature, fruity nose. Some sediment. Decanted three hours. Round, well balanced, good fruit, not unlike a late-bottled Vintage Port without the spice or intensity of true Vintage Port. Still youthful. Very enjoyable.

"EDELKEUR" SUPERIOR, WINE OF ORIGIN 1978, NEDERBURG ESTATE:

❧ March 1992

Bright, deep-golden colour. Lovely botrytis and ripe raisins on both nose and palate. Soft, yet still lively. Excellent dessert wine. This wine was produced by the gifted (and now retired) winemaker at Nederburg, Gunther Bröezel. It is usually made from Steen (Chenin Blanc) grapes. In some vintages, Riesling is added to the blend.

❧ August 1995

On Turnagain Island, with Brad Klein from Los Angeles. Not unlike a rich late-1970s Château St. Jean Riesling BA. Amber, deep orange-gold colour. Spicy, rich, soft, long. Lovely botrytis, luscious, yet not cloying. Good acidity. Very soft and long. Ready. Excellent effort.

"EDELKEUR" SUPERIOR, WINE OF ORIGIN 1979, NEDERBURG ESTATE:

❧ November 1983

9.5° alcohol. Made from botrytized grapes (Chenin Blanc and some Johannisberg Riesling). A rare wine. Made by Günther Bröezel, and purchased originally at the Nederburg wine auction. Date of auction unknown. The Chenin Blanc is called Steen in South Africa.

❧ March 1984

At home, with Peter Sichel (of Châteaux Palmer and d'Angludet), and Joan and Sid Cross. Dark gold, orangy colour similar to a German or California TBA. Fragrant bouquet of raisins, ripe apricots, and peaches. Structured more like a German TBA. Not as cloying and fat as a California TBA. Better acidity. Well balanced, lovely, complex, long on palate. It was the first experience with this wine for our guests, including Peter. Will last for a long time. Try again in four to five years. As is the case in the Loire Valley, Chenin Blanc contributes acidity that is crucial for ageing.

❧ April 1990
Just a bit darker colour. Lovely balance, length. So well balanced and with such good acidity that it will last for many more years. Fine botrytis and ripe fruit extract.

De Wetshof "Edeloes" 1979, "Noble Late Harvest" Superior, Wine of Origin-Robertson:

❧ June 1989
With the panel of *The Wine Consumer*. Made from mostly Sauvignon Blanc and some Riesling. Bottled by Bergkelder Ltd., Stellenbosch. Deep, gold-amber colour, like older St. Jean Late Harvest Rieslings. Honey and apricots on nose, little botrytis. Rich, long, good acidity and herbaceous Sauvignon Blanc character. Round, clean, sweet, and ripe. Very good. A rare treat. !979 was the first vintage of this rare wine.

"Edelkeur" Superior, Wine of Origin 1981, Nederburg Estate:

❧ September 15, 1993
The 20th anniversary of my arrival in Vancouver. Deep amber colour. Ripe raisins; full, rich, honeyed nose. Full, round, very soft on palate, but good acidity. Much more evolved than the 1978 and not quite as great, but lovely extract, botrytis, full, rich, and long.

Nederburg "Noble Late Harvest" Wine of Origin 1991:

❧ February 1996
With the council of the Commanderie de Bordeaux. Excellent wine and great value ($15 per half-bottle). Lovely botrytis nose. Like a fine Beerenauslese. Lovely fruit/acidity balance. Long, complex, spicy, rich fruit, yet not cloying. Very fine and a great buy. Will last well. This is one level below their famous Edelkeur. Now that the embargo on South African wines is over (with the end of Apartheid), our markets are being flooded with very good, and reasonably priced, wines from that country.

SELECTED DRY WHITE WINES FROM AUSTRALIA

Tyrrell's Pinot Chardonnay 1977 "Bin 47":

❧ May 1980
Decanted three hours. Like foamy beer. Almost flat by the time we served it, and very little fizz left. Big, toasty nose of a good white Burgundy. Dark-gold colour. Wine of great distinction and quality. Well balanced, if a bit short on acidity. At its peak, but should last for a few years. Maybe has undergone secondary fermentation in bottle. This wine has evolved quite a bit since last year.

❧ August 1985
Deep, bright gold. Slightly spritzy at first, but that dissipated in the glass. Rich, nutty, toasty, complex. Similar to a mature Corton-Charlemagne. Lovely nose. Full, round, long, well balanced, but forward. Has held better than expected. As this wine matures, it is shedding its California character and it resembles white Burgundy.

❧ January 1989
Tasted against the Tyrrell's 1979 "Vat 47" Chardonnay. Deep gold. Nutty, rich, long, mature, complex. Not unlike a fine, well-aged Corton-Charlemagne. Luscious, rich, solid. Still has fruit, but very mature. At the end of its useful life. Has held very well (12 years). No sign of the foam-fizz so typical of this wine in the past. Very good, and better, in my opinion, than the 1979. An interesting experience.

Tyrrell's Pinot Chardonnay 1979 "Vat 47":

❧ November 1980
Very different in style from the 1977. Lighter colour, clean, crisp nose. Not as big and rich as the 1977 and without the fizz. Fairly high in acidity, good balance. Needs one to two more years. Quite French in style.

❧ August 1981
Had it with a lovely nine-pound barbecued Chinook salmon I had caught that afternoon. Good Chablis/Chardonnay style. Definitely more French than Californian. Good fruit/acidity balance. Ready, and hopefully will hold well. Very pleasant and very different from the 1977.

❧ January 1989
Against the 1977 vintage of the same wine. Medium gold, good depth. Little Chardonnay character. Fairly citrusy, acidic, lean, clean on palate, but lacking fruit. Was better three or four years ago. The 1977 is much more intense and classy. Needs drinking, too.

TYRRELL'S PINOT CHARDONNAY 1980 "VAT 47":

❧ December 1984
Deep bright-gold. Complex, toasty-oaky nose. Full, rich, well balanced. Like a fine Meursault with a touch of California Chardonnay. A very fine bottle. Good fruit, long, clean. Well made.

TYRRELL'S CHARDONNAY "HUNTER RIVER" 1988 "VAT 47":

❧ December 1992
Bright, deep-golden colour. Clean, rich, ripe Chardonnay nose. Not honeyed or oaky. Full, rich on palate, like a rich Corton-Charlemagne (more French than Californian in style), yet simpler finish. Best part was on entry. Good fruit. At its peak, and holding well. Ripe, rich fruit, but fairly low acidity. Good. Went well with lobster.

TYRRELL'S HUNTER RIVER CHARDONNAY 1989 "VAT 47":

❧ November 1994
Bright gold. Lovely oak, Chardonnay nose. Full, rich, fairly acidic. Slight hint of spritz (tiny bubbles). I've encountered that with some older vintages of this wine, notably with the 1977. Long, concentrated. Not very complex, but rich. By now, I have quite a bit of experience with Murray Tyrrell's Chardonnays. They are good, consistent, and reliable.

TYRRELL'S HUNTER RIVER PINOT CHARDONNAY 1991 "VAT 47":

❧ June 1996
Bright, deep, green-gold. Green apples/oak on both nose and palate. Fairly high acidity, even citric, but backed by good fruit. Youthful and intense. Crisp, fresh, long. No rush.

SELECTED RED WINES FROM AUSTRALIA

TYRRELL "RED" 1975:

Made from Shiraz grapes.

❧ July 1982
Some sediment. Deep colour. Good, fruity, sweet nose. No tannins. Long, round, very pleasant on palate. Well made. Ready, but will hold. Excellent value ($4 per bottle).

❧ July 1994
At home, with friends, before a trip to the 1994 World Cup soccer games in Los Angeles. 19 years old. Mature colour; typical "sweaty saddle" bouquet. Rich, long, well balanced. Mature, but still has fruit. Good, chunky wine.

WYNN'S COONAWARRA CABERNET SAUVIGNON 1976:

❧ August 1982
More complex and elegant than Tyrrell's 1978 Cabernet (tasted the same day). Leaner, a bit harder, but overall not as hot and big. Closer to Médoc in structure, but with the unmistakable ripeness on nose of Australian reds. Good. Needs one to two more years.

❧ September 1991
With council of the Commanderie de Bordeaux. Not as fine as the lovely 1973, nor as complex, but soft, delicate, evolved, smooth. Nice fruit. Warm, some sweetness. Long, clean finish. Hint of leather and Shiraz, but not excessively so. Needs drinking. Most enjoyable. Has held very well.

LINDEMAN'S NYRANG HERMITAGE 1976 "BIN 5525," AND LINDEMAN'S NYRANG HERMITAGE 1977:

Both had good, dark colours. The 1976 more evolved. Hot, spicy, sweet, vanilla,

"American oak" nose. Full, alcoholic, spicy Hermitage. Dry, hard finish. Straightforward. The 1977 tighter, leaner, otherwise similar comments. Interesting, but not my type of wines. Slightly rubbery.

TYRRELL'S HUNTER RIVER CABERNET-SHIRAZ 1978 "VAT 94":

50% Cabernet Sauvignon, 30% Hermitage Shiraz, 20% Malbec.

❧ July 1983
Some sediment, fairly deep colour. Soft, round, easy to drink. Clean and well made, if one-dimensional. Lacks the concentration of Tyrrell's Cabernet, but pleasant.

August 1996

On Turnagain Island. At 18 years of age, has held extremely well, but it is a bit astringent. Lost its intense sweetness. Didn't develop any complexity. Some "sweaty-saddle" on nose. Good, but drying up. Now I know that these wines can last, but they don't necessarily develop any complexity with extra bottle-age.

TYRRELL'S HUNTER RIVER CABERNET 1978 "VAT 70":

December 1980

Deep purple colour. Clean, fruity Cabernet nose. Intense. Good fruit/acidity balance. Not too much tannin, but enough intensity, depth, and fruit to last for quite some time. Try again in two years.

August 1983

Not as massive as three years ago. Big, dark, intense, "sweaty saddle" nose, typical of Australian reds. Lots of sediment. Round, full, some tannin. Good fruit. Excellent with game. A bit one-dimensional. Needs two to three more years, but should hold well.

August 1991

Impressive, deep colour. Some maturity at rim. Lots of sediment. Spicy Cabernet nose. Hint of leather, ripe fruit. Full, rich, intense, long. Straightforward, solid. Well balanced. Ready, but no rush.

TALTARNI CABERNET SAUVIGNON 1978, MOONAMBEL, VICTORIA:

December 1984

Very deep, young, rich colour to rim. Intense, open, spicy/sweet Cabernet nose. Full, rich, round on palate, almost sweet. Not a very complex wine, but fleshy and rich, with some tannins to lose. Excellent value ($7 per bottle). Needs two to four more years, and will hold well beyond that.

February 1996

With council of the Commanderie de Bordeaux. Deep colour, especially for its age. Cedar, mint, Cabernet nose. Full, powerful, tannic. Fruit is starting to weaken, though. A big, massive, old California-style Cabernet. In its youth, this wine was hailed as being "Château Latour-like." Well, having tasted this wine several times between 1984 and 1996, I can safely say that this is no Château Latour! However, it is a well-made wine and represents excellent value.

SOME AUSTRALIAN DESSERT WINES

SAMUEL WYNN PORT N/V "SERIES 5":

April 1981

At home, with a group of tasters from Le Tastevin. 18.5° alcohol by volume. Mature, late-bottled Vintage Port style. Not too sweet, good flavour. Slightly brown-orange colour. Good nose. Not too much depth, yet very pleasant. An experience. There is also some rare Tourriga grape in this Port (known for its finesse). Plastic cap and cork. No corkscrew needed; heavy layer of red sealing wax on neck.

MUSCAT BLANC "LATE-PICKED" 1980, BROWN BROS., MILAWA, VICTORIA:

(5° residual sugar)

May 1982

Weight and sugar resembles an Auslese, but unmistakable spicy Muscat nose. Well balanced, good acidity. Clean and well made.

BOTRYTIS SEMILLON "NOBLE LATE HARVEST" 1983 DE BORTOLI WINES, HALF-BOTTLE:

November 1994

Brilliant deep gold. Botrytis/slightly herbaceous on both nose and palate. Sweet, but with good acidity; hint of bitter-almond finish. Sauternes-like, rich, ripe, yet not quite Sauternes. Too herbaceous for that. Good concentration and fruit. Not unlike a very good Ste. Croix-du-Mont, but more intense.

WINES FROM ITALY, SPAIN, LEBANON, AND ISRAEL

ITALY

CHIANTI CLASSICO 1959 "RISERVA," FOSSI:

❧ May 1986

Typical Italian, mature, yet well-balanced wine. Showing some age, complex, forward, leathery-ripe nose. Good acidity; long, clean finish. Very good; has held surprisingly well. Lovely bottle.

SPANNA "MONTALBANO" 1966, ANTONIO VALLANA:

"Spanna" is the name of the Nebbiolo grape (unclassified Piedmont). The difference is that Spanna is planted in large crystallized soil rather than Barolo's and Barbaresco's chalky clay soil.

❧ November 1983

During the International Wine and Food Society's convention in Vancouver. Dark colour, some age, but the colour seemed young for a 17-year-old. Sweet, open, complex, ripe nose. Soft, long on palate. Lovely flavour. Very good. This wine, oddly enough, does not rate as a DOC, yet it is better than many DOC Piedmontese wines.

❧ May 1985

At home, with Bruce Guimaraens, the gifted owner-winemaker of Fonseca's Ports. Good wine, as on past occasions. Bruce has never tasted this wine before, and has little experience with Italian wines.

❧ April 1986

With *The Wine Consumer* panel. Decanted one-and-a-half hours. Served blind. Deep, dark colour. Full, rich on palate. Long, complex. Very rich, ripe, mature wine. At its peak, but no rush. A bit pruny. Tasters thought it was a younger, big Bordeaux or California Cabernet. Has held extremely well for a 20-year-old wine.

❧ August 1988

On Turnagain Island, with Harry and Prue Waugh. Harry has never tasted this before. Fair bit of sediment. Best bottle so far. Rich, yet Claret-like, but the spice, leather, and wood of Italy. Full, round, cedar-mint. Complex, rich. Ready, but no rush. Very good!

SPANNA "DEL PIEDMONTE" 1966, ANTONIO VALLANA:

❧ January 1984

(Against the Montalbano 1966 which was a bad bottle: off, unpleasant nose, acidy, and lean, yet full. Opened a 1966 Gruaud-Larose to replace the Montalbano.) Full, dark colour; sweet, intense Amarone style. Good fruit. Needed more breathing time. Sweeter, it seemed, than the "Montalbano."

BAROLO 1967 "RISERVA," BORGOGNO:

❧ October 1984

Decanted two hours (it needed two hours airing time to round up. At first it was harsh). Some sediment. Medium colour, good depth, showing some age. Elegant, yet a bit spicy and leathery on nose. Full, fairly hard on palate. After two hours, it got rid of some of its harshness. Fairly long, well made. A rather masculine wine. Impressive wine at 17 years of age.

❧ February 1986

Tasted against 1967 Château Latour. Round, elegant, complex, and long. Well balanced. Softer than when tasted previously in 1984. Very good.

AMARONE, RECCIOTO DELLA VALPOLICELLA 1971, CLASSICO SUPERIORE, BERTANI:

❧ November 1979

An intense, big, dark wine, not unlike a Late Harvest Zinfandel. Big, powerful. Pleasant now, but will last for a long time. Ripe, leathery, full, lots of ripe fruit. A big wine. Too intense for my taste.

❧ December 1981

Smells like Port, tastes like a big Zinfandel. I am not a fan of Amarone. A matter of taste.

BAROLO 1971, MONTANELLO:

❧ February 1981

Very big, quite dark. Lots of tannin. Needs three to five more years. Nose opened up a bit, some fruit-sweetness, some tar. Very big and dry on palate. Big "meaty" wine.

❧ November 1995

This wine is now 24 years old. Fair bit of sediment. Decanted one hour. Good, dark colour. Mature rim. Ripe, tar, and candied fruit on nose. Much more evolved than in 1981, of course. Sweet, rich, round, even a bit tannic. A solid, rich wine that has reached its plateau. Full, sweet, long, and well balanced.

BARBARESCO 1974 "RISERVA," PRUNOTTO, CANTINA S. CASSIANO:

❧ August 1986

On our 12th wedding anniversary. Little sediment. Mature amber colour. Open, spicy, leathery, complex nose. Good acidity, well balanced, mature, round, and long. A very good, typical Barbaresco from a good vintage.

❧ February 1995

At over 20 years of age, little sediment. Evolved colour with good depth. Spicy, wet straw, classic tar, Nebbiolo nose. Round, complex. Fairly acidic, no tannins left, but backed by good, round fruit. At its peak, with a good, clean, long finish. Decanted one hour. Very nice wine.

BAROLO 1974 "RISERVA," PIO CESARE:

❧ October 1990
Decanted two hours. Some sediment. Deep colour, mature orange rim. Fruity, delicate, yet full; a bit leathery, complex, rich, well balanced. At its peak. No harshness. Very nice wine. Ready, but will hold four to five more years.

TAURASI 1974, MASTROBERARDINO:

❧ May 1983
Full, dark colour, a bit "cheesy" nose (similar to this producer's white Greco di Tufo). Flavourful. Needed airing for an hour.

GATTINARA 1978 "MONSECCO," LE COLLINE:

A blend of 70% Nebbiolo and 30% Vespolina.

❧ January 1990
Decanted two hours. Bright red. Some sediment. Spicy Nebbiolo, expansive, warm nose. Full, round, almost sweet. Very good balance and length. Good fruit. Clean and long. Getting ready, but no rush.

❧ November 1994
With the council of the Commanderie de Bordeaux. Bright red colour. Some sediment. Decanted one-and-a half hours. Very dry, tight, "old style" wine. Not bad, fairly acidic, lean; too tight, losing its fruit. Drink up.

LACRIMA CHRISTI DEL VESUVIO 1978, MASTROBERARDINO:

❧ April 1981
Pale-golden colour. Fairly neutral on both nose and palate. Not very complex, but well made, clean, easy to drink; lacks personality.

GRECO DI TUFO 1978, MASTROBERARDINO:

❧ October 1981
Pale-golden colour. Interesting, unusual pasta/parmesan nose (said to improve with age). Well balanced, well made. Very unusual, good flavour. Not great, but interesting.

BAROLO 1978 RISERVA "GINESTRA DI MONFORTE D'ALBA," PRUNOTTO:

❧ February 1991
Very little sediment. Medium dark colour, slightly orangy rim. Well structured, good fruit, backbone, a bit tannic, rich. Approaching its peak. Very good.

BAROLO 1978 RISERVA, "BUSSIA DI MONFORTE D'ALBA," PRUNOTTO:

❧ November 1994
Decanted two hours. No sediment. Very good, deep colour. Youthful. Fruity, spicy nose. Full, rich, excellent balance, and ripe fruit, unlike many older-style Italian reds that are too dry and acidic. Rich fruit, long, complex. This is very good. No rush, even though it is already 16 years old.

BARBARESCO 1978 RISERVA, "MONTESTEFANO," PRUNOTTO:

❧ January 1995
Decanted one-and-a-half hours. No sediment. Bright red colour. Some orange at rim. These 1978s are now quite rare and expensive. Retails in the US for US$50 per bottle. (I acquired a few bottles of this wine in Seattle in 1983, and paid $9.50 per bottle.) Good depth. Clean, fruity, losing its hard edge, yet still lively. Fairly high acidity, typical of Italian reds, but backed by lovely fruit, and has a mellow, yet rich finish. Ready, but no rush. Needs breathing for two hours.

SASSICAIA 1978, TENUTA SAN GUIDO-BOLGHERI:

A rare and expensive wine made from 100% Cabernet Sauvignon grapes. This 1978 is fabulous and a sleeper, and one of their biggest, and most concentrated wines ever produced.

❧ July 1986
At home, with the panel of *The Wine Consumer*. Served blind at the end of an extensive wine tasting. Very deep, young colour. Fair bit of sediment. Much younger-looking than its age would indicate. Complex, rich, spicy, full nose, not unlike a California Cabernet Sauvignon (which is what most tasters thought it was). Long, rich, full, fruity, tannic, intense. Needs at least three to five more years to round up a bit. Great concentration. Purchased a case of this wine in Seattle in 1984. Paid $11.75 per bottle.

❧ September 1989
With Haskell and Rae Norman. Superb wine. Great. Comments as three years ago. No sign of ageing.

❧ April 1991
I opened a bottle, knowing that it was not ready, simply because it was mid shoulder level and that worried me. Full, youthful, purple-red colour of a much younger wine. Fruity, spicy, rich, concentrated; very good fruit/acidity balance. Will reach its peak in five years (if well stored), and last for many more.

❧ October 3, 1993
A Middle Eastern dinner, at home, with friends, against 1978 Côte-Rôtie (Guigal), 1978 Torres "Black Label," and 1962 Vega Sicilia "Unico," and followed by a 1945 Rebello Valente Port.

The 1978 Sassicaia is now very rare. Sells at auction (in 1993) for US$150 to $200 a bottle. Low neck level. Very good, deep colour. Not ready yet. Very good extract. Like a 1970 Montrose! Solid, full, rich, long. Spicy Cabernet nose. Austere, tannic, but ripe berries hidden there. No rush. Some tasters think this wine is too dry. I think it needs time. Very good. Solid, serious wine.

❧ January 1996
At home, with friends. Decanted one-and-a-half hours. Intense, very dark colour to rim. The structure of a 1970 Montrose and the minty, spicy nose of a California Cabernet. Complex, tannic, long. Loads of fruit. No rush. A big, powerful wine. Full, serious. Very different from modern Sassicaia which has more new oak/vanilla flavours, and is more accessible. A classic.

❧ January 1997
My contribution to a vertical Sassicaia 1978 to 1989 (11-vintage) tasting. Magnificent. The star of the evening. (The 1985 was close behind.) Big, rich, "old style." Lots of depth, extract, ripe tannins, and fruit. Will last well for another five to ten years or more. Great bottle. At this tasting, it became obvious how much the style of Sassicaia has changed since the magnificent 1978 was produced.

TIGNANELLO 1979 "RISERVA," ANTINORI:

❧ August 1993
Medium dark, maturing colour. Clean vanilla, oak, fruity nose. Round, complex, long. Delicate, not as powerful as a few years ago. Sweetish on palate. Very good balance. Lovely.

SASSICAIA 1981, BOLGHERI, ANTINORI:

❧ November 1989
Deep, youthful colour. Spicy Cabernet nose. Leaner style, a bit acidic, but backed by good fruit. Not as rich or intense as the 1978, but quite nice. Drink now to 1995.

❧ November 1990
With the council of the Commanderie de Bordeaux. Decanted one hour. Some sediment. Lovely, complex wine. Quite rich, like a 1982 red Bordeaux. Raspberries, oak, vanilla, cassis nose. Full, tannic, yet round. Lots of class and elegance. Not ready, but most enjoyable. Excellent balance. Very good.

❧ June 1995
With council of Le Tastevin Wine Club. Deep purplish colour. Very youthful-looking. Unmistakable Cabernet nose. Spicy, ripe black fruit, hint of oak. Lovely, fruity nose. Full, rich, very good acidity. Structured like a fine, rich St. Julien rather than a heavy or ripe California or Australian Cabernet, yet has this "un-French," sweet fruit. Long, complex. Slight sharpness at finish, but very good overall, and holding extremely well. No rush.

TIGNANELLO 1982, ANTINORI:

❧ March 1994
This wine is ready now. Elegant, subdued, complex, delicate, nice fruit, well balanced. Classy. Well made. Hint of new oak.

SASSICAIA 1982 "TENUTA SAN GUIDO-BOLGHERI," ANTINORI:

❧ January 1993
Decanted two hours. Some sediment. Still-purplish, deep, bright colour. Very youthful appearance. Oak, vanilla, sweet cherries, fresh nose at ten years. Slight hint of straw, rubber (typical Italian). Rich, round, loads of ripe fruit. Excellent balance and length. Very good backbone. Will reach its peak around 1996 and last well past 2000. Very good potential. Not harsh or hard. Enjoyable now, but really too young. Not nearly as big or intense as the magnificent 1978, though.

BARBARESCO 1982, ANGELO GAJA:

❧ December 1988
With panel of *The Wine Consumer*. Medium to deep colour. Tight, clean nose. Some spice. Leaner, tannic. Tight fruit, yet clean and long. Very good quality; new oak predominates at this stage. Classy wine. Needs six extra years. Clean and impeccably made.

VENEGAZZÚ 1982 "BLACK LABEL," VILLA LOREDAN:

A rare wine, especially the "Black Label," a monopole of Loredan. Made from a blend of Cabernet and Merlot.

❧ August 1987
Quite similar style to Sassicaia, but with less depth and fruit. Clean, spicy nose. Well balanced. Needs two to four years.

❧ September 1987
With the panel of *The Wine Consumer*. A bit leaner than Sassicaia, and more American oak rather than French. Some sharpness, but quite good. Try again from 1989 onward.

❧ July 1993
On Turnagain Island, with Jean-Claude Berrouet, the winemaker of the Moueix properties, including Petrus, Trotanoy, etc., and his wife Nelly, kids, and friends. Ripe, fairly acidic, full, concentrated. Good fruit, a bit leathery. Lacks complexity, but holding well. It has not evolved nearly as well as the superb 1978 Sassicaia.

CABREO "PREDICATO DI BITURICA" 1983, RUFFINO:

(Predicato is Cabernet Sauvignon.)

❧ September 1996

Bright, deep-red colour. Straw/fruit, classic Sangiovese nose. Clean, lovely fruit, balance, depth, length. All there. At its peak. No sharp edges. Little sediment. A mouthful of lovely, elegant fruit. Very long, clean finish. Extremely well made.

MORMORETTO "PREDICATO DI BITURICA," 1983, FRESCOBALDI:

❧ July 1995

Bright, dark red. "New wave" Italian wine. Fresh, fruity Cabernet with hint of vanilla, oak. Round, good depth. Nice fruit. Well balanced. Surprisingly fresh. Long. Good wine.

SPAIN

VEGA SICILIA COSECHA 1962 "UNICO," RIBERA DEL DUERO:

❧ October 30, 1993

Middle Eastern dinner with friends.

(I also served a 1979 Chave Hermitage Blanc, and the following 1978s: Côte-Rôtie Guigal, Sassicaia, and Torres "Black Label."

With dessert, I served this Port.

1945 REBELLO VALENTE VINTAGE PORT:

Perfect now. Good, dark, mature colour. Subdued, woody, spicy nose. Round, silky, yet great extract. Long, complex, elegant. Excellent balance. Lots of class here. A guest found it too acidic, yet I didn't find it acidic at all, but rather elegant and long. Lovely wine. Best Spanish wine I've ever tasted. Retails now for US$170 a bottle. Great wine!

MARQUÉS DE RISCAL 1970, RIOJA:

❧ 1976 and 1977

Tasted several times. Powerful, dry wine. Medium colour, dry taste. Improved after two hours. A bit thin, but good quality.

❧ May 1979

Fading; has this heavy oak flavour of big older Riojas. Where are the great wines this property used to produce in the past five decades?

TORRES GRAN CORONAS 1970 "RESERVA," PENEDÉS:

❧ September 1979

70% Cabernet Sauvignon in the blend. Deep, fruity, intense wine. Needs two to three more years. Excellent quality.

❧ May 1981

Tasted blind against 1970 Sterling Cabernet Sauvignon and 1970 Château Beaumont. This was the most complex of the three and the lightest in colour. Touch of orange-brown. Good, oak-vanilla nose. Good flavour and long aftertaste. A well-made wine.

❧ February 1987

Good depth, mature. A bit sharper than above. Very good complexity, Claret style, yet some leather and wood, typical of Spanish mature reds. Quite good. Needs drinking.

TORRES GRAN CORONAS 1978 "BLACK LABEL" RESERVA, PENEDÉS:

❧ September 1989

Decanted 45 minutes. Medium to dark still youthful colour. Some sediment. Spicy, oaky, black currant nose. Quite "American oak" on nose. Medium-bodied, good depth, clean, long finish; oak predominates. A well-made wine. Drink now to 1993.

❧ October 30, 1993

Tasted against 1978 Côte-Rôtie Guigal and 1978 Sassicaia (also 1962 Vega Sicilia "Unico"). Most forward of the three 1978s. Medium palish red. Pronounced American vanilla-oak nose. Round, woody, a bit dry. Forward. Round and elegant. Very Spanish. Slightly leathery. Good, but needs drinking.

LEBANON

VIN NAKAD, VIN VIEUX ROUGE 1963, CHTOURA, NAKAD ET FILS:

❧ February 1987

Mature pale-red colour. Slightly woody, clean nose. Soft, forward, getting tired. Lean with noticeable acidity; short, and low fruit. Needs drinking. Not bad, though. Soft, forward, with some elegance.

CHÂTEAU MUSAR 1970:

❧ September 1991

Dark, mature colour. Some sediment. Leathery, mature, spicy, sweet, American oak on nose. Round, yet rich/ripe on palate. Long, complex, round, slightly woody. Rioja-like but slightly sweeter. Very nice.

❧ CHÂTEAU MUSAR 1977:

December 1990. Musty-dirty nose (a bit corked?). Old style, woody, yet nice fruit; spicy, round, forward on palate. Complex, delicate finish. A combination of Cabernet and Rhône style. Ready. Nose was unclean, though.

ISRAEL

YARDEN CHARDONNAY "GALIL" 1987:

❧ March 1991

(First commercial vintage) Pale gold; clean, delicate, subdued nose. Hint of oak and delicate fruit. Light, fair on entry, but short, acidic finish. Young vines. Not a bad first effort

CARMEL CABERNET SAUVIGNON 1974:

❧ Spring 1978

For the price ($4), a good value. Delicate nose, not too intense; lacks depth, and is a bit too sweet. Overall, decent quality.

CARMEL CABERNET SAUVIGNON 1976 "VINTAGE SELECTION":

❧ September 1979

Medium-dark colour. Clean nose, not very complex. Clean taste with Cabernet Sauvignon characteristics (oaky, earthy flavour). Needs another year or two. Not too much tannin left.

❧ April 1987

On Turnagain Island, with Joan and Sam Fromowitz, the US Consul General to Vancouver. Mature colour, some sediment. Pruny, leathery nose, similar to a mature Rioja. Round, forward, a bit too acidic, but good complexity, too. Has held well, but needs drinking.

CARMEL CABERNET SAUVIGNON 1978 "VINTAGE SELECTION":

❧ February 1985

Medium-dark colour. Spicy Cabernet nose. Dry, yet mature on palate, like a Cru Bourgeois. Not bad. Clean aftertaste.

YARDEN CABERNET SAUVIGNON "GALIL" 1985:

This wine was a gold medal winner at the Bristol Wine Fair.

❧ October 1988

Deep, rich, ripe fruit; new oak, intense. California style, yet better acidity, like French Cabernet Sauvignons. Very good effort. Try around 1991 to 1993.

❧ November 1990

Medium-deep, youthful colour. Comments as above, but slightly more forward. Rounder, silky, elegant, oak, vanilla, and cherries, all in harmony.

❧ September 1991

Very deep red. Very intense, youthful. Zinfandel-like, but leaner Bordeaux structure. Needs time. Fruity, spicy, some oak, ripe cherries. Try again in 1995. Intense. Lacks elegance at this stage.

❧ July 1992

Deep, youthful, ruby-red colour. Spicy, scented. More Australian than California style. Very good depth, fruit extract, and length. Needs two to four extra years. As this wine ages, it seems to change—not only in terms of evolution but in style, too.

❧ October 1994

Before a tasting of Châteaux Mouton-Baron-Philippe, Pontet-Canet, and Malescot, all 1959s. Served double-blind. Most people thought it was a California or Australia Shiraz, or Washington State Cabernet. Deep red. Spicy, oaky, "hot country" nose. Very "New World," yet leaner acidity (similar to a Washington State Cabernet). Approachable, but no rush. Quite good.

SEGAL'S CABERNET SAUVIGNON "UNFILTERED" 1988, ISRAEL:

❧ February 1996

With council of the Commanderie de Bordeaux. Appearance, smell, and taste of a cheaply made "foxy" California Pinot Noir. Fruity/nail polish nose. Spicy, decent fruit. No Cabernet Sauvignon character at all. Odd wine.

INDEX *of* PEOPLE & WINES

INDEX of PEOPLE

A

Aaron, *Christine: 403*
Michael: 403
Accad, *Guy: 438*
Achille-Fould: *18*
Adams, *Peter: 58*
Agam, *Yakov: 556*
Alba, *Dominique: 70*
Allan, *David: 229, 260*
Alper, *Simon: 8*
Anderson, *Doug: 504, 527*
Arbel, *Dafna: 563*
Menashe: 6, 7, 33, 151, 153, 154, 193, 194, 545, 563, 576, Photos
Aubin, *Marie-José: 455, 474, 505, 512, 514, 519, Photos*
Avenali, *Joan: 110*
Peter: 110
Avery, *John: 528*

B

Bacigalupi, *John: 34*
Baggio, *Roberto: 393*
Baker, *Mark: 162*
Ball, *Cathy: 245*
Chuck: 245
Bannerman, *Gary: 64*
Baranzini, *Joe: 139*
Barateau, *Mr. H.: 83*
Bardot, *Brigitte: 192*
Baresi, *Franco: 393*
Barnes, *Chris: 54*
Linda: 54
Barolet, *Dr.: 392*
Baron, *Daniel: 139, 166, 310, 370, 371, 378, 389, 403, 549, 597, 631, 642*
Barriaux, *Mr.: 7*
Barrière, *Jacques: 30, 125*
Barton, *Anthony: 67, 190, 191, 272, 296, 429, 491, 502, 510, 519*
Ronald: 41, 67, 191, 491, 502, 510, 519, 543
Thomas: 296
Baruch, *Sir Bernard: 214, 374, 419*
Batista: *266*
Belland, *Adrien: 292*
Bender, *John: 408*
Bennion, *Dave: 28*
Berkley, *David: 231*
Diana: 231
Berman, *Dr. Steven: 522*
Bernhard, *Anna: 387*
Stan: 387
Bernhards, *the: Photos*
Berniau, *Maryse: 589*
Berrouet, *Jean-Claude: 123, 189, 378, 431, 432, 517, 561, 656, Photos*
Nelly: 561, 656
Berry, *Charles Walter: 397*
Bettane, *Michel: 468, 469, 470, 482*
Biondi-Santi, *Dr. Franco: 126, 127, 128*
Bishop, *John: 390*
Bizot, *Christian: 353*
Guy: 353
Blondin, *Raoul: 67, 70, 121, 302, 495, 511*
Blumberg, *Martin: 247, 441, 465, 466*
Bocuse, *Paul: 6*
Boirie, *Mme.: 43*
Boothe, *Barry: 408*
Joan: 408
Borderie, *Jean-Jacques: 576*
Borie, *Bruno: 13*
Jean-Eugene: 13, 191, 431, 507
Bouchard, *Paul: 8*
Boudot, *Gerard: 293, 294, 442*
Bouteillers: *184*
Boyer: *353*
Bradshaw, *Dick: 270*
Val: 270
Brajkovich, *Mr.: 215*
Bretzenheim: *112*
Brincko, *John: 264, 339*
Broadbent, *Bartholomew: 282, 326, 327*
Daphne: 55
Michael: 13, 55, 57, 66, 68, 130, 132, 134, 149, 182, 184, 185, 186, 187, 191, 264, 282, 326, 327, 342, 353, 394, 414, 478, 526, 593
Bröezel, *Gunther: 464, 521*
Bronfman: *73*
Brossier, *Charles: 15, 588*
Brother Timothy: *29, 389, 564*
Brounstein, *Al: 51, 52, 53, 466, 469, 470, 471*
Buchan, *Beth: 338*
Russ: 338, 339
Bucher, *Peter: 357*
Buehler, *George: 217*
Burgundy, *Duke of: 526*
Burnett, *Dr. John: 73*
Burr, *Dr. Larry: 313, 429, 430, 434, 603*

C

Cain, *Marcia: 389*
Campbell, *Ian Maxwell: Intro vii*
Cantona, *Eric: 420*
Capdemourlin: *117*
Carmagnac, *Philippe: 187*
Carpenter, *John: 118, 162*
Carruthers, *Alastair: 105, 177, 186, 233*
Jean: 177
Casey, *Dr. Bill: 101, 196*
Casteja, *Philippe: 14, 71*
Castro, *Fidel: 266*
Cathelin, *Bernard: 529*
Cathiard, *Florence: 457*
Cazenaves: *118, 119, 297, 298*
Cazes, *André: 16, 17, 75, 76, 430*
Jean-Michel: 16, 75, 97, 98, 99, 100, 124, 130, 132, 133, 151, 154, 181, 182, 183, 184, 222, 295, 296, 309, 430, 431, 434, 510, 558, Photos
Marie-Therèse: 100, 125, 183
Michel: 185
Sylvie: 16, 76, 124, 431
Chardon, *Claude: 42*
Pierre: 14
Yves: 14, 42, 190, 294
Chartron, *Jean: 597*
Chave, *Gerard: 9, 10, 154, 156, 243, 294, 312, 502, 521, 529, 617, 619*
Jean-Louis: 9

Chen, *Cherise* (see Moueix, *Cherise*): *390, 391, 572, 626, Photos*

Chevillon, *Robert: 149*

Choppin, *Mlle.: 286, 287*

Christiansen, *Dr. Arnold: 90*

Chroman, *Nathan: 217*

Churchill, *Sir Winston: 214, 373, 609, 611*

Clair, *Bruno, 290: 447, 503*

Clark, *Nick: 19*

Clauzel: *16*

Clavelin, *Michel: 33*

Cloverie, *Madeleine: 123*

Coates, *Clive: 186, 187, 382, 383, 384, 550*

Cobb, *Peter: 361, 362, 363*

Coche-Dury: *293*
Jean-François: 148, 149, 167, 189, 292

Collingwood, *Norm: 29*

Collins, *Bill: 245*

Colonel Mota Gur: *Intro i*

Conroy, *Mike: 15*

Conte, *Jean-Yves: 273, 615*

Cordier, *Mr.: 121*

Corti, *Darrell: 29, 257*

Couasnon, *Mr.: 182*

Crawford, *Justin: 151*

Crocker: *174*
Mr.: 203

Cropsal, *Jean-Paul: 7*

Cross, *Barb: 58, 425*
Joan: 27, 37, 149, 283, 327, 356, 370, 403, 532, 557, 563, 585, 619, 639, 650, Photos
Ken: 24, 58, 75, 86, 97, 274, 358, 365, 425, 552
Sid: 1, 27, 29, 37, 38, 55, 58, 64, 75, 80, 82, 86, 88, 89, 90, 97, 105, 108, 126, 137, 145, 147, 148, 149, 162, 170, 178, 180, 217, 225, 245, 251, 257, 263, 266, 269, 274, 283, 309, 323, 327, 328, 356, 358, 370, 403, 422, 443, 446, 483, 532, 553, 557, 563, 578, 585, 594, 603, 619, 621, 627, 628, 639, 650, Photos

Crosses:
Ken Crosses, the: 3, 34, 60, 235, 332, 426, 552

Croy, *Marcena* (see Levine, *Marcena*): *425, Photos*

Cruse, *Hermann: 414*

D

d'Aramon, *Laure: 432, Photos*

d'Estaing, *Giscard: 589*

d'Ezaguire, *Xavier: 46, 70, 138*

d'Ollone, *Comte Gildas: 429*

da Vinci, *Leonardo: 438*

Daniel, *John: 44, 139, 631*

Danko, *Gary: 415*

Danskin, *Richard: 266, 267*
Sherry: 266

Darracq, *Mme.: 15*

Davidson, *Jim: 425*

Davies, *Jack: 38, 460*

Day: *190*

Dayan, *General Moshe: Intro i*

de Beaumel, *Mr. and Mrs.: 427*

de Bellinex, *Mr.: 4*

de Ferrer, *Hervé: 146, 147*

de Gaulle, *Charles: 192, 276, 508*

de Lalande, *Comtesse: 212*

de Lencquesaing, *Général: 42, 161, 162, 296, 428*
May (Eliane): 41, 122, 161, 162, 163, 164, 191, 193, 210, 301, 399, 428, Photos
Sophie: 429

de Loach, *Mike: 95*

de Lur Saluces, *Count: 355*

de Mallet-Roquefort, *Count: 18*

de Pontac, *Vicomte: 604*

de Rothschilds, *the: 70, 204*

de Rothschild, *Alphonse: 551*
Baron: 209
Baron Philippe: 67, 70, 112, 191, 221, 414, 469, 495, 511
Baronesse Philippine: 67, 138, 556, Photos
Edmond: 551
Eric: 414
Gustave: 551
James: 551

Delacote, *Pierre: 406, 499*

Delaforce, *Richard: 74*
Victor: 166

Delbeck, *Madeleine: 123, 188, 433, 434*
Marie-Amandine: 188
Pascal: Intro vi, 17, 42, 43, 69, 71, 122, 123, 188, 189, 298, 299, 301, 408, 432, 433, 434, 438, 453, 470, 510, 517, 571, Photos

Delmas, *Jean: 67, 271, 337, 491*

Delon, *Mr.: 121*
Michel: 41, 120, 161, 182, 184, 193, 213, 399, 566

Derbalian, *George: 409*

Derksen, *Monte: 169*

Dervieux, *Albert: 157*

Desai, *Bipin: 91, 97, 100, 108, 124, 126, 130, 184, 185, 210, 216, 222, 243, 248, 275, 276, 309, 310, 339, 340, 346, 348, 375, 376, 381, 410, 412, 413, 414, 466*

Deschamps, *Jeanne-Marie: 289*

Dodson, *Charles: 14*

Doise, *Pierre: 525*

Dorfler, *Ernst: 501*

Doudet-Naudin, *Yves: 7*

Dougdale, *David: 243, 622, 634, 638*
Kate: 622, 634, 638

Downs, *Pete: 94*

Draper, *Paul: 28, 294, 530, 547*

Drouhin, *Joseph: 436*
Robert: 7, 202

Duboeuf, *Georges: 149*

Dubois-Chalon, *Mme.: 42, 71, 188, 189, 432, 433, 453*

Dubray, *Jean-Pierre: 452*

Ducasse, *Mr.: 17, 41, 118, 187, 300, 579, 580*

Duckhorn, *Dan: 173, 314, 442, 463*
Margaret: 314, 315, 366, 424, 428, 442, 463, 503, 632

Dunn, *Randy: 38, 89, 90, 503, 507*

Dupin, *Mr.: 191*

Dupuis: *13*

Dyer, *Dawnine: Photos*

E

Eberlin: *149*

Eisele, *Barb: 231*
Milt: 231, 232, 245, 309

Engerer, *Frederic: 431, 443*

Escano, *Jean-Pierre: 8*

F

Faiveley, *François: 88, 232, 272, 525, 526, 529*

Father Don: *174*

Feenie, *Rob: 450, 480, 482, 494, 505*

Ferrand, *Pierre: 406*

Fetzer, *Jim: Photos*

Ficklin, *David: 196*
Walter: 175, 196

Finnigan, *Robert: 383, 468*

Fitzgibbons, *Jim: 32*

Fitzpatrick, *Moira: 4*

Fleming, *Dr. Dick: 409*
Tom: 365

Foley, *Dennis: 91, 169, 383, 384, 385*

Fonteyn, *Margot: Intro iv*

Forman, *Rick: 89, 459*

Fouquet, *Francis: 364, 427, 540, 600, 605, 613, 631, Photos*
Mr.: 424
Mrs.: 631

Fournier, *Eric: 71, 72, 118, 189, 298, 432*

Franco, *Francisco: 341*

François, *Mme.: 151*

Fredericks, *Marcia: 79*
Pete: 79

Freeman, *David: 202, 229, 234, 243, 356, 365, 495, 616, Photos*

Freemans, *the: 32, 34, 80, 235, 579, 585, 587, 629*

Frericks, *H.: 391*

Frescobaldi, *Marchesi: 455*

Fromowitz, *Joan: 200, 332, 374, 505, 581, 659*
Sam: 200, 332, 374, 505, 581, 635, 659

G

Gaby, *Jim: 409*

Gagey, *Pierre-Henri: 284*

Gaja, *Angelo: 143, 144, 258, 421*

Garcia, *Mr.: 182*

Gardère, *Jean-Paul: 70, 76, 191, 192, 193, 260, 276, 508*

Gautreau, *Mr.: 124*

Getty, *Gordon: 433*

Ginestet: *44, 71, 449, 510, 563, 564, 577*
Fernand: 562

Girardet, *Freddy: 470*

Gismondi, *Tony: 37, 80, 105, 181, 187, 188, 190, 192, 425, 541, 545, 577, 588, 641, 642, Photos*

Givton (McGregor), *Carol: Intro v, vi, 3, 5, 6, 10, 13, 14, 15, 16, 25, 44, 47, 60, 67, 70, 71, 73, 74, 89, 164, 172, 177, 230, 246, 252, 253, 267, 309, 310, 327, 328, 346, 351, 352, 354, 356, 372, 395, 409, 411, 439, 454, 462, 463, 492, 532, 533, 534, 535, 537, 541, 544, 545, 546, 547, 549, 552, 553, 555, 556, 558, 562, 563, 568, 569, 571, 573, 574, 580, 582, 584, 585, 586, 587, 588, 592, 597, 599, 600, 601, 602, 607, 608, 612, 614, 617, 632, 639, Photos*
Michael: Intro vi, 4, 16, 47, 158, 231, 349, 391, 422, 426, 454, 462, 463, 523, 525, 534, 538, 560, 572, 574, 578, 586, 588, 589, 599, 601, 603, 607, 614, 637, Photos
Orly: 4, 10, 28, 41, 47, 231, 349, 422, 428, 429, 436, 439, 449, 450, 454, 462, 488, 512, 521, 533, 534, 538, 541, 542, 550, 574, 575, 586, 587, 588, 589, 599, 600, 601, 607, 608, 611, 614, 617, 642, Photos

Godin, *Mr.: 193, 301*

Goldstein, *Buck: 245*

Gordon, *Jim: 128*

Gosset, *Antoine: 272, 352, 353, 608*

Gottardi, *Bruno: 72*

Gouges, *Henri: 273*

Grady, *Ingo: 625*

Grancey: *31*

Grandma Jenny: *598, 631, Photos*

Grath, *Bob: 54*

Greene, *Kenneth: 252*

Grgich, *Mike: 334, 335, 453, 475*

Grillet, *Mr.: 427*

Groom, *Darryl: 368*

Grunewald, *Wolfgang: 339*

Guerard, *Michel: 68*

Guigal, *Etienne: 156*
Marcel: 156, 157

Guimaraens, *Bruce: 57, 73, 74, 102, 103, 124, 136, 149, 166, 398, 399, 400, 495, 544, 549, 595, 613, 616, 628, 633, 648, 654*
Debbie: 544, 613, 616, 628, 648
Fred: 400

Guiter, *Henri: 42*

H

Haas, *Robert: 145, 293*

Hager, *Beth: 342*

Hallay, *Robert: 44*

Hampson, *Dirk: 310*

Hanson, *Craig: 161*

Hare, *Alan: 275*

Hart, *John: 217, 279*

Hatchet: *266*

Healy, *Maurice: 458*

Hebrard, *Jacques: 187, 364, 432, 540, 600, 605, 613, 631, Photos*

Heitz, *Alice: 37, 52, 83, 89, 100, 101, 172, 174, 195, 196, 198, 215, 231, 245, 247, 266, 311, 312, 315, 325, 335, 395, 414, 415, 424, 434, 460, 488, 503, 556, 577, 579, 584, 610, 620, 622, 638*
David: 100, 174, 196, 247, 325, 394, 415, 460, 488
Joe: 37, 38, 52, 77, 83, 89, 100, 101, 166, 172, 174, 175, 195, 196, 198, 199, 203, 215, 231, 232, 239, 245, 246, 247, 258, 263, 266, 267, 281, 282, 311, 312, 313, 315, 323, 325, 326, 335, 366, 386, 390, 394, 395, 414, 415, 424, 434, 439, 460, 466, 488, 496, 503, 506, 507, 528, 529, 530, 531, 543, 547, 556, 573, 577, 579, 584, 609, 610, 619, 620, 622, 626, 634, 636, 638, 641, 645, 647, Photos

INDEX *of* PEOPLE

Kathleen (see Ryan, *Kathleen*)*: 37, 83, 100, 101, 174, 196, 247, 282, 325, 394, 460, 488, 543, 573, 609, 619, 645*
Rolly: 89, 174, 196, 247, 312, 325, 394, 395, 460, 488
Ryan: 89
Sally: 89

Hegedus, *Zoltan: 306*

Helmers, *the: 587*

Hemphill, *Alan: 64, Photos*

Henrikson, *Peter: 326*

Hochar, *Serge: 193, 194, 258, 538, 554, 611, 629, 638*

Hoeter, *Dr. Bernard: 365, Photos*

Hoffmanns*: 328*

Hollowell, *Jay: 304*

Hoover, *Herbert: 342*

Huet, *Johnny: 478*

Hugel, *Etienne: 308*
Jean (Johnny): 5, 36, 196, 197, 308, 382, 383, 524, 621

Huntley, *Ian: 368*

I

Ichinose, *Dr. Ben: 112, 381*
George: 112

Isert, *Merv: 425*

J

Jaboulet, *Gerard: 6, 8, 9, 153, 155, 243, 248, 249, 254, 294, 308, 353, 453, 458, 472, 521, 618*
Paul: 153, 154

Janin, *Mrs.: 116*

Jayer, *Henri: 291*

Jeanty, *Philippe: 498*

Jeffersons*: 356*

Joguet, *Charles: 188*

Johnson, *Hugh: 64, 65, 425, Photos*
Nat: 342

Jordan, *Ehren: 488*
Michael: 349

Juillot, *Michel: 153, 292, 295*

K

Kagele, *Joy: 94*

Kanke, *Bud: 4, 27*

Kaplan, *Stephen: 279, 315, 332, 333, 338, 349, 350, 360, 362, 544, 629*

Keenan*: 248*

Keller, *Hubert: 356, 442*
Thomas: 382, 393, 466, 519, 527

Kester, *Dr. Harold: 365*

Khouri, *Toufiq: 76, 95, 169*

Kidd, *Scott: 494*

Killas, *Kostie: 105*

King Farouk*: Intro iv*

King Hussein*: Intro i, ii*

Klausner, *Willette: 582*

Klein, *Dr. Brad: 76, 90, 126, 135, 140, 207, 214, 216, 219, 237, 239, 262, 263, 266, 279, 309, 317, 318, 327, 338, 367, 371, 372, 381, 393, 410, 413, 439, 498, 512, 544, 559, 565, 587, 605, 633, 650, Photos*
Stephen: 339

Koetter, *Uwe: 386*

Kolasa, *Jay: 304*
John: 191, 303, 330

Kongsgrood, *John: 123*

Konsgaard, *Tom: 245*

Kornell, *Hans: 312*

Kramer, *Mat: 472*

Krug, *Henri: 242, 348*
Rémy: 158, 159, 241, 267, 346, 347, 348, 349, 352, 371

L

La Gardère, *Mr.: 14*

Laborde, *Mr.: 295*

Lacoste*: 518*

Ladoucette*: 145*

Lafon, *Mr.: 16*

Lail, *Robin: 139, 378, 389, 631*

Lake, *David: 94, Photos*

Latour, *Louis: 30, 31, 151*

Lawson, *John: 26, 47, 52, 54, 64, 79, 83, 84, 95, 642, Photos*
Renée: 52, 54, 79, 83

Lawton, *Mrs. Hughes: 427*

Lazarus, *Ed: 56, 76, 90, 140, 204, 207, 216, 318, 319, 332, 333, 338, 339, 340, 346, 367, 371, 384, 544, 582, 629*
Laurie: 90

Le Melletier, *Mr. and Mrs.: 119*

Le Sommer, *Christian: 139, 275, 295, 303, 431, Photos*
Malou: 295, 296, 430, 431

Ledun, *Bernard: 273, 331, 552, 557, 564, 583, 589, 603, 608, 618, 629, 631, 639, 644, Photos*

Lefèvre*: 6, 12*

Leflaive, *Olivier: 294*
Vincent: 274, 282, 294, 295, 392

Lehman, *Ted: 145*

Leighton, *Dr. Terry: 94, 230, Photos*
Frances: 230

Lemelletiers, *the: 16, 40*

Lemelletier, *Mrs. Roger: 71*
Roger: 76, 122, 301

Lemisiano, *Armand: Intro iv*

Lench, *Andy: 403, 443, 473, 598*

Levines, *the: 3, 34, 200, 332*

Levine, *John: 29, 46, 64, 80, 105, 312, 333, 346, 358, 393, Photos*
Marcena (see Croy, *Marcena*)*: 29, 346, 393*

Lichine, *Alexis: 145, 181*

Light, *Dr. Ron: 248*

Lincoln, *Abraham: 209*

Linton, *George: 91*

Lollobrigida, *Gina: 73*

Lopez, *Mr.: 69*

Loren, *Sophia: 192*

Luceau, *M.: 13*

Luper, *Jerry: 469*

Lurton, *Lucien: 19*
Pierre: 432

Lynch, *Kermit: 521, 598*

M

McClelland*: 342*

McConville, *Charles: 45*

McFee, *Dorothy: 425*

McLaren, *Archie: 309*

McWatters, *Harry: 64, 430, Photos*

Mähler-Besse*: 42, 44*

Maltz, *Nathan: 326*

Mandela, *Nelson: 385*

Mandreau, *Jean-Louis: 16, 19, 68, 69, 121, 122, 123, 139, 192, 275*

Manoncourt, *Blondie: 118*
Marie-France: 71, 76, 118, 187
Mathilde: 71
Thierry: 18, 41, 71, 76, 118, 187, 432, 573, 575

Marly, *Jacques: 116, 117, 118*
Mr.: 616

Marti, *Bruno: 31, 32, 34, 93, 94, 96, 202, 242, 269, 346, 425, 426, 495, 529, 556*

Martin, *Henri: 16, 42, 191, 551*

Martini, *Louis: 394, 476*

Matignon, *Jean-René: 430*

Matisse: *438*

Maurèze, *Françoise: 434*
Jean-Marie: 403, 434

Medeville, *Andrée: 75, 76, 119, 120,*
Christian: 76, 119, 120, 390

Meir, *Menachem: Intro iv*
Prime Minister Golda: Intro iv

Mendoza, *Sonny: 444*

Menghi, *Umberto: 457*

Mentzelopoulos: *510, 533*
Corinne: 428, 429, 446, 448, 449, Photos

Méo, *Jean-Nicolas: 291, 292*

Meyer, *Justin: 389*

Miailhe, *Jean: 19, 182*

Miron, *Marc: 449*

Mitchener, *James: 386*

Mommessin, *Isabelle: 12*

Mondavi, *Michael: 345*
Robert: 44, 46, 52, 83, 138, 139, 270, 642
Tim: 69, 84, 138, 259

Monroe, *Marilyn: 192*

Montouroy, *Bernard: 17, 44, 72*

Moreau, *Mr.: 121, 187*

Morrison, *Fiona: 429*

Mottershead, *Ian: 80, 105, 230, 271, 281, 333, 342, 356, 358, 427, 446, 448, 449, 451, 453, 458, 487, 590, 627, Photos*
Rosemary: 356

Mottersheads, *the: 34, 60, 62, 332, 557, 583, 628*

Moueix, *Cherise* (see Chen, *Cherise*): *403, 431, 434, 519*
Christian, 17, 44, 45, 72, 73, 123, 139, 154, 166, 188, 189, 190, 200, 243, 294, 299, 300, 301, 309, 310, 311, 312, 326, 368, 370, 378, 389, 390, 391, 403, 431, 432, 434, 435, 442, 469, 506, 517, 518, 519, 520, 523, 529, 572, 612, 626, 631, Photos
Edouard: 434
Jean-François: 517
Jean-Pierre: 139, 299, 326, 391, 517
Marie-Laure: 72, 189, 200, 299

Mulroney, *Brian: 549*
Mila: 549

Murray, *Bill: 80, 105*

Mussy: *287*

N

Nadeff, *Philippe: 289*

Nader, *Ralph: 437*

Naus, *Hubert: 284*

Navarre, *Laurent: 517*

Neiret-Gachet: *10*
Mr.: 619

Newton, *Mrs.: 301*

Nickel, *Gil: 309*

Noble, *Michael: 436*

Noblet, *André: 146, 164, 494, 584*

Norman, *Dr. Haskell: 76, 91, 106, 168, 169, 170, 195, 217, 255, 267, 270, 271, 282, 309, 317, 328, 360, 362, 439, 363, 416, 426, 452, 528, 621, 655, Photos*
Rae: 270, 328, 621, 655

Nugent, *A.: 566*

Nureyev, *Rudolph: Intro iv*

O

Olivier, *Joan: 540, 611*
Marcel: 540, 611

Orlando, *Ellen: 606*
Jack: 606

Overstreet, *Dennis: 217*

Overton, *Dr. Marvin: 315, 363*
Sue: 315

P

Paes-Braga, *Ruy: 366, 629*

Parker, *Robert: 121, 122, 186, 187, 264, 287, 291, 299, 301, 303, 333, 378, 382, 383, 384, 394, 433, 436, 437, 438, 440, 443, 436, 441, 452, 453, 464, 470, 482, 495, 496, 510, 522, 526, 560*

Pascaud, *Pierre: 116*

Passot, *Roland: 356, 409*

Pauli, *Georges: 76, 121, 187*

Pauly, *Mr.: 15*

Penning-Rowsell, *Eddie: 13, 67, 408, 409, 414, 553*
Meg: 408

Peppercorn, *David: 185, 419*

Peterson, *Dick: 469*
Heidi: 469

Peynaud, *Emile: 19, 22, 405*

Phelps, *Chris: 299, 310*
Joseph: 172, 232, 245, 309, 403

Pic, *Albert: 44*

Picasso: *208, 438*

Pinault, *M: 373*

Pinski (Pinsky), *Babette: 283, 426*
Miriam: 356
Paul: 96, 108, 110, 169, 215, 216, 252, 283, 319, 356, 370, 378, 426, 458, 459, 498, 571, Photos
Sara: 252, 283, 370, 426, 458, 571
Steve: 283, 426

Pol Roger, *Christian: 203, 352, 353, 354, 355, 505, 614*

Pontallier, *Paul: 301, 428, 449*

Portet, *Bernard: 44, 50, 72, 440, 441*
Dominique: 50, 51

Poschel, *Bill: Photos*

Potel, *Gerard: 287, 288, 291*

Pottier: *13*

Prats: *44, 505*
Bruno: 42, 71, 182, 404, 405, 407, 427, 428, 430, 437, 510, 563, 564, 577, 588, 601, 628, 642
France: 404, 407, 427, 601, 628
Jean-Guillaume: 427, 577, 588, 642

President Reagan: *231*

President Roosevelt: *215*

Price, *Terry: 8, 10, 11*
Prieur, *Jacques: 144*
Prime Minister Levi Eshkol: *Intro ii*
Prince Charles: *472*
Prince Philip: *472, 549*
Princess Diana: *472*
Procter, *Frank: 54*
Puck, *Wolfgang: 375*

Q

Quady, *Andrew: 95*
Queen Elizabeth II: *549*
Queen Mother: *472*
Querre, *Theophile: 576*

R

Rainbird, *George: 67*
Lena: 67
Ramonet: *459*
Raymond, *Walter: Photos*
Reid, *Robin: 73, 470*
Reynaud: *10*
Rhodes, *Dr. Barney: 91, 92, 139, 166, 172, 185, 195, 196, 245, 255, 258, 270, 283, 309, 311, 315, 316, 317, 334, 361, 364, 393, 400, 408, 409, 415, 416, 467, 468, 506, 507, 528, Photos*
Belle: 166, 172, 195, 196, 270, 311, 315, 334, 393, 408, 424, 467, 468, 506, 528
Dr. and Mrs.: 76
Ribereau-Gayon, *Professor: 405*
Ricard: *116*
Claude: 117
Richard, *Michel: 219*
Rinaldi, *Tom: 173*
Rion, *Daniel: 291, 292*
Patrick: 90, 291
Rival, *P: 425*
Robarts, *Terry: 190, 472*
Roberts, *Jeremy: 42*
Robin, *Mesdemoiselles: 72*
Mrs.: 431
Robinson: *217, 309, 338, 339*
Frank: 217, 309, 338, 339
Roddis, *Bill: 53*
Rodenstock, *Hardy: 111, 187, 211, 212, 278, 279, 301, 327, 353, 391, 414, 526, Photos*
Rolland, *Michel: 41, 193, 433, 438, 453, 470*
Rombauer, *Koerner: 139*
Rondeau, *René: 544, 565*
Roumier: *289*
Alain: 145
Christophe: 146, 288
Jean-Marie: 288
Mr.: 145
Rousseau, *Charles: 151, 152*
Rubyn, *Jack: 452, 528*
Ruelle, *Mr.: 16, 18*
Ryan, *Kathleen* (see Heitz, *Kathleen*): *89*
Rychlewski, *Alex: 186*

S

Salama, *Raoul: 184, 351*
Salinger, *Tary: 95, Photos*
Sarazin, *Mr.: 81*
Saunders, *Caryl: 386, 387, 388, 506, Photos*
Saunier, *Martine: 256, 291*
Scholefield, *Dave: 541*
Schonfeld, *Dr. Mark: 162, 391, 590*
Tracy: 162, 391, 590
Schroeder, *Mick: 368*
Schubert, *Max: 368*
Schwartz, *Dr. Stan: 172, 248, 309, 342, 387, 582, Photos*
Helene: 172, 248, 309, 387, Photos
Schÿler, *Guy: 70*
Mr.: 431
Scotland, *Bruce: 459*
Sears, *Kerry: 262*
Selvaggio, *Piero: 126*
Sichel, *Diana: 27, 70, 182, 327, 411, 428, 429, 475, 534*
James: 176, 177
Peter: 14, 15, 19, 20, 27, 42, 44, 69, 70, 161, 163, 173, 176, 177, 182, 184, 327, 344, 411, 428, 429, 475, 478, 507, 532, 534, 535, 615, 619, 627, 629, 639, 650, Photos
Rebecca: 69
Sacha: 181
Siefer-Gaillardin, *Alfred: 354*
Signorello, *Ray: 475, 486, 528*
Ray Jr.: 475, 476, 498, 527
Simon, *André: Intro vii, 55, 67*
Sinclair, *Bob: 65, 555*
Roger: 388
Stella: 388
Smith, *Dr. Lee: 409*
Jim: 378
Marcia: 139
May: 409
Soulasse, *Mr.: 302*
Soussotte, *Mr.: 18*
Spence, *Doug: 80*
Spichal, *Joachim: 380, 506*
Spohn, *Bill: 439, 482, 483*
Spurrell, *Alice: 57, 271, 325*
Dave: 57, 80, 235, 324, 325, 333, 425, Photos
Spurrells, *the: 327, 332, 423, 579*
St. Pierre, *Brian: 29*
Stelling, *Doug: 310*
Stone, *Dr.: 83*
Stuart, *Lee: 263*
Sultan, *Patsy: 613, 628*
Randy: 217, 338, 368, 613, 628
Sutcliffe, *Serena: 410, 412, 413, 414, 419, 468, 469, 470, 472, 561*
Symington, *Amos: 74*
James: 74
Paul: 135, 136
Szabo, *Daniel: 305, 306*

T

Taylor, *Simon: 284*
Tchelischtcheff, *André: 53, 89*
Tesseron, *Michel: 458*
Tesserons: *80*
Thienpont: *18, 118, 524*
Alexandre: 297, 432, 433
Leon: 297, 432
Tilson, *Jeff: 333*
John: 90, 216, 225, 265, 332, 333, 338, 339, 367, 384, 385, 544, 597, 629
Laurie: 332, 333, 367

Tobe, *Dr. Allan: 2, 3, 20, 25, 28, 34, 51, 58, 76, 80, 86, 101, 105, 170, 193, 198, 229, 274, 346, 358, 365, 404, 446, 450, 599, Photos*
Sally: 101, 346
Stuart: 101, 105

Tobes, *the: 34, 48, 60, 78, 137, 356, 370, 403, 421, 543, 573, 609, 619, 629, 645*

Togni, *Begita: 25*
Philip: 21, 22, 25, 39, 53, 248, 442, 505, 629

Tollot-Beaut, *Mrs.: 147*

Touchais, *Monsieur: 56*

Trapet, *Jean: 145*

Travers, *Bob: 174, 180, 247, 636, 640*
Mary: 174

Troisgros, *Jean: 75*
Pierre: 149

Troy, *Alexandra: 217*
Jane: 371
Jeffrey (Geoffrey): 204, 207, 217, 266, 371

Trudeau, *Pierre: 81, 434, 555*

U

Uhlen, *Gerald: 7*

Uren, *Bill:* (see Wren, *Bill*)

V

Valadas, *Dr.: 135*

Valette, *Mr. and Mrs.: 119*
Mr.: 374

Van Gogh: *438*

Van Vloten, *Walter: 37, 80*

Van Zellers, *the: 430*
Christiano: 326

Vauthier: *470*
Mr.: 453

Veniat, *Michel: 11*

Verdi: *Intro iv*

Vernay, *Daniel: 10*
Georges: 10

Veyssière, *François: 189*

Viader, *Delia: 424, 440, 441, 442, 448, 449, 460, 498, 521, 572, 625*

Viallard, *Jacques: 43*

Vigoda, *Ken: 94*

Villars, *Bernadette: 122, 181, 182, 297, 374, 445, 566*
Claire: 374
Philippe: 566

Voisin, *Christophe: 232*

Vrinat, *Jean-Claude: 267*

Vuillier, *Albert: 119*

W

Wagner, *Charlie: 38, 90, 393*
Chuck: 38, 90

Wallace, *Clarie: 342*

Warre, *Bill: 282*

Washington, *George: 107, 112*

Water, *Alice: 39*

Waugh, *Harriet: 47, 67, 248, 309, 373, 507, 528, 598, 611*
Harry: Intro vi, viii, 28, 29, 30, 32, 47, 67, 68, 70, 76, 77, 78, 97, 98, 99, 100, 121, 130, 134, 139, 140, 141, 151, 184, 185, 191, 196, 209, 210, 214, 215, 247, 248, 262, 263, 266, 270, 275, 277, 279, 284, 301, 309, 311, 317, 360, 362, 373, 374, 378, 392, 414, 419, 492, 506, 507, 528, 538, 543, 544, 545, 546, 547, 553, 556, 563, 564, 573, 574, 577, 578, 587, 592, 594, 596, 598, 603, 609, 611, 616, 619, 620, 621, 629, 631, 636, 644, 645, 650, 654, Photos
Jamie: 47, 67, 248, 309, 373, 507, 598, 611
Prue: 47, 67, 76, 209, 214, 248, 309, 360, 362, 373, 538, 544, 545, 556, 577, 592, 596, 598, 603, 611, 616, 619, 620, 621, 629, 644, 654, Photos

Webb, *Gyles: 386*

Weir-Jones, *Ian: 80*

Wente, *Eric: Photos*

Wermuth, *Dr.: 83*

Wheelan, *Marcus: 410*

Whitney, *Jarvis: 64*

Wilbrensinck, *Alex: 93*

Wilson, *Val: 426, 550*

Wilson, *Warren: 74*

Winiarski, *Mrs.: 172*
Warren: 69, 76, 88, 172, 312, 506, 630

Woltner, *Fernand: 516*
Henri: 516

Woltner-Dewarvins: *121*

Woltners: *271, 335, 337, 414*

Wong, *Debbie: 426*
Dr. Eugene: 426, 522

Woodward, *Phil: 95*

Wren, (Uren)*Bill: 58, 89, 95*

Z

Zuger, *Paul: 18*
Roger: 18

INDEX *of* WINES

Acacia Pinot Noir "Lund Vineyard" **1979:** 64
Acacia Pinot Noir "Lund Vineyard" **1980:** 64
Aloxe-Corton "Les Chaillots" **1979,** Louis Latour: 12
Aloxe-Corton "Les Chaillots" **1982,** Louis Latour: 151
Aloxe-Corton **1966,** Leroy: 150
Aloxe-Corton **1979,** Louis Latour: 12
Aloxe-Corton **1984,** Tollot-Beaut: 147
Alto Cabernet Sauvignon **1969:** 142
Alto Cabernet Sauvignon **1970:** 650
Alto Cabernet Sauvignon **1984:** 386
Alto Cabernet Sauvignon **1986:** 387
Alto Cabernet Sauvignon" Select" **1965:** 143
Amarone, Reccioto della Valpolicella **1971,** Classico Superiore, Bertani: 654
Anderson's Cabernet Sauvignon Estate Reserve "Conn Valley Vineyards" **1994,** Napa Valley: 486
Araujo Cabernet Sauvignon "Eisele Vineyard" **1995,** Napa Valley: 519
Araujo Syrah "Eisele Vineyard" **1995,** Napa Valley: 528
Arbois-Vin Jaune **1972,** Domaine de la Pinte: 48, 179
Arger Cellars Napa Cabernet Sauvignon **1985,** "Fay Vineyard": 247
Armagnac "Avery's Special Selection" **1934:** 106
Arrowood Cabernet Sauvignon **1985,** Sonoma Valley: 359
Arroyo Cabernet Sauvignon **1974,** Sonoma Valley: 198
Au Bon Climat Chardonnay **1996,** Santa Barbara County: 488
Aureo "Reserva Especial Privado," Muy Viejo, Tarragona: 40
Auxey-Duresses **1985,** Faiveley: 232
Auxey-Duresses Blanc **1978,** Louis Latour: 56
Bacigalupi Pinot Noir **1979,** Sonoma County: 34, 635
Backsberg Estate Cabernet Sauvignon **1969:** 142
Backsberg Estate Cabernet Sauvignon **1971:** 142
Backsberg Estate Cabernet Sauvignon **1976:** 650
Barbaresco "Costa Russi" **1983,** Angelo Gaja: 144
Barbaresco "Riserva" Prunotto **1974,** Cantina S. Cassiano: 654
Barbaresco "Sori San Lorenzo" **1983,** Angelo Gaja: 144
Barbaresco **1961,** Angelo Gaja: 105, 144
Barbaresco **1978,** "Riserva" Prunotto, Montestefano: 655
Barbaresco **1978,** Angelo Gaja: 462
Barbaresco **1982,** Angelo Gaja: 656
Barbaresco **1983,** Angelo Gaja: 144
Barbaresco **1985,** Angelo Gaja: 485
Barolo "Bussia Soprana" **1964,** Aldo Conterno: 54
Barolo "Gromis" **1970,** Angelo Gaja: 421
Barolo "Riserva" "Bussia Di Monforte d'Alba" **1978,** Prunotto: 655
Barolo "Riserva" "Ginestra" **1978,** Prunotto: 475, 655
Barolo "Riserva" **1945,** Aldo Conterno: 412
Barolo "Riserva" **1945,** Borgogno: 412
Barolo "Riserva" **1945,** Rinaldi: 412
Barolo "Riserva" **1952,** Borgogno: 454
Barolo "Riserva" **1955,** Borgogno: 236
Barolo "Riserva" **1964,** Giacomo Borgogno: 54
Barolo "Riserva" **1967,** Borgogno: 54, 236, 502, 654
Barolo "Riserva" **1974,** Pio Cesare: 655
Barolo "Riserva" **1977,** Borgogno: 236
Barolo "Spress" **1989,** Angelo Gaja: 421
Barolo **1945,** Marchesi Castellana: 412
Barolo **1971,** Montanello: 654
Barolo **1990,** Bussia "Vigna Cigala," Aldo Conterno: 496
Bas Armagnac "Château La Brise" **1912:** 216
Bâtard-Montrachet **1970,** Henri Clerc, Avery's: 256
Bâtard-Montrachet **1971,** Joseph Drouhin: 78
Bâtard-Montrachet **1973,** Gagnard-Delagrange: 593
Bâtard-Montrachet **1973,** L. Gros: 593
Bâtard-Montrachet **1976,** Coron Père et Fils: 107
Bâtard-Montrachet **1978,** Louis Latour: 333
Bâtard-Montrachet **1978,** Vincent Leflaive: 74, 202, 388, 487, 594
Bâtard-Montrachet **1979,** A. Rodet: 63
Bâtard-Montrachet **1979,** Ropiteau: 62
Bâtard-Montrachet **1982,** Blain-Gagnard: 367
Bâtard-Montrachet **1982,** Joseph Drouhin: 56, 597
Bâtard-Montrachet **1982,** Remoissenet: 270
Bâtard-Montrachet **1982,** Vincent Leflaive: 235, 274
Bâtard-Montrachet **1983,** Henri Clerc: 300
Bâtard-Montrachet **1983,** Louis Latour: 244, 325, 598
Bâtard-Montrachet **1983,** Remoissenet: 244
Bâtard-Montrachet **1983,** Vincent Leflaive: 317
Bâtard-Montrachet **1985,** Louis Latour: 325, 439, 599
Bâtard-Montrachet **1985,** Ramonet: 356
Bâtard-Montrachet **1985,** Vincent Leflaive: 415, 426
Bâtard-Montrachet **1986,** Jadot: 487, 600
Bâtard-Montrachet **1988,** Louis Latour: 601
Bâtard-Montrachet **1988,** Ramonet: 459
Bâtard-Montrachet **1992,** Joseph Drouhin: 453
Bâtard-Montrachet Grand Cru **1983,** Pierre Morey: 361
Beaulieu Vineyards "Tapestry" **1991,** Napa Valley: 474
Beaulieu Vineyards Burgundy **1964,** Napa Valley: 174
Beaulieu Vineyards Georges de Latour Cabernet Sauvignon "Private Reserve" **1946,** Napa Valley: 89
Beaulieu Vineyards Georges de Latour Cabernet Sauvignon "Private Reserve" **1961,** Napa Valley: 627
Beaulieu Vineyards Georges de Latour Cabernet Sauvignon "Private Reserve" **1966,** Napa Valley: 2
Beaulieu Vineyards Georges de Latour Cabernet Sauvignon "Private Reserve" **1968,** Napa Valley: 262, 530
Beaulieu Vineyards Georges de Latour Cabernet Sauvignon "Private Reserve" **1969,** Napa Valley: 627
Beaulieu Vineyards Georges de Latour Cabernet Sauvignon "Private Reserve" **1970,** Napa Valley: 101, 262, 262, 263, 350
Beaulieu Vineyards Georges de Latour Cabernet Sauvignon "Private Reserve" **1971,** Napa Valley: 627
Beaulieu Vineyards Georges de Latour Cabernet Sauvignon "Private Reserve" **1974,** Napa Valley: 1, 22, 162, 198, 248, 404, 628
Beaulieu Vineyards Georges de Latour Cabernet Sauvignon "Private Reserve" **1975,** Napa Valley: 2, 21
Beaulieu Vineyards Georges de Latour Cabernet Sauvignon "Private Reserve" **1978,** Napa Valley: 248
Beaulieu Vineyards Georges de Latour Cabernet Sauvignon "Private Reserve" **1979,** Napa Valley: 630
Beaulieu Vineyards Georges de Latour Cabernet Sauvignon "Private Reserve" Vintage Unknown, Napa Valley: 175
Beaulieu Vineyards Georges de Latour Cabernet Sauvignon "Private Reserve" **1985,** Napa Valley: 359
Beaulieu Vineyards Pinot Noir "Los Carneros" **1976,** Napa Valley: 634
Beaune "Bressandes" **1966,** Leroy: 150
Beaune "Bressandes" **1987:** 287
Beaune "Cent Vignes" **1966,** Leroy: 149

Beaune "Champimonts" **1966,** Leroy: 150
Beaune "Clos de la Feguine" **1969,** Domaine Prieur, Calvet: 591
Beaune "Clos de la Mousse" Premier Cru **1949,** Bouchard Père et Fils: 354
Beaune "Clos de la Mousse" Premier Cru **1964,** Bouchard Père et Fils: 590
Beaune "Clos des Mouches" **1969,** Joseph Drouhin: 591
Beaune "Clos des Mouches" Blanc **1976,** Joseph Drouhin: 82
Beaune "Clos des Mouches" Blanc **1978,** Joseph Drouhin: 7
Beaune "Clos des Mouches" Blanc **1985,** Joseph Drouhin: 599
Beaune "Clos des Mouches" Premier Cru **1988,** Joseph Drouhin: 419
Beaune "Clos des Mouches" Rouge **1969,** Joseph Drouhin: 80
Beaune "Clos des Mouches" Rouge **1977,** Joseph Drouhin: 7
Beaune "Clos des Ursules" **1988,** Jadot: 285
Beaune "Clos du Roi" Premier Cru **1966,** Coron: 174
Beaune "Clos du Roi" Premier Cru **1984,** Tollot-Beaut: 147
Beaune "Grèves" **1987,** Albert Morot: 287
Beaune "Les Teurons" Premier Cru **1988,** Albert Morot: 419, 592
Beaune "Montée Rouge" Premier Cru **1945,** Leon Violland: 498
Beaune "Teurons" **1983,** Albert Morot: 287
Beaune "Teurons" **1987,** Albert Morot: 287
Beaune "Toussaints" **1983,** Albert Morot: 287
Beaune "Toussaints" **1987,** Albert Morot: 286
Beaune "Toussaints" Premier Cru **1987,** Albert Morot: 592
Beaune "Vigne de l'Enfant Jesus" Premier Cru **1959,** Domaine du Château de Beaune, Bouchard Père et Fils: 354
Beaune "Vigne Franche" **1979,** Louis Latour: 12
Beaune **1966,** Leroy: 149
Beaune du Château N/V, Bouchard Père et Fils: 592
Beaune Hospices de Beaune "Cuvée Nicolas Rolin" **1983,** Mommessin: 229
Beaune Premier Cru **1966,** Leroy: 149
Beaune Premier Cru **1978,** Leroy: 459
Beaune-Grèves Premier Cru **1969,** Ropiteau: 591
Benedictine **1880:** 114
Beringer Cabernet Sauvignon "Knights' Valley" **1985,** Sonoma Valley: 359
Beringer Cabernet Sauvignon "Private Reserve" **1986,** Napa Valley: 238
Beringer Cabernet Sauvignon "Private Reserve" **1990,** Napa Valley: 441
Beringer Cabernet Sauvignon "Reserve" **1985,** Napa Valley: 486
Bienvenues Bâtard-Montrachet **1978,** Louis Latour: 334
Bienvenues Bâtard-Montrachet **1978,** Vincent Leflaive: 74
Bienvenues Bâtard-Montrachet **1982,** Ramonet: 333
Bienvenues Bâtard-Montrachet **1982,** Vincent Leflaive: 274
Bienvenues Bâtard-Montrachet **1983,** Remoissenet: 244
Bienvenues Bâtard-Montrachet **1986,** Jaffelin: 599
Bienvenues Bâtard-Montrachet **1986,** Ramonet: 459
Binger Scharlachberg Riesling Eiswein **1983,** Weingut Villa Sachsen, Rheinhessen: 649
Blanc d c Lynch-Bages **1995:** 430
Blanc de Lynch-Bages **1983:** 124
Boberg Crusted Vintage Port "Wine of Origin Boberg Superior" **1963,** KWV, South Africa: 521, 650
Boberg Superior Muscadel "Late Bottled Vintage" "Wine of Origin" "Bin B-14" **1930,** KWV, South Africa: 143, 650
Boberg Superior Tawny Port **1956,** KWV, South Africa: 231
Bodegas Berberana "Gran Reserva" Rioja **1952:** 27
Bonnes Mares "Vieilles Vignes" **1988,** Georges Roumier: 289
Bonnes Mares **1964,** Pierre Ponnelle: 39
Bonnes Mares **1969,** Avery's (Bristol): 585
Bonnes Mares **1969,** Domaine Clair-Daü: 585
Bonnes Mares **1971,** Drouhin-Larose: 219
Bonnes Mares **1972,** Joseph Drouhin: 586
Bonnes Mares **1978,** Robert Groffier: 483, 587
Bonnes Mares **1983,** Clair-Daü: 314
Bonnes Mares **1985,** Georges Lignier: 221
Bonnes Mares **1987,** de Vogüé: 393
Bonnes Mares **1988,** Domaine Georges Roumier: 289, 288
Bonnes Mares **1989,** Jadot: 447
Bonnes Mares Grand Cru **1983,** Louis Latour: 589
Bonnes Mares Grand Cru **1985,** Georges Roumier: 146
Bonny Doon Vineyards Viognier **1996,** Central Coast: 465
Boschendal Gewürztraminer "Jean Gardé Vineyard" **1990:** 387
Botiglia Particolare **1981,** Vino da Tavola di Greve, Castello di Verrazzano: 457
Botiglia Particolare **1986,** Vino da Tavola di Greve, Castello di Verrazzano: 457, 516
Botiglia Particolare **1994,** Vino da Tavola di Greve, Castello di Verrazzano: 456
Bouchaine "Carneros" Chardonnay **1987,** Napa Valley: 315
Brown Bros. Milawa Spätlese Rhine Riesling **1970:** 23
Brunello di Montalcino "Sugarille" **1990:** 421
Brunello di Montalcino Biondi Santi "Riserva" **1945:** 128, 412
Brunello di Montalcino Biondi-Santi "Riserva" **1891:** 128
Brunello di Montalcino Biondi-Santi "Riserva" **1925:** 128
Brunello di Montalcino Biondi-Santi "Riserva" **1946:** 128
Brunello di Montalcino Biondi-Santi "Riserva" **1951:** 128
Brunello di Montalcino Biondi-Santi "Riserva" **1955:** 128
Brunello di Montalcino Biondi-Santi "Riserva" **1957:** 128
Brunello di Montalcino Biondi-Santi "Riserva" **1958:** 128
Brunello di Montalcino Biondi-Santi "Riserva" **1961:** 127
Brunello di Montalcino Biondi-Santi "Riserva" **1964:** 127
Brunello di Montalcino Biondi-Santi "Riserva" **1967:** 127
Brunello di Montalcino Biondi-Santi "Riserva" **1968:** 127
Brunello di Montalcino Biondi-Santi "Riserva" **1969:** 127
Brunello di Montalcino Biondi-Santi "Riserva" **1970:** 127
Brunello di Montalcino Biondi-Santi "Riserva" **1971:** 127
Brunello di Montalcino Biondi-Santi "Riserva" **1975:** 127
Brunello di Montalcino Biondi-Santi "Riserva" **1977:** 127
Brunello di Montalcino Biondi-Santi Anata **1971:** 127
Brunello di Montalcino Biondi-Santi Anata **1973:** 127
Brunello di Montalcino Biondi-Santi Anata **1975:** 127
Brunello di Montalcino Biondi-Santi Anata **1977:** 126
Brunello di Montalcino Biondi-Santi Anata **1978:** 126
Brunello di Montalcino Biondi-Santi Anata **1979:** 126
Brunello di Montalcino Biondi-Santi Anata **1980:** 126
Brunello di Montalcino Biondi-Santi Moscatello **1969:** 127
Brunello di Montalcino Pertimali **1988:** 496
Burgess Cabernet Sauvignon "Vintage Selection" **1975,** Napa Valley: 629
Burgess Chardonnay "Winery Lake Vineyard" **1977,** Napa Valley: 102
Burgess Chardonnay **1981,** Napa Valley: 53
Burgwerbener Herzogsberg Gutedel **1989,** Doge Winzer Genossenschaft: 312
Burrowing Owl Vineyards **1997,** Okanagan Valley, BC: 505
Cabreo "Predicato di Biturica" **1983,** Ruffino: 657

Cabreo Chardonnay "Vigneto La Pietra" **1984,** Ruffino: 195
Cakebread Cabernet Sauvignon "Reserve" **1992,** Napa Valley: 441
Calera Zinfandel Essence **1976:** 641
Callaway Vineyard Chenin Blanc "Sweet Nancy" Late Harvest **1977,** Temecula, California: 642
Carmel Cabernet Sauvignon "Select" **1978:** 40
Carmel Cabernet Sauvignon "Select" **1979:** 40
Carmel Cabernet Sauvignon "Vintage Selection" **1976:** 659
Carmel Cabernet Sauvignon "Vintage Selection" **1978:** 659
Carmel Cabernet Sauvignon **1974:** 659
Carmel Petite Syrah N/V: 40
Carmignano "Riserva" **1975,** Villa di Capezzano: 57
Carruades de Château Lafite **1966:** 446
Casa di Sonoma "California Cabernet" N/V, Napa Valley: 175
Caymus Pinot Noir **1980,** Napa Valley: 90
Caymus Vineyards "Liberty House" Cabernet Sauvignon **1982,** Napa Valley: 90
Caymus Vineyards "Liberty School" Chardonnay **1979,** Napa Valley: 38
Caymus Vineyards Cabernet Sauvignon "Special Selection" **1984,** Napa Valley: 476
Caymus Vineyards Cabernet Sauvignon **1979,** Napa Valley: 38
Caymus Vineyards Cabernet Sauvignon **1981,** Napa Valley: 90
Caymus Vineyards Cabernet Sauvignon **1982,** Napa Valley: 475
Caymus Vineyards Chardonnay "Special Selection" **1976,** Napa Valley: 393
Caymus Vineyards Chardonnay "Special Selection" Late Harvest **1976,** Napa Valley: 642
Caymus Vineyards Chardonnay **1980,** Napa Valley: 38
Caymus Vineyards Chardonnay **1983,** Napa Valley: 90
Caymus Vineyards Fumé Blanc Sauvignon **1981,** Napa Valley: 38
Caymus Vineyards Pinot Blanc "Oeil de Perdrix" **1980,** Napa Valley: 38
Caymus Vineyards Pinot Blanc "Oeil de Perdrix" **1983,** Napa Valley: 90
Caymus Vineyards Pinot Noir "Special Selection" **1982,** Napa Valley: 90
Caymus Vineyards Pinot Noir **1977,** Napa Valley: 634
Caymus Vineyards Pinot Noir **1978,** Napa Valley: 635
Caymus Vineyards Pinot Noir **1979,** Napa Valley: 38
Caymus Vineyards Sauvignon Blanc **1983,** Napa Valley: 90
Caymus Vineyards Zinfandel **1979,** Napa Valley: 38
Caymus Vineyards Zinfandel **1980,** Napa Valley: 90
Cervaro Della Sala **1995,** Castello Della Salla: 457
Chablis "Blanchots" Grand Cru **1979,** Raveneau: 69
Chablis "Grenouilles" "Tête de Cuvée" Grand Cru **1966,** Remoissenet: 55
Chablis "Grenouilles" Grand Cru **1979,** Château de Grenouilles: 68
Chablis "Grenouilles" Grand Cru **1983,** Château de Grenouilles: 343
Chablis "Les Clos" Grand Cru **1971,** Domaine Robert Vocoret: 106
Chablis "Les Clos" Grand Cru **1971,** Joseph Drouhin: 97
Chablis "Les Clos" Grand Cru **1976,** Pierre Ponnelle: 13
Chablis "Les Clos" Grand Cru **1979,** Joseph Drouhin: 62
Chablis "Les Clos" Grand Cru **1993,** William Febvre: 490
Chablis "Les Preuses" Grand Cru **1981,** René Dauvissat: 351
Chablis "Vaillon" Premier Cru **1983,** Moreau: 598
Chablis "Valmur" Grand Cru **1982,** Raveneau: 597
Chablis "Vaudésir" Grand Cru **1976,** Moreau: 92
Chablis Albert Pic **1981:** 44
Chablis Premier Cru **1979,** Louis Latour: 29
Chalone Vineyards Chardonnay **1979,** California: 34, 638
Chalone Vineyards Pinot Blanc "Reserve" **1980,** California: 641
Chalone Vineyards Pinot Blanc **1980,** California: 506
Chalone Vineyards Pinot Blanc **1981,** California: 318
Chalone Vineyards Pinot Noir **1978,** California: 513
Chalone Vineyards Pinot Noir **1979,** California: 522
Chalone Vineyards Pinot Noir **1985,** California: 475
Chambertin "Clos de Bèze" **1980,** A. Rousseau: 374
Chambertin "Clos de Bèze" **1987,** A. Rousseau: 436
Chambertin "Clos de Bèze" **1989,** Bruno Clair: 590
Chambertin "Clos de Bèze" **1989,** Jadot: 436
Chambertin "Clos de Bèze" **1995:** 526
Chambertin "Collection du Docteur Barolet" **1921:** 112
Chambertin "Cuvée des Héritiers Latour" **1959,** Louis Latour: 31, 229, 583
Chambertin "Cuvée des Héritiers Latour" **1964,** Louis Latour: 228
Chambertin "Cuvée des Héritiers Latour" **1966,** Louis Latour: 228
Chambertin "Cuvée des Heritiers Latour" **1985,** Louis Latour: 589
Chambertin **1945,** Camus: 320
Chambertin **1945,** Faiveley: 320
Chambertin **1945,** Rémy: 320
Chambertin **1945,** Rodet: 237, 320
Chambertin **1955,** Avery's: 90
Chambertin **1955,** Leroy: 389
Chambertin **1966,** Leroy: 151
Chambertin **1969,** A. Rousseau: 585
Chambertin **1971,** Bouchard Père et Fils: 357
Chambertin **1978,** A. Rousseau: 350
Chambertin **1982,** Joseph Drouhin: 230
Chambertin **1984,** Trapet: 145
Chambertin **1985,** Leroy: 225
Chambertin Clos de Bèze **1969,** General Rebourseau, Piat Père et Fils: 585
Chambolle Musigny **1989,** Georges Roumier: 288
Chambolle-Musigny "Charmes" **1969,** Nicolas: 585
Chambolle-Musigny "Charmes" **1971,** Chanson Père et Fils: 40
Chambolle-Musigny "Les Amoureuses" **1966,** Leroy: 150
Chambolle-Musigny "Les Amoureuses" **1969,** Grivelet: 335
Chambolle-Musigny "Les Amoureuses" **1971,** Comte de Vogüé: 140
Chambolle-Musigny "Les Amoureuses" **1985,** Georges Roumier: 146
Chambolle-Musigny "Les Amoureuses" **1985,** Georges Roumier: 146
Chambolle-Musigny "Les Amoureuses" **1988,** Georges Roumier: 289
Chambolle-Musigny "Les Amoureuses" **1989,** Georges Roumier: 288
Chambolle-Musigny "Les Amoureuses" **1989,** Joseph Drouhin: 504
Chambolle-Musigny "Orveaux" **1988,** Faiveley: 420
Chambolle-Musigny **1925,** Martenot: 392
Chambolle-Musigny **1934,** Martenot: 392
Chambolle-Musigny **1949,** Caves de la Busserolle: 582

Chambolle-Musigny **1951,** Martenot: 392
Chambolle-Musigny **1952,** Martenot: 392
Chambolle-Musigny **1966,** Leroy: 150
Chambolle-Musigny **1971,** Joseph Drouhin: 6
Chambolle-Musigny **1976,** Joseph Drouhin: 7
Chambolle-Musigny **1978,** Joseph Drouhin: 7
Chambolle-Musigny **1988,** Georges Roumier: 288
Chambolle-Musigny **1988,** Yves Chaley: 420
Chambolle-Musigny **1989,** Georges Roumier: 288
Chambolle-Musigny **1993,** J. F. Mugnier: 427
Champagne Alfred Gratien Brut **1976:** 69
Champagne Alfred Gratien Brut **1979:** 126
Champagne Ayala "Reserve" Brut **1973:** 46
Champagne Ayala Brut **1964:** 60
Champagne Ayala Brut **1971:** 16
Champagne Ayala Brut **1979:** 190
Champagne Ayala Brut N/V: 344, 367
Champagne Batiste Pertois 100% Grand Cru Blanc de Blancs **1985:** 484
Champagne Batiste Pertois Premier Cru "Blanc de Blancs 100%" **1979,** Cramant: 611
Champagne Batiste Pertois Premier Cru "Blanc de Blancs 100%" **1985,** Cramant: 283, 615
Champagne Billecart-Salmon "Cuvée NF Billecart" **1979:** 169
Champagne Billecart-Salmon "Cuvée NF Billecart" **1990:** 518
Champagne Billecart-Salmon "Cuvée NF Billecart" Brut **1966:** 95
Champagne Billecart-Salmon "Cuvée NF Billecart" Brut **1975:** 215
Champagne Billecart-Salmon "Cuvée NF Billecart" Brut **1978:** 611
Champagne Billecart-Salmon "Cuvée NF Billecart" Brut **1989:** 463, 615
Champagne Billecart-Salmon "Reserve" Brut N/V: 445
Champagne Billecart-Salmon Blanc de Blancs Brut **1982:** 239
Champagne Billecart-Salmon Brut **1976:** 52, 169
Champagne Billecart-Salmon Brut N/V: 256, 276, 278
Champagne Billecart-Salmon Rosé Brut N/V: 194, 225, 263
Champagne Bollinger "Grande Année" **1976:** 229, 610
Champagne Bollinger "Grande Année" **1982:** 614
Champagne Bollinger "Grande Année" **1983:** 300
Champagne Bollinger "Grande Année" **1985:** 397, 461, 487, 494, 500, 520, 354
Champagne Bollinger "Grande Année" **1988:** 522
Champagne Bollinger "Grande Année" **1989:** 450
Champagne Bollinger "R.D." **1961:** 112
Champagne Bollinger "R.D." **1964:** 112
Champagne Bollinger "R.D." **1969:** 332
Champagne Bollinger "R.D." **1970:** 408
Champagne Bollinger "R.D." **1973:** 609
Champagne Bollinger "R.D." **1975:** 106, 202, 215, 610
Champagne Bollinger "R.D." **1979:** 487, 612
Champagne Bollinger "R.D." **1982:** 354, 372, 421, 453, 613
Champagne Bollinger "R.D." Tradition Brut **1973:** 55
Champagne Bollinger "Special Cuvée" Brut N/V: 245, 267, 273, 354, 405, 607
Champagne Bollinger "Vieilles Vignes Françaises" "Blanc de Noirs" Brut **1979:** 346. 612
Champagne Bollinger "Vieilles Vignes Françaises" "Blanc de Noirs" Brut **1981:** 613
Champagne Bollinger "Vieilles Vignes Françaises" "Blanc de Noirs" Brut **1988:** 523
Champagne Bollinger Brut **1945:** 222, 225
Champagne Bollinger Brut **1973:** 175
Champagne Bollinger Brut **1975:** 242, 610
Champagne Bollinger Brut **1976:** 67
Champagne Bollinger Brut **1985:** 425
Champagne Canard-Duchêne "Charles VII" Brut N/V: 86, 608
Champagne Canard-Duchêne Brut N/V: 96
Champagne Charbaut "Certificat" Blanc de Blancs **1982:** 318, 332, 333
Champagne Charbaut "Certificat" Rosé **1982:** 319
Champagne Charbaut Brut N/V: 460
Champagne Charbaut Rosé Brut N/V: 225, 236
Champagne Charles Heidsieck **1945** "Extra Dry": 219
Champagne Charles Heidsieck **1962** "Extra Dry": 128
Champagne Charles Heidsieck Brut **1975:** 610
Champagne Charles Heidsieck Brut **1976:** 125
Champagne Charles Heidsieck Brut **1985:** 614
Champagne Charles Heidsieck Brut **1990:** 489, 499, 525, 615
Champagne de Venoge Blanc de Blancs **1990:** 514
Champagne de Venoge Cordon Bleu "Champagne des Princes" **1975:** 235
Champagne de Venoge Cordon Bleu N/V: 429
Champagne Deutz "Cuvée William Deutz" **1975:** 79
Champagne Deutz "Cuvée William Deutz" **1979:** 195
Champagne Deutz "Cuvée William Deutz" **1985:** 400, 420
Champagne Deutz Blanc de Blancs **1979:** 166
Champagne Deutz Brut N/V, Napa Valley: 77, 169, 172, 238, 315
Champagne Deutz Montana N/V, Marlborough, New Zealand: 335
Champagne Dom Pérignon **1962:** 415
Champagne Dom Pérignon **1966:** 267
Champagne Dom Pérignon **1970:** 25, 609
Champagne Dom Pérignon **1971:** 77, 609
Champagne Dom Pérignon **1973:** 609
Champagne Dom Pérignon **1975:** 610
Champagne Dom Pérignon **1980:** 612
Champagne Dom Pérignon **1982:** 417, 446, 527, 613
Champagne Dom Pérignon **1988:** 434
Champagne Dom Pérignon Rosé **1976:** 72
Champagne Dom Ruinart Blanc de Blancs **1979:** 611
Champagne Dom Ruinart Blanc de Blancs **1981:** 613, 332
Champagne Dom Ruinart Blanc de Blancs **1982:** 365
Champagne Dom Ruinart Brut **1979:** 178
Champagne E. Barnaut "Grande Reserve" Brut N/V: 607
Champagne Gosset "Grand Millésime" **1976:** 141, 161, 611
Champagne Gosset "Grand Millésime" **1982:** 272
Champagne Gosset "Grande Réserve" Brut N/V: 272, 353, 607
Champagne Gosset "Naissance de l'Europe" Brut N/V: 608
Champagne Gosset "Réserve" Brut N/V: 272
Champagne Gosset Rosé Brut N/V: 272
Champagne Gosset Vintage Brut **1983:** 272
Champagne Heidsieck Monopole "Diamant Bleu" **1979:** 223
Champagne Heidsieck Monopole "Diamant Bleu" **1989:** 512
Champagne Henriot (Rothschild) **1969:** 20
Champagne Henriot (Rothschild) **1973:** 45
Champagne J. Lasalle Blanc de Blancs "Chigny" **1983:** 283
Champagne J. Lasalle Blanc de Blancs Premier Cru Brut **1976,** "Chigny": 610
Champagne Jacquart Brut **1982:** 267

Champagne Jacques Selosse Blanc de Blancs Grand Cru Brut N/V: 607
Champagne Jacquesson "Signature" **1982:** 381, 411
Champagne Jacquesson "Signature" **1985:** 444
Champagne Jacquesson "Signature" Rosé **1989:** 439
Champagne Julien Tarin Blanc de Blancs Brut **1977,** Le Mesnil sur Oger: 611
Champagne Krug "Clos du Mesnil" Blanc de Blancs **1979:** 158, 241
Champagne Krug "Clos du Mesnil" Blanc de Blancs **1982:** 352
Champagne Krug "Clos du Mesnil" Blanc de Blancs **1985:** 458
Champagne Krug "Collection" **1928:** 347
Champagne Krug "Collection" **1929:** 349
Champagne Krug "Collection" **1937:** 348
Champagne Krug "Collection" **1938:** 347
Champagne Krug "Collection" **1942:** 347
Champagne Krug "Collection" **1945:** 347
Champagne Krug "Collection" **1947:** 347
Champagne Krug "Collection" **1949:** 348
Champagne Krug "Collection" **1952:** 347
Champagne Krug "Collection" **1953:** 348
Champagne Krug "Collection" **1955:** 348
Champagne Krug "Collection" **1959:** 348
Champagne Krug "Collection" **1961:** 158, 348
Champagne Krug "Collection" **1962:** 241, 347
Champagne Krug "Collection" **1964:** 348
Champagne Krug "Collection" **1966:** 267, 347
Champagne Krug "Collection" **1969:** 158, 241, 269, 348
Champagne Krug "Collection" **1971:** 48, 347
Champagne Krug "Collection" **1973:** 348
Champagne Krug "Collection" **1976:** 347
Champagne Krug "Collection" **1979:** 348
Champagne Krug "Collection" **1981:** 348
Champagne Krug "Collection" **1982:** 347
Champagne Krug "Cuvée Réserve" **1976:** 91
Champagne Krug "Cuvée Spéciale" N/V: 82
Champagne Krug "Grande Cuvée" N/V: 3, 35, 91, 137, 158, 180, 195, 217, 231, 241, 244, 270, 282, 303, 317, 322, 347, 352, 356, 358, 394, 608
Champagne Krug "Special Reserve" **1961:** 58
Champagne Krug Rosé N/V: 158, 198, 241, 271, 607
Champagne Krug Vintage **1955:** 195, 207
Champagne Krug Vintage **1961:** 317
Champagne Krug Vintage **1969:** 57
Champagne Krug Vintage **1975:** 350
Champagne Krug Vintage **1976:** 315, 611
Champagne Krug Vintage **1979:** 158, 225, 231, 235, 241, 274, 328, 370, 388, 403, 612
Champagne Krug Vintage **1982:** 328, 352, 356, 426
Champagne Krug Vintage **1985:** 459, 505
Champagne Lanson "Black Label" N/V: 79, 96, 258, 607
Champagne Lanson "Cuvée Noble" N/V: 79
Champagne Lanson "Red Label" **1976:** 79
Champagne Lanson "Red Label" **1982:** 324, 613
Champagne Lasalle "Imperial Preference" Brut N/V: 167
Champagne Laurent-Perrier "Cuvée Grand Siècle" **1970:** 237
Champagne Laurent-Perrier "Cuvée Grand Siècle" **1978:** 110
Champagne Laurent-Perrier "Cuvée Grand Siècle" **1979:** 222
Champagne Laurent-Perrier "Cuvée Grand Siècle" Brut N/V: 338
Champagne Laurent-Perrier L.P. Brut N/V: 311
Champagne Lechère "Orient Express" Brut N/V: 177, 275, 608
Champagne Leclerc-Briant "Special Club" Brut **1978:** 140, 611
Champagne Louis Roederer "Brut Premier" N/V: 169, 425, 503
Champagne Louis Roederer "Cristal' **1975:** 610
Champagne Louis Roederer "Cristal" **1974:** 609
Champagne Louis Roederer "Cristal" **1975:** 22
Champagne Louis Roederer "Cristal" **1976:** 29, 177
Champagne Louis Roederer "Cristal" **1978:** 611
Champagne Louis Roederer "Cristal" **1979:** 113, 124, 388, 611
Champagne Louis Roederer "Cristal" **1981:** 216
Champagne Louis Roederer "Cristal" **1983:** 311, 321, 364, 489, 500, 614
Champagne Louis Roederer "Cristal" **1990:** 513
Champagne Louis Roederer "Cristal" Rosé **1988:** 399
Champagne Louis Roederer "Cuvée Marc Meneau" Brut N/V: 169
Champagne Louis Roederer "Jamin" Theophile Brut N/V: 207
Champagne Louis Roederer Brut **1971:** 56, 341
Champagne Louis Roederer Brut **1973:** 128
Champagne Louis Roederer Brut **1979:** 192
Champagne Louis Roederer Brut N/V: 129, 135, 169, 183, 310, 450
Champagne Louis Roederer Carte Blanche (Demi Sec) N/V: 78
Champagne Massé Brut **1945,** Massé Père et Fils: 217
Champagne Mercier Réserve Brut N/V: 66
Champagne Michel Noirot Brut N/V, "Cuvée du Clos St. Roch-Les Riceys": 322, 608
Champagne Mumm **1973,** René Lalou: 609
Champagne Mumm **1975,** René Lalou: 33
Champagne Mumm **1979,** René Lalou: 611
Champagne Mumm Blanc de Blancs "Crémant de Crémant" N/V: 47
Champagne Mumm Cordon Rouge Brut N/V: 204
Champagne Mumm N/V, Napa Valley: 238
Champagne Paul Bara "Bouzy" 100% Grand Cru Brut **1986:** 519
Champagne Paul Bara "Bouzy" Brut **1979:** 66, 159, 612
Champagne Paul Bara "Bouzy" Brut **1982:** 314
Champagne Perrier-Jouët "Blason de France" **1976:** 109, 169
Champagne Perrier-Jouët "Fleur de Champagne" **1973:** 92
Champagne Perrier-Jouët "Fleur de Champagne" **1976:** 361
Champagne Perrier-Jouet "Fleur de Champagne" **1985:** 494
Champagne Perrier-Jouët "Fleur de Champagne" **1988:** 403
Champagne Perrier-Jouët Brut N/V: 40, 207, 262, 497
Champagne Perrier-Jouët Grand Brut N/V: 54, 361
Champagne Piper-Heidsieck Brut **1973:** 16
Champagne Ployez-Jacquemart Brut N/V: 607
Champagne Pol Roger "Brut Extra Cuvée de Réserve" N/V: 203
Champagne Pol Roger "Cuvée Réserve" Brut N/V: 80
Champagne Pol Roger "Cuvée Sir Winston Churchill" **1979:** 203, 219, 611
Champagne Pol Roger "Cuvée Sir Winston Churchill" **1985:** 355
Champagne Pol Roger "Cuvée Sir Winston Churchill" **1988:** 505
Champagne Pol Roger "Extra Cuvée de Réserve" Brut **1982:** 613
Champagne Pol Roger "Private Reserve" **1975:** 68, 202, 357
Champagne Pol Roger "Private Reserve" **1982:** 327, 358, 401, 614
Champagne Pol Roger "Private Reserve" Brut **1973:** 609
Champagne Pol Roger "Réserve Spéciale" **1982:** 355
Champagne Pol Roger "Réserve Spéciale" **1985:** 355, 480
Champagne Pol Roger "Réserve" **1975:** 6, 610
Champagne Pol Roger "Reserve" Brut **1921:** 203

Champagne Pol Roger "Rosé" **1975:** 62
Champagne Pol Roger "Rosé" **1985:** 355
Champagne Pol Roger Blanc de Chardonnay **1966:** 3
Champagne Pol Roger Blanc de Chardonnay **1969:** 608
Champagne Pol Roger Blanc de Chardonnay **1971:** 609
Champagne Pol Roger Blanc de Chardonnay **1973:** 27, 609
Champagne Pol Roger Blanc de Chardonnay **1975:** 59, 64, 88
Champagne Pol Roger Blanc de Chardonnay **1979:** 203, 252
Champagne Pol Roger Blanc de Chardonnay **1982:** 336, 613
Champagne Pol Roger Blanc de Chardonnay **1985:** 355, 614
Champagne Pol Roger Blanc de Chardonnay **1988:** 473
Champagne Pol Roger Brut **1976:** 137
Champagne Pol Roger Rosé Brut **1979:** 203
Champagne Pol Roger Vintage Brut **1986:** 353, 354
Champagne Pommery Brut N/V: 90, 452
Champagne Pommery et Greno Rosé **1945:** 223
Champagne R et L Legras Blanc de Blancs Premier Cru **1979,** Chouilly: 612
Champagne René Lalou Brut **1973:** 102
Champagne Salon "Le Mesnil" Blanc de Blancs **1971:** 164
Champagne Salon "Le Mesnil" Blanc de Blancs **1982:** 338, 393, 409
Champagne Taillevent Blanc de Blancs **1980,** Philipponat: 107
Champagne Taillevent Blanc de Blancs Brut **1983,** Philipponat: 267
Champagne Taillevent N/V Rosé: 268
Champagne Taittinger "Collection" **1981:** 236
Champagne Taittinger "Comtes de Champagne" Blanc de Blancs **1975:** 240
Champagne Taittinger "Comtes de Champagne" Blanc de Blancs **1981:** 307, 612
Champagne Taittinger "Comtes de Champagne" Blanc de Blancs **1988:** 427
Champagne Taittinger "Comtes de Champagne" Rosé **1976:** 99
Champagne Tarlant Père et Fils Tradition Brut N/V, Oeuilly, Près Epernay: 214
Champagne Veuve Clicquot "Carte Or" **1982:** 229, 246, 312, 613
Champagne Veuve Clicquot "Carte Or" **1983:** 614
Champagne Veuve Clicquot "Carte Or" **1985:** 371, 387, 406, 614
Champagne Veuve Clicquot "La Grande Dame" **1978:** 62
Champagne Veuve Clicquot "La Grande Dame" **1979:** 126, 254, 270
Champagne Veuve Clicquot "La Grande Dame" **1985:** 454, 476, 615
Champagne Veuve Clicquot "Reserve" **1989:** 449, 513
Champagne Veuve Clicquot Brut N/V: 40, 102, 136, 230, 422, 607
Champagne Veuve Clicquot Rosé **1985:** 448, 614
Champagne Veuve Clicquot Rosé **1988:** 500
Chante Alouette, Hermitage Blanc **1957,** Chapoutier: 96
Chante Alouette, Hermitage Blanc **1970,** Chapoutier: 66
Chante Perdrix Châteauneuf-du-Pape **1978,** J. Nicolet: 329
Chapelle-Chambertin **1966,** Leroy: 150
Chapelle-Chambertin **1984,** Trapet: 145
Chappellet Cabernet Sauvignon **1976,** Napa Valley: 170
Charbaut Champagne Brut N/V: 334
Chardonnay **1984,** Gaya & Rey: 143
Chardonnay **1986,** Pol Roger: 353
Chardonnay **1991,** Salmon Creek, Los Carneros "Bad Dog Ranch": 378
Chardonnay **1994,** Gaya & Rey: 421
Charles Krug "Reserve" Cabernet Sauvignon **1969,** Napa Valley: 627
Charmes-Chambertin "Tasteviné" **1945,** Giroux: 320
Charmes-Chambertin **1929,** Joseph Drouhin: 35, 202
Charmes-Chambertin **1945,** A. Rousseau: 320
Charmes-Chambertin **1945,** Leroy: 236
Charmes-Chambertin **1945,** Prosper Mofoux: 237
Charmes-Chambertin **1949,** Avery's: 90
Charmes-Chambertin **1961,** Joseph Drouhin: 33
Charmes-Chambertin **1966,** Leroy: 151
Charmes-Chambertin **1969,** Faiveley: 35
Charmes-Chambertin **1972,** Joseph Drouhin: 587
Charmes-Chambertin **1982,** Maume: 588
Charmes-Chambertin **1988,** Moillard: 420
Chartreuse, White: 219, 279
Chartreuse, Yellow: 221, 279, 396
Chassagne-Montrachet "Boudriotte" **1979,** Gagnard-Delagrange: 63
Chassagne-Montrachet "Chaumées" **1986,** Jean-Marc Morey: 357
Chassagne-Montrachet "La Romanée" **1979,** Labouré-Roi: 86
Chassagne-Montrachet "Les Caillerets" **1976,** Remoissenet: 594
Chassagne-Montrachet "Les Caillerets" **1979,** Delagrange-Bachelet: 62
Chassagne-Montrachet "Les Caillerets" **1982,** Jean-Marc Morey: 235
Chassagne-Montrachet "Les Caillerets" **1989,** Blain-Gagnard: 513
Chassagne-Montrachet "Les Caillerets" **1992,** Delagrange-Bachelet: 528
Chassagne-Montrachet "Les Chaumées" **1982,** Michel Colin Deleger: 137
Chassagne-Montrachet "Les Chaumées" **1983,** Bouzereau-Gruere: 181
Chassagne-Montrachet "Les Vergers" **1979,** Michel Niellon: 86
Chassagne-Montrachet "Les Vergers" **1985,** Mme. François Colin: 425
Chassagne-Montrachet "Morgeot" **1961,** Marquis de Laguiche: 86
Chassagne-Montrachet "Morgeot" **1970,** Georges Deleger: 408
Chassagne-Montrachet "Morgeot" **1978,** Domaine du Duc de Magenta: 446
Chassagne-Montrachet "Morgeot" **1982,** Albert Morey: 137
Chassagne-Montrachet "Morgeot" **1983,** Bernard Morey: 231
Chassagne-Montrachet "Morgeot" **1988,** Domaine du Duc de Magenta: 285
Chassagne-Montrachet "Ruchottes" **1973,** Ramonet: 593
Chassagne-Montrachet **1984,** Louis Latour: 151
Chassagne-Montrachet Rouge "Morgeot" **1970,** Joseph Drouhin: 322
Château Ausone **1914:** 188
Château Ausone **1920:** 25
Château Ausone **1926:** 241
Château Ausone **1928:** 25, 66
Château Ausone **1942:** 434
Château Ausone **1945:** 131, 218, 571
Château Ausone **1955:** 240
Château Ausone **1961:** 25, 66, 82, 108, 194
Château Ausone **1962:** 129
Château Ausone **1964:** 571

Index of Wines

Château Ausone **1966:** 267
Château Ausone **1970:** 65, 408, 571
Château Ausone **1973:** 188
Château Ausone **1976:** 43, 571
Château Ausone **1979:** 43, 53, 274, 453, 462, 571
Château Ausone **1980:** 43
Château Ausone **1981:** 122
Château Ausone **1982:** 122, 160, 463
Château Ausone **1983:** 122, 434
Château Ausone **1985:** 244, 394, 464
Château Ausone **1990:** 434
Château Ausone **1993:** 434
Château Bâlestard-La-Tonnelle **1945:** 46, 118, 217
Château Bâlestard-La-Tonnelle **1983:** 118
Château Bâlestard-La-Tonnelle **1984:** 118
Château Bâlestard-La-Tonnelle **1989:** 427
Château Batailley **1945:** 134, 223
Château Batailley **1966:** 28, 559
Château Batailley **1970:** 481
Château Batailley **1978:** 32, 493
Château Batailley **1979:** 63, 273
Château Batailley **1982:** 400, 422
Château Batailley **1985:** 246
Château Beaumont **1970:** 479, 565
Château Beau-Rivage, Macau **1961:** 83
Château Bel Air Sauternes **1967,** Larronde Frères: 80
Château Belair **1939:** 188
Château Belair **1982:** 122, 391, 434
Château Belair **1983:** 122
Château Belair **1993:** 434
Château Belair **1995:** 434
Château Belair **1996:** 517
Château Belair Marquis d'Aligre **1848**, Margaux: 113
Château Belair St. Georges **1959,** Calvet Sélection: 350
Château Belgrave **1945:** 222
Château Belgrave **1970:** 66
Château Belle Grave **1975:** 2
Château Beychevelle **1945:** 133, 220
Château Beychevelle **1959:** 545
Château Beychevelle **1961:** 125, 137
Château Beychevelle **1966:** 21, 171, 312
Château Beychevelle **1970:** 30, 137, 235, 479
Château Beychevelle **1971:** 103, 549
Château Beychevelle **1978:** 19, 32, 230, 493
Château Beychevelle **1986:** 519
Château Beychevelle **1989:** 515
Château Bon-Pasteur **1985:** 228
Château Bouscaut **1923:** 4
Château Bouscaut **1964:** 4
Château Bouscaut **1966:** 4
Château Bouscaut **1967:** 4
Château Bouscaut **1969:** 4
Château Bouscaut **1970:** 4, 234
Château Bouscaut **1971:** 4
Château Bouscaut **1973:** 4
Château Bouscaut **1974:** 4
Château Bouscaut **1975:** 4
Château Bouscaut **1976:** 4
Château Bouscaut Blanc "Extra Sec" **1945:** 219
Château Boyd-Cantenac **1978:** 231
Château Branaire-Ducru **1945:** 133, 220
Château Branaire-Ducru **1970:** 479
Château Branaire-Ducru **1975:** 402, 550
Château Branaire-Ducru **1982:** 400, 422, 486
Château Branaire-Ducru **1986:** 519, 458
Château Branaire-Ducru **1989:** 515
Château Brane-Cantenac **1926:** 450
Château Brane-Cantenac **1928:** 264
Château Brane-Cantenac **1945:** 132, 223
Château Brane-Cantenac **1961:** 48, 125, 535
Château Brane-Cantenac **1964:** 535
Château Brane-Cantenac **1966:** 20, 120, 171, 537
Château Brane-Cantenac **1967:** 537, 539
Château Brane-Cantenac **1971:** 537
Château Brane-Cantenac **1983:** 157, 489
Château Broustet **1982:** 298
Château Caillou **1937:** 102
Château Caillou **1945:** 221
Château Calon-Ségur **1916:** 417, 561
Château Calon-Ségur **1918:** 339, 366, 417, 450, 525, 561
Château Calon-Ségur **1926:** 339
Château Calon-Ségur **1928:** 107, 265, 339, 418, 562
Château Calon-Ségur **1929:** 339
Château Calon-Ségur **1934:** 339, 417
Château Calon-Ségur **1943:** 417, 562
Château Calon-Ségur **1945:** 131, 218, 219, 338, 417, 562
Château Calon-Ségur **1947:** 86, 339, 401, 417, 562
Château Calon-Ségur **1948:** 339, 417, 562
Château Calon-Ségur **1949:** 339, 417, 562
Château Calon-Ségur **1952:** 338, 368, 417, 562
Château Calon-Ségur **1953:** 338
Château Calon-Ségur **1955:** 240, 338
Château Calon-Ségur **1959:** 417
Château Calon-Ségur **1961:** 81, 125, 338, 417, 563
Château Calon-Ségur **1962:** 338
Château Calon-Ségur **1966:** 20, 29, 81, 417, 563
Château Calon-Ségur **1970:** 81
Château Calon-Ségur **1975:** 339, 564
Château Calon-Ségur **1982:** 339, 400, 423, 565
Château Calon-Ségur **1989:** 420
Château Canon **1945:** 218
Château Canon **1947:** 136
Château Canon **1961:** 119, 178
Château Canon **1962:** 178
Château Canon **1964:** 178
Château Canon **1970:** 298
Château Canon **1979:** 298
Château Canon **1981:** 119, 487, 575
Château Canon **1982:** 119, 330, 351, 462
Château Canon **1983:** 119, 330, 464
Château Canon **1984:** 119
Château Canon **1985:** 228
Château Canon **1986:** 258, 271
Château Canon de Brem **1996:** 517
Château Canon La Gaffelière **1975:** 76
Château Canon La Gaffelière **1988:** 458
Château Cantemerle **1945:** 124, 133, 222
Château Cantemerle **1955:** 102
Château Cantemerle **1961:** 535
Château Cantemerle **1964:** 246, 535, 536

Château Cantemerle **1970:** 540
Château Cantemerle **1983:** 373, 489, 501
Château Cantemerle **1985:** 246, 542
Château Cantemerle **1989:** 420
Château Cantenac-Brown **1945:** 132, 222
Château Cantenac-Brown **1955:** 534
Château Cantenac-Brown **1988:** 296
Château Cap de Mourlin **1982:** 117
Château Cap de Mourlin **1983:** 117
Château Cap de Mourlin **1984:** 117
Château Carbonnieux **1945:** 221
Château Carbonnieux **1966:** 20
Château Carbonnieux **1970:** 477
Château Carbonnieux **1990:** 525
Château Carbonnieux Blanc **1971:** 615
Château Carbonnieux Blanc **1978:** 24
Château Carbonnieux Blanc **1979:** 32
Château Carbonnieux Blanc **1981:** 76, 125
Château Carbonnieux Blanc **1982:** 172
Château Certan-de-May **1979:** 85, 350, 514, 580
Château Certan-de-May **1985:** 524
Château Certan-de-May **1996:** 518
Château Certan-Guiraud **1978:** 230
Château Certan-Guiraud **1982:** 351, 400
Château Certan-Guiraud **1985:** 228
Château Chalon Vin Jaune **1966,** Bouvret: 478
Château Chalon Vin Jaune Arbois **1982,** Henri Maîre: 366
Château Chambert-Marbuzet **1986:** 258
Château Chasse-Spleen **1970:** 115, 235, 479, 567
Château Chasse-Spleen **1975:** 567
Château Chasse-Spleen **1982:** 422
Château Chasse-Spleen **1989:** 475
Château Chasse-Spleen **1990:** 374
Château Cheval-Blanc **1926:** 241
Château Cheval-Blanc **1934:** 343
Château Cheval-Blanc **1945:** 131, 218
Château Cheval-Blanc **1947:** 3, 17, 79, 86, 108, 136, 344, 346
Château Cheval-Blanc **1948:** 343
Château Cheval-Blanc **1949:** 167, 343
Château Cheval-Blanc **1952:** 343
Château Cheval-Blanc **1953:** 343
Château Cheval-Blanc **1955:** 194, 333, 343, 572
Château Cheval-Blanc **1959:** 343
Château Cheval-Blanc **1961:** 343, 411
Château Cheval-Blanc **1962:** 129
Château Cheval-Blanc **1964:** 343
Château Cheval-Blanc **1966:** 33, 268, 343, 454, 572
Château Cheval-Blanc **1967:** 33, 343
Château Cheval-Blanc **1970:** 65, 343, 349, 408, 481, 572
Château Cheval-Blanc **1971:** 343, 572
Château Cheval-Blanc **1975:** 300, 343, 452, 572
Château Cheval-Blanc **1978:** 342, 572
Château Cheval-Blanc **1979:** 53, 342, 572
Château Cheval-Blanc **1982:** 104, 160, 343, 351, 463
Château Cheval-Blanc **1985:** 228, 244, 394
Château Cheval-Blanc **1986:** 259
Château Cheval-Blanc **1988:** 484
Château Chevalier Cabernet Sauvignon **1980,** Napa Valley: 631
Château Chevalier Merlot **1978,** Sonoma Valley: 633
Château Cissac **1966:** 44
Château Cissac **1970:** 567
Château Cissac **1973:** 44
Château Cissac **1977:** 43
Château Cissac **1978:** 43
Château Cissac **1979:** 43
Château Cissac **1980:** 43
Château Clerc-Milon **1978:** 231
Château Clerc-Milon **1983:** 372
Château Climens **1949:** 4
Château Climens **1962:** 169
Château Climens **1964:** 373, 604
Château Climens **1967:** 170, 331, 344, 406
Château Climens **1976:** 68, 76, 82, 489, 507, 605
Château Climens **1983:** 331, 501, 605
Château Climens **1986:** 259, 525
Château Clos Fourtet **1928:** 264
Château Clos Fourtet **1945:** 131, 217
Château Clos Fourtet **1947:** 108
Château Clos l'Eglise **1945:** 132, 226
Château Clos l'Eglise **1982:** 201
Château Clos René **1945:** 132, 226
Château Clos René **1970:** 66
Château Clos René **1979:** 85
Château Clos René **1982:** 201
Château Clos René **1985:** 228
Château Cos d'Estournel **1870:** 256
Château Cos d'Estournel **1926:** 126
Château Cos d'Estournel **1928:** 265
Château Cos d'Estournel **1945:** 131, 219
Château Cos d'Estournel **1947:** 562
Château Cos d'Estournel **1955:** 428
Château Cos d'Estournel **1959:** 563
Château Cos d'Estournel **1961:** 33, 81, 125
Château Cos d'Estournel **1966:** 81, 564
Château Cos d'Estournel **1970:** 81, 235, 256, 425, 478, 564
Château Cos d'Estournel **1971:** 44
Château Cos d'Estournel **1975:** 427
Château Cos d'Estournel **1978:** 34, 493
Château Cos d'Estournel **1979:** 34, 273
Château Cos d'Estournel **1981:** 44, 410
Château Cos d'Estournel **1982:** 44, 104, 330, 410, 495
Château Cos d'Estournel **1983:** 158, 330, 373, 404, 410, 502
Château Cos d'Estournel **1985:** 183, 243, 350, 492, 509
Château Cos d'Estournel **1986:** 183, 258, 442, 445, 492, 509
Château Cos d'Estournel **1989:** 404, 509
Château Cos d'Estournel **1990:** 404
Château Cos d'Estournel **1992:** 404
Château Cos d'Estournel **1993:** 404
Château Coutet **1961:** 35
Château Coutet **1962:** 274
Château Coutet **1971:** 247
Château Coutet **1975:** 15, 46, 96, 493, 605
Château Croizet-Bages **1945:** 224
Château Croizet-Bages **1970:** 481
Château Croque-Michotte **1947:** 136
Château d'Angludet **1970:** 235
Château d'Angludet **1971:** 69
Château d'Angludet **1973:** 19
Château d'Angludet **1978:** 177, 231, 493
Château d'Angludet **1979:** 163, 177, 273

INDEX of WINES

Château d'Angludet **1981:** 163, 176
Château d'Angludet **1982:** 163, 176
Château d'Angludet **1983:** 157, 163, 176
Château d'Angludet **1984:** 176
Château d'Angludet **1985:** 246
Château d'Issan **1955:** 534
Château d'Issan **1966:** 537
Château d'Issan **1985:** 228
Château d'Issan **1986:** 271
Château d'Yquem **1847:** 380
Château d'Yquem **1864:** 380
Château d'Yquem **1865:** 380
Château d'Yquem **1869:** 380
Château d'Yquem **1870:** 379
Château d'Yquem **1874:** 380
Château d'Yquem **1893:** 380
Château d'Yquem **1900:** 380
Château d'Yquem **1921:** 381
Château d'Yquem **1928:** 266
Château d'Yquem **1929:** 318, 381
Château d'Yquem **1937:** 379
Château d'Yquem **1945:** 225, 237, 379, 412
Château d'Yquem **1947:** 379
Château d'Yquem **1949:** 237, 409
Château d'Yquem **1955:** 194, 379
Château d'Yquem **1958:** 97
Château d'Yquem **1959:** 114, 379, 476
Château d'Yquem **1961:** 126, 243, 32
Château d'Yquem **1962:** 129, 380
Château d'Yquem **1966:** 61, 268
Château d'Yquem **1967:** 34, 96, 216, 318, 346, 380, 395, 504, 602
Château d'Yquem **1970:** 27, 33, 229, 270, 408, 494, 504
Château d'Yquem **1971:** 504, 602
Château d'Yquem **1975:** 325, 380, 415, 424, 451, 504, 513, 602
Château d'Yquem **1976:** 16, 165, 380, 460, 504, 602
Château d'Yquem **1979:** 216
Château d'Yquem **1980:** 177, 429, 462, 484, 487, 503, 603
Château d'Yquem **1982:** 504
Château d'Yquem **1983:** 326, 355, 356, 379, 504
Château d'Yquem **1984:** 603
Château d'Yquem **1985:** 355
Château d'Yquem **1986:** 379, 355, 504
Château d'Yquem **1987:** 355, 484, 503
Château d'Yquem **1988:** 379, 504
Château d'Yquem **1989:** 504
Château d'Yquem **1990:** 504
Château Dauzac **1970:** 478
Château de Bellegarde, Graves Blanc **1982:** 70
Château de Fargues **1945:** 225
Château de Fargues **1967:** 523
Château de Fargues **1971:** 21, 137, 332
Château de Fargues **1975:** 360, 370, 494, 605
Château de Fargues **1976:** 162, 357
Château de Fargues **1980:** 322, 365
Château de Fargues **1983:** 355, 490
Château de Fargues 1985 355
Château de Fargues **1986:** 355
Château de Fargues **1987:** 355
Château de Fieuzal **1978:** 230
Château de Fieuzal Blanc **1986:** 258
Château de Fonsalette **1978,** AOC Côtes du Rhône, Paynaud: 329
Château de l'Hôpital **1982:** 7, 76
Château de Lucques **1924,** Barsac-Eschenauer: 446, 604
Château de Marbuzet **1985:** 183
Château de Marbuzet **1986:** 183
Château de Marbuzet **1992:** 404
Château de Marbuzet **1993:** 404
Château de Pez **1966:** 563
Château de Pez **1970:** 478, 564
Château de Pez **1982:** 252
Château de Rayne Vigneau **1917,** Vicomte de Pontac: 603
Château de Rayne Vigneau **1933,** Vicomte de Pontac: 604
Château de Rayne Vigneau **1945,** Vicomte de Pontac: 227, 412
Château de Ricaud **1920,** Loupiac: 604
Château de Ricaud **1986,** Loupiac: 606
Château de Sales **1982:** 581
Château des Coulinats **1959,** Ste. Croix-du-Mont: 49
Château Desmirail **1928** Margaux: 264
Château Doisy-Daëne **1945:** 219, 412
Château Doisy-Daëne **1982:** 57
Château Doisy-Védrines **1945:** 219
Château Doisy-Védrines **1955:** 194
Château du Domaine de l'Eglise **1970:** 479, 578
Château du Domaine de l'Eglise **1982:** 201
Château du Tertre **1979:** 542
Château du Tertre **1982:** 324
Château Ducru-Beaucaillou **1945:** 133, 220
Château Ducru-Beaucaillou **1955:** 544
Château Ducru-Beaucaillou **1959:** 233
Château Ducru-Beaucaillou **1961:** 48, 60, 125, 233, 446, 453, 546
Château Ducru-Beaucaillou **1962:** 234
Château Ducru-Beaucaillou **1964:** 60, 233, 547
Château Ducru-Beaucaillou **1966:** 21, 60, 181, 233
Château Ducru-Beaucaillou **1967:** 181
Château Ducru-Beaucaillou **1970:** 29, 55, 60, 181, 210, 234, 446, 479, 548
Château Ducru-Beaucaillou **1972:** 550
Château Ducru-Beaucaillou **1973:** 180
Château Ducru-Beaucaillou **1975:** 180, 233, 475, 496
Château Ducru-Beaucaillou **1976:** 233
Château Ducru-Beaucaillou **1978:** 153, 180, 435, 550
Château Ducru-Beaucaillou **1979:** 233
Château Ducru-Beaucaillou **1981:** 87, 180, 233
Château Ducru-Beaucaillou **1982:** 180, 233, 401
Château Ducru-Beaucaillou **1983:** 233, 373
Château Ducru-Beaucaillou **1985:** 243, 516
Château Ducru-Beaucaillou **1986:** 271, 519
Château Ducru-Beaucaillou, Faiveley: **1978:** 233
Château Duhart-Milon **1945:** 223
Château Duhart-Milon **1966:** 171
Château Durfort-Vivens **1928:** 92
Château Durfort-Vivens **1966:** 537
Château Durfort-Vivens **1990:** 374
Château dY'quem "Mountain Crest" N/V, Livermore, Sonoma Valley: 175
Château Ferrière **1970:** 349
Château Feytit-Clinet **1982:** 201
Château Figeac **1961:** 18
Château Figeac **1964:** 71, 573
Château Figeac **1966:** 573

Château Figeac **1970:** 41, 55, 210
Château Figeac **1971:** 71
Château Figeac **1975:** 71, 118, 188
Château Figeac **1976:** 18
Château Figeac **1978:** 493, 575
Château Figeac **1980:** 71
Château Figeac **1981:** 41
Château Figeac **1982:** 104, 351, 423, 442, 462, 464, 575
Château Figeac **1983:** 118, 432
Château Figeac **1985:** 188
Château Figeac **1986:** 188, 271
Château Figeac **1988:** 374
Château Figeac **1989:** 501
Château Figeac **1990:** 374
Château Filhot **1928:** 604
Château Filhot **1929:** 316
Château Filhot **1945:** 221
Château Filhot **1975:** 27, 605
Château Fonplégade **1970:** 480
Château Fourcas-Hosten **1961:** 48
Château Fourcas-Hosten **1983:** 158
Château Franc-Mayne **1970:** 480, 574
Château Gazin **1945:** 226, 236
Château Gazin **1971:** 579
Château Gazin **1990:** 458
Château Gazin **1996:** 518
Château Gilette "Crème de Tête" **1949:** 120
Château Gilette "Crème de Tête" **1950:** 120
Château Gilette "Crème de Tête" **1953:** 120, 172, 176, 342
Château Gilette "Crème de Tête" **1955:** 75, 120
Château Gilette "Crème de Tête" **1959:** 119
Château Gilette "Crème de Tête" **1967:** 390
Château Gilette **1929:** 120
Château Gilette Les Justices "Doux" **1950:** 119
Château Gilette Les Justices **1975:** 119
Château Gilette Les Justices **1979:** 119
Château Gilette Les Justices **1982:** 119
Château Giscours **1945:** 222
Château Giscours **1961:** 535
Château Giscours **1964:** 535
Château Giscours **1966:** 29, 171, 537
Château Giscours **1967:** 196
Château Giscours **1970:** 355
Château Giscours **1978:** 231
Château Giscours **1983:** 372
Château Gloria **1970:** 479, 548
Château Gloria **1982:** 104
Château Gloria **1986:** 518
Château Grand Corbin d'Espagne **1945:** 131
Château Grand La Lagune **1926:** 338
Château Grand La Lagune **1945:** 133, 222
Château Grand-Barrail-Lamarzelle-Figeac **1945:** 217
Château Grand-Puy-Lacoste **1945:** 134, 223, 179
Château Grand-Puy-Lacoste **1955:** 179
Château Grand-Puy-Lacoste **1961:** 75, 180, 247, 558
Château Grand-Puy-Lacoste **1964:** 559
Château Grand-Puy-Lacoste **1966:** 82, 179
Château Grand-Puy-Lacoste **1970:** 82, 179, 235, 481, 560
Château Grand-Puy-Lacoste **1975:** 179
Château Grand-Puy-Lacoste **1978:** 179, 450
Château Grand-Puy-Lacoste **1979:** 179, 273, 358
Château Grand-Puy-Lacoste **1981:** 179
Château Grand-Puy-Lacoste **1982:** 104, 179, 324, 330, 401, 495, 525, 561
Château Grand-Puy-Lacoste **1983:** 158, 179, 331, 502, 525
Château Grand-Puy-Lacoste **1985:** 394, 525
Château Grand-Puy-Lacoste **1989:** 466, 525
Château Grillet **1971:** 617
Château Grillet **1978:** 22, 79, 328, 617
Château Grillet **1979:** 79, 102, 248, 617
Château Grillet **1980:** 79, 620
Château Gruaud-Larose **1865:** 113
Château Gruaud-Larose **1870:** 113, 256
Château Gruaud-Larose **1905:** 1
Château Gruaud-Larose **1916:** 450, 543
Château Gruaud-Larose **1921:** 107
Château Gruaud-Larose **1928:** 264, 316, 388, 543
Château Gruaud-Larose **1945:** 67, 133, 220, 262, 328, 360
Château Gruaud-Larose **1949:** 245, 262, 544
Château Gruaud-Larose **1953:** 231, 422
Château Gruaud-Larose **1955:** 240, 261
Château Gruaud-Larose **1957:** 261
Château Gruaud-Larose **1958:** 322, 544
Château Gruaud-Larose **1961:** 48, 202, 255, 261, 332, 370, 496, 529, 546
Château Gruaud-Larose **1962:** 261, 407, 547
Château Gruaud-Larose **1964:** 327, 547
Château Gruaud-Larose **1966:** 29, 171, 231, 255, 261, 483, 512, 547
Château Gruaud-Larose **1967:** 261
Château Gruaud-Larose **1970:** 255, 256, 261, 479, 548
Château Gruaud-Larose **1971:** 261, 549
Château Gruaud-Larose **1973:** 255, 261
Château Gruaud-Larose **1975:** 255, 261, 352, 402
Château Gruaud-Larose **1976:** 255
Château Gruaud-Larose **1978:** 254, 261, 493, 550
Château Gruaud-Larose **1979:** 75, 187, 254, 261, 273, 364, 515
Château Gruaud-Larose **1980:** 254
Château Gruaud-Larose **1981:** 87, 187, 255, 261, 364, 515, 551
Château Gruaud-Larose **1982:** 254, 261, 324, 515
Château Gruaud-Larose **1983:** 158, 254, 261, 373, 515, 551
Château Gruaud-Larose **1984:** 121
Château Gruaud-Larose **1985:** 121, 246, 254, 261, 515
Château Gruaud-Larose **1986:** 445, 486, 519
Château Gruaud-Larose **1989:** 450
Château Guiraud **1967:** 20, 425
Château Guiraud **1970:** 36
Château Guiraud **1979:** 49
Château Haut-Bages-Avéroux **1961:** 48, 557
Château Haut-Bages-Avéroux **1987:** 296
Château Haut-Bages-Avéroux **1994:** 431
Château Haut-Bages-Avéroux **1995:** 431
Château Haut-Bages-Libéral **1976:** 40
Château Haut-Bages-Libéral **1982:** 104
Château Haut-Bages-Libéral **1984:** 122
Château Haut-Bages-Libéral **1985:** 246
Château Haut-Bages-Libéral **1986:** 445
Château Haut-Bailly **1928:** 265
Château Haut-Bailly **1945:** 105, 131, 221
Château Haut-Bailly **1955:** 568

Château Haut-Bailly **1964:** 569
Château Haut-Bailly **1970:** 477, 570
Château Haut-Bailly **1979:** 273
Château Haut-Batailley **1945:** 223
Château Haut-Batailley **1970:** 66, 481
Château Haut-Batailley **1975:** 25
Château Haut-Batailley **1982:** 104
Château Haut-Brion **1858:** 113
Château Haut-Brion **1926:** 20, 107
Château Haut-Brion **1929:** 108
Château Haut-Brion **1945:** 131, 221
Château Haut-Brion **1953:** 109
Château Haut-Brion **1955:** 47, 194
Château Haut-Brion **1959:** 22, 109, 274, 368, 397, 567
Château Haut-Brion **1961:** 10, 349, 397, 411, 567
Château Haut-Brion **1962:** 129, 567
Château Haut-Brion **1964:** 196, 266, 397, 567
Château Haut-Brion **1966:** 196, 268, 274, 397, 567
Château Haut-Brion **1967:** 568
Château Haut-Brion **1969:** 568
Château Haut-Brion **1970:** 30, 65, 397, 408, 477, 568
Château Haut-Brion **1972:** 568
Château Haut-Brion **1975:** 397
Château Haut-Brion **1976:** 266, 568
Château Haut-Brion **1978:** 266, 397
Château Haut-Brion **1979:** 15, 53, 266, 273, 397, 523, 568
Château Haut-Brion **1981:** 87, 266, 396, 397
Château Haut-Brion **1982:** 104, 160, 266, 396, 514
Château Haut-Brion **1983:** 158, 266, 396, 514
Château Haut-Brion **1985:** 244, 266, 396, 514
Château Haut-Brion **1986:** 259, 396, 514
Château Haut-Brion **1989:** 514
Château Haut-Brion **1990:** 514
Château Haut-Brion Blanc **1928:** 263
Château Haut-Brion Blanc **1945:** 219
Château Haut-Brion Blanc **1975:** 109
Château Haut-Brion Blanc **1982:** 236
Château Haut-Brion Blanc **1983:** 236, 273
Château Haut-Brion Blanc **1988:** 397
Château Haut-Marbuzet **1982:** 484, 565
Château Kirwan **1945:** 132, 222
Château Kirwan **1966:** 537
Château Kirwan **1978:** 31, 231
Château Kirwan **1979:** 63
Château l'Angélus **1945:** 217
Château l'Angélus **1970:** 57
Château l'Angélus **1988:** 374
Château l'Angélus **1990:** 374
Château l'Arrosée **1961:** 2, 37, 58, 328, 333, 451, 573
Château l'Arrosée **1966:** 2, 28, 35, 37, 96, 333, 451, 574
Château l'Arrosée **1967:** 2, 37
Château l'Arrosée **1970:** 2, 37,57, 96, 234, 333, 480 574
Château l'Arrosée **1971:** 2, 37
Château l'Arrosée **1973:** 37
Château l'Arrosée **1976:** 37
Château l'Arrosée **1978:** 493
Château l'Arrosée **1982:** 351, 462
Château l'Arrosée **1985:** 228, 246
Château l'Arrosée **1986:** 271
Château l'Arrosée **1989:** 420
Château l'Eglise-Clinet **1945:** 226
Château l'Eglise-Clinet **1961:** 3, 48
Château l'Enclos **1945:** 131, 226, 372
Château l'Evangile **1928:** 264
Château l'Evangile **1945:** 227
Château l'Evangile **1961:** 577
Château l'Evangile **1971:** 579
Château l'Evangile **1975:** 580
Château l'Evangile **1978:** 230, 580
Château l'Evangile **1979:** 85
Château l'Evangile **1982:** 118, 201, 351, 401, 474
Château l'Evangile **1983:** 118, 463, 581
Château l'Evangile **1985:** 228, 247, 524
Château l'Evangile **1986:** 259
Château La Conseillante **1916:** 214
Château La Conseillante **1945:** 226
Château La Conseillante **1966:** 214
Château La Conseillante **1975:** 579
Château La Conseillante **1979:** 63
Château La Conseillante **1981:** 350, 389, 581
Château La Conseillante **1982:** 104, 201, 351, 454
Château La Conseillante **1984:** 118
Château La Conseillante **1985:** 118, 228, 247, 524
Château La Croix **1982:** 201
Château La Croix Canon **1996:** 517
Château La Croix de Gay **1945:** 131, 226
Château La Croix de Gay **1982:** 201
Château La Dominique **1982:** 464
Château La Dominique **1989:** 420
Château La Fleur de Gazin **1945:** 576
Château La Fleur-Petrus **1945:** 132, 226
Château La Fleur-Petrus **1970:** 55, 480, 578
Château La Fleur-Petrus **1971:** 579
Château La Fleur-Petrus **1979:** 85
Château La Fleur-Petrus **1982:** 201, 351
Château La Fleur-Petrus **1989:** 390
Château La Fleur-Petrus **1990:** 390
Château La Gaffelière **1945:** 218
Château La Gaffelière **1970:** 235, 480, 574
Château La Gaffelière-Naudes **1928:** 135, 264
Château La Gaffelière-Naudes **1945:** 131
Château La Gaffelière-Naudes **1961:** 33, 48, 58, 573
Château La Garde A/C Graves **1953,** Louis Eschenauer: 568
Château La Grande Roche Pinot Noir **1991,** Napa Valley: 459
Château La Grange **1964,** Graves Supérieur Blanc: 90
Château La Grave **1996:** 518
Château La Grave-à-Pomerol **1989:** 390
Château La Grave-à-Pomerol **1990:** 390
Château La Gurgue **1990:** 374
Château La Lagune **1926:** 20
Château La Lagune **1961:** 101, 199, 451, 535
Château La Lagune **1966:** 29, 171, 199, 304, 335, 489, 538
Château La Lagune **1970:** 199, 235, 304, 477, 540
Château La Lagune **1975:** 199, 304
Château La Lagune **1978:** 32, 34, 199, 230, 304
Château La Lagune **1979:** 34, 199
Château La Lagune **1980:** 199
Château La Lagune **1981:** 87, 199, 303,
Château La Lagune **1982:** 199, 303, 324, 401, 422, 542
Château La Lagune **1983:** 158, 199, 303, 489

Château La Lagune **1985:** 246, 303, 394, 445
Château La Lagune **1986:** 303, 445
Château La Lagune **1989:** 420
Château La Louvière **1982:** 201
Château La Louvière **1985:** 227, 247
Château La Louvière **1988:** 419
Château La Mission Haut-Brion **1928:** 265
Château La Mission Haut-Brion **1945:** 131, 221
Château La Mission Haut-Brion **1949:** 79
Château La Mission Haut-Brion **1952:** 336
Château La Mission Haut-Brion **1955:** 336
Château La Mission Haut-Brion **1959:** 336, 569
Château La Mission Haut-Brion **1961:** 279, 336, 411
Château La Mission Haut-Brion **1962:** 39, 129, 349
Château La Mission Haut-Brion **1964:** 336
Château La Mission Haut-Brion **1966:** 268, 274, 336, 388, 569
Château La Mission Haut-Brion **1967:** 336, 569
Château La Mission Haut-Brion **1970:** 336, 477
Château La Mission Haut-Brion **1971:** 336
Château La Mission Haut-Brion **1975:** 336, 402, 452, 462, 516
Château La Mission Haut-Brion **1978:** 274, 336, 570
Château La Mission Haut-Brion **1979:** 336
Château La Mission Haut-Brion **1981:** 87, 336, 505, 571
Château La Mission Haut-Brion **1982:** 160, 336
Château La Mission Haut-Brion **1983:** 502
Château La Mission Haut-Brion **1985:** 228, 244, 491
Château La Mission Haut-Brion **1986:** 259, 271, 491
Château La Montagne **1925:** 255
Château La Pointe **1945:** 132, 236
Château La Pointe **1947:** 576
Château La Pointe **1982:** 201
Château La Pointe: 226
Château La Providence **1982:** 201
Château La Tour Blanche **1861:** 411
Château La Tour Blanche **1945,** "Propriété d'État Mr. Osiris": 222
Château La Tour Carnet **1934:** 245
Château La Tour Carnet **1945:** 133, 222
Château La Tour de Mons **1945:** 133
Château Lafaurie-Peyraguey **1945:** 227, 412
Château Lafaurie-Peyraguey **1983:** 418, 605
Château Lafaurie-Peyraguey **1986:** 516, 606
Château Lafaurie-Peyraguey **1995:** 518
Château Lafite-Rothschild "Grand Vin" N/V (Pre-**1905,** Birkedal-Hartmann, Bordeaux: 358): 551
Château Lafite-Rothschild "Ten Boek" Collection **1870:** 1
Château Lafite-Rothschild **1864:** 318, 415
Château Lafite-Rothschild **1870:** 113, 317, 415
Château Lafite-Rothschild **1874:** 113, 317
Château Lafite-Rothschild **1887:** 113
Château Lafite-Rothschild **1926:** 241
Château Lafite-Rothschild **1945:** 61, 134, 224
Château Lafite-Rothschild **1947:** 1
Château Lafite-Rothschild **1949:** 61, 108
Château Lafite-Rothschild **1953:** 109, 169, 317, 415
Château Lafite-Rothschild **1955:** 195
Château Lafite-Rothschild **1956:** 97, 243
Château Lafite-Rothschild **1959:** 22, 49, 91, 109, 114, 243, 317, 368, 415, 551
Château Lafite-Rothschild **1961:** 49, 51, 94, 109, 203, 243, 411, 452
Château Lafite-Rothschild **1962:** 129, 243, 254, 358, 552
Château Lafite-Rothschild **1965:** 113
Château Lafite-Rothschild **1966:** 49, 243, 268, 552
Château Lafite-Rothschild **1967:** 552
Château Lafite-Rothschild **1968:** 552
Château Lafite-Rothschild **1970:** 30, 48, 65, 243, 408, 481, 523
Château Lafite-Rothschild **1971:** 552
Château Lafite-Rothschild **1975:** 243, 460, 552
Château Lafite-Rothschild **1976:** 242, 397, 552
Château Lafite-Rothschild **1978:** 242
Château Lafite-Rothschild **1979:** 53, 242, 553
Château Lafite-Rothschild **1980:** 242
Château Lafite-Rothschild **1981:** 242
Château Lafite-Rothschild **1982:** 104, 160, 242
Château Lafite-Rothschild **1983:** 242, 373, 553
Château Lafite-Rothschild **1984:** 242
Château Lafite-Rothschild **1985:** 242, 244, 553
Château Lafite-Rothschild **1986:** 259, 304
Château Lafite-Rothschild **1988:** 484
Château Lafleur **1945:** 132, 226, 237
Château Lafleur **1970:** 480, 578
Château Lafleur **1975:** 580
Château Lafleur **1985:** 524
Château Lafleur-Gazin **1945:** 132, 226, 450
Château Lafon-Rochet **1945:** 130
Château Lafon-Rochet **1970:** 229, 235, 425, 478
Château Lafon-Rochet **1982:** 324
Château Lagrange **1966:** 403
Château Lagrange **1989:** 515
Château Lanessan **1970:** 234, 256, 479, 567
Château Lanessan **1975:** 452
Château Lanessan **1978:** 493
Château Langoa-Barton **1928:** 543
Château Langoa-Barton **1945:** 133, 220
Château Langoa-Barton **1961:** 546
Château Langoa-Barton **1971:** 549
Château Langoa-Barton **1979:** 63
Château Langoa-Barton **1982:** 104
Château Langoa-Barton **1986:** 519
Château Larmande **1985:** 227
Château Larrivet-Haut-Brion **1982:** 162
Château Lascombes **1961:** 48, 535
Château Lascombes **1970:** 478, 540
Château Latour **1847:** 278
Château Latour **1864:** 279
Château Latour **1865:** 279
Château Latour **1870:** 278
Château Latour **1874:** 278
Château Latour **1875:** 278
Château Latour **1881:** 113
Château Latour **1892:** 278
Château Latour **1893:** 278
Château Latour **1899:** 278, 279
Château Latour **1900:** 279
Château Latour **1918:** 278
Château Latour **1920:** 278
Château Latour **1924:** 1, 278
Château Latour **1926:** 241, 278
Château Latour **1928:** 265, 279, 316
Château Latour **1929:** 78, 279

Château Latour **1934:** 78, 278
Château Latour **1936:** 277
Château Latour **1937:** 277
Château Latour **1940:** 277
Château Latour **1942:** 277
Château Latour **1943:** 1, 277
Château Latour **1944:** 277
Château Latour **1945:** 1, 78, 134, 224, 277, 508
Château Latour **1947:** 78, 108, 277
Château Latour **1948:** 78, 277
Château Latour **1949:** 1, 68, 78, 277
Château Latour **1950:** 276
Château Latour **1952:** 77, 102, 276, 553
Château Latour **1953:** 77, 276
Château Latour **1955:** 24, 77, 195, 240, 276
Château Latour **1956:** 277
Château Latour **1957:** 276
Château Latour **1958:** 277
Château Latour **1959:** 23, 77, 114, 276, 278, 316, 365, 444
Château Latour **1960:** 276
Château Latour **1961:** 24, 77, 108, 137, 276, 365, 411
Château Latour **1963:** 277, 508
Château Latour **1964:** 23, 77, 193, 276, 278, 316, 365, 444, 553
Château Latour **1965:** 277
Château Latour **1966:** 23, 77, 268, 276, 303, 365, 422, 444, 553
Château Latour **1967:** 23, 47, 77, 277, 444, 554
Château Latour **1969:** 21, 24
Château Latour **1970:** 24, 30, 65, 77, 193, 210, 271, 275, 350, 365, 404, 408, 444, 481, 508, 554
Château Latour **1971:** 24, 277, 331, 365, 444, 554
Château Latour **1975:** 275, 365, 402, 404, 554
Château Latour **1976:** 75, 275, 554
Château Latour **1977:** 508
Château Latour **1978:** 121, 275, 316, 365, 444, 473
Château Latour **1979:** 53, 275, 365,
Château Latour **1980:** 260
Château Latour **1981:** 275
Château Latour **1982:** 105, 160, 275, 331, 365, 443
Château Latour **1983:** 68, 121, 260, 275, 331, 365, 397
Château Latour **1984:** 121
Château Latour **1985:** 244, 275, 304, 364, 443, 485, 508
Château Latour **1986:** 259, 272, 275, 365, 445
Château Latour **1987:** 275, 303
Château Latour **1988:** 364, 443
Château Latour **1989:** 364, 443
Château Latour **1990:** 443
Château Latour **1991:** 431, 443
Château Latour **1994:** 431
Château Latour **1995:** 431
Château Latour **1996:** 518
Château Latour Musset **1970,** Parsac: 42
Château Latour-à-Pomerol **1945:** 377
Château Latour-à-Pomerol **1947:** 377
Château Latour-à-Pomerol **1949:** 376
Château Latour-à-Pomerol **1952:** 377
Château Latour-à-Pomerol **1953:** 376
Château Latour-à-Pomerol **1955:** 377
Château Latour-à-Pomerol **1959:** 377
Château Latour-à-Pomerol **1961:** 377
Château Latour-à-Pomerol **1962:** 376
Château Latour-à-Pomerol **1964:** 377
Château Latour-à-Pomerol **1966:** 377
Château Latour-à-Pomerol **1970:** 371, 377
Château Latour-à-Pomerol **1971:** 24, 377
Château Latour-à-Pomerol **1975:** 378, 580
Château Latour-à-Pomerol **1976:** 376
Château Latour-à-Pomerol **1978:** 580
Château Latour-à-Pomerol **1979:** 377
Château Latour-à-Pomerol **1981:** 377
Château Latour-à-Pomerol **1982:** 201, 378, 391
Château Latour-à-Pomerol **1983:** 377
Château Latour-à-Pomerol **1985:** 377
Château Latour-à-Pomerol **1986:** 377
Château Latour-à-Pomerol **1988:** 377
Château Latour-à-Pomerol **1989:** 377
Château Latour-à-Pomerol **1990:** 377
Château Latour-Haut-Brion **1945:** 221
Château Latour-Haut-Brion **1966:** 274, 569
Château Latour-Haut-Brion **1970:** 477
Château Latour-Haut-Brion **1975:** 350
Château Latour-Haut-Brion **1978:** 274
Château Latour-Haut-Brion **1981:** 571
Château Latour-Martillac **1984:** 273
Château Latour-Martillac **1990:** 422
Château Latour-Martillac Blanc **1990:** 364
Château Laville-Haut-Brion "Crème de Tête" **1945:** 220, 413
Château Laville-Haut-Brion **1945:** 220, 413
Château Laville-Haut-Brion **1970:** 371
Château Laville-Haut-Brion **1978:** 203, 336, 442, 450, 512, 615
Château Laville-Haut-Brion **1979:** 30, 46
Château Laville-Haut-Brion **1981:** 229
Château Laville-Haut-Brion **1982:** 203, 236
Château Laville-Haut-Brion **1983:** 236
Château Laville-Haut-Brion **1985:** 243, 331
Château Laville-Haut-Brion **1987:** 321, 331
Château Le Canuet **1988:** 296
Château Le Gay **1970:** 194, 479, 577
Château Le Gay **1982:** 201, 351
Château Le Pin **1983:** 463
Château Le Pin **1985:** 524
Château Le Prieuré **1970:** 66
Château Leoville, Nathaniel Johnson and Sons, Bordeaux, vintage unknown: 342, 543
Château Leoville-Barton **1945:** 133, 220, 333, 543, 545
Château Leoville-Barton **1961:** 545
Château Leoville-Barton **1966:** 20, 29, 512
Château Leoville-Barton **1970:** 29, 210, 479, 548
Château Leoville-Barton **1975:** 352, 402
Château Leoville-Barton **1978:** 550
Château Leoville-Barton **1979:** 63
Château Leoville-Barton **1982:** 401
Château Leoville-Barton **1983:** 373, 502
Château Leoville-Barton **1985:** 491, 516
Château Leoville-Barton **1986:** 272, 445, 491, 519
Château Leoville-Barton **1989:** 421
Château Leoville-Lascases **1924:** 1, 107
Château Leoville-Lascases **1928:** 264
Château Leoville-Lascases **1945:** 105, 134, 220
Château Leoville-Lascases **1948:** 135
Château Leoville-Lascases **1953:** 454

Château Leoville-Lascases **1959:** 120, 283, 316, 361, 513, 545
Château Leoville-Lascases **1961:** 179
Château Leoville-Lascases **1964:** 268
Château Leoville-Lascases **1966:** 20, 137, 171, 179, 323, 465, 548
Château Leoville-Lascases **1967:** 137
Château Leoville-Lascases **1970:** 55, 66, 137, 178, 209, 479
Château Leoville-Lascases **1971:** 137, 178, 549
Château Leoville-Lascases **1973:** 137, 178
Château Leoville-Lascases **1975:** 25, 120, 138, 178, 402, 550
Château Leoville-Lascases **1976:** 550
Château Leoville-Lascases **1978:** 32, 34, 120, 137, 178, 492, 528, 550
Château Leoville-Lascases **1979:** 34, 178, 273
Château Leoville-Lascases **1980:** 137
Château Leoville-Lascases **1981:** 87, 178, 410
Château Leoville-Lascases **1982:** 178, 324, 401, 410
Château Leoville-Lascases **1983:** 373, 410
Château Leoville-Lascases **1986:** 519
Château Leoville-Poyferré **1945:** 134, 221, 360
Château Leoville-Poyferré **1961:** 125
Château Leoville-Poyferré **1970:** 479
Château Leoville-Poyferré **1975:** 229
Château Leoville-Poyferré **1978:** 32, 231, 550
Château Leoville-Poyferré **1982:** 423
Château Leoville-Poyferré **1983:** 373, 502
Château Leoville-Poyferré **1985:** 246, 394, 515
Château Leoville-Poyferré **1986:** 391, 409, 445, 474, 498, 519
Château Leoville-Poyferré **1990:** 486
Château Les Carmes Haut-Brion **1947:** 358
Château Les Carmes Haut-Brion **1961:** 358, 569
Château Lynch Bages **1975:** 402
Château Lynch-Bages **1928:** 99
Château Lynch-Bages **1929:** 99
Château Lynch-Bages **1934:** 99
Château Lynch-Bages **1936:** 99
Château Lynch-Bages **1937:** 99
Château Lynch-Bages **1945:** 99, 134, 224
Château Lynch-Bages **1947:** 99
Château Lynch-Bages **1948:** 99
Château Lynch-Bages **1949:** 99
Château Lynch-Bages **1950:** 99
Château Lynch-Bages **1952:** 99
Château Lynch-Bages **1953:** 99, 104
Château Lynch-Bages **1954:** 99
Château Lynch-Bages **1955:** 99, 100, 195
Château Lynch-Bages **1957:** 98, 103, 557
Château Lynch-Bages **1959:** 16, 78, 98, 100, 103, 371
Château Lynch-Bages **1960:** 98
Château Lynch-Bages **1961:** 48, 75, 78, 98, 100, 103, 558
Château Lynch-Bages **1962:** 98, 100, 103, 309
Château Lynch-Bages **1964:** 98, 100
Château Lynch-Bages **1966:** 78, 98, 100, 103, 171, 559
Château Lynch-Bages **1967:** 98
Château Lynch-Bages **1969:** 98
Château Lynch-Bages **1970:** 5, 30, 55, 79, 98, 100, 103, 124, 235, 281, 481, 559
Château Lynch-Bages **1971:** 98, 100
Château Lynch-Bages **1972:** 98
Château Lynch-Bages **1973:** 98
Château Lynch-Bages **1975:** 98, 100, 103, 184, 281, 331, 560
Château Lynch-Bages **1976:** 97
Château Lynch-Bages **1977:** 97
Château Lynch-Bages **1978:** 16, 32, 97, 103, 231, 281
Château Lynch-Bages **1979:** 75, 97, 103, 100, 281
Château Lynch-Bages **1980:** 97
Château Lynch-Bages **1981:** 97, 100, 103, 281, 435
Château Lynch-Bages **1982:** 97, 100, 103, 104, 281, 331, 324, 436, 423
Château Lynch-Bages **1983:** 97, 331, 435, 426, 502
Château Lynch-Bages **1984:** 97
Château Lynch-Bages **1985:** 246, 262, 394, 436
Château Lynch-Bages **1986:** 258, 435, 445
Château Lynch-Bages **1987:** 296
Château Lynch-Bages **1988:** 435
Château Lynch-Bages **1989:** 435
Château Lynch-Bages **1990:** 435
Château Lynch-Bages **1992:** 435
Château Lynch-Bages **1994:** 431
Château Lynch-Bages **1995:** 431
Château Lynch-Moussas **1945:** 224
Château Magdelaine **1945:** 218, 390, 572
Château Magdelaine **1961:** 573
Château Magdelaine **1982:** 351, 463
Château Magdelaine **1988:** 520
Château Magdelaine **1989:** 390, 420, 575
Château Magdelaine **1990:** 390
Château Magdelaine **1996:** 517
Château Magence **1983:** 194
Château Majon **1982,** Mendocino County "Sauternes" (No. "5"), John Parducci: 464
Château Malartic-Lagravière **1928:** 265
Château Malartic-Lagravière **1961:** 569
Château Malartic-Lagravière **1962:** 569
Château Malartic-Lagravière **1966:** 20
Château Malartic-Lagravière **1981:** 76
Château Malartic-Lagravière **1982:** 400, 422
Château Malartic-Lagravière **1983:** 158, 501
Château Malartic-Lagravière Blanc **1982:** 96
Château Malescot-St.-Exupéry **1945:** 132, 222
Château Malescot-St.-Exupéry **1959:** 396
Château Malescot-St.-Exupéry **1961:** 215, 396, 535
Château Malescot-St.-Exupéry **1964:** 395, 536
Château Malescot-St.-Exupéry **1966:** 395, 536
Château Malescot-St.-Exupéry **1970:** 478, 540
Château Malescot-St.-Exupéry **1975:** 541
Château Malescot-St.-Exupéry **1983:** 489
Château Margaux "Harvey's Selection" **1955:** 196
Château Margaux **1924:** 532
Château Margaux **1926:** 241
Château Margaux **1928:** 265
Château Margaux **1943:** 532
Château Margaux **1945:** 133, 223, 225, 429
Château Margaux **1952:** 532
Château Margaux **1953:** 36, 109, 532
Château Margaux **1955:** 1, 195
Château Margaux **1959:** 2, 22, 109, 532
Château Margaux **1961:** 36, 110, 532
Château Margaux **1962:** 129
Château Margaux **1966:** 268, 449, 532
Château Margaux **1967:** 533, 539

Château Margaux **1969:** 533
Château Margaux **1970:** 30, 65, 66, 408, 478
Château Margaux **1978:** 34, 251, 350, 308, 448, 493, 495, 533
Château Margaux **1979:** 34, 53, 251, 308
Château Margaux **1980:** 252
Château Margaux **1981:** 87, 251, 308, 311, 364, 397, 505, 523, 534
Château Margaux **1982:** 104, 160, 251, 308, 333, 449
Château Margaux **1983:** 158, 160, 251, 307, 373, 449, 490
Château Margaux **1984:** 251
Château Margaux **1985:** 244, 251, 260
Château Margaux **1986:** 259, 448
Château Margaux **1987:** 304
Château Margaux **1988:** 448
Château Margaux **1989:** 448
Château Margaux **1990:** 448
Château Margaux **1994:** 448
Château Maucaillou **1970:** 565
Château Mazeyres **1945:** 226, 576
Château Meyney **1961:** 563
Château Meyney **1970:** 478
Château Monbrisson **1989:** 420
Château Montelena Cabernet Sauvignon **1974,** Sonoma Valley: 198
Château Montelena Chardonnay **1973,** Napa Valley: 20
Château Montelena Chardonnay **1975,** Napa and Alexander Valleys: 637
Château Montrose **1869:** 113
Château Montrose **1870:** 256
Château Montrose **1906:** 36
Château Montrose **1926:** 92
Château Montrose **1928:** 265
Château Montrose **1945:** 130, 219
Château Montrose **1953:** 159, 562
Château Montrose **1955:** 240
Château Montrose **1959:** 160, 563
Château Montrose **1961:** 81, 160
Château Montrose **1962:** 159
Château Montrose **1966:** 20, 81, 159, 171
Château Montrose **1970:** 30, 81, 96, 159, 210, 256, 332, 425, 478, 564
Château Montrose **1971:** 159
Château Montrose **1973:** 159
Château Montrose **1975:** 159, 402, 522, 564
Château Montrose **1976:** 29, 159, 564
Château Montrose **1978:** 159, 493
Château Montrose **1979:** 159, 273
Château Montrose **1981:** 159
Château Montrose **1982:** 104, 159, 324, 401, 423, 565
Château Montrose **1983:** 159
Château Montrose **1989:** 421
Château Moulin du Cadet **1996:** 517
Château Mouton-Baron-Philippe **1945:** 223
Château Mouton-Baron-Philippe **1961:** 166, 451, 557
Château Mouton-Baron-Philippe **1970:** 481
Château Mouton-Baron-Philippe **1981:** 302
Château Mouton-d'Armailhacq **1928:** 264
Château Mouton-d'Armailhacq **1945:** 134, 224
Château Mouton-Rothschild **1853:** 209
Château Mouton-Rothschild **1859:** 209
Château Mouton-Rothschild **1865:** 209
Château Mouton-Rothschild **1867:** 209
Château Mouton-Rothschild **1869:** 209
Château Mouton-Rothschild **1870:** 209
Château Mouton-Rothschild **1874:** 209
Château Mouton-Rothschild **1878:** 113, 208
Château Mouton-Rothschild **1889:** 207
Château Mouton-Rothschild **1893:** 207
Château Mouton-Rothschild **1899:** 207
Château Mouton-Rothschild **1900:** 207
Château Mouton-Rothschild **1904:** 208
Château Mouton-Rothschild **1905:** 208
Château Mouton-Rothschild **1906:** 208
Château Mouton-Rothschild **1907:** 208
Château Mouton-Rothschild **1908:** 208
Château Mouton-Rothschild **1909:** 208
Château Mouton-Rothschild **1911:** 207
Château Mouton-Rothschild **1912:** 207
Château Mouton-Rothschild **1918:** 207
Château Mouton-Rothschild **1919:** 207
Château Mouton-Rothschild **1920:** 205
Château Mouton-Rothschild **1921:** 205
Château Mouton-Rothschild **1924:** 111, 205
Château Mouton-Rothschild **1926:** 205, 241
Château Mouton-Rothschild **1928:** 111, 205, 265
Château Mouton-Rothschild **1929:** 111, 205
Château Mouton-Rothschild **1933:** 207
Château Mouton-Rothschild **1934:** 203, 207, 554
Château Mouton-Rothschild **1937:** 207
Château Mouton-Rothschild **1938:** 207
Château Mouton-Rothschild **1940:** 205
Château Mouton-Rothschild **1942:** 205
Château Mouton-Rothschild **1943:** 45, 205
Château Mouton-Rothschild **1944:** 205
Château Mouton-Rothschild **1945:** 45, 111, 134, 206, 225, 326
Château Mouton-Rothschild **1947:** 45, 111, 206
Château Mouton-Rothschild **1948:** 111, 206
Château Mouton-Rothschild **1949:** 111, 206
Château Mouton-Rothschild **1950:** 206
Château Mouton-Rothschild **1951:** 206
Château Mouton-Rothschild **1952:** 45, 111, 206, 326
Château Mouton-Rothschild **1953:** 111, 206, 283
Château Mouton-Rothschild **1954:** 205
Château Mouton-Rothschild **1955:** 111, 195, 205, 240
Château Mouton-Rothschild **1956:** 205
Château Mouton-Rothschild **1957:** 205, 514, 554
Château Mouton-Rothschild **1958:** 204
Château Mouton-Rothschild **1959:** 45, 111, 114, 208, 507, 555
Château Mouton-Rothschild **1960:** 208
Château Mouton-Rothschild **1961:** 45, 82, 111, 125, 137, 208, 326, 349, 411
Château Mouton-Rothschild **1962:** 110, 129, 208, 326, 555
Château Mouton-Rothschild **1963:** 207
Château Mouton-Rothschild **1964:** 204
Château Mouton-Rothschild **1965:** 204
Château Mouton-Rothschild **1966:** 45, 204, 268, 349
Château Mouton-Rothschild **1967:** 204, 555
Château Mouton-Rothschild **1968:** 204
Château Mouton-Rothschild **1969:** 204, 555
Château Mouton-Rothschild **1970:** 45, 65, 208, 281, 323, 408, 481, 516, 555

Château Mouton-Rothschild **1971:** 45, 208, 302
Château Mouton-Rothschild **1972:** 208
Château Mouton-Rothschild **1973:** 207
Château Mouton-Rothschild **1974:** 207
Château Mouton-Rothschild **1975:** 45, 206, 281, 323, 325, 402, 501, 555
Château Mouton-Rothschild **1976:** 26, 206, 555
Château Mouton-Rothschild **1977:** 206
Château Mouton-Rothschild **1978:** 32, 45, 206, 281, 323, 326, 397, 555
Château Mouton-Rothschild **1979:** 54, 85, 206, 281
Château Mouton-Rothschild **1980:** 204
Château Mouton-Rothschild **1981:** 45, 87, 204, 281
Château Mouton-Rothschild **1982:** 105, 160, 204, 281, 324, 401, 423
Château Mouton-Rothschild **1983:** 158, 204, 324, 373, 495, 502, 556
Château Mouton-Rothschild **1984:** 204, 556
Château Mouton-Rothschild **1985:** 204, 244, 323, 395, 445, 524
Château Mouton-Rothschild **1986:** 259, 272, 323, 445, 486
Château Mouton-Rothschild **1987:** 323
Château Mouton-Rothschild Prephylloxera: 208
Château Musar **1964:** 258
Château Musar **1966:** 93
Château Musar **1969:** 80
Château Musar **1970:** 258, 658
Château Musar **1972:** 93, 258
Château Musar **1975:** 93, 258
Château Musar **1977:** 93, 258, 462, 658
Château Musar **1978:** 258
Château Musar White **1989:** 391
Château Nairac **1983:** 352
Château Nenin **1945:** 132, 226
Château Nenin **1971:** 578
Château Nenin **1975:** 580
Château Ormes de Pez **1967:** 16
Château Ormes de Pez **1970:** 15, 235
Château Ormes de Pez **1979:** 124, 183
Château Ormes de Pez **1987:** 296
Château Ormes de Pez **1994:** 431
Château Ormes de Pez **1995:** 431
Château Palmer **1928:** 264, 316, 451, 534
Château Palmer **1945:** 133, 223
Château Palmer **1959:** 56, 345, 534
Château Palmer **1961:** 69, 177, 270, 327, 345, 411, 429, 534
Château Palmer **1962:** 345
Château Palmer **1964:** 344
Château Palmer **1966:** 177, 230, 270, 327, 345, 537
Château Palmer **1967:** 164, 230, 344, 538, 539
Château Palmer **1970:** 30, 55, 344, 176, 177, 235, 269, 327, 334, 344, 451, 454, 463, 478, 492, 539
Château Palmer **1971:** 177
Château Palmer **1975:** 25, 177, 176, 230, 269, 344, 402, 540
Château Palmer **1976:** 75, 177, 230, 269, 344, 541
Château Palmer **1977:** 175
Château Palmer **1978:** 32, 14, 163, 175, 177, 269, 344, 462, 493, 495, 541
Château Palmer **1979:** 14, 163, 175, 177, 274, 344, 542
Château Palmer **1980:** 163, 175, 176
Château Palmer **1981:** 87, 163, 176, 344, 410, 542
Château Palmer **1982:** 163, 176, 230, 344, 410, 423, 475
Château Palmer **1983:** 158, 163, 176, 230, 344, 410, 429, 490, 542
Château Palmer **1984:** 176
Château Palmer **1985:** 190, 344, 394, 491
Château Palmer **1986:** 190, 491
Château Palmer **1989:** 420
Château Pape Clément **1959:** 406
Château Pape Clément **1961:** 125
Château Pape Clément **1975:** 402
Château Pape Clément **1986:** 445
Château Pape Clément Blanc **1979:** 102
Château Pape Clement Blanc **1980:** 616
Château Patache d'Aux **1982:** 492
Château Pavie **1945:** 218
Château Pavie **1947:** 136, 573
Château Pavie **1970:** 235, 406, 480, 574
Château Pavie **1971:** 119
Château Pavie **1982:** 462
Château Pavie **1985:** 228
Château Pavie **1988:** 374
Château Pavie **1990:** 374
Château Pavie-Decesse **1966:** 119
Château Pavie-Decesse **1981:** 119
Château Petit Villages **1987:** 430
Château Petit-Villages **1945:** 226
Château Petit-Villages **1959:** 577
Château Petrus **1945:** 108, 132, 227, 237
Château Petrus **1950:** 523
Château Petrus **1952:** 72
Château Petrus **1955:** 3, 194, 283
Château Petrus **1959:** 109, 112
Château Petrus **1961:** 30, 110, 85, 576
Château Petrus **1962:** 129
Château Petrus **1963:** 109
Château Petrus **1964:** 75
Château Petrus **1966:** 268
Château Petrus **1967:** 576
Château Petrus **1970:** 65, 408, 480, 576
Château Petrus **1971:** 501, 579
Château Petrus **1975:** 311
Château Petrus **1976:** 393
Château Petrus **1979:** 53
Château Petrus **1981:** 45
Château Petrus **1982:** 44, 160, 202
Château Petrus **1985:** 524
Château Petrus **1989:** 390
Château Petrus **1990:** 391
Château Petrus **1995:** 431
Château Petrus **1996:** 518
Château Pibran **1987:** 296
Château Pichon-Lalande **1875:** 212
Château Pichon-Lalande **1892:** 212
Château Pichon-Lalande **1893:** 212
Château Pichon-Lalande **1899:** 212
Château Pichon-Lalande **1900:** 212
Château Pichon-Lalande **1917:** 211
Château Pichon-Lalande **1918:** 211
Château Pichon-Lalande **1920:** 214
Château Pichon-Lalande **1921:** 214
Château Pichon-Lalande **1923:** 214

Château Pichon-Lalande **1924:** 214
Château Pichon-Lalande **1926:** 214
Château Pichon-Lalande **1928:** 214, 265
Château Pichon-Lalande **1929:** 214
Château Pichon-Lalande **1931:** 211
Château Pichon-Lalande **1934:** 162, 211, 308
Château Pichon-Lalande **1937:** 211
Château Pichon-Lalande **1942:** 211
Château Pichon-Lalande **1945:** 134, 211, 224, 399
Château Pichon-Lalande **1947:** 211, 399
Château Pichon-Lalande **1949:** 211, 399
Château Pichon-Lalande **1950:** 211
Château Pichon-Lalande **1952:** 211, 399
Château Pichon-Lalande **1953:** 162, 211, 162, 399
Château Pichon-Lalande **1955:** 102, 211, 399
Château Pichon-Lalande **1957:** 211
Château Pichon-Lalande **1958:** 211
Château Pichon-Lalande **1959:** 210, 399
Château Pichon-Lalande **1961:** 82, 210, 399
Château Pichon-Lalande **1962:** 162, 210
Château Pichon-Lalande **1964:** 55, 122, 162, 210
Château Pichon-Lalande **1966:** 161, 210
Château Pichon-Lalande **1967:** 210
Château Pichon-Lalande **1970:** 161, 213, 399, 481
Château Pichon-Lalande **1975:** 161, 213, 399, 560
Château Pichon-Lalande **1976:** 122, 213
Château Pichon-Lalande **1978:** 32, 34, 161, 213, 308, 399, 493, 495, 560
Château Pichon-Lalande **1979:** 34, 161, 213, 274, 308, 561
Château Pichon-Lalande **1980:** 213
Château Pichon-Lalande **1981:** 87, 161, 213, 308, 332, 410, 561
Château Pichon-Lalande **1982:** 161, 212, 213, 308, 410
Château Pichon-Lalande **1983:** 161, 212, 213, 307, 373, 410
Château Pichon-Lalande **1984:** 212, 213
Château Pichon-Lalande **1985:** 212, 213, 228, 243, 301, 429, 491
Château Pichon-Lalande **1986:** 271, 445, 491
Château Pichon-Lalande **1987:** 301
Château Pichon-Lalande **1988:** 301
Château Pichon-Lalande **1989:** 500
Château Pichon-Lalande **1990:** 374, 399
Château Pichon-Lalande **1994:** 399, 428
Château Pichon-Longueville-Baron **1945:** 134, 224
Château Pichon-Longueville-Baron **1952:** 395
Château Pichon-Longueville-Baron **1953:** 184
Château Pichon-Longueville-Baron **1955:** 67
Château Pichon-Longueville-Baron **1959:** 396, 557
Château Pichon-Longueville-Baron **1961:** 396, 558
Château Pichon-Longueville-Baron **1966:** 171
Château Pichon-Longueville-Baron **1982:** 104
Château Pichon-Longueville-Baron **1987:** 296
Château Pichon-Longueville-Baron **1989:** 421, 500
Château Pichon-Longueville-Baron **1994:** 430
Château Pin-de-Fleurs **1947:** 136
Château Pontet-Canet **1945:** 134, 224, 396, 556
Château Pontet-Canet **1947:** 396
Château Pontet-Canet **1949:** 202, 557
Château Pontet-Canet **1952:** 395, 458
Château Pontet-Canet **1955:** 240
Château Pontet-Canet **1959:** 97, 195, 396, 557
Château Pontet-Canet **1961:** 80, 396, 413, 451, 558, 559
Château Pontet-Canet **1964:** 559
Château Pontet-Canet **1966:** 171, 395
Château Pontet-Canet **1968:** 559
Château Pontet-Canet **1970:** 481
Château Pontet-Canet **1975:** 270
Château Pontet-Canet **1990:** 458
Château Potensac **1982:** 566
Château Prieuré-Lichine **1970:** 478
Château Prieuré-Lichine **1983:** 158, 489
Château Rabaud **1945,** P. Rothschild: 221, 222
Château Rausan-Ségla **1945,** Bordeaux-bottled by Cruse: 223
Château Rausan-Ségla **1945:** 133, 223
Château Rausan-Ségla **1964:** 535
Château Rausan-Ségla **1983:** 158, 489
Château Rausan-Ségla **1986:** 445
Château Rausan-Ségla **1995:** 508
Château Rauzan-Gassies **1945:** 133, 223
Château Rayas **1983:** 495
Château Rayas **1989:** 495
Château Rayas **1990:** 496
Château Rieussec "R" Dry Wine **1979:** 19, 615
Château Rieussec "R" Dry Wine **1983:** 229
Château Rieussec **1945:** 225
Château Rieussec **1970:** 25, 54, 75, 605
Château Rieussec **1975:** 361
Château Rieussec **1976:** 28, 81, 200, 605
Château Rieussec **1979:** 452
Château Rieussec **1981:** 88
Château Rieussec **1982:** 161, 202, 410
Château Rieussec **1983:** 446, 605
Château Rieussec **1986:** 502
Château Rieussec **1988:** 505
Château Rodier **1982:** 117
Château Rodier **1983:** 117
Château Rodier **1984:** 117
Château Rouget **1928:** 264
Château Rouget **1945:** 226, 523
Château Rouget **1959:** 473, 523
Château Roumieu **1978:** 59
Château Saint-Pierre **1961:** 202
Château Saint-Pierre **1982:** 551
Château Saint-Pierre **1983:** 502
Château Saint-Pierre **1986:** 519
Château Senejac **1945:** 222, 407, 565
Château Simard **1970:** 574
Château Smith-Haut-Lafitte **1945:** 221
Château Smith-Haut-Lafitte Blanc **1995:** 457
Château Smith-Haut-Lafitte Rouge **1993:** 458
Château Sociando-Mallet **1979:** 63, 567
Château Sociando-Mallet **1982:** 484
Château Sociando-Mallet **1983:** 500
Château Sociando-Mallet **1984:** 301
Château Sociando-Mallet **1985:** 227, 246, 394, 491
Château Sociando-Mallet **1986:** 272, 491
Château Soutard **1982:** 351, 422
Château Soutard **1985:** 246, 394, 464
Château St. Jean "Belle Terre Vineyard" Chardonnay **1978,** Sonoma Valley: 3
Château St. Jean "Belle Terre Vineyard" Johannisberg Riesling "Select Late Harvest" **1978,** Sonoma Valley: 60, 75, 426, 642

Château St. Jean "Belle Terre Vineyard" Johannisberg Riesling "Select Late Harvest" **1976,** Sonoma Valley: 33, 641
Château St. Jean "Beltane Ranch" Chardonnay **1976,** Sonoma Valley: 637
Château St. Jean "Glen Ellen" Cabernet Sauvignon **1976,** Sonoma Valley: 60
Château St. Jean "Glen Ellen" Cabernet Sauvignon **1977,** Sonoma Valley: 59
Château St. Jean "Hunter Vineyard" Chardonnay **1978,** Sonoma Valley: 2
Château St. Jean "Jack London" Cabernet Sauvignon **1977,** Sonoma Valley: 59
Château St. Jean "Jimtown Ranch" Select Late Harvest Gewürztraminer **1980,** Sonoma Valley: 643
Château St. Jean "Laurel Glen" Cabernet Sauvignon **1977,** Sonoma Valley: 59
Château St. Jean "Les Pierres Vineyard" Chardonnay **1977,** Sonoma Valley: 2, 637
Château St. Jean "Les Pierres Vineyard" Chardonnay" **1978,** Sonoma Valley: 2
Château St. Jean "McRae Vineyard" Chardonnay **1977,** Sonoma Valley: 3
Château St. Jean "McRae Vineyard" Chardonnay **1978,** Sonoma Valley: 2, 65
Château St. Jean "Robert Young Vineyard" Chardonnay **1977,** Sonoma Valley: 3, 637
Château St. Jean "Robert Young Vineyard" Chardonnay **1978,** Sonoma Valley: 2, 199, 637
Château St. Jean "Robert Young Vineyard" Chardonnay **1979,** Sonoma Valley: 57, 638
Château St. Jean "Robert Young Vineyard" Johannisberg Riesling "Individual Bunch, Selected Late Harvest" **1977,** Sonoma Valley: 162
Château St. Jean "Robert Young Vineyard" Johannisberg Riesling Selected Late Harvest **1984,** Alexander Valley: 643
Château St. Jean "Wildwood Vineyard" Cabernet Sauvignon **1975,** Sonoma Valley: 60
Château St. Jean "Wildwood Vineyard" Cabernet Sauvignon **1976,** Sonoma Valley: 170
Château St. Jean "Wildwood Vineyard" Cabernet Sauvignon **1977,** Sonoma Valley: 59, 60
Château St. Jean "Wildwood Vineyard" Cabernet Sauvignon **1978,** Sonoma Valley: 59
Château St. Jean "Wildwood Vineyard" Chardonnay **1977,** Sonoma Valley: 2
Château St. Jean "Wildwood Vineyard" Chardonnay **1978,** Sonoma Valley: 3
Château St. Jean Chardonnay **1978,** Sonoma Valley: 59
Château St. Jean Merlot **1977,** Sonoma Valley: 60
Château St. Jean Pinot Blanc **1979,** Sonoma Valley: 641
Château Suduiraut **1928:** 265
Château Suduiraut **1945:** 227, 412
Château Suduiraut **1959:** 22, 91, 106, 168, 202, 333, 358, 500, 604
Château Suduiraut **1962:** 105, 391, 407
Château Suduiraut **1967:** 75, 80, 323, 327, 604
Château Suduiraut **1969:** 64
Château Suduiraut **1970:** 32, 178
Château Suduiraut **1971:** 75, 236, 605
Château Suduiraut **1975:** 24
Château Suduiraut **1982:** 401
Château Suduiraut **1983:** 364
Château Suduiraut **1988:** 527
Château Talbot **1928:** 264
Château Talbot **1945:** 108, 134, 220, 282
Château Talbot **1949:** 544
Château Talbot **1955:** 544
Château Talbot **1961:** 545
Château Talbot **1966:** 171, 548
Château Talbot **1970:** 14
Château Talbot **1976:** 76
Château Talbot **1981:** 87
Château Talbot **1982:** 330
Château Talbot **1983:** 330, 373, 502
Château Talbot **1985:** 246
Château Talbot **1986:** 519
Château Talbot **1989:** 420, 515
Château Tertre Rôteboeuf **1988:** 464
Château Troplong-Mondot **1947:** 136
Château Trotanoy **1924:** 375
Château Trotanoy **1926:** 375
Château Trotanoy **1928:** 264
Château Trotanoy **1934:** 375
Château Trotanoy **1945:** 132, 227, 237, 376
Château Trotanoy **1947:** 376
Château Trotanoy **1949:** 375
Château Trotanoy **1952:** 375
Château Trotanoy **1955:** 375
Château Trotanoy **1959:** 375
Château Trotanoy **1961:** 24, 376
Château Trotanoy **1962:** 375
Château Trotanoy **1964:** 3, 24, 75, 375, 506, 577
Château Trotanoy **1966:** 375
Château Trotanoy **1967:** 24, 375
Château Trotanoy **1970:** 24, 376, 480, 578
Château Trotanoy **1971:** 24, 376
Château Trotanoy **1975:** 72, 123, 190, 300, 376
Château Trotanoy **1979:** 85, 375
Château Trotanoy **1981:** 375
Château Trotanoy **1982:** 202, 376, 391
Château Trotanoy **1983:** 375, 426
Château Trotanoy **1985:** 375, 524
Château Trotanoy **1986:** 375
Château Trotanoy **1987:** 375
Château Trotanoy **1988:** 375
Château Trotanoy **1989:** 376, 420
Château Trotanoy **1990:** 376
Château Trotanoy **1993:** 474, 493
Château Trottevieille **1945:** 218
Château Trottevieille **1961:** 58
Châteauneuf-du-Pape "Les Cèdres" **1957:** 249
Châteauneuf-du-Pape "Les Cèdres" **1962:** 249
Châteauneuf-du-Pape "Les Cèdres" **1966:** 249
Châteauneuf-du-Pape "Les Cèdres" **1967:** 249, 616
Châteauneuf-du-Pape "Les Cèdres" **1969:** 248
Châteauneuf-du-Pape **1961,** Domaine du Mont Redon: 616
Châteauneuf-du-Pape **1978,** Domaine du Vieux Télégraphe: 329, 512, 521, 617
Châteauneuf-du-Pape **1994,** Château de Beaucastel: 475
Châteauneuf-du-Pape Rouge **1982,** E. Guigal: 156
Chavignol "La Grande Côte" **1982,** Sancerre, Paul Cotat: 623

Chevalier-Montrachet "Demoiselles" **1974,** Louis Latour: 30
Chevalier-Montrachet "Demoiselles" **1978,** Jadot: 393
Chevalier-Montrachet "Demoiselles" **1982,** Louis Latour: 413
Chevalier-Montrachet "Demoiselles" **1985,** Louis Latour: 338, 358, 403, 450, 599
Chevalier-Montrachet "Demoiselles" **1986,** Louis Latour: 358, 413, 404, 599
Chevalier-Montrachet "Demoiselles" **1988,** Louis Latour 435, 601
Chevalier-Montrachet "Demoiselles" **1989,** Louis Latour: 370, 401, 461
Chevalier-Montrachet **1969,** Georges Deleger: 77
Chevalier-Montrachet **1978,** Remoissenet: 202, 254, 269, 327, 328, 342, 521, 595
Chevalier-Montrachet **1978,** Vincent Leflaive: 240
Chevalier-Montrachet **1979,** Joseph Drouhin: 62
Chevalier-Montrachet **1982,** Georges Deleger: 367, 597
Chevalier-Montrachet **1982,** Vincent Leflaive: 274, 322, 598
Chevalier-Montrachet **1986,** Jean Chartron: 529
Chevalier-Montrachet **1986,** Vincent Leflaive: 295
Chevalier-Montrachet **1987,** Vincent Leflaive: 295
Chevalier-Montrachet **1990,** Jean Chartron: 522
Chevalier-Montrachet Grand Cru **1986,** Chartron et Trebuchet: 599
Chianti Castellana Riserva **1945:** 412
Chianti Classico "Riserva" **1959,** Fossi: 80, 654
Chianti Classico "Riserva" **1981,** Castello di Verrazzano: 457
Chianti Classico "Riserva" **1985,** Castello di Verrazzano: 456
Chianti Classico "Riserva" **1988,** Castello di Verrazzano: 457
Chianti Classico "Riserva" **1990,** Castello di Verrazzano: 506
Chianti Classico "Riserva" **1990,** Luciano Bruni: 455
Chianti Ruffina "Riserva" **1994,** Nipozzano: 456
Chinon "Vieilles Vignes" **1978,** Charles Joguet, Loire: 5, 623
Chorey-lès-Beaune **1978,** Joseph Drouhin: 7
Chorey-lès-Beaune **1984,** Tollot-Beaut: 147
Chorey-lès-Beaune **1989,** Tollot-Beaut: 455
Cinsault Landskroon **1978,** Landgoedwyn: 142
Clos Blanc de Vougeot **1983,** Héritiers-Guyot: 273
Clos de la Roche **1934,** Commune de Morey-St.-Denis, Domaine des Grands Crus de Vougeot: 581
Clos de la Roche **1945,** Rémy: 237, 319
Clos de la Roche **1955,** Charles Vienot: 583
Clos de la Roche **1971,** Leroy: 426
Clos de la Roche **1972,** Domaine Dujac: 232
Clos de la Roche **1983,** Joseph Drouhin: 436
Clos de la Roche **1985,** A. Rousseau: 354
Clos de la Roche **1985,** Faiveley: 233
Clos de la Roche **1985,** Georges Lignier: 221
Clos de la Roche **1985,** P. Amiot: 234
Clos de la Roche **1986,** Domaine Dujac: 260
Clos de la Roche Grand Cru **1934,** Société Civile du Clos Vougeot: 245
Clos de la Roche Grand Cru **1983,** Joseph Drouhin: 588
Clos de la Roche Grand Cru **1988,** Joseph Drouhin: 420
Clos de Tart **1989,** Mommessin: 473
Clos de Vougeot "Grand Maupertuis" **1955,** Jean Gros: 583
Clos de Vougeot "Grand Maupertuis" **1959,** Jean Gros: 583
Clos de Vougeot **1945,** Château de la Tour: 320
Clos de Vougeot **1945,** Grivelet: 320
Clos de Vougeot **1945,** René Engel: 311, 323, 582
Clos de Vougeot **1952,** Remoissenet: 64
Clos de Vougeot **1964,** Remoissenet: 59, 311
Clos de Vougeot **1964,** René Engel: 584
Clos de Vougeot **1966,** Leroy: 150
Clos de Vougeot **1983,** Domaine Rebourseau: 452
Clos de Vougeot **1983,** Robert Arnoux: 314
Clos de Vougeot **1985,** Charles Mortet: 234, 589
Clos de Vougeot **1985,** Faiveley: 232
Clos de Vougeot **1985,** Georges Mugneret: 225
Clos de Vougeot **1987,** Meo-Camuzet: 589
Clos de Vougeot **1995,** Faiveley: 526
Clos de Vougeot Blanc **1978,** Héritiers-Guyot: 102
Clos des Lambrays **1934,** Heritiers Cosson: 229
Clos des Lambrays **1945,** Héritiers Cosson: 319
Clos des Lambrays **1946,** Héritiers Cosson: 346, 582
Clos des Lambrays **1950,** Heritiers Cosson: 582
Clos du Val Cabernet Sauvignon "Reserve" **1992,** Napa Valley: 441
Clos du Val Cabernet Sauvignon **1974,** Napa Valley: 198
Clos du Val Cabernet Sauvignon **1977,** Napa Valley: 50
Clos du Val Cabernet Sauvignon **1978,** Napa Valley: 50
Clos du Val Cabernet Sauvignon **1979,** Napa Valley: 50
Clos du Val Cabernet Sauvignon **1980,** Napa Valley: 50
Clos du Val Chardonnay **1978,** Napa Valley: 64
Clos du Val Chardonnay **1981,** Napa Valley: 51
Clos Floridère Blanc **1993,** Graves: 427
Clos Haut-Peyraguey **1976,** Sauternes: 160
Clos Nicrosi Blanc de Blancs N/V, Côteaux du Cap Corse, T. Luigi: 624
Clos Pegase Cabernet Sauvignon **1996,** Napa Valley: 520
Clos Pegase Chardonnay "Mitsuko's Vineyard" **1996,** Napa Valley: 520
Clos Pegase Merlot **1996,** Carneros/Napa Valley: 520
Cockburn's Vintage Port **1896:** 362
Cockburn's Vintage Port **1900:** 362
Cockburn's Vintage Port **1904:** 362
Cockburn's Vintage Port **1908:** 362
Cockburn's Vintage Port **1912:** 362
Cockburn's Vintage Port **1927:** 362
Cockburn's Vintage Port **1935:** 101, 361
Cockburn's Vintage Port **1945:** 361
Cockburn's Vintage Port **1947:** 361
Cockburn's Vintage Port **1950:** 361
Cockburn's Vintage Port **1955:** 361
Cockburn's Vintage Port **1960:** 360
Cockburn's Vintage Port **1963:** 360, 645
Cockburn's Vintage Port **1967:** 360
Cockburn's Vintage Port **1970:** 360
Cockburn's Vintage Port **1975:** 166
Cockburn's Vintage Port **1983:** 360
Cockburn's Vintage Port **1985:** 360
Cognac "Reserve Lafite-Rothschild": 110, 169, 270
Cognac "Reserve" 20 Years Old, Pierre Ferrand: 449
Cognac Circa **1850:** 118
Cognac Delamain "Réserve de la Famille": 96
Cognac Exshaw "Fins Bois" **1961:** 69, 331
Cognac Ferrand "Sélection des Anges" (30 years old): 395
Cognac Taillevent Fine Champagne "Sélection Officielle Bicentenaire de la Revolution Française 1789 - 1989": 268
Cohn Vineyard Merlot **1996:** 503

Condrieu "Château de Rozay" **1981,** P. Multier: 136
Condrieu "Château de Rozay" **1982,** P. Multier: 129, 136
Condrieu "Château du Rozay" **1983,** P. Multier: 136, 620
Condrieu "Côteau de Vernon" **1982,** Georges Vernay: 620
Condrieu "Côteau de Vernon" **1985,** Georges Vernay: 270, 620
Condrieu "Côteau de Vernon" **1987,** Georges Vernay: 282
Condrieu "Côteau de Vernon" **1988,** Georges Vernay: 368, 486
Condrieu **1976,** Delas: 22
Condrieu **1985,** E. Guigal: 156
Condrieu **1985,** Jaboulet: 308
Conn Creek Chardonnay **1983,** Napa Valley: 245
Cooks Chardonnay Private Bin **1986:** 215
Corbans Chardonnay Private Bin **1984:** 215
Cornas **1978,** Delas Frères: 329
Cornas **1978,** Noel Verset: 522
Cornas **1979,** Jaboulet: 9
Cornas **1981,** August Clape: 516
Cornas **1982,** August Clape: 501, 516, 618
Cornas **1985,** Jaboulet: 154
Corton "Bressandes" **1959,** Louis Latour: 11
Corton "Bressandes" **1984,** Tollot-Beaut: 147
Corton "Clos de la Vigne au Saint" **1961,** Louis Latour: 228
Corton "Clos de la Vigne au Saint" **1971,** Louis Latour: 370
Corton "Clos de la Vigne au Saint" **1976,** Louis Latour: 591
Corton "Clos des Cortons" **1983,** Monopole, Faiveley: 385
Corton "Clos des Cortons" **1985,** Monopole, Faiveley: 385, 592
Corton "Clos des Cortons" **1986,** Monopole, Faiveley: 385, 515, 592
Corton "Clos des Cortons" **1987,** Monopole, Faiveley: 385
Corton "Clos des Cortons" **1988,** Monopole, Faiveley: 385
Corton "Clos des Cortons" **1989,** Monopole, Faiveley: 385
Corton "Clos des Cortons" **1995,** Monopole, Faiveley: 526
Corton "Cuvée Charlotte Dumay" **1985,** Hospices de Beaune: 234
Corton "Perrières" **1966,** Leroy: 150
Corton "Perrières" **1979,** Louis Latour: 12
Corton "Pougets" **1971,** Reine Pedauque: 59, 64
Corton "Pougets" **1979,** Louis Latour: 12
Corton "Renardes" **1966,** Leroy: 150
Corton "Renardes" **1983,** Reine Pedauque: 314
Corton "Vigne au Saint" **1979,** Louis Latour: 12
Corton **1959,** Doudet-Naudin: 54
Corton **1961,** Doudet-Naudin: 55, 356
Corton **1962,** Joseph Drouhin: 356
Corton **1966,** Leroy: 150
Corton **1971,** Bonneau du Martray: 591
Corton **1978,** Doudet-Naudin: 7
Corton **1988,** Moillard: 419
Corton Blanc **1980,** Faiveley: 596
Corton Blanc **1988,** Chandon de Briaille: 407
Corton Hospices de Beaune "Cuvée Dr. Perte" **1976,** Bouchard Aîné et Fils: 26
Corton-Charlemagne "Comtes de Grancey" **1971,** Louis Latour: 31, 107, 593
Corton-Charlemagne "Comtes de Grancey" **1973,** Louis Latour: 107, 593
Corton-Charlemagne "Comtes de Grancey" **1976,** Louis Latour: 106, 594
Corton-Charlemagne "Comtes de Grancey" **1978,** Louis Latour: 29, 31, 59, 60, 63, 64, 82, 96, 107, 110, 240, 254, 407, 595
Corton-Charlemagne "Comtes de Grancey" **1979,** Louis Latour: 62, 64, 107
Corton-Charlemagne "Comtes de Grancey" **1981,** Louis Latour: 107
Corton-Charlemagne "Comtes de Grancey" **1982,** Louis Latour: 106, 407
Corton-Charlemagne "Comtes de Grancey" **1983,** Louis Latour: 151, 242, 269, 407, 598
Corton-Charlemagne "Comtes de Grancey" **1985,** Louis Latour: 269, 370, 405, 522, 599,
Corton-Charlemagne "Comtes de Grancey" **1986,** Louis Latour: 269, 407, 600
Corton-Charlemagne "Comtes de Grancey" **1988,** Louis Latour: 407, 493
Corton-Charlemagne "Comtes de Grancey" **1989,** Louis Latour: 370, 401, 406, 484, 461, 602
Corton-Charlemagne "Comtes de Grancey" **1995,** Louis Latour: 512
Corton-Charlemagne "Diamond Jubilee" **1976,** Avery: 216
Corton-Charlemagne "Diamond Jubilee" **1976,** Remoissenet: 216, 283, 405
Corton-Charlemagne "Diamond Jubilee" **1978,** Remoissenet: 60, 82, 103, 140, 252, 254, 407
Corton-Charlemagne "Diamond Jubilee" **1983,** Remoissenet: 343, 370
Corton-Charlemagne "Diamond Jubilee" **1992,** Remoissenet: 405
Corton-Charlemagne "Diamond Jubilee" **1995,** Remoissenet: 524
Corton-Charlemagne "Silver Jubilee" **1978,** Remoissenet: 595
Corton-Charlemagne **1952,** Reine Pedauque: 105
Corton-Charlemagne **1966,** Joseph Drouhin: 80
Corton-Charlemagne **1971,** Tollot-Beault: 593
Corton-Charlemagne **1973,** Bonneau du Martray: 593
Corton-Charlemagne **1976,** Bonneau du Martray: 405
Corton-Charlemagne **1978,** Bonneau du Martray: 194
Corton-Charlemagne **1978,** Jadot: 341
Corton-Charlemagne **1978,** Labouré-Roi, Maldant Père et Fils: 80
Corton-Charlemagne **1978,** Pierre Ponnelle: 8
Corton-Charlemagne **1978,** Remoissenet: 35, 60, 328, 388
Corton-Charlemagne **1979,** A. Rodet: 63
Corton-Charlemagne **1979,** Bonneau du Martray: 167
Corton-Charlemagne **1979,** Reine Pedauque: 54, 63
Corton-Charlemagne **1979,** Tollot-Beaut: 61, 596
Corton-Charlemagne **1982,** Bonneau du Martray: 169, 215, 267
Corton-Charlemagne **1982,** Tollot-Beaut: 311, 598
Corton-Charlemagne **1983,** Remoissenet: 598
Corton-Charlemagne **1985,** Bonneau du Martray: 338
Corton-Charlemagne **1986,** Bonneau du Martray: 399
Corton-Charlemagne **1986,** Chanson: 269
Corton-Charlemagne **1986,** Jadot: 407, 600
Corton-Charlemagne **1986,** Joseph Drouhin: 269
Corton-Charlemagne **1986,** Michel Juillot: 407
Corton-Charlemagne **1986,** Moillard: 269, 308, 600
Corton-Charlemagne **1987,** J. F. Coche-Dury: 405
Corton-Charlemagne **1987,** Tollot-Beaut: 413
Corton-Charlemagne **1988,** Chartron et Trebuchet: 370
Corton-Charlemagne **1988,** Jadot: 285
Corton-Charlemagne **1988,** Tollot-Beaut: 404, 407, 507, 601

Corton-Charlemagne **1989,** Bonneau du Martray: 370, 405
Corton-Charlemagne **1989,** Chartron et Trebuchet: 370, 405
Corton-Charlemagne **1989,** Domaine Maldant: 406
Corton-Charlemagne **1989,** Faiveley: 406
Corton-Charlemagne **1989,** Georges Roumier: 406
Corton-Charlemagne **1989,** Joseph Drouhin: 406, 517
Corton-Charlemagne **1989,** Leroy: 406, 493
Corton-Charlemagne **1989,** Maldant: 505
Corton-Charlemagne **1989,** Tollot-Beaut: 484
Corton-Charlemagne **1990,** Bouchard Père et Fils: 406
Corton-Charlemagne **1990,** Faiveley: 406, 494, 505
Corton-Charlemagne **1990,** Jadot: 427
Corton-Charlemagne **1990,** Marius Delarche: 406
Corton-Charlemagne **1990,** Pierre Bitouzet: 406
Corton-Charlemagne **1990,** Tollot-Beaut: 406
Corton-Charlemagne **1992,** Bernard Amboise: 405
Corton-Charlemagne **1992,** Bonneau du Martray: 466, 519
Corton-Charlemagne **1992,** Clos Frantin, A. Bichot: 405
Corton-Charlemagne **1992,** Jadot: 498
Corton-Charlemagne **1992,** Joseph Drouhin: 473, 516
Corton-Charlemagne **1992,** Michel Voarick: 452
Corton-Charlemagne **1992,** Tollot-Beaut: 405, 516
Corton-Charlemagne **1994,** Jadot: 449
Corton-Charlemagne **1995,** Bonneau du Martray: 512
Corton-Charlemagne **1995,** Tollot-Beaut: 512
Corton-Charlemagne **1996,** Faiveley: 527
Corton-Grancey **1969,** Louis Latour: 31, 228
Corton-Grancey **1971,** Louis Latour: 11
Corton-Grancey **1972,** Louis Latour: 40
Corton-Grancey **1979,** Louis Latour: 151, 228
Corton-Vergennes "Château de Bligny" **1978,** Pierre-Yves Masson: 39, 596
Côte de Nuits Villages **1964,** Pierre Ponnelle: 12
Côteau du Layon, Co-op **1969:** 44
Côteaux de l' Aubance" Botrytized Chenin Blanc **1945:** 81
Côte-Rôtie "Côte Brune" "Font Gent" **1983,** E. Guigal: 157
Côte-Rôtie "Côte Brune" "La Viaillère" **1983,** E. Guigal: 157
Côte-Rôtie "Côte Brune" "La Viaillère" **1984,** E. Guigal: 157
Côte-Rôtie "Côtes Brune et Blonde" **1955,** Chapoutier: 81
Côte-Rôtie "Côtes Brune et Blonde" **1978,** E. Guigal: 246, 330, 521, 618
Côte-Rôtie "Côtes Brune et Blonde" **1983,** E. Guigal: 156
Côte-Rôtie "La Landonne" **1982,** E. Guigal: 156
Côte-Rôtie "La Landonne" **1988,** E. Guigal: 523
Côte-Rôtie "La Mouline" **1900,** E. Guigal: 156
Côte-Rôtie "La Mouline" **1983,** E. Guigal: 157, 465
Côte-Rôtie "La Mouline" **1988,** E. Guigal: 523
Côte-Rôtie "La Turque" **1985,** E. Guigal: 157
Côte-Rôtie "Les Jumelles" **1976,** Jaboulet: 33
Côte-Rôtie "Les Jumelles" **1979,** Jaboulet: 9
Côte-Rôtie "Les Jumelles" **1985,** Jaboulet: 154
Côte-Rôtie **1945,** Vidal-Fleury: 412
Côte-Rôtie **1961,** Jaboulet-Isnard: 254
Côte-Rôtie **1966,** André Passat: 616
Côte-Rôtie **1978** "La Viaillère," Dervieux-Thèze: 330
Côte-Rôtie **1978,** André Drevon: 329
Côte-Rôtie Côte Blonde "La Grande" **1984,** E. Guigal: 157
Côtes de Buzet "Cuvée Napoleon" **1978,** Co-op Vignerons Réunis des Côtes de Buzet: 37
Côtes de Buzet "Cuvée Napoléon" **1981,** Cave Co-op: 70
Côtes de Buzet **1979,** Co-op Vignerons Réunis des Côtes de Buzet: 37
Côtes de Buzet **1980,** Co-op Vignerons Réunis des Côtes de Buzet: 37
Côtes du Rhône Red **1979,** E. Guigal: 520
Côtes du Rhône Red **1983,** E. Guigal: 156
Côtes du Rhône White **1985,** E. Guigal: 156
Cotnari N/V, Monimpex, Roumania: 80
Crighton Hall Chardonnay **1992,** Napa Valley: 393
Criots-Bâtard-Montrachet **1979,** Domaine de Marcilly: 62, 86
Criots-Bâtard-Montrachet **1982,** Fontaine Gagnard: 367
Croft's 20-Year-Old Finest Tawny Port: 649
Croft's Vintage Port **1896:** 257
Croft's Vintage Port **1900:** 257
Croft's Vintage Port **1912:** 257
Croft's Vintage Port **1917:** 87, 257
Croft's Vintage Port **1920:** 257
Croft's Vintage Port **1922:** 257
Croft's Vintage Port **1924:** 257
Croft's Vintage Port **1927:** 257
Croft's Vintage Port **1935:** 257
Croft's Vintage Port **1945:** 257, 414
Croft's Vintage Port **1950:** 256
Croft's Vintage Port **1955:** 256
Croft's Vintage Port **1960:** 255, 644
Croft's Vintage Port **1963:** 46, 61, 82, 203, 254, 255, 328, 339, 388, 445, 645
Croft's Vintage Port **1966:** 646
Croft's Vintage Port **1970:** 255
Croft's Vintage Port **1977:** 255
Croft's Vintage Port **1985:** 255
Crozes-Hermitage "La Mûle Blanche" **1985,** Jaboulet: 154
Crozes-Hermitage "Thalabert" **1978,** Jaboulet: 329, 520, 617
Crozes-Hermitage "Thalabert" **1979,** Jaboulet: 9
Crozes-Hermitage "Thalabert" **1985,** Jaboulet: 154
Crozes-Hermitage **1985,** Jaboulet: 154
Cru Bedat 1943 AOC Graves Blanc: 615
Csopaki Furmint **1921,** Hungary: 279
Cuvaison Cabernet Sauvignon "Signature" **1975,** Napa Valley: 21, 26, 39, 53, 505, 629
Cuvaison Cabernet Sauvignon **1976,** Napa Valley: 170
Cuvaison Chardonnay "Reserve" **1978,** Napa Valley: 25
Cuvée de la Commanderie du Bontemps **1970:** 76
Cuvée de la Commanderie du Bontemps Blanc **1986,** Louis Latour: 303
Cuvée Remoina" **1976,** Remoissenet (Avery's): 591
Dalva Vintage Port **1963:** 67
Darmagi **1983,** Angelo Gaja: 143
De Bortoli Wines Semillon Botrytis "Noble Late Harvest" **1983:** 653
De Loach **1985** Chardonnay, Sonoma County, Russian River Valley: 312
De Wetshof Estate "Edeloes" "Noble Late Harvest Superior" Wine of Origin **1991,** Robertson: 387
De Wetshof Estate "Edeloes" "Noble Late Harvest Superior" Wine of Origin **1979,** Robertson: 651
Delaforce Vintage Port **1963:** 74
Delheim "Edelspatz" Noble Late Harvest **1991:** 388
Diamond Creek Gravelly Meadow "Micro Climate" **1991:** 467
Diamond Creek Gravelly Meadow "Special Select" **1982:** 468

Diamond Creek Gravelly Meadow **1974:** 468
Diamond Creek Gravelly Meadow **1975:** 468
Diamond Creek Gravelly Meadow **1976:** 466
Diamond Creek Gravelly Meadow **1978:** 466
Diamond Creek Gravelly Meadow **1979:** 423
Diamond Creek Gravelly Meadow **1981:** 468
Diamond Creek Gravelly Meadow **1982:** 468
Diamond Creek Gravelly Meadow **1983:** 467
Diamond Creek Gravelly Meadow **1984:** 467
Diamond Creek Gravelly Meadow **1986:** 471
Diamond Creek Gravelly Meadow **1987:** 471
Diamond Creek Gravelly Meadow **1988:** 467
Diamond Creek Gravelly Meadow **1989:** 467, 472
Diamond Creek Gravelly Meadow **1990:** 469
Diamond Creek Gravelly Meadow **1991:** 467
Diamond Creek Gravelly Meadow **1992:** 467
Diamond Creek Gravelly Meadow **1994:** 469
Diamond Creek Gravelly Meadow **1995:** 472
Diamond Creek Gravelly Meadow **1997:** 472
Diamond Creek Gravelly Meadow/Lake Blend **1992:**469
Diamond Creek Lake Vineyard **1978:** 472
Diamond Creek Lake Vineyard **1984:** 467
Diamond Creek Lake Vineyard **1987:** 469
Diamond Creek Lake Vineyard **1990:** 469
Diamond Creek Lake Vineyard **1992:** 467, 472
Diamond Creek Lake Vineyard **1994:** 467
Diamond Creek Red Rock Terrace "First Pick" **1977:** 468
Diamond Creek Red Rock Terrace "Micro Climate" **1994:** 467
Diamond Creek Red Rock Terrace "Second Pick" **1977:** 468
Diamond Creek Red Rock Terrace "Special Select" **1982:** 467
Diamond Creek Red Rock Terrace **1972:** 471
Diamond Creek Red Rock Terrace **1974:** 470
Diamond Creek Red Rock Terrace **1975:** 471
Diamond Creek Red Rock Terrace **1976:** 468
Diamond Creek Red Rock Terrace **1978:** 470
Diamond Creek Red Rock Terrace **1979:** 423, 468
Diamond Creek Red Rock Terrace **1980:** 468
Diamond Creek Red Rock Terrace **1981:** 471
Diamond Creek Red Rock Terrace **1982:** 467
Diamond Creek Red Rock Terrace **1983:** 468
Diamond Creek Red Rock Terrace **1984:** 468
Diamond Creek Red Rock Terrace **1985:** 467
Diamond Creek Red Rock Terrace **1986:** 468
Diamond Creek Red Rock Terrace **1987:** 469
Diamond Creek Red Rock Terrace **1988:** 471
Diamond Creek Red Rock Terrace **1990:** 467
Diamond Creek Red Rock Terrace **1991:** 471
Diamond Creek Red Rock Terrace **1992:** 472
Diamond Creek Red Rock Terrace **1994:** 467
Diamond Creek Red Rock Terrace **1995:** 469
Diamond Creek Red Rock Terrace **1997:** 469
Diamond Creek Three Vineyard Blend "November Picked" **1981:** 468
Diamond Creek Three Vineyard Blend **1981:** 471
Diamond Creek Three Vineyard Blend **1983:** 472
Diamond Creek Three Vineyard Blend **1985:** 468, 471
Diamond Creek Three Vineyard Blend **1989:** 467
Diamond Creek Three Vineyard Blend **1990:** 469
Diamond Creek Volcanic Hill "First Pick" **1979:** 471
Diamond Creek Volcanic Hill "Micro Climate" **1991:** 469
Diamond Creek Volcanic Hill "Special Select" **1982:** 471
Diamond Creek Volcanic Hill **1972:** 471
Diamond Creek Volcanic Hill **1973:** 471
Diamond Creek Volcanic Hill **1974:** 466
Diamond Creek Volcanic Hill **1975:** 466
Diamond Creek Volcanic Hill **1976:** 470
Diamond Creek Volcanic Hill **1978:** 49, 468
Diamond Creek Volcanic Hill **1979:** 24, 423, 466, 471
Diamond Creek Volcanic Hill **1980:** 467
Diamond Creek Volcanic Hill **1981:** 467
Diamond Creek Volcanic Hill **1982:** 471
Diamond Creek Volcanic Hill **1983:** 471
Diamond Creek Volcanic Hill **1984:** 471
Diamond Creek Volcanic Hill **1985:** 471
Diamond Creek Volcanic Hill **1986:** 467
Diamond Creek Volcanic Hill **1987:** 467
Diamond Creek Volcanic Hill **1988:** 467, 468
Diamond Creek Volcanic Hill **1989:** 472
Diamond Creek Volcanic Hill **1990:** 471
Diamond Creek Volcanic Hill **1991:** 469
Diamond Creek Volcanic Hill **1992:** 469
Diamond Creek Volcanic Hill **1993:** 472
Diamond Creek Volcanic Hill **1994:** 472
Diamond Creek Volcanic Hill **1995:** 467
Diamond Creek Volcanic Hill **1997:** 467
Diez Hermanos "Fino Imperial": 397
Domaine Challon "Cuvée du Manoir" **1995:** 433
Domaine Chandon "Tenth Anniversary" Champagne Brut, California: 162
Domaine Chandon Blanc de Blancs Brut: 39
Domaine Chandon Blanc de Noir N/V, Napa Valley: 62, 238
Domaine Chandon Napa "Réserve" Brut N/V: 245
Domaine Comte Peraldi **1997,** Ajaccio A/C, Comte de Poix: 527
Domaine de Chevalier **1945:** 131, 221, 393
Domaine de Chevalier **1959:** 322
Domaine de Chevalier **1961:** 322, 323, 569
Domaine de Chevalier **1962:** 322
Domaine de Chevalier **1964:** 322
Domaine de Chevalier **1966:** 322
Domaine de Chevalier **1970:** 210, 321, 477, 570
Domaine de Chevalier **1975:** 321
Domaine de Chevalier **1978:** 321, 493
Domaine de Chevalier **1979:** 321, 525, 570
Domaine de Chevalier **1981:** 87, 321, 395
Domaine de Chevalier **1983:** 321, 502
Domaine de Chevalier **1988:** 374, 394
Domaine de Chevalier **1990:** 374
Domaine de Chevalier **1995:** 522
Domaine de Chevalier Blanc **1960:** 381
Domaine de Chevalier Blanc **1970:** 371
Domaine de Chevalier Blanc **1976:** 20
Domaine de Chevalier Blanc **1983:** 616
Domaine de Chevalier Blanc **1988:** 461
Domaine de Chevalier Blanc **1990:** 374
Dominus Estate **1983:** 370, 631
Dominus Estate **1984:** 312, 371, 631
Dominus Estate **1985:** 311, 371, 394, 426, 631
Dominus Estate **1986:** 371
Dominus Estate **1987:** 371, 378
Dominus Estate **1988:** 371

Dominus Estate **1989:** 371, 435
Dominus Estate **1990:** 91
Dominus Estate **1991:** 391, 403
Dominus Estate **1994:** 488, 497
Dorfjohannisberger **1904,** A. Koch Sohne, Mainz: 112
Dow's Boardroom Tawny N/V: 86
Dow's Extra Dry White Port N/V: 86
Dow's Late-Bottled Vintage Port **1964:** 61
Dow's Vintage Port **1931:** 227
Dow's Vintage Port **1945:** 413
Dow's Vintage Port **1963:** 61, 83, 102, 231, 645
Dow's Vintage Port **1966:** 495
Dow's Vintage Port **1975:** 166. 647
Dow's Vintage Port **1980:** 86
Duckhorn Vineyards Cabernet Sauvignon "Howell Mountain" **1989,** Napa Valley: 632
Duckhorn Vineyards Cabernet Sauvignon **1980,** Napa Valley: 500, 630
Duckhorn Vineyards Cabernet Sauvignon **1986,** Napa Valley: 441
Duckhorn Vineyards Merlot "Three Palms Vineyard" **1978,** Napa Valley: 103, 463, 633
Duckhorn Vineyards Merlot "Three Palms Vineyard" **1982,** Napa Valley: 89
Duckhorn Vineyards Sauvignon Blanc **1992,** Napa Valley: 389
Dunn Vineyards Cabernet Sauvignon **1979,** Napa Valley: 507
Dunn Vineyards Cabernet Sauvignon **1983,** Napa Valley: 503
Dunn Vineyards Cabernet Sauvignon **1991,** Napa Valley: 501
Echézeaux **1945,** Lupé-Cholet: 320
Echézeaux **1961,** Joseph Drouhin: 35
Echézeaux **1966,** Leroy: 150
Echézeaux **1973,** Domaine de la Romanée-Conti: 587
Echézeaux **1983,** Faiveley: 229
Echézeaux **1983,** Joseph Drouhin: 314
Echézeaux **1983,** Mugneret-Gouachon: 588
Echézeaux **1985,** Faiveley: 232
Echézeaux **1985,** Moillard: 589
Echézeaux **1988,** Emmanuel Rouget: 528
Echézeaux **1988,** Moillard: 420
Edelkeur "Superior" "Noble Late Harvest" Wine of Origin **1986,** Nederburg Estate, South Africa: 387
Edelkeur "Superior" "Noble Late Harvest" Wine of Origin **1978,** Nederburg Estate, South Africa: 143, 350, 367, 650
Edelkeur "Superior" "Noble Late Harvest" Wine of Origin **1979,** Nederburg Estate, South Africa: 650
Edelkeur "Superior" "Noble Late Harvest" Wine of Origin **1991,** Nederburg Estate, South Africa: 651
Edelkeur "Superior" "Noble Late Harvest Wine of Origin **1978,** Nederburg Estate, South Africa: 464, 521
Edna Valley Vineyard Chardonnay, San Luis Obispo **1980:** 107, 639: **1990:** 358
Ehrmann Frères Grande Champagne Vieux Cognac: 175
Eitelsbacher Karthaüler Hofberger (Wachstum) Riesling Beerenauslese **1959,** Hans Wilhelm Rauenstrauch (Mosel-Saar-Ruhr): 512
Elk Cove Pinot Noir "Willamette Valley" **1983,** Oregon: 314
Etude Pinot Noir **1988,** Napa Valley: 315
Far Niente "Dolce" **1986,** Napa Valley: 310
Far Niente Cabernet Sauvignon **1982,** Napa Valley: 310
Far Niente Cabernet Sauvignon **1983,** Napa Valley: 310
Far Niente Cabernet Sauvignon **1984,** Napa Valley: 310
Far Niente Cabernet Sauvignon **1985,** Napa Valley: 310
Far Niente Cabernet Sauvignon **1986,** Napa Valley: 310
Far Niente Cabernet Sauvignon **1987,** Napa Valley: 310
Far Niente Cabernet Sauvignon **1994,** Napa Valley: 513
Far Niente Chardonnay **1985,** Napa Valley: 310
Far Niente Chardonnay **1986,** Napa Valley: 334
Fay Vineyard (Heitz): 83
Felton-Empire "Tepusquet Vineyards" Late Harvest Gewürztraminer **1979,** Santa Barbara: 642
Fenton's Port **1863:** 114
Ferrari-Carano Chardonnay **1995,** Alexander Valley: 488
Ferreira's Vintage Port **1945:** 413
Feuerheerd Vintage Port **1970:** 66
Ficklin California Port **1951:** 175
Ficklin California Port: 196
Fine Old Brown Sherry **1878:** 112
Fixin **1985,** Faiveley: 232
Fonseca's Vintage Port **1912:** 400
Fonseca's Vintage Port **1922:** 400
Fonseca's Vintage Port **1927:** 400
Fonseca's Vintage Port **1934:** 74, 234, 400
Fonseca's Vintage Port **1945:** 400, 413
Fonseca's Vintage Port **1947:** 400
Fonseca's Vintage Port **1948:** 73, 74, 400
Fonseca's Vintage Port **1955:** 400
Fonseca's Vintage Port **1960:** 400
Fonseca's Vintage Port **1963:** 61, 67, 86, 374, 398, 495
Fonseca's Vintage Port **1966:** 398
Fonseca's Vintage Port **1970:** 86, 398, 399, 647
Fonseca's Vintage Port **1975:** 166, 345, 358, 398, 647
Fonseca's Vintage Port **1977:** 398
Fonseca's Vintage Port **1980:** 398
Fonseca's Vintage Port **1983:** 398
Fonseca's Vintage Port **1985:** 398
Fonseca's Vintage Port **1992:** 398
Forman Cabernet Sauvignon **1995,** Napa Valley: 506
Freemark Abbey "Edelwein Gold" Botrytized Johannisberg Riesling TBA **1982,** Napa Valley: 271, 643
Freemark Abbey "Edelwein Gold" Johannisberg Riesling **1973,** Napa Valley: 114
Freemark Abbey "Edelwein Gold" Johannisberg Riesling **1976,** Napa Valley: 641
Freemark Abbey Chardonnay **1987,** Napa Valley: 312
Frog's Leap Cabernet Sauvignon "Reserve" **1989,** Napa Valley: 441
Gallo Bellatore "Gran Spumante" N/V, Modesto, California: 245
Gallo Sauvignon Blanc "Barrelli Creek" **1995,** Sonoma Valley: 488
Gamla (see Yarden)
Gattinara **1978** "Monsecco," Le Colline: 655
Gemello "35th Anniversary" California Cabernet Sauvignon N/V: 334, 366, 529, 626
Gemello California Cabernet Sauvignon **1968:** 627
Gemello California Cabernet Sauvignon **1970:** 627
Gemello California Cabernet Sauvignon **1974:** 628
Gevrey-Chambertin "Clos de la Justice" **1955,** Avery's: 90
Gevrey-Chambertin "Clos du Fonteny" Monopole **1990,** Bruno Clair: 426
Gevrey-Chambertin "Clos St. Jacques" **1966,** Leroy: 150

Gevrey-Chambertin "Clos St. Jacques" **1983,** Clair-Daü: 314
Gevrey-Chambertin "En Pallud" **1982,** Maume: 588
Gevrey-Chambertin "En Pallud" **1993,** Maume: 426
Gevrey-Chambertin "La Combe aux Moines" **1972,** Gesweiler: 40
Gevrey-Chambertin "La Combe aux Moines" **1985,** Faiveley: 232
Gevrey-Chambertin "La Combe aux Moines" **1995,** Faiveley: 526
Gevrey-Chambertin "Lavaux Saint-Jacques" **1982,** Maume: 588
Gevrey-Chambertin "Lavaux Saint-Jacques" **1983,** A. Rousseau: 152
Gevrey-Chambertin "Lavaux Saint-Jacques" **1988,** Jadot: 285
Gevrey-Chambertin "Les Cazetiers" **1966,** Leroy: 151
Gevrey-Chambertin "Les Cazetiers" **1980,** Philippe Leclerc: 587
Gevrey-Chambertin "Les Cazetiers" **1985,** A. Rousseau: 353
Gevrey-Chambertin "Les Cazetiers" **1989,** Bruno Clair: 503
Gevrey-Chambertin "Les Cazetiers" **1991,** Faiveley: 527
Gevrey-Chambertin **1934,** H. de Villamont: 392
Gevrey-Chambertin **1945,** Faiveley: 320
Gevrey-Chambertin **1976,** A. Rousseau: 68
Gevrey-Chambertin **1978,** Doudet-Naudin: 7
Gevrey-Chambertin **1983,** Philippe Rossignol: 588
Gevrey-Chambertin 1984 Trapet: 145
Gevrey-Chambertin **1985,** Philippe Nadeff: 234
Gevrey-Chambertin **1985,** Philippe Rossignol: 589
Gevrey-Chambertin **1988,** A. Rousseau: 420
Gewürztraminer "Bergheim" **1990,** Domaine Marcel Deiss: 395
Gewürztraminer "Cuvée des Folastries" **1992,** Josmeyer, Alsace: 418
Gewürztraminer "Cuvée Laurence" **1986,** Domaine Weinbach, Alsace: 267
Gewürztraminer "Cuvée Tradition" **1979,** Hugel: 36
Gewürztraminer "Reserve Cuvée Emile Willm" **1990,** Willm: 622
Gewürztraminer "Réserve Personnelle" **1979,** Hugel: 36
Gewürztraminer "Sélection de Grains Nobles" **1976,** Fût 28, Hugel: 56, 334
Gewürztraminer "Vendange Tardive" "Réserve Personnelle" **1983,** Hugel: 622
Gewürztraminer "Vendange Tardive" "Selection de Grains Nobles" **1976,** Hugel: 36, 622
Gewürztraminer "Vendange Tardive" **1976,** Dopff et Irion: 621
Gewürztraminer "Vendange Tardive" **1983,** Leon Beyer: 622
Geyser Peak Petite Syrah "Unfiltered" **1976,** Centennial Bottling, California: 476
Ghemme "Collis Breclemae" **1990,** Antichi Vignetti di Cantaluppo, Tuscany: 517
Gigondas **1978,** Jaboulet: 9, 329, 520
Gigondas **1979,** Jaboulet: 9
Gigondas **1983,** E. Guigal: 156
Girard Cabernet Sauvignon **1987,** Napa Valley: 350
Givry "Clos Marceaux" Monopole **1988,** Laborde-Juillot: 295
Golan (see Yarden)
Gonzales-Bias Vintage Port **1970:** 62
Graham's Fine Ruby Port N/V: 86
Graham's Vintage Port **1887:** 168
Graham's Vintage Port **1908:** 168
Graham's Vintage Port **1912:** 168
Graham's Vintage Port **1920:** 168, 316
Graham's Vintage Port **1927:** 168
Graham's Vintage Port **1935:** 168
Graham's Vintage Port **1942:** 168
Graham's Vintage Port **1945:** 20, 168, 274, 379, 414, 644
Graham's Vintage Port **1955:** 178
Graham's Vintage Port **1962:** 644
Graham's Vintage Port **1963:** 645
Graham's Vintage Port **1966:** 646
Graham's Vintage Port **1970:** 88, 392
Graham's Vintage Port **1975:** 166, 647
Graham's Vintage Port **1977:** 380, 428
Graham's Vintage Port **1980:** 647
Graham's Vintage Port **1985:** 485, 506
Grande Champagne Cognac "Abel" of Maison Ferrand: 406
Grande Champagne Cognac "Grande Réserve": 47
Grande Fine Champagne Cognac **1904,** Gaston Briand: 78
Grands Echézeaux **1945,** Domaine de la Romanée-Conti: 320
Grands Echézeaux **1945,** Leroy: 320
Grands Echézeaux **1945,** René Engel: 237, 320
Grands Echézeaux **1963,** Domaine de la Romanée-Conti: 584
Grands Echézeaux **1966,** Leroy: 150
Grands Echézeaux **1971,** Domaine de la Romanée-Conti: 446
Grands Echézeaux **1972,** Domaine de la Romanée-Conti: 40, 102, 105, 334, 483, 499, 528, 586
Grands Echézeaux **1978,** Domaine de la Romanée-Conti: 367
Grands Echézeaux **1979,** Domaine de la Romanée-Conti: 146
Greco di Tufo **1978,** Mastroberardino: 655
Grgich Cellars Cabernet Sauvignon **1990,** Napa Valley: 475
Grgich Hills Chardonnay **1977,** Napa Valley: 64, 248
Grgich Hills Chardonnay **1978,** Napa Valley: 248, 638
Grgich Hills Chardonnay **1984,** Napa Valley: 139
Grgich Hills Zinfandel **1980,** Napa Valley: 160
Grignolino "Private Stock" N/V, Napa Valley: 634
Groot Constantia Cabernet Sauvignon **1968:** 143
Groth Vineyard Cabernet Sauvignon "Reserve" **1985,** Napa Valley: 474
Hallcrest Vineyard Cabernet Sauvignon **1959:** 530
Hanzell Vineyards Cabernet Sauvignon **1959,** Sonoma County: 323
Hanzell Vineyards Chardonnay **1974,** Sonoma County: 27, 238
Hanzell Vineyards Chardonnay **1984,** Sonoma County: 252
Harrison Estate Chardonnay "Unfiltered" **1995,** Napa Valley: 506
Harry Waugh Selection **1970,** Bordeaux Supérieur: 30
Harvey's "Very Fine Old Amontillado" Sherry: 170
Harvey's Bristol Cream: 374
Hattenheimer Wisselbrunnen Riesling Auslese **1976,** Lang, Mosel: 446
Hawthorne Mountain Pinot Gris VQA **1996,** Okanagan Falls, British Columbia, Canada: 487
Heitz Cellars "Alicia" **1989,** Napa Valley: 311
Heitz Cellars "Angelica" **1974,** Napa Valley: 335, 415, 641
Heitz Cellars "Angelica" **1976,** Napa Valley: 395
Heitz Cellars "Bella Oaks" Cabernet Sauvignon **1976,** Napa Valley: 196, 247, 313
Heitz Cellars "Bella Oaks" Cabernet Sauvignon **1977,** Napa Valley: 37, 66, 172, 247, 313
Heitz Cellars "Bella Oaks" Cabernet Sauvignon **1978,** Napa Valley: 269, 313
Heitz Cellars "Bella Oaks" Cabernet Sauvignon **1980,** Napa Valley: 101, 166, 172, 248, 313, 409, 631
Heitz Cellars "Bella Oaks" Cabernet Sauvignon **1981,** Napa Valley: 313
Heitz Cellars "Bella Oaks" Cabernet Sauvignon **1982,** Napa Valley: 313

Heitz Cellars "Bella Oaks" Cabernet Sauvignon **1983,** Napa Valley: 313
Heitz Cellars "Bella Oaks" Cabernet Sauvignon **1984,** Napa Valley: 313
Heitz Cellars "Bella Oaks" Cabernet Sauvignon **1985,** Napa Valley: 281, 313
Heitz Cellars "Bella Oaks" Cabernet Sauvignon **1986,** Napa Valley: 335
Heitz Cellars "Fay Vineyard" Cabernet Sauvignon **1977,** Napa Valley: 37
Heitz Cellars "Fay Vineyard" Cabernet Sauvignon **1978,** Napa Valley: 34, 268
Heitz Cellars "Martha's Vineyard" Cabernet Sauvignon **1967,** Napa Valley: 262
Heitz Cellars "Martha's Vineyard" Cabernet Sauvignon **1968,** Napa Valley: 27, 38, 199, 239, 496, 531
Heitz Cellars "Martha's Vineyard" Cabernet Sauvignon **1969,** Napa Valley: 239, 263, 439, 496, 507, 531
Heitz Cellars "Martha's Vineyard" Cabernet Sauvignon **1970,** Napa Valley: 101, 239, 497
Heitz Cellars "Martha's Vineyard" Cabernet Sauvignon **1973,** Napa Valley: 83
Heitz Cellars "Martha's Vineyard" Cabernet Sauvignon **1974,** Napa Valley: 22, 25, 38, 198, 239, 267, 367, 497
Heitz Cellars "Martha's Vineyard" Cabernet Sauvignon **1975,** Napa Valley: 21, 335
Heitz Cellars "Martha's Vineyard" Cabernet Sauvignon **1977,** Napa Valley: 37
Heitz Cellars "Martha's Vineyard" Cabernet Sauvignon **1978,** Napa Valley: 269, 522, 630
Heitz Cellars "Martha's Vineyard" Cabernet Sauvignon **1979,** Napa Valley: 196, 247
Heitz Cellars "Martha's Vineyard" Cabernet Sauvignon **1980,** Napa Valley: 101, 248, 461, 631
Heitz Cellars "Martha's Vineyard" Cabernet Sauvignon **1984,** Napa Valley: 326
Heitz Cellars "Martha's Vineyard" Cabernet Sauvignon **1985,** Napa Valley: 281, 465, 631
Heitz Cellars "Martha's Vineyard" Cabernet Sauvignon **1986,** Napa Valley: 325, 335, 631
Heitz Cellars "Martha's Vineyard" Cabernet Sauvignon **1990,** Napa Valley: 421
Heitz Cellars "Trailside Vineyard" Cabernet Sauvignon **1991,** Napa Valley: 434
Heitz Cellars Cabernet Sauvignon (**1959** Hanzell Vineyards), Napa Valley: 414, 530, 626
Heitz Cellars Cabernet Sauvignon "Lot C-91" **1969,** Napa Valley: 38, 89, 497
Heitz Cellars Cabernet Sauvignon **1968,** Napa Valley: 27, 529
Heitz Cellars Cabernet Sauvignon **1970,** Napa Valley: 350
Heitz Cellars Cabernet Sauvignon **1977,** Napa Valley: 37
Heitz Cellars Cabernet Sauvignon **1979,** Napa Valley: 83
Heitz Cellars Cabernet Sauvignon **1980,** Napa Valley: 101
Heitz Cellars Cabernet Sauvignon **1985,** Napa Valley: 281
Heitz Cellars Cabernet Sauvignon **1986,** Napa Valley: 335
Heitz Cellars Chardonnay "Heitz Vineyard" **1981,** Napa Valley: 83
Heitz Cellars Chardonnay "Heitz Vineyard" **1983,** Napa Valley: 247
Heitz Cellars Chardonnay "Lot Z-21" **1972,** Napa Valley: 3
Heitz Cellars Chardonnay "Lot Z-41" **1974,** Napa Valley: 3
Heitz Cellars Chardonnay **1980,** Napa Valley: 37, 325
Heitz Cellars Chardonnay **1983,** Napa Valley: 215
Heitz Cellars Pinot Blanc "Lyn Crest Vineyard" **1971,** Napa Valley: 89
Heitz Cellars Pinot Chardonnay "Lot Z-32" (**1973**), Napa Valley: 3, 38, 238, 313, 636
Heitz Cellars Pinot Chardonnay **1975,** Napa Valley: 101
Heitz Cellars Pinot Noir **1979,** Napa Valley: 37
Heitz Cellars Pinot Noir **1982,** Napa Valley: 83
Heitz Cellars Port **1994,** Napa Valley: 460
Heitz Cellars Port N/V, possibly **1973,** Napa Valley: 89
Heitz Cellars Sherry N/V, Napa Valley: 174
Heitz Cellars Zinfandel **1981,** Napa Valley: 83
Hermitage "La Chapelle" **1937:** 251
Hermitage "La Chapelle" **1944:** 250
Hermitage "La Chapelle" **1949:** 251
Hermitage "La Chapelle" **1952:** 251
Hermitage "La Chapelle" **1953:** 250
Hermitage "La Chapelle" **1955:** 251
Hermitage "La Chapelle" **1957:** 248
Hermitage "La Chapelle" **1961:** 6, 251
Hermitage "La Chapelle" **1962:** 250
Hermitage "La Chapelle" **1964:** 250
Hermitage "La Chapelle" **1966:** 248, 251
Hermitage "La Chapelle" **1967:** 250
Hermitage "La Chapelle" **1969:** 250, 325
Hermitage "La Chapelle" **1970:** 250, 458, 616
Hermitage "La Chapelle" **1971:** 154, 250, 309
Hermitage "La Chapelle" **1974:** 249
Hermitage "La Chapelle" **1976:** 250
Hermitage "La Chapelle" **1978:** 9, 249, 309, 330, 366, 521, 617
Hermitage "La Chapelle" **1979:** 9, 154, 249, 309, 618
Hermitage "La Chapelle" **1980:** 249, 309
Hermitage "La Chapelle" **1981:** 309
Hermitage "La Chapelle" **1982:** 249, 309, 618
Hermitage "La Chapelle" **1983:** 249, 308
Hermitage "La Chapelle" **1984:** 249, 308
Hermitage "La Chapelle" **1985:** 154, 249, 474, 308, 485, 618
Hermitage "La Chapelle" **1986:** 249, 308
Hermitage "La Chapelle" Blanc **1937:** 250
Hermitage "La Chapelle" Blanc **1959:** 250
Hermitage "La Chapelle" Blanc **1973:** 249, 250
Hermitage "La Chapelle" Blanc **1975:** 249, 250
Hermitage "La Chapelle" Rouge **1972:** 250
Hermitage "La Sizeranne" **1955,** Chapoutier: 495, 614
Hermitage "La Sizeranne" **1966,** Chapoutier: 507
Hermitage "La Sizeranne" **1971,** Chapoutier: 617
Hermitage "La Sizeranne" **1978,** Chapoutier: 329, 520, 617
Hermitage Blanc "Chevalier de Sterimberg" **1959,** Jaboulet: 417, 617
Hermitage Blanc "Chevalier de Sterimberg" **1979,** Jaboulet: 9
Hermitage Blanc "Chevalier de Sterimberg" **1981,** Jaboulet: 620
Hermitage Blanc "Chevalier de Sterimberg" **1985,** Jaboulet: 154, 250
Hermitage Blanc "Chevalier de Sterimberg" **1989,** Jaboulet: 507
Hermitage Blanc **1969,** Jaboulet: 10
Hermitage Blanc **1978** "Domaine de l'Hermite," Domaine Gray: 329
Hermitage Blanc **1978,** E. Guigal: 329, 520, 619
Hermitage Blanc **1978,** J. L. Chave: 9, 66, 329, 520, 617

Hermitage Blanc **1979,** J. L. Chave: 9, 66, 617
Hermitage Blanc **1980,** J. L. Chave: 620
Hermitage Blanc **1983,** E. Guigal: 156
Hermitage Blanc **1983,** J. L. Chave: 155, 425, 502, 620
Hermitage Blanc **1984,** J. L. Chave: 155
Hermitage Blanc **1985,** J. L. Chave: 155
Hermitage Prephylloxera **1832**, producer or shipper unknown: 112
Hermitage Rouge **1967,** J. L. Chave: 156
Hermitage Rouge **1969,** J. L. Chave: 10
Hermitage Rouge **1970,** Jaboulet-Isnard: 248
Hermitage Rouge **1975,** J. L. Chave: 10
Hermitage Rouge **1977,** J. L. Chave: 10
Hermitage Rouge **1978,** J. L. Chave: 10, 156, 330, 472, 521, 620
Hermitage Rouge **1979,** J. L. Chave: 10, 312, 447, 619
Hermitage Rouge **1980,** J. L Chave: 619
Hermitage Rouge **1981,** J. L. Chave: 155
Hermitage Rouge **1982,** J. L. Chave: 155
Hermitage Rouge **1983,** E. Guigal: 156
Hermitage Rouge **1983,** J. L. Chave: 155
Hermitage Rouge **1984,** J. L. Chave: 155
Hermitages Blanc **1978,** E. Guigal: 329
Hester Creek Pinot Blanc VQA **1996,** Golden Mile, Oliver, British Columbia, Canada: 487
Hinzerling Late Harvest Gewürztraminer **1979,** Yakima Valley: 643
Hoffmann Mountain Ranch Pinot Noir "Paso Robles" **1976:** 328
Holland Gin 1780: 114
Hospices de Beaune "Guigone de Salins" **1966,** Leroy: 150
Hospices de Beaune "Guigone de Salins" **1972,** Beyermann: 40, 591
Hospices de Beaune "Cuvée Estienne" **1966,** Leroy: 149
Hospices de Beaune "Cuvée Nicolas Rolin" **1966,** Leroy: 150
Inglenook Cabernet Sauvignon "Cask J-3" **1954,** Napa Valley: 239
Inglenook Cabernet Sauvignon "Classic Claret" **1958,** Napa Valley: 627
Inglenook Cabernet Sauvignon "Classic Claret" **1959,** Napa Valley: 530
Inglenook Cabernet Sauvignon "Estate-Bottled" **1968,** Napa Valley: 80
Inglenook Cabernet Sauvignon "Limited Cask" "Cask A-1" **1960,** Napa Valley: 239
Inglenook Cabernet Sauvignon "Limited Cask" "Cask A-17" **1974,** Napa Valley: 141, 58
Inglenook Cabernet Sauvignon "Limited Cask" "Cask A-7" **1973,** Napa Valley: 58
Inglenook Cabernet Sauvignon "Limited Cask" "Cask F-19" **1963,** Napa Valley: 141
Inglenook Cabernet Sauvignon "Limited Cask" "Cask F-3" **1962,** Napa Valley: 627
Inglenook Cabernet Sauvignon "Limited Cask" "Cask F-31" **1970,** Napa Valley: 58, 141
Inglenook Cabernet Sauvignon "Limited Cask" "Cask F-9" **1959,** Napa Valley: 239
Inglenook Cabernet Sauvignon "Limited Cask" "Cask G-28" **1966,** Napa Valley: 141
Inglenook Cabernet Sauvignon "Limited Cask" "Cask H-12" **1968,** Napa Valley: 530
Inglenook Cabernet Sauvignon "Limited Cask" "Cask J-46" **1949,** Napa Valley: 140
Inglenook Cabernet Sauvignon "Limited Cask" "Cask J-6" **1959,** Napa Valley: 140
Inglenook Cabernet Sauvignon "Limited Cask" **1961,** Napa Valley: 141
Inglenook Cabernet Sauvignon "Limited Cask" **1978,** Napa Valley: 58, 141
Inglenook Cabernet Sauvignon "Limited Cask" **1980,** Napa Valley: 141
Inglenook Cabernet Sauvignon "Reserve" **1981,** Napa Valley: 141
Inglenook Cabernet Sauvignon **1941,** Napa Valley: 140
Inglenook Cabernet Sauvignon **1943,** Napa Valley: 140
Inglenook Cabernet Sauvignon **1946,** Napa Valley: 140
Inglenook Cabernet Sauvignon **1949,** Napa Valley: 239
Inglenook Cabernet Sauvignon **1955,** Napa Valley: 140
Inglenook Cabernet Sauvignon **1958,** Napa Valley: 140, 239
Inglenook Charbono **1978,** Napa Valley: 58
Inglenook Chardonnay "Special Reserve" **1984,** Napa Valley: 141
Inglenook Gewürztraminer **1985,** Napa Valley: 141
Inglenook Merlot "Limited Bottling" **1980,** Napa Valley: 58
Inglenook Sauvignon Blanc "Reserve" **1984,** Napa Valley: 140
Inglenook-Niebaum "Reserve Claret" **1985,** Napa Valley: 359
Ironhorse Vineyards Cabernet Sauvignon **1985,** Sonoma Valley: 359
Jordan Cabernet Sauvignon **1983,** Napa Valley: 200
Joseph Phelps Cabernet Sauvignon "Backus Vineyard" **1984,** Napa Valley: 173
Joseph Phelps Cabernet Sauvignon "Eisele Vineyard" **1974,** Napa Valley: 232
Joseph Phelps Cabernet Sauvignon "Eisele Vineyard" **1977,** Napa Valley: 245
Joseph Phelps Cabernet Sauvignon "Eisele Vineyard" **1979,** Napa Valley: 232
Joseph Phelps Cabernet Sauvignon "Eisele Vineyard" **1984,** Napa Valley: 173
Joseph Phelps Cabernet Sauvignon "Eisele Vineyard" **1985,** Napa Valley: 503
Joseph Phelps Cabernet Sauvignon "Insignia" **1974,** Napa Valley: 198
Joseph Phelps Cabernet Sauvignon "Insignia" **1983,** Napa Valley: 173
Joseph Phelps Cabernet Sauvignon "Insignia" **1985,** Napa Valley: 359, 483
Joseph Phelps Johannisberg Riesling "Select Late Harvest" TBA **1978,** Napa Valley: 38
Joseph Phelps Sauvignon Blanc, Napa Valley **1980:** 25
Joseph Phelps Syrah **1982,** Napa Valley: 172
Joseph Swan Zinfandel **1974,** Sonoma Valley: 632
Judge's Zinfandel "Konsgaard Vineyards" **1985,** Napa Valley: 245
Kaiser Stuhl "Bin U31" Auslese Rhine Riesling **1976,** Eden Valley: 23
Kalin Cellars Chardonnay "Cuvée W" **1988,** Livermore Valley: 640
Kalin Cellars Pinot Noir "Cuvée DD" **1982,** Sonoma Valley: 635
Kalin Cellars Pinot Noir **1980,** Santa Barbara: 635
Kallstadter Seinacker Sierer-Rebe Beerenauslese **1971,** Rheinpfaltz-Weingut Karl Unckrich und Sohne: 312
Kanonkop Pinotage **1989:** 388
Keenan Cabernet Sauvignon **1978,** Napa Valley: 630
Keenan Chardonnay **1978,** Napa Valley: 65

Keenan Chardonnay **1979,** Napa Valley: 639
Kistler Chardonnay "Cutrer" **1979,** Sonoma Valley: 639
Kistler Chardonnay "Dutton Ranch" **1979,** Sonoma Valley: 639
Kistler Chardonnay "Dutton Ranch" **1989,** Sonoma Valley: 453
Kistler Chardonnay "Dutton Ranch" **1989,** Sonoma Valley: 640
Kistler Chardonnay "Dutton Ranch" **1995,** Sonoma Valley: 501
Kistler Chardonnay "Winery Lake" **1979,** Sonoma Valley: 639
Klein Constantia "Vin de Constance" **1987:** 387
Klein Constantia Chardonnay **1991:** 387
Klein Constantia Shiraz **1987:** 387
Kumeu River Wines Chardonnay **1986:** 215
L'Ormarins Cabernet Sauvignon **1985,** "La Maison du Roi," Franschoek Valley: 387
La Forêt-Mâcon Villages Blanc **1979:** 7
La Quadratura del Cerchio **1995,** "Secondo Viaggio," Tuscany: 516
La Rève de Saxenbourg "Private Collection" 1991 Noble Late Harvest: 388
La Tâche **1942,** Domaine de la Romanée-Conti: 402, 582, 499
La Tâche **1945,** Domaine de la Romanée-Conti: 237, 321
La Tâche **1947,** Domaine de la Romanée-Conti: 499
La Tâche **1951,** Domaine de la Romanée-Conti: 499, 582
La Tâche **1952,** Domaine de la Romanée-Conti: 401, 499, 582
La Tâche **1953,** Domaine de la Romanée-Conti: 499
La Tâche **1955,** Domaine de la Romanée-Conti: 461
La Tâche **1957,** Domaine de la Romanée-Conti: 357, 583
La Tâche **1958,** Domaine de la Romanée-Conti: 499, 583
La Tâche **1959,** Domaine de la Romanée-Conti: 96, 382
La Tâche **1961,** Domaine de la Romanée-Conti: 46, 106, 108, 499
La Tâche **1962,** Domaine de la Romanée-Conti: 106
La Tâche **1963,** Domaine de la Romanée-Conti: 357, 366, 382, 584
La Tâche **1964,** Domaine de la Romanée-Conti: 106, 382
La Tâche **1966,** Domaine de la Romanée-Conti: 357, 499
La Tâche **1969,** Domaine de la Romanée-Conti: 499
La Tâche **1971,** Domaine de la Romanée-Conti: 106, 114, 216, 270, 319, 325, 356, 357, 382, 409, 500, 585
La Tâche **1972,** Domaine de la Romanée-Conti: 102, 357, 499, 587
La Tâche **1975,** Domaine de la Romanée-Conti: 146
La Tâche **1976,** Domaine de la Romanée-Conti: 106, 357, 366, 484, 499, 586
La Tâche **1978,** Domaine de la Romanée-Conti: 342
La Tâche **1980,** Domaine de la Romanée-Conti: 85, 146, 367
La Tâche **1981,** Domaine de la Romanée-Conti: 146
La Tâche **1984,** Domaine de la Romanée-Conti: 146
La Tâche **1985,** Domaine de la Romanée-Conti: 476
La Tâche **1988,** Domaine de la Romanée-Conti: 333, 334
Lacrima Christi Del Vesuvio **1978,** Mastroberardino: 655
Latricières-Chambertin "Tastevinage" **1971,** Faiveley: 56
Latricières-Chambertin **1984,** Trapet: 145
Latricières-Chambertin **1985,** Faiveley: 233
Latricières-Chambertin **1995,** Faiveley: 526
Le Bonheur Cabernet Sauvignon **1982,** Simonsig, Stellenbosch: 386
Le Bonheur Cabernet Sauvignon **1984:** 387
Leonetti Cellars "Reserve" "Seven Hills Vineyard" Cabernet Sauvignon **1990,** Washington State: 475
Leonetti Cellars Merlot **1993,** Washington State: 454
Les Collines de Laure **1994,** Jean-Luc Colomba, Rhodaniennes: 419
Les Tourelles de Longueville **1987:** 296
Les-Forts-de-Latour **1966:** 29, 559
Les-Forts-de-Latour **1970:** 260, 481
Les-Forts-de-Latour **1973:** 260
Les-Forts-de-Latour **1974:** 193
Les-Forts-de-Latour **1975:** 192, 260, 303, 444
Les-Forts-de-Latour **1976:** 68, 121, 260
Les-Forts-de-Latour **1978:** 192, 260, 331
Les-Forts-de-Latour **1979:** 192, 260
Les-Forts-de-Latour **1981:** 192
Les-Forts-de-Latour **1982:** 303
Les-Forts-de-Latour **1989:** 443
Les-Forts-de-Latour **1991:** 431, 443
Les-Forts-de-Latour **1995:** 431
Lindeman's Coonawarra Rhine Riesling "Nursery Vineyard" **1979:** 22
Lindeman's Nyrang Hermitage "Bin 3610" **1967,** Australia: 80
Lindeman's Nyrang Hermitage "Bin 5525" **1976:** 652
Lindeman's Nyrang Hermitage **1977:** 652
Livadia **1945:** 412
London Dock Port (at least 75 years old): 174
London Dock Port "Superior" N/V: 203, 647
Loupiac **1955:** 604
Macallan Single Malt Scotch Whisky: 101
Madeira **1792:** 112
Madeira **1851:** 114
Madeira Bastardo **1969,** Cossart-Gordon: 398
Madeira Terrantez **1795,** Barbeito: 648
Madiran **1981:** 68
Maître d'Estournel Blanc **1986** A/C Bordeaux: 183
Maître d'Estournel Rouge **1985** A/C Bordeaux: 183
Málaga "Solera" **1885**, Scholtz Hermanos, Málaga, Spain: 649
Marcobruner Beerenauslese **1945:** 339
Markko Vineyards Cabernet Sauvignon **1983,** Ohio: 247
Markko Vineyards Chardonnay **1983,** Ohio: 196
Marqués de Riscal "Reserva" **1993,** Rioja: 476
Marqués de Riscal **1970,** Rioja: 657
Marsannay Blanc Chardonnay "Vieilles Vignes" **1992,** Phillipe Nadeff: 452
Martin Ray "Winery Lake" Pinot Noir **1977,** Carneros, Napa Valley: 634
Martin Ray Cabernet Sauvignon **1947,** Saratoga: 530
Martin Ray Cabernet Sauvignon **1976,** California: 170
Martínez-Gassiot White Porto XSR 120: 168, 357, 367, 494, 500
Mas de Daumas Gassac Vin de Pays de l'Herault **1978,** A. Guibert de la Vaissière: 507, 624
Mas de Daumas Gassac Vin de Pays de l'Herault **1980,** A. Guibert de la Vaissière: 624
Mas de Daumas Gassac Vin de Pays de l'Herault **1981,** A. Guibert de la Vaissière: 366, 624
Mas de Daumas Gassac Vin de Pays de l'Herault **1985,** A. Guibert de la Vaissière: 484, 625
Mas de Daumas Gassac Vin de Pays de l'Herault **1991,** A. Guibert de la Vaissière: 625
Mas de Daumas Gassac Vin de Pays de l'Herault **1992,** A. Guibert de la Vaissière: 625,
Mas de Gourgonnier **1981,** Côteaux des Baux, Provence VDQS, Nicolas Cartier: 624
Matanzas Creek Chardonnay **1979,** Sonoma Valley: 638
Matanzas Creek Chardonnay **1987,** Sonoma Valley: 640

Mayacamas **1974,** Napa Mountain: 1, 21, 25
Mayacamas **1975,** Napa Mountain: 21
Mayacamas Cabernet Sauvignon **1970,** Napa Mountain: 263
Mayacamas Cabernet Sauvignon **1974,** Napa Mountain: 198, 628
Mayacamas Chardonnay **1972,** Napa Mountain 3
Mayacamas Chardonnay **1973,** Napa Mountain: 28
Mayacamas Chardonnay **1974,** Napa Mountain: 28, 48, 180
Mayacamas Chardonnay **1975,** Napa Mountain: 25, 28, 180, 636
Mayacamas Chardonnay **1976,** Napa Mountain: 180, 199, 637
Mayacamas Chardonnay **1977,** Napa Mountain: 180
Mayacamas Chardonnay **1979,** Napa Mountain: 199
Mayacamas Chardonnay **1981,** Napa Mountain: 640
Mayacamas Late Harvest Zinfandel **1968,** Napa Mountain: 263
Mayacamas Late Harvest Zinfandel **1974,** Napa Mountain: 632
Mazis-Chambertin **1945,** Gelin: 320
Mazis-Chambertin **1964,** Avery's: 90
Mazis-Chambertin **1966,** Leroy: 151
Mazis-Chambertin **1982,** Domaine Maume: 489, 588
Mazis-Chambertin **1983,** Philippe Nadeff: 588
Mazis-Chambertin **1985** Hospices de Beaune, Leroy: 225
Mazis-Chambertin **1985,** Faiveley: 233
McCrea Cellars "Mariah" **1990,** Don Graves Vineyard, Columbia Valley, Washington State: 488
Mercurey "Clos Oudin" **1985,** Mercurey: 153
Mercurey Blanc **1981,** Château de Chamirey, Jouenne d'Herville: 74
Mercurey Blanc **1982,** Michel Juillot: 598
Mercurey Blanc **1985,** Michel Juillot: 153
Mercurey Blanc **1988,** Michel Juillot: 295
Mercurey Rouge "Champ Martin" **1986:** 295
Mercurey Rouge "Clos Tonnerres" **1985,** Mercurey: 153
Mercurey Rouge "Clos Tonnerres" **1987,** Mercurey: 295
Merlot **1987,** Meerlust: 386
Messias "Quinta do Cachao" Vintage Port **1970:** 166
Meursault "Clos de la Barre" **1992,** Comtes Lafon: 527
Meursault "Cuvée La Barre-Narvaux" **1982,** J. F. Coche-Dury: 149
Meursault "Cuvée Loppin" Hospices de Beaune **1978,** Bouchard Aîné et Fils: 56
Meursault "Désirée" **1990,** Comtes Lafon: 447
Meursault "Désirée" **1993,** Comtes Lafon: 474
Meursault "Le Limozin" **1982,** Michelot Buisson: 153
Meursault "Les Casse Têtes" **1986,** J. F. Coche-Dury: 352
Meursault "Les Casse-Têtes" **1983,** J. F. Coche-Dury: 167, 598
Meursault "Les Charmes" **1983,** J. F. Coche-Dury: 167
Meursault "Les Chevalières" **1987,** J. F. Coche-Dury: 601
Meursault "Les Luraules" **1985,** Monceau-Boch, Mme Guidot: 598
Meursault "Les Narvaux" **1978,** Michelot-Buisson: 174
Meursault "Les Narvaux" **1983,** J. F. Coche-Dury 167, 598
Meursault "Les Narvaux" **1983,** Michelot: 194
Meursault "Les Perrières" **1983,** J. F. Coche-Dury: 167
Meursault "Les Perrières" **1987,** J. F. Coche-Dury: 600
Meursault "Les Rougeots" **1987,** J. F. Coche-Dury: 600
Meursault **1971,** Remoissenet: 21
Meursault **1979,** Jean Michelot: 596
Meursault **1979,** Leroy: 522
Meursault **1981,** Jaffelin: 84
Meursault **1985,** J. F. Coche-Dury: 379
Meursault **1988,** Jadot: 284
Meursault **1992,** Jadot: 436
Meursault N/V, Birkedall Hartmann: 592
Meursault-Blagny **1985,** François Jobard: 356
Meursault-Charmes "Charmes Dessus" **1979,** Domaine de la Guyomière: 63
Meursault-Charmes **1969,** Remoissenet: 59
Meursault-Charmes **1978,** René Monnier: 100
Meursault-Charmes Premier Cru **1945,** Leroy: 316
Meursault-Genevrières "Cuvée Baudot" Hospices de Beaune **1983,** Remoissenet: 425
Meursault-Genevrières **1973,** Louis Latour: 30
Meursault-Genevrières **1978,** François Jobard: 194
Meursault-Genevrières **1978,** Louis Latour: 239
Meursault-Genevrières **1979,** François Jobard: 83
Meursault-Genevrières **1979,** Louis Latour: 31, 55, 62
Meursault-Genevrières **1982,** Jadot: 214
Meursault-Genevrières **1989,** Louis Latour: 422
Meursault-Perrières "Tasteviné" **1979,** J. F. Coche-Dury: 332
Meursault-Perrières **1945,** Leroy: 236
Meursault-Perrières **1962,** Potinet-Ampeau: 129
Meursault-Perrières **1973** Boillot-Buthiau: 88
Meursault-Perrières **1978,** Jacques Prieur: 29, 82
Meursault-Perrières **1979,** Guyon: 63
Meursault-Perrières **1982,** J. F. Coche-Dury: 309:
Meursault-Perrières **1982,** Pierre Morey: 361
Meursault-Perrières **1987,** J. F. Coche-Dury: 459, 522
Meursault-Poruzots **1981,** François Jobard: 76
Meursault-Poruzots **1985,** François Jobard: 378, 487
Meursault-Poruzots **1986,** François Jobard: 501
Meyer's Méthode Champenoise Brut N/V: 89
Michel Tribant N/V California: 238
Mildara Fino Sherry "Winemaker's Selection": 22
Mirassou "Monterey" Petite Syrah Unfiltered **1976:** 636
Mirassou Champagne **1973,** Sonoma Valley: 35
Mirassou Champagne **1974,** Sonoma Valley: 57
Mondavi-Rothschild Opus One **1980,** Napa Valley: 138
Mondavi-Rothschild Opus One **1981,** Napa Valley: 138
Mondavi-Rothschild Opus One **1982,** Napa Valley: 138, 372
Mondavi-Rothschild Opus One **1983,** Napa Valley: 372, 373, 631
Mondavi-Rothschild Opus One **1984,** Napa Valley: 372
Mondavi-Rothschild Opus One **1985,** Napa Valley: 372, 524
Mondavi-Rothschild Opus One **1986,** Napa Valley: 372
Mondavi-Rothschild Opus One **1987,** Napa Valley: 372
Mondavi-Rothschild Opus One **1988,** Napa Valley: 372
Mondavi-Rothschild Opus One **1989,** Napa Valley: 372
Mondavi-Rothschild Opus One **1990,** Napa Valley: 372
Monteiro Vinhos Vintage Madeira LDA "Malmsey Sweet" **1900,** Funchal: 327
Monterey Cabernet Sauvignon **1980,** Maryland: 175
Montesodi **1993,** Castello Nipozzano, Marchesi Frescobaldi: 456
Monthélie **1988,** Jadot: 285
Montrachet "Baron Thenard" **1971,** Remoissenet: 106
Montrachet **1964,** Domaine de la Romanée-Conti: 164
Montrachet **1965,** Domaine de la Romanée-Conti **1966:** 164
Montrachet **1967,** Domaine de la Romanée-Conti: 164
Montrachet **1968,** Domaine de la Romanée-Conti: 164
Montrachet **1969,** Domaine de la Romanée-Conti: 164
Montrachet **1970,** Domaine de la Romanée-Conti: 11, 164
Montrachet **1970,** Fleurot: 593
Montrachet **1971,** Domaine de la Romanée-Conti: 165

Montrachet **1972,** Domaine de la Romanée-Conti: 165
Montrachet **1973,** Bouchard Père et Fils: 2
Montrachet **1973,** Domaine de la Romanée-Conti. 167, 240
Montrachet **1974,** Domaine de la Romanée-Conti: 165
Montrachet **1975,** Domaine de la Romanée-Conti: 165
Montrachet **1976,** Domaine de la Romanée-Conti: 165
Montrachet **1977,** Domaine de la Romanée-Conti: 165
Montrachet **1978,** Domaine de la Romanée-Conti: 165, 240, 334, 494
Montrachet **1978,** Pierre Morey: 240
Montrachet **1978,** Thévenin: 63
Montrachet **1979,** Domaine de la Romanée-Conti: 165
Montrachet **1981,** Domaine de la Romanée-Conti: 165
Montrachet **1982,** Domaine de la Romanée-Conti. 165, 240
Montrachet **1983,** Domaine de la Romanée-Conti: 165, 257, 409
Montrachet **1983,** René Monnier: 257
Montrachet **1984,** Domaine de la Romanée-Conti: 165
Montrachet **1985,** Louis Latour: 346, 370, 439, 463
Montrachet Bourgogne Blanc **1959,** Lebegue-Bichot: 95
Montrachet Marquis de Laguiche **1959,** Joseph Drouhin: 95
Montrachet Marquis de Laguiche **1969,** Joseph Drouhin: 3, 592
Montrachet Marquis de Laguiche **1970,** Joseph Drouhin: 215
Montrachet Marquis de Laguiche **1976,** Joseph Drouhin: 46, 92
Montrachet Marquis de Laguiche **1989,** Joseph Drouhin: 462, 477, 492, 513, 601
Morey-St.-Denis "Clos de la Bussière" **1988,** Georges Roumier: 288
Morey-St.-Denis "Clos de la Bussière" **1989,** Georges Roumier: 288
Morey-St.-Denis "Monts Luisants" Premier Cru **1988,** Domaine Ponsot: 601
Morey-St.-Denis "Monts-Luisants" Premier Cru **1979,** Domaine Ponsot: 596
Morey-St.-Denis **1966,** Leroy: 150
Morey-St.-Denis Blanc "En la Rue de Vergy" **1990,** Domaine Bruno Clair: 447
Morey-St.-Denis Premier Cru **1979,** Louis Latour: 151
Mormoretto "Predicato di Biturica" **1983,** Frescobaldi: 657
Mormoretto **1994,** Castello Nipozzano, Marchesi Frescobaldi: 456
Morris Port **1978,** Sonoma County: 25
Morris Premium Liqueur Muscat: 23
Moscatel **1870,** Osbourne: 257
Moscatel de Setúbal (25 years old), J. M. de Fonseca: 423, 649
Moulin des Carruades de Lafite **1979:** 242
Moulin des Carruades de Lafite **1981:** 242
Moulin Touchais **1928,** Anjou, Loire Valley: 93
Moulin Touchais **1933,** Anjou, Loire Valley: 93, 48, 55, 606
Moulin Touchais **1937,** Anjou, Loire Valley: 93
Moulin Touchais **1945,** Anjou, Loire Valley: 94
Moulin Touchais **1947,** Anjou, Loire Valley: 94, 136, 606
Moulin Touchais **1949,** Anjou, Loire Valley: 94
Moulin Touchais **1955,** Anjou, Loire Valley: 65, 94, 110, 258
Moulin Touchais **1959,** Anjou, Loire Valley: 94, 606
Moulin Touchais **1962,** Anjou, Loire Valley: 94
Moulin Touchais **1964,** Anjou, Loire Valley: 94
Mount Eden Vineyards Cabernet Sauvignon **1974,** Napa Valley: 198
Mount Eden Vineyards Cabernet Sauvignon **1974,** Santa Clara: 1
Mount Eden Vineyards Chardonnay **1973,** Santa Clara, California: 58
Mount Eden Vineyards Chardonnay **1974,** Napa Valley: 77
Mount Eden Vineyards Chardonnay **1978,** Napa Valley: 238
Mount Eden Vineyards Chardonnay **1983,** Napa Valley: 238
Mount Veeder Vineyards Cabernet Sauvignon **1974,** Napa Valley: 1, 198
Mount Veeder Vineyards Chardonnay **1975,** Napa Valley: 25
Mouton **1959:** 368
Mulderbosch Sauvignon Blanc **1995,** Stellenbosch, South Africa: 441
Murfatlar **1978,** Roumania: 40
Muscadet **1986,** Marquis de Goulaine: 247
Muscat "Cuvée Tradition" **1979,** Hugel: 36
Muscat Aszú 4 Puttonyos **1986:** 306
Muscat Blanc "Late-Picked" **1980,** Brown Bros., Milawa, Victoria: 653
Muscat de Beaumes-de-Venise **1978,** Jaboulet: 9
Muscat de Beaumes-de-Venise **1986,** Jaboulet: 250
Musigny "Cuvée Vieilles Vignes" **1945,** Comte de Vogüé: 237, 320
Musigny "Cuvée Vieilles Vignes" **1959,** Comte de Vogüé: 350
Musigny **1945,** Morin Père et Fils: 135, 237, 319
Musigny **1947,** Faiveley: 82
Musigny **1949,** Comte de Vogüé: 170
Musigny **1961,** Jacques Prieur: 513
Musigny **1964,** Comte de Vogüé: 465, 584
Musigny **1964,** Joseph Drouhin: 33, 584
Musigny **1966,** Comte de Vogüé, Coron Père et Fils: 170
Musigny **1966,** Leroy: 150
Musigny **1971,** Jadot: 586
Musigny **1972,** Jadot: 586
Musigny **1985,** Georges Roumier: 146
Musigny Blanc **1935,** Comte de Vogüé: 318
Musigny Blanc **1952,** Comte de Vogüé: 318
Musigny Blanc **1953,** Comte de Vogüé: 318
Musigny Blanc **1969,** Comte de Vogüé: 318
Musigny Blanc **1970,** Comte de Vogüé: 319
Musigny Blanc **1973,** Comte de Vogüé: 319
Musigny Blanc **1976,** Comte de Vogüé: 319
Musigny Blanc **1978,** Comte de Vogüé: 319
Musigny Blanc **1979,** Comte de Vogüé: 319
Musigny Blanc **1982,** Comte de Vogüé: 170, 319
Musigny Blanc **1983,** Comte de Vogüé: 319, 425
Musigny Blanc **1985,** Comte de Vogüé: 319
Musigny Blanc **1988,** Comte de Vogüé: 315
Nederburg Estate Cabernet Sauvignon "Select" **1961,** South Africa: 142
Nederburg Estate Cabernet Sauvignon "Select" **1962,** South Africa: 142
Nederburg Estate Cabernet Sauvignon "Select" **1968,** South Africa: 142
Nederburg Estate Cabernet Sauvignon "Superior" **1974,** South Africa: 232
Nederburg Estate Cabernet Sauvignon **1971,** South Africa: 142
Nederburg Estate Cabernet Sauvignon **1973,** South Africa: 387
Nederburg Estate Cabernet Sauvignon **1976,** South Africa: 142
Nederburg Estate Cabernet Sauvignon **1981,** South Africa: 387
Neethlingshof Gewürztraminer **1993:** 388
Nevers Cabernet Sauvignon **1995,** Napa Valley: 488
Newton Vineyards Cabernet Sauvignon **1985,** Napa Valley: 359
Newton Vineyards Zinfandel **1994,** Napa Valley: 441

Niepoort "Colheita" Porto **1912:** 644
Nuits-St.-Georges "Aux Murgers" **1985,** Méo-Camuzet: 427
Nuits-St.-Georges "Château Gris" Premier Cru Monopole **1978,** Lupé-Cholet: 372, 587
Nuits-St.-Georges "Clos de l'Arlot" **1978,** Jules Belin: 64, 332, 595
Nuits-St.-Georges "Clos de l'Arlot" Blanc Premier Cru **1978,** Jules Belin: 177
Nuits-St.-Georges "Clos de l'Arlot" Blanc Premier Cru **1992,** Domaine de l'Arlot: 430
Nuits-St.-Georges "Clos de la Maréchale" Premier Cru Monopole **1995,** Faiveley: 526
Nuits-St.-Georges "Clos des Argillières" Premier Cru **1987,** Daniel Rion: 590
Nuits-St.-Georges "Clos des Corvées" **1988,** Jadot: 285
Nuits-St.-Georges "Clos des Forêts" **1972,** Jules Belin: 40
Nuits-St.-Georges "Clos des Porrets St. Georges" Tastevinè **1979,** Faiveley: 88
Nuits-St.-Georges "Les Cailles" Premier Cru **1983,** Robert Chevillon: 588
Nuits-St.-Georges "Les Cailles" Premier Cru **1990,** Alain Michelot: 474
Nuits-St.-Georges "Les Didiers" **1988,** Jacques Duret: 454
Nuits-St.-Georges "Les Perrières" **1983,** Robert Chevillon: 314
Nuits-St.-Georges "Les Porrets St. Georges" Premier Cru **1979,** Pierre Ponnelle: 8
Nuits-St.-Georges "Les Porrets St. Georges" Premier Cru **1989,** Faiveley: 527
Nuits-St.-Georges "Les Porrets St. Georges" Premier Cru **1993,** Faiveley: 427
Nuits-St.-Georges "Les Roncières" Premier Cru **1986,** Joseph Drouhin: 500, 589
Nuits-St.-Georges "Les Roncières" Premier Cru **1993,** Robert Chevillon: 427
Nuits-St.-Georges "Les Vaucrains" **1945,** Henri Gouges: 319
Nuits-St.-Georges "Les Vaucrains" Premier Cru **1983,** Robert Chevillon: 588
Nuits-St.-Georges "Murgers" Premier Cru **1985,** Méo-Camuzet: 234
Nuits-St.-Georges **1945,** John Harvey: 582
Nuits-St.-Georges **1950,** Martenot: 392
Nuits-St.-Georges **1955,** Avery's: 90
Nuits-St.-Georges **1983,** Joseph Faiveley: 229
Nuits-St.-Georges Blanc **1986,** Robert Chevillon: 273
Nuits-St.-Georges Villages **1979,** Pierre Ponnelle: 8
Oak Crest Vineyards Cabernet Sauvignon **1971,** Napa Valley: 110
Ockfener Bockstein Riesling Eiswein **1989,** Weingut Gebert, Mosel/Saar/Ruhr: 649
Offley's Vintage Port **1920:** 415
Offley's Vintage Port **1945:** 413
Offley's Vintage Port Boa Vista **1960:** 644
Offley's Vintage Port Boa Vista **1963:** 645
Oksamit Ukrainy **1976:** 80
Oppenheimer Sacktrager Gewürztraminer Trockenbeerenauslese **1976,** Guntrum, Rheinhessen: 271
Ornellaia **1990,** Antinori: 496
Paarl "Roodeberg" **1975:** 650
Paarl "Selected" Pinotage **1964,** KWV: 142
Paarl "Selected" Pinotage **1966,** KWV: 142
Paarl "Selected" Pinotage **1970,** KWV: 142
Paarl Cabernet Sauvignon N/V, KWV: 143
Pandora "Old Sherry" **1933:** 174
Paraduxx **1996:** 503
Pavillon Blanc du Château Margaux **1981:** 88, 203
Pavillon Blanc du Château Margaux **1986:** 448
Pavillon Blanc du Château Margaux **1995:** 428, 448
Pavillon Rouge du Château Margaux **1982:** 449
Pavillon Rouge du Château Margaux **1985:** 228
Pavillon Rouge du Château Margaux **1990:** 449
Penfold's Cabernet-Shiraz "Bin 389" **1983:** 341
Penfold's Cabernet-Shiraz "Bin 389" **1986:** 341
Penfold's Cabernet-Shiraz "Bin 389" **1987:** 341
Penfold's Chardonnay **1988,** Barossa Valley: 341
Penfold's Grange Hermitage "Bin 95" **1966:** 368
Penfold's Grange Hermitage "Bin 95" **1967:** 368
Penfold's Grange Hermitage "Bin 95" **1968:** 59, 368
Penfold's Grange Hermitage "Bin 95" **1969:** 368
Penfold's Grange Hermitage "Bin 95" **1970:** 368
Penfold's Grange Hermitage "Bin 95" **1971:** 368
Penfold's Grange Hermitage "Bin 95" **1972:** 59, 369
Penfold's Grange Hermitage "Bin 95" **1973:** 59, 369
Penfold's Grange Hermitage "Bin 95" **1974:** 59, 369
Penfold's Grange Hermitage "Bin 95" **1975:** 23, 369
Penfold's Grange Hermitage "Bin 95" **1976:** 369
Penfold's Grange Hermitage "Bin 95" **1977:** 369
Penfold's Grange Hermitage "Bin 95" **1978:** 369
Penfold's Grange Hermitage "Bin 95" **1979:** 369
Penfold's Grange Hermitage "Bin 95" **1980:** 369
Penfold's Grange Hermitage "Bin 95" **1981:** 341, 369, 476
Penfold's Grange Hermitage "Bin 95" **1982:** 341, 369, 476
Penfold's Grange Hermitage "Bin 95" **1983:** 341, 369
Penfold's Grange Hermitage "Bin 95" **1984:** 341, 369, 476
Penfold's Grange Hermitage "Bin 95" **1985:** 341, 369
Penfold's Grange Hermitage "Bin 95" **1986:** 369
Penfold's Grange Hermitage "Bin 95" **1987:** 369
Pernand-Vergelesses Ile de Vergelesses **1979,** Louis Latour: 12
Pesquera "Janus" Reserva **1994,** Ribera Del Duero, Spain: 501
Petaluma Chardonnay **1978:** 23
Piesporter Güntherslay Riesling Eiswein Beerenauslese **1975,** Marienhof, Mosel: 334
Pinot Blanc **1979,** Hugel: 36
Pinot Noir **1988,** Jadot: 285
Pinot Noir **1989,** Meerlust: 386
Pinot Noir **1991,** Oregon, Domaine Drouhin: 421
Pinotage Lanzerac **1962:** 142
Piper-Sonoma **1980:** 79
Piper-Sonoma N/V: 238
Pomino Bianco **1996,** Castello di Verrazzano: 456
Pomino Chardonnay **1994,** Castello di Verrazzano: 456
Pomino Rosso **1994,** Castello di Verrazzano: 456
Pommard "Clos de Verger" **1979,** Pothier-Rieusset: 447, 591
Pommard "Clos des Boucherottes" **1983,** Domaine Coste-Caumartin: 314
Pommard "Clos des Epeneaux" Premier Cru **1985,** Comte Armand: 490
Pommard "Clos des Epeneaux" Premier Cru **1988,** Comte Armand: 490
Pommard "Clos des Epenots" **1959,** de Courcel: 590
Pommard "Clos Micault" **1966,** Leroy: 150
Pommard "Epenots" **1928,** H. de Villamont: 392
Pommard "Epenots" Premier Cru **1985,** de Courcel: 267

Pommard "Epenots" Premier Cru **1988,** Jadot: 285
Pommard "Grands Epenots" **1966,** Leroy: 149
Pommard "Les Jarollières" **1987,** Domaine de la Pousse d'Or: 287
Pommard "Les Jarollières" **1988,** Domaine de la Pousse d'Or: 490, 419
Pommard "Les Noizons" **1990,** J. L. Joillot: 490
Pommard "Rugiens" **1939,** Martenot: 392
Pommard "Rugiens" **1959,** Michel Gaunoux: 392
Pommard "Rugiens" Premier Cru **1959,** Michel Gaunoux: 590
Pommard "Rugiens" Premier Cru **1983,** de Courcel: 490
Pommard **1966,** Leroy: 150
Pommard **1990,** J. M. Boillot: 490
Port Circa **1750:** 114
Port Wine N/V: 647
Porto "Special Reserve" **1897,** Barros: 245
Pouilly-Fuissé "Clos La Roche" **1982,** Guffens-Heynen: 598
Pouilly-Fuissé "Clos La Roche" **1994,** Saumaize: 602
Pouilly-Fuissé "Ronchevats" **1994,** Saumaize: 602
Pouilly-Fuissé "Tastevinage" **1981,** Dufouleur: 74
Pouilly-Fuissé "Tête de Cru" **1975,** J. Loron: 593
Pouilly-Fuissé **1988,** Jadot: 284
Pouilly-Fuissé N/V, Bouchard Ainé et Fils: 592
Pouilly-Fumé "Baron de L" **1979,** Ladoucette: 623
Pouilly-Fumé "Baron de L" **1985,** Ladoucette: 525, 623
Pouilly-Fumé **1976,** Ladoucette: 622
Pouilly-Fumé **1978,** Ladoucette: 14
Pouilly-Fumé **1979,** Ladoucette: 26
Pouilly-Fumé **1982,** Ladoucette, Loire Valley: 84
Pouilly-Fumé **1986,** Ladoucette: 259
Prado Enea "Gran Reserva" **1976,** Rioja, Muga: 439
Primitivo **1973,** Azienda Vinicola Amanda, Rosso di Sava, Italy: 61
Prunelle de Bourgogne: 8
Prunier Grande Champagne Cognac **1929,** A/C: 62
Puligny-Montrachet "Champs-Canet" **1983,** E. Sauzet: 343
Puligny-Montrachet "Champs-Canet" **1983,** Etienne Sauzet: 598
Puligny-Montrachet "Clos du Cailleret" **1978,** Joseph Drouhin: 56, 202
Puligny-Montrachet "Clos du Cailleret" **1982,** Joseph Drouhin: 56, 597, 598
Puligny-Montrachet "Clos du Cailleret" **1989,** Jean Chartron: 465, 601
Puligny-Montrachet "Clos du Cailleret" **1990,** Jean Chartron: 436
Puligny-Montrachet "Clos du Cailleret" **1993,** Jean Chartron: 483
Puligny-Montrachet "Les Chalumeaux" **1979,** Ropiteau-Mignon: 62
Puligny-Montrachet "Les Combettes" **1976,** Remoissenet: 33, 92
Puligny-Montrachet "Les Combettes" **1979,** Etienne Sauzet: 67
Puligny-Montrachet "Les Combettes" **1985,** Etienne Sauzet: 422
Puligny-Montrachet "Les Combettes" **1986,** Etienne Sauzet: 422
Puligny-Montrachet "Les Folatières" **1976,** Joseph Drouhin: 20, 46
Puligny-Montrachet "Les Folatières" **1978,** Joseph Drouhin: 7
Puligny-Montrachet "Les Folatières" **1982,** Domaine Henri Clerc: 392
Puligny-Montrachet "Les Folatières" **1982,** Joseph Drouhin: 56
Puligny-Montrachet "Les Folatières" **1982,** Monnier-Vaivrand: 267
Puligny-Montrachet "Les Folatières" **1982,** René Monnier: 88
Puligny-Montrachet "Les Folatières" **1983,** Monnier-Vaivrand: 231, 598
Puligny-Montrachet "Les Folatières" **1983,** Roux Père et Fils: 88
Puligny-Montrachet "Les Folatières" **1986,** Domaine Henri Clerc: 392
Puligny-Montrachet "Les Folatières" **1986,** Jadot: 296
Puligny-Montrachet "Les Folatières" **1986,** Joseph Drouhin: 600
Puligny-Montrachet "Les Folatières" **1994,** Paul Pernot: 512
Puligny-Montrachet "Les Pucelles" **1969,** Henry Boillot: 592
Puligny-Montrachet "Les Pucelles" **1976,** Vincent Leflaive: 46, 92, 594
Puligny-Montrachet "Les Pucelles" **1978,** Henri Boillot: 35, 322,89, 595
Puligny-Montrachet "Les Pucelles" **1978,** Vincent Leflaive: 35, 356, 392, 594
Puligny-Montrachet "Les Pucelles" **1983,** Vincent Leflaive: 282
Puligny-Montrachet "Les Pucelles" **1986,** Joseph Drouhin: 260
Puligny-Montrachet "Les Pucelles" **1986,** Vincent Leflaive: 295
Puligny-Montrachet "Les Pucelles" **1987,** Vincent Leflaive: 295
Puligny-Montrachet "Les Referts" **1979,** Louis Latour: 63, 596
Puligny-Montrachet "Les Referts" **1981,** Jadot: 172
Puligny-Montrachet **1986,** Vincent Leflaive: 295
Puligny-Montrachet **1987,** Vincent Leflaive: 295
Puligny-Montrachet **1988,** Jadot: 285
Puligny-Montrachet **1994,** Etienne Sauzet: 442
Quady Black Muscat **1983,** California: 171
Quady Port "Lot II" **1978:** 57
Quarles Harris Late-Bottled Vintage Port **1979,** Corney and Barrow: 172
Quart de Chaume Château de Suronde **1969,** Loire: 125
Quart de Chaume Château de Suronde **1978,** Loire: 606
QuercIolino **1990,** Castello di Verrazzano: 457
Quinta do Cachao Vintage Port **1970:** 315
Quinta do Noval Nacional **1931:** 129
Quinta do Noval Nacional **1934:** 129
Quinta do Noval Nacional **1947:** 130, 283, 459
Quinta do Noval Nacional **1955:** 130
Quinta do Noval Nacional **1960:** 92
Quinta do Noval Nacional **1962:** 92
Quinta do Noval Nacional **1963:** 92
Quinta do Noval Nacional **1966:** 92, 180
Quinta do Noval Vintage Port **1931:** 129, 241
Quinta do Noval Vintage Port **1934:** 129
Quinta do Noval Vintage Port **1945:** 129, 414
Quinta do Noval Vintage Port **1947:** 130
Quinta do Noval Vintage Port **1955:** 87, 130
Quinta do Noval Vintage Port **1960:** 92
Quinta do Noval Vintage Port **1963:** 92, 401, 646
Quinta do Noval Vintage Port **1966:** 92, 180, 646
Quinta do Noval Vintage Port **1970:** 92
Quinta do Noval Vintage Port **1975:** 167
Quinta do Noval Vintage Port **1985:** 381
Quinta do Sibio Vintage Port **1960:** 644
Rare Amoroso Sweet Sherry "Landed Age" N/V, E. Lustau: 340
Rauenthaler Baiken Riesling Trockenbeerenauslese **1976,** Schloss Eltz: 112
Rebello Valente Vintage Port **1945:** 644, 657
Rémy Martin Louis XIII Cognac: 91
Réserve de la Comtesse **1993:** 429
Respides-Medeville Red Graves **1984:** 120

Richebourg **1937,** Domaine de la Romanée-Conti: 581
Richebourg **1945,** Charles Vienot: 320
Richebourg **1945,** Domaine de la Romanée-Conti: 237, 320
Richebourg **1958,** Domaine de la Romanée-Conti: 499, 583
Richebourg **1959,** A. Bichot: 583
Richebourg **1959,** Avery's: 219
Richebourg **1959,** Domaine de la Romanée-Conti: 95
Richebourg **1963,** Domaine de la Romanée-Conti: 11
Richebourg **1966,** Charles Noëllat: 584
Richebourg **1966,** Remoissenet: 88
Richebourg **1969,** Jean Gros: 585
Richebourg **1972,** Domaine de la Romanée-Conti: 586
Richebourg **1977,** Domaine de la Romanée-Conti: 11
Richebourg **1978,** Chanson Père et Fils: 587
Richebourg **1978,** Domaine de la Romanée-Conti, 367
Richebourg **1982,** Domaine de la Romanée-Conti: 146
Richebourg **1985,** Domaine de la Romanée-Conti: 459, 485, 496, 508
Richebourg **1990,** Domaine de la Romanée-Conti: 496
Ridge Vineyards "Howell Mountain" Cabernet Sauvignon **1982,** California: 324
Ridge Vineyards "Jimsomare" Late Harvest Zinfandel **1970,** California: 263
Ridge Vineyards "Jimsomare" Zinfandel **1970,** California: 239
Ridge Vineyards "Monte Bello" "Holliwood Cuvée" **1968,** California: 262, 263
Ridge Vineyards "Monte Bello" Cabernet Sauvignon **1968,** California: 28
Ridge Vineyards "Monte Bello" Cabernet Sauvignon **1970,** California: 28
Ridge Vineyards "Monte Bello" Cabernet Sauvignon **1973,** California: 28
Ridge Vineyards "Monte Bello" Cabernet Sauvignon **1974,** California: 21, 28
Ridge Vineyards "Monte Bello" Cabernet Sauvignon **1975,** California: 21, 28
Ridge Vineyards "Monte Bello" Cabernet Sauvignon **1976,** California: 28
Ridge Vineyards "Monte Bello" Cabernet Sauvignon **1977,** California: 28
Ridge Vineyards "Monte Bello" Cabernet Sauvignon **1978,** California: 473, 630
Ridge Vineyards "Monte Bello" Ruby Cabernet **1974,** California: 28
Ridge Vineyards "Shenandoah" Zinfandel **1978,** California: 632
Ridge Vineyards "York Creek" Cabernet Sauvignon **1976:** 170
Ridge Vineyards Cabernet Sauvignon N/V, California: 529
Ridge Vineyards Zinfandel "Essence" **1968,** California: 239
Ridge Vineyards Zinfandel "Geyserville" **1973,** California: 632
Ridge Vineyards Zinfandel "Geyserville" **1996,** California: 518
Riesling "Cuvée Tradition" **1977,** Hugel: 36
Riesling "Les Ecaillers" **1985,** Leon Beyer: 622
Riesling "Les Murailles" **1978,** Dopff et Irion: 5
Riesling "Reserve Exceptionnelle" **1971,** Hugel: 621
Riesling "Vendange Tardive" "Selection de Grains Nobles" **1976,** Hugel: 5, 524, 622
Riesling "Vendange Tardive" **1976,** Hugel: 36
Riesling **1978,** Hugel: 36
Riesling Beerenauslese, Rheinpfaltz **1976:** 33
Ritchie Creek Vineyard Cabernet Sauvignon Stony Hill **1987,** Napa Valley: 488
Ritchie Creek Vineyard Chardonnay Stony Hill **1985,** Napa Valley: 238
Robert Mondavi Cabernet Sauvignon "Reserve" **1974,** Napa Valley: 1, 21, 84, 162, 199, 198, 334, 418, 628
Robert Mondavi Cabernet Sauvignon "Reserve" **1975,** Napa Valley: 21, 22, 47, 52, 57, 79, 629
Robert Mondavi Cabernet Sauvignon "Reserve" **1976,** Napa Valley: 27, 26
Robert Mondavi Cabernet Sauvignon "Reserve" **1978,** Napa Valley: 47
Robert Mondavi Cabernet Sauvignon "Reserve" **1979,** Napa Valley: 52, 79, 85, 418
Robert Mondavi Cabernet Sauvignon "Reserve" **1980,** Napa Valley: 84, 418, 631
Robert Mondavi Cabernet Sauvignon "Reserve" **1981,** Napa Valley: 52
Robert Mondavi Cabernet Sauvignon "Reserve" **1982,** Napa Valley: 324
Robert Mondavi Cabernet Sauvignon "Reserve" **1985,** Napa Valley: 260, 304, 359, 418, 485
Robert Mondavi Cabernet Sauvignon "Reserve" **1986,** Napa Valley: 304, 418
Robert Mondavi Cabernet Sauvignon "Reserve" **1987,** Napa Valley: 304, 418
Robert Mondavi Cabernet Sauvignon "Reserve" **1988,** Napa Valley: 418
Robert Mondavi Cabernet Sauvignon "Reserve" **1989,** Napa Valley: 304, 418
Robert Mondavi Cabernet Sauvignon "Reserve" **1990,** Napa Valley: 418
Robert Mondavi Cabernet Sauvignon "Reserve" **1991,** Napa Valley: 489
Robert Mondavi Cabernet Sauvignon "Unfiltered" **1970,** Napa Valley: 105
Robert Mondavi Cabernet Sauvignon **1974,** Napa Valley: 1, 25, 345, 628
Robert Mondavi Cabernet Sauvignon **1975,** Napa Valley: 345
Robert Mondavi Cabernet Sauvignon **1976,** Napa Valley: 170, 345
Robert Mondavi Cabernet Sauvignon **1977,** Napa Valley: 346
Robert Mondavi Cabernet Sauvignon **1978,** Napa Valley: 26, 346
Robert Mondavi Cabernet Sauvignon **1979,** Napa Valley: 346
Robert Mondavi Cabernet Sauvignon **1984,** Napa Valley: 345
Robert Mondavi Cabernet Sauvignon **1985,** Napa Valley: 345
Robert Mondavi Cabernet Sauvignon **1986,** Napa Valley: 345
Robert Mondavi Cabernet Sauvignon **1987,** Napa Valley: 345
Robert Mondavi Cabernet Sauvignon **1988,** Napa Valley: 345
Robert Mondavi Chardonnay "Reserve" **1975,** Napa Valley: 52
Robert Mondavi Chardonnay "Reserve" **1976,** Napa Valley 83
Robert Mondavi Chardonnay "Reserve" **1977,** Napa Valley: 79, 83
Robert Mondavi Chardonnay "Reserve" **1978,** Napa Valley: 22, 83, 35, 47
Robert Mondavi Chardonnay "Reserve" **1979,** Napa Valley: 27, 35, 47, 57, 83
Robert Mondavi Chardonnay "Reserve" **1980,** Napa Valley: 84
Robert Mondavi Chardonnay "Reserve" **1981,** Napa Valley: 52, 79, 84, 640
Robert Mondavi Chardonnay "Reserve" **1982,** Napa Valley: 84

Robert Mondavi Chardonnay "Reserve" **1986,** Napa Valley: 259
Robert Mondavi Chardonnay "Reserve" **1987,** Napa Valley: 640
Robert Mondavi Chardonnay "Unfiltered" **1976,** Napa Valley: 162
Robert Mondavi Chardonnay **1978,** Napa Valley: 35, 65
Robert Mondavi Chardonnay **1983,** Napa Valley: 180
Robert Mondavi Fumé Blanc "Reserve" **1978,** Napa Valley: 26
Robert Mondavi Fumé Blanc "Réserve" **1981,** Napa Valley: 52, 84
Robert Mondavi Fumé Blanc "Reserve" **1986,** Napa Valley: 259
Robert Mondavi Fumé Blanc **1976,** Napa Valley: 84
Robert Mondavi Fumé Blanc **1978,** Napa Valley: 641
Robert Mondavi Fumé Blanc **1979,** Napa Valley: 26
Robert Mondavi Fumé Blanc **1981,** Napa Valley: 52
Robert Mondavi Johannisberg Riesling "Botrytis" **1978,** Napa Valley: 103, 642
Robert Mondavi Johannisberg Riesling "Oak Knoll Vineyards Botrytis" **1977,** Napa Valley: 642
Robert Mondavi Johannisberg Riesling "Special Selection" **1982,** Napa Valley: 52
Robert Mondavi Muscat d'Oro **1982,** Napa Valley: 79
Robert Mondavi Pinot Noir "Reserve" **1975,** Napa Valley: 84
Robert Mondavi Pinot Noir "Reserve" **1976,** Napa Valley: 46, 84
Robert Mondavi Pinot Noir "Reserve" **1977,** Napa Valley: 46, 52, 79
Robert Mondavi Pinot Noir "Reserve" **1978,** Napa Valley: 26, 47, 52
Robert Mondavi Pinot Noir "Reserve" **1979,** Napa Valley: 47, 52
Robert Mondavi Pinot Noir "Reserve" **1980,** Napa Valley: 52, 79, 84, 85, 47
Robert Mondavi Pinot Noir "Reserve" **1981,** Napa Valley: 84
Robert Mondavi Pinot Noir "Reserve" **1986,** Napa Valley: 260
Robert Mondavi Pinot Noir **1968,** Napa Valley: 38
Robert Mondavi Pinot Noir **1979,** Napa Valley: 26
Robert Mondavi Sauvignon Blanc "Botrytis" **1978,** Napa Valley: 47, 52, 642
Robert Mondavi Sauvignon Blanc "Botrytis" **1983,** Napa Valley: 260
Robert Mondavi White **1981,** Napa Valley: 52
Robert Pecota "Moscato d'Andrea" **1996,** Napa Valley: 469
Roddis Cellar Cabernet Sauvignon **1981,** Napa Valley: 53
Romanée-Conti **1945,** Domaine de la Romanée-Conti: 321
Romanée-Conti **1955,** Domaine de la Romanée-Conti: 110
Romanée-Conti **1959,** Domaine de la Romanée-Conti: 96, 382
Romanée-Conti **1961,** Domaine de la Romanée-Conti: 46, 216
Romanée-Conti **1964,** Domaine de la Romanée-Conti: 216, 381
Romanée-Conti **1971,** Domaine de la Romanée-Conti: 216, 382
Romanée-Conti **1973,** Domaine de la Romanée-Conti: 232
Romanée-St.-Vivant "Les Quatres Journaux" **1959,** Louis Latour: 342
Romanée-St.-Vivant "Les Quatres Journaux" **1964,** Louis Latour: 31
Romanée-St.-Vivant **1961,** London-bottled, Bouchard Père et Fils: 584
Romanée-St.-Vivant **1969,** Marey-Monges, Domaine de la Romanée-Conti: 585
Romanée-St.-Vivant **1971,** Domaine de la Romanée-Conti: 140, 270, 487
Romanée-St.-Vivant **1972,** Domaine de la Romanée-Conti: 102
Romanée-St.-Vivant **1978,** Marey-Monges, Domaine de la Romanée-Conti: 342
Romanée-St.-Vivant **1987,** Domaine de la Romanée-Conti: 506
Romanée-St.-Vivant **1990,** Domaine de la Romanée-Conti: 494
Rosemount Estate "Noble Semillon" Hunter Valley "Show Reserve" **1985,** Australia: 338
Rosso di Montalcino **1995,** Ciacci Piccolomini, d'Aragona: 486
Rothbury Estate Individual Vineyard Semillon **1976:** 23
Round Hill "Reserve" Cabernet Sauvignon **1985,** Napa Valley: 359
Royale Club (Four Star Cuvée) **1978,** A/C Bourgogne, Remoissenet: 494
Rubicon **1987,** Meerlust: 386
Ruchottes-Chambertin "Clos des Ruchottes" Monopole **1987,** A. Rousseau: 590
Ruchottes-Chambertin **1953,** Charles Vienot: 583
Ruchottes-Chambertin **1983,** Georges Roumier: 146
Ruchottes-Chambertin **1988,** Georges Roumier: 288
Rully **1988,** Laborde-Juillot: 295
Rully Rouge **1985,** Faiveley: 232
Russian Port Massandra Collection Muscat **1940,** Crimea: 273
Russian Port Massandra Collection Muscat **1945,** Crimea: 480
Rutherford Hill Cabernet Sauvignon **1975,** Napa Valley: 245
Rutherford Hill Gewürztraminer **1987,** Napa Valley: 311
Rutherford Hill Merlot **1979,** Napa Valley: 633
Rutherford Ranch Merlot **1983,** Napa Valley: 200
S. Anderson Sparkling Wine "Blanc de Noir" **1984,** Napa Valley: 232
Samuel Wynn Port "Series 5" N/V: 653
San Giacomo Vineyard Chardonnay **1983,** Napa Valley: 172
Sancerre "Clos du Chêne Marchand" **1983,** Lucien Crochet: 153
Sancerre "Les Perrières" **1978,** Hippolyte Reverdy: 57
Sancerre **1976,** Chavignol, Cotat: 90
Sancerre **1995,** Paul Prieur: 450
Sandeman's Port **1945:** 105, 114
Sandeman's Vintage Port **1945:** 512
Sandeman's Vintage Port **1957:** 73
Sandeman's Vintage Port **1963:** 61, 645
Sandeman's Vintage Port **1966:** 86, 646
Sanford and Benedict Pinot Noir **1978:** 635
Santenay "Gravières" **1987,** Domaine de la Pousse d'Or: 287
Santenay **1969,** Chanson Père et Fils: 40
Santino "El Dorado" Riesling "Dry Berry Select Harvest" **1982,** Shenandoah Valley: 172
Sassello **1994,** Castello di Verrazzano: 456
Sassicaia **1978:** 270, 440, 655
Sassicaia **1979:** 440
Sassicaia **1980:** 93, 440
Sassicaia **1981:** 440, 462, 656
Sassicaia **1982:** 161, 440, 656
Sassicaia **1983:** 440
Sassicaia **1985:** 440, 477, 485
Sassicaia **1986:** 440
Sassicaia **1987:** 440
Sassicaia **1988:** 440
Sassicaia **1989:** 439
Sauvignon Blanc "Alteni de Brassica" **1994:** 421
Sauvignon Blanc **1985,** Napa Valley: 172
Savennières "Clos de la Coulée de Serrant" Grand Cru **1980,** Mme Joly, Loire: 480, 606
Savigny "Champ Chevrey" Premier Cru Monopole **1984:** 147
Savigny "Lavière" Premier Cru **1984,** Tollot-Beaut: 147

Savigny-Fonqueraud "Hospices de Beaune" **1923:** 392
Savigny-lès-Beaune "Guettes" Premier Cru **1971,** Jaffelin: 358
Savigny-lès-Beaune **1966,** Leroy: 150
Savigny-lès-Beaune **1978,** Doudet-Naudin: 7
Savigny-lès-Beaune **1982,** Louis Latour: 151
Savigny-Vergelesses "Bataillère" **1988,** Albert Morot: 419
Schloss Vollrad's Riesling Kabinett **1959,** Rheingau: 108
Schramsberg Brut N/V, Napa Valley: 238
Schramsberg California Champagne "Reserve" **1976:** 38
Seppelt Great Western Hermitage "GW115" **1967:** 23
Seppelt Para Liqueur Port **1933,** Seppeltsfield, Australia: 58
Serriger Wurzberg Riesling Auslese **1975,** Herrenberg, Mosel: 439
Setúbal "Colheita" **1934,** J. M. da Fonseca: 481
Shafer Cabernet Sauvignon **1978,** Napa Valley, Stag's Leap District: 393
Shenandoah Vineyards Zinfandel Port "Lot 2" N/V, Amador County: 61
Signorello Vineyards "110 Year Old Vineyard" Petite Syrah **1995,** Napa Valley: 476
Signorello Vineyards C "Founders Reserve" Chardonnay **1985:** Napa Valley: 312
Signorello Vineyards Pinot Noir "Los Amigos Vineyard" **1995,** Carneros: 476, 498
Signorello Vineyards Pinot Noir "Los Amigos Vineyard" **1997,** Carneros: 527
Signorello Vineyards Semillon **1997,** Napa Valley: 527
Signorello Vineyards Zinfandel **1997,** Napa Valley: 527
Silver Oak Winery Cabernet Sauvignon **1990,** Napa Valley: 403
Simonsig Cabernet Sauvignon **1978:** 142
Sirius White **1993:** 429
Smith-Woodhouse Vintage Port **1977:** 474
Solaia **1990,** Antinori: 486
Sonoma-Cutrer Chardonnay **1984,** Russian River: 172
Souverain Cabernet Sauvignon **1968:** 263
Spanna "Del Piedmonte" **1966,** Antonio Vallana: 654
Spanna "Montalbano" **1966,** Antonio Vallana: 56, 103, 654
Spottswoode Cabernet Sauvignon **1986,** Napa Valley: 476
Spottswoode Cabernet Sauvignon **1990,** Napa Valley: 475
Spring Mountain Cabernet Sauvignon "Les Trois Cuvées" N/V, Napa Valley: 170, 626
Spring Mountain Cabernet Sauvignon "Lot H 68/69 LN," Napa Valley: 325, 366, 390, 529, 626
Spring Mountain Cabernet Sauvignon **1973,** Napa Valley: 453
Spring Mountain Cabernet Sauvignon **1975,** Napa Valley: 629
St. Clement Cabernet Sauvignon **1980,** Napa Valley: 101
St. Clement Chardonnay **1978,** Napa Valley: 65
St. Clement Chardonnay **1979,** Napa Valley: 35
St. Clement Chardonnay **1980,** Napa Valley: 35
St. Clement Sauvignon Blanc **1982,** Napa Valley: 245
St. Hallett Shiraz "Old Stock" **1994,** Barossa Valley, Australia: 486
St. Jean de Bebian **1981,** Vin de Pays de l'Herault, Alain Roux: 196
St. Joseph "Le Grand Pompée" **1985,** Jaboulet: 154
St. Supéry Cabernet Sauvignon "Limited Edition Reserve, Dollaridge Ranch" **1991,** Napa Valley: 441
Staadter Maximiner Prälat Riesling **1976** Auslese, Mosel: 439
Stag's Leap Wine Cellars Cabernet Sauvignon "Lot 2" **1976,** Napa Valley: 630
Stag's Leap Wine Cellars Cabernet Sauvignon "Lot 2" **1977,** Napa Valley: 630
Stag's Leap Wine Cellars Cabernet Sauvignon "Lot 2" **1978,** Napa Valley: 630
Stag's Leap Wine Cellars Cabernet Sauvignon "Lot 23" **1979,** Napa Valley: 630
Stag's Leap Wine Cellars Cabernet Sauvignon "SLV" **1985,** Napa Valley: 359
Stag's Leap Wine Cellars Cabernet Sauvignon **1974,** Napa Valley: 1, 21
Stag's Leap Wine Cellars Cabernet Sauvignon Regular "Lot 1" **1974,** Napa Valley: 198
Sterling Vineyards Cabernet Sauvignon "Reserve" **1973,** Napa Valley: 627
Sterling Vineyards Cabernet Sauvignon "Reserve" **1974,** Napa Valley: 1, 22, 198, 425, 628
Sterling Vineyards Cabernet Sauvignon "Reserve" **1975,** Napa Valley: 21
Sterling Vineyards Chardonnay **1972,** Napa Valley: 3
Sterling Vineyards Chardonnay **1975,** Napa Valley: 25, 637
Sterling Vineyards Chardonnay **1976,** Napa Valley: 637
Sterling Vineyards Chardonnay **1979,** Napa Valley: 322, 638
Sterling Vineyards Merlot **1974,** Napa Valley: 633
Stony Hill Vineyards Chardonnay **1964,** Napa Valley: 238
Stony Hill Vineyards Chardonnay **1973,** Napa Valley: 58, 238
Stony Hill Vineyards Chardonnay **1974,** Napa Valley: 238
Stony Hill Vineyards Chardonnay **1975,** Napa Valley: 238
Stony Hill Vineyards Chardonnay **1976,** Napa Valley: 238
Stony Hill Vineyards Chardonnay **1978,** Napa Valley: 238
Stony Hill Vineyards Chardonnay **1992,** Napa Valley: 409, 488
Stony Hill Vineyards Gewürztraminer **1966:** 238
Stony Hill Vineyards Gewürztraminer **1970:** 238
Sumac Ridge 1988 Gewürztraminer, Okanagan Valley, BC: 313
Surozh **1945:** 413
Sylvaner **1980,** Hugel: 36
Taltarni Cabernet Sauvignon **1978,** Australia: 50, 653
Taltarni Cabernet Sauvignon **1979,** Australia: 50
Taltarni Cabernet Sauvignon **1980,** Australia: 51
Taltarni Shiraz **1978:** 51
Taurasi **1974,** Mastroberardino: 655
Tavel "L'Espiègle" **1979:** 9
Taylor's "Quinta do Vargellas" **1967:** 74, 325
Taylor's Late-Bottled Reserve **1972:** 647
Taylor's Quinta do Vargellas **1967:** 57
Taylor's Vintage Port **1920:** 317, 318
Taylor's Vintage Port **1927:** 60
Taylor's Vintage Port **1945:** 125, 414
Taylor's Vintage Port **1948:** 87
Taylor's Vintage Port **1955:** 56, 86, 644
Taylor's Vintage Port **1960:** 61
Taylor's Vintage Port **1963:** 61, 93, 422, 444
Taylor's Vintage Port **1966:** 73
Taylor's Vintage Port **1970:** 57, 74, 408, 487, 646
Taylor's Vintage Port **1975:** 57, 86, 167
Taylor's Wood Port **1934:** 136
Terrantez **1795,** Barbeito: 418
Thelema Chardonnay **1988:** 386
Tignanello **1979,** Antinori: 656
Tignanello **1982,** Antinori: 505, 656
Tignanello **1983,** Antinori: 313
Tignanello **1985,** Antinori: 505. 528
Tignanello **1990,** Antinori: 505

Tokai Aszú 3 Puttonyos **1969:** 648
Tokai Aszú 3 Puttonyos **1980:** 307
Tokai Aszú 3 Puttonyos **1983:** 306
Tokai Aszú 4 Puttonyos **1981:** 306
Tokai Aszú 5 Puttonyos "Bojta" **1991,** Royal Tokai Wine Company: 465
Tokai Aszú 5 Puttonyos **1961:** 108
Tokai Aszú 5 Puttonyos **1971:** 648
Tokai Aszú 5 Puttonyos **1973:** 648
Tokai Aszú 5 Puttonyos **1974:** 648
Tokai Aszú 5 Puttonyos **1975:** 306
Tokai Aszú 5 Puttonyos **1979:** 305, 307
Tokai Aszú 6 Puttonyos **1966:** 648
Tokai Aszú 6 Puttonyos **1972:** 306
Tokai Aszú Essencia **1957:** 307
Tokai Aszú Essencia **1964:** 396, 648
Tokai Aszú Essencia **1976,** Monimpex, Hungary: 307, 402, 508
Tokai Dry Szamorodny **1983:** 306
Tokai Dry Szamorodny **1984:** 306
Tokai Essencia **1735:** 112
Tokai Essencia **1889,** Zimmerman Lipot es Fiai: 318
Tokai Essencia **1988:** 333
Tokai Szamorodny Sweet **1983:** 306
Torres Gran Coronas "Black Label" Reserva **1978,** Penedés: 657
Torres Gran Coronas "Reserva" **1970,** Penedés: 657
Trefethen Chardonnay **1993,** Napa Valley: 409
Tualatin Oregon Pinot Noir **1979,** Willamette Valley: 635
Tyrrell "Red" **1975:** 652
Tyrrell's Hunter River Cabernet "Vat 70" **1978:** 653
Tyrrell's Hunter River Cabernet-Shiraz "Vat 94" **1978:** 652
Tyrrell's Pinot Chardonnay "Hunter River" "Vat 47" **1977:** 651
Tyrrell's Pinot Chardonnay "Hunter River" "Vat 47" **1979:** 23, 651
Tyrrell's Pinot Chardonnay "Hunter River" "Vat 47" **1980:** 23, 652
Tyrrell's Pinot Chardonnay "Hunter River" "Vat 47" **1988:** 652
Tyrrell's Pinot Chardonnay "Hunter River" "Vat 47" **1989:** 652
Tyrrell's Pinot Chardonnay "Hunter River" "Vat 47" **1991:** 652
Tyrrell's Pinot Hermitage **1978:** 23
Urziger Wurzgarten Riesling Auslese **1975,** Nicolay, Rheingau: 446
Vacqueyras **1978,** Côtes du Rhône, Jaboulet: 329
Vega Sicilia "Unico" **1936:** 340
Vega Sicilia "Unico" **1941:** 340
Vega Sicilia "Unico" **1942:** 340
Vega Sicilia "Unico" **1948:** 340
Vega Sicilia "Unico" **1949:** 340
Vega Sicilia "Unico" **1953:** 340
Vega Sicilia "Unico" **1957:** 340
Vega Sicilia "Unico" **1960:** 340
Vega Sicilia "Unico" **1962:** 314, 340, 461
Vega Sicilia "Unico" **1965:** 506
Vega Sicilia "Unico" **1968:** 476, 506
Vega Sicilia "Unico" Cosecha **1962:** 280, 657
Vega Sicilia "Unico" Cosecha **1965:** 280
Vega Sicilia "Unico" Cosecha **1973:** 280
Vega Sicilia "Unico" Cosecha **1976:** 280
Vega Sicilia "Valbuena" 5 Años **1976,** Cosecha: 388
Vega Sicilia "Valbuena" 5 Años **1982:** 279
Venegazzú "Black Label" **1982,** Villa Loredan: 656
Vergenoegd Cabernet Sauvignon **1970:** 142
Vergenoegd Cabernet Sauvignon **1975:** 650
Viader Vineyards **1989,** Napa Valley: 441
Viader Vineyards **1992,** Napa Valley: 425
Viader Vineyards **1993,** Napa Valley: 425
Viader Vineyards **1994,** Napa Valley: 501
Viader Vineyards **1995,** Napa Valley: 460
Viejo (Burgos) Fino, Vinos Finos Sancho: 167
Vieux Château Certan **1945:** 132, 227, 237
Vieux Château Certan **1959:** 577
Vieux Château Certan **1964:** 75
Vieux Château Certan 1966 371
Vieux Château Certan **1970:** 479
Vieux Château Certan **1979:** 85
Vieux Château Certan **1982:** 104, 201, 351
Vieux Château Certan **1985:** 524
Vieux Château Certan **1986:** 271
Vieux Château Certan **1988:** 474
Vieux Château Certan **1989:** 460
Vieux Château Certan **1993:** 433
Vieux Château Certan **1994:** 433
Vieux Château Certan **1996:** 432
Vigna Flaminio (Brindisi) Rosso **1994,** Agricole Vallone: 486
Villa Mount Eden "Tres Niños Vineyard" Pinot Noir **1978,** Napa Valley: 635
Villa Mount Eden Cabernet Sauvignon **1978,** Napa Valley: 630
Villa Mount Eden Chardonnay **1978,** Napa Valley: 65
Vin Nakad Vin Vieux Rouge **1963,** Chtoura, Nakad et Fils, Lebanon: 80, 658
Vin Santo **1991,** Pomino: 456
Vino Liquoroso "Vecchio Soliento Bianco" **1971,** Croce d'Oro (Golden Cross), Ruffino, Italy: 75
Volnay "Caillerets" "Clos des 60 Ouvrées" **1987:** 287
Volnay "Caillerets" **1972,** Domaine de la Pousse d'Or: 288
Volnay "Caillerets" **1988,** Domaine de la Pousse d'Or: 419
Volnay "Champans" **1985,** Monthélie-Douhairet: 234
Volnay "Clos de la Bousse d'Or" **1984,** Domaine de la Pousse d'Or: 288
Volnay "Clos de la Bousse d'Or" **1986,** Domaine de la Pousse d'Or: 287
Volnay "Clos de la Bousse d'Or" **1987,** Domaine de la Pousse d'Or: 287
Volnay "Clos de la Bousse d'Or" **1988,** Domaine de la Pousse d'Or: 592
Volnay "Clos des Ducs" **1957,** Marquis d'Angerville: 507
Volnay "Clos des Santenots" **1976,** Domaine Jacques Prieur: 29
Volnay "Santenots" "Hospices de Beaune-Cuvée Gauvin" **1972,** Beyermann: 40
Volnay **1985,** J. F. Coche-Dury: 379
Vosne-Romanée "Aux Réas" Premier Cru **1988,** Leroy: 498
Vosne-Romanée "Beaux-Monts" Premier Cru **1985,** Daniel Rion: 589
Vosne-Romanée "Les Chaumes" **1985,** Méo-Camuzet: 234
Vosne-Romanée "Les Suchots" Premier Cru **1990,** Manière-Noirot: 421
Vosne-Romanée **1935,** H. de Villamont: 392
Vosne-Romanée **1974,** Leroy: 216
Vosne-Romanée **1976,** Latour: 31
Vosne-Romanée **1983,** Jean Grivot: 589
Vosne-Romanée **1988,** Jadot: 285

Vosne-Romanée **1993,** Daniel Rion: 426
Vosne-Romanée **1993,** René Angel: 427
Vougeot "Clos de la Perrière" **1985,** Domaine Bertagna: 589
Vouvray "Clos de Bourg" **1992,** A. Huet: 419
Vouvray Moelleux "Le Haut-Lieu" **1947,** A. Huet: 478
Wachenheimer Altenberg Riesling Spätlese **1993,** Weingut Joseph Biffar (Rheinpfaltz): 488
Warre's Vintage Port "Directors' Reserve" **1934:** 447, 323, 644
Warre's Vintage Port **1920:** 284
Warre's Vintage Port **1922:** 284
Warre's Vintage Port **1924:** 284
Warre's Vintage Port **1927:** 284
Warre's Vintage Port **1934:** 284
Warre's Vintage Port **1945:** 135, 284, 414
Warre's Vintage Port **1947:** 284
Warre's Vintage Port **1955:** 283
Warre's Vintage Port **1958:** 135, 283
Warre's Vintage Port **1960:** 135, 283
Warre's Vintage Port **1962:** 283
Warre's Vintage Port **1963:** 135, 283
Warre's Vintage Port **1966:** 135, 283
Warre's Vintage Port **1970:** 135, 282, 462, 647
Warre's Vintage Port **1975:** 135, 166, 282
Warre's Vintage Port **1977:** 86, 135, 282, 449
Warre's Vintage Port **1980:** 135, 282
Warre's Vintage Port **1983:** 136, 282
Warre's Vintage Port **1985:** 282
Warre's Vintage Port Late-Bottled **1974:** 135
Warre's Warrior Finest Vintage Character: 136
Weissburgunder Ruster Beerenauslese **1976,** Morandell, Austria: 649
West Indies Rum, blend of choicest "Grog Americano Palido, Rhum Four Paths," Arturos S.A. "Hecho en Mexico," T. Noirot and Co.: 283
Whitcraft Winery Chardonnay **1985,** Santa Barbara: 247
William Hill Cabernet Sauvignon "Gold Label Reserve" **1985,** Napa Valley: 486
William Hill Cabernet Sauvignon "Silver Label" **1985,** Napa Valley: 359
Windsor Vineyards Select Late Harvest Johannisberg Riesling **1982,** Russian River, Sonoma Valley: 643
Winzerheimer Rosenheer Riesling Beerenauslese **1976,** von Plattenberg: 179
Wynn's Coonawarra Cabernet Sauvignon **1976:** 652
Wynn's Coonawarra Cabernet Sauvignon **1978:** 23
XSR 120 White Porto "Very Finest," Martinez and Gassiot: 255, 360
"Y" d'Yquem **1977:** 100, 106
"Y" d'Yquem **1979:** 169, 477
"Y" d'Yquem **1980:** 230
"Y" d'Yquem **1988:** 355
Yalumba "Chairman's Selection" Cabernet Sauvignon **1976:** 23
Yarden "Galil" Cabernet Sauvignon **1985,** Golan, Israel: 359, 659
Yarden "Galil" Cabernet Sauvignon **1986:** 252
Yarden "Galil" Cabernet Sauvignon **1993:** 455
Yarden "Galil" Chardonnay **1987** "First Release": 252
Yarden "Galil" Chardonnay **1987:** 659
Yarden "Galil" Chardonnay **1995:** 455
Yarden "Galil" Merlot **1986:** 252
Yarden "Galil" Sauvignon Blanc **1987:** 252
Yarden "Galil" White Riesling "Special Release" **1987:** 252
Yarden "Gamla" Chardonnay **1995:** 455
Yarden Cabernet Sauvignon **1986,** Golan: 332
ZD "California" Chardonnay **1977:** 102
ZD "California" Chardonnay **1988:** 315, 640
ZD "California" Chardonnay **1991:** 393
ZD "California" Chardonnay **1996:** 513
ZD "California" Merlot **1979:** 633
ZD "Patusquet Vineyard" Chardonnay **1977,** Santa Barbara: 637
Zinfandel "Monte Rosso" **1979,** Sebastiani, Sonoma Valley: 172
Zinfandel **1983,** Grapes from Parducci Vineyards, California: 502